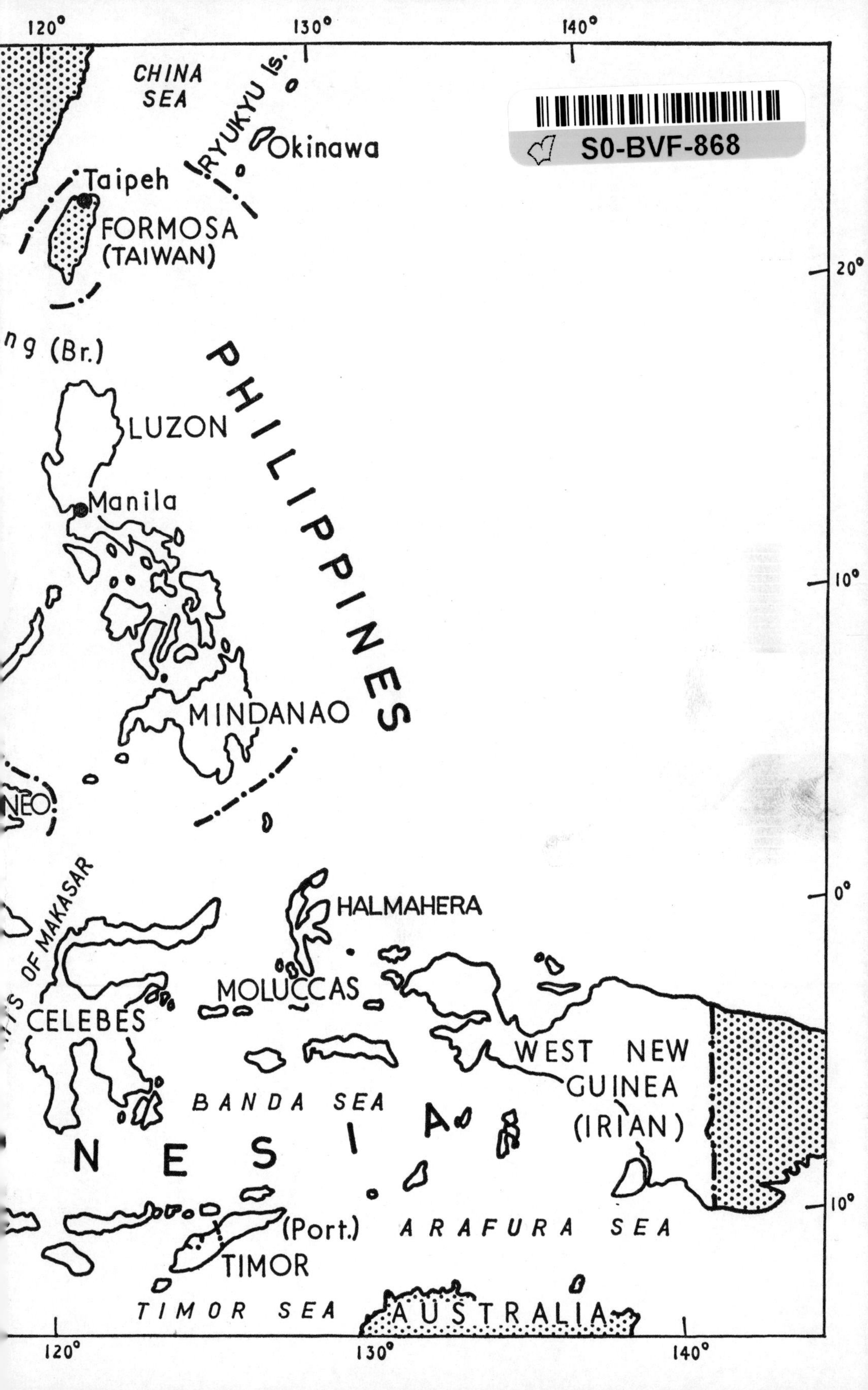

120°
130°
140°
CHINA
SEA
RYUKYU Is.
Okinawa
Taipeh
FORMOSA
(TAIWAN)
20°
ng (Br.)
PHILIPPINES
LUZON
Manila
10°
MINDANAO
NEO
STRAITS OF MAKASAR
HALMAHERA
0°
MOLUCCAS
CELEBES
WEST NEW
GUINEA
(IRIAN)
BANDA SEA
N E S I A
10°
(Port.)
ARAFURA SEA
TIMOR
TIMOR SEA
AUSTRALIA
120°
130°
140°

South-east Asia

SOUTH-EAST ASIA

A Social, Economic and Political Geography

CHARLES A. FISHER

Professor of Geography with reference to Asia
University of London

'Ignorer les facteurs non-géographiques sous le prétexte d'être géographe, nous paraîtrait la pire trahison possible envers la discipline géographique.'

Jean Gottmann: *La Politique des États et leur Géographie*, Paris, Armand Colin, 1952, p. ix.

LONDON: METHUEN & CO. LTD.

First published 1964

Reprinted 1965
Second edition 1966
Reprinted 1967
Reprinted 1969
Reprinted 1971
Printed in Great Britain
by Hazell Watson & Viney Ltd
Aylesbury, Bucks

S.B.N. 416 42480 5

TO IRENE

A candid but constructive critic

Distributed in the U.S.A.
by Barnes & Noble Inc

Preface

When one has already written over 400,000 words on a subject one should if possible resist the temptation to add anything more, but a few comments on the circumstances in which this book has been planned and finally brought to completion nevertheless seem to be called for, if only to explain certain characteristics of its method and approach.

For many years now it has been my conviction that the most effective level at which a geographical synthesis can be made is that of the political unit rather than that of the natural region for, fundamental though the latter concept undoubtedly is to comparative geographical study, it is primarily as a member of a nationally organized society that modern man comes to terms with his physical environment.[1] That such an approach, which I have accordingly adopted in this book, merits the term regional geography I do not propose to contend, though I certainly regard South-east Asia as a major part of the world, possessing a sufficient measure of overall unity to justify its being viewed first as a single entity before its component states are examined in detail. But since such physical and historical material as I have included, besides being largely derivative, is introduced primarily in order to assist the reader to understand the present-day social, economic and political geography, I have worded my title explicitly in terms of these last.

Perhaps the greatest difficulty with which the writer of contemporary geography has to contend is the fact that his subject matter is itself in a state of constant change and, while this problem is in no sense a new one, it is present in a peculiarly intense and compelling form in the newly independent lands of South-east Asia, the whole basis of whose social, economic and political life has been undergoing revolutionary transformation in the twenty-odd years that have elapsed since the outbreak of the Pacific War in December 1941.

Thus if it be true, as Vidal de la Blache has claimed, that it is man who reveals the individuality of a country by moulding it to his own use, we are faced here with a series of personalities most of which are now in the process of being remade, as what, *pace* Riesman, we may perhaps call the 'other-directed' patterns imposed by the colonial powers are replaced by the 'inner-directed' patterns created by independent peoples.

It was against this shifting background that in 1946 I wrote the first chapter

[1] See my 'Economic geography in a changing world', *Transactions and Papers of the Institute of British Geographers*, No. 14, 1948, pp. 69–85, and *The Compleat Geographer*, 1959.

of what was planned to be a large-scale geography of South-east Asia, but as crisis followed crisis in almost every country within that region it was soon borne in upon me that the time was not yet ripe for the kind of study I had envisaged, and although an invitation to make a shorter contribution to *The Changing Map of Asia*[1] provided an opportunity for a reconnaissance survey of the ground to be covered, it was not until the early 1950s that the outlines of the new post-war scene appeared to have achieved a sufficient degree either of clarity or of permanency to justify the writing of a larger geographical study based upon them. And indeed, although the original text of the present book, apart from the epilogue, was written between 1952 and 1959, the scene continued to shift both throughout that entire period and in the years which have followed it, when the maps were being drawn and the text being set, and the consequent modifications which this has entailed have inevitably led to further delays. Thus writing this book has been rather like trying to run up an express escalator going down, and my final reaction on eventually arriving into daylight at the top is one of relief tinged with incredulity that I have ever succeeded in getting there.

In these circumstances I decided at an early stage to abandon any attempt to produce a definitive geographical portrait of the new South-east Asia, and instead have tried to view the present merely as a transitory phase in an evolving pattern, whose significance can only be understood in the light of what has gone before, and whose probable further development can best be judged in terms of such significant trends as may be discerned in the contemporary scene. This method, which has been adopted with only minor variations in all the 'country' sections, is worked out in greatest detail in the first group of these, namely the series dealing with Indonesia which, besides being by far the largest South-east Asian country, has also experienced the longest and most varied period of Western rule, and still presents perhaps the most baffling range of unresolved economic and political problems.

Thus, after an examination of the physical and historical setting in Chapters 7 and 8, Chapter 9 attempts to depict the old 'other-directed' personality of the Indies as this appeared in the final stages of Dutch rule, in the belief that this stage, which is the last for which detailed Census data are yet available, represents a necessary introduction to an understanding of the economic and political problems with which the new regime is confronted. These problems, together with an indication of the distinctive ways in which the Indonesians as an independent people are reacting to them, are discussed in Chapters 10 and 11, and although it is still too early to discern the main features of the new 'inner-directed' economic and political geography which is emerging, an attempt is at least made to assess the processes by which it is being shaped. This method would appear at least to possess the merit of placing in proper perspective the

[1] Edited W. G. East and O. H. K. Spate, and published by Methuen. (First edition 1950.)

inevitable dating of factual information, and if, as no doubt has happened in many parts of the book, my text has failed to keep pace with what has been happening on the ground, this certainly has not been for want of trying on my part, nor should it be regarded as a criticism of the information services of the countries concerned, which in present circumstances have unusually difficult tasks to perform.

By an accident of war it happened that my first experience of South-east Asia, which may perhaps be described as a case of love at first sight, came in the course of military service in Malaya in 1941–2, and not even the ensuing three-and-a-half years of prison camp life succeeded in appeasing my appetite for foreign travel which had thus been whetted. And indeed, while the somewhat unorthodox form of enforced nomadism, which between 1942 and 1945 took me into various other parts of the region, imposed obvious constraints upon the pursuit of geographical research—though it is surprising how much field-work can be accomplished in the absence even of a stout pair of boots—it nevertheless afforded certain invaluable compensations.

For in living for several years at a level little different from that of millions of Asian peasants, and making the best one could of an environment that often seemed to pose more problems than it afforded opportunities, I learned in some degree to look at South-east Asia from within rather than, as I had hitherto done, from without, and this surely is the beginning of geographical understanding. Moreover, in living through the critical period which saw the passing of the old order and the tempestuous birth of the new, I trust that I have deepened my understanding of the motives which are animating the new regimes within South-east Asia today, without falling into the current fallacy of believing that everything in the colonial garden was unlovely.

This, at least, is the spirit in which I have tried to write, and if my criticisms of some of the things that are happening in some parts of the region today may appear severe, I can only say that they are offered out of a deep desire to see that what has so recently been won at such heavy cost shall not unwittingly or needlessly be cast away.

C.A.F.

University of Sheffield, September, 1963.

Preface to the 1965 Reprint

The pace of change in South-east Asia has not slackened during the short time since the first edition of this book went to press, and I have therefore made such alterations and additions, notably in the Chapters on Malaysia and Indochina, as seem to be called for at this stage.

C.A.F.

School of Oriental and African Studies,
University of London, September, 1964.

Preface to the Second Edition

From the vantage point of the future the year 1965 may well appear as a turning point in the evolution of post-colonial South-east Asia. While it is as yet too early to assess the full significance of the new and sombre developments in many parts of the region, I have endeavoured at least to record the more important changes which have taken place, notably in Malaysia/Singapore and the several Indochinese lands.

C.A.F.

School of Oriental and African Studies,
University of London, October, 1965.

Acknowledgements

In the preparation of this book I have drawn extensively on a wide range of sources and, although every effort has been made to acknowledge them appropriately, I wish in advance to apologize for any inadvertent omissions.

What I trust is an exhaustive list of the works on which I have drawn directly or indirectly is found in the bibliography on pages 778 to 811. In addition, the principal works to which reference has been made, and occasionally others of outstanding importance, are listed in the relevant select bibliographies at the end of individual chapters, and in cases where it appears particularly helpful to do so I have also given more specific references in supplementary footnotes. Only in exceptional circumstances, however, have I attempted to give specific references to newspapers and news reports, etc., though my overall indebtedness to these, notably to *The Times*, *Guardian* and *Economist*, is very great.

Inevitably several relevant works now available have appeared too recently for me to have taken their findings into account, but I have tried to include some of these in addenda to the select bibliographies. In this connexion also I should mention the forthcoming publication under the joint auspices of Messrs. George Philip and the *Journal of Tropical Geography* of a selection of the papers presented at the International Geographical Union Regional Conference of Southeast Asian Geographers held at Kuala Lumpur in April 1962.

Immediately following the bibliography, on pages 811 to 812, is an extended note on the sources of maps used in the text, while sources of statistical information are given below most of the tables concerned.

Not the least important of my sources of information have been the innumerable individuals with first-hand knowledge of South-east Asia whom I have been privileged to meet at one time or another during the past twenty years, and who have been kind enough to pass on some of their knowledge to me, in the course of interviews or more informal conversation. To thank them all by name would be almost to write another book, but I trust that in their collective anonymity they will nevertheless accept my sincere thanks.

Among the many official and commercial bodies whose help in providing information I gratefully acknowledge are: the Embassies in the United Kingdom of the non-Commonwealth countries with which this book is mainly concerned, Malaysia House and India House (London), the Sarawak Information Service (Kuching), the International Tin Council, the International Rubber Study Group, Caltex Trading and Transport Coy., the Gulf Oil Corporation, the Shell International Petroleum Coy., Bank Indonesia, the Chartered Bank of

India, Australia and China, the Hongkong and Shanghai Banking Corporation, the Hamburger Kreditbank, and the Nationale Handelsbank N.V. Needless to say none of these bears any responsibility for the use I have made of the information supplied to me.

Most sections of this book have been read by one or more specialists in the various fields concerned, and in thanking the following for their helpful comments I wish at the same time to absolve them of all blame for any errors or omissions which remain: Professor C. D. Cowan, Mr. B. H. Farmer, Dr. D. W. Fryer, the late Mr. G. E. Harvey, Professor T. Herman, Professor B. L. C. Johnson, Professor M. Halim Khan, Mr. Peter Lyon, Mr. E. Paget, Dr. Puey Ungphakorn and Professor Frederick L. Wernstedt. Responsibility for opinions expressed is mine alone.

In addition to these, my especial thanks are due to my colleague Mr. J. L. H. Sibbons who, on reading my original section on climate, volunteered such a wealth of constructive comment, which he subsequently wove into my text, that the greater part of the credit for pages 21 to 42 is now due to him, and only his characteristic modesty has prevented its being listed as such. My sincere thanks are also given to Miss J. M. Wilkes for compiling the index, and to Miss W. Booker for extensive secretarial help.

C.A.F.

In the second edition I have noted, in addenda to some of the select biographies at the end of individual chapters, particulars of a few of the more important works which have come to my attention since the first edition of the book was completed.

C.A.F.

Contents

PREFACE *page* v

ACKNOWLEDGEMENTS ix

TABLES xiii

MAPS xvii

PART I SOUTH-EAST ASIA AS AN ENTITY

1 THE PERSONALITY OF SOUTH-EAST ASIA 3

2 THE PHYSICAL AND BIOGEOGRAPHICAL ENVIRONMENT 11

3 THE INDIGENOUS PEOPLES AND THEIR WAYS OF LIFE 63

4 THE POLITICAL GEOGRAPHY OF THE PRE-EUROPEAN PERIOD 102

5 THE ERA OF WESTERN RULE 126

6 THE LEGACY OF THE WEST 160

PART II THE EQUATORIAL ARCHIPELAGO: INDONESIA

7 INDONESIA: GENERALITIES AND PHYSIQUE 205

8 RACIAL, CULTURAL AND HISTORICAL BASES OF INDONESIAN REGIONALISM 238

9 THE NETHERLANDS INDIES BETWEEN THE TWO WORLD WARS: ECONOMIC AND SOCIAL GEOGRAPHY 275

10 PROBLEMS OF THE NEW INDONESIA: A – ECONOMIC 310

11 PROBLEMS OF THE NEW INDONESIA: B – POLITICAL 360

12 THE PROBLEM OF WEST NEW GUINEA 392
(*with a note on Portuguese Timor*, p. 404)

PART III THE TROPICAL MAINLAND: BURMA, THAILAND AND INDOCHINA

13 THE MAINLAND STATES: PHYSICAL INTRODUCTION 407

14 THE UNION OF BURMA 430

15 THAILAND 484

16 THE STATES OF INDOCHINA 529

PART IV THE FEDERATION OF MALAYSIA; SINGAPORE; BRUNEI

17 MALAYA: THE PHYSICAL AND HISTORICAL SETTING *page* 583
18 MALAYA: ECONOMIC GEOGRAPHY 604
19 MALAYA: SOCIAL AND POLITICAL GEOGRAPHY 633
20 NORTHERN BORNEO 662

PART V THE TROPICAL ARCHIPELAGO: THE PHILIPPINES

21 THE REPUBLIC OF THE PHILIPPINES 691

PART VI EPILOGUE

22 SOUTH-EAST ASIA AND THE WORLD 739

BIBLIOGRAPHY 778
SOURCES OF MAPS INCLUDED IN THE TEXT 811
INDEX 813

Tables

1 South-east Asia: selected temperature and rainfall figures *page* 23
2 South-east Asia: selected climatic data 24–5
3 Area, output and yield per acre of paddy 73
4 World rubber production and consumption, 1953 and 1961 166
5 World tin production and consumption, 1956 and 1961 167
6 South-east Asia: production of mineral oil, 1940–59 167
7 Population growth in South-east Asia, 1824–1958 174–5
8 South-east Asia: area and population 177
9 Ethnic Chinese and Indians in South-east Asia, 1956 181
10 South-east Asia: Europeans, Eurasians and Japanese 184
11 South-east Asia: currencies and estimated national incomes, 1959 190
12 Estimated foreign investments in South-east Asia before the Second World War 191
13 Overseas trade of South-east Asian countries, 1938, 1955 and 1960 200
14 Indonesia: main topographical divisions 209
15 Indonesia: selected temperature and rainfall figures 214
16 The indigenous peoples of Indonesia 240–3
17 Indigenous peoples of Indonesia professing Christianity, 1939 266
18 Netherlands Indies: export production, 1937 278
19 Java and Madura: harvested areas of indigenes' crops, 1916 and 1937 279
20 Netherlands Indies: estate acreage, 1937 280
21 Netherlands Indies: growth and density of population, 1905–30 290
22 Java and Madura: density of population, 1930 291
23 Indonesia: geographical distribution of co-operatives, end of 1956 and 1959 314
24 Indonesia: foreign trade by commodities 316
25 Indonesia: production and export of estate rubber 319
26 Indonesia: export of small-holders' rubber by principal production areas 320
27 Indonesia: rubber exports 321
28 Indonesia: purchase of copra by Jajasan Kopra 321
29 Indonesia: acreage and production of main export crops 323
30 Java and Madura: land classification, 1950 325
31 Indonesia: petroleum and petroleum products, production and trade 326
32 Indonesia: production and export of tin 329
33 Indonesia: main food crop production 332
34 Indonesia: indigenous agriculture 333
35 Indonesia: production, imports and exports of fish 335
36 Indonesia: livestock 336
37 Indonesia: transmigration, 1950–59 340
38 Indonesia: manufacturing industry at end of 1958 346
39 Indonesia: foreign trade by principal ports, 1938 and 1959 347
40 Indonesia: railways, track miles in use 353
41 Indonesia: overseas trade by countries 356–7
42 Indonesia: education 358

43 Indonesia: population, 1954 and 1959 *page* 367
44 Indonesia: population by ethnic origin, 1954 384
45 Indonesia: population by religion, 1954 384
46 Indonesia: towns with over 50,000 inhabitants, 1961 388
47 West New Guinea: overseas trade, 1955 and 1957 402
48 Mainland South-east Asia: selected temperature and rainfall figures 422
49 Burma: rice acreage and export, 1886–1960 436
50 Burma: Eight Year Plan allocation 449
51 Burma: land use, 1937–41 450
52 Burma: agricultural production, 1936–61 454
53 Burma: principal field crops 455
54 Burma: direction of rice exports 456
55 Burma: mineral production 459
56 Burma: production of petroleum and refined products 460
57 Burma: population of main towns, 1953 466
58 Burma: main ethnic and religious groups 468
59 Burma: overseas trade by commodities 479
60 Burma: overseas trade by countries 480–1
61 Thailand: population growth 506
62 Thailand: rice production and export 507
63 Thailand: acreage and production of chief crops 508
64 Thailand: overseas trade by countries 510–11
65 Thailand: direction of rice exports 512
66 Thailand: overseas trade by commodities 513
67 Thailand: manufacturing and processing industries 515
68 Thailand: population of main towns, 1947 519
69 Cochinchina: expansion of rice cultivation, 1880–1939 540
70 French Indochina: overseas trade, 1938 547–8
71 Northern Vietnam, Southern Vietnam, Cambodia and Laos: main ethnic groups 559
72 Northern Vietnam, Southern Vietnam, Cambodia and Laos: selected production data 576
73 Southern Vietnam, Cambodia and Laos: land use 576
74 Cambodia, Southern Vietnam, Laos, Northern Vietnam: overseas trade 577–9
75 Malaya: selected temperature and rainfall figures 587
76 Malaya: Newbold's estimate of population, 1835–9 596
77 Malaya: land use 606
78 Federation of Malaya: rubber production 611
79 Malaya: employment 623
80 Malaya: employment in manufacturing and processing industries 623
81 Federation of Malaya: channels of trade, 1953 629
82 Federation of Malaya: trade 630
83 Singapore: trade 631
84 Malaya: major ethnic groups, 1947 and 1957 634
85 Malaya: Malaysian population, 1947 637
86 Malaya: Chinese population, 1947 640
87 Malaya: Indians and Pakistanis, 1947 644
88 Malaya: changing ethnic composition of population, 1931–57 646
89 Federation of Malaya: vital statistics, 1947, 1953 and 1955 647
90 Singapore: vital statistics, 1947, 1953 and 1955 647
91 Malaya: town and community, 1947 and 1957 649

TABLES

92	Malaya: population of principal towns	*page* 651
93	Federation of Malaysia; Singapore; and Brunei: population	684
94	Northern Borneo: selected data	685
95	Northern Borneo: trade	686
96	The Philippines: selected temperature and rainfall figures	694
97	The Philippines: agricultural production	711
98	The Philippines: land use	712
99	The Philippines: mineral reserves, and production, 1960	716
100	The Philippines: principal towns, 1960	722
101	The Philippines: religions, 1948	723
102	The Philippines: principal languages, 1937 and 1948	730
103	The Philippines: overseas trade by countries	732
104	The Philippines: overseas trade by commodities	733
105	The Philippines: manufacturing industry, 1953–8	734
106	Pre-war trade of South-east Asian countries with certain other countries	753
107	Post-war trade of South-east Asian countries with certain other countries	754
108	International aid to South-east Asia	756–9

Maps

1 South-east Asia and neighbouring lands *page* 4
2 Monsoon Asia: distribution of population 6
3 South-east Asia: structure 13
4 South-east Asia: relief 18
5 South-east Asia: pressure and surface winds 30
6 South-east Asia: annual rainfall 35
7 South-east Asia: climatic pattern 40
8 South-east Asia: biogeographical limits 44
9 South-east Asia: religions of indigenous peoples 97
10 South-east Asia: languages of indigenous peoples 99
11 South-east Asia: political divisions, mid 8th century, A.D. 104
12 South-east Asia: political divisions, late 11th century, A.D. 111
13 South-east Asia: political divisions, late 15th century, A.D. 118
14 Indian Ocean: seasonal winds affecting historic sailing routes 129
15 Indian Ocean: Portuguese possessions and sailing routes, 16th century 129
16 Pacific Ocean: sailing routes used by Spaniards, 16th–18th centuries 132
17 Indian Ocean: Dutch East India Company's possessions and sailing routes, 17th–18th centuries 132
18 Mainland South-east Asia: expansion of European influence in the 19th century 150
19 South-east Asia: economic development 170
20 South-east Asia: distribution of population 178
21 South-east Asia: distribution of Chinese population 180
22 South-east Asia: shipping routes 186
23 South-east Asia: air routes 188
24 Growth of Japanese trade in Eastern Asia 196–7
25 Indonesia: orientation map 207
26 Indonesia: vegetation 212–13
27 Sumatra: geology 218
28 Sumatra: relief 219
29 Borneo: relief 222
30 Java: geology 224
31 Java: relief 225
32 Java: morphology 226–7
33 Celebes: relief 231
34 West New Guinea: relief 233
35 Indonesia: regional languages 246
36 Indonesia: religions 250
37 Indonesia: indigenous states, 17th century 253
38 Indonesia: expansion of Dutch influence 257
39 Java: rice-land and forest 276–7
40 Java: chief crops, 1923 282

41 Indonesia: major Dutch administrative divisions *page* 299
42 Three Javan towns: Djakarta, Surabaja, Semarang 302–3
43 Indonesia: agriculture 318
44 Indonesia: minerals 327
45 Java: transport and production 345
46 Sumatra: roads, railways and towns 348
47 Borneo: roads and towns 349
48 Celebes: roads and towns 351
49 Bali and Lombok: roads and towns 352
50 Eastern Lesser Sundas: roads and towns 352
51 Indonesia: shipping routes 354
52 Indonesia: air routes 354
53 Indonesia: major administrative divisions under the federal system 363
54 Indonesia: major administrative divisions, 1950 365
55 Indonesia: strength of political parties in 1955 elections 374
56 Indonesia: major administrative divisions, 1960 383
57 West New Guinea: products and roads 397
58 West New Guinea: new roads suggested by J. Winsemius 397
59 West New Guinea: air routes 400
60 Mainland South-east Asia: relief 408
61 Mainland South-east Asia: drainage 410
62 Mainland South-east Asia: evolution of drainage, according to J. W. and C. J. Gregory 411
63 Mainland South-east Asia: vegetation 427
64 Burma: natural regions 431
65 Situation of Rangoon 440
66 Burma: rice-land 453
67 Burma: economic development, 1954 458
68 Burma: languages 470
69 Burma: major administrative divisions, 1960 475
70 Thailand: natural regions 485
71 Thailand: roads and railways, 1955 494
72 Thailand: rice-land 498
73 Bangkok 520
74 Thailand: political 524
75 Indochina: natural regions 530
76 Indochina: rivers and railways 536
77 Indochina: economic development 543
78 Indochina: roads 551
79 Indochina: Roman Catholic Church, 1954 558
80 Indochina: languages 563
81 Indochina: political divisions, 1960 568
82 Malaya: geology 584
83 Malaya: relief 586
84 Malaya: political divisions, 1832–1942 594
85 Malaya: rice-land, actual and potential 605
86 Malaya: land use 612
87 Malaya: railways 618
88 Malaya: roads 620
89 Malaya: communal distribution, 1947 635
90 Malaya: Malay reservations 639

MAPS

91 Malaya: urbanization and community, 1911–1947 *page* 650
92 Singapore island 652
93 Northern Borneo: relief 664
94 Northern Borneo: ethnic groups 667
95 Northern Borneo: roads and railways 667
96 Northern Borneo: land use 671
97 Northern Borneo: political divisions 682
98 Federation of Malaysia; Singapore; and Brunei: population by community 688
99 The Philippines: relief 692
100 The Philippines: climatic types 696
101 The Philippines: economic development 707
102 The Philippines: roads and railways 718
103 The Philippines: shipping routes 720
104 The Philippines: air routes 721
105 Manila 723
106 The Philippines: languages 728
107 South-east Asia: imperial alignments, 1939 740
108 South-east Asia: political alignments, 1961 740
109 South-east Asia: strategic alignments, 1954–62 750
110 South-east Asia: A.S.A. and the Federation of Malaysia, as originally proposed in 1962 773

PART I

South-east Asia as an Entity

CHAPTER I

The Personality of South-east Asia

It is only since the Second World War that the term South-east Asia[1] has been generally accepted as a collective name for the series of peninsulas and islands which lie to the east of India and Pakistan and to the south of China. Nor is it altogether surprising that the West should have been slow to recognize the need for some such common term for this area, which today comprises Burma, Thailand, Cambodia, Laos, Vietnam,[2] the Federation of Malaysia,[3] Singapore, Brunei, Indonesia[4] and the Philippines. For, apart from the fact that all of these, with the solitary exception of Thailand, had long formed parts of different imperial groupings, British, French, Dutch or American, the inherent geographical unity of South-east Asia has always seemed somewhat negative in character.

This point is illustrated by two older terms which were sometimes used to describe the area in pre-war times, namely Further India and the Far Eastern Tropics. For according to these, South-east Asia was envisaged either as an eastward extension of India or as a tropical appendage of the Far East proper,[5] and in fact for centuries before the coming of the Europeans, as well as in more recent times, the region has tended to be overshadowed, in one way or another, by these two great neighbours, between which it forms one of the great cultural and political marchlands of the world.

Thus it was not until 1941–5, when the Japanese armies, in a manner strikingly reminiscent of the Napoleonic campaigns in 19th-century Europe, overran virtually the whole of South-east Asia and in so doing kindled to a new intensity the already smouldering fires of nationalism, that the Western powers became conscious of the region as an entity and, in establishing S.E.A.C.[6] for the purpose

[1] The current tendency to dispense with the capital S is unfortunate. South-east Asia is no less readily definable than e.g. the Middle East or the Far East.

[2] Now divided into Northern and Southern Vietnam. See Chapter 16.

[3] Which comprises the former Federation of Malaya, Sarawak and Sabah (formerly North Borneo). Singapore and Brunei are outside the Federation.

[4] Besides the territories of the Indonesian Republic, the Portuguese retain control over the eastern portion of Timor and until 1962 the Dutch administered West New Guinea. Whether the latter belongs geographically with South-east Asia or with the South-west Pacific is considered below, Chapters 2, 7 and 12.

[5] *I.e.* China, Japan, Korea and Formosa. There is much to be said for referring to this area as Eastern Asia, and similarly for using the term Southern Asia collectively to embrace India, Pakistan and Ceylon.

[6] *I.e.* South-East Asia Command. Apparently because the headquarters of S.E.A.C. were in Ceylon, some writers still persist in including the latter as part of South-east Asia, though there is little justification on any other grounds for doing so.

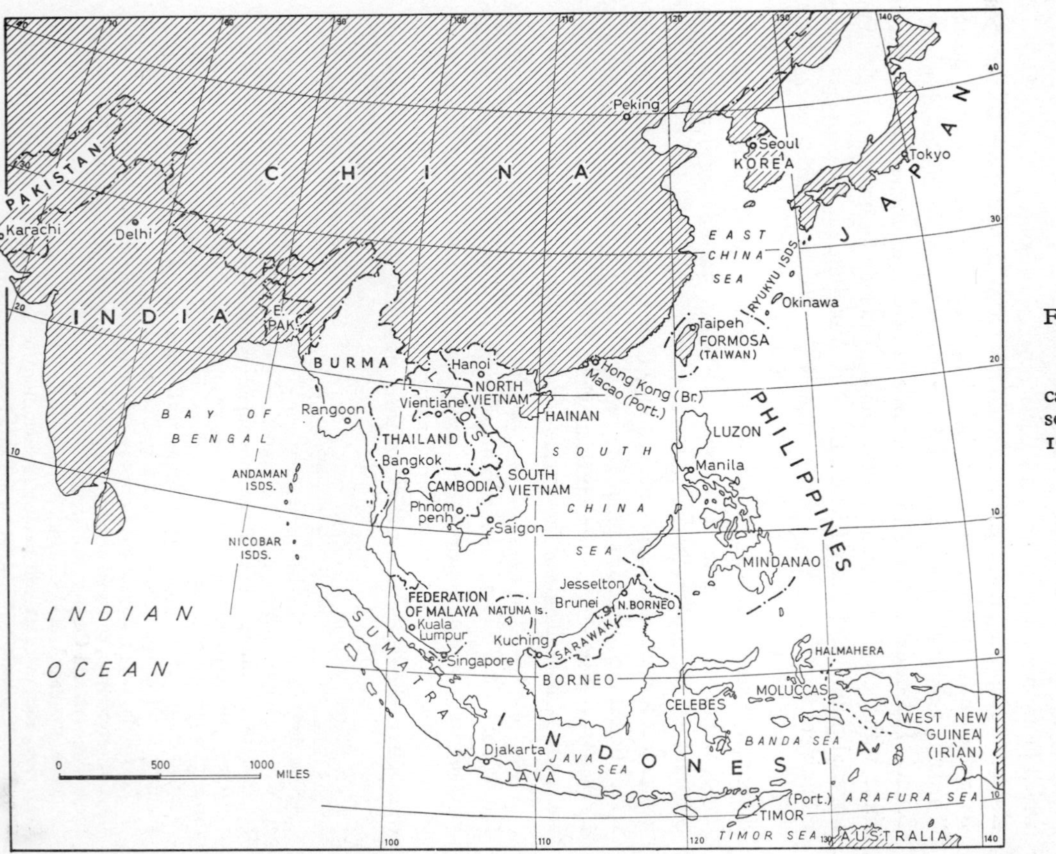

FIG. 1—South-east Asia and neighbouring lands

Note: West New Guinea came under Indonesian sovereignty on 1st May, 1963.

of tackling the immediate military problem, gave to the region the name by which it has since become known.

Nevertheless, from a geographical point of view South-east Asia must be accounted a distinctive region within the larger unity of the Monsoon Lands as a whole, and worthy to be ranked as an intelligible field of study on its own account. Fundamentally this individuality stems from its geographical position and its intrinsic physical character, and in these respects three main points are of decisive importance.

In the first place, whereas practically the whole of the Far East proper lies within the temperate zone and only half of the Indian sub-continent is in the strictest sense tropical, South-east Asia straddles the equator and is almost wholly comprised within the humid tropics. And even though the exclusion of northern India and most of Pakistan from the tropical category may be regarded as little more than a quibble, the fact remains that South-east Asia is markedly different climatically from both its neighbours, being at the same time much warmer than China and appreciably wetter even than the greater part of the Indian sub-continent.

Secondly, while the high mountain barrier along its northern border, which merges with the Tibetan plateau itself, made South-east Asia far more remote than were either India or China from the ancient centres of human dispersal in the continental interior, its position as a great maritime crossroads has exposed it to seaborne invasions, both of peoples and of cultures, deriving in early days mainly from these self-same neighbouring lands, and in recent centuries from the more distant Western world as well.

Thirdly, in striking contrast to the massive, indeed continental lineaments of India and China, South-east Asia is deeply interpenetrated by arms and gulfs of the sea, and further broken up topographically by its intricate and rugged relief. Moreover, to this complexity of outline the abundance of rainfall has added an exceptionally elaborate network of rivers, and in the great deltas of the largest of these, as also in some of the volcanically enriched islands of the archipelago, there exist extensive patches of cultivable land whose fertility is far above the average for the humid tropical zone.

The influence of these various natural traits is evident in many aspects of the region's human geography. Thus the difficulty of entry from the north has greatly restricted the volume—if not the variety—of human migration into South-east Asia overland, and this appears to be the primary reason why South-east Asia today is the only part of the Monsoon lands which is not as a whole seriously overcrowded,[7] even though some of its better endowed agricultural lands—notably Java—have belatedly filled up with astonishing rapidity during the last 150 years and are now densely populated.

[7] The average density of population in South-east Asia (126 to the square mile) is approximately one-third that of the Indian sub-continent (305) and of China proper (350), and one-sixth that of Japan (610). Note, however, the exceptional position of Northern Vietnam, see below, p. 179 and pp. 531–2.

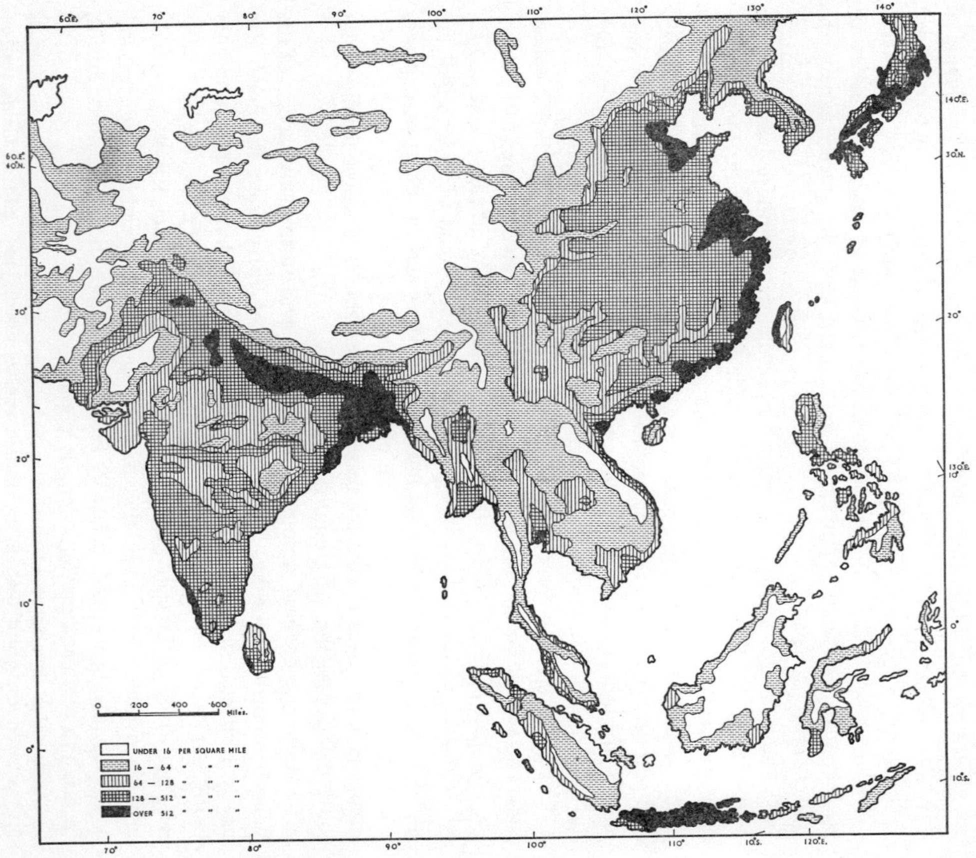

FIG. 2—Monsoon Asia: distribution of population

On the other hand, thanks to its character as a focus of convergence where land and sea routes meet, the region contains a remarkable diversity of peoples and cultures, ranging from the primitive Negrito hunters of the remoter forest interiors, through a wide variety of ethnic groups who still practise shifting tillage in many parts of both the mainland and the archipelago, to the highly skilled lowland rice cultivators who today form the majority populations in every one of its component states.[8]

So far as the lowland peoples are concerned, the ease of movement by sea has greatly facilitated contact of many kinds between the several lands bordering the South China Sea, along whose shores the main clusters are grouped 'like ants and frogs around a pool', as Plato once said of their counterparts in the classical Aegean.

Indeed, notwithstanding important differences, notably in language and religion, between the various national groups, the underlying cultural unity of these lowland peoples, evident in such matters as folklore, traditional architectural styles, methods of cultivation, and social and political organization, still constitutes perhaps the most important common denominator within the region.[9]

Moreover this similarity in culture is accompanied by a general similarity in physical and mental characteristics among the peoples concerned. Thus Burmans, Thais, Cambodians, Vietnamese, Malays, most Indonesians,[10] and Filipinos all show much the same predominantly Mongoloid cast of countenance, yellow-brown skin colour, and rather short stature, as well as a natural elegance of bearing and an apparently innate cheerfulness and good humour. At the same time, however, there is another side to this picture, and although it is impossible to pronounce with scientific accuracy upon the more elusive aspects of racial character, it would be even less scientific to ignore the widespread comments of foreign observers, fellow-Asians as well as Westerners, regarding the existence, if not the cause, of the characteristic insouciance and the addiction to an adagio tempo of living which prevail among these extremely likable people.

Whether or not these particular attributes should be ascribed to the effects of prolonged sojourn in an exceptionally enervating environment, there can be little doubt that they, along with the relative smallness of numbers and the historic sub-division into a series of separate river valley and island kingdoms, have played

[8] Malaya is an exception to this, but only because it has an unusually high proportion of commercial cultivation.

[9] Both the Chinese and Japanese have long been conscious of the unity of South-east Asia, and their traditional names for the region, respectively Nan Yang and Nan Yo, which both mean 'the southern seas', are perhaps indicative of the importance of the maritime element in that unity.

[10] *I.e.* such peoples as the Atjehnese, Menangkabaus, the coast Malays of Sumatra and Borneo, the Javanese, Sundanese, Madurese, Balinese, Makasarese, Menadonese, etc. See Chapter 3.

into the hands of more thrusting outsiders, who have been tempted to exert their influence over the region on account of its diverse natural wealth.

In the event, the nature of such influence has varied greatly, both from time to time and from place to place, and it is necessary to treat with the utmost caution such observations as those of K. M. Panikkar, who has stated that 'from the 1st century A.D. to the middle of the 15th century this entire area with the possible exception of Burma was politically within the Indian sphere'[11] or of Sun Yat-sen and Chiang Kai-shek, who have stressed the closeness of China's historic links with mainland South-east Asia.[12] Nevertheless, there undoubtedly is a sense in which the civilizations of the region were profoundly influenced by one or other—and indeed in most cases by both—of these neighbours, in the days before the lure of the Indonesian spice trade brought first the Muslims and then the Europeans into even more active participation in its affairs.

It is, however, the era of Western dominance[13] which has wrought the most drastic changes of all. Beginning in the island periphery in the 16th century, and extending to the mainland for the most part only during the 19th century, Western enterprise has transformed the political and economic life of the region and forged new and powerful ties between these formerly self-sufficient lands and the major industrial centres of Europe and the United States. Innumerable tin and other mines, huge petroleum wells and refineries, and vast areas of plantations devoted to the production of a wide range of export crops have been established, and roads and railways built to link them with the great port cities which have become the new foci of political and economic power.

It is in these essentially alien cities, where opulence and squalor stand cheek by jowl, the imposing if often brash Western architecture of the European quarter contrasting starkly with the rickety slum tenements nearby, and both seeming equally divorced from the simple palm-fringed fishing villages dotted along the adjacent coasts, that the difference between old and new is displayed in its most glaring colours. But elsewhere there remain great areas where the imprint of the West is far less in evidence, and the traditional self-sufficient way of life continues apparently but little changed. For Western activity has been highly selective geographically, and economic development on a major scale is restricted to a relatively few localities, mostly close to the coast, and usually possessing other significant advantages as well.

But the indigenous populations have also been by-passed in another and more serious sense. For since, at least until recently, they evinced no desire to work regular hours for fixed wages in foreign-owned concerns, many of the latter preferred to rely on immigrant Chinese or Indian[14] labour, and this has led to a

[11] Panikkar, K. M. (A), p. 1. [12] Sun Yat-sen, pp. 34–5 and Chiang Kai-shek, p. 770.
[13] Panikkar, K. M. (C).
[14] In this connexion the term Indian refers to immigrants (or their descendants) from either India or Pakistan.

massive influx of these more astute and hard-working foreigners, many of whom have subsequently risen high in the economic and social scale. In this way, therefore, the age-old process of ethnic diversification has been continued, albeit at a newly accelerated pace, during the last hundred years and, with a total population of some twelve million Chinese and nearly two million Indians, the resultant plural societies, which are found in every country in South-east Asia, form yet another feature which helps to differentiate the region as a whole from the rest of the monsoon lands.

Tropical and maritime, focal but fragmented, ethnically and culturally diverse, plural alike in economy and society, and demographically a low-pressure area in an otherwise congested continent,[15] South-east Asia clearly possesses a distinctive personality of its own and is more than a mere indeterminate borderland between India and China. Nevertheless, the extent to which it has traditionally been overshadowed by its neighbours shows no sign of diminishing. On the contrary, the withdrawal of the Western powers from the region has been followed by a notable growth of Chinese, Indian and Japanese interest in it, and it is an open question whether the newly independent states of South-east Asia will be able to maintain their independence, or whether they will one day fall like the celebrated row of dominoes, before the advent of some new Asian imperialism.

For the distinctiveness which we have recognized in South-east Asia resides in its common diversity rather than in any closely-knit unity, and although we may see a certain anology between South-east Asia and the classical Aegean lands, it is surely the parallel with the latter's Balkan hinterland which is of greater relevance today.[16] Alike in South-east Asia and in South-eastern Europe, internal stability has been impaired as a result of topographical fragmentation and of a geographical position which has encouraged repeated invasions and repeated attempts by external powers to control the all-important 'Straits'.[17] Thus both areas bristle with minority problems, as group after group of lesser peoples have sought refuge in the hills from the attacks of the more powerful plainsmen; and both have been the scenes of innumerable internecine conflicts, bitter memories of which are enshrined in the folk legends which too often pass for history among their peoples, and in consequence pose almost insurmountable obstacles to effective regional collaboration, however desirable this may appear on purely logical grounds.

But it is in respect of external relationships, and in particular of the possible threat of being crushed between the conflicting pressures of the two great neighbours, that the analogy may seem to assume its most portentous significance for the decades that lie ahead. Admittedly, analogies of this kind should not be pressed too far. Thus it would be difficult to imagine a more peaceful and co-operative neighbour than India has striven in recent years to be, and although

[15] The reference here is strictly to what S. K. Datta has called 'Asiatic Asia', *i.e.* the monsoonal half of the continent.

[16] Cf. Broek (D).

[17] The analogy may well be extended to take in the position and character of Istanbul and Singapore in relation to the Bosporous and the Straits of Malacca respectively.

more uncertainty may be felt about the intentions of China, there is reason to believe that its immediate preoccupation is primarily with its own vast economic and social problems.

Nevertheless, if an uncontrollable rate of natural increase should in the future render these problems incapable of acceptable solution, the fateful cry for more *lebensraum* may be raised once again as the prelude to a new and momentous *Drang nach dem Süden*. In the meantime, therefore, it must be hoped that the newly independent states will succeed in stamping out the widespread lawlessness and corruption which still remain in some of them as legacies of the momentous upheavals of the 1940s. For only if this is done will it be possible effectively to raise the living standards of their peoples, to check the drift to further Balkanization, and to prevent the region from becoming, as at times has seemed only too probable, the powder keg of Asia.[18]

SELECT BIBLIOGRAPHY

Broek (D)
Buss (C)
Clifford
Fisher (M) (N) (T)
Furnivall (B)
Hall (B)
Ireland
Mills *et al.*
Panikkar (A) (C)
Van Mook (B)
Wint (C)
Zelinsky

These sources have been supplemented by the atlas by Hudson and Rajchman. Although their relevance is in no way limited to the topics discussed in this introductory chapter, this seems the most appropriate place at which to acknowledge my general indebtedness to such pioneer regional geographies as those by Gourou (K), Lyde, and Stamp (A) on Asia, by Sion, and Spencer J. E. (A) on monsoonal Asia, by Dobby (H) on South-east Asia, and by Robequain (D) on the Malaysian realm.

[18] Note, for example, the comment of Lord Home, the British Foreign Secretary, as reported in *The Times* of 26 July, 1962: ". . . . when I went to the Seato conference it was not just a question of war between North Vietnam and Laos. War between the Seato alliance, including America, and the communist powers, including Russia and China, was so close that it could have turned on the spin of a coin."

CHAPTER 2

The Physical and Biogeographical Environment

As defined on page 3, South-east Asia extends from 28° 30′ N to 11° 00′ S and from 92° 20′ E to 134° 50′ E. Within these extreme limits, however, the sea exceeds the land in the ratio of roughly four to one, and while approximately half the total land surface of *c.* 1,571,000 square miles is accounted for by the single mass of the peninsular mainland, which covers some 795,000 square miles, the remaining 776,000 square miles are divided among the several thousand islands which comprise the two archipelagos of Indonesia and the Philippines.[1]

Diversity and complexity are thus the keynotes of the region's topography which calls for analysis before the related human geography can properly be understood. In this chapter, therefore, an attempt will be made first to examine the distinctive features of each of the major component elements in the physical geography of South-east Asia, and secondly to assess the opportunities and problems which these natural characteristics, both severally and in their totality, present to the peoples who live within the region.

I. STRUCTURE

In its geological structure as in other respects South-east Asia is pre-eminently a focal region, and to this must be attributed both its physiographic complexity and, in considerable measure also, its intricacy of outline. For it is here that the two great axes of Cretaceo-Tertiary folding, the approximately latitudinal Tethys and the predominantly longitudinal circum-Pacific series, come into conflict, and this in turn has given a distinctive alignment to the major relief features of the region as a whole.[2] Thus the majestic E/W sweep of the Himalayas abruptly gives place on the borders of Burma to the N/S trend of the Arakan ranges and, although in the south the great arcs of Indonesia again show a more or less latitudinal alignment through Java and the Lesser Sundas, the islands which lie to the north and east of these present a more controversial pattern as

[1] These figures exclude West New Guinea but include Northern Borneo and Portuguese Timor. If West New Guinea is included the eastern limit of the region is 141° 00′ E and its total area is 1,732,000 square miles, of which the archipelagos account for 937,000 square miles. Malaysia is a collective geographical name for Malaya and the island realms of Indonesia, Northern Borneo, Portuguese Timor and the Philippines. Note, however, the new and more restricted political connotation of this term in the Federation of Malaysia. See above, p. 3 note 3.

[2] See Stauffer, p. 21.

they approach the Pacific. Moreover, while the most recent 'earth storm' has already passed its climax on the mainland, this stage has probably not yet been reached in the Malaysian archipelago and active orogenesis is still continuing, notably in the vicinity of the Banda Sea.

In fact, as Gourou has observed, the whole South-east Asian region may be regarded as having been progressively consolidated from north-west to south-east, and while much the greater part of the mainland east of the central depression of Burma consists of pre-Tertiary formations, at least 70 per cent of the surface rocks of Indonesia are either Tertiary or Quaternary in age, and in Java the figure rises to over 99 per cent.[3]

The oldest portion of all, known to geologists as Indosinia, is a partially exposed fragment of pre-Cambrian folding, roughly comparable in age with the south China massif, the Indian Deccan and west-central Australia, which occupies much of Cambodia and southern Vietnam. It was around this ancient nucleus that the rest of South-east Asia was gradually built up by the formation of successive, and in the main roughly concentric, series of folds on its outer margins in subsequent geological times.

While fairly widespread Primary folding may be traced through the mountains of the Burma-Yunnan border, northern Vietnam and the Shan plateau, no structures of comparable age are found in the Indonesian archipelago proper. But Permo-Carboniferous folding led to the formation of Sahul-land, which thereafter constituted a relatively stable massif represented today by the southern portion of New Guinea and the Sahul shelf linking the latter to Australia, and related earth movements were probably responsible for initiating the great geosynclines between New Guinea and Borneo and along the western edge of the South-east Asian mainland.

Further and more extensive mountain building occurred in Mesozoic times, and structures of this age predominate in northern Vietnam and eastern Laos, over the greater part of Thailand and lower Burma, and throughout Malaya, Bangka, Belitung and south-western Borneo. As a result of this phase of orogenesis the mainland portion of South-east Asia was built outwards approximately to the position of the present-day Shan-Tenasserim highlands in the west, and to the respective eastern and northern margins of Sumatra and Java in the south-east and south. Thus in late Triassic times the great massif of Sunda-land (Fig. 3), much of it now covered by the shallow waters of the Malacca Straits and the South China Seas, first took shape as a coherent whole, and thereafter it has remained generally stable, though its outlines have been intermittently modified by marine transgression, notably in Upper Jurassic and Middle Cretaceous times, and again during the Tertiary mountain-building period when extensive sedimentary accumulation took place on its outer edges.

These inner and older structures of South-east Asia, from the pre-Cambrian Indosinian massif to the Mesozoic folds of other parts of the peninsula and of

[3] See Gourou (K), p. 286, and Robequain (D), pp. 9 and 176.

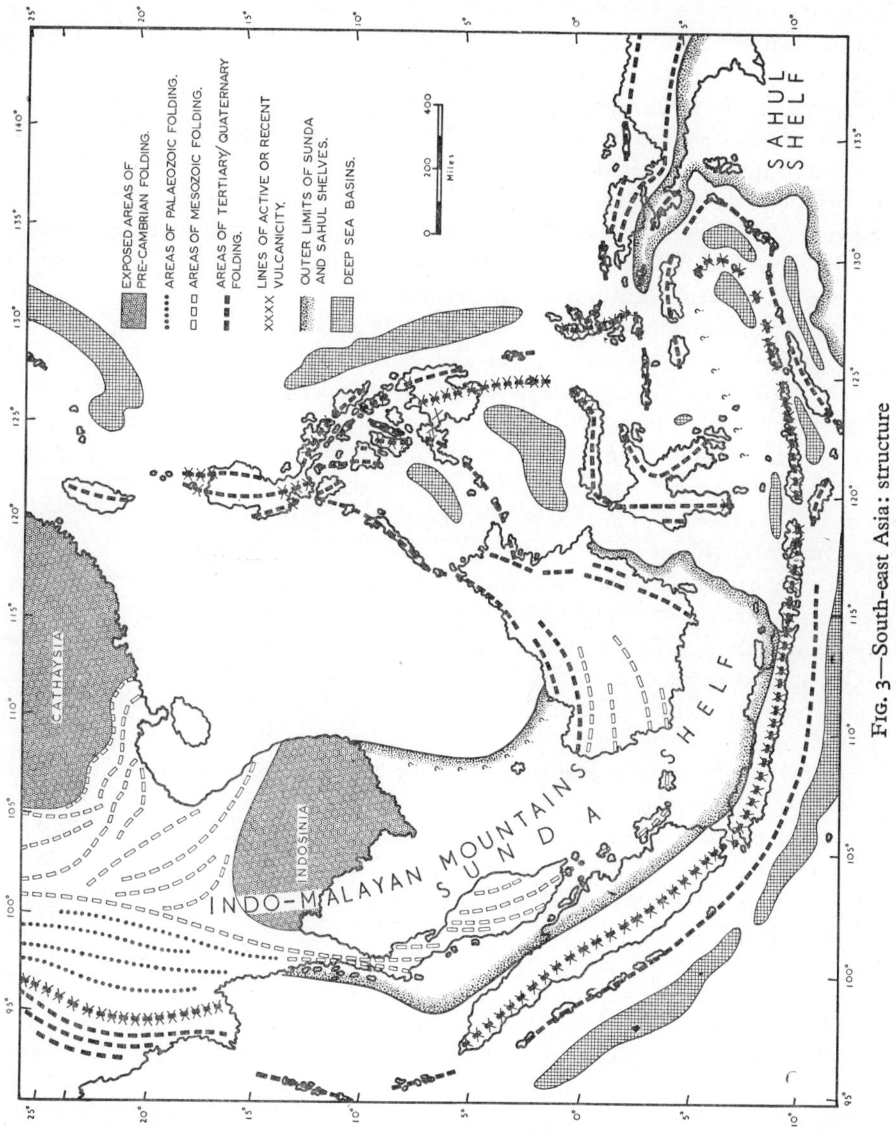

FIG. 3—South-east Asia: structure

its former southward extension into Sunda-land, are sometimes referred to collectively as the Indo-Malayan system, and indeed the contrast between the latter as a whole and the surrounding Tertiary/Quaternary zone to be described below is of fundamental importance in the geography of South-east Asia.

Despite differences in age there is a general consistency of trend throughout this older core, the structural grain on the mainland being almost everywhere longitudinal, while farther south a distinct south-easterly component prevails in some of the islands of the Sunda Shelf, and in south-western Borneo the trend is approximately latitudinal.

It was as a result of compressional movements between this ancient block on the one hand, and the somewhat similar Sahul/Australian massif and the stable floor of the Indian Ocean on the other, that the last major phase of folding took place in Cretaceo-Tertiary and more recent times.

During the Mesozoic era great thicknesses of sediments were laid down in the geosynclines to which reference has already been made. With the onset of the new 'earth storm' in late Cretaceous times, these relatively soft sedimentary rocks were quickly crumpled and raised to produce the first dry land in much of the outer margins of the archipelago, though it was not until well into Tertiary times, after this had been reduced by erosion and sagging, that the first of the two series of folds was formed which in large measure determine the relief of the region today.

Of these two, it is the earlier, dating generally from mid-Miocene times, which is responsible for what may be called the outer line of arcs, running through the western ranges of Burma, the Andamans and the lesser islands south-west of Sumatra, to Seram and Buru in the Moluccas, and probably continuing thence into eastern Celebes, Halmahera and the eastern ranges of the Philippines.

The inner and younger line, which originated in the late Pliocene, runs roughly parallel to its predecessor, and may be traced through the medial hills of Burma and the central axes of Sumatra, Java, and the main line of the Lesser Sundas, to Alor and Wetar. Beyond this point the same structural trend continues through the curve of islets surrounding the Banda Sea, though its continuity thence into western and northern Celebes and the Philippines is no more than conjectural.

Scattered at various points along this inner line, but with a particularly high concentration in the eastern third of Indonesia, are the region's 200 or more volcanoes, of which some 70 in Indonesia and a dozen in the Philippines have erupted within the last 150 years.[4] Likewise it is in and around eastern Indonesia and the Philippines that the most striking examples of recent isostatic movements occur.[5] The same areas also are much troubled by earthquakes, as indeed is the whole zone parallel to the inner arc from Sumatra to the Philippines, the epicentres in most cases lying under the deep seas nearby.

[4] Many of the Indonesian and Philippine volcanoes are extremely violent, as for example Krakatau in the Sunda Strait, whose eruption in 1883 caused 36,000 casualties, and Hibok-Hibok on Camiguin island, whose activity in 1948 caused 35,000 people to leave the island. See also Braak (B), pp. 75–9.

[5] *E.g.* the existence of Pleistocene coral reefs at altitudes of over 4,200 ft. in Timor and over 4,900 ft. in the Philippines. Robequain (D), p. 17.

II. RELIEF

The contrast between the older Indo-Malayan core and the peripheral Tertiary structures is reflected in the generally more subdued and characteristically erosional relief of the former and the bolder and more markedly tectonic lineaments associated with the latter. Even so, however, partly as a result of widespread uplift, notably in Tertiary times, the surviving residual ridges of the older core in many places attain heights of the order of 5–6,000 ft., and in the far north of Burma the relief is considerably more spectacular, though admittedly the highest points of all occur in the Tertiary ranges which branch off from the eastern Himalayas.

Equally fundamental in any consideration of the relief of South-east Asia, however, is a further and largely unrelated contrast, namely, that between the mainland and the insular halves of the region. For while the former of these, though less massive in outline than India or China, is nevertheless comparable in scale to peninsular Europe, the component units of the archipelago are all significantly smaller and among them only New Guinea, Borneo and Sumatra are larger than Great Britain.[6]

On account of its intermediate geographical position and, to some extent also, its transitional character between India and China, the mainland portion of South-east Asia has frequently been referred to as the Indochinese peninsula. But since the name Indochina provides a convenient label for the territories formerly united under French rule, it seems preferable to refer to the mainland collectively as the Indo-Pacific peninsula.[7] Moreover, this term has the further advantage of emphasizing the inter-oceanic character of the peninsula, which is of vital significance in respect of both its climate and of the role it has played as an obstacle to maritime communications.

Thus defined, the Indo-Pacific peninsula has a total length, from the northern tip of Burma to the Straits of Johore immediately opposite Singapore island, of some 2,000 miles. Between the tropic of Cancer and the Bight of Bangkok, *c.* 13° 30′ N, its mean breadth is approximately 750 miles, but farther south it dwindles to a mere 60 miles across the narrow stalk of peninsular Burma and Thailand,[8] and indeed to only half that figure at the Kra isthmus, before again broadening out to form the Malay peninsula which, reaching practically to the equator (Singapore 1° 17′ N), necessitates a vast southerly detour in the shipping routes between India and China.

[6] These three, however, are among the largest islands in the world. (New Guinea 303,092 square miles; Borneo 283,404 square miles; Sumatra 164,129 square miles. Other large islands include Celebes 72,890; Java 51,039; Luzon 40,420; Mindanao 36,537. *Cf.* Great Britain 88,745 and Honshu 88,622 square miles.)

[7] Lyde, p. 492, uses the term 'Indo-Pacific fan'.

[8] The peninsula is divided between Burma to the west and Thailand to the east, as far south as Victoria Point; south of that Thailand occupies the whole width until the Malayan border is reached.

In the north, where its breadth is greatest, the Indo-Pacific peninsula stems from the parent mass of continental Asia in the region of lofty ranges and plateaux which comprise the eastern margins of Tibet and the south-western ramparts of China. Thus it serves to reinforce the separation of China from the Indian Ocean, and the desire to outflank this barrier has been a major source of China's interest in Burma, which goes back many centuries before the time during the last Sino-Japanese war when the Chungking government sought to open the Burma Road as a lifeline to the West.

Throughout most of the Indo-Pacific peninsula the prevailing pattern of relief is one of alternate ridge and furrow, and this is particularly marked in the area north of 13° 30′ where the great master rivers – the Irrawaddy, Salween, Menam, Mekong and Song-koi – occupy roughly parallel structural depressions which they have widened and deepened and also, in their lower courses, floored with great thicknesses of alluvium, to produce the richest and most extensive lowlands of the area today.[9] For thanks to the combination of high temperatures with heavy and often torrential rain, the rivers in all parts of South-east Asia tend to carry extremely heavy loads of sediment, and particularly in the case of the Irrawaddy and the Mekong, which are comparable in size with the Hwang Ho and the Ganges, the formation of deltas has proceeded with great rapidity during historic times.[10]

Although the same ridge and furrow pattern continues south of latitude 13° 30′, the peninsula there is too narrow to engender really large rivers and even in Malaya the extent of alluvial land is relatively small. Likewise along both the eastern and the western margins farther north, the alignment of the main ranges parallel to the shore has been accompanied by a restricted development of coastal plain in Annam and Arakan respectively.

In general, therefore, except for the valleys of the master rivers, the relief is prevailingly upland in character and, alike in the steep and serrated ridges of the Arakan, the deeply dissected plateaux of the Shan/Laos borderlands and the Annamite Chain, and the residual ranges of interior Malaya, it presents serious barriers both to movement and settlement. For although the altitudes are rarely great except in the far north-west, the terrain is characteristically rugged and, more important, the uplands are for the most part densely forested and intensely malarious.

The foregoing observations regarding the negative character of the highlands apply with equal force in most parts of the insular realms to the south and east also, but in other respects the latter present very different patterns of relief.

Together the main island masses of Sumatra, Java and the lesser Sundas in

[9]For the reasons considered below, pp. 412–6, the Salween is an exception in this latter respect.

[10] It has been estimated that the surface level of the Chindwin basin is being reduced by 0·78 mm. a year, and similar rates have been recorded for some of the Javanese rivers. This is more than 100 times as rapid as in comparable parts of the Danube basin. See Dobby (H), p. 49, Stamp (C), pp. 350–1, and also below, p. 414.

the south-west and south, and the Philippines and New Guinea to the north and east, stand like huge breakwaters between the Indian and Pacific Oceans,[11] and the seas within these outer walls are significantly – if by no means uniformly – more placid than those outside them. While climatic factors[12] also help to produce this effect, the influence of topography is fundamental, and the extent to which the latter is broken up has likewise contributed to foster ease of movement within the archipelagos.

Despite the overall intricacy of outline, however, the geographical layout is in no sense haphazard, for all but the smallest islands take their alignment from one or more of the major arcs which traverse the region, and in most cases their relief is dominated, virtually from end to end, by rugged mountain backbones, capped in the volcanic zone by numerous majestic cones, many of which rise to well over 10,000 ft. above sea level.

Apart from the wide differences in size, moreover, there are other dissimilarities between the various island groups. In particular, a major distinction must be drawn between those such as Sumatra, Borneo, Java and New Guinea, which rest wholly or in part on the continental shelves (Sunda and Sahul) and have fairly extensive coastal lowlands fringing shallow seas, and those, between Bali and Borneo in the west and Aru and New Guinea in the east, which rise abruptly, like the isolated peaks of submerged mountain ranges,[13] from depths of anything from one to three thousand fathoms or more, and in many cases have virtually no coastal plain at all. The lowest sea floor recording within the archipelagos, namely 4,267 fathoms, occurs in the eastern part of the Banda Sea, but even greater deeps have been detected in the submarine troughs of the Indian and Pacific Ocean floors immediately to the south and west respectively of Indonesia and the Philippines, where the Java trench descends to over 4,320 fathoms and the Mindanao trench to 6,297 fathoms or over seven miles.

Clearly these exceptional depths are intimately related to the tectonic peculiarities of the two archipelagos, as has already been implied. But of greater significance to the human geography of the region are the factors which more directly affect navigation in these marginal seas. Thus the great coral reefs off the west coast of Sumatra and especially along the edge of the Sunda Shelf in the Makasar Straits and the Flores Sea have played an important part in deflecting shipping routes wherever possible to the generally coral-free seas covering the Sunda Shelf between Sumatra, Malaya, Java and Borneo. In the eastern part of the archipelago, coral atolls and minor reefs are again fairly common though here,[14] notably in the Lesser Sundas, the greatest navigational hazards are the

[11] The series is further reinforced by Borneo along the southern shore of the South China Sea. [12] See below, pp. 21–42.

[13] This should not be taken to imply that the islands are remnants of a former mountain chain which has foundered. On the contrary, the mountain system of which they form part is still only in an embryonic stage. See Brouwer (A), p. 49.

[14] Corals will grow only in clear water, with mean annual sea-level temperatures of at least 58° F, and furthermore cannot live below 25 fathoms. Thus the very thick coral

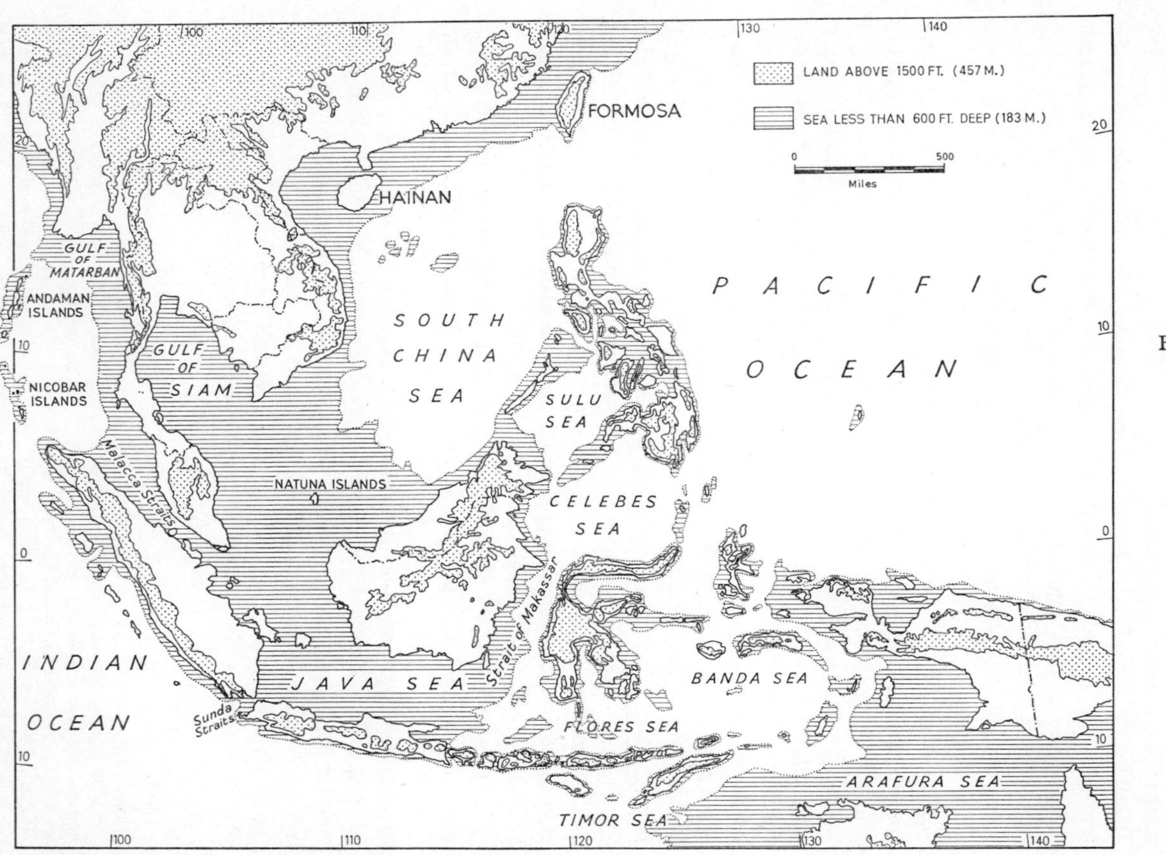

FIG. 4—South-east Asia: relief

swift currents, not infrequently exceeding 15 m.p.h., in the narrower straits between the islands.

As Fig. 3 shows, the great continental shelves of Sunda and Sahul respectively mark the geological limits of Asia and Australasia. Although now covered by from 20 to 45 fathoms of water, both of these areas stood above sea level before the melting of the Quaternary ice elsewhere caused the sea gradually to rise to its present position.[15]

This recent flooding of the continental shelves played a decisive part in shaping the outlines of the region as we know them today. Alike on the mainland and in the several islands of the shelves, wide estuaries were formed by the drowning of river mouths, though these were later at least partially filled in with huge quantities of detritus, deposited by the truncated rivers flowing into the shallow epicontinental seas. For the very process of drowning led to an increase in the rate of sedimentation, and along many of the shallower and less disturbed shores of the archipelago, to wit eastern Sumatra, western and southern Borneo, and south-western New Guinea, vast belts of swamps were built up.[16]

Indeed terrains of this kind constitute the greater part of the total lowland surface within the archipelago though, owing to their waterlogged character, they have hitherto been of far less significance for human settlement than the smaller but better drained and intrinsically more fertile alluvial terrains found in east-central Java, northern Sumatra, parts of the Lesser Sundas and some of the larger Philippine islands, notably Luzon.

Finally, in a wider sense, the flooding of the Sunda Shelf has been of decisive importance in determining the geographical character of South-east Asia as a whole. For in large measure this inundation has been responsible for the region's having a longer coastline, area for area, than any other part of the world of comparable size, with at least half the total surface, including most of the best agricultural lowlands, within 100–150 miles of tidewater. Were the sea once again to recede to its former level, South-east Asia would almost double its total area but, in thus becoming another vast limbless continental mass like Africa or tropical South America, its loss in accessibility would probably more than offset the gain in territorial extent.

This topographical discontinuity is not, however, the only respect in which

formations, to which reference has been made, imply that considerable changes – either eustatic or isostatic – have taken place in the relative positions of land and sea. Eustatic changes were the operative factor in the formation of the barrier reefs along the edge of the Sunda Shelf though on the main surface of that shelf there is too much silt to favour the growth of coral today. In the deeper seas farther east, on the other hand, the atolls rising from depths of 500–1000 fathoms or more provide unmistakable evidence of past subsidence of the sea floor. See Dobby (H), pp. 29–30, and Robequain (D), pp. 16–17.

[15] On the indirect effects of the Quaternary glacial period on South-east Asia, see Dobby (H), pp. 50–55, and Molengraaf, pp. 100–107.

[16] The western shore of Malaya shows a similar development, though on a more restricted scale, thanks to the powerful tidal scour there, and the greater depth of the sea off northern Java has helped still further to reduce the extent of the swamp belt there.

the physique of South-east Asia differs fundamentally from that of most other tropical lands. On the contrary, the proportion of its area which is accounted for by geologically youthful structures is strikingly high in comparison with the inter-tropical zones of both Africa and the Americas, much the greater part of which consists of ancient pre-Cambrian table-lands of considerable altitude and vast extent.

Important economic consequences follow from this difference, in respect of both mineral wealth and types of soil. The latter topic will receive more detailed treatment on pp. 50–53 so that here it must suffice to say that some of the recent volcanic ejecta in the Indies, as well as much of the alluvial material brought down by the great rivers of the mainland, go far to offset the otherwise widespread laterization which is responsible for the characteristically low fertility of most humid tropical soils.

So far as metallic minerals are concerned, regions of Tertiary folding are rarely so favourably placed as the older mountain systems where the deep-seated ore bodies have been rendered more accessible by prolonged denudation, and in South-east Asia most of the principal sources of metals lie within the Indo-Malayan mountain zone.[17] There, in addition to a variety of minerals of secondary economic importance, ranging from the silver and lead of the Shan plateau and the fairly widespread but small deposits of gold in eastern Malaya[18] to the anthracite coal of Tonkin and the high-grade iron ores of Cambodia and Malaya, the region of Mesozoic folding, stretching from Yunnan to the Sunda Shelf, contains the greater part of the world's known reserves of tin.[19] Moreover, a high proportion of this, though deriving originally from lodes located in the intrusive granitic cores of the ranges, has been redistributed in the form of vast alluvial spreads by the rivers flowing into the seas of the continental shelf as a result of the increased sedimentation described on page 19. Such deposits have the combined advantage of being easily worked and readily accessible from the coast, so that although lode tin is mined in many parts of the mainland from Indochina to eastern Malaya, it is the great zone of alluvial tin stretching from Tenasserim through peninsular Thailand and western Malaya to the Indonesian islands of Bangka, Belitung and Singkep which accounts for much the larger share of the output.

The only other South-east Asian mineral which compares in total value with tin is petroleum[20] and this, in contrast to the others already considered, is here associated with the younger geological structures, occurring for the most part in the gentler undulations between the main Tertiary folds and the older Indo-Malayan core. Beginning in the north in the central depression of Burma, the

[17] But there are others, *e.g.* in exposed portions of the basement complex in the Philippines.

[18] These gold deposits are of little significance today, though they played an important rôle in early historic times. See Wheatley (E), pp. 61–78.

[19] And also a considerable proportion of the tungsten.

[20] For some time now the total value of petroleum produced has exceeded that of tin.

series of oilfields continues through eastern Sumatra into northern Java. Thereafter the line splits up, with one branch extending through Seram into the Vogelkop ('Bird's head') of West New Guinea and the others following the southern, eastern and northern edges of Borneo. Again, in all these areas proximity to tidewater is an immense asset and, although the combined yield is nowadays only two per cent of the world total, the South-east Asian fields gain added significance from the absence of large scale production elsewhere in the Monsoon Lands.

Thus, both in its structure and in the related peculiarities of its topography and mineral resources, South-east Asia differs fundamentally from all other regions in similar latitudes, and the only approximate analogue which occurs anywhere else within the tropical belt is to be found in the islands and peninsulas of the Caribbean. In fact the parallel between these two regions is in many respects exceptionally close and, albeit on a smaller scale, the West Indies are characterized by the same youthfulness of structure and fragmentation of form which are so typical of their counterparts in the East.

Nor do the similarities end there, as more than one subsequent chapter will have occasion to point out. But in climate, notwithstanding their common maritime characteristics, the two are by no means identical, for while the Caribbean lies wholly on the northern margins of the tropics and is dominated by the NE trade winds, South-east Asia lies much farther to the south and is pre-eminently monsoonal.

III. CLIMATE

As a climatic term the word 'tropical' has unfortunately come to be used in two different ways and it is essential at the outset to make a clear distinction between them. The former of these usages, which corresponds more closely though by no means exactly with the literal meaning of the word,[21] refers simply to temperature, and is applied to all areas where the mean monthly figure does not fall below 64·4 F.[22] By this definition virtually the whole of South-east Asia, apart from north-eastern Indochina and the higher uplands generally, is rightly regarded as tropical.

But the term is also frequently used more narrowly to describe the type of climate found in those areas within the tropical belt, as defined above, which have neither the monotonously high temperature and humidity which are associated with the equatorial belt (that is approximately between 5° north and south) nor the intense aridity of the desert zone characteristic of the western continental margins between *c.* 15° and 30° (north and south), where the trade winds normally blow off the land throughout the year.[23] In this more restricted usage,

[21] Literally, the tropical belt is the whole zone lying between the tropics of Cancer and Capricorn, respectively 23° 30′ N and S.

[22] This is Köppen's usage. It may be compared with Austin Miller's limit of the 'hot' lands, *i.e.* those having a mean annual temperature of not less than 70° F.

[23] Only a small proportion of the trade-wind deserts lies within the tropics as defined by Köppen, but most is within the 'hot' belt as defined by Miller.

therefore, the 'tropical' climate, with a somewhat wider seasonal range of temperature and much greater variation in rainfall than the equatorial, forms one of the three major climatic types into which the world's hot lands may be subdivided. Of these three, the desert is not represented at all in South-east Asia, thanks to the region's position *vis-à-vis* the main mass of continental Asia and to the related monsoonality which, in its turn, significantly modifies the other two types as they occur here.

An account of the climate of a major world region often hinges on, and builds upon, a discussion of the atmospheric circulation over the area in question. But in South-east Asia the uncertainty that now attaches to some of the fundamental aspects of atmospheric behaviour almost precludes such a treatment. For in recent years various investigations have called in question both the underlying causes and the actual mechanism of equatorial and monsoonal circulations, and thus opened the way for new explanations of these features, or modifications of their classical interpretation.[24] In the account which follows, the main emphasis will be placed on the description and tentative explanation of those aspects of the observed climatic phenomena which are of greatest human significance.

With the exception of northern Vietnam in the north-eastern corner of the region, annual average sea-level temperatures over all parts of South-east Asia are remarkably close to 80°, and the only significant distinctions to note are concerned with the degree of seasonal variation which, though fundamentally a matter of latitude, is considerably modified by the regional disposition of sea and land. Near to the equator the annual range is rarely more than 3° or 4° and, as the Singapore figures (Table 1) illustrate, mean monthly readings fluctuate around 80° from January to December. But to the north and south of this, seasonal variation in temperature becomes progressively more apparent, and at Mandalay, *c.* 20° N, the monthly averages range from 70° in January to 90° in April. Admittedly, this is an inland station,[25] and Akyab on the coast in similar latitudes records a maximum of only 84° (also in April) while at Saigon farther south (10° 14′ N), but nevertheless by definition tropical rather than equatorial, the range is a mere 6°. But it is in the archipelago that the equalizing effect of the sea on temperature is most pronounced. Thus, Kupang in the corresponding (southern hemisphere) latitude to Saigon varies only from 76° to 80° and the great majority of stations in Indonesia show an even smaller annual range than this.

In fact, in equatorial latitudes the daily variation in temperature, usually of the order of 12–15°, is considerably greater than that between the seasons. To an important extent, moreover, the diurnal range itself varies throughout the year, normally showing its greatest amplitude during the driest months. Even so,

[24] For a full treatment of these problems see the authoritative textbook by Riehl, and the review by Palmer of tropical meteorology.

[25] Though, even so, its range is far less pronounced than in a continental interior station like Nagpur (in similar latitudes in the Indian Deccan) where the extreme monthly means are 68° and 95°.

TABLE I

SOUTH-EAST ASIA: SELECTED TEMPERATURE AND RAINFALL FIGURES

Station	*Jan.*	*Feb.*	*Mar.*	*Apr.*	*May*	*Jun.*	*Jul.*	*Aug.*	*Sep.*	*Oct.*	*Nov.*	*Dec.*	*Average*	*Total*
Singapore 1° N, 104° E	78	79	80	81	81	81	81	81	80	80	79	79	80	
10	8·5	6·1	6·5	6·9	7·2	6·7	6·8	8·5	7·1	8·2	10·0	10·4		92·9
Cameron Highlands 5° N, 101° E	65	65	67	67	67	66	66	66	66	65	65	64	66	
c. 4,500	6·0	5·2	6·4	12·3	10·5	5·0	4·8	7·8	8·4	12·9	12·1	9·7		101·1
Akyab 20° N, 93° E	70	73	79	83	84	82	81	81	82	82	78	72	79	
20	0·1	0·2	0·5	2·0	13·7	49·4	53·7	42·5	24·6	11·6	5·0	0·6		203·8
Rangoon 17° N, 93° E	77	79	84	87	84	81	80	80	81	82	80	77	81	
18	0·2	0·2	0·3	1·4	12·1	18·4	21·5	19·7	15·4	7·3	2·8	0·3		99·6
Saigon 11° N, 107° E	79	81	84	85	84	82	81	82	81	81	80	79	82	
near S.L.	0·7	0·1	0·6	1·9	8·7	13·1	12·1	11·1	13·5	10·7	4·5	2·5		79·5
Kupang 10° S, 124° E	78	79	80	80	80	77	76	78	79	80	79	78	79	
48	22·5	14·2	4·2	1·6	0·1	1·7	0·1	0·1	0·1	7·1	4·1	10·5		56·3
Manila 15° N, 120° E	78	79	81	83	84	83	82	82	81	80	79	77	81	
47	0·9	0·6	0·9	1·2	5·1	9·9	16·9	16·3	14·0	7·7	5·8	2·3		81·6
Hanoi 21° N, 106° E	62	62	67	73	80	83	83	83	81	78	71	66	74	
near S.L.	1·2	1·6	1·8	2·8	7·6	9·6	11·4	12·5	12·0	4·4	2·4	1·2		68·6
Lashio 23° N, 98° E	60	63	71	75	77	77	76	76	76	73	66	61	71	
2,802	0·3	0·3	0·6	2·2	6·9	9·8	12·0	12·7	7·8	5·7	2·7	0·9		61·9
Luang Prabang 20° N, 102° E	69	73	78	82	84	83	82	82	82	79	74	70	78	
942	0·6	0·7	1·2	4·3	6·4	6·1	9·1	11·8	6·5	3·1	1·2	0·5		51·5
Victoria Point 10° N, 99° E	79	81	83	84	81	80	79	79	79	79	80	79	80	
147	0·3	0·1	1·3	3·9	17·1	28·3	30·0	25·5	25·9	18·0	5·8	2·7		158·9

NOTE: For each station the position in latitude and longitude is followed by the height in feet above sea-level. The upper line of figures consists of mean temperatures in degrees Fahrenheit. The lower line of figures consists of rainfall totals in inches. Throughout this book temperature readings are given in degrees Fahrenheit and rainfall in inches.

the overall variation is much less than in the outer margins of the tropics. The absolute extremes ever recorded in Djakarta are respectively 96° and 65° but in parts of Luzon during the dry season figures of 100° and 60° are both fairly common,[26] while in the dry zone of Burma the range is still greater and temperatures of 105° are by no means rare immediately before the arrival of the SW monsoon.

The effect of altitude on temperatures is naturally more pronounced, for since

[26] Robequain (D), p. 29.

TABLE 2

SOUTH-EAST ASIA: SELECTED CLIMATIC DATA

A. Temperatures: Mean daily maxima and minima, and mean daily ranges.

Akyab	Max.	Min.	Range	*Bhamo*	Max.	Min.	Range
Jan.	81	59	22	Jan.	76	47	29
Apr.	90	75	15	Apr.	93	67	26
July	84	77	7	July	88	76	12
Mandalay				*Tavoy*			
Jan.	82	55	27	Jan.	89	65	24
Apr.	101	77	24	Apr.	94	75	19
July	93	78	15	July	83	74	9
Hanoi				*Luang Prabang*			
Jan.	68	56	12	Jan.	82	56	26
Apr.	82	69	13	Apr.	96	69	27
July	91	78	13	July	90	74	16
Qui Nhon				*Saigon*			
Jan.	77	69	8	Jan.	89	70	19
Apr.	86	75	11	Apr.	95	76	19
July	93	79	14	July	88	75	13
Nakhorn Ratsima				*Manila*			
Jan.	91	60	31	Jan.	86	69	17
Apr.	98	74	24	Apr.	93	73	20
July	92	74	18	July	88	75	13
Singapore				*Cameron Highlands*			
Jan.	86	73	13	Jan.	71	56	15
Apr.	88	75	13	Apr.	74	57	17
July	88	75	13	July	73	55	18
Pontianak				*Makasar*			
Jan.	87	74	13	Jan.	84	74	10
Apr.	89	75	14	Apr.	86	74	12
July	89	74	15	Aug.	87	69	18
Ambon				*Kupang*			
Jan.	88	76	12	Jan.	87	75	12
Apr.	86	76	10	Apr.	89	73	16
July	81	74	7	July	88	70	18
Oct.	85	74	11	Sept.	81	71	10

TABLE 2 (continued)

B. Relative Humidities.

Mandalay	08.00 hrs.	18.00 hrs.
Jan.	79	52
Mar.	53	31
Apr.	55	33
Aug.	83	72

Tavoy	09.00 hrs.	18.00 hrs.
Jan.	87	67
Apr.	83	73
July	93	91

Luang Prabang	10.00 hrs.	16.00 hrs.
Jan.	80	59
Apr.	67	49
Aug.	80	76

Singapore	09.00 hrs.	15.00 hrs.
Jan.	82	78
July	79	72

Pasuruan	06.00 hrs.	12.00 hrs.
Jan.	91	64
Aug.	82	49

Ambon	06.00 hrs.	14.00 hrs.
Jan.	89	66
July	90	76

Bhamo	08.00 hrs.	18.00 hrs.
Jan.	95	75
Apr.	75	47
Aug.	94	83

Hanoi	10.00 hrs.	16.00 hrs.
Jan.	78	68
Apr.	83	75
Aug.	82	75

Qui Nhon	10.30 hrs.	16.30 hrs.
Jan.	83	82
Apr.	77	81
Aug.	61	63

Pontianak	06.00 hrs.	12.00 hrs.
Jan.	93	67
July	93	63

Kupang	08.00 hrs.	14.00 hrs.
Jan.	85	71
Aug.	62	44

Padang	06.00 hrs.	12.00 hrs.
Jan.	88	67
July	85	62

a rise of 1,000 ft. normally entails a decrease in temperature of approximately 3°, it follows that a considerable proportion of South-east Asia has average temperatures below the tropical norm. Even so, as the hill stations of Baguio in the Philippines and Cameron Highlands in Malaya both show, the seasonal rhythms remain appropriate to the latitude and even at 3–4,000 ft. temperatures are still by no means cool. Moreover, although slight seasonal frosts are common from the Shan plateau northwards and in some upland regions of Indonesia and the Philippines, snow is completely unknown except on a few summits in northern

Burma and New Guinea, and for the most part ruggedness of relief rather than decreasing temperatures is the main physical factor[27] responsible for modifications in land use in the highlands of South-east Asia.

Rainfall

As with temperature so also with rainfall, most readings in South-east Asia are distinctly high, much the greater part receiving over 60 in. annually, and considerable areas two, three or even four times that amount. Again a distinction should be made between those aspects of the pattern which exhibit broad similarity over South-east Asia as a whole and others which manifest characteristic regional differences within it. Thus variations in the total amount of rainfall are usually explicable primarily in terms of local geography, with very high and relatively low readings found in fairly close proximity on the opposite sides of the outer ranges alike of Burma, Indonesia and the Philippines, but over the region as a whole a major distinction exists between the rain-at-all-seasons of the equatorial zone and the characteristic alternation of wet and dry seasons in the areas lying respectively to the north and south of it.

In general, however, the air is extremely damp, and over vast areas its vapour content varies little from day to night or from one season to another. Thus the concentration of water vapour in the air ranges only from 20 to 21 grammes per cubic metre at Pontianak, and from 19 to 24 at Saigon, which is about twice the amount found over southern England in summer. The relative humidity is accordingly high, and its diurnal variation almost the reverse of that shown by the temperature, the values exceeding 90 per cent at night and dropping during the day, though rarely below a level of 65 to 75 per cent.

A dry subsident type of air mass is present over parts of the region at certain times and both absolute and relative humidities are then much lower, the latter showing averages of barely 30 to 40 per cent in the afternoons during the spring in the central districts of Burma and Thailand, and of about 50 per cent in southern Indonesia during the E monsoon. Except in such conditions the cloudiness is also fairly high, yet the annual duration of sunshine exceeds 2,000 hours over virtually the whole of the region and rises slightly above 3,000 hours at Kupang. The northern part of Vietnam stands rather apart in this as in other respects, Phulan recording not quite 1,700 hours of sunshine, a total exceeded by some stations on the south coast of England.

The effects of the dampness of the air both on bodily discomfort and in the form of the damage which it causes to almost every kind of fabric are the most unpleasant features of the climate during the rainy seasons of the year. Thus if clothing is to be preserved for more than a few weeks it will need frequent and systematic airing, and elaborate care is required to prevent fungoid growths in footwear and the sticking together of postage stamps in one's wallet. Wet-bulb temperatures provide perhaps the simplest guide to human comfort, at

[27] Cultural factors are also relevant. See below, Chapter 3.

any rate in the absence of solar radiation, strong wind and air conditioning. Over equatorial South-east Asia the wet-bulb temperatures at sea-level remain above 74° throughout the year. The highest wet-bulb temperatures occur in somewhat higher latitudes, average values remaining above 78° for a period of four to five months on the northern part of the Burmese coast and rising to 80° at Hanoi during July and August.

Notwithstanding the generally high total precipitation, both seasonal and regional variations in its amount are altogether greater than those in temperature, and their effects on land use are, in several cases, of fundamental importance.

The precipitation is derived in four main ways. First, and particularly in equatorial latitudes, the convectional overturning of air gives rise to cumulo-nimbus clouds, often extending through the entire depth of the troposphere, which produce heavy downpours. While local rainstorms are generally due to isolated cumulo-nimbus, these clouds are often observed to form well-defined bands stretching over considerable distances, resulting from the development of convergence lines. These sometimes form along the boundary between two air streams but may also arise in a homogeneous current. In areas of light winds they may persist with little change of position for periods of several days. Some convergence lines develop owing to the disturbance of the regional wind field caused by the growth of a land and sea breeze circulation, the rain falling principally over the land by day and over the sea at night. Recent work suggests that the rain-cooled downdraught from a cumulo-nimbus plays a significant rôle in propagating these disturbances, which are an important feature of Malayan and Indonesian weather, by undercutting the warmer air ahead. The line squalls known in Malaya as Sumatras probably originate in this way.[28]

Cyclonic disturbances of varying intensity constitute a second source of rainfall. These depressions, unlike those of middle latitudes, do not arise from the interaction of warm and cold air currents and are non-frontal. Their growth is strongly influenced by events in the upper portion of the troposphere where, in contrast to the conditions obtaining outside the tropics, the circulation tends to be more disturbed than in the lower layers of the atmosphere. Depressions frequently develop over areas where the surface circulation is weak, the cyclonic flow being most prominent at higher levels. They are observed in the easterly current of the western Pacific, and both along the edges and in the main body of the SW monsoon, the direction of movement in all these cases being predominantly from east to west.[29] While many of these cyclonic eddies give rise only to moderately disturbed weather, others grow into mature tropical cyclonic storms or typhoons, the most violent of all the meteorological phenomena experienced in the tropics, bringing torrential rain and destruction to the areas over which they pass.[30]

While the rainfall associated with the monsoonal air currents, to which

[28] See Watts (A), Chapter 5, and (B), pp. 59–61.

[29] See Palmer (A), p. 873.

[30] See below, pp. 38–39.

reference has already been made, occurs partly as a result of activity along convergence lines and in connexion with cyclonic eddies, orographic, and probably also dynamic, influences are mostly of far greater significance. The precipitation is extremely heavy wherever the monsoonal stream has to rise over a range of hills lying directly in its path because the air arrives in a state of convective instability. Its surface layers have acquired much moisture during their long transit over warm seas but the vapour content decreases fairly sharply with height so that, when the air is lifted, a much greater quantity of latent heat is released by condensation in the lower than in the upper layers of the rising mass. Forced ascent over a relief obstacle thus serves to steepen the lapse rate, producing thereby an unstable vertical temperature distribution in the rising air so that convection is either initiated or greatly strengthened.

The large amounts of rainfall resulting from this process are a direct consequence of the warm air's rapidly diminishing capacity to hold water vapour as it is cooled. Thus the amount of water condensed out of a given volume of air saturated with water vapour when it is cooled by one degree is three times greater with an initial temperature of 77° than with one of 40°.

The occurrence and intensity of rainfall are closely related to the strength of upward vertical motion, which in turn is associated with the presence of convergence in the lower layers of the atmosphere. The controlling influence which upper tropospheric flow may exert on the pattern of convergence and divergence has become increasingly evident, and some reference to the processes involved and their relation to surface climate would appear to be indicated. Two aspects of the question will be examined.

During the northern hemisphere summer the SW monsoon is overlain by an easterly flow, disturbed periodically by the passage of troughs of low pressure and ridges of high pressure. These irregularities give rise to wave-like motion in the current. Riehl[31] invoked Rossby's law, which states that a column of air tends to conserve the ratio of its absolute spin about a vertical axis to its depth, to show that, in such a flow, convergence must take place in areas where the air gains cyclonic rotation and moves towards higher latitudes, while divergence will occur where the motion becomes increasingly anticyclonic and is directed towards the equator. As the maintenance of a divergence field would lead, in the absence of any compensating effect, to much greater variations of surface pressure than are ever observed, areas of upper-air divergence must be situated above those characterized by low-level convergence and rainfall at the ground. The pattern of divergence that develops in connexion with wave-like motion in the upper easterlies can thus assume considerable significance and monsoon depressions and other disturbances may be closely related to their irregularities.

The second aspect of upper tropospheric flow to be considered relates to the vertical circulations associated with jet streams.[32] The latter may be visualized as rather constricted tubes of air moving at very much higher speeds than the

[31] See Riehl, Chapter 9. [32] See Riehl, Alaka, Jordan and Renard.

atmospheric layers around them, the velocity in the core of the tube frequently exceeding 100 knots. A jet stream may be divided into three sections: an entrance zone, a central portion with a maximum transverse pressure gradient, and an exit zone. As air moves into the entrance zone of the tube it encounters a steepening pressure gradient and is forced to accelerate. This it does by moving somewhat towards low pressures which, in the northern hemisphere, lie to the left of the jet axis looking downwind. Accordingly air drifts horizontally towards the left of the entrance zone and this in turn brings about rising motion to the right, and sinking motion to the left of the jet axis. On flowing out of the tube the air meets a weakening pressure gradient and decelerates by moving towards higher pressures. In the exit zone, therefore, the horizontal drift is directed towards the right and the vertical circulation is reversed, air ascending into the jet stream to the left of the axis and sinking to the right.

The vertical motion need only amount to a small fraction of the horizontal motion to have a very considerable influence on the distribution of rainfall, as it is estimated that a sustained upward movement of 1 m.p.h. is enough to lead to appreciable precipitation. During the northern summer an easterly jet stream is found over southern Asia at a height of about 50,000 feet.[33] Its influence on the surface climate of the area is considered below in the context of the regional circulation.

The air which circulates over South-east Asia is drawn from many different quarters including China, India, Australia, the Pacific and the Indian Ocean, and to this source of difficulties there must be added those raised by the nature of flow in low latitudes. The air movements over the region are, not surprisingly, imperfectly understood and only a tentative summary of their principal features can be attempted.

During the northern hemisphere winter, parts of South-east Asia come under the influence of the strong northerly flow, which develops on the eastern flank of the intense though shallow anticyclone formed over Siberia and Mongolia as a result of the excessive radiational cooling of the Asian land mass. This air stream, initially dry and bitingly cold, is profoundly modified during its transit over progressively warmer seas. It is nevertheless still somewhat cooler, on entering the region, than the trade-wind air of the western Pacific or the continental air over India, so that northern Vietnam is the only part of South-east Asia to have winter temperatures appreciably below the average for its latitude. In January Akyab, on the Burmese coast, and Honolulu are respectively 8° and 10° warmer than Hanoi. Cold fronts are responsible for most of the weak winter precipitation in Tonkin, into which they penetrate during the periodic intensifications of the monsoon which follow anticyclonic build-up over China. During these surges of the monsoon the NE trades, which normally reach the east coast of the Philippines, retreat far out into the Pacific. Conversely, when the monsoonal flow weakens, the trade winds may invade even the northern part of the China Sea.

[33] See Koteswaram.

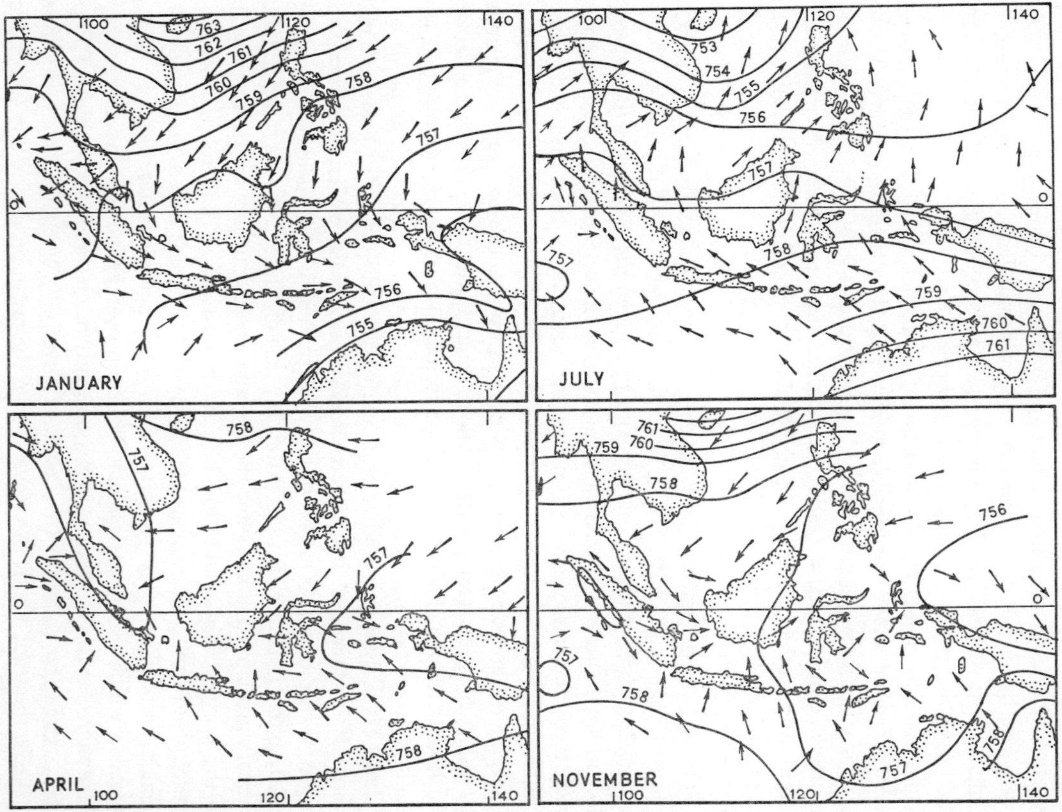

FIG. 5—South-east Asia: pressure and surface winds. Pressure values in millimetres of mercury

The air which reaches the coast farther south, in central Vietnam, has had a longer track over warm seas with the result that the temperature gradient is quite steep. Between Hanoi and Qui Nhon, which are separated by 7° of latitude, the temperature in January rises by 11°. In July the change amounts to little more than 1°. The NE monsoon brings orographic rains to this section of the coast, but the amount of precipitation produced in this way diminishes as the winter progresses owing to the cooling of the sea surface over which the air travels. The process of destabilization which the air undergoes does not therefore proceed as far, while typhoons, which form only over the warmest seas, become less frequent.

Since pressure decreases much more rapidly with height in cold air than in warm, the Asian anticyclone is essentially a surface feature and the monsoonal current, never very deep, becomes ever shallower owing to the sinking motion associated with equatorward flow. Its depth may amount to 8–10,000 ft. when it enters the region but rarely exceeds 5,000 ft. beyond the 15th parallel. Above it the upper westerlies are met at increasingly high levels southwards, and a deepening wedge of trade-wind air separates these two streams. At heights of 30,000 ft. and above, a strong south-westerly stream of equatorial or southern hemisphere origin is found above the Bay of Bengal and Burma,[34] while the subtropical westerly jet stream is situated above the Himalayan crests.[35] The convergence of these currents above the northern parts of Burma and Thailand should result in sinking motion nearer the surface and this is now believed to account for the dryness of the winter in these areas. It is significant that in January Luang Prabang, at a height of 940 ft. in the Mekong valley, has a mean daily maximum of 82°, a value only 1° lower than that of Nagpur in central India and 14° higher than that recorded at Hanoi, while all three stations have similar minima. Over much of Burma, Laos and Thailand the diurnal range of temperature is high, rising inland to 25° or 30°, and humidities are moderately low during the day, indications that the air mass is of a continental type. Conditions are thus reminiscent of India rather than of the Vietnam coast. The temperature gradient is particularly steep in Burma, where a rise of 15° is observed in January over less than 8° of latitude between Bhamo and Rangoon.

In the southern part of the China Sea the monsoonal and trade-wind air are scarcely distinguishable, and conflicting views have been expressed on the subject of their respective contributions to the flow of air across the equator. The northerly current is generally weak and achieves some degree of constancy only between Sumatra and Borneo. Although extending typically to a height of some 5,000 ft. it deepens during monsoonal surges and may then advance several degrees beyond the equator without undergoing deflection. Normally anticlockwise turning occurs, and the current is reinforced by a westerly flow from the Indian Ocean. The resulting air stream, with a varying depth that may attain 20,000 ft., gives rise to the W monsoon of Indonesia, producing copious rainfall

[34] See Ramage (A) and (B).

[35] See Koteswaram, Raman and Parthasarathy.

as a result of both relief and of convergence induced by land and sea breeze phenomena. Cloud development and rain often occur along the boundaries between the W monsoon and the easterly trade-wind streams on either side of it.[36] The southern boundary, which extends to the surface, is the more active of the two.

With the onset of spring the heating of the Asian continent dispels the Siberian anticyclone and the related monsoonal flow, and the inter-monsoon period is one of weak circulation. The Indonesian sector seems to experience a weak easterly flow, perturbed by the passage of cyclonic eddies moving in from the Pacific and interrupted at times by the appearance of westerlies from the Indian Ocean. Because of the absence of well-defined regional currents, land and sea breeze circulations become of great importance and are active in promoting rainfall. On the mainland the interior lowlands experience their hottest and driest weather of the year. Mean daily maxima exceed 95° and rise above 100° in the dry zone of Burma in April and the early part of May. At Mandalay the relative humidity drops at 6 p.m. to 31 per cent in March and 33 per cent in April.

The continuing northward advance of the pressure systems brings Indonesia under the influence of the southern hemisphere trades during May and the months that follow. Generally speaking, no semi-permanent anticyclone of the type found over the eastern parts of the Atlantic and the Pacific forms over the Indian Ocean. The circulatory pattern oscillates rather from periods during which anticyclones migrate eastwards from southern Africa to others when the cells are almost stationary, one being then situated over the Australian continent.[37] The direction of flow, southerly on the eastern flank of the high pressures where it is fed by subsidence, alters to become south-easterly or easterly as the air moves into lower latitudes. As an anticyclonic cell is nearly always to be found above some part of the Australian region the E monsoon of Indonesia is a relatively steady current, though it does not quite show either the strength or the consistency of the winter monsoon in the northern part of the China Sea.[38]

The flow, which brings in air from northern Australia or the Coral Sea, is gently subsident and the temperature inversion that characterizes trade-wind currents is therefore much in evidence. The resulting stability of the air mass is responsible for the pronounced dry season experienced by the southern portion of the archipelago. The stability of the air becomes more marked as the season progresses, and the rainfall minimum is delayed until August or even September. The lower humidities and higher incidence of sunshine strengthen the contrast with the weather of the W monsoon period. At Pasuruan in eastern Java 300 hours of sunshine are recorded during August but only 180 in January, despite the greater length of the days, while the noon relative humidities for these two months amount respectively to 49 and 64 per cent.

The Coral Sea branch of the monsoon is seemingly moister and less stable. It produces extremely heavy rainfall, probably of a mainly orographic nature, on

[36] See Watts (A), Chapter 11. [37] See Garbell, p. 55.
[38] See Crowe (B), pp. 41–3.

south-facing slopes in New Guinea and neighbouring islands. Thus Ambon receives 68 in. of rain during the three months May to July, while stations in eastern Java, Timor and southern Celebes mostly record little more than one inch per month during the same period, and even smaller amounts in August and September. The flow slackens considerably and undergoes a clockwise deflection on approaching the equator, which it crosses with a depth of some 5,000 ft. between the 95th meridian and the Vogelkop in West New Guinea.

Concurrently intense low pressures develop over West Pakistan and western China as a result of the intense radiational heating of the Asian land mass. Penninsular South-east Asia, like the Indian sub-continent, comes under the influence of the air stream which has been termed the SW monsoon or occasionally the Indian westerlies. Crowe's investigations[39] first drew attention to the fact that, in the Indian Ocean, the flow of air across the equator is concentrated in the zone lying to the west of the 65th meridian. This conclusion has been confirmed by Tucker's recent analysis which indicates that the average southerly component of surface flow at the equator for the period June to August decreases from 20 m.p.h. at longitude 50° E to 2 m.p.h. at about 65° E.[40] It appears, therefore, that an appreciable proportion of the vast mass of air carried by the SW monsoon must originate in the northern hemisphere. As the Indonesian monsoon is a shallow current with a southerly component of some 4 to 5 m.p.h. only, the great westerly to south-westerly stream moving across the mainland of South-east Asia must be regarded as essentially a continuation of the flow traversing southern India and the Bay of Bengal.

Over the Burmese coast the westerlies extend to a height of 20,000 ft. and sometimes even 30,000 ft., but their depth decreases appreciably towards the east and north-east, rarely exceeding 10,000 ft. over the northern part of the China Sea. At its maximum extent the SW monsoon penetrates northwards as far as central China and eastwards beyond the Philippines to the 140th meridian, while on its southern margin it overruns to some extent the Indonesian current and abuts on the SE trades which show little sign of deflection above the surface layers. Cloud development and precipitation occur along this equatorial boundary between monsoon and easterlies. The trade winds of the north-west Pacific do not normally affect South-east Asia at this time although they may advance over the Philippines and the China Sea during periods of slack monsoonal flow. As a rule they tend to be deflected around the high pressures of the Pacific, and appear on the east coast of China as the SE monsoon.[41]

The 'burst' of the SW monsoon, which is so prominent a feature of the climate of Burma, as of India, is thought to be closely associated with the onset in the upper troposphere of an easterly flow replacing the westerlies which prevail for most of the year. This change takes place earlier over Burma than over India, where it appears to be delayed until after the main westerly jet stream has been

[39] See Crowe (A) and (B). [40] See Tucker, Chart 4, p. 295.

[41] See Staff Members, Institute of Geophysics and Meteorology, Academica Sinica (A)

displaced to the north of the Tibeto-Himalayan block at the end of May or the beginning of June.[42] Presumably the earlier arrival of the monsoon in Burma is intimately connected with the fact that the upper easterlies appear first over South-east Asia. A jet stream is usually found embedded in them, with its core at a height of 50,000 ft. Various studies have shown that the vertical circulations associated with jet streams can exert a significant influence on the regional distribution of rainfall.[43] The part played by the easterly jet stream in determining the pattern of summer precipitation over South-east Asia, where orographic effects have in the past been regarded as preponderant, is therefore one of the major problems of the climatology of this region.

The axis of the jet stream lies, on the average, close to the 15th parallel during July and August but its position fluctuates from day to day over a zone stretching from 10° N to 25° N, periods of gradual movement away from the equator tending to be followed by a sudden shift southwards.[44] The current generally, but by no means always, accelerates over the Bay of Bengal. Since ascending motion takes place to the right of the axis in the entrance zone, the precipitation induced by this circulation should show a fairly broad peak and should fall away more sharply on the southern than on the northern side.

An examination of the rainfall distribution for the months June to August on the Burmese coast confirms the existence of such a pattern. Along the northern edge of the coastal strip the precipitation for the three months declines from 145 in. at Akyab (20° 08′ N) to 94 in. at Cox's Bazaar (Pakistan, 21° 31′ N) and 65 in. at Chittagong (22° 21′ N). A much more striking diminution of the rainfall is observed in Tenasserim, the totals falling from 129 in. at Moulmein and 141 in. at Tavoy (14° 07′ N) to 93 in. at Mergui (12° 26′ N), 84 in. at Victoria Point (9° 59′ N) and 28·5 in. at Phuket in Thailand (7° 58′ N). These changes are out of all proportion to, and in some districts even contradict, those in the relief. The belt of heaviest precipitation is not unduly wide, and its southern edge seems to correspond quite closely to the mean position of the jet axis.

The SW monsoon is responsible for a very high proportion of the annual rainfall of this coastal strip, and July is the month of maximum precipitation at all the stations listed above, with the exception of the most southerly, Phuket, where May and September are the wettest months, and July and August are distinctly drier. Clearly such a regime would be consistent with the presence of the jet stream in lower latitudes during May and September, a situation that might reasonably be expected at the beginning and end of the summer monsoon. It is perhaps significant in this respect that the rainfall increases from August to September throughout the entire zone lying between 3° 30′ N and 10° N from Borneo to Sumatra. The presumption that this increase is related to the movement of the jet stream appears well founded but needs to be confirmed. The picture is,

[42] See Yin, and Riehl, pp. 256–69.
[43] See Riehl, Alaka, Jordan and Renard, pp. 23–37 and pp. 90–91, and Trewartha.
[44] See Koteswaram.

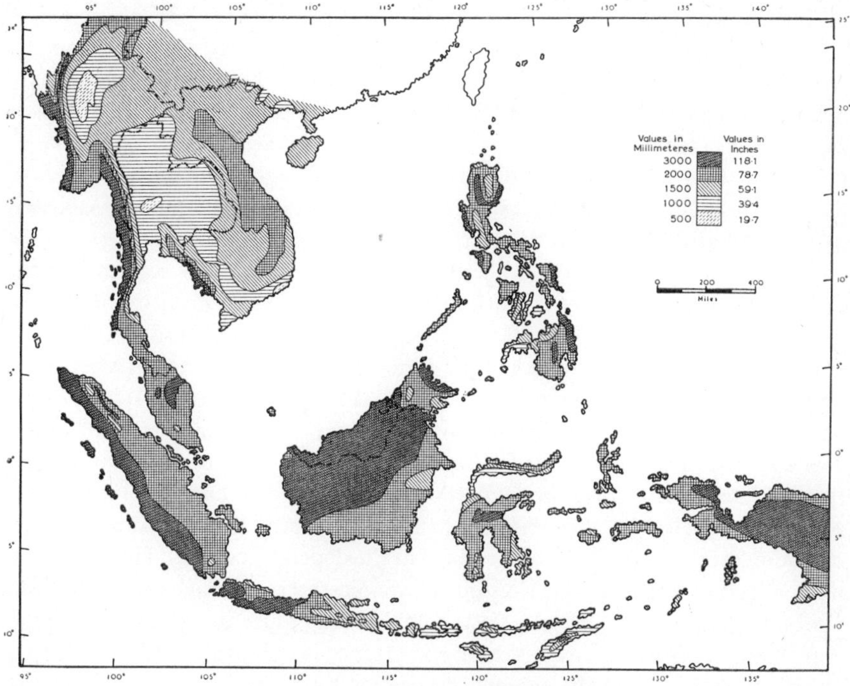

FIG. 6—South-east Asia: annual rainfall

moreover, by no means a simple one, for a similar increase occurs on the mainland up to a latitude of about 18° to 19° N except on the exposed coasts of Burma and Cambodia, the regime changing abruptly to one of pronounced July–August maximum in North Vietnam and northern Laos. This apparent anomaly may well be related to the fact that the inflow which helps to build up the jet stream is associated with an anticyclonic circulation around the Tibetan plateau, with the result that the entrance zone probably displays a NE–SW rather than E–W alignment.

The great influence that the relief of the region exerts upon its summer climate must not be overlooked. The monsoonal air, reaching South-east Asia after a long trajectory over warm seas, is extremely moist in its lower layers and convectively unstable. Consequently forced ascent of even moderate magnitude brings about copious rainfall and this process must make a significant, and perhaps in some areas a dominant, contribution to the vast quantity of rain that falls on the hilly coasts of Burma and Cambodia. Whereas September is a much wetter month than August over the greater part of Thailand and South Vietnam, as was noted above, the reverse is true of the Cambodian coast where Kaskong in fact records its highest monthly total in August with 39 in., a feature which must almost certainly be attributed to the effect of relief.

Similarly the dryness of central Burma, where the rainfall drops sharply during July and August, reflects not merely the loss of the moisture precipitated on the coastal strip and the Arakan range, but also the descent, and therefore warming, of the air in the lee of the hills. In these months the mean daily maximum temperature is 9° higher at Mandalay than at Akyab. The rainfall increases again in September, but in view of the latitude of the area this is unlikely to be associated with jet stream movements. The normal regime in fact reappears on the Shan plateau, the July and August precipitation rising from 7 in. at Mandalay to 25 in. at Lashio. The latter figure provides some support for the suggestion that descent rather than drying out of the air is responsible for the dry zone of Burma. Presumably the position of the driest belt is largely determined by the wavelength of the orographically-induced vertical motion. It is significant that Bhamo, although in the lee of the ranges of the Indo-Burmese frontier and at a height of only 386 ft., receives no less than 47 in. of rain from June to August. It is situated, however, at a greater distance downwind from the principal range than the dry area of central Burma, and not far from the edge of the Yunnan plateau, so that the air is likely to rise rather than sink as occurs over the dry zone. The relative importance of relief and flow configurations in generating the observed pattern of precipitation cannot at present be assessed, but the dependence of rainfall on vertical motion cannot be too strongly stressed. The rainiest areas are almost certainly those where orographic and dynamic effects combine to produce the strongest ascent.

A question of perhaps even greater importance is that of the relief's influence on the general form of the summer circulation over South-east Asia. Observations have shown that the low-pressure cells of West Pakistan and western China do not behave strictly like simple thermal systems, the circulation in these areas remaining cyclonic up to considerable heights. At the highest tropospheric levels the flow is dominated by a vast anticyclone centred over Tibet. This anticyclone forms in somewhat higher latitudes than is usually the case with sub-tropical high-pressure cells of dynamic origin, which are associated primarily with subsidence. It has been suggested[45] that the reason for this is to be sought in the presence of a vast land mass rising into the middle of the troposphere. The greater part of the Tibetan plateau lies above the lowest three-tenths of the atmosphere and its mountainous rim penetrates into levels where the pressure is little more than one-third of that at the earth's surface.

During the summer the plateau surface is strongly heated by solar radiation and its temperature rises well above that of the air in contact with it, the average difference amounting according to a recent view to some 9° or 10° F. The Tibetan plateau is thus a significant source of heat for the atmosphere above it. At Lhasa, at an altitude of 12,000 ft. the mean daily maximum air temperature rises to 75° in June and 74° in July, and the mean for these two months is actually 1° or 2° higher than the characteristic temperature at the same height in the eye of a typhoon! The strong horizontal temperature gradient which develops

[45] Staff Members, Institute of Geophysics and Meteorology, Academica Sinica (B), pp. 71–4, and Koteswaram, p. 56.

around the edges of the plateau leads to the formation of an anticyclonic cell at higher levels, since pressure decreases more slowly with height in a warm than in a cold air column. The great height of Tibet and the intense heating which it experiences in summer are thus probably to a large extent responsible for the existence of a strong southward-directed pressure gradient just below the level of the tropopause, and therefore of the easterly jet stream which exerts so marked an influence on the surface climate of South-east Asia. The vast quantity of latent heat liberated by condensation, and so made available to the atmosphere, as a result of large-scale ascent along the southern edge of the plateau plays, in turn a vital part in the maintenance of the monsoonal circulation.

The renewed cooling of the Asian land mass from September onwards dispels the continental low pressures and causes the monsoonal circulation to weaken and retreat to lower latitudes. By the end of October the westerly current is clearly identifiable only at some distance above the ground; although confined to a relatively narrow belt occupying the equatorial portion of the Indian Ocean, it shows an increasing tendency to advance over Indonesia. Over a wide area at the surface, the winds are mostly light and variable so that land and sea breezes are much in evidence, particularly in the Malay peninsula and the northern and central parts of the archipelago where they contribute significantly to the rainfall. Typhoons frequently form at this season and appreciably increase the precipitation of Vietnam and especially of the Philippines.

South of the equator the Australian and Coral Sea easterlies at first show no sign of weakening, and September ranks with August as the driest month of the year in the southern part of Indonesia. The mainly orographic rainfall of mountainous south-facing slopes shows in some cases a striking reduction; at Ambon 9 in. of rain fall during September as against 16 in. in August. Concurrently a marked increase in precipitation takes place over a broad zone situated from 3° to 10° to the north of the equator and extending from Borneo to Sumatra. This trend is maintained in October[46] and the belt of increasing rainfall is displaced somewhat to the south, spreading beyond the equator. A number of stations, including Labuan in North Borneo and Penang, record their highest total in this month. It has been suggested above that the change which takes place from August to September is probably connected with the retreat of the monsoonal easterly jet stream from its summer position. The question therefore arises of whether the increase in precipitation over equatorial South-east Asia during the inter-monsoon period may not also be related to the movement of this jet. It is not known however whether the easterly jet stream moves into lower latitudes, or re-forms subsequently on the other side of the equator, or whether it simply disintegrates. The occurrence of a similar pattern at the southern tip of India and in Ceylon may appear significant (the rainfall maximum occurs in the same latitude as in north-western Malaya) but in the absence of adequate upper-air data no conclusions, however tentative, may be drawn.

[46] See Dale (B).

Following the reappearance of the Asian anticyclone the NE monsoon, as a rule, becomes established over the northern part of the China Sea late in September or at the beginning of October, although an earlier short-lived burst is often noted after a sudden rise of pressure over north and central China. The monsoon gradually advances into lower latitudes, reaching Singapore towards the middle of November. Its arrival initiates a period of extremely heavy rainfall in the central portion of the Vietnamese coast and eastern Malaya. The shifting of the period of maximum rainfall, which lasts approximately two months, can clearly be related to the advance of the monsoon. At Hué (16° 31′ N) 49 in. of rain fall in the months of October and November, and Kuala Trengganu (5° 20′ N) in its turn receives 46 in. during November and December. The NE monsoon in both areas strikes a mountainous coast almost at right angles so that, as the air stream is convectively unstable, the orographic component of the rainfall is presumably dominant, but the very high totals recorded suggest that an additional factor may be involved.

It appears from upper-air charts that an anticyclonic cell is often present at this time of the year in the upper troposphere over Thailand. On the eastern and south-eastern sides of this cell, above Vietnam and Malaya, the flow will be essentially of a divergent nature with the result that convergence, and hence ascent, should be observed in the surface layers. It is of interest in this respect that the NE monsoon brings quite a heavy rainfall to the western part of Malaya when it firsts sets in, even though the amounts received are smaller than on the east coast. An upper-air situation of the kind envisaged would moreover be consistent with the appearance of convergent upper south-westerlies above Burma, where the precipitation decreases markedly from September to November. The drier conditions during the later part of the NE monsoon are perhaps to be associated with a displacement of the upper anticyclone and the development of a more continuous ridge of high pressure to the east.

An account of the air movements over South-east Asia would not be complete without some reference to the most violent and destructive of their manifestations, namely the typhoons which periodically afflict the eastern tropical margins of the region, particularly the Philippines and the Vietnamese coast and, to a lesser extent, the extreme south-east of Indonesia.[47] Although the cause of these disturbances is not entirely clear, they are known to form exclusively over areas where the temperature of the sea surface rises above a value of about 80° F and to be most frequent in late summer and autumn, when the sea is warmest in relation to the overlying air. Thus in Vietnam and the Philippines the main typhoon season lasts from July to November,[48] and in Melanesia and to the south of New Guinea it is from November to April.

[47] For a full account of typhoons see Riehl, pp. 281–357, and Proceedings of the UNESCO symposium on typhoons.

[48] Dobby (H), p. 42, records the monthly incidence of typhoons in the South China Sea, 1918–29, as follows: January 2, February 0, March 0, April 0, May 4, June 6, July 22, August 17, September 11, October 15, November 15.

The vast quantity of latent heat obtained from the ocean through evaporation, and released by condensation as cloud forms in the rising air spiralling towards the centre of the storm, provides the driving source of energy.[49] The heat gained in this way helps to keep the typhoon materially warmer than its surroundings up to great heights, with the result that, above a level of about 30,000 ft., the pressure is higher inside the typhoon than outside. This makes possible a strong outflow of air at high levels, without which the depression would very soon fill up. Accordingly, when a typhoon moves inland it rapidly dies out, its main source of energy having been cut off, and the worst of the damage inflicted by these storms is restricted to islands and narrow strips of land along the exposed coasts.

While the rate at which the storms advance is generally not more than 10–20 m.p.h., the velocity of the wind spiralling round the central 'eye' of the typhoon commonly reaches 75 m.p.h. and may even touch 100–160 m.p.h. Thus the strip of land and sea over which the storm centre passes may experience devastating damage to buildings, crops and shipping, while a far wider area than this, up to 100 miles or more in breadth, may receive heavy or torrential rain, the record in this respect being a fall of 88 in. within four days in the Philippines.[50] While such a figure is obviously very exceptional it has been estimated that the average precipitation at a station lying directly in the path of the inner core of a typical storm is of the order of 11 in.[51]

In the north-eastern part of the region, some 70 per cent of the typhoons originate to the east of the Philippines and only about 30 per cent over the China Sea. The storms at first move westwards but, after a time, their paths nearly always recurve towards higher latitudes, though this is not invariably the case.[52] Recurvature often occurs when the advance of a trough of low pressure causes upper tropospheric westerlies to appear in a lower latitude than usual, immediately to the west of a typhoon, which is then 'captured' by the westerly current. Many storms begin to recurve on reaching a position to the north-east of Luzon, so that only a very small proportion of those originating east of the Philippines ever reach the coast of Indochina; and still fewer of those in the southern hemisphere have any appreciable effect on areas within the region. While typhoons contribute significantly to the rainfall of virtually all parts of the Philippines and, in a less marked degree, of the seaward fringe of Vietnam during the later months of the year, elsewhere and at other times in South-east Asia their influence on the distribution of precipitation is negligible.

Despite the intricacy of the air movements over the region, and the significance of the local variations induced by their impact on an area of intricate outline and

[49] It is estimated that the condensation of water in a typhoon amounts on the average to 10^9 tons/day releasing 6×10^{17} calories.

[50] See Freeman, p. 16. [51] See Riehl, p. 295.

[52] Many of these storms pass close to Japan. Recurvature is characteristic of tropical cyclones in general. *Cf.* the hurricanes of the Caribbean and Atlantic seaboard of North America.

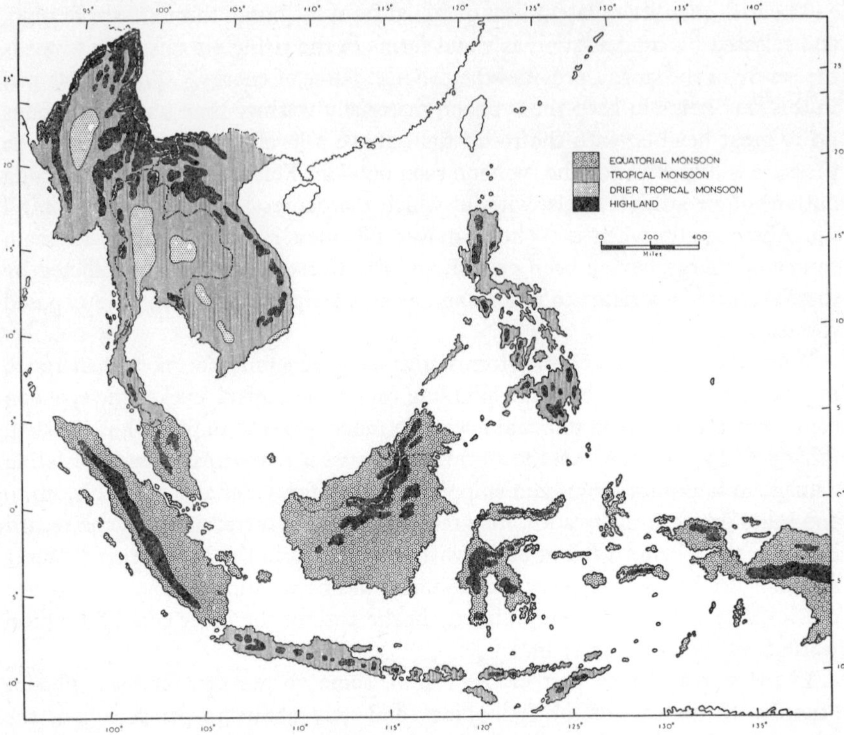

FIG. 7—South-east Asia: climatic pattern

rugged relief, the broader features of the climatic pattern are relatively simple. Two major and two minor sub-divisions may be distinguished.

First the equatorial monsoon type climate, having uniform monthly temperatures around 80° and rain at all seasons, though usually with one or more well defined peak periods, is found throughout those lowlands which lie approximately between 5° north and south of the equator. Moreover, thanks to its slight pressure variations (Fig. 5) this area is further characterized by the remarkable calmness of its atmosphere and hence also of its seas, a fact which has reinforced the sheltering effects of relief as has already been noted.[53]

Beyond the latitudinal limits of the equatorial monsoon climate the remaining lowlands of South-east Asia belong for the most part to the tropical monsoon type and this forms the second main sub-division of the region as a whole.[54] Generally less calm on land and at sea, this type is differentiated from its predecessor mainly on the grounds of its greater seasonal variety in both tempera-

[53] See Braak (A), pp. 56–7 and Robequain (D), p. 27.

[54] While it is sometimes argued that the eastern Philippines have a trade wind rather than a monsoonal climate, there are good reasons for including them within the latter category. See below, p. 695.

ture and rainfall, though the respective annual averages and totals of these do not as a rule fall significantly below those of the equatorial monsoonal type.

It is, however, necessary to place into a separate category those relatively small but nevertheless distinctive rain-shadow areas within the tropical zones of South-east Asia where the total annual precipitation drops below 50 in. For since much of the rain which does fall there comes in the form of torrential showers, a considerable proportion is lost through run-off, and totals of less than 50 in. or so are reflected in important differences in agricultural practices. Moreover, it is in these areas of what may be called drier tropical monsoon climate that variations in rainfall from year to year are both most common and most far reaching in their consequences. All the dry zones of the peninsular mainland (that is in Burma, Thailand and Cambodia) and several lesser areas in eastern Indonesia belong in this category though these last are too small to be shown on Fig. 7.

Lastly it remains to distinguish between the lowlands so far considered, all of which with the possible exception of the Tonkin delta merit the term hot, and the fairly extensive though generally sparsely populated areas in both equatorial and tropical latitudes which are of sufficient elevation to require classification as warm or, in a few cases, cool or even cold. While in theory there is scope for several sub-divisions here, the sparseness of population and the pronounced isolation of most high mountain areas renders such refinement unnecessary for the purpose of the present study, and accordingly it will suffice here to include all areas which have mesothermal or cooler climates in a single highland category.

The resultant climatic pattern shown on Fig. 7 is thus essentially empirical and accordingly less complex than those suggested in the more analytical classifications of Thornthwaite (1933) and Köppen. However it is no less valid on that account. For, apart from such aberrations as Thornthwaite's characterization of the Irrawaddy delta as an area where rainfall is 'adequate at all seasons',[55] both his and Köppen's system inevitably emphasize diversity at the expense of the underlying similarity which is of such tremendous significance in the human geography of the region. In fact, thanks to its situation relative to the equator and to the high ratio of sea to land in its overall extent, South-east Asia possesses a far higher degree of climatic homogeneity than most areas of comparable size and, with the relatively minor exceptions of the sub-humid dry zones, the whole of its effectively settled territory falls within the category of the humid tropics.

Nevertheless, as in its geological structure so also in its climate, South-east Asia is exceptional among the world's major tropical regions. For monsoonal and maritime influences reinforced by the effects of relief help to bring about a significantly higher rainfall in both tropical and equatorial South-east Asia than the respective averages of 30–60 in. and 50–80 in. in the corresponding zones of Africa and the Americas. Thus, besides experiencing mean annual temperatures

[55] Thornthwaite, pp. 433–40. Note also the comment on this in Spate (E), p. 52, note 12.

as high as any in the world, South-east Asia as a whole receives considerably more rain than any other region of comparable size.[56]

This combination of intense moisture and sustained heat is, of course, well suited to swamp-rice cultivation, particularly of the *indica* varieties of rice which were probably domesticated under essentially similar climatic conditions in or near the Ganges lowlands. But although the main rice granaries of South-east Asia today are the great deltas of the peninsular mainland, most – though not all[57] – of which receive characteristically heavy rainfall, historically speaking it was the relatively drier interior valleys of the mainland and the somewhat similar terrains of east-central Java which, together with the Song-koi delta of Vietnam, were probably the first parts of the region to practise wet-rice cultivation.[58]

For the rest, the relative similarity of climate has favoured the development of similar forms of agriculture throughout the lowland areas and, with minor variations in species to suit particular local conditions, the same garden vegetables, palms and fruit trees – notably the durian, mango and banana – are common to most parts of South-east Asia. In commercial agriculture, it is true, more regional specialization may be discerned, with, for example, rice as the dominant export crop in Burma, Thailand and Southern Vietnam, rubber in the equatorial zone proper (particularly in Malaya, Sumatra and Borneo) and copra in the more tropical islands of eastern Indonesia and many parts of the Philippines. However, although these distributions have some foundation in regional climatic differences, they are also in large measure either a reflection of relief or the outcome of historical accident. Thus, the deltas offer much the best terrain for extensive rice cultivation, while the scope for further extensions of rubber production in the tropical countries has been limited ever since the First World War by the original and partly fortuitous concentration of plantations in western Malaya and north-eastern Sumatra. But these are complicated topics, and further consideration of them is best deferred to the appropriate regional chapters.

IV. VEGETATION

Few aspects of the South-east Asian scene are more striking than the richness of the natural life, animal, vegetational and micro-organic, which thrives in its hot humid climate. And while the typical rain forest, with its gigantic soaring trees and its wealth of shrubs and smaller plants, is renowned for its remarkable stillness, broken only by the occasional chatter of monkeys and the sudden swish of a snake, the more open landscapes abound in wild life and when, during the brief tropical twilight, the buzzing of myriads of insects, the trilling of cicadas

[56] While heavier totals have been recorded in isolated places elsewhere, such as Cherrapunji in nearby Assam, there is no other part of the world in which so much rain falls over so extensive an area as in South-east Asia.

[57] The Menam delta is the main exception to this generalization. See below, pp. 424 and 486.

[58] This matter is discussed more fully in Chapter 3.

and the hideous croaking of frogs combine in one great crescendo of sound, the very air itself seems to teem with life. Yet this same exuberance of organic growth is also the bringer of death or decay, alike to animals, to man, and to inanimate matter. For in such an environment microbes and bacteria multiply with a rapidity unknown in more temperate latitudes, and insects, fungi and huge climbing plants quickly destroy all but the most solid structures.[59]

In respect, first, of its vegetation South-east Asia exhibits an abundance and diversity of forms which are without parallel anywhere else in the world. Nor is this surprising when it is recalled that, besides possessing both a climate and a degree of topographical fragmentation which are conducive to such profusion and variety, the region is focally situated between the main Asian and Australian centres of plant dispersal.

Thus, just as the Malay archipelago has been described as an ethnographic museum, so Merrill has called it a botanical paradise, with its flora numbering, according to his 'reasonably conservative estimate', some 45,000 different species.[60] But Malaysia is only half of South-east Asia and indeed South-east Asia itself forms but a part of the major Indo-Malayan plant realm,[61] which stretches from India to New Guinea and Formosa and is thus roughly coextensive with the humid tropics of southern Asia. Moreover, in mainland South-east Asia the higher mountain ranges introduce yet another element of complexity in that their flora represents a southward extension of that of the Himalayas, and accordingly contains numerous genera more characteristic of the cool temperate zone.[62] In the century which has elapsed since A. R. Wallace first attempted to divide the flora and fauna of Asia from those of Australia by a line drawn immediately to the west of Celebes and Lombok, it has become increasingly evident that Asian types of vegetation have been much more widely disseminated to the east than Wallace supposed, and notwithstanding the many Australian varieties which have spread westwards, particularly into eastern Indonesia and the Philippines, the former group is overwhelmingly preponderant in nearly all parts of the region.

In its primeval state almost the whole of South-east Asia must have been forested, and even today, in contrast to India and China proper, only a relatively small proportion of its area, mainly in Java, west-central Luzon, western Malaya and the better riverine and coastal lowlands of the Indo-Pacific peninsula, has been permanently cleared for cultivation. On the other hand, the natural vegetation of much of the remainder has in varying degree been modified by human

[59] This fact presents great difficulty to the historian and archæologist in their attempts at reconstructing the past. At Angkor, for example, all but the large stone and laterite structures have disappeared, and even some of these have been undermined and crushed by the growth of giant creepers and tree roots. See Roberts, G. (A), p. 350.

[60] Merrill, pp. 67–9.

[61] The area embraced by this term as used by the botanists is of course much more extensive than that covered by the geological term Indo-Malayan mountains.

[62] Campbell, p. 194.

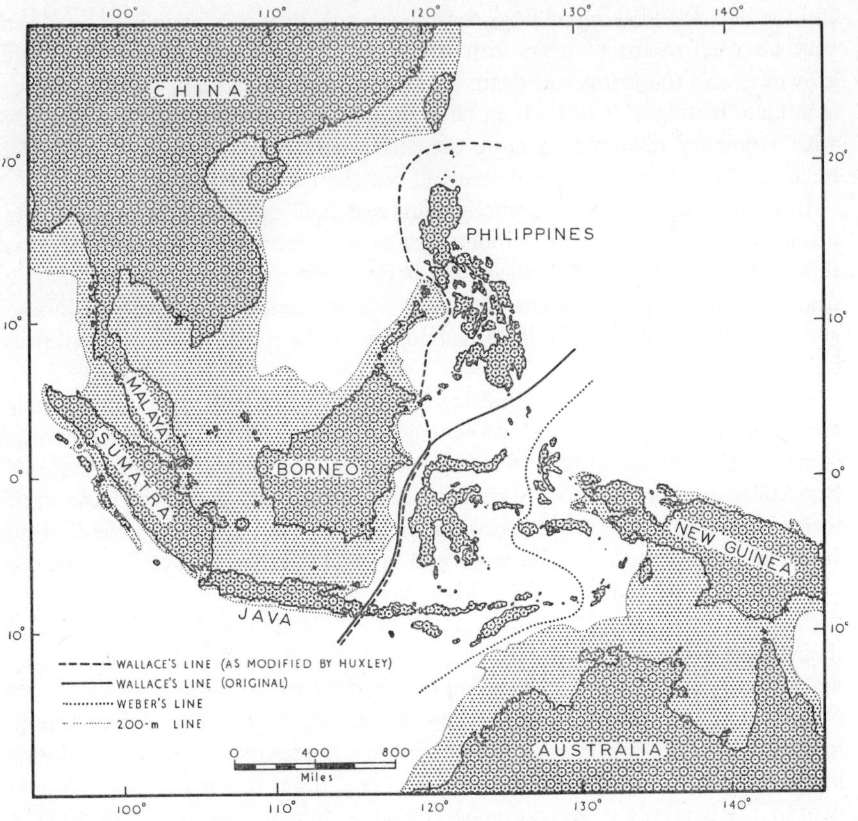

FIG. 8—South-east Asia: biogeographical limits

activity, particularly in the extensive areas in both the mainland and the islands where the activities of shifting cultivators have led to the replacement of virgin forest by *belukar* or secondary jungle.

Although the whole of South-east Asia forms part of one great vegetational realm, it nonetheless exhibits considerable regional variety which closely reflects the salient features of its climatic pattern. In this respect the most important distinction to be drawn is that between the tropical evergreen rain forest of both the equatorial lowlands and much of the wetter tropical zone to north and south, and the more open type of tropical deciduous or 'monsoon forest', as it is often called, in areas of definite seasonal drought. While in a general way this division follows that between the equatorial and the tropical monsoonal climatic types already considered, it will be seen that the evergreen rain forest extends in places well beyond the limits of the strictly equatorial climate, though the factors which determine the boundary between it and the deciduous forest do not appear to be everywhere the same. Thus, for example, while in the peninsular mainland total annual rainfall affords a fairly good guide, and most areas up to about 3,000 ft. or so which receive over 80 in. of rain in the year carry evergreen rain forest, in eastern Indonesia, which is subjected to strong desiccating winds between April and September, the length and intensity of this dry season seem to be the decisive factors,[63] and practically the whole of the forests in southern Celebes and the Lesser Sundas belong in the deciduous category.

The true evergreen rain forest, though not perhaps as overpowering and 'impenetrable' as it is sometimes painted, is certainly extremely dense and exhibits a remarkable profusion of plant growth. Frequently three separate storeys may be recognized, the tallest trees, 100–180 ft. high, rising as relatively isolated specimens above a more or less continuous roof formed by the closely spaced crowns of the second layer, 50–75 ft. from the ground, while below this in turn stand the younger trees and the whole range of shrubs and lesser plants which carpet the forest floor.

Among the larger trees, members of the *Dipterocarpaceae* are particularly noteworthy, their straight white trunks, which may rise to as much as 100 ft. before the lowest branch appears, standing out clearly against the prevailing heavy greens of the forest foliage. But although it has been estimated that dipterocarps of one kind or another[64] account for at least half of the forest trees in the equatorial lowlands of South-east Asia, continuous stands of single species (of these or of other families) are rare, and the marked heterogeneity of tropical rain forests generally presents great difficulty to the economic exploitation of their potentially vast reserves of timber.[65]

The profusion of tangled undergrowth and especially of lianes, thick woody creepers which climb upwards from tree to tree towards the light, add to the difficulties alike of lumbering and even of simple movement, though on the other hand rattans (climbing palms) are prized by many local people who use them as ropes and, along with various resins, gums and camphor, they figure prominently among the lesser forest produce which enters international trade. To the indigenous peoples, on its borders and within, the forest also provides useful sources of fuel and rough timber for tools and buildings, and in the latter connexion both bamboos and the leaves of some of the palms are particularly important. Neither of these two groups is in any sense limited to the rain-forest belt but both are usually well represented there. All-told there are over 250 varieties of bamboo (a member of the *Gramineae* or grass family), some of them growing to 130 ft. or more, though 30–40 ft. is a commoner size, and in addition to their value as building material they are used in the manufacture of a wide variety of objects, ranging from hunters' blowpipes and domestic utensils to

[63] Though the porosity and drainage of the soils also have important effects locally.

[64] Some 4,000 different species of dipterocarps are recognized in the Indo-Malayan region, to which they are unique.

[65] In the long run the greatest economic value of the tropical rain forests may be found to lie in the use of their quick-growing timbers for pulp and cellulose. See Broek (K), p. 5.

smiths' bellows and minor aqueducts to carry irrigation water. Similarly there are some 150 species of palms in South-east Asia, several of which, notably the sago, coconut, and various sugar palms, are valuable sources of food, while the sap of the palmyra is made into toddy and the nut of the areca provides the local counterpart of chewing tobacco. Palms of many kinds are particularly characteristic of the swamp forest which extends over wide areas behind the mangrove zone along the coasts of much of Indonesia and Malaya.

Deciduous monsoon forest is found at lower altitudes within two main areas of South-east Asia, namely the south-eastern portion of Indonesia and those parts of the mainland north of about 7° where the annual rainfall does not exceed 80 in. or so. While in marginal areas the one type of forest may grade very gently into the other, and in general appearance the difference between the two is not very striking during the rains, the true monsoon forest has a distinctively bare and almost wintry aspect in the dry season, when most of the trees shed their leaves and the danger of fire is very great. Moreover, while undergrowth is again fairly profuse, and many kinds of bamboo, including some giant varieties, are common, the main trees are normally more widely spaced and less high than those of the rain forest, the place of the dipterocarps being taken by such trees as pilang (*Acacia leucophloea*) and species of *Albizzia*.

Again, as in the rain forest, a wide variety of species is normally the rule, but some large tracts do exist in which the natural resistance of particular species to forest fires has led to their achieving a marked predominance. Particularly important in this respect is teak (*Tectona grandis*), one of the largest trees of the monsoon forest, which frequently attains a height of 100–130 ft. It occurs in much of central and eastern Java, as well as in many parts of Burma and Thailand and to a lesser extent in Laos, and is highly valued commercially because of its great density and durability. Likewise in eastern Indonesia and the Philippines, eucalypts, which came originally from Australia, are not infrequently found in single stands, and the same applies to bamboo, though only in the wake of shifting cultivation. In the dry zones of Burma and Thailand, the monsoon forest is markedly thinner than elsewhere, and with careless handling easily degenerates to scrub or even semi-desert.

As a general rule secondary forest is much lower, but also far more tangled and congested, than the primary growth, for until new trees have had time to grow to maturity the smaller plants, which normally constitute the undergrowth, are free to run riot. Although many observers have commented on the rapidity with which secondary vegetation establishes itself, the very profusion of such growth delays the process of complete reversion to the original type. Even today, five hundred years after the forest reconquered Angkor, the flora there is still distinguishable from that of the surrounding countryside.[66] So long as shifting cultivation continues, however, any long respite is out of the question, for the cultivator is concerned only with allowing a sufficient covering of vegetation to develop to

[66] Gourou (H), p. 50.

ensure that the fertility of the soil will not be permanently lost. Thus, after clearing and burning, and then cultivating a patch for a year or two, he will rarely leave it fallow for more than 15–20 years before renewing the process. In these circumstances the secondary vegetation will never advance beyond the stage of young *belukar*, with an initial covering of tropical grass followed by clumps of bushes and tangles of lianes, and finally by a few spindly trees, none of them exceeding 30–40 ft. in height. Indeed too frequent burning, especially of the thinner type of monsoon forest in exceptionally dry areas, may well lead to an apparently permanent change from forest to something like a savanna vegetation[67] usually of *lalang*[68] (*Imperata cylindrica*), a tussocky grass which, except when young, is too coarse and sharp edged to be of any use for grazing animals. Certainly much of the more or less open savanna-scrub, interspersed with clumps of bamboos and thorny bushes, which today occurs sporadically in the dry zones of the peninsula and several parts of eastern Indonesia, is man-induced, and whatever may be the origin of the savanna association in other continents, it is doubtful whether true natural grassland exists anywhere at all in South-east Asia.[69]

Besides these two basic types of forest, corresponding to the two major climatic sub-divisions of the region, other regional variations in vegetation reflect its topographical diversity, and in this connexion the coastal and highland associations call for particular consideration.

Throughout South-east Asia, wherever the land surface is being extended seawards by the deposition of silt, the shoreline is characteristically fringed with a belt of mangroves which, thriving in half-consolidated mud, help in turn to consolidate the latter more fully and thus to build the land still farther out to sea. Such conditions occur along all the more sheltered stretches of the gently shelving shorelines of the Sunda and Sahul platforms, as well as near the mouths of many of the larger rivers elsewhere.

About thirty species of mangrove are known, all of them in varying degree adapted to marine inundation, and collectively they are of considerable economic value both for firewood, charcoal and building material, and also for the tannin obtained from their bark. Commonly associated with them is *Nipa fruticans*, a palm which is adapted to brackish conditions and whose leaves are particularly favoured for thatch. All-told the width of the mangrove belt may be anything from 100 yards to a couple of miles or even more, beyond which it is frequently succeeded by freshwater swamp before firmer ground is reached. As has already been noted, swamps of this kind cover vast areas in eastern Sumatra and in southern and western Borneo.

Elsewhere, on non-sedimenting and more exposed shores, mangroves are

[67] A similar effect may also be produced in wetter areas if the soils are particularly acidic.

[68] This is the Malay name; it is known as *alang-alang* in Indonesia, *cogon* in the Philippines and *tranh* in Vietnam.

[69] According to P. W. Richards (p. 335) there is no evidence that any of these South-east Asian grasslands is a climatically-determined climax community.

generally absent, and instead of repellent and evil-smelling swamps are found stretches of sandy beach and often great spreads of shingle, with various salt-tolerant plants such as the grass *Spinifex squarrosus*. Frequently the shore is lined with a narrow fringe of graceful casuarinas[70] but more common still is the coconut palm, which thrives in such sandy coastal margins and likewise imparts a distinctive beauty to them.

Especially in equatorial latitudes where the frost line is highest, dense forest extends several thousand feet up most of the mountain slopes, though between 1,500 and 3,000 ft. a gradual change begins and various northern types make their appearance among the more characteristic tropical trees. This is particularly marked on the mainland, where maples, oaks and magnolias are found, but oaks are also fairly common at such altitudes even in Indonesia. Between 3,000 and 6,000 ft. in the equatorial zone, there is a further and more pronounced change to moss or mist forest, in which the predominantly gnarled and stunted trees are draped with huge masses of clammy moss. Away from the equatorial zone, however, mist forest is less common, and in many drier areas it is replaced by pine forest[71] with much bracken and grass. Finally, apart from the small patches of Alpine flora at the highest elevations in New Guinea and the Yunnan border, the uppermost slopes beyond the tree line, *c.* 10,000–14,000 ft., support a vegetation of grasses and shrubs typically including gentians and rhododendrons.

V. FAUNA

The several factors which account for the exceptional abundance and diversity of the flora of South-east Asia likewise in large measure explain the richness of the regional fauna, though it should perhaps be stressed that the denser rain forests in general support a lighter animal population than do the more open monsoon forest and the secondary jungle.

Notwithstanding its shortcomings as a guide to plant distribution, Wallace's line, especially as extended by Huxley to the west of the Philippines, has considerable validity as a zoogeographical divide. For while plants may be easily dispersed by both winds and currents, animals tend to be more restricted in their movements and even relatively narrow seas may constitute major obstacles to migration.

Thus Wallace's line, approximately following the edge of the Sunda shelf, does mark the natural eastern limit of many of the larger Asian mammals, including the tiger, elephant, rhinoceros and orang-utan.[72] On the other hand

[70] *Casuarina equisetifolia*. As a family the casuarinas, which originated in Australia, are rather similar in appearance to conifers.

[71] Another species of casuarina, *Casuarina Junghuhniana*, forms extensive forests at intermediate altitudes in central and eastern Java.

[72] Not all of these are equally widely dispersed however. Thus the orang-utan is limited to Sumatra and Borneo, the tiger occurs in all mainland countries plus Sumatra, Java and Bali, and the rhinoceros exists in many parts both of the mainland and the islands though

several Asian types, particularly of insects, butterflies, birds and reptiles, extend much farther eastwards and even some of the monkeys are found as far afield as Timor, Celebes and the Philippines. For this reason Weber's line, which represents another attempt to delimit the eastward extent of Asian fauna, was drawn much farther to the east, approximately along the edge of the Sahul shelf. In effect, therefore, it marks the separation between the Asian poisonous snakes and those of New Guinea and, more important, the western limit of many of the most characteristic marsupials and monotremes, two ancient forms of animal life which in origin were unique to the Australian continent.

Once again, however, there are many anomalies, such as the presence of various lemurs (marsupials) in Celebes, and it is clear that no hard and fast line can be drawn between the fauna of the two continents. Thus there is a growing tendency to accept Wallace's and Weber's lines as marking the respective primary limits of Asian and Australian forms and at the same time to regard the intervening area, sometimes called *Wallacea*, as a transitional zone in which the two intermingle. For, as has been noted, this is a structurally youthful and markedly unstable area, and the repeated changes in outline which it has experienced have profoundly affected the sequence of animal colonization there.

As a general rule birds and insects have been far less impeded by breaks in the land bridges than have the other animals, and there is a tremendous profusion and diversity of both throughout the region as a whole. Nevertheless there are important regional variations, and one of the most striking features in this regard is the abundance in eastern Indonesia and New Guinea of birds with exceptionally brilliant plumage, notably parakeets, cockatoos and birds of paradise.[73]

The least restricted of all, of course, are the various forms of marine life, fish, crustaceans and molluscs, in which the warm and generally placid seas of South-east Asia abound. Again the variety of forms is great, and mackerel, anchovy, sardines, various tunas, threadfins, sharks and rays, as well as prawns, shrimps, cuttlefish, squid, octopus, bêche-de-mer, clams, crabs and oysters[74] are all of some economic importance. Indeed there is evidence to suggest that the shallow seas, particularly of the Sunda shelf, are among the world's richest fishing grounds, though hitherto the difficulty of preserving the freshness of the catch in a region subjected to such high temperatures has hindered the development of commercial fisheries, as opposed to subsistence fishing which is well-nigh ubiquitous. But, with growing realization of the need to find new sources of food and also to diversify the predominantly vegetarian diet of the great mass of the population, considerable expansion is already taking place both in sea and river fishing, and

it is rarely seen. The elephant is found all over the mainland countries and in Sumatra. See Robequain (D), p. 57. Note also the water buffalo, which is probably indigenous to South-east Asia, where it appears to have been first domesticated. It is kept in all parts of the region from Burma and Vietnam to Sumatra, Sumbawa and the Philippines.

[73] The plumage of such birds has formed an item of trade since ancient times.

[74] See Morgan, pp. 172–4.

also in the breeding of fish in natural water bodies, artificial ponds and rice-fields, in which practice Java in particular has an old-established tradition.[75]

VI. SOILS

Of the many popular myths which Westerners still entertain with respect to the humid tropics, none is so fundamentally erroneous as the belief in the abounding fertility of their soils. For, despite the abundance and rapidity of plant growth in the equatorial forest zone, experience has all too often shown that the soil on being cleared for cultivation is surprisingly poor, and moreover apt to degenerate still further in the space of a few years to such an extent as to be incapable of supporting anything more than meagre scrub.

The key to this apparent paradox is two-fold. In the first place it is the climate, in effect the natural equivalent of a hot-house, which explains the profusion of vegetation and, secondly, these same conditions of abundant heat and moisture greatly intensify the rate of bacterial action and chemical weathering. Thus, Vageler[76] has estimated that over the year as a whole the rate of weathering in the tropics is at least ten times as rapid as that in temperate latitudes, and where soil temperatures exceed 75° the rate of accumulation of humus at the surface is more than offset by the speed with which it is broken down and removed. In fact, however, virgin forest does not demand a great deal from the soil and normally lives in a state of equilibrium, organic material from falling leaves being quickly broken down into humus and subsequently reabsorbed as plant food by the growing trees.[77]

Nevertheless this equilibrium is very precarious. If the vegetation cover is removed, the supply of humus disappears, the temperature of the unshaded soil increases as does the intensity of chemical and biochemical activity and, perhaps most important of all, the characteristically torrential rains cease to be broken in their fall and instead beat down direct on the ground with a violence rarely experienced in temperate latitudes. As a result, the soil is leached of its soluble nutrients and its texture may well be seriously damaged, a state of affairs which prepares the way for sheet and gully erosion by wind and heavy rain, especially after periods of prolonged drought. For although a well-established covering of *lalang* will provide adequate safeguard against erosion on level land, the immediate consequences of burning[78] can be disastrous and, particularly on steep slopes, the whole of the soil layer may be swept away to expose the bare surface of the bed rock itself.[79]

To return to the main theme, however, it is evident that, primarily as a result

[75] Particular success has been achieved in recent years with the fast-breeding *Tilapia* fish. See Calder, pp. 79–83.

[76] Vageler, p. 16, cited in Spate (E), p. 90.

[77] See Gourou (H), Chapter 3, especially pp. 13–14.

[78] Or of over-felling, *e.g.* of teak.

[79] The terracing of hillsides, *e.g.* in parts of Indonesia and the Philippines, though designed to facilitate irrigation, also serves to check soil erosion.

of the great intensity of leaching which prevails in the humid tropics, the soils of this zone are generally very deficient in the main plant foods, that is the assimilable bases, phosphorus, and humus, and in consequence are for the most part noticeably less fertile than those of cooler latitudes.

Until recently it has been customary to refer to the type of leaching found within the humid tropics as laterization, in contra-distinction to podsolization, which it was assumed was limited to the cooler humid regions. But while it is clear that a distinction does exist between the prevailing leaching process associated with the higher temperatures of the humid tropics, which leads to the removal of silicates into the lower horizons of the soil, leaving residual oxides nearer the surface, and that normally occurring in cooler latitudes, which involves the downward removal of the sesquioxides and the survival of residual silicates, the mutual geographical exclusiveness of these two types is no longer generally accepted, and considerable doubt exists as to whether the formation of laterite proper can be explained wholly in these terms.

As first employed by Francis Buchanan in 1807, the name laterite referred to a reddish mottled clay, consisting almost entirely of hydroxides of iron and alumina, whose most distinctive trait was its tendency to solidify on exposure to the air, and hence to make useful building material.[80] In practice such building material is usually derived from the characteristic pan,[81] commonly but not invariably found at depths varying from 2 to 9 feet below the surface layer of friable sandy or clayey soil. In cases where the iron content is particularly high (20 to 30 per cent) it may be mined for the ore itself, as in the lateritic iron deposits of the Philippines, while elsewhere, notably in the Riau archipelago, laterites with high concentrations of alumina are worked for bauxite.

The factors governing the formation of the impermeable horizon are not entirely clear. For while intense leaching postulates a prolonged and intense rainy period, the existence of a pan near the surface implies an upward movement of soil water for at least a substantial part of the year, and it has accordingly been widely assumed that true laterites must necessarily be associated with tropical rather than equatorial climates. However, while laterite is certainly common in parts of Burma, Thailand and Indochina it has also been found in equally mature form within the equatorial zone, particularly in Malaya, Borneo and other islands of the stable Sunda Shelf. Some scientists have sought to explain this apparent anomaly in terms of climatic change, but opinion on this matter is still divided and further consideration of the arguments involved is beyond the scope of the present study.

Be that as it may, however, what has commonly been referred to as laterization is the normal determinant of soil type in almost all parts of the humid tropics,

[80] From *later* (Latin) = a brick. Laterite is very resistant and has been widely used as a building stone, notably at Angkor. It also makes good road metal for secondary roads in the humid tropics. See Pendleton (A), pp. 177–202.

[81] See Dobby (H), p. 80.

except at higher altitudes where podsolized bleached earths are typically found. And in general, owing to the rapidity with which the process has operated, the effect on soil composition of differences in the parent rock have in large measure been obliterated except in the case of very recently formed soils.[82]

Nevertheless, while nearly all South-east Asian soils are thus at least partially laterized, the commonest types, namely the so-called tropical red and yellow earths, are by no means identical with pure laterite as described above. The difference in colour between these two types results merely from differences in the degree of hydration of the iron oxides in the soil, though in general the yellow earths correspond roughly with the areas having no dry season at all while the red earths are more characteristic of the monsoon-forest zone.

In both cases, however, the soils are moderately to severely leached and accordingly deficient in soluble bases, though their texture is often reasonably good and may even approximate to that of a loam.[83] Thus, especially in relatively dry areas, tropical red earths may yield good crops for a few years though, like all tropical soils, they tend to be quickly exhausted by leaching and are easily eroded unless well protected by vegetation.

In general, therefore, all the soil types so far considered, namely laterites, upland bleached earths and tropical red and yellow earths, which together cover the greater part of the humid tropics, South-east Asia included, are agriculturally poor and sometimes indeed virtually useless.[84] But fortunately this is not the whole of the picture, and two other major groups of soils remain to be considered, both of which are generally of much greater value to the cultivator.

The first of these comprises the tracts of recently deposited alluvium in the lower courses and particularly the deltas of the larger South-east Asian rivers. Since much of the soluble plant food which has been leached or removed by surface erosion from the soils throughout the whole catchment area ultimately finds its way downstream the deltas are often extremely fertile, and notwithstanding the tendency towards laterization which prevails there as elsewhere, the constant replenishment by fresh silt brought down by the river[85] serves to prevent deterioration even under continuous cropping.

Moreover, these soils occur in precisely those parts of the peninsular mainland which are also most favoured for cultivation on the grounds of both relief and proximity to the sea. In the larger Indonesian islands, on the other hand, the greatest lowlands – if such they can be called – are the vast coastal swamps

[82] But see below, p. 53, on the fertility of young volcanic and alluvial material.

[83] Intense chemical weathering favours the formation of clay.

[84] In a few small and exceptionally dry parts of central Burma and eastern Indonesia the upward movement of water in the soil has given rise to a distinctive type sometimes known as a tropical black earth. However, such soils do not normally compare in fertility with the true chernozems.

[85] Much of this material is derived from the dry zones and also from upland areas outside the tropics altogether, where different processes govern the formation of sedentary soils. Dissolved plant nutrients contained in the river water itself are at least equally important to agriculture in flooded or irrigated areas.

fringing the Sunda Shelf. Here, owing to the check which waterlogging of the soil imposes on bacterial action within it, dead vegetation tends to accumulate at the surface, often in the form of thick layers of peat. Until, therefore, this can be removed and the swamps themselves systematically drained, their potential fertility is of little practical account.

The second major exception to the characteristic infertility of tropical soils occurs in other parts of Indonesia and the Philippines where vulcanism has continued into historic times. Again contrary to popular belief, volcanic material, even when of recent origin, is not everywhere conducive to the formation of fertile soils, the more acid types normally yielding soils which contain a great deal of silicic acid and very inadequate quantities of any plant nutrients. But where the volcanic ejecta are neutral or basic rather than acid, the soils derived from them may well be quite exceptionally rich, and this applies in some parts of Sumatra, extensive areas in central and eastern Java, much of Bali and Lombok, and also in various more scattered localities in Celebes and the Philippines.

In respect, therefore, of the proportion of its area which has soils of relatively high fertility, South-east Asia as a whole is much more favourably placed than any other major tropical region, not excluding the Caribbean. Moreover, soil erosion, though serious in some parts of the region, is on balance probably less severe than elsewhere in the inter-tropical belt, largely as a result of the comparatively high level of skill displayed by the indigenous cultivators, both shifting and sedentary.

On the other hand, however, comparatively little has been done positively to improve the quality of South-east Asian soils by deliberate human effort. Thus, for example, in contrast to the mixed farming areas of western Europe, where the relatively poor podsolized soils have over many centuries been steadily improved by means of careful tillage and the practice of rotations involving the production of both vegetables and animal manure, the dominant farming system in South-east Asia has involved the continuous use of the same fields for wet-rice cultivation, and livestock rearing has been largely neglected.

While rice is unique among the cereals in that it can be grown year after year, and even century after century, on the same plot of land so long as adequate water is available,[86] nevertheless without some application of fertilizer in one form or another even the best land will ultimately deteriorate under such treatment. Thus, except in the Annamite lands where the Chinese system of agronomy has long been in operation, soil impoverishment of this kind constitutes one of the most widespread problems encountered within South-east Asia today.

[86] Many factors are involved here. In particular the water itself, most of which comes from the lower courses of the rivers, contains many valuable plant-foods, and, furthermore, the presence of a protective layer of water covering the soil reduces the temperature of the latter and so helps to reduce the rate at which plant nutrients are removed from it. See above, p. 52, and Gourou (H), p. 100.

VII. HEALTH AND DISEASE

As the foregoing pages have shown, the popular view regarding the fertility of tropical soils is in large measure erroneous but the same unfortunately cannot be said of the general belief in the unhealthiness of the humid tropics. Admittedly, much of what has been assumed in the past concerning the direct effect of climate on health has gradually been proved false as, one by one, the spine-pad, the cholera-belt and the pith helmet, all of which until recently were regarded as essential for the white man's very survival in the lower latitudes, have been discarded without any catastrophic consequences.

For while the climate of the humid tropics is undeniably enervating and monotonous, it is not in itself a major cause of acute bodily discomfort,[87] still less of disease, and in the writer's opinion even its psychological effects have been much exaggerated.[88] That is not, of course, to pretend that the mental and bodily vigour, whether of the indigene or the European, are likely to be as great in South-east Asia as in more temperate latitudes. But a desire to take things easily in hot weather need not be equated with ill-health and, provided that the daily routine of work is adjusted to avoid the period of highest temperature, no adverse effects need ever be felt even from sustained physical effort in these conditions.

Nevertheless, even if the direct effects on human health of the humid tropical climate are thus of relatively minor importance, its indirect consequences arising from the related profusion of insects – flies, fleas, lice and mosquitoes – and of innumerable varieties of parasites and microbes, are an entirely different matter. Moreover, in a climate which favours the rapid growth of bacteria, both on land and in water, the prevailing practice in South-east Asia of using the rivers at one and the same time as bathing places, sources of drinking water and the normal repositories of sewage is even more pernicious than it might be elsewhere, and accordingly both floods and droughts all too often lead to calamitous epidemics of various kinds.

As a general rule the humid tropics show a moderate to high incidence of most of the main diseases familiar in temperate latitudes, as well as of many others which, nowadays at least, are more or less restricted to the warmer parts of the globe. So far as South-east Asia in particular is concerned, all the major tropical diseases are prevalent with the exception of yellow fever and sleeping sickness, but these absences are in large measure counterbalanced by the high incidence of cholera which is not endemic in either Africa or South America.

Although less immediately virulent than many other diseases in South-east

[87] So long as a commonsense diet is adopted. But the Englishman's traditional breakfast lies heavily on the stomach in Singapore, and the gargantuan repasts of the Dutch in the Indies were scarcely appropriate to the climate.

[88] The sun is rarely invisible for more than a very few days at a time, and nothing in the tropics is as depressing as a typical English November. The so-called tropical hysteria is usually limited to those persons who, for reasons other than the climatic, have too much time on their hands. But See Robequain (D), p. 36.

Asia, malaria is undoubtedly the greatest scourge of all, both because of its widespread distribution and also because the recurrent attacks of high fever which it entails steadily reduce the individual's vitality and weaken his capacity to resist other more deadly diseases. That does not mean, however, that malaria itself cannot be fatal, and indeed the annual number of deaths directly attributable to it in the region as a whole cannot be far short of a million, a high proportion of which are of very young children. But, according to Gourou,[89] every death corresponds to at least 2,000 days of sickness, and the general debility and lethargy of a malaria-ridden population is quickly reflected in a deterioration in farming standards and indeed in almost all aspects of its bearing and behaviour. Such a decline, both physical and mental, has been adduced as a major contributory factor to the downfall of Greece and Rome[90], and similar conditions may well have played a significant rôle at more than one stage in South-east Asian history.

Formerly attributed to 'noxious exhalations' from coastal swamps, malaria is now known to be caused by parasites which are carried by mosquitoes of the *anopheles* family, but owing to the varying habitats of the several species of these which may act as vectors[91] no ready generalization is possible concerning the geographical factors which govern its distribution.

Thus, for example, *Anopheles umbrosus* formerly swarmed in the coastal swamps of Malaya, but wherever the swamp forest was felled another but no less efficient vector, *Anopheles sundaicus*, was found to take its place. However, both of these disappeared when the swamps were embanked and drained, and in this way much of western Malaya has been practically cleared of malaria. But such treatment cannot avail in the uplands where *Anopheles maculatus*, which appears whenever the forest is felled, breeds in running water including even the most swiftly flowing streams, and has only been exterminated by systematic spraying with oil.

Accordingly in Malaya it is the lower hill country, up to about 2,000 ft.,[92] which is the most intensely malarial of all, and this is also true of many other parts of South-east Asia, notably the Annamite Chain, the ranges between Thailand and Tenasserim, and the northern and western 'hills' of Burma, including the deadly Hukawng valley. In most of Vietnam and Thailand, as also in Java[93] and the Philippines, *Anopheles minimus* is the principal vector, and since this species avoids the muddy stagnant water of the rice fields the main lowlands are largely free from malaria. In Sumatra, on the other hand, the low-lying coastal swamps show the highest incidence, and conditions there are

[89] Gourou (H), p. 7.

[90] Jones, W. H. S.

[91] The three main vectors in South-east Asia are *Anopheles umbrosus*, *A. minimus* and *A. maculatus*. There are some thirty other species of anopheles within this region, most of which do not act as vectors. See Watson, pp. 161–72. In addition various other mosquitoes act as vectors for dengue, another exhausting fever which is very common all over South-east Asia.

[92] *Anopheles* are rare above this altitude.

[93] Ninety-five per cent of the densely populated areas of Java are free from malaria. Watson, p. 165.

generally similar to those which formerly obtained across the Straits in western Malaya.

These differences of habitat, together with the tendency of new species of *anopheles* to take the place of others which for one reason or another have been eliminated, have combined to make the prevention or even the control of malaria an extremely difficult task. In the decade immediately following the Second World War spraying with DDT achieved spectacularly successful results in many parts of the region, as also in other malaria-infested lands, but as early as 1951 it was found that some species of *anopheles* had developed an effective resistance to this new insecticide. However, the more recent discovery that systematic spraying can virtually eliminate malaria from a specific area in three to four years has encouraged the World Health Organization to launch a crash programme for the world-wide eradication of this, 'the world's most expensive disease', during 1958–62.[94]

Hardly less widespread than malaria is dysentery, both bacillary and amœbic, a chronic intestinal complaint which results mainly from polluted drinking water and is spread by flies. Its elimination depends primarily on the introduction of efficient systems of garbage disposal which, except in a few of the larger towns, are still virtually non-existent. Besides dysentery, another intestinal complaint, ankylostomiasis (a form of hookworm), the various other worm infections known collectively as filariasis and the deficiency diseases, among which yaws[95] and beri-beri[96] are the most important, all belong like malaria to the group of diseases whose most common effect is a slow but steady deterioration in the general health of the affected person.

Of the deadlier diseases, most of them tending to occur in more or less seasonal epidemics, cholera is probably the greatest single killer, though both typhus, which is carried by a variety of mites, fleas and lice, and plague, can also be great scourges in many parts of South-east Asia. In modern times serious outbreaks of cholera have been almost eliminated from Indonesia and the Philippines but frequent epidemics still occur on the mainland north of Malaya, especially in the river valleys where the disease is apt to flare up with great intensity at the time of low water immediately before the rains begin.

Moreover, it seems that former periods of national disaster in several South-

[94] *Malaria eradication*, pp. 7–12.

[95] Yaws or *frambœsia* is particularly common in Indonesia where 12 million people (15 per cent of the population) were said to be infected. It is characterized by huge red swellings and sores which are both painful and unsightly, but it can be relatively easily cured with penicillin injections, and WHO and UNICEF have already done much to assist in this respect. See Calder, Chapter 2.

[96] Beri-beri is caused by vitamin B deficiency, and the incidence has risen in many areas with the spread of the 'genteel' habit of eating polished rice instead of the whole grain. It can be prevented by fortifying the rice with a synthetic mixture of vitamins, as is done notably in Japan and in the Philippines. Another method is that of parboiling, but this detracts from the appearance of the rice and is not popular outside India. Both parboiled and polished rice store much better than under-milled rice. See Pelzer (G), p. 6.

east Asian countries were associated with spectacular outbreaks of cholera, a relationship which, however, may well have been more complex than that of a single chain of causation. Thus, for example, the neglect of drainage and irrigation channels in time of war might precipitate an epidemic of cholera and/or favour the proliferation of new malaria vectors, and in this way the population could be so reduced in numbers and vitality as to be incapable of effective resistance to further attacks from its neighbours.[97]

To complete the list of the commoner complaints in South-east Asia it remains first to include a mass of skin infections, the ubiquitous tropical ulcers, which quickly develop from even a minor bamboo scratch when a person is in poor health and may easily lead to the loss of a finger or even a limb, and leprosy which, perhaps because of its very prevalence, is locally regarded with far less horror than the mere mention of its name suggests to the Westerner. Finally, both tuberculosis and venereal disease have very high incidence rates, particularly but by no means exclusively in the overcrowded slums of the great cities.

The general state of physical health among the peoples of South-east Asia thus presents an extremely sombre picture, but no worthwhile assessment of the region's human geography can be made without taking it into account. Nevertheless, although Westernization is often, and rightly, blamed for the introduction, or at least the rapid increase in the incidence of some diseases, the balance is unmistakably tipped in the opposite direction, and Western hygiene and medicine together have won many notable victories in South-east Asia during the present century. Thus in every country the death-rate is now showing a steadily downward trend, and indeed in some of the better-run towns it has fallen during the last decade to a level which compares favourably with many parts of western Europe. But, as yet, this is only a beginning, and vast expenditures on drugs, equipment and trained personnel, and equally far-reaching changes in many established habits of sanitation and diet will be necessary before the vicious circle of disease, debility, inefficiency, malnutrition and more disease is finally wiped away from the rural areas in which the great majority of the people live.[98]

In this connexion it may not be out of place briefly to summarize the medical experience of the 46,000 or so Allied prisoners of war whom the Japanese employed on railway construction and maintenance between Thailand and Burma during 1942–5. Compared with the various groups of Asian labourers who were likewise engaged, these British, Dutch and Australian prisoners were generally both healthier and stronger at the time when the assignment began, and accordingly were able to work much more energetically, to such an extent, indeed, as to cast serious doubts on the belief that white men are less fitted than

[97] Something of this sort may well have been responsible for the sudden decline of Angkor. See also Murphey (A), who points out, p. 199, that malaria first became virulent in Burma, Thailand and Cambodia some time after the 13th century A.D.

[98] Animals are also subject to many diseases, particularly insect-borne and parasitic types. But since livestock-rearing plays only a minor part in the South-east Asian economy this does not call for detailed comment.

the indigenous peoples for sustained manual labour in tropical climates. Contrary to general expectation, hardly any cases of heat stroke were recorded, although the prisoners worked hatless and usually shirtless throughout wet and dry seasons alike. Moreover, in spite of the heavy tasks and long hours (10–12 hours a day, 6 or 7 days a week) remarkably good health was maintained so long as the working parties stayed in the settled lowlands of western Thailand, where the diet was reasonably well balanced[99] and malaria comparatively rare.

But once the prisoners were moved up into the remoter hills, where malaria was rife, rations deteriorated, working hours increased and medical supplies were almost unknown, the sickness rate quickly reached catastrophic proportions. Even so, attacks by one disease alone rarely caused death, and the great majority of fatalities occurred only when a person, long debilitated by recurrent malaria, fell a victim also to dysentery or avitaminosis, or developed acute tropical ulcers. In such circumstances, as might be expected, the occasional epidemic could take a swift and terrible toll, and in this respect by far the most deadly were the seasonal outbreaks of cholera in the upper Gweinoi valley.

Thus, while in the space of two to three years death removed over 30 per cent of the total labour force, particular groups which were suddenly exposed to virulent epidemics lost far more heavily than this, and in one case one-third of a total force of 10,000 died within a period of less than six months. Yet it is also noteworthy that among the Asian workers, who consisted predominantly of Tamils brought up from the rubber estates of Malaya by the Japanese, the death-rates were even higher than those among the Europeans, and some 40 per cent of a total of 150,000 Asian workers never returned to their homes.

These facts have been cited because in the writer's opinion they serve to bring home the intensity of some of the natural forces with which the peoples of South-east Asia have had to contend down the centuries before modern medical science began to offer some hope of alleviation. For although the conditions of work under the Japanese were certainly exceptional, and notwithstanding the fact that the local peasantry have long since learned to shun the more malarial terrains, the jungle is never neutral and tyranny was not unknown in South-east Asia before the days of the Co-prosperity Sphere.

VIII. ENVIRONMENT AND MAN

How, then, is the physical character of South-east Asia to be assessed in respect of the opportunities and difficulties which it affords to human settlement? Certainly this region is strikingly different, both intrinsically and in its spatial relationships with the outside world, from the vast and comparatively undifferentiated tracts of continental Africa and South America which lie in similar latitudes.

Thanks to the vagaries of its geological evolution the territory is broken up

[99] *I.e.* it contained plenty of local green vegetables, as well as a little meat or fish, in addition to the basic daily ration of ± 16 oz. rice (normally polished).

into a series of much more easily manageable units than the great African and Brazilian plateaux or the immense lowlands of Amazonia, the Congo basin and the Guinea coast and, because of the position and the fertility of its larger deltas and other alluvial plains, many of these provide excellent *points d'appui* for settlers and other pioneers coming into the region via the sea routes which lie across it. Moreover, virtually all these key areas of better soils, while receiving enough moisture from rain or flood to support wet-rice cultivation, are not subject to such exceptionally high precipitation as occurs over much of the rest of South-east Asia, and their climate is not noticeably more enervating or unhealthy than that normally associated with the humid tropics.

To what extent these relatively favourable natural circumstances help to explain the much greater cultural achievements of South-east Asia, compared with those of the African and South American[100] tropics, however, it is extremely difficult to say, if only because the region's geographical position between the two main foci of Oriental civilization has for so long exposed it to altogether more powerful external stimuli than any which have impinged upon the other two continents during the greater part of their history. And in this respect the West Indian islands, though possessing many physical advantages similar to those of South-east Asia, were hardly less isolated in pre-Columban times than the Amazon basin notwithstanding their relative proximity to the homeland of the Mayan civilization on the Central American mainland.

On all these grounds, therefore, it is not inherently surprising that South-east Asia should have been the scene of a distinctly higher level of human advancement than anything in the other inter-tropical regions, with the sole exception of India[101] which in any case lies both farther to the north and much nearer to the ancient centres of Middle Eastern civilization.

But beyond this tentative and rather nebulous conclusion, is it possible at the present stage to say more? If the indigenous civilizations of South-east Asia are more advanced than those of Africa or South America, they nevertheless lag behind those of its nearer neighbours. Can this and the perhaps associated insouciance of South-east Asian peoples also be attributed to anything in their physical environment?

Such questions in their turn give rise to others. For the most part the population of South-east Asia today is descended from a succession of Mongoloid invaders who came in from outside the tropics, and their nearest kinsfolk still remaining in the temperate zone, namely the peoples of southern China, are among the most vigorous and hard working to be found anywhere in the world. Yet in South-east Asia only the Vietnamese appear in this respect to match the Chinese, and moreover within Vietnam itself it is a traditional belief that the inhabitants of Cochinchina in the south, despite the fact that this is the pioneer zone, are effete and indolent compared with those of Tonkin which, as

[100] *I.e.* in pre-Columban times.

[101] And possibly also the Mayan civilization of Central America. See below, note 103.

has been seen, is the only lowland area in South-east Asia whose tropicality is open to question. Likewise, among the immigrant Chinese in Malaya, it is commonly said that the second and especially the third generation lack the drive and energy of their predecessors and of more recent arrivals from the mother country.

Admittedly, these popular beliefs must be subjected to careful scrutiny and it is possible that, even should they prove to contain a significant measure of truth, the explanation may lie in fields other than the physical environment.[102] Nonetheless it is interesting to note that here in eastern Asia, as in western Europe, the local population is conscious of a connexion between human vigour and terrestrial latitude.

Whether, however, the available evidence in Asia and elsewhere is sufficient to warrant Gourou's formulation of what he specifically styles 'the rule that hot, wet lands do not spontaneously give rise to high civilizations but require civilizing influences brought from extra-tropical regions'[103] is another matter though, on the face of things, it does seem that in South-east Asia and perhaps in India also, successive waves of immigrants and invaders, after infusing a new dynamism into the region, have gradually lost their original élan and slowly succumbed to degeneration.[104]

But even if this proposition be accepted, the cause still remains to be determined. Is the adoption of a slower tempo of daily life the result of gradual adjustment to more enervating and more continuous heat, in the same way that the siesta has come to be regarded as a virtual necessity on the Mediterranean lands? Gilberto Freyre, the Brazilian sociologist, has argued persuasively that the 'slow ... pleasant ... and suave rhythm of existence' in his country, where 'leisure is not regarded as a vice' is in part the result of such an adaptation, and it would not seem unreasonable to assume a generic relationship between the prevalence of 'mañana' in Latin America and of 'tidapathy' in South-east Asia.[105]

Or is prolonged exposure to the multifarious debilitating diseases of the tropics the root cause of the alleged indolence and insouciance of the South-east Asian peoples? Certainly it would appear that disease alone provides a substantial part of whatever explanation is needful and, if so, the implication is unmistakable

[102] The original Chinese immigrants were driven by the lash of poverty and worked hard. Later generations born in South-east Asia had a better start and were less conscious of the need to struggle. Nevertheless even third- and later-generation Chinese still retain much of the traditional Chinese attitude to work.

[103] Gourou (H), p. 51. The Mayan civilization undoubtedly presents something of a problem to acceptance of this statement, though Gourou's observations on this are interesting. *Ibid.*, pp. 43–52.

[104] Note Gourou's observation: 'India is endowed with a high civilization ... But much of that civilization came from without – perhaps the better parts ... Germs of culture from lands outside the tropics have been needed to develop a high civilization in this hot, wet country.' *Ibid.*, p. 108.

[105] See Freyre, pp. 3 and 12. The term mañana (Spanish = tomorrow) is also used in the Philippines, to denote the habit of putting off until tomorrow whatever it is not absolutely essential to do today. 'Tidapathy' is Anglo-Malay for the same sort of attitude. Tidak apa (Malay) = it doesn't matter. In Laos the equivalent phrase is Bo pen nhang.

that the conquest of tropical disease might make possible a revolutionary transformation in the national life of every state in southern Asia.

The economic factor also needs to be taken into account. For, so long as serious population pressure and a consequently acute struggle for survival do not develop in the humid tropics, there is little inducement to do more than the necessary minimum of work, and in many parts of South-east Asia, where nature, if respectfully handled, is relatively bountiful, such problems have as yet been slow to develop.[106] But where, as in India or China the devil of overpopulation has driven, people have been prepared to migrate to South-east Asia and to work far harder there than the indigenes in order to stave off literal starvation. Moreover, there is some, though by no means conclusive, evidence to suggest that the emergence of similar pressures in certain parts of South-east Asia itself in recent years has induced among the indigenous peoples a greater self-reliance and willingness to submit to more rigorous working conditions.

Finally, the question arises as to whether any aspect of the physical character of South-east Asia explains its relatively low population density. Here, again, the virulence of many of the common epidemic diseases might of itself seem adequate to account for the difference in density between this region and China, though the fact that in India also, where the same tropical diseases are no less rampant, the population density is roughly three times as great as in South-east Asia calls for further examination. Clearly, the problem is extremely complex and many more factors will need to be considered before even a tentative answer can be ventured.

Nevertheless, questions of this kind need to be asked, and the geographer is neglecting his duty if he refrains from posing them out of fear of being dubbed an environmentalist or – still worse – a determinist. In the writer's experience a three-year sojourn in the jungles of Thailand went far to counter the optimistic possibilism which appeared so eminently reasonable in the air-conditioned clubs of Singapore. And if the possibilists seriously maintain that the rigours of the humid tropical environment are a wholly inadequate explanation of the retarded development of these regions, does their philosophy really amount to anything other than a re-formulation, however unintentional, of the old doctrine of white supremacy?

SELECT BIBLIOGRAPHY

Academica Sinica
Braak (A) (B) (C)
Brouwer (A) (B)
Calder
Campbell
Chapman
Chhibber
Crowe (A) (B)
Dale (A) (B)
Dobby (D) (E) (H)
Freyre
Garbell
Gourou (H) (K)
Gregory, J. W.
Gregory, J. W. and C. J.
Hare
Hudson and Rajchman
Kendrew
Koteswaram
Koteswaram, Raman and Parthasarathy
Lobeck
Mayr
Merrill

[106] Though the quality if not the quantity of the diet often leaves much to be desired.

Miller, A. A.
Mohr (C)
Molengraaf
Murphey (A)
Oliver
Palmer (A) (B)
Pelzer (C) (G) (H)
Pendleton (A)
Prescott and Pendleton
Ramage (A) (B)
Richards, P. W.
Riehl
Riehl, Alaka, Jorden and Renard
Robequain (D)
Roberts, G. (A)
Rutten (A) (B)
Rutter (A) (B)
Scrivenor (A) (B)
Simmons *et al.*
Sion
Spencer, J. E. (A)
Stamp (A)
Stauffer
Suess
Thompson, B. W.
Trewartha
Tucker
Umbgrove (A) (B)
Vageler
Van Bemmelen
Van Steenis
Van Vuuren
Wallace
Watson
Watts (A) (B)
Yin

Chambers's Encyclopædia
Encyclopædia Britannica
Indo-China (*N.I.D.*)
Netherlands East Indies, I (*N.I.D.*)
Malaria eradication (*W.H.O.*)

These sources have been supplemented by the atlas by Hudson and Rajchman.

On structure and relief Umbgrove, Molengraaf, Brouwer, Stauffer, Lobeck, Rutten and the two N.I.D. volumes are particularly useful. Braak (C) (in German) is the basic work on the climate of South-east Asia as a whole; Braak (A) (in English) is a useful shorter statement with particular reference to Indonesia. The seminal work on the Indo-Malayan vegetation is that by Van Steenis (in Dutch). A very useful English account is contained in *Netherlands East Indies, I* (*N.I.D.*); Merrill also provides an excellent introduction to the subject, while P. W. Richards' book may be recommended for the specialist. On soils, again, *Netherlands East Indies, I* (*N.I.D.*) is particularly useful, as also are the works by Pendleton and by Prescott and Pendleton.

On medical geography and the problems of the humid tropical environment in general, Gourou (H) is a classic, and further valuable data are also contained in the two N.I.D. volumes.

Note: As mentioned in Acknowledgements, Section III of this Chapter owes much to the work of Mr. J. L. H. Sibbons.

Addendum: A useful account of the problems posed by the humid tropical environment is contained in the inaugural lecture by Ho, Robert.

CHAPTER 3

The Indigenous Peoples and their Ways of Life

I. INTRODUCTION

As in relief so also in human geography South-east Asia is characterized by great diversity and complexity, and these traits are intimately related to its position and configuration which have made the region both a bridge and a barrier to the movement of peoples and ideas.

During prehistoric times, and more especially during the stage before the continuity of the Pleistocene land surface was slowly broken down by the post-glacial flooding of the Sunda Shelf, the bridging function was clearly the more important; and even after the main islands had assumed something like their present outlines[1] shortly before the dawn of recorded history, they continued to serve as a series of stepping stones which helped to determine the direction of the major migrations through the archipelagos.

The southward drift of peoples, which continued on the mainland well into historic times, has indeed been a principal *leit-motiv* in the evolving human pattern of the region as a whole. But although the process shows remarkable continuity in time, the volume of movement has in general been relatively small, for the extreme unhealthiness and the forbidding relief of the northern uplands have combined to limit the flow of migration,which in effect has been little more than a fluctuating overspill from the vast human reservoir of east-central Asia.

The consequent retardation of settlement in South-east Asia, by comparison with that of China and India, helps to explain why in historic times greater importance has been attached to the character of the region as a barrier between these two more densely peopled lands, and hence to such opportunities as nature affords for crossing or circumventing it. In this respect the choice has been virtually limited to two main alternatives, namely the direct but extremely difficult route across the northern plateaux and ranges, from Assam through upper Burma to south-western China, and the more circuitous but less hazardous sea route through the Malacca or Sunda Straits and the South China Sea, which offered the further advantage to early mariners of the monsoonal system of winds, which could be relied upon for both the outward and the homeward voyage in alternate halves of the year.

[1] However, significant changes have continued into historic times as, for example, the sedimentation of the east coast of Sumatra and the seaward growth of the large deltas of the mainland.

Accordingly, although the northern land route was used from very early times and has never since entirely lost its significance,[2] the sea route – including the variation of it which made use of short cuts overland across peninsular Siam – has been by far the more important of the two. Thus while South-east Asia as a whole has formed a great historic marchland between India and China, those parts of it which flank the main sea lanes have lain open to culture contact on the grand scale, and the effect of this has ultimately extended far beyond the immediate coastal fringe.

It is from the resultant meeting and mingling of diverse races and cultures which have entered South-east Asia by these various routes that the region has come to acquire its present character as a veritable ethnographic museum. In this and the following chapter attention will be confined to the indigenous peoples and their traditional civilizations, while chapters 5 and 6 will analyse the further complications that have been produced in the human pattern of the region as a result of Western imperial control and the associated influx of Chinese, Indians and other alien Asians. But it is not only the diversity of the contemporary population which is of such surpassing interest alike to the geographer and the anthropologist. For in addition South-east Asia also provides important information regarding the ancestry of the human species, and it will be appropriate to begin this chapter with a brief consideration of what this evidence reveals.

II. RACIAL ORIGINS

It was in 1891 that the fragmentary skeletal remains of *Pithecanthropus erectus* ('Java man') were found in the Solo valley and in the last thirty years several other finds of pithecanthropoid remains have been made in the same vicinity. All of these, with the possible exception of *Pithecanthropus modjokertensis*, which may be still earlier, are now dated at mid-Pleistocene, approximately half a million years ago, and it appears that these earliest hominids in South-east Asia were near kinsfolk of Peking man (*Sinanthropus pekinensis*).

The next group of remains to note are the eleven late Pleistocene skulls of *Homo soloensis*, which were likewise discovered in the Solo Valley of Java at Ngandong. These, although more advanced in type than those of the earlier Pleistocene, seem nevertheless to have belonged to individuals too primitive to be classed as *Homo sapiens*, and the first remains of unmistakably *sapiens* type known in South-east Asia are the two Wadjak skulls from the upper Brantas valley of eastern Java, which belonged to peoples living there perhaps 10,000 years ago.

For many years it was widely believed that the occurrence of *Pithecanthropus* and *Sinanthropus* in south-eastern and eastern Asia pointed to this part of the world as the critical region in which evolution took place from the anthropoid apes into the earliest sub-men. But more recently considerable evidence has

[2] This route from eastern India to south-western China acıoss the 'hump' acquired a new importance during the Second World War.

accumulated to suggest that this development and the further advance to *Homo sapiens* occurred much farther to the west, probably in the vicinity of Arabia, the Sahara[3] or the adjacent parts of eastern Africa. According to this interpretation the south-eastern and eastern margins of Asia[4] in the remoter peripheries of the Old World land-mass were both areas in which archaic forms survived until a comparatively late stage after more advanced types had established themselves nearer the Middle Eastern-African crossroads. Thus it is argued that *Homo sapiens* had already emerged in eastern Africa before *Pithecanthropus* and later *Homo soloenis* appeared in South-east Asia.

If, as has been suggested, the earliest known *sapiens* types in Java (as represented by the Wadjak skulls) were of proto-Australoid race, there would be strong grounds for believing that Australoid man originally evolved in this part of the world. However, it is still not wholly clear whether Australoids preceded Negritos in South-east Asia, though the probability seems to be that Negritos were not aboriginal to the region but migrated thither from the Indian sub-continent.

For the rest it may be assumed that the peopling of South-east Asia has been brought about by the series of southerly migrations to which reference has already been made. In the main these have probably come from the continental interior through the Indo-Pacific peninsula and thence into Indonesia, though there have also been subsidiary currents along the line of the offshore island arcs. Moreover, some of the movements continued far beyond the region into Australasia and the Pacific island world, leaving only scattered and often problematical traces in South-east Asia itself. In general, however, at least during the more recent stages of the process which have occurred since the invention of agriculture, successive waves of invaders have seized the better coastal and riverine lowlands for themselves, and in so doing have sought to push the earlier inhabitants either into the mountainous interiors or the remoter islands of the extreme south-east. But at the same time considerable intermixture has taken place between successive immigrant peoples and those already in occupation, and in several instances conquest has amounted to little more than the superimposition of a new aristocracy – and perhaps also its language – on an already established population.

The effect of this sequence is apparent in the contemporary racial pattern which is seen to be composed of two main layers. These include, first, a primitive component, which is rarely recognizable except in a few relatively isolated places, though its presence may be inferred over a far wider area, and secondly a more recent layer, which is now almost everywhere dominant and is particularly evident among the more advanced peoples.

In more detail the lower layer includes at least three distinct strands, of which

[3] During glacial times when these areas had a climate roughly similar to that of the Mediterranean lands today.

[4] As also of Europe and southern Africa.

the Australoid and the Negrito already noted form the first two. The true Australoid type is dark-skinned, dolico-cephalic[5], cymotrichous[6] and further characterized by beetling brows, generally coarse features, and low stature, which averages between 5 ft. and 5 ft. 2 in. in the adult male. The Negrito (or dwarf negro) which forms the second strand in the primitive substratum is equally dark and even shorter (4 ft. 10 in. to 5 ft.), but differs from the Australoid in being brachy-cephalic[7] and ulotrichous[8]. Thirdly the Melanesoid, though again dark-skinned, is considerably taller (5 ft. 5 in. to 5 ft. 6 in.) and while in respect of head-form, which is long and narrow, it is closer to the Australoid, in hair type it is ulotrichous like the Negrito. Thus it seems likely that the Melanesoid type is the result of mixing and subsequent development of these two more primitive stocks.

In the present population of South-east Asia the Australoid type in the strict sense is no longer represented, though traces of it may be recognized among many of the primitive hill peoples and the inhabitants of some of the eastern islands of Indonesia, notably the Flores-Timor group which lies opposite the northern coast of Australia.

However, several distinct groups of true Negritos, all of them extremely primitive peoples, still survive in isolated localities in the interior uplands of several parts of the region; these include the Semang of Malaya and the very similar Orang Akit of Sumatra, the Aëta of Luzon and the Tapiro of New Guinea.[9] Moreover Negrito blood is almost certainly present to a significant degree among many other relatively backward peoples, such as the Badui of Java and more especially among the interior folk of the Moluccas and eastern Lesser Sundas.

The present distribution of Melanesoids in South-east Asia is, on the other hand, more compact. For while no representatives of this type occur on the mainland or in the western islands, they become progressively commoner from west to east through the Lesser Sundas and are much in evidence among the Alfurs[10] of the Moluccas, and still farther east in New Guinea the hairy, long-legged Papuan representative of the Melanesoid type predominates over most of the interior.

Nevertheless much the greater part numerically of the present indigenous population of South-east Asia derives in the main from the later immigrants, who form the upper stratum already referred to. Two main components may be recognized here, sometimes referred to as Proto- and Deutero-Malays but perhaps less confusingly termed Nesiot (or Indonesian) and Pareœan (or southern Mongoloid) respectively. Both are of modest height (5 ft. 2 in. to 5 ft. 6 in.) though, if anything, the Nesiots tend to be the shorter of the two, but there are

[5] Long-headed.
[6] Wavy-haired, *i.e.* hair of elliptical cross section.
[7] Broad-headed.
[8] Woolly-haired, *i.e.* hair of flat cross section.
[9] The Andamanese also belong in this category.
[10] A collective name for the interior peoples of the Moluccas.

considerable differences in other respects. Thus the Nesiots tend to be dolichocephalic and cymotrichous, and their physiognomy, which sometimes shows a surprising resemblance to that of Europeans, suggests that there is a distinct Caucasoid[11] element in their make-up. The Pareœans, on the other hand, brachy-cephalic and flat-faced, leiotrichous[12] and yellow-brown in skin colour, are unmistakably Mongoloid in appearance and in some cases almost undistinguishable from the southern Chinese.

Both the Nesiots and the Pareœans were comparatively late-comers to South-east Asia and, according to Kunst, their arrival in Indonesia occurred between 2000 and 1500 B.C. While some scholars, who have regarded the Nesiots as related to the Caucasoid-Mediterranean peoples, have further postulated dispersal *via* the sea routes around the southern margins of Asia, it is usually held that these peoples came into South-east Asia overland from the north, probably via the Assam/Burma borderland. From there southwards their migration routes must have been very similar to those followed shortly afterwards by the Pareœans, who entered the peninsula from the high plateau country lying between Tibet and south-western China. Indeed it may well be misleading to think in terms of two clear-cut migrations, and the probability is rather of a whole series of related southward movements of progressively more Mongoloid peoples spreading down the main valleys of the peninsula and thence into the Indonesian archipelago. Meanwhile subsidiary movements also extended into the Philippines from the north, via southern China, and from the south via Borneo and other more easterly Indonesian islands.

The present geographical distribution of ethnic types seems consistent with such an interpretation. Thus Nesiot characteristics are very marked among many of the hill peoples of the mainland, such as the Wa and Palaung of Burma, the Kha and Moi farther east in Indochina, and the Jakun of the Malay peninsula. In the islands again the type is much in evidence among the Bataks and Gajo of interior Sumatra, the Tenggerese of the eastern uplands of Java and the Sasaks of Lombok, as also among the 'inlanders' of Borneo and Celebes, respectively known as Dyaks and Toradja, and the Bontoc, Ifugao, and other relatively backward groups in the Philippines.

Elsewhere, however, the Pareœan type predominates, and it is clear that peoples of this stock have been in occupation of most of the main coastal and riverine lowlands of South-east Asia at least since the time when recorded history begins there in the early centuries of the Christian era. Moreover, so far as the Malaysian realm is concerned, no major new components have been added to the indigenous pattern since that time, though there has undoubtedly been some minor Indian, Arab and Chinese admixture, as well as a great deal of inter-insular movement and associated mingling within the archipelago since very early times.

[11] However, most of the peoples classed as Nesiot today show at least as many Mongoloid as Caucasoid characteristics; in colour they are usually a darker brown than most Pareoeans.

[12] Having lank, straight hair, of round cross section.

Thus the present-day distinctions between such peoples as the Atjehnese, Menangkabaus and the Malays of eastern Sumatra, Malaya and the Bornean coasts, the Javanese and their near neighbours the Sundanese and Madurese, the Balinese, the Makasarese, Buginese and Menadonese of Celebes, the coastal peoples of the Moluccas and the Timor group and, in the Philippines, the Tagalog, Visayan, Ilocano and Moros, are essentially cultural in origin, for racially all are predominantly Pareœan in character and scarcely distinguishable in appearance one from another.

In mainland South-east Asia, however, the situation is more complex, for there the southward drift of peoples from the Tibeto-Chinese border has continued well into historic times. For this reason a distinction must be drawn between the early Mons (also known as Peguans or Talaings) of lower Burma and the Menam valley, the Khmers[13] of the Mekong valley, and the Chams of the central and southern coastlands of Annam, all of whom were essentially similar to the Pareœan peoples of the islands,[14] and the more recent arrivals from the north who include the Annamites,[15] the Tibeto-Burmans,[16] and the Thai-Lao-Shan peoples. Of the earlier Pareœan peoples only the Khmers survive in strength as a national group today, though small minorities of both Mons and Chams have preserved their identity in Burma and Indochina respectively. But undoubtedly much intermingling occurred between all these early Pareœan peoples and the later invaders whose descendants today form the dominant elements in Burma, Thailand, Laos and Vietnam. Furthermore, since these later arrivals were themselves of related Pareœan stock, the bulk of the modern populations of the mainland are not markedly different in physical type from their counterparts in the islands, though the skin colour of most of the mainlanders is perhaps a shade lighter and their features more obviously Mongoloid than those of contemporary Malaysians.[17]

Besides the major ethnic groups already mentioned, many lesser groups were caught up from time to time in the great historic currents of southward migration into the Indo-Pacific peninsula, and it is in the main from these – again predominantly Mongoloid – invaders that a majority of the present hill peoples, notably the Karens, Chins, Nagas and Kachins of Burma, and the Mans, Miaos and Lolos of Laos and Tonkin, are descended. While the Karens who mostly occupy the

[13] Khmer is the vernacular name for Cambodian.

[14] Though it is thought that during the Funan period in the first few centuries A.D. the inhabitants of the lower Mekong valley were Nesiots, who were later submerged beneath the Khmer invasion. See below, pp. 103–5.

[15] The Annamites were in occupation of the Song-koi delta before the dawn of the Christian era, but their advance southwards did not take place until much later. See below, pp. 113 and 122–3.

[16] Of whom he Pyus, who spread into lower Burma around the beginning of the Christian era, were probably the first wave. Later, the Pyus were submerged beneath the main advance of the Burmans proper.

[17] This difference in skin colour and features is most evident among the Annamites who are very similar to the southern Chinese. There has certainly been more mixing with Chinese stocks in some parts of the mainland than in the islands.

lower hill country along the Burma/Siam border seem to have moved in from the north-east well before the end of the first millennium A.D., many of the other hill peoples arrived much more recently, and it is this fact rather than any inherent inferiority on their part which probably explains their relegation to the poorer upland terrains.[18]

Finally, to complete this outline of the racial geography of South-east Asia it remains to add that within the last few centuries, and especially during the era of European dominance, the pattern has been further complicated by the great influx of Chinese and, to a lesser extent, of Indians and Arabs. While for the most part these have remained as distinctive minority groups, considerable miscegenation has also taken place. Likewise, particularly in the lands originally under Spain and Portugal, European admixture has been common, and the resultant Eurasian population includes mixtures of European with both indigenous and immigrant Asian stocks. But as the present chapter is concerned essentially with the indigenous peoples of South-east Asia, further discussion of this latest phase of racial diversification will be deferred to Chapters 5 and 6.

III. TRADITIONAL WAYS OF LIFE

In general the cultural divisions in South-east Asia run parallel with the outlines of the racial pattern described in the foregoing pages. And while the details of the picture are in many places complex and puzzling, it is nevertheless possible once again to discern order amid the variety.

At least 90 per cent of the indigenous population of South-east Asia today must be classed as rural in habitat, but within this broad category three distinct modes of life[19] can be recognized as in some degree common to the whole region. The first of these, namely that of the food gatherers, is much the least important economically and in the numbers involved, but is nevertheless represented by widely scattered groups, including besides the Negrito Semang, the Senoi-Temiar,[20] Kubu and Toala (respectively of interior Malaya, Sumatra and Celebes), all of whom seem to be at least partially Australoid in origin, the Nesiot Punan of Borneo, and various groups in the interior of New Guinea. Among these isolated and very backward peoples little or no regular cultivation is practised even today, and since their livelihood is obtained almost entirely by the hunting and collecting of jungle animals and plants, their mode of existence is basically nomadic.[21]

In such communities social organization is limited to the banding together of large family groups extending over two or three generations and commonly comprising some 40–50 individuals. These groups normally have customary

[18] For by this time the lowlands and lower plateaux were occupied in strength by the earlier arrivals already considered. Some of the hill peoples have migrated into their present areas within living memory.

[19] *I.e.* the traditional modes of life. In addition most of the commercial cultivators and estate workers must also be classed as rural.

[20] See below, pp. 90, 590 and 633n.

[21] Some of the less inaccessible of these peoples have in recent times begun to modify their mode of living in various ways, *e.g.* by obtaining metal tools, usually by barter.

rights over a particular stretch of territory, perhaps 20–30 square miles in extent, and this, in effect, implies an average density of population of at the most two or three to the square mile.

All-told, therefore, the number of people in South-east Asia who live in this extremely primitive way cannot be more than a few hundred thousand, but in contrast to this the second category, that of the shifting cultivators, includes several million people, who are widely distributed over the interior uplands of the Indo-Pacific peninsula and the Philippines, and also in the highlands and in many of the lowlands of the outer islands of Indonesia.

Although known by many different regional names – *taung-ya* in Burma, *tam râi* in Thailand, *hay* in Laos, *ray* in Vietnam, *caiñgin* in the Philippines, *humah* in Java, and *ladang* in the rest of Indonesia and in Malaya – the system is basically the same throughout and, moreover, is obviously akin to the methods which are extensively practised both in India and Ceylon, and in the African and American tropics as well. Indeed shifting tillage is still by far the commonest type of agriculture in use in the humid tropics as a whole and, in Gourou's opinion, 'there are few such clear instances of identical response by man to similar environment.'[22]

Wherever it occurs, this system 'of rotation of fields rather than of crops'[23] aims at maintaining the fertility of the fragile tropical soil under cultivation by means of long fallowing, designed as far as possible to preserve the protective cover provided by the natural vegetation. As practised in South-east Asia the usual method is to clear a patch of forest or secondary jungle by felling and burning, and then to cultivate this for one or two years before abandoning it in favour of other successive patches, leaving each in turn to rest for a long enough period to allow the forest substantially to replenish itself. After the original burnt-over clearing has been made, the stumps of the larger trees are left in the ground, only very limited weeding is undertaken in the first year[24], and cultivation may amount to little more than inserting tubers or yams into holes made by a digging stick. However, in most parts of South-east Asia such root crops have been largely replaced by millets and, more recently, by dry rice and maize,[25] though taro and yams, along with the sago palm remain very important in the eastern part of the Indonesian archipelago, and sugar and coconut palms, as well as various fruit trees, are almost ubiquitous.

Despite its obvious limitations and its prevailing appearance of untidiness, which originally called forth unfavourable criticism from Western observers,

[22] Gourou (H), p. 32.

[23] Pelzer (C), p. 17.

[24] Though if the plot is cultivated for a second year more extensive weeding will be necessary.

[25] The distinction between upland (or dry) and lowland (or wet) rice is by no means clear cut; many varieties of the former can be grown in areas usually associated with the latter, and *vice versa*. For further details see below, pp. 74–6. Maize has spread very widely over South-east Asia since the Spaniards introduced it into the Philippines from the Americas in the 16th century.

shifting cultivation is nowadays recognized as representing a serious attempt to utilize the poor laterized soils which are typical of much of South-east Asia as of other humid tropical regions.[26] Thus the link between the protective vegetation and the preservation of a healthy soil structure is implicit in the system and both the use of wood ash as a fertilizer after burning and the avoidance of excessive weeding are eminently sound.[27] So also is the practice of restricting the extent to which the soil is turned up either by digging or for the removal of tree stumps, for burning exaggerates the innate friability of most tropical soils and to disturb them more than is absolutely necessary in such circumstances may easily cause serious damage to their structure. However, if a plot is cultivated for more than one season, some breaking up of its surface will be necessary before the second and successive plantings take place, and for this purpose the hoe which is now in common use represents a distinct improvement on the digging stick.

Provided, therefore, that population does not rise above the level which can be maintained while at the same time allowing each plot of land an adequate period of fallow in relation to cultivation, the system can be continued indefinitely. But if pressure becomes too great, the ratio of fallow to cultivation is liable to fall, and when this happens both the fertility and the structure of the soil quickly suffer, and erosion may follow with devastating consequences for the whole surrounding countryside.

While the capacity of shifting tillage to support population obviously varies greatly according to local conditions of soil and climate, the calculations made in respect of the outer islands of Indonesia by Van Beukering in 1940[28] provide a rough guide to the density which the system may be expected to maintain. In brief he estimated that a shifting cultivator and his dependants normally occupied about $2\frac{1}{2}$ acres of land a year and, allowing nine years fallow for every year under crops, this would mean that an average size family of five persons would need to have some 25 acres of suitable land at its disposal. This would therefore permit a maximum possible density of 130 persons to the square mile, though since these figures make no allowance for the proportion of any given tract of country which is either physically unsuitable for use or needs to be left permanently under forest, the normal practicable density over extensive areas is unlikely to be more than about half this figure and in many cases may well be very much lower.

Nevertheless it is clear that this system represents an enormous advance in efficiency over that of the hunters and collectors previously considered, and the social organization which is associated with it is correspondingly more elaborate. Thus the village is commonly the unit of settlement and often functions collec-

[26] On the pros and cons of shifting cultivation see Pelzer (C), pp. 21–24, (H), pp 5–10, Gourou (H), pp. 31–33, and Farmer, pp. 48–50.

[27] Pelzer (G), p. 12 also points out that the decomposition of the tree stumps by fungi, moulds, termites, etc., is good for the soil, and at the same time presents no problem to cultivators using a digging stick or hoe.

[28] See Van Beukering, A.J., *Het ladangsvraagstuk* (unpublished), quoted in Pelzer (C), p. 23.

tively, as in the task of clearing the forest and in ownership of land. Owing to the wide area over which its operations extend as the years go by, the village may need to be moved from time to time, and among many of the peoples in question the whole village community lives together in a single 'long house' as, for example, among some of the Dyaks of Borneo, the Toradja of Celebes and the Malayan Sakai.[29] In other cases the multi-family house of various other shapes seems to be intermediary in character between this and the single-family house favoured by many of the sedentary cultivators, and both these communal types of dwelling are widely associated with matrilineal forms of social organization which survive in many parts of the region. Despite many variations in architectural style, there is a broad similarity throughout in the use of bamboo as the main structural material, along with the leaves of various palms for thatching, and also in the practice of building on piles or stilts.

The last of the three ways of life to be considered is that of the sedentary cultivators, who today form the great majority of the South-east Asian peasantry and include nearly all the main Pareœan peoples listed on p. 68.

With few exceptions wet rice cultivation provides the basis of subsistence among all these peoples, though they may in addition cultivate various dry crops, nowadays often for cash, and many of them also maintain garden plots of varying size immediately surrounding the individual house or village. Such plots[30] are particularly well developed in the densely peopled parts of Java in which island they account for some 15 per cent of the total cultivated acreage, but they are also found in many other parts of the region, including the eastern islands of the Indonesian archipelago where they achieved renown as the earliest centres of spice cultivation. Whether or not it is true, as Ochse and Terra maintain,[31] that this type of cultivation represents a survival of primitive grainless hoe cultivation, in which all the useful plants of the forest have been concentrated in compact and accessible plots, the latter do in effect reproduce something closely parallel to the natural pattern of forest vegetation.

Thus it is often possible to distinguish three storeys, first of low growing plants which tolerate the shade, such as yams, arrowroot, sweet potatoes and taro, then a middle layer of higher plants like cassava, papaya and the banana, and finally an upper level of tall palms and other fruit trees including the coconut, pomelo, jackfruit and tamarind. While again, as with the lands of the shifting cultivators, the appearance of these garden plots is at first sight confused, untidy and un-

[29] However, this should not be taken to imply any direct correlation between the distribution of shifting cultivation and that of communal dwellings. See Loeb and Broek pp. 414–25.

[30] Nowadays these garden plots are often at least partially used for cash production, especially near towns. This however should not be confused with the more extensive market-gardening practised by many Chinese.

[31] Ochse, J. J., and Terra, G. J. A., *Geld-en-producten-huishonding, volksvoeding en gezondheid in Koetowinangoen, Part I: Het onderzoek naar den economischen en landbouwkundigen toestand en het Voedselverbruik te Koetowinangoen* Buitenzorg, 1934, quoted in Pelzer (C), p. 44.

weeded, the system has an eminently sound ecological basis, and the wide variety of vegetables and fruits produced help materially both to balance and to flavour the otherwise monotonous rice diet on which the peasants subsist.[32]

Lowland or wet rice is of many varieties which have been bred in the course of several thousands of years mainly in response to the diverse range of climates and soils found within the monsoon realm. Thus, for example, although the normal length of stalk is some three or four feet, the so-called floating rice which has been evolved in the deeply flooded plains of Cochinchina may reach as much as fifteen feet in height, while elsewhere salt-tolerant varictics are adapted for cultivation near the coast and in brackish water, and all-told the length of time required for growth ranges from as little as 60 to as much as 300 days.

TABLE 3

AREA, OUTPUT AND YIELD PER ACRE OF PADDY (*i.e.* UNHUSKED RICE)

All figures are annual totals or annual averages.
Areas in thousand acres, outputs in thousand metric tons and yields in bushels per acre.

Country	*Area under paddy*		*Output of paddy*		*Yield per acre*	
	1934/5 1938/9 av.	1954/5	1934/5 1938/9 av.	1954/5	1934/5 1938/9 av.	1954/5
Burma	12,184·6	9,577·8	6,971	5,568	28·0	28·7
Thailand	8,327·0	11,179·3	4,357	5,709	25·9	25·1
Vietnam*	10,828·6	5,342·2	5,434	2,707	24·7	24·9
Cambodia	1,806·4	2,767·4	767	850	20·9	13·9
Laos	1,047·7	1,235·5	297	400	13·9	15·9
Federation of Malaya ..	733·9	867·4	530	662	35·4	37·6
Brunei	4·9	7·4	2	4	19·9	26·4
North Borneo	81·5	71·7	20	42	12·0	28·8
Sarawak	595·6	—	148	—	12·1	—
Indonesia	15,619·9	16,341·1	9,987	11,747	31·5	35·2
Philippines	4,917·4	6,560·9	2,179	3,203	21·9	23·9
Japan	7,830·5	7,506·9	11,501	11,336	72·3	74·3

* 1954/5 data refer to Southern Vietnam only. Japan is included for comparison.

Source: Based upon *Economic Survey of Asia and the Far East* (U.N.) Bangkok annual.

Likewise in respect of its soil requirements rice shows considerable tolerance, though under intensive wet cultivation a heavy soil undoubtedly gives the best results, and a heavy clay subsoil is a great asset in preventing excessive loss of water through percolation.

[32] Coconut oil, widely used for frying, is the principal source of fat in the diet; fish is the chief source of animal protein. See below, p. 78.

Although over a thousand varieties of rice (*Oryza sativa*) are recognized, the most important of those now in cultivation can be divided into two major groups known respectively as *indica* and *japonica*.[33] As may be inferred from its name, the former group is most commonly associated with tropical Asia, and is adapted to give good yields under conditions of abundant heat and moisture (even on relatively infertile soils), particularly if there is a long period available for growth. The *japonica* group on the other hand seems to be a later development in response to mid-latitude conditions, and benefits markedly both from the longer hours of sunshine available there during the summer months, and also from the application of natural and artificial fertilizer.

Thus in Japan and other temperate countries *japonica* rice will give significantly higher yields than are commonly obtained from the *indica* varieties grown in the tropics. (Table 3) Nevertheless, provided that adequate water can be obtained either directly in the form of impounded rainfall or else by means of irrigation, which is usually necessary in some form or another if the annual rainfall is less than 50 in. or so, most parts of lowland South-east Asia are capable of yielding 20–35 bushels per acre of *indica* rice, which does not compare unfavourably with the average yield of wheat in Western countries.

However both the preparation and maintenance of rice fields are laborious tasks, the former of which involves levelling the land and surrounding it with a retaining wall of earth to hold the water required for cultivation. Usually the best natural facilities for such construction are found in the alluvial lowlands where the ground is at least partially levelled by nature, the soil often inherently suitable for rice cultivation, and river water is available either by direct seasonal flooding or by means of irrigation channels which can normally be dug there without great difficulty.

In all these respects the relatively small lowlands of east-central Java are almost ideal for *sawah* (wet-field) construction and cultivation, and furthermore the relatively lighter forest cover, associated there with the long dry season, was doubtless more easily cleared in early days than was the dense tropical rain forest elsewhere in the region. Somewhat similar geographical conditions to those of east-central Java are also to be found in certain parts of the mainland dry zones, where again wet rice cultivation has been practised for a considerably longer period than in most other parts of South-east Asia. But in the lower courses of the great peninsular rivers the problems of water control have been much more formidable, and, except in the Annamite lands,[34] were never fully solved until recent times.

In other areas shortage of natural lowland has frequently led to extensive terracing along the edges of the uplands in order to increase the acreage of flooded fields, and notably in parts of Java, Bali and Luzon such works, extending like

[33] See Calder, pp. 134–5, Grist, pp. 302–3, and Pelzer (H), pp. 11–12.

[34] The Song-koi delta was first subjected to Chinese methods of water control approximately 2,000 years ago. See below, pp. 88–9 and 531–2.

huge flights of steps far up the mountain sides, have been built and maintained at a prodigious cost in human toil.

While there are many regional variations in the technique of cultivation, it is common practice in most parts of South-east Asia to plant the seeds close together in nursery beds and then, some four to six weeks later, to transplant the seedlings to the main fields which have meanwhile been thoroughly soaked with water and worked into a fine soft mud by repeated hoeing, ploughing or trampling, coupled with systematic harrowing and weeding. After transplanting has taken place the level of water in the fields needs to be carefully regulated so that the upper part of the growing plant is not submerged, and when the rice is approaching maturity the fields are drained in preparation for harvesting, which is also carried out by hand.

Like the other forms of cultivation which have already been considered, this traditional system of wet rice agriculture is the outcome of a long process of painstaking adaptation to the peculiar local conditions of climate and terrain[35] and since, moreover, it involves an altogether more intensive form of land use than that of shifting tillage, the achievement is all the more remarkable. Thus in the first place the levelling, dyking and, where necessary, terracing of the rice fields together provide a high degree of protection against the ever-present threat of soil erosion and, furthermore, in many areas cultivation has continued for hundreds if not indeed thousands of years without any serious loss of fertility. This is notably the case where the irrigation or flood waters contain abundant mineral matter and, in particular, where they deposit a seasonal layer of fertile silt as, for example, in much of the volcanic country of Java and in the valleys of the great peninsular rivers which rise beyond the limits of the severely laterized zone.

Nevertheless even in these areas continued cropping without any long fallowing often calls for some further replenishment of the soil, and although the buffalo and ox[36] are widely used for ploughing, the quantity of manure so derived is not large. Accordingly such practices as leaving a substantial portion of the rice stalks in the soil,[37] or raising various leguminous manure crops have been adopted in certain cases, and in this latter respect again the Annamites have hitherto been the most enterprising of all South-east Asian peoples. Otherwise, however, it must be admitted that away from the richer alluvial terrains there are many signs of soil impoverishment in almost all parts of the region, and while the problem could be at least partially solved by wise and adequate use of chemical fertilizers, most of the cultivators are either too poor or too ignorant to adopt this remedy.

[35] Though, with the possible exception of Java, all the main rice-growing areas of South-east Asia acquired their basic methods by cultural borrowing from either India or China.

[36] The buffalo is more useful for ploughing heavy swamp soils, but in areas of drier climate and lighter soils the ox commonly takes its place. However, although cattle are fairly widely distributed throughout the region, more especially in the drier parts, they are usually of only very minor importance as sources of meat or milk. The goat is fairly common in many areas, and is generally valued more for its flesh than for milk.

[37] By cutting not far below the ear. See Pelzer (C), p, 49.

In addition to the wet fields and garden plots a certain amount of generally inferior land is commonly used by the sedentary cultivators for the raising of supplementary dry crops, both of grains and of other kinds, including various perennials. In most parts of the region this has traditionally been of relatively minor importance, but in modern times it has taken on a new meaning in many areas with the increasing participation of peasant farmers in cash crop production. In Java, where such activities are of long standing and population pressure is acute, recourse to the so-called *tegalan* system is very common and the same applies with even greater force in the nearby and notoriously congested island of Madura where a high proportion of the surface consists of low limestone uplands. But despite the considerable skill and industry of the local peasant cultivators, soil erosion tends to be a serious problem on much of this land, which is often strained to the limits of its productive capacity, and although terracing and other remedies have been fairly extensively practised, notably in Madura, the intrinsic value of the land is often too low really to justify them.

For the most part, however, subsistence sedentary cultivation in South-east Asia remains pre-eminently the cultivation of wet paddy and, as has already been implied, this system simultaneously demands a high expenditure of labour and provides a correspondingly high output of food in relation to the area cultivated. While it is by no means easy to distinguish which came first in what seems to be a vicious spiral of cause and effect, the fact remains that wherever wet-rice cultivation is practised in South-east Asia today the density of population is several times higher than that supported elsewhere in the region by shifting tillage.[38] (See Figs. 6 and 20.)

Nevertheless two further observations are called for at this stage. First, except in Java and the northern Annamite lands, where rural densities of 1,000 and more to the square mile occur over extensive areas, the average density remains well below those in the corresponding parts of India, China and Japan. And secondly, all cultural differences apart, it seems beyond dispute that the areas in South-east Asia which support the heaviest densities of agricultural population are with few exceptions those which possess the most intrinsically fertile soil. While the first of these points can perhaps be explained largely in terms of the more recent settlement and agricultural development of South-east Asia compared with neighbouring regions, the second automatically poses the further question of what the carrying capacity of the lands at present under shifting tillage would be if they also were to change over to wet rice cultivation. More detailed consideration of this problem must be deferred to later chapters, but beyond any doubt it is a matter of the utmost importance for the future of the whole of South-east Asia.

The social organization which is found in association with sedentary rice cultivation in South-east Asia exhibits many interesting variants in different parts of the region, though in general settlement tends to be at least partially

[38] And far above the average for the humid tropics as a whole.

concentrated in relatively large rural agglomerations[39] and a rich development of village life is almost everywhere typical. Indeed, notwithstanding the often quite elaborate political structure, especially in many parts of the lowland areas where some form of urban life has been in existence for well over a thousand years, the village community still remains by far the most significant social unit so far as the great mass of the population is concerned, and there are widespread and deeply rooted traditions of democratic election to the various village offices, of communal ploughing and ownership of land, and of mutual aid[40] among the members of the community. In an economic sense also the village was traditionally an almost completely self-contained unit, for besides producing their own requirements of food[41] most of its members engaged in various handicraft industries during the slack periods of the agricultural year, and among some of the more advanced groups individual villages might also contain a number of whole- or part-time craftsmen skilled in such trades as carpentry, metal-work and boat building.

As regards dwellings a wide variety both of architectural forms and related social customs can be traced, from the ornate communal houses of the Menangkabaus, who have an elaborate matriarchal organization, to the single-family houses common among the Javanese, the coastal and peninsular Malays, and many of the mainland peoples farther north. Like their more primitive neighbours who practise shifting tillage, nearly all the sedentary cultivators also rely largely on bamboo and palm leaf as construction materials[42] and, moreover, apart from the Annamites whose dwellings are similar to those of the Chinese, and the Javanese who nowadays favour houses with the floor resting on the ground, all adopt the familiar practice of building on piles.

Though pile dwellings have certain advantages even in inland localities in the tropics,[43] it is probable that they were originally designed to give protection against flooding in coastal and riparian areas. And certainly the great majority of indigenous settlements are concentrated in such areas, for, as we have seen, waterways provide the only natural routes through the tropical rain forest and well-water is often virtually unobtainable in maturely laterized country.

Indeed one of the outstanding common denominators in South-east Asia is the widespread prevalence of almost amphibious ways of life, a fact which is in no way surprising in view of the characteristically waterlogged nature of so much of the region's coastal plains and the seasonal flooding by huge and swollen

[39] With or without subsidiary hamlets.

[40] Known in Indonesia as *gotong rojong*. See below, pp. 296, 313, 381 and 448n.

[41] From a nutritional point of view the traditional diet, of unpolished rice, vegetables, fish, eggs and coconut and palm oil, was adequate and reasonably well balanced.

[42] The houses of sedentary cultivators are usually more substantial and often more elaborately finished than those of shifting cultivators.

[43] Building on piles gives a cool draught under the house, affords protection against snakes and other animals, and allows fires to be made to keep away mosquitoes. Poultry, and in non-Muslim areas pigs, are often kept under the house and live off the refuse which collects there. See Hodder (D), pp. 60–73.

rivers of most of the main interior valleys. Thus virtually all the peoples in such areas show considerable skill both in boat-building and in navigation, whether on inland waterways or on the sea, while fishing, with the aid of a great variety of traps, nets, lines and stupefying poisons, is well-nigh ubiquitous. Almost without exception fish provides the main source of animal protein in the diet, and the strong-tasting, and even stronger smelling fish-pastes, which are known under a variety of local names, are commonly esteemed by most of the coastal peoples alike on the mainland and in the archipelago.[44]

However, most of these apparently aquatic traits are also found among the shifting cultivators as well, many of whom nowadays live in upland or even mountainous areas far removed from the coast. Nor are these the only cultural characteristics which are in a significant measure common to both the relatively backward and the more advanced peoples within the region as a whole. Thus, as has already been suggested, the garden plot, which is now most typical of the regions of intensive farming, may well represent a survival of a much more primitive form of cultivation, and the practice of raising poultry is almost equally common among shifting cultivators and sedentary agriculturists.[45]

Similarly the matrilineal organization of society overlaps the divide between settled and shifting cultivators, and almost certainly its distribution in former times was much more extensive than it is today. Closely associated in origin with this trait is the high social status of women which, again, seems to be common to the region in its entirety and to have survived with almost equal success in Buddhist Burma, Islamic Indonesia and the Christian parts of the Philippines.

All these and many parallel lines of evidence[46] would seem to suggest, first, that a common indigenous culture existed, probably over the greater part of South-east Asia at an early stage in the human story and, secondly, that in the process of successive invasion and cultural colonization from outside two important developments repeatedly occurred. On the one hand, peoples who had originally inhabited the coastlands and river valleys, but were later driven into the interior uplands or the remoter islands of the east, continued in the relative isolation but often quite different physical circumstances of their new abodes to practise the ways of life to which they had traditionally been accustomed.[47] And secondly, the new-comers in the coastal and riverine lowlands, besides bringing traditions and techniques of their own, also acquired many of the cultural habits of the previous populations, often as a result of extensive inter-marriage, and in their turn were subjected to further acculturation from outside as a result of the maritime trading links which later grew up with neighbouring lands.

[44] See Spencer, J. E. (A), Chapter 6, and Firth for further details on fishing.

[45] Moreover in many parts of South-east Asia both shifting and irrigated cultivation are carried on side by side by the same peoples, for example, with *ladangs* on hillsides and *sawah* in the valleys.

[46] See Furnivall (B), p. 16.

[47] For example Pelzer (C), p. 17, points out that shifting cultivation is often thought to be particularly adapted to uplands, though in reality shifting cultivators prefer flat country if it is available.

Thus while the interior uplands and the outlying islands are typically areas of cultural continuity in which older ways of life have been preserved, often with surprisingly little modification for thousands of years, the coastal fringes and the principal riverine lowlands, especially in the western part of the region, are pre-eminently areas of cultural change and replacement.

IV. CULTURAL ORIGINS

Any attempt to trace the relationships beween the existing modes of life and the racial pattern as it has gradually evolved within South-east Asia is beset with many pitfalls. Nevertheless certain hypotheses have been advanced which make it possible to attempt a reconstruction of the sequence of cultural evolution in the region during prehistoric times.

Leaving aside the many complex problems that arise over the interpretation of the crude artefacts apparently associated with the early sub-men of South-east Asia, we may reasonably assume that their successors, the first truly human inhabitants of the region, eventually evolved a form of Palæolithic hunting and gathering culture not strikingly different from that of the present-day Negritos and other similarly primitive peoples described on pp. 69–70.

This in turn was succeeded over much of the region by the more advanced Bacson-Hoabinhian (Mesolithic) culture, which takes its name from the two provinces in Tonkin where the most numerous remains have been found.[48] These artefacts, consisting of not very highly finished stone implements, bone utensils, fishing tackle and pottery, were probably the work of early Australoid and Melanesoid peoples, and it has been inferred that their economy, though based on hunting, collecting and especially fishing, was also characterized in some cases by supplementary cultivation of a rudimentary kind.

It is to the Mesolithic peoples of South-east Asia that Carl Sauer has attributed one of the most decisive advances in the progress of the human race, namely the development of the earliest form of agriculture ever practised by man.[49] In support of his contention that South-east Asia was the hearth of this first fishing-planting culture,[50] in which yams, aroids and bananas, together with various palms and spices were the first cultivated plants, and such small household animals as the dog, pig, fowl, duck and goose were domesticated, Sauer stresses the region's natural advantages of 'high physical and organic diversity . . . reversed monsoons giving abundant rainy and dry periods, of many waters inviting to fishing, of location at the hub of the Old World for communication by water or land.'[51]

Since this is as yet only one possible hypothesis, it must suffice here merely

[48] Though related finds have been made in many other parts of South-east Asia.

[49] Sauer, Chapter 2.

[50] *I.e.* planting as opposed to the seeding of plants, which did not take place till Neolithic times.

[51] Sauer, p. 24.

to record the salient features of the culture as Sauer has envisaged it. Thus '. . . the men built the boats and fished; the women had domain over the tilled land and the homes. Women were cooks and cultivators, domestics and domesticators. These societies were largely developed and organized by their women . . . The *Kulturkreis* school seem to have a valid generalization in equating its "Old Planter" complex with matrilineal societies, and in linking to them multi-family houses . . . providing living and storage space for the extended household and often built on platforms set on posts.'[52]

Whether or not Sauer's thesis be accepted, there is now a substantial measure of agreement that one of the most ancient centres of agriculture did develop within the tropical monsoon zone of southern Asia, though whether South-east Asia itself was involved is much less clear. The *vittatus* species of pig and various fowls are indigenous to the area, and it seems that they as well as the water buffalo were domesticated here in very early times. The same argument also applies in the case of most of the cultivated plants mentioned by Sauer, and as a group these differ completely from the plants first cultivated in the better known hearth of Neolithic agriculture in the Middle East/Caspian region.

This difference is fundamentally a reflection of the profound climatic differences between the two areas and these in turn explain why in Monsoon Asia, with its seasonal rhythm, such Western-type grains as wheat and barley, which require a relatively dry summer, have never been adopted. Instead, however, millet and more especially rice gradually replaced the other indigenous starch foods, and it is now widely held that rice was first domesticated somewhere in southern Asia, probably in Neolithic times. In order to practise such cultivation the tropical forest vegetation must first have been cleared, and it seems reasonable to assume that this was done primarily by the slash and burn technique which still survives among the shifting cultivators of the region today.

Whether, however, either mainland South-east Asia or, as some have suggested, parts of Indonesia participated in this earliest phase of rice cultivation is still an open question. And whether or not South-east Asia was in the forefront of human progress in these remote times, it seems clear that no such cultural lead was maintained. On the contrary, the Neolithic stage seems to have persisted over most of the region until much later than in India and China, and in the closing centuries B.C., when the Bronze Age agrarian civilizations of these two neighbouring lands[53] had already reached a high level of advancement, the lowland peoples of South-east Asia were only just beginning to learn from them the use of metals.

It has been customary to attribute the introduction of Neolithic culture into South-east Asia to the Nesiot peoples, and the earliest use of metals there, both bronze and iron, to the Pareœans who later followed them into its coastal and riverine plains. But it was only during the last few centuries B.C. that the so-

[52] *Ibid.*, p. 28.

[53] As also of the still earlier centres in the Middle East.

called Dongson (iron and bronze) culture[54] began to spread southwards across South-east Asia and gradually to supersede the older Neolithic cultures in the lowlands. There its diffusion was greatly facilitated by the navigational skill of the early Pareœan invaders, who not only travelled extensively over the more or less enclosed seas of South-east Asia itself, but also ventured beyond to India and China, and the contacts which they thus established had already become the means of further cultural enrichment before the great era of Indianization and Sinicization began.

Already, therefore, as the mists of prehistory begin to disperse in the light of the first fragmentary historical records shortly after the dawn of the Christian era, South-east Asia appears in its most characteristic rôle as the meeting ground of cultural influences from India and China. This is not, of course, to pretend that its peoples were untutored savages, incapable of any initiative, and in fact their Austro-Asiatic civilization had developed many distinctive traits of considerable refinement. Nevertheless, in view of the severe restraints imposed by the humid tropical environment, some measure of cultural retardation *vis-à-vis* India and China is surely to be expected, and the surprising thing is not that South-east Asia progressed more slowly than its neighbours, but rather that a region in such latitudes had attained so high a level of civilization at so early a date.

According to the pioneer historian in this field, Georges Cœdès,[55] the Austro-Asiatic civilization was characterized *inter alia* by a distinct group of languages, a matrilineal organization of society, worship of ancesters and of the soil god, with shrines located on high places, and a mythological dualism in which the interior uplands were opposed to the sea. Furthermore he postulates irrigated rice cultivation as the agricultural basis of this civilization, a view which appears to be derived from the philological arguments of Kern and other Dutch scholars who were primarily concerned with Javanese sources.[56]

But this philological line of reasoning is not wholly convincing and there is a growing volume of evidence to suggest that, wherever in southern Asia rice was first domesticated, the advance to irrigated cultivation of this grain was first made in India and/or in China, and the introduction of such methods in South-east Asia did not take place until much later times.

Thus at the time when their homeland was incorporated into the Chinese empire in the 2nd century B.C., the Annamites were still practising a system of shifting tillage and, to judge from contemporary Chinese accounts, the same was probably true of the inhabitants of Funan, in the Mekong delta, prior to Indianization in the early centuries A.D.

Moreover, although some of the Thai and Burman invaders certainly brought

[54] This name also comes from Vietnam, after a village where many finds have been made. The Dongson culture was probably introduced into South-east Asia from China; the early Dongson art style appears to be closely related to that of central-southern China in the 4th and 3rd centuries B.C.

[55] Hall (B), p. 8, and Cœdès, p. 26.

[56] See Schrieke, Pt. I, pp. 232–4.

with them a limited knowledge of Chinese methods of irrigated rice cultivation, which they introduced to several parts of the interior of the Indo-Pacific peninsula before the 10th century A.D., and some of their coastal neighbours had learned to use the Indian wet-farming techniques at a still earlier date, there are strong arguments for believing that as late as the 15th century the great Khmer city of Angkor depended heavily on food obtained from shifting tillage, even though wet-rice cultivation was practised near to the city itself, with the aid of large water storage tanks and distributing channels.[57]

As regards the archipelago, again, the evidence is conflicting. Thus wet cultivation may have been carried on in some parts of east-central Java from even earlier times than in Annam, and the terraced rice fields of the Bontoc and Ifugao in Luzon are likewise of great antiquity, but there is no reason to believe that irrigated cultivation was at all widely practised in Malaysia before the era of Indian acculturation, and the adoption of this technique in some areas, such as the Preanger district of western Java, did not take place until well into the period of European rule.[58]

In short, while some rudimentary wet-rice cultivation may have been practised in a few favoured localities in South-east Asia before the dawn of the Christian era, and if so perhaps as a result of indirect contact with India or China, the system must have remained relatively limited in its distribution until much later, and the dominant position which it occupies today is of comparatively recent origin.

Nor, in spite of the obvious advantages which the system entails compared with other more primitive forms, is this delay in its general acceptance altogether surprising. For besides requiring a distinctly high level of skill on the part of its practitioners as well as a fairly elaborate form of territorial organization if major water resources are to be satisfactorily controlled,[59] wet-rice cultivation calls for a far greater expenditure of human effort than do the somewhat casual methods of the shifting tillers, and in these circumstances both the generally enervating climate and the lethargy induced by recurrent malaria and other diseases may have been potent forces making for conservatism.

Thus it is possible that in many cases only the threat of hunger arising out of mounting population pressure would provide the necessary stimulus to bring about such a change and, in view of the relative recency of the main currents of migration and the high death rate due to both disease and internecine warfare, this problem has been slower to emerge in most parts of South-east Asia than in either India or China. Moreover, even when the challenge has arisen, it has not necessarily elicited this particular response. Thus, for example, the increase of

[57] See Pelzer (C), p. 20, who quotes Pendleton, R. L.: 'Some inter-relations between agriculture and forestry particularly in Thailand', *Journal Thailand Research Society, Natural History Supplement*, Vol. 12, 1939, Bangkok, pp. 33–52.

[58] According to Scheltema rice did not become the principal food for a large part of the population of Java until after the early 19th century. Cited by Pelzer (C), p. 75.

[59] See below, pp. 93–4.

population in upland Burma in the 19th century and that in interior Sarawak today[60] have both led instead to the dangerously attractive alternative of merely shortening the period of fallow within the traditional system, and Pendleton has suggested that a similar sequence of events was the root cause of the decline of the Khmer empire in the 15th century.[61]

Finally it remains to add that the skill of some South-east Asian wet-rice cultivators appears to have declined rather than improved within historic times. Thus for example the Siamese, who first learned about irrigated cultivation from the Chinese in Yunnan, must then have been familiar with the art of hill-side terracing, but this has apparently been completely lost in the course of their migration into the Menam lowlands. Similarly the peninsular Malays, who presumably acquired their wet-farming techniques from the upland peoples of Sumatra, where again terracing is widespread, have no knowledge of this practice.

While in both these instances the existence of adequate expanses of flat alluvial land in past times is perhaps a sufficient explanation for the loss of interest in a labour-consuming technique which had become a stark necessity in upland regions, the growing pressure on the land today, at least in Malaya, makes it a cause for concern that this particular skill has died out there.

V. THE CULTURAL INFLUENCE OF INDIA AND CHINA

With the beginning of recorded history the influence of India and China upon the cultural evolution of South-east Asia emerges with greater clarity. And although present-day scholars rightly stress the importance of the indigenous element in the civilizations which arose within the region during the first fifteen hundred years of the Christian era, the fact remains that all the greatest achievements there, whether in the realm of art or statecraft, were made under the stimulus of an inspiration which derived ultimately from one or other of these two great neighbours.

So far as India is concerned, the effectiveness of the mountain barrier separating Assam from the Indo-Pacific peninsula has limited overland contact to the minimum, and the historic links have in consequence been almost entirely by sea. But on the other hand Indian civilization had come to terms with a humid tropical environment long before the Chinese had settled in what are now their southern coastal provinces, and to explore eastwards across the Bay of Bengal presented no major climatic problems to the early mariners of the Coromandel coast. Thus by the 6th century B.C. explorers and traders were edging their way along the coast to Burma, the Malay peninsula and the western islands of Indonesia, probably in search of gold and other precious metals.[62]

[60] For a detailed account of the problem in Sarawak see Hodder (B), pp. 76–7.

[61] For further consideration of this problem see below, pp. 114–5.

[62] See Wheatley (E), pp. 65 and 67. Wheatley accepts the view that the Golden Chersonese of Ptolemy was in the Malay peninsula.

Moreover, owing to its midway position in the Indian Ocean, peninsular India was well placed to take a leading part in developing the trade of the great sea route which skirts the southern shore of Asia all the way from Egypt to the China coast. And although many other peoples, notably the Arabs and Persians and later, also, the Chinese themselves assumed a larger share in the exchange of textiles and other manufactures against the metals, aromatic woods, ivory, camphor, spices and other forms of primary produce from South-east Asia, the commercial links between the latter and India were maintained with great persistence until the coming of the Europeans.[63]

Nevertheless the volume of this traffic underwent significant fluctuations from time to time, and a connexion may be traced between periods of exceptional maritime activity and the temporary closing of the land routes across the continental interior as a result of disturbed conditions among the nomadic peoples of Central Asia. Certainly some such increase seems to have occurred during the first two centuries A.D., and this in turn may have been partially responsible for inaugurating the great era of Indianization which began in South-east Asia about this time.

This interpretation would accord with the views of those historians who, while rejecting the earlier hypothesis of a mass migration of southern Indians to South-east Asia, nevertheless believe that a series of small colonies of Indian merchants grew up at key points along the sea route during the early centuries A.D. Thereafter, according to this view, some of the more enterprising settlers established themselves as territorial rulers, perhaps by marrying the daughters of local indigenous chieftains, and subsequently the Hindu and Buddhist religions, following in the wake of commerce, were actively propagated from these early centres. In this way, therefore, Indian civilization gradually spread over the greater part of the coastlands of Indonesia and the Indo-Pacific peninsula as far as western Celebes and southern Annam respectively.[64]

More recently, however, this interpretation has been challenged by several scholars, notably by van Leur who claims that the Indianization of South-east Asia was merely a continuation overseas of the Brahmanization of India, a process which had begun in the north-west and later spread over the Deccan. Thereafter, just as the various princes of southern India had aided this advance by enlisting the services of Brahmans,[65] skilled in writing and administration, to legitimize their rule and to organize their states according to the Hindu code, so in the first centuries A.D. South-east Asian chieftains, who were by this time

[63] The Chola attacks on Sri Vijaya in the 11th century (see below, pp. 115–6) were the outcome of an attempt by southern Indian trading peoples to keep control over a substantial share of such trade. But the character of Indian participation in South-east Asian trade changed after the 13th century. See below, pp. 91–2.

[64] Indian influence is much less evident in Borneo and Celebes than in Java and Sumatra. In the Philippines the traces are even weaker and are mostly if not entirely due to indirect contact via Indonesia.

[65] *I.e.* Hindu priests. On this subject as a whole see van Leur Chapter 3, especially pp. 96–8.

beginning to learn something about southern India through contact with Indian or other traders, sought to gain similar advantages by summoning Brahmans to their courts. Thus, while van Leur accepts the continuity of Indian trade with South-east Asia since very early times, he does not regard it as the key to the diffusion of Indian culture in that region, and furthermore his theory attributes a much more positive rôle to the indigenous peoples than was usually admitted by earlier scholars.

Be that as it may, there is general agreement that the primary media of Indianization were the Hindu and Buddhist religions which, though profoundly different from each other in origin and emphasis, did in fact co-exist peacefully in the pioneer lands of South-east Asia for many centuries, and indeed appeared rather as complementary facets of the same basic Indian civilization.[66] Through the dissemination of a literate culture and the introduction of far more elaborate systems of political organization than any which had previously existed there before them, the priests and teachers of the new religions prepared the way for the subsequent growth of a series of major kingdoms and empires, as well as numerous lesser Indianized states, in many parts of the region. Although none of these was ever a political dependency of India, all in greater or lesser degree rested on the aristocratic concepts of monarchy and the social order which derived from India, and were in large measure common to both Hinduism and Buddhism.

[66] Hinduism arose in India many centuries before the Christian era and, thanks to its great capacity for absorbing the teachings of other faiths, subsequently developed an exceedingly heterogeneous body of doctrine. In India itself it has been traditionally associated with the caste system, and is often referred to as Brahmanism, after the name of the priests who comprise the highest caste. But while Hinduism as introduced into South-east Asia retained its markedly hierarchic character, it is significant that the caste system was never generally adopted there outside court circles, and today is found only in Bali, and even there only in a much diluted form. The Hindu religion recognizes a large number of minor deities, but in general either Vishnu or Siva is regarded as the supreme being.

The rise of Buddhism in northern India after 560 B.C. was in part a reaction against the excesses of Hinduism, manifest for example in the power of the Brahman caste and the proliferation of deities. Thus it eschewed caste and had no priests (though monks played a major rôle as teachers), and in its original form it had no place for any deity. After the first century A.D., however, it split into two branches, and though one of these, the Hinayana (or Lesser Vehicle) preserved much of the original purity of doctrine, the Mahayana (or Greater Vehicle) elevated the founder, Gautama Buddha, to the status of a god who, together with a host of lesser deities, was worshipped in a manner reminiscent of the popular Hindu cults of Vishnu and Siva.

It was the Mahayana branch, traditionally using Sanskrit as its sacred language, which became accepted in China, Korea and Japan, though in all these countries, as in the Annamite lands (see below, p. 87), it has survived for the most part only in association with other beliefs, whether Taoist, Confucian or Shinto. Both Mahayana and Hinayana Buddhism were introduced into various parts of South-east Asia during the early centuries of Indianization, but only the Hinayana form (which uses the Pali script) remains alive there today. For this reason the practice has grown up of referring to Mahayana as 'northern' and Hinayana, which is now virtually limited to Ceylon, Burma, Cambodia and Laos, as 'southern' Buddhism. In these last areas the term Theravada Buddhism (*i.e.* the Buddhism of the Theras or teachers) is nowadays preferred to Hinayana Buddhism. See Harrison, pp. 13–16, and Hall (B), p. 12.

Thus the king and his entourage of nobility and high officials in the state capitals were sharply divided socially from the great mass of the people,[67] though subordinate territorial rulers – usually hereditary chieftains – provided some form of administrative link with the inhabitants of outlying regions.

Almost certainly the creation of the first true towns and cities in South-east Asia, as opposed to a mere expansion in the size of particular villages, must be attributed to the introduction of Indian forms of political organization. As Heine-Geldern has shown, Hindu-Buddhist practice in this regard was based on a belief in 'the parallelism between Macrocosmos and Microcosmos, between the universe and the world of men' and harmony between the empire and the universe was obtained 'by organizing the former as an image of the latter, as a universe on a smaller scale'. To this end elaborate capital cities were built as models of the Hindu-Buddhist cosmology, each with its principal temple situated on a central hill (natural or artificial) which was regarded as the abode of the gods. The city itself was surrounded by a square wall and parallel moat, symbolizing the universe with its enclosing wall of rock and ocean, and within this outer frame the streets were arranged in rectilinear pattern.[68] These features are strikingly illustrated, for example, in the two successive cities of Angkor, that is Yasodharapura, which was nearly two and a half miles square, and Angkor Thom[69] which was somewhat smaller, but essentially similar features have been found elsewhere, notably in the remains of various Indonesian cities and in the early Burmese capitals described by Kirk.[70]

Apart from the state capitals, however, urban development was relatively unimportant, and indeed only the major kingdoms could afford either to build or to maintain large cities even for this purpose. Moreover, while in Angkor and the other great capitals massive stone and laterite buildings of great magnificence were erected for religious and royal use, the ordinary dwellings even there were of wood or bamboo, and the lesser towns were built almost exclusively of such non-durable materials and accordingly in most cases have virtually disappeared with the passage of time. But in part this impermanence is also related to the frequency with which early capitals were moved, often for magical or religious reasons, and unless this is borne in mind an exaggerated impression is easily obtained of the degree of urbanization in the region at any given time in the pre-European period.

[67] Whose services were nevertheless required for building and maintaining the court cities.

[68] This symbolism probably originated in the Middle East and was well established in Babylon by the 3rd millennium B.C. See Heine-Geldern (A), p. 15, from which the above quotations are taken. See also Harrison, pp. 32–5.

[69] Angkor Thom was reputed to have contained over a million people, though this is probably an exaggeration. See below, p. 110.

[70] On Indonesian cities see Wertheim (C), p. 169, and on the Burmese capitals see Kirk (A), pp. 20–5. Note also that the concept of the city came to South-east Asia from China as well as from India (see below, p. 91). To what extent the symbolic significance of these ancient cities was understood by their inhabitants is by no means clear.

In these circumstances the extent to which Indian culture really touched the ordinary people outside immediate court circles and the effective orbit of the state capitals must obviously have been severely limited, and even in the courts themselves neither Hinduism nor Buddhism ever fully displaced the older animistic beliefs but tended rather to blend syncretically with them.[71] Nevertheless, in the course of time the lives of all the Indianized peoples were affected and animated by contact, however indirect, with the higher civilization, and even though its more elaborate refinements were doubtless limited to the relatively small court circles of rulers and nobility, much of the literature of Hinduism and Buddhism filtered through to the common people among whom it still lives on in folklore, the puppet theatre and the shadow play.

In the more mundane field of material culture the extent of the Indian legacy is harder to assess. Nevertheless the prevalence of the Indian-type plough throughout the greater part of lowland South-east Asia[72] strongly suggests that, whether or not the introduction of wet-rice cultivation there is to be attributed to Indian initiative, its further development within historic times owes much to that source. Similarly such well-nigh ubiquitous crafts as the carving of wood and precious metals, though undeniably of earlier origin, were probably carried to a new pitch of refinement by the techniques and traditions introduced by early Indian temple artificers. But this, again, is a subject on which the older and newer schools of thought are at variance and as yet there is little conclusive evidence to be adduced by either side.

In contrast to the wide-ranging but necessarily somewhat tenuous influence of Indian civilization which reached the western two-thirds of South-east Asia along the sea lanes, the influence of China was in the main exerted overland, and although the area so affected was smaller, the imprint, at least in the Annamite lands, was deeper and more enduring. But while the Indian contribution was primarily concerned with the things of the spirit, China never sought to export its religious beliefs beyond the confines of its own empire. Indeed during Han times (206 B.C.–214 A.D.) when its interests first began to extend into South-east Asia, China was itself coming under the influence of Indian Buddhism *via* the trade route across Central Asia, and by the 6th century A.D. Mahayana Buddhism seemed to have become the dominant religion of the Middle Kingdom. Thus Chinese pilgrims began to frequent the established centres of learning and devotion in India, not infrequently travelling by the southern sea route and so incidentally contributing to China's knowledge of the South-east Asian lands through which they passed. From T'ang times (618–907 A.D.) onwards, however, Buddhism as such gradually declined in China, though in fact much of its content became absorbed in the amalgam of Confucian, Taoist, and animist beliefs which has since come to be regarded as the 'Chinese' religion.

[71] Note also that the two Indian religions themselves fused, with further local accretions, in the cult of the Siva-Buddha. See below, pp. 98 and 116n.

[72] Though not in the Annamite lands.

For a variety of reasons China's influence was much later than that of India in making any significant impression on South-east Asia, apart from the northern Annamite lands which lay on its own doorstep. Until well into the second millennium B.C. the orbit of Chinese civilization was virtually restricted to the area north of the Yang-tze, and meanwhile the lands to the south of this were inhabited by the ancesters of the modern Thai peoples who, though culturally less advanced than the Chinese, were not strikingly different from them in physique. After about 1000 B.C. the Chinese advanced southwards into this tribal territory, founding colonies and at the same time both mixing with the local population and driving others farther south.[73] But it was not until the Imperial Age[74] (255 B.C.–A.D. 214) that the Yang-tze lowlands were fully assimilated, and only then was it possible for Chinese political power to be extended still further afield to the shores of the South China Sea.

The Thai tribes at that time occupying the present-day provinces of Kwangtung and Kwangsi were known to the Chinese as Nan Yüeh, and immediately to their south essentially similar peoples had already inter-married with earlier Pareœan types in the Song-koi delta and the coastlands of northern Annam to produce the ancestors of the modern Annamites or Vietnamese. After an abortive attempt at controlling this whole region in Ch'in times, the Chinese effectively subdued it in 111 B.C., thus extending their teritories virtually to the Porte d'Annam, near the eighteenth parallel, where the Annamite Chain reaches down to the coast.

It is possible that this conquest helped to stimulate Chinese interest in opening up a new overland trade route to India across the north of the Indo-Pacific peninsula,[75] but whatever the motive the event was followed by the complete absorption of the Nan Yüeh territories within the centralized administrative system which thereafter came under the all-pervasive influence of the Chinese empire.[76] As a result, an influential minority of Annamites began to receive schooling in the classical Chinese fashion and, perhaps even more important, both the traditional beliefs and the material culture of the ordinary peasantry were in varying degrees transformed.

In particular the primitive hoe cultivation of the Annamites was superseded

[73] There is a large Shan element in the ancestry of the modern inhabitants of southern China which helps to blur the ethnic distinction between them and their neighbours in many parts of mainland South-east Asia.

[74] This term is used to cover both the Ch'in (255–206 B.C.) and the Han (206 B.C.–A.D. 214), when China first expanded to something like its modern boundaries.

[75] However. no such route was in fact opened. But Chinese trade had already begun to find its way across the Yunnan plateau to the Ganges delta even earlier, and in A.D. 69 China established the prefecture of Yung ch'ang, with its headquarters some 70 miles south-west of Tali, to control this route. In later periods the route fell into disuse, but it became important again under the aegis of Nan Chao in the 8th century. See Hall (B), p. 22.

[76] Thenceforward the name Nan Yüeh (or in its Annamite form Nam Viet) was restricted to the area lying south of China proper, *i.e.* to an area at first almost identical with that of the present-day (Communist) Republic of (Northern) Vietnam.

by the much more advanced agricultural methods of the Chinese which, by means of elaborate systems of water-control, dyke-building and skilful use of both night soil and vegetable manure, made possible a far more intensive utilization of the land, and hence a greatly increased capacity for supporting population. These innovations, which were much more far-reaching than the sporadic introduction of the southern Indian form of wet-rice cultivation in other parts of South-east Asia,[77] were destined ultimately to give the Annamites a decisive advantage over the other Indochinese peoples with whom they came in contact. Thus, although Chinese tutelage was resented and eventually in 939 A.D. thrown off, the benefits which it conferred proved to be of lasting value.

By comparison with the Annamite lands which were thus subjected to a process of direct assimilation for over a thousand years, the imprint of Chinese civilization elsewhere in South-east Asia is much less in evidence. Nevertheless many cultural traits of Sinitic origin were later introduced into other parts of the Indo-Pacific peninsula as a result of the migrations of the Thais and Burmans, both of whom lived for centuries along the fringe of the Chinese œcumene before being driven southwards as the latter expanded under the pressure of increasing population.

Thus the Thais, though expelled at an early date from the lower-lying areas to the east, successfully resisted the Chinese advance in the high plateaux of what are now Kweichow, Yunnan and the northern parts of Siam and Burma. During the middle of the 7th century A.D. they organized there the powerful kingdom of Nan Chao which, despite a continuing drift of population down the great river valleys to the south, was able to maintain its integrity until 1253–4 when its capital, Tali, was sacked by the Mongol armies of Kublai Khan. It was this event which precipitated the final exodus of Shans to the south, though several millions still live on the Chinese side of the border, notably in Yunnan.[78] During their long contact with the Chinese the Thais learned much of value from their more advanced neighbours, and in turn passed on some of this knowledge to the Burman tribes who lived for a time along their own western borders before migrating down the Irrawaddy valley between the 9th and the 11th centuries.

[77] The most elaborate Indian-style irrigation system in South-east Asia was that of Angkor (see below, pp. 93–4), which relied heavily on artificial storage lakes (*baray*) analogous to the tanks of peninsular India. (Sion, II, p. 406, and Groslier and Arthaud, pp. 25–6.) The largest of these were some 5 × 1¼ miles in extent, and the scale of some of the related canals was equally impressive. But although – or perhaps because – the Annamites never built any great monuments comparable to those of the Khmers, their economy seems to have been basically stronger and certainly much more permanent. Although irrigated rice cultivation was probably first practised in India the Chinese later developed the art to a higher level of refinement, and their traditional agronomy (see King, F. H.) was much further advanced in recent times than that of the Indians. It is possible that the use of night soil was less offensive and less injurious to health in the Chinese climate than in that of India. Certainly the practice has not been adopted anywhere in South-east Asia outside the Annamite lands, except by some immigrant Chinese farmers.

[78] Though Chinese now form the majority of the population in Yunnan as a whole.

Thus both the Thai-Lao-Shan peoples[79] and also the later Burmans[80] brought a smattering of Chinese culture with them into South-east Asia, and though this was subsequently overlain by the veneer of Indian civilization which they acquired at second hand from the Mons, Pyus and Khmers who preceded them in the southern lowlands of the Indo-Pacific peninsula, such occasional features as the walled towns of Siam and both the Burmese and Siamese methods of water-control bear witness to the Chinese element in their cultural heritage.[81]

Beyond the Indo-Pacific peninsula, however, Chinese cultural influence is altogether more superficial and sporadic, thanks in the main to the relative tardiness of the Chinese in taking to the sea. Nevertheless, although their achievements in this respect remained markedly inferior to those of the Indians and various Middle Eastern peoples until the time of the Southern Sung (1127–1279), Purcell asserts that 'by the fourth and fifth centuries Chinese ships were feeling their way along the coasts and over the seas to meet the Arabs, Persians and Indians part way'[82] and some of their vessels seem to have sailed as far as the Malay peninsula at an even earlier date.

For, despite a strongly felt sense of material as well as cultural self-sufficiency,[83] the Chinese early evinced an interest in the more exotic tropical produce of the Nan Yang and certainly under the T'ang dynasty there was a substantial volume of trade in aromatic woods, swallows' nests[84] and the plumage of kingfishers and birds of paradise, which were obtained in return for Chinese textiles, metal-ware and porcelain.

Moreover, this early trade between China and South-east Asia was accompanied by a form of diplomatic relationship which ultimately brought virtually all the more important kingdoms of the Nan Yang at least nominally within the Chinese political orbit. Since it was a cardinal principle of traditional Chinese political philosophy that the Middle Kingdom constituted the only sun in the Oriental sky,[85] the rulers of what it chose to regard as the lesser barbarians surrounding it were expected to pay their respects to the Emperor by periodically despatching envoys with token gifts of their countries' produce. As China would trade only with those countries which conformed to this usage, the practice of sending such tribute-bearing missions was gradually adopted by most of the South-east Asian states during the first millennium A.D.

The exact significance of this tributary relationship is not easy to assess, though the rights which the Chinese normally claimed on the basis of it amounted

[79] These all belong fundamentally to the same ethnic group. Thai is their own name; Lao comes from the Chinese name for them, Ai-lao; and Shan is the Burmese form of it.

[80] *I.e.* as opposed to the earlier arrivals, beginning with the Pyus. See above, p. 68n.

[81] Though in neither case was the agricultural and hydro-technical skill nearly as advanced as that of the Annamites.

[82] Purcell (D), p. 17.

[83] Which was related to the great diversity of resources within their own territories, which extend from cold continental to tropical latitudes.

[84] Used respectively in the making of coffins and soup.

[85] The phrase is from a Chinese proverb, quoted by Fitzgerald, p. 18.

to little more than a vague and generally beneficent patronage. Certainly they did not imply any direct control over the tributary country's affairs, though at least one alien dynasty, namely the Yuan or Mongol (1279–1368), perhaps through failure to appreciate the subtler points of the relationship, sent its armies as far afield as Burma, Annam and Java in unsuccessful attempts to enforce more rigid submission.

On the other hand, even the native Chinese emperors never liked to see any neighbouring states become exceptionally powerful, and accordingly they frequently endeavoured to play off one against another and so, in effect, to reinforce the tendency to political fragmentation which is inherent in the geography of South-east Asia. Thus Cœdès has observed that the periods of maximum growth of the major South-east Asian states, such as Funan, Cambodia and the kingdoms of Java and Sumatra, correspond to epochs of Chinese dynastic weakness and, conversely, whenever the regime in China was strong it was apt to pursue a more positive policy in the Nan Yang.[86]

This desire on the part of China to play an influential part in the affairs of South-east Asia seems to have grown with the expansion of maritime commerce between the two areas from about the 13th century onwards, a development which moreover was accompanied by the founding of permanent settlements of Chinese traders in various parts of the Philippines, Indonesia and perhaps also the Malay peninsula.[87]

In the meantime the nature of the ties between South-east Asia and India were undergoing a no less significant change. Whether or not the initial phase of Hindu/Buddhist proselytization in the early centuries A.D. was accompanied by any significant Indian settlement, it is certain that in later centuries, during which the two religions gradually established themselves in various parts of the region, no such movement took place. Thus in the course of time these imported Indian beliefs underwent considerable modification in coming to terms with the indigenous customs and traditions, though for the most part they remained limited in their appeal to a small élite.

In the 12th century however, a decisive change began on the mainland with the introduction into Burma of the new Mahavihara sect of Theravada Buddhism from Ceylon. Both in Burma and Siam there was a long tradition of Theravada Buddhism going back at least to the 5th and 7th centuries respectively, but in the 13th century the beliefs of the new sect spread also to Cambodia where they completely undermined the established state religion based on Hinduism and Mahayana Buddhism. For, in contrast to these, the new Sinhalese version of Theravada Buddhism was a popular religion, and wherever it spread throughout the peninsula it struck deep roots among the common people.[88]

An even more spectacular change followed in the archipelago with the advance

[86] See Cœdès, p. 6.

[87] See Wheatley (E). Many Chinese traders and artisans also settled in various mainland countries at least as early as this.

[88] See Hall (B), p. 114 and below, p. 115.

of Islam along the maritime trade routes. Since the 7th century A.D. Muslim merchants from the Middle East had frequented the ports of South-east Asia but it was not until Islam became accepted by Indian peoples, such as the Gujaratis and Bengalis, that it began to make converts in South-east Asia, and the prestige enjoyed by wealthy Indian Muslim traders probably explains the initial desire of local rulers to accept the new faith in much the same way as their ancesters had adopted Hinduism and Buddhism.[89] Be that as it may, Marco Polo records that by 1292 Islam had become the official religion of the small kingdom of Perlak in northern Sumatra, and thereafter the faith spread eastwards along the seaways through the Indonesian archipelago and into the Philippines, where it was eventually checked by the even more vigorous missionary enterprise of Spanish Dominican friars after the 16th century.

Like the new Sinhalese form of Buddhism, Islam owed much of its success to its character as a popular faith in a region hitherto dominated by more exclusive creeds. But while this gave it an immense advantage in the archipelago, it was of no particular significance in the Theravada Buddhist lands farther north and, mainly for that reason, Islam won no permanent foothold on the mainland north of the Malay peninsula, except, interestingly, among some of the surviving Chams of Cambodia, who were already in a state of decline.

Taken together, these religious changes implied a gradual but unmistakable weakening of the spiritual ties between South-east Asia and India. This was particularly marked among the Islamized peoples to whom the holy places of Arabia became the new focus of veneration, and India lost its former place as a kind of mystical motherland. Admittedly, the commercial link with India survived, albeit with modifications, for both the great Muslim trading system which had meanwhile grown up in the Indian Ocean region and the Portuguese empire which subsequently replaced it maintained close contact between the Deccan ports and those of Malaysia. But the waning of Indian influence was real enough, and the religious transformation alike in the archipelago and on the mainland was followed by far-reaching changes in the organization of state and society.

For neither Islam nor Sinhalese Buddhism required the same elaboration of court ritual which had been a principal *raison d'être* of the great capital cities and the hierarchic organization of the organized kingdoms.[90] And while the change took different forms and proceeded at varying rates in different parts of the region, it would seem that by the time the Europeans arrived on the scene the era of the great cities was already on its way out and, notwithstanding the considerable splendour of such capitals as Ava and Ayuthia, nothing comparable in size or

[89] See Harrison, pp. 50–1. Here again, however, van Leur puts the emphasis somewhat differently, stressing in particular the political motive (*Op. cit.*, p. 88). The increase in Muslim sea trade about this time has been related by some historians to interruptions in overland trade across central Asia as a result of the early raids of the Mongols.

[90] See Hall (B), p. 114.

magnificence to the former Angkor survived as a living entity anywhere in the region.

The significance of this reversion to a more simplified way of life, which occurred most dramatically in Cambodia but also had its counterparts in Indonesia and elsewhere, has been variously assessed. From one point of view it has been seen primarily as evidence of the great vitality of the indigenous South-east Asian civilization, whose essential ethos is thus regarded as having survived despite a thousand years of Indianization. As we have noted on page 77, this civilization was primarily village-centred, and it is above all the traditions of village democracy and mutual self-help within the village community which contemporary nationalist leaders[91] like to stress as the distinctive characteristics of their people's way of life.

Whether in fact these particular traits are exclusive to South-east Asia may perhaps be doubted, and indeed some of them bear so close a resemblance to the Indian rural tradition as to suggest that even at village level the Indian cultural legacy is all-important. But be that as it may, the prevailing character of South-east Asian life, at least since the beginning of direct European contact with the region, has in most respects been far removed from the kind of authoritarianism which Wittfogel in his recent study of Oriental despotism associates with the hydraulic type of agrarian civilization.

According to Wittfogel's thesis the task of constructing and maintaining elaborate irrigation works has led in several parts of the Old World, from Egypt to China (an also in parts of pre-Columban America) to the growth of a rigidly centralized and despotic organization of society, completely opposed to the individualist traditions of the West. To what extent the more advanced South-east Asian lands should be regarded as coming within Wittfogel's category of Oriental despotisms is perhaps arguable, though his references to Siam and Bali, and his more general concluding observations, seem to imply that he himself would include at least some of them.[92]

In fact, however, there are very few cases in South-east Asia outside the Annamite lands and the immediate vicinity of Angkor, where really large-scale hydraulic works were ever established in pre-European times[93] and most, if not all, of the other ancient irrigation installations known in the region – notably in the interior valleys of Burma and Siam, in east-central Java, Bali, parts of Sumatra and Luzon – would seem to belong rather to Wittfogel's lower category of hydroagriculture, in which the smaller scale of the water works does not call for centralized political control. Admittedly the lines here are not easy to draw, and perhaps Java and Burma might be ranked as truly hydraulic, though it is doubtful whether the magnitude of their irrigation works was any greater than those of

[91] Particularly in Indonesia. See, for example, the views of Sukarno cited below, p. 378, note 44.

[92] Wittfogel, pp. 32, 53, and Chapter 10.

[93] In none of the large mainland deltas, except that of the Song-koi in Annam (a true Oriental despotism) was there any major system of water control prior to the 19th century.

Japan, which Wittfogel specifically excludes from the true hydraulic category.[94]

On the other hand, however, there is no denying that the great monuments and palaces built at various times in Burma, Siam and parts of Sumatra, and above all in Java and Cambodia, are characteristic examples of the kind of spectacular non-utilitarian construction frequently undertaken by Oriental despots, and indeed could not have been executed at all without despotic methods of mobilizing labour on a massive scale. Furthermore, the elaborate court ceremonial in most of these countries, and such practices as crawling in the presence of the monarch, which survived in Burma and Siam until as recently as the 19th century, also fit unmistakably into the same pattern.

Clearly these are problems on which much more detailed research needs to be done, but *prima facie* there would seem to be good grounds for regarding the presence of these various 'despotic' traits in South-east Asia as being, in most cases at least, the result of 'institutional transfer',[95] either from China or India, rather than as truly indigenous examples of hydraulic despotism.

In any case, however, it is surely of greater importance that the elaborate hierarchical ordering of society, centred in the great capital cities of former times, had already begun to give place to a simpler and more localized way of life in all parts of South-east Asia, the Annamite lands alone excepted, before the first traces of European influence were felt anywhere in the region.

In the writer's opinion this decline of Indianized civilization in South-east Asia would seem to provide substantial confirmation of Gourou's thesis that the highest forms of civilization are not indigenous to the tropics and can be maintained there only as a result of vigour imported from outside.[96] Thus, whether one accepts the interpretation of Coedès or of van Leur, the great flowering of civilization in the humid tropical fringe of south and south-eastern Asia during the millennium which preceded the impact of the West may not unreasonably be viewed as the outcome of such a tide which, after sweeping over the Indian sub-continent from the north-west, ultimately petered out in ripples of ever diminishing intensity across the peninsula and archipelagos beyond.

Whatever the truth in this respect, however, it was against the background of religious and political change in the Nan Yang that the rulers of the early Ming dynasty (1368–1644) attempted not merely to repair the damage done to China's prestige by the disastrous miscalculations of their Mongol predecessors but also to extend their country's influence in the region on a hitherto unprecedented scale.

With this in mind they despatched armies to re-occupy the Annamite lands

[94] Java displays the same kind of topographical fragmentation which Wittfogel cites as being not conducive to hydraulic agriculture in Japan (*Ibid.*, pp. 197–200.). For further details on indigenous irrigation in the countries concerned see the appropriate regional chapters below.

[95] Wittfogel (Chapter 6 E) advances this explanation to cover conditions in other parts of the world.

[96] See Gourou (H), p. 51.

from 1407 to 1428, and between 1405 and 1431 sent seven major naval expeditions under Cheng Ho to patrol the Nan Yang and to persuade the local rulers to resume payment of the customary tribute to the Middle Kingdom. But although this initiative met with considerable response, it came to a sudden end as a result of renewed Chinese preoccupation with the attacks of nomadic tribesmen along their north-western frontiers. By the 1430s China had reverted to a predominantly continental policy and this was continued with greater singleness of purpose by the Manchu dynasty which succeeded the Ming in 1644 and remained in power until the revolution of 1911.

Under the later Ming and the Manchu dynasties, therefore, the Chinese made no further attempt to take an active part in the affairs of South-east Asia, except for an abortive overland invasion of Burma in 1766, which arose out of the Emperor Chi'en Lung's policy of strengthening and extending his hold along virtually the whole length of China's land frontiers. Moreover, so far from playing a positive political rôle overseas, the Manchus sought by means of a series of enactments to put a stop to the trickle of emigration which had already begun to the Nan Yang several centuries earlier.

In part, this lack of official interest in overseas affairs may have been a reflection of the essentially landward outlook of the Manchu rulers, but it was also dictated by a desire, so far as possible, to avoid contact with the Europeans who by this time had achieved a dominant position on the seas of eastern Asia. A similar introvert attitude likewise came to prevail among the Japanese who after at last beginning to show an interest in the Nan Yo[97] during the 15th century, suddenly reversed their policy in this respect early in the 17th century. But whereas the Tokugawa seclusionist laws of 1631–9 were so rigorously enforced that no coherent Japanese settlements survived in South-east Asia,[98] the Chinese edicts seem to have been honoured more in the breach than in observance, with the result that the number of Chinese residents in the region already ran into hundreds of thousands before the main exodus from the Middle Kingdom began in the 19th century.

VI. RELIGIOUS AND LINGUISTIC PATTERNS

In their different ways, therefore, both India and China exerted a profound influence over South-east Asia during the first millennium and a half of the Christian era. Yet while in a sense the whole region formed a great frontier zone in which the cultures of both these neighbouring lands met and inter-penetrated,

[97] Nan Yo is the Japanese equivalent of Nan Yang or 'southern seas'. (see above, p. 7). The Japanese became interested in trading as well as in piracy and buccanneering. It has been estimated that by the 17th century there were *c.* 15,000 Japanese living in the Philippines and 8,000 in the towns of Siam, as well as smaller concentrations in Annam, Cambodia and other parts of South-east Asia. Ishii, p. 188.

[98] It has been suggested that the Menadonese of northern Celebes show evidence of considerable Japanese admixture. The Japanese are known to have traded along a route via the Philippines to eastern Indonesia, and there were Japanese as well as English victims of the Massacre of Amboyna. See below, p. 136.

the line of the Annamite Chain marks a major divide between the relatively small but intensely Sinicized zone to the east and the much larger area to the west and south in which Indian influence, though usually in a more dilute form, is generally predominant.

Significant as this difference undoubtedly is, however, the more fundamental contrast remains that between the coastal and riverine lowlands on the one hand, and the interior uplands and the remoter Indonesian islands on the other. For, in continuance of the pattern which can be traced back to prehistoric times, the impact of Indian and Chinese civilization was confined almost exclusively to the former areas, and while the great part of their inhabitants down to the humblest peasants bear the unmistakable stamp of a higher civilization, the majority of the peoples in the remaining parts of the region have not as yet attained to that level of advancement.

Apart from their effect on material culture the twin processes of Indianization and Sinicization achieved their most lasting results in the transformation they wrought in respect of religion, language and political organization. While the third of these requires a chapter to itself, it seems appropriate to conclude the present chapter with a consideration of the geographical distribution of the main religious and linguistic groups within the region as summarized in Figs. 9 and 10.

In the first place Fig. 9 shows the survival of primitive animistic beliefs to be characteristic of a very extensive area in the remoter parts of both mainland and archipelago, while for the rest the most notable features are the area of so-called 'Chinese' religion in the Annamite lands, the preponderance of Theravada Buddhism over most of the rest of the peninsula, and the almost complete ascendancy of Islam in most parts of the archipelago. In the latter area, however, two important exceptions call for comment, namely the survival of Hinduism in Bali[99] where a nucleus of its adherents took refuge after the overthrow of the last Hindu dynasty in eastern Java, and secondly the prevalence of Christianity in the northern two-thirds of the Philippines and in a few parts of eastern Indonesia where Islam had not succeeded in establishing itself firmly before Western missionary activity began.[100]

Nevertheless the map needs to be read with caution, and few if any of the religions which it shows can be regarded as quite the same as their nominal equivalents in other parts of the world. Thus, for example, except in Atjeh, Pasundan and Bandjarmasin, the Indonesian version of Islam, notwithstanding the sincerity with which it is practised and the high proportion of its followers who make the pilgrimage to the holy places of Arabia, has little of either the militancy

[99] This is perhaps best regarded as a composite form of Hinduism and Buddhism.

[100] There are also many other pockets of Christianity which are too small to be shown on this general map, though they are mentioned in the appropriate regional chapters. Most of the groups concerned, such as the Bataks and Karens, are hill peoples who had not come under the direct influence of any of the other higher religions before Christian missionaries arrived in recent centuries.

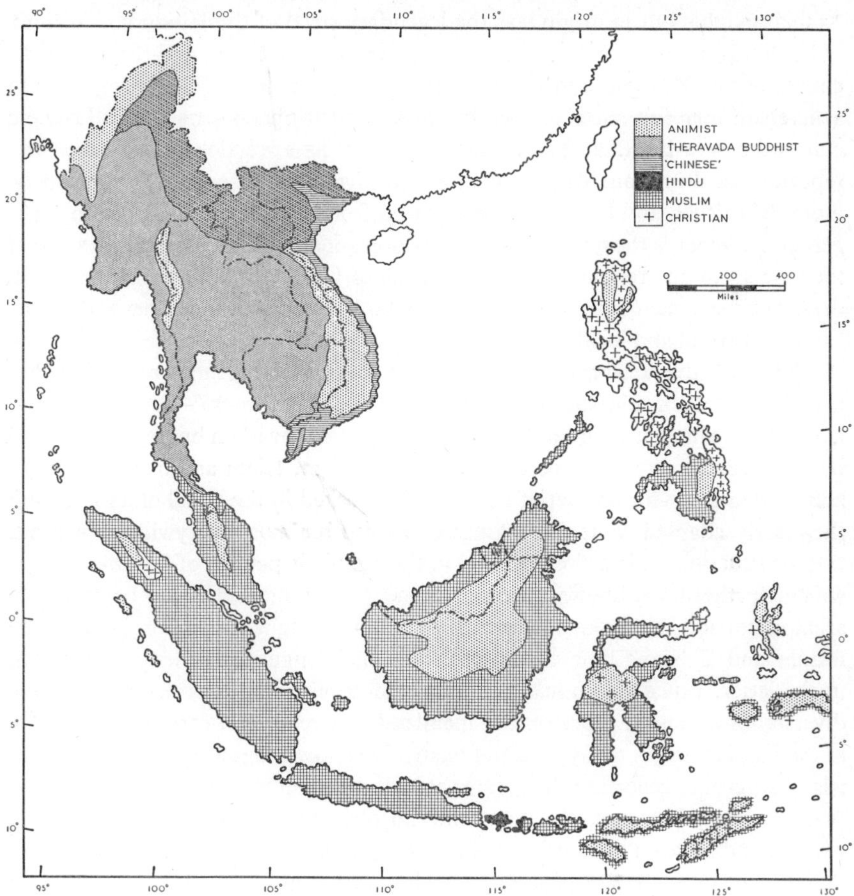

FIG. 9—South-east Asia: religions of indigenous peoples

or the puritanical zeal which have traditionally characterized the faith in its Middle Eastern homeland. While this comparative softness has often been attributed to the long-term effect of an enervating climate, Cœdès is no doubt right in stressing also the moderating effect of a thousand years of Hinduism and Buddhism on the mores at least of the Javanese prior to their conversion to Islam.[101]

Moreover many of the early mosques were built in the style and often on the sites of the previous Hindu or Buddhist temples, and these in turn may well have perpetuated a pre-Indian pattern of location based upon the sanctity of high places.[102] In like manner, also, the ancient Indian epics were recast and some of their heroes renamed, and today a predominantly Muslim Indonesia has as its national emblem the garuda bird, which appears as the 'roc' in the Tales of the

[101] See Cœdès, pp. 421–2. [102] See above, p. 81.

Arabian Nights but in origin was the legendary steed of the Hindu god Vishnu.

In all this, as in the curious sects of contemporary Vietnam and the Aglipayan church of the Philippines, may be discerned the ingrained regional propensity to syncretism manifest since very early times in such phenomena as the Javanese cult of the Siva-Buddha,[103] and clearly representing a reaction to prolonged and repeated acculturation. And indeed, as Furnivall has observed, 'if religion be more than ritual, and belief may be deduced from conduct, it is hardly an exaggeration as regards the great mass of the people (of all South-east Asia) to say that they are all of one religion, and in the name of Christ, Buddha or Muhammad, drive out the same devils as the hill folk who have not advanced beyond a conception of tribal and local spirits.'[104]

Thus, as in the racial ancestry of the more advanced Pareœan peoples there has usually been a considerable admixture of several other stocks – both earlier and later – so also in their religion the pagan substratum is overlain but rarely obscured by more recent accretions of Buddhism, Hinduism, Islam and/or Christianity, and the tendency for one set of beliefs to be cloaked in the ritual of another and then freely adapted to fit the dogmas of a third is almost everywhere apparent.

This situation finds a close parallel in the linguistic pattern of South-east Asia which, furthermore, shows a similar broad geographical division between the archipelago and the mainland, with Austronesian languages predominant in the former and Tibeto-Chinese monosyllabic tonal languages generally prevalent in the latter. Equally significant in this connexion is the contrast between the diversity of linguistic types on the mainland, where several early forms survive as distinct languages today, and the relatively simple geographical pattern of the island languages reflecting the greater ease of diffusion by sea.[105]

Once again, however, the map tends to obscure more than at first sight it reveals, and in reality the present linguistic geography of South-east Asia is the outcome of an elaborate process of evolution, much of which has taken place within comparatively recent times.

At the beginning of the Christian era most of the more advanced mainland peoples spoke Mon-Khmer languages belonging to the Austro-Asiatic group, though the Chams of south-eastern Indochina used an Austronesian (Malayo-Polynesian) language akin to those which were already widespread in the archipelago by this time. According to the pioneer scholar W. Schmidt, the affinities between these two major groups, that is the Austronesian and the Austro-Asiatic, are sufficiently close to warrant their being classed together as the Austric family. This, however, does not include the various Sino-Tibetan languages which, during the last two thousand years, have been introduced into most of the penin-

[103] See below, p. 116n. [104] Furnivall (B), p. 14.

[105] See Broek (D), p. 40. But this contrast is largely a matter of degree. Thus there are several distinct regional languages within the Indonesian group (see below, pp. 238–246), though the differences between them are relatively small as can be seen by the rapidity with which the new national language *Bahasa Indonesia* is being learned in the various areas involved. See below, pp. 368–9.

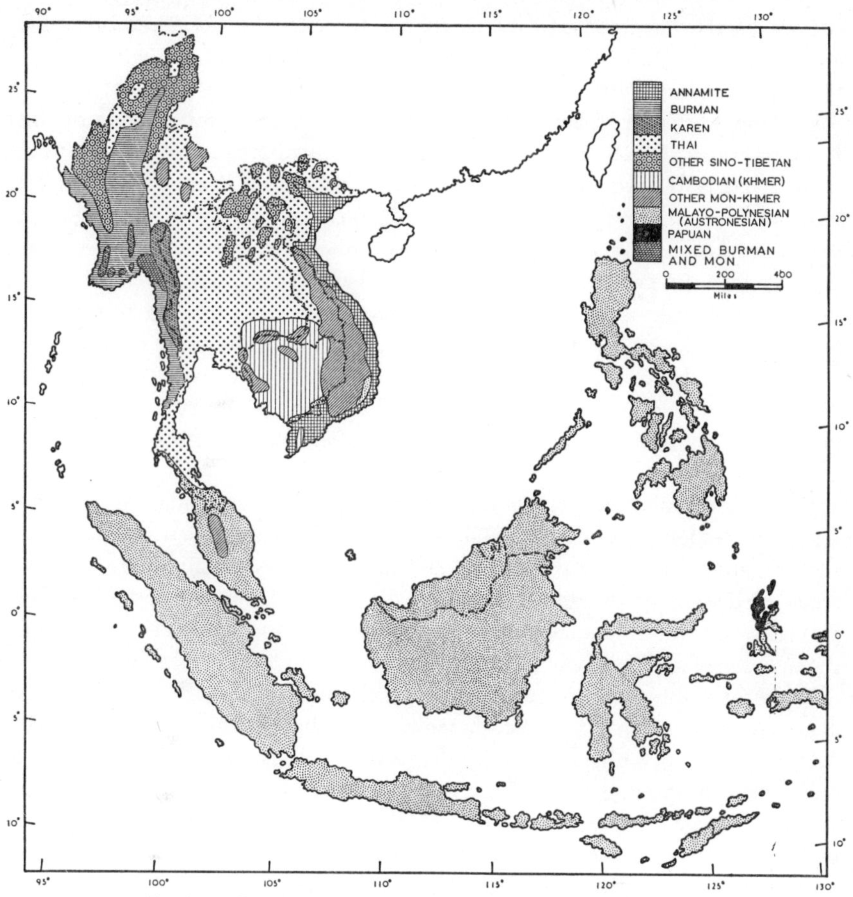

FIG. 10—South-east Asia: languages of indigenous peoples

sular lowlands by the immigrant peoples from the north. Three main sub-divisions may be recognized here, namely the Tibeto-Burman in the west, the Thai group in the centre and Vietnamese in the east, though Austro-Asiatic languages still survive in Cambodia (Khmer) and among such lesser peoples as the Wa, Palaung, Moi, Semang, Senoi-Temiar, Jakun and Besisi.[106]

In the archipelago, on the other hand, the absence of further large-scale immigrations enabled the Austronesian languages to hold their ground, though there has, of course, been considerable subsequent evolution and regional specialization within historic times. Two main sub-divisions should be noted, namely the Indonesian and the Oceanic or Melanesian, the latter of which is found only in and around New Guinea. But the Papuan languages, which are also represented in New Guinea and in parts of the Moluccas, are entirely distinct and do not belong within any branch of the great Austric family.

[106] However most, though not all, of the Mon peoples of Burma today speak Burmese.

Both on the mainland and in the islands the effect of Indianization on linguistic evolution was of fundamental importance. For besides enriching the vernacular speech with many new words and grammatical forms of Sanskrit origin, the process of Indianization was also responsible for introducing the first forms of writing into South-east Asia and these contributed immeasurably to the stabilization and development of the principal languages there.[107] Such scripts were adapted with varying success to both tonal and non-tonal languages and they still remain in normal use among the Cambodians, Burmans, Shans, Thais and Laotians. Likewise many of the regional languages of Indonesia have traditionally employed scripts of Indian origin, though some of these have been superseded by the Arabic script as, for example, in Atjeh and among the coast and peninsular Malays.

Today the Roman alphabet is widely known among the educated minority in all these countries, though it is only in Indonesia, the Philippines, Malaya and, more recently in Vietnam, (where it has replaced a system based on the ancient Chinese ideographs) that it has been adopted as the standard form for the respective national languages. While in every South-east Asian country today such a national language does exist, and in most cases is gaining ground as a result of deliberate governmental policy, there are also numerous other more localized indigenous languages which are more than mere dialects even though the number of speakers may in some cases amount to only a few thousand.

Notwithstanding the many other cultural traits which are in some sense common to the region as a whole, therefore, the indigenous peoples of South-east Asia exhibit a much higher degree of diversity in both language and religion than might reasonably be expected from their numbers alone. Indeed on both these scores the range of variety far exceeds that in either Europe or China, and while the Indian sub-continent provides a closer parallel, it also is now in process of achieving a much greater measure of cultural unity than seems likely to be attained in South-east Asia in any foreseeable future.

SELECT BIBLIOGRAPHY

Broek (D)
Buxton
Calder
Cœdès
Cole, F-C.
Coon
Firth (B)
Forde
Furnivall (B)
Gourou (H)
Grist
Groslier
Groslier and Arthaud
Haddon
Hall (B)
Harrison
Heine-Geldern (A) (B)
Hodder (B) (D)
Ishii
Kennedy (A) (B) (C)
Kirk (A)
Kleiweg de Zwaan
Kunst
Lasker (A)
Le May
Linton
Loeb and Broek
Pelzer (C) (G) (H) (K)

[107] In Vietnam Sinicization was equally important and led, *inter alia*, to the introduction of a modified form of the Chinese ideographs.

Purcell (D)
Quaritch Wales
Robequain (D)
Roberts, G. (A) (B)
Sauer
Schrieke
Skeat and Blagden
Spencer, J. E. (A)
Van der Kroef (C)
Van Helsdingen and Hoogenberk
Van Leur
Weidenreich
Wertheim (C)
Wheatley (E)
Wickizer and Bennett
Wiens
Wittfogel
Wormser
Zelinsky

Chambers's Encyclopædia
Encyclopædia Britannica
Indo-China (N.I.D.)
China, I (N.I.D.)
Netherlands East Indies II (N.I.D.)

Among the pioneer anthropological studies may be noted those by Skeat and Blagden, Haddon, and Buxton. More recent accounts, on which my section on the racial pattern of South-east Asia is largely based, are to be found in *Netherlands East Indies, II (N.I.D.)*, Chapter 1, in *Chambers's Encyclopædia*, I, pp. 679–81, in Kennedy (A), Chapter 2, and in Lasker (A). The section on traditional ways of life is likewise much indebted to Pelzer (C), Chapters 1–3, and Pelzer (H). The two papers by Roberts provide a geographical introduction to the problems of early relations with India and China, which topics form the subject matter of the two important studies by Wales and Wiens respectively.

On general cultural matters the standard histories by Cœdès, Hall (B), and Harrison, are invaluable. These may be supplemented by the more specialized papers by Wheatley (E), and Heine-Geldern (A) and (B), and also by Wittfogel's pioneer study of Oriental despotism. Wickizer and Bennett's book is a standard work on rice economies, and an interesting unpublished study of rice cultivation in South-east Asia is contained in the thesis by Lim, J. J.

Addenda: Reference should also be made to the excellent recent study in historical geography by Wheatley (K). Note also the important article by Terra, G.J.A., 'Farm systems in South-East Asia', *Netherlands Journal of Agricultural Science*, 6, 1958, pp. 157–182.

CHAPTER 4

The Political Geography of the Pre-European Period

In no respect was the influence of India and China upon South-east Asia of more lasting significance than in the transformation which it effected in the region's political geography. Under the higher forms of administration which these two more advanced civilizations introduced, the particularism of local clans and tribes gave place to more extensive territorial groupings, and although the latter rested on personal authority, qualified by customary obligations and sanctified by the new religions, the ties were sufficiently strong to permit the growth of states and even empires, some of which by the standards of the time were large and powerful.

Nevertheless, conditions in this respect were by no means uniform, and in particular the nature of the terrain and the degree of Indian and Chinese cultural penetration combined to present very varied prospects for political unification in different parts of the region. Thus it was above all in the valleys of the great rivers and in the more accessible and fertile coastal lowlands that the most powerful states emerged, thanks to the relative ease of communication, the higher density of population, and the superior facilities which these together provided for the development of regional trade. But in the uplands, and especially in the severely dissected plateaux in the interior of the Indo-Pacific peninsula, movement across the grain of the country was extremely difficult. For this reason, although repeated attempts were made to unite large tracts under the ægis of one ruler or another, they rarely achieved lasting success, and the uplands have tended rather to remain divided among a series of petty kingdoms, more often than not in some degree subordinate to the stronger lowland states.[1]

This contrast between the degree of political cohesion in mountains and plain has not been without its advantages, however, for the loosely organized principalities of the former areas have often served as useful shock absorbers in the struggles between the more highly developed lowland kingdoms, and to some extent also between the latter and China. And just as most of the lowland states were in the habit of paying tribute to China, so many of the lesser upland principalities in turn paid tribute to them, and indeed not infrequently to two or more of them simultaneously and perhaps also to China as well, in the hope of thereby insuring themselves against trouble from all possible quarters.

[1] See Furnivall (B), pp. 17–18.

During the 1,500 years which preceded the coming of the Europeans many changes took place in the political geography of South-east Asia, most frequently as the result of new movements of peoples and ideas into the region. Yet the strong hand of topography never ceased to exert its influence over the course of this evolution, and there was in consequence much repetition in the patterns which emerged at successive stages.

I. THE FIRST INDIANIZED STATES OF THE MAINLAND

At the earliest epoch for which reliable evidence survives, all the more important states occupied coastal situations. These included, besides the southward extension of Imperial China into the Annamite lowlands, the three Indianized kingdoms of Funan, Champa and Langkasuka, all of which date from the first two centuries A.D. and were located at key points along the sea route between India and China (Fig. 11).

Whether at this time the direct route through the Malacca Straits was used is uncertain, but the early importance of Langkasuka, which appears to have been based near the modern Patani on the Bight of Bangkok and to have maintained close overland ties with the Kedah plain on the opposite side of the Malay peninsula,[2] suggests that an overland short cut was already in use, probably as a means of avoiding the ravages of pirates in the Malacca Straits. For the frequent calms descending on these narrow waters through the doldrum belt could place small sailing ships at the mercy of marauders, skilled in oarsmanship, for whom the fringing mangrove swamps provided excellent cover, and this menace was never entirely overcome until steam-powered patrol boats were introduced in the 19th century.

Of the other two states, Champa occupied the series of small but fertile plains along the Annamite coast between the Col des Nuages and Camranh Bay, and had its original capital in the vicinity of the modern Quang Nam (near Tourane), while Funan was centred immediately to the south of this in the plains of the Mekong delta. While all these localities offered obvious advantages for maritime pursuits, only Funan was well placed to expand on land, and moreover had a sufficiently large territorial base to sustain imperial ambitions. In the event these were quick to develop, and Funan accordingly rose to a pre-eminent position among the peninsular states. From a 3rd-century Chinese account it seems that its inhabitants were excellent seamen though, unlike the people of Champa and Langkasuka who were probably Pareœans, they appear to have been of Nesiot stock. Their ruler, who claimed descent from an Indian Brahman prince, bore the imperial title of 'King of the Mountain', but had nevertheless already begun to send periodic embassies to China.

[2] On the relations of Langkasuka with Kedah, however, see Wheatley (A).

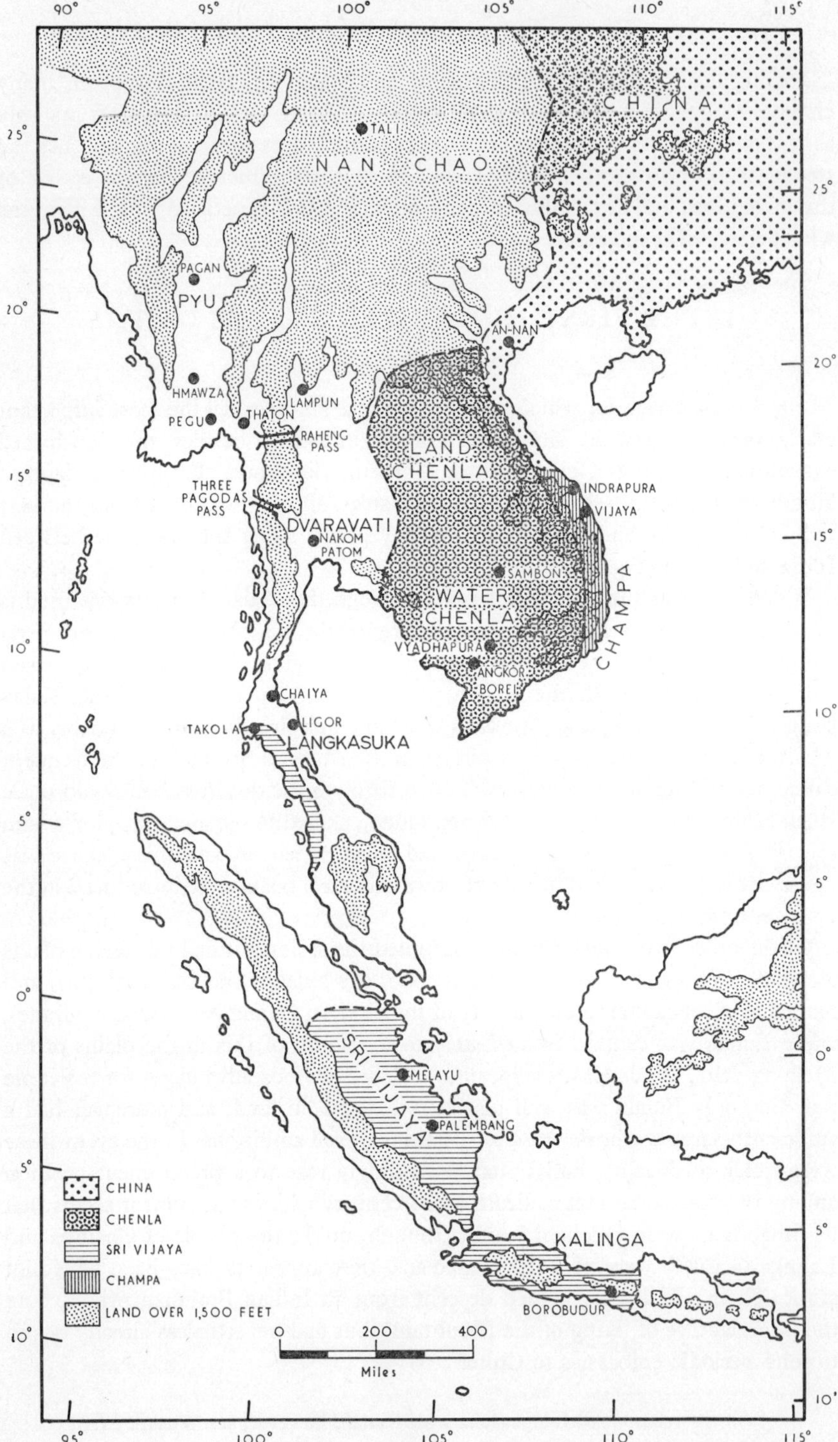

FIG. 11—South-east Asia: political divisions, mid 8th century, A.D.

For some time the Funan capital was at Vyadhapura[3] near the apex of the delta, and at that time approximately 20 miles from the sea, that is some 40–50 miles less than at the present day. Thanks to its geographical position and to the considerable agricultural resources of the delta, Funan was able to expand both coastwise to the east and north, and also up the Mekong valley into the fertile Cambodian basin from which, in turn, movement into the Menam basin has always proved comparatively easy. In this way, therefore, Funan came to establish its hegemony over a series of lesser states which had meanwhile grown up around the Gulf of Siam, and at its zenith in the 5th century, by which time the Hindu cult of Siva had become firmly established side by side with Mahayana Buddhism, its territories stretched from the borders of Champa to the Malay peninsula, and included a frontage on the Indian Ocean in what is now Tenasserim.

In the 6th century, however, the power of Funan weakened, and one of its former vassals, Chenla, revolted and attacked it. Chenla was a Khmer kingdom, originally occupying the inland area immediately to the north of Funan proper along the middle Mekong, with its capital at first near the present Bassac and later at a site about 100 miles farther downstream. As the population of Chenla increased, in part through the influx of further migrants from the north, the balance of power tipped more and more in its favour until, probably in the year 627, it defeated Funan and thereafter succeeded to its cultural heritage.

This event which marks the beginning of the pre-Angkor period of Khmer history, provides a typical example of the recurrent 'drive to the south'[4] by new Pareœan peoples coming into the peninsula via the Yunnan-Tibetan borderland and later both overthrowing their Indianized predecessors and at the same time absorbing much of their civilization. An essentially similar sequence can also be traced in the western and central parts of the peninsula where, by the 5th or 6th century A.D., several Indianized Mon kingdoms had grown up along the coastal margins.

Notable among these was the powerful state of Dvaravati whose capital, Nakom Patom, about 40 miles west of the present Bangkok, was probably built as a coastal port though the town is now 30 miles inland. In the 8th century Dvaravati ruled over most of the Menam basin, though the southward migration of the Thai/Lao/Shan peoples had already begun and, indeed, a small Lao kingdom had been established at Lampun (Haribunchai) just south of the modern Chiengmai in or around the year 570. Further settlements followed, notably in the 9th century, but it was not until after 1254 that the Thais became the dominant element in the Menam lowlands.

Still farther to the west, around the shores of the Gulf of Martaban, the Indianized Mon kingdoms of Thaton and Pegu had grown up probably well before the beginning of the 6th century, by which time the Pyus had reached the

[3] Vyadhapura, which was close to the present Banam, was one of several walled towns within the country.

[4] Harrison, p. 22.

Irrawaddy delta where they had set up their capital at Hmawza (Prome), and were fast becoming Indianized through contact with their Mon neighbours. Further southward migrations of Burmans into the dry zone of the middle Irrawaddy followed, and there, fifty years after the fall of Prome at the beginning of the 9th century, a new Burman kingdom succeeded in establishing itself with its capital at Pagan near the Chindwin/Irrawaddy confluence.

These complex movements of peoples were to lead eventually to the emergence of the great riverine states of Burma and Siam, respectively occupying the Irrawaddy and Menam basins, as well as of the congeries of lesser Shan and Laos principalities in the adjacent plateaux, though many centuries elapsed before this process of crystallization was complete.

II. EARLY STATES AND EMPIRES OF THE ARCHIPELAGO

In the meantime equally significant developments were taking place in the archipelago to the south. Already by the 5th century A.D. several small Indianized kingdoms had grown up along the coasts of Sumatra, Java and Borneo, a pattern which suggests that by this time improvements in navigational skill and increases in the size of ships were beginning to give somewhat greater immunity from piratical attacks, and that the all-sea routes, either through the Malacca Straits and the South China Sea, or via the Sunda and Makasar Straits and the Java Sea, were in more or less regular use.

In most parts of the archipelago, however, the opportunity for such centres to develop into states of more than local significance was severely restricted by geographical circumstances. For, except in Borneo and eastern Sumatra, the river valleys are built on a much smaller scale than their counterparts in the Indo-Pacific countries, and in these two islands the extent of the alluvial lowlands is offset by the width of the swamp belts which cover their coastal margins.[5] Thus, although small kingdoms did spring up at or near the mouths of many of the larger rivers, which, as on the mainland, provided the only practicable routes through the dense tropical forests originally covering the greater part of the region, the agricultural resources at their disposal were in most cases very small.

On the other hand, however, the sea lanes, which provided even more useful means of communication than the inland waterways, were also potential sources of wealth of another kind, and at an early date many of the coastal kingdoms began to develop inter-insular trade and to levy lucrative tolls on such foreign shipping as they could compel to put in at their ports. From these beginnings, therefore, there grew up throughout the greater part of the Malaysian archi-

[5] Though significantly narrower in early historic times the swamp belts must have been of considerable extent even then. See Dobby (H), p. 58, Roberts G. (A), p. 355, and below, p. 220.

pelago a geopolitical pattern remarkably similar to that of maritime Europe in medieval times, with political power organized in units of sea rather than of land, so that a state's territory consisted of a series of scattered ports and bases, strategically placed on both sides of the waterway or waterways which it sought to dominate.[6] Until the introduction of modern European political forms in recent centuries such thalassic patterns predominated in nearly all parts of the archipelago, applying equally to the small units built up around minor channels or straits and to the great kingdoms which, from the more productive land bases, succeeded in absorbing whole series of lesser principalities in order to gain exclusive control over the major sea lanes traversing the region.

Nevertheless, in one part of the archipelago geographical conditions did make possible the growth of powerful states on the basis of agricultural wealth, soccage,[7] and a related system of bureaucratic administration essentially similar to that of the major land states of the peninsula. That area was east-central Java whose river basins, though comparatively small, enjoyed such exceptional fertility as to be capable of supporting large and compact concentrations of population.[8] While it is impossible to estimate what such densities might have been in the first few centuries A.D., there is considerable evidence to suggest that from even earlier times the figure for east-central Java was markedly higher than that for the outer islands, and it is clear that by the 7th century, if not indeed earlier, it was sufficient to sustain significant political power and *inter alia*, as van Leur points out, to provide labour for massive building programmes comparable with those of the great land states of the mainland[9] but without parallel elsewhere in the archipelago.

This contrast and the related struggles between the land powers of interior Java and the maritime states, both of the outer islands and of the northern coast of Java itself, together form one of the dominant themes of Indonesian history from the 7th century onwards, when two such kingdoms, respectively representing these two geopolitical types, each acquired a new importance following the fall of Funan on the mainland.

The first of these was the Sumatran kingdom of Palembang, which probably dates from the 5th century but first rose to a position of real eminence only after the disappearance of the fleets and the commercial influence of Funan some two hundred years later. Early Palembang has been described as a 'city on rafts' and although today it lies some 50 miles upstream, its original distance from the mouth of the Air Musi must have been much less than this. Virtually from the outset of its expansionist career, Palembang was aided by the growing volume of trade

[6] See Roberts, G. (A), p. 352. For an account of the medieval sea state in Europe see Darby.

[7] The word soccage is expressly used by van Leur in his brilliant analysis of Javanese society, p. 105 *et seq.* Several of the ideas expressed there may be compared with Wittfogel's portrayal of the hydraulic society. See above, p. 93.

[8] On the climatic and vegetational aspects see above, pp. 41–2 and 46–7.

[9] Notably the Khmer empire. See below, pp. 110 and 112.

passing through the Straits of Malacca[10] and the increase in Chinese exports of bronze, silk and pottery under the T'ang dynasty. Thus, thanks to its position close to the place where the Malacca and Sunda Straits and the Java and South China Seas all converge, Palembang was almost ideally situated to serve as both a way-station along the all-sea routes, and a centre for the collection and exchange of Malaysian primary produce against the manufactures of India and China.

It was from this nucleus and by such means that the great maritime empire of Sri Vijaya, which is first mentioned as sending an embassy to China in 670, was built up. Between 689 and 692 it absorbed the neighbouring kingdom of Djambi (Melayu) and thereafter quickly advanced its rule over most of the eastern and southern coasts of Sumatra. But its power and wealth rested above all on its ability to compel all ships using either the Malacca or the Sunda Straits to call at one or other of its ports, and accordingly in the 8th century it extended its hegemony over most of western Malaya and also over the western tip of Java (Fig. 11). Although one result of these monopolistic policies was to promote a new interest in the overland routes avoiding the Straits, notably through Kedah and Singgora and across the Kra isthmus from Takua Pa to Chaiya,[11] the Malacca Straits route maintained its importance and Sri Vijaya continued to grow in renown as a centre both of commerce and of Mahayana Buddhist learning.

In the meantime a further consequence of the fall of Funan had been the attempt by an ambitious new dynasty in central Java, probably in the Sivaite (Hindu) kingdom known to the Chinese since 640 as Ho-ling,[12] to lay claim to the former's Imperial title of 'King of the Mountain' or, in its Sanskrit form, Sailendra. Whatever the precise reason for this assumption of the old Funan title, the rise of the Sailendra dynasty in Java during the 8th century was marked by a great cultural renaissance associated with the introduction of Mahayana Buddhism and finding its highest expression in the many temples and monuments which date from this time. The most magnificent of these, the great stupa of Borobudur in the Progo valley to the north-west of Djokjakarta, was probably begun in the year 772.

But although the Sailendra power was based on the agricultural resources of the lowlands of interior Java, the dynasty seems later to have obtained a controlling interest in the coastal ports in the north-east of the island, and, with their fleets at its disposal, it began to extend the range of its influence overseas, along the east coast of the Malay peninsula and even to Cambodia itself. Much uncertainty surrounds these latter events but it is clear that the southern coast of Indochina was twice raided from Java, in 774 and 787, and there is a persistent Khmer

[10] Which in turn was primarily the result of the expansion of Persian and other Muslim trade between India and China. See Harrison, p. 23.

[11] See also Wheatley (E), pp. 74–5. Other routes, via the Three Pagodas pass and the Raheng Pass were also being increasingly used at this time.

[12] Also known as Kalinga, perhaps implying Kling or Tamil.

tradition of a period of Javanese overlordship during the latter half of the 8th century.

Of more lasting significance, however, was the establishment of Sailendra rule over Sri Vijaya, perhaps as the result of a dynastic marriage, in the mid-9th century. For this involved a permanent shift in the seat of Sailendra power to Palembang, and with its prestige thus further enhanced Sri Vijaya was able to maintain its position as the greatest and most influential empire in the archipelago for upwards of another two hundred years.

The vacuum created in Java by the removal of the Sailendras to Sumatra was quickly filled in the closing years of the 9th century by the growing power of Mataram, and with this in turn came a revival of both Hinduism and the ancient Javanese traditions which by this time had in large measure fused. After 929 Mataram moved its capital to the eastern interior of Java, from where it also was in a position to dominate the coastal ports and to develop an extensive trade, particularly with the eastern islands of the archipelago. Indeed, towards the end of the century its commercial and political prowess had become so great that it attempted to challenge Sri Vijaya and, although this resulted in a temporary defeat, a new division of spheres was tacitly agreed upon, whereby Mataram was left supreme in the east of the archipelago while Sri Vijaya's ascendancy in the west was not contested. Moreover, the essentials of this arrangement survived the partition of Mataram in 1045, into the two kingdoms of Janggala and Kadiri, and although eastern Java remained disunited until early in the 13th century, when the new kingdom of Singhasari in effect replaced both these successor states, the trading links with the eastern islands continued to develop under the stimulus of the growing demand of foreign merchants for the nutmegs of Banda and the cloves of the Moluccas.

III. THE INDO-PACIFIC PENINSULA FROM THE EIGHTH TO THE FIFTEENTH CENTURY

While Sri Vijaya maintained its pre-eminence in the archipelago from the 8th to the 11th centuries,[13] a new imperial power of comparable stature was emerging under the Khmers on the mainland. Following their acquisition of the metropolitan territories of Funan, the Khmers of Chenla established a new capital at a site considerably farther inland, some twelve miles north of Kompong Thom, and from there proceeded to consolidate their hold over the area around Tonlé Sap and the lower Mekong valley. In 706 Chenla split into a northern and southern kingdom, respectively known as Land- and Water-Chenla.[14] It was the latter which in effect became the successor of Funan, but despite its name it was not a sea-power in the sense that Funan had been. And after the founding of the

[13] Though from the 12th century onwards the various kingdoms which successively dominated eastern Java were probably its equals.

[14] With capitals respectively at Sambor (north of Kratié) and at Angkor Borei (50 miles south of Phnom-Penh).

Angkor dynasty by Jayavarman II[15] in 802 the two Chenlas were reunited and the kingdom became definitively focused in the Tonlé Sap basin, whose abundant resources of both fish from the lake and rice from the seasonally flooded lowlands surrounding it were to provide the economic basis of the formidable power which the kingdom soon came to wield.

The first city of Angkor,[16] situated near the northern tip of the lake, was founded towards the end of the 9th century and, to judge from both its remains and contemporary accounts, was probably larger than ancient Rome. While estimates that its population was of the order of a million are almost certainly exaggerations,[17] there can be no doubting the lavish and magnificent scale on which the city was planned, or the remarkable skill of the engineers who provided it with a water supply by diverting the Siemreap river and building an elaborate system of channels and storage reservoirs.[18]

Except for a brief interlude during the 10th century, Angkor remained the Khmer capital until 1432, and in the meantime the kingdom revived to the full the territorial ambitions of Funan. In this connexion both the economic resources and the geographical position of the Cambodian basin, well protected by natural defences and at the same time commanding easy routes to the upper Mekong, the Korat plateau, the Menam basin and the coastlands to the south and east, were immense assets. By exploiting these to the full, and taking advantage of the weakness of Sung China in the latter part of the 11th century, the Khmer kingdom expanded to reach its zenith under Suryavarman II (1113–50), the builder of the superb funerary temple of Angkor Wat.[19]

To the north the Khmer territories marched with those of China itself, while to the east they bordered on Champa which, indeed, was completely subdued for a time in the latter part of the 12th century. But the kingdom's most spectacular gains were made along its western frontiers, where between the 10th and the 12th centuries it absorbed the Mon territories of Dvaravati, thus extending its hold from Sawankalok and Sukothai in the north-west to the Tenasserim coast, and even down the narrow neck of peninsular Siam as far as Grahi, which lay

[15] Who according to legend delivered the kingdom from its subjection to Javanese (Sailendra) rule. See above, p. 109.

[16] Originally called Yasodharapura. It covered a larger area than the later Angkor Thom (which was founded at the end of the 12th century, see below, p. 112) though the two overlap.

[17] Such views appear to be based on false analogies with European cities but Angkor was a monument of religious and symbolic significance rather than a city in the Western sense, modern or medieval. *Cf.* Farmer's comments (*op. cit.*, p. 16) on Anuradhapura in Ceylon. Groslier and Arthaud, p. 25, estimate that the population of the 'region of Angkor' probably exceeded one million.

[18] Besides supplying the city's own requirements, these installations provided irrigation water for the surrounding plains. For an interesting account of the irrigation works see Groslier, especially pp. 101–3, and Groslier and Arthaud, pp. 24–5; see also above, p. 89.

[19] This was dedicated to the Hindu God Vishnu, worship of whom was the official religion.

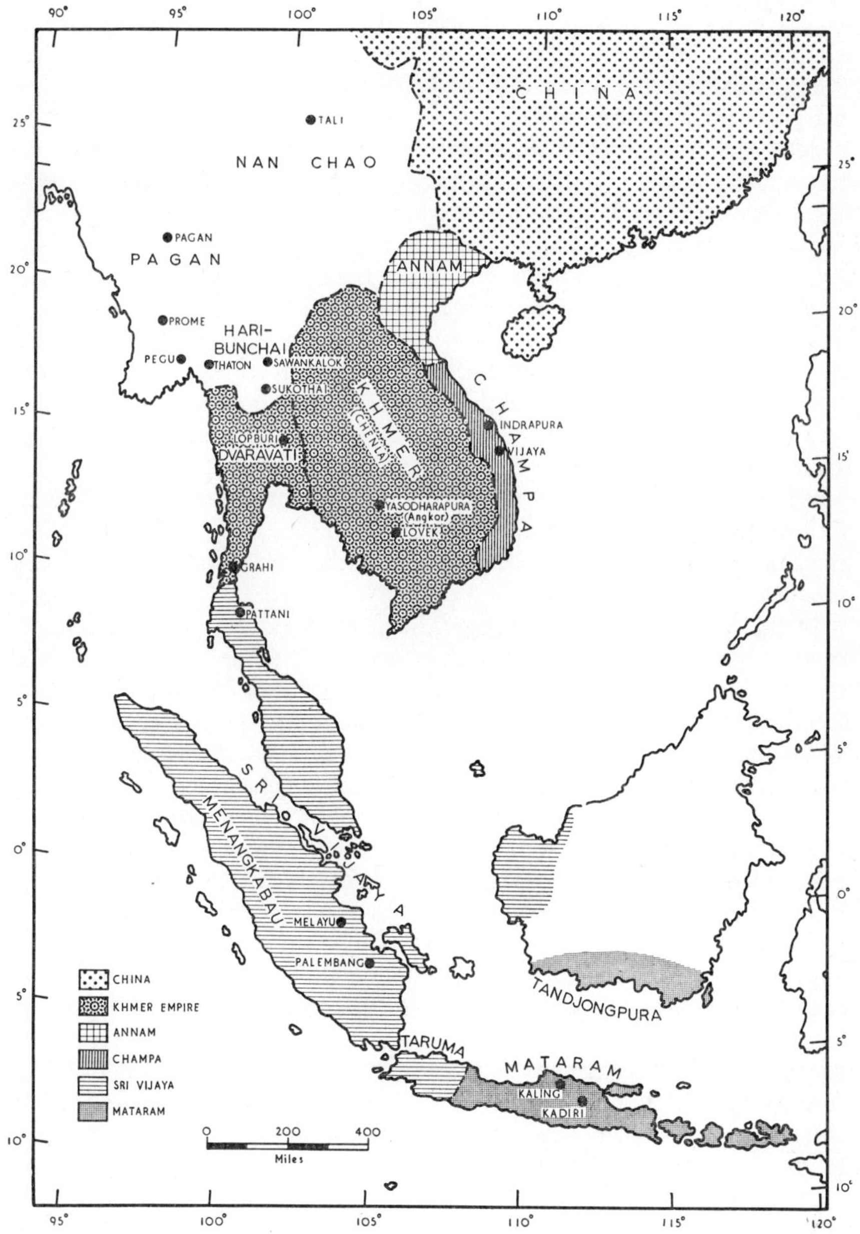

FIG. 12—South-east Asia: political divisions, late 11th century, A.D.

immediately to the north of the modern Patani. Since the last-named area was still at this time a dependency of Sri Vijaya, the spheres of the two greatest empires of South-east Asia, the one on the mainland and the other based on the seaways of the western archipelago, seem to have met along this critical northern margin of the Malay peninsula.

After a serious setback at the hands of the Chams who, after attacking by sea, put Angkor to the sack in 1177, Cambodia experienced a remarkable revival under Jayavarman VII (1181–1219) who restored the capital city, thereafter known as Angkor Thom, and also built an impressive system of roads radiating from it. Indeed to all outward appearances the Khmer kingdom continued in full glory for a further two hundred years, and a fabulous account of its splendour was given by Chou Ta-kuan, a member of a Chinese diplomatic mission under the Mongol dynasty, shortly before the end of the 13th century.[20] But already by this time it was beginning to feel the strain of growing pressure from the Thais, on its outlying territories in the Menam basin and the Korat plateau, which ultimately was to play a major part in its downfall.

Before dealing with this final episode in the history of the ancient Khmer civilization, however, it is desirable first to consider the march of events in other parts of the Indo-Pacific peninsula where further movements of people had meanwhile been taking place.

In the Annamite lands Chinese rule had produced the necessary material conditions to support a steady growth of population in the Song-koi delta and the adjacent coastal lowlands, though under the Chinese no attempt was made to extend the frontier beyond the Porte d'Annam, which formed an obvious natural limit. But in 939 the Annamites, whose distinctive language and traditions had served to foster something akin to a rudimentary sense of nationality, revolted against Chinese rule and established their own kingdom of Dai-co-viet.[21]

From the outset Dai-co-viet, probably under the pressure of an expanding population, sought to extend its territory and, in view of the obstacles presented by China to the north and by the fever-ridden uplands to the west, the south was the obvious direction of least resistance. South of the Porte d'Annam its territories adjoined those of Champa, which still ranked as one of the major Indianized states on the mainland and had attained to a level of civilization not recognizably inferior to its own.[22] But in geographical resources Champa was poorly endowed. For a time it had extended its influence over much of the highland country along its western borders, but this was extremely unhealthy and sparsely populated, and although the lowlands fringing the coast were more fertile, their total area was not large and the way in which they were broken up

[20] See Briggs (E), pp. 244–50.

[21] After their failure to retake this kingdom under the Sung dynasty the Chinese subsequently called it An-nan or 'pacified south' [*sic*]. Notwithstanding the break with China, the new Annamite kingdom was in many respects modelled on the Chinese.

[22] The Chams left some very fine monuments and are known to have practised irrigated rice cultivation, though not of the Chinese pattern adopted by the Annamites.

into a series of small compartments by spurs branching off from the main Annamite Chain constituted a serious impediment to political unification.

In these circumstances, therefore, the Annamites found no great difficulty in pushing southwards little by little at Champa's expense. In 1069 the Chams lost the country between the Porte d'Annam and the modern Hué; attempts to retake this met with no lasting success and, crushed between the advancing Annamites from the north and the Khmers in the rear, Champa embarked upon a long drawn out and eventually unsuccessful struggle for its very survival.

In the Irrawaddy valley, meanwhile, further southward migrations of Tibeto-Burman peoples reinforced the earlier settlements around Pagan, and under Anawratha, who founded a new dynasty there in 1054, the Burmans proved strong enough to conquer the two seaboard kingdoms of Thaton and Arakan and so to extend their rule over an area which roughly foreshadowed that of the modern Burmese state.

But the most extensive migrations within the Indo-Pacific peninsula at this time were those of the Thai/Lao/Shan peoples which, following the Mongol destruction of Nan Chao in the mid-13th century, culminated in a series of parallel thrusts down all the larger river valleys leading southwards from the Yunnan table-land.

Under the Pagan dynasty the Shans of Burma had been contained within the north-eastern plateaux by a line of forts in the foothill country, but in the latter part of the 13th century the new influx from the north enabled them to break through these defences and to overrun the plains. Pagan fell to their attacks in 1287,[23] and thereafter a Shan dynasty established itself in the heart of the dry zone, eventually making Ava its capital, and remained in control there until 1531. During this interlude of some two and a half centuries the unity achieved under Pagan disappeared. Arakan reasserted its independence, and the central lowlands lapsed into a state of chaos, with the Mons of Pegu and a new Burman kingdom centred at Toungoo on the Sittang contending with each other and with the Shans of Ava for the mastery.

Farther to the east the advance of Lao tribes down the Mekong valley likewise led to the growth of a series of small states in the area of present-day Laos. In 1353 these were united under one of their chiefs, Fa Ngoun, as the kingdom of Lan Chang, so named after its capital which later became known as Luang Prabang. With the gradual withdrawal of Khmer power from the middle Mekong basin and the Korat plateau, Lan Chang acquired control over the greater part of this area, and for a time ranked as one of the largest states of the peninsula though, owing to the agricultural poverty of much of its territory, its population was never very large.

[23] Murphey (A), p. 199, has suggested that the fall of Pagan, as also of the Lao kingdom of Lampun towards the end of the 13th century (and of Angkor in the 15th century) may have been partly due to internal weaknesses arising from the spread of malaria into the Indo-Pacific peninsula for the first time around that date.

It was, however, in the centre of the peninsula, that is in the territory which forms the heart of modern Thailand, that the Thai peoples achieved their greatest successes. For in contrast to the dissected plateaux and semi-arid lowlands to east and west, the basin of the Menam is one of the most fertile agricultural lowlands in the whole of South-east Asia, and after the 13th century neither the Mons nor the Khmers were sufficiently powerful to prevent the Thais from gaining control over this region in its entirety.

In the far north, hitherto under Mon control, a number of Thai groups coalesced under a single leader and established the kingdom of Chiengmai in 1296. Some years prior to this the two towns of Sawankalok and Sukothai, immediately to the south, had been wrested from the Khmers by local leaders who had thereupon established the Thai kingdom of Sukothai, and after Ram K'amheng succeeded to its throne in 1275 he extended his territories at the expense of the Khmers southwards to Nakhornsrithamrat beyond the isthmus of Kra. But although Sukothai remained an independent state for over another hundred years it was eclipsed by the new kingdom of Ayuthia, founded according to tradition in 1350 by a Thai prince from U'tong (Supanburi) who, with his followers, had abandoned the latter town after a devastating epidemic of cholera. By the end of the 14th century Ayuthia's domains had been extended to include not only Sukothai and its erstwhile dependencies but also Moulmein, Tavoy, Tenasserim and much of the Malay peninsula, all of these last being particularly prized on account of the maritime trade route which ran close to their shores but by-passed the Gulf of Siam.

This southward advance of the Thais over the Menam lowlands was repeatedly contested by the Khmers, and at the same time the Mongols, after acceding to power in China in 1279, encouraged the Thais to further attacks in order to undermine the strength of Cambodia, which still remained by far the most powerful state on the mainland. With each successive advance the Thais became better placed to carry the struggle into Cambodia itself, and from the end of the 14th century onwards Angkor was almost constantly under the threat of attack. The decisive blow was struck in 1431 when a Thai army captured Angkor, and the following year the Khmers finally abandoned the city, thereafter withdrawing their capital eastwards to a less exposed situation at Lovek. Although the Cambodian territories of the kingdom remained intact, its era of greatness was at an end, and its spectacular achievements were never repeated. Angkor itself was completely deserted and engulfed by the tropical forest, and by comparison Lovek and its successor Phnom-Penh were little more than minor provincial towns. By the 19th century Angkor and all it stood for evoked no memory among the surviving Khmers, a people for the most part of unsophisticated villagers, who were accounted of little consequence by either their Siamese or Vietnamese neighbours.

The swiftness and thoroughness of this decline have inevitably prompted much speculation, to which several references have been made in preceding chapters. Probably a number of factors contributed to the collapse, though the details of the story still remain to be unravelled. Certainly, however, the urban superstructure of the Khmer empire, represented above all by Angkor itself, must have been disproportionately large for the resources of the state, and its upkeep must have imposed a heavy burden on the local peasantry. And if, as Pendleton implies, the majority of the latter beyond the immediate vicinity of the Tonlé Sap lowlands were shifting cultivators, the possibility that the growing demands of the capital eventually led to excessive pressure on the land, and hence to soil impoverishment and erosion, may be significant. Moreover, apart from the problems entained by a dwindling food supply, soil erosion might well have had disastrous indirect effects on health, for the clogging of natural and artificial water courses by dust and silt lead to the formation of swampy tracts which would provide breeding grounds for malaria vectors in areas hitherto free from infection.[24] Admittedly, this is still a matter of speculation, but there would seem to be fairly strong *prima facie* reasons for suspecting that the vigour of the Khmer people had already begun to decline before the attacks of the Thai armies administered the *coup de grâce*. Whether the widespread adoption of Theravada Buddhism contributed to such a decline is perhaps more doubtful, though on the other hand, once Angkor had fallen, the necessary support for any attempt to rebuild along the old lines was probably ruled out by this change in popular mores. Whatever the causes, however, the facts are not in dispute. The Khmers, who in the 7th century had come down from the hills to conquer Funan, themselves succumbed to the southward drive of the Thais eight centuries later. In truth, the wheel had come full circle.

IV. THE RISE AND FALL OF MADJAPAHIT

The period from the 12th to the 15th centuries which witnessed these great changes on the mainland was likewise marked by a major transformation in the archipelago. Although the growing volume of trade – especially in spices – through the Straits enabled Sri Vijaya for a time to recover its fortunes after the setback of the Chola attack in 1025, the empire was clearly in a state of decline by the latter part of the 13th century, and from 1256 onwards Palembang itself was reduced to the level of a Javanese dependency.[25] This decline of the once powerful Sumatran kingdom may well have been caused by continued sedimentation along the greater part of the eastern coast of the island. Though this process must have been at work throughout historic times, it only began seriously to affect Sri Vijaya in the second millennium A.D., possibly because of a temporary increase in the silt load of the rivers following upon a period of exceptional volcanic activity in the western highlands. In part, no doubt, the

[24] See Note 23. It is also possible that the rapid process of delta formation by the Mekong caused some modification in the drainage pattern farther upstream and so contributed to an increase in the extent of such swampy terrains.

[25] Though it needed to be disciplined again in 1377.

disadvantages caused by the resultant widening of the swamp belt along the Sumatran coast were offset by the possession of outposts on the Malayan side of the Straits; and in this connexion it is significant that the Chola raiders went to considerable lengths to destroy Sri Vijaya's ports in the Dindings, Johore, and Tumasik.[26] But in the long run the increasingly serious drawback from which Palembang itself suffered must certainly have contributed to the empire's decay.

The decline of Sri Vijaya in the west of the archipelago was balanced by the steady growth in the power and influence of eastern Java, and in some measure at least this was aided, albeit unintentionally, by the efforts of the Mongol dynasty of China. For whether or not the rapid expansion of Singhasari's influence over the outer domains of the disintegrating Sri Vijaya during the reign of Kertanagara (1268–92) was due to the latter's desire to build up a strong defensive confederation of Indonesian states against a possible Mongol attack,[27] Mongol forces certainly helped Kertanagara's son-in-law, Vijaya, to regain the Singhasari throne in 1292 after an internal upheaval in that kingdom. And this restoration prepared the way for Vijaya's founding of the new empire of Madjapahit which, during the 14th century, came to represent the final and most magnificent flowering of Indo-Javanese civilization.[28]

Like the earlier land powers of east-central Java, Madjapahit, whose capital lay in the extremely fertile Brantas valley, proved strong enough to manipulate such powerful port kingdoms as Tuban, Gresik and Surabaja[29] to serve its own ends and to help by means of their fleets in extending its influence farther afield. Under the guidance of Gaja Mada, the chief minister who held office from 1330 to 1364, Madjapahit is said to have encompassed the final downfall of Sri Vijaya,[30] and thereafter to have succeeded to the latter's territories in Sumatra and in the Malay peninsula as far north as Patani, besides ruling over the Lesser Sundas, Celebes, and most of Borneo and the Moluccas.

Such at least is the account given by the contemporary court poet Prapança, and until comparatively recently it has been accepted as substantially true. But since C. C. Berg first cast doubts upon this interpretation,[31] which implied that Madjapahit ruled over a vast empire almost identical in extent with that of the modern Netherlands Indies, a growing body of evidence has accumulated to

[26] On the site of the modern Singapore. On silting, see Dobby (H), p. 58. See also Roberts, G. (A), p. 355.

[27] As has been suggested by C. C. Berg. See Hall (B), p. 66, and Wertheim (C), pp. 51–2.

[28] Like Singhasari, Madjapahit adhered to the syncretic cult of the Siva-Buddha.

[29] From these ports local seamen used to sail with the E monsoon to the Straits of Malacca, Sumatra, Borneo, Pattani and Siam, and with the W monsoon to Bali, Timor, Buru, the Moluccas, Seram and even to Mindanao. Tuban was the main port of Madjapahit until late in the 14th century. Schrieke, Pt. I, pp. 20–2.

[30] As early as 1286 the Malay royal house of Palembang withdrew to the Menangkabau highlands, which thereafter became the main focus of the Malay world in the narrower sense of that term. See Schrieke, Pt. I, p. 16.

[31] See Hall (B), pp. 78–81, and Wertheim (C), pp. 51–2.

confirm his suspicions. Thus, it is now believed that while the Madjapahit kingdom attained great brilliance in east-central Java and may also have maintained a measure of hegemony over some of the lesser islands to the east, the other parts of the Malaysian world remained outside its effective control and their relationships to it were at most limited to the formal payment of tribute.

V. SOUTH-EAST ASIA ON THE EVE OF THE IBERIAN CONQUESTS

Nevertheless, Madjapahit was undoubtedly the strongest power in the archipelago during the 15th century, and with the Thais by this time victorious over the Khmers on the mainland, South-east Asia exhibited a somewhat similar geopolitical division to that which had characterized the earlier era of Angkor and Sri Vijaya, and once again the two spheres met within the confines of the Malay peninsula.

Indeed, Malaya, as a part of the Indo-Pacific peninsula which nevertheless belongs climatically and ethnically with the archipelago, would at first sight appear to be the master key to South-east Asia. For, in addition to its obvious centrality, it holds a commanding position in relation to both the all-sea route through the Malacca Straits and the alternative trans-isthmian route through Kedah and Pattani. Moreover, as Wheatley has emphasized, the fact that ships from India and China sailed to South-east Asia with one monsoon and returned with the other meant that they had to wait for the change of wind in some sheltered harbour at or near the southern tip of the land-mass. This in turn favoured the early growth of such entrepôt centres as Ptolemy's Takola and Sabora, which Wheatley suggests were situated in the vicinity of Phuket and modern Singapore respectively.[32]

On the other hand, however, the general sterility of Malaya's predominantly lateritic soils and its lack of any really large alluvial lowlands have greatly restricted its capacity for exploiting the undoubted potentialities which the geographical position affords. Yet such an attempt was made during the 15th century and, thanks to a peculiarly favourable combination of circumstances, it achieved for a time a remarkable measure of success.

Although the processes of coastal sedimentation which entailed such disastrous consequences for Sri Vijaya extended over most of the Sumatran side of the Straits, they did not trouble either the northern end of that island, where the adjacent seas are much deeper, nor the western coast of Malaya where powerful tidal scour prevents excessive accumulation of silt. Thus, following the downfall of Sri Vijaya in the 14th century, both of these areas were in a position to take over some of that empire's former seaborne trade, though admittedly for several

[32] See Wheatley (E), pp. 74–5. In addition, Pahang gold seems to have been an important item of commerce from before the Christian era until the 17th or 18th century A.D., and it seems probable that the Malay peninsula was the Golden Chersonese referred to by Ptolemy. *Ibid.* See also Wheatley (K).

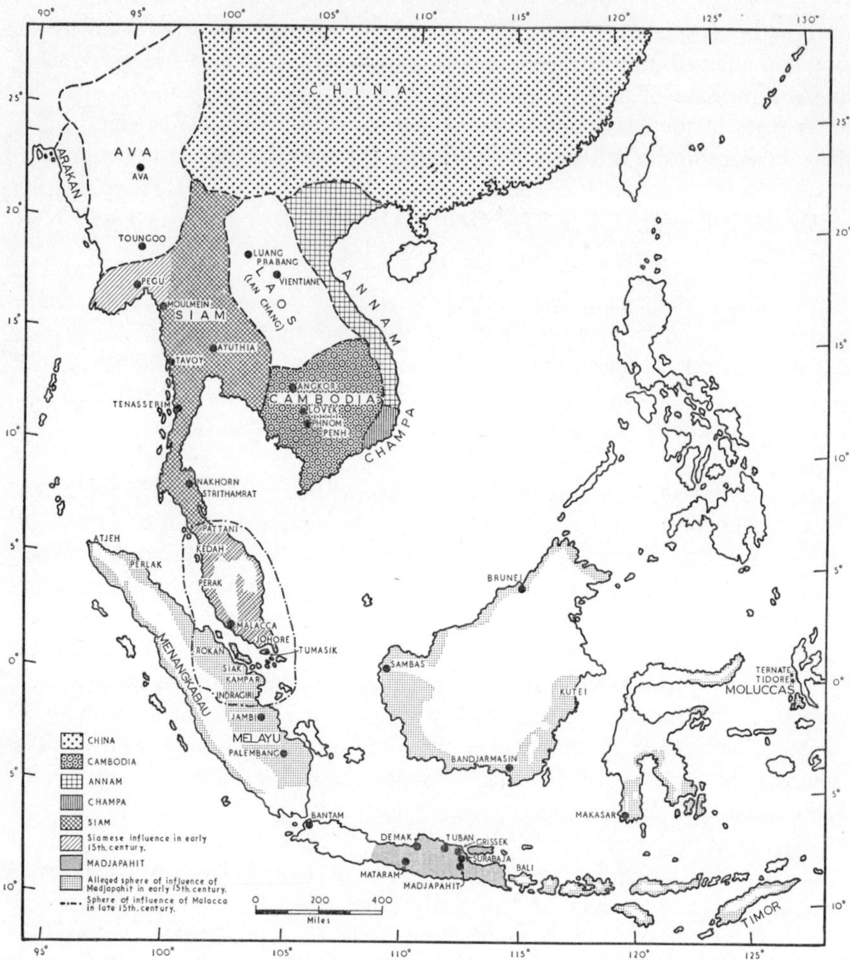

FIG. 13—South-east Asia: political divisions, late 15th century, A.D.

decades the depredations of pirates – particularly the notorious Chinese bands who installed themselves in Palembang itself – caused many Persian and other traders to avoid the Malacca Straits by sailing first to Atjeh, and then *via* the west coast of Sumatra and the Sunda Straits to the spice-collecting ports of northern Java. Perhaps for this reason it was the ports near the northern tip of Sumatra (Passei) which were the first to benefit most from the fall of Sri Vijaya, but by the middle of the 15th century the lead had passed to the newly established kingdom of Malacca on the opposite side of the strait which bears its name.

According to tradition Malacca was the effective successor of Tumasik (Old Singapore), which had been founded by Palembang but was eventually destroyed late in the 14th century owing to the combined pressures of Siam and Madjapahit, both of which sought to control this strategic point and hence to dominate the sea route past its shores. The Palembang prince who had established himself as the local ruler of Tumasik was forced to move, and about the year 1400 he founded a new kingdom some 130 miles farther up the coast at the mouth of the small Malacca river.[33]

Nevertheless, had it not been for the intervention of China at this juncture, it is unlikely that Malacca would have been able to survive against the rival threats of Siam and Madjapahit. In the event, however, Cheng Ho's fleets[34] provided the requisite protection, and in the two decades following 1409 when it passed under Chinese suzerainty the Malacca kingdom succeeded in taking firm root.

Moreover in 1414 its ruler accepted the Islamic faith, and this event at once strengthened the port's links with the Indian and Middle Eastern Muslim merchants, who by this time monopolized the spice trade in the Indian Ocean and from their ports on the Persian Gulf and the Red Sea supplied at fabulous prices the Venetians and other traders of the Mediterranean. Thus, particularly after the accession of Muzaffar Shah as Sultan in 1445, Malacca moved into the lead as the chief entrepôt for Indonesian spices and the main centre for the further diffusion of Islam throughout the archipelago,[35] a process which was accompanied by a rising tide of rebellion among the coastal kingdoms of northern Java against the overlordship of Hindu/Buddhist Madjapahit.

Meanwhile, as its confidence grew, Malacca also extended its grip both on the peninsula as far north as Kedah and Patani and also, in true sea-state fashion, over the island kingdoms of the Riau and Lingga archipelagos and the small riverine states of Siak, Rokan, Kampar, and Indragiri in eastern Sumatra. Farther south, however, its influence was checked by Demak, which had come to dominate most of the north Javan ports as well as the southern tip of Sumatra, and in 1518 was responsible for dealing the decisive blow against Madjapahit.[36] Nevertheless, it was Malacca which had benefited most from the decline of Madjapahit, and from the middle of the 15th century until the coming of the Portuguese it continued on the crest of the wave of commercial and Islamic expansion to become the leading maritime power in the whole of South-east Asia.

[33] This position may be related to the overland route to Pahang, via the Muar river nearby. See also Harrison, pp. 56 and 63, and Wheatley (E), p. 66. Schrieke, Pt. I, pp. 16–17, implies that although the reigning dynasty first at Singapore and later at Malacca was related to the Palembang royal house, the initiative in developing trade there came from Hindu Javanese who formed the dominant element in Malacca's population until that kingdom was converted to Islam by Gujarati traders.

[34] See above, p. 95.

[35] There were usually at least 1,000 Gujarati traders living in Malacca, as well as other Indians, Persians, Arabs, Chinese and Indonesians. At its hey-day the port probably counted 10,000 to 15,000 Arab traders. Van Leur, p. 132.

[36] After 1518 survivors of the Madjapahit dynasty continued a precarious existence in the extreme east of Java until 1639 when they transferred to Bali. *Ibid.*, p. 173.

It was, of course, no accident that the first foothold acquired by the Europeans in South-east Asia was Malacca itself and, in thus seizing the focal point of Muslim sea-power there, the Portuguese effectively ruled out any possibility of the region's at last becoming politically united under local leadership. In fact, however, such a possibility had always been remote, owing to the geographical fragmentation of South-east Asia as a whole, and to the shortage of good agricultural land in the Malay peninsula which alone might conceivably have bridged the gap between the mainland and the archipelago. Indeed, notwithstanding its rapid rise to a position of commanding influence, Malacca was consistently dependent on imported rice from Java, and even before 1511 its power was apparently waning. Nevertheless, the Portuguese victory in that year marked the definitive end of an epoch. For thereafter, without interruption until the present day, the nearby maritime crossroads which form the natural focus of South-east Asia have remained in alien hands, and the whole course of the region's history has been profoundly altered as a result.

VI. THE INDO-PACIFIC PENINSULA FROM THE SIXTEENTH TO THE NINETEENTH CENTURY

From the early 16th century onwards the political systems of the archipelago came increasingly under European influence, and indeed can only be properly understood in that context, which forms the subject of Chapter 5. But on the mainland north of the Malay peninsula, European influence, though certainly not negligible, did not become of decisive importance until the 19th century and in the meantime geopolitical evolution there continued along the lines which have already been sketched. Thus, in the course of the 15th to the 19th century political unification was gradually achieved within the central valleys of Burma and Siam and throughout the eastern coastal strip of Vietnam, while at the same time the Shan and Laos peoples lost their hold over all but the plateau country which lies between these several lowlands, the territory of the Khmers was gradually whittled away to leave only the core of the former kingdom intact in the eastern part of the Cambodian basin, and Champa disappeared entirely from the map.

The reunification of Burma was brought about under the Burman kingdom of Toungoo which, in the Sittang valley, commanded a more productive rice-growing region than the Dry Zone held by the Shans. Thus, Toungoo was able little by little to encroach into the south-eastern territories of Ava, and eventually in the early 16th century to conquer both it and the Mon kingdom of Pegu.[37] In 1539 it made Pegu its own capital, and thereafter developed a considerable overseas trade through the port of Syriam. The struggle against the Shans[38] was carried farther afield, with incursions into the territories of both Lan Chang

[37] Toungoo was helped by artillery obtained from the Portuguese.

[38] The distinctions between the various Thai/Lao/Shan peoples and principalities were even more blurred at this time than they have been in more recent centuries.

and Ayuthia, and in 1556 Chiengmai was captured and reduced to the status of a vassal kingdom.

However, the unity of Burma was maintained only with difficulty in the face of the continued hostility of the Mons and the counter-attacks of the Siamese from Ayuthia, which *inter alia* were responsible for the decision to move the capital back to Ava. Indeed from the second half of the 16th century until the beginning of the 18th the strife was well-nigh unbroken, but after 1740 a new leader arose in the person of Alaungpaya, who succeeded in imposing effective control over the whole country apart from Arakan, and in 1752 founded a new dynasty which lasted till 1885.[39] Even so, intermittent warfare continued against Siam, culminating in the destruction of Ayuthia in 1767, and, although Burma was thus victorious, the war entailed a heavy drain on its resources. Moreover, the Alaungpaya dynasty followed a brutally repressive policy towards its non-Burman subjects. In particular the Mons were savagely treated and many of them accordingly migrated to Siam, leaving the Irrawaddy delta partially depopulated by the beginning of the 19th century, and after Arakan was conquered in 1784–5 a similar exodus began from there into the adjacent parts of India.

The evolution of Siam during the centuries following the Thai defeat of the Khmers in 1431 was closely bound up with the course of events in Burma described in the preceding paragraphs. For a time in the latter part of the 16th century, Burmese pressure seemed to threaten the extinction of the Siamese kingdom of Ayuthia but, beginning in 1590 under King Phra Naret, the tables were turned, and after subduing both Lan Chang and Cambodia, Siamese forces successfully carried the struggle against Burma into the latter's home territory with two attacks on Pegu.

Nevertheless, the unification of Siam was not completed until after the further humiliation brought about by the Burmese sack of Ayuthia in 1767 which, surprisingly, led to a spectacular national revival under the leadership of P'ya Taksin, a man of mixed Thai and Chinese blood. Under Taksin the Burmese were driven out, and the northern provinces, including Chiengmai, now recovered from Burma, were brought firmly under the control of the new capital which he established at Thonburi on the right bank of the Menam some 50 miles below Ayuthia. His successor, P'ya Chakkri,[40] who shifted the capital to Bangkok on the opposite side of the river, achieved further notable victories, and by the time of his death in 1809 the Siamese again ruled over Tenasserim and Tavoy, and were in process of extending their authority deep into the Malay peninsula. Likewise, to the north-east Siam had come to exert a controlling influence in Laos (Lan Chang) and important territorial gains had also been made along the western frontiers of Cambodia.

[39] Both the British and French were involved in long-term intrigues in Burma at this time. See below, p. 141. Much of Alaungpaya's success was due to his chance acquisition of a large supply of French arms. See Pearn, pp. 9–10.

[40] The founder of the present dynasty.

In contrast to Siam, which was thus markedly in the ascendant at the beginning of the 19th century, both Laos and Cambodia were by this time clearly in a state of decline. For geographical reasons the political unification of the Laos plateau had proved exceedingly difficult to achieve, and after the beginning of the 18th century Lan Chang had split into two separate states, Luang Prabang and Vien Chang (Vientiane) whose internecine struggles played into the hands of both the Siamese and the Annamites. After Vientiane had been virtually destroyed as an independent kingdom, following the Siamese invasion of 1827, Luang Prabang strove hard to avoid a similar fate and to this end paid tribute to Annam as well as to Siam.[41]

Cambodia likewise was long subjected to pressure from both the Siamese and the Annamites and, although its royal house survived in office and claimed to have avoided permanent subjection to either, the status of the kingdom nevertheless sank lower and lower. In 1795 the Siamese occupied the two western provinces of Battambang and Angkor, and thereafter remained in possession of these until 1907.

More serious, however, was the encroachment of the Annamites on the opposite side of the kingdom, which led ultimately to the loss of the whole of the Mekong delta. The Annamite advance to the south, which had begun with the attack against Champa in the 10th century, continued throughout the period under discussion here. In 1402 the Chams were forced to give up all territory north of Quang Nam, and four years later Vijaya, their capital city, fell to the Annamite attackers. By the end of the 15th century only a few Cham districts maintained their independence, and Annamite power reached south as far as Cap Varella.

In extending their territories in this way, however, the Annamites, like the Chams before them, soon encountered serious difficulties in holding together the long, narrow and fragmented strip of coastal plain which lies between the Annamite Chain and the sea. During both the 15th and the 16th centuries local territorial families in various parts of the country strongly resisted the centralizing efforts of the monarchy, and for a time the latter was fairly effectively relegated to the background. Particularly important in this connexion was the growing power of the Nguyen family in the south, which was considerably helped by arms obtained from the Portuguese. To strengthen their defences against the north the Nguyen rulers built two great walls across the waist of the country, one near Dong Hoi and the other at Truong Duc.[42] Thus, the divide between north and south, thereafter known to the West as Tonkin and Cochinchina respectively, became complete, and while the imperial title was retained by the Le dynasty in the north, the heads of the Nguyen family also arrogated to themselves the style of independent monarchs.

[41] After the French had declared Annam a protectorate they seized upon this practice as a pretext for extending their rule over Laos. See below, pp. 154–5.

[42] *I.e.* just to the north and south respectively of the Geneva partition line of 1954.

Moreover, although the southern kingdom was a new and in a sense a colonial territory, it created an administrative system basically similar to that of the north, and continued to push the frontier of Annamite settlement still farther along the coast. In 1692 the remaining territories of Champa were finally absorbed, though a Cham ruler maintained nominal independence until 1822, and in the meantime Cochinchina continued the southward advance at the expense of Cambodia.

From the early 17th century Annamite deserters and adventurers had begun to settle in the eastern fringes of the Mekong delta, and between then and the closing decades of the 18th century virtually the whole of this area, hitherto only sparsely occupied by the Khmers,[43] passed into the hands of Cochinchina, thus leaving Cambodia with no outlet to the sea, except for a short and neglected stretch of coast along the Gulf of Siam.

These extensive territorial gains in the south added substantially to the power and prestige of Cochinchina before a dynastic quarrel broke out in the 1770s which, by a strange turn of fortune, was to lead to the reunification of all the Annamite lands under the house of Nguyen. For although in the resultant confusion, during which the Le emperor managed to escape to China, the Nguyen family was almost wiped out, their legitimate heir, Nguyen Anh, survived in the south, where in 1789 he received the support of a small French task force, thanks to the intervention on his behalf of the French missionary priest Pigneau de Behaine. Thus aided, the Nguyen forces won a series of victories in the south, and eventually, after a protracted struggle, succeeded in capturing Hué in 1801 and Hanoi in 1802. Despite the Annamites' long-standing tradition of hostility to Chinese overlordship, the new emperor, henceforward known as Gia Long, thought it prudent in the circumstances to request the official recognition of China, which was granted in 1803, in return for Vietnam's undertaking to send tribute to Peking every two years.

With a sound sense of geographical realities Gia Long selected Hué, in the ancestral territory of the Nguyen, to be the new central capital of Vietnam, and both the northern and the southern deltas were administered through imperial Governors-General, from Hanoi and Saigon respectively. This arrangement marked the beginning of the three-fold division of the Annamite lands, which was later confirmed by the French establishment of the Colony of Cochinchina in the south and the Protectorates of Annam and Tonkin in the centre and north.

Before any European annexations had taken place on the mainland, therefore, the broad outlines of the modern political map had already made their appearance just as, at an earlier stage, Madjapahit had in some measure anticipated the unity which the Dutch eventually achieved in Indonesia. This correspondence is not

[43] Who had never developed a really satisfactory technique for rice cultivation in the extensive parts of the delta which are annually flooded to a depth of several feet. See below, p. 533.

fortuitous but reflects rather the permanent realities of the region's geography. For while in the islands the ease of movement by sea has served since the earliest times to promote cultural and political unification, the severity of the natural barriers on the mainland has impeded the development of comparable links between the principal riverine and coastal lowlands. Nevertheless, the element of continuity in the pattern must not be overstressed, for, as the foregoing pages have shown, successive movements of peoples have necessitated repeated readjustments in the relations between state and territory within the region.

Indeed at first glance the history of the mainland seems to consist of little more than a series of ding-dong struggles between successive invaders, each contending for as much as possible of the more attractive lowlands. This process was arbitrarily arrested by the imposition of Western rule in its various forms, as described in Chapter 5, but it remains to be seen whether the removal of such external restraints will presage a return to the rivalries of former times.

Meanwhile, both on the mainland and in the archipelago, the record of past achievements is a powerful factor in moulding contemporary national consciousness. While within limits this may be all to the good, it is nevertheless a matter which needs to be treated with restraint by the politicians. For since, almost without exception, the several states of the region can look back to periods when, in one direction or another, their territories were more extensive than they are today, it is not difficult to quote supposedly valid precedents for expansionist policies. In these circumstances, moreover, myth tends to be more persuasive than reality and the 'glorious past' of chauvinist politicians is usually a purely imaginary epoch into which have been telescoped all the nation's most spectacular achievements but none of its equally numerous setbacks. Here, as we have already seen, the parallel with the Balkans is both geographically and historically valid, and it is to be hoped that the statesmen of South-east Asia are fully alive to the lessons which it teaches.

SELECT BIBLIOGRAPHY

Briggs (A) (B) (C) (D) (E)
Coedès
Credner
Duyvendak
Furnivall (A) (B)
Groslier
Groslier and Arthaud
Hall (A) (B)
Harrison
Harvey (A) (B)
Le May
Majumdar (A) (B)
Panikkar (A) (B) (C)
Parkinson (A)
Pearn
Purcell (C) (D)
Roberts, G. (A) (B)
Schrieke
Sokol (A)
Steel and Fisher
Thompson, V. (A) (B) (C)
Tibbetts
Van Leur
Vlekke (A)
Wales (A) (C)
Wheatley (A) (B) (C) (D) (E) (F) (G) (H)
Winstedt (A) (B) (C) (D) (E)
Wood
Zelinsky

Chambers's Encyclopædia
Encyclopædia Britannica
Indo-China (*N.I.D.*)
Netherlands East Indies, II (*N.I.D.*)

The definitive historical-political geography of South-east Asia has yet to be written, though the papers by Sokol and Zelinsky, the pamphlet by Furnivall (B) and the books by Wales (A) and (C) provide much useful material, as also do the two N.I.D. volumes, and the series of papers by Wheatley (A)—(H) are invaluable contributions to the historical geography of the Malay peninsula.

For the rest I am much indebted to the standard regional histories, notably the monumental work by Hall (B) and the shorter but very readable book by Harrison, and to the histories of particular countries, notably Hall (A), Harvey (A) and Pearn (Burma), Wood (Siam), Briggs (E) and Groslier (Indochina), Winstedt (E) (Malaya), and Furnivall (A), Vlekke (A) and Van Leur (Indonesia).

These sources have also been supplemented by various historical atlases, notably Herrmann's *Historical and Commercial Atlas of China*, Sellman's *An Outline Atlas of Eastern History*, and *Westermanns Atlas zur Weltgeschichte*.

Addendum: See also Wheatley (K).

Note: Although, as has been made clear in the foregoing pages, the coastline of various parts of South-east Asia has undergone substantial change within historic times, lack of precise data has made it impossible to show such changes on Figs. 11–13.

CHAPTER 5

The Era of Western Rule

I. INTRODUCTION

The coming of the Europeans in the 16th century marked the beginning of a revolutionary change in the spatial relationships of South-east Asia. Whereas during the preceding 1,500 years or so the main emphasis had lain on the region's geographical position between India and China, from now onwards the Bay of Bengal and the South China Sea slipped into wider perspective as mere annexes of the Indian and Pacific Oceans, and the fate of South-east Asia itself became increasingly bound up with the course of events in still more distant parts of the globe. For it was the lure of the Moluccan spice trade which impelled Spain and Portugal to take the lead in exploring the oceanic highways of the world and, in so doing, to usher in the four and a half centuries of Western dominance in Asia which began with the arrival of Vasco da Gama at Calicut in 1498 and ended with the departure of the British from India in 1947.[1]

In the long drawn out process whereby Western political control was extended over nearly the whole of South-east Asia, three main stages may be distinguished. In the earliest phase, corresponding roughly to the 16th century, European activity was essentially peripheral, and amounted to little more than the acquisition of a few key footholds on certain strategically placed islands. In the second phase, however, which followed the establishment of Spanish settlements in Cebu towards the end of the 16th century and the arrival of the Dutch in Indonesia early in the 17th century, European control, though still restricted to the island fringe of South-east Asia, was gradually extended at least over the greater part of Java and the northern two-thirds of the Philippines. But it was not until the 19th century, with the growing Western demand for markets and materials, the invention of the steamship, and the cutting of the Suez canal in 1859–69, that the final parcelling out took place, and Britain, France and the United States joined the Netherlands as the principal Western powers controlling the destinies of South-east Asia.[2]

Nevertheless, although in early times the hold of the Europeans, operating as

[1] Panikkar (C), p. 11. Note, however, that the British, French and Dutch still remained in various parts of South-east Asia for some years after 1947, though it was undoubtedly the withdrawal from India which marked the end of the epoch.

[2] Britain and France had certain interests in the area prior to the 19th century (see below, pp. 139–142) but their main activities there came after 1800.

they were with relatively limited technical superiority at enormous distances from their home bases, was often precarious, and both Indian and other Muslim merchants offered stubborn resistance to all attempts to destroy their trade, the presence of the Westerners had from the outset a far greater effect than their numbers alone would seem to imply. For their very weakness encouraged them whenever possible to foment local disagreements in order to strengthen their own position, and since the whole of the island fringe was still in a state of political confusion arising from the spread of Islam[3] and the break-up of Madjapahit, the scope for such disruptive activities was great.

In this respect, moreover, the Moluccas, which provided the greatest attraction of all, were particularly vulnerable, alike on account of the backwardness of their population and their equivocal position in relation to the Tordesillas[4] division of 1494, which laid them open to the simultaneous advances of the Portuguese from the west and the Spaniards who approached from the opposite direction across the Pacific.

The countries of the Indo-Pacific peninsula, on the other hand, though far from stable internally and frequently at war with one another throughout the period under discussion, were in better condition to resist Western pressure than were the Malaysian lands; and, in any case, thanks to their position away from the main sea routes[5] and the absence of any specific attraction comparable to that of the spice trade, they received far less attention from the West during the early Oceanic period. Moreover, since the presence of Portuguese shipping and naval power in the South China Sea played a decisive part in weakening China's maritime links with the Nan Yang after the 16th century, the activities of the Feringhi[6] served virtually from the outset to sharpen the cultural divide, already apparent since the coming of Islam, between the mainland and insular halves of South-east Asia.

II. THE PORTUGUESE AND SPANISH POSSESSIONS IN THE SIXTEENTH CENTURY

The growing demand in Europe for oriental spices during late medieval times arose out of the desire for condiments to flavour salted and pickled meat which figured prominently and monotonously in the popular diet until the 18th century, when the practice of cultivating root crops as winter feed put a stop to the whole-

[3] This process continued throughout the early colonial period.

[4] Whereby Spain and Portugal agreed to divide the world's newly discovered lands respectively to the west and east of a line drawn 370 leagues west of the Cape Verde Islands. It was not, however, clear which of these islands provided the point of reference, and this gave rise to further confusion when the line was projected through 180° to the East Indies. By the Treaty of Saragossa in 1529 Spain sold its doubtful claims over the Moluccas to Portugal.

[5] At this era their capitals were in most cases well inland.

[6] *I.e.* 'Franks', the name applied by Asians first to the Portuguese and later to Westerners in general. Its origin goes back to the time of the Crusades.

sale slaughtering of cattle each autumn. Among the spices in greatest demand, pepper and ginger (the 'heavy spices') were grown over a fairly wide area including India, Ceylon and various parts of the East Indies, notably Sumatra, but the more expensive cloves and nutmegs were at first restricted to the small Moluccan island groups of Ternate, Tidore, Amboyna and the Bandas, where a few Muslim Malay Sultans had established their rule over the rather primitive indigenous peoples and organized the cultivation of these two highly saleable commodities, both of which were native to the islands.[7]

As described on page 127, the business of transporting Indonesian spices to Europe had in the later Middle Ages become a jealously guarded monopoly of the Muslims and Venetians. Besides striving to break this, by finding a direct sea route round Africa to the Moluccas, the Portuguese were concerned also to carry the struggle against Islam a stage further by making a great outflanking movement which would cut off the most valuable part of the Muslim world's seaborne trade at its source.[8] Accordingly, having discovered the Cape of Good Hope route to India in 1498 and established themselves at various points along the Deccan coast in succeeding years, the Portuguese defeated the combined Egyptian and Gujarati fleets at Diu in 1509, and were then free to press on to the Spice Islands. Following the ancient sea route through the Straits they seized Malacca, the chief spice market, in 1511 and thereupon despatched an expedition to open up relations with the Moluccas.

Notwithstanding the continued resistance of the peninsular Malays from 1511 to 1526 and the even more severe opposition of Atjeh after 1537, the Portuguese managed during the 16th century to establish a network of bases along the main sea routes through the archipelago as far as Timor and the Spice Islands, though Malacca never lost its pre-eminence as the key to the western approach through the Straits. Meanwhile in 1530 the Sultan of Ternate was forced to pay an annual tribute of cloves, and other potentates both in the Moluccas and elsewhere in the archipelago were prevailed upon to grant monopolies of their spices and other produce.

Thus, although at an early stage after their arrival in 1511 the Portuguese set up several trading posts along the coasts of Siam, Burma and Cambodia, and later extended their activities still farther afield in an attempt to trade with China and

[7] Nutmegs are obtained from the seed of *Myristica fragrens*, an evergreen tree growing to a height of 50–60 ft. and native to the Moluccan-New Guinean region. Cloves come from the buds of another tree, *Eugenica aromatica*, which grows to about 40 ft. and is also native to the Moluccas. Geographically there was no reason why both these should not be grown in many other tropical lands, though the fact that the local rulers in the Moluccas were prepared to organize production there was an advantage which could not readily be repeated elsewhere. It was not until 1770 that the clove monopoly was completely broken, but in that year the French introduced the tree into Mauritius and later it spread to the Guianas, Brazil, the West Indies and Zanzibar, the last of which is now the main producer. Nutmegs were eventually cultivated with varying success in Penang, Bengal, Réunion, Brazil, French Guiana and the West Indies, but the Moluccas are still the main source of supply.

[8] Harrison, p. 70.

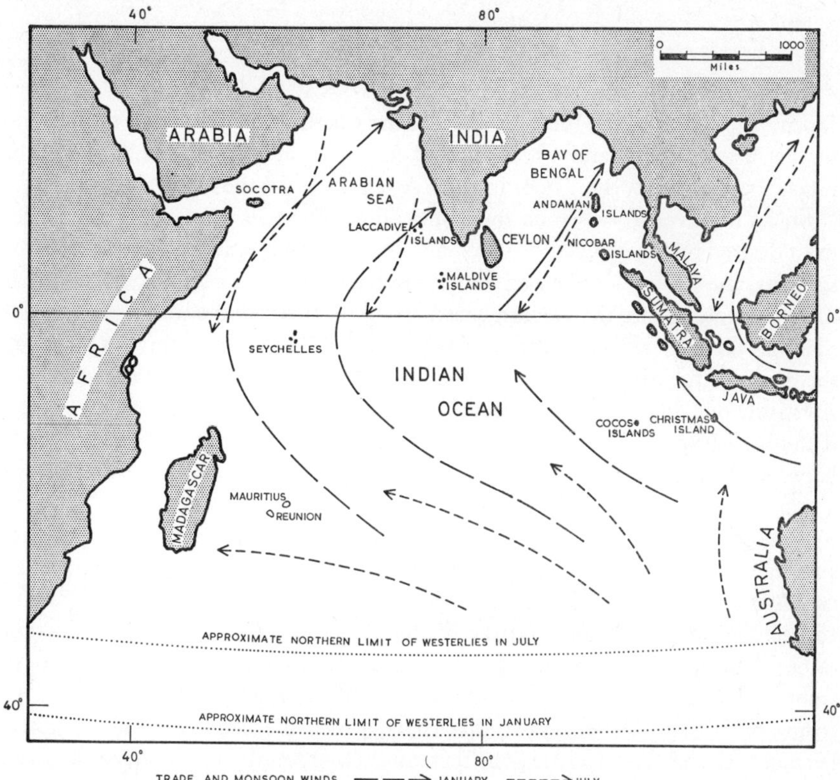

Fig. 14—Indian Ocean: seasonal winds affecting historic sailing routes

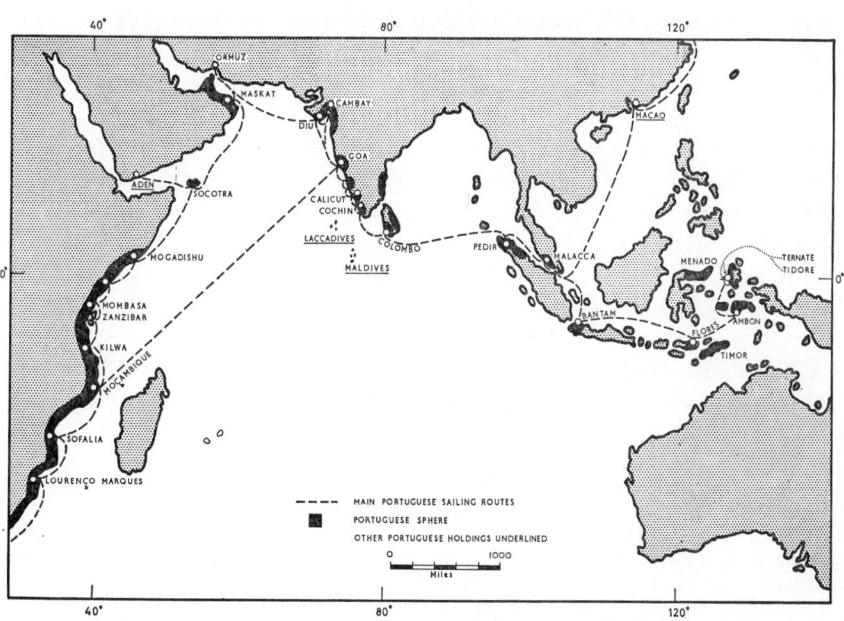

Fig. 15—Indian Ocean: Portuguese possessions and sailing routes, 16th century

Japan,[9] the spices of the Indies, thanks to their high value in relation to bulk and to the insatiable demand which existed for them in Europe, continued to be much the most important item in their Asian trade for the rest of the century.

Since, however, it was soon found that Indian textiles were the commodities most desired by the Moluccan rulers in exchange for the spices produced by their subjects, the Portuguese had an added motive for retaining and extending their early footholds along the Deccan coast, and thus preserving under new management an already familiar pattern of trade. Indeed, in their attempts to destroy the power of the Muslim traders in the East, the Portuguese policy was simply to substitute one monopoly for another. For such a system was considered essential if the high price of spices was to be maintained, and even at its peak the trade between the Indies and Portugal amounted only to some ten to twenty shiploads a year.[10]

Because of these relatively limited aims, which in part reflected the acute shortage of man-power in the mother country, the Portuguese hold on South-east Asia was restricted to a few vital points in the archipelago, and such trading and soldiering as took place on the mainland was a matter of individual action rather than of official policy. Thus the whole eastern empire of the Portuguese amounted to little more than a series of fortified posts centring in Goa and strung out along the seaways from Ormuz, which blocked the entrance to the Persian Gulf, to Ceylon, Malacca, Bantam, Timor, Ambon (Amboyna) and the Moluccas, and ultimately also to Macao on the China coast. Except in so far as it was linked to the West by a further series of bases fringing the shores of the African continent, this system, which depended on the maintenance of close commercial and other links between southern India and South-east Asia through the Straits of Malacca, had much in common with the earlier geopolitical pattern of Muslim sea power in the Indian Ocean.[11]

In such a 'garrison empire' contact with the indigenous peoples was necessarily limited though, thanks to a notable absence of colour prejudice, the Portuguese were not averse from intermarriage with local women in the few centres where they settled, and the resultant half-caste population went some way towards solving the persistent problem of inadequate man-power. Moreover, this Eurasian community, which was strongly Portuguese in culture and Roman Catholic in religion, has maintained its identity ever since, and forms perhaps the most important surviving legacy of the Portuguese era in South and South-east Asia. But among the indigenous peoples, Roman Catholic missionary work did

[9] The first two Portuguese arrived in China from Malacca in 1516 and 1517. The Portuguese were later allowed to set up a trading post at Macao in 1557, where they developed a valuable entrepôt trade foreshadowing that of Hong Kong in the 19th century.

[10] See Harrison, p. 84, and Hudson, p. 8. The Portuguese also obtained supplementary income by continuing the traditional Malay policy of making all passing ships put in at Malacca and pay tolls for the privilege of doing so.

[11] See Roberts, G. (C), p. 475, and Parry, pp. 40–43.

not begin on a large scale until after 1542,[12] and even then made little or no significant headway against Islam, though many of the more backward peoples, notably in the Moluccas where Islam had scarcely penetrated, were converted.

In view of the reputedly fabulous wealth to be derived from the spice trade it is understandable that Spain, even after having obtained almost exclusive rights in the Americas, should nevertheless have wished to discover its own private route to the Moluccas as well. This was the reason for Magellan's expedition which, after first navigating the straits that bear his name and then sailing west with the trade winds to discover the Philippines, arrived at Tidore towards the end of 1521.[13] And even after it became clear that the main spice islands lay within the Portuguese half of the world, Spain continued to press its claim to a place in the Moluccas by virtue of its prior discovery of Tidore.

In the meantime, however, the Portuguese were already established in nearby Ternate, and the petty rivalries between these two small Malaysian sea-states offered almost unlimited scope for the intrigue and counter-intrigue of Spain and Portugal. Nor did this struggle end with the Treaty of Saragossa (1529), whereby Spain nominally relinquished its dubious claim to the Moluccas, and it was not until 1545 that it finally ceased interfering in that area.

But in the 1550s the Spaniards, after having virtually neglected the Philippines since Magellan had originally claimed them in 1521, began to consider more seriously the possibilities which the islands afforded for colonization, and the conquest of Cebu by Legaspi in 1565 marked the beginning of this new phase of Spanish interest in South-east Asia. Moreover, an added incentive was provided by Urdaneta's discovery in the same year that the track of the westerlies between latitudes 31° and 44° N afforded a reliable return route across the Pacific to Acapulco in Mexico, thus complementing the more southerly trade wind route between latitudes 10° and 14° N which had been used since Magellan's time for the westward journey.[14] Accordingly control was quickly extended to both north and south, and Manila in Luzon was made the capital in 1571.

From a geographical point of view this alignment of the Philippines with Mexico was an innovation of the utmost importance, even though Spain never regarded the islands as anything more than a minor appendage of its Central American territories until the latter made good their independence early in the 19th century. Before the end of the 16th century the influx of Mexican silver into the Philippines encouraged the many Chinese merchants, already by that

[12] Under St. Francis Xavier, the (Spanish) Jesuit 'apostle of the Indies', who was sent by John III of Portugal as a missionary to the East in 1542. This Portuguese missionary effort was aimed at winning allies and sympathizers against the local Muslim potentates. But in the event it goaded the Muslims to wage a religious counter-offensive, and Islam thus spread with even greater rapidity in the 16th century than in the 15th. Schrieke, Pt. II, p. 235.

[13] Magellan was a Portuguese sailing in Spanish service. He was killed in the Philippines in 1521 but the expedition continued the journey back to Spain under his second-in-command.

[14] Jones and Mehnert, pp. 360–61.

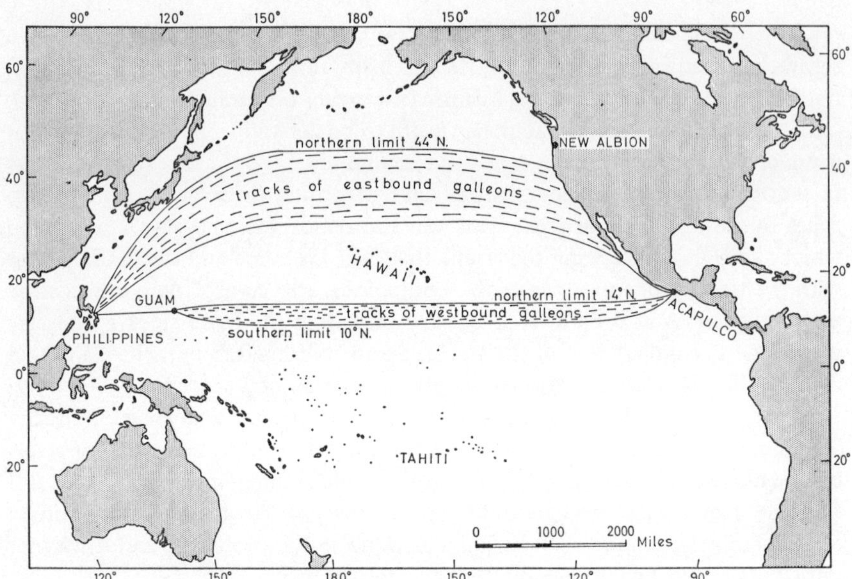

FIG. 16—Pacific Ocean: sailing routes used by Spaniards, 16th–18th centuries

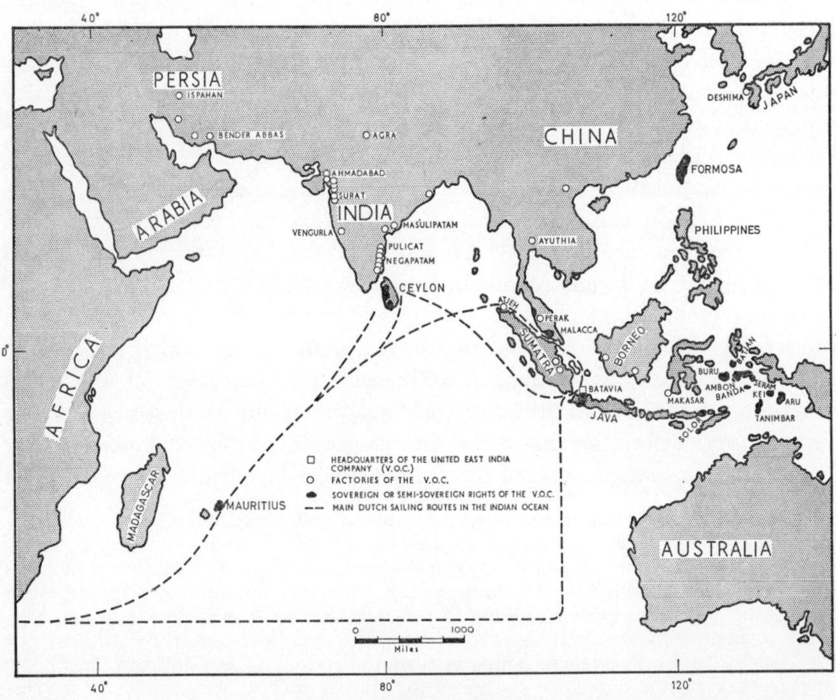

FIG. 17—Indian Ocean: Dutch East India Company's possessions and sailing routes 17th–18th centuries

time established in Manila, to build up a new and lucrative entrepôt trade which quickly rivalled that of the Portuguese in Macao. Thus, by means of the annual Manila galleons, silk and porcelain from China were exported to Central America and Europe, and paid for by Mexican silver dollars, which in this way became the accepted international currency in the ports of eastern Asia.[15]

In spite of the islands' apparently great potentialities, however, Spanish rule did little to promote their economic development, though various American crops, such as tobacco, maize, sweet potatoes and peanuts, were introduced and ultimately found their way thence into most parts of the Orient. As in the New World so also in the Philippines, the Spaniards scarcely concerned themselves with commerce and aimed rather at establishing a system of landed estates on the feudal pattern of the mother country.[16]

In this way, therefore, Spanish control in the Philippines did not remain restricted, like that of the Portuguese in the Indies, to a few bases along the coast, and furthermore the introduction of colonial administration into the interior was everywhere accompanied, if not indeed preceded, by the advent of the missionary priest. And since, moreover, the Filipino population had been barely touched by Indianization, and only superficially affected by Islam except in Sulu, Mindanao and Palawan in the south, the relatively unsophisticated tribal society and animistic beliefs offered little resistance to this organized acculturation at the hands of the friars. Thus, long before it came to an end in 1898, the era of Spanish rule in the Philippines had transformed the northern two-thirds of these islands into a predominantly Christian region and an outpost of Latin-American civilization on the fringe of the Asian continent.

Compared with that of Spain in the Philippines, the Portuguese hold over most of their scattered bases in the Indies was much less secure and, in consequence, of much shorter duration. Owing to the weakness and poverty of the mother country, few of Portugal's Asian posts could be adequately manned, and the attempt to enforce monopolistic restrictions provoked strong local resentment. Thus, as early as 1574 the Portuguese were driven out of Ternate and thereafter, although they managed to hold on to Malacca for a further 67 years, their position in other parts of the archipelago became steadily more precarious.[17] As the 16th century gave place to the 17th, maritime supremacy passed from the Iberian powers to the new nation states of north-western Europe, and while the Philippines, which were reckoned of lesser account by the latter, remained in Spanish hands, both India and the Indies, thanks to the continuing importance of the spice trade, came increasingly under the control of the English and the Dutch.

[15] China was a great exporter of manufactures, including textiles, until after the beginning of the industrial revolution in the West. Purcell (E), p. 10. In the later 17th century trade via Manila declined, and never recovered during the rest of the Spanish period.

[16] In both areas the Spaniards, like the Portuguese, intermarried extensively with the indigenous population.

[17] On the decline of Portuguese power in Asia, see Parry, pp. 93–7.

III. THE ESTABLISHMENT OF DUTCH POWER IN THE INDIES

Like the Portuguese and the Spaniards before them, the English had sought to discover their own routes to the Spice Islands, and it was only after the North-east Passage was seen to offer little prospect of success that the English began openly to challenge the Iberian powers' monopoly of the established sea routes.[18] Thus in 1577 Drake began his voyage around the world, following the approximate route of Magellan, and in 1579 he anchored off Ternate. By the time a second English voyage to the East Indies was made in 1586 under Thomas Cavendish, who used a similar route, the war between England and Spain which was to lead to the defeat of the Armada in 1588, had already broken out.

Soon after this decisive English victory, a group of London merchants, interested in the direct purchase of spices and the marketing of English woollen cloth, decided to send a trading expedition to the Indies via the shorter route around the Cape of Good Hope in 1591, and in 1600 the East India Company was founded to further these ends.

In the meantime, however, the Dutch had become very active and soon proved to be much the more important of the two new rivals of the Iberian powers in South-east Asia. During the second half of the 16th century the Dutch, who had built up a highly profitable trade in northern Europe by redistributing the spices brought to Lisbon by the Portuguese,[19] became increasingly interested in obtaining direct access to the Spice Islands for themselves and, with this in mind, they also had played a major part in the search for the North-east Passage. Moreover, many individual Dutchmen had visited the Indies in Portuguese service, and were familiar with both the sailing routes and the local harbours, a lengthy account of which was embodied in the treatises of van Linschoten, first published in 1595–6.

Accordingly, when in 1594 Philip II[20] closed the port of Lisbon to the Dutch and the English, the challenge was quickly taken up, and in the following year the first Dutch expedition, under de Houtman, sailed to the Indies via the Cape of Good Hope. Its success was immediate, and between then and 1601 a total of 65 Dutch ships made the journey, normally sailing first to Bantam, where they obtained cargoes of pepper, and then to the Moluccas, where supplies of the more valuable nutmegs, mace and cloves were purchased from the local rulers.[21]

Thus by 1600, when the (English) East India Company was founded, the

[18] The attempt to find a North-west Passage, which began seriously under Frobisher in 1576, was likewise to prove a disappointment.

[19] The Portuguese needed all their large ships for the Eastern trade. See Harrison, p. 87.

[20] *I.e.* of Spain and Portugal, whose thrones were united from 1580 to 1640, though their respective colonial territories remained distinct.

[21] Harrison, p. 89. Some of these early ventures used the Magellan route in the opposite direction, but this practice, which involved sailing against the prevailing winds for great distances, was soon seen to be less satisfactory than the approach via the Cape of Good Hope.

number of Dutch ships sailing to the Indies was already much greater than that of their English rivals, and Dutch enterprise there formed a major part of the national struggle against the Iberian powers in a theatre where the latter were most vulnerable.

In particular, the over-extended position of the Portuguese in the Indies offered great scope to the already superior seamanship of the Dutch, who were prepared to sail direct across the southern Indian Ocean along the track of the westerlies instead of hugging the coast in the traditional Portuguese fashion.[22] And while Malacca was strongly defended, the Portuguese post at Bantam was quite incapable of preventing the Dutch from using the alternative entry to the archipelago through the Sunda Straits, and so by-passing the main Portuguese bases in India and the Malaya peninsula.[23] In 1602 the Dutch won a decisive naval battle over the Portuguese off Bantam, and in the same year the States-General amalgamated the separate trading organizations into a single concern, the Vereenigde Oostindische Compagnie (United East India Company). Thus, although a French Company was founded in 1604[24] and the Danes set up another in 1616, the main struggle for control of the Indies trade lay between the English and the Dutch companies and, thanks to the greatly superior resources of the latter, the issue was virtually decided from the outset.

In 1605 the Dutch seized Amboyna, the last important Portuguese stronghold in the archipelago east of Malacca,[25] and by 1616 they had a total of fifteen posts at various points in the islands, notably in Tidore, Ternate and Banda, where they obtained a monopoly of the local spice output,[26] and at Bantam which served as a collecting centre for Sumatran pepper and as a *pied à terre* close to the Sunda Straits. Like the Portuguese, moreover, they carried on some marginal trade with the South-east Asian mainland, arriving in Cambodia for this purpose as early as 1602, and subsequently extending their range to Burma and Siam later in the century. Meanwhile, the E.I.C., though operating on a smaller scale, established

[22] The usual route after 1619 was to sail across the southern Indian Ocean to about 100° E and then to turn northwards to the Sunda Straits. (See Fig. 17, and Eldridge, p. 250.) As a result of some ships overshooting this longitude the Dutch discovered the western shores of Australia and other Dutch navigators later explored around that continent from East Indian bases. But as the Dutch were interested in trade rather than settlement they had no use for this almost empty land. See also Roberts, G. (C), p. 477, Vlekke (A), pp. 96–7, and Parry, p. 157.

[23] See Roberts, G. (C), p. 477 and Parry p. 100.

[24] The French chartered a series of companies for Eastern trade, respectively in 1604, 1611, 1615, 1642 and 1664. Only the last achieved much success. See below, p. 140. In the following pages the English and Dutch companies are referred to as the E.I.C. and V.O.C. respectively.

[25] Timor, originally valued for its sandalwood, may constitute a partial exception to this statement. Despite a succession of struggles with the Dutch, the Portuguese managed to retain the eastern half of the island, together with the so-called Okussi enclave. See Sowash, pp. 227–35.

[26] After the Dutch had gained control of the world's supplies of nutmeg and mace by getting a monopoly of Banda's production in 1623, they attempted similarly to restrict the production of cloves to the single island of Ambon. See below, p. 255.

its agents in various Indonesian ports from Atjeh (where pepper was obtained) to Makasar, as well as at Patani and Ayuthia in Siam, and tried hard to break into the closely guarded clove and nutmeg trade of Banda and Ambon.

However, with the appointment of Jan Pieterszoon Coen as Governor-General in 1618 the Dutch determined to force the British out of the archipelago. In 1619 Coen set up his headquarters at the small port then known to the Europeans as Jacatra, but later (1621) renamed Batavia,[27] and in 1623 matters were brought to a head by the so-called 'Massacre of Amboyna' in which ten Englishmen, nine Japanese and one Portuguese were executed for plotting to seize the fortress of Amboyna.

This event marked the turning point of the E.I.C.'s relationship with the Dutch in the Indies and thereafter, while the Dutch proceeded without much difficulty to take over the remaining Portuguese factories there and to establish others of their own, the English, who had already abandoned their stations in Siam, gradually withdrew from the archipelago between 1628 and 1682. And although, admittedly, a new fort was opened at Benkulen in 1685 and remained in British hands until 1824, its position on the remote west coast of Sumatra served only to emphasize the exclusion of the E.I.C. from the vital inner seas of the region which, for all practical purposes, had become a Dutch lake by the middle of the 17th century.[28]

Having thus been driven out of Malaysian waters, the E.I.C. fell back on peninsular India where it had maintained a factory at Surat since 1609, and in 1632 it opened a second factory at Masulipatam on the eastern coast of the Deccan.[29] The Dutch, on the other hand, never extended their holdings very widely in India, though in the final stage of their struggle against the Portuguese they became the effective masters of Ceylon (1640–56), which proved to be one of their most valuable possessions until its cession to the British in 1798. It was the acquistion of a foothold in Ceylon which enabled the Dutch to break the link between the Portuguese bases in India and Malacca, and in 1641 they finally succeeded in conquering this strongly defended port which had long been cut off from the greater part of its former Malaysian trading sphere.

From the early 17th century until the middle of the 20th century, therefore,[30]

[27] Although Batavia could be reached from Europe via the Sunda Straits, it was nevertheless near enough to the Malacca Straits to command the trade route between Malacca and the Moluccas via the Java Sea. (See Sokol (A), p. 348.) In addition, Eldridge, p. 235, citing Admiral G. A. Ballard's *Rulers of the Indian Ocean*, points out that since Batavia lay within the southern trade-wind belt, the V.O.C.'s fleets based there enjoyed the great strategic advantage of being able at all seasons to get to windward of the Portuguese bases on the west coast of the Indian Ocean.

[28] Benkulen was valued for pepper, then the most important export of Sumatra (as also of Borneo). See also Wertheim (C), p. 56. Note that Benkulen is nowadays spelt Bangkahulu by the Indonesians.

[29] Others followed, *e.g.* in Madras (1639) and in Bengal (1650).

[30] Apart from two relatively brief periods of foreign occupation, namely by the British during the Napoleonic Wars and by the Japanese during the Second World War. See below, pp. 144–5 and 194–8.

the Dutch were left as the dominant European power in the Indonesian archipelago, completely supplanting the Portuguese except in the eastern half of Timor which, by a curious irony, still survives, along with Macao, and until recently Goa, as a vestigial remnant of the old Portuguese empire. But although in a real sense the Dutch empire, not only in Indonesia but throughout the whole maritime fringe of southern and eastern Asia, was built upon Portuguese foundations and consciously or unconsciously preserved many of the characteristics of its predecessor, the Dutch nevertheless introduced several changes of lasting significance.

In the first place, the V.O.C. concerned itself exclusively with material affairs, and the Indies were regarded simply as a *bedrijf* (a business concern) whose sole purpose it was to make profits for the Dutch and to take them away from their rivals. In this respect, moreover, Coen was quick to appreciate that, owing to excessive foreign competition, the price of spices in Europe had already fallen to a level which offered scant prospect for maintaining the solvency of the Company. Accordingly he proposed to extend the range of its activities by exploiting the focal geographical position of the archipelago in the marginal seas of southern Asia, so as to develop a great inter-Asian trading concern under Dutch auspices.[31]

In effect, such a policy was a logical continuation of the traditional monopolistic control, exerted in turn by Sri Vijaya, Malacca and the Portuguese over the maritime commerce passing between the Indian Ocean and the South China Sea, though under the Dutch the flow of trade was more effectively controlled, thanks to their command over major sources of many of the principal commodities involved. Thus, besides Javanese rice, sandalwood from Timor, the cloves and nutmegs of the Moluccas and the pepper of Borneo and Sumatra, the Dutch controlled the supply of cinnamon from Ceylon and of copper from Japan, and were also in a position to obtain Persian gems, Indian cloth and Chinese silk and porcelain. From the start Coen sought to centre this extremely lucrative and wide ranging entrepôt trade in Batavia and, thanks to Dutch command of the sea routes, his plans were in large measure realized by the middle of the 17th century.[32]

In concentrating its attention on trade the V.O.C. hoped, like its Portuguese predecessors, to avoid direct territorial expansion, but this policy called for some modification as time went on. To begin with, the need to check illicit spice production, smuggling and piracy led the Dutch to establish control over the most important islands in the Moluccas, and repeated threats to the safety of Batavia also caused them gradually to widen the perimeter around the town, until by the end of the 17th century they ruled over most of the western third of Java. In taking over this area, the Company assumed the rights formerly exercised by native princes to receive tribute from local chiefs, and this arrangement

[31] Sokol (A), p. 346. Note also that Coen had originally proposed to establish a system of Dutch-run spice plantations, using slave labour, the latter to be obtained, if necessary, by kidnapping Chinese. Vlekke (A), p. 119.

[32] Vlekke (A), p. 120.

later proved to be a useful standby when, towards the end of the century, the Asian coastal trade began to decline, mainly as a result of changing political circumstances in many of the countries most directly involved.

Eventually, as the decline continued, the Company was compelled to find alternative sources of income and two of these came to be of lasting importance. Soon after the founding of Batavia, Chinese settlers had established sugar plantations and mills in the vicinity of the town, and by the early 18th century the price of sugar in Europe had become sufficiently high to make it worthwhile developing this as an export crop. About the same time also, the cultivation of coffee was introduced from India, and shortly afterwards the idea was conceived of demanding the payment of tribute in place of the traditional rice in several areas under the Company's control. This was the origin of the system of taxation by 'forced deliveries' and 'contingents' which, by transforming Java from an entrepôt centre into an outstanding producer of tropical commodities,[33] gave a new lease of life to the Company and provided a fresh motive for the extension of the latter's authority over other parts of the island.

Meanwhile, as their territorial commitments increased, the policy of the Dutch underwent significant changes in other respects. Thus, although they were less troubled than the Portuguese had been by the man-power problem, the remoteness of the archipelago from Europe and the difficulty of maintaining health in its humid tropical climate presented great obstacles to the residence of white women there,[34] and for this reason the Dutch adopted the practice of miscegenation which had been introduced by the Portuguese. In this way the Eurasian community grew in numbers in all the main areas under Dutch control, though during the 17th and 18th centuries its members continued to speak a debased form of Portuguese which also served as the *lingua franca* between Europeans and Asians generally throughout the archipelago.[35]

However, even in Java both Dutch and Eurasians together were far outnumbered by the Chinese who since Portuguese times had formed a significant community, composed mainly of traders, shopkeepers and skilled craftsmen. During most of the 17th century, and particularly under the Governor-Generalship of van Diemen (1636–56), the V.O.C. favoured the further immigration of Chinese, whose industry, self-reliance and peaceful behaviour appealed to the Dutch far more than did the allegedly lazy and unpredictable habits of the Indonesians. Thus, especially when the Manchu conquest of China was followed by civil war in Fukkien, from which the bulk of the Chinese emigrants to the Nan Yang traditionally came, the flow increased rapidly in volume and by 1733

[33] See Vlekke (A), Chapter 9. Sugar and pepper remained the two most important in the first half of the 18th century, but in the second half coffee became the largest single source of revenue. Other commodities included tea, indigo and teak.

[34] In the days before modern hygiene and sanitation Batavia, in particular, was extremely unhealthy, owing to its Dutch-style canals. Beginning in 1732 it experienced a series of epidemics of malignant malaria and other fevers. Vlekke (A), p. 175.

[35] Wertheim (C), p. 291.

the total number in Java was of the order of 100,000, of whom 80 per cent lived in or around Batavia.[36] But this sudden influx soon led to extensive unemployment, and when as a result the Dutch decided in 1740 to deport large numbers to Ceylon, a revolt broke out and in a sudden panic thousands of Chinese were killed.

Nevertheless this incident, which psychologically had much in common with the hysterical massacres of Chinese in the Philippines in 1603 and 1639, did not put a stop to further immigration, for the Chinese were too persistent and too useful to the Europeans – in both the Indies and the Philippines – to be permanently excluded. Owing to the peculiar structure of the colonial society the Chinese were able to serve as intermediaries of many kinds between the European officials and the indigenous peasantry, and thus to form a kind of middle class analogous to that formed by the Jews in many parts of central and eastern Europe.

Like the latter, moreover, the Chinese remained essentially a community apart, and although many married local wives they continued to preserve their own traditions and the language of their homeland, and brought up their children to do the same. While such immigration was not unknown elsewhere in South-east Asia, it was for the most part on a very limited scale outside Java and the Philippines, where the presence of the Europeans produced the necessary conditions of stability in which Chinese enterprise could reap its reward.

From a geographical point of view the most significant consequence of Dutch rule in Indonesia during the 17th and 18th centuries was that the centre of gravity of the Malaysian world moved back from the former commercial focus of Malacca in the western approaches to the South China Sea to Java which, though more distant from the main sea routes, had other and in many ways more permanent assets in its great agricultural resources. However, although both Dutch and Spanish political power thus remained confined to the island periphery of South-east Asia, the countries on the mainland were not entirely ignored by the Europeans even at this stage. And while the Dutch had been the first to supplant the Portuguese traders there also, the English and French later came to play the leading rôles even though, in both cases, their activities were subsidiary to those in the Indian sub-continent.

IV. ENGLISH AND FRENCH ACTIVITIES IN THE INDO-PACIFIC PENINSULA DURING THE SEVENTEENTH AND EIGHTEENTH CENTURIES

As the E.I.C. acquired more bases and wider interests in India during the 17th century it began to concern itself in a minor way with Burma and Siam as well, partly on account of the trade which these countries had to offer and partly out of fear lest the Dutch or the French should instal themselves at strategic points along the eastern coast of the Bay of Bengal and so menace its own position on

[36] Purcell (D), p. 466; Furnivall (A), pp. 45–8; and Cator, p. 11.

the opposite shore. In the middle 17th century the E.I.C. maintained a post at Syriam, and in 1661 it opened a new factory at Ayuthia, though neither of these ever became of much commercial significance.

The French likewise had dabbled in Eastern affairs since the early years of the 17th century, but it was only after the founding of a new French East India Company by Colbert in 1664 that their activities became of any real importance.[37] Four years later they opened two Indian depôts, at Surat and Masulipatam, and these were followed by the establishment of a strong post at Pondicherry which thereafter became their principal station in the East. Finally, in 1690, a French naval expedition was despatched to the Bay of Bengal for the purpose of establishing commerce with Burma and Siam.

Even so, however, the French remained more interested in political than in commercial gains, and a similar political motive seems to have been associated with their early missionary activity in South-east Asia which also dates from approximately the same period. The first Roman Catholic missions in the Orient (apart from those of the Spaniards in the Philippines) had been run mainly by Portuguese Jesuits who ventured as far afield as Tonkin, southern China and Japan. Accordingly, the first two bishoprics in the East, namely Malacca and Macao, were both held by Portugal, but after 1650 the French took the lead in missionary work in Indochina, and French priests were appointed to two new bishoprics in Siam.

During the following two or three decades French missionaries won particular influence in that country, partly through their ability to supplement religious evangelism with the teaching of Western military science,[38] and partly also through the intermediary of the Greek adventurer, Constantin Phaulkon, who for a time occupied an extremely important position in Siamese government service. But this brief interlude came to an abrupt end in 1688 with the execution of many French nationals and the expulsion of the remainder.

In Annam and Tonkin also, French missionary and trading interests went hand in hand during the 17th century, but in the 18th century the Annamites became so hostile that French activities were brought almost to a standstill. In these discouraging circumstances Pigneau de Behaine established contact with the refugee Nguyen Anh, as described on page 123, and by a treaty of 1787 promised him French assistance; in return, France was to be rewarded by the cession of Pulo Condore[39] and further territory in the Bay of Tourane, but these claims lapsed as a result of the French Revolution.

[37] As early as 1631 the French regarded Madagascar as of particular value for extending their trade with southern Asia; and in 1638 the island of Bourbon, later renamed Réunion, was claimed by the Frenchman Gaubert, and was formally annexed in 1643 as a *point d'appui* in the Indian Ocean.

[38] See Harrison, p. 122.

[39] Pulo Condore is a small island, with several good anchorages, some 58 miles from the coast of the Mekong delta. Its strategic position in relation to the trade routes of the South China Sea had led the English to occupy it in 1702, but they abandoned it three years later. See Hall (B), pp. 364 and 369.

Meanwhile, however, the main activities of the French in Asia were concentrated in India and the Indian Ocean theatre where, in the 18th century, they began in earnest to play for bigger stakes.[40] As events moved forward to the inevitable collision between the English and the French in India, both sides conducted rival intrigues in Burma, whose reserves of teak had a high strategic value as material for naval shipbuilding. In the event it was the Burmans, whom the British had backed, and not the French-supported Peguans, who emerged victorious in the internal struggle for supremacy in Burma during the middle 18th century. And with Clive's victory at Plassey in 1757 and the surrender of Pondicherry in 1761 the French dreams of empire in India faded,[41] though it was not until after the battle of Baxar in 1764 that the British decisively consolidated their position in the sub-continent.

Thereafter French interest in South-east Asia languished for the next three-quarters of a century or so. But the British, having become a great territorial power in India, were conscious both of new strategic problems and new commercial opportunities, and these together led to a revival of British interest not only in the Indo-Pacific peninsula but also, and more immediately, in the Malaysian archipelago.

In the first place the recent struggle against the French had underlined the strategic weakness of the E.I.C.'s position in India during the period of the NE monsoon (October–January), when its naval vessels were liable to be cooped up in the Coromandel coast ports by rough weather, thereby leaving the whole of that coast at the mercy of foreign raiders. Thus the need was felt for a naval base on the eastern side of the Bay of Bengal, to which units of the fleet could retire during this season so as to be ready for action should the need arise.[42]

Furthermore, there were important commercial reasons for the revival of British interest in South-east Asia at this time. For not only were the British, like the French, interested in obtaining territories of their own in which to cultivate spices and other tropical produce, but they were also developing a valuable trade with China, exporting opium from Bengal in exchange for tea from Canton, and hence desired to safeguard the rights of British shipping through the Malacca Straits and the South China Sea.[43]

It was against this background that in 1786 the E.I.C. took possession, by

[40] The French East India Company, which had seemed on the point of collapse in 1713, was reorganized in 1720. The key islands of Mauritius and Seychelles were acquired in 1715 and 1744 respectively, and a whole series of factories was set up in peninsular India in the years which followed.

[41] Though for a short time the French were very active economically. They broke the Dutch clove monopoly by introducing these and other spices into Seychelles in 1770, and also built up sugar, clove and nutmeg plantations in Mauritius. These islands, which were used as bases for numerous attacks on British shipping in the subsequent wars, were finally ceded to Britain by the Treaty of Paris, 1814, though Réunion remained French.

[42] Wright and Reid, Chapter IV. Cf. also note 27, above.

[43] By the Treaty of Paris, 1784, all the seas of the archipelago were declared open to the British, but the monopolistic habits of the Dutch were slow to die.

somewhat devious methods, of the island of Penang situated close to the Malayan shore at the northern entrance to the Malacca Straits. And while, in origin, this acquisition represented little more than a widening of the Company's strategic perimeter in the Indian Ocean, the British were already finding new and compelling reasons for edging their way back into the Malaysian archipelago from which they had been virtually excluded since the 17th century.[44]

At the same time, moreover, the British were beginning to encroach into the Dutch sphere from the opposite extremity as a result of their new-found interest in the sea approaches to Australia, and several years before this culminated in the founding of the Botany Bay settlement in 1788, the presence of British ships off New Guinea was causing concern to the Dutch. Further emphasis on the Pacific approach to the archipelago likewise resulted from the arrival of the first American trading vessel at Batavia in 1786, an event which suggested to some of the V.O.C.'s representatives the disturbing possibility of a reorientation of the Indies' trade with the U.S.A. at the expense of the Netherlands.[45]

As on other occasions, Dutch fears regarding foreign advances towards their cherished possessions in the East, though not entirely groundless as subsequent history was to show, were certainly premature. Nevertheless, the Dutch were faced with real problems, arising on the one hand from the loss of naval supremacy and the growth of British and French commercial competition,[46] and on the other hand from the widespread corruption[47] within the Company itself. The high level of profits which had characterized the late 17th and early 18th centuries had become a thing of the past and by the time the United Provinces were invaded by the Jacobins in 1795 the situation was beyond repair. Four years later, under the Batavian Republic, the Company was finally dissolved and in 1800 the Government itself assumed responsibility for the administration of its territories.

V. ANGLO-DUTCH RIVALRY IN THE ARCHIPELAGO DURING THE FIRST HALF OF THE NINETEENTH CENTURY

The gradual extension of Dutch control over the interior of Java, which had been the most important European achievement in South-east Asia during the 17th and 18th centuries, was a natural consequence of the changing character of the Western demand for tropical produce and, in particular, of the shift in emphasis from high-value spices, whose production required only a very limited

[44] The British made various attempts to found new stations there in the 18th century, the most successful being at Natal (1751) and Tapanuli (1755), both of which, like Benkulen, were on the west coast of Sumatra.

[45] Vlekke (A), p. 218.

[46] Following the defeat of the Dutch navy at Dogger Bank in 1781.

[47] Van Leur, p. 287, states that maritime impotence was the sole cause of the V.O.C.'s downfall.

amount of land, to sugar and coffee, which were consumed in much larger quantities and entailed a great increase in the acreage of land under cultivation. Yet despite the very substantial quantities, notably of coffee, which were shipped to Europe by the V.O.C. during the second half of the 18th century, this enterprise was not a financial success, and while corruption may provide a partial explanation for the failure, the high cost of transport arising from the enormous distance involved was undoubtedly a serious handicap.

Indeed, although the East Indies had been the first tropical region to attract the attention of the Europeans, it was the Caribbean which had engrossed the greatest attention as a plantation region during the 17th and 18th centuries. For in addition to such assets as fertile soils and easy access from the sea, in both of which respects it was essentially similar to South-east Asia, the Caribbean region possessed the further inestimable advantage of being much closer to Europe, and its deficiencies in labour were fairly easily overcome by the importation of slaves from western Africa.

On this basis, therefore, the Caribbean region and the adjacent coastlands of Brazil became by far the most important source of tropical produce for Europe during the 17th and 18th centuries, with sugar, followed by coffee, cocoa and indigo as the principal crops involved, and against this part of the world the more distant Asian tropics could not hope to compete on equal terms.[48] But as the 18th century gave place to the 19th a series of apparently unrelated developments combined to bring about a diversion of European interest from the American to the Asian tropics and, in so doing, to inaugurate the third and final stage in the extension of Western control over South-east Asia.

In the first place, the amount of suitable land in most of the West Indian islands was small, and from the early 18th century onwards the problem of soil exhaustion had begun to give cause for concern. By the end of the century little scope remained for further expansion in many of the islands and when, in the 1830s and 40s, the British, French and Danes abolished slavery, the region lost one of its main competitive advantages. But more important than either of these factors was the effect of the Industrial Revolution, which both spectacularly increased the European demand for tropical materials and, through the application of steam power to ocean transport, greatly reduced the disabilities of distance from which the remoter parts of the world had hitherto suffered.

In such circumstances, therefore, Europeans concerned with production and trade in tropical commodities began to turn to South-east Asia – a veritable Caribbean writ large – as the most promising field for future expansion, and this change in outlook was already becoming apparent by the middle of the 19th century.[49]

[48] Even though Java was for a time the world's largest single supplier of coffee, the total value of all tropical produce from the West Indies was much greater than that from the East Indies.

[49] The Europeans also turned to Africa, though for the most part the physical barriers to penetration inland delayed developments there until later.

In the meantime, however, the even greater preoccupation of European industrialists with the search for overseas markets had led to a prior concentration of interest on such densely peopled lands as China and Japan (as well, of course, as India) and it was not until the main positions had been taken up in relation to such trade that official attention began to focus more specifically on the immense economic potentialities of South-east Asia as a producing region.[50] But from the 1850s onwards, and especially after the opening of the Suez canal in 1869, the imperial forward movement gathered momentum throughout the region, and one by one all its remaining territories, Siam alone excepted, passed under Western control.

In this activity Great Britain, which was the prime mover in the Industrial Revolution and had emerged from the Napoleonic Wars as the world's leading sea power, set the pace, and in the opening years of the 19th century the British attempt to find new markets in China for Lancashire textiles[51] gave an added incentive to those servants of the E.I.C. who were anxious to extend the Company's influence in the areas bordering upon the Straits of Malacca.

As on many other occasions the course of events in South-east Asia was in large measure determined by the vagaries of European history. With the French invasion of the Netherlands in 1794–5, the British proceeded to occupy the Dutch possessions in the Cape of Good Hope, Ceylon, Malacca, the Moluccas and the west coast of Sumatra, though it was not until after the annexation of Holland by Napoleon in 1810 that they took the decisive step of invading Java, which they held from 1811 to 1816. But while in the eyes of the E.I.C. the British action in Java was designed merely to eliminate Dutch power from the region for the duration of hostilities, the official who was charged with the administration of Java, Thomas Stamford Raffles, viewed his task in much more grandiose terms.

Ever since his arrival at Penang several years earlier, Raffles had been completely captivated by the charms of the 'unspoiled' Malaysian peoples, and this state of mind was largely responsible for his desire to better the lot of the Javans,[52] both by substituting British for Dutch rule and, more immediately, by putting an end to compulsory labour services and encouraging the peasants to cultivate whatever crops they wished. However, although most of his criticisms of traditional Dutch methods were amply justified, and indeed endorsed by many of the Dutch administrators themselves, Raffles' championing of the interests of the indigenous peoples was not entirely disinterested. As a representative of Britain

[50] See Sokol (A), p. 350.

[51] Between 1700 and 1780 the value of Britain's annual exports to Asia rose from £100,283 (representing 1½ per cent of the total exports) to £909,033 (or 6 per cent). Van Leur, p. 28. On the activities of British shipping in the early 19th century see Allen and Donnithorne, p. 210.

[52] Since the term Javanese strictly refers to the inhabitants of only part of Java (see below, p. 239) the term Javans is used here to cover the indigenous people of that island as a whole.

which, unlike Holland,[53] had cheap manufactures to sell and, moreover, had every reason to believe that in conditions of free competition it could undersell any competitor, Raffles tended to look upon Asian peoples not as mere producers of tribute but rather as potential customers, whose living standards it was sound policy to raise. Furthermore, his pioneer researches in Malaysian history caused him to appreciate, as did few if any of his contemporaries, the immense geo-political significance of the archipelago, and this served to strengthen his desire to bring it permanently under British control. In particular, his imagination was fired by the story of Madjapahit,[54] and by the possibility of re-creating, under the protection of a British governor in Java, a great Malaysian realm stretching from Sumatra to Mindanao and New Guinea, which might form a bridge between the established centres of British naval power in the Indian Ocean and the new settlements in Australia.

This ambitious proposition met with little sympathy in Britain itself, however, which was more concerned to see a friendly Netherlands in the heart of western Europe than to indulge in a further flurry of empire building on the periphery of Asia. Thus, in 1814 Britain agreed to restore to the Netherlands all the latter's possessions and rights in Indonesia, as of 1803,[55] and though some minor delays and disputes took place, this restitution was eventually made in full.

Despite this setback and his own recall from Java in 1816, Raffles continued to work for the advancement of British power in the archipelago and eventually, after failing to elicit support for a proposal to set up a post in Atjeh, he succeeded in getting the Governor-General in Calcutta to 'authorize the establishment of a station beyond Malacca such as may command the southern entrance to the Straits'. Accordingly, in 1819, with the agreement of the local *de facto* ruler, he planted a settlement on the sparsely inhabited island of Singapore, of whose significance as a trading post in ancient times he was already aware from his studies.[56] Although this move aroused Dutch fears lest the British might now seek to extend their rule over the whole archipelago, it soon became clear that, whatever Raffles' motives might be, his action in acquiring Singapore was being officially supported not on account of the Malaysian significance of the island but rather because of the means it afforded of securing the British right of way from the Indian Ocean to the South China Sea.

Thus a basis existed for an acceptable division of spheres between the British

[53] See Wright and Reid, Chapter 7; Vlekke (A), Chapter 12; and Furnivall (A), Chapter 3. In the 18th, and indeed well into the 19th century, the Dutch had concentrated on finance and the carrying trade, and were much slower than the British (or even the French) in industrializing. Lack of coal played an important part in this.

[54] See, for example, van Leur, p. 277, and Boulger, p. 92, cited in Emerson.

[55] Though the Cape of Good Hope, Ceylon (and Demerara) were not restored.

[56] It is probable that Raffles, relying on the semi-legendary sources which were the only ones then available, over-estimated the importance of Singapore ('the lion city of Sinhapura') and perhaps also of Madjapahit. He knew nothing of Sri Vijaya, whose achievements had been forgotten by the indigenous population until 20th-century European scholars rediscovered them.

and Dutch, and effect was given to this in the Treaty of London of 1824. Britain, which no longer needed to use the Sunda Straits, relinquished Benkulen in exchange for Malacca, and undertook to make no further settlements in the archipelago south of Singapore. In keeping with this proviso, moreover, the rights acquired by the E.I.C. over Belitung (Billiton) in 1812 were transferred to the Dutch who, in their turn, agreed to respect the independence of Atjeh.[57]

This arbitrary political division, however reasonable it might seem to Europeans, was completely at variance with the Malaysian concept of the unity of the seas through which it ran. Already the British occupation of Singapore had brought about the final dismemberment of the Johore/Riouw kingdom,[58] into a peninsular portion lying within the British sphere and an island realm which remained under Dutch protection. But from 1824 onwards this division took on a wider meaning as the territories on the British side of the new international boundary were subjected to radically different policies of colonial administration from those which were applied in the rest of the Malaysian world with which they had hitherto belonged.

Nevertheless, in the decades which followed, the course of events in the region suggested that the decisions of 1824 were neither ill-conceived geopolitically nor entirely without historical justification. For, although Penang had been obtained as a strategic outpost of India, and Singapore had at first been regarded as a forward base for the opium and textile trade with China, the Malaysian affinities of both these islands quickly asserted themselves and, after the British acquisition of Hong Kong in 1842, Singapore as well as Penang began to concentrate predominantly on South-east Asian as opposed to Far Eastern trade.

For this rôle its geographical situation was ideal[59] and, as a free port in an area traditionally bound by monopolistic practices, it rapidly drew to itself the indigenous trade of many parts of Indonesia which was meanwhile beginning to revive after nearly two centuries of suppression by the V.O.C. Thus, besides attracting large numbers of Chinese, and to a lesser extent Indian and Arab traders, Singapore also became the great centre for the Buginese merchants, whose *prahus*, sailing each year with the monsoon, used to bring the produce of the eastern archipelago, much of it ultimately destined for the China market, before returning to Makasar with cargoes of British manufactures. Later both Chinese and Arabs, using large European schooners, took over more and more of this trade and indeed by 1850 had reached a dominant position in the inter-island traffic of the archipelago, which by this time focused primarily upon

[57] The Dutch also ceded their remaining factories in India.

[58] A survival of the old Malay power (formerly centred in Malacca) whose territories included the southern part of the peninsula and the islands immediately to the south of it.

[59] In the changed conditions of the 19th century the offshore islands of Singapore and Hong Kong, close to the continental mainland and hence to the shortest sea route to the East, were much better placed as entrepôts than were Batavia and Manila in the outer island fringe.

Singapore and thus had the effect of relegating Batavia to the level of a provincial harbour.

For obvious geographical reasons the trading links which developed between the Straits Settlements' ports and both eastern Sumatra and northern Borneo were particularly close and, since in the latter though not the former area the 1824 Treaty also gave scope for British territorial expansion,[60] political developments followed before very long. The expedition of James Brooke to Borneo led to his being installed as Rajah of Sarawak in 1842, and shortly afterwards in 1846 the island of Labuan was ceded to the British by the Sultan of Brunei, to be used as a naval base, coaling station and local entrepôt between Singapore and Hong Kong.[61]

Thus, in addition to controlling the eastern shore of the Malacca Straits from the Straits Settlements, the British gradually established their influence along the Bornean shore of the South China Sea. In a strategic sense the parallel with the Mediterranean later in the century is suggestive, and the series of British footholds at Penang, Singapore, Labuan and Hong Kong may be compared with Gibraltar, Malta, Suez and Aden.[62] Within the South China Sea only the minor island groups of Natuna, Anamba and Tambelan remained under Dutch jurisdiction, and although in theory their strategic potentialities are considerable, no serious use has ever been made of them.[63]

In effect, therefore, although Raffles' attempt to re-create the empire of Madjapahit under British auspices was a failure, he succeeded in laying the foundations of a new British domain in South-east Asia which, in both its territorial layout and its concentration on trade rather than production,[64] strikingly resembled that of Sri Vijaya. Admittedly its nucleus lay on the opposite side of the Straits from Palembang which, together with the rest of Sumatra south of Atjeh, formed part of the Dutch political sphere. But in forbidding the Dutch to occupy Atjeh,[65] the British had tightened their grip on the Straits, and their position was further reinforced by the spectacular expansion of Singapore's entrepôt trade.

Thus, the division of spheres between the British and the Dutch came to reflect the fundamental geographical realities of the situation, and while Britain was pre-eminently concerned with sea-borne commerce, both locally and with

[60] The wording of the treaty was vague, but nevertheless when in 1857 the free-lancer Wilson tried to establish a British vassal state in Siak (north-eastern Sumatra) the British government refused to support him on the grounds that such action would contravene the treaty.

[61] China had ceded Hong Kong to Britain in 1842.

[62] Though of the Asian footholds only Singapore and Hong Kong were ever developed.

[63] In 1886 the Sultan of Johore put forward a claim to these three island groups, arguing that they had belonged to the Sultan of Riau who, however, had ceded them to the Dutch in 1857. But the British Colonial Office declined to support this claim and the matter was dropped. *Holland: East Indies Colonial Possessions*, pp. 158–9.

[64] At least until the end of the 19th century when the tin (and later the rubber) production of the F.M.S. became more important than the trade of the S.S. See below, pp. 592–9. [65] Van Vuuren (A), pp. 7–8.

China, the Dutch were left to continue their established practice of developing the Indies as a primary source of tropical produce.

This contrast in the 19th-century policies of the British and Dutch in South-east Asia was also, however, in large measure an outcome of the great differences in economic development between the two metropolitan countries. Since Holland was much slower to industrialize than was Great Britain, it had shown little sympathy with the economic reforms which Raffles had introduced into Java during his tenure of office there. Moreover, the problem had later been aggravated both by the severe economic setback in the mother country as a result of the Napoleonic Wars, and by the heavy expenditure incurred in suppressing the widespread revolt which greeted the Dutch resumption of authority in Java. Thus, while the Java War which followed (1825–30) marked the final advance of direct Dutch control over the whole of the island, apart from the residual principalities of Djokjakarta and Surakarta, its conclusion left the Dutch gravely weakened financially and anxious to recoup their losses with all possible speed.

It was in these circumstances that Johannes van den Bosch put forward a plan which, in effect, represented a reversion to the old V.O.C. policy of compulsory production. Under this so-called *cultuur stelsel*[66] which he introduced immediately after his assumption of office as Governor-General in 1830, the Javan peasantry, instead of paying taxes as Raffles had laid down, were compelled to set aside one-fifth of their land for the cultivation of export crops – in the initial stages principally coffee, sugar and indigo – as prescribed by the Dutch.[67] These commodities were then collected and despatched to Europe by the Nederlandsche Handels Maatschappij (N.H.M.), a government-sponsored trading company which had been founded in 1825, and sold under official auspices at Amsterdam.

Out of the proceeds of this enterprise the Dutch were able, in the course of the next few decades, not merely to make good their former losses, but also to accumulate the necessary capital to build up the third-largest merchant navy in the world and to establish important textile and other manufacturing industries in the metropolitan country.[68] The effect on Java, however, was by no means as beneficial and although, with the later addition of tea and cinchona cultivation, the system led eventually to a useful diversification of cash-crop production there, it nevertheless lent itself to all kinds of abuses and imposed a heavy burden on the peasantry. Furthermore, while in view of both the great natural fertility of Java and its established position as the main centre of Dutch influence in the archipelago, it was understandable that the authorities should have concentrated these activities almost exclusively in that island, their policy in so doing was largely

[66] Usually translated 'culture system' though 'system of forced cultivation' is a better rendering. On this see Furnivall (A), Chapter 5.

[67] This system was still regarded as preferable to the plantation system as practised in the West Indies. In particular, it was cheaper to run since the local people were skilled cultivators who did not need costly supervision.

[68] As the British had done (though perhaps less self-consciously, a century earlier) on the basis of their trade with India.

responsible for bringing about the serious lack of economic balance between it and the outer territories which poses a peculiarly intractable problem in Indonesia today.

VI. ANGLO-FRENCH RIVALRY IN THE INDO-PACIFIC PENINSULA DURING THE SECOND HALF OF THE NINETEENTH CENTURY

Both economically and politically events on the mainland took a different course from those in the archipelago. Following the acquisition of Singapore in 1819, the British strove to reach a territorial agreement with Siam which might serve as a counterpart to the 1824 Treaty with the Dutch. For while at this stage the British, owing to their preoccupations with maritime commerce, had no inclination to control or to exploit the interior of the Malay peninsula, they were anxious to prevent the small and weak Malay Sultanates bordering on the Straits Settlements from the chaos which a threatened Siamese invasion would entail.[69] Accordingly, after much preliminary haggling, a treaty was eventually signed in 1826[70] which limited Siamese suzerainty to the states north of Perak and Pahang.

In the meantime, however, more important developments had been taking place farther north in Burma. Since the latter part of the 18th century the Burmese kingdom under the Alaungpaya dynasty had been pursuing expansionist policies, and after its invasion and conquest of Manipur and Assam in 1813–16, it became clear that the Burmese, in complete ignorance of the strength of British power in India, were planning further advances in that direction. Thus, when in 1824 Burmese forces in Arakan began preparations for an invasion of the Chittagong frontier, the British themselves seized the initiative, and in the First Burmese War which followed they forced Ava to cede both Arakan and the coastal strip of Tenasserim (1826) and to give up its claims to Manipur and Assam.[71]

While economic considerations played a subsidiary rôle in bringing about this first British annexation of Burmese territory, the main motive, as in the earlier acquisition of Penang, was to secure the eastern defences of India. This policy was carried a stage further by the annexation of the intervening delta region after the Second Burmese War (1852), which was precipitated by continued Burmese hostility to British merchants and to the British Resident at Ava. Thereafter, only the short stretch of Siamese coast from Victoria Point to Province Wellesley broke the continuity of British control over the eastern shore of the Bay of Bengal, and the security of this non-British strip had already been provided for by the Treaty of 1826.

[69] Siam was pursuing an expansionist policy at this time. See above, p. 121.

[70] The British also hoped that this treaty would lead to an extension of trade with Siam, but the latter had different views and no significant developments took place until after the further treaty of 1855. See below, p. 490

[71] These and the other Burmese territories which Britain annexed in 1852 and 1886 were added to the Indian Empire.

FIG. 18—Mainland South-east Asia: expansion of European influence in the 19th century

By the time of the Second Burmese War, however, a new interest was attaching to the Indo-Pacific peninsula as a possible back-door approach to China. The idea of making a short cut to south-western China via the Mekong had interested the Dutch in the 17th century, but the expedition which they had sent under van Wuysthoff proved a failure, and the matter was not pursued further at that time.[72] But after the British obtained their first territorial foothold in Burma in 1826, they also became concerned to find a profitable overland route to Yunnan, and this interest continued to grow as progress in railway construction in other parts of the world suggested that not even the rugged relief of the peninsular interior need prove an insuperable obstacle to similar developments there.

In this connexion the proposals which were put forward, and the decisions subsequently taken regarding them, should be viewed against the wider background of British policy towards the China trade as a whole. During the first half of the 19th century the British, conscious of their great head start in industrialization, feared little serious Western competition in their attempts to dominate the China market. Thus all that appeared necessary was to obtain safe bases for trade on the China coast, preferably near the mouths of the great rivers, and the commerce of the interior would then automatically gravitate to these centres, where British merchants could skim off the cream. This, in effect, had been the basis of the agreements over Hong Kong, the treaty ports and the system of extra-territoriality which had been secured as a result of the Opium War (1839–42) but, in the decades which followed, more intensified Western competition began to give point to suggestions that a shortening of the long sea route via Singapore might repay consideration.

In these circumstances, therefore, and at a time when the geography of the interior of the Indo-Pacific peninsula was still very imperfectly known, the realization that the upper reaches of the Yang-tze were at one place only just over 600 miles from Calcutta, compared with a sea distance of 4,300 miles from the latter to Shanghai, inevitably gave rise to a whole series of attempts to find practicable railway routes from the peninsular coast to the China border, along one or other of the great N/S rivers whose upper courses lie in such close proximity to that of the Yang-tze itself.

Between 1852 and 1900 innumerable projects of this kind were considered in Britain,[73] and meanwhile several Frenchmen were quick to see in similar ventures a possible means of overtaking the British lead in the China trade.[74] But while the greatest saving in distance overland would clearly be effected by means of an approach from the shores of the Bay of Bengal, the French were virtually precluded from using either the Irrawaddy or the Salween routes as a result of Britain's

[72] See Hall (B), p. 565.
[73] See Christian (A), p. 278 and (B) Chapter 4; and Hallett, p. 178.
[74] There was also some German interest in the possibilities of railway building here, though nothing came of it.

prior acquisition of the territory through which their lower courses ran, and accordingly they were driven to look farther east for alternatives.

In the meantime, moreover, the French were evolving other and more grandiose plans for short-circuiting the British route to the East. Ever since Talleyrand had argued that the opening of a sea route via Suez would react on England in the same fatal way as the discovery of the Cape route had ruined Venice and Genoa in the 16th century,[75] French speculation on the possibility of cutting such a canal had continued, and in the 1850s it began to take on an altogether more practical shape as a result of the specific proposals put forward by Ferdinand De Lesseps. Moreover, while De Lesseps himself was primarily concerned with the benefit to world commerce as a whole which would result from the realization of his scheme, the initial opposition with which this was greeted by the British served to rally widespread French support behind it, and work was put in hand in 1859.

It was against this background that the French imperialists, mindful of their country's former interests in the Annamite lands, began to seek an overland route to China via the Mekong valley and Yunnan. In 1856 France joined with Britain in a second war against China, and although this, like the Opium War, was undertaken with the primary object of extending facilities for trade, the official reason for French participation was the murder of a French missionary priest in Kwangsi. Thus one of the terms of the ensuing Treaty of Tientsin (1858) was that China undertook to tolerate Christianity, and when the Emperor of Annam, which the Chinese claimed was a tributary state (see p. 123) intensified the traditional hostility to French missions in his territories, the French seized this pretext to bombard Tourane in August 1858. Thereafter the attack shifted to Saigon, near the mouth of the Mekong, which was captured in 1859. The eastern half of Cochinchina was ceded by the Annamites to France in 1862, and in 1863–4 the latter proclaimed a protectorate over nearby Cambodia.[76]

This acquisition by France of a territorial foothold in the Mekong delta was quickly followed in 1866–7 by an expedition under Doudart de Lagrée and François Garnier to explore the middle and upper courses of the river. Much to the disappointment of the French, however, their findings made it clear beyond any doubt that, owing to the number and extent of the rapids and the length of the dangerous gorges along its course, the Mekong offered no possibility of through navigation to China, and for this reason, after a short hiatus occasioned by the Franco-Prussian War, French interest in the peninsula shifted to Tonkin where it was hoped that the Song-koi might afford better prospects for a route to Yunnan.

[75] Siegfried, p. 54.

[76] Cambodia had hitherto claimed to be an independent kingdom, though both Siam and Annam aspired to suzerainty over it. Siam's resentment at the French protection of Cambodia was mollified for the time being by the French decision to allow it to retain the two Cambodian provinces of Battambang and Siemreap (Angkor) which it had occupied since 1795. In 1867 the French annexed the remainder of Cochinchina.

Coupled with this, moreover, a new plan now came to the fore, namely to steal a further march on the British by following Suez with a similar canal across the isthmus of Kra[77] and so by-passing Singapore. Such a proposition had, in fact, been considered by the British themselves at an earlier stage, and in 1863 the Indian Government had sent a survey party to Kra under Captains Fraser and Forlong. But these two military gentlemen had concluded that the construction of a canal was impracticable though, apparently in complete ignorance of the costs entailed by a double break of bulk, they had urged the construction of a trans-isthmian railway on the twin grounds that it would effect a useful shortening of the route to China, for freight as well as for passengers, and that if the British did not build it the French undoubtedly would.

In the event, the British authorities did not accept this recommendation and, as had been forecast, the initiative passed for a time to the French. In 1882–3 French engineers surveyed what they considered to be a feasible route for a canal across the isthmus, and on June 8, 1883 De Lesseps presented his plan for the canal to the King of Siam as '*la route française au Tonkin*'.[78] Meanwhile Tonkin itself had become the scene of further and more intensive French activity. In 1873 Jean Dupuis, after exploring the Song-koi route to Yunnan, had concluded that it offered better promise than the Mekong. But despite the Franco-Annamite Treaty of 1874 which opened the river to navigation, little or no use could be made of it owing to the hostility of the local population and of the marauding bands of Chinese, notably the so-called 'Black Flags', who were active along almost its entire course.

It was to put an end to this state of affairs that the French in 1882[79] sent a major military expedition to Tonkin which compelled Annam to accept a French protectorate for itself and another for Tonkin. These arrangements called forth a strong protest from China as the suzerain power, but by the Convention of Tientsin, 1884, and a further treaty of 1885 it finally agreed to respect the treaties concluded between France and the Annamite Court of Hué.

These expansionist activities of the French produced immediate and far-reaching repercussions on British policy in Burma. All through the 1860s the Manchester Chamber of Commerce had urged the British Government to open up the so-called Moulmein route[80] to China, and in 1867 the British Chief Commissioner at Ava obtained a treaty establishing British extra-territorial rights in upper Burma and guaranteeing navigation rights for British steamships on the Irrawaddy river. By this time Garnier's actions had produced acute fears of an

[77] *I.e.* following a route which had been in intermittent use since the beginning of history. See Fisher (A), pp. 85–6, and Loftus.

[78] Christian (A), p. 281.

[79] The French had already sent an earlier expedition under Garnier in 1873. Although this was successful to the extent of getting the 1874 agreement noted above, Garnier himself was murdered by the Black Flags. See Hall (B), p. 569.

[80] *I.e.* via the Karenni Hills to Kianghung on the upper Mekong and thence to Szemao (Esmok). See Hall (B), Chapter 33, for a full account of this question.

impending French advance via the Shan country to Mandalay, and when later the French switched their activities to Tonkin these and similar anxieties were intensified. Matters came to a head in 1885 when the Burmese King Thibaw, after outrageously penalizing the (British) Bombay and Burma Trading Company, concluded a far-reaching agreement with France.[81] This, together with evidence of Burma's intention to import French arms via Tonkin, precipitated the Third Burmese War of 1885, which ended with the British annexation in 1886 of all the remaining territories under the control of the Burmese monarchy. As with the recent French annexations in the Annamite lands, the British found it expedient to sign an agreement with China (The Convention of Peking, 1886) whereby the latter formally recognized the British as rulers of Burma and the two countries agreed to delimit the Sino-Burmese boundary.[82]

During the last decade of the century further complications arose out of the French decision to round off their territories in Indochina, by establishing a protectorate over the series of small Laotian states which occupied the plateau country adjoining, and in places straddling the middle and upper courses of the Mekong. As virtually the whole of this area had long formed a political no-man's-land between Annam and Siam in the south and between Burma and China to the west and north, the attempt of the French to lay claim to it by virtue of their new position as rulers of Annam[83] provoked serious repercussions.

Closely related, both ethnically and historically, to the Laos principalities were the geographically similar Shan states which, since the 16th century, had owed allegiance to Burma. After the annexation of Upper Burma in 1886 the British had shown some hesitation over the policy they should adopt towards these territories for, while military opinion was in favour of accepting the Salween as the boundary, some of the Shan states lay to the east of this river and indeed two of them, Kengtung and Kiang Hung, even claimed territory east of the Mekong. Again, although there seemed to be strong arguments for limiting the extent of the British domain so as to leave a strip of neutral (that is Chinese and Siamese) territory between Burma and French Indochina, it was clear that the ineffectiveness of the Siamese hold over this mountainous region might well tempt the French to advance their claims to the Salween. In these circumstances, therefore, the British decided to secure control over all of the Shan states which had hitherto been subject to Ava.[84]

[81] Which provided, *inter alia*, for the establishment of a Bank of Burma with French capital, a line of French steamships on the Irrawaddy, and the construction of a railway. Christian (A), p. 279.

[82] Although the immediate Burmese resistance had been slight in 1885, the campaign was followed by protracted guerrilla warfare. The Shan States submitted to British rule in 1890, but the Chins held out until 1896.

[83] According to Hall, Chapter 37, the Siamese claims were much stronger than those of the Annamites, and both ethnically and linguistically the local ties with Siam were close. Further, there was little ground for the French claims that Siam was planning to seize the opportunity created by the French defeat of the Annamites in order to drive to the sea at Vinh. *Ibid.*

[84] *Ibid.*

Shortly afterwards, in 1893, the French compelled Siam to cede all its remaining territories east of the Mekong.[85] These lands, though no less fragmented politically than the Shan states, were made into the single protectorate of Laos, and this was immediately incorporated within the Union of Indochina which had meanwhile been set up in 1887. These developments caused an acute crisis in Anglo-French relations, but in 1895 the British agreed to forego all claims to territory east of the Mekong, in return for French participation in a joint declaration of January 1, 1896 which, in effect, established what was left of Siam as a buffer state between India[86] and French Indochina.

Thus, partly as a result of Anglo-French rivalry, partly through the astute policy of its own ruling house, and not least because of its relatively isolated geographical position away from the main sea lanes, Siam alone among the states of the Indo-Pacific peninsula succeeded in preserving its independence from Western control. Nevertheless, a price was exacted for this privilege for, besides the actual losses of territory already noted, Siam was forced to acquiesce in the establishment of rival British and French spheres of influence over important outlying portions of the kingdom.[87]

The mutual suspicions of Britain and France on the mainland of South-east Asia were, of course, only one manifestation of rivalry which ranged over the whole colonial field from Africa to the South-west Pacific, until brought to an end by the *Entente Cordiale* of 1904. And while the French modification of the boundary between Laos and Siam in their favour in the same year provoked no serious complaint,[88] their annexation of Battambang and Siemreap in 1907 caused a revival of British suspicions, as well as much bitterness in Siam, though it was naturally well received in Cambodia.

Thereafter, however, as the probability increased that few of the proposed overland routes to China would ever materialize, the local basis of Anglo-French discord in the peninsula gradually disappeared. In the event, France did succeed in opening one important link with China, namely the railway from Haiphong to Kunming, which was completed in 1910. But the plan for linking this line with the Burma railway system across the extremely rugged country north-east of the Shan states was ruled out as 'midsummer madness' by Lord Curzon, and no modern communication was ever developed between Burma and China until after the outbreak of the Sino-Japanese War in 1937.[89]

[85] Since 1827 Vientiane (the southern half of the old Lan Chang) had been effectively Siamese.

[86] India by this time included Burma. See above, note 70. Note the analogy with Afghanistan, the buffer state between India on the west and Britain's other great rival, namely Russia.

[87] See Fig. 18. By this time 90 per cent of Siam's foreign trade was in British hands and seven-eighths of this was with the Menam valley. Hall (B), p. 610, note 2.

[88] Laos obtained some territories of Luang Prabang on the right bank of the Mekong, and Siam renounced sovereignty over Luang Prabang.

[89] *I.e.* first the Burma Road and later also the Ledo Road. On Curzon's views see Christian (B) p. 224.

The Kra canal scheme likewise died a natural death, which was scarcely surprising in view of the relatively small saving in distance which it could offer. Nevertheless, British concern to retain command of the sea-way between the Indian and the Pacific Oceans led them to insist on a guarantee in the Anglo-Siamese Treaty of 1909 that no third party should acquire concessions of strategic significance on the west coast of the Gulf of Siam.[90]

VII. ECONOMIC AND POLITICAL EXPANSION IN SOUTH-EAST ASIA, 1870–1941

By the turn of the century, therefore, European interest in the Indo-Pacific peninsula as a possible means of access to China had largely evaporated, but in the meantime the region had acquired a new importance in its own right as a major centre of rice production. This development must be numbered among the many indirect consequences of the opening of the Suez canal, for although the great deltas of the Irrawaddy, Menam and Mekong were intrinsically suited by both their physique and their absence of population pressure to become major exporters of rice, it was not until after 1869 that it became a paying proposition to import heavy milling machinery or to export so bulky a commodity to Europe.[91] But thereafter rice quickly became by far the most important cash crop, alike in Burma, Siam and Indochina, and this pre-eminence has been maintained ever since, notwithstanding the considerable developments that have taken place in the production of teak, rubber, and minerals of many kinds.

In the island realm to the south the economic and political consequences of the opening of the Suez canal were, if anything, even more revolutionary in character. For besides greatly improving the prospects for the export of the bulkier tropical products to the West, the new route made it possible for shipowners, both European and Asian, to buy up large numbers of small and often second-hand steamers, which would have been incapable of reaching the East via the longer and rougher Cape route, but were nevertheless able to fulfil an invaluable function in developing local shipping lines throughout the normally placid Malaysian seas.[92]

Thus, just as the greater part of Burma and Indochina had been absorbed into the rival empires of Britain and France between 1826 and 1886, so in Malaysia after 1870 the British and the Dutch extended their authority from their original bases over virtually the whole of the respective spheres which had been agreed upon in the Treaty of 1824.

Prior to 1874 Britain's territorial interest in the Malay peninsula had stopped short at the four Straits Settlements (Singapore, Penang, Malacca and the

[90] See Jones, Borton and Pearn, p. 299. On renewed interest in a Kra canal, see below, p. 526.

[91] Later the greater part of the rice found markets in nearby parts of Asia.

[92] Many of the novels of Joseph Conrad deal with this epoch. See Van Helsdingen, p. 119.

Dindings[93]) which flanked the sea route through the Malacca Straits. But, beginning in that year, a form of protection was extended over four of the interior Sultanates which seemed to be particularly rich in tin or gold and during the early years of the 20th century the desire to obtain new land for rubber prepared the way for the further extension of British rule over Johore (1914) and the four northern Malay states which had remained under Siamese jurisdiction until 1909. Likewise in northern Borneo the British extended their authority inland from the original offshore foothold of Labuan, and in 1888 Sarawak, Brunei and the territory of the British North Borneo Company were all brought under protection.

Within the Dutch sphere as defined in 1824 even greater changes took place, and as the revolution in communications transformed the East Indian seas from a remote and isolated cul-de-sac into a great meeting place for the ships of many nations, the last lingering vestiges of monopoly and mercantilism were swept away and the whole of the archipelago was drawn into the stream of international commerce.

Under the pressure of the new liberal middle class in the mother country[94] the *cultuur stelsel* was abolished in Java and the new Agrarian Law enacted in 1870, and together these two events led to a rapid increase of the plantation acreage in that island. But even before this date other enterprising planters had begun to appreciate the potentialities afforded by the rich coastal lowlands of north-eastern Sumatra, flanking the Straits seaway, and their activities,[95] together with the search for coal, oil and other minerals in many parts of the archipelago, went hand in hand with the gradual establishment of effective Dutch control over the outer islands.

For the most part this process was achieved without serious opposition, though an important exception occurred in the case of Atjeh.[96] Under the 1824 Treaty the Dutch were precluded from intervening in the affairs of this intensely Muslim state occupying the northern tip of Sumatra, but when the increased volume of shipping in the Straits after 1869 was followed by an even more rapid growth of Atjehnese piracy the British waived the relevant clause in the Treaty, and in 1873 the Dutch attacked. The Atjehnese proved an extremely difficult foe to defeat, and it was not until 1903 that organized resistance came to an end.

At the opposite extremity of the archipelago, fear of British encroachment northwards and westwards from Australia had led the Dutch in 1826 to proclaim

[93] The Dindings was a small coastal territory in Perak acquired as a base for anti-pirate patrols. Penang also included Province Wellesley on the mainland coast, acquired from Kedah in 1800.

[94] This new middle class was largely associated with the trading and industrial activities described above (p. 148), and thus indirectly owed much of its prosperity to the *cultuur stelsel*. See Furnivall (A) Chapter 6.

[95] Tobacco was the first major crop produced here, followed later by coffee, rubber, palm oil, etc.

[96] There was also some resistance elsewhere, most notably in Bali.

their sovereignty as far as the 141st meridian in New Guinea. However, little was done to substantiate these claims until much later, but after the shock occasioned in 1884–5 by the British and German annexations of south-east and north-east New Guinea respectively, the Dutch purchased the claim of the Sultan of Tidore over the western half of that island, and finally in 1898 brought it within the administrative framework of the Indies.

To the north-east also, Dutch anxieties had been aroused, for after the Japanese annexation of Formosa in 1895 the possibility of a further southward advance by Japan seemed to be encouraged by the condition of decadence into which Spanish rule in the Philippines had sunk during the latter part of the 19th century.[97] In addition to Japan, Germany was also casting covetous eyes on the Spanish possessions in the western Pacific, but in the event it was the United States which, temporarily departing from its anti-colonial traditions, obtained the Philippines after the Spanish-American War of 1898–9.[98]

Although United States' commercial interest in the Philippines had begun on a small scale much earlier in the century, and even for a time seemed likely to extend from there into northern Borneo, in a manner foreshadowing that of the later British North Borneo Company, the establishment of political control over the Philippines was dictated far more by strategic than by economic considerations, for even at this stage the growing strength of Japan was viewed as a potential threat to the United States' position in the Pacific. Thus the Philippines became a kind of forward defensive screen for the Californian coast, and as a result of this policy and of the new cultural and economic ties which developed with the United States, the islands were once again more closely aligned with the opposite side of the Pacific than with the remainder of South-east Asia.

By the end of the 19th century, therefore, the political map of South-east Asia had assumed the form it was to maintain with only minor adjustments until the Japanese occupation during the Second World War. In the space of less than a hundred years Western control had advanced from a few scattered positions in the Malaysian archipelago to embrace the whole of the region, apart from a much-reduced Siamese kingdom whose independence was further compromised by Western spheres of influence and the principle of extra-territoriality.

Notwithstanding occasional setbacks, among which only that caused by the world economic crisis of the 1930s was either severe or prolonged, the first four decades of the 20th century saw a spectacular expansion of production and trade in every country within the region, and at the same time the achievements of Western rule in such fields as medicine, education and public works were generally far superior to those in other tropical dependencies. This, then, was

[97] A Dutch writer, Professor Schlegel, suggested in 1896 that Holland should curb possible Japanese aggressive designs on the Indies by taking possession of Formosa. Stoddard, p. 20.

[98] Germany was able to buy some of the lesser Spanish islands elsewhere in the Pacific, but not Guam which was a staging point between the United States and the Philippines. The United States also annexed Hawaii in 1899.

the situation when the Japanese drive to the south in December 1941 put an end to the era of Western domination and prepared the way for the new national states of today.

SELECT BIBLIOGRAPHY

Allen and Donnithorne
Baker
Baring-Gould and Bampfylde
Boulger
Clifford
Coupland
Davies
Eldridge
Emerson (A)
Fisher (A)
Furnivall (A) (B)
Hall (A) (B)
Hallett
Harrison
Harvey (A) (B)
Hyma
Jones and Mehnert
Lattimore
Loftus
Mills
Muir
Panikkar (A) (B) (C)
Parkinson (A)
Parry
Pearn
Pelzer (K)
Purcell (C) (D) (E)
Raffles
Reclus
Robequain (D)
Roberts, G. (C)
Roberts, S. H.
Siegfried
Sokol (A)
Sowash
Swettenham
Thompson, V. (A) (C)
Unger
Van Helsdingen and Hoogenberk
Van Leur
Van Vuuren (A)
Wertheim (C)
Williamson
Winstedt (A) (B) (C) (D) (E)
Wint (C)
Wright and Reid
Wood
Wurzburg

Chambers's Encyclopædia
Encyclopædia Britannica
Indo-China (N.I.D.)
Netherlands East Indies, II (N.I.D.)

The principal historical sources on which this chapter is based consist of the standard regional histories of South-east Asia and of its constituent countries listed elsewhere (see bibliographical notes following Chapters 4, 8, 14, 15, 16, 17 and 21). On early Western contact with the region, Baker, Parry and Williamson are useful sources, as are Roberts, S. H., and Siegfried on the 19th century, while Eldridge and Panikkar (A) (B) (C) are important studies of the rôle of sea-power in this context.

These sources have also been supplemented by various historical atlases, notably Davies's *An Historical Atlas of the Indian Peninsula*, Herrmann's *Historical and Commercial Atlas of China*, *Philip's Historical Atlas, Medieval and Modern*, Sellman's *An Outline Atlas of Eastern History*, *Stanford's London Atlas of Universal Geography* (1904), *Geschiedkundige Atlas van Nederland—De Kolonieën*, and *Westermanns Atlas zur Weltgeschiechte*.

CHAPTER 6

The Legacy of the West

I. THE RE-DRAWING OF THE POLITICAL MAP

Viewed in its true historical perspective the age of Western domination in South-east Asia is seen to have been of relatively brief duration. Except for a few small portions of the Malaysian archipelago and the coastal fringes of Burma, effective European occupation has been at most a matter of barely a single century. Yet the period of Western rule has witnessed a revolutionary transformation alike in the economic, social and political life. And although with the post-war granting of independence to the Philippines (1946), Burma (1947), Indonesia (1949), Indochina (1954) and the Federation of Malaya (1957), the imperial age is now effectively at an end, its imprint is still apparent in every aspect of the human geography of the region.

In the first place it is evident in the political map, for with few exceptions the national boundaries of today are identical with those agreed upon by the Europeans in the course of the 19th-century scramble for territory. This arbitrary parcelling out of the region into a veritable patchwork of rival colonies, protectorates and spheres of influence marked a further stage in the process of regional diversification, and today the several states of South-east Asia, like the republics of Latin America, 'face the world, turning their backs to one another'.[1]

Admittedly some of the new territorial units established by the Europeans, notably Burma and perhaps also Indonesia, corresponded fairly closely to older indigenous groupings, though this can hardly be claimed of either the Philippines or French Indochina. But even where such historical precedents did exist, the administrative patterns imposed by the West were essentially alien; the new linear boundaries had a precision and permanence hitherto unknown in South-east Asia, and the usual practice of establishing the seat of government in coastal ports rather than inland towns represented a complete break with the accepted traditions in many parts of the region.

Moreover, each of these various dependent territories was tied to a different part of the outside world, so that each became Westernized through different linguistic media and according to widely varying concepts of colonialism, which in turn were reflected in both social policy and political evolution. Nor was this solely a matter of the direct relationships with the metropolitan powers them-

[1] Broek (D), p. 188.

selves. Thus, for example, Burma was administered as part of British India, and from the middle of the 19th century until the separation of 1937 its communal structure, its pattern of trade and ultimately also its advance towards self-government were decisively shaped by this fact. On the other hand British Malaya, though likewise originally envisaged as an outpost of India, later came to be regarded rather as the gateway to the Pacific, an outlook which found expression in the establishment of the great naval base at Singapore in the 1920s. Similarly, Indochina was cast for the key rôle in the wide-ranging, if in the end ineffective, imperial strategy of the French in the Far Eastern and Pacific theatres, while the Netherlands Indies, as the preserve of one of the lesser European powers, maintained a degree of detachment and even obscurity which ill accorded with their wealth, but was nevertheless not without its advantages to Dutch commercial interests. Even more isolated from the rest of South-east Asia was the Philippines, whose character as a cultural outlier of Latin America was only partially altered by its 20th-century alignment with the United States, and whose subsequent evolution as a colony of a traditionally anti-colonial power was without parallel in other parts of the region. Only Siam retained political independence, but from the 1860s onwards it was intimately linked economically with British South-east Asia, and experienced the revolutionary impact of the West in only a slightly less intense form than its neighbours.

II. ECONOMIC CHANGES

The re-drawing of the political map symbolizes the introduction of law and order, the West's greatest single contribution to South-east Asia. Coupled with this was the provision of sound money which, as Allen and Donnithorne have stressed,[2] was of almost equal importance in making possible the economic development which was the principal motive for Western intervention in the region's affairs.

The forms of economic activity with which the West concerned itself were governed by the outlook of the age in question, that is first in the Indies by mercantilism, but far more important, both there and elsewhere, by the liberal capitalist doctrines of the 19th and early 20th centuries. In either case, however, the Westerners were concerned primarily with making profits for themselves, and only secondarily with the need to develop the territories for the benefit of the indigenous inhabitants.[3] Thus the colonial dependencies of South-east Asia were viewed as *Ergänzungsräume* for the European metropolitan powers,[4] and from this point of view the most profitable lines of development were the extraction of such materials as were readily accessible, and, more important, the cultivation of whatever forms of tropical produce were in greatest demand in temperate markets.

Such development of course was not without very real benefit to the South-

[2] Allen and Donnithorne, p. 265.

[3] This attitude changed considerably after the early 20th century. See below, p. 192.

[4] See Pelzer (K), p. 314.

east Asian lands. For although the Portuguese had been content to trade in those spices which were native to the archipelago, and the various crops brought in from the New World by the Spaniards achieved importance mainly within the framework of subsistence cultivation, the other European rulers, particularly the Dutch and the British, subsequently introduced a wide range of new commercial plants which were drawn from all over the tropical world, and included all the major cash crops of today apart from rice, sugar and coconuts. In this process, as we have seen, there has been a gradual shift of emphasis from high-value commodities to the cheaper and bulkier forms of tropical produce, while at the same time constant attention has been given to the task of adapting the imported plants to the peculiarities of the South-east Asian environment and to introducing or breeding new varieties better able to resist the diseases which thrive there.

Thus, for example, during the 17th century, Arabian coffee (*Coffea arabica*) was introduced by the Dutch into Java, where it remained the most important cash crop until the 1880s, by which time cultivation had also been extended on a smaller scale to Celebes, Sumatra and the Malay peninsula. Thereafter, however, it proved to be extremely susceptible to the rust fungus (*Hemileia vastatrix*) which virtually brought production to an end in Malaya but led the Dutch in Java to experiment with other more resistant African types. Hence, today Indonesia is still an important coffee producer, but mainly of the *liberica* variety, which grows on heavy lowland soils, and of the *robusta* which prefers the better-drained soils of the lower hill slopes up to about 2,500 ft.

However, largely because of the great increase in output of cheaper Brazilian coffee after the 1880s, attention shifted to other crops, and by the last decade of the 19th century[5] cane sugar had already replaced coffee as the leading export crop of Java whose central and eastern districts were almost ideally suited to its cultivation. Similarly favourable physical conditions likewise encouraged commercial sugar production in many parts of the Philippines, but the early hopes for developing successful cultivation in western Malaya were never realized, except on a minute scale in Malacca and Province Wellesley.

Following a serious setback caused by the ravages of *sereh*, a parasitic disease of the vascular tissues of the cane, Dutch plant breeders in the present century perfected a series of new varieties which were both more resistant and substantially more productive, and one of these, POJ 2878, was giving the astonishingly high average yield of over 120 cwt. per acre by 1929.[6] But although Java, owing to the combination of optimum natural conditions, cheap labour and the intensive researches of Dutch scientists, was able to produce sugar more cheaply than any other part of the world, the industry has never fully recovered from the great depression which began in 1929 and lasted well into the 1930s. For, in

[5] See Allen and Donnithorne, p. 90.

[6] POJ 2878 accounted for 90 per cent of Java's sugar production in 1938, when the average yield for the island was 124 cwt. per acre. See also Robequain (D), p. 342.

contrast to most of the other major cane producers, Java had no large protected market for its exports and, although some improvement in production occurred just before the outbreak of the war, the latter caused an even more serious setback and led to a great expansion of production in the rival centres in the Western hemisphere.[7]

Besides coffee and sugar, several lesser but nevertheless very profitable cultures were developed during the 19th century, again mainly in Indonesia. Of these, tea, originally introduced from China and Japan, made a promising start in the uplands of western Java early in the century, though in response to a growing demand for Indian-type teas new varieties were brought in from Assam after 1873 and these have since become the more important. Likewise, the Andean cinchona tree, from whose bark quinine is obtained, was successfully planted in the same vicinity in the 1850s, and proved an astonishing success prior to the recent advent of synthetic anti-malarial drugs,[8] while North America provided the first tobacco plants to be cultivated in Sumatra, and kapok was a native of the Latin-American tropics.

But undoubtedly the most spectacular progress was that achieved by rubber, and since the history of this commodity in South-east Asia also illustrates many of the problems which have been encountered in the cultivation of other plantation products there, it is worth considering in some detail.

Rubber is obtained from the sap of the tree *Hevea brasiliensis*, and until the early years of the present century the main commercial supply came from Brazil, where itinerant Amerind labourers used to wander through the Amazon jungle tapping the scattered *hevea* trees which grew there in their natural state. But in 1876, at a time when the new electrical and bicycle industries were creating a growing demand for rubber in the United Kingdom, the Englishman Henry Wickham smuggled a stock of *hevea* seeds out of Brazil and succeeded in germinating them in Kew Gardens. From there seedlings were taken to Ceylon and thence to Singapore, but it was not until around the turn of the century that some of the former Malayan coffee estates, which had recently been ruined by the blight and growing Brazilian competition[9], began to experiment with rubber as a possible alternative.

It was at this juncture that the coming of the motor-car suddenly led to a totally unexpected expansion in the demand for rubber,[10] with the result that in

[7] Fryer (C), p. 171.

[8] Cinchona is not ready to yield its bark before the tree is 15 years old, so that heavy capitalization is necessary. By the early 20th century Java had almost a monopoly of production, but since then various synthetic drugs, such as atebrin, mepachrine and paludrine, have largely ousted quinine from its principal use in the prevention and treatment of malaria, and this has led to a catastrophic fall in demand. In 1955 Indonesian exports of cinchona bark were only 1,207 tons, compared with 6,957 tons in 1938.

[9] It is ironical that Brazil's rise to pre-eminence as a coffee producer should have been a contributory factor to South-east Asia's replacement of Brazil as the world's leading producer of rubber.

[10] By 1897 Britain was already importing 20,000 tons of rubber a year. Chaloner, p. 8.

the first two decades of the present century it established itself as by far the most important export crop in Malaya. From there production quickly spread to Java, Sumatra and Borneo, and by the end of the 1920s rubber had become the leading export of the Netherlands Indies, besides having been taken up on a smaller but nevertheless significant scale in Burma, Thailand and Indo-china.

For besides the relatively high price which it normally commands,[11] rubber offers many other advantages to the cultivator. Being indigenous to the Amazon jungle, it is naturally adapted to the hot humid climate of much of South-east Asia and thrives even on maturely laterized soils. Moreover, while tapping, which involves making an incision in the bark and allowing the latex to drain into a small collecting cup, provides steady employment all the year round with no seasonal fluctuations, the tree is not in fact damaged if for any reason tapping is suspended for a considerable period.[12] From this point of view, therefore, rubber is equally suited to estates, which prefer to maintain a permanent labour force in regular employment[13], and to the peasant cultivator who wishes to combine cash-crop production with subsistence farming which makes much more variable demands on his time.

Although during the last 30–40 years the rôle of the small-holder has become extremely important, particularly in Indonesia and Malaya, the essential pioneer work in rubber cultivation was carried out almost exclusively by the estates and the research institutes which were established in conjunction with them. In the main this was because only large Western-run concerns could afford the heavy capital outlay needed to pay for the initial clearing of the forest, the provision of transport facilities and processing factories,[14] and to cover operating charges during the initial six or seven years between planting and the first production from the trees.

In the early days plantations were laid out like Western orchards, with the *hevea* trees in regular lines and the intervening ground surface kept free from weeds. But this so-called 'clean-weeding' quickly led to the deterioration and erosion of the soil, to guard against which the practice was accordingly evolved in the inter-war years of growing various cover crops which would provide protection from the direct action of sun and rain.

Even more important has been the increase in productivity which resulted from the development of bud-grafting and the use of clonal seeds during the same period.[15] The former of these practices was in fact first successfully tried in 1913 and subsequently became widely adopted on the big estates. Clonal seeds on the other hand only came into regular use in the 1930s, but have since then been extensively adopted by the small-holders as well, and together these

[11] Though this is subject to much fluctuation. See p. 165.

[12] As happened, for example, during the Japanese occupation.

[13] One tapper can look after 6 acres on an average estate. Dobby (H), p. 113.

[14] In which latex is coagulated and formed into sheets, and then dried by smoking.

[15] Robequain (D), p. 334, and Mills.

improved methods have been responsible for something like a three-fold increase in output per acre wherever they have been introduced. At the same time the invention of latex foam for use in upholstery opened up a new range of demand for rubber after 1929, and in 1961 the Malayan export of natural rubber latex amounted to the equivalent of 102,260 tons of dry rubber.

In spite of these striking developments in production, however, the future prospects for rubber are by no means certain. Largely because of the slowness with which supply can be adjusted to demand, the price of rubber has been marked in the past by extreme instability, varying in the inter-war years from as little as *4d.* to as much as *4s. od.* per lb. It was because of a severe drop in price following the First World War that in 1922 British rubber producers in Malaya and Ceylon set up the 'Stevenson' restriction scheme which, however, the Dutch refused to join, because of the difficulties it might be expected to cause to Indonesian small-holders in Sumatra and Borneo.[16] Later, as prices rose to a peak in 1925, both the Dutch and the French in Indochina greatly expanded their rubber acreage, and as it became clear that the Stevenson plan was merely playing into their hands, it was called off in 1928. But in 1930–31, during the world-wide economic crisis, the price dropped to the lowest figure ever recorded, and again the British producers took the initiative in setting up a restriction scheme which eventually, after much hesitation and long drawn out negotiation, the Dutch, French and Siamese agreed to join.[17] Thereafter the combination of international agreement among the major producers, the recovery from the world crisis and the beginning of stock-piling for military needs brought renewed prosperity to the industry until the time of the Japanese invasion of 1941–2.

Nevertheless, experience of the wide fluctuations in rubber prices had already encouraged the belief that such a crop was perhaps better suited to small-holders, who have only minor overhead expenses, than to the great estates with their heavy standing commitments in both plant and labour. However, the estates have so far held their ground, mainly by virtue of the superior quality of their finished product,[18] but co-operative processing has meanwhile done much to improve the standard of small-holders' rubber.

Since 1945 a new threat has appeared on the horizon in the form of growing competition from synthetic rubber. Thus, whereas even in the late 1930s the only general-purpose synthetic rubber in regular use was a heavily subsidized German product, at that time of somewhat doubtful durability, today as a result of the West's success in developing substitutes after Japan over-ran South-east Asia during the Second World War, some 73 per cent of the rubber consumed in

[16] The Stevenson scheme caused U.S. companies to develop new sources of supply in Liberia and Brazil, and it also led to the growth of a new reclaiming industry. Allen and Donnithorne, p. 123.

[17] In 1934 the International Rubber Restriction Agreement was ratified by the British, Dutch, French and Siamese governments to run for four years. *Ibid.*, p. 125.

[18] Since the Second World War estates have been trying to reduce labour costs by employing a higher proportion of local personnel in management. *Ibid.*, p. 129.

TABLE 4

WORLD RUBBER PRODUCTION AND CONSUMPTION, 1953 AND 1961

Figures in thousand long tons

Natural rubber

Production	1953	1961	*Consumption*	1953	1961
Indonesia	695	671	United States	553	427
Malaya	574	739	United Kingdom	220	166
Thailand	96	182	France	115	126
Ceylon	99	96	Germany (Federal Republic)	106	136
Vietnam	52	78	Japan	89	176
Cambodia	22	39			
Sarawak	24	47			
Total (incl. others)	1,728	2,090	Total (incl. others)	1,655	2,113

Synthetic rubber

Production	1953	1961	Consumption	1953	1961
United States	848	1,404	United States	785	1,102
Canada	81	164	Canada	36	63
Germany (Federal Republic)	6	86	Germany (Federal Republic)	11	120
United Kingdom	—	105	United Kingdom	5	121
Italy	—	87	France	13	96
			Japan	2	84
Total (excl. U.S.S.R.)	936	1,978	Total (incl. others)	872	1,918

Source: Based on *Rubber Statistical Bulletin*, Vol. 16, No. 9, June 1962.

the U.S.A., by far the world's largest single market, was home-made synthetic and in the entire non-Communist world synthetic accounted for 54 per cent of consumption in 1961.

Admittedly the total world demand is still growing fast[19] and, at least as yet, the synthetic product is not a complete substitute for natural rubber. Nevertheless, when one recalls the crippling blow which synthetic substitutes have already dealt to such commodities as indigo, quinine and silk, it is difficult to be confident about the long-term prospects for natural rubber. Indeed, it would seem that, as a general rule, the economic advantage will lie increasingly with the synthetics, for not only can they be tailored much more closely to fit particular

[19] Though such events as the Korean War, with its sudden encouragement of stockpiling, make it difficult to evaluate long-term trends.

TABLE 5

WORLD TIN PRODUCTION AND CONSUMPTION, 1956 AND 1961

Figures in thousand long tons

Production (tin in concentrates)	1956	1961	*Consumption (primary tin metal)*	1956	1961
Malaya . .	62·3	56·0	United States .	60·5	49·7
Indonesia . .	30·1	18·6	United Kingdom .	21·8	20·2
Bolivia . . .	26·8	20·7	Germany (Federal Republic	8·4	25·8
Thailand . .	12·5	13·2	Japan . . .	9·8	14·3
Nigeria . .	9·2	7·8	France . . .	10·4	10·1
Total (incl. others)	166·0	137·0	Total (excl. Soviet bloc)	150·0	165·6

Source: *International Tin Council, Statistical Bulletin*, July 1962.

TABLE 6

SOUTH-EAST ASIA, PRODUCTION OF MINERAL OIL, 1940–59

Figures in thousand metric tons

	1940	1946	1956	1963 (*preliminary*)
Indonesia	7,900	300	12,700	21,323 (Indonesia and West New Guinea)
West New Guinea . .	nil	nil	400	
Brunei and Sarawak .	1,000	300	5,800	3,526
Burma	1,100	negligible	200	*c.* 600

Source: *Petroleum Information Bureau*, and *Petroleum Press Service, etc.*

demands, but their costs of production should tend to decline as capital costs are paid off, while the natural commodities, whose price depends so largely on labour costs, will face growing difficulty as the demand for better living standards becomes effective throughout the former colonial lands. However, rubber may prove an exception to this rule, owing partly to the importance of peasant cultivation of the natural product and partly[20] to the likelihood of a steady rise in

[20] Improved higher-yielding varieties of natural rubber may also enable the latter to continue to compete effectively. But Table 4 shows the extent to which synthetic is catching up.

the cost of the oil-derivatives, styrene and butadiene, from which the synthetic form is made. Nevertheless, the outlook remains extremely uncertain, and in these circumstances it is understandable that much thought is now being given in South-east Asia to possible alternative crops which might, at least in some degree, replace natural rubber as a source of cash.

Of these, oil-palm products are probably the most promising, though in spite of an apparently assured demand for both the oil and the kernels at the present time[21] it would be rash to assume that they could do more than provide a partial solution to the problem. The oil palm, *Elæis guineensis*, is a native of West Africa and was first introduced into Malaya and north-eastern Sumatra in the 19th century. But it was not until about 1910 that any extensive cultivation was attempted there, and it has never attained an acreage comparable with that of rubber in either country.[22] Like rubber, it is well adapted to the climate and soils of both these areas, and although the best yields have been obtained on fairly well-drained alluvials it is certainly successful on the much commoner sedentary lateritic material, and even there gives a cash return per acre which compares favourably with that from rubber.

In its natural state the oil palm attains a considerable height, and the task of harvesting its fruit, which grows in a cluster at the top of the bole, involves much wastage of time both in seeking out the scattered palms within the forest and in climbing them to reach the fruit. Moreover, the latter is easily bruised by falling, and unless it is then quickly transported to the processing centre, the quality of its oil will be seriously impaired.

For these reasons, and also because of the expensive machinery required for extracting the oil,[23] cultivation in South-east Asia has hitherto been virtually restricted to estates. There the method followed is to plant continuous stands of selected palms with much shorter trunks, which enables the fruit to be cut from ground level by means of a knife attached to a long pole. Processing takes place with the minimum delay on the estate itself, the palm oil being extracted from the mesocarp of the fruit though the inner kernel is commonly exported intact to be crushed for palm-kernel oil in the country of import.

Fundamentally, there would seem to be no reason why the oil palm should not be as successfully cultivated by the small-holder as rubber now is,[24] especially if production and processing are organized on a sound co-operative basis. But as yet

[21] The demand for vegetable oils is very great and there is a high degree of interchangeability between the various oils and fats used for food and industrial purposes. Nevertheless, some anxiety has been aroused among oil-palm growers by the increasing popularity of synthetic detergents and the declining use of palm oil in the manufacture of tinplate. Palm oil, which is very rich in vitamins A and D, is of great value in the indigenous diet and should be encouraged for that reason. See Jarrett, p. 55.

[22] See below, pp. 323 and 614.

[23] Plus the need for capital for jungle clearing and tiding over the long period before production begins.

[24] The oil palm is cultivated by small-holders in West Africa, though the yield there is much less. See Jarrett, p. 53 and Robequain (D), pp. 345–6.

not much has been done in this respect, and for the present by far the most widely cultivated source of vegetable oil in South-east Asia is the coconut.

Although the inter-island copra trade came into existence in the East Indies during the 17th century, large-scale production did not begin until the early 20th century, after German discoveries had solved the problem of deodorizing the oil, and the big increase in the world demand for fats had made it worth while to organize production for export on a massive scale.[25]

Compared with Sumatran oil palm, which in 1940 yielded an average of 2,880 lb. of oil per acre,[26] Malayan coconut plantations averaged only 631 lb. in 1953. On the other hand, however, the coconut makes much smaller demands on labour, and this is in fact one of the principal reasons for its popularity as a small-holders' crop, particularly when grown as an adjunct to subsistence farming. Moreover, as we have already observed, the coconut is indigenous to the region, and the use of both its flesh and still more of its oil in the traditional styles of cooking[27] is very deeply ingrained. For commercial use the flesh is converted into copra by drying in the sun or smoking, and from this the oil is later expressed at the local ports or overseas.

For the most part the coconut palm is a plant of the coastal zone, and it does best in climates without a pronounced dry season. But because of the relatively slight demands which it makes on the cultivator, it is today most characteristic of eastern Indonesia and the Philippines,[28] some parts of which do in fact experience a very well-marked dry season.

With the exception of a small percentage of the rubber, the various cash crops referred to in the preceding pages are cultivated almost exclusively within the Malaysian lands, that is Malaya, Indonesia and the Philippines, though of these only Indonesia is seriously concerned with more than two or three of them. In Burma, Thailand and Indochina, on the other hand, commercial agriculture is completely dominated by the production of rice, a crop which is ideally suited to the seasonal rhythm of their tropical monsoonal climates and to the nature of the terrain in the great deltas which constitute the best part of their available land within easy reach of the coast.

So far as the technique of rice cultivation is concerned the West contributed very little during the colonial period, and the methods followed in these three countries (which are described in detail in Chapters 14, 15 and 16) are still essentially traditional. But in such matters as drainage, irrigation and flood

[25] Allen and Donnithorne, p. 248.

[26] Though in 1955, following the disturbances of the War and the struggle for independence, yields in Sumatra were down to 1,900 lb. of oil per acre. Both oil palm and the coconut are very efficient producers of vegetable oil when compared with temperate oil-bearing plants such as the soya bean, which in the U.S.A. yields an average of about 200 lb. of oil per acre. Mountjoy, p. 44.

[27] Coconut oil is also very important as a domestic illuminant, though it is rapidly being replaced by electricity in the more accessible villages.

[28] Partly because of the lower population density and partly because of the relative backwardness of eastern Indonesia.

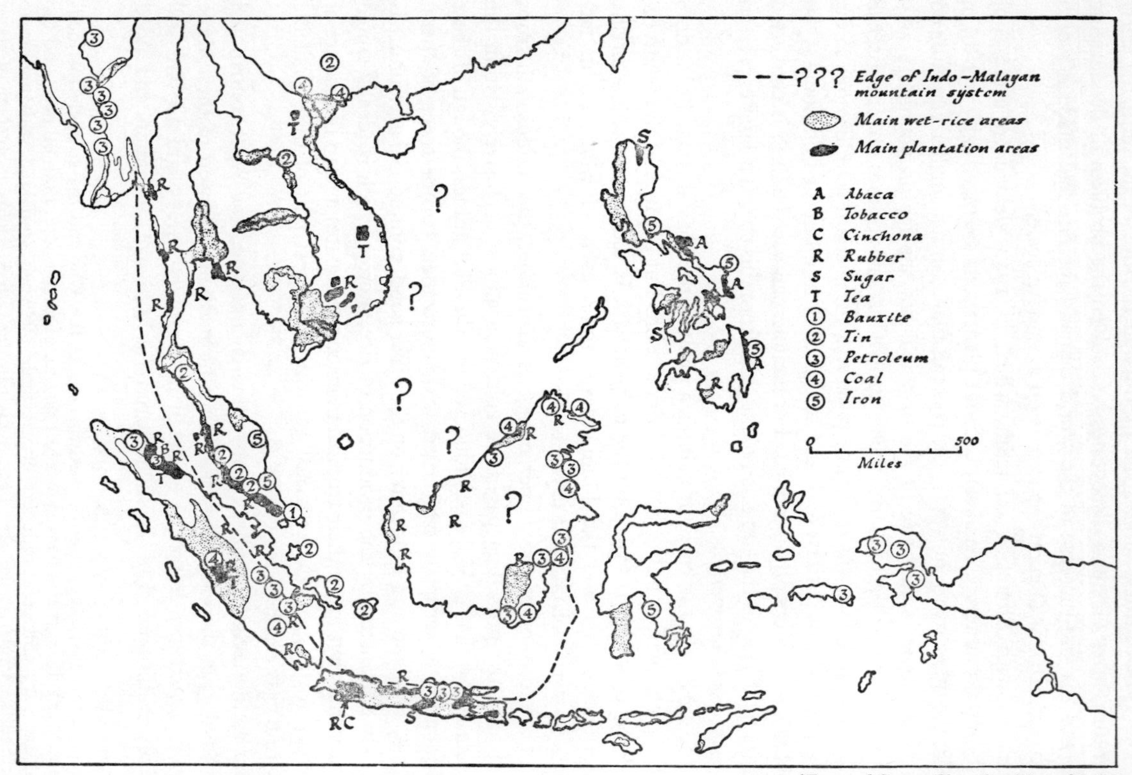

(*East and Spate:* Changing Map of Asia)

FIG. 19—South-east Asia: economic development

control, as well as in the wider field of economic organization, the West has made vital contributions,[29] without which the export economies would never have evolved in anything like their present form. Since the Second World War, moreover, a new interest has been shown in increasing the output of rice, both by means of more effective water utilization, particularly in Burma and Thailand, and also by developing better-yielding varieties of rice. In the latter connexion F.A.O.[30] is sponsoring a research programme aimed at producing new hybrids of *japonica* and *indica* rice, which will combine *japonica's* ability to respond to the application of fertilizer with *indica's* tolerance of the short hours of daylight in the tropical growing season. A successful outcome of this work might have revolutionary effects on the agriculture not only of the mainland rice-exporting countries, but of South-east Asia as a whole, though as yet it is only in the experimental stage.

Besides its share in the development of commercial agriculture, Western initiative has also played the decisive rôle in both forestry and mining. Admittedly, it was Chinese enterprise which first revealed the potentialities of the alluvial tin belt in Malaya and adjacent areas, but the subsequent introduction of large-scale machinery there, as well as the creation of the petroleum industry in Burma, Indonesia and British Borneo and the mining of coal and various metals in other parts of the region, have been due essentially to the Europeans.[31]

The total results of all this enterprise were indeed spectacular and in several of the most important items of tropical produce, South-east Asia in the inter-war years contributed well over half the world's commercial supply. Thus, in the late 1930s it produced 93 per cent of the rubber, 90 per cent of the rice, 90 per cent of the cinchona, 75 per cent of the copra, and 55 per cent of the palm oil, and also 60 per cent of the tin entering the stream of international trade.[32] Moreover, since a high proportion of these products were sold in the United States they played a vital part in balancing the trading accounts of the metropolitan powers, notably Britain and the Netherlands, both of which normally bought far more from North America than they sold to it direct. It was for this reason that Malaya came to be known as 'the Empire's dollar arsenal', while Indonesia was variously dubbed 'the cork by which Holland floated' and 'the tail which wagged the Dutch dog' with what at times amounted to a positively transatlantic vigour.

[29] The Chinese (and in Burma the Indians) also have played important, though unpopular, rôles in the marketing and milling of rice.

[30] *I.e.* the Food and Agricultural Organization of the United Nations which in 1949 established the International Rice Commission to study problems of production and consumption of rice. See Pelzer (G), pp. 11–12, and (H), pp. 10–12. The research into possible hybrids of *indica* and *japonica* rice is being carried out in India. See also Calder, pp. 134–5, and Grist, pp. 302–3.

[31] The Chinese had in fact discovered and mined several of these minerals before the Europeans arrived, though in most cases their operations were only on a small scale.

[32] Note that, like rubber, tin also was subjected to international restriction of production during the 1930s.

III. THE GROWTH OF POPULATION

Hand in hand with the transformation which the West has wrought in the political and economic structure of South-east Asia have gone equally profound changes in its social geography. Of these the most striking has been the phenomenal increase in population which has taken place during the past 150 years.

If we may accept the contemporary estimates of Crawfurd,[33] South-east Asia in or about the year 1830 had a population of some 25,824,000, which is almost exactly one-seventh as large as the United Nations' estimate of 181,709,000 for the year 1954. When compared with the approximate doubling of the population of China or even with the trebling of those of the Indian sub-continent and Japan during the same period, the rate of increase in South-east Asia which these figures imply is astonishingly high, and for this reason the validity of Crawfurd's estimates may perhaps be called in question.

Nevertheless, there is a great deal of circumstantial evidence to suggest that Crawfurd did not seriously err on the side of under-statement, and in the area which has witnessed the most spectacular increase of all, namely Java, fairly reliable supporting data had been provided by the census carried out under Raffles in 1815 which recorded a total for the island of approximately 4,800,000. Moreover, as the authorities in other parts of the region began one by one to take censuses of the population within their territories, the findings seem to confirm the essential soundness of Crawfurd's figures, when due allowance is made for the differential spread of Western influence within the region during the 19th century.

On the generally accepted assumption that the first major factor leading to an increase in population in South-east Asia during the period under review was the drop in the death-rate resulting from the suppression of internecine warfare and the establishment of law and order by the Western powers, it is reasonable to expect that Java and the Philippines would show the greatest total growth. For in both cases European control had been fairly effectively established over the greater part of the territory by the early part of the 19th century, whereas in Burma, Indochina, the interior of Malaya and most of the outer islands of Indonesia a comparable stage was not reached until fifty to a hundred years afterwards. But once such control was established in these latter areas similar results followed, so that while the populations of both Java and the Philippines show something like a ten-fold increase between 1820 and 1954, that of Burma rose from 8,500,000 in 1891 to 19,242,000 in 1954, Indochina from 15,859,000

[33] John Crawfurd's estimates for most of the mainland countries appear in his *Journal of an embassy to the courts of Siam and Cochin-China* (2nd edition, 1830). His *History of the Indian archipelago* (1820) does not give any comparable data for Malaysia but Hugh Murray's *An Encyclopaedia of Geography* (1834), besides citing Crawfurd's figures for the mainland countries (except Burma) on page 1015, also includes on page 1126 estimates by Crawfurd (apparently based on a personal communication) for the major islands and island groups. All these Crawfurd estimates may thus be dated c. 1830, and with them may be included Murray's estimate of the population of Burma. These are used in Table 7.

in 1906 to 31,460,000 in 1954, and the outer territories of Indonesia from 7,670,000 in 1905 to 27,100,000 in 1954.

Besides the process of internal pacification a further factor contributing to a decline in the death-rate during the 19th century was the creation by the Westerners of new economic opportunities as described on pp. 161 to 171. For the opening up of new land for subsistence farming and the development of commercial agriculture, mining and other new means of livelihood, all directly or indirectly helped to reduce the number of mortalities from malnutrition, while improvements in transport virtually eliminated the danger of outright famine.

Finally, and more especially during the 20th century, the spread of Western hygiene, sanitation and medical facilities has continued this downward trend to the present day,[34] and though much still remains to be done in all these respects the present crude death rate of approximately 23/1,000 in Burma and Indonesia is a distinct improvement on the probable 30–40/1,000 prior to 1800, while in more favoured areas, such as the Federation of Malaya (11·5/1,000) and especially in the larger cities (Singapore 8·7/1,000) the figure was down virtually to Western levels by 1953.[35]

On the other hand, so far as can be inferred from the fragmentary vital statistics which are available, the birth-rate has undergone no comparable change, and indeed it is doubtful whether any significant decline has taken place in this respect during the past 150 years in any part of the region. Thus Carr-Saunders has calculated that in Java the crude birth-rate must have averaged 38/1,000 over the whole period from 1815 to 1930,[36] and more recently Warren S. Thompson has cited a figure of 32·4/1,000 for the Philippines during 1938–42.[37]

For the fact remains that throughout South-east Asia (as also in most of the neighbouring lands) the large-family system is an essential part of the traditional way of life among all settled cultivators, and doubtless this tradition has grown up at least in part as a means of making good the losses entailed by the very high death-rates which prevailed in earlier times. In western Europe it has taken from the 17th to the 20th century to complete the change from a similar wasteful demographic balance, based on a high death-rate and a high birth-rate, to the modern balance in which both figures are down to between a half and a third of the levels prevailing in medieval times, and it remains to be seen how long it will take to effect a comparable revolution in the Orient, and to what extent the total population there will increase in the meantime before the birth-rate is finally brought into step with the diminished death-rate.

As yet the only significant declines in Asian birth-rates have occurred in

[34] This factor operated on a significant scale in the Netherlands Indies during the 19th century also. See Furnivall (A), p. 362, and Wertheim (C), p. 92.

[35] This is in part the result of a very high proportion of young people in the population. But although in the long run this proportion may be expected to fall, continuing improvements in public health are likely to prevent the death-rate from rising in any foreseeable future.

[36] Carr-Saunders, p. 282.

[37] Thompson, Warren S., p. 162.

TABLE 7

POPULATION GROWTH IN SOUTH-EAST ASIA, 1824–1958

Burma

1834	Murray	4,000,000
1891	Estimate based on census*	8,500,000
1901	Census	10,490,624
1921	„	13,212,000
1931	„	14,667,000
1941	„	16,800,000
1954	U.N. estimate	19,242,000
1958	„ „	20,255,000

* 1891 census recorded 7,722,000 but omitted parts of the Shan and Chin hills.

Thailand

c. 1830	Crawfurd	2,730,000*
1850	Ingram	5–6,000,000
1911	Census	8,266,000
1919	„	9,207,000
1929	„	11,506,000
1937	„	14,464,000
1947	„	17,317,000
1954	U.N. estimate	19,925,000
1958	„ „	21,474,000

* Including Laos territories later incorporated into French Indochina q.v.

Indochina

c. 1830	Crawfurd	5,194,000*
1906	Smolski	15,859,000
1921	„ and Annuaire statistique	18,800,000
1926	„ „ „ „	20,500,000
1931	„ „ „ „	21,450,000
1936	„ „ „ „	23,030,000
1954	U.N. estimate	31,460,000
1958	„ „	33,423,000

* Excluding Laos territories.

*Malaya**

1826	Crawfurd	350,000
1835-9	Newbold	400,000
1911	Census	2,644,490
1921	"	3,326,695
1931	"	4,347,704
1947	"	5,848,910
1954	U.N. estimate	7,054,000
1958	" "	8,030,000

* *I.e.* present Federation of Malaya and Singapore.

Indonesia

		Java and Madura	*Outer Islands*	*Total*
1802	Engelhardt	3,500,000	—	—
1815	Raffles	4,800,000	—	—
c. 1830	Crawfurd	6,000,000	5,000,000	11,000,000
1845	Bleeker	9,400,000	—	—
1860	Official estimate	12,690,000	—	—
1880	" "	19,803,000	—	—
1900	" "	28,753,000	—	—
1905	Census	30,366,000	7,670,000	38,036,000
1920	"	34,977,000	14,367,000	49,344,000
1930	"	41,718,000	19,009,000	60,727,000
1954	Official estimate	54,000,000	27,100,000*	81,100,000*
1958	U.N. estimate			87,300,000*

* Excluding West New Guinea.

Philippines

1800	Zuñiga	1,500,000
c. 1830	Crawfurd	2,500,000
1850	Buzeta	3,857,000
1891	Official estimate	5,682,012
1881	Census	5,984,727
1903	"	7,635,426
1918	"	10,314,310
1939	"	15,984,247
1954	U.N. estimate	21,440,000
1958	" "	24,010,000

Sources: As stated. Engelhardt and Bleeker, etc. are cited in Pelzer (B) and Zuñiga and Buzeta, etc. in Kolb.

association with urbanization and the related breakdown of the traditional family system, notably in Japan, though perhaps a new era in this respect is about to begin in India as a result of deliberate governmental action to popularize family planning. But in South-east Asia, where the urban percentage is much lower[38] and the age-old insouciance still widespread, there is so far no indication of any slackening in the birth-rate among the great mass of the population.[39]

Thus every advance in welfare and public health is apt to be reflected in a quickening of the rate of natural increase, and today this has reached an average figure of 22/1,000 for the region as a whole. While this is undoubtedly a very high rate it is not by any means unique in the contemporary world, and at least equal figures are found in many parts of Africa and Latin America. What, however, does seem to be without parallel anywhere else in the world is the persistence of such high rates of increase as, for example, those of Java (fluctuating between 15/1,000 and 26/1,000) *over a period of several generations*. And while it may be only in Java and the Philippines that this rate of increase has continued unbroken for 130–150 years, there are few parts of South-east Asia which have not witnessed as rapid a rate of growth for at least the past 50–75 years.

Yet despite this prodigious pullulation, South-east Asia in 1961 had an average density of only 142 to the square mile which, as has already been noted, was little more than a third that of the Indian sub-continent or China proper and only a sixth that of Japan. This state of affairs raises two points of great interest. In the first place it is clear that in the not distant past the discrepancy in density between South-east Asia and its neighbours must have been even greater than it is today and one is accordingly led to speculate on what the demographic situation in the region must have been in the centuries preceding the advent of the West. So far as India is concerned, Kingsley Davis[40] has cited strong evidence to suggest that the total population in 1820, which he puts at some 120 million, was not significantly higher than it had been in 300 B.C., though in China a slow and irregular growth can be traced from *c.* 65 million in A.D. 1400 to 150 million in 1600–1700, and 313 million in 1794.[41] While much less evidence is available concerning the early demographic history of South-east Asia, it seems probable that the situation there had more in common with India than with China.

Indeed one may go further and add that, in view of the virtually continuous political instability of South-east Asia during early historic times, it is by no means unlikely that very large fluctuations occurred in the size of the population prior to the 19th century, and it is possible that some of the great kingdoms of the past may have carried a higher density of population in their hey-day than

[38] See below, p. 185.

[39] Note, for example, the very high birth-rate of Singapore, 48·7/1,000 in 1953 and 42·5/1,000 in 1957, reflecting in part the age-structure of the population. See below, pp. 646–8.

[40] Davis, Kingsley, pp. 23–9.

[41] Ho Ping-ti, pp. 264–78.

they did in 1800.[42] Nevertheless, when all this has been conceded, it seems difficult to resist the conclusion that the average density in such times was much lower than might be inferred from many accounts of early South-east Asian history, and that this relative sparsity was fundamentally the result of the region's retarded and frequently interrupted settlement,[43] and the associated lateness of the change-over from shifting to sedentary cultivation in many parts of it.

TABLE 8

SOUTH-EAST ASIA: AREA AND POPULATION

Country	*Area (sq. miles)*	*Population mid-1953 (thousands)*	*Population mid-1958 (thousands)*	*Population mid-1961 (thousands)*	*Density per sq. mile 1961*
Burma . . .	261,760	19,272	20,255	21,527	86
Siam . . .	198,454	19,556	21,474	27,181	137
Northern Vietnam .	59,938	—	15,000	16,690	278
Southern Vietnam .	65,951	—	12,800	14,520	220
Cambodia . .	66,610	—	4,740	5,335	81
Laos . . .	91,425	1,445	1,690	1,850	20
Federation of Malaya	50,697	5,706	6,515	7,137	140
Singapore . .	224	1,192	1,515	1,687	7,531
Brunei . . .	2,225	52	77	87	39
Sarawak . . .	47,498	592	655	760	16
North Borneo . .	29,387	355	409	460	16
Indonesia* . .	575,852	79,500	87,300	95,655	166
Portuguese Timor .	5,762	456	490	520	90
Philippines . .	115,708	21,211	24,010	28,727	248
South-east Asia .	1,571,491		196,930	222,136	142

* Excluding West New Guinea (area 160,617 sq. miles, population 700,000).
Based on *U.N. Statistical Year Book 1962*, Table 1.

A second observation follows from this conclusion. During the last 150 years a beginning has been made in making up the leeway, and in this process the distribution map has been substantially modified, notably by the flocking of peoples from up country into the Irrawaddy, Menam and Mekong deltas, and by the filling out of the settlement pattern in both Java and the northern and central Philippines. Thus the coastal fringes of the region have taken an ever-increasing share of the population, and today more than six-sevenths of its inhabitants are concentrated in approximately one-sixth of the total area. Yet, even so, few

[42] There is, however, no reason to assume that this was generally the case, and it seems highly improbable that the population of the region as a whole was ever significantly higher in earlier centuries than it was in 1800. Note, for example, that the V.O.C.'s *Daghregister* 1631–4 estimated the population of Mataram (then embracing over 80 per cent of Java) at 2,500,000, which Schrieke, Pt. II, p. 139, regards as an overestimate.

[43] See also Zelinsky, pp. 135–45.

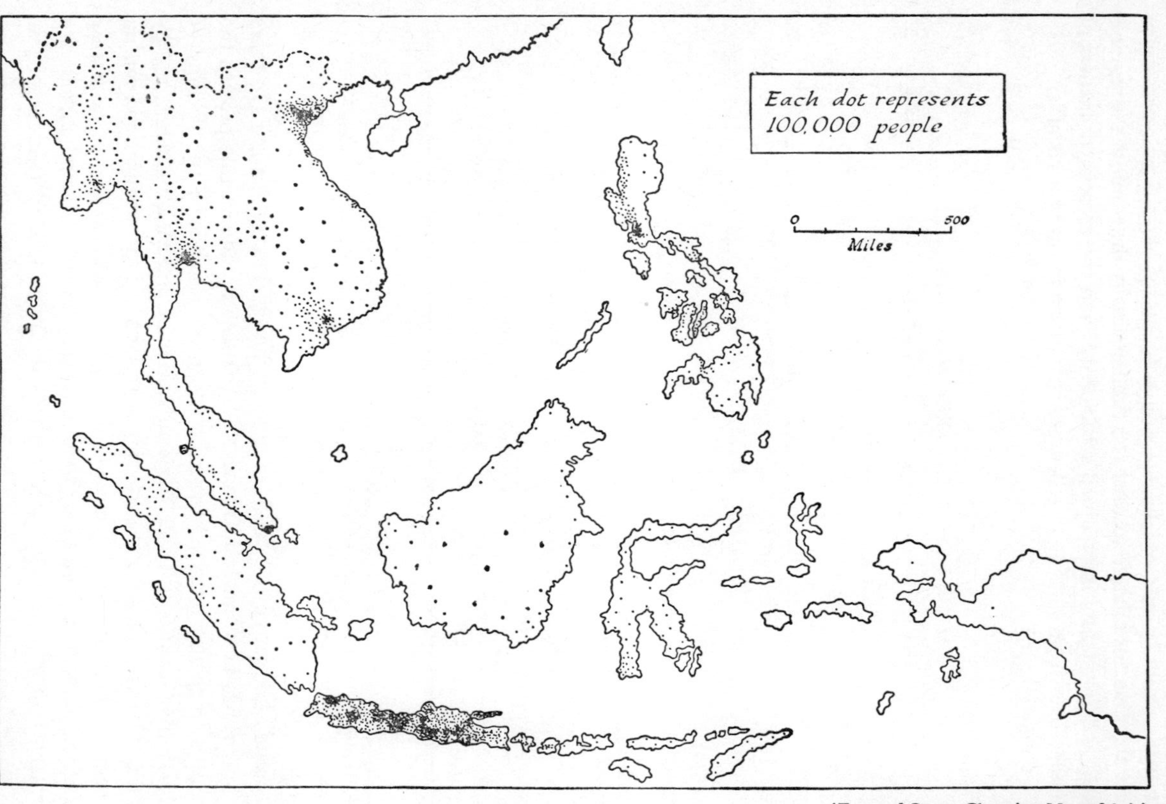

(*East and Spate:* Changing Map of Asia)

FIG. 20—South-east Asia: distribution of population

parts are as yet overcrowded, and in contrast to the figures of well over 1,000 to the square mile which are common in much of the Ganges and Yang-tze deltas, the densities in the Irrawaddy or Mekong deltas only in rare instances exceed 500 to the square mile.

Nevertheless, some important exceptions to this general pattern do exist, notably in Tonkin which may be regarded as a demographic extension of southern China, and in Java and a few parts of the Philippines where, as we have seen, the influence of the West has been of longest duration. Indeed Java, with its astonishingly high average density of 1,168 to the square mile (1959) has become one of the classic examples of congestion, and the rapidity with which this problem has developed during the last century provides an obvious warning of the danger which in the future may face other parts of South-east Asia if the present high birth-rates are not reduced.

For the time being, however, this is still largely an academic question in most parts of the region and, although many of the governments are conscious of the maldistribution of population within their national territory, it is probably true to say that most of them are more worried by the relative emptiness of their lands which it is feared may arouse the cupidity of overcrowded neighbours.

IV. IMMIGRATION AND THE PLURAL SOCIETY

Besides the natural increase arising from the excess of births over deaths among the indigenous peoples, the immigration of Chinese and Indians[44] has also contributed a significant share to the growth of population in South-east Asia during the past 150 years. The respective size of these two communities in the several territories today is indicated in Table 9, though it should be noted that in addition to the figures given for ethnic Chinese there are considerable numbers of Chinese mestizos in many of the countries concerned.[45]

As we have already seen, both Indian and Chinese migration to South-east Asia can be traced back to very early times. But whereas the former had already ceased before the end of the first millennium A.D., if indeed it had ever amounted to more than a trickle in earlier times, the flow of Chinese emigration first became important only during the period of European control. For paradoxically the coming of the Europeans, which helped to undermine China's political influence in the Nan Yang, simultaneously created in the region an economic and social climate which was exceptionally favourable to Chinese settlement there.

These two seemingly opposite tendencies both reached their culmination in the closing decades of the 19th century, when the British and French finally

[44] Throughout this section the term Indians refers to indigenes of the whole Indian sub-continent.

[45] The degree of mestization has varied from time to time and from place to place. Its effects are greatest in the areas of older Chinese settlement, notably Java and the Philippines, and in such mainland countries as Thailand and Vietnam, but there is very little in Malaya or the outer islands of Indonesia. There are very few Indian mestizos.

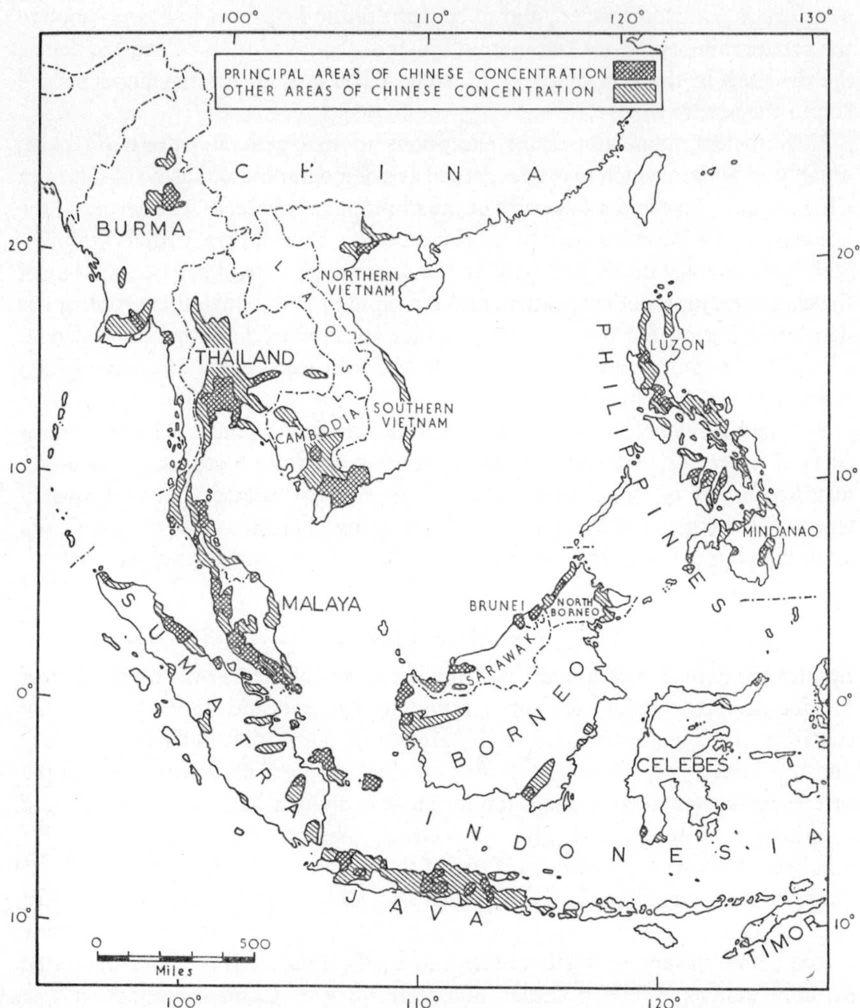

FIG. 21—South-east Asia: distribution of Chinese population

forced China to forego its claims to suzerainty over Burma and the Annamite lands, while at the same time the great commercial expansion following the opening of the Suez canal was providing unprecedented opportunities for immigrant labour throughout the Nan Yang. From the 1860s onwards the Chinese authorities were brought to recognize the right of their nationals to emigrate,[46] and thereafter the volume of migration to the south rose to a veritable

[46] A proviso to this effect was first included in a treaty in 1870; this was the Burlingame Treaty with the U.S.A. Purcell (D), p. 37.

TABLE 9

ETHNIC CHINESE AND INDIANS IN SOUTH-EAST ASIA, 1956

	Chinese	Per cent	Indians*	Per cent
Burma	350,000	1·8	800,000	4·1
Thailand	3,000,000	15·0	50,000	—
Cambodia	180,000	4·1	200	—
Laos	15,000	1·1	—	—
Northern Vietnam	100,000	0·8	—	—
Southern Vietnam	800,000	6·2	6,000	—
Federation of Malaya	2,300,000	38·0	691,000	11·4
Singapore	920,000	75·8	91,000	7·5
British Borneo	250,000	23·8	5,000	—
Indonesia	2,200,000	2·7	40,000	—
Philippines	200,000	0·9	1,300	—
TOTAL	10,315,000	5·6	1,694,500	0·9

Source: Based mainly on *The Times*, April 10, 1956, and May 8, 1956.
*Throughout this section the term Indians covers peoples from the whole Indo-Pakistan Sub-continent.

flood, second only in scale to that of the contemporary exodus from Europe to the Americas.[47]

The situation has been aptly outlined by Unger as follows: 'Western capital and management were available in most places but there was a lack of adaptable cheap labour to do the work, of clerical and supervisory personnel, and of traders and merchants to set up the services and provide the goods needed in remote or newly developing areas.'[48] For, with few exceptions, the familiar insouciance of the indigenous peoples rendered them unresponsive to the stimuli of a money economy, and notably reluctant to abandon their established way of life in order to work the long and regular hours which the Europeans regarded as essential for the successful running of their enterprises.

In these circumstances, millions of Chinese, driven by the lack of opportunity in their overcrowded homeland, were only too eager to emigrate to the new pioneer fringe which beckoned them southwards. While the various govern-

[47] The modern stream of Chinese migration to the Nan Yang may perhaps be said to begin with the flow to Singapore in the 1820s. But after *c.* 1870 the scale increased and migrants were transported mainly on Western-owned steamships, under conditions which can be imagined from the local name – 'the pig business' – by which the traffic became known. For a vivid picture see Joseph Conrad's short story *Typhoon.*

[48] Unger, p. 201.

ments of South-east Asia did not all view the prospect of Chinese immigration with such whole-hearted enthusiasm as did the British in the Straits Settlements, few serious obstacles were placed in their way prior to the economic crisis of the 1930s, except in the Philippines which came under the United States' immigration laws early in the present century.[49]

So far as the Chinese themselves were concerned their motives in emigrating were almost exclusively economic, and their present distribution reflects alike their sublime indifference to the cultural, linguistic and religious divisions within the Nan Yang, and their readiness to undertake any kind of work including the lowest paid and most arduous. Hence have arisen the great concentrations of workers in the mining centres and the larger towns, on the outskirts of which others of their compatriots are engaged in market gardening. In general their superior agricultural skill compared with the indigenous cultivators has caused the Chinese to avoid subsistence farming (though an important exception occurs in western Borneo) in order to specialize on the production of the more lucrative cash crops. But the adaptability which they display in abandoning their centuries-old peasant methods for others which skim both profits and fertility from the soil, in conformity with the reckless spirit of the frontier, constitutes a serious menace to the more conservative indigenous peoples among whom they have settled.

However, neither agriculture nor manual labour has normally satisfied more than a fraction for very long, and either they have returned to China, as most of them originally intended to do, or else, having acquired the necessary capital, they have established themselves as craftsmen, money-lenders or petty traders. From such humble beginnings not a few have subsequently risen to spectacular heights as business-men, industrialists, bankers and entrepreneurs of all kinds, while still others have achieved equal distinction in medical, legal and other professions. Some indication of their total economic stake in the region can be gleaned from Table 12, to which it may be added that perhaps their most conspicuous and disturbing success has been the measure of control which they have obtained over the marketing and milling of rice, particularly but by no means exclusively in the exporting countries.[50] Thus it has been variously estimated that 80–90 per cent of the rice mills in Siam, over 80 per cent of those in Indochina, and 75 per cent in the Philippines were Chinese owned immediately before the Second World War.[51]

In respect of employment the position of the Indian immigrants is similar to that of the Chinese, apart from an almost complete neglect of mining, but the total numbers are much smaller, and geographically the main concentrations are confined to those areas which were formerly under British rule. For the modern

[49] Purcell (D), p. 620.

[50] Besides the money they invested locally, the Chinese communities in South-east Asia also remitted large sums to relatives in China.

[51] Indian immigrants occupied a comparable position in Burma. See below, pp. 439 and 474–6.

phase of Indian emigration did not begin until 1834, and although the Indians have been motivated by essentially the same considerations as the Chinese they have in general shown less economic initiative. Thus they have mostly ventured abroad only for very short periods and in many cases under recruitment schemes which provided for their subsequent repatriation. Nevertheless, in Burma[52] large seasonal migrations took place in pre-war days, and the Indian community there remains much larger than the Chinese. In Malaya, on the other hand, the relative strength of the two alien groups is reversed, and competition between them in manual, clerical and professional work is very strong.

It is, however, misleading to think of either the Chinese or the Indians in South-east Asia as homogeneous groups, for in both cases there are numerous cleavages based upon length of domicile, economic status and also on more fundamental cultural differences brought with them from their respective mother countries. Thus the Indians include both Hindus and Muslims and a diversity of linguistic groups,[53] while the Chinese, coming as they do mainly from the southern provinces of Kwangtung, Fukien and Hainan, are divided into Hokkien, Tiuchiu, Cantonese, Hakka and Hailam, to name only the most numerous of the various dialects or 'tribes' represented.

Nevertheless, such differences gradually lose their importance with the passage of time, and especially since the 1930s the tendencies to more permanent domicile and to a more normal sex ratio among the immigrant communities have become increasingly evident. Meanwhile the growth of nationalism, both in China and India and among the indigenous peoples of the several South-east Asian countries themselves, has been paralleled by a growing sense of solidarity among the Chinese and Indians resident there.[54]

Besides these two principal minority communities other alien Asians are numerically insignificant, though the populations of all the main ports are typically cosmopolitan,[55] and in Indonesia and Malaya there are small but influential colonies of Arab traders and middlemen.

To complete the list of the main exotic components in the plural societies of South-east Asia it remains to mention the Europeans and the Eurasians (Table 10). Apart from a section of the Dutch population in Indonesia, the European official and commercial class has always been essentially transitory, and this

[52] Which until 1937 was administratively a part of India.

[53] Nevertheless the great majority derive from the specifically Indian part of the Subcontinent. Perhaps best known are the Chettyars, a money-lending caste who operate all over southern India, and many parts of South-east Asia, especially Burma. See Mende, p. 118.

[54] Among the Chinese a major rôle has been played by the teaching of the new national language, Kuo Yü, in Chinese schools throughout South-east Asia, as well as in the mother country, since the late 1920s.

[55] There were a few Japanese traders etc. in the larger towns but, except in the Philippines (which is the nearest part of South-east Asia to Japan) the number of Japanese residents was much smaller than that of Europeans prior to the Second World War. See Table 10.

impermanence has been heightened by the several transfers of sovereignty since 1945. Thus, while some Europeans are likely to continue working in South-east Asia for several years to come, their main function now, whether in government service, industry or commerce, is to train local personnel to take their places as quickly as possible.

The Eurasians on the other hand are in a fundamentally different position for, notwithstanding their European admixture, such roots and opportunities as they possess lie in the country of their birth and in most cases they have little option but to remain there. In the territories formerly under British or French rule the number of Eurasians has in fact been very small, but in Indonesia and the Philippines the so-called 'Indo-European' and mestizo communities have been much more numerous and have played important – though by no means identical – rôles in the national life.

TABLE 10

SOUTH-EAST ASIA: EUROPEANS, EURASIANS AND JAPANESE

Country	*Year*	*Europeans**	*Eurasians*	*Japanese*
Burma . . .	1931	10,000	19,000	465
	1957	?	23,000	?
Thailand . .	1937	2,176	?	522
	1947	6,284	?	?
Indochina . .	1936	28,000	15,000	241
Malaya . .	1931	17,700	16,000	8,000
	1947	18,958	19,171	225
Indonesia . .	1930	40,000	200,000	6,500
	1954	250,000		?
Philippines . .	1939	16,000	*c.* 900,000	29,000
	1956	8,000	*c.* 1,000,000	?

*Note: European is used in the ethnic sense. Members of armed services are not included.

Sources: Various.

The term plural society may be taken to connote 'a society comprising one or more elements or social orders which live side by side yet without mingling, in one political unit'.[56] Such societies are found in many parts of the world, but in all cases they appear to have been produced by colonialism in one form or another.

[56] Furnivall (A), p. 446

In South-east Asia some aspects at least of pluralism would seem to antedate the coming of the Europeans, but nevertheless the highly complex plural societies which exist there today, with their European, Eurasian, Chinese, Indian and indigenous components, are clearly to be included among the legacies of the period of Western domination.

Moreover, although the relative proportions and the mutual relationships obtaining between these various elements have differed widely from one territory to another, the great mass of the indigenes have always remained at the bottom of the economic pyramid, while the alien Asians and Eurasians together supplied the bulk of the middle class, and a handful of Europeans directed affairs and endeavoured to hold the balance between the other communities by the familiar process of divide and rule.

Thus, while the Dutch devised the system of 'like over like',[57] other governments such as the British in Malaya established special departments to supervise the affairs of the immigrant communities but, with the exception of the Americans in the Philippines, none was ever conscious before 1939 of the need to educate the whole population to a sense of common nationhood.

So long as dependent status persisted these policies were generally successful in preventing serious friction between the various communities, but with the introduction of self-government their inadequacy has quickly become apparent. For while the ending of European rule has automatically led to the assumption of political authority by indigenous leaders,[58] it is often the Chinese who emerge as the most powerful economic group in the newly sovereign states, and their preponderance in most of the professions is equally pronounced. And while in the past the great majority of the Chinese have shown little interest in political affairs, it remains to be seen whether this particular trait will undergo any change as the result of the Communist victory in their mother country.[59]

V. URBANIZATION

It is above all in the great towns that the problems of the plural society are seen in clearest outline. For although, as noted in Chapter 5, South-east Asia has had its great capitals in the past, all its leading cities today, apart from Bangkok, are relatively recent creations of the West and, alike in appearance and function, are essentially alien phenomena.

While at most 15 per cent of the total population of South-east Asia can be classed as urban, and in Indonesia the figure drops to less than 10 per cent,[60] at least 30 per cent of the alien Asians are town dwellers and the proportion of Europeans and Eurasians so resident is even higher. The alien composition of the population is particularly evident in the primate cities of each territory, the Chinese alone accounting for 77 per cent of the total in Singapore, over 50 per

[57] See below, pp. 268 and 270–3. [58] In Singapore this means, in effect, the local Chinese.

[59] See below, pp. 768–772. [60] Ginsburg (A), p. 455. But here, as elsewhere in the region, the percentage is now increasing fast. See below, p. 388.

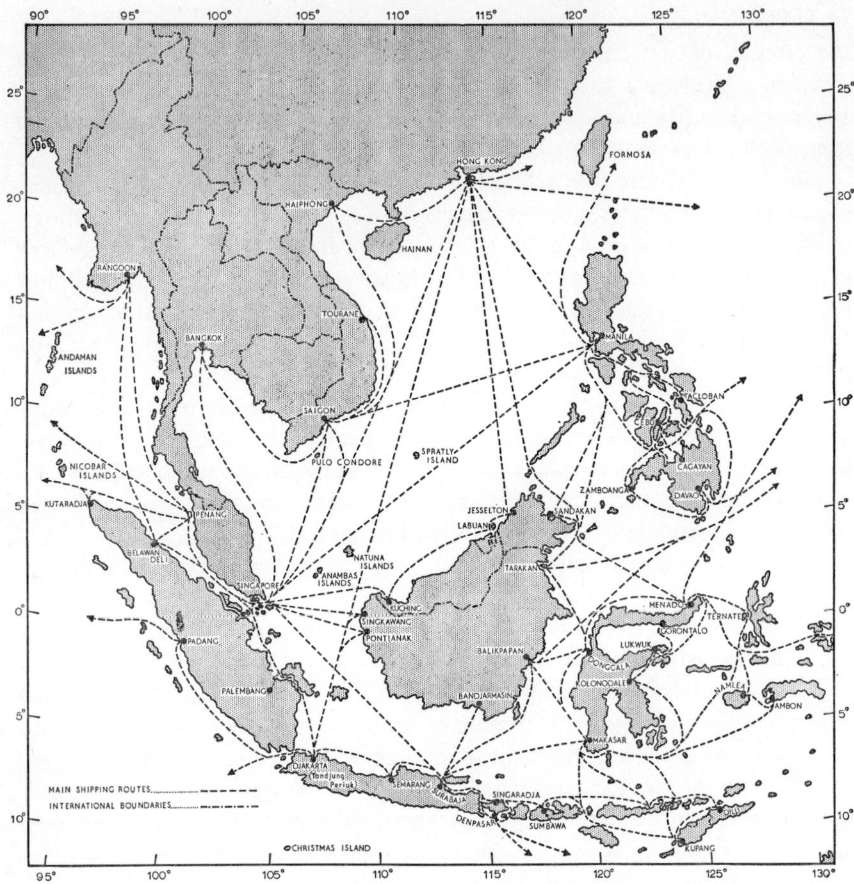

FIG. 22—South-east Asia: shipping routes

cent in Bangkok, probably 30 per cent in Saigon-Cholon, and even 5–10 per cent in Manila and Djakarta.[61]

All these cities, as also Rangoon, are ports[62] and all of them except Bangkok originated as the coastal bases from which the Europeans subsequently organized both the economic exploitation and political administration of the respective interiors. And although Bangkok was founded in 1782 as the last of the series of Thai forward capitals, whose proximity to the sea was largely fortuitous, it also has subsequently developed as a port and as the headquarters for Western and Chinese economic enterprise throughout the hinterland to which it is the gateway.

Indeed in most of the South-east Asian countries the original Western port of

[61] Fryer (A), p. 493. Note also that in Rangoon Indians were the largest single group before the War and may still be so today.

[62] Though their harbours are mostly poor, in part as a result of silting. All the ports in use today are artificial. See Fryer (A), p. 488, and Ginsburg (A), p. 460.

entry has maintained a position of unchallenged supremacy alike as the commercial, administrative and social centre, for as Ginsburg observes, 'there are in effect only a limited number of services to be performed by cities within a predominantly village and folk society, although it may be industrializing slowly, and the great cities continue to possess a virtual monopoly of these services'.[63]

This is clearly so in Burma, Thailand and the Philippines, in all of which the capital city is at least five times as large as its nearest rival, though political divisions in Malaya and Indochina, and the sheer size and diversity of Indonesia have led to a somewhat greater sharing of functions there. Thus, while there is a fair sprinkling of small provincial towns, most of them merely overgrown villages or mining camps, the low proportion of towns of middle grade is a characteristic feature of all South-east Asian countries. Besides Djakarta, Surabaja, Manila, Saigon, Bangkok and Singapore, all of which have now passed the million mark, only about 25 others in the entire region exceed 100,000 and only four of them have more than 500,000. Most of these middle-grade towns, particularly such regional ports as Haiphong, Semarang and Medan, are almost as alien in character and population as the capital cities themselves, though others, like Mandalay, Djokjakarta and Phnom-penh, all significantly well away from the coast, preserve a certain continuity of indigenous traditions, even though they have also acquired some new functions in recent times.

Nevertheless, it is the village rather than the town, whatever its size, which remains the prime focus of South-east Asian life, and in these circumstances the rôle of the great port cities in the new national states is bound to be somewhat equivocal. So far, at least, in spite of the inspiration which all the national movements have drawn from the memory of their respective country's achievements in pre-colonial times, there have been no attempts since independence to emulate the Turks or the Russians of a generation ago in symbolizing the change of regime by abandoning Western-oriented capitals in favour of others which more fittingly epitomize their historic traditions.[64]

In part, no doubt, the present attitude is indicative of a healthy common sense in recognizing that only in the existing primate cities are anything like adequate facilities available for the maintenance of an efficient national administration, and furthermore that all these cities are excellent 'head-links'[65] with the outside world, however much external political alignments may have changed in recent years. Nevertheless, the danger does exist that the exotic character of such capital cities will be reflected in a growing isolation of the central government from the every-day preoccupations and problems of the peasantry, who still constitute the overwhelming majority of the population.

Admittedly the repatriation of Western officials and the rapid post-war drift

[63] Ginsburg (A), p. 457. Kuala Lumpar, however, is an inland city.

[64] Thus Ankara replaced Constantinople (now Istanbul) and Moscow replaced St. Petersburg (now Leningrad). And more recently the Chinese have abandoned Nanking in favour of Peking for similar reasons.

[65] Spate (B), p. 628.

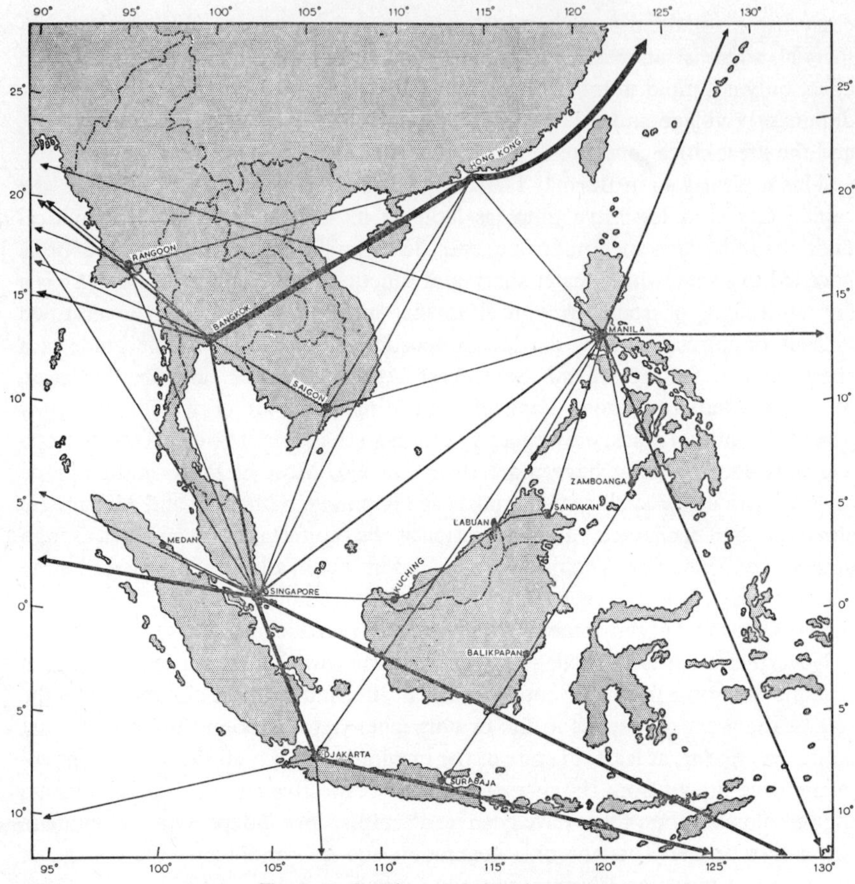

FIG. 23—South-east Asia: air routes
Thickness of lines is proportionate to frequency of flights

of indigenous peoples from the countryside to the big cities are gradually modifying both the composition and the character of the latter and, if industrialization proceeds as rapidly as is hoped, it will doubtless help to accelerate this trend. But for all that, the relationship between capital and nation is likely to remain peculiarly difficult in all the South-east Asian countries, and so long as the loyalty of the alien communities is in doubt the presence of major concentrations of these close to the centres of political and economic power is bound to give cause for concern.

VI. ECONOMIC AND PSYCHOLOGICAL BASES OF NATIONALISM

In the foregoing pages various consequences of the period of Western rule in South-east Asia have been considered and it remains now to attempt a more general assessment of the legacy which the West has bequeathed.

While it is beyond the scope of such a study as this to describe in detail the educational, social and cultural achievements of the colonial powers, though these topics will receive some consideration in the appropriate regional chapters, it is right to point out that not all the criticisms – whether on grounds of commission or omission – that have been levelled against these powers can seriously be sustained. Moreover, when one considers the extent of princely tyranny, oppression of minority peoples, debt slavery and internecine warfare under the pre-European regimes, it is clear that South-east Asia was by no means an earthly paradise prior to the advent of Western rule.

For when all is said and done, the decline in the death-rate and the astonishingly rapid increase in population during the last 150 years are unmistakable evidence of some improvement at least in the material conditions of life. Admittedly, in a few areas this increase has itself induced new problems, and notably in Java there are indications that the living standards of the peasantry have declined rather than improved during the present century. But outside the recognized centres of over-population in Java, central Luzon, Cebu and Northern Vietnam, the living standards of the ordinary villager in pre-war days were visibly higher than those of his counterpart in India or China and, although in all conscience there remained much room for improvement, there was far less in South-east Asia of the obvious and degrading poverty which was such an outstanding feature of these two neighbouring lands.[66]

Nevertheless, it would be absurd to deny the immense discrepancy in material well-being between the indigenous peoples on the one hand and both the Europeans and many of the immigrant Asians on the other. And while some of the profits obtained from commercial production were ploughed back into the colonies in schemes for jungle clearance, reclamation and irrigation for subsistence farming, as well as into the provision of education, health and other social services for the benefit of an ever-growing percentage of the population, the fact was plain for all to see that many of the non-natives were there primarily for what they could take away, and whether in the profits of Western businesses, the pensions paid to European personnel or the innumerable remittances home of the Chinese and Indians, wealth was being pumped out of the region in a seemingly unending stream.

Nor was that all. At least until very late in the day Western economic exploitation was undertaken with no sense of obligation to build up healthy and balanced economies in the South-east Asian dependencies, and such attempts as were belatedly made to redress the resultant damage were too short-lived to have much effect on the overall pattern.

[66] While this statement may seem to conflict with the income figures shown in Table 11, it should be borne in mind that most of the South-east Asian countries suffered a great setback in this respect as a result of the Second World War and the post-war chaos, from which Indochina, Indonesia and Burma in particular had by no means recovered in the late 1950s. Furthermore, these are average figures, and in India the level is raised by the very high incomes of the not inconsiderable indigenous merchant, industrial and princely groups, which have no real counterparts in South-east Asia.

Thus, while it may be true that, by and large, material standards of living rose as a result of Western activities in the region, much unnecessary hardship and dislocation were also occasioned by the same processes. Outstanding in this respect was the great damage done to the traditional handicraft industries, particularly the manufacture of clothing, agricultural implements and domestic utensils, as a result of the flooding of the local market with cheap Western manufactures. And while outside Java and the Annamite lands such indigenous industries were much less advanced than those of India or China, the harm done was real enough, in that subsistence manufacturing of this kind traditionally provided useful employment during the slack seasons of the agricultural year.

TABLE II

SOUTH-EAST ASIA: CURRENCIES AND ESTIMATED NATIONAL INCOMES, 1959

Country	Units of national currency per U.S. dollar		National Income: In national currency (millions)	National Income: In U.S. dollars (millions)	Population (millions)	National Income per head U.S. dollars
Burma	kyat	4·790*	4,722	986	20·5	48
Cambodia	riel	35·000†	14,689	420	4·8	88
Federation of Malaya	Malayan dollar	3·060*	4,232	1,383	6·7	206
Indonesia	rupiah	36·000‡	202,900	5,636	90·3	62
Philippines	peso	2·015 –2·519*	10,015	4,650	24·7	184
Thailand	baht	21·190*	47,419	2,238	21·9	102

Notes on exchange rates:

* Selling rate (in case of Philippines conversion to U.S. dollars is at former rate, i.e 2·015).

† Official rate.

‡ Principal export rate (principal import rate 1959 was 45·000–67·500; other import rates 90·000–135·000).

The piastre of Southern Vietnam and the kip of Laos each has the same nominal value as the riel of Cambodia.

Source: Based mainly on *United Nations' Statistical Yearbook, 1961*, Tables 163 and 165

Moreover, although in times of prosperity both labourers and small-holder producers of cash crops were sure of at least a survival income, such prosperity was nevertheless precarious and unpredictable. For the economic well-being of all the South-east Asian countries depended almost exclusively on the export of primary produce, the demand for which was apt to fluctuate wildly in response to circumstances entirely beyond the power of the producers to control. While this pattern of primary production was in large measure rooted in the facts of geography, and in particular in the general shortage of nearly all the physical

TABLE 12

ESTIMATED FOREIGN INVESTMENTS IN SOUTH-EAST ASIA BEFORE THE SECOND WORLD WAR

Figures in million U.S. $

(*A*) *Western and Japanese Investments*

Country	*Year*	*Entre-preneur invest-ments*	*Rentier invest-ments*	*Total*	*Of which*
Netherlands Indies	1937	1,411	853	2,264	Dutch 1,040 British 200 U.S. 95 French 35 Japanese 12 German 10 Italian 10
British Malaya .	1937	372	83	455	British 320 Also much U.S., Dutch, French & Japanese.
Thailand . .	1938	90	34	124	British and Australian 90–100 Also Danish, U.S., Swiss & Japanese.
Philippines . .	1935	315	61	376	Entrepreneur only: U.S. 163 Spanish 90 British 35 Japanese 27
Burma . .	1939	225	8	233	British 200+
Indochina .	1938	302	82	384	French 370+

(*B*) *Chinese Business Investments in late* 1930*s*.

Netherlands Indies . . .	150	Philippines	100
British Malaya . . .	200	Indochina	80
Thailand	90	Burma	10–15*

* Note that in Burma, Indian investments were of the order of 250.

Source: Based mainly on Callis.

resources necessary for the establishment of heavy industry, it is also clear that the colonial powers were extremely slow to foster the development of textile and other consumer goods industries for which the long-term prospects were by no means so unfavourable.

The lack of balance which characterized the economic structure of the South-east Asian dependencies was equally typical of their economic geography. Since virtually any form of economic development within the region involved heavy capital outlay on jungle clearing, road, railway and harbour construction, and often on malaria- and pest-control, it normally paid to concentrate such exploitation within as small an area as possible, instead of attempting to spread it more or less evenly over the area as a whole. Thus, not only are nearly all the estates and many of the mines, for obvious reasons, within 75 miles of tide-water, but even within that relatively narrow zone much the greater part of the export economy is concentrated in a few compact localities, notably in Java, north-eastern Sumatra, western Malaya and the deltas of the Irrawaddy, Menam and Mekong.

In all of these intensively developed patches, export production is highly organized and the whole way of life intimately geared with the machinery of world trade. But over the rest and by far the greater part of the region, subsistence agriculture and traditional ways of life have survived with altogether less modification.

The resultant contrast between a few areas, some of which may in the long run prove to have been over-exploited agriculturally, and a generally under-developed periphery, is inevitably reflected in stark contrasts in population density and in degrees of economic and political maturity which present serious obstacles to healthy social evolution within every one of the South-east Asian lands. And when to these are added the related but nevertheless distinct cleavages between alien and indigene, and between town and countryside, it is clear that the human legacy of individual and largely uncoordinated ventures in economic development by outside enterprise leaves much to be desired from the point of view of the local population.

In the final analysis it was the conviction that local interests were rarely considered, except as incidentals to the satisfaction of Western wishes, which caused the deepest resentment on the part of the South-east Asian peoples, and these feelings were too profound to be eradicated by the various reforms introduced during the final stages of the colonial period.

While most Westerners find no difficulty in understanding the bitterness occasioned by the humiliations and not infrequent brutality of the earlier phases of their rule, the almost equally complete rejection of the paternalistic policies of more recent times has come as a shock to many Europeans, whose natural reaction is all too often to chide their former wards for base ingratitude. Yet whether in pursuing the goal of cultural assimilation in Indochina, or seeking to preserve the traditional societies virtually intact, as in much of Indonesia and the protected states of Malaya, the Western powers were bound in the end to be disappointed. For the fact remains that the local peoples wanted to become neither synthetic Europeans nor moribund museum pieces, but only – and most understandably – to advance in their own way and to make their own response in their own good time to the new ideas and opportunities which, willy-nilly, were being thrust upon them.

That is not to deny that economic motives were present, even though these operated differently at different levels within the community. Thus the nationalist leadership came almost entirely from the educated few who were rarely impecunious, and even though their desire to step into the place of the Western ruling class may in some cases have been motivated by personal ambition, it also rested on a genuine belief that the spiritual as well as the economic well-being of their countrymen would be furthered by such a change. Among the mass of the population, on the other hand, willingness to follow this lead was sometimes based on resentment against poverty, though outside the towns the sense of being treated as social inferiors was probably more important.

Unfortunately, the European authorities, partly from an obvious self-interest in preserving the *status quo*, but partly also out of a sincere concern for the well-being of their South-east Asian subjects, too often sought to postpone any major political change to an indefinite future when the colonies should in some unspecified way have proved their fitness for self-government. Yet, misguided though much of this paternalism may have been, it was by no means as uniformly dishonourable as is often assumed. For while the great majority of European officials had a real affection for the extremely likable people among whom they spent their working lives, they also had abundant experience of the extent to which the latter in their naïveté needed protection, for example, against exploitation by Indian or Chinese money-lenders and middlemen, many of whom were only too ready to batten on the unsuspecting villagers whenever opportunity afforded. Nor was such exploitation limited to the remote countryside, as the grip of the aliens on almost every form of non-agricultural activity makes clear, and even today it is still an open question whether the indigenous peoples have acquired a sufficient degree of worldly wisdom to be a match for the foreign Asians within their midst.

Nevertheless, the desire for independence grew. And although it must be regarded as a spontaneous reaction in almost every part of the region, it undoubtedly owed much to outside example. Thus, for instance, both Indonesian and Burmese leaders in large measure sought to emulate the more mature and better organized *swaraj* movement in India, while the Annamite nationalists took their cue first from the Kuo Min Tang and later from the Communists in China next door. But perhaps more important than either of these was the inspiration derived from Japan, for it was the latter's victory over a great Western power in the Russo-Japanese War of 1904–5 which first really convinced the prophets of nationalism in all parts of Asia that their cause was not an idle dream.

Thus from 1905 onwards Japan came to be regarded in a special sense as the champion of Asia as a whole *vis-à-vis* the West, and it is interesting to note that the first suggestion for a Monroe Doctrine for the Far East came from a Burmese newspaper in that year, in an editorial suggesting that the dependent lands of

Asia would welcome Japanese initiative in curbing Western colonialism and ultimately expelling it from the Orient.[67]

VII. SOUTH-EAST ASIA UNDER JAPANESE RULE

These sentiments were fully reciprocated by the Japanese, though ultimately this was to lead to a form of intervention very different from that originally envisaged in South-east Asia.

By comparison with India and China, Japan had few historic links with South-east Asia though, as noted in Chapter 4, a beginning had been made in respect of trade and settlement before the Tokugawa Seclusion put an end to such activities for over two hundred years. With the reopening and subsequent modernization of Japan after 1853, this interest in South-east Asia revived, and although the United States' acquisition of the Philippines imposed an unexpected obstacle to Japan's aspirations, the latter continued to increase and, in the view of the military expansionists who dominated the political scene after 1931, 'the inevitability of Nippon's southward expansion always remained'.[68]

To the Japanese, South-east Asia appeared as that part of the tropical zone in whose trade they had the most obvious right to share. One of their most strongly reiterated propaganda themes in the 1930s and 40s concerned the supposed complementariness of the temperate and tropical lands. Thus, so the argument ran, just as the United States had traditionally concentrated its attention in this respect mainly on the Caribbean and Latin-American tropics, so Europe should limit its activities to Africa, the part of the tropical zone nearest to it, and leave South-east Asia to Japan.

This of course fitted in excellently with Japan's demand for a 'Monroe Doctrine for East Asia', which in the late 1930s gave place to the more grandiose plan for establishing the so-called 'Greater East Asia Co-prosperity Sphere'. In this sphere, alongside Japan itself, which was to serve as the managerial and industrial nucleus, and the nearby 'continental arsenal' of Manchukuo and northern China, South-east Asia had a vital part to play as the 'Southern Resources Area', which would provide both materials and markets for the metropolitan country and also absorb much of the latter's superfluous population.

Long before the outbreak of the Pacific War the Japanese expansionists had begun to prepare their drive to the south, and, faithful to the doctrines of Clausewitz, they drew no sharp distinction between economic, political and military means of penetration. Thus, besides the psychological success of their slogan 'Asia for the Asiatics',[69] their ability to supply the sort of consumer goods which the local population wanted, at prices far below those of the corresponding European articles, created an extremely favourable impression, as also did the

[67] Stoddard, p. 23.
[68] *Sakura*, Vol. 5, No. 2 (undated), p. 11. See also Fisher (F), p. 18.
[69] 'Asiatics' is now non-U in Asia, but the term 'Asians' had not been invented at this time.

willingness of Japanese firms to train and employ indigenes as assistants in their various South-east Asian branches.[70] Moreover, while in Western eyes Japanese aggression in Manchukuo in 1931 and in the rest of China after 1937 exposed the hollowness of their claims, these acts did little damage to their reputation in South-east Asia owing to the widespread popular hostility there towards the local Chinese.

Yet, although the Japanese had good reason to expect a friendly reception from the local populace in most parts of South-east Asia, their military preparations were far from complete when the early successes of the German armies in the Second World War presented them with an opportunity which seemed unlikely ever to occur again. In the event, the temptation proved irresistible, and after the collapse of France had opened the way for the Japanese occupation of French Indochina in 1941, the defensive strategy of the Western powers in South-east Asia was fatally undermined.

In so far as the strategy of the A.B.C.D.[71] powers had been co-ordinated at all, it was based upon the primary concentration of defensive power in Singapore and the Philippines. While this pattern reflected the rôles of these two areas in the Commonwealth defence system of the British and the Pacific Ocean strategy of the United States respectively, it also implicitly recognized that South-east Asia was a unit which would inevitably stand or fall together. For any power striking southwards through the region must have the strength to advance simultaneously along both the Indo-Pacific peninsula and the Philippine islands, since it would otherwise expose an extended flank to lateral attack from the Indian or the Pacific Ocean theatre. Somewhat to the surprise of the West, the Japanese did possess sufficient strength to carry out such a vast two-pronged attack, and in the absence of adequate Allied forces to hold it, the whole effective territory of South-east Asia passed into Japanese hands in a matter of months.

The material devastation which resulted from the Japanese invasion, the long years of occupation and the eventual successful counter-offensive of the Allies was prodigious, and even today rehabilitation is by no means complete in many parts of the region. Nevertheless, the psychological and political consequences were of far greater significance, and to future generations Japan's drive into South-east Asia may well rank as one of the great turning points in human history.

In the early stages of the war, the Japanese were widely welcomed as liberators from Western oppression, and many of the leading nationalist politicians openly collaborated with them[72] during part or the whole of the occupation. Yet although in due course Burma, the Philippines, Indonesia and Indochina were all granted

[70] This was one of the few ways in which the young indigenes could get commercial training in view of the preference alike of Europeans, Chinese and Indians for their own kind and their low opinion of the commercial aptitudes of the indigenes.

[71] *I.e.* Americans, British, Chinese and Dutch.

[72] The Japanese began by releasing nationalist internees, of whom there were a particularly large number in the Netherlands Indies. See Fisher (B), p. 301. Even so, by no means all such nationalists co-operated with the Japanese after their release.

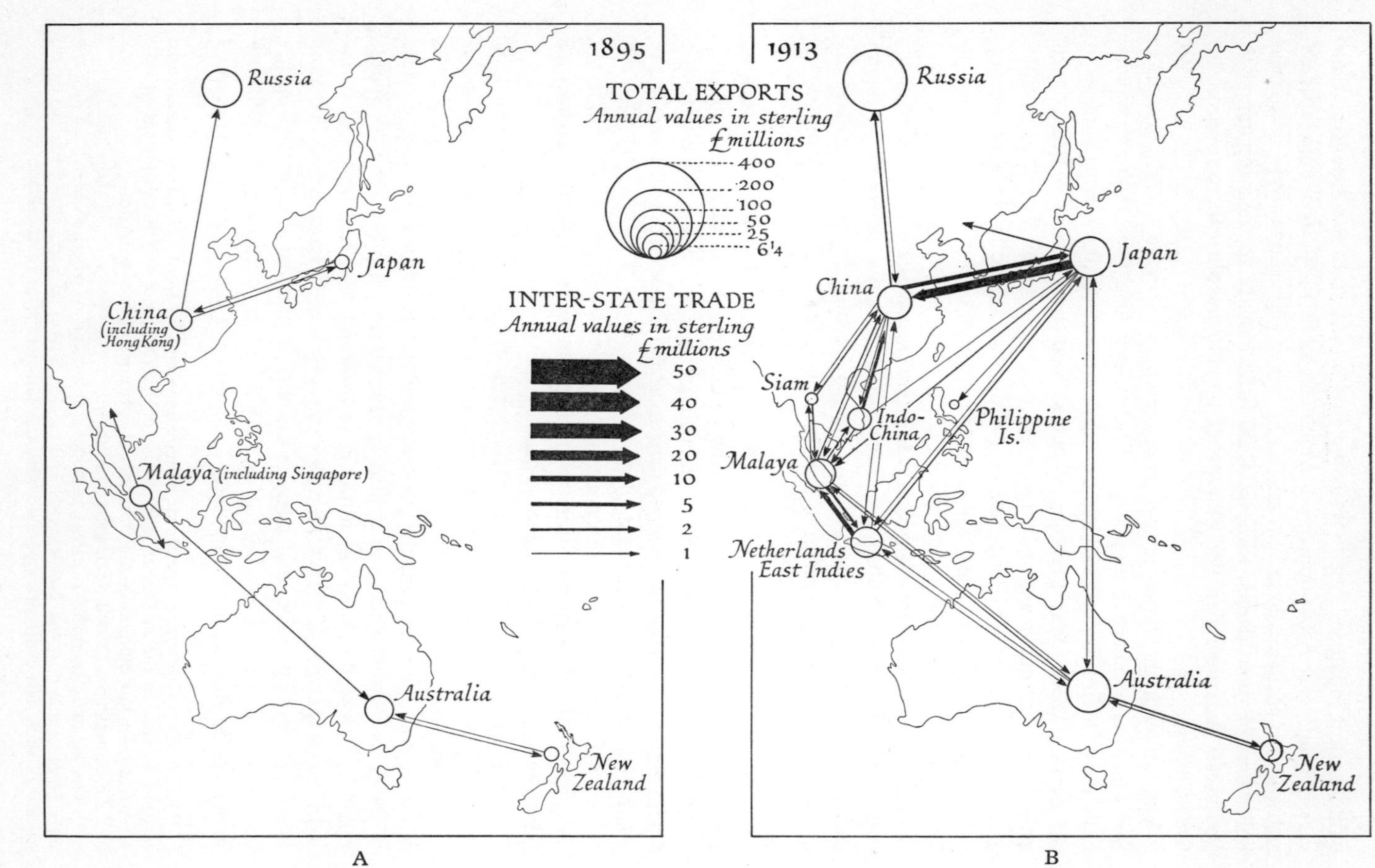
1895
Russia
Japan
China
(including Hong Kong)
Malaya (including Singapore)
Australia
New Zealand
A
1913
TOTAL EXPORTS
Annual values in sterling
£ millions
400
200
100
50
25
6¼
INTER-STATE TRADE
Annual values in sterling
£ millions
50
40
30
20
10
5
2
1
Russia
Japan
China
Siam
Indo-China
Philippine Is.
Malaya
Netherlands East Indies
Australia
New Zealand
B

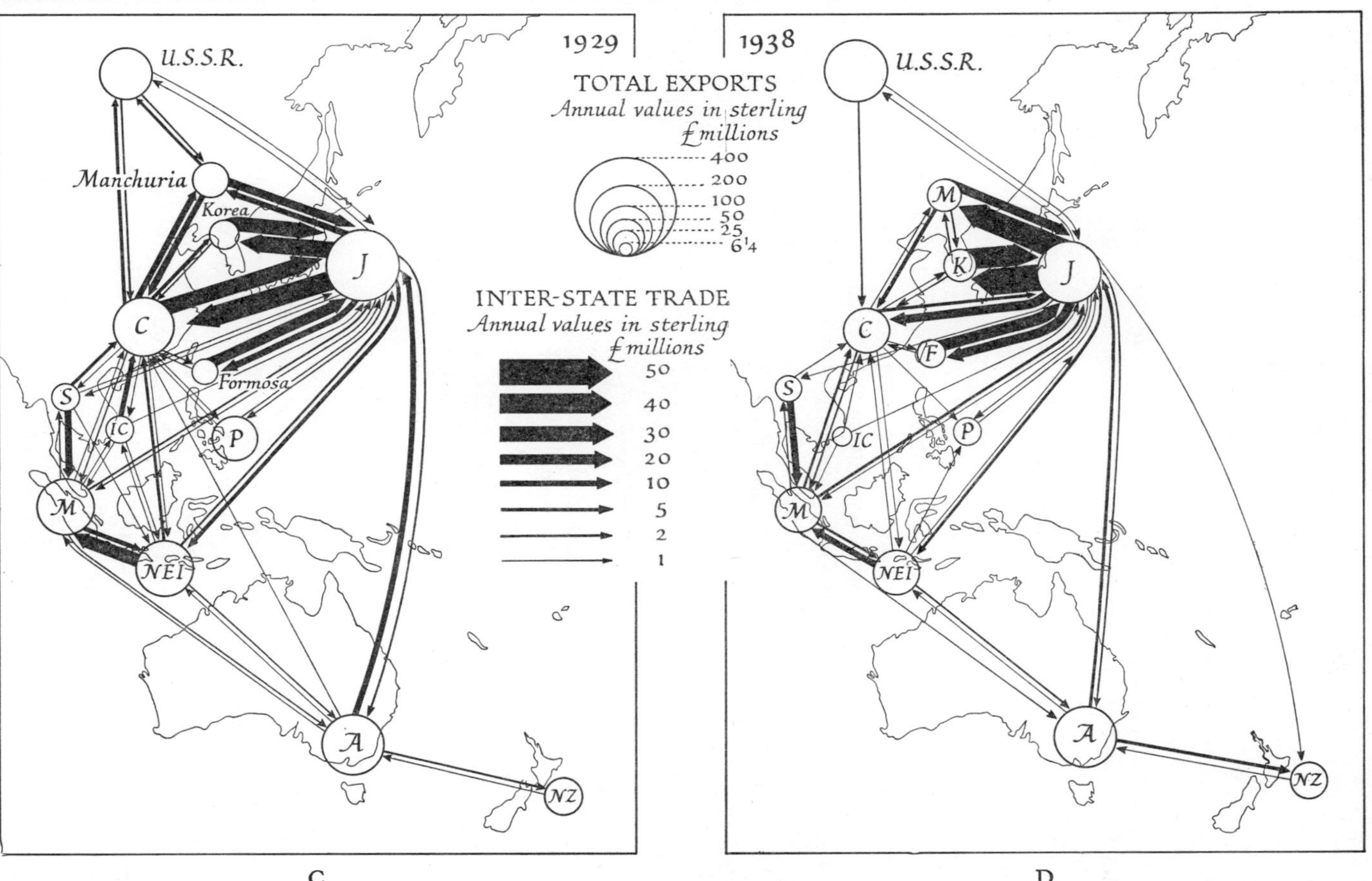

C

D

Fig. 24—Growth of Japanese trade in Eastern Asia: A. 1895; B. 1913; C. 1929; D. 1938

or promised 'independence within the Co-prosperity Sphere', experience of Japanese rule inevitably brought disenchantment. In brutality and high-handedness Japanese behaviour far exceeded anything that could be remembered against the West, and in particular the appalling losses of life among forced-labour gangs left a widespread sense of bitterness which has since constituted a serious obstacle to the resumption of normal Japanese commercial relations in many parts of the region. Before the end of the war many nationalists, notably the A.F.P.F.L. in Burma,[73] had changed sides and many more had lost all faith in their former heroes.

This disillusionment, however, did not mean that the old colonial regimes were wanted back, or that the subsequent armed opposition to their return was merely, as the Dutch claimed, the result of a 'time-bomb left by the Japanese'. On the contrary, nationalism had been matured in the forcing house of the occupation, and for better or worse had now become the driving sentiment throughout all the more advanced parts of the region. This fact was fairly quickly sensed by the Americans and the British, but only tardily recognized by the Dutch and French governments. Nevertheless, once India, Pakistan, Ceylon, Burma and the Philippines had been granted their independence, colonialism had no hope of survival in the lands in between, and in the years which followed they also obtained their freedom.

VIII. THE PROBLEMS FACING THE NEWLY INDEPENDENT STATES

In spite of many local differences in the political and economic situations in different parts of the region, the new nationalist governments which today control most of South-east Asia are all faced with essentially similar problems. By its very nature South-east Asian nationalism is opposed to Western rule, and deep and exaggerated suspicions often remain regarding Western intentions. Moreover, the nationalists are understandably resentful of the wealth and power already acquired by alien and indigenous minority groups, whether Chinese or Indian, within their midst.

In these circumstances the temptation to continue the struggle against such Western influence as still survives in European plantations, mines and business concerns is strong, as also is the urge severely to restrict the share, both economic and professional, which the alien minorities are to have in the national life.

Yet to pursue either of these courses is to court even greater dangers. For while there are certainly some nationalists in South-east Asia who, like Gandhi, desire above all else to revive a more simple and supposedly more Asian way of life, a growing number would undoubtedly prefer to see a speedy improvement in material standards, to be obtained by means of industrialization, modernization of agriculture and the application of Western science in all appropriate fields.

[73] *I.e.* Anti-Fascist Peoples Freedom League. See below, pp. 447–8.

But if these desirable economic goals are to be achieved by the new states within any foreseeable future, three conditions at least will need to be satisfied. First, the maximum possible use will have to be made of the existing very limited reserves of skilled and experienced personnel, regardless of the fact that a high proportion of these are not indigenes.[74] Secondly, it will be necessary both to attract more outside investments, which will involve granting reasonably favourable treatment to the foreign capital already there, and also for many years to come to earn as much foreign exchange as possible by the export of primary produce, even though in the long run it may be wise to reduce the present excessive dependence on such unstable sources of income.

Thirdly, the countries of South-east Asia will need to cut their coats according to their cloth, and resist the temptation to indulge in an orgy of factory building merely in order to remove the stigma supposedly implied by the term 'underdeveloped'. For so long as the pattern of world economy remains tied to the established forms of energy, South-east Asia must be regarded as among the less suitable areas geographically for major industrial development, though there are few technical obstacles to the introduction of more electrical or oil-powered machinery. Moreover, now that India and China, to say nothing of Japan and the Western powers, are already much farther advanced along the technological road, the South-east Asian countries, with their small internal markets, cannot hope to compete in any but the simpler and cheaper forms of manufacturing, except at excessive cost to themselves in protective tariffs. In short, both geography and history combine to make primary production the most profitable export line for South-east Asia, and its peoples will have to realize, as nations like Denmark and New Zealand have already learned, that such a state of affairs is not necessarily incompatible with a reasonable standard of living.

Nevertheless, none of these conditions, all of which appear to smack of continued 'colonialism' in one form or another, will prove palatable to the local population. But however much the era of Western rule may be resented, the economic and social conditions which it has left provide the only realistic basis on which to start building now, even if the new architects aspire to erect structures of a very different kind in the years that lie ahead.

Much the same considerations apply also in the political field where again certain fundamental problems are common to the region as a whole. Thus, for example, each of the new states is confronted with the task of welding an indigenous majority group[75] and various minority communities, indigenous as well as exotic, into a single self-conscious nation. However, while this three-fold ethnic division occurs in all the South-east Asian states, the groups concerned are found in different proportions, and in varying degrees of mutual rivalry, in each individual state, and the situation is further complicated by the great geo-

[74] Non-indigenes include principally Chinese, Indians and Eurasians.

[75] Malaya presents an exception in this respect since the Malays do not form an absolute majority there.

graphical contrasts between the compact riverine states of the mainland and the scattered insular territories of the Indonesian and Philippine archipelagos.

Moreover, there are deep-seated linguistic and historic affiliations which run counter to the contemporary political divisions inherited from the era of Western rule, and it remains to be seen whether the several successor states have retained or will develop sufficiently powerful *raisons d'être*[76] to enable them to survive within their present boundaries, or whether, as has already happened in Indo-china, the age-old tendency to political fragmentation will gradually reassert itself now that the West has relinquished control.

TABLE 13

OVERSEAS TRADE OF SOUTH-EAST ASIAN COUNTRIES, 1938, 1955 and 1960

All figures in million U.S. $

Country	*Imports c.i.f.*			*Exports f.o.b.*		
	1938	1955	1960	1938	1955	1960
Burma	77·7	179·9	260	178·3	225·4	226
Thailand	56·9	297·6	453	88·6	360·8	410
French Indochina*	56·8			82·9		
Laos		18·9	12		1·4	1
Cambodia		44·0	95		33·9	70
Southern Vietnam		263·2	240		69·0	86
British Malaya†	314·9	1,248·5		334·2	1,357·7	
Federation of Malaya			703			956
Singapore			1,332			1,136
Brunei	1·6	30·5	22	3·8	99·1	88
North Borneo	3·6	28·6	64	14·0	34·3	73
Sarawak	12·8	144·3	138	14·3	156·0	159
Indonesia	247·9	604·2	574	379·5	931·4	840
Philippines‡	132·1	536·2	604	116·1	416·6	560

* French Indochina figures for 1938 do not include trade between the three territories which are listed separately for 1955 and 1960, or between these and Northern Vietnam.

† British Malaya figures for 1938 and 1955 do not include trade between the two territories which are listed separately for 1960.

‡ Philippines imports are f.o.b.

Source: *United Nations Statistical Yearbooks, 1957 and 1961.*

[76] See Hartshorne, p. 110.

In this sense, therefore, South-east Asia provides a fascinating politico-geographical laboratory, and the success or failure of the series of experiments in state-building which are now in progress there will be of lasting significance, not only to the local inhabitants themselves, but also to millions of interested spectators in many other parts of the world.

SELECT BIBLIOGRAPHY

Allen and Donnithorne
Bowen
Buss (C)
Broek (D) (F) (H)
Callis
Carr-Saunders
Clark, C.
Clark, W. D.
Crawfurd (A) (B) (C)
Davis
Del Tufo
Dobby (H)
Du Bois
Emerson, Mills and Thompson
Field
Fisher (F) (G) (N) (T)
Furnivall (A)
Ginsburg (A)
Greene and Phillips
Ishii
Jacoby
Jarrett
Kondapi
Mills *et al.*
Mountjoy
Murphey (B)
Murray
Naunton
Pelzer (A) (B) (C) (G) (H) (K)
Purcell (D)
Robequain (D)
Roberts, G. (B)
Rowe
Schrieke
Sokol (A)
Spate (B) (C)
Stoddard
Thompson, W. S. (A) (B)
Unger
Vaile
Vandenbosch and Butwell
Van Mook (A) (B)
Vlieland (A)
Wertheim (C)
Wickizer and Bennett
Wint (C)
Zelinsky
Zinkin (A)

'The rubber industry', *Manchester Guardian*, January 15, 1957
Proceedings of the Fourth Pacific Science Congress, Java, 1929, Vol. IV
Volkstelling 1930 (Census of Netherlands India)
Indo-China (N.I.D.)
Netherlands East Indies, II (N.I.D.)

Two excellent short introductions to the problems of South-east Asia on the eve of independence are Broek (D) and Furnivall (B). Robequain (D), Parts III and IV, deals at greater length with many related topics, and I have also made extensive use of some of my own earlier work, Fisher (F) (G) and (N) in this connexion.

On general economic topics Rowe, and Allen and Donnithorne are indispensable, while on specifically agricultural problems three contributions by Pelzer (G) (H) (K) are outstanding, and may be supplemented by the two papers by Mountjoy and Jarrett respectively.

As regards population studies also, Pelzer has made several major contributions, notably (A) (B) (C), to which should be added the more general works by Thompson, W. S., and the important paper by Zelinsky. The standard work on the Chinese in South-east Asia is the monumental study by Purcell (D), and the earlier paper by Unger is also useful. Kondapi may be consulted on Indian migration, and Thompson and Adloff on minority problems in general. On urbanization three excellent papers are those respectively by Fryer (H), Ginsburg (A) and Murphey (B).

The book by Du Bois is a seminal work on social change, while the three studies, respectively by Emerson, Mills and Thompson, by Mills and associates, and by Vandenbosch and Butwell, deal with nationalism and governmental problems from the standpoint of the political scientist.

Addendum: See also *Future population estimates by sex and age, Report III The Population of Southeast Asia* (*including Ceylon and China: Taiwan*) 1950–1980 (United Nations).

PART II

The Equatorial Archipelago: Indonesia

CHAPTER 7

Indonesia: Generalities and Physique

I. INTRODUCTORY

The Indies-born writer Multatuli[1] was perhaps guilty of a certain poetic exaggeration in respect of both the size and the richness of his homeland when he described it as 'the magnificent empire of Insulinde encircling the equator like a girdle of emeralds'. Nevertheless, its extent is indeed great and if, as must be conceded, the living standards of a majority of its peoples are among the lowest in Asia, the fundamental cause is to be found not in any intrinsic lack of resources but rather in an excessive concentration of population in certain areas of exceptionally fertile soils.

Both in the extent of its surface, 575,852 square miles,[2] and in the size of its population, approximately 91,700,000 in 1959, Indonesia accounts for nearly half of the sub-continental total and, although such peripheral parts of the Malaysian realm as the the Philippines, Portuguese Timor, British Borneo and Malaya are politically distinct from it, the country nevertheless embraces at least four-fifths of the archipelago, and includes what historically have been its two principal cultural foci, respectively in Java and Sumatra.

Thanks to the early attraction exerted by the spice trade of the Moluccas and the more varied agricultural potentialities of Java, European influence has been of much longer duration in Indonesia than in most other parts of South-east Asia, and in this respect a more fitting comparison is to be found with the Indian sub-continent. Moreover, the former British India and the Netherlands Indies, each with a population roughly seven times as large as those of the respective metropolitan powers, were by far the most important components in the dependent empires of Britain and Holland, and both in the economic benefits which the two European powers derived from these relationships and in the degree to which the outlook and institutions of the former have consciously or uncons-

[1] Pseudonym of E. Douwes Dekker. See below, p. 385 and van Helsdingen, p. 1.

[2] This figure excludes West New Guinea whose status prior to 1962-3 was disputed by the Netherlands and Indonesia. In this and the four succeeding chapters West New Guinea is treated as part of the archipelago wherever it seems appropriate to do so; the question of its status and development is more fully considered in Chapter 12. The area of West New Guinea is 160,617 square miles, and if this is included the total area of Indonesia is 736,469 square miles. On the other hand, West New Guinea contains only approximately 700,000 people, which makes an insignificant addition to the Indonesian total. See Fig. 25.

ciously been inherited by the newly independent successor states in Asia today, the parallel between India and Indonesia is remarkably close.

Yet despite this similarity Indonesia belongs ethnically, and culturally, as well as geographically, not to South but to South-east Asia, and many of the most pressing problems which it faces today, arising as they do out of the character of its indigenous peoples and the disproportionate influence of the more go-ahead aliens in their midst, have more in common with those of its lesser neighbours, Burma, Indochina, Malaya and the Philippines, than with the South Asian Commonwealth Republics of India and Pakistan. For this reason, and also because of its primacy in area and population, its success or failure in coming to grips with these problems will have profound consequences for the whole of the region of which it forms part.

As befits its great extent and the complexity of its outlines, Indonesia is a land of wide diversity and striking contrasts. Nowhere else in the world has civilization flourished at so high a level so near to the equator as in Sri Vijaya and Madjapahit,[3] yet still today primitive forms of shifting cultivation are widely practised in Sumatra and even in some isolated parts of Java, while at the opposite extremity of the archipelago the majority of the inhabitants of New Guinea have not advanced beyone the stone age. Intimately related to these sharp cultural contrasts are the astonishing differences in population density between Java and Madura, with 1,168 persons to the square mile, and the remainder of the archipelago[4] for which the average figure is only 62 to the square mile, though this in turn covers a wide range from *c.* 750 in Bali, 93 in Celebes and 80 in Sumatra to a mere 18 in Indonesian Borneo and 6 in West New Guinea.

Put in another way these facts are even more remarkable for, if Bali and Lombok are grouped together with Java, something like 70 per cent of the total population are seen to be living in less than 9 per cent of the country's total land area, or in less than 7 per cent if West New Guinea is counted in. Even by South-east Asian standards this is an exceptional figure, and suggests a serious unbalance between a congested nuclear region and an under-developed periphery. This indeed constitutes one of the most difficult problems facing Indonesia today, and in its turn it serves to aggravate the manifold local rivalries which are almost inevitable in so large and dispersed a territory. To what extent these numerous and in many cases striking differences between the several parts of Indonesia are a reflection of geographical conditions is a matter on which opinions differ, but clearly both the relative positions and the physical characteristics of the component islands must be taken into account in any attempt at appraising the situation.

[3] The reference here is to pre-colonial times. See pp. 307–8 for comments on the Dutch achievements in the Indies compared with those of the Portuguese and their descendants in Brazil.

[4] The areas outside Java and Madura may collectively be referred to as the 'outer islands' or 'outer territories' (Dutch *Buitengewesten*) though these terms have no political or administrative significance. The figures quoted here are estimates for 1959.

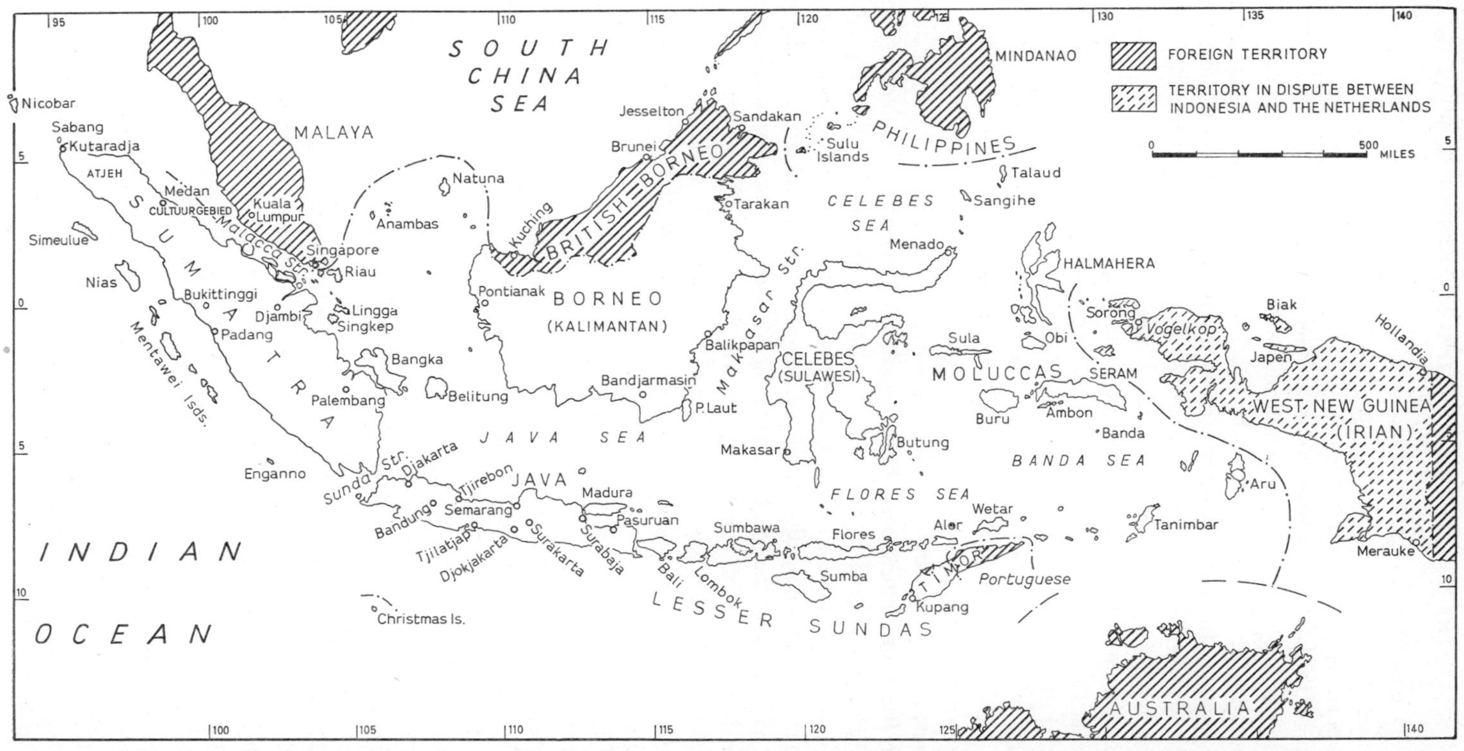

FIG. 25—Indonesia: orientation map. Note: West New Guinea came under Indonesian sovereignty on 1st May, 1963.

In its geographical position Indonesia undoubtedly enjoys many potential advantages, though these do not apply by any means uniformly to the country as a whole. As was implied in Chapter 3, Indonesia represents the discontinuous portion of the land bridge between continental Asia and Australia, and the major gaps in this line – the Malacca, Sunda and Makasar Straits and the South China Sea – form the natural sea routes between India and China. Thus, in general, those parts of Indonesia lying closest to the South-east Asian mainland, and especially those fringing one or other of the main seaways, have received the strongest and most frequent cultural stimuli from outside, and have benefited commercially from their proximity to the great inter-oceanic trade routes. Conversely, whatever their intrinsic character, the remoter islands of the east have all tended to suffer from the drawbacks of isolation, a situation that is seen in its most extreme form in New Guinea which, at least until the time of the Second World War, seems always to have constituted the dead end of the archipelago.

In respect of the country's internal geography, generalization is much more difficult, though, as Vandenbosch has pointed out, Indonesia is doubly distinctive as the most important equatorial country and the largest insular territory in the world.[5] The outer limits of the archipelago are separated by over 2,500 miles from east to west and 1,250 from north to south so that, superimposed on more familiar western maps, the outlines of Indonesia would stretch from the west coast of Ireland to the south shore of the Caspian or from Portland (Oregon) to the Bermudas. And even though nearly four-fifths of the intervening area is covered by sea, the total land surface of Indonesia, now that it includes West New Guinea, is nevertheless sufficient to make it the tenth largest political unit in the world today.[6]

All-told the country includes some 3,000 islands,[7] and these exhibit the widest variations in both size and character. Thus, at the one extreme New Guinea (303,092 square miles) and Borneo (283,404 square miles) are accounted the world's second and third largest islands respectively, though Indonesia embraces only about two thirds (208,298 square miles) of Borneo and is to have only just over half of New Guinea. Of the remaining islands, all of them except Timor wholly under Indonesian rule,[8] Sumatra (164,129 square miles) is approximately equal in size to Sweden, Celebes (72,890 square miles) is nearly as large as Great Britain, and Java (51,039 square miles)[9] slightly exceeds the area of England alone. Compared with these five, the other islands are all very much smaller, but there is nevertheless a wide range between, for example, Timor, which is roughly the size of Ireland, and the hundreds of minute islets which stud the Banda Sea.

These islands can be grouped in various ways. According to the popular

[5] Vandenbosch, p. 1.

[6] In number of inhabitants it is now the fifth largest state in the world.

[7] Though not all of these are inhabited.

[8] The eastern part of Timor remains Portuguese territory. See below, p. 404.

[9] These figures include the lesser adjacent islands in each case.

topographical terminology of the Dutch[10] the archipelago was sub-divided into four main components. Thus, apart from New Guinea which constituted a unit in itself, the four largest islands, Borneo, Sumatra, Celebes and Java, were known as the Greater Sundas, in contradistinction to the Lesser Sundas, which extended from Bali to Timor inclusive, and the Moluccas, a name originally applied to the five small volcanic islands of Tidore, Ternate, Motir, Makian and Batjan, together with their immediate dependencies, but later extended to ambrace all the islands between West New Guinea, the eastern Lesser Sundas end Celebes.

TABLE 14

INDONESIA: MAIN TOPOGRAPHICAL DIVISIONS

English name	*Dutch name*	*Indonesian name*
Greater Sundas	Groote Soenda-eilanden	Sunda Raja
Java	Java	Djawa
Sumatra	Sumatra	Sumatera
Borneo	Borneo	Kalimantan
Celebes	Celebes	Sulawesi
Lesser Sundas	Kleine Soenda-eilanden	Sunda Ketjil or Nusa Tenggara
Moluccas	Molukken	Maluku
West New Guinea	West Nieuw-Guinea	Irian Barat (popularly Irian)

Despite various changes in names, for the most part reversions to older indigenous usages, the Indonesians still retain this four-fold Dutch topographical division in everyday speech, though in certain respects it seriously confuses the more fundamental geographical realities. Thus, for example, Celebes, which lies to the east of Wallace's line, has no direct affinities with the Sunda shelf and in consequence differs profoundly from the other three Greater Sundas, while conversely the two westernmost of the Lesser Sundas, particularly Bali, have more in common geographically with Java than they have with the rest of the series to the east.

As was explained in Chapter 2, the Indonesian archipelago embraces parts of both the Sunda and Sahul shelves, together with the extensive series of Tertiary/Quaternary island arcs which have developed in the adjacent portions of the Tethys and Circum-Pacific geosynclines. Within the country as a whole three main

[10] This terminology should not be confused with that of the administrative divisions. See below, Chapters 9 and 11.

morphological divisions may be recognized. The first of these comprises the large western islands, Sumatra, Borneo and Java, along with the numerous lesser groups between, such as the Riau and Lingga archipelagos and the tin islands of Bangka, Belitung and Singkep, all of which are linked together by the Sunda shelf. Admittedly this province includes portions of the older Indo-Malayan core, alike in south-western Borneo, eastern Sumatra, northern Java and in the lesser islands which represent a former southward continuation of the coulisses of the Malay peninsula,[11] as well as the more recent Tertiary and Quaternary structures which predominate in most parts of Sumatra and Java, and in northern and eastern Borneo. But an important element of unity derives from the extent of the alluvial plains which in all cases[12] fringe the shallow seas of the Sunda shelf, and provide a major contrast between the western islands and those which lie between Wallace's and Weber's lines.[13]

The second division, consisting of New Guinea and the adjacent Aru and other islands of the Arafura Sea, is in many respects analogous to the one just described. Thus here again we are dealing with an ancient stable surface (Sahul land), along whose northern edge extensive Tertiary folding has taken place so that the resultant relief today presents a somewhat similar contrast between the young and lofty mountains of the interior and the wide alluvial plains fringing a shallow sea.

The unstable area between these two constitutes the third and structurally the most confused of the major morphological regions of the Indonesian archipelago. Here the structural axes of all the main islands correspond to one or other of the two lines of Tertiary folding already apparent farther west, *i.e.* the outer and earlier line running through the Nias, Mentawei and Enggano islands south-west of Sumatra, and continuing via the submarine ridge south of Java into Sumba, Timor, Tanimbar (Timor Laut), Kai, Seram and Buru, and the inner volcanic line which runs from end to end of Sumatra and Java and can thereafter be traced through Bali, Lombok, Sumbawa, Flores, Alor and Wetar to the arc of lesser islets, of which Damar and Banda are the best known. But, whereas in Java and Sumatra the Tertiary structures are, as it were, welded on to the outer edge of the older massif of Sunda-land, here the several islands appear as a series of isolated and much smaller fragments of dry land which have only recently emerged above the surface of the deep seas of the geosyncline.

While no direct connexion can be traced between either of these lines and the roughly contemporaneous folding in northern and eastern Borneo and in central and northern New Guinea, it seems probable[14] that both continue into Celebes, with the outer series forming the axes of the south-eastern and eastern limbs,

[11] See Fig. 3, p. 13.

[12] Even the small islands of the Sunda shelf, such as Bangka, Belitung, Singkep, Natuna, etc., have a much higher proportion of plain than have the small islands of the eastern archipelago.

[13] *I.e.* the modified lines. See above, Fig. 8, p. 44.

[14] Though this is disputed by some geologists.

and the inner series correspondingly running through the south-western (Makasar) and north-eastern (Minahasa) peninsulas.

Certainly it is only in the last two parts of Celebes that evidence of current or recent volcanic activity exists, and this is in accordance with conditions elsewhere in the archipelago, where continuing or recently dormant vulcanism is found only along the inner line. Even so, the portion of the archipelago whose soils have been affected by such activity is considerable, including as it does much of Sumatra and extensive parts of Java, many of the Lesser Sundas, Moluccas and the aforementioned parts of Celebes.[15] As noted on p. 53 this does not necessarily imply that the material in question is everywhere of high fertility, for the original chemical composition of the ejecta, the length of time since eruption, and the extent to which the various soil-forming processes have been able to operate are all significant variables. But where, as in much of Java and in a few scattered localities in the outer islands, there has been continuing eruption of intermediate or basic lava or ash, which has subsequently been broken down and redistributed by river and wind action, the soils exhibit a level of fertility which is without parallel in equatorial lands elsewhere.

The term equatorial, however, calls for some qualification so far as climate is concerned, for with a latitudinal range from 6° N to 11° S Indonesia extends beyond the limits normally accepted under this heading.[16] Admittedly it would be pure pedantry to exclude either the northern tip of Atjeh (6° N) or for that matter west-central Java (6° – 8° S) from the equatorial zone and in fact, as the figures for Djakarta and Bandung[17] show, temperatures in the latter area are remarkably constant throughout the year, thanks in the main to the equalizing influence of the surrounding seas. But eastwards of this limit the line of island arcs extends progressively farther south, and this fact, aggravated by increasing nearness to the sub-arid and desert zone of Australia, has given rise to a tropical rather than an equatorial climatic regime in the part of Indonesia which lies to the south and east of the Rembang plateau of Java.

This indeed is the only extensive regional variation,[18] other than the altitudinal, in the climate of Indonesia which is sufficiently pronounced to give rise to a major difference in vegetation type from the tropical rain forest which prevails elsewhere. And in this context the presence of extensive limestone tracts in eastern Java serves, by intensifying the effects of seasonal drought, to extend the range of casuarina, teak and other types of monsoon forest farther to the west than might otherwise have been the case. Be that as it may, the proportion of evergreen forest declines notably to the east of central Java, and in Sumba,

[15] The Vogelkop (*lit.* bird's head) of West New Guinea, as well as much more extensive parts of eastern New Guinea, also come within this category.

[16] See above, p. 21.

[17] Bandung represents an upland variant, but the regularity of its mean monthly temperatures is even more pronounced than that of Djakarta.

[18] Though in a country of such intricate relief there are innumerable local anomalies even within the lowlands. See Braak (A), p. 52.

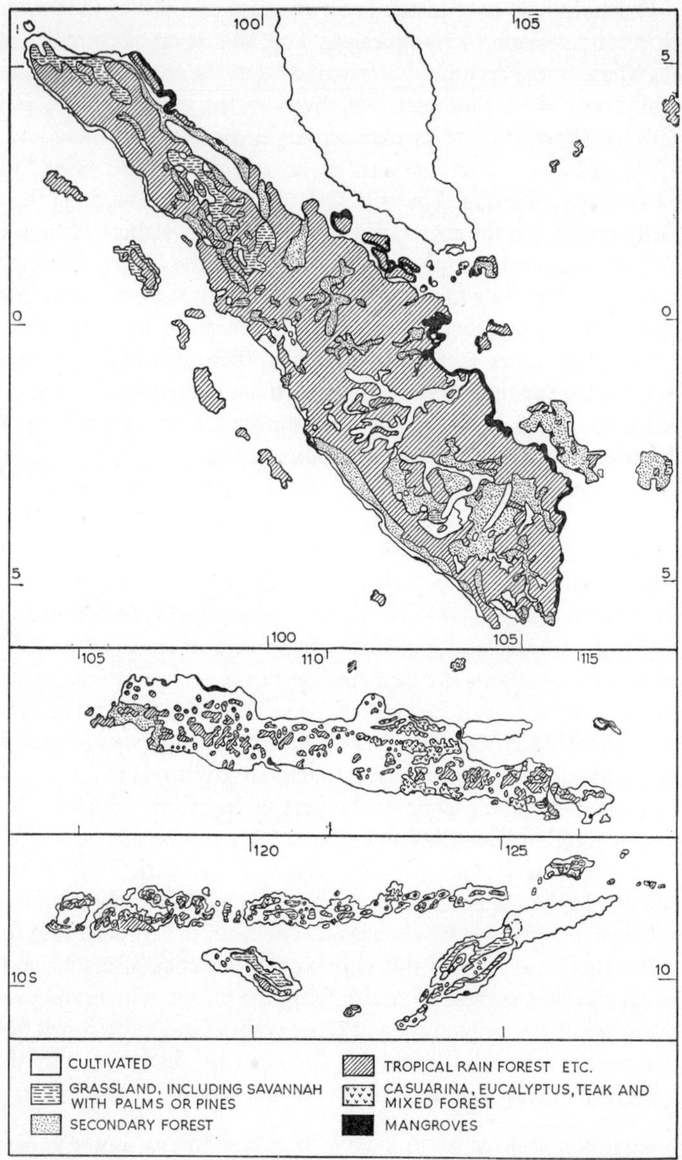

CULTIVATED
GRASSLAND, INCLUDING SAVANNAH WITH PALMS OR PINES
SECONDARY FOREST
TROPICAL RAIN FOREST ETC.
CASUARINA, EUCALYPTUS, TEAK AND MIXED FOREST
MANGROVES

FIG. 26—

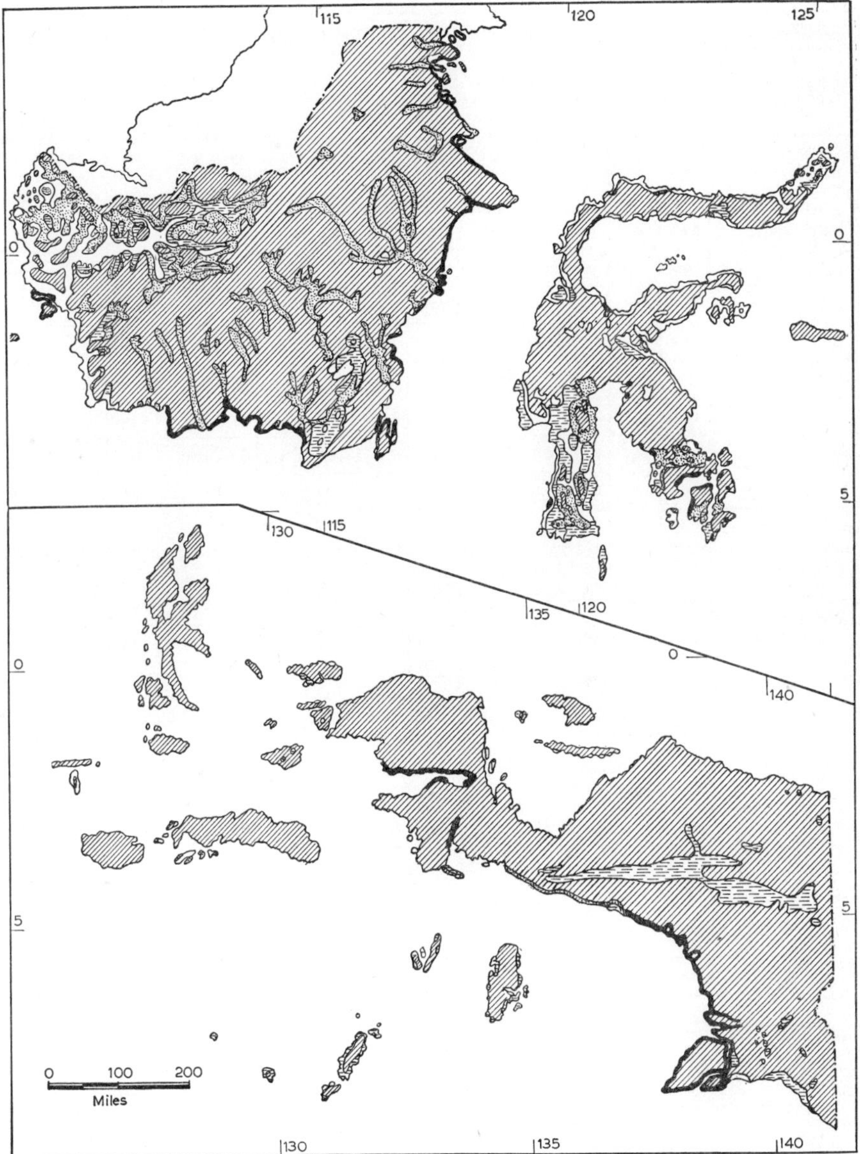

Indonesia: vegetation

TABLE 15

INDONESIA, SELECTED TEMPERATURE AND RAINFALL FIGURES

Station	*Jan.*	*Feb.*	*Mar.*	*Apr.*	*May*	*Jun.*	*Jul.*	*Aug.*	*Sep.*	*Oct.*	*Nov.*	*Dec.*	*Average*	*Total*
Ambon 4° S, 128° E	81	81	81	79	79	78	77	78	78	79	80	81	80	
10	5·6	4·5	5·4	10·9	20·5	23·9	23·2	16·0	9·1	6·9	4·1	5·7		135·8
Bandung 7° S, 108° E	72	72	72	72	72	72	72	72	72	73	72	72	72	
2,360	7·6	7·1	9·6	9·0	5·2	3·6	2·6	2·3	3·6	6·7	8·9	8·5		74·7
Bukit Tinggi 0°, 101° E	69	69	70	70	71	70	69	69	69	70	69	69	69	
3,500	9·2	7·0	9·2	10·2	7·6	5·6	3·8	6·4	6·4	9·0	9·0	10·4		94·0
Djakarta 6° S, 107° E	78	78	79	80	80	79	79	79	80	80	79	79	79	
23	13·0	12·8	7·8	5·1	4·0	3·7	2·6	1·7	2·9	4·5	5·5	8·5		72·1
Djokjakarta 8° S, 110° E														
335	13·9	13·2	12·3	8·3	5·0	3·5	1·6	1·0	1·2	3·7	9·0	13·4		86·1
Kupang 10° S, 124° E	78	79	80	80	80	77	76	78	79	80	79	78	79	
48	22·5	14·2	4·2	1·6	0·1	1·7	0·1	0·1	0·1	7·1	4·1	10·5		56·3
Kutaradja 6° N, 95° E														
0	5·9	3·5	3·5	4·2	6·1	3·6	4·3	4·4	6·8	7·2	7·2	8·3		65·0
Makasar 5° S, 119° E	79	79	79	80	80	79	78	78	78	79	80	79	79	
6	27·0	21·1	16·7	5·9	3·5	2·9	1·4	0·4	0·6	1·7	7·0	24·0		112·2
Menado 1° N, 125° E	77	77	78	78	79	79	79	80	80	79	79	78	79	
28	18·6	14·4	10·3	8·0	6·6	6·5	4·9	3·8	3·4	4·8	8·6	14·7		104·6
Padang 1° S, 100° E	79	80	79	80	80	79	79	79	79	79	79	79	79	
3	13·5	9·9	11·9	14·0	12·6	13·0	11·8	13·7	16·1	20·0	20·7	19·4		177·6
Pasuruan 7° S, 113° E	81	81	81	81	80	79	78	78	80	81	82	81	80	
16	8·9	11·0	8·4	5·4	3·7	2·2	1·0	0·2	0·2	0·7	2·4	6·5		50·6
Pontianak 0°, 109° E	78	79	79	79	80	80	80	79	79	79	78	78	79	
10	10·8	7·9	9·8	10·8	10·7	8·7	6·3	8·9	8·4	14·8	15·7	13·2		125·9
Surabaja 7° S, 112° E	79	79	79	80	80	79	79	79	80	80	80	80	80	
16	12·3	11·5	10·5	7·4	4·3	3·5	1·9	0·5	0·5	1·5	4·6	9·8		68·3
Tosari 8° S, 113° E	63	62	62	62	61	60	59	60	62	62	62	62	62	
5,692	12·4	14·6	10·8	6·9	4·6	3·3	1·5	1·1	1·0	3·4	7·8	11·8		79·2
Sandakan* 5° N, 118° E	79	79	81	82	82	81	81	81	81	81	80	79	80	
98	19·4	9·9	7·8	4·1	5·1	8·6	10·0	6·9	9·5	10·2	16·4	19·3		127·2
Manokwari 1° S, 134° E	79	79	79	79	80	79	79	80	80	80	80	80	80	
62	11·3	9·8	13·3	10·9	8·0	7·6	5·7	5·5	4·9	4·3	6·4	10·6		98·3

*Sandakan is in North Borneo but is included here for comparison.

Flores and Timor eucalyptus- acacia- and other types of savanna are widespread.

The accompanying figures for Pontianak on the west coast of Borneo provide a typical example of the sea-level climate found within the relatively sheltered inner zone of Indonesia, that are in areas not directly exposed to the full force of either monsoon. Mean monthly temperatures vary only from 78° in November–January to 80° in May–July, humidity is intense, and the very heavy rainfall (125·9 in.) shows two well-marked peaks, in April and November respectively. An upland variant of the same basic type is provided by Bukit Tinggi (Fort de Kock), 3,500 ft. above sea level in the Padang highlands of western Sumatra, at a point which to some extent lies in the rain shadow of the higher mountains along both the eastern and western edges of the plateau.

Nevertheless, even in the relatively sheltered inner zone of the archipelago the rainfall regime is nowhere that of the equatorial type in its purest form. For in almost every case the influence of one or both of the monsoons is apparent, bringing more than the usual amount of rain between the two convectional peaks so that, for example, in Pontianak no month has less than 6·3 in. And in more exposed localities the effect of the monsoons on the rainfall pattern is altogether more pronounced as, for example in Padang and Sandakan[19] or even in Djakarta and Bandung.

Thus from December to March the prevailing wind direction is from southern and eastern Asia towards Australia, the winds in question blowing from the NE across the South China Sea towards the northern coasts of Borneo and Celebes, and thence swinging round across the equator to blow from the NW to WNW over the rest of Indonesia where, indeed, they are often called the 'W monsoon'. The vernal equinox is followed by a period of light and variable winds until by June/July the E monsoon takes over and the prevailing winds blow from the SE south of the equator, veering to SW as the line is crossed. The cycle is completed by another transitional season around October and November comparable to that experienced earlier in the year.

As explained in Chapter 2, the W monsoon which approaches Indonesia saturated with moisture from its long transit across the South China Sea and South-west Pacific is a great rain-bringer, whereas the E monsoon, a descending wind coming direct from the arid interior of Australia is predominantly dry over all but the south-western corner of the archipelago.[20]

The effects of the two monsoons on the rainfall pattern can be clearly seen by comparing the amounts and seasonal incidence at Sandakan and Djakarta, both of them exposed to the W but sheltered from the E monsoon,[21] with those at

[19] Sandakan is in (British) North Borneo.

[20] *I.e.* in particular the western side of Sumatra. See the data for Padang, Table 15. As explained in Chapter 2, both the direction and the character of the original E monsoon have changed by the time it reaches this part of Indonesia. Thus the winds approach western Sumatra from the SW, and are heavily laden with moisture from the southern Indian Ocean.

[21] NE and SW respectively at Sandakan.

Padang, Djokjakarta and Kupang, which are all at least partially sheltered against the latter[22] and successively more and more under the dominating influence of the former.

The area outside the equatorial monsoonal limit certainly includes eastern Java, Madura, the Lesser Sundas and the southern fringe of New Guinea. In their rainfall figures, Surabaja and Pasuruan on the north-western edge of this area already reveal the existence of a recognizable dry season, though even so, eastern Java has a fairly high total rainfall and only a small proportion receives less than 50 in. in the year.[23] Kupang, the most south-easterly station on the list shows a longer and more intense dry season, though again the total annual rainfall is considerable – 57·8 in. – which may be compared with the 61·8 in. of Darwin in northern Australia.

The northern limit of the zone of tropical monsoonal climate in Indonesia is not easy to determine. Thus, for example, Makasar, which lies only 5° south of the equator and has the high annual total of 113·3 in. of rain, nevertheless experiences a pronounced dry season of four to five months, two of which have less than an inch of rain apiece. Indeed the desiccating influence of the E monsoon normally makes itself felt over most of the south-eastern and south-western limbs of Celebes, and even to a lesser extent over parts of south-eastern Borneo, while in exceptional years the effect may be apparent almost to the equator in Celebes. In these areas, moreover, the presence of rain shadows can lead to surprising anomalies and, as Braak observes, it is at the head of the Palu Gulf in Celebes, only one degree south of the equator, that the lowest annual rainfall of any station in Indonesia is recorded, namely 21 inches.[24]

This fact serves to emphasize what must be our concluding observation on the climate of Indonesia, namely that the variations in both temperature and rainfall which can arise within even a small portion of its area as a result of local topographical features are far greater than those which can be attributed to differences of latitude and longitude over the archipelago as a whole. For owing to the fact that the country straddles the equator and is elaborately interpenetrated by the sea, it exhibits a remarkable measure of climatic homogeneity for so extensive an area. Thus the highest and lowest monthly mean temperatures recorded at any of the sea-level stations shown in Table 15 range only from 82° (Sandakan, April–May) to 77° (Ambon and Kupang, July, and Menado, January–February) and, despite significant variations in seasonal incidence, well over nine-tenths of the area has an annual rainfall exceeding 50 inches. But in the uplands of many of the islands, even within quite short distances from the coast, altitudes are sufficient to cause reductions of 10°–20° in temperature, as shown by the figures for Bandung and Tosari in Java and for Bukit Tinggi in Sumatra, while at the

[22] But in central and eastern Java the discontinuity of the uplands means that only very limited rain-shadow effects are produced.

[23] The driest part of Java lies north-west from Tjirebon, where the total annual rainfall is below 40 in.

[24] Braak (A), p. 59, and (C), p. 17.

same time both the heaviest and the lightest rainfall totals are explicable primarily in terms of the alignment of ranges and valleys *vis-à-vis* the two monsoons.

Such then, in brief, are the factors which determine the physical character of Indonesia. But each of the several islands presents its own individual combination of traits, in morphology, climate, vegetation and soils, and these must now be examined in greater detail.

II. THE SEVERAL ISLANDS

Sumatra stretches some 1,100 miles in a NW/SE direction from 6° N to 6° S and its climate and vegetation are characteristically equatorial throughout, except in so far as the island's extensive uplands cause significant departures from this norm. Though built on a massive scale, the relief exhibits a simple overall pattern; the impressive mountain backbone which stretches uninterruptedly from Atjeh to the Sunda Straits being flanked by occasional strips of coastal plain on the west and by much more extensive lowlands to the east.

Despite the name Bukit Barisan (*i.e.* the mountain range) by which the highlands are collectively known except in the northern part of the island, the system consists in general of two more or less parallel ridges separated from each other by a structural trough and surmounted at fairly frequent intervals by numerous active or extinct volcanoes, most of which are immediately adjacent to the depression. While the summit levels of these volcanic cones are commonly of the order of 8,000 ft., several of them are much higher, for example Gunong Leuser (11,092 ft.), G. Ophir (9,546 ft.), G. Kerintji (12,470 ft.) and G. Dempo (10, 364 ft.), and the mountain system as a whole forms a tremendous barrier to lateral movement of any kind.

The earth movements which produced this great mass of highlands extended from Tertiary into Quaternary times, and as a result of the most recent uplift there is an almost continuous and generally precipitous mountain wall along the whole western side of the island facing the Indian Ocean and only a limited development of coastal lowlands there, except where some of the larger rivers have built extensive alluvial fans which increase its width at a few key points.

From north to south four main regional divisions may be recognized within the uplands as a whole, namely the Atjeh ranges, the Batak plateau, the Padang or Menangkabau highlands and the Benkulen mountains of the south. While these divisions are partly based on cultural and historical considerations, there is nevertheless an unmistakable physical contrast between the splayed-out ranges and valleys of Atjeh, the wide expanse of continuous lava and tuff plateau in the Batak country, the ridge and basin topography of the Menangkabau highlands and the generally narrower and simpler pattern presented by the two main ranges of the south.

Although the effects of vulcanism are evident in all parts of the highlands their significance is perhaps most arresting in the Batak[25] and Menangkabau

[25] See van Vuuren (C).

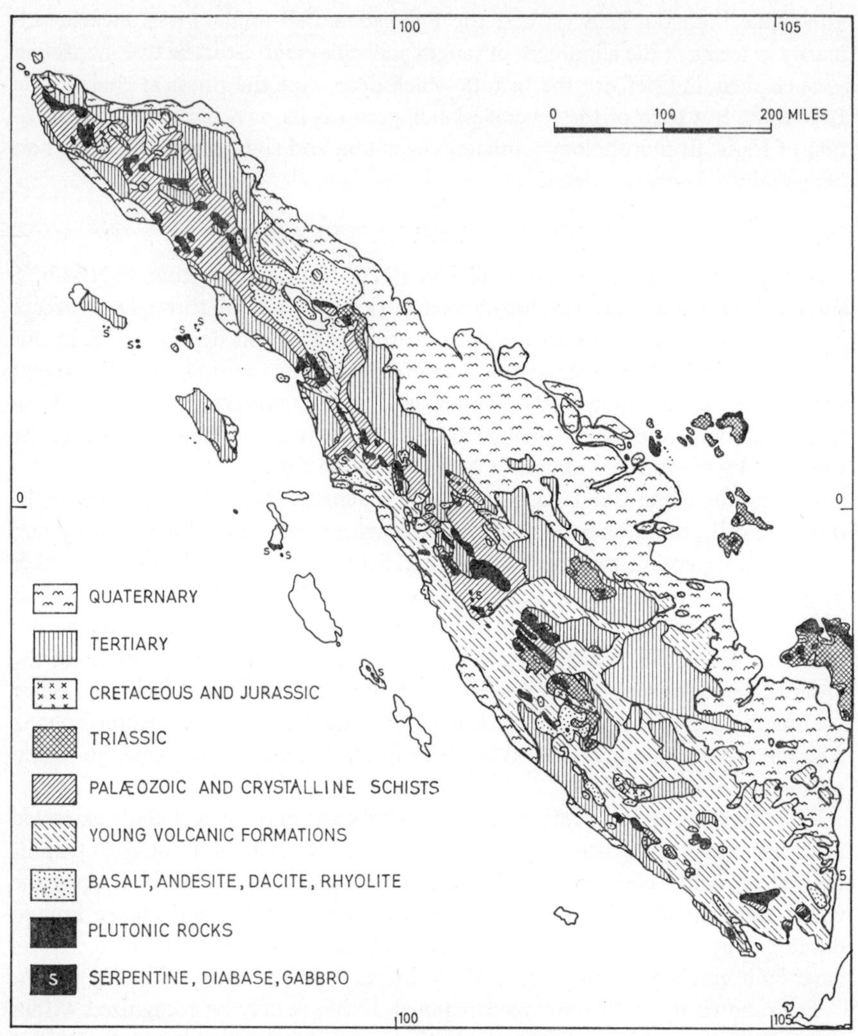

FIG. 27—Sumatra: geology

lands. In the former, which centres in a great subsided tract partially occupied by Lake Toba, the porosity of the predominantly acid volcanic soils, together with an intermont position and an altitude of over 3,000 ft., have given rise to a modified savanna vegetation instead of the tropical rain forest more typical of the surrounding regions.

These areas of acid volcanics are not particularly productive, but in the northern Batak lands, and also in parts of the Menangkabau and Benkulen highlands farther south, the recent ejecta are mainly neutral-basic, and these

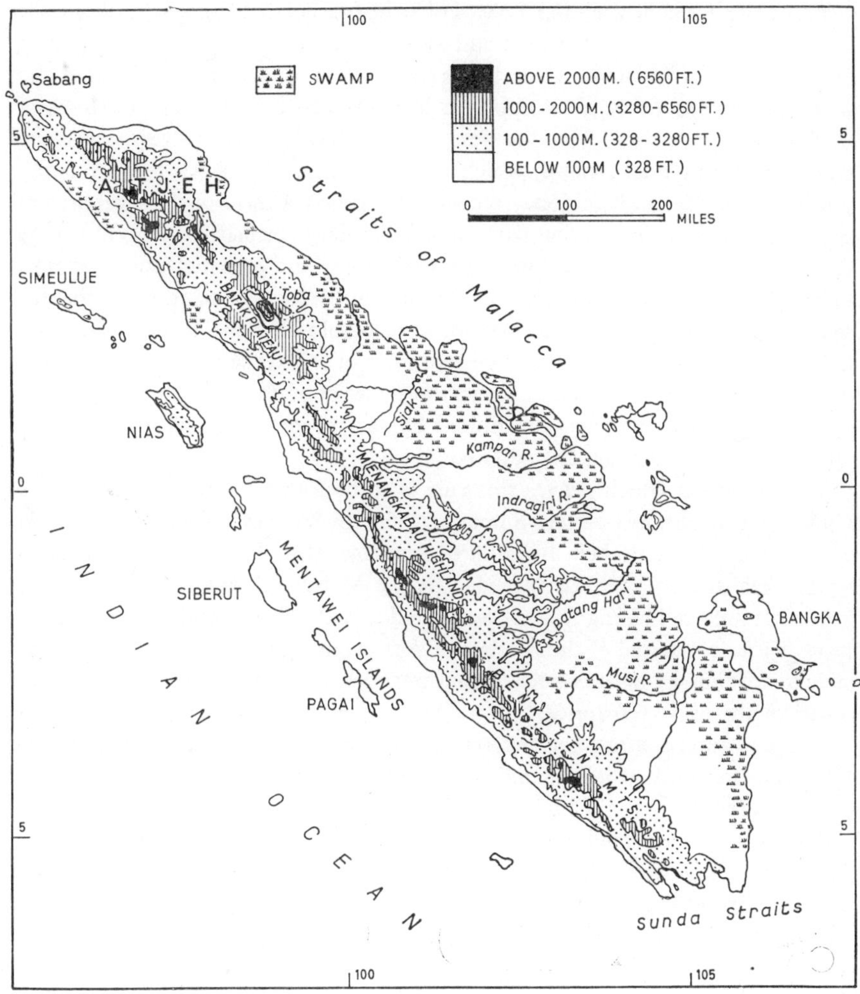

FIG. 28—Sumatra: relief

have given rise to local patches of much greater fertility then is typical of the island as a whole.

Along their entire eastern flank the highlands descend rapidly to a foothill zone corresponding to a belt of Tertiary strata, which is by no means devoid of agricultural potential. Unfortunately, however, except in the far north in Atjeh, this zone is separated from the coast by a belt of swamps some 850 miles long, and though this is only a few miles wide opposite the Cultuurgebied,[26] its breadth is greatly increased farther south, where in places it attains as much as 150 miles.

[26] *I.e.* plantations district. See below, pp. 260–1.

From the Asahan, draining Lake Toba, in the north to the Seputih in the south, a whole series of sluggish and swollen rivers, notably the great Batang Hari and the Air Musi, on whose banks the historic principalities of Djambi and Palembang respectively grew up, have brought down prodigious quantities of easily eroded materials[27] from the western highlands to form this vast expanse of fresh-water and tidal swamp, which almost completely masks the Sumatran portion of Sunda-land and today accounts for nearly a third of the total area of the island. Except in the few parts where Tertiary (primarily Neogene) rocks break the surface this is a region of drab monotony and extremely low economic value, the great thickness of very acid peat – in places over 20 ft. – and the unmanageable seasonal floods posing almost insoluble problems to the indigenous cultivator. Moreover, the natural unhealthiness of this terrain and the associated obstacles which it has placed in the way of penetration into the interior from the eastern coast have hitherto constituted by far the most serious liability from which Sumatra as a whole has suffered.[28]

The exception which proves this rule is to be found in the lowlands of the Cultuurgebied of north-eastern Sumatra, where the Sunda shelf recedes to the east and the coastal swamp belt dwindles to a narrow strip. Thus, within a few miles of the great natural highway provided by the Malacca Straits there is a readily accessible area containing fertile transported soils derived from the intermediate-basic volcanic material of the northern Batak country, and here it has been possible to develop the most important concentration of plantation agriculture in the whole of the outer territories.

The structural contrast between the highland and lowland portions of Sumatra is sharply reflected in its mineral wealth, which is considerable. Thus metallic minerals are limited to the highlands, the best known being the fairly widespread though mostly very small deposits of gold, mainly in the Menangkabau plateau. Much more important, however, are the series of oilfields which occur in the north, centre and south of the eastern foothill zone. In addition, Tertiary brown coal is found, both at Umbilin in the Menangkabau country and at Bukit Asam near the eastern flank of the Benkulen mountains. Finally in this connexion may be noted the predominantly alluvial tin of the nearby islands of Singkep, Bangka and Belitung, and the lateritic bauxite of Bintan in the Riau archipelago farther north.

At first glance it might seem that the advantages of geographical position enjoyed by Sumatra would apply with almost equal force to the neighbouring island of Borneo, which also has an extended coastline fringing the interoceanic seaway. But in fact the greater distance of Borneo from the continental mainland

[27] Derived from the predominantly acid volcanic ejecta noted above.

[28] See Dobby (H), p. 199. It is, however, true that the rivers have provided routes of historic importance and even of considerable significance at the present day. Thus, *e.g.*, the Air Musi is navigable, though its course is extremely tortuous, virtually to the foot of the Barisan, and both the Kampar and the Indagiri provided historic routes to the Menangkabau highlands.

and the exposed nature of its shores facing the South China Sea have combined to reduce these advantages very greatly, so that Borneo as a whole has tended usually to be much more remote from the main streams of world trade than have Sumatra or the nearby Malay peninsula.

In any case, moreover, the northern strip of Borneo lies within the British sphere, dealt with in Chapter 20, and the parts of the island which belong to Indonesia are mostly still further from the main sea lanes. This relative isolation is perhaps the most striking feature of the geography of Indonesian Borneo, and though in several other respects broad similarities with Sumatra are apparent, the differences are probably of greater significance.

Like that of eastern Sumatra the coasts of Indonesian Borneo display the typical characteristics associated with post-glacial submergence, and along both the western and southern shores, which look out onto the shallow seas of the Sunda shelf, essentially similar and almost equally repellent swamps are found, though in general the peat layer is less acid and less thick than its Sumatran counterpart. Together with the even greater size and compactness of the island, the width of the swamp belt goes far to explain its retarded development, though other factors must also be taken into account. Like Sumatra, again, Borneo lies across the equator, and the greater part of its surface is covered by dense tropical rain forest. Under such conditions rivers provide virtually the only natural routes, but the Borneo rivers are far from ideal in this respect. For in addition to the sinuosity of their courses through the insalubrious peripheral swamps, all the main ones are closed to large craft because of bars across their mouths, and furthermore all suffer from great unevenness of flow and an associated liability to seasonal flooding.

Nevertheless, the larger rivers, notably the Kapuas,[29] Barito and Mahakam (as also the Rejang in Sarawak) do provide routes, by means of which country boats penetrate far inland. For Borneo is predominantly low-lying, and wide alluvial plains surround the interior uplands on all sides, most extensively to the outh, west and north-west.

Except in the extreme north-east, Borneo contains no high mountains, and within the Indonesian two-thirds of the island G. Raja (7,472 ft.) in the Schwaner Gebergte is probably the highest point and few other summits attain 6,000 ft. Nor indeed do the uplands form markedly continuous ranges, and it is the absence of through waterways rather than the presence of great mountain masses which so effectively isolates the various coastal fringes from one another, and explains why British Borneo facing the South China Sea seems to belong to a different world from that of the rest of the island which looks out onto the inner seas of Indonesia.

[29] There are two quite separate major rivers of this name in Borneo. The larger one flows out to the west coast near Pontianak and the other (sometimes known as the Dajak Ketjil or Lesser Dyak) merges with the Barito in the swamp belt to the north of Bandjarmasin. With a length of 650 miles the (western) Kapuas is the longest river in Indonesia.

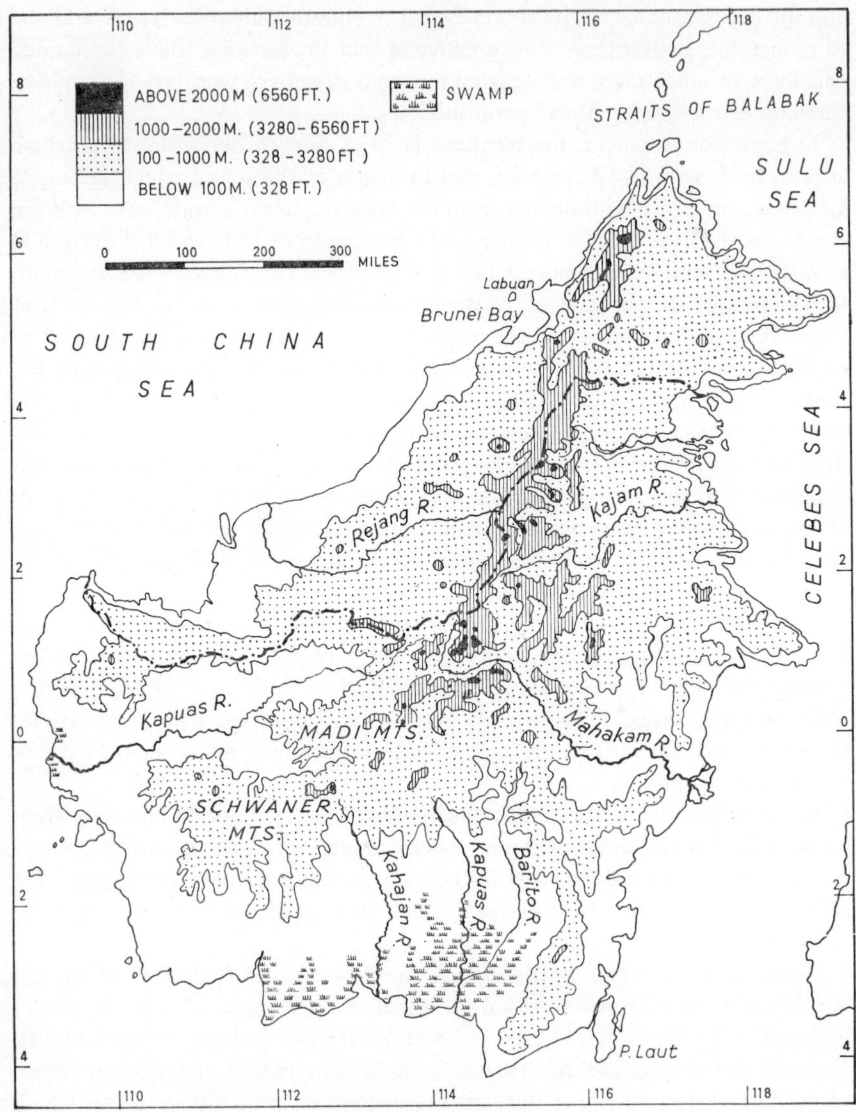

FIG. 29—Borneo: relief

In origin the predominantly latitudinal ranges in the south-west and centre of the island are approximately contemporary with the ranges of Malaya and their offshoots in Bangka and Belitung, and like them are characterized by granitic cores, now exposed over wide areas, and somewhat subdued outlines. Whether any comparable mineral wealth exists here, however, remains unproven though gold, diamonds and iron have all been found in small quantities within this area.

To the north and east these older mountains are flanked by Tertiary beds including both coal- and oil-bearing formations, which have been worked at various easily accessible points along the northern (British Bornean) and eastern coasts. The ranges marking the frontier between the British and Indonesian parts of Borneo, and also the main longitudinal uplands towards the eastern coast of the island, show evidence of folding both in late Triassic and again in late Pliocene times. For the most part their summit levels do not exceed 5–6,000 ft., but in the north-east corner[30] where the two series coalesce, the isolated granite peak of Mt. Kinabalu reaches the exceptional height of 13,681 ft. Although this is not of volcanic origin, some traces of recent volcanic activity are found in nearby parts of British Borneo as mentioned on p. 679. But these have no counterpart in Indonesian Borneo, and in their absence the prevailing equatorial climate, with heavy and well-distributed rainfall amounting in most places to well over 100 in. a year, has resulted in advanced laterization and consequent impoverishment of the soil. Only in the south-east is there any notable dry season, corresponding with the period of the E monsoon.

Of the three main western islands, Java is much the smallest but at the same time by far the most intrinsically attractive as a home for man. In shape it is long and slender,[31] stretching some 620 miles from west to east and ranging in width from rather over 100 miles near both ends to a mere 60 miles at its central waist, and to even less at the eastern extremity where the post-glacial rise in sea level has separated the island of Madura from the main body.

Taken together, Figs. 30–32 suggest something of the fineness and symmetry of the physical features of Java, and in fact the island must be ranked among the loveliest regions on earth. In nearly every part its scenery is dominated by the series of great volcanic cones which, continuing the line of the Sumatran volcanoes, lie mostly within the structural depression running lengthwise through the island from west to east.[32] All-told Java contains 121 such volcanoes, 17 of them still active and 14 of them exceeding 10,000 ft. in altitude, with the highest, G. Mohomeru in the Semeru mountains rising to 12,061 ft., which is almost the equivalent of G. Kerintji in Sumatra.

In the vicinity of Bandung in western Java a series of such high volcanic peaks cluster together to form a great tangle of upland which constitutes a formidable barrier to movement in all directions. But over the central and eastern parts of the island the larger peaks become more widely spaced – roughly one every 20–30 miles – and here they are separated one from another by broad valleys, for the most part covered with volcanic débris.[33] Accordingly the range of relief is particularly impressive, while at the same time the system as a whole does not

[30] *I.e.* in (British) North Borneo. See Rutter, p. 4.

[31] Sion, *op. cit.*, p. 489, refers to its shape as being '*d'une sveltesse élégante*'.

[32] Although most of these volcanoes lie along clearly recognizable E/W lines, this sequence is interrupted in several places as, *e.g.*, in the Tengger-Semeru area, as a result of deep-seated cross disturbances. Stauffer, p. 322.

[33] See van Vuuren (C), p. 14, and Robequain (D), p. 174.

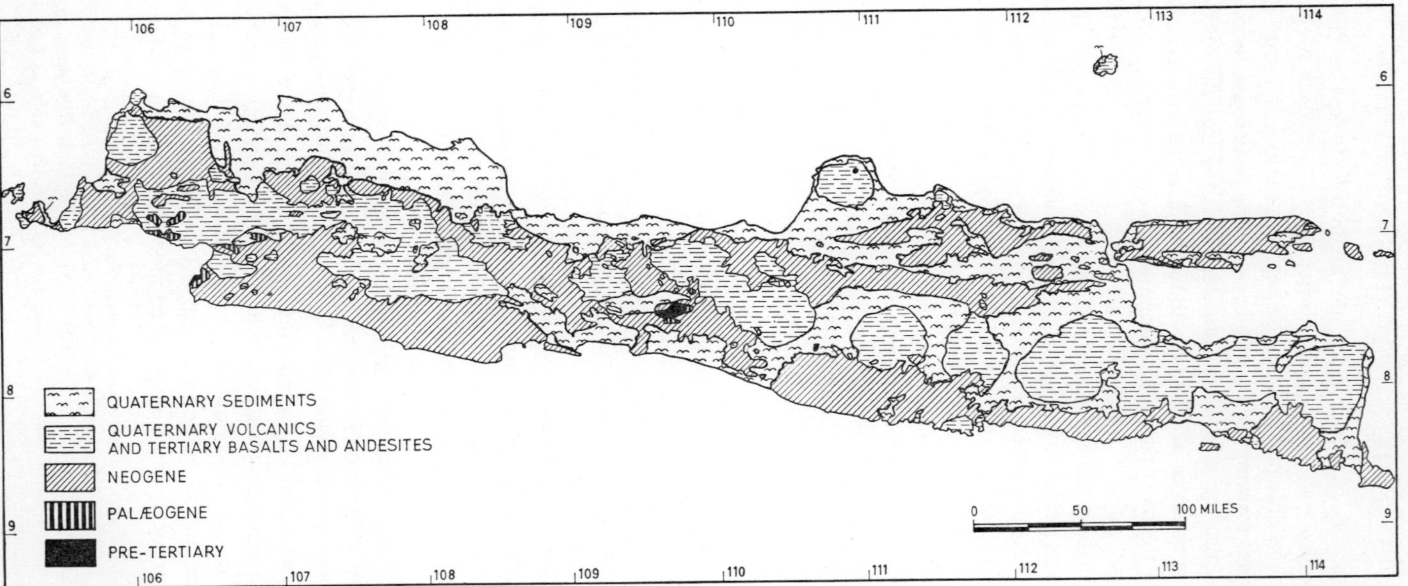

FIG. 30—Java: geology

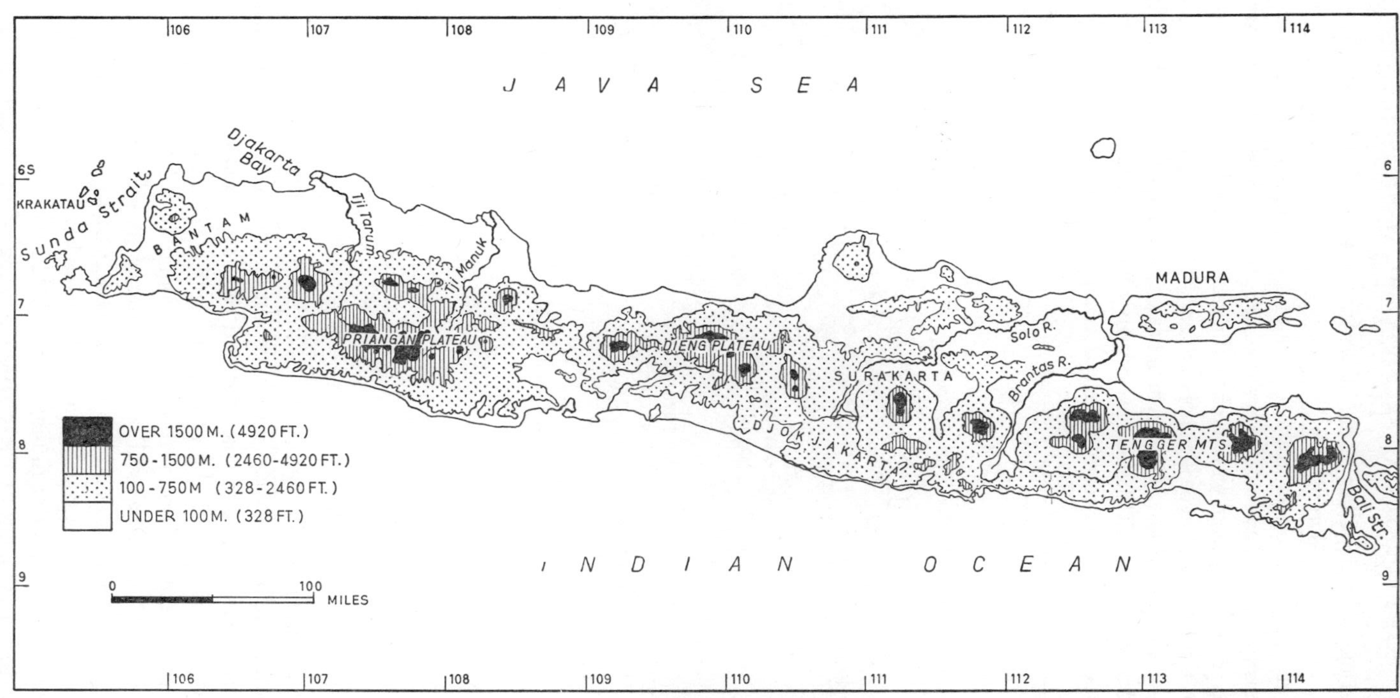

FIG. 31—Java: relief

afford a serious obstacle either to the movement of air streams or to N/S communications east of G. Merapi.

Moreover, the recent ejecta in most parts of east-central Java, both lava and ash, are mostly neutral-basic in composition. It is the repeated replenishment of the fertility of the soil over wide areas with such material, together with the capacity of the latter for retaining moisture on the upper slopes and thus facilitating irrigation in the plains below, which has enabled the island in recent times to support what is probably the highest density of agricultural population in the world. These conditions are seen to perfection in the magnificent series of basins

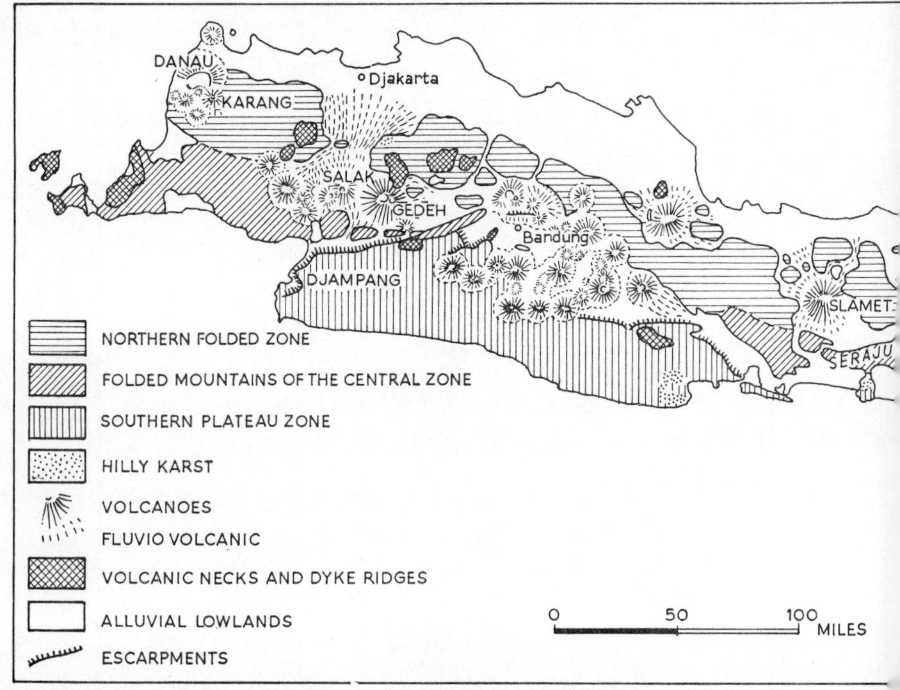

FIG. 32

– Surakarta, Madiun, Kediri and Malang – in the eastern half of the island. But in the Priangan region of western Java an exception occurs, for much of the volcanic material there is acid in character and this fact is reflected in the lower densities of population which this part of the island supports. Indeed, from many points of view western Java, with its more continuous highlands and wider coastal plain (*c.* 30 miles), as well as the nature of its soils, is intermediate in character between Sumatra and the rest of Java, and this difference between the western third and the eastern two-thirds of the latter has made itself felt in innumerable ways since the beginning of recorded history.

Besides this major contrast the physical division of the island into a large number of lesser but nevertheless distinct compartments has given rise to an elaborate regional variety in some ways reminiscent of France and, as Schrieke points out,[34] such *pays* as Kedu, Mataram, Kediri, and others, show a remarkable degree of continuity within historic time. But, again as in France, the general absence of serious barriers to internal movement has meant that, with the exception of the western end of the island, these various centres have not developed in isolation one from another, and the unity of the whole transcends the diversity of the parts.

To the south of the volcanic belt there is a discontinuous series of plateaux,

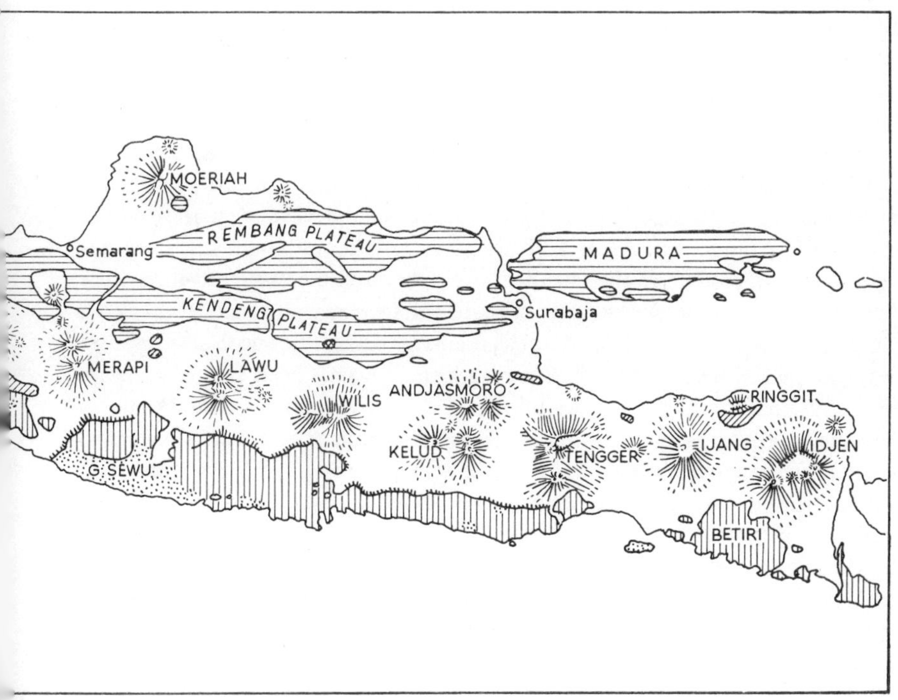

va: morphology

rarely reaching much above 1,000 ft. in height and consisting predominantly of almost horizontal or gently folded Miocene limestones on which there has been developed a characteristic example of tropical karst landscape,[35] whose surface becomes progressively more barren towards the drier east. In the central section of the island a major gap occurs in this plateau series, and there the coastal lowlands are as much as 15 miles wide. But in both eastern and western Java the plateaux extend for well over 100 miles along the coast, and present an uplifted and precipitous edge to the southern Indian Ocean.

[34] See Schrieke, *op. cit.*, Vol. II, p. 211.
[35] See Pannekock, *op. cit.*, p. 12 and Dobby (H), p. 217.

On the northern flank of the main volcanic belt is a further zone of Tertiary/Quaternary folding in which the surface rocks are predominantly of middle and late Tertiary age and include extensive tracts of Neogene marls which support soils of only moderate fertility. However, this zone is interrupted at several points by wide alluvial valleys and is further diversified by a few recent volcanic cones, notably in the far west (G. Karang, etc.), in Tjirebon (G. Tjarene) and in the centre (G. Slamet and the peaks of the Dieng plateau), while farther east it is present as the Kendeng and Rembang highlands and the extension of the latter beyond the Pintu Barat (Westervaarwater) in the limestone massif of Madura. In general character the plateaux of Rembang and Madura resemble the Miocene massifs of the south, and since the prevailing barrenness of their limestone terrains is exaggerrated by a seasonally dry climate, they stand out in marked contrast to the highly fertile coastal plain which elsewhere constitutes the northernmost zone of Java.

For the most part this northern plain varies in width from 10 to 20 miles in central Java, and apart from the immediate coastal margin its surface deposits consist mainly of transported volcanic material comparable with that of the Sumatran Cultuurgebied. As in Sumatra so in Java recent tectonic history has caused the greater part of the island to drain towards the sheltered inner seas of the archipelago, that is in this case towards the Java Sea, and such rivers as the Solo and Brantas have extended their drainage basins by successive capture deep into the southern uplands.[36] But here again Java has been altogether more favoured by nature, in that the usefulness of these rivers and of their valleys as routes has not been reduced by the presence of a wide belt of coastal swamps. Admittedly, mangrove swamps do fringe the northern shore for a few miles, and even over the last 350 years sedimentation has added approximately a mile of mud flats between the old harbour of Batavia (Djakarta) and the present sea coast.[37] But, partly because of the appreciably greater depth of the southern Java Sea compared with the Straits of Malacca, swamp formation along the edge of the Sunda shelf in northern Java has been much less pronounced than that in the comparable zone of Sumatra.

With the exception of the eastern third of the island, practically the whole of Java receives an abundant, but rarely excessive rainfall. Thus Djakarta has 72·1 in. and Bandung 74·7 in. a year, though many of the more exposed uplands get more than double this amount, as, for example, Bogor with 160 inches. Thanks to its latitude between 6° and 9° south of the equator, Java avoids the extreme climatic monotony characteristic of most of Sumatra and Borneo, and all parts of the island have at least an approximation to a dry season. Besides providing a welcome element of variety and being more suited to grain crops than

[36] See Robequain (D), p. 179.

[37] The rate of sedimentation of the Java rivers has varied considerably in historic times, in response both to the extent of volcanic activity and the progress of deforestation. In early historic times such rivers as the Brantas and Solo were probably of much greater use for navigation than they are today. See Schrieke, Vol. II, p. 113.

is the true equatorial régime, this has the added advantage of materially reducing the rate of leaching though, except in the limestone areas,[38] desiccation is rarely severe enough to prevent the land from being intensively cropped throughout the year.

Indeed, practically the whole of the lower lying tracts of the island, as well as most of the gentler slopes in the volcanic uplands are eminently suited for cultivation. And although really efficient utilization of much of the coastal plain had to await the introduction of modern water-control works by the Dutch, the more easily manageable terrains of the interior valleys and basins of east-central Java whose original vegetation cover was predominantly monsoon rather than strict evergreen forest, have been in virtually continuous use as rice lands for well over a thousand years.

In contrast to its great agricultural potential, Java, as might be inferred from its structure, has only a very limited store of mineral wealth. This includes a little oil, occurring in the folded zone of the north-east under conditions roughly analogous to those of the Sumatran fields, and for the rest consists mainly of sulphur, obviously associated with vulcanicity, and a few deposits of phosphate.

To the east of Java and Borneo the Sunda shelf comes to an end, and wide coastal lowlands, so characteristic of the western islands, are conspicuous by their absence in the eastern archipelago. Thus the bony outlines of Celebes recall the mountain spines of Borneo, though with the significant difference that here they are unclothed by peripheral plains, and the several Lesser Sunda islands, like a column of separate vertebrae, display in more extreme form the articulated character of the relief of east-central Java.[39]

This topographical splintering reaches its climax in the Moluccas, for although Halmahera, Buru and Seram are all over 3,000 square miles in extent, the remaining islands here are mostly much smaller, and the best known – such as Ambon, Banda, Tidore and Ternate – range downwards from 300 to a mere 25 square miles respectively.

Moreover, the presence of coral reefs reinforces the geographical remoteness of these islands, and in the eastern Lesser Sundas there is the further disadvantage of a very long and intense dry season which is reflected in the scrub-like vegetation so different from the characteristic equatorial verdure found, for example, in Banda and Ambon, both of which receive over 100 in. of rain in the year. In view of all these considerations, therefore, it is not surprising that the Moluccas and the eastern Lesser Sundas are today among the least developed parts of Indonesia, the former renown of the Spice Islands and the more recent production of oil in Seram notwithstanding.

However, while some of the foregoing remarks do apply to Bali and Lombok, and also to Celebes, these three islands are all in a sense marginal in character,

[38] In fact many parts of the limestone country are extremely densely settled, though only at the price of intense poverty. Madura in particular is notorious in this respect.

[39] See Robequain (D), p. 227, and van Vuuren (C), p. 14.

and hence of much greater economic importance than the remainder of eastern Indonesia.[40] Indeed, the strait between Java and Bali is only 1¼ miles wide, compared with the 1½ miles which separate Java from Madura and, with its fertile volcanic foothills and plains, Bali has as much in common with the smiling and productive countryside of central-southern Java as Madura has with the less attractive plateaux of the north. Somewhat similar physical conditions are also found in Lombok, though there the area of lowland is smaller, but farther east the differences from Java decisively outweigh the resemblances.

The great spread-eagled island of Celebes, so aptly described by Tomlinson as 'a handful of peninsulas tied in the middle and flung into the ocean'[41] owes its distinctive layout and relief to two main sets of factors, namely the collision of several axes of Tertiary folding and the occurrence both in Tertiary and more recent times of extensive uplift, faulting and subsidence.

As a result of its peculiar structural evolution Celebes presents many distinctive features which are relatively unfamiliar in other parts of Indonesia. Most striking is the general angularity of much of its relief, and the widespread occurrence of lakes, of which the largest are Towuti, Poso and Matana, formed within the maze of rift valleys in various parts of the island. Moreover, in many of these characteristically trench-like *graben* small but often very severe dry zones occur, and in such areas the combination of exceptionally steep slopes and a climate in which the prevailing seasonal dryness is periodically broken by sudden and extremely heavy downpours is conducive to soil erosion, especially where, as in most of Celebes, shifting cultivation is still the prevailing type of land-use. Not surprisingly, some of the most severe soil erosion is found in the Palu Gulf, which, as noted above, has an exceptionally low total rainfall.

Although in a general sense the centre of the island is the highest part and relief tends to become more subdued towards the extremities of the several peninsulas, the highest single peak is in fact Bukit Rantemario near the head of the south-western peninsula. Its altitude of 11,286 ft. is of very nearly the same general order as that of the highest summit levels in the other large islands farther to the west.

The Minahasa region at the north-eastern tip of Celebes has several active volcanoes, notably G. Saputan, and the associated soils are generally fertile. Another area of comparable richness also accurs at the opposite extremity of the island near Makasar, though the great volcano there, G. Lompobatang (Piek van Bonthain) has shown no sign of activity in recent centuries. Both these are areas of long-established agricultural settlement, and it is probably as a result of greater familiarity with them than with the rest of the island that there was much talk in certain Dutch circles during the inter-war years of preparing Celebes to become another Java.

Such ideas, however, were based on serious misconceptions. Apart from the two relatively small areas already noted, the island has experienced no important

[40] Cf. Dobby (H), p. 251. [41] Quoted in Stamp (A), p. 449.

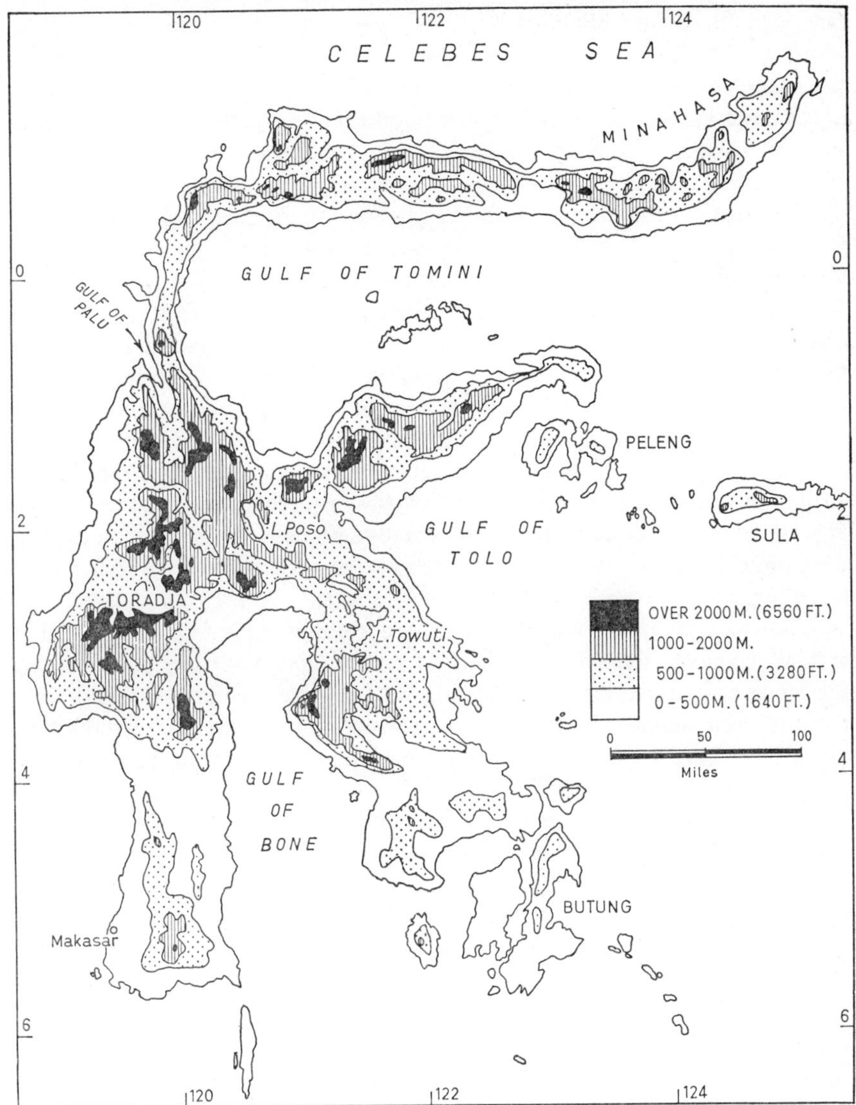

FIG. 33—Celebes: relief

volcanic activity since Tertiary times and its soils are subjected to intense leaching under a climate of consistently high temperatures and an annual rainfall in most parts above rather than below 100 inches. Thus agricultural potentialities are in general far from encouraging, quite apart from the pronounced shortage of flat or low-lying land. Except for a narrow and far from continuous coastal plain, occasionally broadened, as at the head of the Gulf of Bone, by alluvial fans, and the valleys occupied by Lake Tempe and the Sampar river in the south-western and south-eastern peninsulas respectively, virtually the whole of the island is rugged upland more than 1,500 ft. above sea level, and several of the peaks in the predominantly metamorphic and crystalline mountains of the interior are over 8,000 ft. in altitude.

Moreover, although occasional good anchorages are found, the coastline is characteristically forbidding and often extremely dangerous and this, together with the widespread and treacherous coral reefs offshore, goes far to nullify the apparent advantage of its great length (some 3,000 miles) in relation to the total surface area (72,890 square miles). Admittedly, movement by sea is much easier than by land, but with each of the four peninsulas facing in different directions, and ways into the interior impeded by high ranges and deep tectonic trenches, Celebes is an area of extreme compartmentalism and isolation.[42]

Nevertheless, the potentialities of the island should not be underestimated. Its known mineral wealth includes gold, silver, nickel and iron, and though the fertility of its soils, as a whole, is less than was formerly presumed, the absence of wide belts of unhealthy and agriculturally useless swamps helps to explain why, notwithstanding its relative remoteness, the average density of population is the highest of all the larger islands outside Java.

Compared even with the uncertainty that surrounds our knowledge of Celebes and still stands in the way of an entirely reliable appraisal of its potentialities, the ignorance concerning the geography of West New Guinea has until very recently been infinitely greater, and in these circumstances wildly conflicting views have been expressed and still remain current regarding the economic prospects which this territory affords.

In size New Guinea is comparable with Borneo, and in many other respects, notably in the size of its swamps along the shallow south-western shores which fringe the Sahul shelf, there are significant similarities between these two great equatorial islands. But the lofty series of Tertiary fold mountains, running NW/SE from the Vogelkop peninsula to the Owen Stanley range in south-eastern Papua, and broadening in the Nassau Range of the western half of the island to well over 100 miles in total width, is a far more spectacular feature than the uplands of central Borneo and indeed may more nearly be compared with the Alps in the general character of both its structure and its relief. Thus, notwithstanding their latitude, the highest peaks – Idenburg-top (15,750 ft.) and Carstenz-top (16,400 ft.) – in the Nassau Range extend above the snow line, there about 14,000 ft., and the system as a whole forms an immense barrier to communications.

On the southern side of these mountains the swamp belt, imperfectly drained by the Eiland, Digul and other rivers, extends virtually from the sea coast to the foot of the central ranges,[43] though in the area around Merauke more solid

[42] Robequain (D), p. 231.

[43] However, in the eastern half there is a wide intermediate zone of foothills.

ground and a drier climate are reflected in a change from equatorial swamp vegetation to more or less typical savanna. To the north of the central ranges, east of latitude 136°, there is a deep structural trough, the Meervlakte, roughly comparable morphologically to the central valleys of California and Chile. This valley is drained by the twin E/W rivers Tariku (Rouffaer) and Taritatu (Idenburg) which unite to form the northward-flowing Tarikaikea or Mamberano, and

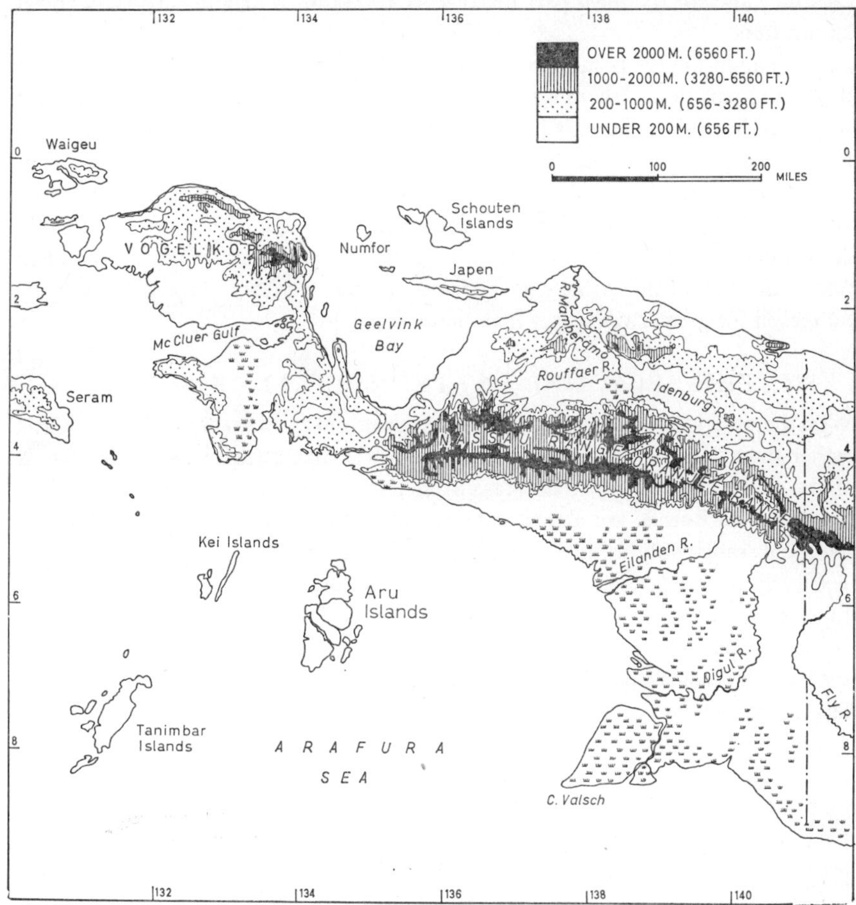

FIG. 34—West New Guinea: relief

this in turn breaks through the series of intensely folded ranges, 3,000 to 7,000 ft. high, running parallel with the recently uplifted Pacific coast.

Although most of the lowest lying areas north of the central ranges are clothed with dense equatorial forest, the vegetation cover thins out at higher altitudes, and between 12,000 ft. and 14,000 ft. a modified tropical grassland is the predominant type. Even at much lower levels, however, many of the rain-shadow areas within the mountain belt support a covering of savanna, and it seems to be on this account that the legend has grown up in recent decades that West New Guinea contains extensive areas of 'rolling grasslands' capable of being developed as 'white highlands' on the East African model.

Unfortunately, however, practically the whole of West New Guinea with the exception of a small area in the Vogelkop lies outside the range of recent vulcanism,[44] and for the most part its soils are now known to suffer from advanced laterization.

From almost every point of view, indeed, the Vogelkop appears to be the most promising part of an otherwise not very attractive territory. Both petroleum and coal have been found in this north-westerly corner of West New Guinea which also, in contrast to most of the remainder of the area west of the 141st meridian, apart from the nearby Bombarai peninsula, is well provided with natural harbours. But even here remoteness from the main sea routes has directly and indirectly constituted a tremendous obstacle to cultural and economic progress, and such minor developments as have taken place in the territory since 1945 suggest no reason for greater optimism than heretofore.

III. THE REGIONAL PATTERN: ISLANDS AND SEAS

With the exception of New Guinea, whose structural affinities are with Australasia rather than with the rest of the archipelago, the size of the Indonesian islands shows a general tendency to decrease from north-west to south-east, so that while Sumatra and Borneo are almost continental in scale the Lesser Sundas and the Moluccas range only from the small to the minute.

Clearly on grounds of size alone, to say nothing of the various climatic and topographical disadvantages from which many of them suffer, none of these lesser islands could ever of itself sustain the population necessary to play more than a very localized rôle in human affairs for any length of time. But the largest islands also suffer from obvious and serious drawbacks, New Guinea above all from remoteness, Celebes from the shortage of flat land, Borneo from the general sterility of its soils, and all of them, including also Sumatra, from the inhospitable nature of their coasts, arising out of either the great width of the fringing belts of swamps or, as in the case of Celebes, the presence of offshore coral reefs and a generally precipitous shoreline.[45]

Thus it is almost as much by contrast with the defects of its neighbours as by virtue of its own great positive advantages that Java, the golden mean in both size and location, stands out as much the most favoured island for human settlement in the whole archipelago.

In the foregoing analysis of the physique of Indonesia, attention has necessarily been focused on the individual islands. But equally important to an under-

[44] Though recent vulcanism is widespread in the eastern half of New Guinea.

[45] This also applies to western Sumatra, and indeed for that matter to southern Java as well.

standing of the country's human geography is the rôle played by the intervening bodies of water for, owing to the way in which relief and vegetation combine to impede movement in the interiors of almost every island, the seas and the lower courses of the larger rivers have normally constituted the main avenues of communication.

On both its northern and southern flanks the archipelago as a whole lies exposed to the full force of the monsoon winds which give rise to tempestuous seas, notably off northern Borneo and Celebes, and along the Indian Ocean coasts of Sumatra and Java. Moreover, because the structural nature of these shorelines makes good anchorages few and far between, it is all the more natural that maritime activity should concentrate in the inner 'Mediterranean' seas of the archipelago. And finally it is to these latter, which are at the same time more sheltered, liberally studded with islands capable of serving as intermediate points of call, and better provided with capacious estuaries, that much the greater part of all the larger islands drains.

Thus, while one may seek in vain for any sense of cultural or historic unity in such islands as Sumatra, Borneo, Celebes or New Guinea[46], in all of which there is a well-marked antithesis between the coastlands and the interior, the regional pattern based upon the three main inner seas of the archipelago has been remarkably persistent throughout historic times.

The first of these regional units may be taken to comprise the lands bordering the Straits of Malacca and the adjoining parts of the South China Sea. Since as noted in Chapter 3 the shortest sailing route between India and China lay through these two seas, many attempts have been made by far-sighted rulers to establish their authority over both sides of the trade route in order to control the shipping which passed along it. Thus the eastern parts of Sumatra[47] have repeatedly been linked politically with Malaya and the Riau-Lingga archipelagos, though admittedly this region has had a turbulent history and its centre of gravity has changed on many occasions.[48]

At the opposite extremity of the archipelago, the eastern seas between Wallace's and Weber's lines constitute another great geographical unit, whose remoteness from the Asian mainland has been reinforced in many places by the hazards of approaching its steep and coral-girt shores. Thus, in spite of the ancient renown of its spice-producing islands, the eastern archipelago has more generally assumed the rôle of a cul-de-sac and has been largely by-passed, alike by the civilizing influences emanating from mainland Asia – whether Hindu, Buddhist, or Islamic –

[46] As has been noted above (p. 227) there is a much greater degree of unity in Java, though even there the contrast between the western third and the remainder has been evident throughout historic times.

[47] *I.e.* Melayu, Djambi, Palembang and sometimes Atjeh, but significantly not the Batak and Menangkabau highlands which tended to be rival centres of power.

[48] In this connexion the progress of sedimentation along the Sumatran side has been of the greatest significance for, other things being equal, it is clear that this island would have provided the best base from which to command the western approaches.

and by the main streams of international commerce since the industrial revolution. Nevertheless, here also the relatively greater ease of movement by sea than across the wild and rugged interiors of all but the smallest islands has helped to encourage maritime exploits, and indeed the Makasarese and Buginese of southern Celebes have historically ranked among the most outstanding seafarers of the whole archipelago.

Finally, between these two lies the Java Sea which constitutes the all-important link in the series. By comparison with the main route through the Malacca Straits and the South China Sea, the Java Sea may be regarded as a secondary highway in respect of through traffic though, owing to the many drawbacks associated with the infertility and hazards of the lands fringing the Malacca route, the alternative route via the Java Sea and the Sunda and Makasar Straits has sometimes been preferred. But it is above all in relation to the internal communications of Indonesia that the importance of the Java Sea resides, and in this context its relative seclusion compared with the Straits of Malacca and the South China Sea has been an asset rather than a liability, and still remains a vital fact in the strategic and political geography of the present day.

This historic rôle of the Java Sea as the central artery of Indonesia is, of course, intimately bound up with the fact that Java itself lies along its southern shore. For the absence of serious obstacles to movement, either in the form of extensive swamps along the coast or continuous mountain ranges in the interior favoured the precocious development of Java, and the great fertility of its volcanic and alluvial tracts made possible the support of a population so much denser than that of the outer territories, that from early times it was able to exploit its position as a maritime focus to become in a real sense the metropolitan island of the archipelago.

These remarks apply more especially to the eastern two-thirds of Java for, as noted above, most of the area west of the Priangan highlands is less fertile country and has owed its importance more to its position *vis-à-vis* the western approaches and in particular the route through the Sunda Strait which it directly overlooks. For these reasons the interests of western Java have frequently been more closely aligned with southern and eastern Sumatra than with the rest of the island of which geographically it forms part.[49]

Whatever may be the truth concerning the traditional belief that Madjapahit in the 14th century was able to unify the whole archipelago[50], there is no denying that the strength of that kingdom rested upon the combination of the great agricultural wealth of east-central Java and the maritime supremacy which this sustained in the critical region of the Java Sea. And although the Portuguese were never in a position to apply this same strategy effectively, it was again exploited by the Dutch as the essential basis of their power in the Indies from the early decades of the 17th to the middle of the 20th century.

Today, under the newly independent republican regime, the degree of political

[49] As shown, for example, in Figs. 12 and 34. See also Furnivall (A), p. 3.
[50] See above, pp. 116–7.

centralization in Java is as great as ever, and the geographical focality of the Java Sea remains unchanged. But in the last hundred years many other things have changed profoundly. The metropolitan island, having suffered the penalties of its own intrinsic productiveness, is now congested and impoverished, and the primary centres of the country's wealth are no longer the rich grain-, sugar- and coffee-growing districts of Java, but the vast rubber-, petroleum-, tin- and copra-producing territories of the outer islands, notably Sumatra, Celebes and Borneo, in which, moreover, the greatest potentialities for further expansion alike of agriculture, mining and hydro-electric-power production clearly lie.

In these circumstances the continued political ascendancy of Java is essentially a matter of geographical momentum. But geographical momentum is not necessarily permanent, and in view of the centrifugal tendencies which have become apparent in the last few years a high level of statesmanship will assuredly be needed if Indonesia is to be maintained as a single going concern instead of disintegrating into a confused series of petty island states.

SELECT BIBLIOGRAPHY

Braak (A) (B) (C)
Brouwer (A) (B)
Douwes Dekker
Dobby (H)
Fryer (E)
Helbig (B)
Honig and Verdoorn
Kendrew
Lobeck
Miller, A. A.
Mohr (A) (C)
Pannekoek
Posewitz
Robequain (D)
Rutten (A) (B)
Rutter
Schrieke
Scrivenor (A) (B)
Sion
Stamp (A)
Stauffer
Suess
Umbgrove (A) (B)
Van Bemmelen
Van Helsdingen
Van Vuuren
Wallace

Handbook of the Netherlands Indies, 1930
Vademecum voor Nederlands Nieuw Guinea
Chambers's Encyclopædia
Handbook on Netherlands New Guinea
Encyclopædia Britannica
Netherlands East Indies, Vol. I (*N.I.D.*)

Van Vuuren (C) provides an excellent introduction to the physical geography of Indonesia, and Pannekoek is particularly useful on the geomorphology of Java. The most detailed account of the physical geography of Indonesia known to the writer is that contained in *Netherlands East Indies, I* (*N.I.D.*), while Douwes Dekker's book gives an excellent descriptive account of the country with some superb photographic illustrations. Very useful works on geology and structure are those by Brouwer (A) and (B) and Stauffer, while Van Bemmelen may be recommended for the advanced specialist. Braak (A) is a standard work on the Indonesian climate and much other useful material is also contained in the two symposia edited respectively by Rutten (B) and by Honig and Verdoorn. Of the standard regional geographies, Dobby (H) and Robequain (D) are particularly full in their treatment of the physical geography of Indonesia.

CHAPTER 8

Racial, Cultural and Historical Bases of Indonesian Regionalism

I. INTRODUCTION

In the diversity and complexity of its human geography Indonesia is probably unequalled and certainly unsurpassed by any other state in the world of comparable size. Thus, besides the immigrant Chinese, European, Indian and Arab communities, the indigenous population includes speakers of at least 25 different languages and 250 lesser dialects[1] and adherents of three of the world's major religions,[2] while profound racial, cultural and demographic contrasts exist between coast and interior, between the eastern third and the western two-thirds, and between Java and the outer islands as a whole.

This great intricacy of pattern derives on the one hand from the varied succession of ethnic and cultural invasions to which the country has been subjected, and on the other from the elaborately fragmented character of its territory which has at all times affected the course of racial dispersion and cultural diffusion. Moreover, both the sheer size of the archipelago and the barriers to communication presented by the existence of negative tracts of fever-ridden swamps and uplands have meant that the mingling and subsequent evolution of peoples and cultures have proceeded more or less independently in a whole series of separate centres, in each of which the several ingredients have been present in varying proportions and have combined in different ways.

These centres have not, of course, been completely isolated one from another and, in general, movement has been considerably easier by sea than overland. In turn this state of affairs has given rise to the characteristic thalassic pattern of the traditional linguistic and political units (Figs. 35 and 37) and has also facilitated the diffusion of many common cultural traits throughout the coastal lowlands of many parts of the region.

Yet notwithstanding the benefits which the omnipresence of the sea has conferred, both in this respect and also, as noted in Chapter 7, in its effects upon climate, the division of the Indonesian territory among 3,000 islands has undeni-

[1] *Cf.* above, p. 98, note 105.

[2] Viz. Islam, Hinduism and Christianity, as well as surviving traces of Buddhism in the Indianized parts of the country.

ably been a principal cause of the extreme diversity of custom and outlook which today constitutes so serious a threat to internal stability and to the preservation of national unity.[3]

It is the purpose of the present chapter to explain this diversity by reference, first to the indigenous racial and cultural patterns, and secondly to the modifications which have been produced in these as a result successively of Indian and Islamic acculturation and Portuguese and Dutch colonial rule.

II. PRE-EUROPEAN COMPONENTS

The main features of the racial and cultural geography of Indonesia are summarized in Table 16,[4] and at first sight the complexity which this suggests appears baffling. However, when each of the ethnic and cultural layers which have been superimposed upon Indonesia is examined in turn, the significance of the various permutations and combinations of these in different parts of the country is more readily comprehended.

First, then, as regards racial geography, the contrasts between coast and interior and between the western and the eastern islands are all-important. Of the various stocks involved, the Pareœans, who represent the last prehistoric arrivals from the continental mainland, now form the principal element in the western two-thirds of Indonesia, that is as far east as Bali and Celebes inclusive. Throughout the coastlands of this entire area, and particularly in Java and Sumatra, such peoples were firmly established at the time when recorded history begins and, partly because in these generally well-favoured areas they have tended to multiply more rapidly than have the inhabitants of the interior uplands, they have since been driven to expand both eastwards along the coasts of the remaining Lesser Sundas and the Moluccas, and in varying degrees up the major river valleys of the western islands as well. Indeed, in Java the relative ease with which such movement into the interior could be effected has led to the almost complete absorption of earlier stocks, and though the Pareœan peoples[5] of the island themselves fall into three main groups, namely Javanese, Sundanese and Madurese,[6] the differences between these are not great, and the total number of the Badui and Tenggerese survivals of earlier stocks is only a few thousand. Likewise in nearby Bali, Pareœan predominance is almost complete,[7] and the Balinese, who are mostly descended from immigrants from the adjacent parts of eastern

[3] It may be noted that the outer territories of Indonesia have a population roughly as large as that of Thailand spread over an area two-and-a-half times as great.

[4] Although an attempt has been made to bring this up to date, the basic information comes from the last census which was taken in 1930. See *Volkstelling*, 1930, 7 volumes.

[5] All such Pareœan peoples are in varying degree mixed with earlier stocks.

[6] See below, p. 264. The Badui are in south-western Java and the Tenggerese in the Tengger uplands of eastern Java.

[7] The aborigines who survive in a few isolated spots in Bali, the so-called Bali Aga, are predominantly Melanesoid.

TABL

THE INDIGENOU

Group	*Predominant racial stock*	*Home area*	*Number and density per square mile*	*Religion*
1. Atjehnese	Deutero-Malay	Atjeh, N Sumatra. Predominantly coastal but also interior	1,600,000 40–100	Strongly Muslim
2. Bataks	Proto-Malay	Uplands N interior Sumatra and adjacent W coast	2,300,000 70–200	N Animist C Christian S Muslim
2a. Gajo	Proto-Malay	Between 1 and 2	70,000	
3. Menangkabau Malays	Deutero-Malay	Uplands C Sumatra and adjacent W coast	2,600,000 150–500	Strongly Muslim
4. Sumatran Coast Malays	Deutero-Malay	E coast Sumatra between 1 and 6 and nearby islands	2,300,000 15–35	Muslim
5. Redjong-Lebonger	Deutero-Malay	Uplands SW Sumatra and adjacent W coast	400,000 15–35	Lax Muslim
6. Lamponger	Deutero-Malay	S Sumatra	300,000 25–100	Muslim
7. Minor Peoples of Sumatra	(*a*) Orang Akit – Negrito – Sungei Mandau – Animist (*b*) Orang Laut – Proto-Malay – Parts of Riau archipelago – nominal Muslim (*c*) Sakai, Talang, Utan, Rawar – Proto-Malay – Parts of E coast – nominal Muslim (*d*) Orang Mamak, Kubu, Lubu – Proto-Malay – Interior – Animist/Muslim (*e*) Islanders of Simeulue, Nias, Mentawei, Enggano – largely Proto-Malay – 300,000 – Menta			
8. Javanese	Deutero-Malay	C and E Java	35,000,000 750–2,000	Muslim but stron Hindu-Buddhi survivals
9. Djakartans (Batavians)	Mixed	In and around Djakarta	1,300,000	Predominantly Muslim
10. Sundanese	Deutero-Malay	W Java (Pasundan)	11,000,000 450–1,000	Strongly Muslim
11. Madurese	Deutero-Malay	Madura and adjacent parts of E Java	5,600,000 750–2,000	Muslim
12. Minor Peoples of Java	(*a*) Tenggerese – Proto-Malay – E Java – degenerate Hindu – 16,000 – very sparse (*b*) Badui – Negrito-Proto-Malay – Preanger uplands – degenerate Hindu – 1,700 – v			
13. Borneo Malays	Deutero-Proto-Malay	Coastal areas of Borneo	700,000 2–10 in East 1–5 in South 10–30 in West	Muslim

16

PEOPLES OF INDONESIA

Language *M.P. = Malayo-Polynesian*	*Economy*	*Distinctive traits*
Atjehnese (M.P.) Arabic script	Wet rice	Formerly series of tribes which were welded into quasi-national unity by Atjeh war. Skilled craftsmen. Very able traders.
Batak (M.P.) Indian-type script	Wet rice in valleys and terraced slopes. Otherwise shifting cultivation	Vigorous hill people. Multi-family houses. Central group much influenced by German Lutheran missions. Much emigration, largely because of population pressure.
Menangkabau (M.P.) Arabic script	Skilled wet-rice cultivation in valleys and terraced slopes	Matrilineal society, elaborate long family houses. Most advanced peoples of Sumatra, highest percentage school attendance in Indonesia. High level of craftsmanship, very keen traders.
Malay (M.P.) Arabic script	Mainly shifting cultivation; some poor-quality wet-rice cultivation	Keen seafarers who have ventured widely over archipelago. Close affinities with peninsular Malays. Note that population of Cultuurgebied is predominantly immigrant of diverse origin.
Redjangese (M.P.) Indian-type script	Largely shifting cultivation	Some affinities with 3 and 4 but generally more retarded.
Lampong (M.P.) Indian-type script	Mainly wet-rice cultivation; some shifting cultivation	Some affinities with 4. Much influenced by contacts with West Java in past. Note that there are many transmigrants from Java in this area.
45,000, very sparse 10 per sq. m. Nias 75–175	Hunting, fishing, collecting, with some shifting cultivation	
Javanese (M.P.) Indian-type script. Leading literary language of Indonesia	Skilled wet-rice cultivation in lowlands and terraced slopes	Generally considered most advanced people of Indonesia. Individual houses, large nucleated villages. Aristocratic and hierarchical social order. High level of craftsmanship but little interest in trading
Malay (M.P.)	—	Descendants of very heterogeneous groups of peoples who settled outside city walls of old Batavia in early days of V.O.C. Now largely urbanized.
undanese (M.P.) ndian-type script	Wet-rice cultivation in plains; various forms of upland cultivation	Originally hill peoples but now predominantly lowland in habitat. Less sophisticated and less skilled in craftsmanship than Javanese, but reputedly more hardworking.
adurese (M.P.) ndian-type script	Little land suitable for wet cultivation. Skilled dry cultivators. Cattle rearing	Originally limited to Madura but now also found in large numbers in adjacent parts of Java. Less sophisticated than Javanese. Reputedly dour and hardworking.
arse	Shifting cultivation	
alay (M.P.) rabic script	Largely shifting cultivation. Some wet rice	Similar to 4, but not identical with them, owing to extensive Javanese, Buginese and Arab admixture.

TABLE 16—

Group	*Predominant racial stock*	*Home area*	*Number and density per square mile*	*Religion*
14. Bandjarese	Deutero-/Proto-Malay	Coastal areas around Bandjermasin, S Borneo	1,200,000 70–175	Strongly Muslim
15. Dyaks (and minor peoples of Borneo)	Proto-Malay etc.	Interior Borneo	1,300,000 1–10	Animist
16. Balinese	Deutero-Malay	Bali and W coast Lombok	1,700,000 500–1,200	Hindu, with strong Buddhist survivals
17. Sasaks	Proto-Malay	Lombok	1,000,000 250–500	Lax Muslim
18. Makasarese	Deutero-Malay	SW Celebes around Makasar	1,000,000 200–700	Muslim
19. Buginese	Deutero-Malay	SW Celebes	2,200,000 125–350	Muslim
20. Menadonese (Minahasans)	Deutero-Malay (akin to Filipino)	E half of N limb of Celebes	400,000 35–350	Christian
21. Other Coastal Peoples of Celebes	Deutero-/Proto-Malay	(*a*) W half N Celebes (*b*) W Celebes (*c*) E and SE Celebes and nearby islands	Gorontalese: 400,000 Mandarese: 300,000 Others: 1,200,000 35–200	Muslim
22. Toradjas (and minor peoples of Celebes)	Proto-Malay etc.	Interior Celebes	700,000 10–20	Animist/ Christian
23. Coastal Peoples of Eastern Lesser Sundas	Deutero-Malay much mixed with 24	Belunese, Atonis } Timor Bimanese, Sumbawans } Sumbawa	2,500,000 35–250 (23 and 24)	Muslim
24. Inland Peoples of Eastern Lesser Sundas	Melanesoid, Australoid and Negrito	Sumbanese – Sumba Manggaraians, Sikkanese, Lionese } Flores		Animist an Christian i Flores, Timo Sumba etc.
25. Coastal Peoples of Moluccas	Deutero-Malay much mixed with 26	Ambonese – Ambon	800,000 7–250 (25 and 26)	Muslim an Christian i Ambon, Bur Seram etc.
26. Alfurs	Various, largely Melanesoid	Ternatese – Ternate Halmaherans – Halmahera		Animist/ Christian
27. Peoples of West New Guinea	(*a*) Coastal fringes W and N W. Some Indonesian settlement – Muslim (*b*) NE coast – Melanesian languages and cultures – Animist/Christian (*c*) Interior – Papuan – Animist/Christian		1,000,000 0–10	

Continued

Language *M.P.=Malayo-Polynesian*	*Economy*	*Distinctive traits*
Malay (M.P.) Arabic script	Wet-rice cultivation	Similar to 13 but Javanese influence more in evidence. Individualistic and enterprising emigrants.
Dyak group (M.P.)	Shifting cultivation, hunting, fishing, collecting	A collective name covering a wide range of cultural differences. Most live in communal long houses.
Balinese (M.P.) Indian-type script	Skilled wet-rice cultivation	A highly advanced people whose culture represents a survival of Hindu-Javanese traditional civilization. Very high level of craftsmanship and artistry.
Sasak (M.P.) (closely akin to Balinese)	Wet-rice cultivation	Much more backward than 16 but appreciably influenced by contact with 16, who were formerly their overlords.
Makasarese (M.P.) Indian-type script	Wet-rice cultivation	Ethnically related to 4 and 8. Skilled seamen and enterprising traders. Less skilled as cultivators.
Buginese (M.P.) (closely akin to Makasarese)	Wet-rice cultivation	Closely similar to 18.
Menadonese (M.P.) (akin to S Philippine group)	Wet-rice cultivation	Various affinities with peoples of southern Philippines but strongly influenced by Dutch Protestant missions. High percentage of school attendance.
Various, M.P. (akin to 18 and 19)	Wet-rice and shifting cultivation	Similar to 18 but with less interest in seamanship; more stay-at-home.
Toradja (M.P.) group	Mostly shifting cultivation; some sedentary cultivation	A collective name covering many separate tribes. Most live in communal family houses. Some groups much influenced by missions.
Bima-Sumbawa group (M.P.)	Wet-rice/shifting maize cultivation	Deutero-Malay element most marked in coastal fringe.
Timor group (M.P.)	Shifting maize cultivation/ hunting and collecting	Very mixed ethnically. More and more backward from W to E, grading from Indonesian to Papuan cultures. Some islands much influenced by missions.
Sulu-Batjan group Ambon group (M.P.)	Wet-rice/shifting cultivation	Deutero-Malay element largely from Celebes. In many islands much modified by European (Portuguese and Dutch) influence, including miscegenation.
S. Halmahera group (Melanesian) N. Halmahera group (Papuan)	Mainly hunting, fishing, collecting—largely sago	A collective name covering great diversity. Generally very primitive. Some islands much influenced by missions.
	Shifting cultivation but mainly hunting, fishing and collecting—largely sago	

Java,[8] have in turn subsequently spread also into the western coastal fringe of Lombok.[9]

In Sumatra again the Parecean advance has proceeded far inland, notably in the middle of the island, where the Menangkabau Malays occupy the Padang highlands and much of the western coast as well, though there nevertheless remain several large groups of pre-Parecean peoples such as the Nesiot Bataks[10] and Gajo of the northern uplands, the various island peoples off the western coast, again mainly Nesiot, and isolated groups of diverse origin, ranging from the Negrito Orang Akit to the Nesiot Sakai, amid the swamps and jungles of the eastern littoral.

In origin the Menangkabau and Coast Malays were closely related, though numerous distinctions gradually grew up between them after the former had settled in the western uplands and the latter had become established along the eastern seaboard where they constitute the predominant group today. And although there was some early, as well as more recent, migration of Menangkabaus into western Malaya,[11] it was above all the Sumatran Coast Malays, with their strong seafaring traditions, who played the leading part in the settlement of the Malay peninsula, as also of coastal Borneo and various eastern islands, in all of which areas they appear to have intermingled both with earlier stocks and with other Parecean immigrants, notably from Java and Celebes.

Certainly in Borneo and Celebes Parecean stocks are again predominant, though in both islands physical obstacles to movement into the interior are more severe than in Java and Sumatra, and accordingly a larger proportion of the total area is still occupied by peoples of mainly Nesiot stock, namely the Dyaks and Toradjas respectively. But whereas in Borneo the coastal peoples, though variously derived from Malay, Javanese and Buginese[12] admixture with earlier Nesiot stocks, have maintained close contact among themselves, the corresponding peoples of the several peninsulas of Celebes have remained much more isolated one from another, and today some seven separate groups may be distinguished among them.

By contrast to the Greater Sundas and the adjacent island of Bali, the islands which lie farther to the east bear a much more superficial Parecean imprint. Thus here, even among the relatively recent[13] coastal settlements traditionally attributed to seafaring peoples from the western islands[14], there is much evidence

[8] Such migrations occurred notably in the 9th and again in the 16th–17th centuries.

[9] Lombok came under the domination of Bali in 1740. There were 30,425 Balinese in Lombok in 1930, in addition to the majority people, *i.e.* the Nesiot Sasaks, and a small number of Bodha (Melanesoid) in the interior.

[10] The name Batak was the Coast Malays' term for the peoples of the interior in general. *Cf.* Dyak, Toradja and Alfur, which are the coast peoples' names for the interior peoples respectively of Borneo, Celebes and the Moluccas. See also above, p. 67.

[11] See below, p. 592.

[12] The homeland of the Buginese is in south-western Celebes.

[13] *I.e.* during the last thousand years or so.

[14] Particularly Java and Celebes.

of intermixture with earlier stocks, notably the Melanesoid, and this strain becomes increasingly prevalent eastwards to form by far the most important component in the Alfur peoples of the Moluccas and the Papuan indigenes of New Guinea.[15] Although it is impossible to draw any hard and fast line between the areas of Pareœan and those of Melanesoid predominance, it is none the less abundantly clear that such a division does exist, and that both the whole of New Guinea, together with several of the remoter islands of the Moluccas, belong ethnically with the South-west Pacific rather than with the Indonesian realm.

In respect of spoken language and material culture a roughly parallel gradation to that in racial type may be discerned, both from west to east and from coast to interior, over the archipelago as a whole. Thus all the Pareœan groups speak closely related Malayo-Polynesian languages, and the majority of the coastal peoples in western Indonesia likewise practise irrigated rice cultivation,[16] though admittedly shifting tillage survives in several places either as a result of geographical isolation or local difficulties of terrain. But east of Lombok and south-western Celebes wet cultivation is much less common, and in so far as it does occur it is for the most part limited to areas where the Pareœan element is well represented. Elsewhere in the eastern islands dry cultivation of maize and upland rice is interspersed with hunting, fishing and collecting,[17] which together form the main occupations of the more primitive Melanesoid peoples, both in the Moluccan and New Guinean interiors.

Nevertheless, even in the limited sense considered above, the correlation between racial and cultural distributions is by no means exact, and in particular many of the more accessible non-Pareœan peoples have learned much through contact with their more advanced neighbours. Thus, for example, such peoples as the Bataks and Sasaks are now expert cultivators of wet paddy, and especially in recent years knowledge of this method of cultivation has advanced among many of the hitherto most backward peoples in the eastern archipelago as well.[18] Similarly all the major inland peoples of the western islands speak Malayo-Polynesian languages which are not fundamentally dissimilar from those of their coastal neighbours,[19] and such languages likewise prevail over practically the whole of the eastern archipelago, save only for Halmahera and New Guinea, where the Melanesoid branch of the Austronesian family is represented over most of the coastal fringe, and the completely unrelated but as yet virtually unclassified Papuan family is found in interior New Guinea and the northern extremity of Halmahera.

[15] Also in these eastern islands there are traces of Negrito, a type which is found relatively pure in the Tapiro of New Guinea, and of Australoid, notably in Timor which lies closest to Australia.

[16] Though in many of these areas irrigated rice cultivation has been introduced only during the last few centuries.

[17] The last includes much collecting of the pith of the sago palm, which grows wild.

[18] Particularly under Dutch governmental and missionary tuition.

[19] But many of these inlanders have no literate culture of their own.

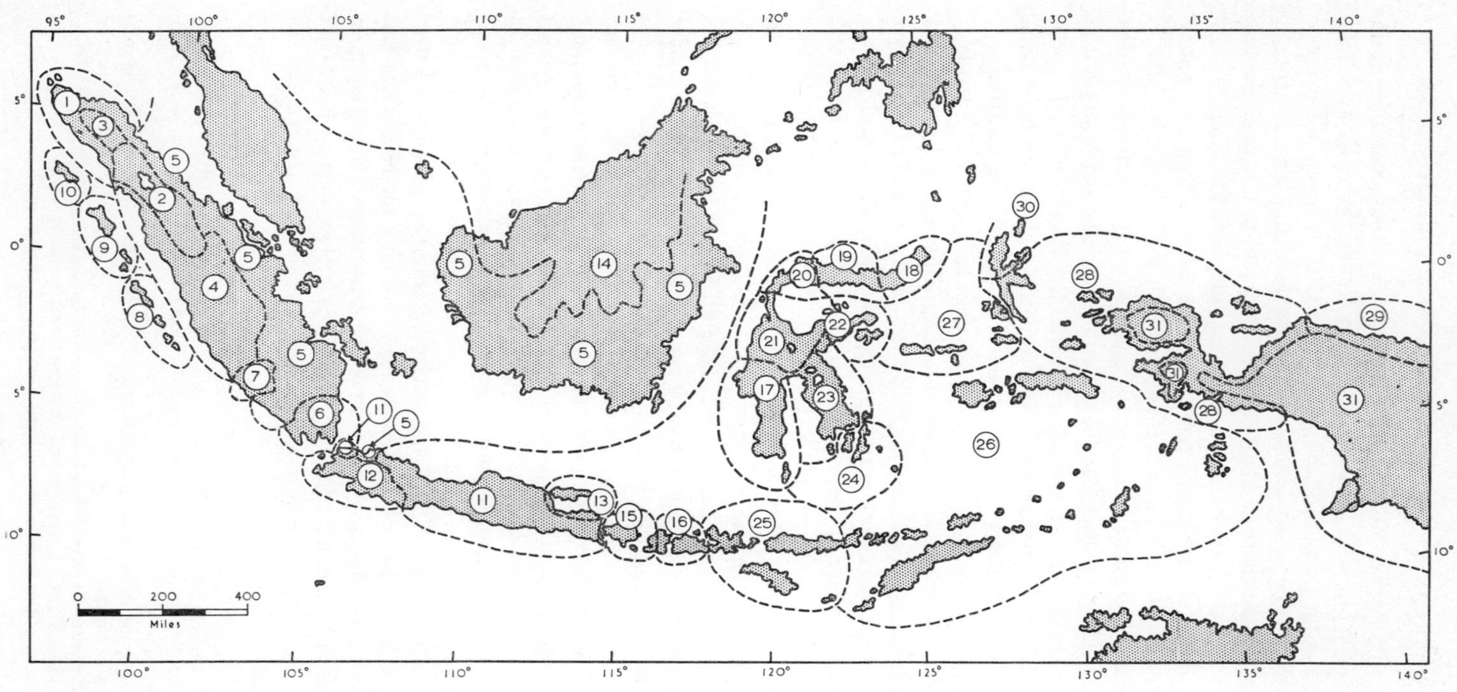

FIG. 35—Indonesia: regional languages

1. Atjehnese. 2. Batak. 3. Gajo. 4. Menangkabau. 5. Malay. 6. Lampong. 7. Redjangese. 8. Mentawei. 9. Nias. 10. Simeulue. 11. Javanese. 12. Sundanese. 13. Madurese. 14. Dyak group. 15. Balinese. 16. Sasak. 17. Makasarese – Buginese. 18. Menadonese. 19. Gorontalese. 20. Tomini. 21. Toradja group. 22. Loinang group. 23. Bungkus – Laki group. 24. Munaas – Butung group. 25. Bima – Sumbawa group. 26. Ambon – Timor group. 27. Sula – Batjan group. 28. S. Halmahera – W. New Guinea group. 29. N. New Guinea group. 30. N. Halmahera group. 31. Interior New Guinea group.

The great era of Indianization during the early centuries A.D. marked a further stage in the process of regional differentiation within the archipelago, and from this time forward two key areas began to stand out as cultural and political foci of more than local significance.[20] The first of these comprised the lands bordering the great maritime crossroads of the west, where the Straits of Malacca and Sunda meet the Java and South China Seas, and here, particularly in the lowlands of eastern and south-eastern Sumatra, Indian acculturation can be traced back at least to the 5th century. The other major focus of early Indianization was in the interior valleys of eastern and central Java, areas whose importance rested primarily on the comparatively large population which their fertile soils were able to support, and to a lesser extent on the excellent network of river communications provided respectively by the Solo and Brantas systems.

By the second half of the first millennium A.D. Indian cultural influence had begun to spread farther afield, ultimately reaching eastwards to the coasts of Timor and the Moluccas, and inland to the highlands of western Sumatra by the 12th–14th centuries. In all of these areas its imprint is still evident in a wide range of features, from Indian-style scripts and methods of political organization to the occasional *kraton* (court) town and the remains of Hindu or Buddhist temples.

Nevertheless, south-eastern Sumatra and more especially east-central Java long retained their pre-eminence, and in both areas powerful kingdoms had already arisen as early as the 7th century. Thus in the west the great maritime power of Sri Vijaya, centred in Palembang and controlling the whole eastern coast of Sumatra and the western shores of the Malay peninsula and of Borneo, remained supreme despite many vicissitudes until the 12th century. Meanwhile a whole succession of powerful kingdoms rose and fell in east-central Java, beginning with Ho-ling (Kalinga) in the Upper Progo and Solo valleys during the 7th century, and followed later by Mataram, which, after moving its capital east to the Brantas valley in 929, established close ties with Bali and other islands still farther to the east. This alignment between eastern Java and the eastern archipelagos achieved a new significance under Janggala-Kediri[21] and later, in the 13th century, under Singhasari, when the port cities of the north Java coast[22] began to thrive on the spice trade with the Moluccas,[23] a region which first entered the main stream of Indonesian history about this time. Indeed, from then until the 18th century or so when the spice trade declined, the Moluccas came to form a third main focus of interest within the archipelago though, owing to the smallness of the component islands and the insignificant number of their inhabitants, they rarely constituted a major seat of political power in their

[20] See Furnivall (A), pp. 2–3.

[21] Janggala was in the Brantas delta and Kediri in the upper Brantas valley.

[22] First Tuban, later also Gresik, Surabaja, Djapara and Demak.

[23] Various timbers, notably sandalwood, and other forest produce also formed items of trade.

own right, but tended rather to be treated as satellites by the various Javanese kingdoms.

Following the decline and ultimate collapse of Sri Vijaya in the 14th century,[24] the new kingdom of Madjapahit, which had meanwhile succeeded Singhasari in eastern Java and built up an even more extensive sphere of influence than its predecessors in the islands to the east, established its power also over most of the western territories formerly ruled over by Palembang. Thus, if the traditional view be accepted, both of the key seats of political power, as well as the third centre of economic significance in the Moluccas, were all united for a brief spell in the 14th century under a single authority, whose sphere of influence included virtually the whole of modern Indonesia from northern Sumatra to Timor and Halmahera.

Admittedly the nature of Madjapahit's suzerainty over these outlying territories has been much exaggerated and indeed in most cases now seems to have been no more than nominal.[25] Nevertheless, the Madjapahit period did mark the emergence of Java as the prime focus of the archipelago and, notwithstanding many and far-reaching changes which were to follow in later centuries, the memory of this golden age of Indonesian unity – whether real or fictitious – has never since been allowed to die.

Besides setting the stage for the ascendancy of Java within the archipelago as a whole, the decline of Sri Vijaya was followed by a shift in the political and cultural centre of gravity within Sumatra itself. After the 12th–14th centuries the south-eastern coastlands began to recede into relative obscurity and, although Palembang survived as a locally important *kraton* town, the peasant peoples of the surrounding countryside are today among the least skilled cultivators of any Pareœan group in the western archipelago, relying for the most part on shifting tillage interspersed with occasional and rather inefficient wet-paddy growing. But in the meantime both the northern tip of Sumatra, which was not seriously affected by sedimentation, and more particularly the fertile plateaux in the west of the island achieved a new importance.

It was in the latter area that the Hindu-Malay kingdom of Menangkabau[26] rose for a time after the late 13th century to a position of great eminence, and to this day the Menangkabaus are the most advanced people in Sumatra, and indeed are among the best educated and most vigorous groups in all Indonesia. Moreover, the nearby Bataks, although formerly regarded as primitives by the Coast Malays, have also made spectacular progress, which has continued in modern times under missionary influence,[27] and it is nowadays in the Menangkabau and

[24] The focus of Sri Vijaya had in the meantime shifted from Palembang to Melayu (Djambi) in the 12th century.

[25] See above, pp. 116–7.

[26] As noted above, p. 116, note 30, the Malay royal house of Palembang withdrew to the Menangkabau highlands after 1286, and this latter area subsequently became the main cultural centre of the Malay peoples.

[27] The southern Bataks are Muslim, those of the centre largely Christian and the northerners still pagan, though partly influenced by Hinduism.

Batak lands that the highest densities of population and the most skilful irrigated rice cultivation in all Sumatra are found.

In short, since the 14th century a complete reversal appears to have taken place in the relative standing of the East Coast Malays on the one hand and the Menangkabaus and Bataks on the other, and it is tempting to seek an explanation in terms of the increasingly unhealthy and enervating conditions of the swamp-ridden lowlands, and the altogether more stimulating climate, as well as the more fertile soils derived from neutral-basic volcanic materials, in the Padang and Toba highlands.[28] Be that as it may, it is clear that after the decay of Sri Vijaya the main centre of interest in Sumatra shifted to the west and, despite the far rougher seas of the exposed Indian Ocean coast compared with those along the Straits shore, the former for a time assumed greater importance owing to its proximity to the western highlands.[29]

Yet the decline of the south-east Sumatran ports did not mean that the Straits seaway had lost its critical importance and *c.* 1377 Madjapahit carried out a series of attacks to bring Tumasik and Pasei as well as Palembang under more effective control. Nevertheless, Madjapahit's main preoccupation was with Java and the islands farther east, and in these circumstances it was not surprising that a new power should have emerged on the shores of the Straits seaway to challenge the supremacy of the Javanese empire in this vital western region.

That power was medieval Malacca, which grew up on the south-western coast of the Malay peninsula, overlooking the Straits which now bear its name, and in the course of the 15th century became, in effect, the geopolitical successor to Sri Vijaya. Thus, once again the second great regional focus of the archipelago began to stand out as a separate entity, wholly distinct politically from the primary nucleus in east-central Java.

The rise of Malacca and the associated dissemination of the Muslim religion mark the beginning of a further major phase in the cultural evolution and the regional differentiation of Indonesia. As described in Chapter 3, Islam, like the earlier Hindu and Buddhist faiths, was brought to Indonesia from peninsular India, and spread along the sea lanes through the archipelago from west to east. In a broad way, therefore, the pattern of its distribution recalls that of the earlier Indianized culture upon which it became superimposed, and indeed all the main centres of the older Indian religions were sooner or later converted to Islam with the solitary exception of Bali, which in the early 17th century[30] provided a refuge

[28] If virulent malaria did not reach Indonesia until early in the second millennium A.D. (see above, p. 57) it might well have been a major factor, in association with coastal silting, in bringing about the downfall of Sri Vijaya, but the highlands above the limit of malaria vectors would have been largely immune from its ravages. Similar factors may also help to explain the traditional belief that the Sundanese (until recently uplanders) are more industrious than the Javanese.

[29] At a later date Benkulen was also important for similar reasons.

[30] *I.e.* when the last remnants of Madjapahit in eastern Java were conquered by the Islamic principalities of the northern coast.

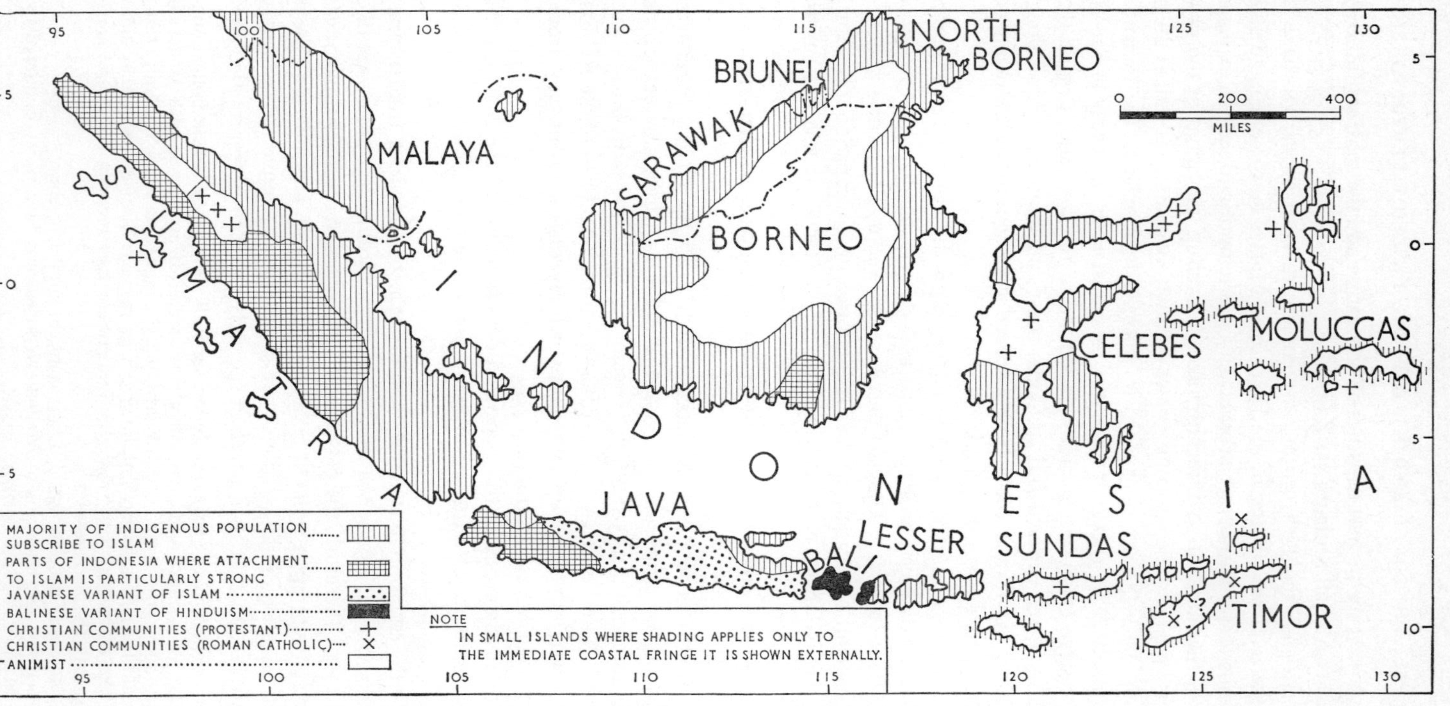
NORTH BORNEO
BRUNEI
SARAWAK
BORNEO
MALAYA
SUMATRA
INDONESIA
JAVA
BALI
LESSER SUNDAS
CELEBES
MOLUCCAS
TIMOR
0 200 400
MILES
MAJORITY OF INDIGENOUS POPULATION SUBSCRIBE TO ISLAM
PARTS OF INDONESIA WHERE ATTACHMENT TO ISLAM IS PARTICULARLY STRONG
JAVANESE VARIANT OF ISLAM
BALINESE VARIANT OF HINDUISM
CHRISTIAN COMMUNITIES (PROTESTANT)
CHRISTIAN COMMUNITIES (ROMAN CATHOLIC)
ANIMIST
NOTE
IN SMALL ISLANDS WHERE SHADING APPLIES ONLY TO THE IMMEDIATE COASTAL FRINGE IT IS SHOWN EXTERNALLY.
95
100
105
110
115
120
125
130
5
0
5
10

FIG. 36—Indonesia and neighbouring areas: religions

for many of the Hindu nobility of Madjapahit in eastern Java, and has since survived as a living museum of the old Indo-Javanese civilization. Moreover, as with the earlier Indianized culture so again with the Muslim religion, a marked falling off in intensity may be observed eastwards from Lombok and Celebes, and inland from the coastal fringes of the latter and Borneo, and in fact among the inhabitants of all these areas, as also among a majority of the Bataks, the traditional animist beliefs have been little disturbed by either Hinduism, Buddhism or Islam.[31]

Nevertheless, in detail the geographical pattern of Islam in Indonesia differs significantly from that of the earlier Indianized culture. For the very fact that east-central Java and parts of south-eastern Sumatra were much more intensely Indianized than the rest meant that Islam, though it was accepted there, became profoundly changed in the process. Indeed, in accepting Islam the Javanese merely added it as yet another component to their syncretic system of beliefs, in which imported Hindu and Buddhist teachings were inextricably intermingled with still earlier elements. Thus the Javanese lands cannot be regarded as the main stronghold of Indonesian Islam and instead this honour has more usually been claimed by Atjeh, the Sultanate which occupies the extreme north-western tip of Sumatra. For, thanks to its geographical position, Atjeh, besides being relatively remote from the main Indianized centres, was both the first part of the archipelago to be converted to Islam and the one which found it easiest to maintain contact with the rest of the Muslim world in subsequent centuries.[32]

Thus in Atjeh the Islamic faith has been practised with an intensity which is remarkable for Indonesia, and the Atjehnese language is written in the Arabic script. This script has also been adopted by the neighbouring Coast and Menangkabau Malays who were converted to Islam by the Atjehnese themselves, but the usage does not extend to either the Bataks or the Islamized peoples of Java and Celebes, who mostly used Indian-style scripts prior to Romanization in colonial times.

Apart from the Atjehnese, the Menangkabaus and the small group of southern Bataks noted above, two other main groups have gained a reputation for the intensity of their devotion to Islam, namely the Sundanese who, as the occupants of the interior uplands of Priangan in western Java[33] were both less intensely Indianized than, and traditionally hostile to the Javanese, and the Bandjarese of southern Borneo, who are the descendants of immigrant Javanese peoples much mixed with Dyak, Malay, Buginese and Arab stocks. But among the remainder of the Indonesian population, the great majority of whom nominally profess Islam today, the faith differs significantly from that which prevails in the Muslim

[31] Islam is still making fresh converts among such peoples as the Dyaks, Toradjas and Alfurs, though in most cases the Muslim veneer is very thin.

[32] Notably with India and Turkey. In 1868 when Dutch pressure became strong, Atjeh sought unavailingly to recognize the overlordship of Turkey.

[33] Later the Sundanese spread also into the plains of western Java.

lands of the Middle East,[34] and in many of the more backward islands it represents little more than a thin veneer upon a scarcely concealed pagan base.

Closely associated with the original diffusion of the Muslim religion was the development of a simplified form of Malay as the *lingua franca* among the maritime trading peoples of the archipelago. As we have already seen, all the more advanced and indeed many of the more backward peoples of the region speak Malayo-Polynesian languages, all of which have numerous words in common and a basic similarity in etymology and syntax. Thus, while as a result of differential evolution in the several parts of the archipelago these languages are not mutually intelligible, and indeed the more elaborate among them, like the highly inflected Javanese, are distinctly hard to master, the colloquial form of speech used by the peninsular Malay inhabitants of old Malacca was easily learned as a medium of mutual intercourse by the merchants who at this time began to flock to the port from all over Indonesia. Moreover, in the course of subsequent centuries, during which it was still further reduced to its bare essentials, it came to be widely known throughout the coastlands of all but the most insignificant islands, and even among the peoples of the remoter interiors most communities have long had one or two members capable of conversing in this local esperanto.[35]

Nevertheless, the period which saw the initial spread of Islam and of the Malay language was marked by growing political disunity. For, as one by one the lesser kingdoms and principalities were converted to the new religion, they broke away from Madjapahit, and although later there were signs of an incipient regrouping under the ægis of Malacca, this process was arrested by the Portuguese conquest of 1511, and thereafter the geopolitical evolution of the Indies took a different turn.

Admittedly the Portuguese, despite their command of the western sea approaches, exerted comparatively little positive effect on Indonesia, and the Muslim advance continued unabated throughout the 16th century. Owing to the limited sea-power at their disposal and to the weakness from which Malacca suffered as a base because of its dependence on imported food, the Portuguese were never in a position to establish themselves firmly in Java, the primary seat of power within the archipelago. But the Dutch who succeeded them in the 17th century were a very different proposition, and under their rule the whole character of the archipelago was gradually transformed.

III. THE EXTENSION OF DUTCH RULE OVER THE INDIES

In contrast to the essentially marginal position of the Portuguese, the Dutch, though also at first attracted by the Spice Islands, were quick to appreciate the

[34] Even though a high proportion of the population make the pilgrimage to the holy places of Arabia. This traffic was highly organized by the K.P.M. (see below, p. 262) which carried a record total of 52,000 pilgrims in 1926–7. In 1960 the number was 10,738.

[35] Malay is the basis of the new national language *Bahasa Indonesia*. See Kennedy (A), p. 8 and below, pp. 368–9.

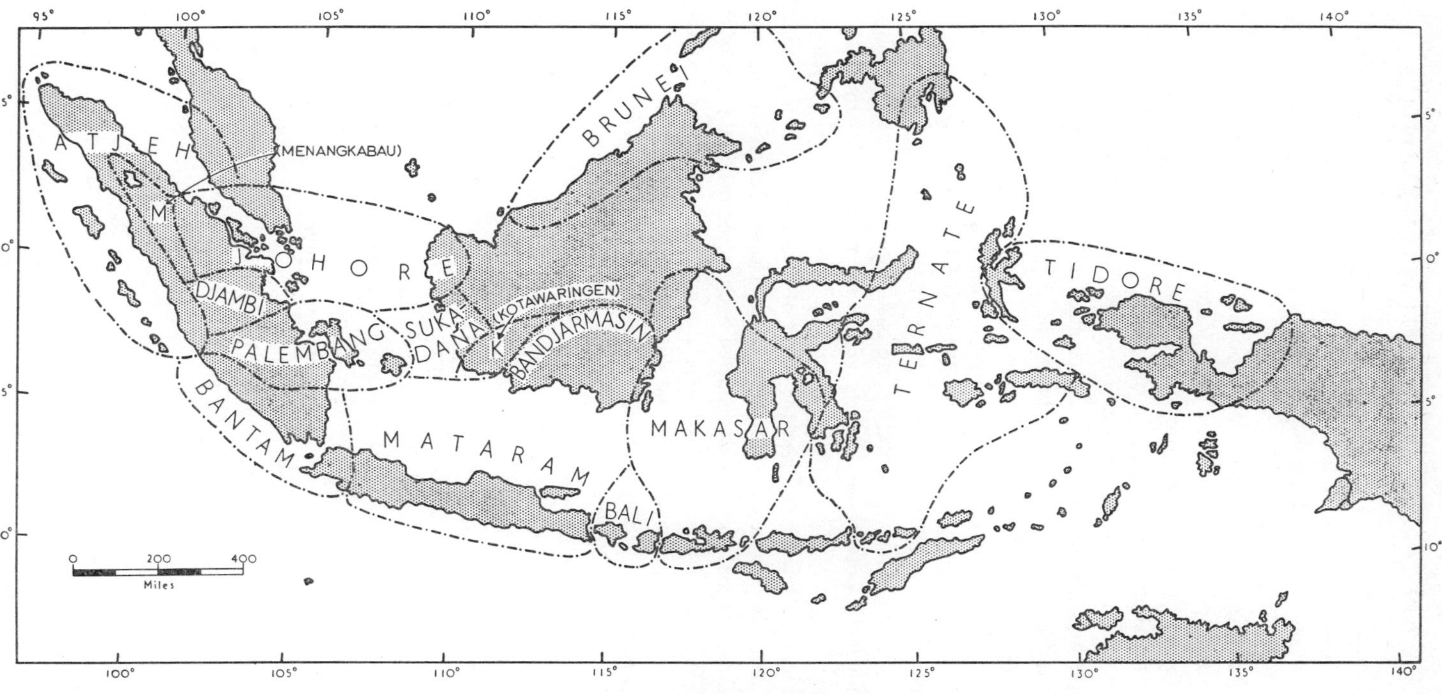

FIG. 37—Indonesia: indigenous states, 17th century

critical importance of Java *vis-à-vis* the maritime arteries of Indonesia, and once Coen had established the V.O.C's headquarters in that island at Batavia in 1621 the chances of any extensive regrouping under indigenous leadership were greatly reduced.

Nevertheless, such a resurgence was a possibility for a time during the 16th and 17th centuries, with first Atjeh and later Mataram as the leading protagonist.[36] Here again the traditional dualism is apparent, for while Atjeh was a maritime and commercial state, which sought to replace Malacca as the leading power in the Straits, Mataram was the latest of the long line of land-based kingdoms in east-central Java which can be traced back at least to the 7th century.

But although during the 16th century the Atjehnese gained a powerful grip on the pepper trade of Sumatra and also seized the portion of the island's western coast which had hitherto been occupied by Menangkabau, the opposition aroused in neighbouring states by Atjeh's ruthlessness ruled out any chance it might otherwise have had of establishing a more wide-ranging hegemony.

In the meantime the Dutch were more preoccupied with the new kingdom of Mataram which, notwithstanding its adherence to Islam, claimed to be the legitimate successor of Madjapahit, and in the late 16th and early 17th centuries extended its territories to embrace the whole of the eastern half of Java including Madura and the ports of the northern coast. Under Sultan Agung (1613–45) during whose reign the capital was shifted back to the original locus of the first Mataram in central Java,[37] a conscious attempt was made to re-establish the Madjapahit empire, but in the event his attempt to drive the Dutch out of Batavia in 1628–9 proved unsuccessful. Moreover, Mataram, which was anxious to curb the influence of the coastal ports, did its best to undermine their seaborne trade, and in thus fatally weakening the indigenous links between Java and the outer islands effectively destroyed the one conceivable means of countering the growing power of the Dutch.

Accordingly the latter, after first extending their foothold around Batavia,[38] and then seizing Malacca from the Portuguese in 1641, were in a position to control both of the principal foci within the archipelago. For the presence of Dutch naval vessels in the Straits constituted a serious obstacle to the revival of Atjehnese ambitions, and the Company likewise lost no opportunity of extending its power eastwards along the northern littoral of Java.

Since the V.O.C. built up its position in Indonesia by a skilful application of the tactics of divide and rule, the period of its ascendancy in the 17th and 18th centuries was marked by an acceleration of the trend towards political disintegration which had begun with the downfall of Madjapahit and the subsequent rise

[36] See Vlekke (A), p. 108.

[37] This was symbolized by his assumption of the title Susuhunan (Emperor) in 1625, a title still borne by the ruler of Surakarta, though the ruler of Djokjakarta is styled Sultan. See below, p. 256.

[38] So assuring it of a better local food supply though it also imported rice from eastern Java.

of Atjeh, Mataram and Ternate as the dominant powers, respectively in the western, central and eastern portions of the archipelago.

In the Moluccas, where the Company founded its first Indonesian settlement at Ambon in 1605, its policy was particularly unfortunate, and local rivalries were deliberately fanned in order to strengthen the Dutch position *vis-à-vis* the Portuguese and the powerful Muslim sultans of Ternate and Tidore who controlled the spice trade. As part of this policy the V.O.C. undertook the conversion to Protestantism[39] of the many Roman Catholic converts which the Portuguese had previously succeeded i making among the indigenous peoples of these eastern islands, notably Ambon, Banda and Saparua, where Islam had scarcely penetrated beyond the range of the sultans' courts. Further, in order to maintain the price of spices, the Company restricted the production of cloves and nutmegs to Ambon and Banda respectively, and in the related attempts to prevent illicit production and smuggling elsewhere it largely destroyed the indigenous commerce of the eastern seas. In 1667 the Dutch seized Makasar, hitherto the headquarters of this trade,[40] and thereafter the Buginese peoples of south-western Celebes, who had played a leading rôle in the inter-island trade, turned instead to piracy and to this end founded a series of settlements along the coasts not only of Celebes but also of Borneo, Bali, Lombok and many lesser islands.[41]

By the time the Company's rule came to an end in 1798 the inhabitants of practically all the eastern islands had been reduced to a state of apathy mingled with hostility against the Dutch. Yet the effective occupation of the latter in this region was limited to a handful of minute islands, notably Ambon and Banda, and a few small enclaves in Seram, Buru and around Makasar and Menado.[42] Only the last named, at the extreme north-eastern tip of Celebes, formed a significant exception, for there the Dutch had been welcomed as deliverers against both the Spaniards and the Sultan of Ternate, when in 1679 they established a post in this, the chief town of the Minahasa district.

In the critical region focusing on the Malacca Straits, at the opposite extremity of the archipelago, the Company's policy was less ruthless but scarcely more constructive. For while the strategically vital Straits were controlled by the Dutch from Malacca, the policy of concentrating all trade on Batavia led to a catastrophic decline in the peninsular port and, so far as Sumatra was concerned, the west coast remained the more important. In fact, although the V.O.C. had established nominal claims over pratically the whole coastline of Sumatra and Borneo, its interests there were limited almost entirely to patrolling the sea-

[39] See Vlekke (A), p. 148. Characteristically, however, much of the Roman Catholic ritual survives in association with Protestant dogma, and Portuguese influence is also apparent in the local speech.

[40] Makasar had inherited this rôle from the north Java ports which had been reduced by Mataram.

[41] Buginese settlement eventually extended as far west as Selangor in the Malay peninsula.

[42] Tidore and Ternate respectively recognized Dutch sovereignty in 1667 and 1683.

ways,[43] and keeping on sufficiently friendly terms with the coastal sultans to obtain regular supplies of pepper, and of small quantities of tin from Bangka, Belitung and Perak in the Malay peninsula.

In contrast to the outlying islands, Java was the scene of steadily expanding activity under the V.O.C., but here again the Dutch followed divisive tactics as, first for security reasons, and later in order to obtain control over lands capable of producing export crops of sugar and coffee, they extended their hold outwards from the original bridgehead at Batavia.

Owing to the town's position between Bantam and Mataram, the two most powerful sultanates of 17th-century Java, the Dutch in Batavia were at first extremely hard pressed to maintain their ground, and were soon involved in conflicts with both of these neighbours. However, in 1677 the V.O.C. acquired a strip of territory lying to the east of Batavia and extending right across the island from the northern coast, through the potentially rich coffee lands of Priangan, to the southern seaboard, and by 1684 Bantam had been reduced to the level of a client state. Thereafter, the Dutch sought to undermine Mataram by cutting it off from the coast; an enclave around the port of Tjirebon was occupied in 1678, and by 1743 the whole of the northern seaboard of Java, except for the extreme east which retained close ties with Bali, was under the Company's control.

After many upheavals and repeated shifts of its capital, Mataram fell apart under continuing Dutch pressure to form the two states of Surakarta and Djokjakarta in 1755, by which time the V.O.C. had become the largest territorial power in the island. But it was not until the conclusion of the Java War in 1830 that Dutch sovereignty was established over the ancient nucleus of Javanese political power in the inland regions of the centre and east. And even then, thanks to the relative isolation of the southern plateaux, Surakarta and Djokjakarta – the former still claiming direct descent from Madjapahit – were able to preserve something of their separate identity in the political geography of the island as the two remaining Vorstenlanden (princely states) when all the rest had come under a more direct form of Dutch rule.[44]

After the liquidation of the V.O.C. in 1798 the Dutch government assumed direct responsibility for the administration of the Indies. Nevertheless, much of the mentality of Company rule persisted, and especially during the period of the *cultuur stelsel* from 1830 to 1870 the country continued to be run as a business concern whose *raison d'être* was to provide profits for the mother country. During the so-called Liberal Era which followed after 1870, private enterprise began to play a much larger part in economic development, but with the introduction of the Ethical Policy in 1901/2 the government again took the initiative in numerous measures aimed at the economic betterment and social well-being

[43] For which purpose they held a few scattered strongposts on the coasts of Sumatra and Borneo, as well as Malacca.

[44] The two smaller principalities, Mangkunegara and Paku Alam, were fiefs respectively of Surakarta and Djokjakarta. See Vlekke (A), pp. 247 and 267.

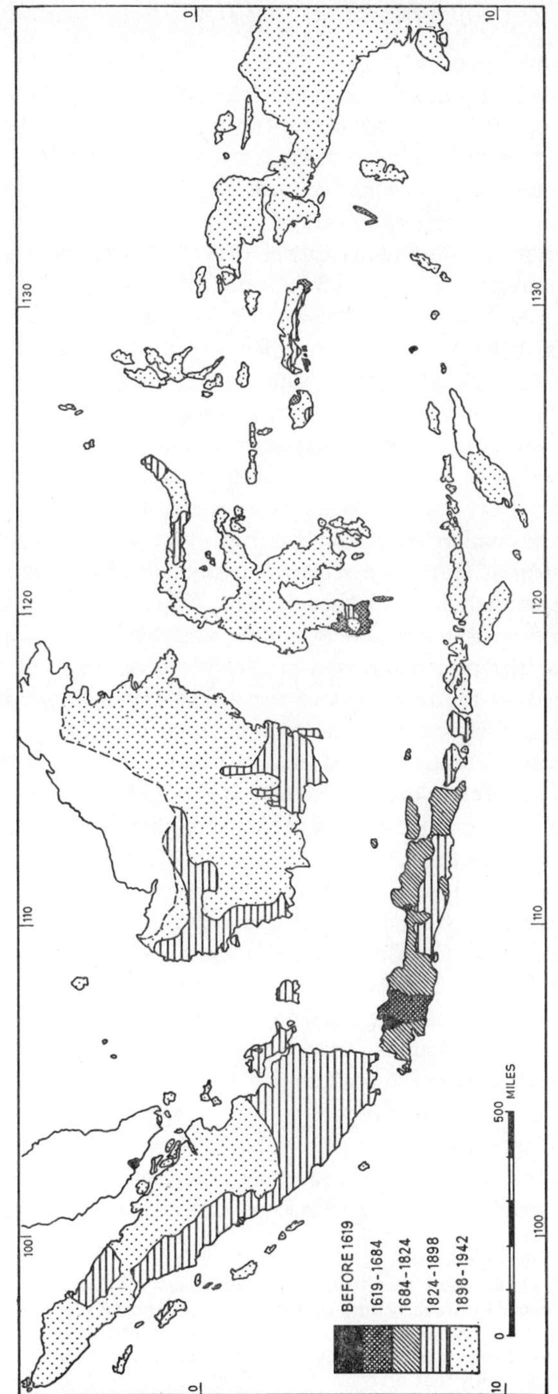

FIG. 38—Indonesia: expansion of Dutch influence

of the indigenous population. Thus the extent of state guidance over the Indonesian economy far exceeded that in most other parts of South-east Asia during much of the 19th and early 20th centuries,[45] but until far into the 19th century there was no reversal of the trends towards a sharpening of the contrasts between Java and the outer territories, and towards social and political disintegration in both, which had characterized the era of Company rule.

Indeed, with the Anglo-Dutch treaty of 1824 the centrifugal tendencies within Indonesia appeared to be intensified for, after the assumption of British control over Malacca, as well as over Singapore and Penang, and the prohibition of Dutch interference in Atjeh, the vital western focus of the archipelago passed almost entirely out of Dutch hands. And since under the *cultuur stelsel* the Dutch continued, with even greater intensity, to concentrate their energies almost exclusively on Java, the rate of population growth in that island far exceeded that in the outer territories, so that its share of the total Indies population rose from some 50 to 75 per cent during the course of the 19th century.

This policy was understandable in that from every point of view Java appeared to offer the greatest immediate scope for economic exploitation at that time. Thanks to the alternation of upland and plains, and the climatic contrast between the almost continuously humid west and the seasonally dry east, the island was well suited for the production of a remarkably wide range of tropical commodities. Aided by the researches of the world-famous Botanical Gardens at Buitenzorg, numerous new crops were developed during the middle 19th century, and among these tea and cinchona early achieved economic importance, though neither was ever a serious rival to coffee and sugar. No less significant was the cultivation of cassava, which the Dutch encouraged as a second food crop on the rice fields,[46] in order to keep pace with the rapid increase in population accompanying the expansion of the export economy.

But in other respects developments under the *cultuur stelsel*, if perhaps less uniformly oppressive than they have sometimes been painted, were far from satisfactory. The heavy demand for compulsory labour did much to undermine the stability of traditional village life,[47] and the abuses to which the system lent itself – as described in Douwes Dekker's novel, Max *Havelaar*[48] – left an abiding sense of bitterness among the peasantry.

Nevertheless, the economic expansion was remarkable. By the 1870s intensive cultivation had spread over the northern half of Java, fanning out in the hinterlands of the three main ports of the north coast, Batavia, Surabaja and Semarang, and the greater part of the island was knit together by a network of roads

[45] See Allen and Donnithorne, p. 50.

[46] Many parts of Java were threatened with famine as a result of the export of rice to Australia and Europe in the early 19th century. See Furnivall (A), p. 121.

[47] However, the indigenous rulers had in the past made similar demands.

[48] The effect of Dekker's book, published in 1860 under the pseudonym of 'Multatuli' has been compared with that of *Uncle Tom's Cabin* in the abolitionist campaign in the U.S.A. See Kennedy (A), p. 43.

far more elaborate than that of any other tropical region and indeed more nearly comparable with those of the advanced countries of north-western Europe.

Throughout the first two-thirds of the 19th century, almost the whole of Indonesia's export crops were produced in Java, on the holdings of the indigenous peasantry under varying degrees of European supervision. But with the abolition of the *cultuur stelsel* the whole pattern of production within the country began to change.

In this respect the Agrarian Law of 1870, which inaugurated a period of almost uninhibited free enterprise, marked a major turning point. Under this law, lands which had hitherto been unoccupied were deemed to belong to the State, and were henceforward to be available to planters on long leases of up to 75 years, which offered ample margin even for the cultivation of slow-maturing perennials. Furthermore, subject to certain regulations, the indigenes were also permitted to lease their land for shorter periods, though, as in the past, they were still forbidden to sell it outright to non-natives.[49]

A great expansion of plantation agriculture followed immediately, and in the first instance Java, thanks to its transport facilities, greater public security and an abundant labour supply, continued to be the principal scene of activity. Nevertheless, in the irrigable lowlands the intensity of indigenous settlement had by this time reached a stage which left little scope for further extension of commercial production, apart from the growth of annuals like sugar and tobacco in rotation with rice, on *sawah* land leased from the local villagers, who could also provide wage labour on a seasonal basis. Thus the cultivation of perennials, since it called for a more permanent system of tenure, was virtually restricted in Java to the hitherto undeveloped areas away from the northern littoral.

Accordingly, except for the concentration around Batavia which represented a carry-over from earlier times, the greatest number of plantations in Java grew up in the highlands in the interior of the island. In these regions natural conditions favoured such products as tea and cinchona, in addition to coffee which was already well established in Priangan. But as more and more of the hill country came under cultivation a re-distribution of these cultures gradually took place so that coffee production became concentrated primarily in the eastern part of Java, on account of its dry season, while the other two came to centre mainly in the west which has remained the most important region of estate cultivation in the island. In most of these new plantation areas labour recruitment initially constituted a problem, though with mounting population pressure in Java as a whole this proved to be capable of solution. Likewise, transport was at first difficult, but both roads and railways were quickly extended to serve the plantation regions, and in this way the communications network of Java became increasingly elaborate.

[49] See Furnivall (A) Chapter 7, Vlekke (A) Chapter 13, and Broek (B) Chapter 1. This law succeeded in preventing the mass alienation of land to non-natives such as occurred in many other parts of South-east Asia.

Yet, in spite of the many advantages which Java offered, the growing congestion of the island as a whole became ever more apparent. It was primarily for this reason that, in the closing decades of the 19th century, many planters began to turn instead to the outer territories, and although as late as 1894 Java and Madura still produced 82 per cent of Indonesia's exports, the outer islands gradually increased their share after that time, and ever since 1925 have produced more than half the total.

In the event the move to exploit the resources of the outer territories had been foreshadowed by various decisions during earlier decades. Thus, for example, coffee cultivation, again under a form of forced labour, was introduced into the Minahasa region of Celebes in 1827, and into various parts of the Sumatran uplands some twenty years later, and after 1854 the system of monopoly which had for so long shackled the trade of the Moluccas was gradually abolished.[50] But it was not until the turn of the century that the economy of these eastern territories really began to revive under the growing world demand for copra, which thereafter became their principal export commodity. In the meantime, further incentives to development outside Java came from the search for bunker coal carried out by the Dutch naval authorities[51] and mining was started at Martapura (southern Borneo), Kutei (eastern Borneo) and Umbilin (western Sumatra) at various dates before 1870. Likewise in 1852, many years after a small production of tin had been forthcoming from Bangka, the Billiton Tin Company started operations in the adjacent island (Belitung) and achieved spectacular results.[52]

But it was above all in the Cultuurgebied (Plantations District) of north-eastern Sumatra that the economic activity of the outer territories began to concentrate after 1870. This area, lying almost immediately behind the coast between the Asahan river and the southern borders of Atjeh, was first occupied by the Dutch in part as a result of their suspicions regarding Wilson's activities in Siak in 1857, but thereafter its immense agricultural potentialities were quickly appreciated. For, as explained in Chapter 7, this part of the eastern seaboard of Sumatra is unique in having only a very narrow swamp belt (from five to seven miles wide), beyond which lies a stretch of extremely fertile alluvial lowland, composed largely of neutral to basic volcanic materials brought down by the rivers from the Batak highlands. Furthermore, it is even better placed geographically than the plantation districts of Java thanks to its direct frontage onto the major shipping route of the Orient, a fact which was underlined by the opening of the Suez Canal in 1869.

[50] In 1846 Makasar was opened to foreign shipping and this arrangement was extended to Menado, Ambon, Banda and Ternate fairly soon afterwards.

[51] Which were widely engaged in the suppression of piracy. On this phase see Vlekke (A), pp. 278–83.

[52] Coal was mined exclusively by government concerns, as also was Bangka tin, and the government had a preponderant share in the Belitung mines. See Allen and Donnithorne, p. 170.

The activities of Jacobus Nienhuys, who first started to grow tobacco along the banks of the Deli river in 1863, drew the attention of other planters to the area, and within less than a decade expansion was in full swing. Until a serious decline in prices occurred in 1891, tobacco was the only important product of the Cultuurgebied, but in that year coffee was added, to be followed in 1907 by rubber and later by tea, palm oil and sisal.[53] Moreover, in addition to the rapidly expanding agricultural production of north-eastern Sumatra this area was also found to contain some of the richest petroleum deposits in the Indies. By the turn of the century its production had outstripped that of the Dordrecht Oil Company in Java, and when in later years the use of oil for shipping began to exceed that for illumination the position of these fields along the Straits seaway further reinforced their advantages.

Thus, notwithstanding the dominance of British political power in the western seaways of the archipelago, the pattern of Indonesia's economic development had begun by the early 20th century to exhibit the familiar geographical dualism, with Java as the primary focus but with the coastlands of Sumatra as a secondary centre of growing importance.

Once begun, the economic advance into the outer territories continued to gather momentum, though for the most part such activity tended to concentrate in a relatively few localities within a short distance of the coast. On the other hand, the parallel and related advance in the political sphere was less restricted in scope, and the Dutch quickly extended more effective control over the interiors as well as the coastlands of the outer territories as a whole. As shown in Fig. 38, much of southern and western Sumatra, south-western and south-eastern Borneo, northern Bali, Lombok, south-western and north-eastern Celebes and various parts of the Moluccas had been brought under formal Dutch administration by 1898, but in Atjeh, parts of the Batak country, and the remoter interiors of Borneo, Celebes, the Moluccas and nearly all of the Lesser Sundas from Sumbawa eastwards, this stage was not reached until the first decade of the 20th century. Surprisingly, in view of its earlier history, the main lowland of Bali[54] was among the last areas to be occupied and indeed only came under Dutch rule in 1908 following protracted resistance which ended with the mass suicide of the remaining Hindu princes and their families. Last of all, practically the whole interior of Western New Guinea remained *terra incognita* until the 1930s, and even at the time of the Second World War Dutch rule was scarcely more than nominal over most of this region a few miles inland from the coast.

This extension of Dutch authority over the outer territories which was formalized by the series of agreements in 1891, 1905 and 1908, respectively defining the international boundaries in Borneo, New Guinea and Timor, was only made possible by the great advances in maritime transport described on pp. 156–8. Yet until late in the 19th century the coming of the steamship and the gradual

[53] On the development of the Cultuurgebied, see Broek (A), p. 196, and Dootjes, p. 45.
[54] The northern fringe of Bali had been occupied by stages during the late 19th century.

triumph of liberal principles in the economic field threatened to operate against, rather than in favour of the unification of the Indies. For, thanks to the established position of Singapore as the point of contact between local Malaysian shipping routes and the major ocean lines to Europe, that port acted as the main trans-shipping centre, not only for the indigenous and Chinese trade with the outlying parts of the archipelago but also for the western plantations growing up in Sumatra, and during the 1870s and 1880s Singapore merchants and ships were far more active even in eastern Borneo and Celebes than were their counterparts from Batavia. In this way the whole of the archipelago seemed destined to become an economic appendage of Singapore, and even mail and passengers from Europe to Java had to change ships at the British port.

Admittedly, the Dutch had become aware of the need for counter action as early as 1850, and in that year the government began subsidizing a small steam-packet service to maintain regular sailings linking Batavia with Sumatra, western Borneo, Makasar and the Moluccas, as well as with Singapore, but the real turning point came with the establishment in 1890 of the Koninklijke Paketvaart Maatschappij, popularly known as the K.P.M.

Despite the great advantage of government backing which the latter enjoyed over private shipping companies, however, it took a long time before the pattern of Indonesian trade could be re-centred in Batavia at the expense of Singapore, and although in the early years of the 20th century the K.P.M., by granting special rates for copra shipment, gradually succeeded in focusing the commerce of the eastern islands on Java, with Makasar as a subsidiary collecting centre, the orientation of the trade of western Borneo and eastern Sumatra towards the Straits Settlements ports continued almost unchecked until the 1930s.[55]

Nevertheless, in the years between the two World Wars, the tendency towards an ever-closer knitting together of the Indonesian archipelago was unmistakable, and with the modernization of Tandjung Periuk harbour (Batavia), the establishment of more and more local processing factories for the rubber and other Indonesian primary produce, and the enactment of various measures to protect Netherlands Indies interests after the outset of the economic crisis and the associated retreat from liberal economic principles in the 1930s, dependence on the Straits ports declined significantly. Moreover, the attempts of the Dutch to solve the problem of over-population in Java, both by 'transmigration' to the outer territories and by developing the metropolitan island as the managerial and industrial nucleus of the whole region likewise served the cause of Indonesian unification.

Thus, by the time the Second World War broke out, the Dutch, with the aid of the K.P.M., whose well-appointed vessels plied regularly across the vast

[55] See Van Helsdingen and Hoogenberk, Chapter 10. The Improvement of Makasar harbour in or der to accommodate ocean ships (1918) and similar action at Belawan (1921) removed the physical need for trans-shipment via Singapore. See Allen and Donnithorne, p. 218. Besides Singapore, Penang also handled much Sumatran trade. See below, Chapter 18.

network of natural waterways 'from Sabang to Merauke', had succeeded in welding the archipelago into a single great sea-state, which represented a veritable realization of the mythical empire of Madjapahit.

IV. UNITY VERSUS DIVERSITY UNDER DUTCH RULE

In effect, therefore, the Dutch, after first taking advantage of the centrifugal tendencies at work in the archipelago following the downfall of Madjapahit, ended by re-uniting the Indies as a single great territorial entity around the traditional focus of Java, though with the significant difference that their power was based primarily on the western tip and not on the east-central regions of that island. For although Batavia, and in a wider sense western Java as a whole, had been selected as the Dutch headquarters because of its position near the Sunda Straits, at a time when the Portuguese were still in command of Malacca,[56] it nevertheless occupied a remarkably fine position for controlling the archipelago, in that it stood roughly mid-way between the two traditional seats of power, namely south-eastern Sumatra and east-central Java, and in some measure was able to combine the rôles of both.

The unification of the Indies, however, was not simply a matter of creating a centralized system of communications and a common administrative authority over the whole area, for in establishing such material links the Dutch inevitably promoted others of a different kind between the inhabitants of the various component islands. Such a process in fact had been at work from the very beginning, even when the V.O.C. was consciously seeking to promote precisely the opposite aim of divide and rule. Thus the mere presence of the Dutch provided a common object against which to unite, and after the series of defeats inflicted by the Company upon Mataram and Bantam towards the end of the 17th century, there was widespread talk throughout the Muslim territories of a Holy War to expel the Infidel.[57] And although the rivalries between the various Indonesian states were too great for such a threat to materialize at that stage, there can be no doubt that a common resentment against the European ruling power continued thereafter to provide a bond between the peoples of various parts of the archipelago, and in the long run this was to prove of decisive importance for the growth of national consciousness.

Similarly the Dutch policy of recruiting troops and police from the outer islands for service in Java, and the practice of drawing upon the population of one area to provide labour of various kinds for the needs of another gradually contributed to the widening of horizons, the spreading of Bazaar Malay and the general ferment of ideas, all of which have also played vital rôles in promoting a sense of national unity in more recent times.

From the early days of Company rule the Dutch relied largely on troops

[56] See also the comments of Sokol (A), p. 348.

[57] See Vlekke (A), p. 162.

drawn from the Christianized east, notably the Ambonese, and later also on the (Muslim) Madurese, who were apt to be willing recruits owing to the acute lack of opportunities in their poor and overcrowded homeland. Likewise, the Batavian police of the 18th century consisted mostly of Ambonese and Balinese, the latter of whom had had a long tradition of service as mercenaries under the Javanese princes.

Even apart from these military and police personnel, the population of Batavia has always been extremely heterogeneous. Originally most of the so-called natives of the city were slaves drawn partly from peninsular India and later to an increasing extent from almost all parts of the archipelago except Java itself. In addition, free men, notably Ambonese, Bandanese, Balinese, Buginese, Makasarese, Malays and Sumbawans, also came in early times to seek employment in the capital, and although at first such peoples settled in 'national' groups outside the city walls they gradually grew together through the medium of Bazaar Malay as the *lingua franca* to form a distinctive 'Batavian' community[58] quite different from the indigenous peoples of Java, and this has ever since been recognized as such by Dutch and fellow-Indonesians alike.[59]

During the 19th century the scale of Christian missionary work was greatly expanded, though such activity still remained restricted for the most part to the non-Muslim areas.[60] From the original centres in Ambon and its environs, and increasingly through the agency of Ambonese missionaries themselves, Protestant Christianity was disseminated in Buru and Halmahera, and in 1855 the field was extended into New Guinea. Likewise in the Minahasa area Protestant mission work began in 1827, at the time of the introduction of coffee cultivation, and virtually the whole population had been converted by 1860, since when, as the self-styled 'twelfth province of the Netherlands', the area achieved renown for the closeness of its spiritual and cultural ties with the Dutch.

Besides the Dutch missions in the foregoing areas and in the Toradja country of Celebes, Swiss and German Protestants were active among the Dyaks of Borneo and the Nias islanders. But the most outstanding successes of the German Lutheran missions were achieved among the Bataks after the middle of the 19th century, and today nearly the whole population of the central Batak lands are professing Christians.

[58] Nowadays known as Djakartan. See Vlekke (A), p. 174, and Volkstelling, Vol. 1, pp. 16–17.

[59] Meanwhile the pattern of the indigenous groups within Java was itself changing. Thus, while the Javanese remained predominant over the eastern and central part of the island, and in Bantam had spread far to the west of the Pemali river (the traditional boundary of Sundanese speech), the Sundanese themselves had spread outwards from the Priangan highlands with the extension of coffee cultivation in western Java during the 17th and 18th centuries, and the Madurese likewise began to stream into the north-east of Java proper when coffee cultivation began there in the 18th and 19th centuries. Thus Java, outside Batavia, came to exhibit a three-fold linguistic pattern, and by 1930 there were 1,940,567 Madurese in Madura and 2,346,709 in the rest of East Java.

[60] For detailed accounts of Christian missions, see van Helsdingen and Hoogenberk, Chapter 9.

Moreover, Roman Catholic missions have also been at work in the Indies, for the Netherlands has a large Roman Catholic minority, which from about the middle of the 19th century onwards began to take a share in the proselytization of the overseas dependencies. For many years the Roman Catholic missionaries confined their attention to areas hitherto neglected by the Protestants, concentrating in particular on Flores and Dutch Timor which adjoined the areas that had already been served by their Portuguese co-religionists, but in more recent times they also have extended their operations into the Batak lands, Minahasa, Borneo and New Guinea.

Aside from its direct religious implications, Christian missionary activity has entailed a rather remarkable reversal in the status of many of the peoples concerned. For while most conversions have been made among relatively primitive and previously pagan peoples, the educational and medical work carried out by the missions was often superior to that provided by the Netherlands Indies government for the more advanced indigenous groups. Thus large numbers of Ambonese, Menadonese and Batak Christians were far better equipped and trained than most Javanese, Malays and other Muslim peoples, and accordingly emigrated to various parts of the archipelago to take up skilled and semi-skilled employment of many kinds. In particular, Menadonese have gone to Java as officials, clerks and accountants, and have also provided a major component in the Netherlands Indies army in modern times, while Ambonese, besides serving in the army, have found employment as teachers and hospital attendants all over the country, and many Bataks have gone as clerks and overseers to the Cultuurgebied and as domestic servants to Batavia.

Such migration has not, however, been limited to the Christianized peoples, and in particular the Menangkabaus, who shared with the Menadonese the honour of being the best educated of all the indigenous peoples, have been successful as traders throughout the whole country. Similarly, large numbers of Buginese have established themselves as seamen and farmers in islands other than Celebes, and Bandjarese have also gone in strength to the pioneer areas of Sumatra and Malaya.

To a considerable extent the more skilled migrants, especially those from the eastern islands, have in the past gone to Java, in part to swell the already large and diverse Batavian community, which between the early 18th century and 1930 increased from a mere 20,000 or so to close on one million.[61] But in the last eighty years or so the movement of manual labour in the reverse direction, that is from Java to the plantation and mining areas of the outer territories, has been on an even larger scale. For although until the 1880s Chinese workers, obtained through brokers in Singapore, provided most of the labour employed in Bangka, Belitung and the early Deli plantations, a preference later developed for Indo-

[61] The total number of Batavians recorded in all Indonesia in 1930 was 980,863. Of these 145,759 and 47,138 were in the twin municipalities of Batavia and Meester Cornelis respectively, and practically all the remainder were in the surrounding countryside.

nesian workers who could easily be recruited from the overcrowded parts of Java. Thus in 1937 most of the 350,000 coolies working in the outer territories were Java-born, and approximately two-thirds of these were in the Cultuurgebied alone.

TABLE 17

INDIGENOUS PEOPLES IN INDONESIA PROFESSING CHRISTIANITY, 1939

A. Protestants

Area	*Approximate number*
Batak lands	400,000
South-eastern Borneo (Dyaks)	12,000
Java	65,000
Lesser Sundas	150,000
Minahasa, Sangihe and Talaud	400,000
Inland Celebes (Toradjas)	100,000
Ambon and nearby islands	200,000
Halmahera and Buru	40,000
New Guinea	60,000
Total (including others)	1,500,000

B. Roman Catholics

Area	*Approximate number*
Batak lands	10,000
Dyak lands	10,000
Java	35,000
Minahasa	25,000
Flores and Timor	280,000
Total (including others)	478,000

Sources: Based mainly on Van Helsdingen and Hoogenberk, pp. 101–15.

Moreover, since a high proportion of the Javanese and Sundanese labourers ended by settling permanently in the Cultuurgebied, either as independent farmers or in various forms of urban employment,[62] and large numbers of Bataks, Menangkabaus and Bandjarese also found opportunities there, the population of the Cultuurgebied in recent years has become almost as diverse in origin, though not so thoroughly intermixed, as that of Batavia. Thus, in 1930 the

[62] Like the Chinese who preceded them. In 1930 there were only 225,000 Java-born labourers out of a total Javan population of 643,000 in the East Coast Residency of Sumatra, and only 10,500 Chinese labourers out of a total of 193,000 Chinese residents there. All-told there were 1,151,000 Javans in the outer territories at this time. See also below, p. 637, note 9.

population of the East Coast Residency of Sumatra,[63] in which the Cultuurgebied lies, included only 19·8 per cent indigenous Malays, compared with 34·8 per cent Javanese, 19·8 per cent Bataks, 3·0 per cent Menangkabaus, 2·6 per cent Sundanese, 1·9 per cent Bandjarese and 11·4 per cent Chinese. As in the Batavian area, so also in the Cultuurgebied and indeed wherever diverse groups of Indonesian peoples lived side by side, the use of Bazaar Malay as the *lingua franca* received a further stimulus and the traditional parochial outlook of the communities concerned was in some measure broadened.

Nevertheless, the extent of this progress should not be exaggerated, and such contacts were often more noteworthy for the animosities and rivalries which they provoked. Certainly there was little love lost between the Christianized minority peoples of the outlying islands and the larger Islamic populations elsewhere, and the fact that in the inter-war years the Netherlands Indies army consisted largely of three distinct groups, namely Ambonese, Menadonese and Javanese/Madurese,[64] the first two of whom could be relied upon to support the Dutch in Java and other Muslim areas, while the Java-born troops could correspondingly be trusted in the Christian and pagan areas, speaks for itself.[65] Moreover, even in the Muslim territories outside Java, much resentment was caused by the growing number of Java-born migrants during the 1920s and 30s, and the Menangkabau traders operating outside their homeland were similarly unpopular.

In addition to these various internal migrations, the period of colonial rule was also accompanied by the rise of several alien minority communities within the Indies. Of these the 30,018 'British Indians',[66] over half of whom were in the Sumatran Cultuurgebied, and the 71,335 Arabs, mostly traders and middlemen living in Java, were too few in number to cause serious concern, but the much larger Chinese and Eurasian communities, from which practically the whole of the small middle class was drawn in colonial times, were a very different matter, and the position they acquired under the Dutch regime has left a legacy of problems for the new Indonesian republic.

Between 1860 and 1930 the number of Chinese residents in the Indies rose from 221,438 to 1,233,214. Nevertheless, despite considerable immigration to Indonesia as a whole during this period of vast economic expansion, 79 per cent of the Indies Chinese population in 1930 were locally born and, of the 582,431 or very nearly half who lived in Java, the great majority were of several generations standing in the country. On the other hand those in the outer territories (448,552 in Sumatra, 134,287 in Borneo and the rest mainly in Celebes) were mostly either immigrants or the children of immigrants, and many of the former

[63] Which had grown from 116,000 in 1880 to 1,675,000 in 1930. *Cf.* the rapidity of growth in western Malaya during the same period. See below, pp. 598 and 634–5.

[64] Officered mainly by Europeans and Eurasians.

[65] *Cf.* the British use of 'hill tribes' in India and Burma.

[66] *I.e.* inhabitants of what are now India and Pakistan. All population figures in this section are taken from the 1930 census unless otherwise stated.

appeared to have no intention of staying for more than a few years. This contrast in length of domicile between the Chinese of Java and those of the rest of the country was reflected also in their economic position, for while three-quarters of the former group were engaged in commerce, transport or industry, nearly half of the latter group were employed in primary production, largely as wage labourers. Thus, although a sprinkling of Chinese traders extended throughout the ports and other towns of virtually the whole archipelago, the great majority of the Chinese in the outer islands were in fact concentrated in three relatively small areas, namely eastern Sumatra (particularly the Cultuurgebied), the tin-producing islands of Bangka and Belitung and lastly in the Singkawang and Pontianak districts of western Borneo, where, most exceptionally, they were mainly engaged in subsistence rice cultivation.[67]

Taken as a whole, however, the Chinese were pre-eminently urban and middle class, and although it has been estimated that in the 1930s their average annual wages fell mostly within the range of $ (U.S.) 160–2,000,[68] there were many whose earnings were far greater than this. Indeed, among the indigenous peoples only the Atjehnese and Menangkabaus were considered a match for them as traders, and nearly all the retail trade in Java and many other areas, as well as the inter-island commodity trade, was in their hands, as was much the greater part of the medium- and small-scale manufacturing industry.

Although considerable intermarriage took place between the Chinese and the indigenous population, the offspring were normally regarded as members of the Chinese community which, socially speaking, kept very much to itself. This marked clannishness, together with a notorious hard-headedness in commercial transactions, made the Chinese unpopular with the indigenous peoples, and for this reason the Chinese tended to align themselves with the colonial power whose presence had created the conditions under which they were able to flourish.[69]

However, this attitude was not fully reciprocated by the Dutch, and although the more exaggerated fears which had led to the massacre of 1740 were never revived, the Dutch always regarded the Chinese with a certain suspicion, which China's insistence on the *jus sanguinis*[70] after 1896 did nothing to alleviate. In accordance with the original V.O.C. tradition of rule by 'like over like', the

[67] These Borneo settlements were of long standing. In the 18th century the Sultan of Sambas brought in Chinese as labour for the gold mines since he considered the local population to be too lazy. Vlekke (A), p. 194.

[68] The corresponding figures for Indonesians were mostly under $50. See Kennedy (A), p. 178.

[69] But Chinese schools taught English, not Dutch, as the first foreign language. In the 1930s some 50 per cent of Chinese males and 15 per cent of Chinese females in the Indies were literate. The average figure for all inhabitants of the country was about 20 per cent and for Indonesians alone about 10 per cent.

[70] The *jus sanguinis* bases the claim to nationality on blood, in contradistinction to the more generally accepted *jus soli*, under which place of birth is the criterion. The Chinese government has insisted since 1896 that persons of Chinese ancestry born overseas are automatically Chinese nationals. See Vlekke (A), p. 330 and Purcell (D), p. xxxi.

Chinese community was left as far as possible under the jurisdiction of its own headmen, and until 1900 the Chinese, like the Jews of medieval Europe, were restricted in their residence to specific areas in several of the towns. Checks and proscriptions on travel within the country continued until an even later date, and although all such limitations were removed by 1926,[71] the Dutch never conceded the demand of the Chinese for legal equality with the Europeans.

While the Chinese thus comprised the greater part of the commercial middle class and were also strongly represented in certain professions, notably medicine, the remainder of the bourgeoisie in colonial times consisted predominantly of Eurasians,[72] though this fact was partially concealed by the Dutch practice of drawing no formal distinction between pure Europeans and those of mixed blood.

As we have already noted, the beginnings of the Eurasian community date back to the Portuguese period, and although under the V.O.C. its numbers grew rapidly and Java replaced the Moluccas as the principal centre of its strength, its members at first continued to speak a debased form of Portuguese and to be treated as social inferiors by the Dutch. But in 1854 a change came about, following a public protest by the 'Indos' against their limited opportunities compared with those of 'imported Dutchmen'. And since Dutch relations with the Chinese had not fully recovered from the shock of 1740, the authorities concluded that it would be dangerous to risk alienating the sympathies of yet another element in this unstable multi-racial society. Accordingly the decision was taken to rank all the descendants of Europeans on the father's side[73] as Europeans, and from that time forward the term Eurasian ceased to have any legal validity.

Between 1870 and 1930 the combined number of 'Europeans' (*i.e.* Europeans and Eurasians)[74] rose from 49,901 to 240,417 and in the meantime Dutch-language educational facilities within the Indies were greatly expanded to meet the needs of this group as a whole. Thus in 1930 apart from the 22,148 'alien Europeans',[75] the remaining 218,269 who were listed as 'Netherlanders' formed a single community, some 80 per cent of whose members lived in Java, mostly in the larger towns. Yet at least two-thirds of these 'Netherlanders' were Eurasians, and the number born in Holland was only 50,885.[76]

With only minor exceptions it is true to say that, in practice as well as in theory, no colour bar existed between Eurasians and *volbloed* Hollanders.

[71] Chinese representatives were also included in the Volksraad. See below, p. 273.

[72] Locally but misleadingly known as Indo-Europeans, often slightingly abbreviated to *Indos*'. On this subject as a whole, see Wertheim (A).

[73] *I.e.* those (which included the great majority) who bore Dutch surnames.

[74] For the remainder of this section 'Europeans' refers to Europeans and Eurasians collectively, while Europeans refers exclusively to pure whites, locally known as *volbloeds*.

[75] For reasons of 'face' Japanese, Filipinos, Thais and Turks were also included in this category.

[76] The total of persons born in Holland almost certainly included many Eurasians; conversely many *volbloeds* were born in the Indies.

Admittedly the majority of the latter were in well-paid jobs mainly in the higher echelons of the administrative and technical services, the professions, commerce, and export production. But there was nothing to prevent Eurasians also from reaching the highest posts, and indeed many achieved real eminence, particularly in government departments and the armed forces. All-told, perhaps 5 per cent of the Eurasians were in appointments which would have been considered first class by Europeans, a further 25 per cent or so held posts which were not beneath the dignity of *volbloed* Hollanders, notably in the middle grades of the administrative and technical services, engineering, teaching and medicine, and the remaining 70 per cent were in lower-ranking jobs, such as locomotive drivers, garage mechanics and junior clerks.

As a result of this non-discriminatory policy most of the Eurasians were staunch supporters of Dutch rule, often indeed *plus royalistes que le roi*, and showed little of the inferiority complex which has been so characteristic of their counterparts in British-controlled territories. Moreover, as the main strength numerically of the administrative and technical services, they were of immense importance in the running of the country, and the high standards of efficiency which were maintained in these respects gave convincing proof of their abilities.

Nevertheless, among the lower-paid and less well-educated Eurasians there were many who were comparable with the 'poor whites' of South Africa or the American South. Such peoples were in constant danger of dropping to the economic level of the indigenous population, and many suffered great hardship during the crisis years of the 1930s when wages for less highly skilled work were apt to be reduced from a 'European' to a 'native' level. Many Indonesians did in fact replace Eurasians for this reason, but the Eurasians, being legally debarred from owning agricultural land in Java, had little opportunity of tiding themselves over by drifting back to the villages until times improved.

V. THE AIMS AND ACHIEVEMENTS OF DUTCH RULE

The Dutch practice of assimilating the Eurasians in the manner described above has often been cited as evidence of unusual tolerance and enlightenment in colonial administration but it nevertheless entailed certain far less fortunate consequences. For, in giving scope to the Eurasians,[77] the Dutch found that they had little left over in the way of rewarding employment to offer to the indigenes, and the resultant frustration cast a lengthening shadow over the closing years of Dutch rule in the Indies.

Even in its final form during the inter-war years, Dutch colonial philosophy owed far more than was generally realized to the early traditions of Company rule.[78] From the beginning the V.O.C., seeking to limit its non-commercial

[77] In this context it is appropriate to include with the Eurasians such Christian minority peoples as the Menadonese and Ambonese, many of whom in any case were of mixed blood.

[78] Which continued in spirit under the *cultuur stelsel*.

commitments as far as possible, had favoured a system of indirect rule, and besides making use of selected Chinese headmen in the manner described above, had relied to a still greater extent on selected Indonesian representatives to handle its day-to-day relations with the indigenous peoples. With minor modifications this principle continued to be followed, both in the older-established centres of Dutch rule and in the newer areas brought under control during the 19th and early 20th centuries. Admittedly, a legal difference existed between those areas in which the indigenous political pattern was retained virtually intact as, for example, in Surakarta and Djokjakarta, and the others where, in the process of pacification, the established order had disintegrated or the local rulers had been deposed by the Dutch on account of their unwillingness to co-operate. But even in such cases the Dutch sought wherever possible to install other indigenous nobles or aristocrats as hereditary rulers, as, for example, the 'Regents' of Java outside the Vorstenlanden, so that the distinction between the two types of administration (which the Dutch rather confusingly came to call 'indirect' and 'direct' rule respectively) was largely a matter of historical accident and less fundamental than might at first sight appear.

Meanwhile, the tradition of rule by 'like over like' was extended during the 19th century, ultimately to give rise to an elaborate system of legal pluralism, under which 'Europeans', 'Foreign Orientals' and indigenes were all governed according to their own legal codes,[79] and to a remarkable civil-service structure with two parallel branches, one of which dealt with matters of primary concern to the 'Europeans' while the other provided the medium through which the Dutch supervised native Indonesian affairs.

An important change in the attitude of the Netherlands towards the Indies occurred with the inauguration of the Ethical Policy in 1901–2. Already for some years prior to that date, considerable misgivings had been expressed about the extent to which Indonesian society, especially in Java, had disintegrated as a result of unscrupulous methods of western exploitation, and the new policy aimed so far as possible to repair the damage, or at least to prevent it from spreading further. Henceforth, therefore, the government was to give much greater attention to the problems of native administration, and in particular to the preservation of the Indonesian way of life and the extension of welfare and educational facilities.

Nevertheless, this enlightened policy of trusteeship did not work out as well in practice as its exponents had hoped, partly it would seem because of a certain psychological antipathy which had always existed between the Dutch and the Indonesians. Thus the former, with their enthusiasm for the Calvinistic virtues of efficiency, hard work and thrift, were singularly unimpressed by the carefree, easy-going and often apparently naïve behaviour of the Indonesians, and this in turn engendered an attitude on the part of the Dutch that was at best paternalistic and at worst both patronizing and excessively cautious.

[79] The Dutch also made an elaborate study of local customary law or *adat*. See Ter Haar.

Hence, while avowedly seeking to strengthen and protect what was best in the indigenous tradition and at the same time to graft on to this whatever was most appropriate of Western ideals and techniques, the Dutch tended to be extremely pessimistic in their assessment of Indonesian capabilities. In these circumstances, therefore, the preservation of indigenous traditions came in effect to mean the perpetuation almost as museum pieces of the traditional regional cultures within the country, rather than the encouragement of a wider national outlook, and similarly the insistence on vernacular rather than western-language education for all but a handful of Indonesians[80] meant that the indigenes were relegated to a position of permanent economic inferiority relative to the Eurasians and Chinese.

In economic matters also significant changes took place after the turn of the century.[81] Thus, as rubber, tin and other commodities came to replace the coffee and sugar of earlier times as the principal exports of the Indies, the direction of the export trade changed, the United States gradually replacing the metropolitan country as the largest purchaser of Indies produce. And since in the meantime the Netherlands had built up large textile and other consumer-goods industries, a growing proportion of whose products were marketed in the Indies, the latter came to play a vital part in balancing the trading accounts of the metropolitan country with the United States.[82]

Thus, notwithstanding fundamental changes in both the nature and direction of the Indies' overseas trade, the prosperity of the Netherlands remained no less dependent upon it than it had been in the 19th century, and indeed it was variously estimated in the 1930s that the salaries, pensions and profits of all kinds accruing to Dutch citizens in consequence of their connexions with Indonesia, accounted for 15–30 per cent of the total income of the mother country.

Besides this economic dependence, Dutch national prestige in the inter-war years was likewise in large measure dependent on possession of the Indies. For it was above all the right to speak on behalf of this vast and highly productive domain, with its 60–70 million inhabitants, which lifted metropolitan Holland, with its 7 million people out of the ranks of the minor European powers and added weight to its representations in the counsels of the nations.[83]

For all these reasons, therefore, Dutch colonial philosophy differed in important respects from those of the other Western powers. So long as Holland believed that its world position and economic well-being depended on retaining

[80] According to Kennedy (A), p. 138, only about 2 million Indonesian children attended schools of any kind in the 1930s, and of these only about 300,000 got beyond village-school level.

[81] The annual surplus (*batig slot*) which the Indies contributed to the mother country was abolished in 1877, and in 1912 the finances of the two countries became completely separate.

[82] This pattern was nevertheless built up under a policy of free trade, from which the Dutch retreated very reluctantly in the 1930s. See also above, p. 171.

[83] See Gerbrandy, p. 117. The population figures here refer to the 1930s.

control of the Indies, the British type of colonial policy, with its emphasis on training for self-government, was regarded as unsuitable for the Netherlands Indies. But at the same time the traditional French approach to colonialism was equally inapplicable to the Indies. For the large Eurasian population blocked the way for the cultural assimilation of the Indonesians, and reliance on the triangular trade with the United States ruled out the possibility of assimiliation in the economic field.

Instead, therefore, the Dutch evolved the ingenious doctrine of 'synthesis'. The polyglot population of the Indies were neither to be educated for self-government nor were they to be culturally assimilated to the West. But, just as the Dutch and Indonesian economies were both alleged to flourish by virtue of their 'symbiotic relationship' with each other[84] so, in the political sense, the professed aim was to build up what Professor Gerbrandy[85] has called 'a new pattern of life which would be a synthesis of East and West'.

Whatever may have been the theoretical merits of such a policy, its application in practice involved the continuance of a markedly Java-centred administrative system, which it had been among the professed objectives of the Ethical Policy to change. Thus the powers of the various local councils set up after 1903 were extremely limited, and even the much publicized Volksraad or Peoples Council, which met in Batavia after 1917, never graduated to the status of a true legislative chamber. Moreover, although a new administrative pattern was introduced after 1925, both the provincial units and their major sub-divisions cut right across the traditional divisions within the country (Fig. 41), and the government flatly rejected the suggestions of Colijn[86] and others that a modified form of federation should be introduced as a means of promoting limited self-government from the bottom upwards. Thus to the end the pre-war administration remained essentially paternalistic in spirit, and both unitary and centralized in structure,[87] and these characteristics have left a legacy of problems which still await solution.

SELECT BIBLIOGRAPHY

Allen and Donnithorne
Barnouw
Bertling
Boeke (A) (B)
Bousquet
Broek (A) (B) (E)
Cator
Coedès
Cole, F.-C.
Collet
Dootjes
Emerson, Mills and Thompson
Fisher (B) (C) (L)
Furnivall (A)

[84] See Hart, G. H. C. (A), p. 91.

[85] Gerbrandy, p. 34.

[86] However, in other respects Colijn's policies were even more conservative than those of the Government itself. See Vlekke (A), p. 345.

[87] Notwithstanding the so-called decentralization policy of 1925 which, though giving considerable responsibility in purely local matters to the Provincial Councils of West, Central and East Java, granted only advisory powers to the Representative Councils of the Governments of Sumatra, Borneo and the Great East.

Gerbrandy
Hall (B)
Harrison
Hart, G. H. C. (A)
Honig and Verdoorn
Hyma
Kennedy (A) (B) (C)
Kleiweg de Zwaan
Kunst
Loeb and Heine-Geldern
Nooteboom
Palmier (A) (C)
Purcell (D)
Robequain (D)
Schrieke
Sokol (A)
Ter Haar
Thompson and Adloff
Van der Kroef (C)
Van Helsdingen and Hoogenberk
Van Leur
Van Mook (A) (B)
Van Nieuwenhuize (A)
Van Vuuren (A)
Vlekke (A)
Wertheim (A) (B) (C)
Widjoamidjojo
Wormser

Volkstelling 1930 (Census of Netherlands India) *Vols. I–VII*
Netherlands East Indies Vol. II (N.I.D.)
Chambers's Encyclopædia

On all aspects of the human geography van Helsdingen and Horgenberk, the N.I.D. volume, and Kennedy (A) are very useful sourves. More specifically on ethnography and demography the seven volumes of the 1930 Census (Volkstelling) are a mine of information. (This was the last census to be taken in Indonesia, though another is expected shortly.) Vlekke (A) is a standard work on Indonesian history, while Furnivall (A), Boeke (A) (B), Broek (A) (B) (E) and Allen and Donnithorne are all extremely useful on economic aspects, as are Schrieke, van der Kroef (C) and also Furnivall (A) on social aspects of the problems discussed in this chapter.

Addenda: Note also the major new work by Geertz, Clifford: *Agricultural Involution—the process of ecological change in Indonesia*, Berkeley and Los Angeles, 1963.

CHAPTER 9

The Netherlands Indies between the Two World Wars—Economic and Social Geography

I. INTRODUCTION

The final phase of Dutch rule under the Ethical Policy of 1901 may be said to have reached its apogee during the period 1935–41, and by any standards its material achievements were striking.[1] As in all other dependent territories, the pattern of development in the Netherlands Indies bore the imprint of the distinctive national ethos of the metropolitan power, and while in technical efficiency and thoroughness the Dutch were unsurpassed among the European colonial powers, the abundance and diversity of Indonesia's resources, both human and material, offered immense scope for their organizing genius. Thus it is not perhaps surprising that, in the years immediately preceding the Second World War, the Netherlands Indies should have been widely regarded in the West as perhaps the best administered of all dependent territories, not only in Southeast Asia, but in the tropical world as a whole.

The pre-war pattern of Indonesian economic development which, despite recent upheavals has not fundamentally changed since that time, was one of great complexity. Two major contrasts should be noted at the outset, the first between the densely settled nuclear area of Java and Madura and the generally far more sparsely peopled outer territories (Table 21), and the second between the subsistence and the commercial economies which existed side by side throughout the archipelago. Yet in neither case was the distinction as clear cut as the foregoing statement might seem to imply. Thus the outer territories in fact contained a great range of diversity, from such an island as Bali with 503 people to the square mile and an extremely intensive system of native agriculture, to the undeveloped wastes of New Guinea where the population density was said to be only two per square mile.[2]

[1] As noted in the preface, the period dealt with in this chapter is the last for which detailed census data are available for Indonesia. However, although the past tense is used throughout, much of the description still applies today, and an attempt is made in Chapters 10 and 11 to bring the account up to date, so far as existing sources of information permit.

[2] Unless otherwise stated population figures quoted in this chapter are based on the 1930 Census. Though in general extremely thorough, the latter almost certainly underestimated the population of West New Guinea, whose density is nowadays estimated at about six per square mile.

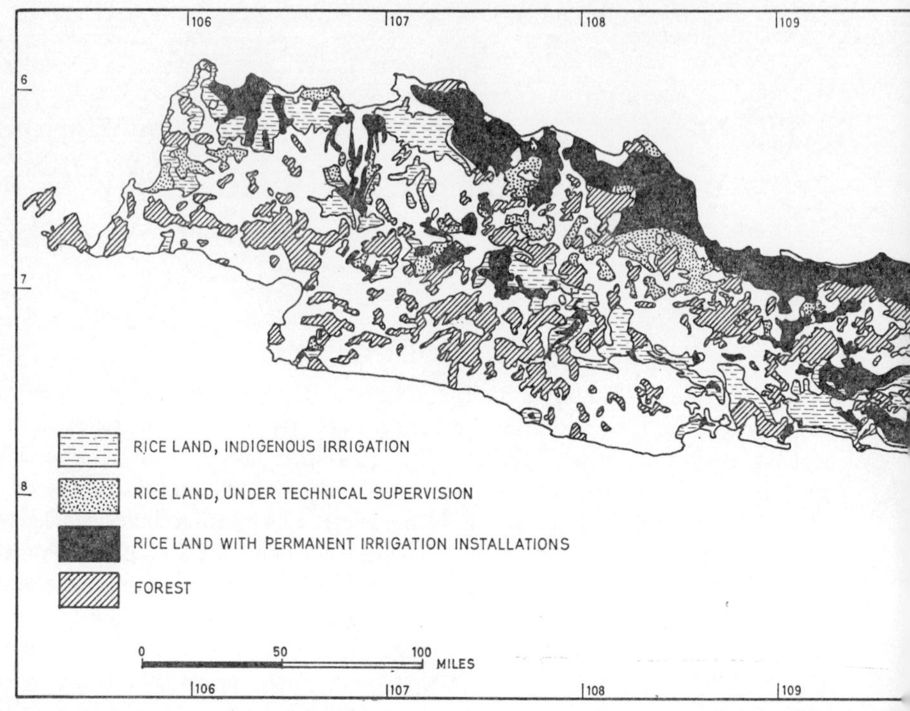

FIG. 39—Ja

Moreover, while the subsistence economy of the Indies, with its emphasis on rice in the west and on various other starch foods in the east, together with coconuts, vegetables and fish, was essentially the concern of the indigenes, production for cash was becoming less and less the sole preserve of the Western-run estates. Indeed, by 1937 46 per cent of the total agricultural exports (by value) were grown by Indonesian peasant cultivators as an adjunct to their own subsistence farming, a development which was particularly important in the outer territories.

While accurate figures for subsistence production have never been available it is clear that rice was much the most important crop grown in the Indies, and the average annual production of nearly 9 million tons during the period 1934–9[3] may be compared with the (1937) data for export crops shown in Table 18. This, together with Figs. 39, 40, 43 and 44, will serve to illustrate the short regional account of East Indian primary production which follows.

II. PRIMARY PRODUCTION IN JAVA

Intense pressure on the land and a relatively high level of productivity per acre were the outstanding features of the agrarian economy of Java. These conditions

[3] Nearly two-thirds of the rice was grown in Java and Madura.

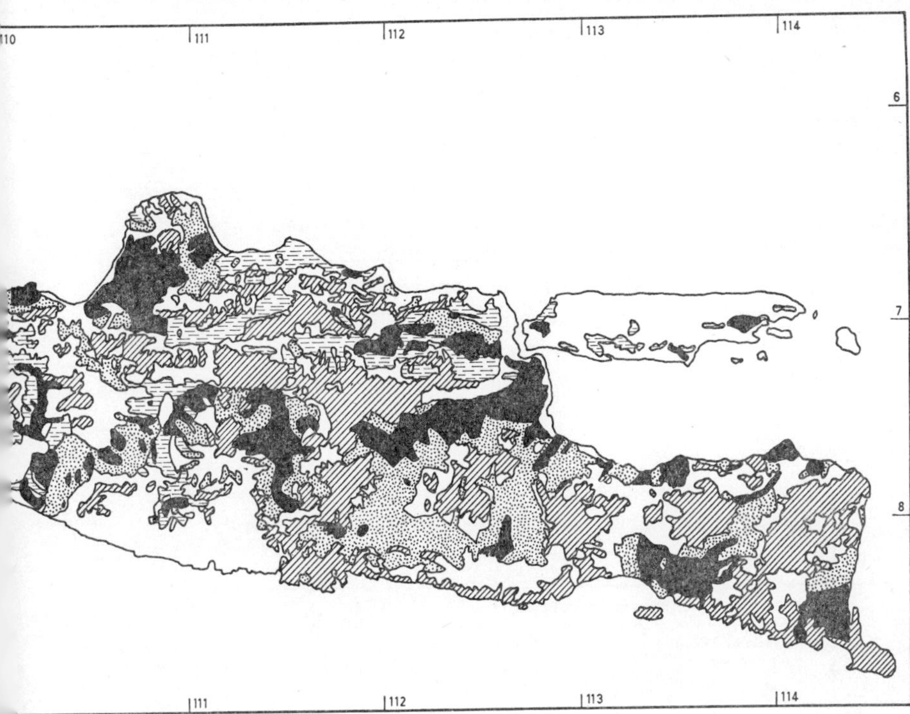

ce-land and forest

resulted from the combination of great natural fertility, an impressive cultural legacy and inherited skill on the part of the native cultivators, and the application of Dutch gardening methods and hydro-technical experience to a tropical island which afforded at least as much scope for them as did the European motherland itself. All-told, nearly two-thirds of the island was under cultivation,[4] a remarkably high figure in view of its largely mountainous character, and the great diversity of crops produced (see Tables 18 and 19) was indicative of a mature economy carefully adjusted to make the fullest use of a richly varied terrain.

By contrast with many parts of the outer territories, native cultivation in Java was almost entirely on a sedentary basis, with a marked emphasis on wet paddy (*sawah*) farming. According to tradition, land was held communally by villages (*desas*), but for many years there had been a distinct trend towards individual ownership, and even where this had not yet become the rule the periodical redistribution of lands usually took place much less frequently than in earlier times.

Nevertheless rice cultivation was still carried out along predominantly tradi-

[4] In the western uplands arable formed less than 50 per cent, but in central and eastern Java it comprised over 80 per cent and in Djokjakarta over 90 per cent. State forests covered 23 per cent of the total area of Java. See Broek (E), p. 124.

tional lines, though to keep pace with the growing population the Dutch had encouraged greater intensification and, wherever practicable, the raising of a second food crop, either of rice or, especially in the drier areas, of maize or cassava. In 1937 some 3,707,000 acres out of the total 8,322,000 acres of *sawah* were irrigated by peasant methods and a further 1,632,000 acres depended solely on rain water directly impounded in the fields.[5] For the most part the traditional methods of irrigation were practised in the inland valleys and on adjacent terraced slopes, the most usual system being that of impounding the water in a river valley by means of an artificial obstruction and leading it off through channels and bamboo pipes direct to the *sawahs*.[6] Especially in the fertile volcanic zone of east-central Java, man-made terraces of this kind extend in great flights up the hillsides and the same irrigation water could thus be used many times over, passing successively from the highest to the lowest fields in the series.

TABLE 18

NETHERLANDS INDIES: EXPORT PRODUCTION, 1937

A. AGRICULTURE

Commodity	*Quantity (in 000 tons)*					*Value*		
	Java & Madura		*Outer Territories*		*Netherlands Indies Total*	*Total export (000 guilders)*	*Order of importance*	*Percent. of world total production* (P) *or export* (E)
	Estate	*Small-holder*	*Estate*	*Small-holder*				
Rubber	85,452	—	130,857	208,550	424,859	287,618	1	38 E
Coconut products	4,289	102,983	27,776	470,894	605,942	72,113	4	29 E
Sugar	1,342,002	8,861	—	1	1,350,864	51,108	5	5 P
Tea	38,988	12,170	15,588	—	66,716	49,061	6	17 E
Tobacco	22,118	14,777	11,887	264	49,046	41,070	7	
Palm oil	10	—	238,356	—	238,366	29,051	8	19 E
Coffee	22,033	—	8,368	67,998	98,399	25,868	9	7 E
Tapioca	90,144	351,124	—	5	441,273	18,383	10	
Sisal, cantala, agave and other fibres	31,803	114	56,950	1	88,968	15,269	11	25 E
Cinchona	5,751	—	802	—	6,553	10,300	12	82 P
Kapok	7,122	47,060	68	5,359	59,609	8,899	13	70 E
Pepper	95	—	70	31,118	31,283	6,993	14	79 E

Approximately 60 per cent by weight and 35 per cent by value of agricultural exports were from Java and Madura. Approximately 54 per cent by value of agricultural exports were from estates.

B MINERAL

Commodity	*Places of production*	*Amount (tons)*	*Value (000 guilders)*	*Order of importance*	*Percent. of world production*
Petroleum	Sumatra 65%, Borneo 20%, Java 10%, Seram 5%	7,262,000	166,615	2	2·8 P
Tin	Bangka 59%, Belitung 35%, Singkep 6%	39,391	84,113	3	20 P

Source: Based mainly on *Indisch Verslag*, Vol. II, pp. 274–5, 287, 291, 331 and 332, 1938.

[5] These figures, from Pelzer (C), pp. 54–5, do not include Djokjakarta and Surakarta.
[6] This method is similar in principle to the tank irrigation of peninsular India.

Although these indigenous methods still prevail over much of Java they tend to suffer from two main drawbacks, namely the danger of damage from heavy floods during the wet season, and the liability to fail when water is most needed during the dry season, especially if the latter is abnormally severe. For these reasons the Dutch had been gradually replacing them by modern irrigation works wherever conditions were suitable, and had also built large-scale works of this kind in many areas, particularly along the coastal plain and in the lower courses of some of the larger rivers, where the problems of drainage and water control had hitherto defied the technical skill of the indigenous peasantry.

Thus by 1937 some 2,728,000 acres in Java were irrigated by modern methods, and in all cases the water was supplied free of charge to the indigenous cultivators. It was primarily by these means, and through the construction of large storage reservoirs (*waduks*),[7] that in the first four decades of the present century the total area of *sawah* in Java and Madura had been increased from 6,672,000 to 8,278,000 acres.

Such land was of course much more productive, acre for acre, than dry fields (*tegalans*) whose total area, however, had meanwhile been increased to an even greater extent, from 7,166,000 to 11,367,000 acres. These dry fields were interspersed with *sawah* throughout the whole length of the island, but the proportion which they formed of the total cultivated area was much higher in such regions as western Java, with its poorer soils and rugged relief, the often parched lime-

TABLE 19

JAVA AND MADURA: HARVESTED AREAS OF INDIGENES' CROPS, 1916 AND 1937

Figures in 000 *acres*

	1916	1937
Wet rice	6531	8590
Dry rice	966	966
Maize	3910	5113
Cassava	1122	2348
Soya beans	403	872
Ground nuts	472	581
Sweet potatoes	400	447
Tobacco	403	371
Total harvested area (including other crops)	n.a.	21,503

Sources: Based on Van Hall, p. 216, and *Pocket edition, Statistical Abstract of the Netherlands Indies*, 1940, p. 37.

[7] *Waduks* were largely intended for the use of sugar cultivators. See Pelzer (C), p. 70.

stone plateaux of the south and north-east, and above all in Madura where over 80 per cent of the cultivated area consisted of *tegalans*, mostly on hill-slopes.[8]

TABLE 20

NETHERLANDS INDIES, ESTATE ACREAGE, 1937

Figures in 000 acres planted

Crop	*Java Madura*	*Outer Territories*	*Total*
Rubber	561·6	905·4	1,466·0
Tea	259·0	84·5	343·5
Coffee	223·1	41·7	264·8
Palm oil	2·0	203·8	205·8
Coconut	17·0	104·4	121·4
Tobacco	72·6	32·1	104·7
Kapok	57·5	3·5	61·0
Cinchona	38·0	4·4	42·4
Nutmeg	4·1	2·7	6·8
Sugar	208·8	n.a.	n.a.
Cocoa	15·0	0·3	15·3
Essential oils	16·5	—	16·5
Pepper	6·1	0·6	6·6

Source: Based on *Indisch Verslag*, Vol. II, 1938, pp. 266–8 and 270.

Significantly it was only in such poorer areas, notably Bantam, Priangan and especially Madura, that cattle rearing played more than a very minor rôle. In any case, however, this was primarily concerned with raising animals for draught, and though a little meat was eaten much the greater part of the very inadequate supplies of animal protein in the peasants' diet was derived from fish. The latter were obtained not only from river and sea fisheries but were also bred under artificial conditions elsewhere. The traditional Indonesian method of fish culture in salt-water ponds is believed to have originated in Madura during the 14th century, and was later introduced into the adjacent coastal lowlands of eastern Java, where in several areas the salinity of the soils rendered them unfit for normal crop cultivation. In modern times the practice has been adopted in various other coastal districts, including those of western and central Java, and the Dutch also

[8] A high proportion of *tegalan* land in Madura is terraced. Though it is doubtful whether this is economically worth while, it certainly helps to reduce soil erosion. Pelzer (C), p. 70.

encouraged the raising of a supplementary 'fish crop' in flooded rice fields in many parts of the island.

A further measure of the intense pressure on the land may be seen in the small size of the average peasant holding, which in 1937 was in the vicinity of 2·2 acres.[9] In these circumstances the scope for cash-crop production over and above the raising of grain (rice or maize), roots, legumes and fruit for direct consumption was obviously very limited. Nevertheless, besides cassava and maize, which were partly produced for sale, the peasant (*tani*) frequently grew other annuals, such as tobacco and ground nuts, in rotation with rice, and might also cultivate perennials like coconuts, tea and, especially in the drier areas, kapok, on the less attractive land. These commodities were sold either to traders, usually Chinese or Arabs, or to the estates, and altogether the peasant cultivators produced about one-fifth by value of Java's total export crops.

The remaining four-fifths came from the 1,177 estates which, averaging about 2,200 acres in size, amounted in sum to over 2,595,000 acres. Of these 1,453,000 acres, or about 7 per cent of the total area of Java, were under crops in 1937.[10] Two main types of estates may be distinguished, namely those on long leases, confined for the most part to the uplands and producing such perennials as rubber, cinchona, tea and coffee, and those on shorter leases from native owners, situated generally in the lowlands and concentrating primarily on sugar and tobacco. Of the latter group, tobacco was normally grown in alternate years with rice, while the sugar crop which occupied the land for 18 months at a time was cultivated only once in 3–4½ years on any given piece of ground. In most cases plantation labour was drawn from nearby villages, and was usually on a part-time or seasonal basis. Moreover, the subsistence and estate economies were further linked by the food and building materials which the peasants supplied to the planters, and the cash crops which they frequently sold to the estates for processing.

An interesting feature of the Java estates, which were predominantly Dutch owned and often of long standing, was that nearly half of them concentrated not on one but on two or more crops, a practice which reduced some of the risks involved in monoculture. Particularly favoured combinations in the west, where approximately half the estates were situated, were rubber and tea, and cinchona and tea, while in the east rubber and coffee were similarly combined.

In contrast to the abundance of agricultural wealth, other sources of primary produce in Java were relatively unimportant. By the 1930s the island's share in the total oil output of the Indies had dropped to 5 per cent, and other minerals were negligible. Teak, however, provided a valuable source of income, especially in the areas of poor soils on the Tertiary ridges of eastern Java.

[9] See Broek (E), p. 123. Although most of the land was owned by Javans, there was considerable variation in the amount held by individuals. Many large landholders had property in several villages, while at the opposite end of the scale there was a growing number of countryfolk who possessed no land at all. See below, p. 291.

[10] Broek (A), p. 194.

The adverse effects of the economic crisis of the early 1930s were keenly felt in Java. For while eventually the restriction schemes in rubber, tea and cinchona caused an improvement in the prices of these commodities, no comparable relief was forthcoming in respect of sugar, coffee or tobacco. This disparity was particularly unfortunate in that the latter group of products came more especially from the eastern part of Java which, because of its less reliable rainfall, tends to be a more precarious place than the rest of the island in which to make a living.

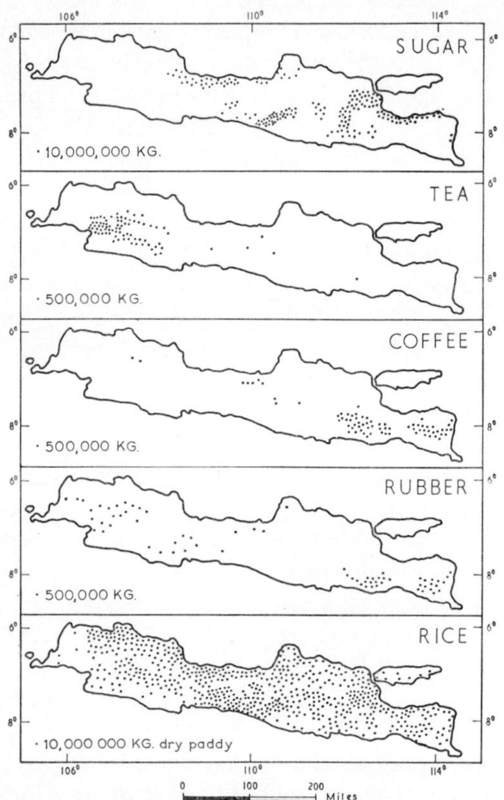

FIG. 40—Java: chief crops, 1923

The most outstanding effect of the depression on Javanese agriculture was the spectacular decline in the importance of sugar, which before 1930 had been the leading cash crop in the island. Within a few years the acreage had fallen to less than a tenth of the former level, and though by 1940 production had begun to recover, it still amounted to only 40 per cent of the 1930 figure.[11] In the meantime, however, the government had wisely encouraged a change-over to food production, and between 1930 and 1937 the rice acreage rose from 7·8 million to 9·6 million. Thus Java had reached the stage of producing an amount of rice equal to 94 per cent by bulk of what it consumed and, by exporting a quantity of better-grade rice mainly to Sumatra, Celebes and Borneo, it was able in effect to pay for its somewhat larger imports, of generally lower quality, from Siam and other parts of the South-east Asian mainland.

[11] The sugar production peak was earlier. In 1920 the sugar export was valued at 1,050 million guilders, in 1925 at 370 million and in 1930 at 254 million. See Allen and Donnithorne, p. 291. See also Fryer (C).

III. PRIMARY PRODUCTION IN THE OUTER TERRITORIES

Owing to the almost exclusive concentration of Dutch effort in Java until the latter part of the 19th century, the economic contrast between it and the outer territories remained very sharp. Equally important, however, was the diversity in both human and natural resources within the outer regions themselves, a state of affairs which was clearly reflected in both subsistence and commercial production there during the inter-war years.

With few exceptions the existence of relatively high population densities, as in the Atjeh plains and parts of the western highlands of Sumatra, in Bali and Lombok, around Bandjarmasin, and in a few areas in Celebes and the lesser islands farther east, could be directly related to the practice of various forms of wet-rice cultivation, and indeed some of the traditional methods employed show evidence of great ingenuity.

Thus, for example, in Bali, both terracing and irrigation practices, while generally similar to those in Java, are even more elaborately organized, and remarkable systems of aqueducts, in some cases carried by tunnels through the hillsides, distribute the water from reservoirs to the *sawahs*. The Menangkabau likewise have a complicated system of irrigation which makes use of water wheels to lift water from the rivers. Elsewhere in the outer territories, however, wet-rice cultivation depends mainly on direct inundation of embanked fields by rain or flood water, and various adaptations in cultivation techniques are called for to meet local peculiarities of climate or relief.[12]

Nevertheless, the most widespread form of indigenous land use in the outer territories is that of shifting cultivation (*ladang*) with either dry rice or maize as the principal crop, though in some of the more backward areas of the east the pith of the sago palm, which is gathered rather than cultivated, forms the staple food.

In general, land hunger is the exception rather than the rule in these areas, and for this reason the Dutch had done very little to develop modern irrigation or water conservancy schemes there, except on a small scale in association with the resettlement of peasant cultivators from Java.[13] Moreover, the absence of population pressure in most parts of the outer territories meant that the incentive to undertake wage labour was much less than in Java, and accordingly the estates and mines relied heavily on imported workers. As has been described in Chapter 8, the emphasis in this respect changed during the last half century of Dutch rule, and in 1937 the total number of Chinese workers employed in the outer territories was only 32,339 as compared with 299,903 of Javan origin.

[12] An interesting example described in Pelzer (C), p. 223, is that of the Bandjarese cultivators in the swamps of southern Borneo. Since the land is too deeply inundated to be cultivated during the wet season, rice is first transplanted when the flood waters have dropped to a depth of about 8–10 in. and meanwhile the seedlings are prepared in floating seedbeds.

[13] See below, pp. 293–4.

Alike in number (1,212) and in total area (3,476,000 acres) the estates of the outer territories had already overtaken those of Java by 1937, though the area actually under crops, namely 1,390,000 acres, was slightly below the figure for Java in that year. The particularly large average size (7,900 acres) of the estates in the Sumatran Cultuurgebied was in the main due to the greater ease of obtaining land in that originally sparsely peopled area. Furthermore, partly because of the shortage of local labour in these newer plantation regions, the main emphasis there was on tree crops,[14] notably rubber and oil palm, which respectively accounted for 65 and 15 per cent of that total estate area in the outer territories. Altogether, therefore, the range of products involved (Table 18) was smaller than in Java, and most estates concentrated on a single commodity.

Although the local population of the outer territories had been comparatively little attracted by the idea of working on the estates, the presence of the latter had already had important repercussions on the indigenous economies. Thus in many areas the peasants had taken to cultivating various tree crops on patches of waste land and also on *ladangs* which, having been cropped for a few years, would otherwise have been left to revert to jungle. In this respect the most spectacular developments were in rubber, especially in Sumatra and Borneo, with the result that before the war the native output of rubber in the Indies was approximately equal in quantity to that grown on estates. And although the quality of this *bevolkingsrubber* (native rubber) was lower than that from the estates, the peasant, who normally relied solely on his family for labour, was able to make a very useful cash income from it. In the eastern parts of the archipelago the coconut played a somewhat analogous rôle but, despite the larger quantities involved, the much lower value of the product meant that the return to the individual cultivator was usually less.

Both native cash-crop production and especially estate cultivation were very patchily distributed in the outer territories and, notwithstanding a certain degree of correlation between particular economic developments and the natural potentialities of the areas in which they took place, the adjustment was altogether less mature than in Java.

In respect of agricultural production,[15] Sumatra was much the most important of the outlying islands. This was primarily due to the development of the Cultuurgebied, which had spread beyond the East Coast Residency into the adjoining parts of Atjeh and Tapanuli, both of which have similarly fertile soils. Rubber alone comprised two-thirds of the estate production, and was followed by palm oil, tea and tobacco, in all of which except the last a considerable proportion

[14] These require much less attention in relation to value of output than do most of the smaller 'garden crops' or tobacco. Though tobacco had been the chief crop initially, its relative importance declined in the 20th century. Besides the heavy demand it made on labour the best cigar wrapper could be grown only once every 8 years or so on a given piece of land. See Broek (A), p. 195, and Pelzer (F), p. 155.

[15] As also of mining. See Broek (A), pp. 197–8, and below, p. 285.

of foreign capital was invested.[16] The geographical distribution of the various crops in the Cultuurgebied was a reflection more of historic sequence than of any important variations in physical conditions, except in so far as the belt of copra production along the coast and the area of tea plantations in the interior uplands towards the Batak country formed part of the region. Thus tobacco, the first cash crop to be grown there, remained pre-eminent in the Deli valley around Medan, while beyond this to both north and south was the rubber zone, developed after 1907, and on the peripheries of this in turn the more recent oil-palm and sisal districts.

Elsewhere in the island plantations were much less extensive, though the Lampung district had several rubber estates, and tea was important in the rainier West Coast Residency. Owing to the demands of the large labouring population of the estate areas, Sumatra as a whole used to import considerable quantities of rice, but the decline in the labour force resulting from the depression, together with governmental measures to increase food production locally, were combining in pre-war years to lessen this dependence on outside supplies.

In addition to its great output of agricultural produce, Sumatra was also the most important supplier of minerals in the whole of the Indies. In particular, 65 per cent of the petroleum came from this island and, for reasons already considered, all the principal fields were situated close to tidewater as also were those of Borneo, Java and Seram. This ease of access was an asset of major importance, and although the country's total output of petroleum amounted to only 2·8 per cent of pre-war world production, it formed 82 per cent of that of the whole of Asia to the east of India.

Next in order of importance among the minerals exported from the Indies were tin and bauxite, and in both cases Sumatra[17] was the sole producer. As regards tin, the combined output of Bangka, Belitung and Singkep amounted to some 20 per cent of the world's total, and gave the Indies third place, after Malaya and Bolivia. As in Malaya, the earlier rather primitive methods of the Chinese had given way in the 20th century, first to hydraulicking and then to gravel pumping; by the 1930s two-thirds of the tin was obtained by dredging, though some deep lode mining was undertaken in Belitung. Bauxite, occurring in lateritic deposits in the Riau archipelago, had been worked only since 1935 but already, with an output of 275,000 tons in 1938, the Indies were listed as the sixth producer in the world.

In the remaining islands of the archipelago economic development was, for various reasons, much less advanced.[18] Borneo, for example, with its extensive swamps, generally poor non-volcanic soils and sparse and mostly rather backward population, had little to attract the planter. Nevertheless, many parts of the island

[16] The amount of foreign capital invested in the East Coast Residency of Sumatra was about as great as that of the Dutch.

[17] *I.e.* in the administrative sense of the term Sumatra, which included the adjacent islands where tin and bauxite were produced. See Broek (E), p. 127.

[18] Broek (E), pp. 127–8.

were becoming active centres of native rubber production, and the oilfields, situated mainly along the eastern coast, were second only to those of Sumatra and accounted for 20 per cent of the total Indies output.

With the exception of fairly large areas in the vicinity of Pontianak and Bandjarmasin, shifting cultivation had not been replaced by more advanced methods, and accordingly some rice had to be imported for the working population. Conditions in the deep interior were still more primitive, but nevertheless the total output of such forest produce as resins, rattan, wild rubber and beeswax constituted a significant item of commerce. Indeed, the forest resources of Borneo are potentially immense and already a beginning had been made by Japanese firms in developing a modern lumbering industry at various points along the east coast.

Bali, and to some extent Lombok also, were areas of intensive subsistence agriculture, and, as we have seen, their irrigated rice cultivation was of a high order. But mainly for historical reasons, and in more recent times from a desire (perhaps not entirely unconnected with the profits drawn from tourism) to preserve unspoiled the Hindu/Buddhist culture of the Balinese, the Dutch showed little inclination to develop the area economically. However, Bali was known for its small-holder coffee production and the breeding of pigs and cattle, while in Lombok tobacco was the main cash crop of the peasantry.

Eastwards from Borneo and Lombok, physical and human factors combined to retard economic development. Here good agricultural land is generally limited in amount, and with only a few exceptions notably in Makasar, the Minahasa district of Celebes and the once 'preferred' spice islands of Banda, Ambon and Seram, the indigenous population has never fully recovered from the state of apathy and mental torpor engendered by centuries of monopoly punctuated with bloodshed.

Remoteness from the main stream of commerce has also played a part in inhibiting progress, but nevertheless a considerable expansion in native coconut production had taken place especially in Minahasa before the Second World War, and in the east as a whole copra had far outstripped the once famous cloves, nutmegs and mace which, however, were still grown on a few estates. Elsewhere plantations, notably of coffee, were mainly confined to north-eastern and south-western Celebes, which likewise were the only areas where wet-rice cultivation was practised by the indigenous peoples.

In many parts of the eastern archipelago the introduction of a money economy had led to a change-over to rice – largely imported – as the staple article of diet. But in the more backward islands maize or wild sago still provided the basic foodstuffs, and after the depression there was a fairly widespread reversion to self-sufficiency in many other areas as well.[19] Among the more interesting local specialities which were beginning to develop in the inter-war years as a result of improved transport may be mentioned the rearing of cattle and horses in the drier eastern parts of the Lesser Sundas.

[19] See Allen and Donnithorne, p. 249.

The only important mineral produced in the eastern archipelago was petroleum, of which Seram contributed 5 per cent of the Indies total before the war. Prospects for nickel mining were known to exist in Celebes and operations on a small scale began there just before the outbreak of the Second World War.

Although, economically speaking, the most retarded of all, Dutch New Guinea was believed even in pre-war days to be of greater potential significance than most other parts of the eastern archipelago. Owing, however, to its extreme remoteness, to the wide and repellent fringe of coastal swamp, and also to the very sparse and backward population of the interior, little had been done to assess, let alone to exploit the resources of this vast territory, and for all practical purposes it had been left as a negative frontier zone marking the eastern limit of the Dutch sphere.

But in the early 1930s, precisely because of its virgin character, the territory began to attract the attention of the Indies Eurasian community, many of whom having been badly hit by the economic crisis were contemplating agricultural colonization overseas. Although it was widely believed that some of the lowlands and especially the interior plateaux offered great prospects, the settlement scheme undertaken by the Indo-Europeesch Verbond failed ignominiously, in part through inadequate planning and lack of capital.[20]

Meanwhile, however, the old suspicion of covert foreign penetration reappeared, occasioned this time by the Japanese who had obtained concessions for cotton and rubber planting along the northern coast. Partly in order to keep an eye on these activities the Dutch began to consider opening up the territory systematically. The Netherlands New Guinea Oil Company started prospecting in the Humboldt Bay area in 1936,[21] but nothing of importance had been achieved in this or other respects, apart from missionary work by both Protestants and Roman Catholics, before the outbreak of the Pacific War.

IV. THE EFFECTS OF UNEVEN ECONOMIC DEVELOPMENT AND POPULATION DENSITY

From a geographical point of view the outstanding feature of inter-war primary production in the Indies was its extraordinary unevenness. Roughly at the centre of the archipelago lay the congested island of Java, full to overflowing with people and cropped to capacity, much of it indeed growing two distinct crops each year. Outside Java, however, conditions were completely different. A few areas of intensive development of one kind or another were to be found scattered up and down the archipelago, but the greater part of the outer islands was still essentially undeveloped territory. And while it is true that the two areas of greatest agricultural importance in the Indies as a whole, namely Java and the East Coast of

[20] Other similar schemes, notably at Giesting in southern Sumatra, also failed.

[21] The main oil companies operating in the Indies collaborated in prospecting in West New Guinea shortly before the Second World War. See Ter Braake, p. 68.

Sumatra, are physically the two best endowed parts of the archipelago,[22] the degree of difference in development between them and the remainder was far too great to be explained solely in such terms.

Thus, for example, the northern boundary of the Cultuurgebied is not determined by physical conditions and much of Atjeh is naturally well suited to intensive agricultural production, as can be seen from the high quality of the rice lands along the coast. Other instances of good land could be cited elsewhere in the archipelago, notably in other parts of Sumatra and in Bali and Lombok, which under the Dutch were almost completely neglected. Clearly the astonishing development of Java is to be explained by an extreme concentration of effort on what was obviously a richly endowed island. Later, when a growing demand for tropical produce led to a search for new areas to develop, an almost equally productive tract of country had been found in north-eastern Sumatra, which was even better placed in relation to shipping routes.

Indeed, as is borne out by the great economic expansion in western Malaya and the lack of comparable developments in both British and Dutch Borneo and beyond, it is probable that accessibility was at least as important as soil fertility in promoting the development of the Cultuurgebied.[23] By the 1930s, however, supplies of most types of tropical produce were beginning to outstrip effective demand, and expansion of the plantation area accordingly ceased. The best areas had been taken up and, despite some serious fluctuations, remained in production. But no occasion arose to justify the expensive task of developing new plantation areas elsewhere and, in view of the high overhead costs involved in estate production, the indigenous small-holder began to come into his own. Thus the native share in the cash-crop production of the Indies as a whole rose from 24 per cent in 1913 to 46 per cent in 1937, and it was this, together with the precipitous decline of sugar production in Java, which explained the relative growth in the agricultural importance of the outer territories[24] during the same period, notwithstanding the difficulties from which the plantations suffered.

Both the great variations in the intensity and duration of European enterprise, and the equally great diversity in the cultural levels of the various indigenous peoples, were reflected in the exceptionally wide range of population density found within the confines of the Netherlands Indies in the 1930s (Table 21). As was noted in Chapter 6, three factors, namely the ending of internecine warfare, the creation of new means of livelihood and the reduction in the incidence of various diseases, have combined to lower the indigenous death-rates in all those parts of South-east Asia which have been brought under effective

[22] Bali may also be included here, though its dry season is more pronounced than that even of eastern Java.

[23] Good soils were certainly needed for the first crop developed there, viz. tobacco, but many of the tree crops which later became important would have thrived on less fertile soils.

[24] The outer territories' share of agricultural exports rose from 35 per cent to 65 per cent during the same period. See Broek (A), p. 189.

European control in the past 150 years. So far as the Indies were concerned, the operation of all three was limited almost entirely to Java during the greater part of the 19th century, with the result that the island's population increased from less than 5 million in 1815 to over 30 million in 1905, compared with an increase in the outer territories of only 3 million, from *c.* 4·7 million to 7·7 million, during the same period.

Striking as this contrast is, however, it is scarcely more remarkable than the fact that even in 1815, before the main era of Dutch exploitation had begun, Java, which accounted for only 7 per cent of the total area of the Indies,[25] already contained half the total population. Presumably this was due to the combination of a high level of agricultural skill, associated with the former status of Java as the leading focus of Indianized civilization in the archipelago, and the intrinsic fertility and other geographical advantages of the island which had doubtless played a large part in establishing its ascendancy in early times.

Nevertheless, in 1815 only a relatively small portion of Java was under cultivation,[26] and the great increase of population which took place in the 19th century went hand in hand with a rapid extension of the cultivated acreage during that period. But during the first three decades of the present century the scope for further expansion of this kind decreased virtually to zero, and in respect of purely agricultural population the island may be said to have reached saturation point. Thus the differences in density within Java by 1930 corresponded very closely with the variations in the carrying capacity of its soil, the greatest concentrations of all occurring in the north-central lowlands and in parts of the Vorstenlanden where soil fertility and the percentage of land under sawah cultivation were both at their highest. (Table 22.)

Of the outer territories only nearby Bali, with a density of 503 in 1930,[27] approached the Java average of 817, and undoubtedly this figure is to be explained in terms of the very close similarities, both physical and cultural, between Bali and the adjacent parts of Java. Yet in respect of the intensity and duration of Dutch influence the two areas were strongly contrasted, and innovations brought about under Dutch rule could have contributed little to reduce the deathrate in the Balinese lowlands until the beginning of the present century. Thus it seems reasonable to assume that prior to 1815 Bali may have been more densely populated than Java, a state of affairs which suggests that the old Indo-Javanese civilization survived in a more vigorous form in Bali than on the parent island itself.[28]

Elsewhere in the outer territories, however, densities were altogether lower,

[25] *I.e.* if West New Guinea was included, as it then was. Otherwise the figure should be *c.* 9 per cent. On population distribution generally see Pelzer (B), pp. 53–60.

[26] Approximately 3,750,000 acres. Zinkin (A), p. 127.

[27] South Bali returned an average of 670 and the figure for the Gianjar sub-division thereof was 1,174.

[28] This is borne out by the greater efficiency of the Balinese cultivators who are the most skilled of any indigenous people in the archipelago.

averaging only 28 for the whole area, and although the local concentrations of population in parts of the western highlands and the east coast of Sumatra, in north-eastern and south-western Celebes, and in some of the Moluccan islands could all be explained partly in terms of better-than-average soils, the facts remain that only in the Menangkabau lands did the level of indigenous cultivation approximate to that of Java and Bali, and only in the Cultuurgebied was western enterprise on a comparable scale with that of the metropolitan islands.[29]

In short, whereas in Java (and Bali) the local resources were being utilized to the very utmost, the agricultural potentialities of the outer territories, which, though generally inferior to those of Java, area for area, are by no means negligible, had received far less systematic attention. And while a policy of concentrating

TABLE 21

NETHERLANDS INDIES: GROWTH AND DENSITY OF POPULATION 1905–30

Region	Area (sq. miles)	Population 1905	Population 1930	Density per sq. mile, 1930
Java and Madura	51,039	30,366,000	41,718,364	817
Sumatra and Dependencies	184,222	4,294,000	8,254,843	44*
Borneo	208,298	1,234,000	2,168,661	12
Celebes	72,890	902,000†	4,231,906	56
Moluccas	32,318	208,000	579,129	18‡
Lesser Sundas	28,420	832,000	3,460,059	180§
New Guinea	159,381	200,000	314,271	2
Outer Territories	687,529	7,670,000	19,008,869	28
Total	738,568	38,036,000	60,727,233	83

*Sumatra included some individual districts with densities up to 900 in the Padang highlands and over 200 in the Cultuurgebied.

†1905 figures for Celebes were almost certainly seriously underestimated.

‡Moluccas includes *inter alia* Ternate 580, Tidore 500, Banda 275.

§Lesser Sundas includes Bali 750, Lombok 500, Sumba/Sumbawa 200, Flores 200, Timor (Dutch) 104.

Source: Based on *Volkstelling*, 1930

[29] The high densities in certain of the Moluccan islands were related to the early establishment of European rule there.

TABLE 22

JAVA AND MADURA: DENSITY OF POPULATION, 1930

Gewest or District	*Density per square mile*
West Java	632
(Ploembon	2,784)
Middle Java	1,026
(Adiwerno	4,242)
Djokjakarta	1,274
(Kotagede	2,331)
Surakarta	1,101
(Klaten	2,852)
East Java	818
(Probolinggo	2,665)
All Java	817

(Gewesten are shown in capitals, and the most densely populated predominantly rural district in each is shown in parentheses below.)

Source: Based on *Volkstelling*, 1930.

first on the better areas is readily understandable, there can be little doubt that the Dutch had carried this too far. Certainly by the 1930s the harmful effects of the extreme congestion in Java could no longer be gainsaid. Thus, in the words of Dr. G. H. C. Hart,[30] the average native diet in that island, already barely adequate at the beginning of the century, 'had definitely deteriorated in food value, if not in actual volume' during the decades immediately preceding the Second World War, a condition which was intimately related to the steady decline in the amount of cultivated land per head of population in that island.[31] Moreover, according to Dr. J. H. Boeke, although 90 per cent of the inhabitants of Java could still be classed as rural in the 1930s, only 65 per cent of the working population were directly engaged in subsistence agriculture, and the remaining 25 per cent led a precarious existence, depending mainly on casual labour for a livelihood.[32]

In contrast to those in Java, living conditions were distinctly better in many parts of the outer territories, particularly where cash-crop production, for example of rubber, was combined with subsistence farming, and over the outer

[30] Hart, G. H. C. (A), p. 94. Dr. Hart was the Netherlands Indies Director of Economic Affairs.

[31] In 1922 the average amount of land per tax-paying landowner in Java was 2·84 acres, but in 1938 it had fallen to 2·13 acres. Pelzer (C), p. 161.

[32] Boeke (B), p. 399.

islands as a whole, De Meel records that in 1935–9 the average *per capita* consumption of rice was 249 lb. a year as opposed to only 181 lb. in Java.[33]

Already by this time the differential was becoming reflected in the vital statistics for, to quote De Meel, 'the continued pressure exerted by an increasing population on the food supply (*i.e.* of Java) pushes the death rate and particularly the infant mortality rate upwards'.[34] And since in the meantime the extension of effective Dutch rule over the outer territories had led to a fall in death-rates there comparable to that in Java during the 19th century, the population of the outer territories had begun to make up some of the leeway it had lost during the earlier period.

Nevertheless, although the percentage rate of increase between 1905 and 1930 was appreciably higher in the outer territories than in Java,[35] the absolute rate of increase in the latter, which averaged *c.* 600,000 per annum between 1920 and 1930, was dangerously high, and indeed had already been causing growing concern to the Dutch before the unemployment resulting from the depression of the 1930s brought matters to a head. Perhaps because of their own retention of the large-family system, to an extent which was unusual elsewhere in Western Europe, the Dutch seemed never to have given serious thought to birth control as a possible solution to the demographic problems of the Indies.[36] But in three other directions their search for an answer to the problem of providing a livelihood for the people of Java was extremely thorough, and each of these will now be examined in some detail.

V. DUTCH ATTEMPTS TO SOLVE THE POPULATION PROBLEM OF JAVA

As we have already seen, the first possibility, namely that of increasing local food production, had been under active consideration since the beginning of the century. So far as Java was concerned, reclamation, irrigation and water conservation, the encouragement of new crops and the application of scientific research to both commercial and subsistence farming had all been undertaken with characteristic Dutch thoroughness, and together had achieved remarkable results.

Thus, although it was estimated that only 1 per cent of the cultivated land

[33] De Meel (B), p. 274. The difference in weight was largely made up by consuming more cassava, which however contains only 0·87 per cent protein as against 9·85 per cent in the case of rice.

[34] *Ibid.*, pp. 273–4. These conditions must have contributed to lethargy and insouciance among the peasantry.

[35] In the Indies as a whole the average annual increase for 1920–30 was 19/1000, but for Central Java alone it was only 7/1000 and for the outer territories 32/1000. See De Meel (B), p. 267. In Java the birth-rate was estimated in 1940 at 38/1000, death-rate 22/1000 and natural increase 16/1000.

[36] De Meel believes that birth-rates have remained more or less uniformly high in Indonesia over the last 150 years, and hence that 'the influence of bad economic conditions on the death-rate is the sole determinant of the rate of population increase in the different regions of Indonesia'. *Ibid.*, p. 273.

received any regular treatment with commercial fertilizer, the peasant relying almost exclusively on the incidental excreta of the water buffaloes used in ploughing to manure his fields, the yield of paddy per acre was the highest in all South-east Asia.[37] This, of course, was in large measure a reflection of the fertility of the island's volcanic soils, though it was clear that long continued cropping had taken its toll in many areas, and approximately 2½ million acres of the rice lands were considered to be seriously deficient in phosphates and another 1¼–2½ million acres similarly deficient in nitrogen. Without doubt still higher yields could have been obtained if the peasant cultivators had been taught to use chemical fertilizers and, more important, had been able to afford to buy them. But the extreme poverty, resulting from what was probably the most intense pressure of population on the land anywhere in the world, ruled out the latter possibility, and virtually no margin existed for further extension of the cultivated area.

Indeed, any widespread depletion of the remaining forests, situated as these were in the upland catchment regions, would almost certainly have been followed by serious soil erosion, which hitherto had been largely prevented, thanks to well-organized water control and skilful methods of cultivation. On the other hand, however, abundant opportunity existed for expanding the food production of the outer territories and, mainly as a result of developments there, the rice import of the Indies as a whole fell from 8 to 4 per cent of total consumption between 1930 and 1939, and by the outbreak of war virtual self-sufficiency in this, the basic foodstuff, had been achieved.

Clearly, however, the most effective way of utilizing the agricultural resources of the outer islands was by moving at least part of the surplus rural population of Java to some of the more promising areas, and this 'transmigration' as the Dutch called it, came to form the second line of attack.[38] The earliest Dutch proposals for transferring part of the rural population of Java to selected areas in the outer parts of the archipelago date from 1903, and two years later the first colonists were settled at Gedongtataän in the Lampung district of southern Sumatra. This pioneer activity was necessarily on a small scale, and for many years afterwards the difficulties experienced, resulting partly from inadequate surveys and consequent poor agricultural returns, partly from epidemics, and not least from the prejudices of the Javanese themselves, seemed to suggest that such ventures could never be economically carried out on a sufficient scale to contribute significantly to a solution of the problem. By comparison with the considerable migration of Javan labourers to various parts of the outer territories, which besides involving much larger numbers made no financial calls on the government, the results were insignificant, and interest in agricultural colonization gradually waned. When, however, in the early 1930s the depression caused

[37] As shown in Table 3, the average paddy yield for all Indonesia was 31·5 bushels per acre, but the figure for Java alone was about 30 per cent higher than this.

[38] For further details of the Dutch 'transmigration' programme see Pelzer (C), Chapters 6 and 7, and Peekema, pp. 145–53.

thousands of unemployed workers to return to the overcrowded *desas* of Java, the authorities began to re-examine the possibilities of transmigration. Thus, in the light of experience at Gedongtataän, new and much more effective methods were devised, which in fact had much in common with those which were being adopted in Holland itself in the settlement of the North-east Polder reclaimed from the Zuyder Zee, and between 1936 and 1940 the number of Javan colonists[39] in the outer territories rose from 68,000 to 206,000.

Under this new *systeem van kernvorming* (*i.e.* the establishment of nuclei of pioneer settlers who would prepare the area for later arrivals) preference was given to young peasant couples, but it was often found that to move a whole village (by stages) was in the long run the most effective procedure. First attention was directed to the areas of greatest congestion, notably in east-central Java, including Djokjakarta and Surakarta, and all-told about 60 per cent of the colonists went to the Lampung district, some 18 per cent to Palembang, a further 4 per cent to other parts of Sumatra, over 16 per cent to central Celebes and 2.5 per cent to southern and eastern Borneo. In all cases the authorities strove to preserve as much as possible of the Javan pattern of agriculture in the new settlements, and colonists usually received one hectare of land (2·47 acres) per family to be used solely for subsistence crops. Thus, freed from debts and other hardships resulting from the long-continued decline in the size of holdings in Java, the colonists were quickly able to attain a higher standard of living than they had been accustomed to at home. Nevertheless, there was force in Pelzer's criticism that, notwithstanding the greater capital outlay which would have been required, better results and a safer margin for the future would have been obtained by providing larger holdings, and promoting the cultivation also of cash crops along the lines already followed by many of the indigenous inhabitants of the outer territories.[40]

So far as the latter were concerned, Javanese colonization, though much resented, often had beneficial results in that it fostered a change from shifting to permanent cultivation on the part of those who witnessed the superiority of Javanese methods and whose land could sometimes be irrigated under the schemes introduced for the colonists. Indeed, some modification of the indigenous agriculture in the outer territories was a necessary concomitant of any large-scale settlement there by peasants from the overcrowded parts of Java, though, as will be considered in Chapter 10, other ways of effecting this may prove to be more appropriate.

By the time the Pacific War broke out real progress had been made, and the Dutch were within sight of achieving the goal they had set themselves of moving 100,000 people a year. On the assumption that the population of Java had been

[39] The term colonists here refers exclusively to persons taking part in the 'transmigration' schemes and not to estate labourers, mineworkers, etc.

[40] The standard amount of one hectare (2·47 acres) was only a little larger than that of the average holding in Java, *i.e.* 2·2 acres.

increasing during the 1930s by approximately 600,000 per year, however, even this figure would have been inadequate, and the official view was that an annual migration of about 250,000–300,000 persons, consisting mainly of young people in their 'procreative period', would have been necessary to prevent the population of Java from continuing to grow.[41]

Whether transfers of population on such a scale could ever have been achieved, let alone sustained, was in Pelzer's opinion extremely doubtful, and already signs of congestion were appearing in several parts of the outer territories, notably in the better volcanic areas of upland Sumatra and Celebes. In any case, however, transfers of population on this scale were out of the question in the immediate future so that, notwithstanding the important contribution which transmigration was beginning to make towards solving the problem of over-population in Java, it was necessary to consider other means as well if disaster were to be avoided.

It was in these circumstances, therefore, that industrialization, which since the beginning of the century had been the subject of intermittent discussion and investigation, began for the first time to make really significant progress. To understand the nature of the developments which took place between 1930 and 1942, however, it is necessary to consider something of previous attempts to promote industrial enterprise in Indonesia.

In common with those of a great many other parts of Asia, the traditional subsistence handicraft industries of the Indonesian countryside had suffered a severe decline as a result of the introduction of cheap Western manufactures in the 19th century, and the consequent loss of income on the part of many members of the village community had been a major factor in causing rural impoverishment. For this reason one of the earliest themes to be stressed under the Ethical Policy had been the need for promoting industrialization as a means of raising living standards in the Indies.

As to how this could best be done, however, there was wide disagreement, and although a start was made with the establishment of a rubber factory in Java in 1904, it quickly became apparent that Western investors were not impressed by the possibilities which such enterprises afforded. Still less could be hoped for in the way of investment by the local population, for there was no large indigenous capitalist class and the Chinese and Arabs, who preferred to operate on a smaller and more intimate scale, were not at this stage interested in setting up Western-style factories.

Thus very little progress was made until the First World War, when the Indies were cut off from many established sources of Western manufactures as well as from important markets for their own exports. These conditions prompted the government to send an expert, Van Kol,[42] to study industrial development in Japan and to consider the relevance of Japanese experience to Indonesian conditions. In addition, some provision was made to supply the demand of the Indies-

[41] Quoted in Pelzer (C), p. 211.

[42] Furnivall (A), p. 333.

Dutch community for various food products and to manufacture such goods as soap, paper and textiles for a wider market. At the same time the belief that the lack of skilled technicians was the main obstacle to industrial expansion led to the foundation of the Technical Institute at Bandung in 1919. But with the resumption of 'normal' trading patterns after the war, industry again languished, and several of the new concerns were forced to close down. Dutch factory owners in Holland had no desire to create new rivals for the Indonesian market, and until the 1930s Western-style industry remained virtually limited to the initial processing of locally produced raw materials and the provision of maintenance facilities for railways, motor vehicles, shipping, and the machinery used by the mines and estates.

Meanwhile, the growth of 'cultural nationalism' and in particular of the Budi Utomi movement[43] had been accompanied by a notable revival of handicraft industries in rural Java. Here again war shortages, as well as government aid, had provided a further stimulus, and a considerable expansion took place in the production of cigarettes and kapok. In its origins this small-scale Indonesian industry was essentially a domestic activity, but as time went on the practice grew up of establishing industrial 'centrals' on a co-operative basis. In effect these were small factories employing perhaps ten to fifty workers, and usually carrying out only the final stage(s) of the manufacturing process while the rest were performed, as before, in the peasants' homes. As Sitsen pointed out,[44] this system of co-operation was deeply rooted in two traditional features of Javanese life, namely the strong sense of mutual assistance (*gotong rojong*) among the members of the village community, and the distinct seasonal rhythm in employment on the land, which made it desirable to find other occupations during the slack times of the agricultural year.

When, therefore, the economic crisis of the 1930s caused the authorities once again to turn to industrialization as a possible means of combating the distress caused by the catastrophic decline in the country's exports, there were more solid foundations on which to build than had ever previously been the case. Considerable assistance was given to rural industry in general, and the number of co-operative 'centrals' increased rapidly, particularly those engaged in *batik* production[45] and the manufacture of pottery, furniture, cigarettes and hats. By 1939 it was estimated that there were some 2,500,000 workers in small-scale secondary industries, all but 100,000 of whom were Indonesians. In the rapid expansion which took place, however, a fairly large number of concerns, owing to financial failure, passed into Chinese ownership, and an attempt by Indonesian members of the Volksraad to introduce measures, analogous to those of the 1870

[43] Budi Utomo ('glorious endeavour') was founded in 1908 by a small group of young Western-educated Javanese nobles. It was particularly concerned to set up schools for Indonesians.

[44] Sitsen, p. 17.

[45] *Batik* is a way of producing traditional designs, often of great intricacy, on cotton cloth. It normally involves several dippings in different-coloured dyes, during each of which the parts not to be dyed in that particular colour are blocked out with molten wax.

Agrarian Law, to exclude aliens from participating in such enterprises was unsuccessful.

Important developments also occurred in modern factory industry during the period between the depression and the outbreak of the Pacific War. While to a large extent this was the result of active promotion by the Indies government, which was perturbed by both the economic distress in Java and the growing popularity of cheap Japanese manufactures there,[46] it represented also in part a natural outgrowth from the older-established maintenance industries. Thus, in addition to plants manufacturing various consumer goods, notably textiles, footwear and soap, there was also a considerable expansion in shipbuilding, the manufacture of agricultural machinery and other key engineering enterprises. Particularly significant in the former case was the establishment of subsidiary factories by well-established European and American concerns; examples included Goodyear tyres, a Bata shoe factory and Lever and Van den Bergh's soap and margarine factories. Nevertheless, the total volume of factory production in Indonesia was still comparatively small in 1939, and the development of the ensuing two years before the Japanese occupation, though considerable, did not fundamentally alter the picture.

The outstanding feature of the geographical distribution of manufacturing industry, both large and small scale, in Indonesia was its overwhelming concentration in Java. With the exception of a few isolated installations like the large cement works near Padang and some of the chemical plants located on the oil-fields, practically the only important industries in the outer territories were those engaged in the initial processing of export commodities and local foodstuffs. For the rest, the great mass of small-scale industries and some 70 per cent of the registered factories were widely scattered throughout Java. While to some extent this distribution reflected the localizing effect of very high transport costs in industries designed mainly to supply the home market, it was also in large measure the result of the deliberate official policy aimed at providing new sources of employment for as many of the poverty-stricken peasantry as possible, within close range of their home areas. Thus, in addition to a moderately dense sprinkling of government-supported centrals over the Javanese countryside as a whole, the new factories were fairly evenly shared out among the larger towns. The main soap and margarine factories were situated in Batavia, Semarang produced textiles and motor tyres, Surabaja also had a tyre plant as well as a modern shipbuilding industry, Bandung manufactured quinine and textiles, and both Garut and Tegal had large spinning factories.

By the time the Pacific War broke out in 1941 the various measures undertaken by the Dutch for the purpose of alleviating the population problem of Java were still at too early a stage for their long-term prospects to be assessed with any accuracy. Nevertheless, the beginning of a trend towards a better balance between

[46] Between 1929 and 1935 the Japanese share of the Indies' import trade rose from 10·2 per cent to 30·1 per cent.

the several parts of the archipelago could certainly be discerned during the later 1930s. Both Atjeh and the Lampung district of Sumatra had begun to produce rice surpluses and there was a substantial and growing flow of manufactured goods from Java to many parts of the outer territories[47] where, as we have seen, cash incomes were, on the average, much higher.

In short, Java was coming to depend more and more on exploiting its position at the heart of the archipelago and, by means of the services it rendered as the administrative, managerial and industrial nucleus of the whole of the Indies, was providing a livelihood not only for its relatively large 'European' community but also for a growing proportion of the indigenous population as well. Thus, whereas in earlier times, as Lévy has said, the Indies constituted not one economic unit but several,[48] with some areas tributary to the Straits Settlements, others centring upon Java and still others almost completely isolated, the whole territory under Dutch control was at last being progressively welded into a single economic entity.

VI. TRANSPORT AND COMMUNICATIONS

The measure of this integration was to be seen in the steadily improving network of communications, alike on sea, land and in the air. Thanks to the country's physical character, water-borne transport remained the most important of all, and besides the main commercial and mail services, which were almost completely in the hands of the K.P.M., innumerable country boats and small Chinese-owned steam- and motor-powered craft played a very important rôle in both river and coastal trade.

Although it was a private company, the K.P.M. worked in close collaboration with, and was subsidized by, the Netherlands Indies government, and besides operating an elaborate network of coastal and inter-island services, it also owned craft which plied regularly on many of the larger rivers of Borneo, Sumatra and New Guinea. All-told its fleet, which aggregated over 300,000 tons, included some 150 vessels ranging from the large 4,000- to 6,000-ton steam or motor ships used on the main runs between Java, Sumatra and Malaya to the diminutive stern-wheelers on the upper reaches of the big rivers of Borneo.[49]

In 1938 the K.P.M. operated some 70 regular services of at least monthly frequency, and, as might be expected, Batavia was the main focus for the Java-Sumatra-Malaya-Western Borneo routes, and Surabaja for the Java-Lesser-Sunda-south-eastern Borneo services, while Makasar formed the nodal centre for the network of lines covering the remainder of the Great East. Although it was widely criticized on account of its high charges, particularly for freight,[50] the

[47] Between 1935 and 1941 the value of manufactured goods supplied by Java to the outer territories rose from 34 million guilders to 96 million guilders. Sitsen, p. 4.

[48] Lévy (A), p. 163.

[49] Kennedy (A), p. 76.

[50] It should however be realized that the K.P.M. had to maintain many services to the remoter islands which could never be paying propositions.

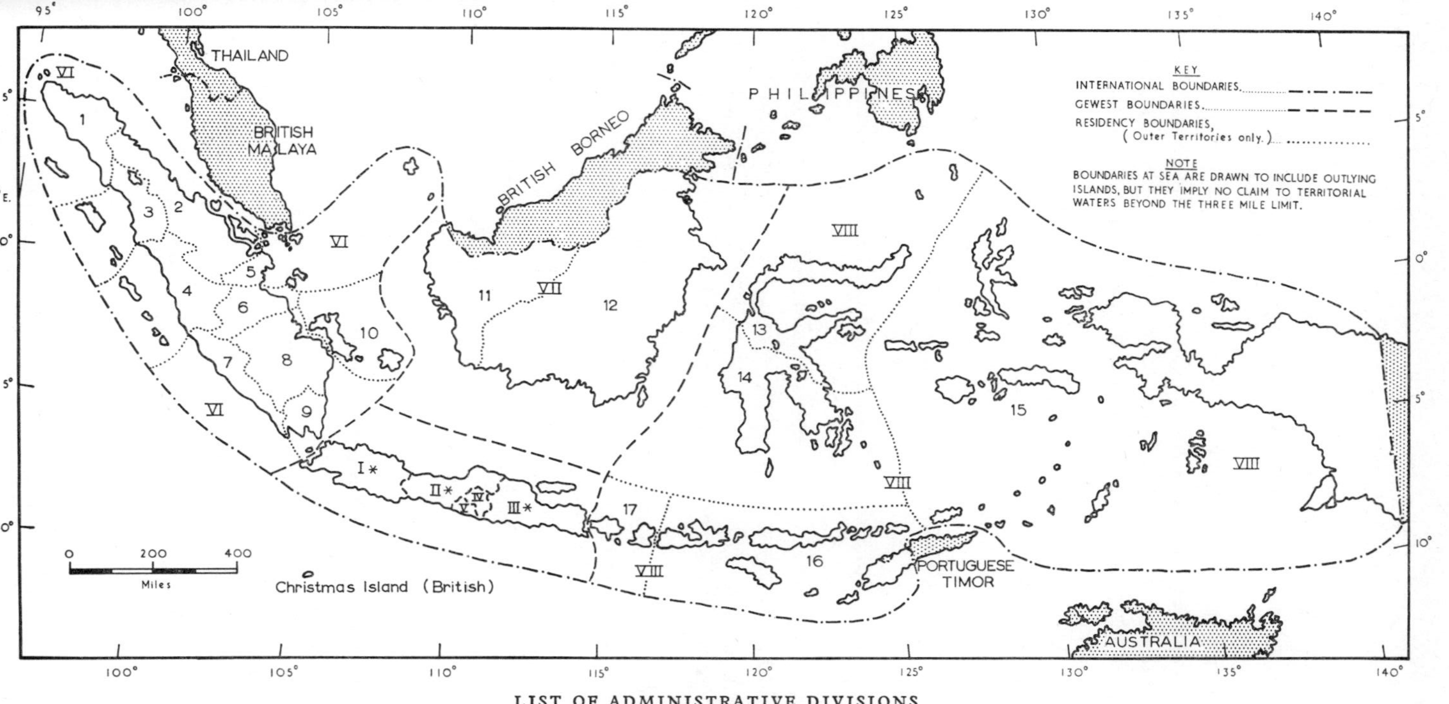

LIST OF ADMINISTRATIVE DIVISIONS

Gewesten in Roman Numerals. Residencies in Arabic Numerals.

Gewesten : I. West Java*. II. Central Java*. III. East Java*. IV. Soerakarta. V. Jogjakarta. VI. Sumatra. VII. Borneo. VIII. Great East.

Residencies: 1. Atjeh. 2. East-coast Sumatra. 3. Tapanoeli. 4. West-coast Sumatra. 5. Riouw. 6. Djambi. 7. Benkoelen. 8. Palembang. 9. Lampoeng. 10. Bangka. 11. West Borneo. 12. South and East Borneo. 13. Manado. 14. Celebes. 15. Moluccas. 16. Timor. 17. Bali and Lombok.

* Province. The remainder were Governments.

FIG. 41—Indonesia: major Dutch administrative divisions

K.P.M. enjoyed a deservedly good reputation for the efficiency with which its wide-ranging services were operated.

In contrast to the shipping network which was conceived on a country-wide basis, the extent and quality of overland communications varied greatly from island to island. This was most strikingly seen in respect of railways, which were limited exclusively to Java and Sumatra, with 3,362 and 1,227 miles respectively, in both cases mainly on the 3 ft. 6 in. gauge. In Java the system was remarkably well developed, no area being as much as 50 miles from a railway line, and some excellent express services linked the principal towns. In Sumatra, on the other hand, the network was much more fragmentary. Thus the three separate 3 ft. 6 in. systems, respectively in the East Coast (Deli), Padang and the far south (Oosthaven-Palembang) were entirely unconnected with one another, while the fourth system in Atjeh, although it made contact with that of the East Coast at Besitang, was on the narrower 2 ft. 6 in. gauge, and through running (by means of a third rail) was possible only as far as Pangkalansusu.

Both the incompleteness of the network in Sumatra and the total absence of railways in the less-developed islands were in part the result of a decision taken in the 1930s to concentrate instead on developing a really good road system in the outer territories. Thus plans for a through railway in Sumatra were scrapped, but by 1940 a N/S road, 1,059 miles long, had been completed from Kutaradja to Oosthaven, and there was also a fairly elaborate network in several other parts of the island.

Java, of course, was even better off in this respect, possessing as it did some 40 per cent of the total Indies road mileage of 42,744 and nearly 70 per cent of the 7,399 system of first-class asphalt roads. The main artery of the Java system was originally the Great Post Road built by order of Daendels between 1808 and 1811 as part of his preparations against the impending British invasion at that time. The road ran from Anjer on the Sunda Strait in Bantam via Batavia to Pasuruan and Panarukan in the extreme east of the island, but partly because of Daendel's fear of sea-borne attack and partly in order to tap the rich and populous agricultural area in the heart of the island it swung inland from the coast east of Batavia, and continued through Djokjakarta and Surakarta, a route which, with certain modifications was later followed by the first State Railway line between Batavia and Surabaja. However, in subsequent years the shorter and less mountainous route via Tjirebon, Semarang and the lower Solo valley was adopted for both the main railway line and the principal trunk road from Batavia to Surabaja.

Outside Java and Sumatra, however, progress in road building was in general much less advanced, and though a few of the smaller islands were fairly well covered, big gaps remained in the interiors of both Borneo and Celebes, while New Guinea had practically no roads at all beyond the coastal ports. Where motor roads were non-existent, coastal and river routes were supplemented by bullock-cart tracks in the more populous areas, but human porterage carried the main share of such traffic as there was in the remoter interiors. And even in Java, where innumerable Chinese- and Indonesian-owned buses and trucks were in regular operation, the indigenous trade, which in effect consisted largely of the exchange of dried and salted fish from the coast against rice from the interior, was still carried mainly by bullock cart along the country roads.

Finally the Dutch had been quick to appreciate the possibilities which air communications afforded for the closer integration of their scattered and largely undeveloped territories in the Indies, and as early as 1928 had set up the K.N.I.L.M.[51] which, like the K.P.M., received an annual subsidy from the Indies Government. By 1938 its regular flights covered 150,000 miles a month and places as far apart as Medan, Tarakan, Makasar and Denpasar were connected with Batavia and Surabaja by weekly or more frequent services.

VII. URBAN GEOGRAPHY

One of the most striking ways in which the Netherlands Indies reflected the distinctive character of the metropolitan power was in the geographical and social pattern of its towns and cities. For Dutch civilization is pre-eminently urban, and the extent to which the refinements and amenities of European town life were transplanted to Java was without parallel in any other part of South-east Asia.

That is not to say, however, that the towns of the Netherlands Indies were exclusively Dutch creations, for Indonesia had an urban tradition of its own, even though this was less highly developed than, for example, those of India, China or Japan. Indeed, some of the old *kraton* towns survived as living entities relatively little changed by Dutch rule, the two most outstanding cases being Djokjakarta and Surakarta, the respective capitals of the two Vorstenlanden of the same names in central Java. But these were undeniably exceptional, and more often the indigenous settlements, whether *kraton* towns or the once more or less independent port cities, were transformed beyond recognition as a result of Dutch activities. Such, in their different ways, were Palembang, Surabaja, Tjirebon and Makasar, to name but a few examples in which the pre-Dutch cores were almost completely submerged by later growth. And finally some of the most important towns, like Batavia, Medan and the oil ports of Borneo, were for all practical purposes the creations of the Dutch and indeed their very existence was based upon economic or strategic factors which had come into operation only during the era of Dutch domination.[52]

[51] Koninklijke Nederlandsche-Indische Luchtvaart Mij. (Royal Netherlands Indies Airways Coy.) Note: Present-day road, rail, sea and air maps are given in Figs. 45–52.

[52] The distinction between the second and third groups of towns referred to here is really one of degree. Thus Batavia itself was built on the site of a pre-existing Indonesian town (Jacatra) though this was less important than pre-Dutch Surabaja or Makasar, and virtually nothing remains of the original Jacatra today.

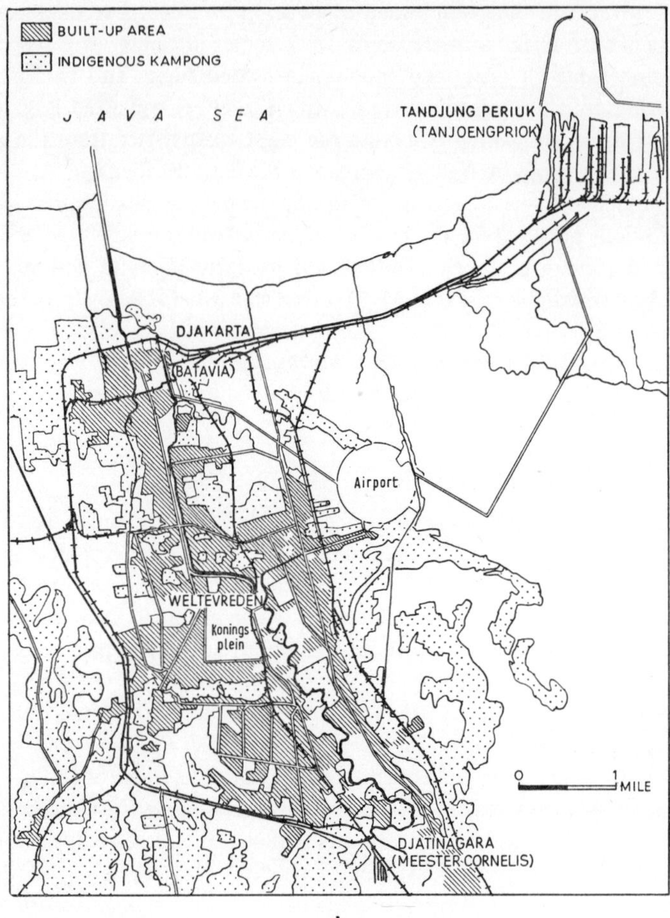

A

Undoubtedly Batavia (533,015),[53] the capital and largest city, was the most outstanding example of all. The old town, founded by Coen in 1619 on the site of the Javanese settlement of Jacatra, originally enjoyed a true coastal location at the mouth of the Tji Liwung but, in the course of the three centuries which followed, a mile-wide belt of alluvium had accumulated between the town and the shoreline. Since the 19th century the old town, though still remaining the chief business district and industrial centre had ceased to be inhabited by Europeans and had become the principal Chinese quarter, the Dutch having moved out to the newer districts of Weltevreden and Meester Cornelis.

One of the less satisfactory aspects of early Dutch urban planning in the Indies

[53] The figure for Batavia is the combined total (1930 Census) for the two municipalities Batavia (435,184) and Meester Cornelis (97,831). For an excellent account of Batavia see Fryer (A), and on urban life generally see Kennedy (A) and Wertheim (C).

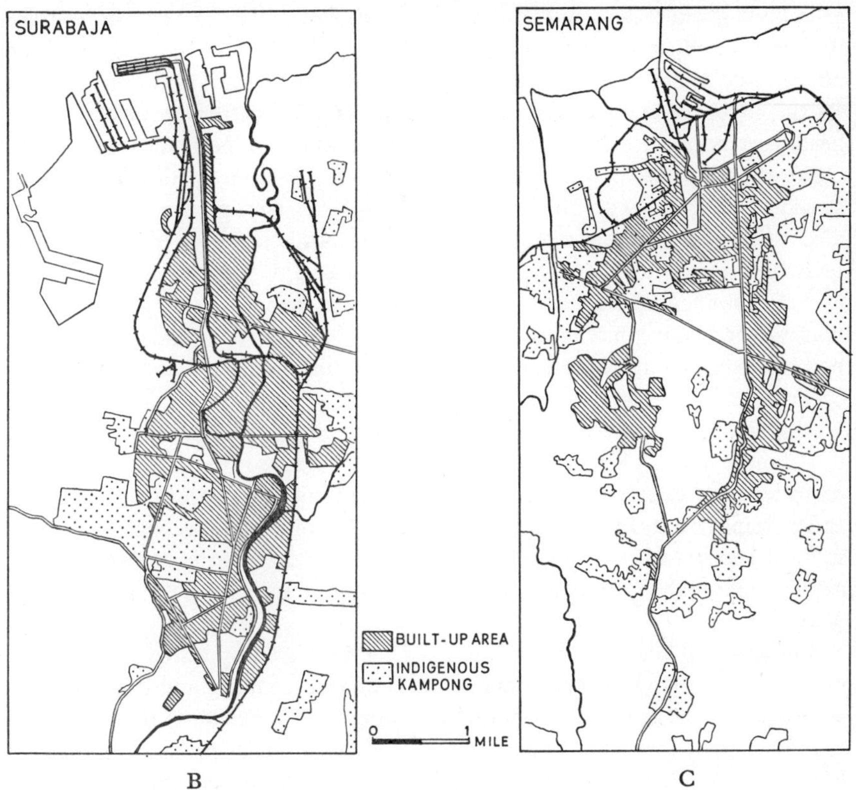

FIG. 42—Three Javan towns: A. Djakarta, B. Surabaja, C. Semarang

had been the practice first adopted in old Batavia of using canals in the manner traditional in the metropolitan country. But while the marshy terrain along the north Java coast was in some respects similar to that of the reclaimed coastlands of the North Sea, the Asian custom of using watercourses indiscriminately for washing, drinking and defecation was even more unsanitary in canals than it was in rivers, and furthermore these artificial waterways became great breeding grounds for disease-carrying insects. Thus in 1732, following the completion of a new canal outside Batavia, virulent malaria suddenly appeared in the villages near which it ran, and from there spread into the city itself. Thereafter for over a century Batavia had one of the highest death-rates of any European settlement in Asia, and despite its magnificence and luxury, was renowned as a 'regular cemetery'[54] of both Europeans and Indonesians alike.

The great amelioration of living conditions in the 19th and 20th centuries resulted primarily from improvements in drainage and preventive medicine, and in the meantime Batavia expanded rapidly towards the south onto the higher

[54] A remarkable contemporary account is given in Harrison, pp. 140–1.

ground of Weltevreden and Meester Cornelis. Both of these new centres were originally developed as part of Daendels' strategic plans to meet British attacks on the coast itself, Weltevreden 3–4 miles inland being chosen as the main centre for the government offices and Meester Cornelis, 6 miles from the shore, as the headquarters of the armed forces. In marked contrast to the Dutch style of the old town, with its stuffy houses and narrow cobbled streets, both districts were spaciously laid out, with fine broad avenues and extensive gardens, and in more recent times many impressive public buildings and hotels were erected in Weltevreden. Meanwhile, Meester Cornelis (now Djatinegara) became the most exclusive residential area, whose numerous and in many cases very ostentatious houses, with their white stucco walls, tiled roofs and floors[55] and great shaded porches, were an apt comment on both the wealth and the mentality of their occupants.

Although with the removal in 1919 of restrictions on their place of residence, the Chinese were no longer confined to any specific parts of the city, the majority remained, for economic reasons in their traditional quarter. Likewise, many Indonesians had their own favourite areas, in the form of indigenous kampong-style settlements which had grown up in the interstices between the major built-up districts of the city where, in Fryer's words, they formed 'a veritable *rus in urbe*'.[56]

As a result of coastal sedimentation and the increase in the size of ships, the need for a new port became acute in the later 19th century, and in 1877 work was begun on the artificial harbour of Tandjung Periuk, 6 miles to the north-east of the old port. During the decades which followed, much expansion and many improvements were made, and by 1938 Tandjung Periuk was one of the best-equipped harbours in the whole of Asia. But although it was the leading port of the Indies in terms of the value of its foreign trade and the tonnage of shipping which entered, it was surpassed in the volume of merchandise handled by both Palembang and Balikpapan, the main oil ports of Sumatra and Borneo respectively, and also by Surabaja in eastern Java.

Geographically speaking, Tandjung Periuk remained separate from Batavia proper, but even so the latter extended N/S for a distance of over 7½ miles on both sides of the Tji Liwung. This attenuated pattern, aligned at right angles to the coast, clearly owed much to the strategic considerations already noted, but the other advantages, particularly in regard to health, which followed from expansion onto the higher ground instead of along the coast were obviously great, and for these reasons an essentially similar pattern of growth was repeated in several of the other coastal towns of northern Java, including besides Surabaja and Semarang such smaller centres as Tegal, Pasuruan and Probolinggo.

In other respects also, most of the larger towns of Java, both coastal and inland, exhibited many of the same characteristics as Batavia, notably in their archi-

[55] Wood was avoided as far as possible owing to the prevalence of termites. Kennedy (A), p. 150.

[56] Fryer (A), p. 482.

tecture, their spacious street patterns and their tradition of communal segregation. In particular the second city, Surabaja (341,675), situated near the opposite end of the island in the lee of Madura, was remarkably similar to the capital in general appearance though, besides possessing growing manufacturing industries and a large commercial harbour, it had its own special importance as the main naval base for the Netherlands Indies fleet. Roughly mid-way between these two was the third largest city, Semarang (217,796), the capital and chief port of Middle Java, and in order of magnitude these three northern coastal cities were followed by Bandung (166,815) an inland town originally founded by the Sultan of Tjirebon in the Priangan highlands, but completely transformed by the Dutch during the 19th and 20th centuries. Thus it became the centre of the quinine industry and the permanent headquarters of the army, and moreover housed several government departments and the chief workshops of the State Railways. Thanks to its elevation (2,300 ft.) and its extremely beautiful surroundings, Bandung was by Western standards the most attractive large town in the whole of the Indies, and this was reflected in the high proportion (over 12 per cent) of Europeans in its population.[57]

By contrast, Surakarta (165,484) and Djokjakarta (136,649) were the least Europeanized of all and, despite the fact that both were on the main E/W road and railway, they still retained much of their ancient character as centres of the traditional Javanese way of life. Each was situated in the midst of the densely populated agricultural plains of the Vorstenlanden and, notwithstanding the large and ornate *kratons* which formed their principal nuclei, both appeared to be essentially overgrown villages rather than cities in the Western sense of the term.

Only after all these urban centres in Java do we come, seventh on the list, to the largest town of the outer territories, namely Palembang (108,145), a long sprawling settlement some fifty miles up the great Air Musi of south-eastern Sumatra. Here the same kind of pile and raft dwellings as were described by the 10th-century Arab writer Bozorg bin Shabriar could still be seen, though the surviving *kraton* dates only from 1780. The main growth of modern Palembang, however, was associated with the spectacular progress of the south-eastern Sumatran oil industry, for which it served as the refining centre and port.

For the rest, while Java had 27 towns of between 20,000 and 100,000 inhabitants, including coastal ports (all except Tjilatjap on the northern coast) and inland marketing and administrative centres widely scattered throughout its teeming countryside, the outer territories had only nine, all but one of which were ports. Thus Sumatra had Medan[58] (76,584), Padang (52,054) and Oosthaven

[57] This was the highest percentage of Europeans in any town in the Indies; a further 10 per cent were Chinese and 77 per cent Indonesians. But as Lehmann has shown, 52 per cent of the residential space was reserved for Europeans, 8 per cent for Chinese and only 40 per cent for Indonesians. Quoted in Wertheim (C), p. 169.

[58] Medan was not a port, this function being performed for it by Belawan (Belawan Deli) some 16 miles away. Similarly, Emmahaven was the port for Padang though the two were often regarded as a single entity.

(25,170), respectively serving the Cultuurgebied, the West Coast and the Lampungs in the extreme south, together with Djambi (22,071), which was very much overshadowed by its near neighbour Palembang. Likewise in Borneo, Bandjarmasin (65,698), Pontianak (45,196) and Balikpapan (29,843) were the principal ports of the southern, western and eastern coasts respectively, while in Celebes, Makasar (84,855), the second largest town of the outer territories, was the great entrepôt of the south-west, with Menado (27,544) as its much smaller counterpart in the north-east. East of Celebes the largest town was Ambon (17,433) whose importance as a port and as the second naval base in the country was, however, rather greater than mere numbers of population might suggest.

Notwithstanding the survival on a limited scale of certain indigenous urban traditions, the larger towns of both Java and the outer territories taken as a whole appeared essentially alien to the surroundings in which they were situated. Whereas only 3·7 per cent of the indigenous population of Java lived in the island's seven largest towns, more than half the Europeans and a third of the Chinese were found in them, and although the combined European and Chinese population in most towns did not amount to more than 15–25 per cent of their total numbers, it was undoubtedly they[59] who ran the administration and controlled all the main economic and other activities which provided the towns with their *raison d'être*.

Moreover, except for Surakarta and Djokjakarta which were the capitals of surviving indigenous states, few of the larger towns were of any real significance as regional foci in the eyes of the ordinary Indonesian peasant,[60] to whom the village of his birth, with its self-contained economy and society, was almost the only focus of interest.

Admittedly the drift of Indonesians, particularly from the overcrowded countryside of Java, to the towns had already reached considerable proportions by the 1930s, and besides the ever-growing urban proletariat, the Indonesian commercial and bureaucratic clerical middle class grew rapidly in numbers, especially after the economic depression had led to the replacement of many Europeans and Eurasians by Indonesians, who were willing to accept lower rates of remuneration. But so far as their incomes permitted, these middle-class Indonesians sought to live in 'European' style, a state of affairs which confirmed the fact that the towns were still run primarily by and for the 'Europeans' to whom they were in almost every respect the main centres of life in the Indies.

With improving communications, the growing numbers of 'European'[61] residents, and various material advances, for example in sanitation and air conditioning, it was possible to provide more and more of the amenities of the

[59] In most of the larger towns 'Europeans' (*i.e.* Europeans and Eurasians) formed between 4 and 10 per cent, and Chinese between 10 and 20 per cent. But in some of the towns of the outer territories the Chinese formed over 30 per cent, *e.g.* Medan, Balikpapan and Tarakan.

[60] Makasar and Palembang were to some extent exceptions to this.

[61] See note 59.

metropolitan country in these tropical outposts. In the early days before the coming of the steamship, when visits home to Europe were extremely few and far between, the Dutch had perforce adopted what has been called a 'mestizo' way of life in the Indies, characterized by a good deal of concubinage, widespread addiction to local customs and dishes and much pseudo-feudal ostentation.[62] But especially in the 20th century these habits had changed almost out of recognition, and no effort was spared to make the expatriate's life as European as possible. Even before the First World War, the Dutch in the Indies had developed an enthusiasm for literary and artistic societies to an extent unknown in British tropical lands, India not excepted, and during the inter-war years such activities multiplied rapidly. Travelling exhibitions of European pictures, frequent visits by world-famous musicians (*en route* to or from Australia or Japan) and the general speeding up in the transit of periodicals and private correspondence from Europe by airmail and of news in general by radio, all combined to make the Indies-Dutch town-dweller less and less conscious of being cut off from home, and correspondingly far more ready to accept what disadvantages there were in return for a far higher standard of living than he could hope to attain in the mother country. Thus, a growing proportion of Dutchmen who had spent their working lives in the Indies chose to retire there, especially in the towns within easy range of one or other of the delightful hill stations of Java. And in this way the snowball effect continued, for the more 'Europeans' there were, the more facilities it paid to provide, as for example the organization of regular supplies of dairy and market-garden produce within the country, and the import of temperate fruit and vegetables by air from Australia.

VIII. THE INDIES-DUTCH WAY OF LIFE

All in all the Indies-Dutch way of life in the 1930s was a remarkable achievement, and as an example of what might be attained in the way of health, comfort and the maintenance of European standards within the humid tropics, its only counterpart was to be found among the wealthier sections of contemporary Brazilian society, a situation which may not have been wholly unconnected with the fact that in both cases many of the 'Europeans' involved were of mixed blood.

Be that as it may, however, the paradox remained that while the 'Europeans' became more firmly attached by residence to the Indies they were nevertheless becoming further and further removed in outlook from the indigenous peoples of the country. For in fact the 'Europeans' were tending to settle more permanently in the Indies only because they were creating there, in a handful of enclaves in the larger towns, an artificial European environment which, by virtue of the great expense entailed in its upkeep, was completely beyond the reach of the ordinary Indonesian. Thus the Indies-Dutchman of the 1930s, though in many cases bred and born in the country and living there until his dying day, was not

[62] See Wertheim (C), pp. 171–2, and also Furnivall (A), pp. 212, 415 *ff*.

infrequently far less in touch with the life of its indigenous peasantry than his predecessor of the 19th century had been.

In this way, therefore, the gulf between the Europeans and the indigenes grew wider, in spite of all improvements in the technicalities of communications, and while in the immediate pre-war years the Indies-Dutch became increasingly desirous of obtaining some form of 'dominion status for the Indies', under which they would have remained the ruling élite, many Indonesian nationalists had already begun to think in terms of a more drastic change in the relationship with the metropolitan power.

This widening political gulf was of course only one aspect of the fundamental problem which, despite the success of the Dutch achievement in other respects, still remained unsolved. For although the Indies ranked as one of the world's leading exporters of primary produce, and as an imperial prize outshone all other territories in South-east Asia, the living standards of the indigenous population were among the lowest in the whole of that region[63] and, at least in Java where two-thirds of them lived, were tending to fall rather than to rise.

While it is fashionable to blame this unfortunate state of affairs primarily on Dutch parsimony, the basic cause of the exceptional poverty in Java was the intense overcrowding in that island. This was only indirectly and unintentionally the result of Dutch activities, and indeed once the seriousness of the situation was realized the authorities had been assiduous in their search for solutions. Moreover, compared with British Malaya, whose exports were nearly two-thirds as large, the Netherlands Indies contained ten times as many people, so that a comparable share of profits ploughed back into social services made a very much poorer showing in the Dutch than in the British dependency. All that, however, is not to deny that the contrast between the wealth of the Europeans (and of many Chinese) and the poverty of the mass of the indigenous people was great, even by colonial standards, and this has inevitably coloured the attitude of the Indonesians to the Dutch in post-war years.

Yet the legacy which the Netherlands bequeathed to the Indonesians in 1949 was by no means as unsatisfactory as the latter have often implied. Whatever its faults, Dutch paternalism was responsible for the Agrarian Law of 1870 which 'conserved the native soil as the national heritage of the Indonesian people'[64] and so left the country almost completely free from the problems of 'disproportionate land concentration and the existence of a landlord class, dangerous for the economic, social and political development of the country'.[65]

Similarly the Dutch policy of relying on indigenous rather than foreign labour has meant that Indonesia today has a far lower proportion of alien Asians in its population than any other country in South-east Asia except the Philippines, and this has meant that communalism is less to the fore than it threatened to be, at least until recently, across the Straits in Malaya.

[63] The numbers of persons paying income tax in Java in 1935 included 51,122 'Europeans' and only 20,384 Indonesians. Zinkin (A), p. 131. [64] Jacoby, p. 69. [65] *Ibid.*

Finally it was Dutch business sense, as well as the inherent geographical diversity of the country, which explained why the Indies export economy was not excessively concentrated on one or at most two major commodities but, on the contrary, covered the widest range of any country in the whole inter-tropical belt. And although the events of more recent years have done much to impair this advantage, the new Indonesia still has far better potentialities for developing a well-balanced range of exports than any other state in South-east Asia.

SELECT BIBLIOGRAPHY

Allen and Donnithorne
Ball
Boeke (A) (B)
Bousquet
Broek (A) (B) (E)
Callis
Coolhaas
Deasey
De Meel (A) (B)
De Neuman
De Waal
Dootjes
Fisher (C) (L)
Fryer (A) (C) (E)
Furnivall (A)
Harrison
Hart, G. H. C. (A) (B)
Honig and Verdoorn
Jacoby
Kennedy (A)
Mills *et al.*
Mohr (B)
Peekema
Pelzer (A) (B) (C) (D) (F)
Purcell (D)
Robequain (D)
Schrieke
Sleumer
Ter Braake
Timmermans
Vandenbosch (A) (B)
Van der Kroef (C)
Van Hall
Van Helsdingen and Hoogenberk
Van Mook (A) (B)
Van Valkenburg
Van Vuuren (A) (B)
Vlekke (A)
Wertheim (A) (B) (C)
Wormser
Zinkin (A)

Economisch weekblad voor Nederlandsch Indië, May 1941
Handbook of the Netherlands Indies, 1930
Indisch Verslag
Proceedings of the Fourth Pacific Science Congress, Java, 1929, Vol. IV
Volkstelling 1930 (Census of Netherlands India), Vols. I–VII
Netherlands East Indies, II (N.I.D.)

On the general economic geography of Indonesia under Dutch rule Broek (B) is the standard work, while Furnivall (A), the N.I.D. volume and Van Helsdingen and Hoogenberk also contain a great wealth of invaluable information. Boeke (A) and Hart (A) (B) are admirable studies from a more specifically economic point of view. In the sections on primary production I have relied extensively on Broek (A) (E), Pelzer (E) and Van Hall, and in those on population and welfare on Hart (B), De Meel (A) (B) and Pelzer (B) (C) (D). On transmigration Pelzer (C) is indispensable, as is Sitsen on industrialization; the former may be supplemented by Peekema and the latter by Furnivall (A) and Timmermans. Kennedy (A) has excellent descriptive accounts of transport and urban life. On urban problems in general Fryer (A), Wertheim (C) and Van der Kroef (C) are most informative.

CHAPTER 10

Problems of the New Indonesia: A – Economic

INTRODUCTION: THE NEW INDONESIA

The independence of Indonesia was first proclaimed by Dr. Sukarno on August 17, 1945, two days after the Japanese surrender, but it was not until December 27, 1949 that the Dutch agreed to transfer sovereignty over the whole of their former East Indian possessions, apart from West New Guinea,[1] to the new republic.

During the eight years which elapsed between the outbreak of the Pacific War and the achievement of independence, the Indonesian economy sustained severe damage and dislocation. In the first brief phase of Allied resistance, numerous installations, especially in the petroleum industry, were subjected to 'scorched earth' tactics and, in the Japanese occupation which followed, the Indies suffered particularly acute hardships. Because of its large population, Java was treated from the outset as the main labour pool of the Nan Yo, and only a minute remnant survived of the 300,000 labourers who were shipped overseas to work on projects of various kinds.[2] Meanwhile, owing to the virtual cessation of foreign trade, multitudes of Indonesians were deprived of their normal livelihood and food supply, a state of affairs which led to much illegal squatting in Java and the Cultuurgebied, and also to dangerous depletion of the forest reserves particularly in the former island. Finally, during the post-war struggle against the Dutch, widespread sabotage and even more general neglect of estates, mines and factories militated against economic recovery, such as was taking place with far less difficulty in many other parts of South-east Asia.

By the agreement of December 1949, Indonesia became an equal partner with the former metropolitan power in the new Netherlands-Indonesian Union, under the titular headship of the Dutch Crown, an arrangement which was clearly modelled on the formula which had previously been devised to keep India and Pakistan within the British Commonwealth. Such a system appeared to entail considerable advantages for both the parties involved. The position of Dutch investments in Indonesia – still very substantial – was safeguarded,[3] and oppor-

[1] See below, pp. 362–4, for an account of the political aspects of the Dutch-Indonesian struggle. It was decided in August 1962 that West New Guinea should come under Indonesian sovereignty on 1st May, 1963. See below, pp. 402–3.

[2] See Wertheim (C), p. 264, and Thompson, Virginia (D), p. 163.

[3] Despite extensive damage to Dutch properties in the Indies after 1941, the total Dutch investments there at the time of the transfer of sovereignty were valued at over 4,000 million guilders. As a result of further losses and considerable though only partially

tunities were preserved for the employment of Dutch skilled personnel in the service of the new state.[4] Since many of these employees, thanks to their special training and unrivalled knowledge of local conditions, were irreplaceable at short notice, the Indonesians stood to benefit no less than the Dutch from this provision.

Nevertheless, the successful operation of the Netherlands-Indonesian Union demanded a degree of mutual confidence which, because of the preceding 'police actions', the hard bargaining of the Dutch over the extent of Indonesia's financial indebtedness, and the continuing dispute over West New Guinea, was not forthcoming. Thus on February 13, 1956 the Indonesian government unilaterally abrogated the Union and in December 1957 it introduced even more drastic measures aimed at excluding all surviving Dutch interests from the country.[5] It is against this background that the economic problems of the new Indonesia will be examined in the present chapter; the political and social problems will be considered in Chapter 11.

With its productive capacity reduced by 1949 to barely half that of 1941, Indonesia began its independent existence under severe economic handicaps. Moreover, the national government's writ has only recently been made effective throughout all the territories nominally under its control, and centres of sporadic disaffection have existed in some of the outer islands and even in parts of western Java within a short distance of Djakarta (formerly Batavia), the capital city, until very recently.

Clearly, economic rehabilitation – if not a complete restoration of the pre-war economic pattern – was a *sine qua non* for the survival of the new regime, and in particular it was necessary to rebuild roads and railways, to repair the essential services of town and countryside (the latter including irrigation works, many of which had suffered severe damage) and to restore the productive capacity of mines, estates and factories.

Furthermore, the new state now has to provide both the funds and the

successful attempts at repatriating Dutch capital since then, the figure had been much reduced by December 1957. Even so, most of the large-scale business enterprises and plantations (the latter responsible for 44 per cent of total exports) were still under Dutch control, though Americans held the lion's share of the investments in the oil industry. Transfers of profits to foreign investors in 1956 (Rp. million) were 447·2 to U.S.A. (62·2 per cent), 165·4 to the Netherlands (23 per cent) and 95 to the Sterling Area (13 per cent).

[4] The new government also assumed responsibility for Indonesia's pre-independence debts to the Netherlands, but this provision constituted a continuing source of friction between the two countries. In April 1950 the Netherlands government granted the Indonesian government a loan of 280 million guilders.

[5] In 1956 the Indonesian government repudiated all its pre-war debts to the Netherlands, and in December 1957, in protest against the Dutch refusal to transfer sovereignty over West New Guinea, it stopped payments on the 1950 loan and subsequently nationalized all Dutch property remaining in the country. A recent Dutch estimate (December 1958) of Indonesia's outstanding debts to the Netherlands put the total at 846 million guilders (552 million to private investors, 98 million balance outstanding of pre-war government debts, and 196 million balance outstanding of 1950 loan). See also below, notes 10 and 82 and Chapter 11.

personnel to maintain many services, such as the civil administration, foreign service, and fighting forces, which were formerly in whole or in part the responsibility of the metropolitan power, and this has imposed an added burden on both its strained financial resources and on its even more limited reserves of educated man-power.[6]

Nor is this all. The old problem of the acute imbalance between congested Java and the predominantly underdeveloped outer islands has become even more pressing as a result of eight years of neglect for, notwithstanding the forced migration and deaths of labou rers under the Japanese occupation, the density of population in Java (1,168 per sq. mile in 1959) is now higher than ever, and the total population of the island is believed to be increasing by over a million a year.[7]

For all these reasons it is apparent that even to restore the pre-war standards of living would have been a task of major proportions for the new regime. Yet in the very nature of the case it was inevitable that the great majority of the population would expect much more than this. For although independence was not sought primarily on these grounds by the small Indonesian intelligentsia, it is clear that in depressed Java the concept of *merdeka* (freedom) had come to be equated with the millennium, and a rapid improvement in living standards would be regarded as the surest touchstone of the new régime's success.[8]

In these circumstances the paramount need was for a hard and sustained national effort to restore and expand productive capacity in the shortest possible time, but partly because of the very limited education in practical affairs previously vouchsafed to the Indonesians and partly, perhaps, out of an innate insouciance, popular demand has instead led to the introduction of a seven-hour working day, and a mass of crippling legislation against foreign capitalists, which has seriously reduced the scale of their activities in the country. Fundamentally this attitude is based on the popular beliefs that Indonesia is the 'third richest raw material country in the world',[9] and therefore that the poverty of its peoples has been due primarily to the excessive profits extracted by the foreigners.

While the better-informed minority realize that, in relation to the total population, the country's natural wealth is by no means superabundant, and that the acute maldistribution of population creates further economic problems of an extremely intractable character, they also are none the less resentful of the colonial past, and have been unable entirely to resist popular clamour for cheap if unavailing panaceas.

Nevertheless, in intention at least, Indonesian economic policy since independence has not been wholly unrealistic. Thus, in the first place it has aimed at

[6] The reasons for the extreme shortage of skilled man-power are discussed above, pp. 272–3.

[7] In addition, the population of the outer islands is increasing by over half a million a year.

[8] See above, Table 11.

[9] *Report on Indonesia*, 8, August–September 1956, p. 15.

reducing the hitherto excessive dependence on the export of a few primary products, whose prices are notoriously unstable, while at the same time building up a much wider range of processing and consumer goods industries and increasing the local production of foodstuffs. And secondly, it has sought to encourage small-holder production at the expense of the estates, and indeed it is clearly the intention that the share of the large foreign-owned concerns in all branches of the country's economy should be reduced as rapidly as possible.

Here, however, a dilemma arises, for these same enterprises are the largest and most efficient producers of export commodities, and it is primarily from the foreign exchange which they earn that all the proposed new economic developments must in the long run be financed. Moreover, if the foreign concerns are led to believe that their existence will be tolerated only for a brief interim period, they cannot be expected to make the further heavy investments, for example, in rubber replanting and general rehabilitation, which are already overdue. And even apart from this, their chances of continuing to operate efficiently are gravely jeopardized by absenteeism, strikes, excessive taxation and a host of pettifogging regulations, all of which are at bottom expressions of a nation-wide resentment against what are regarded as the surviving vestiges of colonialism.

In its present transitional stage, the country's economy exhibits a three-fold pattern, with large-scale capitalist undertakings remaining in control of most of the estates and mines,[10] as well as of much of the factory industry, while state enterprise is gradually taking over a larger and larger share of all these activities, and both peasant agriculture and small-scale rural industry are being organized increasingly on co-operative lines. In a broad way this pattern recalls that of the contemporary Indian economy, though with the important differences, first that the industrial sector of the Indian economy is proportionately much more important and, secondly, that much the greater part of the large-scale capitalist industry in Indonesia remains in alien, that is either European, American or Chinese, as opposed to indigenous, hands.

The present emphasis on co-operatives in the countryside owes much to the former Vice-President, Dr. Mohammad Hatta, and it was mainly as a result of his activities that the government proclaimed its belief in the co-operative as the basic form of Indonesian enterprise[11] and has striven to build the new national economy as far as possible on the old and stable traditions of the countryside.

Ever since his founding in 1932 of the Indonesian Co-operative Movement, after close study of Dutch and Swedish practice, Hatta has argued that it represented a modernized version of the traditional Indonesian *gotong rojong* (mutual assistance or, more freely, village socialism).[12] From a total of 624 co-operatives, mostly credit organizations, immediately before the War the movement has

[10] However, as mentioned above (note 5) the Indonesian government has nationalized all such enterprises owned by the Dutch, and has stated its intention of paying no compensation for these until the West New Guinea dispute is settled in its favour. See also below, p. 378.

[11] See Higgins, Benjamin (A), p. 122.

[12] *Cf.* above, p. 296.

grown rapidly under the new regime, and today there are over 16,000 co-operatives in the country as a whole, with an aggregate capital of over Rp. 1,200 million.[13]

These co-operatives are of many varieties, producer organizations of various kinds predominating in the villages, while consumer-credit co-operatives are commonest in the towns. According to Hatta a healthy development of co-operatives in the countryside could eliminate usury and contribute greatly to an increase in food production (by financing local improvements in irrigation, promoting the use of better seeds and building more village granaries), and could prove equally helpful to both the peasant producer of export crops and the small-scale factories, by improving and standardizing the quality of their products and introducing more efficient methods of marketing. In his view development along these lines, leading to a general raising of living standards and the concentration of the people's capital, should precede any wholesale attempt at nationalizing the large foreign enterprises or at establishing more than a limited range of large-scale manufacturing industries.

TABLE 23

INDONESIA: GEOGRAPHICAL DISTRIBUTION OF CO-OPERATIVES, END OF 1956 AND 1959

	1956	1959		1956	1959		1956	1959
Greater Djakarta	251	464	South Sumatra	317	272	Borneo	575	1,210
West Java	2,747	3,969	Central Sumatra	830	1,179	Celebes	717	521
Central Java	2,550	3,242	North Sumatra	714	1,072	Rest of		
East Java	2,984	3,937	All Sumatra	1,861	2,523	Indonesia	216	736
All Java	8,532	11,612						

	1956	1959
All Indonesia	11,901	16,602

Source: Based on Service for Co-operatives,* and on *Statistical Pocket Book of Indonesia*, 1960, p. 210.

(* Throughout this chapter the asterisk denotes data quoted in *Bank Indonesia, Annual Reports*. The last such report known to the author was for 1957. Wherever possible more recent data have been noted from other sources, *e.g.* United Nations, Colombo Plan, Embassy of Indonesia, and the 1960 *Statistical Pocket Book*, etc.)

Nevertheless, with a total membership of only 2,678,006 and an average subscribed capital of approximately Rp. 450 a head, the co-operative movement has barely touched the fringe of the problem as yet and indeed, even though Hatta has stated that the people are capable of creating a capital of Rp. 300 million a year (old rate) he has never pretended that the co-operative move-

[13] Prior to August 1959 the official rates of exchange were Rp. 31 = £1 (Sterling); Rp. 11·36 = $1 (U.S.). But in August 1959 the rate was changed to Rp. 45 = $1 U.S.

ment could provide more than a partial answer to the country's needs.

So far as larger scale planning is concerned the record to date is less satisfactory. After various development plans, such as the Ministry of Agriculture's Prosperity Plan and the Sumitro Plan for industrialization, had been in partial operation for some years, the all-embracing Five-Year Plan for 1956–60 was submitted to Parliament in 1957 but political instability and disturbances combined to delay its implementation, and it was eventually superseded by the First Eight Year National Overall Development Plan which came into force in 1961.

According to official estimates the Five Year Plan was to have involved an expenditure of Rp. 12,500 million,[14] to be allocated under five headings, as follows: communications, 25 per cent; mining and industry, 25 per cent; power and irrigation, 25 per cent; agriculture, fishing, transmigration and forestry, 13 per cent; and social welfare, 12 per cent. But while the financing of a programme of this magnitude was already causing considerable difficulty to the government, most Western authorities were of the opinion that a much higher rate of investment was called for. Indeed, in the opinion of Dr. Higgins, in order 'to launch and maintain a process of steady economic growth' Indonesia would need a net annual investment of Rp. 8,000–12,000 million which was approximately double the total rate of investment, public and private, then contemplated. Even assuming a much greater effort than has hitherto been forthcoming from the Indonesians themselves, Higgins estimate that there would remain a gap of some Rp. 2–3,000 million (*i.e.* $ U.S. 150–250 million) a year to be filled from abroad.[15] Be that as it may, the new Eight Year Plan envisages a total expenditure of Rp. 240,000 million,[16] which is to come mainly from domestic resources, though foreign assistance will also be sought.

For the most part the private Western investor is interested only in further development of the extractive industries, notably oil, and under present conditions would be reluctant to finance the kind of utilities and factories which Indonesia is most desirous of obtaining, especially since ample scope exists for investment in other more stable countries where there is little likelihood of arbitrary nationalization or expropriation.

So far as assistance at the governmental level is concerned, the United States has repeatedly expressed its willingness to help, and in the post-war decade provided very substantial aid. Thereafter the ideological gulf between the two countries led to a marked falling off in American assistance, though since 1958

[14] See Higgins, Benjamin (C), p. 51. The total plan calls for an investment of Rp. 30,000 million over a period of five years, but details are given only for the Rp. 12,500 million to be invested by the central government. Of this, Rp. 1,000 million is expected to come from foreign aid. *Ibid.*, p. 179. These figures refer to the old rates of exchange.

[15] Higgins, Benjamin (A), p. 117. But see also Higgins' more recent comments referred to below (ch. 11, note 72). Meanwhile the government's attitude towards the local Chinese is causing the latter to invest in Hong Kong and Singapore rather than in Indonesia.

[16] Note, however, the decline in the value of the rupiah since 1959. See above, note 12.

this trend has again been reversed. Meanwhile, in characteristically 'uncommitted' fashion, Indonesia, which has long been receiving small-scale but useful assistance via the Colombo Plan and various United Nations agencies, has also accepted aid worth $110 million from the U.S.S.R.[17]

TABLE 24

INDONESIA: FOREIGN TRADE BY COMMODITIES*

A. Imports

	Value, Rp. million						*Weight in thousand metric tons*		
	1938	*Per cent*	1955	*Per cent*	1959	*Per cent*	1938	1955	1959
Cotton piece goods†	61·2	13·0	912·0	13·0	320·9	6·0	51·7	50·7	20·2
Oil and oil products	5·0	1·0	396·5	6·0	356·5	7·0	130·8	1,456·4	1,419·7
Cotton yarns	10·1	2·0	272·4	4·0	241·3	5·0	9·1	18·0	20·4
Paper and manufactures thereof	6·9	1·4	278·4	4·0	163·5	3·0	54·1	89·0	60·8
Rice	22·1	4·6	246·6	3·5	864·4	16·0	334·2	127·0	604·2
Iron and steel rolled products‡	14·8	3·0	207·2	3·0	493·0	9·0	114·3	104·7	263·5
Motor vehicles and accessories	13·2	2·8	192·4	2·6	224·5	4·0	14·5	15·2	15·7
Wheat flour and meal	7·7	1·5	135·5	2·0	96·5	1·8	85·3	120·1	93·3
Fertilizers (manufactured)	7·5	1·5	116·0	1·7	156·1	3·0	122·4	147·6	254·6
Building cement	1·6	0·3	114·7	1·7	83·3	1·6	121·0	356·8	303·9
Total (including others)	478·6	—	6,887·67	—	5,228·7	—	2,002·8	3,256·6	n.a.

† 1959 values are for cotton fabrics
‡ 1959 values are for iron and steel manufactures

B. Exports

	Value, Rp. million						*Weight in thousand metric tons*		
	1938	*Per cent*	1955	*Per cent*	1959	*Per cent*	1938	1955	1959
Rubber: Estate	84·0	13·0	1,931·0	18·0	n.a.		157·0	237·0	n.a.
Small-holder	71·0	10·0	2,957·0	28·0	n.a.		147·0	465·0	n.a.
Total	155·0	23·0	4,888·0	46·0	4,765·5	48·0	304·0	702·0	718·9
Petroleum and petroleum products	163·0	24·0	2,421·0	23·0	2,637·5	27·0	6,067·0	9,473·0	10,368·5
Tin and tin ore	34·0	5·0	683·0	6·5	402·2	4·0	27·0	46·0	25·9
Copra and copra cakes	43·0	6·3	483·0	4·5	363·1	4·0	659·0	389·0	254·0
Tea	57·0	8·0	355·0	3·5	230·6	2·0	72·0	29·0	33·3
Tobacco	39·0	5·5	316·0	3·0	275·3	3·0	49·0	13·0	15·8
Palm oil and kernels	19·0	2·9	305·0	3·0	273·4	3·0	268·0	155·0	136·4
Sugar	45·0	6·5	210·0	2·0	34·5	0·4	1,175·0	174·0	39·5
Coffee	14·0	2·1	182·0	1·8	215·3	2·0	68·0	23·0	38·9
Pepper and other spices	18·0	2·8	158·0	1·5	140·7	1·4	131·0	26·0	30·8
Forest products	7·0	1·0	84·0	0·3	n.a.		429·0	183·0	n.a.
Tapioca and tapioca products	9·0	1·4	68·0	0·7	n.a.		250·0	184·0	n.a.
Total (including others)	687·0	—	10,618·0	—	9,944·2	—	10,994·0	12,189·0	n.a.

Sources: Central Bureau of Statistics and *Yearbook of International Trade Statistics* (U.N.)

[17] It is estimated that Indonesia has received approximately $1,000 m. in aid of various kinds since independence, of which total the U.S.A. has provided $470 m. and the U.S.S.R. $118 m. In February 1960 the U.S.S.R. granted new credits amounting to $250 m. *The Observer*, February 21, 1960. On Dutch loans see above, notes 4 and 5.

Finally, on January 20, 1958, the long overdue peace treaty was concluded with Japan whereby, *inter alia*, the latter undertakes to supply Indonesia with goods and services valued at $223,080,000 over a period of twelve years. If wisely spent these reparations could make a valuable contribution to Indonesian development in many directions. Further consideration of the political aspects of these problems must be deferred to Chapter 11, and in the remainder of this chapter an attempt will be made to assess the various economic-geographical changes which have taken place in the country since the Second World War.

II. EXPORT PRODUCTION

Table 24 shows the volume of Indonesia's principal exports in 1938, 1955 and 1959, but owing to the wide variations in pre- and post-war prices, as well as the decline in the value of the rupiah, comparison in monetary terms is of little use. Nevertheless, as the tonnage figures show, it is clear that, with the exception of the first two items on the list, namely rubber and petroleum, all the commodities in question still fell short in 1959 of the pre-war level of production. Thus Indonesia is now more than ever dependent on these two key commodities, which together account for some three-quarters of its total exports and, like all the other items on the list, fall within the broad category of primary produce.

Notwithstanding the severe setback occasioned by the Japanese occupation[18] and the difficulties of the immediate post-war period, rubber production reached an all-time peak in 1951 at the time of the Korean War boom, when 755,000 tons were exported. Since then declining prices have led to some falling-off in production, and some of the land formerly under rubber has been turned over to the cultivation of various food crops. Even so, however, Indonesia maintained its position as the world's first source of natural rubber until 1958, but thereafter it has consistently taken second place to the Federation of Malaya.

Coupled with the great fluctuations in the market price of rubber[19] has been growing anxiety regarding the intensified competition of the synthetic product, as described in Chapter 6. Until quite recently, it is true, the estates as a group seemed to be holding their own, mainly because much of their acreage had already been replanted with modern clonal seed and bud-grafted plants immediately before the Second World War, and it was this which explained the increase in their output despite a decrease in total estate acreage. Nevertheless, their future prospects are far from bright. Already rising wage costs have caused many

[18] In a short-term sense the enforced period of rest during the occupation made possible a higher yield when tapping was resumed, but the ageing of the trees and the lack of replanting over many years will have adverse effects on Indonesia's ability to compete with Malaya during the next decade or so.

[19] In 1951 small-holders' rubber fetched an average of Rp 8,350 per ton; in 1953 the corresponding figure was Rp. 3,660.

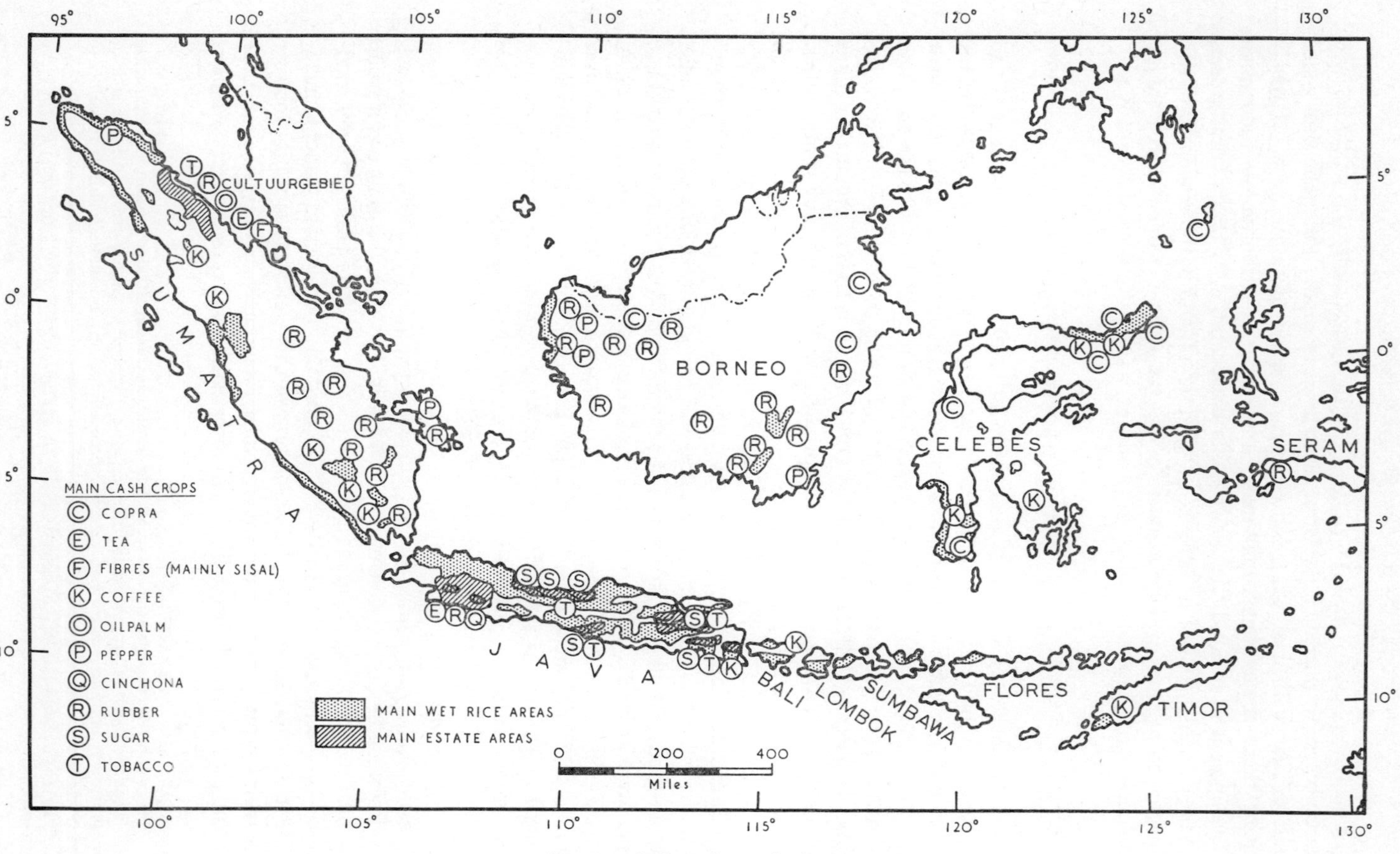

FIG. 43—Indonesia: agriculture

to close down, and the great uncertainty regarding the extension of their long-term leases prevents others from risking the heavy outlay involved in replanting.[12]

TABLE 25

INDONESIA: PRODUCTION AND EXPORT OF ESTATE RUBBER

Figures in metric tons

	Production	*Export*
1938	175,066	156,758
1950	177,938	177,528
1951	226,107	205,173
1954	287,551	237,975
1955	265,648	237,308
1961	219,291	223,312

Source: Based on Central Bureau of Statistics and *Rubber Statistical Bulletin*.*

Meanwhile, the small-holders have increased their output to an even greater extent than have the estates, and in 1960 the former accounted for 65 per cent of the total rubber export, compared with 45 per cent in 1938.[21] Geographically there has been no major change in the overall pattern of small-holder production, though the increased share of the small-holders as a whole implies a continuation of the pre-war trend of the outer islands to forge ahead of Java as producers of export commodities.

In contrast to the estates, the Indonesian small-holdings, run largely on a family and co-operative basis, are much less concerned with overhead costs, and their main problems are, first to improve yields by extensive replanting with high-grade material and more skilful tapping, and secondly to raise the quality of their finished product by means of better processing. At present the indigenous product usually commands a lower price than that from the estates, the respective average figures in 1955 being Rp. 6,273 and Rp. 8,150 per ton. But in this respect the co-operatives are doing much to remove the discrepancy, and the government is now striving to get all small-holder 'slab' rubber remilled before export.[22]

[20] So far the Indonesian government has been prepared to consider only 30-year extensions of these leases. Pelzer (F), p. 152. All-told 36 per cent of the concessions are due to expire by 1970. Fryer (B), p. 181. Fryer also points out that Indonesia is lagging behind Malaya in the promising field of latex production. *Ibid.*, p. 181.

[21] Sixty-five per cent by volume, 60 per cent by value. Hitherto small-holders' rubber has been exported mainly via Singapore. In 1955 26 per cent of Indonesia's total rubber exports went to the U.S.A., 18 per cent to the U.K. and 19 per cent to Singapore. Much of the rubber exported to Singapore goes eventually to the U.S.A., but Indonesia receives payment for this in U.S. dollars. In 1959 31 per cent went to the U.K., 25 per cent to the U.S.A., and 21 per cent to Singapore.

[22] This development, if successful, will significantly reduce the volume of exports via Singapore.

TABLE 26

INDONESIA: EXPORT OF SMALL-HOLDERS' RUBBER BY PRINCIPAL PRODUCTION AREAS

Figures in tons of dry rubber

Area	1938	1951	1954	1956	1961
West Borneo	30,354	68,375	74,125	74,166	n.a.
South and East Borneo	27,390	67,157	55,568	52,664	
Palembang	23,964	89,193	86,446	77,645	
East Sumatra	20,280	82,406	85,345	35,019	
Djambi	22,206	60,621	54,276	56,283	
Tapanuli	4,044	16,991	3,492	9,254	
Lampung	5	43,330	34,036	28,883	
Others	18,333	121,897	80,351	79,346	
Total reported exports	146,596	549,970	471,639	413,346	429,732

Sources: Central Bureau of Statistics, *Rubber Statistical Bulletin.**

For all these reasons, therefore, and in view of the clear nationalist preference for small-holder production, it would seem that, even though in many ways this may be a less efficient method by Western standards, it will continue to increase its share in the country's total output of rubber, as indeed of most other branches of agricultural production.

However, as regards the proportion – at present very nearly half – which rubber as a whole will assume in Indonesia's future export pattern, the outlook is altogether more problematical. And so long as the country's leading export is liable to fluctuate so wildly in price as rubber has done since 1950, effective budgeting and long-term planning on a national scale will remain beset with difficulties.

The second most important agricultural export is copra, but the total amount at present exported is only two-fifths that of pre-war days and in value this is equivalent to less than one-twelfth as much as the rubber export. However, this decline in exports is partly a result of growing local consumption of coconut oil, mainly for cooking, and of copra for soap and other manufactures in Indonesia itself, and in spite of all this the latter still supplies about one-quarter of the world's total demand. Although no accurate production figures are available for copra, at least 95 per cent of which is now grown by small-holders, the statistics showing purchase by the government's Copra Foundation, Jajasan Kopra, and

TABLE 27

INDONESIA: RUBBER EXPORTS

	1952	1953	1954	1955	1959
Total weight 000 metric tons	745	667	710	702	719
Total value, Rp. million .	4,778	3,080	3,013	4,889	4,766
Average value per ton, Rp.	6,407	4,618	4,244	6,964	6,072

Sources: As Table 24.

since 1953 also by the local Jajasan Kelapa Minahasa,[23] indicate that there has been some overall increase during recent years, particularly in the Minahasa district of northern Celebes.

As a cash crop copra is to the eastern part of the archipelago what rubber is to the west, the two areas overlapping in western Borneo which is an important producer of both. This state of affairs is more a reflection of the economic backwardness of the east than of any inherent intrinsic physical differences between the two, and in view of the much lower value of copra compared with

TABLE 28

INDONESIA: PURCHASE OF COPRA BY JAJASAN KOPRA

Figures in 000 metric tons net

Year	*East Indonesia*	*West Borneo*	*Other Areas*	*Total*
1950	325·9	59·7	12·8	398·4
1953	406·0	55·3	—	461·3
1954	351·8†	50·0	—	401·8
1955	309·7†	56·1	—	365·8
1956	281·3†	44·2	13·6	339·1

† Note. Since 1953 an important part of Jajasan Kopra's activities has been taken over by Jajasan Kelapa Minahasa (*i.e.* the Minahasa Coconut Foundation) which in 1955 purchased 59,000 tons of copra.

Source: Based on Jajasan Kopra.*

[23] This body was set up owing to the growing resentment in Minahasa about the extent to which profits made by the national Jajasan Kopra were spent in Java rather than in the copra-producing areas. See below, p. 377.

rubber it follows that, so long as the east continues to depend primarily on the former as a cash crop, its economic importance will remain far behind that of the western islands.[24]

Although world prices have remained fairly steady in recent years and consumption in many parts of Asia has risen substantially, the future prospects of the industry are uncertain. For it also is faced with serious competition, both from other vegetable oils, especially those grown in temperate latitudes, and also from the various synthetic detergents which are already being widely produced in Europe and the U.S.A. Meanwhile, however, the Indonesian government is endeavouring to stimulate copra production and to promote local processing prior to export, and in this connexion a large desiccated-coconut factory was opened at Sukur in Minahasa in 1953. Until 1956 the Netherlands remained the largest purchaser of Indonesian copra exports, apart from Singapore, but in recent years this place has been taken by Germany.

The decline in the export of palm oil and kernels since the War is comparable in scale to that of copra, and again, although the market appears satisfactory at the present time and the world demand for oils and fats in general continues to rise, future prospects are clouded both by the increasing use of synthetic detergents and the decline in the use of palm oil in the manufacture of tin-plate.[25]

Coffee production likewise still stands well below the pre-war level, and with rising local consumption the amount available for export is just over half that of 1938. In general, estates have suffered far more severely from the effects of internal insecurity than have the small-holdings, and accordingly the latters' share in total production has risen from 60 to 80 per cent. Tea presents a close parallel to coffee in the relationship between current and pre-war exports, in the relative increase in the importance of small-holder production, which now accounts for about two-thirds of the total, and in the fact that both used to be destined primarily for the Netherlands market. In view of the large increase in world consumption of both these commodities, and also of cocoa[26] which Indonesia as yet produces only on a very minor scale, the prospects for future expansion appear better than with most other agricultural staples, and here at least there is little fear of competition from synthetic substitutes.

No commodity has been more affected by the change-over from estate to small-holder production than has tobacco. So far as the estates are concerned the Deli area seems to have suffered most, partly as a result of direct war damage but more on account of illegal squatting, mainly by subsistence cultivators.[27]

[24] In this respect eastern Indonesia resembles the Philippines.

[25] Palm-oil production has suffered particularly badly from war and post-war damage to expensive processing plant.

[26] Since 1945 some attempt has been made to develop cocoa production in northern Celebes, in order to reduce that region's dependence on copra. Allen and Donnithorne, p. 146.

[27] Some 285,000 acres of estate land (all crops) in the Cultuurgebied were still illegally occupied by squatters in January 1957. For a full discussion of the problem see Pelzer (F), pp. 151–9.

Moreover, increased labour costs have severely handicapped those plantations which have survived, so that in 1956 the Deli plantations supplied only 3,700 tons compared with 13,786 in 1938, and the Java estates had fared even worse with a decline from 20,924 to 4,300 tons over the same period. In both cases the European tobacco concerns are paying their way only by concentrating almost exclusively on the highest grades; by far the greater part of their exports goes to Germany, though formerly the Netherlands headed the list.

On the other hand the Indonesian government is doing its best to stimulate small-holder cultivation of tobacco, especially in Java, and today this accounts for nearly half of the total export, apart from the large quantities which are consumed in Indonesia itself. In addition to local varieties of tobacco which are

TABLE 29

INDONESIA: ACREAGE AND PRODUCTION OF MAIN EXPORT CROPS

Crop		*Harvested area* (000 *acres*)		*Production* (000 *metric tons*)		
		1938	1954	1938	1954	1958
Rubber	(estate)	1,307·0	1,112·0	175·0	288·0	244·7
"	(small-holder)	864·0	2,790·0	146·6	471·6	451·0
"	(total)	2,171·0	3,912·0	321·6	759·6	695·7
Copra	(estate)	96·0	?	35·0	?	?
"	(small-holder)	1,719·0	2,174·0	723·3	973·5	1,050·0
"	(total)	1,815·0	?	758·3	?	?
Palm oil	(estate)	185·0	?	227·0	169·0	147·6
"	(small-holder)	?	?	?	?	?
"	(total)	?	?	?	?	?
Coffee	(estate)	237·0	106·0	46·0	14·0	12·6
"	(small-holder)	1,186·0	178·0	46·3	10·6	54·0
"	(total)	1,423·0	284·0	92·3	24·6	66·6
Cocoa	(estate)	12·0	10·0	2·0	1·0	—
"	(small-holder)	0·2	4·0	—	6·6	—
"	(total)	12·2	14·0	2·0	7·6	—
Tea	(estate)	339·0	166·0	68·0	39·0	48·5
"	(small-holder)	188·0	41·0	19·0	13·2	23·0
"	(total)	527·0	207·0	87·0	52·2	71·5
Cane sugar	(estate)	213·0	119·0	1,400·0	718·0	771·1
"	(small-holder)	51·0	66·0	90·8	198·4	?
"	(total)	264·0	185·0	1,490·8	916·4	?
Tobacco	(estate)	104·0	?	35·0	?	7·0
"	(small-holder)	276·0	346·0	77·9	72·8	61·0
"	(total)	380·0	?	112·9	?	68·0

Sources: Estate figures, Central Bureau of Statistics, Small-holder figures, Agricultural Extension service*; 1958 data from E.C.A.F.E.

used in the manufacture of spiced *kretek* cigarettes,[28] Indonesians have developed a taste for cigarettes made from Virginia tobacco, and the annual consumption of the latter was recently *c.* 17,000 tons. In order to save foreign exchange the government has encouraged local production of Virginia-type tobacco, notably in the Lengkong, Djateng, Djatim and Surakarta districts of Java, on land formerly given over to dry-rice cultivation, and indeed has hopes of ultimately developing Virginia-type tobacco as a strong export crop. While such exports are still a thing of the future, Indonesia succeeded in reducing its tobacco imports from Rp. 144 million in 1956 to Rp. 19 million in 1959.

Among the fibres kapok and sisal remain relatively important, though exports of both in 1959 were less than one quarter of those in 1938, a decline which is partly attributable to greater Indonesian consumption and partly offset by an increased export of kapok seeds, notably to Japan. So far as the future is concerned, two other fibres, namely ramie and cotton may perhaps become of greater significance. For the most part their importance in Indonesia dates only from the Japanese occupation, when various experiments in their cultivation were carried out. More recently, experimental planting of ramie, a tough fibre with a silky lustre, which could be widely used as an alternative to cotton, has begun under the auspices of the Bank Industri Negara in northern Sumatra, where a processing plant is being set up at Siantar. Similarly, the government has plans for mechanized cultivation of cotton in Sumatra, where the crop has long been grown for local consumption, though, as the Japanese discovered, the eastern islands, thanks to their more pronounced dry season, are better suited for its production, and a project for extending its cultivation in Sumbawa is now well under way in an area of some 12,500 acres. In view of the government's plans (below pp. 341–7) for a substantial increase in the manufacture of cotton textiles, there is an added incentive to expand local production of the raw material.

Sugar is still in many ways the most problematical of all Indonesia's agricultural export commodities. The very great fluctuations in production during the early 1930s have already been considered (above p. 165), and though immediately before the outbreak of the Pacific War some recovery had taken place, the gains were wiped out by the war and only minor increases have been recorded in recent years. Thus in 1955 total production amounted to 851,012 tons (*cf.* 1,400,340 in 1938), of which 174,087 were exported (*cf.* 1,175,292 in 1938). Of the post-war export, approximately 80 per cent comes from estates,[29] though the small-holder's share is tending to rise, and approximately half is sold to Japan.

While for internal political reasons[30] the desire to revive Javanese sugar

[28] Approximately 700 factories, employing 80,000 workers, manufacture 260 million cigarettes daily.

[29] Almost exclusively Dutch or Chinese owned; the former are now nationalized. See Fryer (C), p. 173.

[30] See below, pp. 377–381. But in fact the government itself has done little to assist the recovery of the sugar industry. Fryer (C), p. 171.

TABLE 30

JAVA AND MADURA: LAND CLASSIFICATION, 1950

	Acres	*Per cent*
Small-holders' land		
Irrigated rice fields . .	8,109,000	25
Dry fields	7,867,000	24
Compounds, nipah groves etc. .	3,500,000	11
Tidewater fisheries . . .	171,000	1
Total	19,647,000	61
Estate Land†		
Cultivated	1,501,000	5
Uncultivated	1,149,000	3
Total	2,650,000	8
State forests		
Teak	2,032,000	6
Other	5,605,000	17
Total	7,637,000	23
Other land		
Villages, roads, water bodies, etc.	2,726,000	8
Grand total	32,660,000	100

† Based on pre-war figures.

Source: John E. Metcalf, *The Agricultural Economy of Indonesia* (U.S. department of Agriculture, Washington, 1952, p. 14.

Quoted in Van der Kroef (C), II, 94.

production is understandable, it is doubtful whether Indonesia's post-war aspiration to become once again a major sugar exporter is wisely conceived. For it was only because of a widespread change-over from sugar to cereal growing after the early 1930s that Java was able to continue feeding itself even to the extent that it did, and in the still greater congestion of the present time it would appear a risky policy to devote a higher proportion of the island's severely limited *sawah* land to the production of an export crop for which once again the market is far from certain.

On the other hand, since even the so-called estate sugar is grown in rotation with rice on *sawah* land, the heavy application of fertilizer provided by the estates for the sugar crop helps to maintain the quality of the soil in such areas, and may thus offset the loss in the acreage under rice. Nevertheless the drop in sugar exports to less than 40,000 tons in 1959 seems to mark the end of the story.

Spices, once the most sought-after products of the archipelago but already low on the export list before the Second World War, have declined still further in importance. In particular, the export of pepper in 1959 was only a quarter that of 1938, and although there has been an appreciable increase in the production of cloves these have been mainly for home consumption. Even so, Indonesia in 1955 grew only one-third of the cloves required by its *kretek* industry, and for this reason the government has been stimulating local production, notably by means of import restrictions, with a view to achieving self-sufficiency.[31]

In contrast to the general decline[32] in agricultural exports, there have been significant increases in the output of minerals as a group since 1938, and in this respect petroleum, which forms the country's second most important export, has been outstanding.

TABLE 31

INDONESIA: PETROLEUM AND PETROLEUM PRODUCTS, PRODUCTION AND TRADE

Figures in 000 metric tons

Year	Crude oil			Petroleum products	
	Production	*Imports*	*Exports*	*Imports*	*Exports*
1938 .	7,398	—	68	158	5,999
1950 .	6,816	1,575	8	69	6,091
1954 .	10,775	2,131	2,303	88	7,584
1955 .	11,790	2,626	3,028	185	6,445
1958 .	16,295	1,258	7,343	460	6,024
1959 .	18,218	n.a.	4,444	n.a.	6,125

Sources: Central Bureau of Statistics, Ministry of Economic Affairs,* and *Yearbook of International Trade Statistics*, and *Statistical Pocket Book of Indonesia*, 1960.

The oil of the East Indies was perhaps the most important single strategic objective of the Japanese in the campaigns of 1941–2,[33] and for this reason many

[31] Indonesia now produces only 2 per cent of the world's cloves; its imports come mainly from Zanzibar, the leading producer.

[32] In most cases apart from rubber the figures show some recovery after 1949, though not to pre-war levels, followed by a further decline since 1955. Cinchona, however, has shown a more continuous decline and is now of negligible importance. See above, p. 163, n. 8.

[33] Before the War the industry produced a wide range of commodities, including petroleum, aviation spirit, kerosene, diesel and lubricating oils, paraffin, paraffin wax and

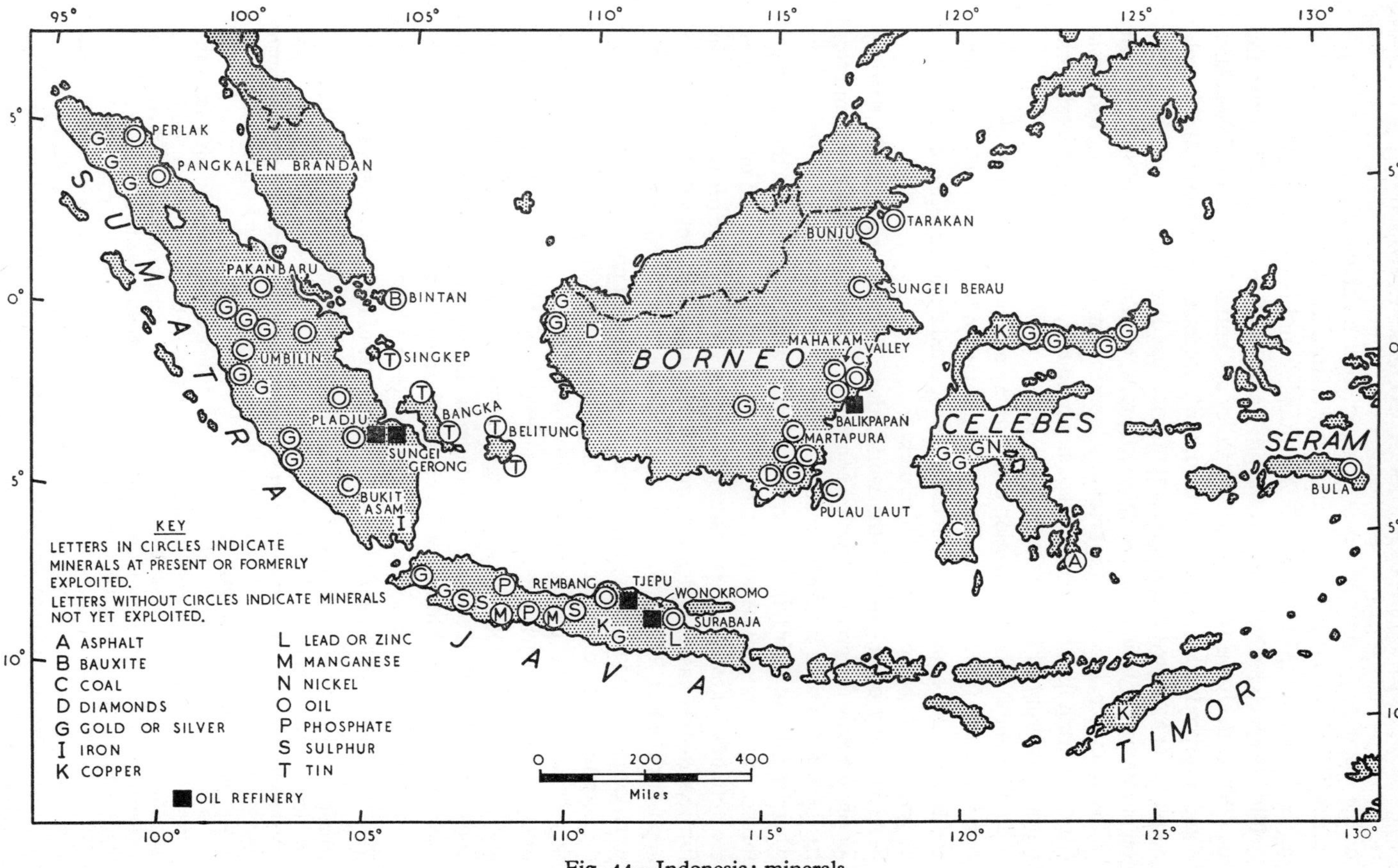

Fig. 44—Indonesia: minerals

of the installations suffered severe damage from bombing and scorched-earth tactics. Rehabilitation has proved extremely costly and is still incomplete, notably in the former B.P.M.[34] fields of North Sumatra and in the Central Java fields, neither of which has yet regained the pre-war level of production. However, the new Minas fields, operated in the Siak valley in Central Sumatra by Caltex, have come into production since 1952, and, with others more recently, this largely accounts for a marked rise in total output since that date. Thus in 1963 the crude-oil production of Indonesia, *i.e.* 21,325,000 tons, was double that of 1938, though in the meantime, thanks to the great developments in the Middle East, Indonesia has fallen from fifth to eleventh place as a producer, and its share of total world output has dropped from 2·6 to 1·7 per cent.

In addition to local production a further 2½ million tons of crude oil are imported annually from Northern Borneo to be refined in Indonesia, but this is balanced by a roughly equal amount of crude oil exported from the Minas fields where, as yet, Caltex has not installed a refinery.[35]

As in many other parts of the world, there is considerable latent hostility locally towards the great foreign oil companies operating in Indonesia, and this has been aggravated by the agreements made before the transfer of sovereignty whereby much of their foreign-exchange receipts are not included in the country's foreign-exchange pool. Again, although it is understood that the oil companies are to train local technicians to take over more and more of the necessary tasks in future, progress has been delayed, mainly because of a lack of suitably educated applicants. Thus, of the 6,000 working at the Pladju refinery, nearly 1,000 were Europeans and only 170 Indonesians had salaried posts in 1952/3.[36]

Accordingly there is a strong popular sentiment in favour of nationalization, though initially the government limited its activities in this respect mainly to the North Sumatran fields. At the same time, however, it has sought to negotiate new and more favourable agreements with the major oil companies as opportunity has afforded, and it is estimated that nearly half of the total profits derived from the exploitation of oil nowadays accrue to the government directly or indirectly in the form of taxes and duties of one kind or another. Moreover, the experience of both the Iranians at Abadan and of the Indonesians themselves

asphalt. Damage to the Palembang refineries, the only major producers of high-octane aviation spirit, necessitated big imports of this for many years after the War but these installations are now in operation again. Other principal refineries are at Balikpapan (Borneo) and Wonokromo (E. Java). The smaller refinery at Pangkalen Brandan (not shown in Fig. 44) is now working again.

[34] These B.P.M. fields were taken over by the Indonesian government after independence. B.P.M. (Bataafsche Petroleum Mij) forms part of the Royal Dutch/Shell group, henceforward referred to as Shell. Stanvac (formerly operating here as the Nederlandsche Koloniale Petroleum Mij) and Caltex (formerly Nederlandsche Pacific Petroleum Mij) are the two main U.S. oil companies now operating in Indonesia.

[35] Production of these Caltex fields is expanding, and a pipeline is being built from Pakanbaru, the main centre of production, to Dumai on the coast. Much of the oil is now shipped to the Caltex refinery opened at Batangas in the Philippines in 1954. See below, p. 719, n. 51.

[36] See Mende, p. 32.

on a smaller scale in North Sumatra suggests that it would be unwise to force the pace of nationalization, especially since it is believed that total reserves are not spectacular, and if the present companies were edged out, new investment capital might not be forthcoming.[37] For many years after the Second World War the Indonesian government's reluctance to grant new concessions seriously held up the work of further prospecting. Since 1959, however, several exploration agreements have been made with various independent groups—Japanese, American and Canadian—and in 1963 with Shell, Stanvac and Caltex, which are now exploring new areas as contractors to state companies.

The production of tin (in Bangka, Belitung and Singkep) rose slightly between 1938 and 1955, but has since fallen again. Since the Bangka smelter went out of production during the War most of the smelting has taken place either at Arnhem, Penang-Butterworth or at Texas City in the U.S.A.[38] It is this fact which accounts for the apparently much larger export of tin in 1955 compared with 1938, for in the earlier year 7,207 tons of the total was refined tin metal as against only 196 tons of refined metal in 1955. (See Table 32.)[39]

TABLE 32

INDONESIA: PRODUCTION AND EXPORT OF TIN

Figures in long tons

	Production of tin in concentrates	*Exports of tin (a) In concentrates*	*(b) Metal*
1938	29,728	13,699	7,207
1950	30,102	31,349	4
1954	35,862	33,941	994
1955	33,368	31,865	196
1958	23,200	18,184	215
1961	18,574	16,788	1,797

Sources: Based on International Tin Study Group, Ministry of Economic Affairs, and *International Tin Council, Statistical Bulletin*, July, 1962.

Owing to its high metal content (*c.* 75 per cent), Indonesian ore is much sought after, and has weathered world fluctuations in tin prices since 1950 reasonably well. Thus Indonesia's share of world production, 13·6 per cent in 1961, is virtually the same as in 1939, and this commodity seems likely to retain its position as the country's third export for the foreseeable future.[40]

[37] See Allen and Donnithorne, p. 179.

[38] It is now proposed to build a new smelter at Muntok in Bangka.

[39] Most of the metal is now exported to Japan.

[40] However, the accumulation of tin stockpiles during and after the Korean war led to the re-introduction of international restriction of tin production in 1957. See Courtenay (B).

Other minerals present a less satisfactory picture than tin and petroleum. Shortly after the War, Indonesian bauxite appeared to have a promising future, and the mines on Bintan island (Riau) were already the largest of their kind in Asia. Most of the output (644,000 tons in 1951 compared with 245,000 in 1938) was exported unrefined to the United States and Japan, though plans were afoot to establish a local refining industry in connexion with the Asahan project in Sumatra (See below, p. 343). Since then, however, the tendency of the United States to prefer Surinam (Dutch Guiana) bauxite, which has a somewhat higher aluminium content, led to a decline in production, and though new markets have been found in western Europe and Japan the total Indonesian output in 1959 was only 387,300 tons.

Coal mining likewise has not yet regained the pre-war level. This admittedly, does not apply to the Bukit Asam fields of South Sumatra which produced 647,000 tons in 1954 and are scheduled for modernization, or to the Mahakam valley mines of South-east Borneo, which have also virtually regained their pre-war position. But the Umbilin mines of Central Sumatra, which were badly damaged during the War, have recently been producing only about 80,000 tons annually, which is a mere eighth of the pre-war amount. Although there is a small export (45,000 tons in 1954), mainly to Hong Kong and Thailand, Indonesia's own railway system is suffering from a continued shortage of coal, and a further expansion in output would be most desirable. Total reserves of coal are estimated at 200 million tons, with a further 2,017 million tons of brown coal; total production in 1959 was 637,600 tons.

The remaining minerals are of small consequence, at least as yet, though two United States concerns have shown some interest since 1945 in the possibility of exploiting nickel in Celebes,[41] and manganese production has varied between 39,064 tons in 1955, 107,827 tons in 1956 and 42,794 tons in 1959. Finally, the exploitation of the sulphur deposits of the Dieng plateau of central Java has been resumed, and the government proposes to carry out more detailed surveys of the low-grade iron-ore deposits known to exist in south-eastern Borneo, central Celebes and the Moluccas.

As regards timber, total authorized fellings had at last regained the pre-war level by 1955, though the export of most kinds of forest produce – copal, damar and rattan – as well as of firewood, charcoal and lumber has fallen appreciably, owing in part to increasing consumption at home. In fact, however, there is much clandestine felling, and especially in Java this is aggravating the already serious situation caused by excessive cutting during the Japanese occupation,[42] when deep inroads were made into the reserved forests, whose preservation is essential to prevent soil erosion in the main upland catchment areas.

[41] Plans for exploiting Celebes nickel had been drawn up by the Dutch before the War, and some sporadic mining was undertaken during the Japanese occupation.

[42] The Japanese cut much teak and other timber for shipbuilding, and many Javanese squatters, especially displaced persons from the towns, cleared forest land for cultivation. Hardly any teak over 30 years old now remains standing.

Recognizing the seriousness of the present situation the government has drawn up a reforestation programme, under which 340,000 acres were replanted in 1950–52 and a further 99,000 in 1953. Theoretically, with 65 per cent of its area under forest, Indonesia would appear to have vast reserves of timber. But aside from the drier areas of eastern Java and the Lesser Sundas, much the greater part consists of equatorial evergreen forest, only a small fraction of whose mixed stands of timber has any commercial value. At present, therefore, exploitation is limited to a few relatively favoured localities where suitable transport facilities make it an economic proposition. Nevertheless, in the long run, as Broek has pointed out, the quick-growing forests of such islands as Sumatra and Borneo may become of far greater importance if the Asian demand for pulp, cellulose and related products continues to expand with a growing consumption of newsprint and the development of the wood plastics industries.[43]

All-told, therefore, as Table 24 implies, Indonesian export production, despite considerable advances since 1950 in certain sectors, still remains below the pre-war level. Moreover, most of the agricultural commodities on the list now have to contend with strong competition from synthetic substitutes, and nowhere is the uncertainty which this causes more apparent than in the case of rubber which is the most important of all, accounting for 48 per cent by value of the country's total exports in 1959.

But if the future is still overhung with uncertainty, two important trends, both of which can be traced back to pre-war days, are clearly operative at the present time. In the first place, partly as a result of greater damage to plantations and partly because of the government's ideological preference for small-holders, the latter are contributing an ever larger and in most cases already a predominant share in the production of the main commercial crops, while the total estates area in the country has fallen from 6,071,000 acres in 1937 to 4,443,000 in 1958. Whether widespread nationalization, as many Indonesians advocate, will be the ultimate fate of all estates is far from clear, but for several years now more and more European planting concerns have been seeking to wind up their affairs in Indonesia, and many of the more badly devastated estates have been sold, at very low prices, to local Chinese who thus obtained control of extensive areas of potentially valuable agricultural land.

At the same time, and for closely related reasons, the share of the outer territories in export production is continuing to grow at the expense of that of Java.[44] Thus, of the commodities whose total output has risen since the war, namely rubber, petroleum and tin, all are predominantly produced in the outer territories, while conversely the most spectacular declines have taken place in sugar and cinchona in the cultivation of which Java was supreme. Admittedly there are exceptions to this rule as, for example, in the production of

[43] Broek (E), p. 131.

[44] In 1954 approximately 66 per cent of the estates acreage was in the outer territories, compared with 57 per cent in 1937.

pepper and coffee, but the overall trend is unmistakable. And of the outer islands it is above all Sumatra[45] which today is making the most rapid progress as a centre of primary production, both for the export market and also to supply the needs of Java and other parts of the archipelago itself.

III. FOOD PRODUCTION

Notwithstanding the great importance of Indonesia as an exporter of primary produce, the country's subsistence agriculture occupies some three times the acreage devoted to export crops, and with increasing population pressure and the policies favoured by the new régime this proportion is likely to rise in the years ahead.[46]

TABLE 33

INDONESIA: MAIN FOOD CROP PRODUCTION

Figures in 000 metric tons

		Irri-gated rice†	*Non-irri-gated rice†*	*Total rice†*	*Maize*	*Cassava*	*Sweet Pota-toes*	*Gro-und -nuts*	*Soya beans*
Java & Madura	1937	3682	223	3,905	2,037	7,637	1,182	181	269
Java & Madura	1955	4,279	144	4,423	1,448	6,475	983	177	307
Outer islands	1955	2,130	572	2,702	434	2,905	883	39	38
Total Indonesia	1955	6,409	716	7,125	1,882	9,380	1,866	216	345
Java & Madura‡	1959	4,711·8	168·8	4,880·6	1,455·6	9,048·0	1,483·8	197·8	375·2
Sumatra	1959	1,163·8	449·3	1,613·1	56·3	749·2	363·5	15·3	13·8
Borneo	1959	302·5	131·0	433·5	10·5	472·7	34·2	1·3	1·4
Celebes	1959	467·4	55·0	522·4	257·6	819·0	180·7	14·9	1·7
Moluccas & W. New Guinea	1959	—	2·3	2·3	3·1	59·0	25·0	1·1	—
Lesser Sundas	1959	410·1	88·0	498·1	317·6	784·5	632·1	24·4	39·2
Total Outer islands	1959	2,343·8	725·6	3,069·4	645·1	2,875·4	1,235·5	57·0	56·1
Total Indonesia‡	1959	7,055·6	894·4	7,950·0	2,100·7	11,923·4	2,719·3	254·8	431·3

† i.e. cleaned rice. For rough paddy production see above, Table 3, p. 73.
‡ Preliminary data.

Sources: Based on Central Bureau of Statistics and Service for Indigenous Agriculture*, and *Statistical Pocket Book, of Indonesia*, 1960, pp. 52–3.

In 1941 the Indies were virtually self-sufficient in the production of rice, by far the most important food crop, and in the decade which followed the acreage devoted to this crop increased considerably, as a result of both the change-over from export to subsistence production on many estates, and widespread illegal

[45] With which for administrative purposes Bangka, Belitung and Singkep are still included.

[46] Between 60 and 65 per cent of the 42 million acres under crops in all Indonesia are under food crops. Of the total cultivated acreage approximately 60 per cent is in Java and Madura. *Report on Indonesia*, 8, 1, p. 16.

squatting in forest reserves and other previously uncultivated areas. Yet despite the large area under rice in 1951, Indonesia was able in that year to produce only 95 per cent of the amount it needed, for in the meantime population had risen by some 7,000,000, and in many areas yields per acre had fallen because of damage to irrigation works.

Thus, in 1952 Java and Madura were compelled to import 565,000 tons of rice, and the outer islands a further 194,000 tons. Since then, however, the government, which has tended to give subsistence agriculture priority over the cultivation of export crops, has made a vigorous effort to increase food production with a view to wiping out this deficit as quickly as possible.

In the short run, and working through the co-operative organizations and the Service for Indigenous Agriculture, it has attempted to do this, so far as Java is concerned, by promoting more efficient production on the existing acreage. This in turn involves repairing and extending local irrigation works, and popularizing the use of fertilizers and better seed selection. As a result of establishing a series of new seed farms, the area planted with high quality rice in Java increased from 2·5 million acres in 1952 to 3·7 million acres in 1955, and meanwhile the area growing green manure was raised to 247,000 acres, though this is still far from adequate for the island's needs.

TABLE 34

INDONESIA: INDIGENOUS AGRICULTURE

Figures in 000 acres harvested

		Irrigated rice	*Non-irrigated rice*	*Total rice*	*Maize*	*Cassava*	*Sweet Potatoes*	*Ground nuts*	*Soya beans*
West Java	1959	3,705	304	4,009	185	667	245	168	67
Djakarta Raya	1959	47	2	49	2	12	5	5	—
Central Java	1959	3,061	109	3,170	1,209	1,053	185	215	317
Djokjakarta	1959	198	89	287	72	126	10	35	47
East Java	1959	3,012	171	3,183	2,676	1,077	193	319	882
Total Java & Madura†	1959	10,023	675	10,698	4,143	2,935	638	742	1,313
Sumatra	1959	2,068	1,196	3,264	138	153	94	52	47
Borneo	1959	914	623	1,537	40	114	12	5	5
Celebes	1959	969	203	1,172	643	173	42	37	7
Moluccas & W. New Guinea	1959	—	7	7	10	17	7	2	—
Lesser Sundas	1959	739	368	1,107	727	230	151	59	126
Total Outer Islands	1959	4,690	2,397	7,087	1,558	687	306	155	185
Total Indonesia†	1959	14,713	3,072	17,785	5,701	3,622	944	897	1,498
Java & Madura	1955	9,701	652	10,353	3,894	2,165	435	625	1,132
Outer Islands	1955	3,907	1,925	5,832	1,137	484	250	119	143
Total Indonesia	1955	13,608	2,577	16,185	5,031	2,649	685	744	1,275

† Preliminary data

Source: Based on Service for Indigenous Agriculture* and *Statistical Pocket Book of Indonesia*, 1960, pp. 50–51.

In the outer islands the percentage increase in food production has been greater than in Java, and has resulted mainly from the action of small-holders in devoting less of their land and time to such crops as rubber and copra, and more to the growing of rice,[47] though a further contribution has also come from various experimental schemes of mechanized rice cultivation on a larger scale in northern Sumatra. As a result of all these developments, Indonesia came close to achieving overall self-sufficiency[48] in rice production in 1954, and the imports of 253,000 tons in that year were required largely to maintain reserve stocks. But although imports fell still further, to 128,000 tons in 1955, this progress has not been maintained, and in 1959 they were again over 600,000 tons.

Since 1949 attempts have also been made to raise the output of various subsidiary foodstuffs. In the outer islands the production of maize, cassava, ground nuts and soya beans has risen considerably during this period,[49] though in Java, where pressure on the land has reached the danger point, increases in the cultivation of the more nutritious foods, such as maize, ground nuts and soya beans, have taken place mainly on land formerly devoted to the less nutritive cassava and sweet potatoes.[50] Recent sample surveys showed that on the typical Javanese peasant holding, 95 per cent of the land was devoted to six main food crops: rice (47 per cent), maize (22 per cent), cassava (16 per cent), soya beans (5 per cent), ground nuts (3 per cent) and sweet potatoes (2 per cent); in addition various local vegetables and many kinds of fruit are grown.

Fish remains by far the main source of animal protein in the Indonesian diet though, notwithstanding the country's obvious natural advantages as an archipelago whose surrounding seas teem with fish, production in 1954 still needed to be supplemented by imports of over 90,000 tons, and consumption per head was only 20·7 lb. Yet these figures represented a marked improvement on those of pre-war days, and by 1959 production had risen to over 753,000 tons, and imports had dropped to around 16,000 tons.

So far as sea-fishing is concerned, there is much leeway to be made up, for the Dutch traditionally discouraged the Indonesians from anything more than small-scale activities carried out from country boats, owing to their fear of competition from Indonesian craft in the inter-island carrying trade. Although this policy was abandoned shortly before the War, few advances had in fact taken place before 1949, but since then the Indonesian government has shown keen interest in promoting sea-fishing and seamanship generally. While its long-term plans aim at very large increases in both the size and the number of sea-going fishing vessels, it has hitherto concentrated almost exclusively on

[47] A similar tendency is also apparent on a smaller scale in Java.

[48] This still involves a considerable inter-island traffic. Borneo is a large importer, while Java exports high quality rice and imports the poorer grades.

[49] Sago output has meanwhile declined.

[50] Similarly, both irrigated- and dry-rice production increased in the outer territories, but in Java the increase in irrigated rice was made possible largely by a reduction in the acreage under dry rice.

TABLE 35

INDONESIA: PRODUCTION, IMPORTS AND EXPORTS OF FISH

Figures in 000 metric tons

		Production of fish			Imports	Exports
		Sea Fisheries	Inland Fisheries	Total		
Java & Madura	1959	105,600	94,858	200,458	14,109	2
Sumatra	1959	138,498	49,419	187,917	2,016	858
Borneo	1959	59,386	146,953	206,339	9	—
Celebes	1959	37,181	60,062	97,243	—	20
Moluccas & W. New Guinea	1959	39,000	7	39,007	—	—
Lesser Sundas	1959	20,661	1,739	22,400	—	—
Total Indonesia	1959†	400,326	353,038	753,364	16,134	889
Total Indonesia	1955	411,775	258,127	669,902	24,590	1,832
Total Indonesia	1940‡	315,000	147,000	462,000	68,519	5,861

† Preliminary data. ‡ 1940 production figures are estimated.

Source: Based on *Statistical Pocket Book of Indonesia*, 1960, pp. 83–4.

purchasing small motorized fishing boats and on installing imported engines in locally made craft, the equipment in both cases being purchased primarily from Japan.[51] Even by such means, however, it is possible to extend the range of operations far beyond the 10–15 miles of inshore fishing that has hitherto been the rule.

While coastal villages in most parts of the archipelago engage in fishing to some extent, more specialized activity is characteristic of two main areas, namely northern Java, and eastern Sumatra, where the port of Bagan Siapiapi alone had an annual catch of 80,000 tons.[52] More recently the Sea Fisheries Service has inaugurated a project with ICA (International Co-operation Administration) aid to Kota Baru on Pulau Laut (off south-eastern Borneo) which should be of considerable economic importance. The plan provides for the establishment of plants for the drying, salting and canning of fish, and the manufacture of fish meal and fishing nets, and also of a training centre for fishermen.

Inland fisheries are of several distinct kinds, and although their total output is still below that of the sea fisheries they are growing rapidly in importance as a result of the activities of the Inland Fisheries Service. Many of the natural water bodies of the larger islands, notably the great rivers of Sumatra and Borneo, contain an abundance of fish which is of great importance to the

[51] In 1954 there were 799 motorized fishing vessels and 96,843 sail fishing vessels registered in the country. In 1959 these totals had risen to 1,462 and 175,575 respectively.

[52] The Bagan Siapiapi fisheries have hitherto been virtually a Chinese monopoly.

preodminantly riparian settlements there, and the Celebes lakes, notably Tempe, are thought to have even greater potentialities in this respect. In Java, on the other hand, the chief interest centres in fish breeding in artificial ponds and flooded rice fields, another characteristic expression of the intensity of land use in this crowded island.[53]

All-told there are some 200,000 acres of cultivated fishponds in Java, mostly along the northern coast, and the total output of fish is *c.* 20,000 tons a year. The raising of fish in flooded rice fields on the other hand is mainly concentrated in West Java where over 75,000 acres of *sawah* are involved. It is estimated that 350 lb. of fish can be satisfactorily raised in an acre of rice field without reducing the rice yield, though this total is as yet obtained only in a few areas.

Stockbreeding continues to play a very minor rôle in Indonesian food production, with only about one-third of the amount of animal products per head that Western food experts regard as the necessary minimum for maintaining good health. By 1959 the number of cattle (and likewise of buffaloes required for *sawah* ploughing) had surpassed the pre-war level, and in Madura, the most important single cattle-breeding area, the breeding stock was appreciably larger than before the war.

In 1954 Madura exported nearly 34,000 head of cattle to other parts of the archipelago and abroad. Furthermore, the government has set up seven artificial insemination centres, in Madura, West and Central Java, and in Bali, and 53

TABLE 36

INDONESIA: LIVESTOCK

Figures in 000 head

		Cattle	*Buffaloes*	*Horses*	*Sheep*	*Goats*	*Pigs*
West Java (1)	1959	129	788	40	1,207	1,058	64
Central Java (2)	1959	1,057	637	77	653	1,948	56
East Java	1959	2,678	324	69	365	1,371	29
Total Java	1959	3,864	1,749	186	2,225	4,377	149
Sumatra	1959	211	263	46	36	406	403
Borneo	1959	88	38	1	2	49	411
Celebes, Moluccas & W. New Guinea	1959	196	479	214	121	319	359
Lesser Sundas	1959	517	293	224	62	215	621
Total Indonesia	1959†	4,876	2,822	671	2,446	5,366	1,943
Total Indonesia	1955	5,059	2,888	584	2,782	7,174	1,469
Total Indonesia	1940	4,356	2,417	711	1,462	3,777	1,224

(1) including Djakarta (2) including Djokjarkarta † Preliminary data.

Source: Based on *Statistical Pocket Book of Indonesia*, 1960, p. 80.

[53] But the Inland Fisheries Service is meeting with considerable success in its plans to increase the number of fishponds in the outer territories, especially Borneo. *Sepat Siam* is the most popular fish there.

cattle-breeding stations which are fairly well distributed over most of the more important islands. While the production of meat and draught animals is more typical of East Java (including Madura), the breeding of dairy cattle is in future to be concentrated more markedly in Central Java because of its more suitable soils; on the other hand, the main privately owned dairy herds are in West Java where they cater for the markets of Djakarta, Bandung and other nearby towns. At the present time Indonesia has four government milk centres, in Djakarta, Bandung, Malang, and Bojolali (Central Java), but total production is minute in relation to the size of the population, and in the interests of better health, particularly among young children, every effort should be made to expand it as rapidly as possible.

IV. POPULATION AND LIVELIHOOD

From the foregoing account it would appear that by 1959 Indonesia had approximately regained its pre-war position of near self-sufficiency in foodstuffs. But while this gives some cause for satisfaction, various qualifications must nevertheless be made. Thus, although accurate comparative data are lacking, it is probable that *per capita* consumption is still below the 1939 level, and since much of the increase in food production has been made possible by a decrease in the acreage devoted to cash crops, living standards as a whole have fallen in a majority of cases, particularly in Java. Furthermore, the position is made more serious in Java by the virtual certainty that recent increases in the cultivated area have passed beyond the safety limit. Thus the encroachment of cultivation into the forest reserves is already resulting in intensified soil erosion in the uplands, and it was the consequent clogging of drainage and irrigation works in the more densely populated areas downstream which was mainly responsible for the damaging floods of 1955.[54]

At best, therefore, increases in food production are barely keeping pace with the growth of population in the country as a whole, while the more specific problem of overcrowding in Java is becoming steadily more acute.[55] Thus although the percentage growth in the outer islands continues to be greater than in Java itself, the absolute increase of over a million a year in the latter presents a truly alarming prospect in view of the degree of congestion that has already been reached. Thus, although there may be room for differences of opinion as to whether Indonesia as a whole could support a substantially larger population than it carries today without any lowering of living standards, the seriousness of

[54] See above, p. 293. Reportedly the Head of the Indonesian Forestry Service stated at Bandung in January 1956, that some 500,000 hectares (1,236,000 acres) of forest had been illegally felled since 1945. Against this only 270,000 hectares (667,000 acres) had been reforested.

[55] The average holding in Java in 1955 was officially stated to be 0·6 hectare (1·48 acres) and over 50 per cent of farm families in Java held less than one hectare (2·47 acres), which is the minimum necessary to feed a family of five. See Tohir, p. 49, and *Social Welfare in Indonesia.*

the situation within Java is plain for all to see. Beyond any doubt this is the transcendental economic problem facing Indonesia today, and unless real and immediate progress can be made towards solving it the outlook for the country will be bleak indeed.

While birth control would clearly offer at least a partial answer to the problem, the Indonesian government has not followed the Indian policy of seeking to encourage this practice,[56] and hitherto has concentrated its search for solutions along the three lines pioneered by the Dutch in pre-war days.

First among these is the possibility of increasing still further the production of food in Java itself. Clearly the only scope here now lies in raising the yield from the existing acreage and, although Java stands well above the South-east Asian average level of agricultural efficiency, there is certainly room for further improvement in both seed selection and the use of fertilizer. Indeed, it has been estimated that adequate fertilizing, particularly with superphosphates and organic manures, could raise the total rice output of Java by from 20 to 40 per cent,[57] and even more spectacular increases are hoped for if current research in India succeeds in producing a satisfactory cross-breed of the *japonica* and *indica* strains of rice.[58]

Perhaps the most hopeful approach to the problem is to be found in the new Community Development Programme, prepared with the help of Indian advisers, which aims at teaching better techniques of farming and handicraft industry, as well as raising the level of education, health, housing and sanitation in the villages. But as yet this has not got significantly beyond the preliminary stage of training Indonesian instructors.

Improvements in drainage and irrigation could also help in some parts of Java, and in recent years the government has been spending substantial sums annually on such work. Hitherto the most important new project undertaken since the war has been the storage dam at Tjabatjan near Tegal, which will irrigate over 100,000 acres of paddy land besides providing a new source of hydro-electric power for Central Java. More spectacular, however, is the Djatiluhur undertaking, Indonesia's first multi-purpose project, which is designed to provide a new water supply for Djakarta, to improve navigation between the latter and Tjirebon (130 miles) and also to produce some 150,000 kW of hydro-electric power and to irrigate an extensive area of nearly 200,000 acres of the coastal lowlands to the east of Djakarta. Preliminary work began in 1954, and the project was scheduled for completion by the end of 1962.

[56] See Fischer, pp. 149–50, for Sukarno's comments on birth control. But note also that editorial comment in the *Indonesian Spectator* of September 1, 1958, (pp. 7 and 9) approved the recent formation of a Family Planning Association in Djakarta, and pointed out that the practice is not forbidden by the Muslim religion.

[57] Financial stringency has led to a reduction in the already very small import of fertilizers since 1954, and any increase in their use must depend mainly on an expansion of local fertilizer manufacture. See below, p. 343.

[58] See above, p. 171.

Nevertheless, in the long run the greatest scope for increased food production in Indonesia lies in the outer islands, where the much lower density of population[59] and the absence, in many areas at least, of complicated problems of land tenure provide opportunities for extensive mechanized cultivation, particularly of rice. Although the experiments so far carried out along these lines have been only on a comparatively small scale,[60] it is clear that modern machinery has revolutionized the technique of jungle clearing, and that many of the hitherto underdeveloped coastal and riverine lowlands in the outer islands could be turned into productive paddy lands.

In this connexion particular interest attaches to the scheme devised by the Dutch engineer, H. J. Schophuys, for draining and reclaiming the swamp lands of southern Borneo. At the present time the whole of Indonesian Borneo contains a total of only 914,000 acres of *sawah* land and much of this is frequently subjected to devastating floods. Schophuys claims that, besides solving the flood problem over a wide area, his scheme would provide a further 2½ million acres of good paddy land in the areas at present imperfectly drained by the Barito, Kapuas and Kahanjan rivers. While the project would entail heavy expenditure on major dykes, canals and pumping stations, much of the smaller-scale work could be carried out on co-operative lines by the cultivators themselves, and for this reason the total cost would be less than that of clearing a comparable area of virgin jungle in the Borneo interior. Moreover, in view of the potential fertility of the alluvial soils to be reclaimed, he estimates that the area could produce at least 1½ million tons of rice, which would be more than enough to solve the country's basic food problem for decades to come.[61]

The scheme, which dates from 1929, was eventually taken up by the Indonesian government and, with the help of a few tractors, bulldozers, pumps and also of foreign technicians, variously supplied under the auspices of TCA, FAO[62] and the Colombo Plan, a start was made in 1953 on reclaiming a pilot area of some 75,000 acres of polder land in the vicinity of Bandjarmasin. In relation to the total project this represents only a very small beginning but, even so, lack of funds has already reduced the expected rate of progress, and for the time being the scheme remains little more than a pipe dream.

In its early stages the Schophuys scheme proposed to concentrate on making new land available for cultivation by the local population of southern Borneo, but were it to progress further it would undoubtedly create great opportunities

[59] In 1959 the average density in the outer territories was 62 per square mile, compared with 1,168 in Java. See Table 43.

[60] According to the *Bank Indonesia Report* 1955–6, p. 118, the country possesses a total of only 225 tractors 'which are spread over the archipelago as rationally as possible'.

[61] There are even larger areas of swamp in Sumatra, though the greater thickness of peat there would make their reclamation much more difficult. The *Colombo Plan Eighth Annual Report* (London 1960), p. 78 records that reclamation of tidewater marshland in Borneo and Sumatra had so far made available over 24,700 acres of irrigated land.

[62] Technical Co-operation Administration (U.S.A.) and Food and Agricultural Organization (U.N.O.) respectively.

for settlement by immigrant cultivators from Java. At present, however, Sumatra continues to be the main outlet for such peoples under the transmigration scheme started by the Indonesian government in 1950.

In effect this also represents a continuation of the work carried out by the Dutch before the War, though the present scheme is less elaborately organized. Nevertheless, the government does attempt to cover the expenses of migrating families for the first six to eight months, and provides credits for tools, clothing and housing. In view of the need to avoid repetition of the old congested conditions typical of Java in the centres of resettlement, the government originally aimed at giving each family a minimum of 2 hectares of land, but in practice this standard has not been maintained, and the average size of recent transmigrants' holdings is only 1·2 hectares or approximately 3 acres.

All-told nearly 90,000 people, mostly labourers and their dependants, were moved from Central, East and to a smaller extent West Java between 1950 and 1954, and as Table 37 shows, although the most important receiving area, as in pre-war days, was southern Sumatra many other parts of the outer territories

TABLE 37

INDONESIA: TRANSMIGRATION, 1950–59

Receiving area	1950	1951	1952	1953	1954	*Total* 1950–54	1959
North Sumatra .	—	—	—	—	1,364	1,364	845
Central Sumatra .	—	—	—	1,246	395	1,641	—
South Sumatra .	77	2,365	16,487	31,410	21,277	71,616	43,279
West Borneo .	—	—	—	—	521	521	512
South Borneo .	—	—	—	2,593	671	3,264	736
East Borneo .	—	—	—	—	447	447	164
South Celebes .	—	99	338	—	—	437	} 298
North and Central Celebes . .	—	—	—	310	1,078	1,388	}
Moluccas . .	—	—	—	—	411	411	—
West Java . .	—	400	682	3,868	80	5,030	—
Total . .	77	2,864	17,507	39,427	28,254	88,079	46,096

Figures are numbers of persons moved by the Department of Transmigration, and on their own account. They do not include the agrarian resettlement of demobilized soldiers, or movement of workers from Java to the estates of the outer territories. 1959 figures include 262 to Western Lesser Sundas and 25 others.

Sources: *The Population of Indonesia*, Djakarta, 1956, and *Statistical Pocket Book of Indonesia*, 1960.

were also involved. However, the actual number moved fell far short both of the pre-war figures and of the proposed total of 200,000 for the period in question. Since 1954 the shortfall has been still more pronounced, despite the statement of a spokesman of the Ministry of Social affairs on January 15, 1954 that it was the government's aim, by means of organized transmigration, ultimately to reduce the population of Java from 52 to 30 million.

In the opinion of the Canadian demographer, Dr. Nathan Keyfitz, 500,000 of Java's total annual increase should be regarded as 'the potential for opening up the unsettled lands outside of Java'.[63] But if transmigration is to make a permanent contribution to the solution of the population problem, the flow must be carefully regulated to prevent the growth of excessive densities, in effect new 'Javas', in the outer territories. Ideally the density in the receiving areas should be kept low enough to permit of the production of a considerable surplus of food, which could then be exchanged against manufactured goods of various kinds from Java.

In this connexion, as Fryer has observed, the present pre-occupation with *sawah* cultivation in the resettlement areas may call for reconsideration. For although it yields at least 20 per cent more per acre than dry-rice cultivation, the irrigated method is less widely applicable, less suitable for mechanization and requires a much heavier initial outlay on water control and field construction. Dry-rice growing with mechanical equipment is nowadays regarded as the most promising means of raising food production in the Australian-administered parts of New Guinea, and it is probable that similar methods would give the best available results in most of the outer territories of Indonesia.[64]

This leads in turn to the third approach to the problem, namely the promotion of further industrial development within the metropolitan island. As has been seen in Chapter 9, the need to mop up rural unemployment in Java, especially during the slack periods of the agricultural year, was one of the principal factors which led the Dutch shortly before the War to embark on a policy of fostering industrialization in the Indies. This motive certainly continues to operate in independent Indonesia today, and moreover is strongly reinforced by the desire on both material and psychological grounds to achieve a more balanced national economy. At an early stage in its existence, therefore, the new regime drafted an ambitious industrialization programme which, in a somewhat modified form, subsequently became known as the Sumitro Plan.

In broad outline the plan fell into two main sections, the first of which aimed at an expansion of small-scale and domestic industries, principally in rural Java, while the second envisaged the establishment of several large-scale projects

[63] Keyfitz (B), p. 6. When Keyfitz wrote this (1953) he estimated the total at 770,000, but it now appears to exceed a million a year. But the *Indonesian Spectator* of September 1, 1958 commented, p. 7, 'It becomes obvious that at the utmost 50,000 people could be transmigrated annually to new resettlements'.

[64] See Fryer (B), p. 180. The Schophuys scheme would, of course, be an exception to this.

sponsored industries it was also hoped that private concerns would establish factories on their own initiative.

So far as the small-scale and domestic industries are concerned a considerable measure of success has been achieved, particularly through the setting up of more central workshops operating in close association with local producer co-operatives in the area which they serve. It is their task to organize collective purchase and to carry out preliminary processing of raw materials, to advise on new and better techniques of production and, finally, to standardize the finished products and to arrange for their marketing. According to the original plan, 23 of these 'centrals' or *induks* were to be set up,[65] the first four of which included a ceramics shop at Plared, a forge at Tjisaät, a tannery at Magelang, and an umbrella works at Djuwiring (all in Java). Among the remainder, most of which were in operation by the end of 1955, were units specializing in ceramics, porcelain, iron- and copper-ware, woodwork, hardboard, ramie, tiles and slates.

While the *induks* have had some success in popularizing the use of improved tools and machines, and providing a better and more standardized finish for the goods manufactured in the homes and small factories of the Javanese countryside, the quality of these articles still leaves much to be desired, and even when helped by the import restrictions imposed in recent years against various non-essential manufactured goods they have often experienced great difficulty in finding a market.

In the promotion of these small industries – frequently referred to nowadays as 'people's industries' – the initiative since 1949 has come essentially from the Indonesian government, and the movement is in complete harmony with the co-operative ideal which permeates official thinking in economic matters today. Nevertheless, very great help has also been received from such outside organizations as the Foreign Operations Administration (U.S.A.), the Technical Assistance Organization (U.N.O.) and the Colombo Plan, particularly in the provision of technical training.

The second part of the Sumitro Plan was concerned with setting up larger-scale industries either to process major export staples or to provide certain specific goods of which the country's economy stood in exceptional need. In more detail two series of projects were envisaged under this heading, the first group to be undertaken as a matter of urgency and the remainder to be embarked upon at a later stage.

The more immediate projects included six printing plants (primarily for newspapers) in Medan, Palembang, Djakarta, Semarang, Surabaja and Makasar; seven remilling units (to process small-holders' rubber) at Pontianak, Sampit and Bandjarmasin in Borneo, and at Palembang, Djambi, Sibolga and in the Asahan district of Sumatra; a second cement factory at Gresik in East Java;[66] a second tyre

[65] Sixteen in Java and 7 in the outer territories. This again represents a continuation of the pre-war Dutch policy described above, pp. 295–7.

[66] Besides the existing one at Padang, which produces 160,000 tons a year. The new factory, now completed, has a capacity of 375,000 tons a year.

factory also in East Java;[67] a large cotton-spinning factory at Tjilatjap (Central Java);[68] a gunny-bag factory at Surakarta and a knitting plant (location unspecified).

The later group, on which preliminary work was expected to begin in 1951–2, included a caustic-soda plant at Waru[69] (East Java), a scrap-iron processing plant at Semarang, a desiccated-coconut factory at Sukur (in the Minahasa district of Celebes) and several more spinning and knitting plants in various parts of Java. Most ambitious of all under this heading, however, was the proposed Asahan multi-purpose scheme in northern Sumatra. The idea of harnessing the Sampuransegara and Sampuranhariman falls on the Asahan river for the generation of hydro-electric power, which in turn would provide the basis of a new aluminium-smelting industry using bauxite from the Riau archipelago, was first put forward by the Dutch administration before the war. Under the Sumitro Plan, however, a much more extensive project was suggested, with fertilizer plants, steel mills, pulp and paper factories and several lesser industrial units such as sawmills in various parts of northern Sumatra, as well as the aluminium smelting originally proposed, all making use of the vast quantity of electricity which it was hoped to generate from the falls. But the recent uncertainty regarding the fortunes of the Riau bauxite industry may call for some modifications in the scheme as a whole, on which, after some delays occasioned by the prevailing insecurity, work was restarted late in 1959.[70]

Similar delays have also overtaken some of the other projects listed above, including even some of those in the supposedly urgent category, though the printing establishments, the gunny-bag and coconut factories, and the cement plant have been completed, and fair progress has been made with the construction of the rubber remilling units and the Tjilitjap spinning factory.

In part this is a reflection of the general instability which has prevailed in Indonesia ever since 1949, but a more specific cause has been the failure of successive governments to work out an adequate policy for financing large undertakings on the scale originally envisaged. And in this connexion more recent indications are even less encouraging. Thus proposals outlined in the summer of 1955 recommended that foreign capital should be entirely excluded from the most vital projects,[71] and that in less essential industries, including consumer-goods factories in the private sector not covered by the Sumitro Plan, at least 51 per cent of the shares should in future be held by Indonesian citizens.

[67] Besides the existing (Goodyear) factory at Bogor (the former Buitenzorg).

[68] With an annual capacity of 3,000 tons of yarn. Indonesia's total production of manufactured textiles has risen from 150 million metres in 1951 to 445 million metres in 1960.

[69] To supply raw materials for soap, etc. More recently work has begun on establishing a nail factory at Waru, with a capacity of 12,000 tons annually.

[70] See *The Colombo Plan, Ninth Annual Report*, London, 1961, p. 72. The total power potential available in the Asahan gorge is estimated at nearly 1 million kW, which is approximately equal to that of the Hoover dam site at Boulder Canyon. Higgins, Benjamin (A), p. 116. The present project will develop 240,000 kW.

[71] These include railways, telecommunications, inter-island shipping, airways, electrical and atomic power, armaments, etc.

While, however, the government goes to great lengths in defining the terms on which foreign capital may be admitted, it appears to be unmindful of the fact that many local phenomena, such as the seven-hour day, restrictions on the purchase of materials, the inadequacy of water and power supplies for existing factories, the difficulties of obtaining admission permits and accommodation for Western staff, and indeed the whole atmosphere of muddle and inefficiency[72] are all tending to frighten away the foreign investor.

Yet it is on the private and largely foreign-owned concerns that Indonesia must for the time being continue to depend for a large part of its industrial output. And, in the absence of any large Indonesian capitalist groups comparable to the Tatas and Birlas of India, it would seem that many of the circumstances which now operate to discourage Western participation in this field will lead simply to the replacement of Western by local Chinese interests. Certainly, both openly and in more devious ways[73] the Indonesian Chinese are playing a leading part in the establishment of small consumer-goods factories, which are nowadays springing up all over the country, especially in the towns of Java.[74]

That this large and growing share in the country's industry should be under the control of such a minority community, which has traditionally been extremely reluctant to employ Indonesians in any but the most subordinate capacities, can scarcely be welcome to the present administration. On the contrary, it would seem that the most effective way of building up an Indonesian commercial and industrial class would be by actively encouraging Western concerns to open branches in Indonesia, providing they are willing to undertake the training of Indonesian personnel to take over as soon as is practicable. In theory the force of this argument may now be widely admitted but, as in so many other aspects of Indonesian life, practice is apt to lag a long way behind.

Table 38, which summarizes the main features of Indonesian industrial geography at the end of 1958, shows the overwhelming predominance of Java in the consumer-goods industries, and indeed in all kinds of industrial activity other than the processing of export raw materials produced in the outer islands. Within Java itself the main industrial concentrations, as would be expected in view of the emphasis on consumer goods, have grown up around the largest towns. Djakarta in particular has a wide range of such manufactures, from toilet requisites and textiles to bicycle and car assembly, together with shipbuilding nearby at Pasir Ikan, while Bandung is noted for textiles and ceramics. Similarly, Bogor has textiles, footwear and tyres, and Surabaja, in addition to its large

[72] As well as the possibility of nationalization.

[73] *E.g.* operating in the name of an Indonesian 'front' man.

[74] This process began during the Japanese occupation, when Indonesia was cut off from the usual suppliers. But more recently the attitude of the Indonesian government has led many Chinese to invest outside Indonesia and indeed to become increasingly anxious about their personal future within the country. See above, note 16, and below, page 386.

[75] Philips, who established this plant, have also set up another at Bandung. Allen and Donnithorne, p. 260.

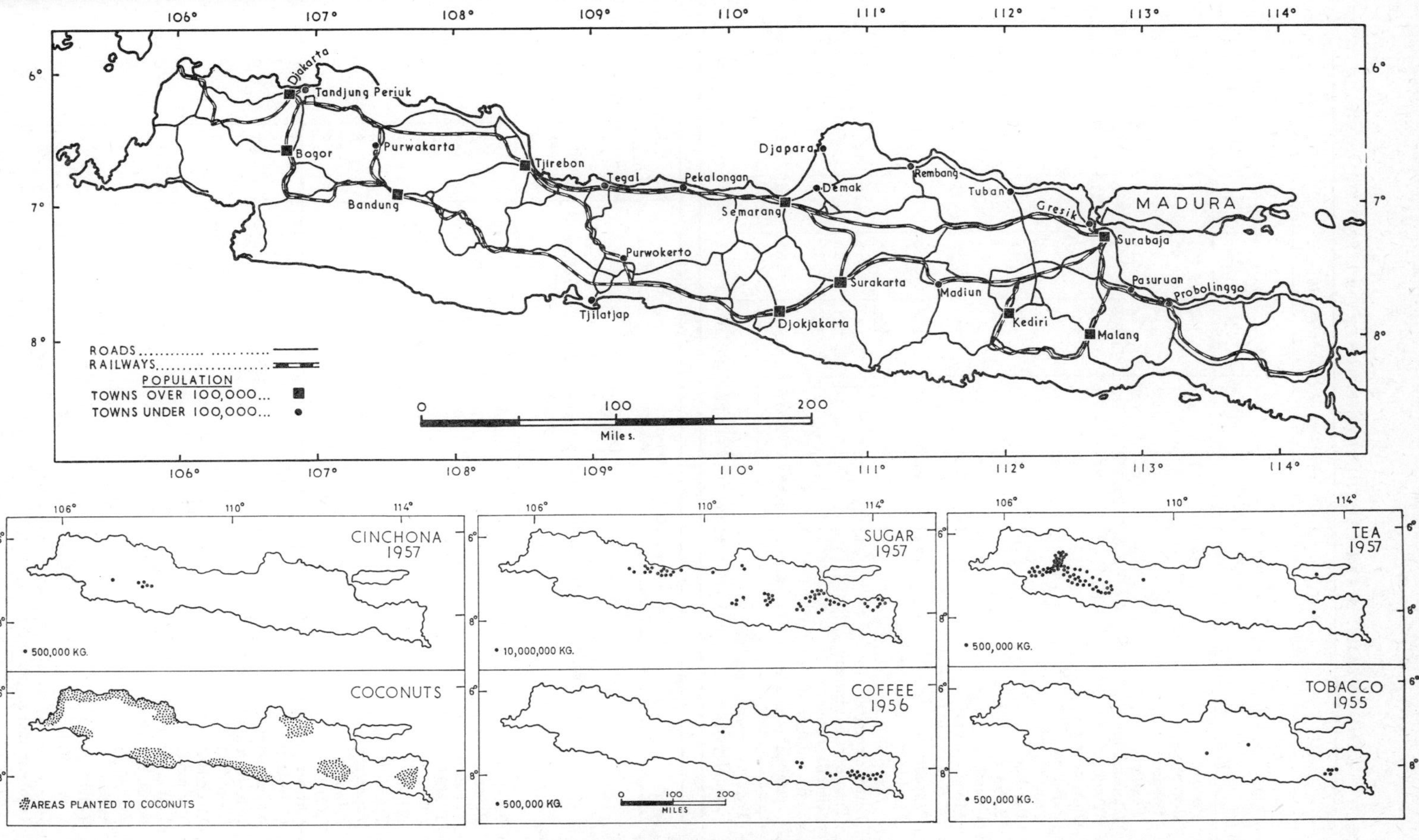

FIG. 45—Java: transport and production

TABLE 38

INDONESIA: MANUFACTURING INDUSTRY AT END OF 1958

Number of establishments

Industrial Group	*Java*				*Sumatra*			
	W	C	E	Total	N	C	S	Total
Food	587	337	568	1,492	199	20	91	310
Beverages	96	39	71	206	50	8	19	77
Tobacco	13	231	271	415	24	0	3	27
Textiles	349	306	129	784	15	4	2	21
Clothing etc.	646	1,260	292	2,198	4	0	2	6
Wood	42	37	70	149	70	11	48	129
Furniture etc.	135	82	84	301	13	2	7	22
Paper etc.	27	9	25	61	6	1	0	7
Printing	211	121	127	459	46	9	13	68
Leather	238	57	71	366	11	2	3	16
Rubber	91	15	50	156	32	43	26	101
Chemicals	203	67	161	431	31	13	8	52
Metal Goods	177	76	99	352	27	5	6	38
Non-metallic mineral products	133	62	73	268	20	4	17	41
Machinery, manufacture & repair (non-electrical)	71	15	36	122	7	0	7	14
Ditto, electrical	15	4	9	28	1	0	0	1
Transport equipment	135	60	86	281	20	9	30	59
Miscellaneous	124	112	94	330	16	8	16	40
Total number of establishments	3,293	2,890	2,316	8,499	592	139	298	1,029
Total number of persons employed	146,504	124,263	124,712	395,479	17,821	5,377	10,064	33,262

Industrial Group	*Number of Establishments*					*Number of establishments which employed*	
	Borneo	*Celebes*	*Moluccas & W. New Guinea*	*Lesser Sundas*	*Total Indonesia*	*100 persons or more*	*1000 persons or more*
Food	63	63	—	19	1,947	51	0
Beverages	13	15	1	7	319	6	0
Tobacco	0	1	0	18	561	196	16
Textiles	1	7	6	2	821	178	10
Clothing etc.	0	5	0	0	2,209	12	0
Wood	30	9	0	2	319	16	0
Furniture etc.	3	19	2	2	349	4	0
Paper etc.	0	1	0	0	69	8	0
Printing	11	12	2	6	558	55	2
Leather	7	8	0	6	403	18	1
Rubber	90	1	0	0	348	54	1
Chemicals	12	17	1	18	531	65	2
Metal goods	5	12	0	1	408	35	0
Non-metallic mineral products	4	8	0	3	324	39	1
Machinery, manufacture & repair (non-electrical)	9	2	0	0	147	15	0
Ditto, electrical	0	0	0	0	29	11	0
Transport equipment	19	23	1	12	395	33	5
Miscellaneous	29	18	2	19	438	24	0
Total number of establishments	296	221	15	115	10,175	820	38
Total number of persons employed	8,181	4,394	314	5,639	447,269	240,673	57,613

Source: Based on *Statistical Pocket Book of Indonesia*, 1960, pp. 90–93

TABLE 39

INDONESIA: FOREIGN TRADE BY PRINCIPLE PORTS, 1938 AND 1959

Figures in Rp. million

Ports	1938			1959 (*preliminary data*)		
	Imports	*Exports*	*Total*	*Imports*	*Exports*	*Total*
Tandjung Periuk . .	134·7	93·7	228·4	1,966·7	686·7	2,653·4
Surabaja	100·2	46·9	147·1	757·4	265·0	1,022·4
Semarang . . .	53·0	31·1	84·1	398·4	97·7	496·1
Total* Java & Madura .	312·4	221·5	533·9	3,300·4	1,295·5	4,595·9
Belawan	35·1	91·5	126·6	510·9	1,676·7	2,187·6
Padang	8·7	8·6	17·3	39·4	64·5	103·9
Palembang . . .	28·0	96·5	124·5	402·7	2,081·1	2,483·8
Total* Sumatra . .	120·8	332·2	453·0	1,512·5	6,786·9	8,299·4
Pontianak . . .	6·1	15·5	21·6	39·1	434·2	473·3
Balikpapan . . .	10·3	46·6	56·9	254·3	518·3	772·6
Total* Borneo . . .	23·7	95·0	118·7	332·5	1,565·1	1,897·6
Makasar	16·8	23·5	40·3	79·2	171·0	250·2
Menado	2·5	2·3	4·8	3·6	39·2	42·8
Total* eastern Indonesia .	21·5	37·4	58·9	83·3	296·6	379·9
Total Indonesia . .	479·4	773·7	1,252·1	5,228·7	9,944·1	15,172·8

* Including others.

Source: Based on *Statistical Pocket Book of Indonesia*, 1960, pp. 109 and 111.

textile, electric bulb[74] and shipbuilding plants, has been selected as the location for the Borguin car assembly factory, whose capital (6 million Deutschmarks) is owned on a 49/51 basis by Borgward of Bremen and an Indonesian company known as Udatin. This important new undertaking is planning ultimately to cater not only for the Indonesian market but also for the rest of South-east Asia, and with this in mind intends to set up its own steel factory at Surabaja within the next six years.

In spite of the present extreme concentration in Java of such manufacturing industry as there is, considerable developments have been projected for the outer territories and it is obvious that at least the initial processing of such export commodities as rubber, coconuts and petroleum would be most economically carried out near the centres of production in Sumatra, Borneo and Celebes. Nevertheless, although the outer territories have been promised major developmental schemes like the Asahan project and the Schophuys plan,[76] these seem to be relegated to an uncertain future, and some years ago it was officially stated[77]

[76] The Schophuys plan is not, of course, concerned with industrial development but its fate has been similar to that of the Asahan project. Other industrial proposals for the outer islands include a steel plant in S.E. Borneo, and a tin smelter in Bangka. Work has begun on a fertilizer plant and a second tyre factory, both in Palembang.

[77] *Bank Indonesia Report*, 1955–6, p. 149.

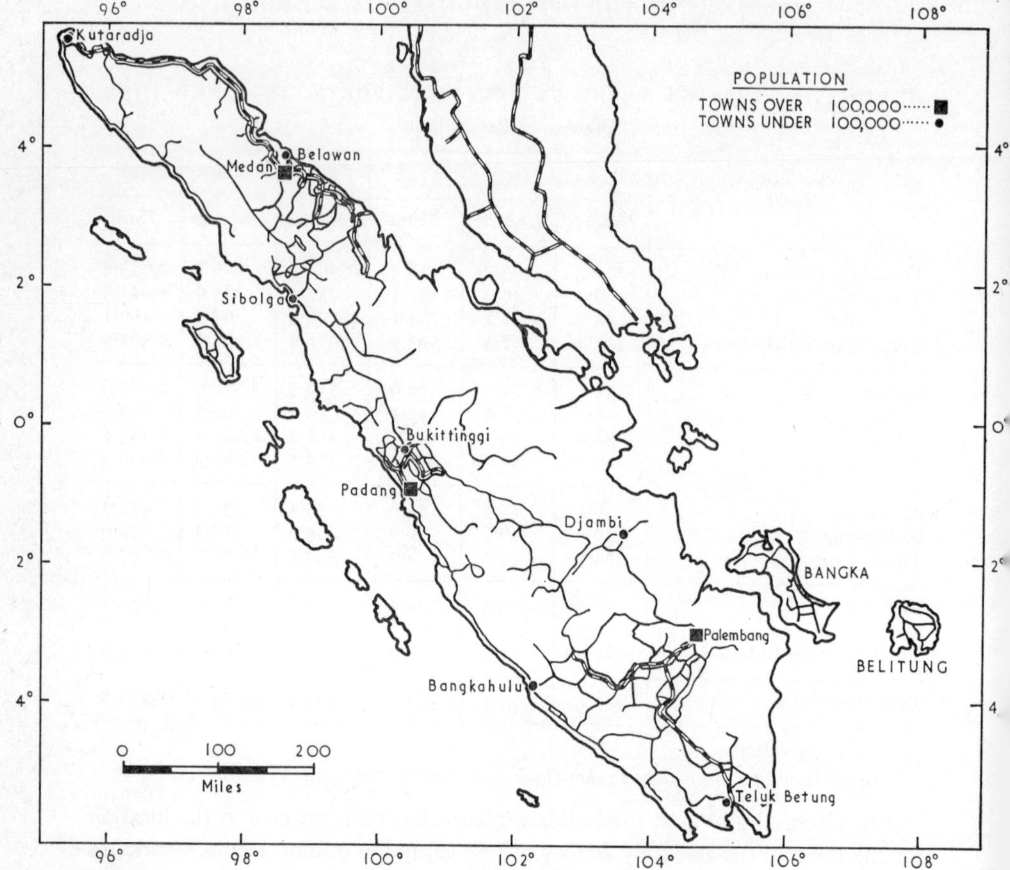

FIG. 46—Sumatra: roads railways and towns

that the Five Year Plan would have to give priority in industrial development to East and Central Java owing to the acute unemployment which now exists there.

While the socio-political reasons for this decision are valid, from a purely economic point of view the best immediate prospects probably lie in a further expansion of the processing industries, and it is to be hoped that this will not be long delayed. So far as consumer goods are concerned, few of them, apart from furniture and other wooden articles, rubber tyres and coarse-fibred goods, have the benefit of adequate local supplies of raw materials, but a substantial expansion may nevertheless be looked for in the production of such items as textiles, footwear, clothing, soap, biscuits and margarine, as well as in the manufacture of synthetic fertilizers and the assembly of bicycles and cars.

As the Borgward project implies, Indonesia should have a considerable advantage over its near neighbours[78] in the manufacture of such articles, by virtue of

[78] Though not over India or China (let alone Japan), which are much further advanced industrially than any of the South-east Asian states.

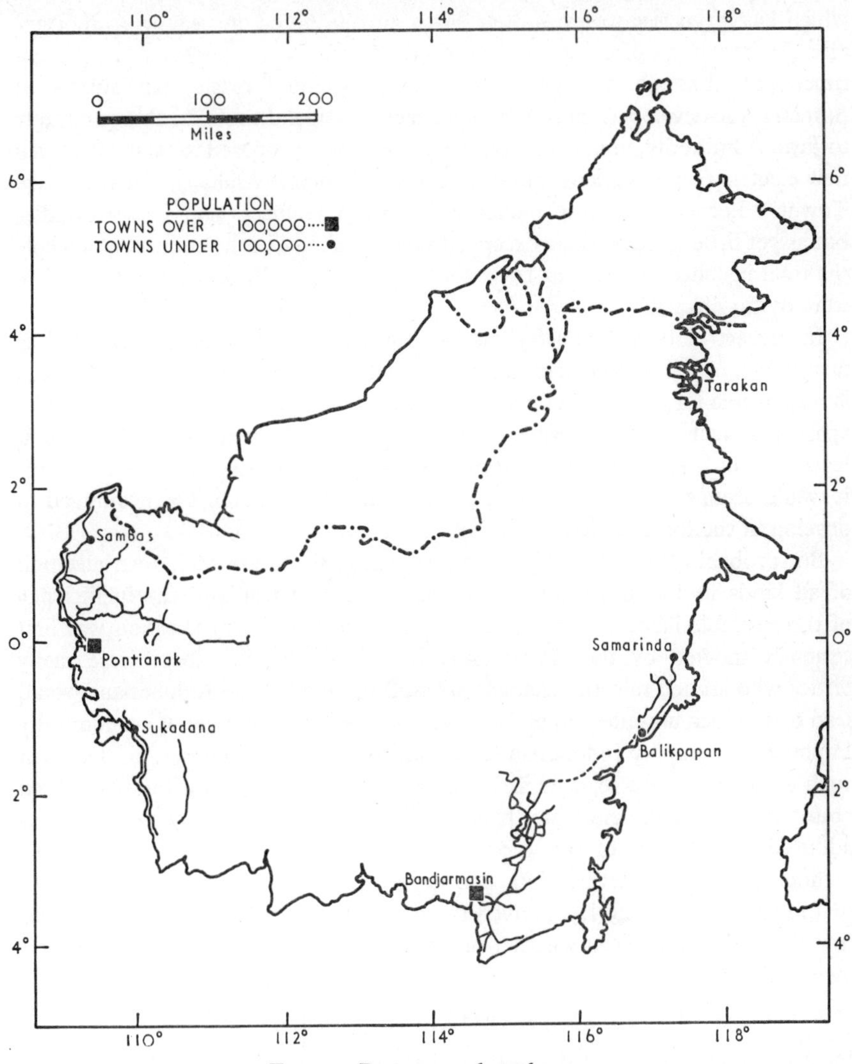

FIG. 47—Borneo: roads and towns

the much larger potential market within its own national territory, and in catering first for its own population, which is more than three times as large as that of any other South-east Asian state, it might be able so to reduce costs as to compete effectively in these neighbouring countries as well, even assuming a substantial measure of tariff protection on their part.

Against this, however, must be set the greater poverty of the potential Indonesian purchasers compared with those in many other parts of South-east Asia at the present critical phase, and also the present governmental policy which has given rise to the various snags already noted on page 312. Shortage of coal, though not of oil, presents serious obstacles to expansion at the present time, and although a large hydro-electric potential exists, particularly in Sumatra, the developed capacity is as yet very small and confined almost entirely to Java. Admittedly, under the Five Year Plan it was proposed to establish eleven new electric power stations, notably in Java, Sumatra (Asahan), Celebes (Lake Towuti), Borneo and, on a smaller scale, in the Moluccas and Lesser Sundas, but as yet little is being done except in Java itself, and in the country as a whole the total installed capacity in 1959 was only 363,000 kW, of which 143,000 kW were hydro-electricity.

In respect of heavy industry the raw material basis cannot be regarded as favourable, owing to a geological structure which in general, like that of Japan, is responsible for a paucity of good-quality iron ore and coking coal. Thus, quite apart from technological backwardness and a type of climate which hitherto at least has not been regarded as propitious for heavy industry on a major scale,[79] it would seem that this is not a line which Indonesia should be encouraged to develop in the foreseeable future.

But probably the greatest problems affecting the future of industrialization of all kinds in Indonesia are the shortage of technicians and the inefficiency of the available labour. In the 1930s when extensive industrialization was first seriously mooted by the Netherlands Indies government, there were many critics who argued that the characteristic insouciance of the Indonesians would lead to so much absenteeism and general inefficiency as to make it economically impossible to employ Indonesian labour in Western-style factories. In the event such arguments were rejected as being unduly pessimistic, and the undoubted ability of some of the graduates from the Technical University of Bandung was adduced as evidence of the Indonesians' capacity to play their part in the technological age.[80] Nevertheless, the experience of many industrial concerns in Indonesia since 1949 has revived the doubts expressed in pre-war days, and it still remains to be seen whether or not the Indonesians will really hold their own in this respect.

V. TRANSPORT AND TRADE

Nothing is more essential for the economic development and political stability of Indonesia today than the maintenance and further extension of the transport network built up by the Dutch before the Second World War. Yet no sector of the country's economy has suffered more acutely than this from the ravages of war, occupation and continuing unrest, and in no other respect has Indonesia been so obviously dependent on foreign nationals for its very survival.

In respect of the two principal forms of overland transport, the pre-war contrast

[79] The experience of Jamshedpur (India) and Volta Redonda (Brazil) suggests that the climatic factor is probably not of great importance. It is now claimed that economically worth while iron ore exists in southern Sumatra, Java and Borneo.

[80] Timmermans, p. 126.

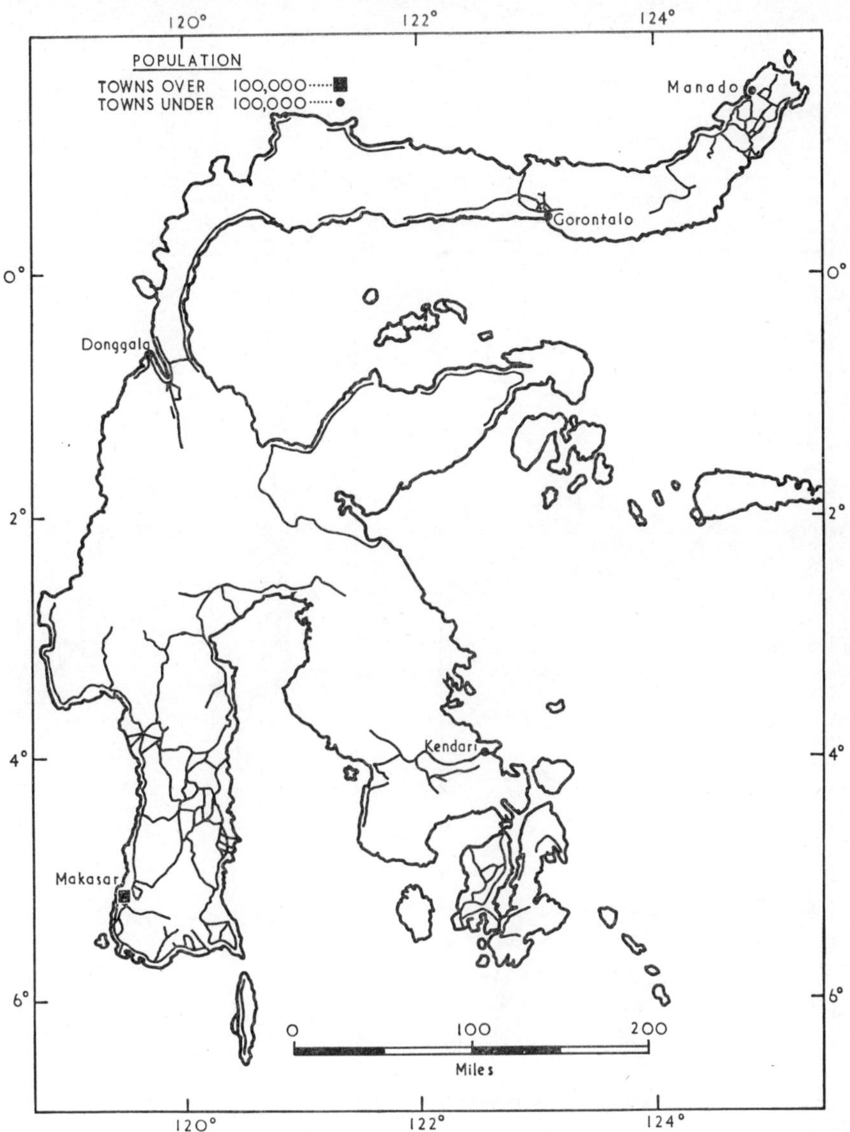

FIG. 48—Celebes: roads and towns

between Java and the outer territories remains undiminished. Indeed, while rehabilitation of roads has made fair progress in Java, the corresponding needs of the outer territories have received much less attention, and financial difficulties have led to the indefinite postponement of plans for building new trunk roads in Sumatra, Borneo and Celebes.

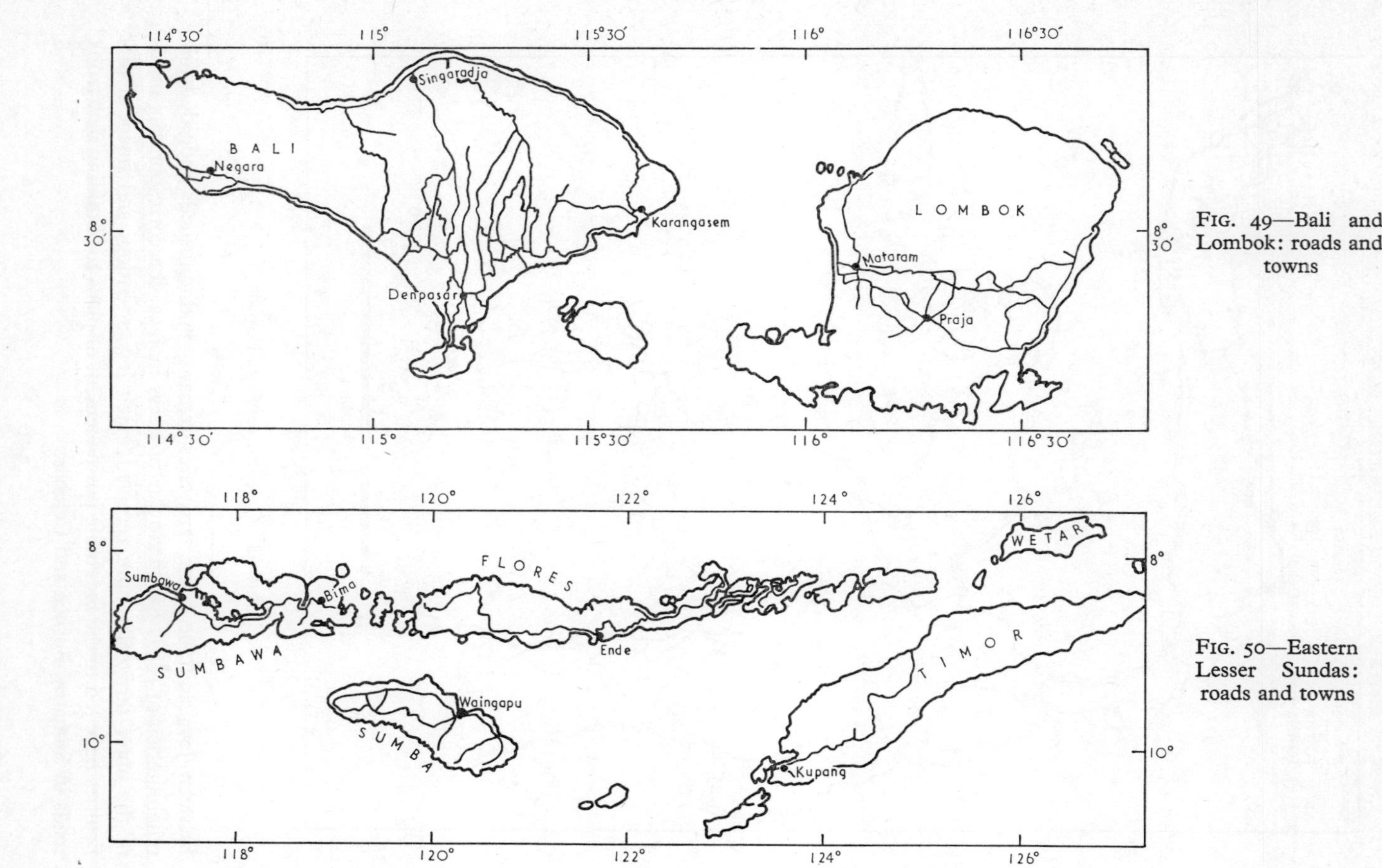

FIG. 49—Bali and Lombok: roads and towns

FIG. 50—Eastern Lesser Sundas: roads and towns

As Table 41 shows, much remains to be done before the railway system can be regarded as back to normal, and although the number of passengers carried has more than trebled since 1938 the volume of freight traffic is still below the pre-war level.

TABLE 40

INDONESIA: RAILWAYS, TRACK MILES IN USE

	1938	1959
Java and Madura	3,362	2,920
Sumatra	1,227	1,102
Total	4,589	4,022

Recently the government[81] has made heavy purchases of rolling stock from abroad, including a number of diesel locomotives for the main lines in Java, but apart from establishing a new rail-ferry link between Merak (West Java) and Pandjang (South Sumatra), no extensions have been made to the system, and the Atjeh line in Sumatra as well as several branch lines in Java have yet to be restored to working order. Under the Five Year Plan the government started to carry out improvements to some 1,250 miles of existing track and to purchase further much-needed replacements of locomotives and rolling stock, but for the time being the acute shortage of fuel is probably the most serious problem with which the railways have to contend.

Owing to its inherent geographical dependence on sea communications Indonesia's continued reliance on the Dutch-owned K.P.M. for inter-insular transport and on other foreign shipping companies for overseas services has been a principal source of national chagrin. Admittedly under the transfer agreement of 1949 the K.P.M. no longer retained its former monopoly, but in practice it met with little competition. Thus in 1955 its fleet of 100 ships with a total displacement of 190,000 B.R.T.,[82] though substantially smaller than before the War, was still able to maintain 44 regular routes covering 182,000 nautical miles, and in so doing it provided some 70 per cent of the total inter-insular transport. The remainder was accounted for mainly by various Indonesian shipping concerns, of which the largest was Pelni, with 39 vessels totalling 22,700 B.R.T.

However, as part of the anti-Dutch action of December 1957,[83] the Indonesian government peremptorily cancelled the operating licence of the K.P.M. and thereafter sought to replace its services by chartering ships from Japan, and by purchasing others, notably from Japan, Poland and the U.S.S.R. While these developments have greatly profited the small indigenous shipping lines, they have led to a drastic reduction in the facilities available to the country as a whole,

[81] The government now operates all the railways.

[82] Including 74 freighters, totalling 116,000 B.R.T., and 26 passenger vessels, totalling 74,000 B.R.T.

[83] See above, note 5.

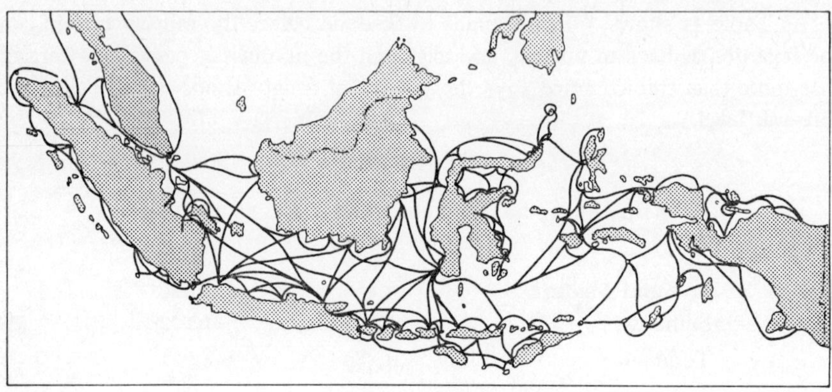

FIG. 51—Indonesia: shipping routes

and unless the situation is quickly restored the economic consequences may well become disastrous.[84]

In respect of air transport the situation since 1949 has been somewhat less embarrassing to Indonesian prestige. From the outset the Indonesian govern-

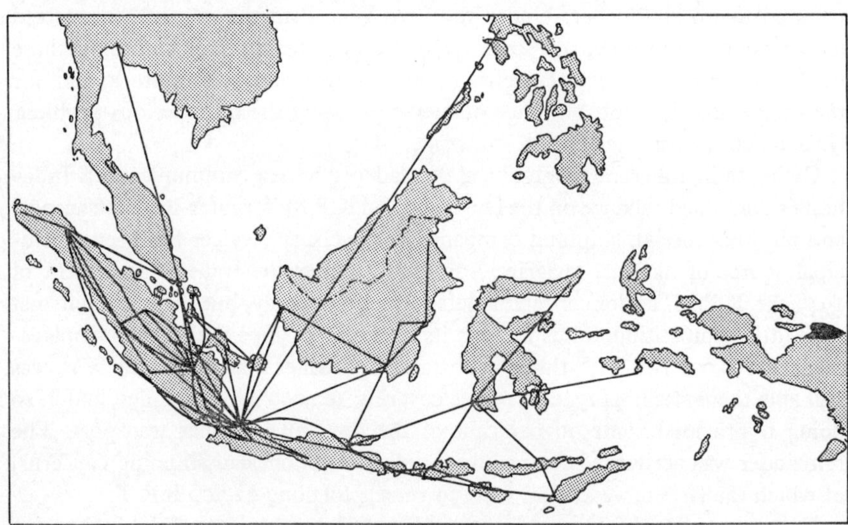

FIG. 52—Indonesia: air routes

ment was quick to appreciate the revolutionary contribution which the great post-war advances in civil aviation could make in linking together the vast and scattered territories under its rule, and with this end in view it determined to

[84] Besides cancelling the K.P.M.'s licence the Indonesian government took over its harbour installations and attempted to seize its ships, though most of these managed to get away to non-Indonesian ports. In 1959 Indonesia had 116,039 tons of its own shipping and chartered a further 138,772 tons of foreign shipping for inter-insular services. The corresponding figures for ocean shipping were 20,686 tons and 152,769 tons respectively.

develop an altogether more elaborate network of air services than that which had been maintained by the old K.N.I.L.M.

Accordingly, under the 1949 agreements, a joint Netherlands-Indonesian concern, Garuda Indonesian Airways, was established and provision made for the training of Indonesian pilots and technicians. Although it was not until 1955 that the first five pilots were ready to assume duties, the Indonesian government in 1954 bought out the Dutch share of the corporation and thus became its sole owner.[85] In 1955 8,185,000 air miles were flown, 308,000 passengers carried and 15,800 tons of mail and freight transported, but owing to civil disturbances these figures had fallen in 1958 to 4,785,000 air miles, 275,000 passengers and 10,301 tons respectively.

The extent of the present airways system is shown in Fig. 52, and in this respect very great developments have taken place since the Second World War. In international aviation also, Indonesia plays an important rôle, for the great arc of islands stretching from Sumatra to Timor provides a convenient series of landing grounds on the route from mainland Asia to Australia. But despite the aspirations of Djakarta to become the air cross-roads of South-east Asia, the country as a whole lies too far south for this to be practicable and, as described in Chapter 18, even Singapore is being displaced from this coveted position by Bangkok.

Tables 42 and 43 provide the basis for a comparison of the overseas trading pattern of Indonesia today with that of pre-war times. Even in 1955, the second year for which figures are given the actual volume of overseas trade was certainly larger than that recorded in the official statistics, though the stage had not yet been reached when *The Economist* was moved to declare (May 18, 1957) that 'the bulk of Indonesia's external trade now seems to consist of smuggling, especially between Sumatra and Singapore, and between Celebes and the Philippines'.[86]

Apart from such illicit activities, however, the legitimate trade via Singapore is sufficient to conceal the ultimate destination of nearly one-fifth of Indonesia's exports. For, as noted in Chapter 18, Singapore, which has risen from second to first place among the countries of destination, is essentially a processing and trans-shipping centre, and retains for its own use only a minute proportion of the goods it obtains from Indonesia. In respect of trade in the reverse direction, on the other hand, Singapore's share has declined very sharply (from fifth to eleventh place), for in the new nationalist era Indonesia prefers to import direct through its own ports.

[85] Under the agreement then negotiated the Dutch airline K.L.M. continued to supply some 300 skilled personnel and to train Indonesians to take their places. This agreement also was terminated in December 1957, by which time approximately one-third of the qualified pilots were Indonesians.

[86] *The Economist*, May 18, 1957, p. 572. Even before this date many parts of the outer territories had been seeking to avoid the central authorities in order to keep control over their own export earnings. See below, pp. 377–381.

Likewise related to changed political circumstances is the decline in the volume of Indonesian trade with the Netherlands, which had dropped from first to third place in both imports and exports by 1955. So far as imports to Indonesia are concerned, the weakening of Dutch commercial influence in the country was doubtless the main explanation, though the drop in Indonesian exports to the Netherlands was largely due to the fact that most of the main items which the Dutch habitually purchased were those which had seen the greatest falling-off of production in Indonesia. But since 1957 trade with the Netherlands has declined to a much lower level.

In the main the decline in trade with the Netherlands has been counterbalanced by an increase in the proportion of trade with the United States, which now (thanks in part to its various assistance programmes) ranks as the leading supplier of Indonesia's imports as well as being a large purchaser of its exports,[87]

TABLE 41

INDONESIA: OVERSEAS TRADE BY COUNTRIES

Figures in Rp. million

A. Exports

Country of destination	1938	*Per cent*	1955	*Per cent*	1959	*Per cent*
Singapore .	116·65	17·0	2,102·66	20·0	2,260·45	23·0
U.S.A. .	97·88	14·0	1,904·49	18·0	1,484·81	15·0
Netherlands	137·49	20·0	1,719·59	16·0	105·29	1·0
U.K. . .	37·32	5·0	1,048·08	10·0	2,176·73	22·0
Japan .	21·43	3·0	834·42	7·0	379·35	4·0
Germany† .	25·46	4·0	471·08†	4·0†	592·18†	6·0
Australia .	28·89	4·0	227·16	2·0	349·43	4·0
Federation of Malaya	11·21	1·5	310·16	3·5	365·28	4·0
Philippines .	6·02	0·9	153·58	1·5	209·49	2·0
France .	12·00	2·0	102·58	1·0	32·55	0·3
Italy . .	9·73	1·5	89·48	0·8	72·46	0·7
Thailand .	2·76	0·4	89·42	0·8	92·62	0·9
China .	9·88	1·5	73·67	0·7	605·03	6·0
Total (inc. others)	687·05	—	10,779·45	—	9,944·15	—

[87] Note that a considerable volume of goods goes to the U.S.A. and the U.K. from Indonesia via Singapore. Since 1955 the U.K. has taken a much larger share of Indonesian exports.

B. Imports

Country of origin	1938	*Per cent*	1955	*Per cent*	1959	*Per cent*
U.S.A. .	60·21	13·0	1,089·77	16·0	830·09	16·0
Japan .	71·83	15·0	987·38	14·0	782·77	15·0
Netherlands	106·17	22·0	808·80	12·0	196·20	4·0
Germany† .	49·05	10·0	701·77†	10·0†	608·19†	12·0
U.K. . .	38·16	8·0	396·99	6·0	346·44	7·0
Hong Kong	6·47	1·5	363·65	5·0	147·81	3·0
India .	11·17‡	2·0‡	362·53	5·0	125·62	2·0
Belgium and Luxemburg	13·19	3·0	223·60	3·0	127·88	2·0
Czecho-slovakia .	4·75	1·0	192·33	3·0	34·05	0·7
Burma .	7·20	1·5	173·52	2·5	324·79	6·0
Australia .	13·24	3·0	142·68	2·0	95·29	1·8
France .	9·41	2·0	141·24	2·0	88·40	1·7
China .	8·25	2·0	114·73	1·6	697·63	13·0
Italy . .	5·05	1·0	125·77	1·5	52·31	1·0
Singapore	36·18	8·0	101·55	1·5	95·77	1·8
Thailand .	2·58	0·5	104·13	1·5	59·84	1·0
Total (inc. others)	478·46	—	7,195·19	—	5,228·66	—

† Federal Republic only.

‡ India and Pakistan.

Source: Central Bureau of Statistics* and *Yearbook of International Trade Statistics* (U.N.)

notably rubber, petroleum and tin, the three export commodities which have seen the greatest advances in output since 1949.

For the rest, the pattern of external trade shows only one major change since the war. Thus while Japan has regained its former position as the second largest supplier of goods to Indonesia and has risen slightly from seventh to fifth place as a purchaser of Indonesian exports, China has jumped from relative obscurity to become the third supplier of Indonesian imports and the fourth outlet for the country's exports.

VI. CONCLUSIONS

When the current state of Indonesian production and trade is compared with that of the pre-war period it is difficult to avoid the conclusion that, for all the talk of building up a new national economy, the major result so far achieved has been rather to allow the once efficient machine created by the Dutch to run down. Despite a 30–35 per cent increase in the country's population since 1941, total recorded production today is still below the pre-war figure, and real *per capita* income has probably fallen by 15–30 per cent in the meantime.[88]

When all possible allowance has been made for external circumstances, there remains little doubt that the primary cause of this decline is the shortage of adequately trained and experienced men, alike in administration, commerce and industry. While the Indonesians are naturally loath to admit this in so many words, they are nevertheless striving to rectify the situation in the most obvious way, by a vast extension of education at all levels. Indeed the progress in this respect is the most encouraging fact in Indonesia today, which already claims a four-fold increase in the number of children at school and a much greater increase in the number of secondary school pupils, as compared with 1941. At the university level the proportionate increase is even greater, and despite the educational problems involved in so rapid an expansion, it may nevertheless be hoped that, given time, the country will succeed in making good the very serious deficiencies in trained man-power from which it now suffers. But whether, in the event, such time will be granted is another matter, which needs to be considered against the background of the political problems discussed in Chapter 11.

TABLE 42

INDONESIA: EDUCATION

		1940	1956	1958/9
Primary Schools	Number of schools	18,091	30,231	34,124
" "	" pupils	2,021,990	6,908,968	7,380,734
Junior Secondary Schools	" schools	114	1,655	3,685
" " "	" pupils	21,875	430,876	579,247
Senior " "	" schools	27	268	968
" " "	" pupils	4,362	68,765	149,680
Universities and Academies	" institutions	5	40	299
" "	" pupils	1,693	23,357	41,000

Source: Based on Moerdowo, p. 25.

[88] Opinions differ on the extent of the decline. See, *e.g.*, Higgins, Benjamin (A), pp. 110–11, and Vlekke (C), p. 68.

SELECT BIBLIOGRAPHY

Allen and Donnithorne
Bro
Broek (E) (G) (K)
De Meel (A) (B)
De Neuman
De Waal
Donnithorne
Fischer
Fruin
Fryer (B) (C) (D) (E) (F)
Furnivall (C)
Higgins (A) (C)
Keyfitz (A) (B)
Khan
Mende
Metcalf
Mills *et al.*
Mintz
Moerdowo
Ormeling
Pelzer (C) (F)
Timmermans
Tohir
Vandenbosch and Butwell
Van der Kroef (C)
Vlekke (C)
Wertheim (C)
Woodman
Zinkin (A)

Bank Indonesia Annual Reports
Economic review of Indonesia
Economisch Weekbled voor Indonesië
Garuda Indonesian Airways Plan 1951–1955
Hamburger Kreditbank: *Wirtschaftlicher Lagebericht Indonesien*, July 1952
Hamburger Kreditbank: *Die Wirtschaftliche Lage Indonesiens*, November 1954
'The industrialization of Indonesia', *I.R.*, I, 1951
Indonesia, Review of commercial conditions
Indonesian Spectator
Report on Indonesia
The population of Indonesia
Social welfare in Indonesia
Colombo Plan Reports
Economic Surveys of Asia and the Far East
Indonesian News
Statistical Pocketbook of Indonesia
Petroleum Press Service

Much of the basic factual material for this chapter has been obtained from the excellent series of reports of Bank Indonesia, published annually (in English) until 1958. In addition to these and to the other reports listed above, the articles by Fryer and Pelzer on various aspects of the economic geography, and by De Meel and Keyfitz on population problems are all extremely useful.

The four general works dealing with post-war Indonesia, by Bro, Fischer, Van der Kroef and Woodman respectively, all contain a good deal of interesting information on economic matters. The most thorough analysis of the post-war economic problems of Indonesia known to the author is that made by Higgins (C), which was preceded by a useful shorter statement from the same author (A). For an interesting geographical contribution to the study of developmental problems as exemplified by Indonesia, the thesis by Fryer should also be consulted.

Addenda: Note the papers by Mackie and by Parker (B); and McVey, Ruth T. (ed.), *Indonesia*, New Haven, 1963.

CHAPTER II

Problems of the New Indonesia: B-Political

I. GEOGRAPHICAL IMPEDIMENTS TO UNITY

While the new rulers of Indonesia have been striving simultaneously, if with limited success, to raise living standards and to reorganize the whole pattern of the country's economy on a 'national' as opposed to a 'colonial' basis, they have been confronted in the political field with the no less difficult task of welding the widely scattered and culturally diverse population of the archipelago into a coherent and united nation. For although the events of 1945–9 made it clear that the majority of the Indonesian population were at one in their desire for *merdeka*,[1] the final achievement of independence has inevitably brought to light the many acute differences which still remain to be resolved within the body politic.

Moreover, the geographical character of the archipelago itself, with its 3,000 islands scattered over vast distances of sea, presents the state-maker with an extremely difficult task, which indeed is without parallel elsewhere in the modern world except for the now defunct British West Indian Federation. Admittedly in historic times the sea has often acted as a unifying factor in Indonesian life, and in more recent decades the efficient weekly or fortnightly services of the K.P.M. brought every major outlying town within twelve days' travelling time from Batavia, though contact with the lesser islands and remoter interiors was much more tenuous. But while such communications sufficed for the transaction of administrative business between the central government and its provincial subordinates under a paternalistic colonial régime, they are scarcely adequate for the proper functioning of a democratic system in which the central government must keep in close touch with public opinion throughout the national territory.

In this connexion it may be noted that, although the total land area of Indonesia is only about one-fifth as great as that of the continental United States, the outer limits of the two are equally far apart and, owing to the slowness of maritime transport, effective distances in Indonesia are in fact still greater. Thus, except for the comparatively small numbers of 'transmigrants' from one island to another, the great majority of the Indonesian peasantry have exceedingly little knowledge of people or conditions beyond their immediate home areas, and each of the main concentrations of population has tended to be a little world unto itself, with its own regional language and sometimes distinctive religious beliefs,

[1] *I.e.* freedom.

and its own preoccupation with some particular cash crop or other localized economic activity.

The constraints imposed by effective distance were well illustrated in the first national elections in September 1955, for while voting was almost everywhere completed within a few days, the results from many of the outer islands were not available in Djakarta for several weeks, and it was physically impossible to assemble the new parliament before the following March. Such circumstances are reminiscent of the pre-railway age in the West, and for a comparable example of the difficulties imposed by geography on the working of a democratic constitution one may turn to the situation which faced the founding fathers of the United States in the late 18th century.

True, there are important differences between the two cases, and while economically and politically the 92 million inhabitants of contemporary Indonesia are mostly at a much lower level of advancement than the three and a half million citizens of the original American republic, Indonesia today nevertheless possesses certain assets, notably in its airways and telegraphic and radio communications, which were not available at all in the earlier period. However, while these 20th-century media are of immense value in the purely technical aspects of administration, the fact remains that in a country of such low living standards as Indonesia they are of very limited significance to the mass of the population, who can neither afford to travel by air, nor to buy newspapers carried by air, nor even in a great many cases to own a radio set.

Thus in Indonesia the gulf, present in some degree in all countries at a similar level of development, between a handful of people at the top, who live in the 20th-century world of rapid communications and international contacts, and the mass of the population, who still for the most part live according to the established tempo and narrowly limited horizons of the pre-industrial era, is particularly marked.

These basic facts, of sheer overall size, geographical fragmentation, regional diversity, with which may also be included the contrasted development of Java and the outer territories, and the mental gulf between rulers and ruled, provide the framework within which the architects of the new Indonesia have had to work in devising a form of government which should give expression to the national will to independence. On the assumption, originally avowed by all political leaders, that a democratic form of government was essential to the well-being of the new state, there would seem at first sight to have been the strongest possible reasons for adopting a federal system, such as has provided a working answer to some at least of these problems in other parts of the world. Such a course, however, was rejected by the Indonesian leaders, mainly because of their suspicions regarding the particular federal system which the Dutch had sought to establish in the Indies after 1946, and a brief consideration of this experiment forms a necessary introduction to an examination of the contemporary situation.

II. THE FEDERAL EXPERIMENT, 1946–9

When the Republic came into being on August 15, 1945, it was at once apparent that it commanded strong support in the more accessible parts of Java and Sumatra. Moreover, when the return of the Dutch to the main coastal cities of Java later in that year led Dr. Sukarno to withdraw his headquarters from Batavia to the relatively remote 'grass roots' capital of Djokjakarta, he quickly consolidated his support in the countryside of east-central Java as well.[2]

But in the remoter and more backward islands farther east the local reaction to the nationalist revolution was not immediately clear, and early in 1946 the Dutch were able to set up an administration in Celebes which aimed initially at controlling all the territories outside Java and Sumatra. Thereafter the Dutch, reversing their pre-war attitude towards federalism, and resuscitating the argument advanced before the war by Colijn[3] that a centralized administration would favour the Javanese at the expense of the lesser peoples, particularly the Christian minorities, of the outer territories, proposed that the Republic and the Dutch-administered territories might together form a federal Commonwealth of Indonesia.

To this end they established the new state (*negara*) of East Indonesia,[4] together with five autonomous districts (*daerahs*) in Borneo. And when, after seeking to break the deadlock which had meanwhile arisen with Djokjakarta, they seized a series of key areas in Republican territory in July 1947, they adopted a similar policy there also, setting up further *negaras* and *daerahs* with the support of members of the local aristocracy, whose position was closely bound up with the continuance of Dutch rule.

It was on this basis that the Dutch eventually agreed in 1949 to transfer sovereignty over all their former East Indian possessions, except West New Guinea, to what at the time was understood to be a federal Republic of the United States of Indonesia. But whatever the rights and wrongs of the decision to exclude New Guinea from the new R.U.S.I., the latter was clearly a politico-geographical monstrosity. As Fig. 53 shows,[5] it consisted of seven *negaras* and nine *daerahs*, with Batavia, officially renamed Djakarta, as the federal capital, while Djokjakarta remained the capital of the Republic of Indonesia. In status the *daerahs*, all but one of which contained less than one million inhabitants each, were inferior to the *negaras*, whose population ranged from 1·5 million (South Sumatra) to the 31 million of the Republic of Indonesia (*i.e.* the Djokjakarta republic), whose territories extended over much of both Java and Sumatra. Yet all these sixteen oddly assorted units were to have equal representation in the

[2] For a detailed account of this period see Kahin (C).

[3] See Schiller, pp. 15–18.

[4] Originally East Indonesia embraced the whole of the former Great East, but later it was decided to exclude West New Guinea from it. See below, pp. 394–5, and Fisher (K), pp. 195–7.

[5] See also Kahin (C), Chapter 14.

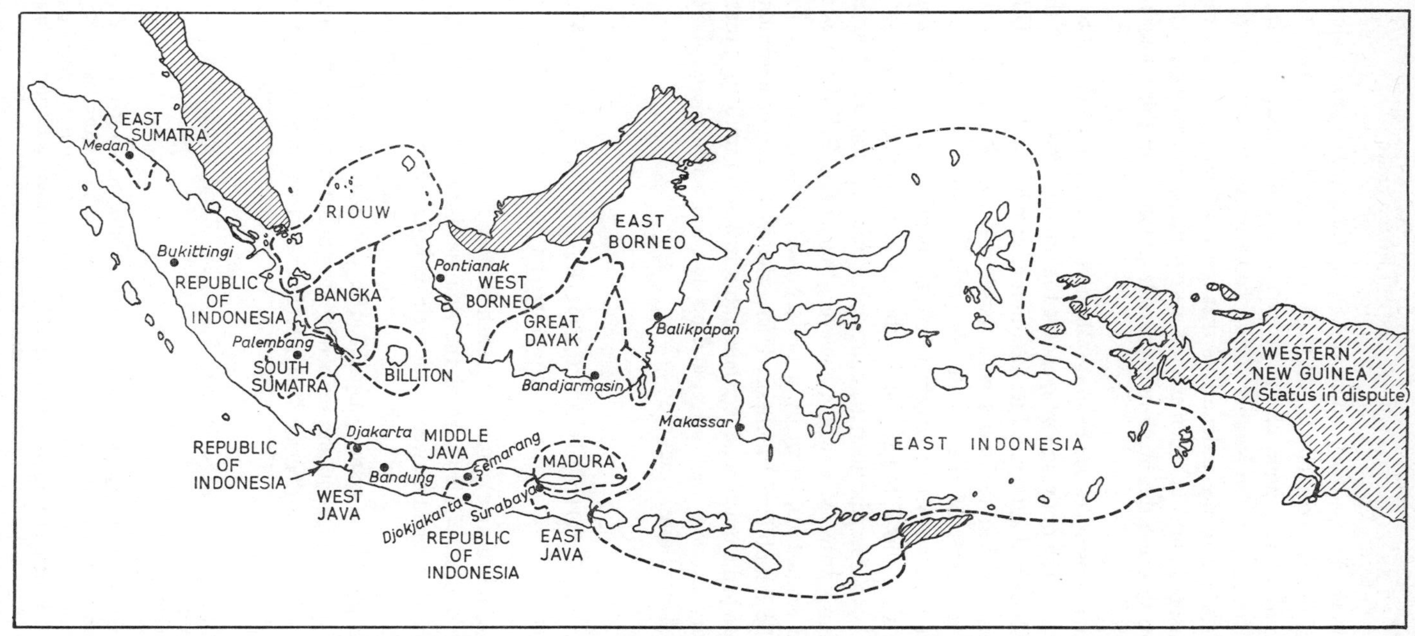

FIG. 53—Indonesia: major administrative divisions under the federal system

Senate, and even in the lower house the Djokjakarta republic was allotted only one-third of the Representatives although it contained nearly half of the total population. Moreover, none of the sixteen units, with the possible but unimportant exception of the Bandjar *daerah*, had any linguistic or historical validity, and it seemed to the Indonesians that the real bases on which the fifteen Dutch-sponsored units had been erected were political and economic expediency and a desire to exert the maximum possible pressure on the Djokjakarta Republic.

In these circumstances the federal system proved short lived, and by the end of May 1950 all the outlying units, except the self-styled Republic of the South Moluccas which had announced its intention of seceding from the R.U.S.I., had agreed to merge their territories with those of the Djokjakarta republic. Undoubtedly the aims of the South Moluccan republic commanded general approval in Ambon, whose largely Christian population retained close sentimental ties with the K.N.I.L.,[6] and although resistance there was crushed in November 1950, sporadic guerrilla fighting continued in the neighbouring island of Seram until 1956. Meanwhile, however, the federal R.U.S.I. was formally replaced on August 10, 1950, by a unitary state, henceforward to be known simply as the Republic of Indonesia. Under the provisional constitution of 1950 the new state had a unicameral legislature, but it was not until 1955 that the first parliamentary elections took place, and no decision was made on the constitution to be adopted until August 1959.[7]

III. THE POLITICAL GEOGRAPHY OF UNITARY INDONESIA

The new administrative pattern established after August 1950 showed several interesting features. While Djakarta, the vital 'head-link'[8] both between Java and the outer territories and between Indonesia and the rest of the world, remained the national capital, and as such was constituted a separate Metropolitan Area outside the provincial system, Djokjakarta, which after November 1945 had acquired a special affection and influence[9] in nationalist circles, was also given a privileged status as a Special District (*Daerah Istemawa*) distinct from the provinces.

[6] Koninklijke Nederlandsche Indische Leger, *i.e.* Royal Dutch East Indies Army. See above, p. 267.

[7] But see below, note 68.

[8] See Spate (B), pp. 628–9.

[9] Besides the rôle of Djokjakarta town as capital of the 1945–9 Republic of Indonesia, the principality, together with Surakarta, was influential in a more lasting respect. For since these two Vorstenlanden maintained an elaborate indigenous system of government throughout the colonial period, they were able to contribute a disproportionately large share of the very small number of experienced officials available to the national administrative machine set up after independence. See below, note 22, and Mysbergh, pp. 38–42.

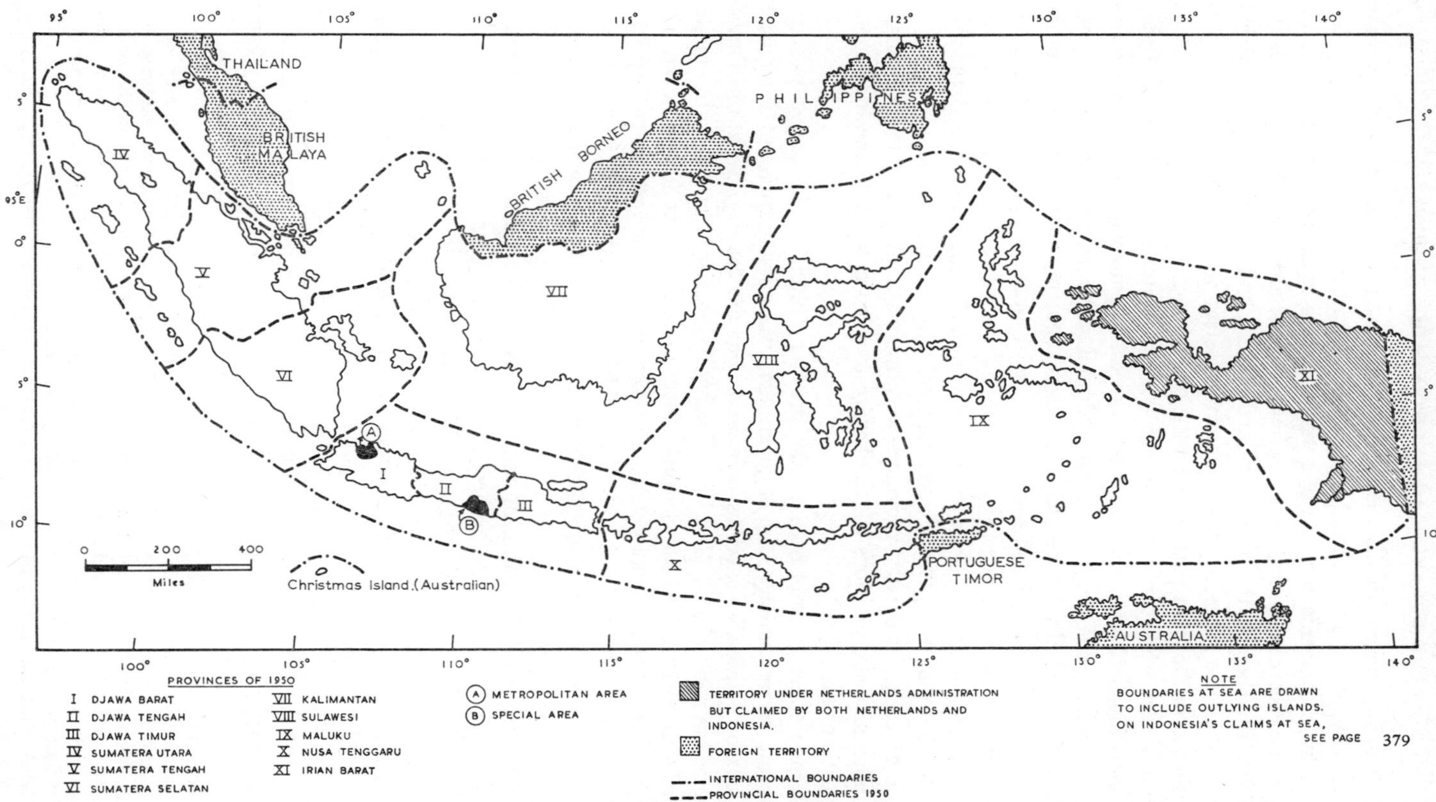
THAILAND
BRITISH MALAYA
BRITISH BORNEO
PHILIPPINES
PORTUGUESE TIMOR
AUSTRALIA
Christmas Island (Australian)
IV
V
VI
I
II
III
VII
VIII
IX
X
XI
A
B
0
200
400
Miles
95°
100°
105°
110°
115°
120°
125°
130°
135°
140°
5°
95°E
0°
5°
10°
PROVINCES OF 1950
I DJAWA BARAT
II DJAWA TENGAH
III DJAWA TIMUR
IV SUMATERA UTARA
V SUMATERA TENGAH
VI SUMATERA SELATAN
VII KALIMANTAN
VIII SULAWESI
IX MALUKU
X NUSA TENGGARU
XI IRIAN BARAT
A METROPOLITAN AREA
B SPECIAL AREA
TERRITORY UNDER NETHERLANDS ADMINISTRATION BUT CLAIMED BY BOTH NETHERLANDS AND INDONESIA.
FOREIGN TERRITORY
INTERNATIONAL BOUNDARIES
PROVINCIAL BOUNDARIES 1950
NOTE
BOUNDARIES AT SEA ARE DRAWN TO INCLUDE OUTLYING ISLANDS.
ON INDONESIA'S CLAIMS AT SEA, SEE PAGE 379

FIG. 54—Indonesia: major administrative divisions, 1950

This rather curious dualism is symbolic of the conflict which is felt in some measure by all the new national states of South-east Asia. For while in part the nationalist movements arise out of a wish to return to the traditional way of life represented by the old indigenous capitals, they are also motivated by a desire to step into the shoes of the former colonial powers, and to maintain under Asian direction all the panoply of a 20th-century state which the Europeans had established in the great port cities on the coasts.

And in fact, while formally decrying what the Dutch have created, the Indonesian nationalist leaders seem bent on perpetuating many of its most characteristic features. Thus the new unitary administrative pattern established since 1950 was as markedly centralized in Djakarta as the pre-war Netherlands Indies government had been,[10] and the ten provincial areas (*propinsi*) into which the country was divided were clearly modelled on the purely arbitrary divisions of the same era. Indeed in Java, apart from the two special areas already noted, the pre-war division into West, Centre and East remained virtually unaltered,[11] while in the outer territories the new provinces were mere assemblages of former Dutch administrative sub-divisions which likewise took no account of the indigenous linguistic or historical groupings.

Despite these resemblances to the pre-war Dutch administrative pattern, however, the new unitary form of government was initially approved of by most sections of politically conscious opinion within the country. Since the Dutch remained in possession of West Irian,[12] many Indonesians feared that they might actively support the dissident South Moluccan Republic next door and even, if a suitable pretext arose, seek by this means to overthrow the Indonesian Republic itself. Thus too much local initiative could prove disastrous, and while it was understood that some measure of provincial autonomy would be granted in due course, there might be a positive advantage in retaining a provincial pattern which so completely flouted traditional cultural divisions as to give scant opportunity for the growth of regional loyalties. Furthermore, the acute shortage of experienced Indonesian administrators made it impossible to fill the much larger number of governmental posts which a federal system would entail, and it was felt that the national interest demanded the concentration of the best available talent at the centre.

Nevertheless, during the years that have followed, the validity of these arguments has been increasingly questioned as experience has seemed to vindicate Colijn's prophecy, and the growing demand of the provinces for a much greater

[10] See Finkelstein, pp. 286–7.

[11] Except that Surakarta was absorbed into Central Java. Note that the three *propinsi* do not correspond with the three-fold linguistic division between Sundanese, Javanese and Madurese. On the assumption that there has been no significant change in the overall distribution of these three groups since 1930, Javanese form 16 per cent of the population of the West (where 75 per cent are Sundanese), 98 per cent of the Centre, and 70 per cent of the East (where Madurese account for 29 per cent).

[12] Irian is the Indonesian name for New Guinea. See below, Chapter 12.

TABLE 43

INDONESIA: POPULATION, 1954 AND 1959

Administrative area *		*Population*		*Density per sq. mile*
English name	*Indonesian name*	1954	1959	1959
West Java	Djawa/Barat	15,100,000	16 500,000	923
Greater Djakarta	Djakarta Raja	2,700,000	2,800,000	12,950
Central Java	Djawa Tengah	15,800,000	17,600,000	1,333
Jogjakarta	Djokjakarta	2,200,000	2,100,000	1,717
East Java	Djawa Timur	18,400,000	20,600,000	1,113
All Java		54,200,000	59,600,000	1,168
North Sumatra	Sumatera Utara	4,900,000	n.a.	n.a.
Central Sumatra	Sumatera Tengah	3,800,000	n.a.	n.a.
South Sumatra	Sumatera Selatan	3,200,000	n.a.	n.a.
All Sumatra		11,900,000	14,600,000	80
Borneo	Kalimantan	3,700,000	3,900,000	18
Celebes	Sulawesi	6,200,000	6,800,000	93
Moluccas	Maluku	1,800,000	900,000	28
South-east Islands (former Lesser Sundas)	Nusa Tenggaru (Sunda Ketjil)	5,300,000	5,900,000	207
Total Outer Islands	Tanah Sabrang	27,900,000	32,100,000	62
Total Indonesia	Indonesia	82,100,000	91,700,000	158

* All of these are provinces except Djakarta Raja (metropolitan area) and Djokjakarta (special area).

measure of autonomy has become one of the two major issues in contemporary Indonesian politics.

Even more fundamental than, though in fact closely related to this has been the question of what is to constitute the unifying force or *raison d'être* of the new state now that the struggle for independence has been brought to a successful conclusion. For, despite President Sukarno's recourse to what he chooses to call the 'science of geopolitics'[13] it does not follow that mere geographical propinquity and a common desire not to be ruled by the Dutch afford any very compelling reason for the several islands of Indonesia to remain together as a single political unit.

IV. THE BASES OF NATIONAL UNITY

Clearly the historical argument is of very limited validity. The Indies were not a united country when, little by little, the Dutch extended their rule over them between the 17th and the 20th centuries. And although the Indonesian govern-

[13] Sukarno, pp. 11–17.

ment, which is understandably loath to admit that the country's unity derives in any meaningful sense from the Dutch,[14] has gone back still further and invoked the unity – real or mythological – under Madjapahit, by taking the *garuda* bird as the national emblem and the device *Bhinneka Tunggal Ika* as the national motto, [15] this symbolism cannot be pressed very far without giving rise to awkward questions about Javanese dominance.

On the other hand there is a firm substratum of cultural unity, embodied notably in the local *adat* and in the use of closely related Malayo-Polynesian languages throughout a wide area, which corresponds roughly, if by no means identically, with the present national territory of Indonesia. And in promoting the use of *Bahasa Indonesia*, a modernized and Romanized form of Bazaar Malay, the Indonesian nationalists have begun to give a new meaning to these ancient cultural ties within the country.

The deliberate propagation of *Bahasa Indonesia* as a national language began in the early 1930s though, as noted in Chapter 8, the old basic Malay as used in Malacca had already been serving as a commercial *lingua franca* for hundreds of years prior to that date. Partly because it is easy to learn and closely related to the main regional languages spoken within the archipelago, and partly because the teaching of Dutch was far too restricted for the latter to serve as the normal medium among the educated classes in the way that English did in India, this basic Malay came into common use during the inter-war years as a medium of communication among the small but growing Indonesian middle class, concentrated in Batavia and the other large towns of Java, but drawn to a considerable extent from various parts of the outer territories as well as from Java itself.[16] This practice led naturally to some attempts at standardization, and in order to emphasize the potential rôle of this modified Malay as the common language of the whole country the nationalists called it *Bahasa Indonesia*, that is, Indonesian language. During the Japanese occupation *Bahasa Indonesia* replaced Dutch as the main official language for day-to-day administration, both in the towns and the countryside, and eventually the proclamation of independence was made in it.

[14] Though, as noted below, p. 394, this is the main basis of the Indonesian claim to West Irian.

[15] These words, which are taken from the *Sutasoma*, a Javanese poem of the Madjapahit period, mean 'unity in diversity'. In the early days of the republic's existence the similarity between this motto and the U.S.A.'s '*E pluribus unum*' was frequently commented upon, and some observers even suspected a family resemblance between the *garuda* bird (the legendary steed of the Hindu god Vishnu, used as a symbol by Madjapahit) and the American eagle.

[16] Wertheim (C), p. 294. As noted on p. 264, Malay has for centuries been the standard speech of the Djakartan (Batavian) community. It may also be noted in passing that the absence of any widespread education in a major Western language helped to isolate the Indonesian nationalists from the main currents of both Western and Asian political thinking throughout the Dutch period, and it is significant that since independence English has replaced Dutch as the first foreign language taught in Indonesian schools. *Cf.* the Chinese attitude on this matter, above, p. 268, note 69.

Although the number of people who speak *Bahasa Indonesia* is still exceeded by the 35–40 million or so whose mother tongue is Javanese, the character of the latter as a regional language and its complex and highly inflected structure combine to make it much less suitable for general use, and for this reason the government's bold decision to adopt *Bahasa Indonesia* as the official language from the very outset of the new regime was politically sound. Nevertheless, the lack of well established literary traditions hitherto in *Bahasa Indonesia* means that it is at present a rather imprecise instrument, and much attention still needs to be given to rationalizing its spelling and grammar, and extending its vocabulary to include new terms needed by administrators, scholars and technologists.[17]

In the meantime, therefore, the lack of precision involved in the use of this relatively undeveloped medium by officials and others, whose own knowledge of it is often far from perfect, has contributed to the decline in efficiency throughout the country at large. But providing that this is only a temporary phase, the price is probably well worth paying, and it is encouraging to note that the government has coupled its drive for the use of *Bahasa Indonesia* with a nationwide literacy campaign directed towards the adult as well as the juvenile population. As yet the results of the latter are difficult to assess, and although is has been claimed that 65 per cent of the Indonesian people are now literate, as compared with 4 per cent in 1942, only a small percentage of the total population are as yet accustomed to read a daily newspaper whether in *Bahasa Indonesia* or in any other language.[18]

In the long run the contribution which *Bahasa Indonesia* may be expected to make to the cause of national unity should be immense, and, however much one may relish the rich cultural diversity enshrined in the old regional languages, there can be no doubt that the increased range of inter-communication which the new language brings represents a real social advance in accord with the realities of a shrinking world. But for the present a majority of villagers, and probably of all Indonesians, still use the regional languages, and it will take at least another decade or two before these are wholly replaced by *Bahasa Indonesia*.

For the time being, therefore, some other bond of unity is required, and in these circumstances the suitability or otherwise of the Muslim religion to provide that link has become a subject of national controversy.

With some 75 million, or over 80 per cent of its total population, professing at least nominal allegiance to the Shafi'i sect of Islam,[19] Indonesia contains the greatest single concentration of Muslims in the world. But while a large proportion of these advocate the setting up of an Islamic state in one form or another, this concept is strongly opposed by numerous other Indonesians, including many Muslims, who favour a secular state, ostensibly for the reasons expressed by President Sukarno:

[17] See Moerdowo, pp. 22 and 35; Alisjahbana, pp. 388–92; and Wertheim (C), p. 294.

[18] The total daily newspaper circulation in September 1955 was only 821,560. Feith (B), p. 24, but Mintz now puts it at 3 million, *op. cit.*, pp. 110–111 and 114.

[19] One of the four Sunni sects.

'If we erect a state based on Islam many regions whose people are not Muslim will secede, for example: the Moluccas, Bali, Flores, Timor, Kai, Celebes. And West Irian which is not yet within Indonesia will not wish to form part of the republic.'[20]

Yet there is here a curious paradox, in that this wider secular view, which seeks to be acceptable to all parts of the country, in fact commands a much smaller range of support geographically than that of the avowedly narrower Islamic view. The key to this anomaly lies in the wide regional variations in the intensity of the traditional attachment to Islam, and in the related variations in the reponse to the Western challenge especially during the past sixty or seventy years.

For the reasons already considered in Chapter 8, Islam is generally most firmly entrenched in the more accessible parts of the western two-thirds of the archipelago, but within that area it is the Atjehnese, Menangkabaus, Sundanese and Bandjarese who are its staunchest devotees, while the Javanese, though nominally Muslim, are characteristically less orthodox in their beliefs.

This equivocal attitude of the Javanese towards Islam is particularly evident in *kraton*[21] circles in Djokjakarta and Surakarta, where strict adherence to the faith is usually frowned upon, and greater significance is accorded to Javanese tradition and culture. An essential aspect of the latter, which distinguishes it from that of all the other islands (except Bali) has been the elaborate hierarchical structure of society, and to an important extent this has been preserved by the former Dutch practice of giving to many members of the aristocracy a formal status, as regents and subordinate officials, in the colonial administration.[22]

On the other hand commerce played only a very minor rôle in the essentially self-contained agrarian economy of medieval Java, and the fact that Muhammad himself had been a trader did little to break down the traditional contempt in which this occupation was held by the Javanese. Thus the most favoured means of social and economic advancement among them has been to enter government service,[23] and though until the beginning of the present century such opportunities were virtually limited to the aristocracy, the subsequent extension of higher educational facilities to Indonesians gradually opened the door to commoners as well. And, since both higher education and the administrative machine itself were markedly centralized in Java, the inhabitants of that island had much greater opportunities for governmental employment than were generally available in the outer territories.

Similarly it is Java, with its numerous towns and large European population,

[20] From a speech made on January 27, 1953. Quoted in Palmier (D), p. 110.

[21] The *kratons* (courts) were the supreme centres of religious worship in the Hindu-Javanese system.

[22] As implied above, note 9, this practice was carried much further in Djokjakarta and Surakarta than elsewhere. For fuller discussion of the effects of cultural change on the growth of nationalism see Wertheim (C), Van der Kroef (C) and Feith (B).

[23] Palmier (D), p. 102.

which has been the main centre for the dissemination of new and socially disruptive ideas, while at the same time the intense pressure of population in its rural districts has resulted in a much greater degree of landlessness and poverty there than in most of the outer islands.

For all these reasons Java today exhibits much the widest range of socio-economic diversity, and in this connexion at least four main groups may be recognized. First and very powerful is the governmental group, which has expanded to over five times its pre-war strength mainly by the recruitment of hordes of often very superficially educated young men, predominantly of Javanese origin. Nevertheless, in general outlook these are still much influenced by the aristocratic governmental élite or *pryayi*, especially the Djokjakarta element, and their allegiance to Islam is apt to take second place to their belief in Java as the supreme repository of Indonesian culture.

At the other end of the traditional scale is the great mass of the Javanese peasantry, until recently little affected by outside currents of thought, but nevertheless growingly resentful of the poverty in their overcrowded countryside. Because of their inferior social status the peasantry have absorbed the Hindu-Javanese culture in a more dilute form than that which prevails among the nobility, so that, especially in those areas most distant both from the *kraton* centres and from the modern coastal towns, the influence of the old-style Muslim teachers remains strong.[24]

Thirdly there is the large and rapidly growing group who have been driven by land hunger to become casual workers, estate coolies or urban wage labourers, and are apt to display the typical characteristics of a deracinated and impoverished proletariat. And now that this group is at last becoming literate its potential importance politically is growing rapidly.

Finally there are those who, with greater enterprise than the rest, have broken most completely with established Javanese traditions by seeking advancement through commerce and the professions, in both of which they have in the past had to face severe competition from the already entrenched Europeans and Chinese. While the professional element has necessarily obtained a Western-style education, the larger commercial and land-owning group are more obviously self-made men, often with little formal schooling but much innate ability. It is from this group, whose native Islamic faith has been little influenced by either *kraton* traditions or Western education, but who have nevertheless been forced through day-to-day contact with the Western scale of values to reconsider the relevance of their traditional beliefs, that the main drive for Islamic reform has come. Outstanding in this respect has been the Muhammadiyah movement[25] which, rejecting asceticism and fatalism as outmoded, has sought to emulate the social-reformist practices of Western Christianity, and to reconcile the teachings of the Koran with the everyday demands of life in a modern state.

[24] Van der Kroef (D), pp. 16 and 17.

[25] See Wertheim (C), p. 208, and Palmier (A), pp. 255–62.

In the outer territories, which under both pre-European and colonial rule were essentially provincial in character, the pattern of social stratification remains less complex. Thus, except in Bali, Hindu influence was far less deeply rooted, and although in many areas the old territorial chieftains were confirmed in power by the Dutch, their numbers were fewer and the socio-religious cleavage between rulers and ruled was much narrower than in east-central Java. Thus nothing really comparable with the Javanese *pryayi* class exists in the outer territories, and a high proportion of the abler young men who have sought to enter government service and the professions have found it necessary to go to Java, both for training and for subsequent employment. On the other hand, outside the Javanese lands there is little or no traditional antipathy to commerce, and many peoples such as the Atjehnese and Menangkabaus enjoy a deservedly high reputation as traders. Moreover, owing to the extensive development of small-holder cultivation, especially in Sumatra, Borneo and Celebes, there is more ready cash there than in the congested rural districts of Java.

In short, in most parts of the outer territories contact with the West is of a more superficial nature and has generally entailed a far less drastic undermining of the traditional social order than has occurred in the Javanese lands. For this reason the main differences in outlook within the outer territories are between the relatively prosperous, who usually favour continued modernization, and the less successful, who tend to blame Westernization for their difficulties and hence hanker after a return to traditional ways of life. Except, therefore, in the specifically Hindu, Christian or pagan areas, this difference is still expressed largely within the Islamic framework, in the rivalry between reformists and old-style believers.[26]

However, outside the areas of subsistence agriculture and small-holder cash-crop cultivation, there are a few centres where Westernization has produced much more sweeping changes, notably in the Cultuurgebied and the larger oil-fields. Among the masses of low-paid workers there, a condition of deracination comparable to that in the Javanese cities is found, and indeed a high proportion of these wage labourers in the outer territories are themselves of Javanese origin. But as yet the proletarian element in the outer islands, with their paucity of cities and modern transport, is numerically very small, and this is perhaps the most important of all the socio-economic contrasts between them and Java at the present time.

In respect of contemporary social and religious patterns, western Java once again occupies an intermediate position between the outer territories and the Javanese lands proper. For while in urbanization and in rural overcrowding,[27] both of which are directly or indirectly the outcome of the Dutch connexion,

[26] See Feith (B), p. 33 *et seq.*

[27] The average density of population in West Java (including Djakarta) is 1,061 per square mile, compared with 1,365 in Central Java (including Djokjakarta), and 1,113 in East Java. In purely rural density the difference between West Java and the rest of the island is rather greater than these figures suggest. See the 1930 figures shown in Table 22.

the area more nearly resembles the rest of the island, the indigenous traditions of western Java dating from pre-colonial times have more in common with those of the outer territories. And this applies not only to the intensely Muslim Sundanese, whose hostility to the Javanese is proverbial, but also to the so-called Djakartan population which has been drawn more from the various outlying islands than from Java itself. Moreover, the economic position of West Java as both a rice-surplus area and by far the most important rubber-producer of Java, makes for a relatively higher standard of living there than in the Centre and East.[28]

V. THE GEOGRAPHY OF PARTY POLITICS

The various strands of opinion within the Muslim four-fifths of Indonesia are reflected in major political differences, and indeed since practically the whole of the Indonesian population tends to equate capitalism with colonialism and hence favours an avowedly socialist economic policy it is primarily along socio-religious lines that the post-war party divisions have arisen.[29]

Among the parties explicitly based on Islam, Masjumi was much the largest, and in the elections of 1955 ran a close second to the Nationalist Party (P.N.I.)[30] in the total number of votes which it received. With its nucleus drawn from the new commercial and largely urban group and reinforced by many of the more prosperous elements in the countryside of Indonesia as a whole, Masjumi was modernist and only mildly socialistic in outlook, though it derived much support from the more conservative Muslims as well. In advocating that the state should be founded on Islamic but not theocratic principles, Masjumi may be regarded as a political expression of the ideology represented by Muhammadiyah.[31] As Fig. 55 shows, it enjoyed much the widest range of support geographically, being generally in the lead in nearly all the Muslim areas of the outer territories as also in western Java, including Djakarta itself. Moreover, although it ranked only fourth among the parties in east-central Java, it nevertheless obtained over 25 per cent of its votes there, mostly in the towns and the villages nearest to them.[32]

A second major current of Muslim opinion, that of the extremist Darul Islam,[33]

[28] Fryer (D), p. 203.

[29] Since Indonesia inherited the Dutch addiction to both proportional representation and confessional politics, the number of parties which have emerged is very large. All-told 28 different parties or factions were represented in the first elected parliament (*i.e.* after 1955) though only 10 of these won more than two seats. Feith (B), pp. 58–9.

[30] The strength of the four main parties in 1955 was: P.N.I. 8,434,653 votes and 57 seats; Masjumi 7,903,886 votes and 57 seats; N.U. 6,955,141 votes and 45 seats; P.K.I. 6,176,914 votes and 39 seats. Feith (B), p. 58. All election figures quoted below are from this source. These are the only parliamentary elections that have so far been held in Indonesia, and the results are of great interest to the political geographer. However, since the constitutional changes of 1959/60 (see below, note 68) the figures quoted no longer represent the distribution of seats in the Indonesian parliament, and the Masjumi and Socialist parties have both been dissolved.

[31] Though there is no formal connexion between the two. See Palmier (A), pp. 255–62.

[32] Feith (B), p. 32.

[33] For a fuller account of Darul Islam see Van Nieuwenhuize (A).

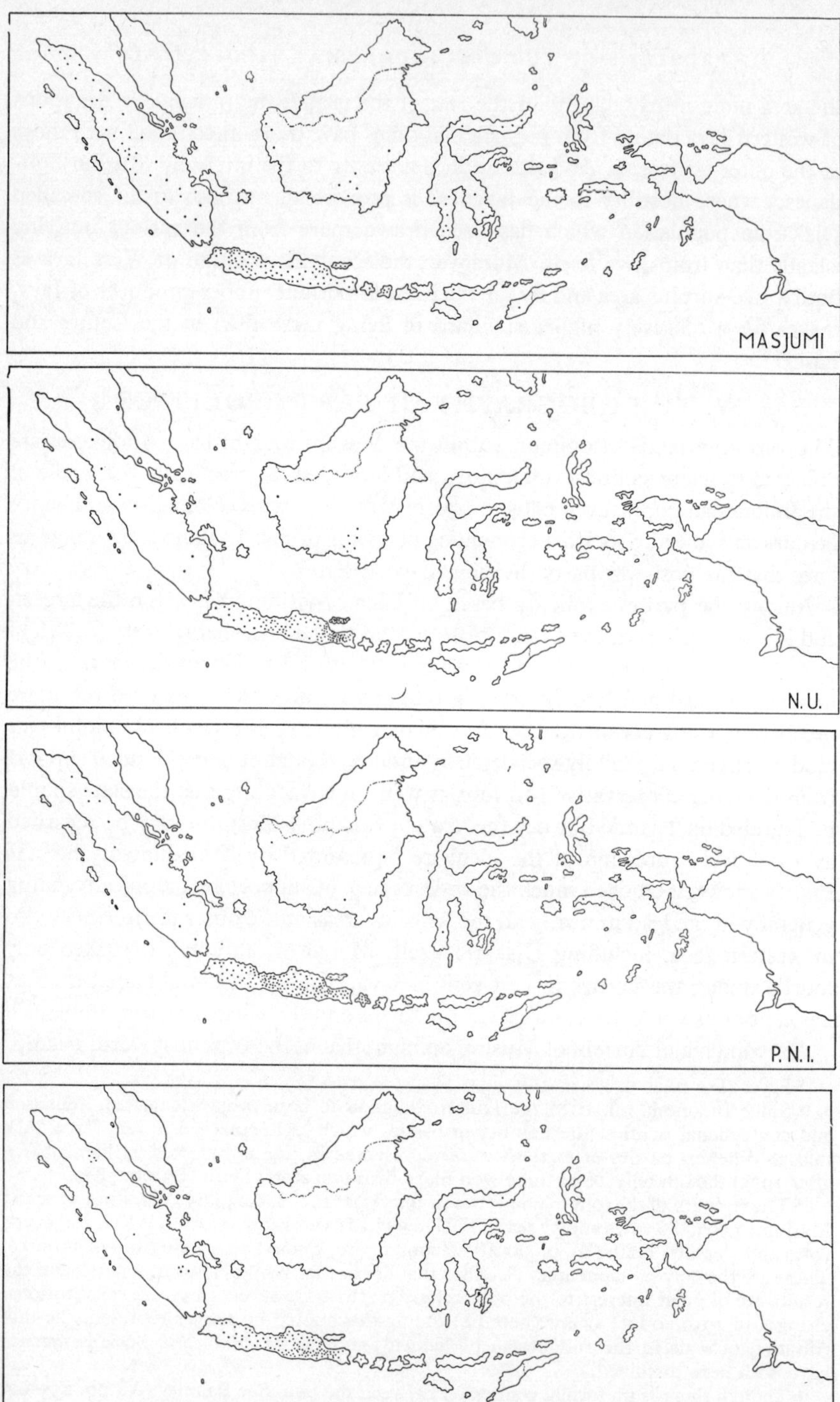

FIG. 55—Indonesia: strength of political parties in 1955 elections.
Each dot represents 50,000 votes

likewise draws its support essentially from the outer islands and western Java, though within these areas its main strength is limited to a few localities with serious grievances, economic or otherwise, to wit the Sundanese districts around Bandung, Atjeh and parts of southern Celebes and southern Borneo. In all of these places it has for several years pursued active guerrilla warfare, at the total cost of thousands of lives and immense material damage. Moreover, it is probable that the movement, which advocates the extension of its own strict theocratic state over the whole of Indonesia, enjoys the tacit support of many of the less contented Muslims in other areas as well, though since it is outside the law and hence did not contest the elections, the precise extent of its following is uncertain.

The other major Islamic party is the Nahdatul Ulama (N.U.) or Muslim Teachers' Party, which is by contrast almost exclusively Javanese. Depending for its support overwhelmingly on the peasantry of east-central Java, N.U. is at once economically radical and doctrinally conservative, a combination which reflects the opposition of the old-style Islamic schoolmen of the Javanese villages to the economic and spiritual leadership of the urban and land-owning middle-class Muslims as represented by Masjumi. In the 1955 elections N.U. emerged as the third largest party in the country, though outside Java it obtained almost negligible support, except in those parts of southern Sumatra with large numbers of Javanese transmigrants.

In contrast to these and various other minor Muslim groups,[34] all of which advocate the establishment of an Islamic state of one kind or another, the remaining parties all explicitly favour a secular state. Among these, for obvious reasons, are the Christian minority parties, namely the Protestant Parkindo and the Catholic Party,[35] whose support comes almost entirely from the scattered areas in the outer territories where a high proportion of the population has adopted one or other form of Christianity. Despite the secessionist aims of the erstwhile South Moluccan Republic, most of these peoples now seem to be loyal supporters of the Indonesian republic, though they would certainly view the establishment of an Islamic state with real concern.

Much the most important of the secular parties hitherto however, has been the P.N.I., which carries on the tradition of the pre-war party of the same name, whose leader was Dr. Sukarno, and it generally supports the policies which he advocates, despite the fact that as President he is now above party politics.

In rejecting Islam as the basis of the Indonesian state, allegedly for the reasons given by Dr. Sukarno,[36] the P.N.I. has put in its place the latter's now famous *Pantja Sila*, first enunciated in June 1945. When it is recalled that these five

[34] The largest of these, the Islamic Association Party, ranked fifth with 1,091,160 votes and 8 seats.

[35] Parkindo, with 1,003,325 votes and 8 seats, and Partai Katolik (R.C.) with 770,740 votes and 6 seats, came respectively sixth and seventh. Sjahrir's Socialist Party came eighth.

[36] See above, p. 370.

principles (nationalism, humanism, democracy, social justice and belief in God) which bear an obvious resemblance to Sun Yat-sen's *San Min Chu I*,[37] were propounded by a professing Muslim of mixed Javanese/Balinese parentage who claims to admire 'what is positive in all great men, whether it is Jesus Christ, Marx or Adolf Hitler',[38] it may not be fanciful to conclude that they constitute a contemporary example of the characteristic syncretism which has for centuries been the hallmark of Javanese thought. And certainly the nucleus of the P.N.I.'s support is to be found in the predominantly governmental group, together with other members of the new Indonesian middle class, particularly in the towns of east-central Java.[39]

Since this group has only been able to rise to its present position by ousting the former Dutch personnel from their posts, its hostility to the Dutch is particularly strong. And since the vagueness of the *Pantja Sila* renders them somewhat ineffectual as a rallying force, the P.N.I. has resorted to the simple tactics of artificially prolonging the struggle against the Dutch as a means of winning popular support. In the event this has taken the form of endlessly reiterating Indonesia's claim to West New Guinea, and insisting on the need to complete the 'unfinished revolution' by 'breaking the Dutch monopoly in trade and finance'.[40]

While these policies elicit an almost instinctive response in many parts of Java, where resentment of Dutch rule is deep-seated, their appeal in the outer territories, most of which came under effective Dutch rule only during the relatively enlightened liberal era since 1870, is altogether weaker. Thus P.N.I. suppor in the outer territories is very small except among the Hindu Balinese, and to a lesser extent the various Christian minorities, and in the plantation and mining districts.

Finally, among the major non-Islamic parties is the Communist P.K.I., which follows the orthodox Moscow line and came fourth in the 1955 elections. Led by a group of urban intellectuals and obtaining its strongest support from the impoverished proletariat in general and the trade unions in particular, the P.K.I. is in fact the most Java-centred of all, and the 11·4 per cent of its votes which were won outside that island came mostly from the Cultuurgebied and the Palembang oilfields. This very close correspondence between the areas supporting the P.K.I. and those supporting P.N.I. is not accidental. For all the main P.N.I. policies, anti-Westernism, secularism, and centralized state planning, are also advocated, in a more intense form, by the P.K.I. And with mounting economic distress the P.K.I. stands to gain at the expense of the P.N.I. not only

[37] *I.e.* the 'three principles of the people', viz. nationalism, democracy and people's livelihood. Sukarno, *op. cit.*, pp. 11–17, makes repeated reference to *San Min Chu I*.

[38] Quoted in Mende, p. 86.

[39] The P.N.I's obsession with nationalization may be partly motivated by the desire to provide bureaucratic employment for the growing number of university graduates. Palmier (D), p. 117.

[40] See the remarks of Premier Ali Sastroamidjojo, quoted by Josey, *op. cit.* p. 23.

in the towns, but also in the countryside of Java, as the 1957 provincial elections showed in no uncertain way.[41]

VI. JAVA VERSUS THE OUTER TERRITORIES

From the foregoing analysis it can be seen that the main Indonesian parties are roughly evenly divided between those which favour and those which oppose some form of Islamic state. On the other major political issue, that of centralization versus greater regional autonomy, an equally strong division exists, but here the difference is between the parties whose main strength lies in Java, namely the P.N.I., P.K.I. and N.U., which for obvious reasons wish the central government to retain the maximum possible measure of control over the outer territories, and those whose support comes predominantly from the latter areas, namely Masjumi and the two Christian parties, which deeply resent the Javanese domination which this policy has come to imply.

This doubly divided state of political opinion, coupled with the fact that no single party has ever commanded a majority, soon reduced government to a matter of ever-shifting coalitions, which perforce confined their activities to tinkering with the country's problems instead of devising and putting into effect long-term plans for their solution. In practice this meant that successive governments, which during the 1950s became increasingly dominated by the P.N.I., concerned themselves almost exclusively with stop-gap measures to meet the problem which lay most immediately to hand, namely the growing poverty and unemployment in the metropolitan island. And in these circumstances the outer territories have been deprived not only of the various development projects described in Chapter 10, but even of urgently needed funds for rehabilitation, education and medical services.

This state of affairs has inevitably revived the latent hostility of the outer territories against the Javanese in general and the Djakarta government in particular. And such resentment is intensified by the fact that since independence, to a greater extent than ever before, it is the outer territories which have provided the bulk of the country's resources.

Thus in 1955–6 approximately 71 per cent of Indonesia's foreign-exchange earnings came from Sumatran exports, and a further 17 per cent from those of the rest of the outer territories, yet over 80 per cent of these were spent on purchasing consumer and capital goods, food and raw materials for the population of Java.

The dissatisfaction of the outer territories regarding this treatment first came to a head in 1956/7,[42] after the national elections had failed to break the political

[41] In the provincial and municipal elections of 1957 the P.K.I. emerged as the strongest party in East and Central Java, and even in Djakarta jumped from fourth to second place.

[42] There had been many earlier indications of such dissatisfaction, *e.g.* the protests in Minahasa about the policy of Jajasan Kopra. See above, p. 321, note 23; for further details see also Fryer (D).

deadlock. Thus, on December 20, 1956 the Military Commander of Central Sumatra announced that he had taken over full control of that area, which he was administering with the help of a council of army officers. Henceforth only 30 per cent of the local revenues would be allowed to go to Java, the remainder being retained for expenditure on schools, hospitals, roads and irrigation works within the region. This action was followed by similar moves successively in North and South Sumatra, East Indonesia and Borneo,[43] and on March 14, 1957, President Sukarno declared martial law throughout the country.

While the action of the military commanders was partly the outcome of disputes within the army itself, the fact remains that, because of its strong local roots, the Indonesian national army commands general support in the regions and there is no doubt that the action of the military appeared fully to accord with local civilian wishes. Nevertheless, this action did not represent a move for secession on the part of any of the outer territories, whose only desires were to achieve greater provincial autonomy and to put a stop to the corruption and inefficiency of the central government.

However, instead of seeking to solve these problems, Sukarno attempted to divert attention from them, first by setting up a National Advisory Council to 'guide' Indonesian democracy,[44] and secondly by intensifying the demand for West New Guinea. And in December 1957, after Indonesia had failed to get a United Nations resolution in its favour on the New Guinea question, the government took drastic vindictive measures against the remaining Dutch interests and citizens within the country.

Thus all Dutch businesses and plantations were seized, the K.P.M.'s licence was cancelled and the K.L.M.'s contract with Garuda Indonesian Airlines terminated, and all Dutch citizens were told to leave the country, except for a few

[43] By the middle of 1957 Central and South Sumatra and North Celebes had achieved *de facto* autonomy. There were also indications of unrest in the Sundanese districts of West Java.

[44] In part 'guided democracy' was Sukarno's riposte to the demand for an upper house giving greater regional representation. The National Advisory Council which was set up in 1957 consisted mainly of representatives of 'functional groups' (such as trade unions, youth movements, religious leaders, foreign-born citizens, etc.) sitting together with members of the Cabinet, the armed forces and members from various islands, but despite the last named it gave very little weight to specifically regional representation. Moreover, Sukarno tried at the same time to set up what he called a *gotong rojong* Cabinet, in which *all* parties would be represented in proportion to their numbers in Parliament. This proposal was abandoned because of most of the other parties' opposition to the inclusion of P.K.I. representatives in the Cabinet. While it would certainly have had this effect, Sukarno justified his proposed Cabinet as being rooted in the indigenous traditions of *gotong rojong* (mutual assistance) and *musjawarat desa* (the practice of discussing the problems of the village until a solution acceptable to everyone is reached). Thus he claimed that it represented a truly Indonesian form of democracy, though the Westerner may be permitted to wonder whether the procedures of village administration have much relevance to the running of a state of over 90 million people, and indeed whether any major national issue would ever be resolved at all under such a system.

key personnel listed as experts, who were ordered to remain.[45] Though the government claimed that the seizure of Dutch enterprises was undertaken in order to protect them from damage by the populace, it subsequently announced that no compensation would be paid until the Dutch government agreed to re-open discussions on the status of West New Guinea.

Moreover on December 13, 1957, the Indonesian government proclaimed territorial rights over all the seas around and between the country's 3,000 islands, within an outer limit of 12 nautical miles 'measured from straight base lines connecting the outermost points of the islands'. Taken literally, this claim extended right to the southern shore of the Malay peninsula and placed Singapore island within Indonesian territorial waters, though in advancing it, the Indonesians were primarily concerned to obtain supposedly legal rights to intercept Dutch shipping *en route* for West New Guinea.[46]

In the event these various acts by the Djakarta government have damaged the Indonesian economy even more than they have penalized the Dutch, and once again the outer territories were particularly hard hit. Accordingly, in February 1958 a group of dissident military and political leaders, who had gathered together in Padang (Central Sumatra), issued an ultimatum demanding that the existing central government be replaced by a new one under the premiership of former Vice-President Hatta.[47]

When this ultimatum was rejected, the rebel leaders, with the support of the two provinces of Central Sumatra and North Celebes,[48] set up their own provisional government for the whole of Indonesia, with its capital at Padang. But despite the considerable political stature of some of its members, the rebel government possessed few other assets. Thus, after a few weeks of fighting, the central government's forces succeeded in bringing organized resistance to an end in the two rebel provinces, and though guerrilla activity continued in both for some time, the central government had fairly effectively reasserted its authority by 1961. In the interests of all Indonesians it must be hoped that the threatened disintegration of the state may now be averted.

[45] See above, pp. 310–11. As of December 1957 there were at least 8,500 Dutch-born residents with jobs in Indonesia and a total such population, with dependants, of about 25,000. This total (which does not include Eurasians) was reduced in the year which followed to about 5,000 and has since dwindled even further. On the accompanying exodus of Eurasians, see below, p. 386, note 59.

[46] In the present confusion over maritime limits there is no general admission of this claim. Meanwhile the Indonesian government has declared that it will guarantee the peaceful passage of foreign ships through the archipelago so long as they do not threaten its security. But it is not clear how these terms would be interpreted if, in the event of a crisis, Australian or New Zealand naval units sought to cross the zone in support of their S.E.A.T.O. partners Thailand and the Philippines.

[47] Hatta is a Sumatran Muslim, well known for his opposition to the P.K.I., and he commands great respect in the outer territories.

[48] *I.e.* the homelands of the Menangkabaus and the Menadonese respectively. It is noteworthy that these two peoples had the highest literacy rate in the whole country in colonial times. See *Atlas van Tropisch Nederland*, Plate 9 A.

So far as Java's dependence on the outer territories is concerned the facts cited on page 377 speak for themselves. No doubt the policy of concentrating the manufacture of consumer goods as far as possible in the metropolitan island, with its greater technical facilities and its superabundance of cheap labour, would be in the long-term interests of the country as a whole, providing, first that the outer territories *per contra* get the lion's share of the processing industries, and secondly that the goods manufactured in Java for sale in the outer territories are worthy competitors of foreign imports, a state of affairs which has not obtained of late.[49] Thus, were the outer territories entirely free to purchase where they chose, Java would certainly lose much of its present sales of consumer goods, with consequent aggravation of its acute unemployment problem, though this would be vastly exceeded by the volume of redundancy in the transport, clerical and administrative sectors if Java were to cease to be the centre of government of the country as a whole. In short, Java without the outer territories would be like a head without a body, and it is difficult to see how its present population of 60 million could continue to survive on what the island could provide if left purely to its own resources.

But the importance of Java to the outer territories is little less fundamental. On all grounds Java is the obvious focus for both the inter-island shipping and airways systems, and even if alternative sea- and airport capacity could eventually be made available elsewhere, it would be impossible to hold the rest of the archipelago together as a single state, separate from and therefore opposed by Java, which is in a position completely to dominate the vital Java Sea.

Geographically, Java remains the keystone of the Indonesian arch and, were it to be removed, the country would almost certainly fall apart into a series of separate island states. While the larger of these, such as Sumatra and perhaps also Borneo and Celebes, might be economically better off on their own than they have been as *de facto* satellites of Java, they would nevertheless be only minor powers in their own right. As by far the largest state in the vast political marchland between India and China, Indonesia, were it to be effectively united, might play a major rôle in international affairs. This indeed has already been foreshadowed in the Afro-Asian Conference at Bandung in 1955, but the prestige which Indonesia as a whole derived from this event could scarcely be inherited by any of its potential successor states if the republic were to disintegrate in the manner referred to above.

It is, however, possible to envisage some other pattern of political grouping within at least part of the archipelago. Thus, instead of Java, the maritime crossroads where the Malacca Straits meet the South China Sea might again provide a focus of political power, and some form of closer association between the western islands of Indonesia and the Malay peninsula, in effect a sort of modern Sri Vijaya, is not as fanciful as it might seem.

Ever since 1945 there has been a significant body of unofficial Malay

[49] See Fryer (D), p. 202.

nationalist feeling in favour of a political link with Indonesia, and though this has been largely motivated by a desire to strengthen the Malays' position *vis-à-vis* the local Chinese,[50] it is also encouraged by the close cultural ties between Malaya, Sumatra and Borneo. Thus the ordinary Malay speech of the peninsula is fundamentally similar to *Bahasa Indonesia,* and the decision to make Islam the state religion in the Federation of Malaya suggests that religion could provide a unifying force for a new Malacca Straits grouping in a way that is ruled out from contemporary Indonesia by the strength of Javanist opposition. Moreover, such a group, free from the burden of supporting Java, while itself controlling over three-quarters of the world's supply of rubber and over half of the tin, as well as petroleum and other produce, would command substantial economic bargaining power.

One great obstacle to such an association, however, is the strength of the Chinese in the Federation of Malaya and their overwhelming predominance in Singapore, which is the supreme commercial focus of the area in question. Notwithstanding the unofficial *Indonesia Raya* movement, which aims ultimately at the incorporation of the entire archipelago within the republic, most Indonesian politicians have until recently been very cautious in their attitude towards closer association with Malaya and British Borneo, partly from a desire to avoid trouble with the British, but also because of deep misgivings about the prospect of more than doubling their country's Chinese population. But if Sumatra and Indonesian Borneo had to choose between subordination to a poverty stricken and communist dominated Java, and membership of a new federation with Malaya and northern Borneo, it is not wholly certain that they would prefer the former.

VII. THE PROSPECTS FOR MAINTAINING THE UNITY OF THE STATE

Nevertheless this choice is at present merely hypothetical, and undoubtedly most Indonesians, however much they may differ on other matters, strongly desire to preserve the unity of their state within its present boundaries. But if this is to be done, some working agreement must be reached on the basic problems of internal organization which have hitherto divided the nationalists from the moderate Muslims, and while one need not assume that P.N.I. any more than Masjumi must survive in its present form, no policy that is unacceptable to either of the great groups of opinion which they have represented is likely to achieve permanent success or for that matter to accord with the ideals of *gotong rojong* and *musjawarat desa.*[51]

Notwithstanding the failure of the 1958 rebellion, the nationalists in general and the Djakarta government in particular have now received clear demonstra-

[50] The total number of Chinese in the Federation of Malaya in 1956 was about 2,300,000, plus a further 920,000 in Singapore and 250,000 in British Borneo. The total number in Indonesia was about 2,500,000. See also below, pp. 386–8 and 684.

[51] See below, page 389, note 68.

tion of the strength of the demand in the outer territories for greater local autonomy, and a thorough refashioning of the governmental structure to give effect to this, perhaps along federal lines, is urgently needed.

In this connexion some modification of provincial boundaries might be desirable, and indeed some such changes have already taken place in response to local demands. Thus in 1956 the central government created the province of Atjeh in an area which had been in a state of chronic unrest since 1953, and shortly afterwards Borneo was split into three new provinces, respectively East, South and West. Further sub-division was also foreshadowed for Central Sumatra, to meet the demands of both Djambi and Riau for separation from the Menangkabau lands, but it was not until August 1957, that is eight months after the autonomous military regime had been set up in Central Sumatra, that this change came into force.[52] Meanwhile in June 1957 the military régime in East Indonesia announced its intention of establishing six separate provinces there, in place of the existing divisions into Celebes, the Moluccas and the Lesser Sundas, and one of the new units, namely North Celebes, was proclaimed shortly afterwards.

In so far as there is a real basis in language, tradition and/or religion for some of these new provinces, and also for others such as Bali which have since been established, their emergence may facilitate the growth of democracy at the regional level within the country. Nevertheless, as reference to Figs. 35 and 36 will show, any system of provinces which attempted rigidly to follow such cultural divisions would be excessively cumbersome, and the great diversity in size and population of the component units would pose further problems of various kinds. Moreover, in view of the growing use of *Bahasa Indonesia*, and the proposed extension of the road network in the interiors of the larger islands, which will ultimately bring about a change from maritime to overland routes as the basis of regional alignments in many areas, any attempt to establish linguistic provinces on the contemporary Indian model would probably be retrograde.

However, as long as the outer territories have cause to be dissatisfied over the extent of Javanese domination, such resentment may well find expression in demands of this kind, and it is thus imperative that agreement should be reached on the crucial matter of the financial relationship between the existing provinces and the central government. Hitherto the provincial claims for control over 70 per cent of the funds earned by their exports have been rejected out of hand by Djakarta, but in the light of the data cited on p. 377 the latter's counter-suggestion of 30 per cent seems hardly less unreasonable.[53]

If in spite of these difficulties a satisfactory basis for greater regional autonomy

[52] See Legge, p. 17 and Van der Kroef (D), p. 18.

[53] Obviously if the central government were to show more interest in development schemes for the outer territories its case for controlling the greater part of the revenues would be strengthened. (See Higgins, Benjamin and Jean, p. 160.) But it is dangerous to assume that demands for greater autonomy, whether at the national or the regional level, are motivated solely by economic considerations, and that is certainly not the case here.

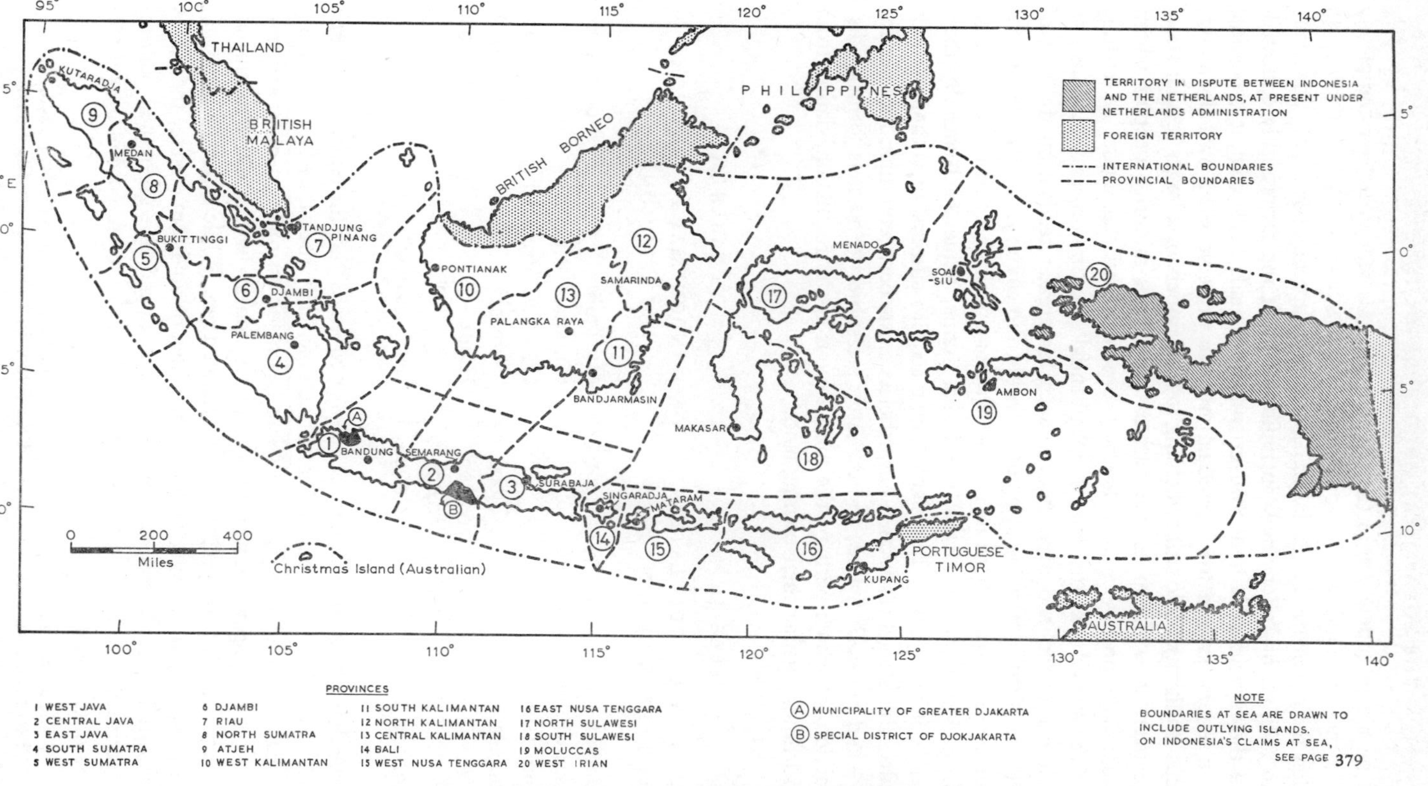

FIG. 56—Indonesia: major administrative divisions, 1960

Note: In August 1962 it was agreed that West New Guinea would come under Indonesian sovereignty on 1st May, 1963.

could be agreed upon before the latent fissiparous tendencies get completely out of hand, it would then become easier for the more moderate Muslims to abandon their demands for an Islamic state, a concept which is clearly unacceptable to millions of Indonesians, including many of the most highly educated. For, as the experience of both Switzerland and Canada has shown, it is possible under a federal system for individual areas to preserve their own distinctive religious traditions while still remaining loyal members of a larger secular state.

Moreover, in addition to the various indigenous minority peoples whom President Sukarno has cited as likely to become disaffected under an Islamic state,[54] the attitudes of the large and influential alien minorities should also be taken into account, and here there is need for greater realism on the part of virtually all shades of political opinion within the country. Under the present law, all non-Europeans born in Indonesia automatically become citizens (*warga negara*) unless they specifically reject that status, while local-born 'Netherlanders' – in fact mostly Eurasians – may acquire citizenship without serious difficulty. But a legal distinction nevertheless exists between ethnic Indonesians – *asli* – and non-*asli* citizens, and the latter are subject to various forms of discrimination, of which perhaps the most serious is the regulation, dating from colonial times, against their owning land.[55]

TABLE 44

INDONESIA: POPULATION BY ETHNIC ORIGIN, 1954

Indonesian	79,000,000
European/Eurasian (of whom Dutch nationals 95,000)	250,000
Chinese	2,200,000
Arabs	70,000
Indians and Pakistanis	40,000

TABLE 45

INDONESIA: POPULATION BY RELIGION, 1954

Muslim	66,000,000
Christian (R.C.)	1,600,000
Christian (Protestant)	1,700,000
'Chinese'	2,000,000
Hindu	2,000,000

Rest: animist

Of the three main alien minorities, the 85,000 Arabs[56] are the only group which presents no serious problem. Although commercially they may be as grasping as any Chinese, their allegiance to Islam has made assimilation easy, and now that most of the 90 per cent who were born in Indonesia have accepted its citizenship this process is taking place at an accelerated rate. While generally conservative in outlook and strongly favouring the idea of an Islamic state, the Arabs have shown little inclination to support Darul Islam and have given their political allegiance mainly to N.U., a fact which is related to the presence of over three-quarters of their number in Java.

[54] See above, p. 370.

[55] Van der Kroef (C), Vol. II, p. 298.

[56] *Ibid.*, p. 250. Note that most of the Arabs in Indonesia are Shafi'ites.

In contrast to that of the Arabs, the position of the predominantly Christian Eurasian community in Indonesia is tragic. Although in the early days of the present century, when E. F. E. Douwes Dekker[57] founded the Indische Partij in 1912, it seemed as though the Eurasians would play a leading rôle in the Indonesian nationalist movement, fear of economic competition from the small but growing Indonesian intelligentsia later inclined most of them to identify their interests with those of the Dutch, and the essentially conservative Indo-Europeesch Verbond (I.E.V.) of 1920 was a characteristic expression of that outlook.

This alignment of the middle and upper strata of the Eurasians with the Dutch was consolidated by the Japanese occupation, when all who considered themselves Netherlanders were interned with the latter, though most of the remainder whose way of life was not far removed from that of the indigenes, were allowed to remain free. Thus the former group played no part in the creation of the republic, and with the transfer of sovereignty their country – the Netherlands Indies, not Indonesia – ceased to exist. Even before this time many had suffered acutely for their openly pro-Dutch sympathies, and some in desperation had already begun to emigrate to the Netherlands. All-told, not far short of 100,000 had eventually done so before December 1957, though not before their mounting antipathy to the new regime had intensified the Indonesians' distrust of the community with what have since proved to be disastrous consequences for those who had chosen to remain.

In view of the lack of opportunities and the problems of settling down in unfamiliar European surroundings, a small group of the die-hards sought a solution in the immediate post-war years by emigrating to West New Guinea. This attempt received strong backing from various unofficial quarters in the Netherlands, and the sentiment in its favour was one of the main reasons for the 1949 decision of the States-General to retain control over West New Guinea. Nevertheless the Dutch government has never officially sponsored such Eurasian resettlement schemes, partly because of the general unsuitability of the urban-minded Eurasians for the pioneer life, which contributed much to the failure of the I.E.V. project in the 1950s, and partly because the presence in West New Guinea of large numbers of Eurasians, known to be hostile to the republic, would have added unnecessarily to the strain of Dutch/Indonesian relations.

Theoretically the 100,000 or so Eurasians who remained in Indonesia were faced with the difficult choice between seeking to preserve their identity, of which in the past they were extremely proud, or throwing in their lot irrevocably with the Indonesian people and ultimately merging with them.[58] Altogether some 30–40,000 were believed to have opted for Indonesian nationality before

[57] Douwes Dekker, a great-nephew of 'Multatuli' (see above, p. 205), was a Eurasian. Wertheim (C), p. 314.

[58] An outstanding example is Douwes Dekker (above, note 57) who has taken an Indonesian name and adopted the Muslim faith. Van der Kroef (C), Vol. II, p. 299.

December 1957, in most cases because it was only by this means that they could hope to obtain or continue in employment as government servants. Nevertheless, many of those who took this step found that the hostility against them was not significantly diminished as a result, and after the anti-Dutch outbursts of 1957–8 many more of the surviving Eurasian population migrated to Holland.[59]

While the Arabs present no problem to anyone, and the plight of the Eurasians is apparently of direct concern only to themselves, and to the Dutch,[60] the Chinese, who are at once more numerous, more influential, more alien and potentially backed by a more powerful outside state, are the cause of much greater anxiety to the Indonesian government.

Despite heavy and often illegal immigration since the Second World War, the great majority of Indonesia's 2¾ million Chinese are locally born. Like the Eurasians the Chinese sustained severe loss of life and property during the violent phase of the revolution, and at least in small-scale village trading their position suffered a serious setback. On the other hand, the urban Chinese appear to have maintained their ground, and their extensive purchases of factories, businesses and estates[61] from despairing European owners suggest that they still have considerable confidence in their ability to withstand whatever pressures the new regime may put upon them.

While in theory a majority of the Chinese should automatically have acquired Indonesian citizenship, in practice this has been complicated by the old problem of dual nationality, resulting from China's traditional insistence on the *jus sanguinis*. Owing to the deep uneasiness caused by Communist China's continuance of this policy, its representative, Chou En-lai, took the initiative at Bandung in 1955 in proposing a new arrangement with Indonesia, whereby all Chinese living in the country should be called upon to choose within two years which of the two nationalities they wished to adopt. By May 1956 approximately 800,000, or rather less than one-third, had formally accepted Indonesian citizenship.

Again eligibility for various opportunities, notably places in the universities, facilities in commerce and employment in government service, have played an important part in bringing about this result, and some doubt still remains concerning the fundamental loyalty even of those who have accepted Indonesian citizenship. Thus, for example, the common practice of one member of a family opting for Indonesian citizenship while another member, jointly engaged in the same family business, retains Chinese citizenship suggests a desire to have the best of both worlds.[62] And while it is certain that many of the old-established

[59] Besides the 20,000 European Dutch who left Indonesia in the twelve months following December 1957, a larger number of Eurasian Dutch citizens went as refugees to Holland, which most of them had never seen before. Only a remnant still live in Indonesia.

[60] Though Indonesia is the greatest loser of all.

[61] Often at prices representing a minute fraction of their true value. For further information about more recent anti-Chinese measures, see below, note 66.

[62] Allen and Donnithorne, p. 283.

middle-class Chinese[63] have no love for the new Communist regime in China, most of them remain convinced of Chinese superiority, which is reinforced by the growing prestige of the new China. Many of these older-generation Chinese have little more than a smattering of any Indonesian language, and nearly all send their children to local Chinese schools, despite the fact that many of the latter are to a significant extent under Communist influence. But so long as the Chinese, even if they opt for Indonesian citizenship, are treated as second-class citizens, their desire to hold together as a separate community is bound to continue, if only for reasons of mutual preservation.

As in other parts of South-east Asia, the concentration of the Chinese in the more important economic centres inevitably gives rise to anxiety about their possible future use as a fifth column, and similar fears have also been expressed in a different context in respect of the Eurasians.[64] However, the proportion of Chinese (2·6 per cent), and indeed of all alien minorities combined (3·0 per cent), is much lower in Indonesia than in most other South-east Asian states, and on purely numerical grounds the problem of absorbing such a relatively small alien element would not appear insuperable. Moreover, owing to the educational policies pursued by the Dutch, Indonesia probably stands in greater need of the skills of its alien communities than do any of the neighbouring countries apart from Malaya, and for this reason also it would seem wise to seek by all reasonable means to win their allegiance.

Undoubtedly such a policy would meet with strong opposition from many of the large and influential group of Indonesians who have stepped into the places of the Europeans, without being adequately equipped to do so. But unless the maximum use is made of all the limited reserves of professional and administrative talent within the country, regardless of race, the very survival of Indonesia as an independent state may be in jeopardy.

Thus, although there are difficulties and risks involved in offering complete equality of opportunity to all who are willing to accept Indonesian nationality, it would seem that the present policy of treating the Chinese and Eurasian *warga negara* as inferior to *asli*[65] citizens entails even greater risks, without offering any compensating advantages. And while the problem would not be automatically solved by the establishment of a secular state, the task of winning the allegiance of the Chinese and Eurasians to an Islamic state would be very much more difficult.[66]

In trying to forecast how the plural society of Indonesia will evolve now that

[63] The Chinese still predominate in medicine and hold a commanding position in small- and medium-scale industry and commerce.

[64] See below, p. 395.

[65] *I.e.* citizens of non-Indonesian and of Indonesian race respectively. See Van der Kroef (C), Vol. I, p. 298 *et seq.*

[66] However, the Indonesian government now seems to be no more favourably disposed towards the Chinese minority than it has been towards the Dutch and Eurasians. Thus, as from January 1960, non-Indonesian shopkeepers (the vast majority of them Chinese) have been debarred from rural areas, and while this step is said to be taken in order to promote Indonesian retail and co-operative trading in the countryside, it has already

the colonialism which gave rise to it is at an end, the contemporary observer can derive little guidance from past experience in other parts of the world. However, owing to the predominantly urban distribution of the aliens it is clear that the outcome will be determined primarily in the towns, which are already the decisive centres of change within the country, and whose peoples provide the leadership of all the main political parties with the possible exception of N.U.

TABLE 46

INDONESIA: TOWNS WITH OVER 50,000 INHABITANTS, 1961

Java and Madura	1952	1961	*Sumatra*	1952	1961
Djakarta Raya (formerly Greater Batavia)	2,500,000	2,913,436	Palembang	237,616	528,297
Surabaja	925,617	1,318,930	Medan	190,831	359,681*
Bandang	724,249	1,020,082	Padang	120,121	325,000
Semarang	334,959	520,565	Telukbetung	n.a.	115,198*
Surakarta	340,455	451,480	Djambi	n.a.	103,570*
Malang	265,372	376,595	Pematangsiantar	n.a.	101,678*
Djokjakarta	244,379	312,000	Bukittinggi (formerly Fort de Kock)	n.a.	90,000
Kediri	144,466	161,384	Pakanbaru	n.a.	56,030
Tjirebon	141,279	144,530			
Madiun	n.a.	130,276	*Borneo*		
Bogor (formerly Buitenzorg)	119,648	118,624	Bandjarmasin	150,000	268,680
Pekalongan	n.a.	100,927	Pontianak	120,126	130,095
Tegal	n.a.	98,576	*Celebes*		
Magelang	n.a.	88,620	Makasar	265,263	310,239†
Sukabumi	n.a.	77,073			
Probolinggo	n.a.	73,290	*Moluccas*		
Pasuruan	n.a.	67,352	Ambon	n.a.	62,960
Salatiga	n.a.	64,128			
Blitar	n.a.	63,524			
Modjokerto	n.a.	55,484			

* 1960 † 1959

Sources: Based on *Social Welfare in Indonesia* and *Petermanns Geographische Mitteilungen*, 106, 1962, p. 66.

Since the achievement of independence the former position of the Indonesians as merely the lowest social stratum in the towns has undergone a great change. The proliferation of governmental and other jobs[67] has brought a mass of newcomers into the towns, and a prodigious amount of former Dutch property –

resulted in the return of some thousands of Chinese to mainland China. According to the *Straits Times* of 5 May, 1962, 100,000 Chinese returned to China from Indonesia in 1960. This organized repatriation may thus mark the beginning of a reversal of Chinese migration trends, but it remains to be seen what the long-term reaction of Peking will be to the new Indonesia policy towards the Chinese minority.

[67] It has been estimated that between 1939 and 1955 the numbers of the bureaucracy had risen from under 250,000 to 1,273,000. Van der Kroef (E), p. 51.

civic, business and residential – has passed into Indonesian hands. Meanwhile, although the standards of urban management and particularly of cleanliness have declined severely, the glamour of the Western-style but Indonesian-run city has exerted an increasing magnetism on the rural population at large, and the drift to the cities continues apace, especially to the largest which are growing most rapidly of all.

These conditions undoubtedly pose many serious social problems, and in particular the gulf between the traditionalist habits of the peasantry and the often brashly Westernized outlook of the urban Indonesians is in danger of becoming almost as great as that which once divided the former from the Dutch ruling caste. In these circumstances it may be argued that a policy of assimilating such of the Chinese and Eurasians as are willing to throw in their lot with Indonesia might serve to increase the cosmopolitanism of the Indonesian ruling class in the towns, and hence to separate the latter still further from the countryside. But such an outcome is not inevitable, and in any case it would seem to entail a smaller risk than is to be expected from a policy which gives these extremely useful peoples little option but to place their allegiance elsewhere.

VIII. CONCLUSION

If, in spite of the difficulties noted above, the Indonesian state were to be remodelled in such a way as to meet the wishes of both the Muslim and the Nationalist elements in the population, the problem would still remain of providing a positive unifying force to draw its diverse peoples more effectively together.[68]

As we have already seen, the continued reluctance of the leaders in the outer territories to think in terms of secession is evidence that there exists a strong desire in all important parts of the country to 'belong together', a sentiment which is of the essence of nationalism, and in this case undoubtedly derives from the sense of common – if none the less recent – history in which all have shared through participation in the struggle for independence.

Up to a point this is sound and healthy enough, but nevertheless Hartshorne's observation that '. . . inevitably a structure that has lost its original *raison d'être*, without evolving a new one, cannot hope to stand the storms of external strife or internal revolt that sooner or later will attack it'[69] carries a real warning for Indonesia today.

It is in this context that the policy of so many of its leaders, from President Sukarno downwards, seems to be most seriously at fault. For many years now the tactics of artificially prolonging the struggle against the Dutch have ceased to

[68] On August 17, 1959, Indonesia reintroduced the revolutionary constitution of 1945. In March 1960, a new parliament was set up, only 130 of whose 261 members were drawn from the political parties, Masjumi being completely excluded. See *The Times*, March 29, 1960. In August 1960 the Masjumi and the Socialist parties were dissolved by Presidential decree. See Palmier (E), p. 167.

[69] Hartshorne, p. 111.

possess even the limited relevance which they may once have had. Thus, while it is possible to understand the motives behind the abolition of the Netherlands-Indonesian Union, the abrogation of the national debt to Holland,[70] the weakening of Dutch financial and commercial influence and the acquisition of Dutch rights over West New Guinea, all of these have at most been secondary issues compared with the pressing need to counteract internal corruption, inefficiency, mismanagement and above all political disintegration.

Instead of continuing to live in the past, the Indonesians should turn their new-found independence into a springboard for a further advance. Thus, to cite a not wholly dissimilar precedent, the United States, after obtaining its freedom from colonial rule, resisted the temptation to break all ties with Britain and accepted the fact that the latter was supremely well placed to supply the capital equipment which it needed in order to develop its young economy which, one may add, continued for many decades thereafter to rely heavily on the export of primary produce. But at the same time, in turning to the great problems and opportunities that awaited them on their own doorstep, the Americans found in the mystique of the frontier a new *raison d'être*, which was to prove a far more dynamic force in nation-building than any lingering vestiges of anti-colonialism which remained.

This surely is the way in which Indonesia should be looking today. A concerted and successful attack on the great problems of national reconstruction, centering in the industrialization of Java and the development of the untapped resources of *tanah sabrang*,[71] by such schemes as the Schophuys plan and the Asahan project[72] would do more to inspire the Indonesian people with a sense of common purpose and national self-confidence than would any amount of political diversions, whether at home or abroad.

And while, in the irresponsible period of militant confrontation against the Federation of Malaysia[73] and deepening estrangement from more and more hitherto friendly powers during 1964–5, such prospects seemed to be fading beyond recall, initial reactions to the new regime headed by General Suharto, which took over following the abortive *coup* of September 30, 1965, suggest that substantial outside help would still be forthcoming if Indonesia were now at long last to turn its attention to this task.

[70] The Union was unilaterally abrogated by Indonesia on February 13, 1956, and in August of the same year Indonesia unilaterally repudiated its pre-war debts to the Netherlands. See above, pp. 310–11.

[71] *I.e.* 'the land beyond' = the outer territories. See Pelzer (C), p. 184.

[72] In their article, 'Indonesia: now or never' in *Foreign Affairs* (October 1958), Benjamin and Jean Higgins have urged the need for greater American economic aid for Indonesia. They argue that Indonesia has the capacity effectively to use at least $100 million a year for the next few years, half of this to be spent on providing food and textiles for Java until new ways of absorbing surplus Javan labour can be worked out, and half on 'highly visible "impact projects" in the outer islands', such as the Asahan scheme, transport improvements in Sumatra, Borneo and Celebes, and land reclamation and mechanized dry-rice farming in Borneo, etc. *Op. cit.*, pp. 161–2.

[73] See below, Chapter 20.

SELECT BIBLIOGRAPHY

Alisjahbana
Allen and Donnithorne
Bousquet
Burger
Cowan (A)
Cutshall (B)
Feith (A) (B)
Finkelstein
Fischer
Fisher (C) (H) (K)
Fryer (A) (D) (E)
Gerbrandy
Hatta (A) (B)
Higgins (A) (B)
Higgins, B. and J.
Josey
Kahin (B) (C)
Kattenburg
Legge
Logemann
Mende
Metzgemaekers
Mintz
Moerdowo
Mysbergh
Palmier (A) (B) (C) (D)
Pelzer (F)
Schiller
Schrieke
Sjahrir
Spate (B)
Sukarno
Supomo
Thompson and Adloff
Vandenbosch (B)
Vandenbosch and Butwell
Van der Kroef (C) (D) (E)
Van der Veur
Van Goudoever (A) (B)
Van Nieuwenhuize (A) (B)
Van Riper
Van Wijnen
Verdoorn
Vlekke (B) (C)
Wehl
Wertheim (A) (B) (C)
Willmott
Wolf
Woodman

Indonesian News
Indonesian Spectator
Report on Indonesia
Round Table Conference at the Hague, Facts and Documents (1949)
Social Welfare in Indonesia

For an insight into the views of three leading Indonesian politicians see the works by Hatta (A) (B), Sjahrir, and Sukarno.

Of the several substantive works by Western authors dealing with various aspects of Indonesian political problems since 1945, Wehl, Wolf and Kahin (C) are standard sources for the formative period of the new Indonesia, while Schiller deals with the Dutch federal proposals. More recently the books by Wertheim (C) and Schrieke are outstanding contributions in the sociological field, as is Vlekke (C) in the political.

Three more wide-ranging studies, written from somewhat contrasted viewpoints are provided by Van der Kroef (C), Woodman, and Fischer.

In addition to a wide range of periodical literature, among which I have found the papers by Finkelstein, Fryer (D), Mysbergh, Palmier (A) (B) (C) (D), Wertheim (A) (B), Van der Kroef (D), Van der Veur, and Van Niewenhuize most useful, I wish particularly to emphasize the outstanding contribution made to the study of this area by the Cornell Modern Indonesia Project under the direction of Professor G. McT. Kahin. Among the works published in this series, I have relied extensively on those by Burger, Feith (B), Legge, and Willmott.

Addenda: Palmier (E) is an important new study of Dutch-Indonesian relations. Note also, McVey, Ruth T. (ed.): *Indonesia*, New Haven, 1963.

CHAPTER 12

The Problem of West New Guinea

When in December 1949 the Dutch finally agreed to the transfer of sovereignty to Indonesia, an exception was made of West New Guinea, which they insisted on keeping under their own control.[1] From that time onwards, however, the Indonesians have never ceased to urge their claim to the territory, and in December 1957, after the Dutch had announced plans for closer collaboration between their administration in West New Guinea and those of the Australians on the other side of the purely arbitrary boundary along the 141st meridian,[2] the dispute came to a head, as described in Chapter 11. However, although the Indonesians took action against Dutch interests in their own territory, they were in no position to eject the Dutch from West New Guinea, which accordingly remained, *de facto* as well as *de jure*, under the control of the Netherlands until 1962.

As has already been seen,[3] New Guinea is geologically and geographically more closely related to Australasia than to Indonesia, and whether one accepts Wallace's or Weber's line the whole of the island must on botanical and zoological grounds be excluded from the Asian realm. Ethnically also, New Guinea stands completely apart from the Malaysian lands, properly so called. For the indigenous Papuans[4] form a branch of the Melanesoid peoples which, though related to the Melanesoid strain present in some of the inhabitants of the Moluccas and the eastern Lesser Sundas, is quite distinct from the Pareœan and Nesiot stocks farther west.

Moreover, none of the indigenous languages of New Guinea belongs to the Indonesian group, and although again there are certain affinities between the coastal languages of the north-western tip of the island and those of southern Halmahera, both of which belong to the Melanesian branch of the Malayo-

[1] In order to prevent a breakdown of the Round Table Conference of 1949 between the Dutch and the Indonesians it was agreed that a decision on the status of West New Guinea should be deferred for a year. But the joint Dutch-Indonesian Committee which met to consider the matter in 1950 completely failed to reach agreement, and discussions finally broke down on December 27, 1950.

[2] This announcement was made on November 6, 1957, and it was further stated in the Hague that the new policy marked the first step towards the creation of an independent Papuan nation. The Australian areas include the Australian Trust Territory of New Guinea in the north-east, and Papua in the south-east of the island.

[3] See above, Chapter 2.

[4] The Dutch use the term to include all the indigenous peoples of West New Guinea, though there are certain differences between those of the coast and those of the interior uplands. There are also a few Negrito peoples in remote parts of the interior.

Polynesian family, the astonishingly diverse languages of the interior of New Guinea are grouped together in the Papuan category which is totally unrelated to the Malayo-Polynesian.[5]

Nevertheless, it remains to add that the very linguistic diversity of West New Guinea has favoured the use of Malay as a *lingua franca* between the various coastal settlements which, in recent centuries, have been brought into contact with the adjacent parts of eastern Indonesia, and this tendency has become more marked during the last fifty years.

Although it is extremely doubtful whether West New Guinea was ever in direct contact with Sri Vijaya or Madjapahit, as the Indonesians have frequently claimed, the Sultan of Tidore was in process of establishing his sovereignty over the north-western coastal region of the island at the time when the first Europeans arrived in the archipelago, and the Dutch recognized, and subsequently inherited his claims there. But while certain ties thus developed between the coastal fringes of West New Guinea and various parts of the Moluccas, the links between the former and the rest of Indonesia were extremely tenuous. The Muslim religion never gained more than a few tentative footholds in this remote region and, although its almost complete absence left the door open to Christian missionary activity at a later date, the great majority of the population in the interior have still been left virtually untouched by the outside world and remain culturally in the stone age.

Until the 1930s, the Dutch, who regarded the territory as a negative frontier zone, made no attempt to develop it economically and, apart from their well-known internment camp at Boven Digoel,[6] appeared to have no use for it at all. Then, precisely because of its virgin character, West New Guinea began to attract the attention of members of the Eurasian community in Java who, having been badly hit by the world economic crisis, were contemplating agricultural colonization overseas. Owing to the lack of capital and inadequate planning, the settlement scheme undertaken in the 1930s by the Indo-Europeesch Verbond[7] failed ignominiously. But in the meantime suspicion of the activities of the Japanese, who had obtained concessions for cotton and rubber planting along the northern coast in 1931, led the Dutch authorities to contemplate a more systematic opening up of the territory. It was in these circumstances that some 2 million guilders were spent on a fruitless search for gold and, more important, that the Nederlandsche Nieuw Guinea Petroleum Mij. was set up in 1935.[8] Although the first oilfield, at Klamono near Sorong, had not come into commercial production when the Pacific War broke out, it was already clear that the prospects were not entirely negligible.

[5] Some related Papuan languages are spoken in parts of northern Halmahera.

[6] This has a certain symbolic significance to Indonesian nationalist leaders, many of whom were interned there in the past.

[7] See above, p. 385.

[8] A joint venture of the B.P.M. (Royal Dutch/Shell), Standard Vacuum (Stanvac), and Far Eastern Pacific Investments, which participated in the ratio of 40:40:20 respectively.

The rival claims of the Dutch and the Indonesians to West New Guinea were not easy to assess, in part because the two have argued from entirely different premisses. In brief, the Dutch have asserted that the responsibility for the territory has been theirs all along and, as the indigenous peoples were far too immature politically ever to have demanded independence, there could be no justification whatever for handing them over to Indonesia. Moreover, in so far as these peoples have been Westernized, they have been much influenced by Christianity,[9] and might suffer in various ways from being transferred to the rule of a predominantly Muslim country. And as regards the much larger numbers who, as yet, have had little or no contact with alien civilizations, the greatest care will be needed to guard against the tendency, which they seem to share with some other Melanesian and Polynesian peoples, of succumbing to a falling birth-rate and perhaps ultimate extinction, when their traditional way of life is disturbed.

Thus the Dutch have argued that it was essential that the handling of the Papuans at this critical time should be left to experienced colonial administrators and not to the Indonesians who, it was said, had failed effectively to administer many of their own minority peoples. And furthermore such administration should be co-ordinated with that of the Australians, French and British in the ethnically and culturally related areas nearby, under the auspices of the South-West Pacific Commission.

In contrast to these arguments the Indonesians have based their claim on two assumptions, first that European rule over non-Europeans was unjustifiable in any circumstances and, secondly, that since West New Guinea was part of the old Netherlands Indies, it should automatically have been handed over to the new Indonesian régime in 1949, and until such a transfer takes place the 'revolution will not be complete'. Thus, in the words of their official spokesmen:

> '. . . the territory which the Indonesian People claims its own, is exactly the same territory not more and not less as the territory which formerly, before the Round Table Conference, was called the Netherlands-Indies territory.'[10]

Stated thus baldly the Indonesian arguments would seem to be purely emotional in character, though that in no way prevents them from serving as a political rallying cry in Indonesia itself, or from winning widespread support among other Asian countries.

In fact, however, there are deeper and perhaps more powerful motives on both sides. Thus the very large number of Dutchmen who had struggled hard to keep for their country a place in the Indonesian sun, and had been profoundly disturbed at the thought of handing over the Christian minorities of eastern Indonesia to the Djakarta régime, were determined to retain control at least over West New Guinea, where possession gave them the proverbial nine points

[9] Both Protestant and Roman Catholic missions have been active in West New Guinea. The number of Protestant indigenes (mainly in the north) was over 60,000 in 1939; Roman Catholics, largely in the south, numbered about 50,000 in 1955.

[10] *Report of the Committee New Guinea (Irian)* 1950, Part III, p. 30. See above, note 1.

of the law. Moreover, it was claimed that West New Guinea might provide a refuge for those Eurasians who found it impossible to remain in the new Indonesia, and retention of Dutch control there would at the same time give the opportunity to vindicate the good name of the Netherlands as a colonial power.[11] Finally, since many believed that the Djakarta government would never be able to win the loyalties of the outer territories, it was felt that New Guinea might provide a base from which to save something from the wreckage, if the new Indonesia eventually disintegrated.[12]

In 1949–50 these feelings were so strong that it was only by insisting on the retention of West New Guinea, at least for the time being, that the Dutch government was able to muster the necessary two-thirds majority in parliament to ratify the transfer agreement of December 1949, even though the government itself had few illusions about the economic value of the territory.

However, the very tenacity of the Dutch in retaining control over West New Guinea served to arouse both the suspicions and the cupidity of the Indonesians. Thus wild rumours began to circulate regarding the 'sea of oil' on which the territory was supposed to float and, more important, the fact that the Dutch position in West New Guinea represented a survival of the old federalist project was regarded as a continuing threat to the security of the republic. In this connexion it should be remembered that the Djakarta regime had never felt wholly sure of the loyalty of the Christian minorities of the Moluccas, and the eastern Lesser Sundas, who may be regarded as ethnically and culturally transitional between the peoples of New Guinea and those of the Islamic Malaysian lands of the western archipelago. Moreover, Ambonese Christians played a major rôle in missionary work in New Guinea, and it was likewise Ambonese Christians who set up the dissident Republic of the South Moluccas, which remained in open rebellion against Djakarta from 1950 to 1956.

Thus it was perhaps not wholly unreasonable of the Indonesian government to fear that the continuance of Dutch rule in West New Guinea might provide a focus there for potentially disloyal East-Indonesians, as well as for equally hostile Eurasians, and that so long as this danger existed the unity, and perhaps even the safety, of the republic might be in jeopardy. Nevertheless, there is no evidence whatever to suggest that such subversive ideas were entertained by Dutch officials, though some at least of the 8,000 Eurasians in the territory did not conceal their sympathies for the South Moluccan Republic.[13]

So long as Indonesia itself remains seriously deficient in financial resources and skilled man-power, however, it is clear that it cannot easily undertake the administration, let alone the systematic economic development of West New Guinea, and for this reason alone the interests of the latter's indigenous population would probably have been better served by their remaining under Dutch administration.

[11] On the latter point, see Gerbrandy, p. 190.

[12] See Douglas Wilkie, *Manchester Guardian*, October 22, 1954.

[13] *Ibid.*

Even so, progress in both respects has hitherto been very limited in scale. For although in the past the extreme remoteness of West New Guinea was regarded as the main reason why economic development had passed it by, more detailed examination has since shown that geographical isolation is by no means the only disadvantage from which it suffers. Thus, in the first place, while there is certainly some good agricultural land within the territory, the presence of an almost continuous series of rugged mountain ranges a short distance inland from the northern coast, and the great expanse of swamps in the south make penetration into the interior an extremely costly process.

Accordingly, the only areas under effective administration to date are the coastal regions which in 1955 contained 288,353 out of the estimated total of 700,000–1,000,000 Papuans within the territory. Besides these indigenes there were some 15,800 Asians (mostly Indonesians and a few Chinese traders) and 16,677 Europeans (including Eurasians) in the administered area, whose largest single settlement, Hollandia, contained a total population (all races) of only 16,700.

Even accepting the highest estimated figure for the interior, the average density of population for the territory as a whole is a mere six to the square mile, and over vast areas, notably in the southern coastal swamps, the figure is still lower. This sparseness of the population, together with its extreme backwardness, constitutes the greatest of all the obstacles to the territory's economic development. So far as is known the highest densities of indigenous population are along the northern coastal fringe and in some of the nearby islands, in the Vogelkop, and in the interior uplands farther east where several hundred thousand Papuans live in virtually complete isolation from the outside world. At present, however, the only centres of even embryonic Western-style development are at the three geographical extremities, namely the north-west (including the Vogelkop and some of the offshore islands), Hollandia in the north-east and Merauke in the south-east, mutually separated from each other by distances of many hundreds of miles and entirely unconnected by any form of land transport.

Indeed the total length of roads in this vast area, almost equal in size to Sweden, is under 300 miles, and in view of the sparseness of population and the immense cost of road building in most parts of the territory no great advances can be looked for in this respect. While both the helicopter and more normal air services can do much to help pioneering in such country, coastal shipping will inevitably remain by far the most important form of bulk transport for many years to come.[14]

Even more serious, however, is the ineffectiveness of the Papuans as labourers.

[14] The K.P.M. has run fortnightly shipping services connecting Sorong, Manokwari, Biak, Seroei, Sarmi and Hollandia in the north, and Steenkool, Fakfak, Kaimana and Merauke in the south, with Singapore via Timor Dili in Portuguese Timor, thus avoiding direct contact with the Republic of Indonesia. The Royal Interocean Lines also started a service (approximately monthly) between Sydney and Melbourne, various West New Guinean ports, Sandakan (North Borneo) and Bangkok, some years ago.

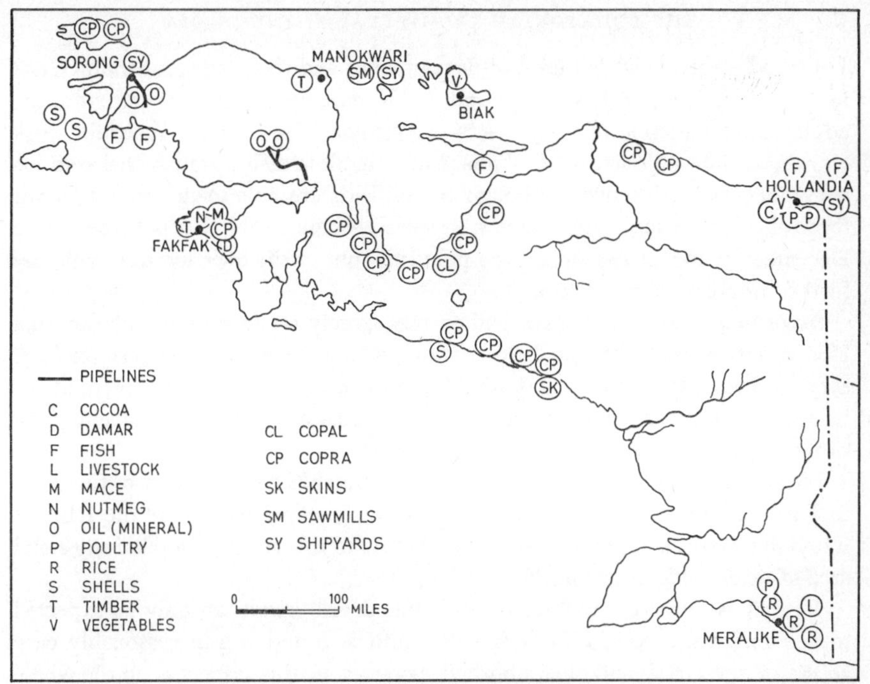

FIG. 57—West New Guinea: products and roads

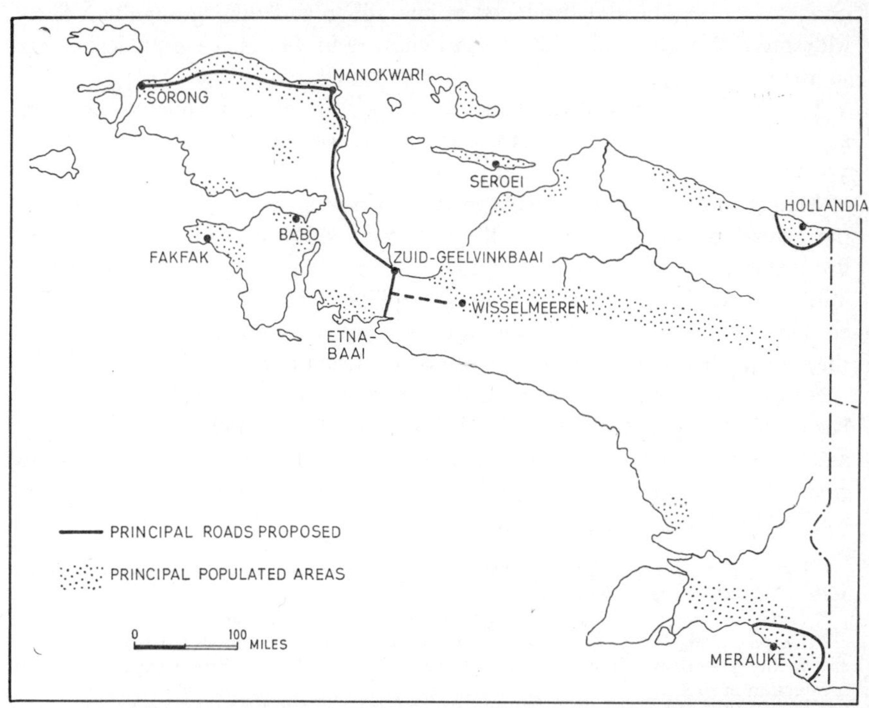

FIG. 58—West New Guinea: new roads suggested by J. Winsemius

For besides their retarded level of development and their apparent indifference to monetary stimuli, it has been found that if more than about 10 per cent of the adult male population in a given area is recruited as temporary labour for work elsewhere, the whole structure of village life is liable to disintegrate with disastrous consequences.[15] Moreover, although the oilfields are able to draw on a labour force of some 10,500 Indonesians who were brought in for that purpose before December 1949,[16] it has since been politically out of the question to recruit any further workers from that source.

Accordingly the Dutch have had to rely largely on European and Eurasian labour, and while with the help of modern machinery and modern medical services such a system may no longer be intrinsically impracticable, it could not be adopted on anything more than a very limited scale without contravening the professed aims of Dutch policy in the territory.

Finally, it remains to add that the soils[17] of much the greater part of the territory are maturely laterized and hence extremely unproductive, as the I.E.V.[18] found to its cost, and the only known exception to this rule is in a relatively small area of recent vulcanicity in the Vogelkop.

Thus it is now clear that major economic development can only be expected to occur if really spectacular mineral wealth is found within reasonably easy access of the coast, and the published evidence in this respect is on the whole disappointing. The search for gold (which is found in parts of eastern New Guinea) has been tacitly abandoned as unavailing, and although lignite is fairly widespread the only coal so far worth mining is in the small Horna field in the southern Vogelkop.

The most important of the minerals worked to date is petroleum, but here again the prospects do not seem to be as great as was once supposed. Since 1946 a 35-mile road and an 8-in. diameter pipeline have been built from the new harbour of Sorong to the Klamono oilfield in the north-western Vogelkop, and in 1955 the annual production reached 485,624 tons, which by value accounted for five-sixths of the total exports. But unless this production can be increased manyfold there would appear to be scant possibility of its giving rise to any major economic development within the territory, and so far from this coming about the output fell to 363,731 tons in 1956 and to an estimated 245,000 tons in 1959.[19]

For the rest, Dutch plans have understandably been tentative. Attempts have been made to encourage the production of cocoa both by indigenous cultivators and by European/Eurasian small-holders, and while initially only 660 acres were planted, mostly near Hollandia, further extensions there and near Manokwari in the Vogelkop raised the total to 2,288 acres in 1959. Manokwari is like-

[15] By 1954 about 10,000 Papuans have been recruited for labour on various projects. Wilkie, *Manchester Guardian*, October 22, 1954.

[16] *Ibid.* [17] See above, p. 234. [18] See above, p. 393.

[19] Despite plans for opening a second oil centre in the Wasian-Mogoi district farther east in the Vogelkop it now seems that the prospect for any significant expansion of oil production is slight.

wise the locus of a new sawmilling establishment and a shipyard, both opened in 1957, while in the area of post-war Eurasian settlement near Merauke an attempt has been made to develop livestock rearing and mechanized rice cultivation as a first step towards reducing dependence on imported foodstuffs.

Apart from the possibility of developing cocoa as a cash crop, the Dutch have sought to improve the standard of indigenous peasant cultivation in the more accessible areas, and minute quantities of copra, mace and nutmegs are beginning to be exported, together with such exotic commodities as shells and crocodile skins, from a few coastal regions. At present the Papuan population is self-supporting in foodstuffs, mainly sago, yams and fish, though at a very unsatisfactory dietetic level, but virtually all food for the non-indigenous population requires to be imported, along with consumer goods and capital equipment of various kinds. As yet, however, the total exports have amounted to less than one-half the value of imports in every year since 1949, and in the opinion of one Dutch expert West New Guinea, which was recently being run at an annual loss to the Dutch of some 80 million guilders, would not cease to be a financial liability for at least another fifty years.

Nevertheless, considerable thought has been given to long-term planning for the future. Thus, for example, Dr. J. Winsemius[20] has urged that an integrated development plan should be drawn up to cover all parts of the territory and all aspects of its economy. Among other things, Winsemius recommended that the capital should be moved from its present eccentric position at Hollandia to a place on the western shore of Geelvink Bay. This would have the advantage of reasonable proximity to the Vogelkop, which is likely to remain the principal centre both of mining and of other commercial production in the foreseeable future, and would also be well placed for establishing contact with the main centres of 'Mountain Papuans' in the interior.

Whether the potential returns would really warrant any such elaborate planning, however, may well have been doubted by the Dutch, and in any case once they had decided on a policy of closer collaboration with Australian New Guinea the arguments for retaining Hollandia as the seat of administration were automatically strengthened.[21]

Apart from thc obvious advantages of co-ordinating development plans with those in the considerably more advanced portion of the island under Australian rule, there are also important strategic considerations involved in this new alignment. During the Second World War New Guinea was revealed as the last line of Australia's external defences to the north, and after the Japanese drive had been halted in the east of the island, Hollandia served for a time as General MacArthur's headquarters, and became the jumping-off ground from which the

[20] Winsemius, pp. 118–29.

[21] Hollandia is linked to Lae in Australian New Guinea by the fortnightly air service of Quantas Empire Airways. Biak is the point of contact between the internal and long-distance air routes. See Fig. 59.

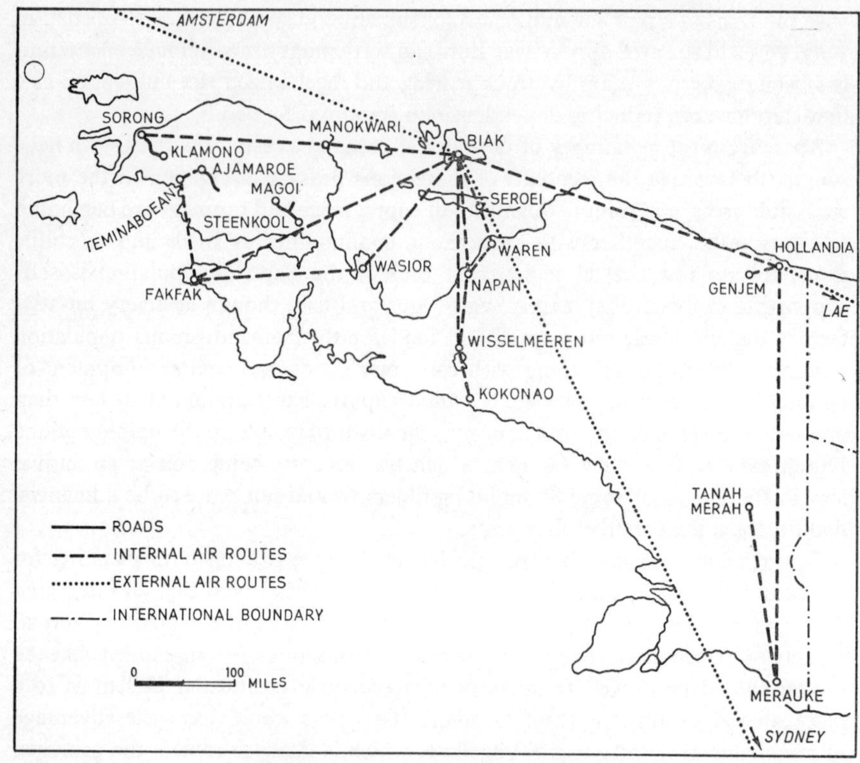

FIG. 59—West New Guinea: air routes

counter-offensive against Japan was eventually launched. After the war, with the withdrawal of Dutch power from Indonesia, New Guinea acquired an enhanced significance in relation to the American/Australian line of bases in the western Pacific, and the Australians were understandably anxious that nothing should prejudice its security against outside attack. Thus, Australia, after strongly championing the Indonesian demand for independence in the early post-war years, subsequently swung round, at least for a time, to favouring the continuance of Dutch rule in West New Guinea, primarily on the grounds that the Dutch were more likely than the Indonesians to keep the territory under effective surveillance.

Originally this attitude arose from continued Australian suspicions regarding the long-term intentions of the Japanese towards the Nan Yo. In this connexion one may cite the Tokyo *Oriental Economist* which claimed in 1949 that Japanese wartime surveys showed that West New Guinea could support 20 million Japanese, and further suggested that facilities for emigration to this area should be granted in order to help in solving Japan's post-war population problem.[22]

[22] See *The Economist*, June 11, 1949, pp. 1096–7.

While this particular estimate was greatly exaggerated, it is undoubtedly true that West New Guinea's greatest deficiency is in skilled labour, and if the Japanese, or for that matter the Chinese, were free to persuade their nationals to go there as labourers or agricultural colonists the territory could certainly be made to support many times its present numbers. Undoubtedly this capacity of the territory to support more people, combined with the present inability of its own sparse and for the most part extremely retarded population effectively to control potential immigration from other parts of Asia, poses a very serious problem, and it was by no means clear that this would be solved by the 1957 plans for preparing West New Guinea (in step with the Australian-administered half of the island) for ultimate home rule, commendable though such an intention may have been on other grounds.

Again, during recent years the Dutch have done much to improve the health and educational services in West New Guinea, but in the latter connexion they have encountered yet another problem in respect of the language to be used as the medium of instruction. Since the numerous local languages were considered too primitive and in any case each is spoken by only a very small number of people, the possibility of using English was seriously considered, not least because of the advantages it offered for closer links with the Australian territories nearby.[23] In the end, however, it was decided to employ Dutch at all levels, but this has proved exceedingly difficult in view of the fact that virtually none of the elementary teachers speak the language, having hitherto been in the habit of using Malay. And while for political reasons the reluctance of the Dutch to adopt Malay was understandable, it has long seemed likely in view of the ease with which it can be learned that Malay would continue to spread as the *lingua franca* with possible long-term political consequences which could not be ignored.

The uncertainty over the language question has been symbolic of the greater uncertainty which has overhung the whole future evolution of West New Guinea. Short of some entirely unexpected development, the territory could not be run on an economically profitable basis for decades to come, so long as the Dutch remained true to their avowedly humanitarian reasons for retaining control. Yet it is only on such grounds that the Dutch have had any valid reason for staying. Indeed, Dutch interest in West New Guinea has been no less a matter of sentiment than is that of the Indonesians, and from a purely material point of view the policy of retaining control over this territory, at the cost of placing the huge Dutch investments in Indonesia in jeopardy, has been completely incomprehensible.

How long the Dutch would have been prepared to carry this singularly thankless and unremunerative burden is now an academic question,[24] though already

[23] Many of the coastal peoples in some areas have acquired a smattering of English as a result either of contacts with the territories farther east or of contacts with Allied forces during the Second World War.

[24] However, the Dutch have received some help from the European Common Market's special fund for underdeveloped territories, and there have been plans for investing

in 1961 they speeded up their plans for the political education of the local population, and have already instituted a New Guinean Council as a first step towards virtual self-government by 1970.[25]

Since the summer of 1961, however, and particularly after India's seizure of Goa, the whole situation began to change. As Indonesia's military strength increased, its demands for control over West New Guinea became more bellicose and, rightly or wrongly, the conviction grew in the United States and elsewhere that it was probably in the best interests of the West to permit a transfer of sovereignty to take place rather than run the risk of a deterioration of relations with the Indonesian government.

It was in these circumstances that, with the help of the United Nations and an American mediator, agreement on the future ownership of West New Guinea was eventually reached in August 1962 between the Dutch and the

TABLE 47

WEST NEW GUINEA: OVERSEAS TRADE, 1955 AND 1957

A. Exports (in 000 guilders)	1955	1957
Crude oil	25,756·4	20,831·8
Copra	1,752·6	2,194·2
Copal	968·1	844·5
Crocodile skins	739·6	1,782·9
Shells	457·8	409·2
Scrap	431·5	385·0
Mace	337·9	702·6
Nutmeg	275·2	2,069·2
Damar	126·2	n.a.
Wood	52·5	5·0
Total (including others)	30,908·0	29,242·6
B. Imports (in 000 guilders)		
Food products	26,221·7	31,087·6
Machinery	21,732·0	23,968·3
Metal products	10,770·6	14,820·8
Textiles and footwear	8,892·4	9,974·3
Oil products	7,884·4	8,998·4
Total (including others)	93,222·6	114,782·2

Source: *Vademecum voor Nederlands-Nieuw-Guinea*, 1956.

$100 million (half U.S. and half Dutch private capital) in nickel and chrome mining in the Cycloops mountains in the east and in Waiego island in the north-west. *The Observer*, May 10, 1959, p. 6.

[25] See 'Perilous half-island', *The Economist*, May 6, 1961, pp. 526–7.

Indonesian governments. According to its terms the Dutch began to hand over the territory to an interim United Nations administration in October 1962, and the United Nations in its turn handed over to the Indonesian government on 1st May, 1963. In addition it was agreed that the local Papuan population would have the opportunity to decide in a plebiscite, to be held under United Nations supervision not later than 1969, whether it wishes to become independent or to remain with Indonesia.[26]

Whether this agreement has been a wise one for all concerned only time will tell. If, with this outstanding territorial problem now settled, Indonesia turns more wholeheartedly to the solution of its own internal economic and political problems, and at the same time achieves an improvement in its relations with Holland, both will benefit materially from it. But if the rule of one race by another is an anachronism in the world of today it is Indonesia, not Holland, that will have to justify it from now on in West New Guinea.

SELECT BIBLIOGRAPHY

Fisher (K)
Gerbrandy
Higgins, B. and J.
Klein
Metzgemaekers
Winsemius

Mededelingen Nieuw Guinea Instituut
'Nederlands Nieuw Guinea en de wereld', *Internationale Spectator*, October 18, 1950
Report on Netherlands New Guinea for the year 1953
Report of the Committee New Guinea (Irian) 1950
Vademecum voor Nederlands-Nieuw-Guinea
Handbook on Netherlands New Guinea
Two articles on West New Guinea, by Douglas Wilkie, in *Manchester Guardian*, October 18 and 20, 1954.
See also Spate (F) (G) for details of conditions in the Australian-administered half of New Guinea.

[26] On 1st May, 1963 the Indonesian Foreign Minister, Dr. Subandrio, stated that Indonesia 'planned no special links with Australian New Guinea'. (*The Times*, 2 May, 1963). Meanwhile Australia is accelerating the advance of the Trust Territory and Papua towards self-government. On 24 May, 1965 President Sukarno was reported to have stated that a plebiscite had become superfluous because the people of West Irian were in favour of Indonesia.

A NOTE ON PORTUGUESE TIMOR

The final elimination of Dutch rule from South-east Asia, foreshadowed by the Netherlands/Indonesian agreement of August 1962, inevitably draws attention to the apparently anomalous survival of Portuguese rule in eastern Timor, on the opposite side of the Arafura Sea. For here, just as, until 1961, in Goa in the Indian sub-continent, a fragment of the earliest European empire in Asia has outlasted that of the vastly more powerful empires which began to supplant it in the 17th century.

In fact the Portuguese had been ousted from all their more important posts in Indonesia before 1655, when the first Resident was appointed to the parts of Timor which remained under their jurisdiction. For much of its history Portuguese Timor was linked administratively with Macao, but in 1926 effect was given to an earlier decision to constitute it a separate province which, in common with all Portugal's remaining territories overseas, is ranked legally as an integral part of the mother country. Under such a system, of course, there has been no intention of preparing the territory for independence, but in view of recent developments in other parts of Portugal overseas it remains to be seen what the future holds for Timor.

From a geographical point of view this small and rugged half-island, with an area of 5,762 square miles and a population of about 500,000, represents the easternmost and hence the driest extremity of the Lesser Sunda islands. As such, its economic potentialities are very limited, and in 1959 the value of its exports, consisting mainly of coffee and sandalwood, amounted to only £570,000, as against an import bill of £716,000. Its capital and chief port, Dili, a town of only 7,000 inhabitants, is connected by regular air service to Djakarta and Darwin.

PART III

The Tropical Mainland: Burma, Thailand and Indochina

CHAPTER 13

The Mainland States: Physical Introduction

The area to be considered in this and the following three chapters is that which today comprises the territory of the political units Burma, Thailand, Laos, Cambodia, and Northern and Southern Vietnam. Together these six states cover 94 per cent of the total 795,000 square miles of the South-east Asian mainland, the remaining six per cent being accounted for by British Malaya which is dealt with in Chapters 17–19.

I. STRUCTURE AND RELIEF

From an average altitude of approximately 10,000 ft., and summit levels almost twice as great in the celebrated 'hump' between India and China, the relief of the Indo-Pacific peninsula gradually falls away southwards until, near the lagoon of Talé Sap in southern Thailand it is possible to cross from the Indian Ocean to the South China Sea over a divide only a few hundred feet above sea-level.[1] Thus, as Eduard Suess observed half a century ago, 'the mighty swell of the Altaides in Thibet subsides and is dispersed. The whole continent becomes lower. Many coulisses disappear. Only a few long branches are continued: on the east into the cordillera of Annam; on the west, always giving rise to fresh coulisses, through the Malay peninsula, and still farther, to Java and beyond.'[2]

In spite of the modifications which more recent research has entailed to some of its details, this pioneer analysis still remains a stimulating guide to the physical geography of the region. Nevertheless, it is nowadays recognized that the structures referred to above belong to at least two and probably more quite distinct phases of mountain building. Moreover, though it has often been claimed that the trend of the Himalayan folding can be traced eastwards through the series of high ridges separating the several major N/S river valleys immediately to the east of Theing Wang Razi (19,578 ft.) at the extreme northern tip of Burma, it is now more generally believed that the main line of Tertiary folding makes a right-angled bend in this vicinity, beyond which it is prolonged, via the Patkai, Naga and Chin hills, into the Arakan Yoma.

To the east of the resultant series of mid-Tertiary fold mountains, swinging as it does in a huge arc from the Hukawng valley to southern Arakan, lies the

[1] Though south of this in the Malay peninsula there are several ranges with summit levels of 5,000–6,000 ft.

[2] Suess, Vol. 3, pp. 231–2.

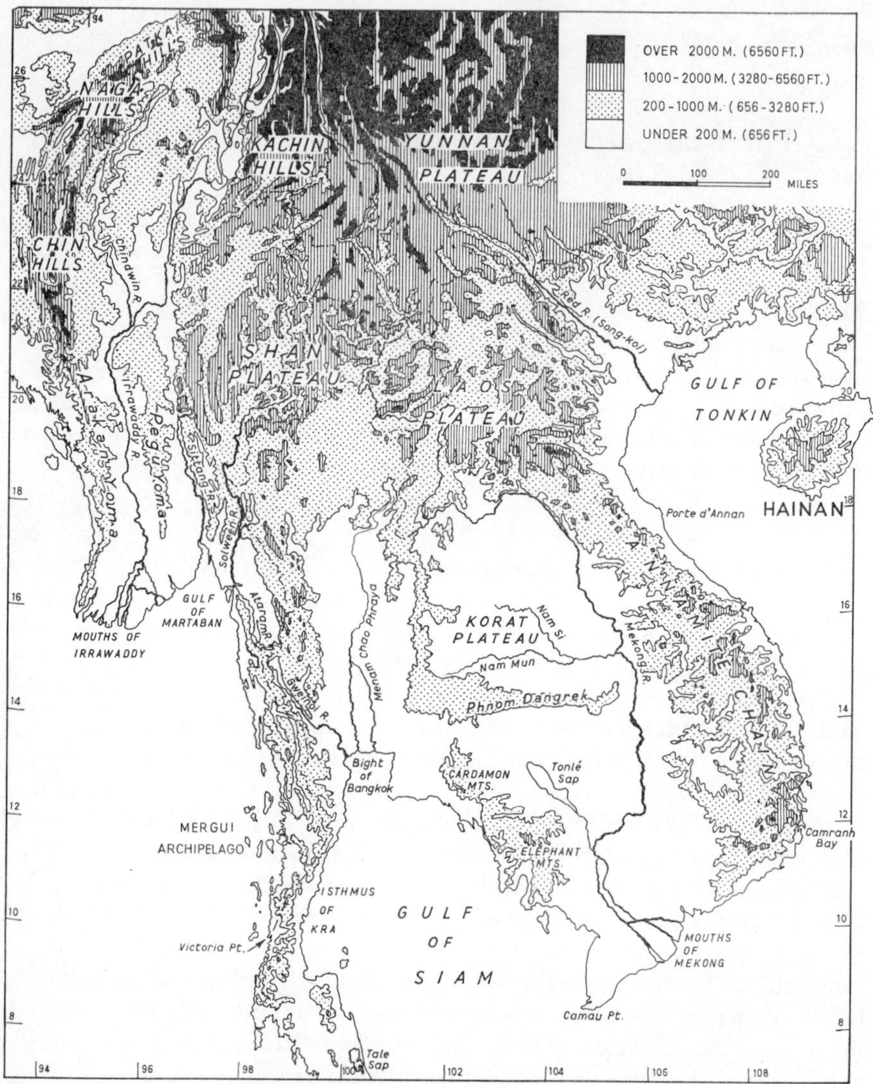

FIG. 60—Mainland South-east Asia: relief

related structural trough of central Burma. This is occupied by a vast longitudinal lowland, floored for the most part with Tertiary sediments and more recent alluvial material laid down by the Irrawaddy-Chindwin-Sittang river system. For much of its length the otherwise low-lying surface of this basin is broken by a discontinuous series of ranges, from the high Kumon mountains in the north to the Pegu Yoma in the south. These uplands, which include a number of recently extinct and now much dissected volcanic cones, notably Mt. Popa, near the Irrawaddy bend, mark the approximate position of a line of late Tertiary folding which runs generally parallel to that of the mid-Miocene Arakan series already described.

The Tertiary zone as a whole thus covers approximately the western two-thirds of Burma, and farther south it is continued beneath the sea to Sumatra and the northern entrance to the Malacca Straits. To the east of this the predominant peninsular structures are of greater antiquity, dating in the main from Mesozoic or earlier times, and the whole of the area in question, stretching from the faulted western edge of the Shan plateau and Tenasserim to the eastern slopes of the Annamite Chain, where another line of fracturing marks the coast of southern Indochina, together forms part of the Indo-Malayan mountain system as described in Chapter 2.

Over much of its extent in the peninsula, notably throughout the Shan plateau, Tenasserim, Malaya and Laos, the dominant folding of this system is Mesozoic in origin and, among a wide diversity of country rocks, massive limestones and sandstones, together with gneisses and granites (the last mainly in the form of long intrusive masses whose remnants frequently survive as upstanding ridges), are particularly characteristic.

Whether the structures of the high and rugged Kachin country to the north of the Shan plateau are similar in age is less certain, and there appears to be some evidence there of a major Palæozoic component in the folding. Moreover, the southern portion of the Annamite Chain does not represent a prolongation of the Mesozoic structures of Laos, but, on the contrary, comprises the most ancient portion of the whole Indo-Malayan system, namely the pre-Cambrian massif of Indosinia. Thus, despite a superficial similarity of relief, which derives in the main from widespread uplift in Quaternary times, the Annamite Chain is of very diverse structural origin. Associated with the Quaternary tectonic movements, extensive outpourings of basaltic lavas have covered many parts of the chain and flanking areas, notably in Darlac, Kontum and the Bolovens plateau.

Notwithstanding the wide differences in the age of the various mountain systems of the Indo-Pacific peninsula, however, the dominant trend lines throughout are roughly longitudinal in direction, though southwards from the Yunnan plateau there is a tendency to spread out somewhat, with the result that in Laos and northern Vietnam the prevailing direction is more nearly NW/SE. These broad structural trends are clearly reflected in the alignment both of the major rivers, whose generally constricted valleys are basically tectonic in origin, and also of the main intervening uplands and the higher residual ridges.

As has already been observed, it is in the extreme north, in the little-known borderland between Tibet, Burma, and Yunnan, that the culminating relief occurs, and by any standards this affords some of the most spectacular and forbidding country in the world. Within a belt less than 120 miles across, the upper waters of the Irrawaddy, Salween, Mekong and Yang-tze plunge and swirl seawards in tremendous gorges, separated one from another by towering and

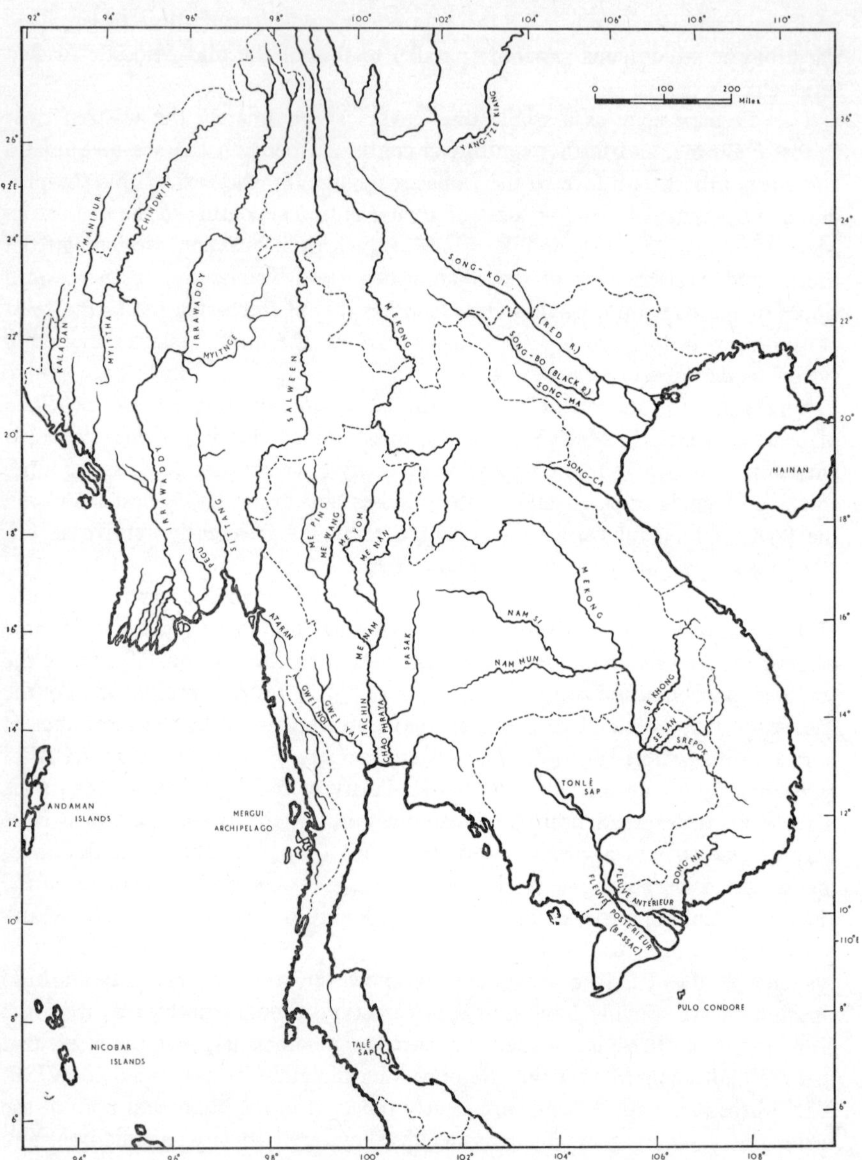

FIG. 61—Mainland South-east Asia: drainage

precipitous ranges whose crests in many places exceed 16,000 ft. in altitude. Farther south the rivers begin gradually to fan out and, although around latitude 27° the Yang-tze swings away more or less due eastwards, the Song-koi takes its place in the series and continues in a generally south-easterly direction, along what is believed to be the former course of the Yang-tze, to the Gulf of Tonkin.

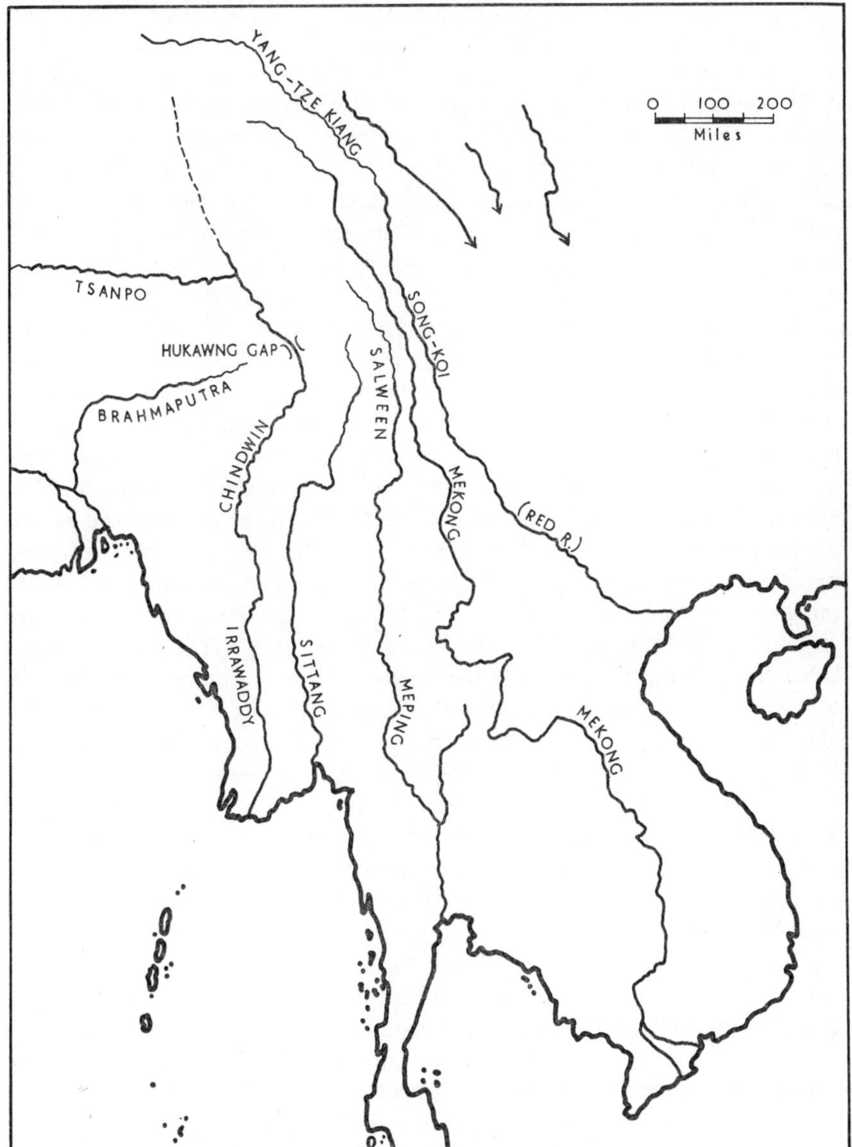

FIG. 62—Mainland South-east Asia: evolution of drainage, according to J. W. and C. J. Gregory

The headstreams of the Menam, the last and shortest of the peninsula's five master rivers, do not rise until another 500 miles farther south, but even so the main stream alone is some 500 miles long, and the system as a whole has built up one of the most extensive alluvial lowlands in the peninsula.

An explanation of this apparent anomaly may be found in Gregory's suggestion that the much greater Salween formerly reached the sea via the present Me Ping and Menam. And indeed, though much remains to be elucidated, there are strong indications of major changes in the courses of nearly all the larger rivers of the region within late Tertiary and Quaternary times. In Gregory's view the great Chinese rivers Tsan-po, Yang-tze and Si-kiang have old-established latitudinal courses, but the Himalayan uplift initiated a predominantly longitudinal drainage pattern over mainland South-east Asia, where the principal river valleys correspond to longitudinal ruptures which enabled the drainage from south-eastern Tibet to escape southwards over the plateau of western Yunnan.[3]

This immediate post-Himalayan pattern is shown in Fig. 62 but thereafter various adjustments have taken place, as a result of river capture aided by local subsidences and no doubt also by the very great differences in the regional incidence of rainfall. The present drainage pattern of the Indo-Pacific peninsula is shown in Fig. 61. In the far north the divides between the main rivers are so narrow as virtually to preclude the development of any tributaries other than short mountain torrents, but south of latitude 25° or so the general character of the relief becomes less congested. To the west the Patkai hills comprise the loftiest and most northerly portion of the series of closely parallel ranges which continue southwards through the Naga and Chin hills and the Arakan Yoma.[4] Together these form the divide between Burma and the Indian sub-continent and, on account of their dense and frequently malarial jungle, as well as the ruggedness of their relief, they have at all times constituted a formidable barrier. Indeed, the only major breach is that provided by the transverse Hukawng valley, which may represent the route by which the Tibetan Tsan-po flowed into the upper Irrawaddy in Tertiary times, before being captured by the Brahmaputra.[5] But although the valley has been suggested as a possible route for a railway to link Burma with India, the extremely high incidence of malaria there has long been a byword, which the experience of the Second World War served forcibly to confirm.

Thus, in the absence of any easy overland routes to the east, the Arakan coast, with its patches of deltaic lowland built up by the short torrential rivers rising in the western flanks of the mountain ranges, has historically been very remote from the main centres of Burmese life, and has often tended to look instead towards nearby Assam and the other lands fringing the Bay of Bengal.

Immediately to the east of the Irrawaddy-Sittang lowlands rises the steep edge, 500 miles long, of the vast upland which embraces the Shan State of Burma, the northern and western provinces of Thailand and the adjacent areas of upper Laos. In effect this wide expanse of highland represents an extension to

[3] Gregory, J. W. and C. J., pp. 171–4.

[4] The highest peak in the Patkai hills is Saramanti, 12,663 ft.; in the Naga-Chin hills summits range from 6,000 to 8,000 ft., and in the Arakan Yoma from 3,000 to 6, 000 ft.

[5] See Stamp (C), pp. 329–56, and Gregory, J. W. and C. J., p. 172.

both south and west of the great Yunnan plateau of south-western China, though that is not to suggest that the region exhibits uniformity of either structure or relief (Figs. 3 and 60). On the contrary, while the plateau surface maintains an elevation generally above 6,000 ft. in Yunnan, the average altitude of the Shan-Laos country is only about half that figure and, moreover, the relief is elaborately diversified by the innumerable deep river gorges which dissect it and by the longitudinal ranges rising above the level of the plateau proper. While the massive limestones, which account for a high proportion of the surface area, support only a relatively light vegetation, the wider valleys and the higher ridges normally carry continuous forest and this, together with the broken nature of the terrain, presents great difficulties to communication across the prevailing longitudinal grain of the country.

In its central portion in northern Thailand the plateau begins to break down into a series of detached and more subdued hills between latitudes 20° and 18°, but to both the west and east of this the main highlands continue south, respectively as the Tenasserim ranges which extend to the Kra isthmus and even beyond, and as the Annamite Chain which stretches almost to the Mekong delta.

Admittedly the saw-like ranges of Tenasserim have lost the plateau character of the uplands farther north, from which they stem, and moreover are traversed by a series of NW/SE valleys. The latter include those of the Ataran-Gweinoi and the Tenasserim rivers, which provide fairly easy routes[6] between the heavily forested and island-studded coast of lower Burma and the more open country along the north-western shores of the Gulf of Siam. But the Annamite Chain, notwithstanding its name, is in general a much broader and more continuous stretch of uplands, with summit levels exceeding 6,000 ft. at several points. Throughout most of its length the chain presents a steep front to the coast and tilts gradually down towards the Mekong valley. Its surface is deeply dissected and this, together with an exceptionally high rate of malaria infestation, has made it an almost insuperable barrier to movement between the coast of Vietnam and the valley of the Mekong.

Immediately to the north of the chain proper, in the country forming the divide between Laos and Tonkin, the uplands continue as a series of NW/SE ranges, composed largely of Uralo-Permian limestone. The latter has given rise to an intensely craggy karstic landscape offering scant possibility for human settlement, and in fact this is one of the most sparsely populated areas in the whole of South-east Asia.

By contrast, the coastal lowlands of Annam, though no wider than those of Arakan and frequently interrupted by a series of lateral spurs branching off from the main chain, contain numerous patches of fertile alluvium brought

[6] Easy, that is, as regards relief, though the region is very malarious. Both of these are very ancient trade routes; more recently the Ataran-Gweinoi route was followed by the Thailand–Burma railway built during the Second World War. See below, pp. 464, 517 and 523.

down by short but well-nourished streams, and this has provided a potent attraction to settlement since very early times.

One final tongue of highland projecting from the Yunnan plateau remains to be mentioned, namely that which forms the watershed between the Song-koi drainage system of Tonkin and the Yu-kiang/Si-kiang systems of southern China. Here again the predominant trend in the relief is NW/SE, but the ranges are generally subdued and their continuity breaks down before the coast is reached. Thus, except in so far as much of the watershed zone consists of poor limestone country incapable of supporting more than a relatively light population, the uplands here do not present any great obstacle to movement between the two countries. Between the wide Tso-kiang valley on the China side and Lang-son on the Tonkinese there is only a minor divide, and along the immediate coastal strip also movement is comparatively easy.[7]

Although the ranges and plateaux already described account for the greater part of the surface area of the peninsula, human activity is concentrated pre-eminently in the lowlands and in particular the middle and lower courses of four great rivers, the Irrawaddy, Menam, Mekong and Song-koi, have from time immemorial constituted the main demographic foci of the South-east Asian mainland.

Many factors combine to place the master rivers of the peninsula among the most actively eroding streams in the world. Thus the great altitude at which most of them and many of their major tributaries rise clearly plays a part, as also do the heavy monsoonal rains, which feed them in their upland reaches and in most cases nearer the coast as well, so giving rise to tremendous volumes of water at the time of the seasonal floods. Moreover, particularly in the dry zones of the interior, the sudden torrential downpours in the rainy season quickly scour the soil into the rivers, and whenever shifting cultivation or indiscriminate felling of the forests leads to the removal of too much of the protective vegetation this effect is magnified out of all proportion. Thus the rivers become clogged with silt, which in turn raises their beds farther downstream and so increases the extent of the flooded area in the lower parts of the valleys.[8]

For all these reasons, therefore, the rivers exhibit an unusually high capacity for sedimenting their lower reaches, and this applies both to the tributary streams which build large alluvial fans where they enter the main valleys, and especially to the main rivers themselves, whose deltas are extending seawards by amounts varying from 50 to 100 yards a year. Indeed, early Chinese records show that when Hanoi was first made the capital of Nan Yüeh over 2,000 years ago, the town which is now 60 miles inland was then on the coast, and although such precise data are not available for the other deltas, all of them have apparently undergone changes of comparable magnitude in historic times.

[7] Ethnically, however, this watershed zone represents a wedge of Thai territory between the Chinese and the Annamites of the lowlands proper. See below, pp. 534–5.

[8] For a vivid account of the problems so created see Calder, pp. 85–9.

As a result of this rapid sedimentation several of the large river-mouth ports of the peninsula are now faced with the need to undertake costly dredging operations to keep their channels clear. In this connexion it is interesting to note that Rangoon and Saigon are situated not on the Irrawaddy and Mekong respectively, as is often stated, but on much smaller rivers whose mouths in each case adjoin the larger delta. Such locations were chosen in pre-colonial times to exploit the benefits of water nodality while avoiding the severe seasonal floods close to the main rivers, but in modern times these ports have suffered less from the effects of sedimentation than have Haiphong and Bangkok which grew up directly on the banks of the Song-koi and Menam respectively.[9]

As has already been seen, the Irrawaddy river system occupies a major structural depression which stretches from northern Burma to the Gulf of Martaban. Perhaps the most striking feature of the Irrawaddy is the great bend between Mandalay and Pakokku in the heart of the dry zone, which is the result of river capture on a spectacular scale. Originally this central trough was drained by two roughly parallel rivers, of which the more westerly is now represented by the Chindwin and the Irrawaddy below Pakokku, while to the east the upper course of the present Irrawaddy formerly continued seawards via the valley of the modern Sittang.

The process whereby a former left-bank tributary of the western river was enabled to capture the upper waters of its neighbour to the east seems to have been initiated in post-Pliocene times by crustal movements in the vicinity of the zone of weakness still marked by Mt. Popa and the earthquake line along the Sittang valley. As a result, the catchment area of the western system was greatly extended, and today the Irrawaddy drains a total of some 158,000 square miles, while the Sittang, which is altogether smaller both in volume and length, nevertheless occupies a valley almost as wide as that of the Irrawaddy itself.

The name Irrawaddy does not apply to the main river north of Myitkyina, the upper limit of all-year navigation for small boats, and beyond this point there are two principal headstreams, known respectively as the Mali Kha and Nmai Kha. Between Myitkyina and the bend, however, navigation is impeded by a series of three gorges. The 'first defile' (*i.e.* the southernmost) at Thabeikkyin is not normally dangerous, but the second and the third – a narrow cleft only 50 yards wide – are progressively more hazardous, and Bhamo situated between the two is the effective limit for steamboats. Nevertheless, this is still some 870 miles from the sea and Ava, only 200 miles farther south, at the eastern end of the bend, is the sole place at which the Irrawaddy has yet been bridged.

In this middle section below the defiles the Irrawaddy meanders across a flood plain some three to ten miles wide which is bordered by a series of Pleistocene terraces rising in steps to several hundreds of feet above the river-level. Thereafter, in its lower reaches between Pakokku and Myanaung where, some

[9] Nevertheless, in all these ports extensive dredging is necessary today to keep the main channels clear. On sites, see Dobby (H), p. 304.

180 miles from the coast, the delta begins, the river broadens out, in places to as much as two miles in width, and forms a magnificent natural highway. The delta itself, with its eight main distributaries[10] and an intricate maze of minor channels, is almost classical in shape and has a sea frontage of approximately 150 miles. Its generally dead flat surface, standing only a few feet above sea-level, is broken by occasional higher ridges of older alluvium providing valuable sites for settlement beyond the reach of the seasonal floods. To the east the deltaic character is continued in the lowlands of the Hlaing and Pegu rivers, though beyond the latter the Sittang has not succeeded in building a delta owing mainly to the intensity of the tidal scour in the Gulf of Martaban.

The length of the depression drained by the Irrawaddy, Chindwin and Sittang rivers is approximately 700 miles, and its overall breadth averages about 100 miles. But, owing to the presence of the series of longitudinal ridges between the eastern and western rivers, the width of continuous lowlands does not exceed 40–50 miles, except in the delta and in the vicinity of the bend which links the two across the middle of the dry zone. Despite the very great differences in climate and vegetation between the delta and the dry zone, it is thus not surprising that these two regions have together constituted the main foci of population in Burma within historic times.

The next major river to the east, the Salween, likewise flows for the best-known part of its course through Burmese territory, but in almost all other respects it stands in marked contrast to the Irrawaddy. Notwithstanding its considerably greater length (1,750 miles, compared with the Irrawaddy's 1,250) its valley contains scarcely any extensive lowlands, and the river itself is of only minor use for navigation. For, apart from the short final stretch before it reaches the Tenasserim coast at Martaban, the Salween, flowing in a long and narrow tectonic trench, cut deep into the wild and wooded plateaux of the Burma-Thailand border, is more a torrent than a river. Indeed, as Chhibber[11] points out, this is the longest defile or canyon anywhere in the world, and although its general trend is longitudinal, it is remarkable for its succession of westward lurches which eventually bring the river out to the Indian Ocean instead of, as formerly, to the Gulf of Thailand. But though on account of its many rapids and its great volume of water it might appear to offer immense prospects as a source of hydro-electric power, the seasonal variation in its level, amounting to as much as 65 ft., is a serious liability in this respect.

Moreover, in the absence of any well-developed plains along even its lower course, the area drained by the river offers little to attract agricultural settlement, and no large clusters of population have ever grown up within it. Finally, while the Salween has not formed a true delta, its mouth is so clogged with silt as to make it virtually inaccessible to coastal steamships and, apart from its value as a

[10] Including the Bassein River, though this is only in part a distributary, and carries comparatively little water from the Irrawaddy to the sea. Stamp (C), p. 340.

[11] Chhibber, *op cit.* See also Spate (C).

chute to bring teak from the surrounding plateaux to tidewater, the river has hitherto proved almost completely useless to the inhabitants of the area through which it flows.

The Menam, on the other hand, though a much smaller system, is of far greater significance to man. Strictly speaking the river usually referred to by this name should be called the Chao Phraya, though the fact that it is more familiar as the Menam, which is simply the vernacular word for river, is a measure of its importance in the life of Thailand.

It originates in four roughly parallel streams which flow southwards from the belt of upland linking Shan State with north-western Laos. At first all four valleys are narrow and steep sided, but they gradually broaden out southwards and ultimately merge near Pitsanulok to form the central plain of Thailand. This lightly wooded[12] alluvial lowland, stretching some 300 miles from north to south and rather more than 100 miles from east to west, is for the most part very flat and low lying, broken only by a few residual limestone hills, and bounded to the west by the foothills of the Shan-Tenasserim ranges and to the east by the scarp face of the Korat plateau.

Only approximately 50 miles south of Paknampo, where the main river is joined by its large tributary, the Me Ping, it sub-divides into two, the Tachin to the west and the Chao Phraya proper to the east. From this point, some 120 miles from the coast, the character of the lowlands becomes deltaic, and since the main distributaries are raised by their own accretion well above the level of the plain and are heavily choked with silt, flooding is very widespread during the rainy season. In the south the Menam delta unites with those of the Srakeo on the left bank and of the Meklong[13] on the right to give a combined frontage of some 120 miles along the shores of the Bight of Bangkok which is steadily being filled in by detritus.[14] Although, on account of its much shorter length and smaller volume the Menam is far less useful as a natural highway than the Irrawaddy in Burma, it has nevertheless played an analogous rôle as the principal artery of Thailand, whose population is predominantly concentrated in the lowlands through which it flows.

With a total length of some 2,600 miles and a proportionately immense volume of water, the Mekong is by far the largest river in the peninsula and its drainage basin contains the greatest expanses of low-lying land in the whole of that region. Indeed, southwards from the point above Vientiane where it emerges from the Laos plateau, approximately 1,000 miles from the sea, its valley floor, though still narrowly hemmed in for several hundreds of miles between the Annamite Chain and the northern and eastern edges of the Korat plateau, does not exceed 600 ft. above sea-level. Furthermore, between Vientiane and the sea

[12] Much of it, of course, has long been cleared for cultivation.

[13] *I.e.* the combined Meklong Gweinoi and Meklong Gweiyai of western Thailand. The seaward margin of the lowlands here is strictly speaking, a marine plain.

[14] Besides the sandbanks which choke the mouth of the Menam (see below, pp. 517–8) the Gulf of Siam is noted for the muddiness of its waters.

the river and its tributaries successively drain most of Korat, the wide basin of Cambodia and the vast sprawling delta which covers the greater part of Cochin-china.

Nevertheless, both the wide seasonal fluctuations in its flow and the general immaturity of its development impose serious limitations to its usefulness and it is only below Kratié that there is any extensive development of true flood plain. As a result of the recent tectonic movements already referred to in connexion with the formation of the Annamite Chain, the middle course of the Mekong, between Luang Prabang and Kratié, consists of a series of calm reaches interrupted by rapids or falls at no less than nine points.[15] Of these the lowest, at Kratié itself, is only 250 miles from the sea, but much the most serious obstacle is provided by the Khone falls, a further 100 miles upstream, where the Mekong crosses a transverse layer of basalt. In so doing it divides into a series of channels spreading over a total width of several miles, and drops a matter of 45 ft. in a succession of cataracts. In terms of volume of flow, Khone ranks as the second greatest waterfall in the world, with 2½ million gallons per second, which is nearly double that of Niagara. Above this point the worst rapids occur in the sandstone gorge near Khemarat, where in places the current reaches a speed of ten knots. But north of Savannakhet the course of the river is unimpeded for over 300 miles and steamboats can navigate without difficulty as far up as Vientiane.

The Korat plateau is a remarkable region of some 60,000 square miles, developed upon an almost horizontal bed of Triassic sandstone which lies between the Menam lowlands of Thailand and the south-central portion of the Annamite Chain, and apparently rests unconformably on a floor of granite and ancient sedimentary rocks akin to those of the adjacent parts of the chain itself. The plateau, which has an average elevation of only about 500 ft., shows a very gentle tilt away from its west- and south-facing edges, the Dawng Phya Fai and the Phnom Dang Rek. Except in the south-western corner where they meet to culminate in the summit of Kh. Khiow (4,175 ft.) these Tertiary fault scarps, respectively overlooking the valley of the Pasak[16] and the great basin of Cambodia do not exceed 1,500–2,000 ft. in height, but thanks to their continuity and the denseness of their forests they have served fairly effectively to isolate Korat from the rest of Thailand.

The plateau itself is drained to the east by two major tributaries of the Mekong, namely the Nam Mun and the Nam Si, which have built wide flood plains extending deep into the heart of the region. However, owing to the blocking of their combined outlet into the main river when the latter is in flood, both the Nam Mun and the Nam Si are themselves prone to very extensive flooding, and large stretches of their valleys are prevailingly swampy, a condition which

[15] See Robequain (C), pp. 113–16.

[16] The Pasak is the easternmost large tributary of the Menam, and probably represents a former and more direct course of the Mekong from the Laos plateau to the sea.

tends to offset their advantages as areas of adequate water supply in a generally parched countryside.

It is, however, in the Tonlé Sap lowlands of Cambodia that the consequences of seasonal variation in the flow of the Mekong are most striking. In effect Tonlé Sap (lit. the Great Lake) represents the last vestiges of a wide inlet of the sea, which formerly occupied the south central portion of the Cambodian lowlands and is now being filled in by the rapid silting of the lower Mekong system. At the season of low water in the main river (November to June) the lake drains via the Tonlé Sap river, or Bras du Lac, into the Mekong, but during the period of high water (June to October) the flow of the Tonlé Sap river is reversed, and a substantial part of the Mekong floodwaters is diverted into the lake. Thus, at this time of year the latter may double or even quadruple its dry-season area of about 1,000 square miles and increase in depth from a mere six to over 40 ft. at the centre.[17] In this way Tonlé Sap acts as a natural regulator for the Mekong, and without such action the extent and depth of the seasonal floods in the delta would be very much greater even than in fact they are.

Immediately below Phnom Penh where the Tonlé Sap river joins the Mekong, the latter divides into two major distributaries, of which the more easterly is known as the Fleuve Antérieur, while the other is referred to either as the Fleuve Postérieur or the Bassac. Below Vinh Long, the Fleuve Antérieur subdivides again into four main branches, and the deltaic lowlands extended northwards and eastwards to merge with the alluvial lowlands of the lower Vaico and Saigon rivers. The Bassac on the other hand flows almost directly from Chau Doc to the sea as a single great stream, which exceeds twelve miles in width at its mouth but, owing to the enormous quantity of silt which it brings down, is of little navigational use except for small vessels. To the south the huge triangular peninsula of Camau with sides ranging from 110 to 130 miles in length, is as uniformly flat as the central delta, though it lacks a comparable network of distributaries and owes its peculiar configuration mainly to longshore drift which has carried great quantities of the deltaic material southwards to form a giant spit.

The Song-koi (or Red river) of Tonkin is a much shorter stream than the Mekong and flows for most of its length in a narrow structural trench somewhat reminiscent of that of the Salween, though on a smaller scale. Accordingly its plains are very restricted in total extent, and only below Yen Bay, 140 miles from the coast, do they broaden out in any significant degree. This trench-like character of much of the main valley is typical also of several of the larger tributaries, particularly the Song-bo (or Black river) which flows in a parallel trough some 40 miles to the south before making a right-angled bend at Cho Bo

[17] Even in maximum flood Tonlé Sap does not now extend to the ruins of Angkor, though it seems likely that the city was originally built on the shore of the lake, which must then have been several times its present size and probably also more easily accessible from the sea. Tonlé Sap is continuing to decrease in extent as a result of the deposition of detritus by the various streams draining into it.

and joining the Song-koi near Hung Hoa.[18] Only a few miles below this confluence is the apex of the delta, approximately 90 miles from the coast, and the lack of any extensive mature reaches between the uplands and the delta helps to explain the severity of the floods in the latter. Thus, at Hanoi the estimated average flow in the dry season (March–May) is some 25,000 cu. ft. per second, but at high water between June and October the figure rises to as much as 812,000 cu. ft. per second, which is double that of the Nile.[19]

In these circumstances, moreover, the delta is extending seawards very rapidly, especially on its southern margins where it directly adjoins the series of smaller deltas of the Song-ma, Song-chu and Song-ka. All-told, therefore, the belt of deltaic country stretches virtually without interruption from the Baie d'Along in the north almost to the Porte d'Annam in the south, beyond which lie the more restricted and patchy coastal plains of central Annam, already described on page 413.

The diversity of the geological structure of the Indo-Pacific peninsula is closely reflected in its mineral wealth, which falls into three or four main divisions. The first of these consists of the mineral oil, found in the series of fields which run lengthwise through the Tertiary depression of central Burma. To the east of this the vast semi-circle of plateaux extending from the Karen-Shan-Kachin country of Burma through Laos into Northern Vietnam has a considerable variety of metallic minerals, notably lead, silver, zinc, tungsten, antimony and lode tin. Moreover, in the south-western prolongation of the Mesozoic uplands into Tenasserim and peninsular Thailand, both lode and alluvial occurrences of tin are widespread. So far as coal is concerned, by far the most important known deposit is the anthracite of the Quang Yen basin of Northern Vietnam, though there are several much smaller deposits of other types of coal and lignite, notably in north-western Burma, Southern Vietnam and central Thailand. As yet very little iron ore has been mined, though the haematite deposits of central Cambodia (near Kompong Thom) and central Thailand (near Lopburi) appear to be promising.

All told, therefore, the Indo-Pacific peninsula is by no means badly placed as regards mineral wealth, though apart from the oil of Burma and the anthracite of Northern Vietnam fossil fuel supplies are very small and scattered, a fact which serves to underline the importance of the very great hydro-electric potential in many parts of the peninsula.[20]

II. CLIMATE AND VEGETATION

With the exception of the predominantly mountainous northern tip of Burma, which reaches to approximately 28° 34′ N latitude, the whole peninsula lies

[18] The line of the upper Song-bo is continued seawards by the Song-huoi, a tributary of the Song-ma.

[19] This represents an increase of over 32-fold. *Cf.* the Menam at Paknampo, with 4,000 cu. ft. per second in the dry season and 54,000 cu. ft. per second at flood, a 14-fold increase.

[20] Unfortunately most, though not all, of the best sites are in relatively inaccessible and sparsely inhabited areas.

within the tropics and its southern extremity in peninsular Thailand, some 5° 42′ N, is barely equatorial, though the climate there does show some approximation to that of Malaya, with rain at all seasons and only minor fluctuations in mean monthly temperatures throughout the year. Elsewhere, however, the peninsula is subjected throughout to the tropical monsoonal rhythm of climate, though clearly a large proportion of the total area is sufficiently elevated for it to experience temperatures well below the appropriate sea-level norms, and in the far north the higher mountains over 10,000 ft. or so may receive up to two months' snowfall in winter.

In general terms the climatic pattern resembles that of peninsular India, which lies in almost identical latitudes, but there are significant differences reflecting both the more intricate relief of the Indo-Pacific peninsula and also the extent to which its surface is penetrated by arms of the sea. Thus, while the N/S alignment of ranges and valleys across the prevailing winds gives rise in the Indo-Pacific peninsula to alternate zones of exceptionally heavy and altogether lighter rainfall, none of its lowlands is sufficiently remote from the sea to be truly continental in character, and even the driest part of the Burmese dry zone is less parched than the worst rain-shadow areas of the Deccan.

Nevertheless, the similarities between these two major regions are much greater than the differences and, as in peninsular India so also in peninsular South-east Asia, the climate is completely dominated by the alternation of SW and NE wind systems in the summer and winter halves of the year. Moreover, the SW monsoon is much the more important source of rain in all but a narrow strip along the east coast of Vietnam where the rainfall régime resembles that of Madras. Thus in both peninsulas rainfall is generally heaviest on the western margins, rather less heavy though still abundant on the eastern edges and significantly lighter in most areas in between.

The mechanism of the monsoons has been described at some length in Chapter 2, so that here it will suffice to consider their effects upon climate during the several seasons of the year. Over most of the Indo-Pacific peninsula the NE monsoon dominates during the least warm season, that is from October to March, in the sense that NE winds tend to prevail throughout that period. In fact, however, these represent an alternation of trade winds and the monsoon proper, the former bringing more humid and oppressive weather and the latter generally cooler and fresher conditions.[21]

This season is marked by rainfall along virtually all the eastern seaboard of Indochina, but such falls scarcely extend inland beyond the edge of the Annamite Chain, and in central Thailand and Burma the period is pleasantly invigorating and sunny, and almost completely dry. Even along the Vietnam coast itself, moreover, winter rainfall varies greatly both in character and amount, the Tonkin delta receiving between 1·2 in. and 2·8 in. a month, largely in the form of drizzle

[21] In the Gweinoi valley of western Thailand less than 500 ft. above sea-level the nights in January and February can be sufficiently chilly to freeze coconut oil.

TABLE 48

MAINLAND SOUTH-EAST ASIA: SELECTED TEMPERATURE AND RAINFALL FIGURES

Station	*Jan.*	*Feb.*	*Mar.*	*Apr.*	*May*	*Jun.*	*Jul.*	*Aug.*	*Sep.*	*Oct.*	*Nov.*	*Dec.*	*Average*	*Total*
Akyab 20° N, 93° E.	70	73	79	83	84	82	81	81	82	82	78	72	79	
20	0·1	0·2	0·5	2·0	13·7	49·4	53·7	42·5	24·6	11·6	5·0	0·6		203·8
Rangoon 17° N, 93° E.	77	79	84	87	84	81	80	80	81	82	80	77	81	
18	0·2	0·2	0·3	1·4	12·1	18·4	21·5	19·7	15·4	7·3	2·8	0·3		99·6
Mandalay 22° N, 96° E.	70	75	83	90	89	87	87	86	85	83	76	71	82	
250	0·1	0·1	0·2	1·1	5·8	5·5	3·3	4·6	5·7	4·7	1·6	0·4		35·1
Lashio 23° N, 98° E.	60	63	71	75	77	77	76	76	76	73	66	61	71	
2802	0·3	0·3	0·6	2·2	6·9	9·8	12·0	12·7	7·8	5·7	2·7	0·9		61·9
Amherst 16° N, 98° E.	78	79	82	84	82	79	78	78	79	81	81	78	80	
71	0·1	0·5	0·3	4·8	23·8	39·2	45·9	42·3	29·2	10·0	1·6	1·3		198·9
Victoria Point 10° N, 99° E.	79	81	83	84	81	80	79	79	79	79	80	79	80	
147	0·3	0·1	1·3	3·9	17·1	28·3	30·0	25·5	25·9	18·0	5·8	2·7		158·0
Phuket 8° N, 98° E.	81	82	82	84	82	82	82	81	80	81	81	81	82	
10	1·4	1·5	2·9	5·0	11·7	10·4	8·5	9·6	12·9	12·4	7·6	3·1		87·0
Bangkok 14° N, 101° E.	77	78	84	87	86	84	84	83	82	82	80	77	82	
near S.L.	0·4	0·7	2·6	1·2	6·3	5·9	6·2	8·2	12·0	9·5	3·0	0·5		56·4
Chiengmai 19° N, 99° E.	72	74	77	82	83	81	80	81	81	79	75	71	78	
1,410	0·4	0·1	1·0	1·6	6·0	5·1	5·7	9·1	9·5	6·7	2·3	0·5		48·0
Nakhorn Ratsima 15° N, 102° E.	75	80	84	86	84	83	83	82	82	80	77	73	81	
594	0·4	1·5	1·6	3·1	7·2	5·3	4·5	6·4	8·7	7·3	1·8	0·4		48·2
Luang Prabang 20° N, 102° E.	69	73	78	82	84	83	82	82	82	79	74	70	78	
942	0·6	0·7	1·2	4·3	6·4	6·1	9·1	11·8	6·5	3·1	1·2	0·5		51·5
Vientiane 18° N, 103° E.	70	74	79	83	81	82	81	81	81	78	75	71	78	
531	0·2	0·6	1·5	3·9	10·5	11·9	10·5	11·5	11·9	4·3	0·6	0·1		67·5
Saigon 11° N, 107° E.	79	81	84	85	84	82	81	82	81	81	80	79	82	
near S.L.	0·7	0·1	0·6	1·9	8·7	13·1	12·1	11·1	13·5	10·7	4·5	2·5		79·5
Nhatrang 15° N, 109° E.	75	77	79	82	83	84	84	84	82	80	78	76	80	
11	2·4	1·1	0·9	0·9	2·4	2·2	2·0	1·5	6·9	10·6	13·9	9·6		54·5
Hué 16° N, 108° E.	69	67	74	80	83	85	84	85	81	78	73	70	78	
23	4·0	4·8	1·8	2·4	3·6	2·8	3·4	4·0	16·2	26·3	22·4	10·2		101·9
Hanoi 21° N, 106° E.	62	62	67	73	80	83	83	83	81	78	71	66	74	
near S.L.	1·2	1·6	1·8	2·8	7·6	9·6	11·4	12·5	12·0	4·4	2·4	1·2		68·6
Qui Nhon 14° N, 109° E.	73	74	77	80	83	85	86	87	83	79	77	72	80	
20	2·1	1·6	1·5	1·0	2·1	2·2	2·7	2·2	9·8	17·1	17·1	5·7		65·1
Cap St. Jacques 10° N, 107° E.	76	77	79	83	82	81	79	79	79	79	78	76	79	
60	0·1	0·1	0·1	1·2	7·8	7·7	8·8	6·0	7·5	8·0	2·8	1·0		51·0

(popularly if inelegantly referred to by the local French ex-patriate as *crachin*) while farther south in central Vietnam, where the seaward edge of the mountains faces the oncoming winds, torrential orographic downpours occur, and the total precipitation is much greater. Thus, for example, Hué receives 26·3 in. in October, 22·4 in. in November and 10·2 in. in December, though thereafter the amount decreases steeply to 4·0 in. in January, 4·8 in. in February and 1·8 in. in March.

The heaviness of the rainfall in central Vietnam at the beginning of the season of the NE monsoon is superficially analogous to the 'burst' of the SW monsoon in India and Burma; the probable causes of this have been discussed in Chapter 2. However, much of the rainfall during the closing months of the year is associated with westward-moving typhoons originating over the South China Sea, and approximately 80 per cent of these occur within the five months June–November inclusive.

It is, of course, primarily as a result of the apparent movement southwards of the sun that the period from November to February is the least warm season in all parts of the Indo-Pacific peninsula, though especially along the eastern seaboard this tendency is reinforced by the cooling effects of the NE monsoon. Nevertheless, it is only in the extreme north-east that mean monthly sea-level temperatures drop even at this time of the year to below 70°, and Hanoi is unique among the stations included in Table 47, in recording a figure as low as 62° for January and February. By late March–early April, however, when the NE monsoon begins gradually to break up over the peninsula and the sun moves north once again, the land becomes extremely dry and progressively hotter. Indeed in most parts of Burma, Thailand and the Mekong lowlands,[22] April and May, between the two monsoons, are the hottest months of all, with mean monthly temperatures averaging mostly from 82 to 87° in coastal areas and reaching as much as 90° in the interior dry zone of Burma.[23]

This period of often almost intolerable heat, punctuated by violent dust storms, when the ground bakes hard and the vegetation appears shrivelled and burnt by the sun, comes to an end with the advent of the SW monsoon, usually in late May. For although the consequent drop in temperature is only a matter of a few degrees, and the monthly sea-level means do not anywhere fall below 80° until October, this great stream of hot and very moist equatorial air at first brings a sudden abundance of rainfall to almost every part of the region except the coast of Annam, and the colour of the landscape changes from yellow-brown to green with astonishing rapidity.

This so-called 'burst' of the SW monsoon is much more pronounced in the west of the peninsula, so that even Mandalay in the Burmese dry zone gets 5·8 in. of rain in May and 5·5 in. in June, though these amounts are not large

[22] Even including the delta. See the figures for Saigon.

[23] As noted above, p. 23, temperatures often reach 105° or so in the dry zone during April and early May.

when compared with Rangoon's 12·1 in. and 18·4 in., which are followed by the even larger 21·5 in. of July. Farther east the onset of the monsoon is progressively more gradual, but throughout the peninsula it continues until September to bring appreciable and generally heavy rain, sometimes indeed in the form of continuous torrential downpours lasting for several days at a stretch, though more usually as an accompaniment to heavy thunderstorms which punctuate otherwise calm and sultry but, in the main, fairly sunny weather.[24]

The decisive effect of relief and aspect on the geographical incidence of rainfall from the SW monsoon can be seen by comparing Akyab's 203·8 in. (183·9 in. of it falling from May to September inclusive) with Mandalay's 35·1 in. (24·9 in. May–September). For, as its name indicates, the prevailing direction of the summer monsoon is SW – or even WSW over the Bay of Bengal – which is almost at right angles to the general trend of the main peninsular ranges, so that most of the Burmese coast from Arakan to Tenasserim receives an annual rainfall of the order of 200 in. But owing to the continuity of the ranges and the relative narrowness of many of the valleys in their lee, the latter derive very little rainfall from the main SW winds, which continue directly across them after depositing extremely heavy falls on the western-facing slopes, and indeed the central valley of Burma suffers appreciably from the desiccating föhn-like effect of such winds descending from the Arakan Yoma.[25] It is not, therefore, surprising that over extensive rain-shadow areas in Burma, Thailand and Cambodia the total annual precipitation is only 40–60 in. and even, in places, less, and in view of the high temperatures and rapid evaporation such amounts leave little or no margin for satisfactory cultivation without some supplementary supply of water.

In fact all these dry zones derive the greater part of their rainfall from offshoots of the main SW-monsoonal airstream, which are drawn into the interior lowlands by the local low-pressure systems developing there during the summer months. In Burma the amount of such rainfall diminishes northwards from the delta as far as the Irrawaddy bend, with the result that while Rangoon, as already noted, receives an annual total of nearly 100 in., Thayetmyo gets only 40 in. and a few areas in the central dry zone have less than 25 in. Farther east, however, the main monsoonal currents lose much of their moisture in crossing successive mountain ranges, so that along the coast of the Bight of Bangkok totals mostly lie between 55 and 80 in. On the other hand, the more subdued character of the relief surrounding the central valley of Thailand means that the latter suffers less from föhn-type winds than does the corresponding region in Burma, and even at Chiengmai, 400 miles from the mouth of the Menam, the annual rainfall is 48 in.

[24] To a limited extent, and more particularly in the east, rainfall during this season may be associated with typhoons. As noted above (p. 38) most typhoons occur in July–November; from July to September their main track lies north of lat. 15° N, whereas in October and November it is between 10 and 15° N.

[25] Föhn-like winds also descend on the Dry Zone from the Shan plateau to the east. See Dobby (H), p. 152.

Broadly similar conditions prevail in the Cambodian basin and that part of the Mekong delta which lies in the lee of the Cardamom and Elephant mountains. Here the annual rainfall is between 40 and 60 in., and similar figures are also typical of the greater part of the Korat plateau.[26] In the latter area, moreover, the porosity of the surface sandstones seriously aggravates the problems arising from the relatively low rainfall, so that except for the wide marshy tracts along the Nam Mun and Nam Si, the plateau is as characteristically waterless as the worst parts of the Burmese dry zone, and is notoriously prone to cholera epidemics during the dry season.

Even as far east as this, however, the more exposed uplands receive very heavy rain from the SW monsoon. Thus the southern and western faces of the Korat plateau have at least 60–80 in. annually, and in places as much as 120 in., while Saigon, virtually at sea-level, receives 79·5 in. since the air streams are recharged with moisture by their passage across the Gulf of Siam.

Indeed, not even the east coast of Indochina is without useful amounts of rainfall all through the period of the SW monsoon,[27] though in central Vietnam this summer rain is very much less than that which occurs during the last three months of the year, as noted on p. 38. But farther north in the lowlands fringing the Gulf of Tonkin the season of the SW monsoon, thanks to the formation then of a small semi-permanent lee depression behind the Annamite Chain,[28] is once again the period of maximum rain, and Hanoi receives 53·1 in. between May and September, out of an annual total of 68·6 in.

Despite the various local peculiarities which have been described in the preceding pages, the data shown in Table 48 serve to emphasize the very considerable degree of similarity between the climates in widely scattered parts of the Indo-Pacific peninsula. However, it should be remembered that while nearly all the stations included in the table are situated in the lowlands, almost half the total area of the peninsula, by virtue of its altitude has temperatures varying from 10 to 30° below the appropriate sea-level norm. Thus, for example, over large parts of the Shan/Laos plateau at least slight night frost is common during the winter months, and the summers are always distinctly cooler than in the nearby plains.

Within the lowlands where at least three-quarters of the population lives, the most obvious distinction is that already drawn on page 41 between the normal tropical monsoonal climate and that of the three main dry zones with less than 50 in. annual rainfall. But the peculiarities of the northern and central Vietnamese coastlands also call for further consideration. For although in view of the relatively small annual range of temperature it matters little whether the heaviest rains occur in the summer or the winter half of the year, it is of far-reaching significance that northern and central Vietnam alone receive enough rain in their driest months to be of real use to the cultivator.

[26] In the rain-shadow area of south-western Korat, *i.e.* immediately behind the highest point of the plateau rim, the annual rainfall is only 34·6 in.

[27] Nhatrang, for example, gets 15 in. during May–September.

[28] Hare, p. 157.

In other respects, however, these two adjacent areas are by no means identical climatically. Thus northern Vietnam, besides having its heaviest rains between April and October, in contrast to the September–February peak of central Vietnam, also shows a wider variation in monthly temperatures (from 62° in January and February to 83° during June–August) than any other part of the Indo-Pacific peninsula. Indeed, in respect of both temperature and rainfall patterns the Tonkin delta has more in common with the adjacent lowlands of sub-tropical China.[29] than it has with the other great deltas of the peninsula, which are all single-harvest regions, and this fact has been of incalculable importance in its effect on the agricultural development of the region.

In view of what has already been stated in Chapter 2 and, *en passant*, earlier in the present chapter, the distribution of vegetation in the Indo-Pacific peninsula (Fig. 63) calls for little further comment. For the most part dense evergreen rain forest is confined to the outer margins of the peninsula, that is to the Arakan ranges and the Annamite Chain,[30] together with a few particularly exposed uplands elsewhere, such as the edges of the Shan and Korat plateaux, and the Elephant and Cardamom mountains, all of which receive 80 in. or more rain annually. As elsewhere in South-east Asia, the character of the vegetation changes above 2,500–3,500 ft., but even so most of these uplands carry a fairly dense tree cover up to their crests.

Nevertheless, very little of this can be classed as virgin forest for, particularly in the western mountains of Burma and in the Annamite Chain, shifting cultivation is widely practised, and most of the rain forest there has long been of the secondary variety. Furthermore, there are many areas within the normal climatic limits of the evergreen rain-forest belt where particularly porous subsoils have instead induced a type of deciduous monsoon forest, similar to that which is generally prevalent throughout most of the rest of the peninsula[31] except at higher altitudes.

In fact, however, the vegetation within the deciduous monsoon-forest belt itself shows considerable variation from place to place, in response to local differences both of rainfall and of soils. Thus the main supplies of teak come from the relatively wetter parts of the monsoon-forest zone, notably the Pegu Yoma, the uplands north of the Irrawaddy bend, northern Tenasserim and the adjacent areas of Karen State, northern Thailand and a small area around Pak Lay in Laos, where comparatively pure stands are found in association with crystalline rocks. But in the drier Menam valley and over much of Cambodia the vegetation is distinctly open in character, with a marked predominance of bamboos in many places.

[29] The extreme south of China lies technically within the tropics, but owing to its position on the eastern side of the world's greatest land mass and the related effects of the NW/NE monsoon it has winter temperatures several degrees cooler than are normally experienced in such latitudes.

[30] The adjacent coastal plains also were once naturally covered with evergreen rain forest though most of this has long been cleared for cultivation.

[31] *I.e.* in areas receiving less than 80 in. of rainfall annually.

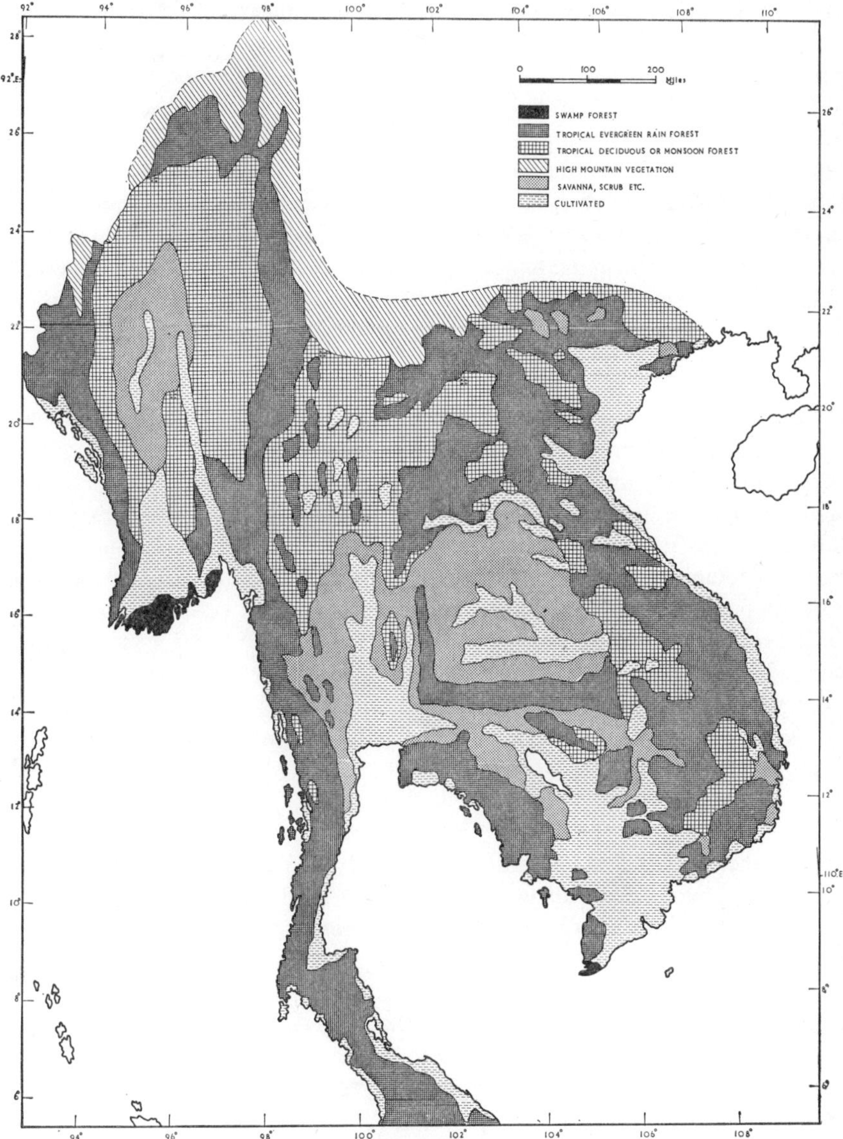

FIG. 63—Mainland South-east Asia: vegetation

In the dry zones proper, the natural vegetation is still lighter, and in both central Burma and the Korat plateau the thorny scrub has a distinctly arid appearance. Moreover, both here and also in many places which would otherwise be under monsoon forest, human interference has led to a deterioration in the vegetation type. Thus, extensive areas in the central valley of Thailand and the

Cambodian basin now support only a cover of savanna grass[32] or parkland, and wide stretches of the Shan and Laos plateaux where the surface is underlain with porous limestones likewise carry a predominantly open vegetation.

Today, of course, most of the alluvial tracts in both the middle and the lower courses of the main rivers, as well as along the coastal margins elsewhere, are kept cleared of their natural vegetation and devoted in the main to wet-rice cultivation.[33] While much of the older alluvium is severely laterized the younger alluvials provide the most fertile soils in the peninsula, and indeed the remainder, apart from some of the *terres rouges* derived from the Quaternary basaltic lavas of southern Indochina,[34] are generally much inferior in quality, suffering as they do from the characteristic defects associated with the humid tropics.[35]

III. CONCLUSION

In attempting to sum up the opportunities which the Indo-Pacific lands afford for human settlement, one's thoughts inevitably focus upon the great river valleys gouged deep into an otherwise mountainous, and in most places exceedingly inhospitable, terrain. Yet within these valleys themselves there are important differences in habitability and agricultural potential. Thus in the middle courses flooding is generally much less severe, and irrigation correspondingly easier to organize than in the lower valleys, and in some cases this contrast is further reinforced by the difference in rainfall between a sheltered interior and an exposed coastal zone.

To peoples equipped with only a limited range of skills[36], the lightly wooded dry zones with their prevailingly lighter soils have normally appeared more manageable than the densely forested and often deeply flooded deltas. But when the latter have been effectively cleared, and their floods in some measure controlled[37], their superior productivity has been plain for all to see.

Nevertheless, while this antithesis between coastal and interior lowlands provides a common denominator in the history of all the great river basins of the peninsula, each of these regions has its own distinctive traits, both physical and human, which it is the task of the succeeding three chapters to portray. Meanwhile it is perhaps appropriate to end the present chapter with a brief reference to the geographical position of the peninsula as a whole, *vis-à-vis* its immediate neighbours, namely China and the Indian sub-continent.

[32] Predominantly *Imperata cylindrica*, known locally as *tranh* in Indochina where it is widely used for thatch.

[33] Even in the Burmese dry zone wet rice is the most important single crop, though it covers only 35–40 per cent of the cultivated area there, as against at least double that proportion in most other lowland areas.

[34] The *terres rouges* vary greatly in quality though the best of them are very fertile. See Robequain (C), p. 188.

[35] This hardly applies to the driest areas, notably in Burma, but the sedentary soils there are not noticeably more fertile and some are apt to suffer from excessive salinity.

[36] *Cf.* Dobby (H), p. 167 and Zelinsky, p. 143.

[37] Or in some cases offset by the cultivation of floating rice. See below, pp. 496, 510 and 533.

Because the general slope of the land exaggerates the normal latitudinal differences in temperature, the transition from the temperate and invigorating climate of the Yunnan-Tibetan borderlands to the sweltering heat of the deep river valleys in the peninsular interior is unusually abrupt.[38] But along the coastal strip from southern China to northern Vietnam the climatic change is so gradual as to be barely perceptible. Furthermore, no serious natural obstacle bars the way southwards until the NW/SE Annamite Chain reaches the coast near the so-called Porte d'Annam, *c.* 18° N, but owing to both its ruggedness and unhealthiness the chain has always formed an extremely effective barrier to movement beyond that point. Thus the lie of the land serves to underline the climatic affinities of northern Vietnam with the southern littoral of China, and so far as physical geography alone is concerned the Annamite Chain may be regarded as the true regional boundary in the east, corresponding to that provided by the Arakan ranges which form the obvious natural limit in the west.

To some extent, also, it is possible to trace an analogy between the intimacy of northern Vietnam's contact with southern China and the way in which Arakan's history has frequently been bound up with that of the neighbouring shores of the Indian Ocean. Yet, despite this local similarity between the north-eastern and north-western frontiers, the wider differences between the peninsula's relationship respectively to China and to the Indian sub-continent remain of far greater significance. For, thanks to the relentlessly longitudinal grain of the relief, the great valleys of the peninsula are more readily accessible from the north than they are from the west, and this fact, which has so largely determined the demographic evolution of the region in the past may likewise entail no less momentous consequences for the future.

SELECT BIBLIOGRAPHY

Braak (A) (B) (C)
Brodrick (B)
Calder
Chhibber
Credner
De Terra
Dobby (H)
Gourou (H) (K)
Graham
Gregory, J. W.
Gregory, J. W. and C. J.
Hare
Lobeck
Lyde
McCarthy
McCune
Miller, A. A.
Morehead
Pendleton (A)
Robequain (C) (D)
Scrivenor
Sion
Spate (C)
Spencer, J. E. (A)
Stamp (A) (B) (C) (D)
Suess
Umbgrove (A)
Zelinsky

Asia's battle against floods
Siam – General and medical features
Siam – Nature and industry
Weather in the China Seas and in the western part of the North Pacific Ocean
Indo-China (N.I.D.)

[38] Kunming (Yunnan) at 6,211 ft. above sea-level has an average annual temperature of 62° and a total annual rainfall of 42·5 in.

CHAPTER 14

The Union of Burma

I. THE REFASHIONING OF BURMA UNDER BRITISH RULE, 1824–1947

With an area of 261,760 square miles, which is rather more than that of France and the Benelux countries combined, Burma is the largest of all the states of mainland South-east Asia. Nevertheless, its total population of 20,255,000 in 1958 is comparatively small, and its average density of *c.* 78 to the square mile is in fact lower than that of most of the other South-east Asian states.[1]

In its geographical layout the country presents a rather simple pattern and, apart from the Tenasserim coastal strip, the national territory is compactly disposed. The core of the Burmese œcumene is formed by the central belt, comprising the main part of the great structural depression drained by the Irrawaddy, Chindwin and Sittang rivers. Although the relief is interrupted by several longitudinal ridges, of which the Pegu Yoma between the Sittang and the lower Irrawaddy is the most notable, it is the distinction between the dry interior and the much wetter coastal zone which represents the all-important regional divide within the central belt. Thus from about latitude 19° to 23° N the dry zone, with less than 40 in. of rain annually, embraces the whole width of the belt, while to the south of this both the lower Sittang valley and the Pegu Yoma may be grouped with the great plains of the Irrawaddy delta as regions of heavy rainfall, generally ranging from 80 in. to 130 in. in the year.[2] Thanks to both the extent of its lowlands and the excellence of its natural waterways, the central belt has throughout history been the focus of Burmese life, though, as noted in Chapter 4, the precise centre of gravity has oscillated between the 'heartland' in the dry zone and the 'entrance area' in the delta.[3] Except along its southern fringe, which lies open to the sea, this central belt is completely surrounded by uplands. To the west, north-west and north, the Tertiary folded ranges of the Arakan Yoma and the Naga and Chin hills effectively separate Burma from the Indian sub-continent, while to the north-east and east the series of plateaux stretching from the borders of Tibet and Yunnan to Tenasserim provides a natural frontier zone against China and Siam. Since in both Arakan and Tenas-

[1] Only Cambodia, Laos and British Borneo have lower densities. See Table 8, p. 177.
[2] Though nearly all of this comes within five months.
[3] Spate (C), p. 10.

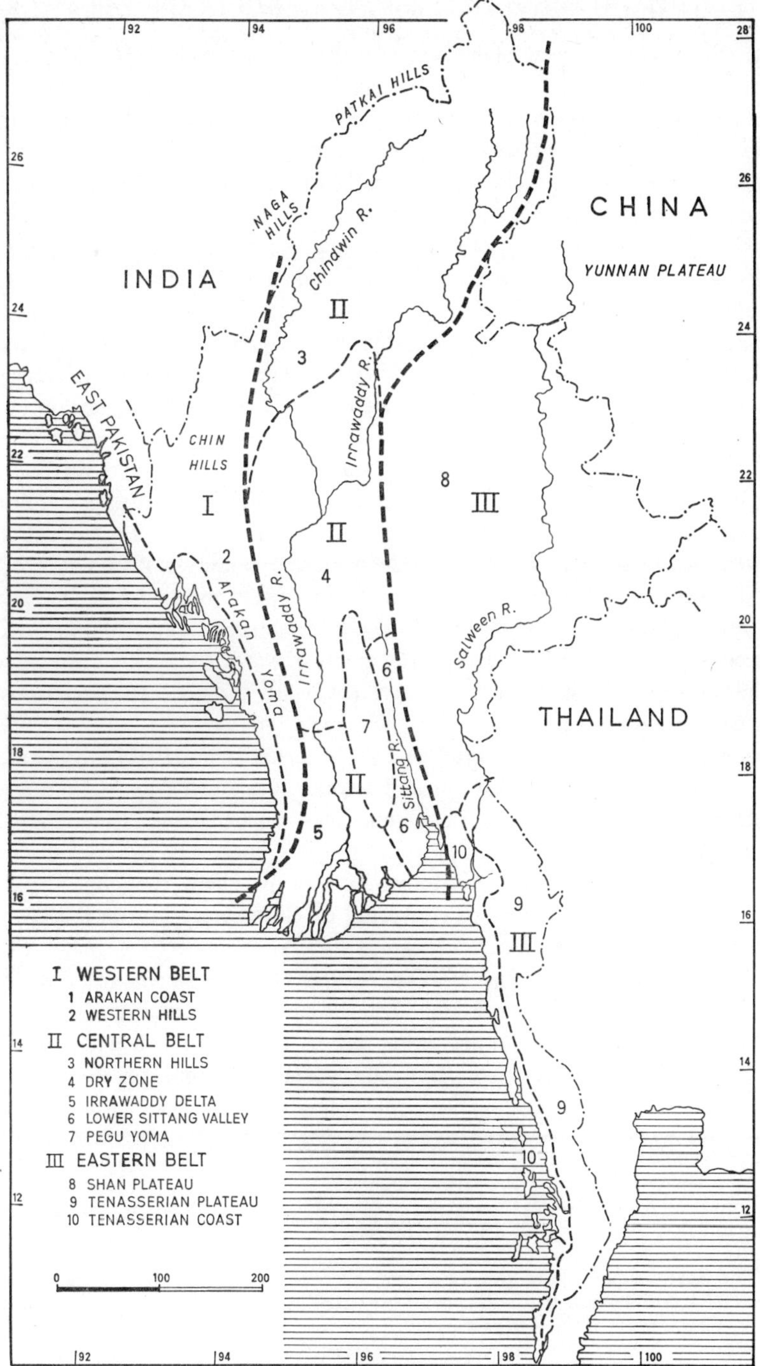
CHINA
YUNNAN PLATEAU
INDIA
EAST PAKISTAN
THAILAND
PATKAI HILLS
NAGA HILLS
CHIN HILLS
Chindwin R.
Irrawaddy R.
Arakan Yoma
Sittang R.
Salween R.
I WESTERN BELT
1 ARAKAN COAST
2 WESTERN HILLS
II CENTRAL BELT
3 NORTHERN HILLS
4 DRY ZONE
5 IRRAWADDY DELTA
6 LOWER SITTANG VALLEY
7 PEGU YOMA
III EASTERN BELT
8 SHAN PLATEAU
9 TENASSERIAN PLATEAU
10 TENASSERIAN COAST
0
100
200

FIG. 6 —Burma: natural regions

serim the narrow coastal plains are immediately succeeded inland by rugged longitudinal uplands, neither of these regions can offer any serious rivalry to the delta as a means of access to the interior, and both are relatively isolated from the main centres of Burmese life.

These broad natural divisions are closely reflected in the racial geography of Burma. Thus, while the dry zone, at the natural focus of riverine communications, is the ancestral home of the Burmans,[4] the latter have spread in historic times into the delta and the coastlands of Arakan and Tenasserim, though not in sufficient strength completely to swamp the Mon (Talaing) peoples of the Pegu region who thus remain as a distinctive ethnic group today. Despite certain superficial differences, notably between the swarthier-skinned Burmans and the rather lighter-coloured Mons, whose language is akin to Khmer (i.e. Cambodian), all the main lowland peoples – Burmans, Arakanese and Mons – are of predominantly Pareœan stock and, more important, all subscribe to the Buddhist religion and are possessors of a literate culture. Indeed, the astonishingly high literacy rate (recently estimated at 72 per cent of the men and 22 per cent of the women)[5] in these areas results directly from the centuries-old practice of the Buddhist clergy of providing free education for boys in village monastery schools. Essentially the same attributes extend also to the Shan people of the east-central plateau region who, from almost every point of view, should be grouped with the plainsmen rather than with the more backward and generally pagan peoples who occupy the hills proper.[6]

Though frequently grouped together as 'hill tribes' these latter include a wide diversity of racial and cultural types. Thus the Was and Palaungs, who occupy the higher uplands of eastern Shan State, show recognizable Nesiot characters and at least among the Was, head-hunting is still practised. On the other hand the Karens farther south are ethnically closer to the Shans, though, except in so far as many of them have been converted to Christianity during the past 150 years, they also are animists.

For the rest the main groups of hill peoples of the west, north-west and north-east are respectively known as the Chins, Nagas[7] and Kachins, but these are vernacular rather than scientific terms and as such conceal a wide variety of dialect and custom. In all three cases, however, the predominant stock is clearly

[4] Originally an ethnic term, the name Burman is now applied to all who habitually speak Burmese, and as such usually covers the Arakanese and Tavoyans as well as the majority peoples of the central lowlands. The term Burmese is nowadays used to embrace all the indigenous peoples of the Union of Burma.

[5] According to the 1931 Census 31·3 per cent of the total population (48·6 per cent of males and 14·1 per cent of females) were literate. *Cf.* rates for Thailand, see below, p. 521, note 85.

[6] The Shans entered later and for a time overran the plains before being eventually driven back into the hills by the Burmans. Nevertheless, the Shans cling wherever possible to the valleys, most of them in fact living at between 1,000 and 4,000 ft. above sea level. According to Tinker (A), p. 327, the Shans appear to have acquired either partial immunity from or an indifference to fevers which others find intolerable.

[7] The Nagas also are head-hunters like the Was.

Mongoloid, and it appears that the Burmans were among these groups on their eastern edge north of Bhamo, before they moved into the plains during the 9th century and thereafter established themselves in the dry zone and began to spread south along the Sittang valley to the coast, and west over the hills into Arakan, in the 11th and 12th centuries respectively.[8] And since the uplands, besides being intensely malarious, never offered anything like such favourable opportunities for agriculture as did the plains, the numerical discrepancy between the minority groups in the former and the majority peoples, particularly the Burmans, in the latter has tended to increase with the passage of time.[9]

Certainly the Burmans were already the leading people well before the introduction of British rule. In the period immediately preceding the First Burmese War (1824–6) their kingdom, which embraced the Arakanese and Mon territories as well as those of Burma proper, was centred at Ava in the dry zone, and the latter was much the most densely peopled part of the country. Admittedly, the very low densities in both Arakan and Pegu[10] were at least partly due to the disastrous effects of recent military action. Thus it has been estimated that as a result of the brutality accompanying the Burmese conquest of Arakan, the population of that province had fallen from 500,000 in 1785 to a mere 100,000 in 1824, and Pegu likewise had witnessed both wholesale slaughter and a continuing exodus of refugees, many of them to Siam, during the long drawn-out wars of the 18th century.

Be that as it may, there is no doubt that the dry zone, the original nucleus of the Burmese state, was much the most highly organized part of the kingdom, and despite the establishment of Burmese rule over the delta, the greater part of the latter had never as yet been brought into cultivation. This prior concentration on the dry zone is understandable, notwithstanding the precarious nature of its rainfall. For apart from its having been the first lowland area to be settled by the Burmans, it afforded considerable scope for small-scale irrigation, particularly in the narrow valleys and on land adjacent to hills from which water is available to supplement the low rainfall.[11]

Moreover, the relatively open vegetation of the dry zone was much more easily cleared, and its generally lighter soils more easily worked than those of the delta. Thus although acre for acre, its potential productivity is lower the initial bringing of the dry zone under the plough presented a much less formidable task than that entailed by the taming of the delta, with its vast jungle-covered swamps and swirling floodwaters during the rainy season.[12]

Indeed, notwithstanding the fact that the volume of the Irrawaddy as it flows through the dry zone is considerably smaller than it is in the delta, no serious attempt was made by the Burmans in pre-colonial times to harness it for irriga-

[8] See Luce, pp. 283–335.

[9] But note that the political ascendancy of the Burmans also gave their culture a prestige value which helped them to absorb other neighbouring peoples.

[10] As a territorial division Pegu at that time included the delta.

[11] See Spate (C), p. 12.

[12] See Dobby (H), Chapter 10.

tion, though rice cultivation has been undertaken since very early times all along its wide flood plains which are subject to direct seasonal inundation.[13] But in the surrounding countryside three main historic irrigation systems, all making use of tributary rivers, still survive, respectively at Kyaukse, to the south-east of Mandalay, in the Mu valley, to the north of it, and in the Minbu district farther to the south-west.

Of these three, the first, which centres in the Myitnge valley, is the largest and this area, which lay within 40 miles of Ava, was traditionally regarded as the nation's principal rice granary. Legend attributes the irrigation works here to the first Burman king, Anawratha, but although he certainly was responsible for the building of many of the canals it seems probable that some of the irrigation works were already in existence at Kyaukse in even earlier times.

The Mu valley system north of Shwebo, on the other hand, was never wholly satisfactory owing to the more severe floods from which it suffered, but British improvements eventually brought some 300,000 acres under fairly effective irrigation there. In the Minbu district the irrigation system differed from both the others in being under popular as opposed to royal control. In this respect it resembled those of northern Siam, around Chiengmai, and indeed it seems to have been built by Shans, and perhaps also Karens, during the 11th–12th centuries.

Besides these three fairly extensive tracts of irrigated land, innumerable small village systems also exist in the dry zone, and indeed wet-paddy cultivation would be almost impossible there if it had to rely on rainfall alone. Nevertheless, the greater part of the cultivated land there consists of dry fields and, this being so, the agricultural system of the dry zone is unusually diversified by South-east Asian standards. Even today only about 40 per cent of the cultivated acreage in the dry zone is devoted to paddy, and millet, peas, pulses, various oilseeds, green vegetables and cotton have all played important parts in the traditional agronomy. Likewise, as in other dry parts of South-east Asia, the rearing of bullocks and buffaloes has received rather more attention than is customary elsewhere in the region.

With such a range of commodities as its base, the subsistence economy of the dry zone, though not rich and always at the mercy of far from reliable rainfall, was capable of sustaining a by no means inconsiderable level of civilization, which found material expression *inter alia* in highly skilled handicraft industries and above all in the architectural splendours of the series of former capitals – Ava, Amarapura, Pagan, Prome and Mandalay – which line the banks of the middle Irrawaddy.

Nevertheless, the carrying capacity of such relatively inferior land under the agricultural techniques of the time was not great, and it may well be that the limits had been virtually reached by the 19th century, if not indeed earlier. For already the Burmese kings had forbidden the export of the small rice surplus

[13] See De Terra, p. 92.

produced in the delta, requiring instead that this be made available for consumption in the dry zone, and the population growth of the latter since its annexation has been at a much more modest rate than that which obtained during the same period in both the delta and the other coastal lowlands.[14]

As was described in Chapter 5, the first British acquisitions in Burma (1824–6) consisted of the two outlying coastal regions of Arakan and Tenasserim, both of which were valued more for strategic[15] than for economic reasons. Nevertheless, the introduction of law and order there was followed by a marked quickening of economic activity. Between 1830 and 1855 the rice acreage in Arakan increased from 66,000 to 350,000 and in Tenasserim from 40,000 to 180,000 and, moreover, since the British annexation put an end to the ban on rice exports the combined total of the latter rose from 73,000 tons in 1840 to 162,000 tons in 1855. However, neither this nor the more valuable export of teak, mainly from the Moulmein district, was of major proportions and it was not until some time after the annexation of Pegu province,[16] following the Second Burmese War in 1852, that any spectacular economic development occurred.

At the time of its annexation the delta was for all practical purposes an almost empty land, for following an abortive rising by the already much-depleted Mon population after the First Burmese War, the majority of the survivors fled into British-held Tenasserim in order to escape further vengeance from the Burmans. Thus only a sprinkling of villages remained, and virtually the sole economic wealth of the province lay in the teak forests of the Pegu Yoma.

Nevertheless, since the British were by this time anxious to develop Burma as a market for Lancashire textiles, it was necessary to provide some means by which the indigenous population could earn a cash income. It was in these circumstances that the great potentialities of the delta as a rice-exporting region[17] were first realized, and with the cutting off of the Carolina supplies to Europe during the United States Civil War, and the opening of the Suez canal shortly afterwards, British merchants turned to the Irrawaddy delta as their principal source of rice.

Thus, whereas in 1855 Pegu province had 563,000 acres under rice out of a total of 1,093,000 in Lower (*i.e.* British) Burma, the total had risen by 1880 to 3,102,000 acres, practically the whole of the increase having come from within

[14] The delta, of course, was almost virgin country prior to annexation, but this did not apply to Arakan or Tenasserim where the population increased respectively 10- and 20-fold between 1824 and 1931. See Harvey (B), p. 14.

[15] *I.e.* in relation to the defence of eastern India and the partial closing of the gap between Bengal and the Straits Settlements. For a time Tenasserim came under the administration of Penang, but later it, like Arakan, became a province under the administration of the Governor-General of the East India Company in Calcutta.

[16] In 1862 the three provinces Arakan, Tenasserim and Pegu were united as the province of Lower Burma, with Rangoon as the seat of the administration. The remainder, *i.e.* what was left of the independent Burmese kingdom, was known as Upper Burma.

[17] Apart from jute, which was already being produced in adequate quantities in the Ganges delta, rice was the only important cash crop really suited to the local conditions of soil and climate.

the delta. After 1869 rice replaced teak as the chief export of Lower Burma and the delta replaced Arakan as the chief source of rice. Within a couple of decades or so the demand of neighbouring Asian lands, notably India, for Burmese rice began to exceed that of western Europe, and this trend continued throughout the first half of the 20th century though the export trade via Rangoon was still carried mainly in British ships.

TABLE 49

BURMA: RICE ACREAGE AND EXPORT, 1886–1960

Year	*Acreage*	*Year*	*Export in tons of cleaned rice*
1886	4,000,000	1881	520,000
1896	5,755,000	1901	1,416,000
1910	9,950,000	1911	1,775,000
1920	10,309,000	1921	2,450,000
1939/40	12,432,000	1941	3,500,000
1945/6	6,945,000		
1953/4	10,398,000	1948	1,271,000
1959/60	10,667,000	1953	1,043,000
		1960*	1,798,000

* Rice and rice products

Sources: *Burma Rice*, pp. 2 and 3, *Economic Survey of Asia and the Far East*, 1956 and Union of Burma, Central Statistical and Economic Department, *Quarterly Bulletin of Statistics, Statistical Paper 2, Second Quarter*, 1961, etc.

In encouraging the opening up of the delta the British authorities sought from the outset to establish a system of peasant proprietorship, and to this end gave the land free to prospective cultivators in plots of about 15 acres per family, a figure well above the average size of holdings in most parts of the monsoon lands. Thus, attracted by the prospects of reliable harvests and a better standard of living, colonists began to pour in from the more precarious dry zone, and it was as a result of this mass migration after the 1860s that within the space of a few decades the delta became the most densely populated region in the whole of Burma.

The methods of farming which developed in the delta differed in important respects from the traditional practices followed in the dry zone. Virtually from the outset the new settlers in the delta concentrated on the production of paddy to the exclusion of almost all other crops, apart from fruit and a few vegetables, and by 1939 some 90 per cent of the cropped area of the delta was under paddy.

Again in contrast to the dry zone, where irrigation is everywhere necessary for successful rice growing, the delta has ample rain for this purpose, and the problem of water control here is rather that of protecting the fields against flood damage when the Irrawaddy is in spate in late July and August, that is roughly two months after the monsoon rains have begun in the delta. For this purpose the natural levees of the river were quite inadequate, and it was not until after 1860 when British P.W.D. engineers, using Indian labour, set about building a series of great embankments along the banks of the main river and its principal distributaries, that effective settlement of the delta began. Apart from the Twante canal, which was cut in 1883 for navigation rather than drainage, the larger British undertakings were limited almost entirely to embankments, while the laborious but more localized tasks of jungle-clearing, reclamation and the building of bunds or *kazins* to enclose individual rice-plots was the work of the Burmese settlers themselves. Truly, in Harvey's words, this colonization is an 'unrecorded epic.[18]

Under the farming system which grew up in the delta[19] the agricultural year began in April, with the repairing of the *kazins* and the clearing of the small drainage channels which lead off the surplus water from the fields. At the same time the light bullock- or buffalo-drawn ploughs and harrows were prepared in readiness for use as soon as the rains had broken in May. By contrast to its Western counterpart, the indigenous plough, which was made of wood and often lacked even a steel tip, was designed to break up the soil rather than to turn over a furrow; while the harrow was merely a wooden beam with half a dozen teeth in its underside.

The first part of the holding to be cultivated was the nursery plot, usually comprising one-tenth or less of the total area of 10–20 acres or so. Here alone was any extensive use made of the limited available supplies of animal manure, and little or no fertilizer of any kind was applied to the rest of the holding, whose fertility thus tended slowly to deteriorate except where there was regular flooding by river water containing both dissolved plant nutrients and fresh supplies of silt.

Nursery plots, which need to be kept under several inches of water, were normally ploughed once and harrowed eight to ten times until the surface was worked to a smooth consistency, and all weeds removed or buried. The standing water was then drained off and the seed, previously sprouted, was sown broadcast. Three or four days later the plot would be covered with an inch or so of water, whose level was gradually raised over the next five or six weeks to keep pace with the growth of the seedlings which, at a height of 18 inches or so, were then ready for transplanting to the main fields.

In the meantime the latter would also have been ploughed and harrowed, though with much less meticulous care than that bestowed on the nursery. Transplanting usually took place by hand, and involved an extremely heavy expenditure of labour, most of it by women working long hours knee deep in leech-infested water. The seedlings were spaced out at from three to ten to the square foot, depending on the fertility of the soil, and thereafter little remained

[18] Harvey (B), p. 49.

[19] This account is based largely on *Burma Rice*. The methods described here are still in normal use today though certain changes are now being introduced as described below, pp. 450–4.

to be done until harvesting, except to regulate the level of water in the fields so that the growing plants were neither drowned nor deprived of adequate moisture.

The harvest season for at least 95 per cent of the delta crop began in November/December, that is several weeks after the cessation of the main rains when the ears had had time to ripen in the sun. Standing water was drained off and the fields allowed to dry out before harvesting began, the latter being carried out by hand. Threshing took place with the use of bullocks or buffaloes on small trampling floors, side by side with winnowing which, again, was entirely a hand operation.

By the beginning of January the bulk of the crop was in transit to the mills, the cultivator having retained perhaps a fifth or a sixth of the total for his own use, while the rest comprised the marketable surplus either for sale elsewhere in Burma or for export overseas.[20] Although the largest rice mills were set up mainly by European firms and located in or near the great export ports, notably Rangoon and Bassein, the present century has seen a rapid growth of smaller mills along the roads, railways and waterways in the paddy-growing area itself. Thus in 1941, out of a total of some 700 mills, 650 or so had a capacity of 100 tons or less of finished rice a day, and most of these then were owned by Burmese, Indians or Chinese. Nevertheless, like the larger European-owned establishments, these country mills were nearly all steam powered, and used rice husks as fuel.

The delta was brought under cultivation not only by Burmans from the dry zone but also by large numbers of colonists from the hills, notably Karens, Chins and Shans. Indians also helped from the outset; in the early stages they even settled on the land, and the seasonal labour force employed by Burmese landlords included many Indians though the chief Indian contribution has been in the financing, marketing and processing of the paddy crop.

Of particular significance in this respect were the Chettyar money-lenders who found abundant scope for their enterprise among the unsophisticated Burmese peasantry. So long as the original rice boom lasted, which it did almost without interruption until 1908, no great harm resulted, and indeed the loans offered by the Chettyars and other money-lenders including some Burmans, did much to stimulate the expansion of production. But in the series of economic crises which followed, the money-lenders came into possession of more and more of the peasants' lands and after 1931, apart from considerable concealed ownership, non-agriculturists – approximately half of them Chettyars – held 56 per cent of the farm land in the delta.[21]

Besides financial and commercial exploitation of all kinds, the Indian immi-

[20] Over two-thirds of the exported rice came from the delta and most of the remainder from other parts of Lower Burma.

[21] This was rented to Burmese cultivators, in many cases to former owners of the land or their descendants. Dobby (H), p. 176, states that over 9 million acres of agricultural land in Lower Burma had changed hands in this way. According to Mende, p. 118, there were *c.* 1,600 Chettyar firms in Burma before the Second World War, and in the delta roughly one Chettyar office for every 5,000 people. See also below, note 51.

grants, whose entry was not formally controlled until after 1937, very largely monopolized the legal, medical and engineering professions. But the largest numbers of Indians were the ordinary workers, employed in the fields, docks, railways and mines, and for the most part domiciled in Burma for periods of not more than two or three years. Nevertheless, Burma gained numerically on balance of migration, as a substantial proportion of the immigrants found the long-term prospects there so much better than they could hope to enjoy at home. After 1924 Rangoon was for many years the greatest immigrant port in the world and, although the flow slackened noticeably after the crisis of the 1930s, the total Indian population in the country, drawn mainly from Madras, Bihar, Orissa and Bengal, stood at over 1 million when the Pacific War broke out in 1941.

Except for large numbers in the Arakan coastlands which adjoined India proper,[22] the Indian population was concentrated overwhelmingly in the delta and in the immediate vicinity of the main railway line to the north, and played much the same rôle in Burma as that of the Chinese in most other parts of South-east Asia. Nevertheless, Burma also had its Chinese minority, which came in during the same period as the Indians and numbered some 194,000 in 1931. Apart from a relatively small number, mostly of seasonal labourers, who spread over the Yunnan frontier into the far north, the Chinese, like the Indians, came mainly by sea, and were principally engaged either in trading in Rangoon and other inland towns along the railway, or in tin mining in Tenasserim.

Both the great influx of immigrants and the spectacular increase in the export trade between 1870 and 1941 were related primarily to the transformation under British rule of the Irrawaddy delta, a region which hitherto had been of relatively minor importance compared with the dry zone of the interior. Meanwhile, following the Third Burmese War, Upper and Lower Burma had been united as a single (British Indian) province in 1886, though it took another five years before the whole of Upper Burma was pacified. Likewise by 1890 the Shan states, most of them hitherto feudatory to the Burmese kings, were brought under effective British rule, but these and the remaining uplands to the north and west were administered separately as the 'backward tracts' later known as the 'Excluded Areas'.[23]

Rangoon, which had served as the original British headquarters in the delta and had long been the country's principal port, was the obvious choice as capital. Thanks to its situation at the southern extremity of the last low spur of the Pegu Yoma, it was in a position to command both the Irrawaddy and the Sittang routes to the interior, though, contrary to popular opinion, the city stands on the banks of neither of these rivers, but at the confluence of the Pegu and Hlaing rivers, some 26 miles from the sea.

[22] Nowadays East Pakistan.

[23] The three small Karenni states also had been feudatory to the Burmese kings, but instead of becoming British territory they were merely brought under British protection in 1875.

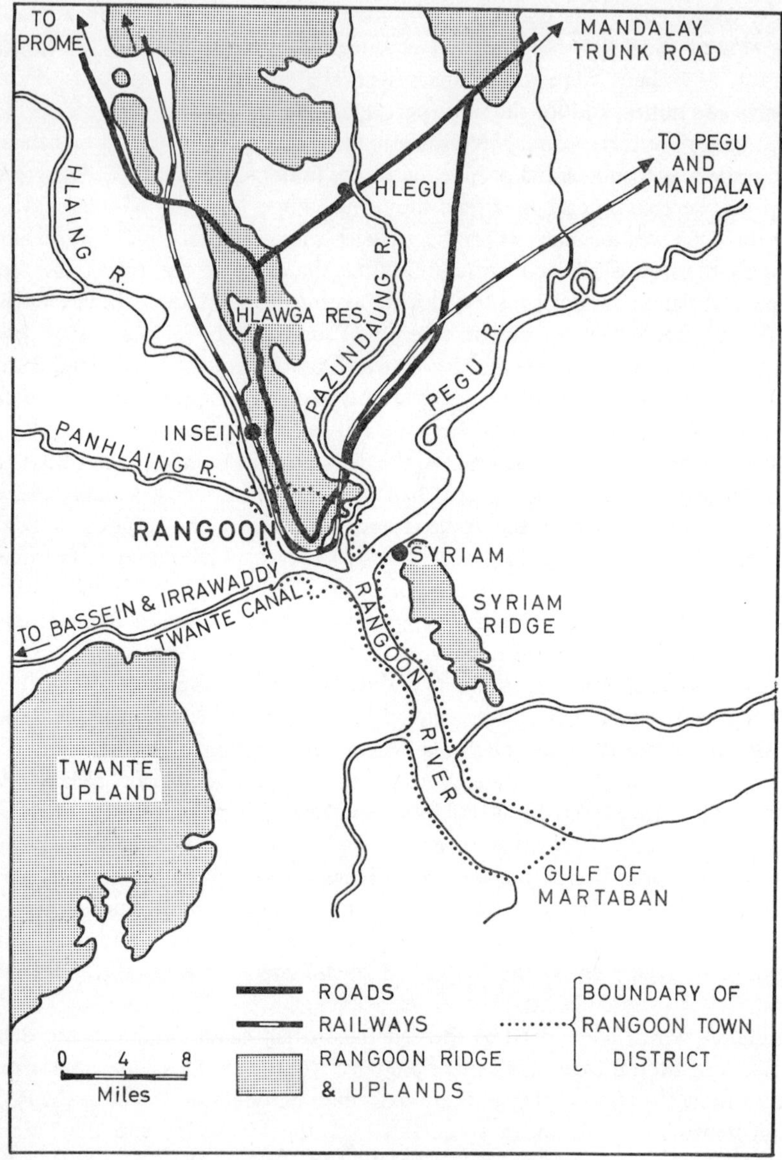

FIG. 65—Situation of Rangoon

In both the dry zone and the hills the pace of economic development following annexation was considerably slower than in the delta. Partly because the ancient nucleus of the Burmese kingdom had already achieved a measure of demographic stability, and partly also because of the exodus to the delta after the 1860s, no spectacular growth occurred in its numbers, and indeed the former capital city, Mandalay,[24] showed an actual decline, from 170,071 in 1891 to 134,950 in 1931, in striking contrast to Rangoon's growth from 92,301 in 1872 to 176,583 in 1891 and to 400,415 in 1931.[25]

These figures epitomize the change which was taking place in the relative importance of the dry zone and the delta during the decades following annexation. For whereas the delta was becoming one of the greatest centres of commercial monoculture in Asia, the dry zone remained predominantly as heretofore a region of diversified but not very lucrative subsistence farming. Nevertheless the economic revolution in the delta reacted also upon the dry zone and, although by the 1930s over half the total rice crop of the former was exported, a considerable proportion also was sold to the dry zone which in turn provided sesamum and ground-nut oil (used in cooking) for consumption in the delta, and cotton both for export to Japan and for use in Burma's domestic textile industry.

But it was petroleum which constituted the main export of central Burma, where indeed hand-dug wells had been in operation on a small scale for centuries. Effective commercial exploitation dates from 1886 when the Burmah Oil Company was founded, and in 1904 the first modern well was sunk near Yenangyaung. By the 1930s exports were worth some £10 million annually, and although this represented only about 0·4 per cent of world production it amounted to over 21 per cent of the British Empire total and found a ready market in nearby India.

Much the greater part of production was in the hands of the Burmah Oil Company and the two other British concerns, namely the Indo Burma Petroleum Company and the British Burma Petroleum Company, though a little still came from country wells and an Indian company was also active. Each of the British companies had refineries on Rangoon river, B.O.C. at Syriam, to which oil was pumped through a 10-in. pipeline 300 miles long, and I.P.B.C. and B.B.P.C. respectively at Seikkyi and Thilawa, both of which depended on river tankers and barges for transport from the oilfields. Besides the export of petroleum, much of the residual oil was made into kerosene and candles, both of which were locally important as illuminants.

In most years prior to the Pacific War, petroleum accounted for over 20 per cent of Burma's total exports, and as such came second to rice which provided over 40 per cent. Teak, still produced mainly in the Pegu Yoma and the hinterland of Moulmein, came third, followed by a variety of metallic minerals. The only other exports of note were the cotton already mentioned from the dry zone, and small quantities of rubber, mainly from Tenasserim, whose climate approximated most nearly to the equatorial type.[26]

[24] Mandalay succeeded Ava as capital under King Mindon in 1857.

[25] 1941 figures: Mandalay, 163,243; Rangoon, 500,800. For 1953 figures see Table 57, p. 466.

[26] The pre-war output of rubber was about 10,000 tons annually, though this was limited by the International Rubber Restriction Agreement (see above, p. 165) and more could otherwise have been produced. The area under rubber in the 1930s was some 110,000 acres, of which 68 per cent was held by estates and 32 per cent by smallholders.

So far as the eastern plateaux were concerned their main commercial wealth lay in metallic minerals, though production of these came mostly from a very few isolated centres. Outstanding among the latter were the rich silver-lead-zinc deposits near Bawdwin in the Shan states, which had been worked for centuries by Chinese from across the border with the help of slave labour. The British first began operations there in 1907, using Indian and Chinese labour since the Burmese were unwilling to work underground, and in 1936 the large smelter which had been erected nearby at Namtu provided 71,915 tons of lead, 76,802 tons of zinc concentrates, 5,952,000 ounces of silver and 1,294 ounces of gold, as well as substantial quantities of copper matte.[27]

The other principal mining centre in the eastern plateaux was that at Mawchi[28] which in pre-war days produced nearly half of Burma's tungsten. The remainder of the output of this metal, of which Burma was the world's second producer after China, came from a series of much smaller mines, mainly Chinese owned, in Tenasserim, from which area also and under similar small-scale organization came virtually the whole of the small tin output of some 4,000 tons annually. The remote village of Mogok in the northern Shan states was for many years the scene of ruby mining but production finally ceased there in 1931.

With the exception of these few and widely scattered mining centres, and the immediate vicinity of the roads and railways which served them, most of the hill country was completely untouched by Western economic enterprise. Admittedly, in the more accessible portions of the Shan plateau, where in any case the indigenous methods of sedentary cultivation, particularly on the terraced slopes of the wider valleys, were relatively advanced, cash cultivation of potatoes, flowers and fruit for Rangoon and the hill stations was developing encouragingly in the late 1930s. But throughout the Chin, Naga and Kachin hills, as also in the higher and remoter uplands of the east, the traditional *taung-ya* cultivation of maize and dry rice continued unchanged.

The extent to which the various parts of Burma had been welded together into a coherent whole can be gauged from an examination of the pre-war communications pattern. Notwithstanding a reasonably good system of roads and railways the 4,000 miles of commercially navigable inland waterways remained the most fundamental component in the country's transport network. In particular, the British-owned Irrawaddy Flotilla Company, founded in 1865, was one of the largest and most influential Western undertakings in Burma, though in addition to this and to the Arracan Flotilla Company (also British owned) innumerable country boats of all kinds carried a great volume of traffic.

In 1867 a treaty with the then independent Burman Government permitted

[27] A private railway linked Bawdwin with the smelter at Namtu and with the Lashio branch of the state railway at Namyao.

[28] Mawchi, the world's largest tungsten mine, is at Bawlake in Kayah State (the pre-war Karenni). The extreme remoteness of this situation was only partly mitigated by the construction before the Second World War of a surfaced road connecting it with Toungoo on the main railway line. See Christian (B), p. 143.

British ships to navigate the Irrawaddy as far as Bhamo, some 900 miles from the coast and only 30 miles short of the Chinese border, a journey which even in the 1930s involved ten days' sailing upstream. The Irrawaddy Flotilla Company's express paddle steamers which were employed on this run were the largest of their type in the world (326 ft. long by 76 ft. beam) and in addition the Company owned a fleet of heavy freighters and barges for service between the oilfields and the delta, as well as numerous smaller craft of all kinds, many of them built in the Company's own dockyards at Dalla near Rangoon.[29] In normal years the I.F.C. and the A.F.C. together carried *c.* 8,200,000 passengers and 1,300,000 tons of cargo, which may be compared with the 18,810,000 passengers and 4,001,000 tons of freight transported by the whole of the Burma Railways in 1939–40.

Besides the Irrawaddy, Sittang and lower Chindwin, the Salween was also used by river vessels for a distance of some 60 miles from Moulmein to Shwegun.[30] Under British rule, moreover, the Twante canal was built to connect Rangoon, at the confluence of the Hlaing and Pegu rivers, with the Irrawaddy proper, and another important canal linked the Pegu with the Sittang. Within the delta region as a whole the maze of distributaries and minor creeks provides an elaborate network of close on 2,000 miles of waterways for country boats and launches, and in pre-war days well over half the rice moving to the mills went by boat.

Indeed the rôle of river navigation in traditional Burmese life can scarcely be exaggerated and, besides the series of former capitals to which reference has already been made, the great majority of villages also occupied riparian sites. On the other hand, the Burmese had never possessed sea-going ships of their own and although the local populations of Arakan and Tenasserim had many small coastal craft the only effective sea links between these two regions and the delta were maintained by larger vessels belonging to either British or Indian concerns.

Under British rule, Rangoon was made into one of the most efficient ports in Asia, capable of handling ships of up to 15,000 tons and 30 ft. draught, and possessing a total of some 15 miles of anchorage in the river and four miles of dockyard.[31] Like Bassein, its neighbour in the delta and the second rice-exporting port, it could be used all the year round, though the Arakan and Tenasserim ports had virtually to close down during the SW monsoon from May to October.

Whereas the traditional pattern of riverine communications centred in the dry zone and has only been refocused in the delta during the past hundred years, the railway network, which was exclusively a creation of the British, was from the outset based upon Rangoon. However, although the first line, opened in 1877,

[29] *Ibid.*, p. 140.

[30] The Irrawaddy may be used for commercial navigation for 874 miles all the year, plus a further 105 miles for 7 months of the year. The Chindwin is usable from its confluence with the Irrawaddy to Homalin (*c.* 400 miles) for 8 months, and the Sittang for 25 miles all the year and a further 30 miles for 3 months only. *Pyidawtha—the new Burma*, p. 63.

[31] See Tinker (C), pp. 280–82.

ran from there to Prome on the Irrawaddy, some 70 miles above the apex of the delta, it was wisely decided that the trunk railway into the interior should not duplicate the main river route but instead should follow the Sittang valley. By 1889 this line had been completed as far as Mandalay, and the extension, from Sagaing, on the opposite bank of the Irrawaddy, to Myitkyina in the hill country north of Bhamo, was opened ten years later. Even more spectacular was the line completed in 1903 from Mandalay to Lashio which, like Myitkyina, was the starting point of an ancient caravan route to China.

Various other branch lines in the delta, the dry zone, the southern Shan States and along the Tenasserim coast to Ye, brought the total railway mileage to 2,058, and in 1934 the gap between Mandalay and Sagaing ceased to exist with the completion of the impressive 4,000 ft. Ava bridge which carried both road and rail.

Since the state-owned railways had enough competition to face from river transport the government had additional reason for delay as regards road building, and although Rangoon had been linked to both Prome and Pegu by the end of the 1850s it was not until after the First World War that anything approaching a countrywide road network was constructed. While the main trunk road from Rangoon to Lashio ran closely parallel to the railway for almost its entire length, an attempt was made elsewhere to build roads as feeders and not as competitors to the latter. In this respect the main effort was directed to the dry zone and the Shan States, rather than the delta which was well supplied with waterways, but the rest of the country, including Tenasserim, received little attention and only a couple of 'adventurously motorable'[32] roads crossed the western hills into Arakan.

Taken as a whole the pre-war transport network was markedly concentrated in the two central regions of the dry zone and the delta, and by comparison with these the peripheral regions were all in greater or lesser degree neglected. But in fact it is misleading to think of the pattern as a single entity, and indeed the rivalry between the older and newer forms of transport was merely one aspect of a division which ran right through the national life. Thus, while the ordinary river villages still remained predominantly Burmese in character, as did most of the old capitals, the series of upstart railway towns, particularly those between Mandalay and the delta, possessed many of the typical characters of the pioneer fringe, and contained a substantial proportion of Indians, and often also of Chinese, in their populations.

This contrast was exemplified on a greater scale between Mandalay and Rangoon, the only two centres in the country which before the war had over 100,000 inhabitants.[33] Thus, whereas the former was little more than a jumble of indigenous dwelling houses and monasteries surrounding the empty palace of the last

[32] Spate (C), p. 8.

[33] Besides these two, the only towns with over 40,000 people in 1941 were Moulmein (71,181) and Bassein (45,662).

of the Burmese kings, Rangoon was a modern Western-style city, with a spacious rectilinear street pattern and imposing buildings, both public and commercial. Though somewhat more provincial than Singapore, it differed little in general character from the other great port cities of South-east Asia except in so far as its atmosphere was more Indian than Chinese, some three-fifths of its population in fact being returned as Indian in the 1931 census.

In short, the contrast between Rangoon and Mandalay represented more than the age-old dualism of the dry zone and the delta. Rather, in Spate's words, it symbolized 'the unresolved contradiction of Burma's polity: the cosmopolitan sea-port, busy and flourishing yet a little shoddy and second-hand, grafted on to the country rather than growing from it; and the overgrown village dreaming of a religious and monarchical past, and for the rest untidily stagnating'.[34]

Apart from a few bridle paths and bullock-cart tracks, no road, let alone rail connexion existed before 1938 between Burma and any of the neighbouring countries. And while in large measure this isolation was the result of the ruggedness and continuity of the surrounding semi-circle of mountains, it was also strongly reinforced by political factors. During the 19th-century era of long-distance rail construction various schemes were discussed, not only for linking Burma with Yunnan but also for building through railways between Rangoon and Calcutta, Bangkok and Singapore respectively.

However, no capital was forthcoming because subscribers required a state guarantee which the government of India was unwilling to give, thinking the projects not only too ambitious but likely to cause political difficulties. This latter objection was regarded at the time as bureaucratic obstruction, but subsequently it appeared in popular form whenever attempts were made, prior to 1937, to revive the Yunnan railway project. In particular, with the example of the Manchu invasions from the north-east in the 18th century and the mass immigration of Indian labourers by sea which began roughly a hundred years later, the Burmese feared that the establishment of railway links with their two great neighbours might well pave the way for either military or demographic conquest.

Thus, although administratively part of India until 1937, Burma was in fact very much a region apart, and alike in its ethnic character, social structure and economic development, as well as its physical geography, it belonged unmistakably with the rest of South-east Asia rather than with the Indian sub-continent. Thanks to the lack of serious population pressure, the average standard of living was appreciably higher than in India, though on the other hand Indian residents held a disproportionately high share of the better-paid posts in Burma. Moreover, Indian capital investments exceeded even those of the British[35] and practi-

[34] Spate (C), pp. 32–3.

[35] Harvey (B), pp. 7 and 67–8 estimates that pre-war Indian investments were over £56 million (two-thirds in agriculture) and British approximately £53 million (oil £18 million, mines £11 million, timber £9 million, transport £6 million, rice £3 million, trade and manufacturing £2·5 million).

cally the whole of the limited range of factory industries – namely textiles, hosiery, footwear, matches, soap and cement, together with most of the rice mills, saw-mills, oil refineries and transport maintenance industries – were owned by aliens, whether Indian, European, Chinese or Japanese.

From many points of view the Indians were more unpopular in pre-war Burma than were the British, and the growing sense of national consciousness during the 1930s was marked by two serious Indian pogroms.[36] The Chinese, on the other hand, appeared less alien and were far less unpopular; intermarriage between Chinese and Burmese was by no means uncommon and the resultant offspring suffered no serious social discrimination.

Besides disliking the Indians in their midst, the Burmese were equally resentful of the political ties which bound their country to the Indian Empire. But while this arrangement was anomalous from almost every point of view, it nevertheless helped materially during the inter-war years to hasten the advance of Burma towards self-government.

In fact a measure of devolution began as early as 1897 when Burma obtained a separate Legislative Council and for the first time began to enact laws appropriate to its own conditions. Moreover, when the British decided to apply the Montagu-Chelmsford proposals for constitutional reform to India, Burma was more or less automatically involved, and thus the system of dyarchy was introduced there in 1923, two years after its introduction in the other Indian provinces. Similarly, when further steps towards self-government were made under the Government of India Act of 1935, Burma again proved a beneficiary, and the decision was taken at the same time to separate the governments of the two countries. Thus in 1937 Burma was granted a cabinet of its own, and in the lower house of its newly reconstituted parliament all the seats were elected.

These arrangements admittedly fell short of complete self-government, for the British Governor and not parliament remained responsible for external affairs, defence and currency, and also for the so-called Excluded Areas which comprised 43 per cent of the territory but included only 16 per cent of the total population. Nevertheless, as the American writer J. L. Christian observed in 1942, 'with the single exception of the Philippines, no tropical appendage of any great power enjoyed a larger degree of autonomy than did Burma',[37] and it was clear that the advance to Dominion status could not be long delayed. Moreover, notwithstanding the excessive concentration on a single export crop and the extraction of large profits by both British and Indian concerns, the economy was fundamentally sound and the standard of living recognizably superior to those of both China and India, and indeed of most colonial dependencies in other parts of the world.

As elsewhere in South-east Asia the Second World War provided the opportunity for a nationalist assumption of power. The assent of Thailand in

[36] After 1937 the Burmese sought to control Indian immigration and in 1941 an agreement was initialed with the Indian government whereby Indian immigrants were required to be in possession of passports.

[37] Christian (B), p. 43.

December 1941 gave the Japanese direct access to the eastern frontiers of Burma, and in the military débâcle which followed, Rangoon fell on March 8, 1942 and soon afterwards the surviving British forces as well as 400,000 Indians escaped across the western hills into Assam. The Japanese were welcomed by the younger nationalist leaders[38] and accepted by the mass of the population, but though the recognition in 1943 of Burma's 'independence within the Co-prosperity Sphere' was gratifying to national sentiment the worthlessness of such an arrangement soon became apparent. In these circumstances the Japanese-sponsored government of Aung San turned against its mentors and in the Allied offensive of 1944–5 the A.F.P.F.L. popular front rendered useful services to the returning British forces. Nevertheless, the A.F.P.F.L.'s total efforts in the Allied cause were small compared with those of the Karens and other hill peoples who had been engaged in anti-Japanese guerrilla fighting from a much earlier stage.

By May 5, 1945 Rangoon was once again in Allied hands. But having been the scene of heavy fighting in both directions Burma had sustained the most severe war damage of any country in South-east Asia, and according to U Kyaw Nyein[39] 'three-quarters of its towns and villages were razed to the ground and its national income reduced to half the pre-war level'. In view of the resultant chaos the British government decided in May 1945 to rule by executive order until such time as new elections could be held and new policies formulated. But the failure of the British[40] to fix a time limit for this procedure aroused nationalist suspicions, and as increasing agitation prevented reconstruction a new approach was called for. Unlike their counterparts in India, Pakistan and Ceylon, the Burmese nationalists insisted on claiming a position of independence outside the Commonwealth, and by the Nu-Attlee Agreement the newly styled Union of Burma became an independent republic on January 4, 1948.[41]

Two main sets of problems confronted the rulers of the new Burma, namely the rebuilding of the country's war-shattered economy and the forging of a true sense of national consciousness among the diverse ethnic and cultural groups within its borders. And when, within a few months of independence, the authority of the new A.F.P.F.L. Government was openly challenged by two rival Communist factions, together with members of the P.V.O.[42] and later also a substantial body of Karens, it seemed almost impossible that it could survive. Nevertheless,

[38] Thirty young nationalists of the so-called Thakin Party, led by Aung San, fled to Japan in 1940 and later returned with the invading Japanese armies. Subsequently Aung San led the A.F.P.F.L. (Anti-Fascist People's Freedom League) against the Japanese. He headed the first post-war Council of Ministers but was assassinated with six of his cabinet colleagues on July 19, 1947 and succeeded by U Nu, Vice-President of the A.F.P.F.L.

[39] *Atlantic Monthly*, Vol. 201, No. 2, February 1958, p. 102.

[40] Both the Churchill government which took this decision and the Attlee government which carried it out.

[41] Burma remained in the Sterling Area, and Britain undertook to help in training its naval, military and air forces.

[42] People's Volunteer Organization, many of whose members sympathized with one or other of the Communist groups.

the tide began to turn towards the end of 1950, and while guerrillas and dacoits remained a serious obstacle to ecomomic recovery, the government was in fair control of the more important parts of the country by 1958. In that year, following the splitting-up of the A.F.P.F.L. into two rival factions, Premier U Nu handed over the government to General Ne Win, whose temporary period of military rule helped further to reduce the scale of guerrilla activity, and also to inject new vigour into the adminstration generally. In the elections of February 1960, U Nu's faction of the A.F.P.F.L. was returned with a clear majority, but in March 1962 his new Pyidaungsu (Union) Party government was supplanted in a coup led by General Ne Win and his Burmese Revolutionary Council, which claimed that they were acting to stop political and economic deterioration.

II. THE UNION OF BURMA: ECONOMIC GEOGRAPHY

Although the repair of war damage, particularly to the railways, water transport services, mining installations, dwellings and commercial property, obviously called for immediate attention, the 1948 government did not propose simply to restore the economy to its pre-war pattern. On the contrary it aimed at setting up a socialist state, and indeed claimed to be following Marxist principles, though the strictness of its adherence to the latter was inevitably tempered by its equally vigorous devotion to Buddhist doctrines. Thus, as time has gone on, the original severity of its policies abated, and its economic programme, which dates effectively from 1952, aimed at the creation of *Pyidawtha*, which has been translated as a 'Happy Land' or, more prosaically, a welfare state.[43]

In the official handbook on the subject, the goal was defined as 'a Burma in which our people are better clothed, better housed, in better health, with greater security and more leisure – and thus better able to enjoy and pursue the spiritual values that are and will remain our dearest possession'.[44]

To this end local self-help was enjoined throughout the countryside for such tasks as the building of roads and the digging of wells, and this kind of activity, aided by discretionary grants from the central government has already achieved useful results.[45] But in recent years the *Pyidawtha* programme has come to be regarded almost as a synonym for the Eight Year Plan for Economic and Social Development which was originally scheduled for completion in the autumn of 1959. According to this plan it was initially proposed to raise the gross domestic product by nearly one-third over the immediate pre-war level, which means rather more than two-thirds above that of 1952. Allowing for a population increase of roughly 13 per cent per decade, this would mean only a 4 per cent increase in *per capita* production over the period 1939–59, but in view of the

[43] But see below, p. 482. [44] *Pyidawtha – the new Burma*, pp. 10–11.

[45] Tinker (B), p. 139. As Tinker points out elsewhere, (C), p. 104, the term *Pyidawtha* is also used to describe such mutual co-operation at the village level. This practice is very close to the Indonesia *gotong rojong* (see above, pp. 296 and 313) and, like it, stems from the common traditions of village life found throughout most of lowland South-east Asia. See above, p. 77, note 40.

reduction in the proportion of the country's income which will henceforth be removed in the form of profits earned by foreign concerns, it has been estimated that living standards would be raised by approximately 9 per cent over the same period.[46]

The full cost of implementing the plan was assessed at 7,500 million Kyats[47] or £562 million, to be allocated as shown in Table 50.

TABLE 50

BURMA: EIGHT YEAR PLAN ALLOCATION

Social and welfare	4,500 m. K.	Manufacturing	230 m. K.
Roads and railways	870 m. K.	Minerals	120 m. K.
Power	780 m. K.	Airways	90 m. K.
Ports and waterways	500 m. K.	Telecommunications	30 m. K.
Irrigation	370 m. K.	Miscellaneous	10 m. K.

Of this total the government proposed to provide approximately 70 per cent, either exclusively out of state funds or in association with private enterprise. Although the larger transport and manufacturing concerns surviving from pre-war days have been nationalized, various forms of joint undertaking have become increasingly popular in recent years, particularly in the extractive industries and in the case of entirely new types of enterprise the government has preferred to contract with Western or other foreign firms to build the necessary installations and to operate these for a number of years, while at the same time training Burmese personnel, before eventually handing over the going concern to government control.

Owing to the continued high cost of fighting the insurgents, which accounted for a large share of total government expenditure, and the unexpectedly severe fall in the price of rice,[48] on which the whole economy turns, the development plan had to be drastically pruned after 1954/5, and in the event the 1960 output fell well short of that of 1939. At the same time, owing to the difficulty in disposing of its growing rice stocks to traditional purchasers, Burma has entered into a series of long-term barter agreements with the Soviet bloc countries, which undertook to provide heavy equipment, consumer goods and the services of technicians in return for fixed quantities of rice, and these arrangements have led to further modifications in the original plan. Nevertheless, the broad outlines of the latter remain unchanged and on the whole it is wisely conceived. It is on this basis that most of the economic changes of recent years have taken place as

[46] Like the Indonesians (see above, p. 312) the Burmese are inclined to believe that their country is exceptionally well endowed by nature and that only 'colonial exploitation' has prevented their enjoying a much higher standard of living hitherto. In this context the Burmese habitually regard the activities of the local Indians as forming part of the process of exploitation. See Tinker (C), pp. 94, 96 and 104.

[47] 1 Kyat = 1 Rupee = 1*s.* 6*d.* Sterling or 21 cents U.S.

[48] Since 1955 the rice export price fell to £36 a ton though the minimum expected had been £45 a ton.

described in the following pages. A note on the new policies since 1962 is included on p. 482.

Employing as it does nearly 70 per cent of the total working population, and contributing some 40 per cent of the national income, agriculture is by far the most important form of economic activity in Burma. And indeed, although agricultural production has barely regained the pre-war level and agricultural exports are still below it, such products form a far higher percentage of total exports than they did in pre-war years, owing to the much more severe dislocation in most other activities, notably mining.[49]

Moreover, since the proposed rate of industrialization is relatively modest, it is unlikely that the numbers of people on the land will be significantly reduced in the foreseeable future. For, compared with such neighbouring countries as India, China or Japan, Burma certainly suffers from no problem of rural overpopulation. Even today the amount of cultivable land per head stands at 2 acres, as against India's 1·1 and Japan's 0·2, although little more than half of the potentially cultivable 24 per cent of the national territory has yet been brought under the plough (Table 51).

TABLE 51

BURMA: LAND USE, 1937–41

Cropped	10%	Uncultivated	12%
Fallow	2%	Unsuited to agriculture ...	25%
Forests	11%	Not yet surveyed	40%

Source: *Pyidawtha – the new Burma*, p. 33.

While, therefore, the demands of a growing population and the necessity for maintaining a high level of agricultural exports as a source of foreign exhange call for increased efficiency in farming and ultimately for an expansion of the cultivated acreage beyond the pre-war levels, which have yet to be regained, these changes can be initiated within the established pattern of Burmese agricultural practice and there is little economic justification at this stage for embarking on costly schemes for wholesale mechanization.

On the other hand the Burmese government has been much exercised over the social problem of land ownership, and one of its earliest enactments was the Land Nationalization Act of October 1948 which limited holdings to 25 – 50 acres, according to circumstances, and provided for government purchase and redistribution to peasant cultivators of land in excess of these amounts. Although this and a subsequent Act of 1953 provided for the payment of compensation, the latter has been at purely nominal rates in the areas so far affected, and it appears that the provision is tacitly being allowed to lapse.[50]

[49] In particular, rice now forms 70–75 per cent of the total exports, compared with about 40 per cent before the Second World War.

[50] Tinker (C), p. 245. Until recently forestry also showed a severe decline, but this has now been reversed.

Owing to insurgency little was in fact done before 1954, but by the end of 1956 some 1,200,000 acres had been redistributed, the greater part of it in the delta where the tenancy problem has been most acute,[51] and considerable further progress has been made since that date. Approximately one-third of the total cultivated area was originally scheduled for redistribution, the immediate result of which is to increase the number of family-held units, mostly of the order of 10 acres or so, though the actual size varies considerably with the character of the terrain and soil. In effect the new holdings are state land, for which a fixed and reasonable rent is payable, but the peasant is promised security of tenure and is in personal control of his holding.

Thus far the system would appear to be much closer to that of Sun Yat-sen's 'land-to-the-tiller' programme than to the more recent 'land reform' of Communist China. But the ultimate aim has been stated to be mechanized collective farming, to be achieved in three stages which closely resemble those adopted by the Chinese People's Republic. Thus redistribution will be followed by the mutual aid system, under which groups of five families will co-operate to work units of about 50 acres, then 200-acre units will be mechanically farmed by groups of twenty families, and finally full collectivization will be introducted on even larger farms.[52]

Such at least were the intentions expressed a few years ago, when the year 1962 was mentioned as the date for the completion of the second phase. But hitherto attention has been mainly concentrated on redistribution and the formation of co-operatives, and it appears to be an open question whether any further increase in the size of the units of production would be economically sound at Burma's current stage of advancement. In particular, the great cost of mechanizing the country's agriculture could only be justified if it led to a substantial increase in the production of marketable crops. And while the low yield of paddy per acre (29 bushels, as compared with 74 in Japan, 38 in Malaya and 25 in Thailand), which is primarily a reflection of the extensive methods of cultivation appropriate to a lower density of population than is typical of most rice-growing lands, suggests that mechanization has more to contribute here than it has in the congested paddy fields of China and Japan,[53] it is by no means certain that in the present state of the world rice market it would prove a paying proposition for the nation as a whole.

Whatever may ultimately be done in this connexion, it seems clear that other and less controversial methods of increasing the efficiency of Burmese farming

[51] Out of 11,120,343 acres cultivated in Lower Burma in 1947, 5,375,000 were owned by non-agriculturists. Of 8,203,498 acres in Upper Burma, 7,125,710 were held by cultivators. Before the War some 3 million acres in Lower Burma had been owned by Chettyars, most of whom fled to India in the exodus of 1942 and now have no prospect of regaining their former holdings or obtaining any compensation for them.

[52] Fairbairn (A), p. 220.

[53] See Fisher (O), pp. 579–84 and (P), pp. 550–51. In 1959–60 the Burmese yield rose to over 30·5 bushels per acre.

are of more immediate importance. These include the provision of rural credit facilities, the setting up of demonstration farms specializing in various lines in different parts of the country, and the dissemination of information about improved strains and more effective techniques via the government's own agricultural extension workers. In particular it is officially estimated that the use of moderate amounts of chemical fertilizer could raise yields by an average of at least 30 per cent and that improved seed selection would add a further 10 per cent to the overall output though, stated thus baldly, such figures have little meaning. But the government is right in stressing that some such increase in efficiency will be required if its various plans for large-scale irrigation are to be economically worth while.

From what has already been stated (pp. 436–8) it will be clear that Burma does not make anything like the maximum possible agricultural use of the water resources available within the country. Although the greater part of the dry zone receives insufficient rain for reliable cultivation, only 1,698,000 acres or approximately 19 per cent of the cropped area in central Burma[54] are irrigated, mostly by traditional small-scale methods of limited efficiency, and it is estimated that another 2,831,000 acres there might be brought into use if the waters available in the Irrawaddy and Chindwin were made available for irrigation. Moreover, while in the delta there is a superabundance of water for cultivation during the summer months, the extremely low rainfall from December to April, when the ground bakes almost as hard as a brick, virtually rules out the possibility of a second crop in the winter half of the year, and the resultant seasonal unemployment constitutes one of the most intractable social problems with which the region has to contend.

In these circumstances it is understandable that the Burmese planners should have given careful thought to the possibility of making much greater use than heretofore of the potential irrigation water available in the main rivers and their larger tributaries, in order to extend the cultivated acreage in the dry zone and to intensify production both there and in the delta. Thus, stimulated by the success of the great multi-purpose projects in many somewhat similar parts of southern Asia and the Middle East, the Nu government proposed to initiate four major schemes during the course of the next decade, and had others in mind for consideration at a later date.

The largest of the four is the Mu River Irrigation Project, in an area in the central dry zone which, despite the existence of an old-established irrigation system, is notorious for its low agricultural productivity. It is claimed that over 1,100,000 acres here will ultimately receive supplemental irrigation during the rainy season, as well as being provided with enough water to grow a dry-season crop of ground nuts, pulses, sesamum or millet. In addition to this, the Yamethin District Irrigation Project, along the Sittang river, from the south-eastern margins

[54] These figures, quoted in *Pyidawtha*, p. 37, are for the ten Districts in which the dry zone lies. See above, pp. 433–4.

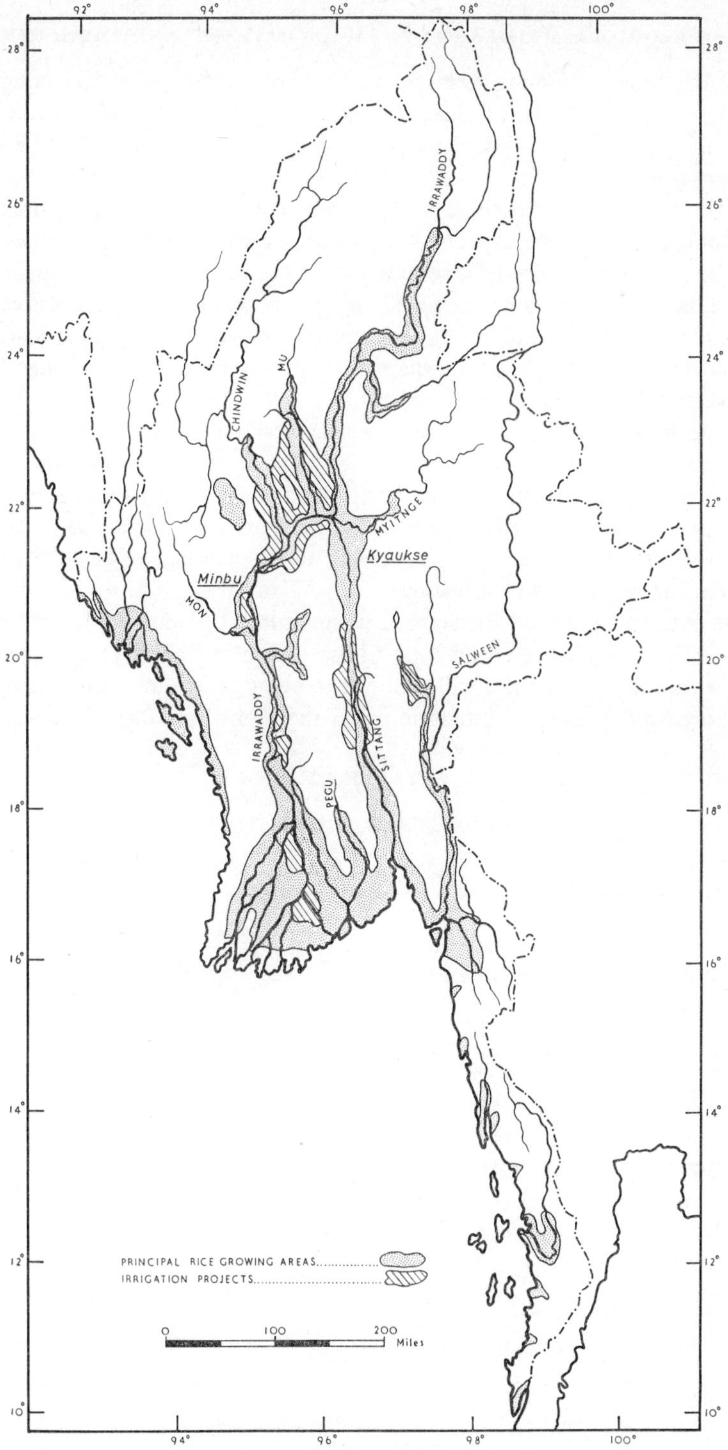

FIG. 66—Burma: rice-land

of the dry zone to Toungoo, is planned to irrigate 609,450 acres, though the Kandaw Village Irrigation Project, also in the dry zone, and the Loikaw Area Irrigation Project in the plateau country of Kayah State are both on a much smaller scale.

As yet, however, despite some local progress, these schemes are still unrealized, and doubts may well be expressed regarding the wisdom of putting them into effect either now or indeed for several years to come. For the fact remains that Burma, in contrast to the various lands whose efforts in this respect it is seeking to emulate, does not suffer from any shortage of readily cultivable land, and until such a problem is in sight it may well expect to get more rewarding returns by investing its capital in other ways.

In the meantime the more urgent task is clearly that of bringing back into cultivation the 2 million or so acres which were in use before the war but are still uncropped as a result of insecurity. And indeed until the insurgency is completely ended many other lands in marginal areas will continue to produce less efficiently than before the war, owing to the shortage of labour[55] and the frequent interruptions to cultivation.

The extent of the post-war setback in agricultural production as well as the degree of recovery achieved by 1960–61 are shown in Tables 52 and 53. From these it can be seen that rice will continue to be by far the most important crop, and indeed it has been the intention under the Eight Year Plan to increase rice

TABLE 52

BURMA: AGRICULTURAL PRODUCTION, 1936–61

Figures in 000 tons

Crop	1936–7 *to* 1940–41 *average annual*	1953–4	1953–4 *as* % *of* 1936–7 *to* 1940–41	1958–9	1960–61 *est.*
Paddy	7,426	5,527	74	6,486	6,682
Pulses	250	201	80	211	342
Ground nuts	181	191	106	284	351
Sesamum	45	44	98	52	64
Cotton	21	22	107	12	12
Tobacco	44	48	109	38	40
Millet and wheat	78	78	100	69	70

Sources: Based on Cooke, p. 48, and *Economic Survey of Burma*, 1960, and 1961, Table 8.

[55] The seasonal immigration of labour from the Indian sub-continent has now ceased.

exports to a total of 2·6 million tons a year, though in fact they amounted to only 1,798,000 tons (rice and rice products) in 1960. These figures may be compared with the pre-war average of *c.* 3 million, out of a total production of 7·4 million tons, but already in 1954 Burma regained its former position as the world's largest exporter of rice. Nevertheless, thanks partly to the Indian drive for self-sufficiency in foodstuffs and partly to the barter agreements recently concluded with the Soviet-bloc countries, the pattern of the Burmese rice export trade, which is now a state monopoly, has undergone a radical change since the Second World War (Table 54).

TABLE 53

BURMA: PRINCIPAL FIELD CROPS

Acreages

Crop	1938–9	1952–3	1959–60 *planned*	1959–60 *actual*	1960–61 *estimated*
	million	*million*	*million*	*million*	*million*
Paddy . .	12·8	10·3	13·3	10·7	10·7
Pulses . .	1·3	1·0	1·3	1·3	1·3
Ground nuts .	0·8	0·7	1·5	1·1	1·2
Sesamum .	1·4	1·3	1·5	1·5	1·5
Cotton . .	0·4	0·3	0·5	0·4	0·4
Total (including others) . .	—	—	—	17·5	17·9

Sources: Based on *Pyidawtha, the new Burma*, p. 47, and *Economic Survey of Burma*, 1961, Table 7.

No other agricultural product ranks as a major export though in 1954/5 rubber exports amounted to 14,000 tons and were valued at £2·85 million, despite the fact that acute insurgency in Tenasserim had led to a reduction in the area under production besides seriously impeding replanting. Short-stapled cotton also continues to be grown in excess of the country's internal requirements but the intention is to change over as far as possible to the production of long-stapled varieties for use in Burma's expanding cotton textiles industry. The possibility of replacing imports of jute from East Pakistan by local production in the delta is also receiving attention now that Burma has established its own jute bag industry near Rangoon.[56]

For the rest, Burmese agriculture is concerned wholly with producing food

[56] 10,000 acres were under jute and some 50,000 under long-stapled cotton in 1954–5. Tinker (C), p. 236. Jute production in 1959–60 was 4,000 tons.

TABLE 54

BURMA: DIRECTION OF RICE EXPORTS

Destination	1934–8 *average*		1955		1956		1960	
	000 tons	%	000 tons	%	000 tons	%	000 tons	%
Indonesia . .	77	3	105	6	342	18	498	28·9
Malaya (including Singapore) .	225	7	241	15	265	14	94	5·5
Japan . .	13	—	239	15	263	14	46	2·7
U.S.S.R. . .	—	—	135	8	212	11	45	2·7
Ceylon . .	335	12	135	8	153	8	251	14·6
India . .	1,652	55	267	16	127	7	318	18·5
China . .	64	2	155	10	85	4	17	1·0
United Kingdom .	58	2	72	5	57	3	4	0·2
Hungary . .	—	—	20	1	40	2	—	—
Yugoslavia .	—	—	13	1	35	2	24	1·4
Czechoslovakia .	—	—	24	2	33	2	6	0·3
Poland . .	—	—	19	1	26	1	—	—
East Germany .	—	—	51	3	20	1	25	1·5
Pakistan . .	—	—	n.a.	n.a.	n.a.	n.a.	197	11·5
Total (incl. others)	3,013		1,671		1,933		1,722	

Sources: Based on Cooke, p. 55, and Union of Burma, Central Statistical and Economic Department, *Bulletin of Export Trade*, Statistical Paper 1, Table 1, pp. 1–3.

for consumption within the country. This, of course, includes well over half the rice-crop, *i.e.* a somewhat larger proportion than before the war, and serious attempts are being made in the dry zone to increase the acreages of vegetable oils, especially ground nuts, substantial quantities of which at present have to be imported from abroad.

Because of the prolonged disorders which have afflicted Burma since 1941, the living standards of its people have dropped below even those of India.[57] Among other things this is evident in widespread malnutrition and a death-rate which is now among the highest in the world. Besides government action to counteract this by measures to increase and diversify food production, Premier

[57] See Table 11. But comparisons of this sort based on average figures are misleading. Thus the Indian average is raised by the considerable indigenous industrial and commercial element in the country but it is disputable whether the average Indian peasant is as well off even today as his Burmese counterpart.

U Nu tried hard to popularize the consumption of unpolished rice which retains most of the original bran covering the grain.[58] Failing this, the practice of parboiling, whereby the rice is steeped and steamed before husking, so that subsequent milling involves less breakage and hence the removal of less of the vitamin content, has much to recommend it. But unfortunately the Burmese people, like the great majority of other Asians, prefer the more palatable but less nutritious form of the grain, and in these circumstances the authorities are resorting instead to widespread distribution of vitamin pills[59] among the poorer sections of the population.

As in most neighbouring countries, fish provides the main source of animal protein, though the average per capita consumption in Burma is only 24 lb. a year, compared with 75 lb. in Japan. Most of the fish at present eaten are fresh-water varieties, but scope exists for a considerable expansion of coastal and deep-sea fisheries, and as a first step the government, in association with a Japanese commercial firm, has set up the Martaban Fishing Company which now operates off the Tenasserim coast.[60]

Today agricultural products comprise about 80 per cent of Burma's exports, as against approximately 50 per cent, of a much larger total, immediately before the war. Of the remainder, timber (largely teak) has risen from 7 to 9 per cent, but metals fell from 11 to 4 per cent, and mineral oil and its derivatives from 22 per cent to practically nothing.[61] These declines, which have served to aggravate Burma's already dangerous dependence on rice, have not been due to any significant increase in local consumption of the commodities in question, though it is the government's intention that an increasing proportion of these should in future be processed within the country. But the present decrease in the shares which metals and oil form of the total exports results directly from greatly reduced production, which in turn is due partly to the more severe war damage sustained by mining as compared with agriculture, and partly to the fact that a high proportion of the sources in question is located in relatively remote areas where insurgency has been particularly troublesome.

Since independence the timber industry has been nationalized and new plans drawn up for forest conservation which *inter alia* allow for an annual production of 450,000 cubic tons of teak. Such an output would be equivalent to the pre-war production, when then represented three-quarters of the world total. As recently as 1958–9 the output was still only 237,188 cubic tons, but since then a marked recovery has taken place.

[58] He argued that the 'heroes of Burma's past, like other Asians of those days', ate *lone dee* (pounded – *i.e.* unpolished – rice). *Atlantic Monthly*, Vol. 201, No. 2, February 1958, p. 102.

[59] These are now being made by Burma's own pharmaceutical industry. See below, p. 462.

[60] The Greater Rangoon Industrial Development Scheme plans to establish a tuna cannery, a fish-meal and fish-oil plant and three cold-storage plants.

[61] Petroleum and petroleum products exported in 1960 accounted for only 0·4 per cent of total exports. Since the Second World War until recently Burma has imported large quantities of oil products.

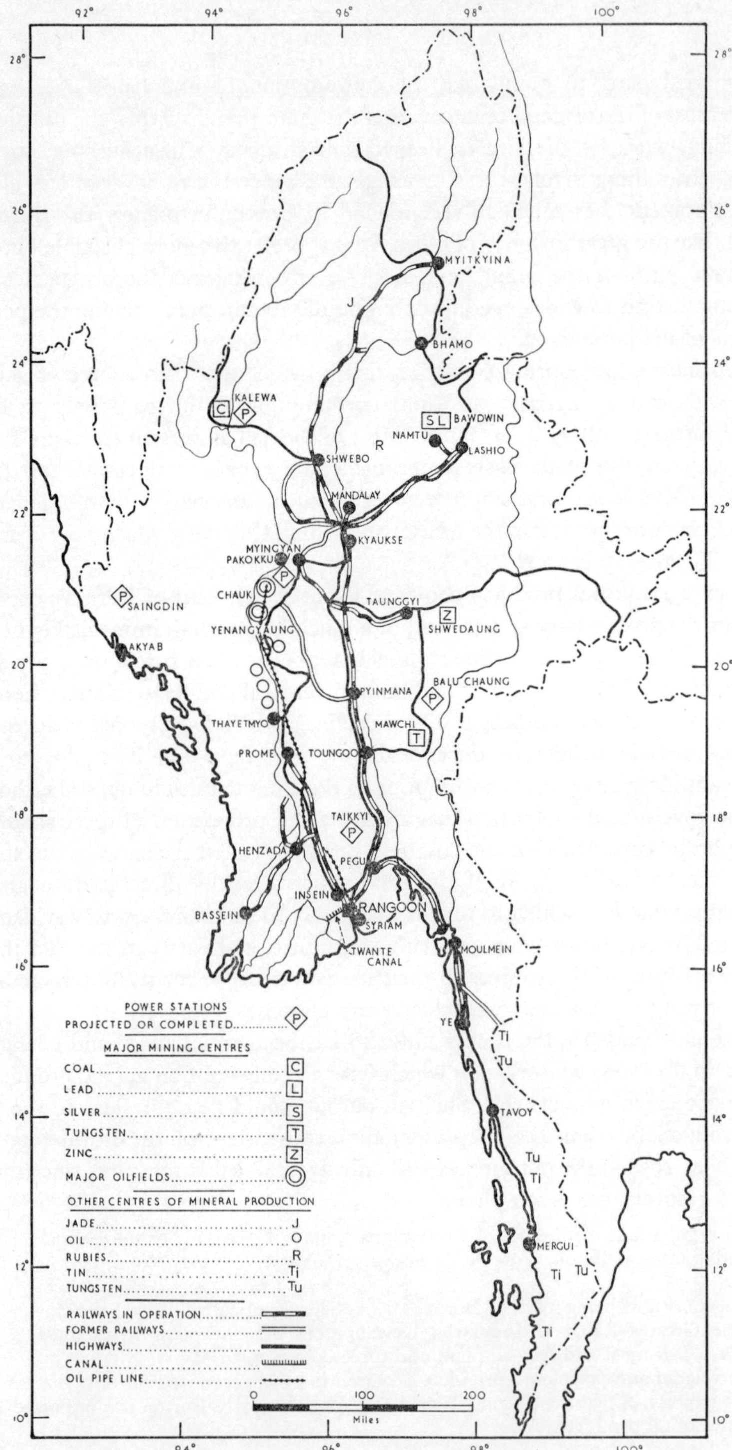

FIG. 67—Burma: economic development, 1954

Other hardwoods, such as pyinkado, padauk and in-kanyin, though at present exploited on a much smaller scale, appear to offer some prospects for development, as also do the t'ung oil, turpentine and resin which were already being commercially produced in the Shan plateau before the war. It is hoped to use this latter group of products as the basis of a paint and varnish industry, and plans also exist for utilizing some of the country's almost limitless supplies of bamboo for the manufacture of paper and pulp.[62]

Table 55 shows that the production of all the principal minerals still stands far below that of 1939. Since 1952 a new concern, jointly owned by the Burmese government and British private enterprise, has been operating the Bawdwin lead-zinc-silver mine in northern Shan State, and rehabilitation is now well under way, although the output is as yet only a fraction of the pre-war figure. On the other hand, the great tungsten-tin mine at Mawchi, which like Bawdwin was subjected to scorched-earth tactics in 1941, has been much slower to recover. From 1950 to 1954 Mawchi was in the hands of the Karen insurgents, and continuing insecurity in the neighbourhood still impedes production. Here also the Nu government favoured a joint Burmese-British undertaking, and a similar approach has been followed in many of the smaller tin and tungsten mines in Tenasserim where, again, insecurity remains the chief obstacle to recovery. Indeed, until this problem is solved there would seem to be little point in the government's proceeding further with its various projects for exploiting new sources of metallic minerals, such as lead and silver in Kachin State, antimony and manganese in Shan State, and the supposedly rich deposits of zinc at Shwedaung near Taunggyi also in Shan State.

So far as the export trade is concerned, the most serious setback has been the decline in petroleum production. With a view to organizing the rehabilitation

TABLE 55

BURMA: MINERAL PRODUCTION

Mineral	1939	1954–5	1960–61
Crude petroleum (million gallons)	275·7	52·4	145·2
Tin ores and concentrates (thousand tons)	5·4	0·8	0·9
Tungsten ores and concentrates (thousand tons)	4·3	0·5	0·4
Mixed tin and tungsten (thousand tons)	5·6	1·5	1·1
Lead ores and concentrates (thousand tons)	77·1	26·1	27·0
Zinc ores and concentrates (thousand tons)	59·3	13·7	12·7

Sources: Cooke, p. 8, and Union of Burma, Central Statistical and Economic Department, *Selected Monthly Economic Indicator*, Statistical Paper 3, January 1962, pp. 13 and 16.

[62] See below, p. 463. Tinker (C), p. 249, pointed out that there had been some change of emphasis from the production of teak for export to that of other timber for local consumption.

TABLE 56

BURMA: PRODUCTION OF PETROLEUM AND REFINED PRODUCTS

Item	*Output* 1955–6	1960–61
Crude petroleum	60·2 million gallons	145·2 million gallons
Motor spirit	11·4 million gallons	43·7 million gallons
Kerosene	16·8 million gallons	24·6 million gallons
Other fuel oil	9·8 million gallons	30·2 million gallons
Wax	8,695 tons	13,021 tons (1960)

Note: Exports 1939/40. Petroleum: 54·7 m. gal., kerosene: 140·5 m. gal., lubricating oils: 7·9 m. gal., wax: 56·218 tons, candles: 4,309 tons. Exports 1955/6. Wax: 600 tons (value K. 400,000).

Sources: Based on Cooke, p. 50, and Union of Burma, Central Statistical and Economic Department, *Quarterly Bulletin of Statistics*, Statistical Paper 2, Second Quarter 1961, Table V (3).

of the industry, the three British oil companies operating in the country pooled their resources in 1945, and later these were formed into a new concern, the Burma Oil Company (1954) Ltd., in which the government has a one-third interest and power to acquire the remainder at an agreed price. But although by 1948 the company had spent £9 million in restoring the oilfields and reopening the pipeline from Yenangyaung to Syriam, the oilfields were overrun, the pipeline cut by insurgents, and rehabilitation ceased in 1949. However, work was continued at Chauk and Lanywa, both of which are now producing satisfactorily, and since 1953 a small refinery at Chauk, with a capacity of 120,000 gallons a day, has provided petroleum, kerosene and fuel oils for central and northern Burma, and has even managed to send a small surplus, and a little wax, for export, by barge to Rangoon. In 1957 a second refinery (capacity 140,000 gallons a day) was opened at Syriam,[63] and this also processes oil brought by river from Chauk and Lanywa.

Thus Burma is now able to satisfy the whole of its own small requirements of petroleum, kerosene and fuel oils, but the resumption of any significant export of these will probably await the restoration of the Yenangyaung fields to production,[64] and meanwhile exploration for new sources of oil has been undertaken in central Burma and the Irrawaddy delta, though so far without spectacular results.

[63] This refinery is a partial reconstruction of the pre-war one destroyed in 1942, but the present capacity is only one-quarter that of its predecessor. It is planned to process aviation turbine fuel there for non-piston aircraft calling at Rangoon. The government hopes to raise Burma's refining capacity from the present 260,000 to 400,000 gallons a day, and work on the expansion of the Syrian refinery is well advanced.

[64] However, Yenangyaung had passed its peak and been overtaken by Chauk before the Japanese invasion. In 1940 the daily output of the four main centres was: Yenangyaung 295,307 gallons, Chauk 377,703 gallons, Lanywa 63,315 gallons, Yenangyat 12,679 gallons. Tinker (C), pp. 282–3.

One important new mining development remains to be mentioned, namely that of the sub-bituminous coal deposits at Kalewa, near the confluence of the Chindwin and Myittha rivers, some 500 miles from Rangoon. The existence of these deposits has been known for many years but, owing to the ease and cheapness of importing coal from Bengal, no attempt was made to work them prior to independence. Now, however, the government's desire to build up a wider range of industry within the country has led it to undertake the exploitation of the coalfield, with the help of British advisers, and it is planned to produce an annual total of 300,000 tons, which should be enough to meet the needs of the railways and thermal-electric power stations. Nevertheless, the remoteness of Kalewa, and the difficulties of navigation along the Chindwin to and from the coalfield during the dry season will continue to keep the price of its product well above that of imported coal.[65]

Owing largely to its former character as a peripheral region of the Indian Empire, Burma before the Second World War was one of the least industrialized countries in the whole of South-east Asia. Thus in 1940 factory workers numbered rather less than 90,000 and nearly 50 per cent of the total were employed in the rice mills, a further 12 per cent in the 100 or so sawmills, and about 10 per cent in the oil industry. By 1951 the figure had shrunk to 43,000 and only a minute fraction of the factory-made goods consumed in the country was locally made.[66]

Thus the desire for rapid industrialization, which has been common to all the new Asian states, was particularly intense in Burma, and a succession of plans to this end followed the achievement of independence. However, after having embarked on the Two Year Plan of 1948, the government called in the American firm of Knappen, Tibbetts, Abbett Engineering Company as consultants, and it is largely on the basis of their findings and recommendations[67] that subsequent planning has taken place, though financial stringency has led to various reductions and postponements in recent years.

According to recent policy, industrialization, while desirable in order to create new forms of employment and to strengthen the country's defence, should nevertheless be undertaken with a careful eye to comparative costs, and the

[65] *I.e.* the price at Rangoon. Were the Myingyan industrial area to be developed Kalewa coal might find a more economic outlet there. See Tinker (C), pp. 305–6.

[66] Of the 1,007 factories registered in 1942, 70 per cent were rice mills and sawmills; of the 692 rice mills (1939), 27 were European owned, 164 Chinese, 190 Indian and 311 Burman, but 80 per cent of them employed less than 100 workers. The largest factories in the country were a cotton spinning and ginning mill at Myingyan, a cement factory at Thayetmyo (which supplied much of Malaya's as well as Burma's needs), a brewery and a match factory at Mandalay (all European owned), a knitting factory near Insein and a sugar refinery at Zeyawaddy (both Indian owned). Besides these there were the Burma Railways workshops at Insein, Myitnge and Kanbalu, but more important employers of industrial labour were the oilfields and mines. See Tinker (C), pp. 283–4.

[67] Knappen-Tibbetts-Abbett Engineering Company, in association with Pierce Management Inc. and Robert R. Nathan Associates Inc., *Comprehensive report on economic and engineering survey of Burma for Ministry of National Planning*, Rangoon, 1953, mimeographed.

primary aim has been to reduce dependence on foreign imports of articles which can be produced economically in Burma itself. Thus during the first phase of four to five years, prior concentration was to be devoted to the provision of technical training and the establishment of a few basic industries, whose products would be required by the various secondary industries which would follow in the second and later phases. But in the event the time allotted for the initial phase has run its course with barely a half of the original projects completed and, while the rest of the programme has also been scaled down, some at least of the secondary industries have already been set up and others are in process of construction.

In theory the programme concentrates on three localities, though in fact the Greater Rangoon Industrial Development Scheme has hitherto received practically the whole attention, owing to the twin problems of insurgency and disrupted transport in other parts of the country. In the Rangoon area, besides the state-owned cotton spinning and weaving factory opened in 1951 at Thamaing,[68] the new Engineering College, Polytechnic and High School have all been completed more recently, as also has the pharmaceutical and drug plant, which was built by a British firm to provide materials required by the Government's public health services.

The most interesting of the basic industries in the Rangoon complex is an electrically operated steel plant of 20,000 tons annual capacity, which has been set up by a German firm at a cost of K. 42 million (£3·15 million), to manufacture such products as bars, rods, sheets, wire and nails. Since no known deposits of suitable iron ore exist in Burma, some doubts have been expressed regarding the wisdom of setting up this plant, which for the time being will rely on the large but not inexhaustible quantities of scrap iron which remain as a legacy of the war.

Other basic industrial activity in Rangoon includes the expansion of the existing sawmill capacity and the development of a whole series of related manufactures, such as plywood, veneers, and wooden fittings, along the waterfront, the establishment of a factory now manufacturing 1·2 million roofing tiles and 12·5 million building bricks a year, and subsequently the erection of a new cement factory with a capacity of 120,000 tons a year.

Besides these the Thamaing cotton factory has been expanded at a cost of K. 17·5 million, and this is being followed by the erection of other cotton spinning and weaving establishments in various parts of the country, though priority in this respect will probably be given to Mandalay in the cotton-growing area.[69] The silk industry likewise has received attention with the setting up of a reeling and spinning mill, costing K. 7·5 million, at Rangoon, and reference has already been made to the large jute bag factory (cost K. 30 million) which, with a production

[68] This large-scale modern plant is designed to use $\frac{7}{8}$-in. staple cotton, but as not enough of this is produced in Burma as yet (which mostly grows $\frac{5}{8}$-in. staple) the factory has to rely in part on imported cotton from Pakistan and the U.S.A. See above, p. 455.

[69] It was announced in 1957 that, as part of the reparations agreement, the Japanese would help in setting up two further cotton mills in Rangoon, and one each in Mandalay and Myingyan, all four to be completed by 1960.

of 10 million gunny bags a year can now supply all that are at present needed in the country. Miscellaneous consumer-goods industries now under consideration or already finished, include paint and varnish, glass, rubber tyres, soap and bottles.

Finally there is the important group of food-processing industries. Besides planning to modernize many of the smaller rice mills in and around Rangoon, the government proposes to set up a rice-bran processing plant and later also a soya-bean milk factory and fish canneries in the city.[70]

In conformity with the traditional geographical dualism of Burma, the second area scheduled for industrial development is centred at Myingyan in the middle of the dry zone. This town is situated on the Irrawaddy, some 60 miles south-west of Mandalay, at the terminus of a railway spur from the main trunk line, and besides being within easy reach of the oilfields is roughly midway between the Kalewa coalfield and the new Balu Chaung hydro-electric power station in Kayah State. Present plans envisage the establishment of zinc smelting and refining, and also of a chemical industry devoted principally to the production of sulphuric acid and fertilizers. As yet, however, all this, together with the proposed textile developments there and at Mandalay and the expansion of the existing cement works at Thayetmyo, is in the planning or the construction stage and the main projects so far completed are a tea-packing plant at Mandalay and a large sugar and alcohol factory, costing K. 18 million, at Pyinmana.[71]

Even less progress has been made in the third proposed industrial area, namely that in northern Arakan. Here the main project under consideration is a large bamboo-pulp and paper factory which, with related units including a saltern and a caustic-soda and chlorine plant, is estimated to cost K. 70 million. The probable site for the scheme is at Ponnagyun, some 13 miles up the Kaladan river, and it is proposed to obtain power from the Saingdin falls 40 miles to the north-west of the town.

Besides these extensive if, as yet, only partially realized plans for large-scale industrialization, the government proposes to expand the existing small-scale industries which are found scattered throughout the Burmese countryside. Such establishments, employing up to 50 workers each, are of great importance in providing temporary work in the slack seasons of the agricultural year, and it is estimated that at least 2 million farm workers are in need of employment of this kind. Moreover, many goods, notably certain types of cotton and silk textiles, pottery, hand-made paper, umbrellas and various foodstuffs, are at present more economically produced in these small concerns than anywhere else and for this reason also the government is anxious to develop them further. In the long run success in this respect will depend largely on improvements in communications, the provision of credit and marketing facilities, the teaching of improved techniques and the spread of rural electrification.

[70] See above, note 60.

[71] There is also another in operation at Namti in the Myitkyina district. A smaller new sugar plant was opened at Bhamo in 1955. Tinker (C), p. 306.

Before the war Burma was very poorly supplied with electricity, the only large generating station being the steam-operated plant at Rangoon which provided 24,000 kW. Elsewhere about 100 small diesel plants supplied the main towns with electric light and some 70 other units provided power for mines and factories.

Under the new regime both industrialization and the raising of rural living standards call for a major increase in supplies and already a chain of new diesel plants is providing electric light to numerous towns and large villages. While further developments along these lines are to be undertaken, the biggest increase in power production is to come from the establishment of a series of large generating stations whose primary task will be to supply mines, factories and irrigation projects.

Apart from the new thermal station recently opened near Rangoon, the main post-war emphasis is on hydro-electric power, for the generation of which many parts of the country have conspicuous natural advantages. Three principal projects are at present envisaged, the largest of them being that at Lawpita (near Loikaw) on the Balu Chaung, a tributary of the Salween, in Kayah State. This plant, whose present capacity is 84,000 kW (but is soon to be expanded to double this capacity), has recently been constructed by Japanese engineers as part of the reparations agreement, and besides supplying the industrial needs of central Burma and various mining centres in the eastern plateaux, it will also cater for the rapidly growing needs of Rangoon.[72] Nevertheless, the latter, together with other parts of the delta, will be the principal consumer of the 15,000 kW to be generated by the Taikkyi project, on the Pegu river, some 40 miles above Pegu itself. As already noted, Arakan will ultimately be supplied by a new power station at Saingdin falls.

Although the Second World War was responsible for the addition of three new components to the Burmese transport network, namely the Burma Road between Lashio and Chungking, the Ledo Road between Mogaung and Ledo in north-eastern Assam, and the Thailand–Burma Railway, between Thanbyuzayat on the Moulmein-Ye branch and Ban Pong via the Three Pagodas Pass, all of these were of strategic rather than commercial importance, and none has survived in active use as a trunk route since the war.[73] Thus they provide no compensation for the severe damage inflicted on the rest of the transport system, and rehabilitation of the latter still remains one of the country's most fundamental needs, without which neither economic development nor political progress can effectively be achieved.

Probably the railways sustained the greatest setback of all, with 48 per cent of their total equipment, including 285 out of 350 locomotives, completely destroyed. By late 1953, 1,649 out of 2,058 miles were again in use, and although the

[72] In view of the government's inability completely to suppress the insurgents the problem of securing long-distance transmission lines against their attacks may become serious.

[73] There has been intermittent talk of reviving the Burma Road and the Thailand–Burma Railway, but the initiative in both cases has come from Burma's neighbours and has not been followed up. See below, p. 523.

considerable stretches running through insurgent territory have remained subject to intermittent attack, progress has continued and the big bridges at Ava and over the Daga river have been repaired. Indeed, though freight traffic is still below the pre-war level, the number of passengers carried is now considerably higher than in 1939, and in recent years much of the track mileage has been restored and much new equipment, including diesels, obtained.

Compared with the railways, roads suffered less from the war but more from the insurgency, and most of them are now in poor condition. On the whole this is a reflection rather than a cause of the relatively low place which motor transport still occupies in the national life, and most of Burma's minute total of 35,100 motor vehicles in 1959 – nearly half of them in Rangoon – are seriously over age. Two new long-distance roads have been under construction, from Prome to Taungup, across the Arakan Yoma (completed in 1955) and from Mindat to Malupi in the Chin Division, and under the local aspect of the *Pyidawtha* programme it is hoped greatly to extend the mileage of minor 'farm-to-market' roads in the countryside at large.

Since independence both inland and coastal shipping have been nationalized, the Irrawaddy Flotilla Company having been taken over by the Inland Water Transport Board and the Arracan Flotilla Company by the Union of Burma Shipping Board. Only 106 of the former company's 600 craft were serviceable by the end of the war, and although there has been some replacement and the construction of 154 new river vessels, including 36 for the oil traffic between Chauk and Syriam, has been largely achieved the volume of freight carried remains well below that of pre-war days and the number of passengers is still only about two-thirds of the former total.

Coastal shipping, on the other hand, has made more progress and the U.B.S.B. now has two passenger ships, each of 2,217 gross tons, which respectively provide a fortnightly service between the Arakan ports and Rangoon, and connect the latter with Tenasserim and Singapore by monthly sailings. In addition the board owns two freight vessels with a cargo capacity of 7,000 tons each, which are used mainly between Rangoon and Calcutta.

Rangoon, which continues to handle *c.* 85 per cent of the foreign and nearly half of the country's coastal trade, still suffers from the wartime damage to its installations so that, although the total volume of its traffic is less than half of that in pre-war days, congestion is now acute. However, re-equipment has been undertaken with the help of a loan from the World Bank.[74] For the rest, Bassein handles 10 per cent of the foreign trade, Akyab (which suffered acutely during the war) less than 4 per cent of the foreign and 15 per cent of the coastal trade, while the corresponding figures for Moulmein are 5 per cent and 15 per cent respectively and Mergui is still responsible for 20 per cent of the coastal traffic.

[74] Substantial progress in the repair of the Rangoon docks was made with U.S. aid during 1951–3, and after the latter ceased the government continued with its own plan for rehabilitation. Tinker (C), p. 290. The new Rangoon circular railway was opened in 1959.

Internal air transport is largely a post-war development so far as Burma is concerned[75] and, as in Malaya, progress has been much stimulated by insurgency. The nationalized corporation, Union of Burma Airways, in 1954 maintained 65 scheduled services per week to 34 towns and handles some 2·5 million passenger miles and 100,000 freight-ton miles each month within the country itself. These internal services were operated by a small fleet of eight Dakotas and three De Havilland Doves, while the corporation's international flights, which began in 1957, are maintained by three Viscounts. The main international airport at Mingaladon on the outskirts of Rangoon has been considerably extended and improved, and besides U.B.A. various foreign companies make regular calls there though the volume of traffic is still below that of most of the other South-east Asian capital cities. Since 1954, moreover, the volume of internal air traffic has declined.

From this outline of the actual and proposed reconstruction of the Burmese economy since 1948, it is apparent that achievement is as yet far below what was originally envisaged. While in the short run this can be largely attributed to such factors as the expense and dislocation entailed by the insurgency and the decline in foreign-exchange earnings resulting from the drop in the export price of rice, it is not wholly clear that these provide the full explanation of the fact that in 1957 the gross national product had still not regained the level reached under British rule in 1939.[76]

For, in common with the other South-east Asian countries, Burma suffers from an acute shortage of trained personnel, and this was notably aggravated by the peremptory dismissal of many Indians, Anglo-Indians and Anglo-Burmans[77] particularly from the railways and customs staffs, as well as of European civil servants and other experts, in the early days of independence.

TABLE 57

BURMA: POPULATION OF MAIN TOWNS, 1953

Rangoon	737,079
Mandalay	185,867
Moulmein	102,777
Bassein	77,905
Henzada	61,972
Pegu	47,378
Akyab	42,329
Tavoy	40,312

Source: Cooke, p. vii.

[75] Though British, French and Dutch lines already called at Rangoon before the war.

[76] It was estimated in 1962 that the average real income per head of the Burmese population was still only 87 per cent of that before the war.

[77] The numbers of Anglo-Burmans (23,000 in 1957) are not large and they present no problem comparable with that of the Eurasians in Indonesia. It is clearly in Burma's interest to make the maximum use of their skills.

Nevertheless, if as now seems possible, internal insecurity begins tc present a less serious drain on the country's energies, the economic prospects for Burma will be by no means discouraging. For, besides having the most favourable ratio of population to agricultural land in the whole of South-east Asia, the country possesses an abundance and diversity of mineral and forest wealth which many of its neighbours have good cause to envy.

Provided, therefore, that its leaders resist the temptation to industrialize for industrialization's sake, and continue to concentrate the greater part of the nation's economic activity on primary production and related processing, the known
Nevertheless, if as now seems possible, internal insecurity begins to present a
resources already ripe for exploitation are capable of sustaining a much higher standard of living than its people have enjoyed hitherto.

III. POLITICAL GEOGRAPHY

In common with the other ex-colonial lands of South-east Asia, independent Burma contains within the boundaries it inherited from the old regime a whole series of minority communities of varying size and differing degrees of self-consciousness.[78] It was with the express purpose of satisfying the aspirations of the more important of these groups for a measure of local automony that a quasi-federal[79] constitution was adopted, under which the Union of Burma is made up of six constituent units, namely Burma proper, the Shan State, the Kachin State, the Karenni State (now Kayah State), the Kawthulay Special Region (now Karen State) and the Special Division of the Chins. Moreover, besides having their own Councils of State, with local control over purely internal matters, all five of these minority groups are also represented in the Upper House of the Union Parliament, which, in imitation of Yugoslav and Soviet practice, is styled the Chamber of Nationalities.[80]

Nevertheless, while these constitutional arrangements were the outcome of a genuine effort to meet the wishes of the principal indigenous minorities, without running the risk of national disintegration, many difficulties have arisen in putting them into effect. In particular the geographical distribution of the various peoples concerned is so complex that no wholly satisfactory units can be devised, and the sometimes arbitrary decisions which have been made in these circumstances have been open to criticism from various quarters.

[78] The original British plan was to grant self-government to Parliamentary Burma only, but at Aung San's insistence the Excluded Areas were also brought into the Union of Burma.

[79] Federal was the official style, though 'not even lawyers seem to be able to say whether the Union is in fact a federal or a unitary state'. Fairbairn (B), p. 309. While the Kayah and Shan States have the constitutional right to secede, the Kachin and Karen States have no such right. But the Ne Win regime seized power in 1962 partly to prevent any further move towards true federalism.

[80] It has 125 members: 25 Shans, 12 Kachins, 8 Chins, 3 Kayahs, 15 Karens and 62 members for the rest of Burma. The Lower House (Chamber of Deputies) has 250 members.

TABLE 58

BURMA: MAIN ETHNIC AND RELIGIOUS GROUPS

Community	1931	1957	*Religions*	1931
Burmans . .	9,627,196	12,800,000		
Karens . .	1,367,673	1,800,000		
Shans . .	1,037,406	1,500,000	Buddhist	12,348,037
Kachins (est.) .	400,000	450,000	Animist	763,243
Chins . .	348,994	400,000	Muslim	584,839
Mons . .	336,728	400,000	Hindu	582,581
Palaung-Wa .	176,382	200,000	Christian (of whom	331,106
Lolo – Muhso .	93,224	100,000	218,790 were Karens)	
Naga . .	70,000	90,000		
Indian . .	1,107,825	800,000		
Chinese . .	193,594	350,000		
Indo-Burman .	182,166	200,000		
Eurasian . .	19,200	23,000		
European . .	11,651			
Total (Inc. others)	15,000,000	20,000,000		

Sources: 1931 Census; 1957 author's estimate.

Except for their scattered distribution which has made it impossible to include them all within a single political region, the Shans would appear to present the fewest problems, for unlike the other frontier peoples of the former Excluded Areas they are not animistic hill-folk, but valley dwellers who profess the same Buddhist faith as the Burmans themselves. However, largely as a result of the topographical fragmentation of the eastern plateaux which have formed the homeland of the great majority of them since the middle ages, they have been organized in a series of some thirty small principalities, varying in size with the character of the terrain from 24 to 11,180 square miles. Each of these states has been under its own hereditary ruler or *sawbwa*, most of whom formerly recognized the overlordship of the Burmese kings, though many, especially those east of the Salween, also recognized the suzerainty of China.[81]

Ethnically and linguistically the Shans are very close to the Siamese, but although during the Japanese occupation two of the states, Kengtung and Möng Pan, were 'retroceded' to Thailand, this decision was reversed after the war, and

[81] Those east of the Salween paid tribute less frequently – or not at all – to the Burmese kings. The latter also exchanged gifts periodically with China and on this basis the Chinese have at times made vague claims to suzerainty over Burma, though these have never been admitted by the Burmese.

in 1948 all the states[82], together with the remote and primitive Wa states, were united to form the new Shan State which has an area of 57,816 square miles.

Nevertheless, in the absence of an adequate corps of trained Shan civil servants the change-over to a modern democratic form of government has not proved easy to bring about. Thus, although the *sawbwas* have been prevailed upon to relinquish some of their traditional power and to agree to half the seats in the State Council's being filled by popular representation, it is still the *sawbwas* who represent the Shans in the Chamber of Nationalities.[83]

From the outset the divergence between traditionalist-minded *sawbwas* and the avowedly socialist aims of the Union government seemed likely to create difficulties. In January 1958 a conference of Shan leaders decided to press for the secession of the Shan State from the Union, and though wiser counsels fortunately prevailed for a time, Shan demands for greater autonomy helped to precipitate the Ne Win coup in 1962.

The Karens, who form the largest of the minority groups, have proved also to be the most difficult of all to accommodate. It is unlikely that they were always confined to the hills, but in the course of centuries those who occupied the plains were absorbed by the Mons and Burmans. The hill Karens remained pagan and, fearful of and despised by the Burmans, who called them 'the wild cattle of the hills', they lived isolated in their remote villages in the south-eastern plateaux and parts of the Pegu Yoma until the coming of British rule brought law and order to Lower Burma. Thereafter they spread with astonishing rapidity into the lowlands around Moulmein and the delta, including the westernmost area around Bassein. At the same time many came under the influence of the American Baptist missions which soon found them far more receptive to their teachings than were the more sophisticated Buddhist Burmans. And, like their counterparts in some of the non-Muslim areas of Indonesia, many of the Karen Christians, having received a useful education in mission schools, were able to obtain employment as policemen, nurses, teachers, doctors and soldiers, including many of commissioned rank in the old Burma Army.[84]

Through all this period the Karens' dislike for the Burmans never abated. In the countryside they kept to their own villages and the religious barrier was intensified rather than diminished as a result of conversion to Christianity. Thus the idea of some form of separate state for the Karens was mooted as early as 1928, and these aspirations were strengthened by the experiences of the Second World War, when many Karens were armed by the British and rendered outstanding service as anti-Japanese guerrillas.

While it was clear to the A.F.P.F.L. leaders from the beginning of the post-war era that some measure of autonomy would have to be granted to the Karens,

[82] These were grouped together as the Federated Shan States in 1922.

[83] See Fairbairn (B), pp. 307–8. It was announced in March 1959 that the *sawbwas* would no longer hold the right of representation in the Chamber of Nationalities after 1964.

[84] *I.e.* under the British. Some also went as Baptist missionaries to the Kachin hills and other animist areas.

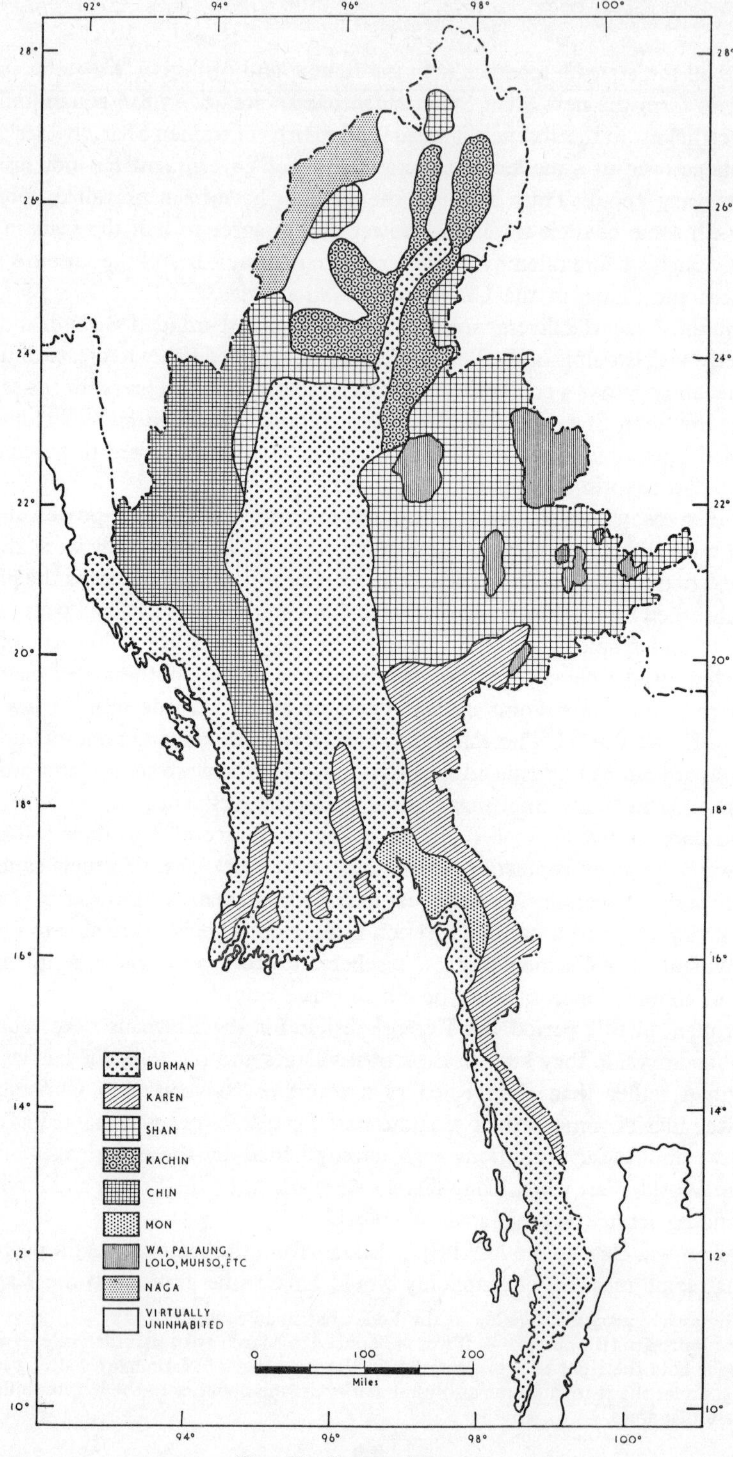

FIG. 68—Burma: languages

in view of the traditional primacy of river communications within the country, this has greatly facilitated the task of national unification.

In common with the other countries of mainland South-east Asia, Thailand has experienced a sequence of population movements from north to south since very early times, and even as recently as the decade 1937–47 the only two provinces which showed a decline in numbers (against a national average increase of *c.* 17 per cent) were Chiengmai and Mae-hongson in the extreme north-west.[6]

As in Burma, the relatively small interior valleys, which were the first areas to be occupied by invaders from the north, offered the least difficulty in respect of water control, and it is accordingly in the vicinity of Sawankalok, Sukothai and Chiengmai that some of the earliest Thai principalities arose after the great dispersal from Nan Chao in the 13th century.[7]

However, the drift to the south was so rapid that by the middle of the 14th century the Thais had become the dominant people over the whole of the central plain and, with the founding of Ayuthia in 1350, the Menam delta was firmly established as the nuclear region of the Siamese kingdom. Thus, in contrast to Burma, where the earlier Mons of the coastal fringe maintained their identity and a separate focus of political power for centuries, their counterparts in the Siamese plains were absorbed by their conquerors, and the old Mon kingdom of Dvaravati disappeared completely from the map.

Nevertheless, the Thai peoples, though all stemming from a common source in the plateau of Yunnan, have never since cohered to form a single national group. Differences both in dates of migration and in the character of the country-sides in which they ultimately settled fostered division into several groups, and while in written language and material culture these continued to preserve many affinities one with another, recognizable distinctions persisted between those who inhabited the plateaux[8] and those who settled in the plains.

Thus, while the latter group were able fairly quickly to build a populous and powerful kingdom in the lowlands focusing on the middle and lower Menam, the others remained divided among a series of smaller and weaker political units stretching from the Shan states in the west through the principalities of northern Siam to the Lao territories of Lan Chang, which prior to the 18th century embraced both the modern Laos and the greater part of the Korat plateau. Moreover, these political divisions were reflected in other ways, and the Thais of the plains, with their higher standard of living and more intensely Indianized culture, came to regard their less sophisticated kinsmen of the up-lands as economically and socially inferior to themselves.

So far as those of the Shan plateau were concerned, the closeness of the

[6] De Young, p. 199.

[7] But note that there was a Lao kingdom at Lampun in A.D. 570 and there were other settlements in the 9th century. See above, p. 105.

[8] Strictly speaking, the Thais usually inhabited the valleys within the plateaux rather than the plateaux proper. *Cf.* Tinker's comments on the Shans. See above, p. 432, note 6.

difficulties at once arose as soon as attempts were made to define the scope of their proposals and the area to which they should apply.[85] Admittedly, so far as the three Karen-ni States were concerned, namely Bawlake, Kyebogy and Kantarawaddy, no problem of demarcation arose, and these tiny principalities, which were ruled over by 'Red Karen' chiefs and had been under British protection since 1875, were reconstituted as the Karen-ni State, later renamed Kayah State.

But this minute territory of some 4,500 square miles contained only a mere 80,000 or so – and those among the most backward – of the total number of well over 1½ million Karens, the rest of whom formed a clear majority in the hill country immediately to the south of Kayah State and a significant minority, interspersed with Burmans and Mons, over most parts of the delta and the lowlands around Moulmein.

In the first flush of their enthusiasm in 1945 some of the Karen leaders made wild claims to the whole of this area, with adjoining parts of Thailand thrown in for good measure. When, a few years later, the Burmese leaders suggested that a much smaller area, to be known as the Kawthulay Special Region, should be established and later built up as a Karen State, the Karens were disappointed. Yet it was not this but the general mistrust between the two peoples which caused the Karens in January 1949 to rise in rebellion against the Union government. Despite the fact that the revolt was supported by numbers of ex-regular Karen officers and men as well as experienced guerrilla fighters, its force was largely spent by 1954,[86] when the new Karen State came into being, more or less as originally planned by the Union government

As can be seen from Fig. 69 the Karen State occupies an extensive area of hill country straddling the lower Salween, but its boundaries stop well short of the coast and the railway line to Tenasserim, and the territory does not include the Ataran valley which the Karens had hoped would be their principal rice granary. All-told not more than one-third of the total Karen population lives within the state, but while this is a cause of much disappointment, the fact remains that to include the remainder would involve bringing in an even larger number of non-Karens, and it is inconceivable that any Burmese government would agree to handing over a part, let alone the whole, of the delta which today, more than ever before, is the supreme focus of the whole country.

By comparison with the Shans and Karens, the remaining peoples of the former Excluded Areas, such as the Chins, Kachins and Nagas,[87] have presented fewer

[85] Although many Karens wished to maintain the British connexion in some form, this was incompatible with the United Kingdom's plans for Burma as a whole. The Karen leaders therefore prepared to negotiate for a Karen State within the Union, and the dispute arose essentially over the area which this should include.

[86] The situation was complicated by the fact that many members of the Union forces were also Karens.

[87] The Naga problem is mainly on the Indian side of the boundary where there are 350,000 of these people, as against only 70,000–90,000 in Burma. The Burmese govern-

problems. This is not because these peoples are numerically smaller and, except in a few isolated Christian missionary areas, animist. Still less is it because they are tribal, for the tribal organization may yet present a further problem. It is because they are so remote and apart, and their contacts with Burma proper few: whereas Burmans and plains Karens live intertwined, with their villages side by side, the more remote of these hill peoples have never seen a Burman. The British ruled them only indirectly, a handful of European officers preventing inter-tribal war and occasionally supervising the chiefs and tribal councils. Hence the British departure made comparatively little difference, and the tribal governments continue to operate under the Union government just as they did under the British. Moreover, the Chins and Kachins have a valuable link with the Union in that, like the less fortunate Karens whose battalions have now been disbanded, these two peoples had for decades served in the British Indian Army and they continue to furnish the Union government with some of its best battalions. Politically the Kachin State, which consists of the former Myitkyina and Bhamo Districts,[88] has a similar status to that of the other semi-autonomous states, but the Chins accepted a closer connexion with the Union government and their territory is designated the Chin Special Division.

While these various arrangements were made to meet the wishes of the main frontier peoples, whose territories had never formed part of Parliamentary Burma under the British regime, the Union constitution clearly implied that no such special provision was needed for any of the lowland peoples. However, this assumption has not been wholly borne out by events since independence, and at one time or another both the Mons and the Arakanese have shown signs of disaffection.

Although the greater part of the descendants of the original Mon population have merged with the Burmans and Karens now inhabiting the southern plains, over one-third of a million persons were returned in 1931 as speakers of the Mon language, and undoubtedly there is a real sense of common identity among many of these. And while this did not prevent them from throwing in their lot with the majority community both before and after independence, some of them joined the revolt against the Union government when the latter seemed on the point of being overthrown in 1948–9.

The Arakanese[89] are Burmans albeit with an admixture of Indian blood, and their language is a somewhat archaic form of Burmese. However, living on the other side of a long mountain chain, they are conscious of their difference from Irrawaddy valley Burmans, and still remember that they had their own kings until 1784. After the departure of the British not only the Arakanese but also the

ment has not attempted to give the latter group any special status and they are administered through the Commissioner of Sagaing. The Nagas in India were given their own administrative unit in November 1957.

[88] This area includes considerable lowland tracts with some 110,000 Burman inhabitants, who in fact play a large part in the running of the Kachin State. See Tinker (A), p. 342.

[89] For a fuller account see Thompson and Adloff, pp. 151–8.

Indians among them developed separatist movements. These latter were strengthened by the large post-war influx of Pakistanis from across the frontier, with the result that in the Akyab region Muslims now outnumber Buddhists, and a group of the former, the so-called Mujahids, have openly advocated a separatist policy and appealed for Pakistani aid to this end. Although no such support has been forthcoming, the situation led to strained relations between the two groups in Arakan, and the inability of the Union government to cope with the problem has in turn caused the Buddhist Arakanese, already resentful of the growing 'Burmanization' of the various services, to put forward demands for regional autonomy. Although the government, understandably perturbed by the threat of fragmentation, was slow to concede these demands, it was announced in April 1961 that both an Arakan State and a Mon State were to be constituted in the autumn of 1962. After the 1962 coup, however, such developments seem less probable.

It is evident, therefore, that Burma is faced, albeit on a smaller scale, with much the same kind of regional minority problems which trouble Indonesia and, as in the latter, the largest ethnic group – in this case the Burman – is anxious to keep within bounds the various fissiparous movements which have become apparent since the successful termination of the struggle for independence.

Nevertheless, the internal problems in Burma have hitherto for several reasons been much less acute than those in Indonesia. In the first place the geographical layout of the country, so far from fostering centrifugal tendencies, is such as to promote fusion, for the links with the outside world across the surrounding semi-circle of hills are few and difficult, and nearly all the internal routes, whether natural or man-made, focus on the central core – that is the dry zone and the delta – which is also the homeland of the dominant ethnic group.

Thus, although the Burmans have been challenged by local uprisings in various parts of the country, the central government's ability to maintain control of the vital lines of communication has helped to prevent any effective co-operation between such dissident groups, and the fact that the territory under its command contains Rangoon, the great port through which nearly all exports must pass, is an immense asset economically. Moreover, since the greater part of these exports come from the Burman areas themselves, the minority peoples have no grounds for the kind of economic grievances which have bedevilled the relations between Java and the outer islands of Indonesia.[90]

In these circumstances, therefore, the nationalist leaders were willing to persevere with the quasi-federal solution[91] to the minority problem, and, although this did not in fact give a very high degree of autonomy to the constituent units, it seemed at least to have gone some way to satisfy their wishes prior to 1962.

Moreover, the cultural forces making for unity are much stronger than in

[90] None of the minority areas can seriously be regarded as capable of standing on its own feet economically. But they have some cause for complaining that most new economic development is taking place in the Burman areas.

[91] This solution has been adopted by the Burmese of their own free will and not bequeathed to them by the former colonial power as in Indonesia. But see above, p. 467, note 79.

Indonesia. Even before the war the Burmese language[92] was habitually spoken by the great majority of the lowland peoples and was familiar to the more responsible or travelled classes in the less inaccessible hill regions, and since independence its use has been encouraged in several of the minority areas. Still more important is the unifying rôle of Buddhism, to which some 86 per cent of the population subscribe. Although there was no official state religion before 1961 the constitution recognized the 'special position' of Buddhism as 'the faith professed by the great majority of the citizens', and much has been done to encourage the propagation of the religion among the non-Buddhist hill peoples. To what extent this activity is based on a desire to make use of Buddhism as a nation-building force is difficult to say, but it seems probable that such considerations played some part in the government's decision to sponsor, at great expense, the holding at Rangoon of the Sixth Great Buddhist Council (1954–6), to which all the leading Theravada centres – Ceylon, Thailand, Laos and Cambodia, as well as Burma – sent delegations.[93]

On balance it would seem that during the 1950s the internal forces conducive to natural unity made real progress in overcoming the traditional hostility of many of the minority peoples towards the Burmans, though considerable resentment remained over 'Burmanization'[94] in some outlying areas.

In addition to the indigenous minorities, however, the builders of the new Burma have also had to contend with the problems posed by the substantial minorities of Indians and Chinese, and in this respect the situation is further complicated by the direct overland contact which exists with the homelands of both these alien groups.

As a result of the great exodus of 1942, the pre-war total of over 1 million Indians in Burma was reduced by at least a third. But movement from India to Burma began again after the war ended, and was not seriously checked until the Union government introduced a new immigration policy which virtually banned the return of former Indian residents.

Today the estimated number of Indians and Pakistanis[95] is approximately 800,000, and while the bulk of these, as in the past, are low-paid wage labourers, many still remain active and influential in commerce and, to a lesser degree, in the medical, legal and teaching professions. Nevertheless, opportunities for Indians are much less extensive than they were under British rule. In particular, the expropriation of absentee landowners has hit the Chettyar community

[92] Burmese is a tonal language written in a script adapted from Pali. Under the constitution, Burmese is the official language but 'the use of English is permitted'. English is widely used in Rangoon and has been the medium of instruction at university level, though it is not intended to continue this practice in future.

[93] This was the first such conference anywhere since 1870; the first four were all B.C. Note that in 1961 U Nu proclaimed Buddhism to be the state religion. This decision caused grave misgivings among the non-Buddhist minorities.

[94] Especially in the form of appointment of Burmans to posts in non-Burman areas. *Cf.* the resentment over 'Javanization' in the outer islands of Indonesia. See above, Chapter 11.

[95] The majority of the 100,000 or so Pakistanis are in Arakan.

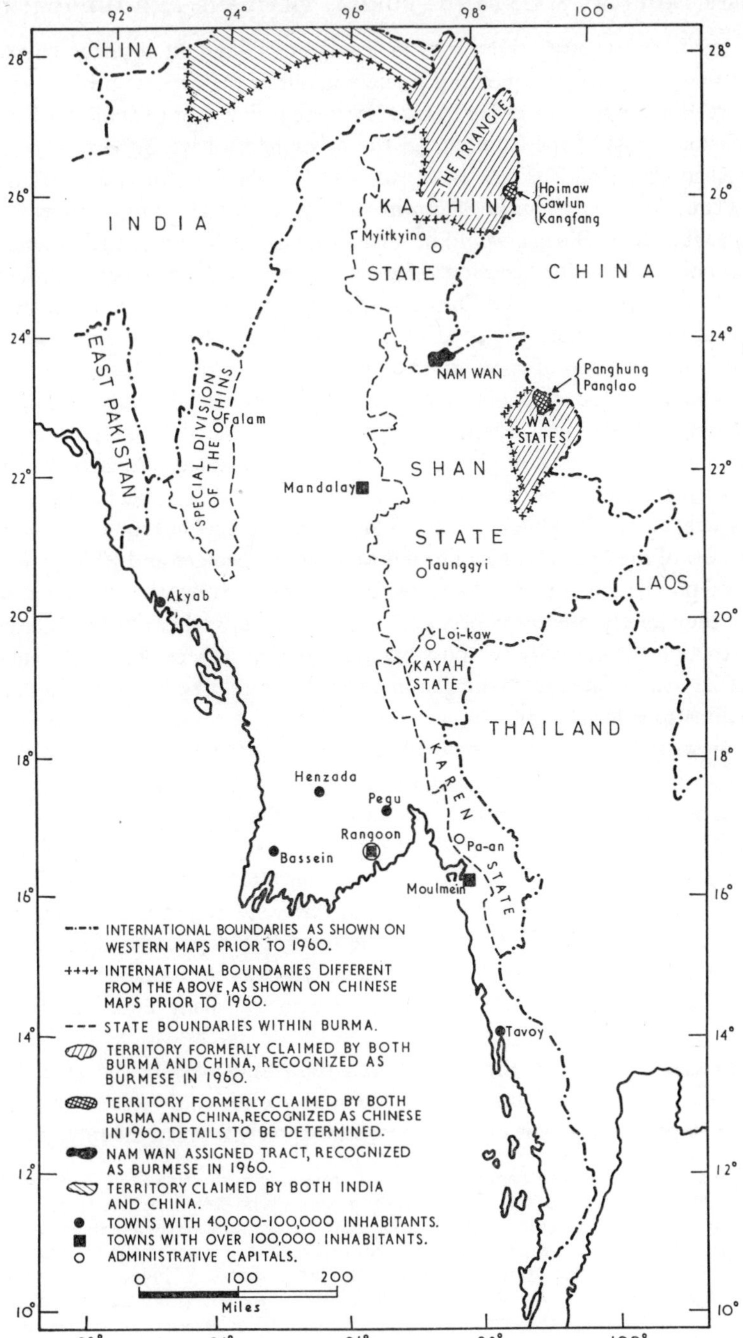

FIG. 69—Burma: major administrative divisions, 1960

very hard, and though there are no legal restrictions on resident aliens, the government's policy of squeezing foreigners out of the export and import trade has forced many Indians either to take Burmese partners or to apply for Burmese citizenship. Most of the Chinese, on the other hand, have hitherto shown less interest in acquiring Burmese nationality, and although in the course of his 1954 visit Prime Minister Chou En-lai promised that the matter of dual citizenship, in so far as it affected Burma, would be settled on his return home, no further clarification has yet been forthcoming. Moreover, whereas the number of Indians in Burma has fallen, that of the Chinese has risen significantly since 1941, and now stands at approximately 350,000. To a considerable extent this appears to have come about as a result of unrecorded movement across the north-eastern borders, and at the same time many of the former Indian commercial interests in Rangoon and elsewhere have been taken over by Chinese. Thus, while the greater part of the Chinese community still consists of miners, market-gardeners and small shop-keepers, there has been some expansion in larger-scale business enterprises which are now able to get loans from the Peking banks.

In view of the relatively small proportions which Indians and Chinese form of the total population (4 per cent and 1½ per cent respectively) the internal problem which they jointly present is probably less than in any other state in South-east Asia, though theoretically the possibility exists that either community could in future be manipulated from outside in a way that might be harmful and perhaps even disastrous for Burma.

So far as Indian policy in this respect is concerned, the Burmese have no fears and indeed, when viewed against the background of pre-war hostility to the Indians in their midst, Burmese relations with that country have become surprisingly cordial. Thus India, whose social philosophy was broadly similar to that of Burma under U Nu, has raised no objections to the various Burmese measures which, in one way or another, have severely penalized individual Indians resident in the country and, in the absence of any outstanding territorial disputes, the two governments have found no difficulty in co-operating to prevent trouble arising among the Naga tribesmen who live along both sides of their mutual frontier.

With China, however, there have been difficulties despite the great efforts which the Burmese government has made to keep on friendly terms.[96] As described in Chapter 4 the whole of the remote and sparsely peopled mountainous tract

[96] The situation has been complicated by the presence in the trans-Salween portion of Shan State of several thousand Kuo Min Tang troops who sought refuge there after the Communist victory in China in 1949. Fearing that this would give the Peking government an excuse for intervention the Burmese government took the matter to the United Nations in 1953. As a result some thousands were withdrawn, with U.S. help, to Formosa, but many still remain on Burmese soil. As late as February 1961 this problem was still embarrassing the Burmese government, not least because of the invaders' encouragement of Shan separatism. See *The Times*, February 23, 1961. For an account of the frontier dispute, see 'The Burma-China frontier dispute', *The World Today*, Vol. 13, No. 2, February 1957, pp. 80–92.

between China on the one hand and the states of mainland South-east Asia on the other has formed a great ethnic and political marchland in which, historically speaking, boundaries have rarely been formulated with any precision or permanence. However, after the British annexed Upper Burma they obtained the agreement of the Chinese to define the boundary line, instead of remaining content with the indeterminate and fluctuating allegiance of such border peoples as the Kachins, Shans and Was.

The boundary was accordingly defined on the map, and by 1900 joint Anglo-Chinese boundary commissions had visited the area to apply this line in detail on the ground. But only in one of the three frontier sectors did the Chinese commissioners concur with the findings of the British and their surveyors – the Chinese brought none – and here there was joint demarcation from a point on the watershed near Myitkyina in the north to the Salween river in the east, and a small area, the Namwan Assigned Tract in the salient south-east of Bhamo, was leased in perpetuity to Britain for Rs. 1,000 annual rent so as to facilitate communication between Bhamo and the northern Shan states. The precise application of the line in the other two sectors, consisting of a largely uninhabited hill area in what is now Kachin State north of Myitkyina and the head-hunting area of the Wa states east of the Salween in the northern Shan states, was not agreed. Here Britain, subsequently finding prolonged discussions useless, ended by issuing a unilateral declaration that the line[97] found by its commissioners was the boundary, and China acquiesced *de facto*.

However, after the Kuo Min Tang had come to power, China began to show more active interest in its western frontiers, and in 1934 contested the right of a British expedition investigating mineral deposits in the Wa states. The dispute was settled in 1941 when both sides accepted the award of a League of Nations Boundary Commission, which gave Britain, with trivial modifications, the line it had claimed in 1900; and Britain, to show goodwill, promised to allow Chinese participation in mining enterprises should the British undertake any. But the question of the 'Triangle', the area north of Myitkyina, remained. It was shown on Kuo Min Tang maps as Chinese territory, in 1946 part of it was occupied by Chinese forces until British troops arrived on the scene, and shortly before Burma received its independence, China reiterated its claim to some 77,000 square miles of territory north and north-west of Myitkyina.

After the Communist victory in China it was soon clear, for example, from the official *Chinese People's Republic Atlas of the Provinces* (1952), that the claim to the Triangle might again be pressed and the 1941 Wa agreement repudiated, and in 1956 the Burmese government protested to Peking that Chinese forces had taken up positions in both areas. Early in 1960 an agreement was at last reached, whereby China relinquished its claim to the Namwan Assigned Tract, but obtained parts of the Wa states and three villages[98] in northern

[97] This was part of the so-called McMahon line (1914).
[98] Hpimaw, Kangfang and Gawlun.

Kachin State. These latter areas were both to be jointly demarcated, but with this proviso China appeared willing to accept the Sino-Burman section of the McMahon line as the boundary between the two countries.

In view of the great disparity in strength of the two contenders, this settlement, which was coupled with a new treaty of friendship between them, whereby each undertook to join no military alliance directed against the other, may seem a very favourable one for the Burmese, though whether it will allay all anxieties remains to be seen. In British times China based its claims solely on former tributary relationships, but the new China appeals to the future as well as to the past. Its method of granting a measure of autonomy to minority groups within the Chinese People's Republic has already been applied to both Thai and Kachin communities in Yunnan since 1953,[99] and many observers have feared that this is but the first stage in a campaign to win the allegiance of related peoples on the Burmese side and hence to bring about the piecemeal disintegration of the Union.

From a long-term point of view control of Burma, besides furnishing China with both *lebensraum* and new reserves of food and other tropical produce, would also provide the direct access to the Indian Ocean which it has long coveted, and in so doing immeasurably strengthen its strategic position *vis-à-vis* India. Whether such developments are seriously contemplated by China remains to be seen, but meanwhile the Burmese like to regard the recent boundary settlement as evidence that their policy of good neighbourliness is justifying itself.

This, of course, is merely one facet of a foreign policy, which, under the style of 'dynamic neutrality' has supposedly aimed at making Burma into the Switzerland, or as some would say, the Yugoslavia of the East.[100] Such a policy rests on the assumption that, for a country in Burma's geographical position, the best hope for continued independence lies in its being accepted as a neutral buffer state between India and China. And certainly, in view of the losses it sustained in the Second World War, its anxiety to avoid becoming another Korea or Vietnam is understandable.

Whether this neutralist policy represents an adequate answer to the strategic problems of the day, which most Westerners prefer to appraise in terms rather of the two great power blocs, only time will show. But already it has given rise to certain difficulties over the acceptance of foreign aid, and for a time Burma refused to accept any such assistance from the U.S.A. More recently, however, it

[99] How far this has gone is not clear. But there is no doubt that activities on the Chinese side of the frontier are attracting the interest of related peoples on the Burmese (and also the Laotian and Siamese) sides. Thus, if these South-east Asian countries are to hold the allegiance of such minority groups in exposed frontier regions, they may have to be prepared to devote much more practical attention to their needs (*e.g.* in respect of education and medical services) than they have done heretofore.

[100] The difference between these two concepts may appear less important to the Burmese than it does to Westerners. The Ne Win regime has reaffirmed Burma's adherence to 'positive neutrality'.

TABLE 59

BURMA: OVERSEAS TRADE BY COMMODITIES

(*Figures in* 000 *Kyats*)

A. Imports

Item	1937–41 *average*	1952–3	1954–5	1960
Machinery and transport equipment .	26,600	93,300	154,500	204,869
Base metals and manufactures thereof	26,800	78,800	107,800	133,593
Cotton piece goods	37,000	144,900	95,300	174,236
Cotton yarns and thread . . .	15,100	50,300	44,200	140,367
Vegetable oils	15,000	n.a.	41,600	37,249
Bags and sacks	15,300	84,500	29,500	27,716
Drugs and medicines . . .	3,100	21,000	28,500	34,166
Milk, condensed and preserved . .	4,200	16,900	27,400	53,672
Mineral oil	5,600	28,500	25,900	23,605
Fish and fish products . . .	5,300	25,700	22,000	21,747
Paper and paper manufactures . .	4,800	14,600	19,600	26,473
Coal and coke	8,900	18,000	14,000	22,353
Tobacco and manufactures thereof .	10,000	9,500	7,900	2,180
Total (including others) . . .	257,300	876,500	905,300	1,238,857

B. Exports

Item	1937–41 *average*	1952–3	1954–5	1960
Rice and rice products . . .	238,800	1,018,700	845,400	703,889
Raw cotton	8,600	54,600	51,500	36,995
Metals and ores	59,000	60,700	48,500	45,062
Raw rubber	6,900	28,300	38,700	41,452
Teak	31,100	26,400	24,200	90,492
Hardwoods	3,400	5,200	3,400	1,221
Hides, skins and leather . . .	2,500	2,400	500	4,523
Petroleum and petroleum products .	108,900	0	0	4,430
Total (including others) . . .	516,400	1,292,400	1,105,800	1,061,769

* 1958–9 figures refer to all timber.

Sources: Based on Cooke, pp. 53 and 56, and Union of Burma Central Statistical and Economic Department, *Bulletin of Import Trade*, 1960, and *Bulletin of Export Trade*, 1960.

has been willing to accept aid from both blocs, though on political grounds the assistance made available via the Colombo Plan and the World Bank has appeared to be more acceptable.[101]

In addition to these sources, and to the not inconsiderable amount of private British and other Western capital invested in the various joint schemes already

TABLE 60

BURMA: OVERSEAS TRADE BY COUNTRIES

A. Imports

(Figures in 000 Kyats)

Country of origin	1937–41 *average*	1956	1960
Japan	18,969	155,370	266,860
United Kingdom	43,310	198,960	171,560
China (mainland)	1,101	105,640	117,820
India	146,505 (India and Pakistan)	93,680	88,210
Pakistan		6,740	59,520
Germany	4,075	64,590†	58,960†
Netherlands	3,585	33,500	47,430
U.S.A.	14,298	27,140	43,150
South Africa	—	390	31,960
Australia	—	28,030	27,380
Yugoslavia	—	7,150	27,120
Hong Kong	3,648	18,470	19,190
Czechoslovakia	—	25,580	18,680
Italy	—	5,130	17,350
Indonesia	964	17,330	14,850
U.S.S.R.	—	14,840	13,910
Federation of Malaya	6,764*	9,040	13,680
Total (including others)	257,275	942,670	1,238,970

[101] In 1950 Britain and other Commonwealth countries jointly granted Burma a loan of £6 million. Beginning in 1950–51 the U.S.A. also offered aid, but this was terminated at Burma's request in June 1953 as a result of the dispute over the Kuo Min Tang troops (see note 96 above). By this time Burma had received some $21 million; more recently U.S. aid has been resumed and from mid-1955 to the end of 1958 the total amount granted was $58 million. Soviet-bloc aid during this latter period totalled $34 million. In 1956 the World Bank granted two loans, one of $14 million for port reconstruction at Rangoon and the other of $5,350,000 for railway rehabilitation. India also offered Burma a loan in 1956 but this has not been drawn upon. Grants under the Colombo Plan up to 1957 were estimated at £1,100,000. On Chinese aid, see below, p. 482.

B. Exports

Country of destination	1937–41 *average*	1956	1960
Indonesia	4,233	137,130	205,070
India	285,861	172,850	163,140
Pakistan		54,010	89,540
Ceylon	30,754	86,510	120,240
United Kingdom	72,614	91,320	102,070
Japan	25,140	178,250	54,400
China (mainland)	7,457	71,770	37,590
Singapore	36,713*	32,930	35,730
Federation of Malaya		72,310	35,240
Germany	12,056	17,360†	34,570†
U.S.S.R.	—	54,370	23,550
Mauritius	—	17,010	20,520
Denmark	—	3,960	16,060
Yugoslavia	—	15,440	12,610
Hong Kong	4,343	27,530	12,020
Netherlands	4,067	10,400	10,440
Italy	708	2,470	8,920
Total (including others)	526,228	1,185,590	1,061,770

* includes Malaya, Singapore and British Borneo.

† Federal Republic only.

Sources: Based on Cooke, pp. 54 and 57, and *Yearbook of International Trade Statistics, U.N.*

noted, Burma has obtained an important part of the foreign-exchange requirements of its capital programme, which have recently been of the order of some £28 million ($78 million) a year, from Japanese reparations. By the agreement concluded in 1954 Japan undertook to pay Burma the equivalent of $20 million a year for ten years in the form of technical services and capital goods, and also to make a total investment of $5 million a year in the Burmese industrial development plan over the same period.[102]

Nevertheless, although the relatively recent but already impressive resump-

[102] In January 1963 Japan agreed to grant Burma additional reparations amounting to $140 million in goods and services and $30 million in loans. In recent years Burma has turned increasingly to Israel for technical advisers of many kinds. These have made a particular contribution to the problems of the dry zone.

tion of Japanese trade with Burma may be expected to continue, the progress of events since 1960 suggests that the economic relations of Burma with China may in the long run become at least equally important. Following the disastrous harvest season of 1960 in China, extensive purchases of Burmese rice were made, and in the meantime China agreed to lend Burma a total of £30 million for the purchase of a wide range of manufactured goods. Indeed if, as seems probable, the expansion of Chinese agricultural production fails to keep pace with both the growth of population and the progress of industrialization, Burma might well find there an adequate outlet for all the rice it is capable of producing.

Whether these trends, if they continue, will really be in Burma's interests is, however, another matter. For if, as appears possible, China becomes a leading purchaser of what is by far the most important of Burma's exports, the already vulnerable strategic position of Burma *vis à vis* its huge neighbour to the north might be still further weakened by the economic pressure which the latter could bring to bear whenever it might choose to do so.

It is largely against this background that the policies followed since March 1962 by the Ne Win regime need to be assessed. Shortly before the latter took over, the new Four Year Plan for 1961/2–1964/5 had already been drafted, with the avowed aim of raising the depressed standard of living, primarily by diversifying agriculture and improving transport and also by extending the range of industrial production, though, so far as the last was concerned, the government's main task was to consolidate what had already been achieved, leaving further developments largely to private enterprise.

Virtually from the outset the new regime showed interest in more radical agricultural policies, though until early February 1963 the main change in this respect had been limited to increasing the number of tractors in the country from *c* 300 to *c* 3,000 and to announcing plans for raising the number still further to 20,000 by importing 2,000 a year from the U.S.S.R. and Czechoslovakia.[103]

However, later in the same month the Minister of Trade and Industry, the moderate socialist half-Chinese Aung Gyi resigned from the Ne Win government,[104] and shortly afterwards a series of moves, including the immediate nationalization of banks, and the nationalization of the milling, marketing and export of rice as from 1964, provided clear indications of a significant swing back towards the more doctrinaire Marxism of the late 1940s. These measures bore particularly severely on the Indian and Pakistani commercial elements, and led to a large-scale return of members of both communities to their respective mother countries. In other ways also, Burma has seemed to be moving beyond mere neutralism towards a virtual withdrawal from the outside world. No doubt if one lives next door to a giant, one is tempted to adjust one's behaviour accordingly.

[103] See *Forward*, 1, 14, 22nd February, 1963, p. 2.
[104] See Dennis Bloodworth: "Burma Turns Left", *Observer*, 24th Feb., 1963.

SELECT BIBLIOGRAPHY

Allen, R. L.
Andrus
Appleton
Ball
Cady
Chhibber
Christian (A) (B)
Cooke
Craw
De Terra
Dobby (H)
Donnison
Fairbairn (A) (B)
Fisher (R) (S)
Hagen
Hall (A)
Harvey (A) (B) (C)
Kirk (A)
Luce
Marshall
Maung
Mende
Morehead
Pearn
Richards
Spate (A) (C) (D)
Spate and Trueblood
Stamp (A) (B) (C)
Stevenson
Thompson and Adloff
Tinker (A) (B) (C)
Trueblood
Vandenbosch and Butwell
Zelinsky
Zinkin (A)

Atlantic Monthly, with special section on Burma, February 1958
Burma facts and figures
Burma petroleum industry
Burma rice
'The Burma-China frontier dispute', *W.T.*, **13**, 1957
Economic survey of Burma
The national income of Burma
Pyidawtha – the new Burma
Colombo Plan Reports
Economic Surveys of Asia and the Far East
Burma Weekly Bulletin
Forward: Union of Burma, Central Statistical and Economic Department publications, notably *Quarterly Bulletin of Statistics; Bulletin of Import Trade;* and *Bulletin of Export Trade.*

There is no major English text on the geography of Burma, but the papers by De Terra, Stamp, (B) and (C), Spate, (A) and (D), and Spate and Trueblood, together with Spate's excellent *Burma Setting* and the other volumes in Longman's series of Burma Pamphlets, go far to remedy this deficiency. Harvey (B) and Christian (B) have been my principal sources of information on social, political and economic aspects of Burma under British rule, and the pamphlets by Appleton, Marshall, Richards and Stevenson provide useful data about peoples and cultures. Section II of this chapter relies largely upon *Pyidawtha—the new Burma*, the *Overseas economic survey* by Cooke, and the *Economic Survey of Burma*, supplemented by Tinker (C) which is also an invaluable source of information on post-war Burma as a whole.

Addenda: Note the papers by Tadaw and Whittam respectively.

CHAPTER 15

Thailand

I. LAND AND PEOPLE

The vernacular name for Thailand is Muang Thai, though Europeans since the 16th century have habitually referred to the country as Siam, a usage derived from 'Shan' which is the Burmese name for the ethnic family also known as Thai or Lao. However, in June 1939 the Siamese government of Pibul Songgram decreed that the Western style of the state should henceforward be Thailand, and although this form was dropped when Pibul was ousted in 1945, it was reintroduced as the official name shortly after his return to power in 1948.

The political significance attached to this terminology by Pibul, the leader of the pre-war Pan Thai movement, springs from the fact that in Siamese the word Thai also means 'free', and certainly Thailand is unique in being the only South-east Asian state which has never formed part of any Western colonial empire. To some extent, therefore, the country may be regarded as a control, in that it provides an indication of the forms which economic and political developments might have taken elsewhere in South-east Asia but for the introduction of Western rule.

In the broad outlines of its relief, on the other hand, Thailand presents a superficial analogue of Burma, with which it shares a common boundary of some 900 miles. Thus, in both countries a semi-circle of uplands, to the west, north and east, partially enclose a great alluvial lowland whose major river is the central artery of the whole territory, and each also has a share of the long and narrow neck of land which extends south ultimately to become the Malay peninsula. All-told Thailand covers an area of 198,454 square miles, as against Burma's 261,760, and its total population of some 21,474,000 in 1958[1] compares with its neighbour's 20,255,000 in the same year.

Nevertheless, the geographical similarities between the two countries should not be allowed to obscure the differences. Thus, in the first place, although Thailand has its upland regions, their average altitude is significantly lower, and the proportion which they form of the national territory is very much less than in the case of the 'hills' and plateaux of Burma. And while this more subdued relief goes far to explain why Thailand is burdened with fewer minority problems than its western neighbour, the related differences in geological character, as described in Chapter 13, mean that in mineral wealth Thailand is

[1] The preliminary report of the 1960 Census gave a total of 25,519,965.

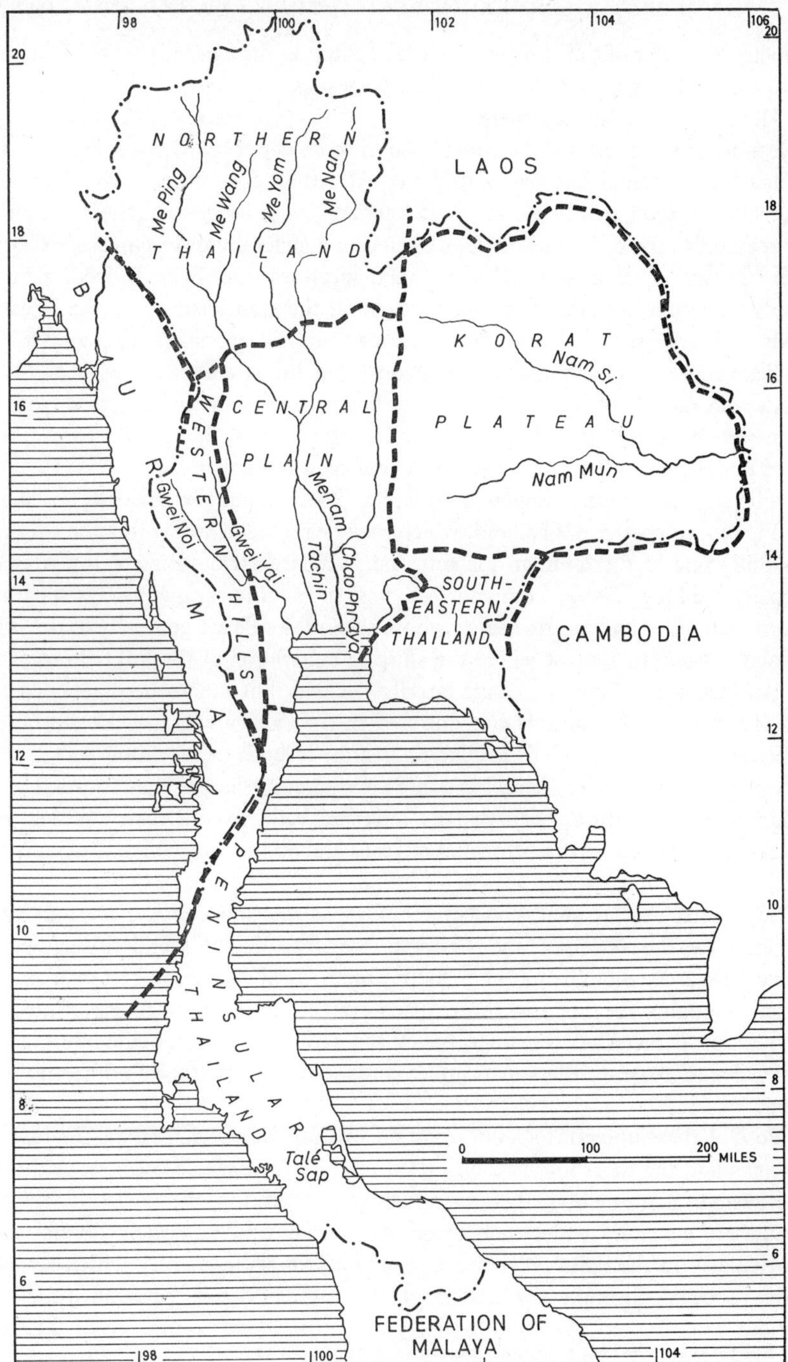

FIG. 70—Thailand: natural regions

much the poorer of the two, and its dependence on the agricultural produce of its alluvial lowlands is thus correspondingly greater.

Here again, however, there are important geographical differences whose effect on productivity will be considered in more detail below. In overall position Thailand lies somewhat nearer to the equator than does Burma (Bangkok being in fact over 200 miles to the south of Rangoon), and its more sheltered situation in relation to the SW monsoon is reflected in a generally drier climate, except in the extreme south and in a few exposed localities elsewhere. Indeed, virtually the whole central plain is to some extent in the rain shadow of the Western hills which form the frontier with Burma, and the annual rainfall at Bangkok is little more than half that at Rangoon (56·4 in. as compared with 99·6 in.). However, no part of the wide Menam valley is so thoroughly blanketed from the rain-bearing winds as is the dry zone of central Burma, though Thailand has its own dry region in the interior of the Korat plateau farther east.

The six main natural regions into which Thailand may be divided[2] are shown in Fig. 70. In northern Thailand, which may be regarded as forming the southern foothill zone to the Yunnan plateau, the four large tributaries of the Menam, namely the Ping, Wang, Yom and Nan, flow in roughly parallel valleys separated from each other by granitic ranges whose summit levels are generally of the order of about 5,000 ft. Except where the shifting cultivation of the hill tribes has led to deforestation, these ranges are heavily wooded, but much the greater part of the Thai population here is concentrated in the valleys which yield good crops wherever irrigation water is available. Thanks to both its elevation and its long dry season, northern Thailand has a more invigorating climate than is found in the plains, and the natural beauty of its hills and valleys, with their swift-flowing rivers, is enhanced by the profusion of roses and orchids for which Chiengmai in particular is renowned.

Somewhat similar conditions of relief are also found in the western hills, drained by the Gweinoi and Gweiyai branches of the Meklong. However, since this area, though marginal to the main Thai migration tracks from the north, contains the historic routes used by the invading Burmese armies, its population density has remained below the national average, being nowadays of the order of 25–50 to the square mile, compared with 50–100 in northern Thailand.

Both of these uplands look out upon the central plain which forms the historic nucleus and the most intensively settled region of the whole country. Although the Menam is a much smaller river than the Irrawaddy, the lowlands which it drains are generally wider than those of lower Burma[3] and their alluvial soils, particularly in the delta proper, are renowned for their fertility which is regularly renewed through the action of the annual floods between June and

[2] See Graham, Vol. 1, p. 6, and Stamp (D) pp. 211-14.

[3] Except in the respective deltas. As noted in Chapter 13, the present Menam is a beheaded stream, representing the former outlet to the sea of the much larger Salween.

December. Even to the north of the delta the inundated zone extends over a width of from 20 to 60 miles, while south of Chainad it gradually broadens out to over 100 miles, and in the central areas nearest to the river the flood water normally reaches a depth of 12–16 ft. Although the full agricultural potentialities of the region cannot be realized until more efficient measures of water control are in operation,[4] the present population density is the highest in the country and for the delta itself the average figure is now over 250 to the square mile.

From many points of view South-eastern Thailand represents an extension of the central plain as far as the Cardamom mountains which mark the frontier with Cambodia. But the rainfall along this west-facing coastal fringe is distinctly heavier than that in the coastal plain, and this is reflected in a more luxuriant natural vegetation, particularly on the numerous hills which diversify the relief.

South of Pechaburi, peninsular Thailand also is characterized by heavy rainfall, and in these more southerly latitudes the range of seasonal variation in both rainfall and temperature is significantly less than in other parts of the country. From the Kra isthmus southwards Thailand occupies the full width of the peninsula, but even so the greater part of it is drained by a series of north-west flowing rivers to the eastern shore, which is easily linked by coastal craft to the Menam delta. Nevertheless, this attractive countryside, with its densely wooded hills, its sandy, palm-fringed beaches and broad alluvial valleys, is very similar to Kedah and Kelantan in nearby Malaya, and this physical resemblance is intensified by the increasing predominance of the Malay element in the population south of Songkhla (Singgora). Both here and farther north, where the region merges with the central plain, peninsular Thailand supports an average density of close upon 100 to the square mile.

In contrast to all the regions so far described is the Korat plateau of the north-east which is climatically analogous to the dry zone of Burma but, in the absence of any great river like the Irrawaddy, is much inferior to its Burmese counterpart in both the character of its soils[5] and the availability of water for irrigation. As a result of the defective drainage across its gently sloping surface, the plateau is waterlogged and muddy in the monsoon season, and desiccated and barren for the rest of the year. While its intrinsic carrying capacity is obviously inferior to that of most other parts of the country, the population density of 50–100 to the square mile is not noticeably below the average for the outlying regions, but it is generally agreed that rural living standards there are the lowest in the kingdom.

With the exception of the Korat plateau, whose only important rivers, the Nam Mun and the Nam Si, drain eastwards to the Mekong, virtually the whole of the present territories of Thailand focus naturally on the Menam delta and,

[4] See below, p. 508 *et seq.*

[5] These are predominantly sedentary lateritic soils, derived from the local sandstone; Korat has no large expanses of alluvium comparable to those of the middle and lower Irrawaddy valley, though the deposits in the valleys of the Nam Mun and Nam Si are not insignificant.

geographical links with the Irrawaddy/Sittang lowlands led at an early stage to political alignment towards Burma rather than Siam, and until very recently it seemed that the peoples of Korat, as well as those of the Laos plateau, would likewise remain politically separate from the Siamese kingdom. For although the western rim of the Korat plateau rarely rises much above 1,500 ft. and can scarcely be regarded as a major physical barrier, the absence of direct river communication with the region was a serious drawback and, notwithstanding the annexation of the Korat territories towards the end of the 18th century and the occupation of Vientiane in 1827,[9] Siamese control over the plateau was little more than nominal until the building of the north-eastern railway early in the present century.[10]

With the northern territories geographical links were certainly closer, and most of the lesser principalities there were absorbed into the Siamese kingdom at a much earlier date, though it was not until the end of the 18th century that the rulers of Chiengmai were fully subordinated to the central government whose headquarters had meanwhile (1782) been shifted south to Bangkok. For although the Menam provides an obvious route to the northern territories, the value of its tributaries as waterways is very limited, especially during the long dry season when they can be navigated only by very shallow craft. Thus the north also remained in large measure isolated from the delta, and it was mainly on this account that the metropolitan Siamese habitually regarded the inhabitants of the north as well as those of the north-east, as Lao and not Thai, though both groups have more commonly referred to themselves by the latter name.[11]

In the southern extremity of the country, on the other hand, the ethnic distinction between Thai and Malay is real enough, and neither there nor in the Cambodian provinces of Battambang and Angkor, which were annexed in 1795, did the Thais succeed in imposing their language or their customs on the indigenous population to any significant extent.

II. MODERNIZATION AND THE DEVELOPMENT OF COMMUNICATIONS

As described in Chapter 4, the great revival of Siamese power, after a succession of defeats at the hands of the Burmese, dates from the closing years of the 18th century, though contact with the industrialized West did not begin on a significant scale until the reign of King Mongkut (Rama IV), 1851–68. Admittedly, the Burney treaty had been signed with Britain in 1826[12], though from the Siamese point of view its main purpose had been to keep the West at arm's length. Meanwhile the British conquests in Burma were not unwelcome in that they severely crippled the power of Siam's most hated rival, but with the advance of the French in Cambodia it was clear that Siam was faced with a new and more

[9] This then became effectively Siamese, but the French compelled Siam to cede all the areas east of the Mekong in 1893.

[10] See below, p. 490. [11] De Young, p. 7. [12] See above, p. 149.

formidable threat in an area over which it had at least some pretensions to suzerainty. However, while this was an important factor in strengthening the Siamese resolve to modernize in order to survive, the decision to pursue such a policy had already been taken by the time Mongkut ascended the throne, and the 1855 treaty with Britain, negotiated by Sir John Bowring, marked the beginning of the new era.

Under this agreement the principle of extra-territoriality was accepted, freedom of trade guaranteed to British subjects, and import duties established at a flat rate of 3 per cent. In effect these provisions represented a modified form of those accepted by China after the Opium War twelve years previously, and the precedent thus established was closely followed in treaties made with most of the other leading Western powers in the course of the next fifteen years, and with Japan in 1898.[13]

The policy of opening the country to Western influence was continued and extended under Chulalongkorn (Rama V) during whose long reign from 1868 to 1910 feudalism and slavery were abolished, a modern civil service created, a Western-style university founded and both railways and large-scale irrigation works introduced. In comparison with many neighbouring countries Siam was fortunate in having two such able monarchs at this critical period in its history, and Chulalongkorn in particular showed great skill in pursuing what may be called a policy of divide and rule in reverse. Thus British pre-eminence in the commercial and financial fields was counterbalanced by the appointment of French experts in the judiciary and Danish officers in the police force. But these tactics broke down when the construction of the Bangkok-Ayuthia-Korat railway was entrusted to a British contractor and a German director, and as a result of the disputes which followed the government had to take over the task in 1896.

Apart from a short privately owned line from Bangkok to Paknam (which was opened in 1893[14]) the Korat line was the first important section of railway to be built in the country, a fact which should be viewed against the background of the French advance into Laos in 1893. But with the completion of the new railway in 1900, the hitherto remote provinces of the Korat plateau were brought into easy communication with the Menam delta, and thereafter the trade of the whole plateau region began to gravitate increasingly towards Bangkok.

The second major railway project was to extend the system from Ayuthia to the north, and here again political considerations were paramount. During the closing years of the 19th century, a substantial volume of trade had developed under the auspices of Chinese merchants between the northern Siamese towns and lower Burma, and indeed the caravan route from Raheng across the Western Hills to Moulmein had far outstripped the traditional but not very efficient river

[13] No treaty was concluded with China until 1946. Today Thailand continues to recognize the Formosa government of Chiang Kai-shek. See below, p. 522

[14] Later incorporated with the State Railway system.

routes from the north to the sea via Bangkok. It was thus in order to prevent the north from drifting into the British Burmese orbit that the northern extension was put under construction in 1898, and further point was given to this decision by a revolt of the northern clans in 1901 by which time the new line had not advanced beyond Lopburi. However, after Uttaradit was reached and a spur built to Sawankalok in 1909, the central government's control over the north was greatly strengthened, though it was not until 1921 that the line was completed as far as the present railhead at Chiengmai.

Meanwhile the first stretch of the south-eastern line was finished (to Shajeungdhrao) in 1908, the year after the French annexation of the two Cambodian provinces of Battambang and Siemreap (Angkor) had caused a renewal of Siamese anxiety regarding the safety of the eastern frontier. This line was eventually extended in 1926 to the border town of Aranya Prades but no connexion existed on the Cambodian side until after the Second World War.

The construction of the southern railway likewise came too late to prevent the loss of valuable peripheral territories. Not long after Pechaburi had been linked with Bangkok in 1903 German proposals were put forward for a further extension to the south. It was on these grounds that the British, who had long been desirous of keeping any third power out of the Kra isthmus, persuaded the Siamese government in 1909 to sign a new treaty. In return for British relinquishment of most of their extra-territorial rights, Siam agreed that the railway should be constructed under a British loan and the four Malay states of Kedah, Perlis, Kelantan and Trengganu, over which Siamese control had hitherto been very tenuous, should be transferred to British protection.

By 1917 a link was effected with the Malayan system at Padang Besar in Perlis, and a further branch was opened to Sungei Golok on the Kelantan border in 1920. The only important lines built by the Siamese between 1920 and 1941 were the two extensions from Korat, respectively to Warindra opposite Ubol in the east, and to Udon in the north-east, and with the completion of these two the total length of the system reached 1,925 miles, all of it metre gauge.[15]

By the time of the Second World War, therefore, Thailand had a fairly extensive railway network, and no part of the kingdom was more than 150 miles from a line. Moreover, although in the total volume of freight and the number of passengers carried the Thai State Railways lagged behind the Burma Railways, their relative importance internally was distinctly greater and they undoubtedly played a decisive part in enabling the central government to tighten its hold over such outlying areas as had not in the meantime been annexed by either Britain or France.

In large measure this state of affairs was a reflection of the marked inferiority

[15] The earliest lines were built on the 4 ft. 8½ in. gauge, but the decision to link up with the Malayan system led to conversion of the whole Siamese system to the metre gauge. Stamp (D), p. 217. Note that Burma and Indochina also use the metre gauge, though the Indonesian railways are mainly on the 3 ft. 6 in. gauge.

of Thailand's natural waterways to those of Burma. Thus the Menam, though navigable by steam launches for some 250 miles during the high-water season, is so reduced in flow during the dry season[16] that the shallowness of its channel and the presence of shifting sandbanks prevent such navigation above Paknampoh, which is only 120 miles from the sea and the other rivers afford even less scope for using large modern craft.

On the lower reaches of the Menam and related rivers, it is true, regular passenger sailings link all the main towns, but even so the vessels concerned are much smaller than those used on the lower Irrawaddy. For the most part cargo is carried in small country boats, which are often towed in long lines, sometimes of 50 or more, by powerful launches, before being dropped off one by one to complete their journeys to particular villages under their own sail, along the tributary streams or canals leading off from the main river.[17]

Such traffic takes place in the delta throughout the year, and even elsewhere small country craft carry a very large share of the total traffic during the wet season. Thus much the greater part of the rice crop moves to the mills by boat in December–January, which is three to four months before the rivers have dropped to their minimum level. Moreover, in most areas the great majority of villages are situated on river (or canal) banks, the houses especially in the central plains being built on stilts of 5–6 ft. high in order to be above flood level, and the older quarters of Bangkok itself are aligned along the river and the numerous intersecting *klongs* (canals), in a manner which has led to the city's being known as the Venice of the East.

By contrast with the Menam, the great Mekong, which flows for over 1,000 miles along the eastern boundary of Thailand, is of small account in the country's transport system, owing partly to the direction of its course and partly to the series of rapids which obstruct it farther downstream.[18]

In respect of road transport Thailand made much slower progress even than Burma before the Second World War. Admittedly, local tracks have served most parts of the countryside since time immemorial, but these become temporarily impassable even to bullock carts for long periods during the rains, and in much of the central plains may be under water for months at a stretch. This problem of the annual flooding of the focal region of the country has constituted a major obstacle to the creation of an effective national road network[19] though it has also been reinforced by the government's reluctance to build roads which might compete with the State Railways. Thus, until recently roads have been built almost entirely as feeders to the latter, notably in northern Thailand and in the

[16] See above, p. 417. The flow at Paknampoh is 54,000 cu. ft. per second in the wet season and 4,000 cu. ft. per second in the dry season. See Dobby (H), p. 267.

[17] In 1949 there were 254 steam launches, with a total gross tonnage of 3,333, and 2,441 motor launches, with a total gross tonnage of 14,099, on the country's inland waterways.

[18] However this situation may be greatly changed if the new Mekong project is implemented. See below, p. 573.

[19] The embankments built as part of water-control schemes can also serve as road beds, and this practice is now being increasingly adopted.

peninsula, where distance from the capital made it particularly desirable to increase the effective range of the government's authority.

In aviation, on the other hand, Thailand has had a more impressive record. In the years immediately following the First World War[20] the government was quick to appreciate that the aeroplane might afford the most effective means of linking up the outlying parts of the country, hitherto separated from one another by jungle-covered hills and seasonally flooded plains. In 1922 military aircraft began a regular service between Korat and Ubol, and later also between Korat and Nong Khai, via Roi-et and Udon, both in effect foreshadowing the railway routes of more recent times. By the 1930s many of the larger towns had regular air connexions with Bangkok, and this helped to offset the isolation resulting from the far from adequate road system.

III. THE REGIONAL ECONOMIES

From the foregoing account of the evolution of the Siamese transport network before the Second World War it is clear that political considerations were more important than economics in determining the policies adopted. Nevertheless, the improvement in ocean transport, together with the conclusion of the Bowring Treaty in 1855, brought about a revolution in the country's economic structure at much the same time as that in most other parts of South-east Asia, and to the successful working out of this the provision of modern internal communications after 1890 made an indispensable contribution.

According to Ingram, the population of Siam in 1855 was some 5–6 million, and the small export trade, notably of sugar, cotton and hides, was already largely in the hands of Chinese merchants. Thereafter the influx of Western textiles and other manufactures provided the stimulus which led Siam, like Burma, to become one of the world's greatest exporters of rice. From an annual export of around 200,000 tons in the 1870s, the total rose to approximately 1½ million tons in the 1930s when Thailand wrested second place from French Indochina. Later, during the period of acute disorder in Burma after the Second World War, Thailand became for several years the largest exporter of all, with a peak figure of 1,637,000 tons in 1951, but more recently the surplus available for sale abroad has fallen to 1,248,000 tons in 1955, and Thailand has again taken second place to Burma.

In many other respects also, the economic and social revolution in Siam since the middle 19th century has followed the pattern set by Burma. Thus the population approximately trebled between 1855 and 1941, and while this was mainly the result of accelerated natural increase on the part of the Thais themselves, it was supplemented by a massive immigration of alien Asians, in this case Chinese.

From the geographical point of view, however, there were important differences

[20] It included an air contingent in its expeditionary force which served on the Allied side in the First World War. On more recent developments in transport see below pp. 516–8.

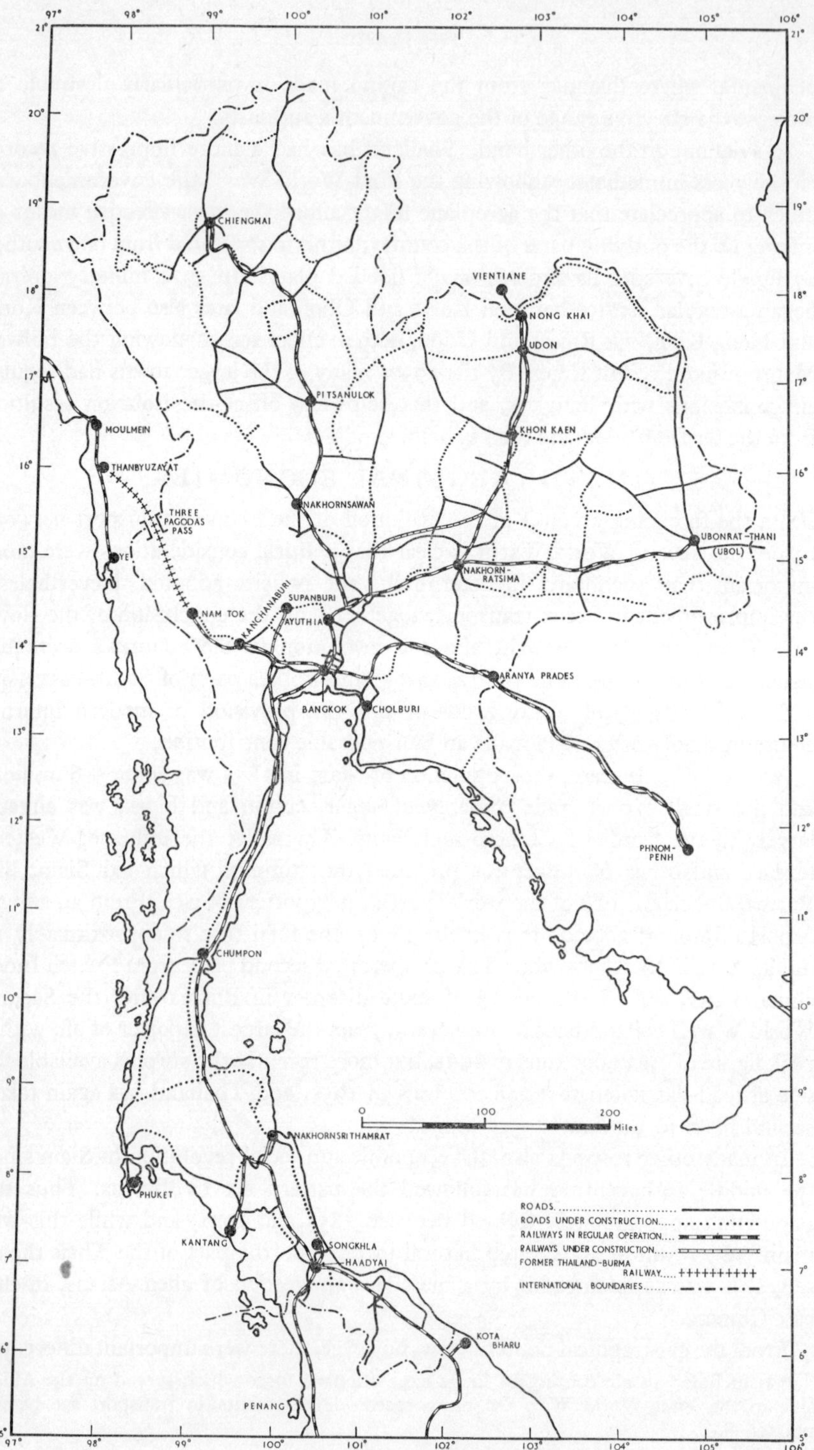

FIG. 71—Thailand: roads and railways, 1955

between the manner in which these changes operate in the two countries. In the first place, whereas the heart of the old Burmese kingdom had hitherto been in the interior dry zone, the Menam delta was already the focus of the Siamese state before the large-scale cultivation of rice for export began. Nevertheless, although the delta was the most densely populated region in the country, the greater part of its surface was still uncultivated in 1855, and there was thus ample scope for extending the acreage under rice in this area which enjoyed the supreme advantage of accessibility to ocean transport.

Moreover, the local peasantry were able to obtain squatter's rights by the simple device of clearing unoccupied land and planting a crop on it. Indeed it was mainly by spontaneous colonization of this kind, involving no great internal migrations of people like those in Burma, that the best parts of the delta[21] were first brought under the plough, and until the beginning of the present century virtually all the export rice came from there. However, after railway links were established with the Korat plateau and the northern part of the central plain, both of these regions also began to contribute their quota. Today the central plain as a whole (*i.e.* including the delta) accounts for some 56 per cent of Thailand's rice production and 75 per cent of its export, the remaining 25 per cent coming mostly from the north-east.

Yet while the central plain is renowned for the high quality of its rice, the region is by no means ideal for paddy cultivation. For the average rainfall there during the growing season is only about 41 in., which provides less than two-thirds the amount of water required for successful paddy growing in these latitudes.[22] But the annual flooding by the Menam is able to make up the deficiency over most parts of the delta normally under paddy, providing that the level of water in the river at Ayuthia is 11 ft. 6 in. above the average level in the Bight of Bangkok for some 2½ months in the year.[23]

Unfortunately, though this represents something like the average flood condition, the variability of rainfall is such that over the 99 years prior to 1930, 30 were so dry that the river level was seriously below the necessary figure and in another 15 it was so much above it as to cause severe damage to crops by excessive flooding. To some extent the problems arising from inadequate flood levels could be offset by the building of large distribution canals, and the earliest irrigation works of modern times, including the big Rangsit scheme of the 1880s, were of this kind. But although the latter opened up a large area of swamp land to the north-east of Bangkok, the problem of water supply there was not effectively solved, and in 1899 the government sought the services of the Dutch engineer J. H. Van der Heide, to devise a more comprehensive and reliable irrigation scheme.[24]

[21] Best, that is, in the sense of having satisfactory natural water supplies. Many other areas still uncultivated today could become equally productive if proper water control were provided.

[22] *Siam – Nature and industry*, p. 187.

[23] Credner, p. 213.

[24] See *Siam – Nature and industry*, p. 192 *et seq.*, and Ingram, p. 81 *et seq.* for fuller details.

In the event Van der Heide's proposals, which centred on the building of a great barrage across the Menam at Chainad, were turned down by the government as too costly, but a series of disastrous years from 1909 to 1912 led to a re-examination of the whole problem. On the advice of a British consultant, Sir Thomas Ward, who considered that the population of the area was not yet numerous enough to justify the construction of so elaborate a project as that recommended by Van der Heide, work began on a series of lesser schemes which could ultimately be linked together. By 1938 the total irrigated area stood at 1·1 million acres[25] but in the absence of large water-storage facilities such as had been envisaged by Van der Heide, crop failure remained an ever-present threat in the years of subnormal flooding.

The type of economy which has grown up in the central plain during the past 60–70 years is essentially monocultural. Particularly in the delta proper where most of the land remains under flood till January or later, the raising of a second crop is virtually impossible, and except for small but intensively cultivated areas of Chinese market gardens in the vicinity of Bangkok and other towns, the region is one vast sea of paddy. Apart from rice cultivation, which is dependent on the water buffalo for ploughing[26], only fishing and the raising of a few ducks[27] are of much importance to the ordinary peasant, though on the outer fringe of the plain a little more variety is apparent, and besides fruit and vegetables there are about 9,600 acres under cotton.

So far as rice cultivation is concerned the best results are obtained from the transplanting method (*dam*) which, as practised here, does not differ very greatly from that in the Irrawaddy delta.[28] But in much of the Menam delta the depth of water is such that floating rice must be grown, and this has to be sown broadcast (*wan*) because the long brittle stalks are too fragile to withstand uprooting when the plant is young. Moreover, the broadcast method is generally adopted with ordinary wet rice wherever family holdings are larger than 10 acres for, in the absence of labour from outside the family circle, transplanting becomes an impossibility.[29]

While the average size of family holding in the central plain is about 12 acres, much of the best irrigated land of the delta, such as that served by the Rangsit scheme, is held in larger units of 15 or more acres, and in the Dhanyaburi district near Bangkok the average holding is 40 acres and 85 per cent of the farmers

[25] Ingram, pp. 84–5.

[26] Most families here have a pair of buffaloes, and this is common in many other parts of the country. In the north and north-east, where soils are generally lighter, however, bullocks are often preferred for ploughing, and the bullock cart is widely used for local transport in nearly all parts of the country. De Young, p. 91.

[27] Mainly by Chinese, who also use duck droppings to fertilize their market gardens. *Ibid.*, p. 99.

[28] At least 80 per cent of the country's rice is *dam*. See De Young, p. 80, and *Siam – nature and industry*, pp. 204–16.

[29] Considerable seasonal labour comes into the delta from the north-east for harvesting. De Young, pp. 85–7.

are tenants, as against 36 per cent for the central plain as a whole. For with the beginnings of organized irrigation, delta land began to acquire a real cash value early in the present century and the old practice of simply squatting on unoccupied land became a thing of the past.

A further feature of the areas of more highly commercialized farming has been the growth of dispersed units of settlement in place of the traditional compact village, and in such circumstances the old co-operative organization of ploughing and harvesting has inevitably disappeared. Again in keeping with the commercialized character of farming in the central plain rents are nowadays paid in cash[30], and it is under these conditions that rural indebtedness reaches its peak. According to Zimmerman 49 per cent of the farm families in the central plain were in debt in 1930, and in Andrews' opinion this represented 80 per cent of the total rural indebtedness in the country.

However, the extent of rural indebtedness even in the delta has remained relatively small in comparison with that in many other parts of South-east Asia, and while much of the total is owed to Chinese shopkeepers and rice dealers, there is no evidence to suggest that these are more rapacious than indigenous Siamese money-lenders. Nevertheless, the hold which the Chinese have gained over the milling and marketing of rice constitutes a social problem of the first magnitude. By 1942–5 between 80 and 90 per cent of all the rice mills in the country were Chinese owned and almost exclusively Chinese staffed, and Chinese middlemen controlled practically the whole of the rice crop from the moment it left the farmer's hands.

Outside the central plain the regional economies are everywhere based primarily upon subsistence farming, and although most of the outlying areas supply one or more commodities for the export market, the more important of these, namely teak, rubber and tin, may perhaps be regarded as secondary developments to the more intensively organized production in either Burma or British Malaya.

The traditional farming system of the north is characterized by skilful adaptation to a shorter growing season, lower rainfall and lighter soils than those of the central plain. In these circumstances wet rice cannot be cultivated without a supplementary water supply, but the comparatively narrow valleys of the northern rivers were well suited to the practice of the simple irrigation techniques which the Thais brought with them from Yunnan. In fact, such methods, co-operatively organized under the supervision of the village headman, have been in regular use there for centuries, and in the small alluvial tracts where they are able to provide water all the year round, a fairly intensive system of agriculture has been evolved, based on rice as the main crops supplemented with beans, vegetables, ground nuts, cotton[31] and tobacco as secondary crops in the dry season.

Owing to the shortness of the summer growing season all the rice here is of

[30] Such tenancy as exists elsewhere is largely on a share-crop basis. *Ibid.*, p. 75 *et seq.*

[31] There were 10,400 acres under cotton in the north in 1948. Ingram, p. 119.

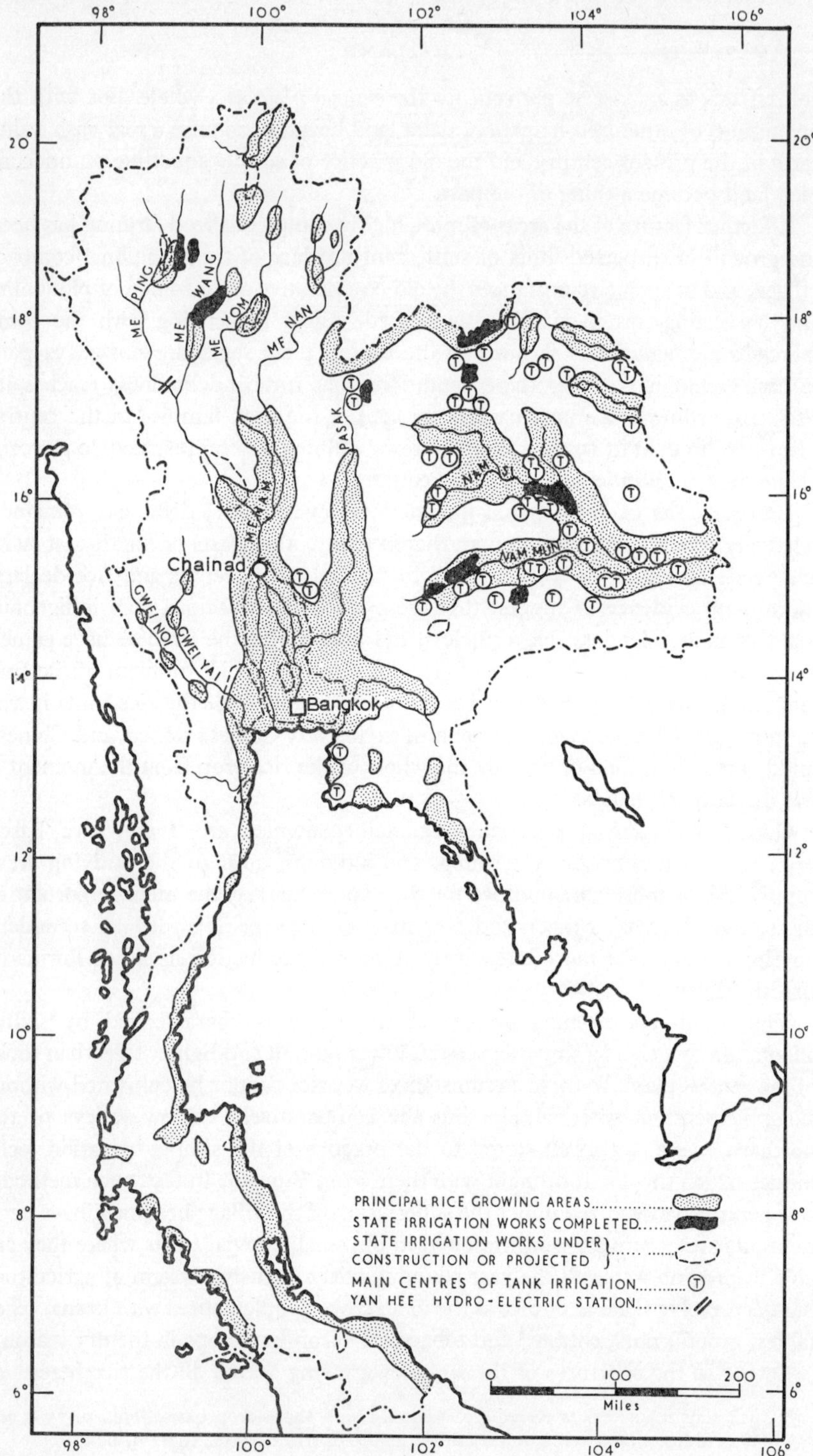

98°
100°
102°
104°
106°
20°
18°
16°
14°
12°
10°
8°
6°
ME PING
ME WANG
ME YOM
MF NAN
PASAK
ME NAM
NAM SI
NAM MUN
Chainad
GWEI NOI
GWEI YAI
Bangkok
PRINCIPAL RICE GROWING AREAS
STATE IRRIGATION WORKS COMPLETED
STATE IRRIGATION WORKS UNDER CONSTRUCTION OR PROJECTED
MAIN CENTRES OF TANK IRRIGATION
YAN HEE HYDRO-ELECTRIC STATION
0
100
200
Miles

FIG. 72—Thailand: rice-land

the fast-ripening glutinous kind, and it is in part because of the small overseas demand for this[32] that no serious attempt has been made to develop export production. However, since the imposition of a 25 per cent import duty on manufactured tobacco in 1927,[33] production of both Siamese and Virginia tobacco has expanded rapidly in northern Thailand and much the greater part of the country's total supplies, which are now enough to meet the internal demand, are grown in this region. In recent years the State Tobacco Monopoly has operated buying stations and curing sheds both here and in the north-east, and seedlings are distributed free to farmers who undertake to sell their crop to the government.

With such a source of cash in addition to a fairly wide range of subsistence crops, poultry, pigs and fish in the local streams, the northern peasant may enjoy a relatively good standard of living on an average-sized holding of 4 acres, and even the 27 per cent of the farmers who have no land of their own are probably better off than the great mass of their countrymen in the north-east.

The foregoing remarks apply only to the valley population of north Thailand, and not to the more primitive uplanders who rely wholly or mainly on shifting tillage. Economically, however, the northern hills are most important as the main centre of the Siamese teak industry which began on a commercial scale at the end of the 19th century, following incipient signs of exhaustion in the teak forests of Burma.[34] In contrast to other productive activities in the north, the teak industry has been largely in alien hands, and besides the four British, one French and one Danish firm whose combined interests were estimated at over £3 million in 1924, local Chinese are also responsible for a part of the production. Though the volume of exports has been declining in recent years, this is partly due to an increase in the use of teak for constructional purposes within the country, and only about one-third of total production is nowadays exported. Individual logs are floated down the northern tributaries of the Menam to such places as Raheng, Sawankalok and Uttaradit, where they are assembled into rafts which continue the journey southwards to the sawmills at Bangkok.

The Korat plateau of the north-east presents an altogether less satisfactory picture than the north. Here the difficulties arising from a similarly short growing season and an even lower average rainfall are further aggravated by the poverty and porosity of the prevailing sandy soils. Thus, except in the wide and seasonally inundated valleys of the two main rivers, the Nam Mun and the Nam Si, little wet cultivation is possible and even in these areas where, as Dobby has observed, even simple forms of water control would seem to offer obvious advantages, no indigenous system of irrigation ever developed in the past.[35]

[32] Plus the high cost of transport by rail.

[33] On tobacco see Ingram, pp. 140–42, and De Young, pp. 95–6.

[34] On teak see Ingram, pp. 105–8. Besides teak, *yang* is also exploited commercially in many upland areas. Sixty-three per cent of Thailand is forested.

[35] Dobby (H), p. 271. But note that tank irrigation is now being introduced there. See below, p. 509.

Away from the rivers, and more especially in the outer foothills, shifting cultivation of dry rice and other crops is commonly practised by the Thais themselves. The area involved is apt to be substantially larger in bad years than in good, but the average figure cannot be far short of half a million acres out of a total of some 5½ million cultivated in the whole region.[36]

Yet although this latter figure represents only 7 per cent of the area of the Korat plateau, and the average size of farm holdings there is a mere 2½ acres, this region provides a considerable export of rice, the area under paddy there having risen from 1,560,000 acres in 1920–24 to 4,800,000 acres in 1948–50.[37] Moreover, non-glutinous varieties now account for 30 per cent of the total crop in what for climatic reasons has traditionally been a glutinous-rice region and some 300,000 tons of the former are exported annually in addition to the sale of a small quantity of glutinous rice to central Thailand. Apart from this 20 or so per cent of the country's rice exports, the north-east has no major cash crop, though the 56,000 acres under cotton and the widespread cultivation of tobacco, kenaf and maize are worth noting. More important than these, however, is the rearing of cattle for sale in other parts of the country as well as for local use. This activity is essentially a part of the ordinary peasant farming system, though it is particularly well developed in northern Korat where the percentage of land under rice is very low. All-told approximately half of the country's 5 million buffaloes and a similar proportion of its cattle are raised in the north-east and this is enough to provide a surplus for sale and also to give a useful – if still pitifully small – amount of animal manure for this region of exceptionally poor soils.[38]

So far as the remaining regions are concerned their subsistence agriculture calls for little comment. Both the south-east and the south obtain below average yields of rice, but coconuts and other fruits, together with coastal fish, give more variety to the staple diet, and living standards are reasonably high. In addition, the south-east produces small quantities of pepper, cardamoms and rubber for cash, but much the greater part of the country's rubber acreage is in the far south, beyond the Kra isthmus.[39]

Since 1920 the area under rubber has risen from a mere 29,000 acres to 362,000 in 1934 and 780,000 in 1950, and of this some 67 per cent is in smallholdings of less than 20 acres and only about 8 per cent is accounted for by plantations of over 80 acres. Official returns show most of the cultivators as Thai, but at least half are ethnically Chinese and most of the others are Malay. By comparison with the standards which obtain in the Federation of Malaya production is inefficient, and although the government Rubber Division now

[36] *Ibid.*, p. 279. [37] Ingram, p. 50.

[38] Without this manure the rice yields there would be even less than they are at present. See below, pp. 28–9. On livestock, which also includes considerable numbers of pigs in the north-east, see Credner, pp. 246–50. Secondary crops in Korat include kapok, tapioca and bananas.

[39] On rubber, see Ingram, pp. 101–5.

provides good-quality material for planting at low cost, overall yields still remain low. Output in 1959 amounted to 10 per cent of the world total natural rubber, and apart from a minute fraction used in the local footwear industry all Siamese rubber is exported.[40]

The peninsula south of the Kra isthmus is also the scene of nearly all the Siamese tin-mining industry.[41] Here, as in western Malaya, the alluvial deposits are extremely easy to work by primitive hand methods, and in fact Chinese mining activity of this kind, centred in Phuket, has a history which goes back several centuries. After 1907, however, when an Australian company began operations with tin dredges in the vicinity of Tongkah Harbour, Western concerns using modern techniques have assumed a growing share of production, and in 1950 25 mines, all but three of them British or Australian owned, accounted for about two-thirds of the output, the remainder coming from some 300 much smaller Chinese mines, most of which used the gravel-pumping method. Practically the whole of the tin output, which represented 9·7 per cent of total world production in 1961, is exported via Malaya, where smelting takes place prior to despatch to Europe and the U.S.A.

IV. NATIONALISM AND INDUSTRIALIZATION IN THE INTER-WAR YEARS

As the preceding pages have shown, several distinctive regional economies, broadly reflecting the main natural divisions of the country, have emerged in Siam with increasing clarity during the past 70 or 80 years. But at the same time the distinction between indigenous and alien economic activity has also grown sharper, with subsistence farming and the cultivation of rice for export remaining in Siamese hands while the production of tin, rubber and teak, together with the milling and export of rice and the import and distributive trade as a whole, have been predominantly controlled by aliens, either European or Chinese.

In this respect, therefore, the experience of independent Siam has not differed fundamentally from that of formerly dependent Burma, and indeed the size and influence of its alien Asian minority are predominantly greater than in any other South-east Asian country apart from Malaya. To a considerable extent geographical propinquity explains the centuries-old history of Chinese settlement in Siam, and well before the growth of regular seaborne commerce between the two countries in the 17th century there was a flourishing caravan trade between Yunnan and northern Siam. By the beginning of the 19th century, Chinese traders occupied an influential position in court circles, and several contemporary

[40] Formerly most of the export was via Penang, but the greater part now goes direct to the U.S.A. In 1955 the government set up a pilot plant at Koh Hongs, Songkhla, to instruct rubber growers in modern methods of making rubber smoked sheets and processing latex.

[41] See *Weekly Overseas Mail*, Special supplement on Thailand, September 15, 1951, p. 10, and Ingram, pp. 98–101.

European travellers estimated that more than half the population of Bangkok was ethnically Chinese.[42]

Nevertheless, large-scale immigration of Chinese did not begin until around the middle of the century and, as in other parts of South-east Asia, the movement was almost entirely by sea, mainly from Hainan and the adjacent coastlands. Throughout the second half of the 19th century the Chinese immigrants concentrated markedly in the delta, as the focus of the country's commercial life, and also in the tin-mining areas of the south where, particularly in Phuket, they formed for many years a virtual *imperium in imperio*.[43]

Despite a considerable filling out of the pattern as a result of continued heavy immigration during the early decades of the present century, these two concentrations are still apparent, but today there are few towns in any part of the country without their Chinese shopkeepers, and the small boats of itinerant Chinese merchants penetrate to the farthest navigable reaches of the principal rivers.

Until well into the present century most of the Chinese immigrants who settled permanently married Siamese wives and, thanks to the ethnic similarity between the two peoples, assimilation was easily effected. Many Chinese, especially the more successful merchants, took Siamese names and the offspring of mixed marriages – the so-called *luk chin* – were often highly esteemed for their mental alertness.

Meanwhile, however, as the power and wealth of the Chinese community grew,[44] the practice developed after 1900 or so of sending home for wives of Chinese race. And with the rise of the Kuo Min Tang after the First World War the process of assimilation was further slowed down, as the Chinese in Siam began to found their own schools and organize their own Chambers of Commerce.[45]

About this time also, the Siamese themselves first became seriously affected by the stirrings of Asian nationalism and though this did not assume so intense a form as in some colonial territories, the small Western-educated Siamese élite were inspired by the Kuo Min Tang in China to press for the termination of the old 19th-century treaties which seriously limited their country's fiscal autonomy and perpetuated various Western extra-territorial privileges. In this connexion the Anglo-Siamese Treaty of Commerce and Navigation (1925) marked an important advance though the British insisted that the tariff on all the more important types of manufactured goods should be limited to 5 per cent for the ensuing ten years.[46]

Before this period had elapsed, however, other changes were ushered in by the bloodless revolution of 1932. This, the first of the series of *coups d'état* which

[42] For details of these reports see Purcell (D), Chapter 11.

[43] *Ibid.*, Chapter 12.

[44] Chinese economic interests in Siam in the inter-war years exceeded those of all the Western powers put together.

[45] See Crosby (A), Chapter 13.

[46] Ingram, p. 181.

have punctuated the recent history of Siam, was led by a group of young army officers and a handful of other professional men, who exploited the local discontent attendant on the worldwide economic crisis in order to replace the old absolutist system by a constitutional monarchy.

Although the revolution succeeded in effecting this constitutional change,[47] differences of opinion soon appeared within the movement and the more radical wing, under Pridi Banomyong, who favoured nationalization of rice production and trade, was defeated. Thereafter, government came increasingly under the control of the army, Pibul Songgram eventually becoming Prime Minister in 1938, and under this regime more conservative economic policies were combined with strong nationalist demands for the termination of Western treaty rights and the curbing of Chinese economic power within the country.[48] In 1937 the 1925 Treaty with Britain had been replaced by another which removed the last vestiges of extra-territoriality and left Siamese fiscal autonomy completely unimpeded. Similar treaties followed with other Western powers and between 1929 and 1939 the British share in Siam's imports fell from 17·6 per cent to 11·3 per cent, while that of Japan rose from 2·8 to 14·8 per cent, a figure which was largely accounted for by Japan's rapid gains in textiles sales.

Nevertheless, while this shift in the source of manufactured goods may have been commercially advantageous as well as politically acceptable, the Siamese government was anxious to build up its own manufacturing industries, and its newly acquired tariff autonomy made it possible for the first time to afford significant protection to this end.

In common with neighbouring lands, Thailand has an old-established tradition of handicraft industry[49] and though some branches of this suffered severely from the competition of imported manufactures after 1855, others have survived surprisingly well, so that in the regions outside the commercialized central plain such industry is probably more important than in any other major part of South-east Asia. Thus Andrews estimated in 1934–5 that handicraft industry was responsible for 32 per cent of the peasants' money income in the north-east, 26 per cent in the north, 30 per cent in the south and even 18 per cent in the central plain.

Before the introduction of Western manufactures, cotton and silk weaving were almost ubiquitous, though both were especially important in the north-east as supplements to the low income obtainable from agriculture there. Sericulture in particular was well suited to such an environment, and even the ordinary peasantry customarily wore coarse silk clothing, while the better-grade fabrics were sold as far afield as Burma. With the improvement in transport after 1900 the influx of cheap European cottons caused a serious decline in the Korat silk industry, and the government's attempts to counteract this with the help

[47] The constitution, which represented a tentative step towards democracy, provided for a single-chamber legislature, with half the members elected by popular vote and the other half nominated, ostensibly by the Crown but in practice by the government of the day.

[48] See below, pp. 512, 514 and 521–2.

[49] See Ingram, Chapter 6, De Young, pp. 102–3, *Siam – nature and industry*, Chapter 15.

of Japanese advisers met with only limited success, though the industry still survives in the villages away from the main lines of communications.

Locally grown cotton is also of some importance in the same area, and to a lesser extent in the north, but the domestic manufacture of cotton textiles declined steadily until well into the present century, and according to Ingram[50] the product of domestic cotton weaving was only half as great as the volume of imported cloth prior to the Second World War.

On the other hand, such activities as the making of tiles and bricks, carts and boats, and plaited bamboo hats and baskets, all of which relied on local materials and catered for local conditions unfamiliar to Western manufacturers, have continued to flourish, as also have certain specialized crafts, notably the production of *niello* ware, that is silver inlaid with a black alloy of lead, sulphur, copper and silver, which is centred mainly in Bangkok and Nakhornsrithamrat.

Before the 1932 revolution the Siamese authorities had been attempting to strengthen the position of the surviving handicraft industries, mainly through the activities of the Arts and Crafts School established for that purpose in Bangkok. But under the nationalist regime attention shifted to the possibility of setting up Western-style factory industries, of which the number hitherto established by public and private enterprise was extremely small.

As in other parts of South-east Asia the main obstacle to the establishment of modern industry in Siam, apart from the small size of the local market, was the absence of an indigenous mercantile class, which had already enabled the Chinese to obtain a preponderant share in the small-scale manufacture of cheap consumer goods in Bangkok.

For this reason, therefore, the government decided in the later 1930s to establish a series of semi-official trading organizations and factories under Thai control. Between 1935 and 1941 a cotton mill was erected at Bangkok, a second paper factory at Kanburi, a modern sugar plant at Lampang and a cannery at Pak Chang, as well as a series of lesser industrial undertakings in other parts of the country, and in 1941 the British-American Tobacco Company's cigarette factories in Bangkok were taken over by the State Tobacco Monopoly.

In this way, therefore, the foundations of a nationalist economic policy were being laid in the years immediately preceding the Pacific War, but, in the absence of any form of external economic assistance, the scale and progress of industrialization still lagged behind those in the neighbouring colonial lands. Moreover, while the favourable ratio of population to agricultural land meant that acute rural poverty was very rare except in the north-east, it would probably be true to describe pre-war Siam as commercially the least developed country in the whole of South-east Asia.[51]

[50] Ingram, p. 119.

[51] Such an assessment is largely subjective and it certainly should not be taken to imply that the standard of living in Siam was the lowest in South-east Asia, for this was assuredly not so.

However, by comparison with these neighbouring countries Siam suffered only minor hardships as a result of the Second World War. After a brief token resistance to the Japanese attack on December 8, 1941, the Siamese forces capitulated, and soon afterwards the government concluded an alliance with Japan and declared war on Britain and the United States.[52] Later, as the tide of war turned, popular opinion in Siam swung against the Japanese, and in 1944 the Pibul government was overthrown, largely through the efforts of the resistance movement led by Pridi, who became Prime Minister after the first post-war elections early in 1946.

Except for the British insistence that Thailand should supply 1,500,000 tons of rice from its accumulated stocks to meet the urgent needs of Malaya[53] the peace settlement imposed no indemnity and, in view of the post-war interruptions to agricultural production in both Burma and Indochina, Thailand enjoyed the advantages of a seller's market for its surplus rice for several years after the ending of hostilities.

Furthermore, notwithstanding the series of *coups* which brought Pibul back to office in 1948 and displaced him again in 1957, there has been no major political unrest in Thailand since the war, and in the absence of any memory of colonial rule the Thais have been prepared to co-operate more explicitly with the West than have any other South-east Asian people except the Filipinos. Thus, paradoxically, the state which before the war was the least Westernized in the whole of South-east Asia has since 1948 become the principal centre of Western influence in the region, and its capital city today houses the permanent headquarters of S.E.A.T.O.[54]

It is against this background that the post-war economic development of Thailand should be seen. Enjoying a far greater measure of stability than any of its neighbours, it has thus been able to devote its main energies to productive ends,[55] which is one reason why its national income had in 1959 reached $88 per head, compared with the Burmese figure of $48 for the same year.

V. CONTEMPORARY ECONOMIC PROBLEMS

Although Thailand's average population density of 109 to the square mile (1958) is greater than that of Burma (78) this difference can be related to the higher proportion of lowland in the former, and in any case the density is below the

[52] Britain recognized this but the U.S.A. did not.

[53] This demand was later modified and eventually cancelled. See Ingram, p. 87. See also Peterson (A), pp. 364–72.

[54] E.C.A.F.E. also has its headquarters in Bangkok.

[55] This statement holds, notwithstanding the considerable proportion of U.S. aid which has been earmarked for military purposes. Between 1945 and 1957 U.S. economic aid totalled about $88 million and since 1956 such aid has been at the rate of $24 million a year; much larger sums continue to be granted in the form of military aid. Other assistance has been provided in the form of loans from the World Bank (see below, pp. 516–7) and under the Colombo Plan.

South-east Asian average of 126. Thus, while there are signs of congestion in the infertile north-east, the country as a whole is by no means overpopulated, and indeed most experts believe that it could without difficulty support substantially more people than it does today.

Be that as it may, population is now growing rapidly as Table 61 shows. Thanks to a comparatively good diet which combines more fish and vegetables with the staple rice than is common in most other Asian lands, the population of Thailand has for many years shown a death-rate below the regional average, and the extent to which this has been still further reduced since the war by anti-malarial measures and the provision of better sanitation has been more than enough to offset the virtual cessation of immigration from China.[56]

TABLE 61

THAILAND: POPULATION GROWTH

	Crude birth-rate per 1,000 *p.a.*	*Crude death-rate* per 1,000 *p.a.*	*Natural increase* per 1,000 *p.a.*
1925–9	29·9	15·5	14·4
1937	36·7	17·8	18·9
1951	29·0	10·1	18·9
1954	34·2	9·7	24·5
1958	36·8	9·7	27·1
1960	32·8	8·2	24·6

Source: *Statistical Year Book of Thailand*, etc.

Moreover, the drop in the death-rate has been accompanied by a continued high birth-rate, and while this may change in the future, the rate of increase is likely to remain high for many years to come.

In these circumstances, therefore, a steady increase in export production will be required if living standards are to be maintained, for even if, in common with most of its neighbours, Thailand now embarks on more extensive industrialization, the process will have to be financed mainly out of export earnings. In this respect the substantial post-war increase in rubber production is offset by the decline in both teak and tin exports, and there is little reason to expect that the small deposits of zinc, antimony and wolfram known to exist in the northern hills will ever be of much account.[57]

[56] See below, p. 521.

[57] Outputs of minerals in 1960 (in metric tons) were: tin ore 16,757; wolfram 407; lead ore 4,600; iron ore 11,475; and lignite 107,783.

Thanks partly to its better prospects on the world market, rubber outstripped rice as Thailand's most valuable export in 1960, though whether this change will be lasting, even if the current scheme for rubber replanting is successful, will depend primarily upon the continuing struggle between the natural and the synthetic product, which has been considered on pages 165–8.

Be that as it may, the combination of subsistence and export production of rice is likely to ensure that it will remain by far the most important single agricultural commodity within the country, even though the present allocation of some 86 per cent of the cultivated area to it may well be regarded as excessive. And in these circumstances the fact that the great expansion in paddy acreage during the present century has been accompanied by a decline in the yield per acre, from 36·6 bushels in 1906–9 to 25·72 in 1952, gives grounds for very serious concern.[58]

TABLE 62

THAILAND: RICE PRODUCTION AND EXPORT

Year	*Acreage (million)*	*Production (million tons)*	*Export (million tons)*
1850 . . .	2·32		
1857–59 average. .			0·059
1905–9 „ . .	3·68		0·879
1915–19 „ . .	5·56	1·92	0·939
1935–39 „ . .	8·48	2·71	1·510
1951–55 „ . .	13·20	4·50	1·331
1959			1·098

Sources: Based on Ingram, pp. 38 and 44, *Agricultural Statistics of Thailand*, 1957, etc.

Two main factors appear to be involved here. First, in the almost complete absence of artificial fertilizer of any kind, continued cropping has led to progressive impoverishment of the soil except in areas where annual flooding provides replenishment in the form of soluble plant foods and fresh silt. And secondly, much of the extension of the area under rice has been on to decidedly inferior land, notably on the poorly watered edges of the central plain and in the north-east.[59] Indeed, in the latter region yields have fallen from 32·25 bushels per acre in 1920–24 to 19·28 in 1952, when 14 out of 15 of its provinces had yields below the national average, the lowest of all being Surin with 7·73 bushels.[60] In the

[58] This has also been accompanied by increased per capita consumption within Thailand. Ingram, p. 53.

[59] *Ibid.*, pp. 48–50.

[60] Seven of the 14 provinces in the south have below-average yields as also have most of those of the south-east and the western hills.

TABLE 63

THAILAND: ACREAGE AND PRODUCTION OF CHIEF CROPS

Crop	*Acreage* 1952	*Production* (000 *metric tons*)				
		1948	1952	1955	1958	1959
Paddy	13,420,302	6,835	6,602	7,712	7,123	7,186
Rubber	800,000*	n.a.	117	132	141	174
Coconuts	238,556	n.a.	694	1,187	1,150	n.a.
Maize	112,306	17	45	67	186	317
Tobacco	109,629	14	42	56	66	66
Ground nuts	175,000†	n.a.	n.a.	64	—	101
Sugar cane	184,204	618	1,476	2,699	4,309	4,147
Sesamum	42,690	6	9	n.a.	17	17
Cotton	96,550	16	24	n.a.	35	37
Beans and peas	321,557	52	121	n.a.	184	n.a.
Kenaf	n.a.	n.a.	n.a.	n.a.	30	50

* = 1951; † = 1950–51 average.

Note: Total cultivated acreage, 1950—16,946,824 = 13·4 per cent of total area.

Sources: *Statistical Year Book of Thailand, Thai News,* etc.

central plain on the other hand, the decline has been much less marked, and whereas yields in this region in 1921–4 were mostly below the then average, all but one of its provinces were above the current average in 1952, as were all seven of the northern provinces.

From these data it would seem that the time has come when Thailand should turn from the pioneer phase of skimming fertility off an ever larger area of newly cultivated land to a more systematic and intensive exploitation of those areas which are by nature best suited to rice growing. Here the question of water-control is all-important for, as noted on page 496, no comprehensive project was ever put in hand for the Menam delta before the war, and as recently as 1931 only 1·1 million acres of paddy land were irrigated, which, according to a more recent E.C.A.F.E. estimate, represents a mere 7 per cent of the potentially irrigable area within the country.

It was in these circumstances that the Greater Menam Project was initiated in 1952, with the help of an $18 million loan from the World Bank. This scheme, which harks back to the plans of Van der Heide and Ward earlier in the century, involves the construction of a major barrage across the Menam at Chainad, together with 14 other large undertakings lower down stream which will link together the existing irrigation works in a comprehensive scheme of water control. When completed this will add 2·3 million acres to the area under effective irrigation, thus making it possible to more than double the rice output of the central delta. Moreover, besides enabling a second crop to be raised during the dry season, the scheme will greatly reduce the risks and increase the efficiency of wet-season cultivation, and by preventing excessive flooding will enhance the prospects for the rearing of livestock and the growing of vegetables and other minor crops.

While the central plain is rightly receiving the principal attention in this respect, some new irrigation works are being undertaken in the north, and in 1952 the Ministry of Agriculture introduced a plan for building some 500 small irrigation tanks, of the peninsular Indian kind, in the north-east. By the end of 1955 100 of these had been completed, and this project, together with the use of mobile pumps to provide emergency irrigation in time of exceptional drought,[61] should do much to reduce the risks of rice cultivation in that region. Nevertheless, it is doubtful whether this part of the country should aim at substantially increasing its production of rice for export, and greater attention to the rearing of livestock, and the growing of cotton for internal consumption would probably be more rewarding in the long run.

Besides irrigation the Ministry of Agriculture has devoted much attention in recent years to rice-seed improvement, and seed strains have been bred which are capable of increasing paddy yields by up to 30 per cent. These strains are now being multiplied on seed farms all over the country in preparation for distribution among the peasantry. But little has yet been done to increase the use of chemical fertilizer, and while for financial reasons this neglect is perhaps understandable, it remains a serious weakness in the present agricultural system.[62]

Finally, it remains to consider the contribution which mechanization might take towards increasing the efficiency of rice cultivation.[63] For over 25 years government experimental stations have used tractors and since 1945 experiments have been carried out to assess the economies which might be obtained from mechanized farming. From these it appears that the buffalo cannot be dispensed with altogether, especially on the smaller farms, for ploughing out field corners and the odd jobs of carting are more economically performed with animals than with tractors.

More important than this, however, is the variation in the seasonal demand for labour. In the areas which practise the intensive transplanting method such labour is required for planting and also for harvesting, so that while a tractor

[61] De Young, pp. 195–6. The political aspects of these developments in the north-east, which owe much to U.S. initiative, are discussed below, p. 525.

[62] The new ammonium sulphate plant opened in 1955 (see below, p. 514) will help, but only to a very limited extent.

[63] See *Weekly Overseas Mail*, Special supplement on Thailand, September 15, 1951, p. 11.

would be useful for ploughing, it would not replace the labour employed in the later stages. But in the 20 per cent or so of the rice lands using the more extensive broadcast method, the quantity of labour needed for harvesting greatly exceeds that for sowing, so that if it were possible to harvest as well as to plant by mechanical means a much smaller labour force would be required. Unfortunately, however, mechanized harvesting is only possible with a standing crop, and though rice will lodge when the stalks are not more than about 18 in. tall, most of the rice grown by the broadcast method in deeply flooded fields is much taller than this and so can only be reaped by hand.

Hitherto, therefore, mechanization has had little to offer to the farmer on smallholdings of less than about 10–12 acres, and has been technically impracticable on most of the larger holdings, where, on economic grounds it would be most beneficial. But with the improvements in water control resulting from the current irrigation schemes it will be possible to replace floating rice by strains with shorter stalks, and this may lead to a major increase in the use of mechanized methods.

Were this to happen, still further changes might follow, for as the benefits of mechanization became apparent the arguments in favour of larger holdings than the average-sized farm (10 acres) of the central plain would be reinforced. As yet,

TABLE 64

THAILAND: OVERSEAS TRADE BY COUNTRIES

A. Imports

Country of origin	1938–9 (*Per cent*)	1951 (*Per cent*)	1956 (*million Baht*)	1959 (*million Baht*)	1964 (*million Baht*)
Federation of Malaya‡	26	33	270·3	231·7	203
Singapore	—	—	603·2	685·4	265
Hong Kong	10	25	1,234·9	690·1	392
U.S.A.	3	9	1,175·3	1,484·7	2,269
China*	4	—	67·2	81·8	—
United Kingdom	11	7	852·7	914·0	1,282
Japan	15	3	1,256·7	2,255·8	4,566
Germany†	7	—	462·1	613·5	1,076
India	6	7	120·0	125·5	—
Switzerland			108·6	104·0	—
Netherlands			403·0	514·2	504
Indonesia			260·6	288·1	473
Total (incl. others)	£12,960,000	£106,000,000	7,562·1	8,984·7	13,971

B. Exports

Country of destination	1938–9 *Per cent)*	1951 *(Per cent)*	1956 *(million Baht)*	1959 *(million Baht)*	1964 *(million Baht)*
U.S.A.	11	31	1,719·2	1,778·0	553
Federation of Malaya‡	57	14	1,004·7	1,136·6	1,845
Singapore . . .	—	—	963·7	1,020·8	899
Japan	1	9	589·1	879·3	2,686
India	1	9	31·9	12·2	—
Indonesia . . .	—	5	437·3	149·9	1,094
Hong Kong . . .	11	3	573·6	644·1	994
Philippines . . .	—	3	54·8	4·0	—
British Borneo . .	—	1	131·3	144·9	—
United Kingdom .	1	—	214·2	221·2	577
Germany† . . .			98·5	181·1	577
Netherlands . .			206·5	132·4	575
Total (incl. others) .	£18,730,000	£128,000,000	6,716·5	7,257·7	12,454

* 1956 and 1958 figures refer to Formosa.
† 1956 and 1958 figures refer to Federal Republic.
‡ 1938–9 and 1951 data refer to all British Malaya; 1964 data to Malaysia.
Source: Based partly on *Yearbook of International Trade Statistics*, and Department of Customs, Bangkok.

in the absence of any very serious problems of rural indebtedness and land hunger[64], there has been little popular pressure for any such change and since it would entail far-reaching social repercussions the authorities have preferred to let well alone. But falling rice prices in recent years have produced some signs of rural discontent, both in the north-east and in the tenant-farming areas of the delta, and were this to become serious or were a more socialistic regime to come to power, the latter might well introduce fundamental changes in the pattern of land tenure as foreshadowed in Pridi's plans of the 1930s.

While the Agricultural Department has been primarily concerned in recent years with increasing the output of rice, the need to expand the production for internal consumption of other foodstuffs and raw materials, notably kenaf, cotton, sugar and tobacco, and to improve the quality of livestock[65] has not been overlooked. Fishing, which remains second only to agriculture in economic importance and is practised along the whole length of the Siamese coastline as

[64] F.A.O. estimated in 1953 that the average size of agricultural holding in Thailand was 10 acres and that 87 per cent of the farmland (the highest percentage in Asia) was owned by the cultivators.

[65] Rinderpest has been almost eradicated from most parts of Thailand since the Second World War, and many breeding animals have been imported.

TABLE 65

THAILAND: DIRECTION OF RICE EXPORTS

Figures in metric tons

Country	1953	1954	1955	1958
British Malaya	376,663	299,557	401,445	350,714
Japan	475,800	331,286	350,801	72,479
Hong Kong . . .	234,966	115,404	171,223	170,982
Indonesia	49,176	77,995	64,641	128,340
British Borneo . . .	15,539	35,830	38,399	2,975
United Kingdom . .	1,325	16,711	8,518	23,624
Philippines . . .	—	—	—	31,357
Netherlands . . .	—	—	—	45,005
Total (including others) .	1,340,588	1,003,757	1,220,552	1,000,188

well as in virtually all inland waterways, has likewise received attention. In particular, concern over the steadily dwindling numbers of river fish has prompted the government to turn some 150 square miles of swamp near Paknampoh into a lake (Bung Borophet) which is now being used as a vast spawning ground, and with the co-operation of W.H.O. and M.S.A. experts, fish-breeding stations have been set up in several parts of the country.[66]

Table 67 shows the principal industries recorded in 1949–50 and although various new factories have been established since that date, rice milling still retains its pre-eminent place on the list. However, by no means all the industries included in the table are modern factory enterprises, and in 1941 only 72 of the rice mills had a capacity of over 100 tons of paddy per day. Nearly all these larger mills, which are mostly steam operated and burn rice husks as fuel, are in the vicinity of Bangkok and are Chinese owned, though the Thai Rice Company operates a dozen or so of the largest of them in an attempt to break the Chinese monopoly.[67] Perhaps more important in this respect, however, has been the growth as in Burma of small country mills in the rice-growing districts, and there are now over 800 such units with an average daily capacity of 30–40 tons. More recently still, the use of small portable mills which handle 8–12 tons a day has become very widespread, and it was estimated that 4,000 of these were in operation in 1952.[68]

Sawmills also show a similar division. The 300 or so powered units, many

[66] De Young, pp. 197–8. Spectacular success has been achieved with *tilapia*. See Calder, pp. 83–4.

[67] See above, p. 503. [68] Ingram, p. 70.

TABLE 66

THAILAND: OVERSEAS TRADE BY COMMODITIES

Figures in million Baht

Imports	1956	1959
Textile yarn and fabrics	1,566	1,455
Iron and steel manufactures	922	1,037
Petroleum products	770	850
Chemicals	654	918
Motor vehicles	408	490
Electrical machinery and apparatus	353	393
Milk products	240	316
Paper and board	169	228
Rubber manufactures	160	182
Instruments and photographic supplies	118	104
Railway vehicles	70	39
Agricultural machinery (including tractors)	65	92
Total (including others)	7,562	8,837

Exports	1956	1959
Rice	2,861	2,591
Crude rubber	1,526	2,336
Tin ore and concentrates	507	434
Timber	384	299
Oil seeds and nuts	196	176
Livestock	77	100
Fish	84	11
Skins and hides	49	71
Eggs	57	44
Total (including others)	6,717	7,273

Source: *Yearbook of International Trade Statistics.*

of them in or near Bangkok, have a total annual output of 700,000 cubic metres, but no figures are available for the numerous smaller hand-operated establishments. Meanwhile the number of government-owned sugar factories has risen to six, though four of these are very small, and the same is true of all the 14 State distilleries except the one at Bang-yi-khan. The two cigarette factories in Bangkok each employ over 1,000 workers.

As table 67 shows, weaving, pottery manufacture and metalwork are all of some importance, but the numbers employed even in these branches are very small relative to the total population. Nevertheless, the proportion of persons in industry is growing, and recent developments include the setting up of a new cement factory at Taklee in connexion with the Yan Hee project, and the opening in 1952 of a state-owned gunny-bag factory relying mainly on local kenaf. At the same time the Thai Cement Company began to work the hæmatite ores in the vicinity of Saraburi and the intention is to produce both pig iron and structural steel, the latter to the tune of about 30,000 tons a year.

In 1953 a five-year industrial development plan was approved for the setting up of 32 more government-operated plants. Besides an ammonium sulphate plant which was completed in 1955, these include an edible-oil extractor and leather, weaving, rope, sugar and more gunny-bag factories. Meanwhile, various private concerns, mostly Chinese owned, have set up new factories, mainly in Bangkok, for the manufacture of such cheap consumer goods as mineral waters, soap and clothing, and in Haadyai and elsewhere in the south for the manufacture of rubber footwear. Largely as a result of the 1953 plan, the total number of factories with over five employees rose from some 1,750 in 1950 to 13,388 in 1959, and whereas all of those in existence in 1950 were in Bangkok – Thonburi, nearly half of the total in 1959 were in other towns.[69]

Although under the new National Economic Development Plan of 1961–6 it is proposed to raise the contribution of industry from 10 per cent to 12 per cent of the national income, Thailand, unlike many of its neighbours, appears to show little alarm at the prospect of remaining dependent on the export of primary produce.[70] In part this is because in Thailand factory industry has been pre-eminently the concern of the Chinese rather than of Europeans. Thus, whereas in other parts of South-east Asia national self-respect demands that the indigenes should now take over and add to the formerly European-run establishments, the Thais seem more concerned with the long-familiar problem of curbing Chinese economic power within the country, and the Thai population displays relatively little inclination to desert agriculture for urban employment.

In these circumstances, therefore, there is much to be said for building up and extending the range of rural handicraft industries which, for a comparatively

[69] The following were the total outputs of certain manufactured goods in 1959: cement 566,000 tons, sugar 80,000 tons, paper 2,600 tons, tobacco 8,400 tons, gunny bags 4, 952,000. See Bunchana, p. 5.

[70] However, this attitude is now beginning to change, and foreign investment is now encouraged.

TABLE 67

THAILAND: MANUFACTURING AND PROCESSING INDUSTRIES

Type	No. of establishments		No. of workers
	1949	1950	1949
Rice mills	908	925	12,837
Flour mills	553	580	2,592
Saw-mills	506	521	7,479
Liquor	76	76	4,456
Beer	1	1	136
Pottery	1,064	1,064	3,666
Metalwork	717	729	3,122
Cigarettes etc.	2	2	2,669
Machine shops	412	403	2,590
Salted goods	447	447	2,427
Vermicelli and noodles	142	147	1,860
Smithies	438	440	1,736
Printing	116	118	1,450
Medicines	119	119	1,255
Cement and cement goods	176	177	1,249
Matches	4	4	1,167
Furniture	308	325	898
Paper	2	2	760
Ice	70	80	734
Rubber goods	62	65	655
Oil extraction	47	48	436
Soap	5	5	433
Tannery	73	73	432
Aerated water	63	67	419
Glass	17	17	350
Dyeing	17	17	167
Water supply	14	14	153
Bus and truck maintenance	5	5	39
Ship repair and building	34	33	1,090

Source: *Statistical Year Book of Thailand.*

small outlay of scarce capital, can materially improve the living standards of the country by simultaneously mopping up seasonal unemployment and providing various types of consumer goods in regular demand.

Whatever the relative importance of factory and domestic industry in the years ahead, however, progress in both will depend largely on improvements in power supplies and transport facilities. Hitherto, in the absence of any known coal deposits, wood and imported oil have been the principal fuels consumed in factories, thermal electric plants and on the railways. Both of these suffer from serious drawbacks, the former on account of the depletion of valuable timber reserves and the accelerated soil erosion which have followed from too rapid cutting, and the latter because of the drain of some £2 million per annum which it imposes on limited reserves of foreign exchange. Thus, since 1955 an attempt has been made to exploit the lignite deposits at Mae Moh near Lampang, and production there is expected shortly to reach 200,000 tons a year.

More important than this, however, are the plans for developing hydro-electric power in various parts of the country. Although it was originally proposed to generate 24,000 kW of electricity as a by-product of the Chainad scheme this idea has since been abandoned and the main power project now under construction is at Yan Hee on the Me Ping some 260 miles north-west of Bangkok. When the first stage, involving the building of a dam 505 ft. high and 1,510 ft. long, is completed in 1963 at an estimated cost of $68 million, the new power station will have a capacity of 140,000 kW but this will subsequently be quadrupled.[71] By this means it is hoped to meet the chief needs of Bangkok as well as to make electric power available to wide areas of the countryside in the northern and central provinces.[72]

Whereas fuel and power projects have accounted for only about 3 per cent of budgetary expenditure in recent years, as against 2 per cent on government-owned industry and 11 per cent on irrigation, transport, with 40 per cent has been by far the largest item of all. While on economic grounds alone the need for improved transport is indisputable, the degree of emphasis on this sector is clearly related to Thailand's strategic rôle in S.E.A.T.O. and the need to strengthen still further the government's control over outlying regions.

In the first place the authorities have attempted to close the gap at the centre of the road pattern, and to build up a system of trunk highways radiating from the capital to all the main provincial towns. Though work began on this national highway project during the 1930s, little was in fact achieved before the Japanese

[71] This may be compared with the total installed capacity of 157,434 kW in all Thailand in 1960, and is greater than that of the proposed Lawpita station in Burma. The Thailand government obtained a loan of $66 million from the World Bank in 1957 for construction of the first part of the project, which is expected to be completed by 1963. The quadrupling of capacity is expected to be achieved by 1975. The consumption of electricity in the Bangkok Electricity Works area in 1952 was 63,193,131 kWh, which represented approximately 93 per cent of the country's total consumption. A thermal electric power station is also being built at Nondaburi, with a capacity of 75,000 kW, to meet the growing demand for power in the Bangkok/Thonburi area, between 1961 and the completion of the Yan Hee project.

[72] Besides providing power the project will also irrigate 2 million acres and help in flood control and navigation.

occupation, and even in 1950 the total length of first- and second-class roads outside Bangkok was only 232 and 3,597 miles respectively, and no direct connexion existed between the capital and either Songkhla or Chiengmai, the second and third largest towns in the country. But in 1952 the government embarked on a four-year plan to build 1,280 miles of trunk highways, and though this was not achieved within the stated time a second plan was initiated to extend the system still further (see Fig. 71). As yet the number of motor vehicles in Thailand remains minute by Western standards, but the total has nevertheless risen from 17,000 in 1951 to 63,700 in 1957 and the rapid growth of country bus services is effecting an immense widening of the peasants' horizons in all parts of the land.

Notable progress has also been made in air transport and in 1952 the aircraft of the government-owned Thai Airways Company flew a total of 1,562,000 miles and carried 37,615 passengers and 719·7 tons of freight. Since then its activities have been considerably expanded, and in 1959 it cooperated with Scandinavian Airlines System in forming the new Thai Airways International for the operation of overseas services. Meanwhile the civil airport at Dom Muang, north of Bangkok has been extended and is now the most important air focus in the whole of South-east Asia. For, unlike the steamship, the aeroplane does not need to make the long détour via the Straits of Malacca and even by 1953 Bangkok recorded 42 international departures per week, compared with only 27 from Singapore.[73]

So far as railway transport is concerned the chief task of recent years has been to repair the extensive damage to bridges, track and workshops sustained during the war, and to replace old and dilapidated locomotives and rolling stock. This has now been virtually completed, with the help of two loans from the World Bank, and the volume of passenger traffic is today approximately seven times that of pre-war days.

In 1945 the Thai government took over the section of the wartime Thailand–Burma Railway between Ban Pong and the frontier at the Three Pagodas Pass, but this proved to be too shoddily constructed for normal peacetime use and, like the other Japanese-built line across the Kra peninsula from Chumphon to Khao Huagang,[74] has since been closed down. On the other hand, improvements have been made in the rail connexions with Thailand's neighbours to the east and north-east. Thus through-running with the Cambodian railway system began in 1954, and the line to Udon has been prolonged to Nong Khai on the north bank of the Mekong almost opposite Vientiane.

As a result of these developments a substantial part of the overseas trade of both Laos and Cambodia began to go via Bangkok instead of the Vietnamese ports and this change was helped by the improvements to the port facilities at Bangkok which were begun in 1953.[74] Before that date the bar at the mouth of the Menam prevented ships of over 4,000 tons from entering the river and the

[73] See Ginsburg (A), p. 462.

[74] But see below, p. 523, note 91.

normal practice was to discharge or take on cargo at the island of Koh Sichang, 19 miles south-east of the bar. But with the dredging of a channel through this obstacle, vessels of up to 10,000 tons can now proceed direct to Bangkok itself, thus saving a journey of several hours by lighter and effecting an annual economy estimated at nearly £2 million in handling costs.[75]

VI. URBAN AND POLITICAL GEOGRAPHY

To the political geographer Thailand is of exceptional interest in that it represents a survival of the traditional riverine state pattern which has not been fundamentally remodelled by a European colonial power. Admittedly several of its peripheral – and ethnically non-Thai – territories were lopped off in the course of the colonial scramble, and the core area of the central plain was meanwhile transformed economically and socially by intrusive forces, both Chinese and European. Nevertheless, the state preserves much more of its indigenous character than do any of the other major South-east Asian countries.[76]

This is evident in the high degree of local self-sufficiency in all the outlying regions and also in the manner in which the railway and more recently the road systems tend to repeat the old pattern of the waterways,[77] so that all the main routes continue to focus on the Menam delta as they have done ever since Ayuthia was founded in 1350. Moreover, notwithstanding the survival of many former capitals, such as Sukothai, Lopburi, Supanburi, Pitsanulok, Ayuthia and in a sense also Chiengmai and Nakorn Pathom,[78] the present capital, Bangkok, enjoys a degree of ascendancy over all the other towns within the country which is unparalleled elsewhere in South-east Asia today, but appears to have been characteristic of the region in earlier times when state capitals fulfilled mythological and religious as well as economic and administrative functions.

While, in common with all the other main port cities of South-east Asia, Bangkok is nowadays expanding rapidly, its pre-eminence within the country is not a matter of recent growth, and as long ago as 1884 Leon de Rosny estimated its population at 404,000.[79] Furthermore, Bangkok's rôle as a port has been largely an accident of history, for the city was originally built in 1782 to succeed Ayuthia[80] as the national capital of an essentially self-contained non-maritime kingdom. In this connexion the main advantage of its position, apart from proximity to the former capital, was the natural protection against further

[75] In 1952 1,074 ships totalling 2,067,357 tons, were recorded as outbound from the port of Bangkok. Plans are afoot to build a new harbour at Songkhla.

[76] Laos and Cambodia are similar in this respect, but scarcely rank as major countries.

[77] Largely because the rivers offered much less scope than those of Burma for the development of modern shipping services.

[78] All these were almost certainly more populous at the time when they were capitals than they are today. For further details on towns, see Credner, Chapter 7.

[79] Quoted in Purcell (D), p. 107.

[80] After the Burmese sack of Ayuthia in 1767 Thonburi, opposite the present Bangkok, was capital from 1768 to 1782. During the Second World War Pibul proposed to shift the capital to Lopburi.

TABLE 68

THAILAND: POPULATION OF MAIN TOWNS, 1947

Bangkok-Thonburi		1,178,881 (1,328,228 1956)
Songkhla	(S.)	40,602
Chiengmai	(N.)	38,111 (95,665 1959)
Nakhorn ratsima	(E.)	34,212
Ubonrat-thani	(E.)	32,779
Nakhornsrithamrat	(S.)	31,644
Cholburi	(S.E.)	26,815
Samutsakhorn	(C.)	25,925
Ayuthia	(C.)	25,272

Sources: *Statistical Year Book of Thailand*, etc.

Burmese attacks afforded by a great loop in the Menam which surrounds it to the north, west and south, and was accounted sufficiently important to offset the obvious drawbacks of an exceedingly swampy terrain.

With the cutting of the Klong Ong Ang,[81] the original royal city, which still contains the Grand Palace, some of the finest *wats* (temples) and several ministries and other public buildings, became effectively an island, and throughout the first hundred years of its existence Bangkok had virtually no roads, depending instead on the network of waterways provided by its innumerable creeks and *klongs*.

Even before the royal city was built, with the help of more than 10,000 Cambodian prisoners of war, Chinese traders already occupied part of its site, and during the 19th century a large Chinese quarter grew up at Sampeng, immediately to the south-east of Klong Ong Ang. From that time onwards Chinese have formed the largest ethnic group within the city, and their present proportion (some 60 per cent) of its population gives too modest an impression of their economic importance within the capital.

The transformation of Bangkok into a modern city was a natural consequence of the opening of the country to foreign trade after 1855, though that is not to minimize the constructive efforts of both Chulalongkorn and Vajiravuhd.[82] Nevertheless, it was not until almost the end of the 19th century that a modern network of roads began to be built, largely along the lines of former *klongs* which were filled in for the purpose, and a new business district grew up in the Bangrak area behind the main waterfront south-east of the old centre. Subsequent expansion has taken place to both north and east, the new administrative quarter of Samsen-Dusit in the former being laid out in spacious fashion as a planned city, while the area east of Sampeng became the favourite residential quarter of the Europeans[83] and also housed universities and hospitals.

[81] Klong = canal. For further details on Bangkok, see also Fryer (A), Ginsburg (A) and Stamp (D).

[82] Also known as Rama VI.

[83] Bangkok had some 1,300 European residents in 1935. Credner, p. 379.

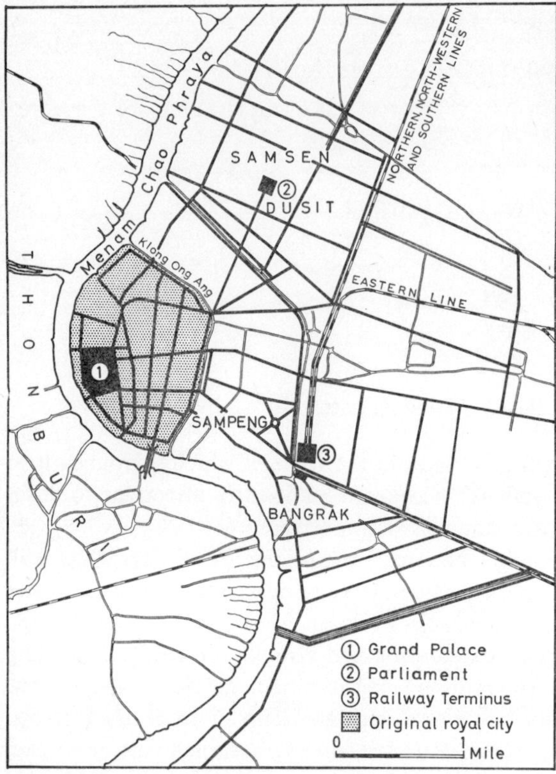

FIG. 73—Bangkok

In contrast to these northern and eastern districts, with their wide tree-lined boulevards and a variety of Victorian-Oriental and more modern architecture, the area west of the Menam has remained truly Siamese, with its network of creeks, its thousands of house-boats and its celebrated 'floating market', and in other parts of the city also innumerable clusters of indigenous atap-thatched pile dwellings are hidden away behind the more recent façade.

Yet though these contrasts between old and new and between alien and indigenous are undeniable, Bangkok has achieved a measure of cultural synthesis which is without parallel in any other big South-east Asian city, and it is this which gives it its unique charm, even if it does occasionally, as in the summer of 1958, entail the hazard of a serious cholera epidemic.

Likewise, in contrast to most of its neighbours, Thailand with its long historical continuity is not a state in search of a *raison d'être*. Apart from the 700,000 Muslim Malays and half-caste Sam-Sams who form the bulk of the population in and around Patani, a smaller number of Cambodians who overlap the eastern frontier along the foothills of the Dangrek Range, and a few scattered hill peoples in the north and west,[84] the indigenous population of Thailand is ethnically homogeneous, and possesses a more than rudimentary national conscious-

[84] The hill tribes of the North and North-west include the Miao, Lahu, Yao, Lisu, Lawa and Lolo, who are related to similar groups in the adjacent uplands beyond the frontiers of Thailand, as also are the Karens of the western hills. Most of these peoples practise non-irrigated forms of cultivation and their settlements are well above the valley floors inhabited by the Thais. Many of the Miaos are engaged in opium cultivation and there is a considerable smuggling trade in this commodity. The total number of hill peoples is *c.* 300,000.

ness, reinforced by loyalty to the ruling house and devotion to Theravada Buddhism which is the State religion.

Admittedly, the inhabitants of the north and especially the north-east have often been thought of as Lao rather than Thai, and for long periods in their history both groups have had closer links with other upland branches of the Thai family than with the plainsmen of the Menam valley. But though in the past this was reflected in significant differences in spoken dialect, these have been considerably reduced in recent decades, as a result of improved communications and the spread of popular state education[85] which adopts the central Thai speech as the standard throughout the country.

However, while the Thais are thus no longer troubled by any important cultural differences among themselves, they still have to contend with the grave problems presented by the large Chinese minority now numbering *c.* 3 million, whose distribution and economic importance have already been considered on pp. 502–3.[86] It was primarily in reaction to the growing solidarity of this minority community that Siamese nationalism developed as an active political force in the inter-war years. And while many of the resultant measures which were taken against the Chinese were understandable enough, as for example, attempts to restrict immigration, insistence on the *jus soli* instead of the *jus sanguinis*, and the prohibition of school teaching in any language other than Thai,[87] the extension of the assimilationist policy to the Malay areas of the south, though perhaps logical, certainly smacked of chauvinism.

Moreover, this soon took other forms. By no means all branches of the Thai family are contained within the Thai state, the main exceptions being the 6–7 million Thais in Yunnan, 1½ million Shans in Burma, and 1½ million Lao peoples in Laos. Since all these were under alien rule, whether Chinese, British or French, Pibul was able to enlist considerable sentimental support for the Pan Thai movement which implicitly aimed at extending the boundaries of Thailand at the expense of neighbouring countries. Further, like so many other *Pan-Ideen*, the greater Thailand movement was not conspicuous for its consistency of principle. Thus, where the ethnic argument broke down, historic claims were advanced instead, and, so far from admitting that the former logically implied renunciation both of Patani and of a small strip along the eastern frontier, Thailand claimed the right to rule over parts of Malaya and Cambodia on the basis of its former rights of suzerainty.

During the Second World War the Japanese pandered to these ambitions by negotiating the transfer of certain Cambodian frontier territories in 1940 and

[85] De Young, p. 7. The 1947 Census returned 41 per cent of the total population as literate.

[86] See also below, pp. 525–6. There are also some 50,000 Indians, mainly engaged in the clothing trade in Bangkok, but they present no problem.

[87] Other measures included restricting certain occupations to Thai nationals and limiting the proportion of aliens who might be employed in factories and other enterprises. See Coughlin, pp. 378–9.

later handing over the Shan States of Möng Pan and Kengtung and the Malay States of Kelantan, Trengganu, Kedah and Perlis to Thai rule[88] (Fig. 74). However, the Thai government restored the former British colonial possessions in 1945, and though popular feeling in favour of retaining the Cambodian territories was strong these also were retroceded to the French in November.

With the return to power of Pibul in 1948 the question arose whether the pre-war Pan Thai movement would be revived, especially as the new regime quickly intensified the assimilationist policy at home. Thus the economic and political activities of the Chinese were further restricted and immigration brought almost to a standstill, the numbers of new arrivals dropping from 67,862 in 1947 to 1,815 in 1950. The Malays of southern Thailand likewise experienced a renewal of assimilationist pressure at this time, and when serious unrest broke out in Naradhivas province in 1948[89] it evoked sympathetic comment from fellow-Malays south of the border. While, however, there is continuing evidence that the Patani Malays wish to preserve their own language and religion, it is less clear whether this community as a whole aspires merely to a greater measure of autonomy within the Thai state or whether it would prefer some form of closer association with the Federation of Malaya or even with the Republic of Indonesia. Following the outbreak of the terrorist movement in Malaya in 1948, British concern to obtain the co-operation of the Thai government in controlling traffic across the frontier took precedence over any interest which might otherwise have been shown in the fate of Patani, and events in Indonesia in the meantime did little to encourage an alignment in that direction. But with the achievement of independence in Malaya in 1957 a new situation has been created, and it remains to be seen whether the question will ever be raised again.

Much greater interest attaches to the Thai attitude to their own kinsmen beyond the border. Here the situation has changed in two ways since 1945, by virtue first of the ending of colonial rule in Burma and Indochina and the breaking up of the latter into its constituent national units, and secondly, of Communist China's minority policy which aims at using the non-Han peoples within its territories to spread Communist influence further afield. Thus, with the establishment in 1953 of the Thai Autonomous People's Government at Cheli in Yunnan, Bangkok was faced with a new rival for the allegiance of the Thai minorities in neighbouring lands. But at the same time Thailand, although it has no direct frontier with China, has inevitably shared in the apprehension which other South-east Asian governments feel at the growing power of their great neighbour to the north, and in Thailand's case this has been intensified by the exceptional strength of its own Chinese community.

Under the Pibul regime from 1950 to 1957 this situation led to a departure from Thailand's traditional foreign policy in the form of open alignment with the Western powers, particularly the U.S.A., and a consequent non-recognition

[88] See above, p. 468.

[89] See Thompson and Adloff, pp. 158–65, and Whittingham-Jones, pp. 4 and 5.

of Communist China. Meanwhile in 1953 Thailand suggested the setting up of a 'Buddhist bloc' including, besides itself, both Laos and Cambodia and perhaps also Burma, to stand together against the further advances of Chinese Communist power.

While this proposal understandably revived memories of the old Pan Thai chauvinism, it nevertheless has strong arguments in its favour. So far as Laos is concerned, ethnic, linguistic and religious links can all be invoked, and the traditional Laotian fear of Vietnamese dominance, which has again come to the fore with the withdrawal of French power, provides an added inducement to closer association with Thailand. Thus the completion of the railway link from Bangkok to the south bank of the Mekong in 1953 was particularly welcome to Laos whose other outlets to the sea had hitherto been through Vietnamese territory. Apart from the linguistic difference and the long-standing territorial dispute already described, much the same arguments may also be cited in favour of co-operation between Cambodia and Thailand, which likewise found expression with the initiation of through railway services in 1954. So far as relations with Burma are concerned, historic antipathies are more deeply rooted, but nevertheless the immediate crisis arising from Thailand's alleged connivance at the presence of K.M.T. troops in the Shan plateau was amicably resolved in 1954, and shortly afterwards Thailand proposed that the Japanese-built railway between Ban Pong and Thanbyuzayat should be re-opened in order to strengthen the links between the two countries.

More serious than the physical obstacles to such a course, however, has been the fact that, whereas Thailand has aligned itself with the West, and indeed became a founder-member of S.E.A.T.O. in September 1954,[90] Burma has sought a solution to the same basic problem in neutralism. And in recent years similar complications have also begun to affect Thailand's relations with Laos and still more so with Cambodia. Indeed, as Cambodian attachment to neutralism has strengthened since 1956, the historic suspicions between it and Thailand have reasserted themselves and relations deteriorated in 1958 because of a disputed claim to the ancient Khmer temple of Préah Vihéar,[91] which lies close to the frontier, and also because of Cambodia's recognition of Communist China.

The internal problems of Laos and Cambodia are considered in Chapter 16, but it is pertinent here to examine the nature of the threat with which Thailand believes itself to be confronted along its northern borders. Notwithstanding Peking's broadcasts recommending the setting up of a 'People's Republic of Ayuthia' to embrace Siam, Shan State, Laos and Yunnan,[92] China's immediate aims here are likely to be limited at most to the fostering of a series of lesser People's Governments wherever local conditions are propitious, though

[90] See below, p. 556.

[91] This dispute, which for a time led to the closing of the frontier between Thailand and Cambodia, was settled in Cambodia's favour by a judgement of the International Court at the Hague in June 1962. [92] Runciman, p. 9.

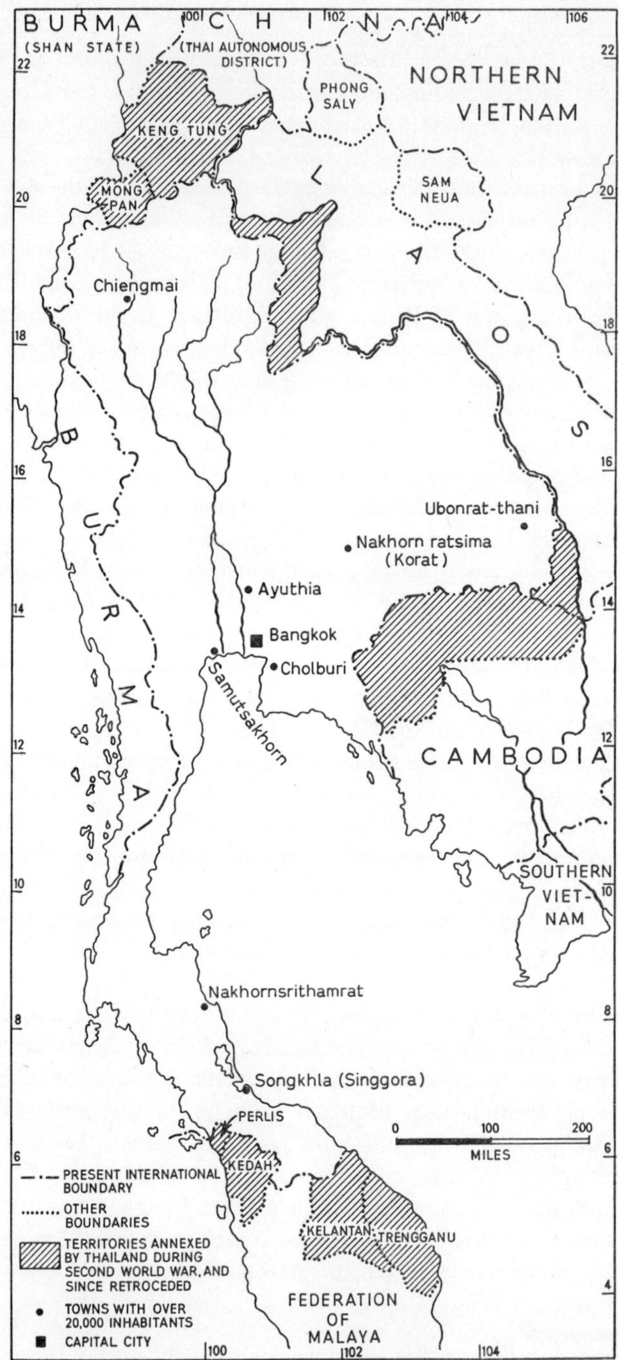

FIG. 74—Thailand: political

that would not rule out the long-term possibility of a greater Thai federation under Chinese patronage. Be that as it may, the Lao Issarak movement, which after the late 1940s represented one potential component in this pattern, expressly aimed not only at taking over the government of Laos, but also at uniting north-east Thailand with the latter and thus, by implication, reviving the geographical pattern of the old kingdom of Lan Chang.[93]

Whether, in view of the recent progress in education and communications already described, the inhabitants of North-eastern Thailand would any longer be susceptible to such overtures, apart from the few dissidents who were involved in the separatist rising at Ubon in 1949, it is difficult to say, though there is no denying the closeness of everyday contacts between the peoples on opposite sides of the Mekong. But undoubtedly, if Laos were to fall within the Communist orbit of Peking, or more probably of Hanoi, north-east Thailand would become a danger spot, and its weakness would be aggravated by the real poverty of the region.

Thus, while it is probably true that there is little really serious discontent in the North-east[94] – and for this the absence of land hunger and of foreign commercial enterprise is largely responsible – the Thai government has recently been at pains to forestall such dangers by devoting much more attention than heretofore to the social and economic betterment of this little-known region.

In this connexion perhaps the most promising step has been the decision to extend the activities of the Community Development Administration into this depressed part of the country, where it will certainly find ample scope for improving such basic rural amenities as wells, irrigation tanks, roads and domestic industries.[95] In contrast to the first important rural development scheme in Thailand, namely that started at Senatburi in the northern part of the Menam delta under Pibul's wartime administration, and later resumed after his return to power in the 1950s,[96] the emphasis in the new Community Development Administration, which began in 1958 under the Sarit regime, is on the village rather than on the individual. In this respect the inspiration behind the new system would seem to have much in common with that of the nationalist revival of mutual-aid traditions in many other parts of rural South-east Asia, a trend which may perhaps prove to be of deeper significance than is at present apparent.

From a purely economic point of view the period 1947 to 1957 was one of considerable progress in Thailand, but the same can hardly be said of the country's political evolution, and the various constitutional changes which occurred represented no consistent advance towards true democracy. After Pibul's fall

[93] For details of the later development of the Lao Issarak movement see below, Chapter 16. See also Thompson and Adloff, Chapter 4.

[94] See Madge, p. 9.

[95] See Tinker (D), pp. 316–7.

[96] This scheme was originally started in connexion with his plan to shift the capital to Lopburi (see above, p. 518, note 80). All-told about one million acres have been earmarked for settlement, with individual lots of the order of 10 acres each. Tinker (D), p. 316.

from power in 1957 his successor, Marshal Sarit, dissolved the National Assembly and later set up a new Constituent Assembly, three-quarters of whose members were drawn from the armed forces, to draft a new constitution.

Like his predecessor, Sarit maintained a strongly anti-Communist line, affirming the continued loyalty of Thailand to S.E.A.T.O., supporting the country's association with the Federation of Malaya and the Philippines in A.S.A.,[97] and even resuscitating the idea of the Kra canal,[98] as a means of strengthening the links between the mainland countries of South-east Asia in the event of Singapore's falling under a neutralist or Communist regime. Furthermore, the policy in force since 1950 of refusing to sell rice or rubber to Communist China has been maintained, despite the fact that with the ending of the seller's market for rice the offers of the Soviet-bloc countries become ever more attractive,[99] and the new government has also imposed drastic restrictions on Chinese business-men and commercial organizations with the result that Chinese capital has been finding its way to Hong Kong and Singapore, instead of being invested in Thailand.[100]

To what extent these policies enjoy the support of the Thai people it is impossible to say, in the absence of any popularly-elected assembly, and in view of the general lack of interest in politics shown by the apparently well-contented peasantry who form the great mass of the population. Nevertheless it seems that increasing political sophistication in the towns, and above all in Bangkok, was the basic cause of the 1957 coup, and sooner or later this may express itsef in more far-reaching constitutional changes than any which have yet taken place.

In the opening paragraphs of this chapter mention was made of the significance of Thailand as a test case of South-east Asian development under indigenous rule, but in the final analysis the measure of the success which it has achieved during the past one hundred years still remains in doubt. For whereas Japan succeeded in keeping the West at bay by positive means, Thailand's method of resisting Western rule by bowing with the breeze has been essentially negative in character, and the price that has been paid is the virtual stranglehold over the country's economy exerted by the second-largest Chinese minority in the whole of South-east Asia.

This fact, which is rendered the more ominous by the geographical proximity of China itself, undoubtedly poses the supreme problem facing Thailand today. Yet nowhere else in South-east Asia is the Chinese question so thoroughly

[97] I.e. the Association of South-east Asian States, see below, p. 659.

[98] The Anglo-Siamese peace treaty of 1946 continued the ban on the cutting of such a canal, though whether the United Kingdom would be prepared to reconsider this matter remains to be seen. The possibility of developing Chumphon as a major port in the vicinity has also been suggested. In October 1964 the Kra canal plan was abandoned.

[99] Cf. the problem in Burma. See above, p. 455. However, the great increase in rubber exports (p. 507) which go mainly to the U.S.A., means that Thailand is making itself less vulnerable than Burma in this respect.

[100] Cf. developments in Indonesia. See above, p. 344, note 74.

obfuscated by lack of precise data. For while, since Thailand follows the *jus soli*, only the 476,588 persons born in China and not subsequently naturalized were returned as Chinese in the 1947 census, the extent of Chinese admixture in the Thai population lends credence to the current semi-official estimates which put the ethnic Chinese total at approximately 3 million.

Somewhere between these two extremes lies the operative number of those who consciously regard themselves as Chinese. Despite the fact that the anti-Chinese measures of post-war years[101] have certainly not been restricted in their application to the smaller total, the Chinese commercial community is still intact, and in addition many persons of at least partial Chinese ancestry occupy influential positions in other walks of national life. Indeed it would appear that, in the absence of European control as well as of religious barriers, a substantial proportion of the established Chinese community in Thailand has become much more closely identified with the indigenous majority people than has happened anywhere else in South-east Asia. Precisely how extensive this identification is, and whether it is strong enough to withstand all the pressures to which it may be subjected in the years ahead, only time will show.

Meanwhile it remains to add that, particularly since General Thanom became Prime Minister following the death of Marshal Sarit in December 1963, Thailand, helped by its modest prosperity and its freedom from anti-colonialist obsessions, has endeavoured to play a positive role as a much needed stabilizing force in the centre of the South-east Asian mainland. Notwithstanding its unresolved difficulties with Cambodia, its friendly relations with both Burma and Malaysia are evidence that neither political nor cultural differences, deep though they may be, need prove insuperable obstacles to mutual co-operation even in this critical corner of Asia.

SELECT BIBLIOGRAPHY

Andrews
Ball
Bunchana
Coughlin
Credner
Crosby (A) (B)
De Young
Dobby (H)
Fisher (A) (R) (S)
Fryer (A)
Graham
Hallett
Ingram
Landon (A) (B)
McCarthy
Madge
Pendleton (A) (B)
Peterson (A)
Purcell (D)
Rawson
Reeve
Runciman (A)
Skinner
Stamp (D)
Thompson, V. (C)
Tinker (D)
Thompson and Adloff
Ungphakorn (B)
Vandenbosch and Butwell
Whittingham-Jones
Zelinsky
Zimmerman (A) (B)
Zinkin (A)

Thai news

International Bank for Reconstruction and Development: *A public development program for Thailand.*

[101] See Coughlin, pp. 378–89.

Hamburger Kreditbank, *Wirtschaftlicher Lagebericht Thailands*, 1954
Miller, D. McIver, 'Communications and transport in Siam, 1918' (MS. in the Library of the Royal Geographical Society)
Siam – General and medical features
Siam – nature and industry
Statistical Year Book of Thailand
Thailand, Review of commercial conditions
Weekly Overseas Mail, Special supplement on Thailand, September 15, 1951
Colombo Plan Reports
Economic Surveys of Asia and the Far East

Credner's magnificent survey of 1936 is still the standard work on the geography of Thailand; much useful geographical material is also contained in the articles by Stamp and Pendleton. Section II of this chapter owes much to Miller's account of pre-1918 transport, and especially to Ingram's excellent study of modernization. The latter has also been extensively used along with De Young's attractive account of contemporary village life, and the earlier works by Andrews, Credner and Zimmerman, and *Siam – nature and industry*, in Sections III–V. The works by Landon and Crosby are illuminating sources of information on social and political matters. The I.B.R.D. study is likely to remain a useful work of reference for many years.

Addenda: Note the paper by Ayal, and the important new study *Thailand, aspects of landscape and life*, by Pendleton *et. al.*

CHAPTER 16

The States of Indochina

I. LAND AND PEOPLE

Alone among the former colonial territories of South-east Asia, French Indochina has ceased to cohere as a single political unit since gaining independence. Thus the term Indochina has become a mere geographical expression covering four entirely separate states, namely Northern Vietnam (59,938 square miles and 15,000,000 inhabitants), Southern Vietnam (65,951 square miles, 12,800,000 inhabitants), Cambodia (66,610 square miles, 4,740,000 inhabitants) and Laos (91,425 square miles, 1,690,000 inhabitants).

This process of disintegration is not altogether surprising when it is recalled that Indochina had at no time formed a political unit before the establishment of European rule. And if the same may also be said of Indonesia – except for the brief and very uncertain unity under Madjapahit – Indochina is undoubtedly the more deeply divided, straddling as it does the fundamental cultural boundary in all South-east Asia, namely that which lies between the predominantly Indianized lands including Cambodia and Laos to the west, and the even more profoundly Sinicized Annamite domains to the east.

These major cultural and historic units correspond fairly closely to the physical divisions of the territory. Broadly speaking, Indochina comprises three longitudinal zones, namely the eastern coastal plains, including the deltas of the Song-koi and Mekong, together with the diminutive but intrinsically similar pockets of lowland along the Annamite coast between; the western alluvial lowlands, along the Mekong and around Tonlé Sap in Cambodia; and the intervening uplands, stemming from the Yunnan plateau in the north and extending south almost to the Mekong delta.

From a purely topographical point of view the Mekong delta might seem to provide the key to control of the whole area, since it is here that the two strips of lowland merge into one. But in fact the natural difficulty of communications along either of these routes, arising from the numerous falls and rapids of the Mekong, and the rough seas of the typhoon season in late summer and the NE monsoon in winter along the exposed Annamite coast, made this a matter of small significance in the days of water-borne transport. Moreover, although the Mekong delta did acquire early pre-eminence under Funan, it was the lowlands around Tonlé Sap which later benefited from the advance down the Mekong valley of new migrants from the north, and after the 6th century A.D. the centre of gravity

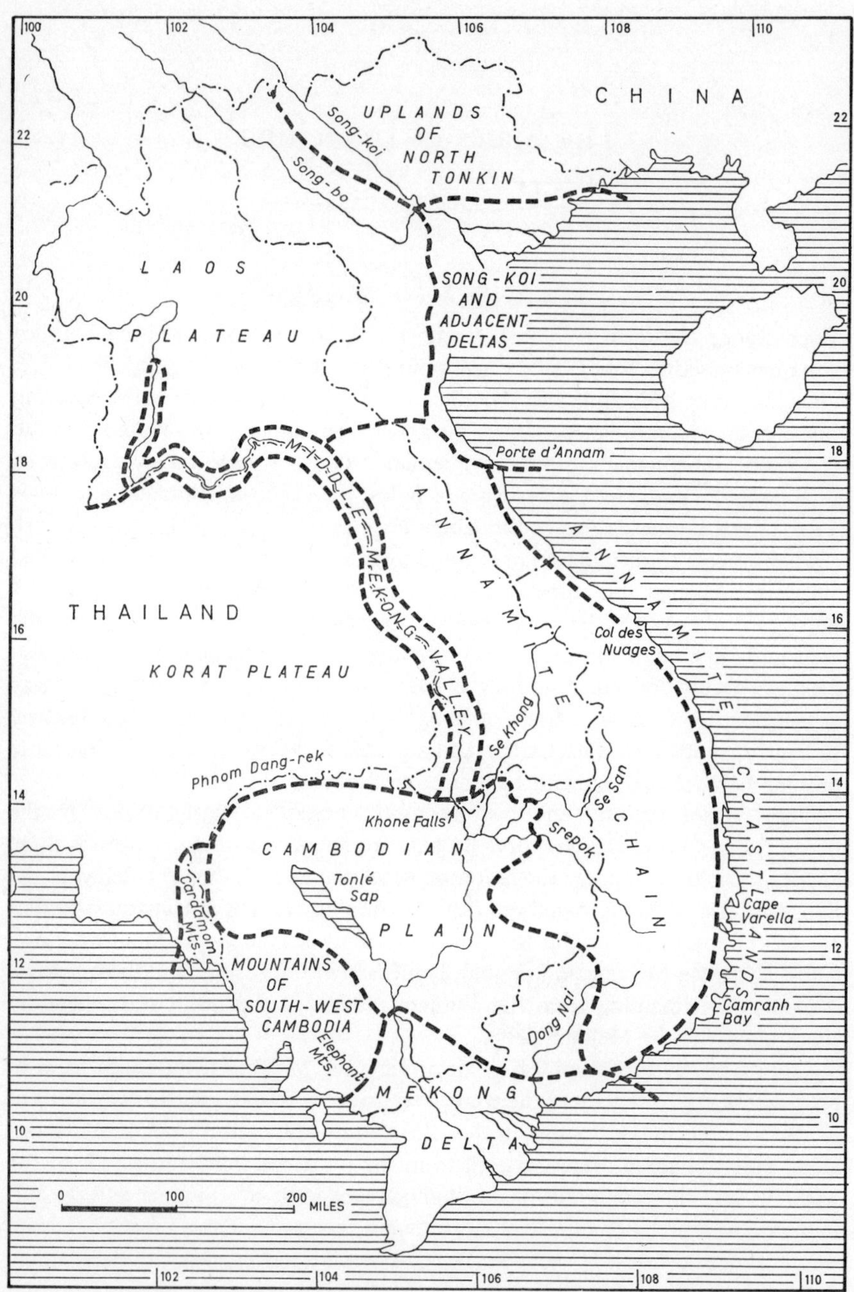

FIG. 75—Indochina: natural regions

shifted from the delta to the Cambodian basin, which remained one of the two great cultural foci of the Indochinese lands until comparatively recent times.

The other main nucleus was the Song-koi delta of the north which, together with the narrowing strip of coastal lowland stretching southwards to the Porte d'Annam, formed the original core of the Annamite empire. Thanks to the physical similarity of this region with what is now Kwangtung province, and the closeness of the early contacts between the two during the period 111 B.C. to A.D. 939 when both formed part of Imperial China, the northern Annamite lands gradually acquired the character of a demographic extension of southern China rather than a typical part of South-east Asia.[1]

For during this long period of forced assimilation Chinese settlers and officials introduced not only their traditional systems of political administration, law, religion and art, but also, and more fundamentally the material basis on which this 'hydraulic civilization', to use Wittfogel's phrase, had been developed in China itself.[2] This included elaborate methods of diking, which made a revolutionary contribution in mitigating – if not entirely overcoming – the effects of the severe seasonal floods of the Song-koi,[3] and also the distinctive Chinese techniques of rice cultivation with the aid of bucket lifts to irrigate the enclosed fields, and the use of animal and human excreta as well as green manure to offset the loss of fertility caused by continued cropping.[4] Moreover, since the northern Annamite lands, though technically within the tropics, nevertheless have four consecutive months when mean temperatures fall below 70°, thereby enhancing the effectiveness of the not inconsiderable total rainfall of 5 to 6 in. during that period (December–March), the practice devised in southern China of raising a second (winter) crop could be applied there also. Today over half the paddy acreage of the northern Annamite lands is double cropped with rice,[5] and much of the rest supports a second 'dry' crop, such as maize, beans or sweet potatoes, while the dikes and bunds between the small fields are characteristically planted with fruit or mulberry trees.

On the basis of this highly intensive agriculture, practised without serious interruption for well over a thousand years, the 5,800 square miles of the Song-koi delta have come to support an average population density today of approximately 1,200 to the square mile, a figure which rises to 2,500 in many places still

[1] See Zelinsky, p.116.

[2] According to Wittfogel's thesis the socio-political organization was itself related to water control. See above, pp. 93–4.

[3] Exceptional floods could burst or overflow the dikes, and in the course of centuries this danger increased as sedimentation raised the water level still farther above that of the fields.

[4] As a result of diking, the bulk of the silt-laden river water flowed direct to the sea without spreading over and replenishing the land.

[5] This high proportion of double-cropped land is largely the result of improvements made in the last 50 years, though some double cropping has been practised since very early times.

almost exclusively rural, and to over 3,500 in the most fertile tracts of recent alluvium close to the main rivers. Such figures indeed are on a par with those of the Si-kiang delta of southern China, but in part they result from innovations made during the French colonial period, and farther south the smaller deltas of the Song-ma and Song-chu carry only about half this density.

For while the Annamites learned much from the Chinese, the process of assimilation was not absolute. In the seclusion of their ancestral villages the Annamites showed great tenacity in preserving their traditional way of life which was distinctly less sophisticated than that of the Chinese, and to this day the Annamites, besides being temperamentally remote from the Chinese, are generally inferior to them as cultivators,[6] even though in most other respects they are more than a match for the rest of the population of Indochina.

This resistance to Sinicization led ultimately to the successful revolt against China in 939, and it was only after that time that the Annamites began their slow but steady advance into the lands first of the Chams and later of the Cambodians, south of the 18th parallel. The resultant difference in dates of settlement is still evident in the landscape, for while several of the more northerly pockets of deltaic plain, such as those around Than Thien, Quang Nam and Quang Ngai, have densities of 500–750 to the square mile, the figure falls off in the even more fragmentary patches of lowland south of Cape Varella, where Annamite settlement dates only from the end of the 15th century.[7]

But it is the Mekong delta of the south which has the lowest overall density of population anywhere within the Annamite lowlands. Over this vast area of 14,000 square miles the average figure today is only 250 to the square mile, varying locally from around 500 in the central portions between My Tho and the Bassac river, to less than 100 in the remoter west, 75 in central Camau and a mere 25 in the swamps of the extreme southern tip.

Thus, taken as a whole, the Mekong delta supports barely one quarter the density of population living in the Song-koi delta, a difference which cannot be attributed to any inferiority in soil fertility, though it is true that the climatic regime virtually rules out the possibility of a second rice crop,[8] since there is less than 1½ in. of rain for the three months January–March, when mean temperatures ranging from 79 to 84° give rise to high rates of evaporation. But undoubtedly the main reason for the comparatively low population density is the recency of Annamite settlement, for although rice cultivation was practised here in the

[6] Although it is claimed that great improvements have been made in this respect under Communist rule since 1954, it may be doubted whether this is really so. See below, p. 560.

[7] Within the coastlands between latitudes 18 and 11° N there is considerable local variation in rainfall patterns (see above, pp. 421–6). Thus around 18° there are harvests in June and November, around 16° in April and November, around 14° in April and September, and around 12° in January and September. But in all cases only the best lands are double-cropped. Throughout this strip only relatively small-scale irrigation systems exist, based mainly on a series of storage dams built at the places where individual rivers emerge from the mountains.

[8] Unless massive storage dams were to be built, which has never yet been attempted.

time of Funan and later of the Khmer empire, the methods adopted were less efficient than those of the Annamites, whose effective occupation did not begin until the 18th century, and was limited to a comparatively small part of the delta prior to the French annexation.

Indeed in 1862 the average density of population in the delta was only about 50–60 to the square mile, and the Annamites had not developed any system of diking corresponding to that in the north. Thus rice cultivation depended mainly on direct and often inadequate rainfall, supplemented by uncontrolled inundation during the flood season. Though less violent than those of the Song-koi, the Mekong floods reach very considerable depths in many parts of the central delta, and it was to cope with this situation that the Annamite pioneers introduced floating rice, which later played an important part in the great expansion of cultivation there under French rule.

By the time the French established themselves in Indochina, therefore, Annamite settlement already extended in a long narrow ribbon from its original core in the Song-koi delta to the coastal fringes of the Mekong delta, a thousand miles to the south. This pattern, which was subsequently filled out in the south, but has not otherwise undergone any fundamental change since then, shows an exceptionally pronounced concentration on alluvial lowland, though it was the fear of malaria even more than the difficulties of upland cultivation which made the Annamites shun the hills. For while the *anopheles* does not flourish in the muddy waters of the rice fields (though other mosquitoes abound there), the zone between 300 and 3000 ft. or so is intensely malarious, and it is this fact more than any other which explains why in 1937 the Annamites, though forming 72 per cent of the total population of Indochina, nevertheless occupied barely 10 per cent of its surface area.[9]

While the problem of maintaining effective communications within this extremely attenuated territory, which has been compared to two bags of rice dangling from a pole, led to the emergence of various political sub-divisions and differences in spoken dialect,[10] the Annamites succeeded in preserving a high degree of cultural unity throughout their domains. Nevertheless, the historic differences between the older north and the newer south were no less pronounced than, for example, those between the Rhi neland and East Prussia. And to this must be added the effect of what is probably the most significant fact in the geography of the Annamite lands, namely that while the north is sufficiently akin to southern China for it to have adopted the essentials of the latter's sub-tropical

[9] See Gourou (H), pp. 101 and 107, and Robequain (C), p. 49.

[10] On the political divisions see above, Chapter 4. The basic vocabulary of the Annamese language appears to be Austro-Asiatic, but a majority of the words today in use are wholly or partly of Chinese origin, and the language is tonal. Until the 13th century it was written exclusively in the Chinese ideographs. Later various modifications of these were made, giving rise to the system known as chu'-nom, but in the 17th century Roman Catholic missionaries introduced a Romanized form of writing called qu'oc-ngu which is now standard usage. See Brodrick (A), pp. 39 and 44.

agronomy, the unmistakably tropical character of the south has given rise to quite different agricultural patterns and a different tempo of life.

Whether it be due to the enervating effects of a winterless climate or to the lack of any serious population pressure in the south, the inhabitants of the latter have long been regarded by the northerners as less industrious and less hard-headed than themselves, a distinction which is in line with that already noted between the Annamites as a whole and the Chinese.

In sharp contrast to the generally well-settled and in places overcrowded lowlands of the eastern seaboard, the uplands enclosing the Tonkin delta, and the extensive plateaux of the Annamite Chain support a population averaging less than 10 to the square mile, and indeed over large areas the density is a mere fraction of this figure. Practically the whole of the scanty upland population consists of minority groups[11] of many different stocks, but mostly organized on a tribal basis and depending for their livelihood on relatively primitive forms of cultivation.

Over the southern two-thirds of the country the hill peoples, who are known to the Annamites as Mois, to the Cambodians as Penongs and to the Laotians as Khas, all of which are merely collective names meaning savages, are predominantly of Nesiot origin and show physical and cultural affinities with the Dyaks of interior Borneo. All-told there are approximately one million such Mois of various tribal groups, many of whom live in communal long-houses; all are animists except for a few recent converts to Christianity, and all practise *ray* or shifting cultivation, principally of dry rice and maize. Similar peoples live in the Cardamom and Elephant mountains and on the Dangrek range, respectively south and north of the Cambodian plains.

On both the eastern and the western flanks of the southern end of the Annamite Chain small groups of Chams, totalling approximately 120,000, occupy scattered villages between the main centres of Annamite and Cambodian population in the plains, and the Moi territories of the uplands. These downtrodden and dispirited survivals of a formerly advanced civilization still practise irrigated rice cultivation, though not very efficiently, and adhere either to Hinduism (in the east) or to Islam (on the Cambodian side). Most of them are clearly of Deutero-Malay origin, though there has also been considerable intermixture with Mois in the uplands where many Chams sought refuge after the 15th century.

In the northern third of the country there is a much greater diversity of hill peoples, and although pockets of Moi/Kha folk are found as far north as the Chinese frontier, these groups are generally outnumbered by other more recent arrivals from the Yunnan-Tibetan borderland, whose distribution exhibits a complex altitudinal zoning.

Throughout the northern interior of Indochina, including the strip of low

[11] The lowland peoples regard the uplands as negative frontier zones. Since the modern political boundaries usually run through the middle of these broad zones there are minorities of hill peoples in all of the Indochinese states.

upland which forms the frontier with China, the valley floors are mostly occupied by Thais who, as already noted, are not strictly hill people at all.[12] Owing to both the topographical fragmentation and the fact that they entered in a series of migrations spread over many centuries, the Thais, though speaking closely related dialects and subscribing to Theravada Buddhism, are split into a number of distinct groups. These include the White and Black Thai, the Tho, Lu, Nung and Nhang, most of whom occupy the upper valleys of rivers draining to the Gulf of Tonkin, and as a result have been in fairly close contact with the Annamites from whom many of them have adopted various cultural traits. But in addition to these lesser Thai groups, today numbering perhaps 800,000 souls, there are some 700,000 Lao Thais occupying the valleys of the Upper Mekong and its tributaries, a region which formed the nucleus of the large principalities of Luang Prabang and Vientiane, and has long been intimately connected with the ethnically similar territories across the Siamese border.

As in the Korat plateau, wet cultivation of glutinous rice is the normal basis of Thai agriculture in most parts of northern Indochina, but even in the upper Mekong valley population density does not average more than 25–100 to the square mile, and over Laos as a whole the figure is only 38.

In the uplands between these several centres of Thai valley settlement live the northern hill peoples proper, all of whom are closely related to tribal communities on the Chinese side of the border, and, while certainly retarded, are generally less primitive than the Mois. Nevertheless, most of them rely mainly on shifting cultivation of rice, maize, beans, sugar-cane and roots, and in some cases – especially among the Meos (Miaos) – the opium poppy,[13] though in view of the severe erosion to the hillsides caused by such practices the French tried hard to induce them to change to sedentary irrigated cultivation on terraced fields.

The first of these peoples to migrate southwards into Indochina appear to have been the Mans (or Yaos) who arrived in the 13th century, after the earliest waves of Thais, and established themselves in the zone above the latter, at altitudes between 1000 and 3000 ft. Of more recent migration are the Meos who live exclusively above the 3000 ft. contour and have apparently proved unable to acclimatize at lower levels. Together with the Lolos, who are also found mostly in the higher uplands, and the Muongs who occupy scattered areas between the latter and the inland limit of Annamite settlement, these various northern hill peoples probably number upwards of half a million, a total which is shared between the modern political units of Laos in the west and Northern Vietnam in the east.

To the south of the Khone falls the Mekong valley merges in effect with the great basin of Cambodia, and the human pattern also changes. For notwith-

[12] See above, p. 432, note 6.

[13] This has long been illicit but still goes on, as in similar areas in Thailand (see above, p. 520, note 84.) The importance of these areas as illicit sources has been enhanced by more rigorous attempts to suppress such cultivation elsewhere, notably in China, in recent years.

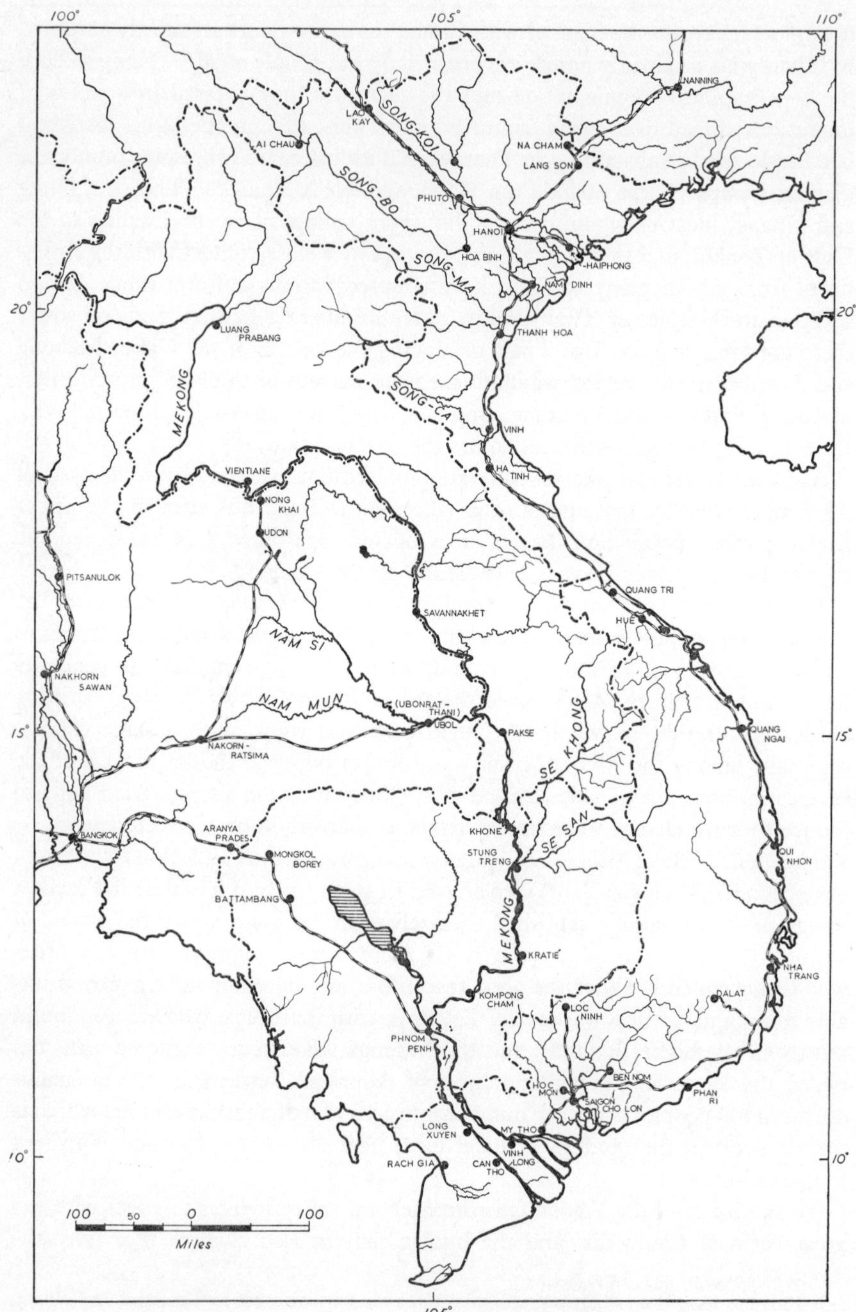

FIG. 76—Indochina: rivers and railways

standing the decline of the ancient Khmer empire after the Siamese sack of Angkor in 1431, the Cambodian population, ethnically Deutero-Malay and culturally Theravada Buddhist, has preserved its identity over most of the basin, though the focus of the kingdom has shifted since the 15th century from the Tonlé Sap lowlands to the banks of the Mekong in the south-east.

The modern Cambodians, who are an essentially unsophisticated and easy-going people, seem strangely remote from the achievements of their ancestors. Although they have abandoned the practice of shifting cultivation, which is believed to have provided the main economic basis of the old civilization away from the nuclear region,[14] their wet-rice cultivation of today is not very efficient, the methods resembling those of the Siamese rather than of the Annamites. As in the Menam basin a relatively low rainfall is supplemented by flood water, both along the banks of the Mekong and in the zone surrounding Tonlé Sap. In the absense of controlled irrigation only one rice crop is possible each year, generally of floating rice in the areas of deepest floods, though a second dry crop – most commonly of maize – is often grown, and lake and river fish are of great importance in the subsistence economy. On this basis population density reaches about 200 to the square mile in parts of the south-east bordering the Mekong, and about 50–75 in the inundated zone around Tonlé Sap, but elsewhere the average drops to below 15, and much of the basin is for all practical purposes uncultivated.

The eastern political boundary of Cambodia does not correspond exactly with the ethnic divide between Annamite and Khmer, for while some 480,000 Cambodians remain in the adjacent parts of Southern Vietnam there is a substantial overlap of Annamites on the Cambodian side of the line. This situation has arisen from the slow but persistent advance of the Annamites into Khmer territory, which continued largely spontaneously throughout the period of French rule but had already been responsible for cutting off Cambodia from its principal outlet to the sea in the 18th century.

Even apart from Cambodia's loss of the delta, however, the Mekong basin had never achieved a measure of political unity comparable with that of the Irrawaddy or the Menam. While a full explanation of this difference in geopolitical evolution involves many factors, including the ease of latitudinal movement which first tempted the Khmers to over-extend their empire into Siam and later facilitated the counter-invasions of Ayuthia, the formidable series of impediments to navigation from the Khone falls northwards has certainly played a significant part in the story.

II. INDOCHINA UNDER FRENCH RULE

Between 1862 and 1907 the French established their rule over the whole of Vietnam, Cambodia and Laos, and the policies they introduced during the decades

[14] There is much uncertainty on this matter. But though there were some large irrigation works and storage tanks in the vicinity of Angkor (see Groslier, pp. 101–8, and see also above, pp. 89n. and 93–4) these were abandoned because of the Thai attacks of the 14th and 15th centuries, and this area has never been intensively cultivated since.

which followed have left an abiding impression on the economic and political geography of these lands.

Unlike the British and Dutch whose nearest colonial possessions were separated by thousands of miles of ocean from the mother country, the French laid the foundations of their second colonial empire much nearer home on the opposite shore of the Mediterranean, and, largely for this reason, tended thereafter to regard their colonies as direct extensions of France overseas.[15] Moreover, the growing disparity in population between France and Germany during the later 19th century led to a desire to redress the balance by recruiting military man-power from the colonies. It was in these circumstances that the doctrine of *assimilation* was born which, notwithstanding an official change to *association* in the 1920s, has coloured and at times dominated French colonial policy ever since the 1880s.

According to the assimilationist view, colonies were to be developed not as individual organisms in their own right but rather as 'limbs' of France. Thus their economies must be intimately related to that of the mother country and in theory, at least, the colonies should produce not whatever paid best (like those of Britain under *laissez faire*), but rather such commodities as were specifically needed by metropolitan France, for whose exports they should in return provide a privileged and closely controlled market. Meanwhile, and again in contrast to Britain it was this which in public received the greater emphasis, France's supreme rôle, like that of ancient Rome, was to act as a civilizing force in a barbarian world, by educating and accepting a growing proportion of the indigenous population as the full equivalents of European-born Frenchmen.

Whatever may prove in the long run to have been the merits of this philosophy as applied to France's African territories, its relevance to Indochina was severely limited by the utter remoteness of the country, both geographically and culturally from Mediterranean Europe. As described in Chapter 5, French interest in Indochina developed from three main origins, namely Roman Catholic missionary activities during the 17th and 18th centuries, the subsequent desire to compensate for the loss of India, and the search after 1850 for backdoor routes to China which should ensure for France a pre-eminent position in the struggle for power in the Far East and Pacific. Notwithstanding the failure to find navigable river routes into Yunnan, the French thus came into possession of the largest single block of territory (272,355 square miles) on the South-east Asian mainland, an area which in its economic potential rated at least as high as that of the rival British sphere in Burma.

Between 1887 and 1899 the various indigenous political units of the Annamites, Laotians and Cambodians were reorganized as the supposedly federal Indochinese Union. The Annamite lands, which in 1802 had been reunited, albeit with local governors-general for the northern and southern deltas, lost their corporate

[15] As implied by the practice of referring to the French empire as *la France d'outremer*. On the character of French colonial rule as a whole see Roberts, S. H., *op. cit.*

identity in the larger unity of Indochina in which they formed the colony of Cochinchina (acquired 1862–7) and the protectorates of Annam and Tonkin (1882), side by side with the protectorates of Cambodia (1863–7–1907) and Laos (1893–1904). But just as the federal character of the Union was no less fictitious than that of the F.M.S., so the difference in status between the colony and the several protectorates was of minor significance. For while the indigenous ruling houses and their administrative hierarchies remained in being in Annam, Cambodia and Luang Prabang, their powers were mainly vestigial, and in Tonkin as also in the other main focus of French economic activity, namely Cochinchina, the system was virtually one of direct French rule. Moreover, notwithstanding the assimilationist doctrine, all but the most junior posts in the civil service throughout Indochina were held by European-born Frenchmen, and although there were indigenous representatives on both State and Federal Councils, these bodies remained purely consultative in character, and effective power rested in the hands of the Governor-General, assisted by the Governor of Cochinchina and the four Residents-Superior of the other states.

To an even greater extent than in the other South-east Asian dependencies, European economic activities in Indochina were concentrated within the coastal fringe, a fact which reflected not only the distinctive topographical layout of the country, focusing in the two great deltas, but also the more ready response of the Annamites than of the Cambodians and Laotians to the stimulus of the Western money economy.

First to be developed were the almost virgin plains of the Mekong delta to the west and south of the Bassac river, which marked the effective limit reached by Annamite settlement at the time of the French annexation. And here at the very outset the French were faced with the conflict between doctrinaire colonial policy and the facts of geography. For this region, closely analogous both physically and demographically to the Irrawaddy and Menam deltas, was obviously suited to become a great rice granary, but offered little scope for the production of other commodities more immediately desired by the mother country.[16] In the event the geographical factor proved decisive, but despite later attempts to popularize a taste for rice in France – the effects of which are still evident in the national cuisine – the mother country could not absorb more than half the Indochinese export, and the latter never rose significantly above half the Burmese figure, notwithstanding the immense agricultural potential of the Mekong delta.

The manner in which the Cochinchina ricelands were opened up also differed considerably from that adopted by the British in Lower Burma. Beginning in 1870 the French constructed a series of major canals, which served both to drain the land and to extend the network of navigable waterways provided by the rivers, and in the course of the seventy years which followed, the area under rice increased more than four-fold (Table 69). But instead of promoting peasant pro-

[16] At various times the French tried to develop the production of silk, cotton and tobacco in Indochina for the French home market, but with little or no success.

prietorship, the French aimed rather at a system of large-scale tenure as offering the best economic return on the heavy capital outlay involved.[17]

TABLE 69

COCHINCHINA: EXPANSION OF RICE CULTIVATION, 1880–1939

Year	*Area (acres)*	*Export (metric tons of cleaned rice)*
1880 . . .	1,282,000	284,000
1900 . . .	2,656,000	747,000
1920 . . .	4,572,000	1,200,000
1939 . . .	5,450,000	1,454,000

Sources: Based on Robequain (C), p. 220, and Chesneaux, p. 164.

Thus, while holdings of 2–12 acres remained typical in the area of pre-French settlement north-east of the Bassac, the new area to the south-west had much larger units, many indeed being between 1,250 and 2,500 acres in size and some even larger. These estates were generally sub-divided into holdings small enough to be worked by an individual tenant and his family, with the help of seasonal labour from the eastern delta at the peak periods. Such tenants, who comprised some two-thirds of the rural population of the delta in the 1930s,[18] normally paid 40 per cent of their crop as rent, and often found it necessary to borrow both rice and cash from their landlords – many of them absentees – at even higher rates of interest.

By South-east Asian standards this was a far from intensive system of farming. In the late 1930s the average rice yield in the trans-Bassac provinces (19·8 bushels per acre) was well below even the unimpressive Indochinese average of 25 bushels per acre, and with some 90 per cent of the land under paddy and the greater part of the product destined for export, the Mekong delta suffered from all the characteristic drawbacks of monoculture. Furthermore, the opening up of the delta did little to help the congested lands of Tonkin and northern Annam, which were not under French jurisdiction when the system was originally devised, and though some spontaneous migration did take place from the north,

[17] The French authorities originally expected that individual landowners would themselves extend the canal network by building a series of secondary and tertiary drainage and irrigation canals on their own land. But owing to the speculation fever this did not come about and only the paddy land along the main canals is irrigated. Robequain (C), pp. 221–2 and Pelzer (C), p. 65.

[18] Nearly one-half of the cultivated area of Cochinchina was in holdings over 250 acres. Dumont, p. 141. The average size of farm units there was about 8½ acres.

much the greater part of the settlers in the trans-Bassac came from the adjacent provinces of Cochinchina itself. Yet though living standards in the Mekong delta were certainly higher than those in the north, landlessness and indebtedness constituted very real problems to which no easy solution existed.

For the most part the great land-holders were themselves southern Annamites, though a few were European-born Frenchmen, and money-lending was likewise principally in the hands of Annamites, together with a sprinkling of Chettyars. But from the outset the transport, milling and marketing of rice were virtually monopolized by the Chinese community, which had dominated the small overseas trade of the Annamite lands[19] since before the arrival of the first Europeans, and had subsequently taken an active part in the Annamite advance into the delta, having *inter alia* founded the market town of Cholon at the focus of the natural waterways some time in the late 1770s.

With the canal-building activities of the French, the nodality of Cholon was further enhanced, and while the French made their own headquarters in the nearby Annamite settlement of Saigon,[20] which they swiftly transformed into a tropical replica of a French provincial town and the largest port in the whole of Indochina, Cholon remained the centre of the rice trade, and the number of Chinese in Cochinchina rose from 45,000 out of a total of 1,250,000 in 1880 to 171,000 out of approximately 3 million in 1936.

Throughout the period of French rule the export of rice remained the mainstay of the economy of southern Indochina, and of the country's total export of *c.* 1·5 million metric tons[21] in the 1930s Cochinchina supplied approximately 1,150,000 tons, which amounted to nearly 60 per cent of that state's production. The remaining 350,000 tons came almost entirely from Cambodia, which also produced most of Indochina's export of about 500,000 tons of maize.[22] Both grains were grown there in traditional fashion by the Cambodian peasantry, though their development as cash crops resulted from contact with the commercial economy built up by the French and Chinese in Cochinchina.

In addition to its pre-eminence as a grain exporter, southern Indochina also became much the most important centre of plantation cultivation in the country, with some 80 per cent of the total estate acreage of 2½ million in 1937. Besides the longer period of French settlement and the greater ease of obtaining land there than in the north, the south also contains most of the basaltic *terres rouges*, and has the further advantage of a winterless climate, which is essential for rubber cultivation and no less suitable for tea and coffee.

[19] This was carried out from the port of Faifo near Tourane. Faifo also had a large Japanese quarter prior to the Tokugawa Seclusion.

[20] Though it was the chief political centre of the newly colonized Annamite territories in the south, Saigon was little more than a village surrounding an imperial fortress. Nothing of the old core remains today. Fryer (A), p. 477.

[21] These figures are for cleaned rice.

[22] As befits its relatively dry climate Cambodia has also to some extent specialized in livestock; it accounted for about half of the 2½ million oxen in all French Indochina in 1940.

Of these three principal estate crops in Indochina, coffee was the first to be developed (1888), but in contrast to the other two the main centres of production were in Tonkin. However, neither coffee (with a total production of 1,500 tons in 1937–8) nor tea (880 tons) which was developed by French planters after 1924 mainly on the southern *terres rouges*, was to be compared in importance with rubber which covered 313,000 acres (242,000 in Cochinchina and 67,000 in Cambodia) and yielded a total output of 76,000 tons in 1941.

Although experimental rubber growing began before the end of the 19th century, very little was done until after the First World War. In the initial stages planting took place on the older alluvials along the northern edge of the Mekong delta, but during the big expansion of the 1920s it spread on to the lower *terres rouges* beyond, mostly at altitudes of less than 600 ft., and also into parts of eastern Cambodia adjacent to the Mekong. Production, which supplied virtually the whole of the mother country's need, was almost exclusively in the hands of European estates, with 94 per cent of the acreage in holdings of over 100 acres and a relatively high proportion of very large and extremely efficient estates. But in the absence of any large surplus of local labour most of the rubber planters in the south relied on northern Annamite workers engaged on three-year contracts, though the tea and other estates in the *terres rouges* recruited their labour mainly from the nearby plains of the Annam coast.

Apart from the processing of agricultural produce, mostly for export, southern Indochina had few large factory industries, the main exceptions being soap, cigarettes and brewing in Saigon and Cholon, which also contained many small Chinese factories making consumer goods. But by far the most important industry of these twin cities was rice milling, and of the 27 mills having over 100 h.p., 4 were French owned and nearly all the rest belonged to Chinese. As elsewhere in South-east Asia, the large mills of Cholon and Saigon began to suffer competition from small country mills during the 1930s, but the Chinese nevertheless continued to hold a pre-eminent position in the trade. Other industries in the delta towns and cities included sugar refining, distilling and sawmilling, while Phu Phong in the centre of a region noted for sericulture had a solitary silk-weaving factory. In Cambodia factory industry was limited to a few sawmills, a dozen or so not very large rice mills, some sugar refineries and a single distillery at Phnom Penh.

The economic development of the northern half of French Indochina followed very different lines from that of the south. For while as a result of its inaccessibility Laos was even more neglected than Cambodia, the acute congestion of the northern Annamite lands ruled out the possibility of substantial agricultural surpluses as in Cochinchina, and instead the French concentrated on other forms of enterprise for which the dense population provided labour or markets, and in some cases both.

In this connexion the considerable mineral wealth of Tonkin, which had long been known to the Annamites and Chinese, attracted their attention at an early

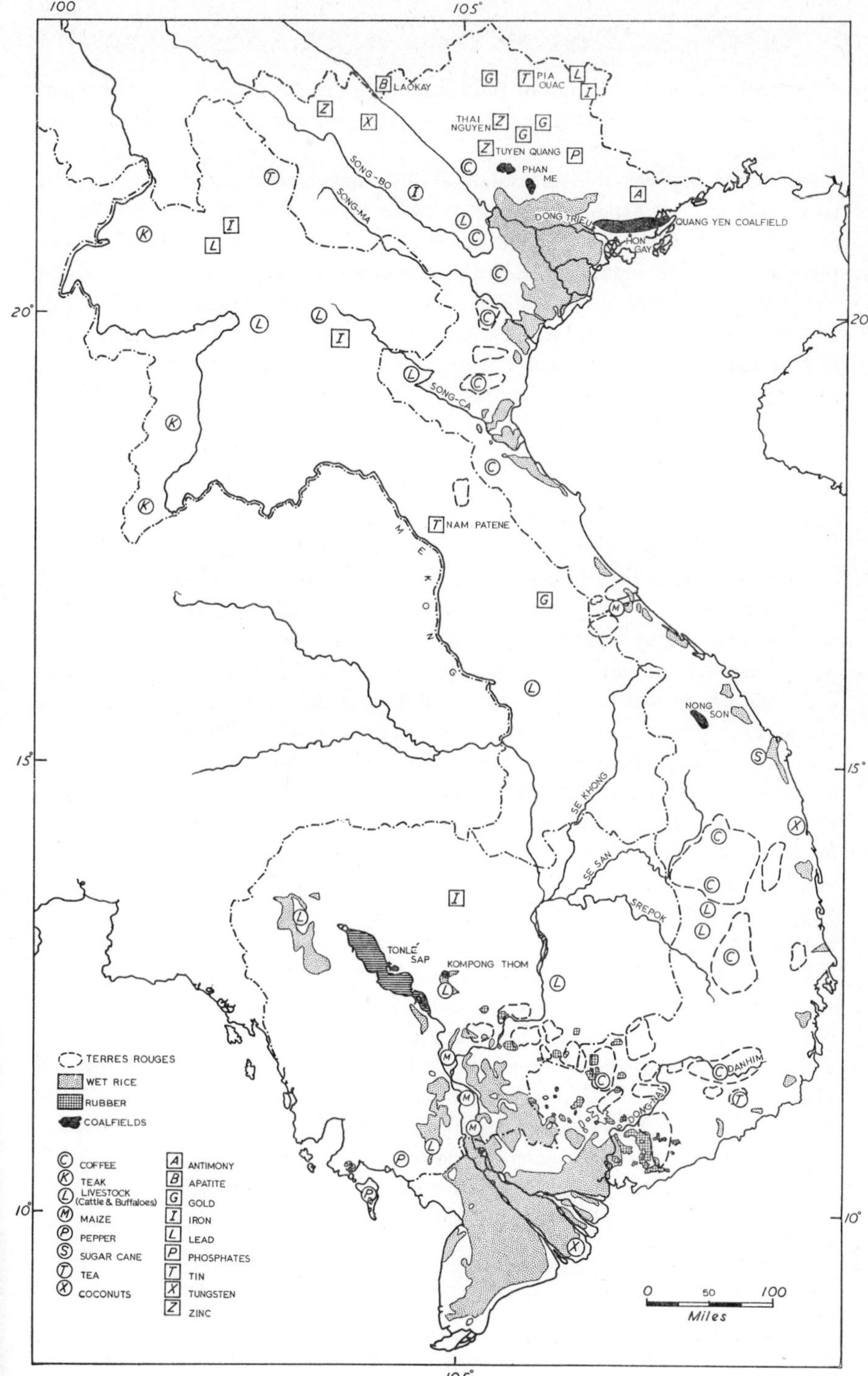

FIG. 77—Indochina: economic development

stage, and in 1940 95 per cent of Indochina's mining was located in the northern half of the country, practically all of it, apart from the Nam Patene complex, being in Tonkin.

Much the most valuable mineral of all is the anthracite coal of the Quang Yen basin, whose beds extend for some 93 miles immediately to the north of the Song-koi delta, from Sept Pagodes to the coast. Two main centres have been exploited since work began in the late 19th century, namely Hon Gay and Dong Trieu, which together produced well over 90 per cent of Indochina's coal output of 2,615,000 tons in 1939. Of this total, which represented only a small fraction of what could readily have been mined, 1,780,000 tons were exported, including 150,000 tons which went via the long sea route to France.

Apart from coal, zinc and tin were the only other important minerals worked by the French. Lode tin mining in the Pia Ouac range of northern Tonkin dates from 1901–2, the main centre being near Tinh Tuc, but this was overtaken in the 1920s by Nam Patene in southern Laos, whose alluvial workings produced 60 per cent of the country's 1,602 tons of tin concentrates in 1937.[23] On the other hand the output of zinc declined from 60,000 tons of ore in 1926 to 10,000 tons in 1940, most of it coming from the Tuyen Quang-Thai Nguyen area of northern Tonkin. Among the other minerals known to exist but never worked on a major scale by the French were wolfram, lead, silver, antimony, gold, phosphate and graphite, as well as the hæmatite and magnetite iron ores discovered in northern Tonkin and near Kompong Thom in central Cambodia.

Besides mining, which took place mainly in the surrounding hill country, the lowlands of Tonkin and northern Annam also contained the largest concentration of factory industry in Indochina. Both in the reservoir of accumulated skills and in the market which domestic weaving offered for factory-spun yarn, the well-developed tradition of handicraft industries in these older Annamite lands played a part in this localization,[24] though proximity to the Quang Yen coal was at least as significant in most cases.

While the factory industries established by the French in the north included some processing of agricultural produce, mainly for local consumption, this region had a much wider range of other manufactures than that of the Mekong delta. Three towns stood out as important industrial concentrations, namely Haiphong (with cement, cotton spinning, ship-building, glass bottles, pottery, building materials, rugs, buttons, candles, oxygen, rice milling); Hanoi (matches, tanning, brewing, building materials, pottery, buttons, rubber, glass, distilling); and Nam Dinh (cotton spinning and weaving, silk weaving, glass, distilling); while other manufacturing included the bamboo pulp[25] and paper factories of

[23] This was exported to Singapore for smelting.

[24] See Gourou (A), pp. 460–505. Gourou estimated that 250,000 persons were occupied more of less full-time in domestic industry in the Tonkin delta.

[25] However, although sawmilling was locally important in many parts of the country, the French did comparatively little systematically to exploit Indochina's forest resources.

Viettri and Dap Cau respectively, the match industries of Ben Thuy and Ham Rong, and the main railway workshops at Vinh.

Among these various industries cement and cotton are of particular interest. The large cement factory built in 1889 at Haiphong, near supplies of limestone as well as of coal, was intended originally to meet the local demand for constructional material, but by 1939 over half its annual product of some 306,000 tons of high-quality cement was exported, mostly to other parts of South-east Asia.[26]

While the production on the spot of such a bulky commodity as cement did not conflict with orthodox French economic policy for the colonies, the establishment of cotton mills was a more controversial matter and was only undertaken after it had become clear that the poverty of the peasantry severely limited their capacity to purchase French textiles and compelled them to buy only the cheapest – mostly Indian-spun – cotton yarn. It was to replace the latter that the French Société Cotonnière de l'Indochine first set up its three large spinning mills, respectively at Hanoi (afterwards closed), Haiphong and Nam Dinh, and only at a later stage did the last and largest of these extend its activities to the production of blankets, towels and other fabrics.[27]

Some indication of the predominance of northern Indochina in mining and manufacturing can be gained from the fact that in 1937 approximately two-thirds of the country's total output of 153 million kW[28] of electric power was generated in Tonkin, practically all of it in thermal stations. But the scale of these activities should not be exaggerated, as it sometimes has been in consequence of the handful of big cotton and cement plants, and in fact the total of around 90,000 factory workers shortly before the Second World War was no larger than that of Burma.

Moreover, if it be assumed that at least 60,000 of the factory workers and nearly all of the 50,000 miners (mostly Annamites, though the total includes some Chinese) were in Tonkin, it is clear that these forms of employment did not in fact make any major contribution to a solution of the problem presented by overpopulation in that state, and the same is true of the temporary migration of labourers (never more than a few tens of thousands at any given time) to the plantations of the south.

As was implied on p. 531 the Song-koi delta must already have shown many signs of incipient overcrowding at the time of the French annexation in 1882, for though statistical data are lacking it may be inferred that the average density was then of the order of 500–600 to the square mile. Thereafter, as in the other lowland regions of Indochina, French medical services significantly reduced the

[26] As noted above, p. 297, one of the earliest large industrial plants in the Netherlands Indies was the cement works at Padang in Sumatra. But Java imported much cement from French Indochina, as also did Siam, the Philippines and Malaya.

[27] In 1937 the Haiphong and Nam Dinh mills together produced over 8,000 tons of yarn. The Nam Dinh mill, which employed 4,000 workers, also produced 702,000 blankets and 2,212 tons of miscellaneous cotton fabrics. Another firm also had a smaller spinning mill at Haiphong.

[28] The total installed capacity was 93,363 kW.

incidence of smallpox, cholera and malaria, and by the 1930s the population had roughly doubled its numbers and was continuing to grow by over 100,000 a year.

In such an area of small peasant holdings the inevitable result was further subdivision, leading to growing poverty and indebtedness, and during the 1930s it was estimated that some 70 per cent of holdings there were less than 1 acre, and only 8 per cent more than 4½ acres in size, while the average per capita consumption of rice was barely half that in Cochinchina.[29]

Faced with this situation it is difficult to see what the French could have done without striking at the very roots of the established order, a process which would have entailed incalculable costs both financially and politically. It is therefore scarcely surprising that in the event they limited their activities to whatever could be accomplished within the existing agricultural and social framework. On the one hand this included the provision of rural credit facilities and the promotion of modern co-operative associations, both of which they also encouraged in certain other parts of the country, notably southern Annam. But undoubtedly their principal contribution was the improvement and extension of the existing hydraulic installations in the Song-koi delta.

French efforts at strengthening dikes as a protection against exceptional floods began in the late 19th century, but their greatest achievements followed the calamitous floods of 1926, after which many of the main dikes were reinforced to a total thickness of 150 ft. with heights of up to 40 ft. in the central delta. Moreover, the traditional irrigation works were supplemented by a series of new dams and canals which permitted control of the water level in the rice-growing basins. Although the earliest works of this kind which date from 1905 were outside the delta proper, the system was gradually extended within it until nearly one-third of the total paddy area of Tonkin was served by modern irrigation works.

As a result of these hydraulic works the hazards of rice cultivation were greatly reduced and the proportion of land capable of giving two crops a year considerably increased.[30] But though in the late 1930s the average yield in Tonkin, namely 28 bushels per acre (for a single crop only) was the highest in Indochina, it is doubtful whether the increase in production was keeping pace with the growth of population and it was often necessary to supplement a poor harvest by substantial imports of rice from the south.[31]

One possible approach to the problem would clearly have been to resettle Tonkinese peasants in the Mekong delta, and in fact a small-scale but unsuccessful attempt to do this had been made as early as 1907. But the shifting of people from one end of the country to the other in the 20th century, which necessitated the learning of a new dialect and a new technique of farming and irrevocable

[29] See Gourou (A).

[30] Of a total irrigated area in the Tonkin delta of some 2,720,000 acres about 1,240,000 acres were double cropped in 1936. Gourou (A), p. 107.

[31] Such imports amounted to about 100,000 tons in 1940 and to approximately double that total in the early post-war years.

separation from the graves of the ancestors, was not to be compared with the gradual advance of the Annamite frontier in pre-French times.[32] Thus, when the economic crisis of the 1930s spurred the French to emulate the Netherlands Indies' plans for transmigration, and the resultant Tonkinese Colonization Commission reserved large areas in Rach Gia and Ha Tien in south-west Cochinchina for the purpose,[33] little enthusiasm was aroused and only a few thousand people were eventually moved.

All things considered, it would seem that the period of French rule intensified rather than weakened the pre-existing social and economic contrasts within the Indochinese lands. For while on the one hand the Annamite territories as a whole were much more deeply penetrated by French influence of all kinds than were Laos and most parts of Cambodia, the great difference in population density between the southern and northern deltas became reflected in the growth of two quite different economies, the one based on the export of agricultural produce and the other predominantly self-contained.

The extent of this economic division can be gauged from Table 70. Thus Indochina's three main exports, rice, rubber and maize, as well as fish which ranked sixth, came almost entirely from the southern Annamite lands and/or the nearby parts of Cambodia, and together comprised 78 per cent of the total; whereas the only important items coming mainly or wholly from the north, namely coal, tin and cement, amounted to a mere 6 per cent.[34]

TABLE 70

FRENCH INDOCHINA: OVERSEAS TRADE, 1938

Imports: £11,680,000

Items (*per cent*)		*Sources* (*per cent*)	
Cotton, silk and jute tissues	23·2	France and French colonies	56·3
Machines, vehicles and parts	9·8	Hong Kong	7·4
Chemicals, etc.	5·5	China	7·3
Petroleum	5·4	U.S.A.	5·0
Food	5·3	Netherlands Indies	4·3
Iron and steel	4·8	United Kingdom	3·2
Miscellaneous metal goods	4·6	Singapore	3·0
Raw cotton	4·1	Japan	2·9
Paper, etc.	3·2	Siam	1·8
Tobacco	2·0		
Wines	1·6		

Viewed against this background of divergent economic development in north and south, the comparatively small value of Indochina's exports (1938) for a

[32] Robequain (C), p. 64 *et seq.*
[33] It was estimated that if necessary 1¼ million acres could be made available there.
[34] See also the figures below, p. 548.

Exports: £17,160,000

Items (per cent)		*Destinations (per cent)*	
Rice	35·0	France and French colonies	53·2
Rubber	21·8	Singapore	9·7
Maize	18·0	Hong Kong	9·6
Coal	4·3	U.S.A.	8·8
Fish	2·8	Japan	3·1
Tin ore and metal	2·6	India	2·8
Cattle, hides and skins	1·2	China	2·7
Cement	0·9	United Kingdom	2·1
Oilseeds	0·8	Netherlands Indies	1·0
Kapok	0·8		
Tea	0·8		
Eggs	0·7		
Timber	0·7		
Copra	0·6		
Pepper	0·6		

Note: Only after the depression of the early 1930s, which strengthened the idea of a self-contained French imperial trading system, did trade with France account for over 50 per cent of Indochina's total external trade.

Source: Based on Greene and Phillips, pp. 185–6.

country of 23 million people, namely £17,160,000 or less than half that of Burma, is more understandable, and the limited scale of export production in the north did not mean that this area was of little economic importance to France. On the contrary, the French had large capital investments there, particularly in Tonkin which was also a heavy purchaser of French manufactures. But it was none the less true that French economic interests in the northern Annamite lands partook rather of the character of Western interests in China, and only in the southern half of the country did the economic pattern show a general conformity with that in the other colonial dependencies in South-east Asia.

This difference between north and south showed itself in other ways besides the export figures. Thus it was estimated in the 1930s that unskilled workers in Tonkin earned an average daily wage of only 0·29 piastres, against 0·38 in Cochinchina, while for skilled workers the rates were respectively 0·53 and 1·20 piastres (1 piastre in 1937 = 1*s.* 2*d.*). Similarly, while the newer and more commercialized south offered considerable scope to the Chinese, there were few openings for them in the north, with its dense population and well-established domestic industries. As a result of this situation, Robequain estimated[35] that *c.* 85 per cent of the Chinese population lived in Cochinchina and Cambodia, where besides rice marketing, milling and other branches of industry, they were prominent in

[35] Robequain (C), p. 34.

fishing, river transport, market gardening and pepper cultivation.[36] Moreover, Cochinchina and Cambodia also contained nearly all of Indochina's 6,000 Indians, mostly Chettyars and other money-lenders, as well as a few descendants of the Javanese plantation coolies who were brought in for a time after 1906.

In short, Cochinchina and the adjacent parts of Cambodia had a more or less typical South-east Asian plural society, with a characteristically high concentration of aliens in the larger towns. Thus legal Chinese alone comprised 66,000 out of Cholon's total population of 134,000, 34,000 out of 122,000 in Saigon and 29,000 out of 96,000 in Phnom Penh, the capital of Cambodia. But in the northern cities the proportion of Chinese was much lower, with 19,000 out of 124,000 in Haiphong, 5,000 out of 128,000 in Hanoi and 1,500 out of 23,000 in Nam Dinh.[37] However, as Robequain points out, the old Annamite lands had absorbed many Chinese in former centuries, both before and after A.D. 939, and it was primarily because of the resultant mingling of bloods and traditions in the past that so few opportunities remained there for the Chinese immigrant in modern times.

Finally, the difference between north and south expressed itself in a form of expatriate rivalry between Saigon and Hanoi, which in some respects recalled that in British Malaya between Singapore and Kuala Lumpur (pp. 651–5). In particular Saigon, which had been the first centre of French administration, deeply resented the decision to make Hanoi the capital of the Indochinese Union in 1902,[38] and from that time onwards felt that the interests of the original colony were being subordinated to those of the newer protectorates. Moreover, whereas Saigon was almost entirely a French creation and preeminently a port city with related commercial and planting interests, Hanoi had been the Chinese and Annamite capital until the 17th century, and though likewise completely rebuilt and greatly extended by the French, was more obviously an administrative and cultural centre, with its imposing government buildings, museums, university and the world-famous École française d'Extrême Orient.

Since the functions of chief port and capital were divided between the two, and each of them also had a nearby associate (*i.e.* Cholon and the port of Haiphong respectively)[39] it is not surprising that neither had so large a population as

[36] Pepper, of which French Indochina was the world's second producer before the Second World War, was grown in the coastal regions on both sides of the Cochinchina/Cambodia frontier.

[37] In 1936 French Indochina had 21 towns with populations of over 10,000. Of these, three were in Cambodia, one (Vientiane) in Laos and the remainder in the Annamite lands. Only 873,000 out of a total population of 23,030,000 lived in these 21 towns.

[38] Various factors were involved in this change: (1) the Tonkin delta had the greatest concentration of population; (2) interest in the overland trade to China, for which Hanoi might become a forward base; (3) the climate of Hanoi, with its winter 'cool' season was more attractive to Europeans than that of Saigon. The climatic factor also led to some consideration of Dalat as a possible Union capital.

[39] In 1937 2,493,563 tons of shipping entered Saigon and 1,054,844 entered Haiphong. Saigon can take ships up to 30 ft. draught and 550 ft. length, but Haiphong suffers badly from silting and can handle only smaller vessels than these. Neither Saigon nor (still less) Haiphong is on the main shipping routes of the South China Sea.

the leading cities of the other South-east Asian countries, apart from the F.M.S. Eventually it was arranged that the Governor-General should reside alternately in each for a part of every year, but though this went some way to meet Saigon's wishes, it did not remove the strong sense of rivalry between these two main foci of French interests.

This situation was not helped by the tardy and inadequate development of modern means of transport, and apart from coastal shipping, which was handicapped by the lack of intermediate ports as well as by rough seas for nearly half the year, the only link between north and south until 1913 was the indigenous 'Mandarin Road', originally built by the Annamite emperors to connect Hué with both extremities of their domains.

Admittedly, as early as 1898 a national railway network had been planned by Governor-General Doumer, involving a through line, the 'Transindochinois' from the Siamese to the Chinese frontiers, via Phnom Penh, Saigon, Hué and Hanoi, together with two main lateral lines, respectively between Yunnan, Hanoi and Haiphong, and between Laos and the Annam coast. However, owing to the continuing preoccupation with the China trade, prior attention was given to the Yunnan line, and notwithstanding the immense difficulties entailed by topography and disease, the latter of which eventually cost the lives of one-fifth of the 60,000 coolies employed, the 290-mile line, with its 172 tunnels and 107 bridges, was opened to Kunming in 1910. Although the high hopes entertained of this route were not wholly realized[40] it did at least prove more profitable than the rest of the system, whose development followed much more slowly.

In particular, the topographical difficulties of the coastal route between Saigon and Hanoi, though less spectacular than those in Yunnan, made for high costs and many delays, and the link was not effected until 1936.[41] Other lines completed about the same time included two branches into the southern uplands (specifically to Loc Ninh in the *terres rouges* and to the hill station of Dalat), and the line from Phnom Penh to Mongkol Borey near the Siamese border. But the gap remained between Phnom Penh and Saigon, and though twelve miles of line were laid from Tan Ap to Xom Cuc on the proposed route to Thakhek in Laos, work was thereafter suspended indefinitely.

Thus both Laos and Cambodia were entirely without railway connexions to the Annamite lands, which contained Indochina's only major seaports. However, Cambodia was fairly well served by roads. The whole length of the Mandarin Road, both there and in the Annamite lands, was improved after 1913 as Route Coloniale No. 1, and No. 6 ran parallel to it through the country to the north of Tonlé Sap. But for many years Laos had to rely on the hazardous navigation of the Mekong, which involves at least four breaks of bulk between Kratié

[40] Besides intending to develop its mineral and agricultural resources, the French hoped to open up the high plateau of Yunnan as a giant hill station for all the Far Eastern tropics. Beyond they they also had their eyes on the possibility of tapping the trade of Szechwan.

[41] The sections Saigon-My Tho and Hanoi-Langson (on the Chinese border) had been completed earlier.

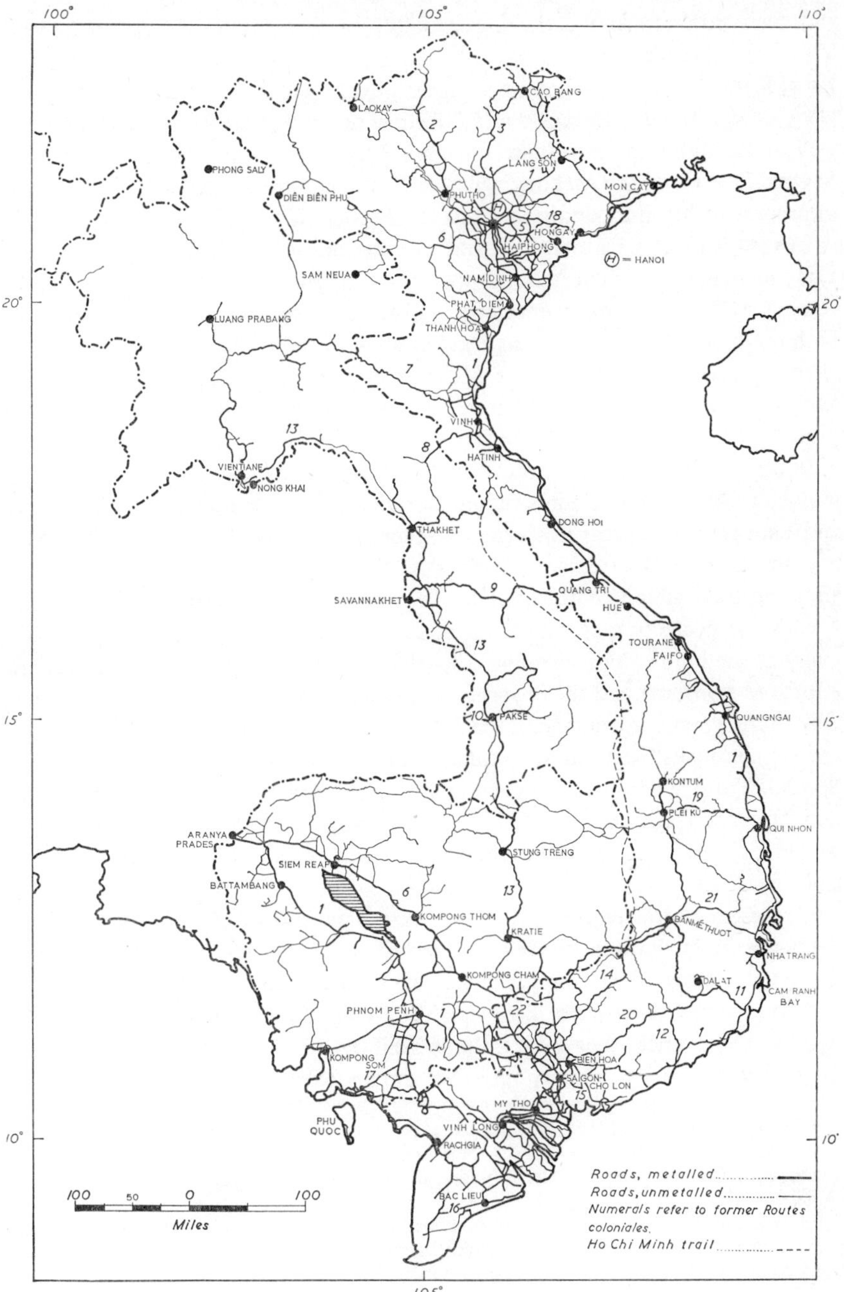

FIG. 78—Indochina: roads

and Savannakhet. Above the latter point, the river is navigable to beyond Vientiane, and it was accordingly to Savannakhet that the first metalled road to Laos, Route Coloniale No. 9, was opened from Quangtri on the Annam coast. Compared with this, Routes 7 and 8 farther north were more tortuous and less well surfaced, but an important new outlet to the south, namely Route 13 from Savannakhet along the Mekong valley to Kratié and thence direct to Saigon, was in process of being modernized when the Second World War broke out.

In sum, Indochina's total road and railway mileages (respectively 16,930 and 2,095 in 1939) were slightly larger than those of Burma[42] but the territory as a whole was by no means so effectively linked together. For a high proportion of both the road and railway mileage was swallowed up in duplicating the not very effective sea route between the Mekong and the Song-koi deltas,[43] and the Mekong above Kratié carried barely one-twentieth the volume of freight transported by the middle and upper Irrawaddy.

In the political sphere, the unity of Indochina existed only on paper and in the minds of the French administration. Socially, as economically, both Cambodia and Laos remained areas of stagnation, though their peoples resented the influx of some thousands of Annamite officials, clerks, traders and professional men after the turn of the century.[44] For this reason they continued to look to the French for protection against these more thrusting neighbours, though in fact many of the innovations introduced by the French, such as Western education, improved transport and the lowering of the death-rate, were working unmistakably to the greater advantage of the Annamites. But whether the absence of any serious nationalist opposition to colonial rule in Cambodia and Laos before the Second World War should be attributed to insouciance or to the lack of population pressure (phenomena which may well have been at least partially interconnected) it was certainly in sharp contrast to the situation in the Annamite lands nearby.

Besides their greater vigour and the immediate spur of more intense poverty, the northern Annamites especially had a tradition of resistance to cultural change and revolt against alien domination (*i.e.* by China), and from the outset did not take kindly to French rule. Believing their own civilization to be at least the equal of the French, they were unimpressed by the theory of assimilation, and the subsequent lack of opportunities for the limited few who acquired a French

[42] Burma had 2,058 miles of railway and 12,422 of road; of the latter 6,811 were metalled as against 11,486 in French Indochina. Note, however, that the Indochina railway mileage includes the Chinese section of the Yunnan railway; the total railway mileage in Indochina alone was only 1,807.

[43] French ships used only one intermediate port of call, namely Tourane, the chief port of Annam. There are many excellent harbours, notably Cam Ranh Bay which has been compared with Sydney and Rio de Janeiro, but all of them suffer from extremely restricted hinterlands and thus have been left virtually undeveloped.

[44] There were 191,000 Annamites in Cambodia and 27,000 in Laos in 1937. A large proportion of those in Cambodia were cultivators in the area bordering on Cochinchina. See above, p. 537.

education made them even less satisfied with it in practice.[45] Thus, from 1905 onwards[46] nationalism showed itself as a force to be reckoned with, and Japanese support for independence was actively sought by Prince Cuong De, the cousin of the Emperor of Annam.

Later, both geographical propinquity and the similarity of the local economic problems to those of China led to greater interest in the aims of the early Kuo Min Tang and then, under Ho Chi Minh of the more drastic solutions propounded by the Communists. While Ho's Vietnamese Revolutionary Association was proscribed by the French, a large and growing proportion of both the traditional and the Western-educated élites had by the 1930s become ardent advocates of independence, which logically had no place in the French scheme of things, and such views were widely held even among the 1½ million Roman Catholics whose numbers had increased rapidly during the period of French rule.[47]

In the last analysis the strength of the Indochinese Roman Catholic community, the largest in all South-east Asia outside the Philippines, may well prove to have been the most important legacy of French rule, and in certain districts in the northern Annamite lands, where four-fifths of its members lived, Roman Catholics comprised over 30 per cent of the population. Moreover, owing to the extensive educational work undertaken by the missions, Roman Catholics formed a disproportionately large part of the local intelligentsia.

In the southern Annamite lands, on the other hand, Roman Catholics were outnumbered by adherents of two new sects which grew up during the inter-war years. The larger of these, Cao Dai, was founded by an Annamite ex-merchant in 1925 and had its headquarters at Tay-Dinh some 50 miles north-west of Saigon. This self-styled 'third amnesty of God in the Far East' which has been enigmatically described as a mixture of Buddhism, Confucianism, Taoism and Roman Catholicism, and *inter alia* includes Joan of Arc, the Jade Emperor and Victor Hugo among its saints, is a characteristic manifestation of South-east Asian syncretism in a period of social disintegration. But whatever the significance of its religious doctrines, and in spite of its generally conservative economic policy, its following of over 500,000 in 1939 (which had grown to over two million by 1954) was sufficiently nationalist and pro-Japanese to have been regarded by the French as subversive. A similar opinion was also held regarding the somewhat smaller but more fanatical Hoa Hao sect, founded in 1939 and likewise centred in Cochinchina, though doctrinally this was quite different in character, representing rather an ascetic and militant variant of Theravada Buddhism.

By the time the Second World War broke out the Annamite lands were among the most strongly nationalist areas in all South-east Asia, and the sequence

[45] Of the 42,000 persons recorded as 'French and *assimilés*' in 1937, 30,000 were European Frenchmen. These included many Corsicans who were not infrequently despised as 'second-class Frenchmen'.

[46] The name Vietnamese is now the preferred nationalist form for Annamite.

[47] It is estimated that there were 82,000 Roman Catholics in the country by the middle of the 17th century.

of events after the fall of France inevitably intensified these sentiments. Towards the end of 1940 the Japanese obtained a foothold in Tonkin[48] and when in July the following year they compelled the whole country to become 'friendly occupied territory' the way was open for them to turn the defences of Singapore and to overrun the rest of South-east Asia.

Later, as the tide of war turned against them, the Japanese withdrew their South-east Asian headquarters from Singapore to Saigon, and in March 1945 replaced the French administration by one of their own. At the same time they created three ostensibly independent national states, namely Vietnam (consisting of the three Annamite *kys* of Tonkin, Annam and Cochinchina), Cambodia and Laos, under the respective rule of Bao Dai (Emperor of Annam) and the Kings of Cambodia and Luang Prabang.

This development proved to be the first stage in the dismemberment of the Indochinese Union. The second followed shortly afterwards with the Potsdam decision that China Command and South-east Asia Command (the latter relying on British Indian forces) should be responsible for taking the Japanese surrender respectively north and south of the 16th parallel.

Historically this division corresponded roughly to the frontier in the early centuries A.D. between the Sinicized domains of the original Annamite kingdom and the Indianized zone occupied by Champa and Funan.[49] Its political repercussions were likewise significant. For many years the Chinese had been interested in Tonkin as an outlet for Yunnan, and accordingly were anxious that the French should not resume exclusive control over the railway from Haiphong. After indulging in extensive pillage, the Chinese occupation forces, under the Yunnanese General Lu Han, were extremely slow to hand over to the French, and only completed their withdrawal late in 1946, when an agreement had been signed whereby, among other things, the French transferred to China the ownership of the Yunnan railway north of Laokay.[50]

Meanwhile, under cover of the occupation, Ho Chi Minh, who had spent the war years in China where he had organized the Vietminh coalition (*i.e.* the League for the independence of Vietnam), established a government in Tonkin to which Bao Dai, and by implication Annam, immediately adhered. Notwithstanding the return of the French to the coastal towns in 1946, the Vietminh thereafter retained effective control of most of the northern countryside.

In the south, on the other hand, French officials accompanied the British Indian occupation forces in September 1945. Thus the French speedily re-estab-

[48] The Japanese demanded this in the first instance so as to prevent military supplies from reaching China via the Yunnan railway.

[49] Though the southern frontier of Nan Yüeh was the Porte d'Annam *c.* 18° N. See also above, pp. 88 and 112.

[50] After the French closed the Yunnan railway in 1940 the Chinese removed much of the track on their side of the border, with the intention (never realized) of relaying it along a new route to link up with the Burma railway system. On the situation in 1945–6 see Hammer, p. 135.

lished their administration in Saigon even though much of the surrounding area was in a chaotic state, with the sects, previously armed by the Japanese, in control of extensive territories and the Vietminh also seeking to organize opposition.

Precisely what form of administration the French proposed to introduce in post-war Indochina was by no means clear at this stage, though it was known that, like the Dutch, they planned to reorganize their empire on federal lines but had no intention of granting complete independence to any part of it.

At the same time it was also apparent that, even apart from the difficulties caused by the Chinese occupation in northern Indochina, the French were not averse from concentrating their activities in the south. One consequence of the old rivalry between Hanoi and Saigon had been that when the administration in the former took its orders from Vichy, Saigon became a centre for local Gaullist sympathizers. Moreover, even before the war, growing pessimism was being expressed concerning the population problem of Tonkin,[51] but the prospects for expanding the production of the south's rice and rubber appeared bright. Finally Saigon commanded the Mekong valley routes to both Cambodia and Laos, with whose rulers the French quickly reached working agreements.

Some basis therefore appeared to exist for a compromise with Ho Chi Minh, and in March 1946 the French signed an agreement with him recognizing the Democratic Republic of Vietnam (thenceforth usually known as Vietminh) as a free state within the Indochinese federation, which in turn was to form part of the proposed French Union. But differences arose over the degree of independence involved, and on whether or not Cochinchina should be included in Vietnam, and in December 1946 war broke out between the two sides.

At first this was regarded as primarily a conflict between colonialism and nationalism, but events after 1949 led to a reassessment. While the Communists gained the upper hand in China, Ho Chi Minh dispensed with the greater part of his non-Communist support, and thereafter the Chinese People's Republic was in a position to give direct support to the Vietminh overland.

In these circumstances the French were able to enlist United States' support for their cause by emphasizing its part in the world-wide struggle against Communist expansion, while at the same time making a bid for local support by setting up the new Associated State of Vietnam (comprising Tonkin, Annam and Cochinchina), under the headship of Bao Dai who had meanwhile broken with the Vietminh. But although the southern sects and most of the Roman Catholic hierarchy regarded the Bao Dai régime as preferable to the Vietminh, the mass of the Annamite population were unimpressed by French intentions. In this connexion the customs and communications union set up at Pau in December 1950, to embrace the three Associated States of Vietnam, Cambodia and Laos, seemed to be merely the old Indochinese Union under a new name, and besides being unpopular in Vietnam it served also to stimulate growing nationalist opposition to French policy in the other two states.

[51] See the observations of Gourou quoted in Dumont, pp. 143–4.

By the spring of 1954 the military position of the French had deteriorated to such an extent that, barring outside interventions on their behalf, they could no longer continue the war. Negotiations were accordingly undertaken which ended in the Geneva agreements signed on July 21 of that year.[52]

The principal provisions were as follows. Vietnam was to be temporarily divided immediately to the south of the 17th parallel,[53] and Vietminh and French Union forces were to regroup respectively north and south of this line.[54] Neither zone was to participate in any military alliance, or to allow any foreign power to maintain bases within its territory. Civilians were free to move into either zone, and elections for the whole of Vietnam were to be held under international supervision within one year. Cambodia and Laos likewise were debarred from membership of any military alliance, except for self-defence, and were not to grant bases to foreign powers. All foreign troops were to withdraw from their territories, and in Laos the local Communist (Pathet Lao) forces were to regroup in the two northern provinces of Sam Neua and Phong Saly.

In the meantime, the United States which had refused to support the Geneva settlement, took the initiative in organizing the S.E.A.T.O. Defence Treaty as a means of stabilizing the situation thus created. The treaty, signed at Manila on September 8, 1954, by Australia, France, New Zealand, Pakistan, the Philippines, Thailand, the United Kingdom and the United States, aimed at resisting armed aggression in 'the general area of South-east Asia, including also the entire territories of the Asian parties, and the general area of the South-west Pacific, not including the Pacific area north of latitude 21° 30′ N'.[55] By separate protocol the signatories 'designated' Cambodia, Laos and Southern Vietnam as areas against which they would regard an attack as 'endangering their own peace and security'.

Finally, on December 19, 1954, the Pau agreements were abrogated, and thereafter the French gradually abandoned the attempt to keep any part of Indochina even nominally within the French Union, which itself eventually followed the Netherlands-Indonesian Union into limbo. Nevertheless the French breach with the Indochinese lands was never quite so embittered or so complete as that between the Netherlands and Indonesia after 1956, and partly for this reason President de Gaulle, has been able since 1963 to resume some political initiative here with his suggestion of neutralizing the whole area as a buffer zone.

[52] The signatories were France, the United Kingdom, the U.S.S.R., (Communist) China, Vietminh, Vietnam, Cambodia and Laos, though Vietnam refused to sign the clause dealing with the armistice in Vietnam.

[53] In detail the line was drawn so as to leave the Quangtri-Savannakhet road to Laos in the French Union sphere. In a broader sense the line is roughly midway between the Potsdam line and the ancient Porte d'Annam frontier.

[54] In the following pages the areas to north and south of this line are respectively referred to as Northern and Southern Vietnam. Strictly speaking North Vietnam and South Vietnam are synonymous respectively for the old Tonkin and Cochinchina, while the corresponding name for Annam is Central Vietnam.

[55] Hong Kong and Formosa were thus excluded from its terms of reference.

III. THE NEW NATIONAL STATES OF INDOCHINA: NORTHERN AND SOUTHERN VIETNAM, CAMBODIA AND LAOS

In less than a century since the first annexations in Cochinchina French rule has come to an end and the ramshackle Union of Indochina has foundered on the rising tide of Asian nationalism. While the final separation of Cambodia and Laos from the Annamite lands was furthered by the Geneva decision to establish these two as neutral buffer states between the Communist bloc and Thailand, the main Western outpost in South-east Asia, popular opinion in Laos and Cambodia endorses this policy and also welcomes the partition of Vietnam which serves to reduce the danger of Annamite pressure on their territories.

From the Annamite point of view, however, partition is a disaster. Although for both geographical and historical reasons they possess a less developed sense of national unity than do the Koreans, whose post-war experience presents an obvious parallel with their own, the Annamites are indubitably one people, and both Ho Chi Minh and Bao Dai, despite their profound differences in other respects, always insisted on the national unity of all three Annamite *kys*.

Nevertheless, it is a mistake to regard partition solely in terms of great power rivalries. For even though these dominated the Geneva negotiations, the internal conflict between the two nationalist concepts represented by the new *de facto* states of Northern and Southern Vietnam is real enough.

In the overcrowded and impoverished North, Chinese ideas of land reform, whether in the form originally propounded by Sun Yat-sen or in that of Mao Tse-tung more recently, have aroused the greatest interest.[56] But against this the Annamites have traditionally regarded the Chinese with hostility, and even among the most radically minded there has been little desire for Vietnam to become a Chinese satellite. Particularly in the South, where the land problem was different both in kind and in intensity from that in the North, and where the numbers of local Chinese were much larger, anti-Chinese feelings were liable to outweigh the economic attractions of Communism. But the difference between North and South provides only part of the explanation, for anti-Communist sentiments have been strongest among the wealthier Annamites, regardless of latitude, and above all among the Roman Catholics, the great majority of whom were in the North.

This latter element provided a formidable hard core of non-Communist nationalists, and had the French been prepared in good time to work with them they might well have succeeded in outbidding the Communists. This policy has

[56] When, after the late 1920s, the failure of the Kuo Min Tang to put Sun Yat-sen's plans for land reform into practice prepared the way for the more drastic Communist approach in China, the Vietnam Quoc Dan Dong (*i.e.* Nationalist Annamite Party, whose name is a translation of Kuo Min Tang) began to lose ground in the Annamite lands to the local Communist movement led by Ho Chi Minh.

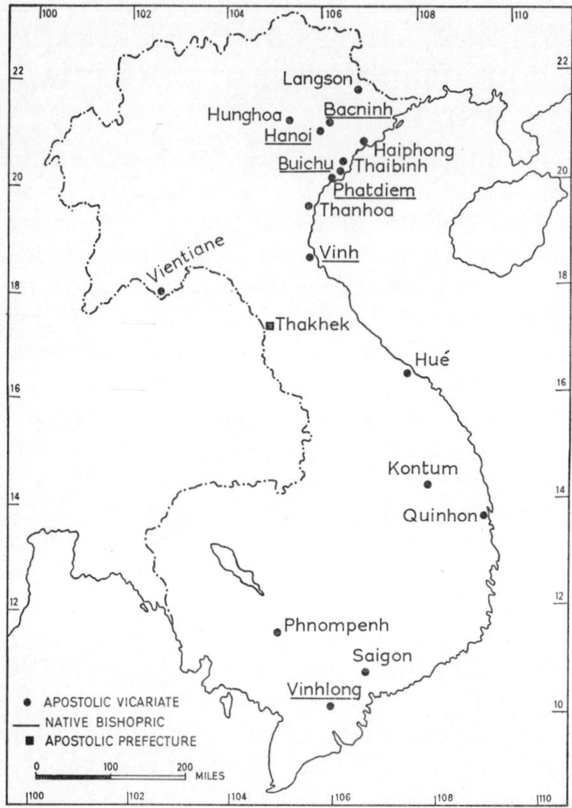

FIG. 79—Indochina: Roman Catholic Church, 1954

since been adopted by the United States, which strongly supported Mr. Ngo Dinh Diem, an energetic Roman Catholic nationalist politician, who replaced Bao Dai as head of the state in Southern Vietnam in October 1955.

Following the Geneva agreement, some 860,000 refugees, most of them Roman Catholics, migrated from North to South,[57] as against perhaps 100,000 who moved in the opposite direction. Nevertheless, Southern Vietnam in 1958 had only 12,800,000 people, compared with 15,000,000 in the North, and in these circumstances Diem has refused to participate in all-Vietnam elections as provided for in the Geneva agreement.[58] Thus the partition, like that in Korea, has hardened into apparent permanence, with the North as a satellite of Communist China and the South as a protégé of the United States. It remains to be seen whether the two regimes can continue to co-exist indefinitely, or whether one or other will eventually provide a nucleus around which the Vietnamese people as a whole will re-unite.

[57] Thus within a few months a vastly greater shift of population occurred from the overcrowded North to the South than the French had been able to achieve in half a century. It may be relevant to note that, as Christians, these refugees were not inhibited by the common Annamite sentiment of unwillingness to leave the ancestral graves. See above, pp. 546–7.

[58] Official grounds for refusal have been that under a Communist regime the elections in Northern Vietnam would not be free.

TABLE 71

NORTHERN VIETNAM, SOUTHERN VIETNAM, CAMBODIA AND LAOS: MAIN ETHNIC GROUPS

1955 estimates

Group	*Northern Vietnam*	*Southern Vietnam*	*Cambodia*	*Laos*
Vietnamese . .	13,000,000	9,750,000	300,000	50,000
Cambodian (Khmer)		480,000	4,000,000	
Cham . . .		40,000	80,000	
Thai (Lao) . .	800,000	25,000	30,000	800,000
Hill peoples . .	300,000	900,000	75,000	600,000
Chinese .	100,000	800,000	180,000	15,000

Northern Vietnam

Of the two Vietnams the North inherited the more difficult set of economic problems. Already a rice deficit area before the Indochina war, it had suffered a serious decline in agricultural productivity through damage to dikes and irrigation channels, and the severance of all ties with the South cut off its established source of rice imports.

Moreover, even apart from the greater damage sustained by the mining and manufacturing industries, the latter had not been developed on a sufficient scale for them to be quickly expanded as earners of foreign exchange, and, in view of the acute and growing pressure on the land, there appeared to be little prospect of a substantial increase in any form of agricultural production other than that urgently needed within Northern Vietnam itself.

To begin with the new Hanoi regime[59] followed the Chinese lead. It began by concentrating primary attention on the countryside and insisted that the food problem could be solved, a belief which was not altogether revolutionary from the Chinese point of view since the rice yield of the Tonkin delta was little more than half that of the pre-war average for the whole of China.

By the end of 1956 the Vietminh had completed the initial stage of their land-reform programme except in certain minority areas. The method adopted, which closely followed that in Communist China, was to divide rural population into five categories: landlords, rich, medium and small peasants, and landless workers, and thereupon to take land mainly from those in the first two and give it to members of the last two groups. As a result the overwhelming majority of Northern Vietnam's farms came to be worked by owner occupiers, the size of holding averaging initially 0·37 acres per person, or 1·85 acres for a family of five, though groups of families were encouraged to work together as 'mutual aid teams'.

[59] Hanoi remains the capital of Northern Vietnam. Its population in 1956 was estimated at 500,000 and that of Haiphong at 180,000.

Although the original land redistribution was carried out in such a way as to antagonize far more than those who could reasonably be classed as landlords, an attempt was subsequently made to 'rectify' this 'error', and on balance it may be that the acquisition of new land acted as a stimulus to production on the part of a majority of the peasantry. Furthermore, virtually all the damaged hydraulic installations have been repaired and even some extensions made, in part with the help of mutual aid teams, and the output of phosphate fertilizers has been restored to its pre-war level of *c.* 30,000 tons. The latter, however, is far below the country's needs, recently estimated at 120,000 tons a year,[60] but a major expansion of production is hoped for from the Laokay apatite deposits, and output from these reached 490,000 tons in 1960.

As a result of these various activities the rice acreage was increased by about one-sixth between 1939 and 1956 and, more remarkably, the yield per acre rose from 28 to 38 bushels, giving an improvement in total output from 2,453,000 to 4,238,000 tons. On the basis of the official rice ration of 300 kg. (661 lb.) per person per year, Northern Vietnam proceeded to claim not merely complete self-sufficiency in rice but also to have produced a surplus of 5 kg. per head, an impressive achievement even when due allowance is made for the fact that the exodus of refugees removed approximately eight years' natural increase of population in the space of a few months. Spurred on by this success, the government pressed on with the introduction of co-operatives in 1958–9, and announced a target of 7,600,000 tons of rice to be produced in 1960. But although a record harvest of 5,200,000 tons was obtained in 1959 this was followed by a drop to 4,400,000 tons in 1960. Allowing for an increase of 500,000 people a year, this meant that food production was not keeping pace with home demand, and the rice ration was therefore reduced.[61]

As yet, Northern Vietnam has not adopted the commune system introduced in China since 1958, nor has any great progress been made in the mechanization of agriculture. And indeed, although some seventeen state farms, with an average size of rather over 1,000 acres, were in mechanized operation in Northern Vietnam in 1956, it may well be doubted whether in so densely populated a country extensive mechanization has much to contribute.

As regards industrial development also, the long-term prospects are somewhat obscure, though extensive rehabilitation of mines and factories has already been carried out. But apart from anthracite, Northern Vietnam has few obvious assets to justify its being developed as a major industrial centre by China (or by other members of the Communist bloc) which would have to supply the necessary capital equipment. Thus, although a few new industrial plants have been installed since 1954, they are not of major proportions, and apparently no very large-scale pro-

[60] By Dumont, p. 147, who also points out that the same amount of nitrogenous fertilizer (which could be produced locally by synthetic means) is needed.

[61] On this and other recent developments in Northern Vietnam, see 'North Vietnam: six years after Geneva', *E. W.*, **14**, 8, pp. 16–18, and *China Quarterly, Special Survey of North Vietnam.*

jects were envisaged at this stage. On the other hand much effort has been devoted to expanding the output of small workshop and handicraft industries which, without heavy outlay, can help to raise living standards and develop useful skills, while at the same time mopping up seasonal unemployment in the countryside. In this last connexion it has been estimated that the average Vietnamese peasant is employed for only 125 days in the year,[62] though it is none the less true that virtually all are fully employed during the peak periods of planting and harvesting, and were there to be a large permanent exodus to the towns the agricultural output would suffer accordingly.

Though the available evidence is scanty, it seems that the economic policies followed in Northern Vietnam until 1960 corresponded to those of the first decade in China after the 1949 revolution, and on this basis it was widely assumed that Northern Vietnam was no more than a Chinese satellite. Doubtless such an arrangement would have suited the Chinese, whose interest there, apart from the possibility of using Haiphong as an outlet, was probably limited in the immediate post-1949 period to keeping the territory, originally valued by the French as a strategic *point d'appui*, out of Western hands.

However, it seems clear that both China and Northern Vietnam originally expected that the nation-wide elections, provided for under the Geneva settlement, would automatically bring the South as well as the North under the control of Hanoi. And while for the latter such a reunification would have provided a far stronger economic base and hence perhaps the choice of greater freedom of action generally, the attitude of China, both at Geneva and afterwards, suggested that it also regarded the prospect of such a reunited Vietnam as consistent with its own interests in this part of the world.

Be that as it may, having already granted aid to the value of 800 million yuan (*c.* $325 million) in 1955, the Chinese announced in 1957 that, despite retrenchment in other respects, they proposed to increase the scale of their aid to certain countries (*i.e.* principally Northern Vietnam). Besides Chinese assistance, the U.S.S.R. supplied 170,000 tons of Burmese rice in the critical year after Geneva and granted 400 million roubles (*c.* $100 million) aid in 1955, which was used *inter alia* to set up a tea factory at Phy Tho, and a machinery plant and a power station at Thanh Hoa.[64]

During the period 1955–61 total Chinese aid to Northern Vietnam amounted to $457·5 million, as against $365 million from the U.S.S.R. and $85 million from eastern Europe. This left China still slightly in the lead, and although the Northern Vietnamese government seemed to swing over after 1960 to support for Moscow as against Peking, and the policies underlying its 1961–5 Plan seemed

[62] Dumont, p. 142.

[63] The Chinese line from Chuchow (on the Peking–Canton trunk line) to Langson was completed in order to supply the Vietminh during the Indochina war. On the Yunnan line the track removed during the Second World War has since been relaid. Shabad, p. 49.

[64] *Ibid.*, p. 51. All-told 14 new industrial plants, mostly for the processing of local produce, were built in 1957, but most of them are very small.

to be modelled on those of the U.S.S.R., a further apparent reversal occurred in 1963.

In respect of internal administration both Russian and Chinese precedents can be cited for the policy of the Northern Vietnamese government, which has wooed the ethnic minorities by setting up two autonomous zones, respectively the Thai-Meo A.Z. and the Viet Bac A.Z., the latter inhabited by a variety of Thai, Tho and Nung peoples.[65] But at the same time it has undoubtedly antagonized the economically more important Roman Catholic community, still not far short of a million strong, and it remains to be seen how the traditional nationalist opposition to China will eventually affect the internal rivalry between those of the Communist leadership who are apt to incline towards Moscow and those whose ideological sympathies lie more with Peking.

Southern Vietnam

In the competition for viability Southern Vietnam, as the richer half, which absorbed 58 per cent of the imports and supplied 82 per cent of the exports of the combined Annamite territories in 1939,[66] would at first sight seem the better placed. Nevertheless, it remains almost entirely dependent on outside sources for all but the simplest kinds of manufactured goods, and the wartime reversion of vast areas of rice land to swamp had reduced its rice surplus almost to zero by 1954. This situation was aggravated by the territorial power wielded over much of Cochinchina by the sects,[67] which continued after the Geneva settlement to defy the authority of the discredited central government, and finally the latter had to cope with the problem of resettling 860,000 refugees, different in dialect and mostly different in religion from the local population.

It was therefore remarkable that the new regime of Mr. Ngo Dinh Diem[68] should have largely succeeded in bringing order out of this chaos within so short a space of time. Thanks to substantial aid supplied by the United States in a determined effort at least to hold the Geneva line, the new government was enabled to concentrate its attention first on political unification before turning to the long-term problem of economic development. Local armed forces were trained and equipped by the United States to replace the French Union troops withdrawn under the Geneva agreement, and by 1956 the government had succeeded in completely crushing the resistance of the sects. Moreover, in October 1956 a new constitution was inaugurated, based largely on the U.S. pattern though with stronger presidential powers, in some ways foreshadowing the system introduced in France by de Gaulle in 1958.

Such a similarity, however, was purely coincidental, for Diem appeared at

[65] A third, the Lao-Hai-Zen A.Z. is to be set up shortly. Note that the Viet Bac A.Z. includes the upland country along the border with China.

[66] Shabad, p. 51.

[67] By this time a third so-called sect was involved, namely the Binh Xuyen; this, however, had no religious basis.

[68] Who became Prime Minister in June 1954 and, after ousting Bao Dai, himself assumed the Presidency in October 1955. See above, p. 557.

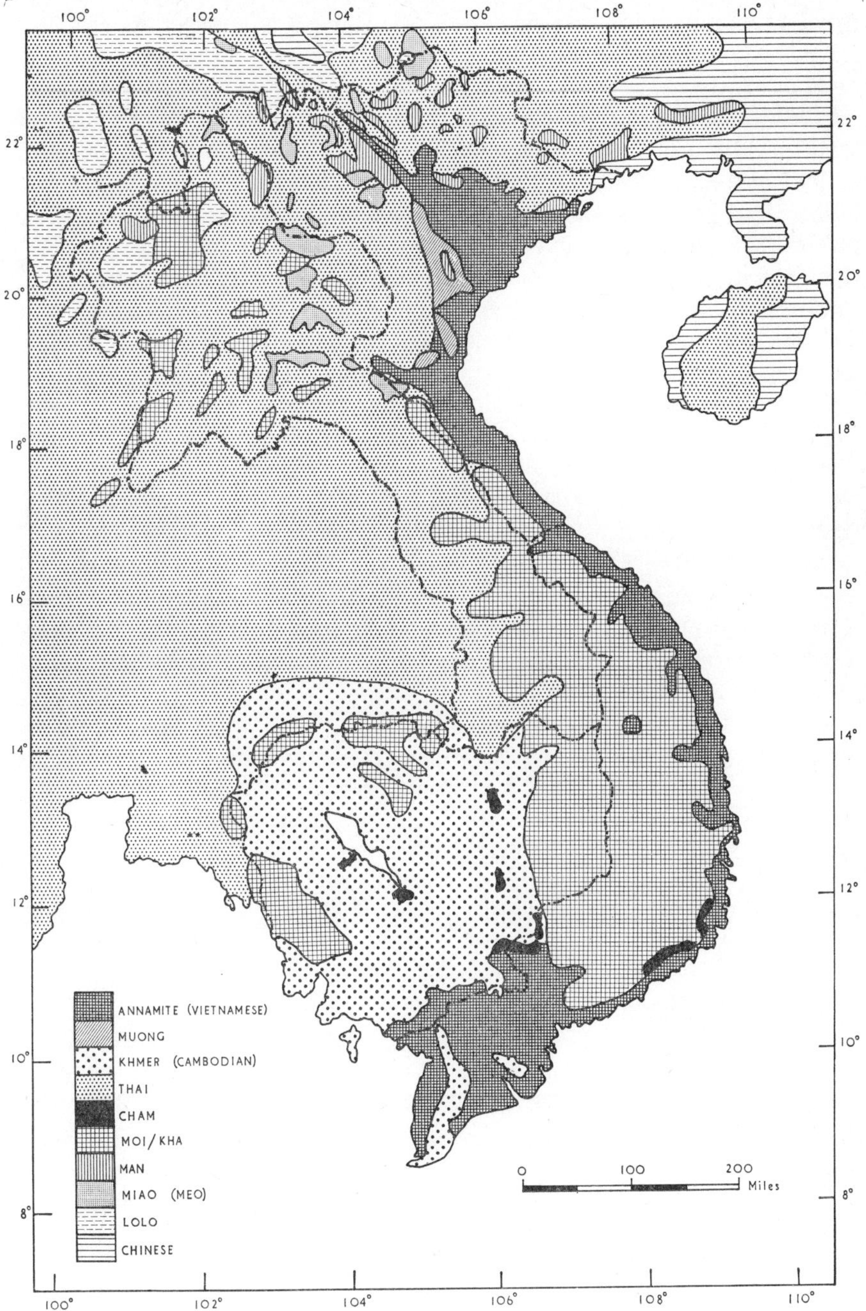

FIG. 80—Indochina: languages

pains to minimize any surviving vestiges of French influence.[69] Indeed, as a French-educated Roman Catholic northerner, he seemed far removed from the local peasantry and his consequent desire to emphasize the nationalist character of the regime may explain one of the most controversial measures it has yet undertaken, namely the attempt to assimilate the Chinese minority.

By a retroactive law of August 21, 1956, all Chinese born in Vietnam were declared to be Vietnamese nationals, and must henceforth take Vietnamese names. This was followed in September by another decree excluding foreigners from eleven professions, the most important of which were the rice and retail trades.[70] Taken together, the new measures effectively permitted all local-born Chinese, that is some 500,000 out of a total of 800,000 ethnic Chinese, to carry on their business unimpeded, and most of the rest would probably be able to do the same under cover of appropriate family arrangements. But the special status which the Chinese enjoyed by virtue of the 1930 Nanking treaty, which gave them most of the advantages of citizenship with few of its responsibilities, was abolished, and the new policy marked a turning point in South-east Asian attitudes towards the local Chinese *imperia in imperiis*.[71]

As such it provoked immediate protest from Formosa (the only China recognized by Southern Vietnam) and stubborn resistance on the part of the local Chinese residents. But in the long run the latter, with their characteristic hard-headedness, may yet rate economics more important than *amour propre*, deeply though this has been offended.

It was not until 1957 that Southern Vietnam's first five-year plan was drawn up, and in view of the controversy it aroused publication was postponed indefinitely. However, the plan, which incorporated various projects already under way since 1954, gave a fairly clear indication of the way the government was thinking, notably in giving priority to agriculture in general, and in particular to extending the cultivated acreage by reclamation of abandoned lands and the opening up of new areas. While mining and manufacturing were not overlooked, the intention was clearly to rely on rice, rubber and other agricultural products as the main earners of foreign exchange.

Four large agricultural development projects were involved, namely Caisan (western delta), Baclieu-Camau (southern delta), Plaine des Joncs (north-central delta) and High Plateaux (mainly on the *terres rouges*). The first three of these schemes originated in part with the need to resettle the refugees from the North, but the settlers in the High Plateaux were drawn mainly from the overcrowded coastal lowlands of Annam. Ultimately it was hoped to establish some 150,000 Vietnamese in this predominantly Moi countryside, lying at an altitude of

[69] There has since been some modification in this respect, and France still remains an important trading partner, though second to the U.S.A.

[70] Chinese account for about 34 per cent of the business in the proscribed categories. These do *not* include manufacturing industry. Fall (F).

[71] However, more drastic steps have since been taken elsewhere in South-east Asia, notably in Indonesia. See above, pp. 387–8, note 66.

1,200 to 3,000 ft., and already more than a third of that number have been settled, mainly in a series of villages around such centres as Pleiku, Banméthuot and Kontum. Each family was granted about 10 acres of land, a portion of which had been cleared in advance by earlier arrivals, and was supported by the state until the first harvest could be gathered.

Besides relieving congestion in the lowlands this project was designed to contribute to the diversification of the country's agriculture by expanding production of tea, coffee, rubber and fruit. But its main objective seemed to be to establish politically reliable nuclei of settlement within the sparsely populated Moi lands which offered an obvious route for Communist infiltration from the North. Associated with this policy was the extensive road-building programme carried out with U.S. aid, which aimed at linking Quinhon–Pleiku, Ninhoa–Banméthuot and Plaiku–Banméthuot in the heart of this region. Nevertheless, the prospective influx of large numbers of Vietnamese into these remote territories produced such intense resentment on the part of the Moi tribesmen as to defeat the main purpose for which the scheme had been devised.[72]

The three lowland projects, on the other hand, were pre-eminently concerned with large-scale rice production, and all-told embraced an area of some 900,000 acres. The most advanced was that at Caisan where it was planned within three years to reclaim 400,000 acres, resettle 100,000 refugees and produce an annual crop of 150,000 tons of paddy, two-thirds of which would be surplus to local needs. By the end of 1956 fourteen large drainage canals, each six to nine miles long, had been dug by hand and the first crop obtained by tractor ploughing and broadcast sowing. For the initial preparation of the first 75,000 acres the U.S. Operations Mission provided over $10 million and 100 tractors,[73] but while the possibilities of developing large-scale mechanized cultivation on a permanent basis were explored, the plan at Caisan was to establish family holdings of about 7½ acres each, which would be supplied with buffaloes for ploughing in the traditional manner.

On the wider question of land reform Southern Vietnam is faced with quite different problems from those in the North, the main difficulties being not so much the size of holdings as high rents, insecurity of tenure and rural indebtedness, especially in the Mekong delta where some three-fifths of the rice land is owned by non-cultivators. To meet this situation the government devised a four-stage programme, providing first for the conclusion of written contracts at reduced rents of 15–25 per cent of the value of the annual rice crop; secondly, the granting of popular credit at annual interest rates not exceeding 6 per cent; thirdly, redistribution to cultivators of some 500,000 acres of state land; and finally, compulsory government purchase of rice land above a maximum of 100 hectares (247 acres) permitted to any single landowner, and the resale of this, on deferred payment terms, to peasant cultivators. However, while fair progress was made in implementing the first two stages of this plan, much less had been

[72] See Fall (G), p. 252 and *New York Times*, April 5, 1959. [73] Fall (G), pp. 251–2.

done in respect of the other two before the need to counter the intensified Communist (Vietcong) guerilla activities became the main preoccupation of the Diem government in the countryside after 1960.[74]

In the meantime the output of rice had been raised from under 3 million tons in 1954 to nearly 5 million tons in 1960, and though the recorded export of 350,000 tons was still only one-third of the normal pre-war amount, a considerable contraband export took place to the North. Rubber exports on the other hand reached 76,611 tons, which exceeded the highest pre-war total, and as in the past were marketed almost entirely in France. Tea and tobacco industries also revived, and in addition big increases were hoped for from the three fibres silk, kenaf and cotton, whose respective totals of 48, 41 and 345 tons (1957) were to be greatly increased to help meet the needs of local industry.

In this last connexion, however, the South's plans have never been very elaborate, the main concern being to extend the pre-existing facilities for processing local primary produce and to establish a few new consumer goods industries to take the place of those in the North, from which the South has been cut off since 1954. Associated with these developments has been the initiation of a major hydro-electric power scheme on the Danhim river near Dalat which, when all its three stages have been completed, will generate 2,716 million kWh per year. Mining remains very unimportant, and the main coalfield, at Nongson, produced only 27,000 tons in 1960.

Notwithstanding the limited development of its industrial sector and the incompleteness of its programme of agrarian reform, Southern Vietnam, thanks both to lavish American aid[75] and to its favourable ratio of population to agricultural resources, undoubtedly enjoyed a much higher standard of living under the Diem regime than that of its Communist counterpart in the North. Indeed, it was its very success in this respect, in contrast to the mounting economic difficulties faced by the overcrowded North, which seems to have impelled the latter, in the words of General Vo Nguyen Giap (1960) to step up 'the revolution in the South'.

In its efforts to counter the rapid increase in Vietcong terrorist activity thereafter, the Diem regime quickly became the victim of what was already its own greatest weakness. Largely because of the influx of refugees, the population of Saigon-Cholon has risen to some two million, or approximately one-sixth of the entire Southern total, and probably nowhere else in all South-east Asia has the

[74] While the U.S.A. sought to persuade the government to make greater efforts in land reform, there was much resistance from local landlords. But by 1958 recognizable progress was at last being made.

[75] U.S. aid from 1950 to 1956 inclusive amounted to $560,430,000 and since then has continued on a very generous scale. There has also been a smaller volume of French aid, which for 1955 and 1956 totalled 63·7 million piastres. On May 13, 1959 an agreement was signed whereby Japan undertook to pay reparations to the value of £19,857,000 to Southern Vietnam. The greater part of these reparations, which will be delivered in the form of goods and services, are to be devoted to the Danhim hydro-electric project (see above). No Japanese reparations are being paid to Northern Vietnam.

contrast between the life of the capital city and that of the surrounding countryside become so pronounced as it has here. In these circumstances the Diem ruling clique, predominantly Westernized and largely Roman Catholic as it was, became increasingly divorced from the down-to-earth realities of the villages, and its failure to provide the South as a whole with a convincing *raison d'être* eventually proved to be its undoing.

But in the time which has elapsed since the murder of Diem in 1963, none of his many successors has appeared any more effective in this respect. While, therefore, the willingness of the Southern population to continue soldiering on in these circumstances suggests that there is no widespread enthusiasm for reunification under the aegis of the Hanoi government, it is equally clear that, but for the massive increase of American military support in 1965, such an outcome could not have been long delayed.

Cambodia and Laos

Compared with the two Vietnams, Cambodia and especially Laos are much less developed economically and less experienced in the ways of the outside world. This situation, together with some miscalculations in Western policy, has weakened their effectiveness in the role of buffer states as envisaged by the 1954 Geneva settlement, with the result that Communist influence in Laos is now much more extensive, and Cambodia, though internally stable, is inclining noticeably towards China in its external relationships.[76]

The predominantly subsistence agricultural economy of Cambodia has not suffered such serious dislocation since 1940 as have the more complex economies of the Vietnamese lands, and the present rice production of some 1,500,000 tons is above the pre-war level, thus permitting of an annual export of about 300,000 tons. Rubber production also has risen, from 17,000 tons in 1938 to over 36,000 tons in 1960, and these two gains may be set against the recent decline in the export of maize and fish.

Notwithstanding the rapid increase in population to a total of 5,740,000, and an average density of 82 to the square mile in 1962, Cambodia still remains relatively empty, with only 10 per cent of its land under the plough,[77] and at least four times this amount potentially cultivable. Indeed the possibility that its extensive open spaces may attract the attention of unwanted neighbours is one of the most serious problems with which Cambodia's rulers have to contend and when in 1956 an agreement was signed permitting 50,000 Japanese to settle in the country within the next five years it was stated that these would constitute far less of a threat than would a similar influx of Vietnamese. For the Cambodians have not forgotten the continuing Annamite encroachment during the period of French rule, and fears are strong that the Southern Vietnam government may seek new land at their expense.

[76] See below, p. 572.

[77] Mostly owned by peasant proprietors; there is no serious land problem.

FIG. 81—Indochina: political divisions, 1960

Distrust of the Vietnamese is primarily responsible also for the decision to build a new port at Sihanoukville, near Kompong Som, in order to provide the more populous south-east of the country with its own outlet to the sea instead of having to rely on Saigon.[78] The new port, which has been linked by a modern highway to Phnom Penh, was opened to ocean shipping in May 1956. Moreover, as noted in Chapter 15, the western provinces were provided with a through railway to Bangkok, and for a time prior to 1955/6 is seemed that in spite of historic enmities, Cambodia was drawing closer, politically as well as economically, to Thailand.

More recently, however, relations with Thailand, as also with Southern Vietnam have deteriorated, and though this has shown itself in the form of border disputes, its root cause lies in growing differences over the alignment of foreign policy as a whole. Thus, while Thailand and Southern Vietnam are clearly ranged with the West, Cambodia argued that open acceptance of S.E.A.T.O. protection was inconsistent with its status as a buffer, and after 1956 adopted a neutralist policy modelled on that of India, and in 1958 recognized the Peking government. Meanwhile, having previously obtained promises of substantial United States' and French aid, the Cambodians emphasized their uncommittedness by accepting further aid from Communist China as well.[79] But in 1963, as a preliminary to an accommodation with China, Cambodia renounced United States aid, and thereafter made a further approach to France for military aid and a loan for the building of a railway to link Sihanoukville with Phnom-penh.

Besides the port development scheme Cambodia has plans for agricultural improvement, an extension of health and educational services, and the building up of at least a nucleus of industries to process its main raw materials. Although several factories have been built recently the total number is still very small, and despite a substantial increase recently the total electric power generated was only 59·6 million kWh in 1960.[80]

Hitherto, such industry as has existed has mostly been run by Chinese and Vietnamese, who likewise dominate the retail trade. These two minority communities together provide the only middle class between the small, mainly aristocratic ruling élite[81] and the mass of the Cambodian peasantry. Thus, while the

[78] Phnom Penh on the Mekong is also a port accessible to ships of 4,000–6,000 tons, depending on the season of the year. But ships using it have to pass through the territory of Southern Vietnam.

[79] Total U.S. aid to the end of 1957 was $117·4 million. French aid, 1955–7 was 9,360 million francs and Chinese aid in 1956 approximately $22·5 million. *Inter alia* the French have built the new port at Sihanoukville, while the Americans built the road linking it with Phnom Penh. Among the projects financed by Chinese aid are a radio station, a plywood factory, a textile factory at Kompong Chom and two others producing cement and paper respectively.

[80] Besides those noted above (p. 569, note 79), there are new privately owned factories for car assembly, canning, and the manufacture of rubber goods and soft drinks.

[81] The 'strong man' is ex-King Norodom Sihanouk, who abdicated in favour of his father in 1955 and is the leader of the Sangkum (Democratic Socialist Community). The Cambodian monarchy, like that of Thailand, is by tradition the spiritual embodiment of the state, and still retains a strong popular appeal.

total Chinese and Vietnamese communities (respectively 250,000 and 350,000 strong) together represent about 11 per cent of the total population, they constitute a majority (respectively 30 per cent and 28 per cent) of the 550,000 inhabitants of the capital city of Phnom Penh.

In these circumstances the authorities, besides refusing equality of civil rights to the local Chinese, have recently excluded the latter from various professions, and would clearly like to promote more Cambodian participation in any further industrial development which takes place. But the fact remains that extremely few Cambodians have either the training or the inclination for such activity, and as yet there is little evidence of any change from the traditional insouciance which permitted the present situation to arise in the first place.

Such remarks apply with even greater force to Laos, which owing to its geographical isolation had been scarcely touched by the forces of modernization prior to the last few years. Even today there are barely a thousand miles of motorable road (motorable, that is, during the dry season) in an area nearly twice the size of England, no major industries, and a total electric power production (all thermal) of only 14·5 million kWh a year. Present population is variously estimated at from 1,500,000 to 3,500,000, but clearly recent growth has been rapid and the local output of some 550,000 tons of rice needs increasingly to be supplemented by imports. The only available exports are minute quantities of tobacco and coffee, some timber, benzoin and stick-lac and a little tin, though the Nam Patene mines, reopened in 1955, at present produce only a fraction of the quantity of ore mined before the war.

However, as one of the most exposed parts of South-east Asia, Laos has been receiving substantial foreign aid, primarily from the United States,[82] and while this has been spent largely on the army and police, it also covers the cost of nine-tenths of the imports and is paying for various much-needed improvements, particularly in transport, both internal and external. Here, as in Cambodia, a change in orientation has taken place recently. Thus while an agreement was made some years ago with Southern Vietnam for Laos to use Tourane as a transit port (via Route 9), the main link with the outside world is no longer through the Annamite lands, but instead via Bangkok and the Nong Khai railway.

Politically Laos is much less unified and less stable than Cambodia. In so far as the country has a geographical nucleus it is the long and narrow valley of the upper Mekong in which the greater part of the Lao people live, surrounded by a variety of hill peoples as shown in Fig. 80. In its general pattern, and in the traditional contempt of the valley dwellers for the uplanders, this situation recalls that of Burma and the other riverine states of South-east Asia, with, however, the

[82] U.S. aid for the period 1950–57 inclusive amounted to $133·6 million; for the year 1956/7 it was $44·4 million. French aid for the two years 1955 and 1956 was 2,800 million francs. If, as it has striven to do since 1962, Laos continues to adopt a neutralist policy it will still remain precariously dependent on foreign aid for any economic progress. In 1957 the value of its imports was 38 times as great as that of its exports. See Table 72.

significant difference that here in Laos the hill peoples together probably account for more than half the population.[83] Furthermore, the Lao themselves, being merely a branch of the greater Thai family, can scarcely be regarded as a true national group. And in fact within the Lao territories historic rivalries are deeply rooted, for prior to 1893 the country had more often than not been divided into a number of petty kingdoms, corresponding roughly to the main and subsidiary valley tracts. Under French rule only one of these kingdoms, namely Luang Prabang, preserved a semblance of its identity, while the more accessible town of Vientiane, a former capital of Lan Chang, and the traditional rival of Luang Prabang, became the seat of the French Resident-Superior. Today this dualism is still evident in that while Luang Prabang is the royal capital,[84] Vientiane is the administrative capital and the two do not always see eye to eye. Most serious of all however is the territorial/ideological division first recognized by the 1954 Geneva requirement that the Pathet Lao forces should regroup in Phong Saly and Sam Neua.[85]

In effect the Pathet Lao was the successor of the Lao Issarak or national independence party, but under its later style the movement was predominantly Communist led and maintained close liason with the Vietminh. Indeed many of the Pathet Lao troops were themselves Vietnamese, and still others were hill tribesmen whom the Communists had trained to be formidable guerrilla fighters. For here, once again, Communist overtures to the minority peoples have been made easy by the latter's age-old resentment against their treatment by the local plainsmen. After regrouping in Phong Saly and Sam Neua, which directly adjoin the Thai Autonomous Region of China[86] and the Thai-Meo Autonomous Zone of Northern Vietnam, the Pathet Lao for several years completely controlled these two provinces, which the Communists apparently wished to hold as *points d'appui* for use against the rest of Laos as opportunity offered.

In November 1957, however, the Pathet Lao agreed to the reintegration of Phong Saly and Sam Neua into the kingdom, in return for the legalization of the Pathet Lao as a political party. As a result of the elections which followed in May 1958 the latter, under the new guise of the New Lao Hakset, obtained more than a third of the seats in the National Assembly, but thereafter the government broke up, to be followed by another which aligned itself clearly with the West and, thereafter pursued an unequivocally anti-Communist policy.

This apparent stability came to a sudden end in 1960 with the neutralist *coup* of Captain Kong Lae, and although a new right-wing government was eventually established in Vientiane under the southern Prince Boun Oum, it seemed clear that the cleavages between the neutralists, supported by the Pathet Lao and the Soviet bloc, and the anti-Communists, backed by Thailand and the U.S.A., were so great as to

[83] See 'Crisis of authority in Laos', *Guardian*, January 28, 1960.

[84] Because of the former division of the territory into separate kingdoms the roya family in Laos is less of a unifying factor than is its counterpart in Cambodia.

[85] See Fig. 78 and note that Phong Saly commands the route via the Nam Hou valley to the royal capital of Luang Prabang.

[86] See above, p. 522.

preclude any possibility of long-term stability under a government of either colour.

Although for a time the subsequent hostilities, into which this situation soon deteriorated, threatened also to involve the Communist powers on the one side and the S.E.A.T.O. alliance on the other, a compromise was eventually arranged. Thus in June 1962 the two extreme factions in Laos were again brought together in a coalition government under the leadership of the neutralist Prince Souvanna Phouma, and in July 1962 at Geneva, 14 nations, including the United Kingdom, the United States, France, the Soviet Union and China, agreed to respect the country's neutrality, and Laos itself formally rejected S.E.A.T.O. protection.[87]

During the 1962 crisis it seemed for a time that a partition of Laos might offer the best solution, but though precedent existed for a latitudinal division between Vientiane and Luang Prabang the effective division now lay between the government-controlled areas along the Mekong and the Pathet Lao-dominated territories to the east. Be that as it may, the precarious internal stability supposedly restored in 1962 soon broke down, and renewed Pathet Lao pressure led to a resumption of fighting in 1963 and again in 1964 in which the Pathet Lao substantially extended its hold. Attempts to re-establish a measure of internal political cohesion had achieved no real success by the autumn of 1965.

In the adjacent but much less exposed buffer state of Cambodia a policy of strict neutrality was followed for several years, though this was severely criticized by its anti-Communist neighbours, Thailand and Southern Vietnam. But while these three regard Cambodia as constituting a dangerous source of weakness[88] to the area as a whole, Cambodia appears to be no less seriously disturbed by the strength of their military forces and by what it regards as evidence of hostile intentions on the part of its two traditional enemies.[89] However its attempts to insure itself against such eventualities by drawing politically closer to China in 1964 seem to entail even greater risks than those it seeks to obviate.

In this connexion one further possibility deserves mention. To a significant extent the political fragmentation and consequent strategic weakness of the Mekong basin, which is divided between China, Laos, Thailand, Cambodia and Southern Vietnam is a result of the series of obstacles which have made the Mekong almost useless as a natural highway. In recent years, however, the last four states have been considering a 20-year plan to improve and develop the lower half of the Mekong, and the proposals are now being investigated under United Nations auspices.

[87] Immediately following the Geneva agreement of July 1962, Cambodia suggested the convening of a conference to consider the incorporation of Laos, Southern Vietnam and Cambodia in an internationally guaranteed neutral zone. See also below, Chapter 22.

[88] As mentioned above, p. 523, note 61, the dispute with Thailand over Préah Vihéar was settled in June 1962.

[89] See 'Cambodia profits from neutrality', *The Times*, June 20, 1960, p. 13, which claims that the basic reason for Cambodia's policy is that its Prime Minister, Prince Sihanouk, is convinced that China will ultimately rule over all South-east Asia. Thus he appears to believe that it may be wisest to begin to come to terms with the inevitable.

Initially five main dual- or multi-purpose projects would be undertaken, respectively at Pa Mong, twenty miles above Vientiane, Khemarat, on the Laos/Thailand border, Khone falls, on the Laos/Cambodia border; Sambor, farther south in Cambodia; and Tonlé Sap. Of these the first four would all include both electrical generating stations and navigational improvements. In addition, irrigation water would be provided at Pa Mong for the Korat plateau and the Vientiane plain, and at Sambor for an extensive area below Kratié, while the Tonlé Sap scheme would regulate water supplies over the entire region surrounding the lake.

Clearly the execution of this imaginative plan would be a momentous task, and the best hope for success, in view of the political as well as economic problems involved, would be for it to be undertaken under the auspices of the United Nations rather than of S.E.A.T.O. or any other regional body. Meanwhile until a thorough survey has been carried out it remains to be proved that the enormous sums which such an undertaking would involve could not in fact be used to better effect in other less spectacular ways within the several countries concerned.[90] However, if the project can be shown to be economically worth while there would be much to be said for attempting to put it into effect. For while it might be argued that the improvement of this great waterway, formerly but mistakenly regarded as an easy route to China, would now serve to increase the risk of Chinese penetration in the reverse direction, the benefits resulting from the economic development and mutual co-operation of the series of lesser states along its course are important considerations to be weighed on the other side.

Viewed against the background of the intensified military struggle between Northern and Southern Vietnam, the Mekong scheme may appear to have become even more of a pipe dream than it was before, but President Johnson's suggestion in the spring of 1965 that the United States might be willing to give massive assistance for a regional development project based upon it shows that Washington is alive to the potential contribution it could make, both economically and psychologically, to a solution of the long-term problems of the region as a whole.

In this connexion, however, it is imperative to see the present struggle in Vietnam in the wider context of that country's geographical position between China and South-east Asia. Although apparently determined solely by the exigencies of contemporary power politics, the redrawing of the map of Indochina at Geneva served to restore preponderant Chinese influence over an area corresponding almost exactly to the Nan Yüeh of the first millennium A.D., and in October 1954, Mr. Nehru let it be known that he regarded Cambodia as lying within the Indian cultural sphere, an alignment which acquired a new significance

[90] As noted on pp. 417–8, the part of the Mekong valley involved in this scheme is relatively narrow, being hemmed in between plateau country to both east and west, and this imposes much more rigorous limits on the extent of potentially irrigable land than some press reports about this project seem to imply.

with Cambodia's adoption of a neutralist policy but has since been called in question by the latter's closer alignment towards China.

Whether this tacit division of spheres, which was not ill-founded historically or geographically could still provide a basis for stabilization is doubtful, not least because the position of Southern Vietnam represents an unprecedented factor in the equation. Thus, while for most of the first millennium A.D. the southern frontier of the Chinese sphere stopped short not far from the present divide between Northern and Southern Vietnam, the frontier of the Indianized lands to the south of this was subsequently pushed back by the Vietnamese themselves after they had won their independence from China in 939, as has already been described in Chapter 4. And today it would seem that, as throughout their past history, the primary focus of nationalist sentiment in the Annamite lands remains in the North rather than the South, and further that the appeal of Ho Chi Minh's regime lies at least as much in its nationalist as in its Communist persuasions. Admittedly in the North, where rural poverty had long been abyssmal, these two go hand in hand, but while conditions in this respect have been different in the South, the events of the early 1960s suggest that mere anti-Communism buttressed by outside economic assistance is not in itself sufficient to counteract the determination of the Northern-inspired Vietcong[91] to see the whole of the the Vietnamese lands reunited under Communist rule.

If this is simply because, as happened for a time in Malaya during its period of Communist-led terrorism after 1948, the ruthlessness of the guerrillas tends to convince the mass of the rural population that resistance is futile, the United States' policy of helping to arm and train the peasants to defend their own villages, as was done successfully by the British in Malaya in the early 1950s[92] may yet enable the South to hold its own.

But in contrast to Malaya, where the great majority of the terrorists were not Malays but Chinese, the Vietcong are members of basically the same Vietnamese nation as the Southern Vietnamese themselves. Thus if any sense of solidarity with their kinsfolk in the historic home of Vietnamese nationalism in the North[93] should ever seriously undermine resistance in the South, which has yet to show that it has found a positive *raison d'être*, the outlook for the survival of the latter as a separate entity would be poor and the inevitable growth of war weariness among many of the population serves to aggravate this problem.

Were the South to be thus absorbed by a Communist North the effects could scarcely be expected to stop there. For although the importance of historical precedents should not be exaggerated, the fact remains that after their first

[91] The Vietcong guerrillas, though largely of Southern origin, have been increasingly strongly supported both in men and materials from the North, in part *via* the so-called Ho Chi Minh trail. See Fig. 78.

[92] On the Malayan 'Emergency' see below, pp. 604, 609 and 657.

[93] In this historic respect the Western-backed part of partitioned Vietnam appears to be in a weaker position than the corresponding parts of Germany and Korea.

attacks on Champa in 1069[94] the Vietnamese peoples advanced steadily but inexorably into the territories of their Indianized neighbours for close upon 800 years, until the political map was temporarily frozen by the French in the latter part of the 19th century, and even then Vietnamese economic penetration continued into both Laos and Cambodia.

Admittedly, much else has changed since then, and in particular the nationalist movement in Northern Vietnam, unlike those in all other parts of South-east Asia, has identified itself with Communism which, notwithstanding the current rift between Peking and Moscow, still has universalist aspirations. What long-term significance this rift will have for Northern Vietnam remains to be seen, but one factor which has not changed in this situation is the age-old contrast between the dynamism of the Vietnamese and the insouciance of their neighbours to the south and west.[95] And in view of the continuing Vietminh penetration into Laos even after the Second Geneva Agreement of 1962, it seems all too probable that the removal of the remaining element of Western power from Indochina, namely that provided by the United States' links with Southern Vietnam, would be followed by further advances of Vietnamese influence, directed from Hanoi and supported by Peking in the states to the south and west. Thus proposals, such as those of President de Gaulle, for neutralizing Indochina[96] need to be subjected to severe scrutiny, though if, perhaps as a result of extensive international participation in the Mekong scheme, a basis came to exist for the effective guaranteeing of such neutrality, it would certainly deserve more serious consideration.

Earlier in this chapter the geographical significance of the Mekong delta as a possible base for the control of Indochina was examined, but it must be admitted that the French attempt to use Cochinchina in this way after 1945 emphasized rather the contrary aspect of its situation, namely that the region lay open to penetration by both the coastal and the interior routes, both of which could equally well be commanded from their northern ends in Tonkin and nearby Laos.

In 1897 the French Marshal Lyautey, then a young officer in charge of operations on the northern border of Indochina, observed: 'Tonkin is a doorway; this door must be kept bolted.'[97] Japanese strategy during the Second World War showed the soundness of this appreciation and doubtless President Eisenhower's famous dictum about the row of dominoes, following the French collapse in 1954, was inspired by similar considerations. *Plus ça change . . .?*

[94] See above, p. 113.

[95] The reasons for this have been considered above, pp. 59, 89–97, 529–534 and 552. See also below, pp. 762–3. For another interpretation see Harris (A).

[96] See above, p. 556.

[97] Lévy (C), p. 36.

TABLE 72

NORTHERN VIETNAM AND SOUTHERN VIETNAM, CAMBODIA AND LAOS: SELECTED PRODUCTION DATA

Item and unit	*Northern Vietnam*	*Southern Vietnam*	*Cambodia*	*Laos*
Rice—paddy (million tons)	3·9 (1957)	3·0 (1957)	1·53 (1956/7)	0·55 (1956)
Rubber (000 tons) . .	—	*c.* 60 (1957)	32 (1956/7)	—
Maize (000 tons) . .	248 (1956)	n.a.	140 (1956/7)	12 (1956)
Tobacco (000 tons) . .	n.a.	11 (1957)	n.a.	0·6 (1956)
Ground nuts (000 tons) .	n.a.	20 (1957)	2·5 (1956/7)	1·8 (1956)
Cattle (000 head) . .	n.a.	659 (1956)	n.a.	300 (1956)
Buffaloes (000 head) .	n.a.	382 (1956)	n.a.	650 (1956)
Pigs (000 head) . .	2,950 (1957)	2,362 (1956)	n.a.	700 (1956)
Fish catch:				
Sea (000 tons) . .	114 (1957)	100 (1957)	130 (1956/7)	—
Inland (000 tons) . .	n.a.	30 (1957)	30 (1956/7)	n.a.
Coal (000 tons) . .	1,230 (1956)	less than 10 (1957)	—	—
Cement (000 tons) . .	230 (1956)	n.a.	—	—
Electricity (million kWh) .	142·3 (1957)	n.a.	37·95 (1957)	8·0 (1957)

Note the following 1960 data for Northern Vietnam.
Rice 4·4 million tons, sugar cane 403,000 tons, pigs 3,600,000 head, coal 2,600,000 tons, cement 450,000 tons, electricity 254 million kWh, textiles 86 million metres, cigarettes 65·9 million packets.

Sources: Various
Northern Vietnam 1960 from Kaye, *op. cit.* and *Vietnam advances*, May 1961.

TABLE 73

SOUTHERN VIETNAM, CAMBODIA AND LAOS: LAND USE

1957 unless otherwise stated. All figures in thousand acres

Crop	*Southern Vietnam*	*Cambodia*	*Laos*
Rice	6,776	3,027	1,500*
Maize	49	346	35 (1956)
Rubber	142	66 (1953–4)	n.a.
Sugar cane	77	n.a.	n.a.
Ground nuts . . .	59	12	2
Dry beans	40	247	n.a.
Soya beans	n.a.	86	n.a.
Tea	22	n.a.	n.a.
Tobacco	22	30	5
Cotton	2	2	2
Sesamum	2	20	n.a.
Jute	2	n.a.	n.a.
Total cultivated (including others)	7,504	4,942	2,520

* signifies estimate.

Source: Based mainly on *Production Yearbook*, Vol. 12, 1958, F.A.O., Rome, Sections I, IV and V.

TABLE 74

CAMBODIA, SOUTHERN VIETNAM, LAOS, NORTHERN VIETNAM: OVERSEAS TRADE

A. CAMBODIA: TRADE BY COMMODITIES, 1959

Values in thousand riels

Imports		*Exports*	
Cotton piece goods	152,253	Rubber	789,985
Iron and steel	159,747	Rice	781,271
Machinery, etc. (not electrical)	155,411	Maize	193,339
Electrical equipment	102,475	Live animals	68,802
Motor vehicles and parts	88,019	Pepper	60,980
Pharmaceutical products	107,883	Lumber	46,863
Chemicals	100,289	Fish	35,687
Paper and cardboard	79,015		
Petroleum products	114,669		
Cement	103,820		
Dairy products	77,382		
Total (including others)	2,446,744	Total (including others)	2,103,806

B. CAMBODIA: TRADE BY COUNTRIES, 1959

Values in thousand riels

Imports		*Exports*	
France	706,007	France	659,575
Hong Kong	334,818	U.S.A.	526,373
Japan	310,986	Hong Kong	331,478
Malaya	293,536	Malaya	202,451
U.S.A.	183,341	Japan	85,380
China	158,410	China	51,986
Indonesia	86,175	Germany (Federal Republic)	25,847
Germany (Federal Republic)	51,054		
Southern Vietnam	46,566		
Total (including others)	2,446,744	Total (including others)	2,103,806

C. SOUTHERN VIETNAM: TRADE BY COMMODITIES, 1959

Values in million piastres

Imports		*Exports*	
Cotton piece goods	491·4	Rubber	1,642·0
Machinery (not electrical)	622·8	Rice, polished	680·2
Electrical equipment	279·5	Rice, broken	132·1
Motor vehicles and parts	337·7	Cinnamon	27·3
Iron and steel	436·1	Tea	17·5
Paper, cardboard, etc.	292·4		
Pharmaceutical products	436·2		
Cement	243·1		
Gasoline	221·7		
Gas oil and fuel oil	204·9		
Dairy products	368·9		
Wheat flour	216·9		
Total (including others)	7,861·4	Total (including others)	2,627·3

D. SOUTHERN VIETNAM: TRADE BY COUNTRIES, 1959

Values in million piastres

Imports		*Exports*	
U.S.A.	2,047·1	France	831·8
Japan	1,668·4	Germany (Federal Republic)	399·1
France	1,416·0	French Overseas Associates	340·6
Indonesia	548·4	U.S.A.	224·0
Germany (Federal Republic)	461·4	Hong Kong	185·2
Belgium—Luxemburg	228·0	Singapore	160·7
Formosa	213·7		
U.K.	207·7		
India	138·9		
Total (including others)	7,861·4	Total (including others)	2,627·3

E. LAOS.

Imports (1957) 1,461 million kips
Exports (1957) 38 million kips

Imports:	Textiles, etc.	21 per cent
	Vehicles and parts	15 ,, ,,
	Metal goods	10 ,, ,,
	Food products and tobacco	10 ,, ,,
Exports:	Tin concentrates	47 ,, ,,
	Benzoin	13 ,, ,,
	Coffee	8 ,, ,,

F. NORTHERN VIETNAM.

No precise data. Approximately 75 per cent with other Communist-bloc states, particularly China, Czechoslovakia and U.S.S.R.

Currency: 1 piastre = 1 riel = 1 kip;
98 piastres = £1 sterling; 35 piastres = $1U.S.
But it is generally agreed that at these rates the piastre is much overvalued.

Sources: The tables for Cambodia and Southern Vietnam are based on *Yearbook of International Trade Statistics, U.N.*, 1959, Vol. 1. Other data have been compiled from a variety of sources.

SELECT BIBLIOGRAPHY

Ball
Brodrick (A) (B) (C)
Chesneaux
Clementin
Condominas
Crozier
Dang Chan Lieu
Dumont
Fall (A) (B) (C) (D) (E) (F) (G)
Fisher (R) (S)
Fryer (A)
Ginsburg (B)
Giscard d'Estaing
Gourou (A) (B) (C) (D) (E) (F) (H)
Greene and Phillips
Groslier
Groslier and Arthaud
Hammer (A) (B) (C) (D) (E)
Honey (A (B)
Jumper
Le Bar and Suddard
Lê Thanh Khôi
Lévy (C)
Limbourg
McCune (A) (B)
Micaud
Miller, E. W.
Mus (A) (B)
Norodom Sihanouk
Purcell (D) (G)
Robequain (A) (B) (C)
Roberts, S. H.
Sasorith
Shabad
Shah
Sion
Smolski
Steinberg *et al.*
Thompson, V. (A) (F)
Thompson and Adloff
Vandenbosch and Butwell
Wittfogel
Wurfel
Zelinsky

Far Eastern Quarterly, special number on French Indochina, 5, 1946
France-Asie: Présence du Cambodge, Nov.–Dec., 1955
France-Asie: Présence du Royaume Lao, Mar.–Apr., 1956
Indo-China – a geographical appreciation
Indo-China (N.I.D.)
'Indo-China – the unfinished struggle', *W.T.*, **12**, 1956
'Indochinas Christen', *Z.G.*, **26**, 1955
'The waning power of France in Vietnam', *W.T.*, **12**, 1956
News from Viet-Nam
Republic of Viet-Nam Information Bulletin
Colombo Plan Reports
Economic Surveys of Asia and the Far East
Atlas de l'Indochine
Atlas des Colonies Françaises
Times of Viet Nam
Vietnam
Vietnam advances

There is a considerable literature by French scholars on the geography of Indochina, beginning with the sections in Sion and followed by the definitive works of Gourou (A) (D) and of Robequain (A) (C), which rank among the great pioneer studies in the wider field of tropical geography. Important historical works include those by Chesneaux, Groslier and Lê Thánh Khôi, which may be supplemented by the more specific studies of French colonial policy in Roberts, S. H., and Thompson, V. (A), while the N.I.D. volume provides an excellent overall survey of Indochina under French rule.

For the chaotic period which followed, documentation is much more piecemeal and it has been necessary to rely largely on press reports, including some useful articles in *The Economist* and in *The World Today*. However there are three excellent books on various aspects of developments in Vietnam, namely Fall (D), Mus (B) and Hammer (C), together with several articles by these same authorities, and a useful chapter in Ball. In addition there is an invaluable series of articles, notably by Hoang Van Chi, Honey (B), Kaye, and Nguyen Ngoc Bich in the *China Quarterly Special Survey of North Vietnam* On Laos and Cambodia the literature is much sparser, but the respective works (Le Bar and Suddard, and Steinberg) on these countries in the Human Relations Area Files series are useful new sources.

Addenda: The book by Lancaster is an important study of the recent history of Indochina, and the articles by Hendry, Leifer and Trued should also be noted. Note also Honey, P. J., *Communism in North Vietnam*, London 1965, Fall, Bernard B., *The Two Viet-Nams*, London 1963, and Schaaf, C. Hart and Fifield, Russell H., *The Lower Mekong: challenge to cooperation in Southeast Asia*, New York, 1963.

PART IV

The Federation of Malaysia; Singapore; Brunei

CHAPTER 17

Malaya: The Physical and Historical Setting

I. THE LAND

By almost any standards Malaya[1] is anomalous. Geographically, ethnically and culturally its affinities are indisputably with the island realm of the Indies, yet at the same time it is physically a part of the great Eurasian land-mass of which in fact it forms the south-eastern extremity. Moreover, situated as it is in the midst of a region rich in historical associations, Malaya itself has relatively little to record prior to the 15th century and its present-day life is a curious amalgam of the unhurried charm of the Malay countryside and the bustle, squalor and brashness of the immigrant Chinese and Indian pioneer fringe. Finally, and perhaps most paradoxical of all, Malaya, with both the highest percentage of urban population and the highest standard of living in all South-east Asia has nevertheless been almost the last country[2] in that region to gain its independence from colonial rule.

To whatever else its great wealth is due, it certainly cannot be attributed to any intrinsic physical advantages for such are conspicuous mainly by their absence. Structurally the Malay peninsula, unlike Java or Sumatra, is made up entirely of a portion of Sunda-land, the old stable core of South-east Asia, and this fact, combined with the rapidity of sub-aerial erosion in these equatorial latitudes, explains both the maturity of its relief and the prevailing poverty of its soils.

In common with the rest of Sunda-land the relief of Malaya is dominated by the effects of late Mesozoic folding, with the principal trend lines running in a roughly N/S direction. Some seven or eight major ranges, with summit levels varying from 4,000 to 7,000 ft., can be traced in the peninsular interior, all of them possessing intrusive granitic cores[3] which have been exposed over wide stretches by subsequent erosion. Of this series the Main Range, extending without interruption from the Siamese border to Negri Sembilan and reinforced in the north by the Larut hills, is the most important single feature in the Malayan landscape, though its highest point, Gunong Kerbau (7,159 ft.)

[1] Throughout Chapters 17 to 19 the term Malaya is used to include both the mainland of Malaya (i.e. the former Federation of Malaya) and the adjacent island of Singapore, while Malaysia is used in the older geographical sense except where it specifically refers to the new Federation of Malaysia. (See p. 660.)

[2] Sarawak and North Borneo (Sabah) joined with Singapore and the former Federation of Malaya in the Federation of Malaysia in 1963, but in 1965 Singapore ceased to be a member of this.

[3] Commonly flanked by Palæozoic limestones and Triassic quartzites and shales.

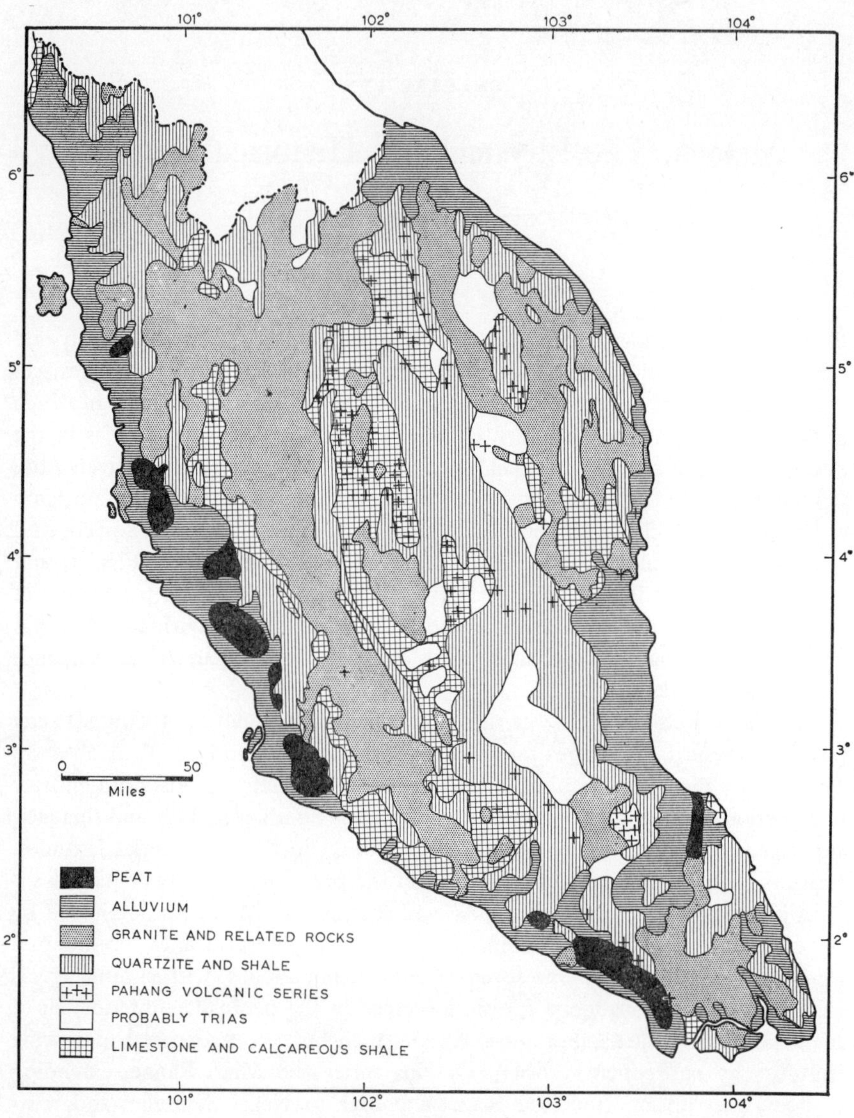

FIG. 82—Malaya: geology

is slightly lower than Gunong Tahan (7,185 ft.), the highest mountain in Malaya, which lies some 60 miles due east in the parallel but much shorter range of the same name.

It is in this latitude, between 4° and 5° N, that the peninsula simultaneously exhibits its greatest width and its most mountainous character, and a cross section from the Perak to the Trengganu coasts would show a succession of four major ridges and deep intervening furrows. In the southern half of the country however the Main Range, lying well towards the western side of the peninsula, preserves its continuity until it also finally peters out near the Malacca boundary. Beyond lies the almost uniformly flat and badly drained lowland of Johore which, together with the structurally related island of Singapore, forms the southern tip of Malaya. Rising above the Johore peneplane at various points, isolated summits, some of them exceeding 3,500 ft., continue the trends of the N/S ranges farther north, and this can likewise be traced in the higher relief features of Singapore and of the Riau, Lingga and Bangka archipelagos which form part of Indonesia.

In addition to the Johore lowlands, the mountainous interior of Malaya is surrounded on its remaining sides by alluvial plains of varying width. Although the peninsula is too small to engender any great rivers like those farther north in Burma, Thailand and Indochina, the abundance of surface water has resulted in an exceptionally elaborate river network and both the Pahang (*c.* 200 miles long) and the Perak (*c.* 170 miles) are large and impressive streams. While these two, as also the Kelantan, and the Muda in Kedah, flow for the greater part of their courses in a longitudinal direction following the structural grain of the country, most of the shorter rivers in both east and west tend to follow a generally latitudinal course from the mountains to the coast, and river capture is a very common phenomenon in many parts of the peninsula.

Thanks to rapid sub-aerial erosion and to the accelerated rate of sedimentation associated with the post-glacial rise in sea-level, the Malayan rivers have built up a virtually continuous fringe of lowland around the coasts, and along the more sheltered western shore this has been extended progressively farther seawards by the steady advance of mangrove swamp. Nevertheless, tidal scour is much greater on the Malayan side of the Malacca Straits than along the opposite shore, and the Malayan swamp belt does not compare in width with that of Sumatra, reaching at most a dozen miles in only a few places. For the same reason also the deep-water channel used by ocean shipping lies nearer to the Malayan than to the Sumatran shore, and is particularly narrow off the Malacca and Selangor coast.

In contrast to the mud and mangroves which form an uninterrupted strip along the western side of Malaya, the eastern coast, subjected as it is to the full force of the NE winds blowing across the South China Sea, is characterized instead by sandy beaches and great shingle spits which are backed in turn by a narrow band of casuarina forest. Moreover, whereas the lack of good harbours, and the persistence of high winds and rough seas during the NE monsoon (from October to March) make the east coast exceedingly dangerous to navigate, the Malacca Straits, blanketed from both the NE and the SW monsoons by the mountains of Malaya and Sumatra respectively, are normally as placid as an inland sea, and form a natural highway which has served to link together the adjoining shores since the dawn of history.

Except perhaps for the extreme northern tip, the whole of Malaya comes with-

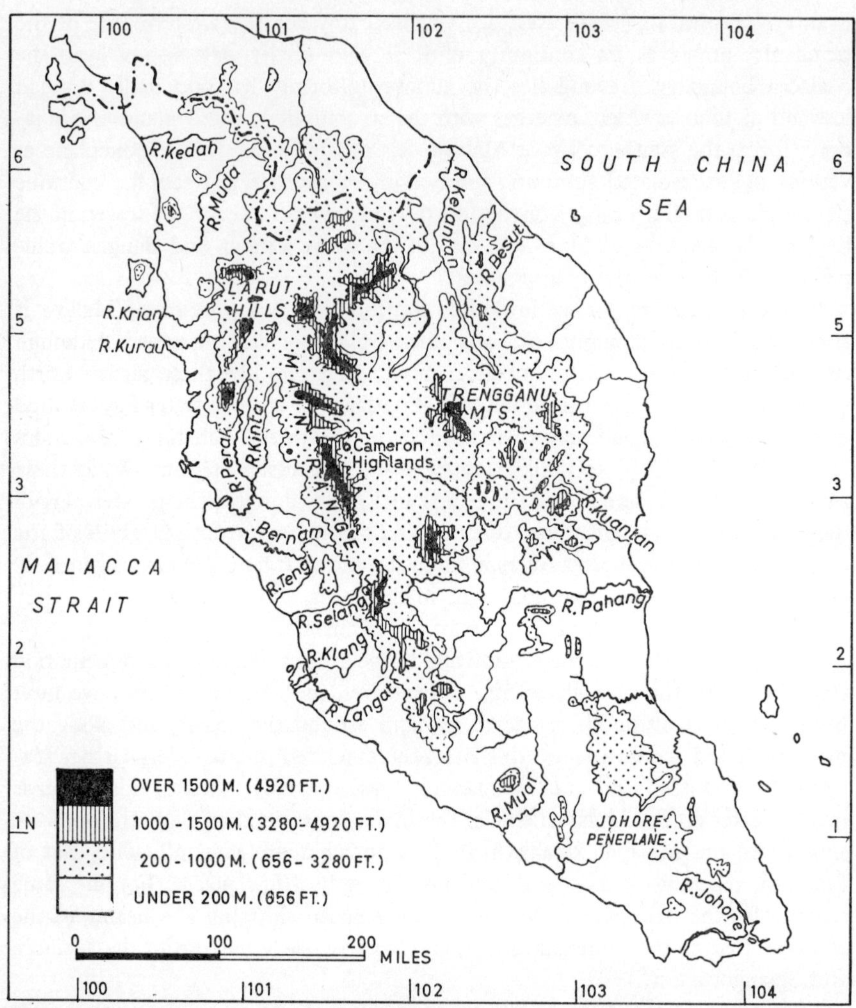

FIG. 83—Malaya: relief

in the area of equatorial monsoon climate as defined on page 40. As such it experiences a typical equatorial temperature régime throughout, though certain broad differences between one area and another are apparent in the seasonal incidence of rainfall. Thus, while on the east coast the period of maximum precipitation coincides with the NE monsoon and the driest month is July, most of western[4] and interior Malaya has two seasons of peak rainfall which correspond not with the monsoons but with the transitional periods between the latter when upward currents of air are dominant.

[4] A small area on the west coast around Malacca and Port Dickson has a rainfall maximum corresponding to the SW monsoon, and its driest month is January.

TABLE 75

MALAYA: SELECTED TEMPERATURE AND RAINFALL FIGURES

Station	*Jan.*	*Feb.*	*Mar.*	*Apr.*	*May*	*Jun.*	*Jul.*	*Aug.*	*Sep.*	*Oct.*	*Nov.*	*Dec.*	*Average*	*To*
Singapore	78	79	80	81	81	81	81	81	80	80	79	79	80	
1° N, 104° E 10	8·5	6·1	6·5	6·9	7·2	6·7	6·8	8·5	7·1	8·2	10·0	10·4		92·9
Penang	80	80	81	82	82	81	80	80	80	80	79	79	80	
5° N, 100° E 23	3·9	3·0	4·7	7·0	11·0	7·2	8·9	12·8	19·0	16·1	10·9	4·8		109·3
Cameron Highlands	65	66	67	67	67	66	66	66	66	65	65	64	66	
5° N, 101° E *c.* 4,500	6·0	5·2	6·4	12·3	10·5	5·0	4·8	7·8	8·4	12·9	12·1	9·7		101·1
Kuala Lumpur	81	82	82	82	82	82	81	81	81	81	81	80	81	
3° N, 102° E 127	62·0	7·9	10·2	11·5	8·8	5·1	3·9	6·4	8·6	9·8	10·2	7·5		96·1
Kuala Trengganu	77	78	80	81	82	81	81	81	80	80	79	77	80	
5° N, 103° E 105	11·5	6·4	6·3	6·1	5·3	4·3	4·6	5·8	7·5	11·0	24·0	21·8		115·0

Interesting as these regional variations are, however, there is a remarkable measure of uniformity in the climate of Malaya as a whole. Mean monthly sea-level temperatures, mostly in the lower 80s, vary by only a few degrees throughout the year, and the daily range is normally nearer 10° than 20°. Rainfall, of course, shows a wider range but, excluding hill stations, the maximum variation is between Taiping with an annual average of 166 in. and Jelebu with 65 in.; much the greater part of the country has between 80 and 120 in., and with few exceptions monthly totals do not normally fall below 3 in.

Thus, although it is theoretically possible to divide the country into climatic sub-regions, this has little vegetational or agricultural significance. Admittedly the north, with its somewhat more marked seasonal variation and greater sunniness, is less unsuitable to paddy cultivation than is the rest of the peninsula, but this does not prevent extensive cultivation of paddy as far south as Johore, and regional variations in climate are even less significant in their effect on the distribution of the other main staples.

So far as natural vegetation is concerned altitude and drainage are everywhere the differentiating factors, and apart from the coastal fringes of mangrove and casuarina, the principal distinction lies between the almost impenetrable freshwater swamp vegetation of the more waterlogged lowlands and the somewhat less obstructive but nevertheless dense equatorial evergreen forest, containing several valuable types of timber, which clothes the remainder of the peninsula up to an altitude of approximately 2,000 ft.[5] Even at higher levels,

[5] Except over the wide areas, particularly of the lowlands of western Malaya, where it has been cleared for subsistence or commercial cultivation.

although recognizable changes appear in the forest cover, whose commercial value here is much less, it is the density of the vegetation[6] far more than ruggedness of relief which has constituted the greatest obstacle to human movement.

Similarly, with respect to soil formation the climatic factor may be regarded as more or less constant throughout Malaya, and in most parts of this old stable land surface the bulk of the soils show clear evidence of laterization and, with few exceptions, are far from fertile. Granite in particular rarely supports a good agricultural soil here, and though the soils derived from quartzites and shales, notably in the foothill zone of the flanks of some of the larger ranges, are somewhat better, they also are by no means ideal and tend to suffer from deficient aeration.

The main exceptions to this general run of poor-quality soils consist of relatively small patches of volcanically derived material in interior Pahang and nearby parts of Johore,[7] and some of the peripheral alluvial soils, provided that these have satisfactory drainage.[8] Among the best of the alluvials are those of the Kedah plain and the Kelantan delta in the extreme north-west and north-east respectively, and, as has already been implied, these areas have the further advantage of a somewhat more favourable climate for rice cultivation than is typical over most of the remainder of the peninsula. But, as Fig. 85 implies, the total extent of even moderately fertile soils is extremely small in relation to the area of the country as a whole.

In sum, therefore, it is clear that the physique of Malaya has been in no sense exceptionally favourable to human settlement. From whatever angle the country was approached the widespread occurrence of both lowland and upland jungle seriously impeded movement any distance inland, and even today such vegetation covers between 70 and 80 per cent of the country. Until very recent historical times virtually the only lines of movement through the jungle were by way of the navigable rivers, and although in this respect the country is well endowed, a high proportion of its riverine lands are rendered both unhealthy and agriculturally unproductive by the widespread prevalence of marsh.

Moreover, the alignment of the mountain ranges, and in particular of the Main Range, provided a major obstacle to E/W movement, and the resultant separation between the two sides was reinforced by the contrast between the ease of maritime access in the west and the great difficulty of navigation along the east coast. And since the Malacca Straits have for many centuries been both a link between Malaya and Sumatra and a highway frequented by the vessels

[6] As noted above (p. 55), malaria is also a major factor in this connexion though it occurs with greatest intensity below 2,000 ft.

[7] This so-called Pahang volcanic series is probably of Mesozoic age and is entirely unconnected with the younger volcanics of Indonesia. There are some patches of basic igneous material within it which have given rise to good soils, but these are in relatively inaccessible areas. See Dobby (H), p. 99.

[8] But in fact the restricted drainage of large areas near the west coast has encouraged the growth of acid peat, commonly some 3 to 4 ft. thick, and this presents a great problem to the cultivator. There are, however, some excellent alluvial soils in coastal Selangor.

of many lands, the western coastline has traditionally been the 'front door' of the peninsula while the east, especially Pahang, has been in Sir Hugh Clifford's telling phrase, 'the further side of silence'.

In addition to the physical obstacles to movement in the interior, the peripheral distribution of the better agricultural soils was a further factor tending to foster localism, for settlement has most consistently concentrated in a few relatively favoured lowland areas, widely scattered round the edges of the peninsula as a whole.

In this respect, as in many others, there is a profound contrast between Malaya and the great river-basin states such as Burma, Siam and Cambodia to the north, and a more obvious resemblance to the larger islands of the Malaysian archipelago. But there also are significant differences for, in contrast to Java or even Sumatra, Malaya's severely limited food-producing capacity has repeatedly proved a handicap to the development of political power.

Only in the possession of vast spreads of easily worked alluvial tin, derived originally from lodes, veins and scattered crystals in the granitic cores of the mountains, and redistributed by the rivers at the break of slope, notably in the western foothill zone flanking the Main Range, does the Malayan natural environment provide any distinctive asset of major importance.[9] But it was not until well into the 19th century that the full significance of this resource was realized and until that time, except for a brief interlude in the 15th and 16th centuries, the Malay peninsula remained a relatively unimportant corner of the much larger Malaysian world.

In contrast to the many shortcomings of its internal physique, however, the geographical position of Malaya is unusually rich in potentialities. In the words of Skeat and Blagden, the peninsula is both 'a causeway of colossal proportions and a breakwater',[10] in effect an almost complete link between the continental mainland and the islands of Indonesia, and at the same time an obstacle round which sea-borne traffic between India and China must make a détour of many hundreds of miles. Such a course, however, is aided by the monsoonal wind systems, and in particular the NE/SW reversal of winds over the South China Sea has greatly facilitated the seasonal movement of sailing ships between the South China coast and the southern entrance to the Straits of Malacca. Moreover, the narrowness of this maritime defile has repeatedly encouraged the inhabitants of the adjacent coasts both in Malaya and Sumatra to attempt to control, and hence to draw valuable profits from, the traffic passing through.

Inevitably such control has depended on sea power, and that in its turn, as Mackinder has shown, has always needed 'to be nourished by land-fertility somewhere'.[11] In this regard, as has been seen, Malaya is badly deficient and

[9] Tungsten, occurring in the form of wolfram and scheelite, is found in association with tin. Other minerals include some coal, iron and bauxite, but none of these is found in large quantities. However, this view may perhaps need to be revised in respect of iron. See below, p. 616.

[10] Skeat and Blagden, Vol. 1, p. 1.

[11] Mackinder, p. 33.

accordingly it has constituted a standing temptation to more powerful outsiders who have sought through control over its shores to wield influence over the adjacent seas. From the dawn of history until the campaigns of 1941–2 Malaya has repeatedly suffered from the weakness of nodality unsupported by commensurate internal strength, and although much is now being done to remedy that situation, the problems to which the country is subjected by virtue of its geographical position are very real.

II. EARLY SETTLEMENT

During prehistoric times the bridging function of the peninsula was of primary importance in determining the movements of people. In turn Negrito and Nesiot groups passed through the peninsula from north to south, and some 30–40,000 descendants of these,[12] the present-day Semang, Senoi-Temiar and Jakun, survive, for the most part in the mountainous interior or in refuge sites amid lowland swamps.

As noted in Chapter 3, the Pareœan Deutero-Malays, the main parent stock of the modern peninsular Malays (as well as of the great majority of the contemporary Indonesian population) were the last major group to migrate from the South-east Asian mainland to the archipelago via the Malay peninsula, probably at some time between 1500 and 2000 B.C. But whereas until recently it was generally assumed that little settlement took place in the peninsula itself at this stage, and that the main Malay occupation began with colonization from Sumatra in the 7th or 8th centuries A.D., it is now believed that at least the more attractive lowlands of the north, in what are now the states of Patani, Kelantan, Trengganu and Kedah, have been continuously occupied from an early stage in the southward migration.

This interpretation would certainly accord with the minor but recognizable differences in physical type between the Malays of the northern and those of the south-western parts of the peninsula and perhaps also with the greater density of Malay settlement in the former area. And, whether, as Winstedt implies,[13] the original Pareœan invaders brought with them the technique of irrigated rice cultivation or whether they acquired it at a later stage through contact with more advanced neighbours, the broad pattern of Malay settlement in the peninsula has long been determined by the distribution of the better alluvial land, from which the aborigines were steadily pushed out. Thus the Malays settled in little clusters along the coast, and in a few favoured riverine lowlands, whose waterways provided the lines of communication on which the later political units,[14] with their 'capitals' at coastal *kuala* sites, were based.

The extent to which Malaya was affected by direct contact with India during the early centuries A.D. is still a matter of uncertainty though there is no doubt that, prior to their conversion to Islam, the Malays had been effectively Indian-

[12] Possibly mixed with Australoid stocks in some cases. [13] Winstedt (E), p. 15.

[14] *I.e.* the sultanates of historic and contemporary times.

ized. But whether the Indo-Malayan kingdom of Langkasuka, founded according to Chinese records about A.D. 100, was in fact centred in the Merbok estuary in Kedah as has been widely believed, is far less clear. Moreover, although there is evidence to suggest that north-eastern Malaya, *i.e.* Kelantan, Trengganu and part of Pahang, reached a high level of civilization as a result of their contacts with the Mon-Khmer lands to the north before the latter were engulfed by the great Thai invasions, the record is nevertheless very fragmentary, and the same observation applies with regard to the medieval trading post of Tumasik on Singapore island, which most authorities agree in attributing to Sri Vijaya.[15]

We are, however, on surer ground with the founding *c.* A.D. 1400, of Malacca, the rôle of which as the emporium of the spice trade and the major centre for the diffusion of Islam throughout the archipelago has already been described on pp. 119–20. In this connexion it is interesting to speculate on what form the political and social evolution of the Malay peninsula might have taken had not the Portuguese seized Malacca in 1511. For the town, though by no means centrally situated along the western seaboard of Malaya, would seem to have been more favourably placed than either Kedah or Singapore for uniting the country and exercising control over the Straits highway, as Sri Vijaya had formerly done from the Sumatra side. And indeed, on the eve of the Portuguese conquest, Malacca had in some measure established its hegemony over all the small river-basin sultanates in the peninsula, even as far north as Patani, as well as over the nearby districts of Kampar, Rokan, Indragiri and Siak in western Sumatra.

Nevertheless, it seems clear that the strength of Malacca was already restricted by the decidedly limited capacity for food production of its immediate hinterland. Thus Ma Huan, who accompanied Cheng Ho, noted that the soil of Malacca was barren and saline, the crops poor and agriculture not in favour;[16] even at that time rice was being imported from Java and throughout the Portuguese and Dutch periods the town's dependence on imported foodstuffs remained a strategic weakness curiously foreshadowing that of Malaya as a whole in modern times.

Throughout the 130 years of their occupation Portuguese interest in the peninsula was virtually limited to their one strategic foothold at Malacca, and the numbers of Portuguese who settled there remained extremely small. To the Dutch, whose main interest in the archipelago quickly became centred in Java, Malacca was never more than a backwater, and although in seeking to secure allies against Atjeh they found it expedient to enter into treaty relations with Johore, the Dutch had little interest in the peninsula for its own sake. Indeed,

[15] There was also a close connexion between Langkasuka and Sri Vijaya, and some authorities who accept the view that Langkasuka was in Kedah believe that Sri Vijaya's interests in it and in Tumasik were bound up with an attempt to control both ends of the Malacca Straits. See above, p. 103, Winstedt (E), p. 28, Steel and Fisher, pp. 278–9 and Wales (B), p. 1. However, the evidence more recently cited by Wheatley (notably (A) and (E)) suggests that the most likely location for Langkasuka is in the neighbourhood of the modern Patani.

[16] See Purcell (C), p. 18.

but for the presence in Malaya today of some 20,000 Eurasians, a majority of whom bear Portuguese or Dutch surnames, these two European powers have left hardly any surviving imprint on the peninsula outside the narrow confines of what is now the quiet provincial town of Malacca.

Nevertheless, the Portuguese conquest of Malacca did mark a major turning point in Malayan history for, with Europeans in control of this key point on the Straits seaboard, the nascent political unity of the peninsula, which depended essentially on coastal communications, was destroyed. The several sultanates, Johore, Pahang, Perak, Kedah, Kelantan, Trengganu and Patani, roughly corresponding geographically to the major drainage units of the peninsula, gradually split apart once more, while in the west Buginese settlers from Celebes carved out a new sultanate (Selangor), during the 18th century, and the descendants of Menangkabau immigrants in the region north of Malacca organized their territories into the 'confederation' known as the Negri Sembilan in 1773.

Already before this time, however, an equally decisive change had taken place in the peninsula with the final forcible conversion of the remaining pagan Malays to Islam at the behest of the Sultan of Atjeh in the 17th century. In this respect, of course, Malaya was not notably different from most other parts of Malaysia. Indeed, as the foregoing paragraphs have implied, many of its sultanates maintained the closest links with the nearby islands, and especially along the west coast its population continued to grow by sea-borne immigration from Sumatra and other parts of the archipelago. Malaya, in short, continued to form a part, though only a minor and essentially peripheral part, of the greater amphibious region whose centre of gravity had been firmly established in Java long before the Dutch made Batavia the headquarters of their island empire.

Yet in one respect at least Malaya was exceptional, for in its geographical connexion with the lands to the north, it was open to overland invasion by non-Muslim neighbours. And in the closing years of the 18th century the revival of Siamese power (after the great defeat of 1767 when the Burmese destroyed Ayuthia) was marked by a resumption of the traditional 'drive to the south' which threatened the complete subordination not only of Patani, Kelantan, Trengganu and Kedah, but also of the larger and more southerly sultanates of Perak and Pahang. Once again, however, the intervention of alien sea-power proved decisive, and with the British acquisition of Penang in 1786[17] a new chain of forces was initiated which was to entail revolutionary consequences for the political and economic evolution of Malaya.

III. THE ESTABLISHMENT OF BRITISH MALAYA

The various factors which led to the extension of British power into the Straits of Malacca, and the subsequent division of spheres between the Dutch and the British by the Treaty of London (1824) have already been considered in Chapter

[17] This did not, however, prevent the Siamese from invading Kedah in 1821.

5. It must suffice therefore to recall that, in establishing themselves first in Penang (1786) and later (1819) in the virtually uninhabited island of Singapore, the two obvious insular *points d'appui* along the western Malayan seaboard, the British were concerned first with the naval defence of India and later with securing the right of way through the Straits which provided the shortest sea route between the Indian Ocean and the South China Sea. And although three small strips of the adjacent mainland, namely Province Wellesley, Malacca and the Dindings, were soon added to the British holdings in Malaya, which in 1829 became known as the Straits Settlements, there was no intention at this stage of forging any closer ties with the peninsular hinterland. Province Wellesley provided a defensive strip and a supplementary source of foodstuffs for Penang; the Dindings, a rocky promontory and an associated group of small islands off the Perak coast, were obtained as a base from which to stamp out piracy in the Straits;[18] and Malacca, whose trade had meanwhile dwindled to insignificance,[19] was occupied by the British mainly because it had previously been held by the Dutch.

This essentially maritime outlook was summed up in the treaty of 1824, by which, in the words of Sir Richard Winstedt, 'all the land right of the East Indiamen's course to China now fell within the Dutch sphere, and all land to the left of that course fell within the British sphere'.[20] And although, as events in Borneo were later to demonstrate, the permitted sphere of British influence was wider than this statement implies, there can be no doubt that Britain's primary concern was with command of the maritime trade routes. Thus in Raffles' own words:

> 'You may take my word for it, Singapore is by far the most important station in the East; and as far as naval superiority and commercial interests are concerned, of much higher value than whole continents of territory.'[21]

Indeed Raffles was fond of calling Singapore 'the Malta of the East',[22] a clear reference to its ability to command the passage between the Straits of Malacca and the South China Sea, as its European prototype controls the narrows between the eastern and western basins of the Mediterranean. From another point of view, however, the similarity of Singapore's position to that of Gibraltar is perhaps more significant, for although the island was separated by less than a mile from the mainland, it was viewed almost exclusively in its maritime context and no more regarded as a stepping stone to the supposedly valueless Malay peninsula[23] than was Gibraltar to the rest of Iberia.

[18] Though they were never in fact used for this purpose.
[19] As a result of the establishment first of Penang and then of Singapore.
[20] Winstedt (A), p. 85.
[21] Quoted in Vlieland (A), p. 1, and Pelzer (A), p. 68.
[22] Coupland, p. 106.
[23] With an estimated population of only 350,000 in 1826 (Crawfurd) the peninsula was accounted of negligible economic importance at this time.

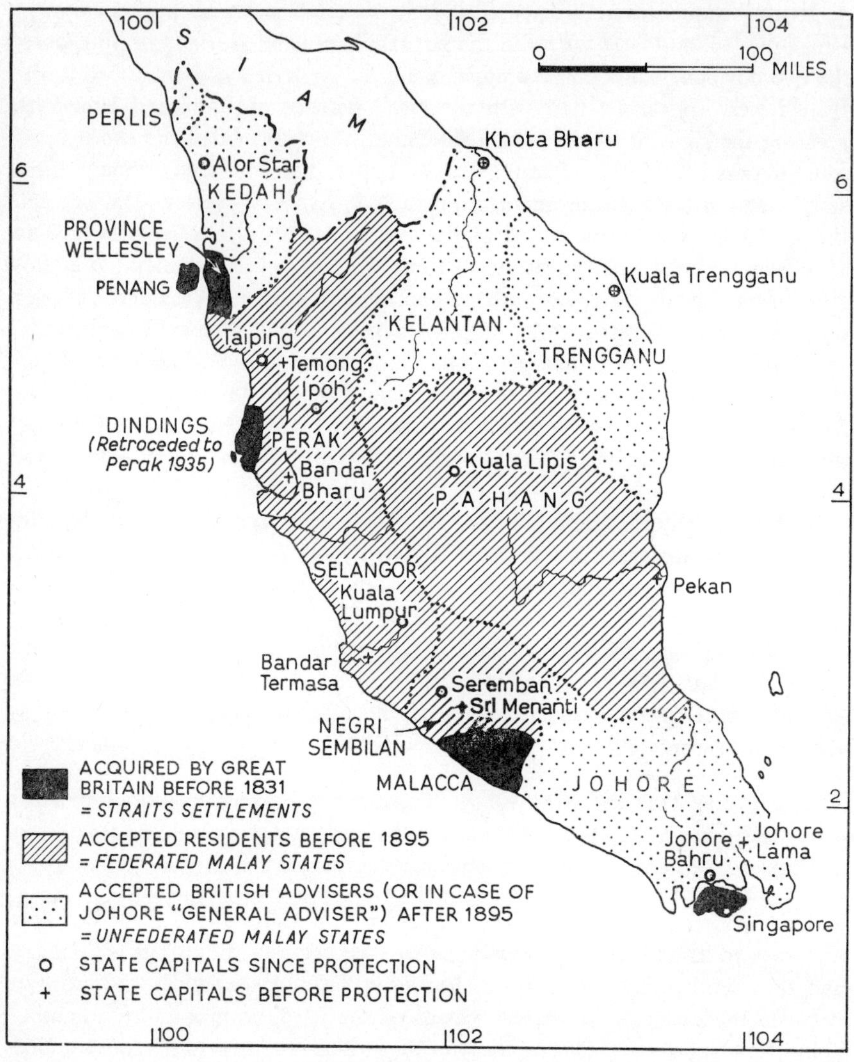

FIG. 84—Malaya: political divisions, 1832–1942

On the other hand, Singapore was never envisaged primarily as a naval station, and indeed from the naval point of view it remained little more than a coaling station and port of call on the way to Hong Kong and Australia until after the First World War. But its superb geographical position and its commodious and sheltered anchorage,[24] combined with the enlightened free-port

[24] The deep-water harbours of Singapore and Penang (and also – though never developed – of Lumut in the Dindings) are situated at the seaward ends of major coulisses. Otherwise the coast is predominantly flat.

system introduced by Raffles, enabled it within a few years to become the greatest entrepôt in the whole of South-east Asia.

The spirit of *laissez faire* likewise permeated British policy in respect of immigration to the Straits Settlements. Penang, as an outpost of the East India Company, had from the first been the scene of considerable Indian settlement, to which Chinese were soon added and, notwithstanding a marked predilection for the Malays – apparently in the light of subsequent history an instinctive reaction of British proconsuls in this part of the world – Raffles welcomed the immigration to Singapore of peoples of all races, especially the Chinese whose energy and commercial acumen he greatly admired. Thus to the enlightened liberalism which so sharply distinguished the early Straits Settlements from the contemporary Netherlands Indies, with their parochial and restrictive outlook, may be traced the origin of the profound ethnic difference between present-day Malaya and Indonesia, whose populations contain respectively the highest and lowest proportion of foreign Orientals to be found in the whole of South-east Asia.

Between 1819 and 1824 the total population of Singapore rose from *c.* 150 to over 10,000, and by 1850 to over 60,000.[25] Meanwhile, within a year of its founding, the city's trade had grown from zero to over $4 million in value – already more than the total trade of Malacca – and by 1823 the figure had increased to over $13 million.[26] Penang, whose promising initial growth had been recognized by the settlement's being made the Fourth Indian Presidency in 1805, was likewise rapidly overtaken by Singapore,[27] mainly because its more northerly position offered less scope for the development of trade with other parts of Malaysia, at least until the closing years of the 19th century when the Dutch began systematically to open up north-eastern Sumatra. Accordingly in 1832 Singapore succeeded Penang as capital of the Straits Settlements, and thereafter local pressure in favour of freeing the Straits Settlements from the control of the India Office increased until 1867 when the territories were constituted a separate Crown Colony.[28]

In view of the great expansion in the trade of both Singapore and Hong Kong and the continuing interest in the coastlands of northern Borneo, it might well have been expected that this change in administration, together with the opening of the Sucz canal two years later, presaged a much more active interest by the British in the lands bordering the South China Sea. And in a commercial sense at least this proved to be the case, for both Singapore and Hong Kong greatly

[25] In 1824 Singapore's estimated population of 10,683 included *inter alia* 3,317 Chinese, 1,925 Buginese, 756 Indians, 580 Malays, 74 Europeans and 15 Arabs. By 1860 50,043 out of its total of 80,792 were Chinese.

[26] These figures are in Straits $ (now Malayan $); $1 = 2*s.* 4*d.* (sterling).

[27] Penang's population in 1795 was estimated at 20,000, of whom over a quarter were Chinese. An estimate of 1812 gave a total of 24,000 inhabitants.

[28] In 1886 the Cocos (Keeling) Islands became part of the Straits Settlements, as did Christmas Island in 1889, and Labuan in 1905. The first two of these are in the southern Indian Ocean; Labuan lies off the coast of North Borneo.

extended the scale of their entrepôt trade as a result of the new economic developments which followed in Siam, French Indochina, the Philippines and the outer islands of the Netherlands Indies.

But there was also another side to the picture. Although the unpropitious physique of Malaya and the unimpressive character of the scattered Malay settlements along its coasts and the lower courses of its rivers had originally led the British to regard the peninsula as an area of very limited potentialities,[29] they had reacted unfavourably to the Siamese conquest of Kedah in 1821, and had taken the precaution of sending an envoy to Bangkok in 1826 to persuade the Siamese to relinquish their claims over all areas south of Kedah and Patani.

TABLE 76

MALAYA: NEWBOLD'S ESTIMATE OF POPULATION, 1835–9

Patani	54,000	Negri Sembilan	27,680
Kelantan	50,000	Johore	25,000
Trengganu	31,000	Pahang	40,000
Kedah*	21,000	Singapore	29,984
Perak	35,000	Penang and Province Wellesley	86,009
Selangor	12,000		
Malacca	37,706		

* According to Crawfurd's *Descriptive dictionary of the Indian islands,* London, 1856, the population of Kedah before the Siamese conquest of 1821 had been *c.* 50,000.

Source: Based on Newbold.

Nevertheless, British economic activity on the mainland, apart from Province Wellesley and Malacca, remained very slight until the closing decades of the 19th century, and it was Chinese pioneers from the Straits Settlements who first revealed the prospects which the peninsula had to offer. The widespread deposits of alluvial tin in the foothills of western Malaya had been known to the Malays for centuries though the amounts which they mined were small. To the more alert and hard-working Chinese immigrants however, Malayan tin seemed to constitute a vast source of potential wealth sufficiently close to the west coast to be commercially worth exploiting and, thanks to its mode of occurrence, requiring a minimum of capital equipment for the task.

Thus, following the discovery of the rich Larut field in 1848, what Dobby has called a 'tin rush' of major proportions began,[30] resulting, in the course of the next few decades, in the creation of a new and entirely alien economy in the western foothills of Perak and Selangor and to a lesser extent of Negri Sembilan.

[29] See Table 73, and note that the areas of greatest population lay within the Siamese sphere. [30] Dobby (D), p. 46.

In these regions, notably in the vinicity of the modern Taiping, Ipoh and Kuala Lumpur, Chinese tin miners, for the most part practising primitive but ingenious methods of extracting the tin from the gravels, lived in their own villages and were ruled over by their own headmen. And although this Chinese settlement pattern did not seriously overlap that of the Malays, most of whose villages lay lower down-stream, disputes between the two peoples became increasingly prevalent and faction fights between different groups of Chinese proved beyond the powers of the Malay rulers to suppress.

It was ostensibly with the purpose of restoring order out of this growing chaos[31] and hence of enabling Singapore and Penang to reap the many direct and indirect advantages which an expansion of tin mining in the interior would bring, that the British finally reversed their declared policy of not interfering in the Malay states, and in 1874 established protectorates over Perak, Selangor and Sungei Ujong.[32] All of these states, to which the remainder of Negri Sembilan was added in 1889, were situated on the western side of the Main Range, and with only a few exceptions the tin-mining areas in them were not more than fifty miles from the coast. On the other hand, Pahang, which also became a protected state in 1888, lay to the east of the Main Range, and contained no important centres of tin mining, though it was incorrectly thought to be extremely rich in gold. So far as the remaining Malay states were concerned, Kedah, Perlis, Kelantan and Trengganu to the north were recognized as being within the Siamese sphere, while Johore in the south, which, on account of its physical structure seemed unlikely to contain any major mineral deposit and was moreover ruled by an exceptionally astute sultan, came under a much looser form of protection than the central states in 1885.

Under the system of protection which was adopted in Perak, Selangor, Negri Sembilan and Pahang, the respective rulers agreed to accept a British Resident, whose advice would be followed on all matters except those relating to Malay custom and the Muslim religion. In effect this constituted an inexpensive form of indirect rule whereby the British provided the minimum administration necessary for ensuring that economic development could be undertaken without interruption. But the rapidity with which trade and immigration proceeded after 1874 was so great that a more elaborate governmental structure seemed essential for the co-ordination of policy, particularly with respect to road and rail construction and the supervision of the Chinese immigrants, in the area as a whole. Accordingly in 1895–6 the four states were united to form the so-called F.M.S. (Federated Malay States) with the mining town of Kuala Lumpur in central Selangor as its capital. Within a few years the outlines of a federal road and railway system began to emerge as the early lateral lines from the west coast to the mining belt were linked together by a longitudinal trunk railway and

[31] But the movement was also part of the wider general European struggle for positions in South-east Asia following the opening of the Suez canal. See Parkinson (A), p. 16.

[32] Sungei Ujong was the key area of Negri Sembilan.

a new E/W road was built from Port Swettenham via Kuala Lumpur to Kuantan on the remote east coast of Pahang.

In fact, if not in name, the F.M.S. was an entirely new political structure deliberately superimposed on the four pre-existing states, and its establishment was proof – if such were needed – of the extent to which the Malays even at this stage had ceased to be masters in their own house. For already, in spite of continuing Malaysian immigration from Sumatra and other parts of the archipelago,[33] the Chinese were well on the way to becoming the largest ethnic group in the three western states (though not in Pahang) and the British had shifted the state capitals from the traditional coastal location favoured by the Malays to upstart Chinese towns in the interior mining belt.

Yet although the F.M.S. was no less a British creation than was its precursor, the S.S., the two administrations remained entirely separate entities. The reason for preserving this separation was partly that the Malay states were not British territory and partly that the free-trade policy of the S.S. trading community was thought to be irreconcilable with the best interests of the primary producing economy of the F.M.S.[34]

Until the turn of the century, tin mining, which remained almost entirely a matter of innumberable small-scale Chinese concerns, was the mainstay of the F.M.S. economy, though various attempts at planting, mainly of coffee, tea, sugar and spices, had been made in a limited way and, owing to the prevailing poverty of the soils, with little success by both Europeans and Chinese. But in the closing years of the 19th century a disastrous fall in coffee prices, combined with a sudden and spectacular increase in the demand for rubber, first for electrical purposes and then for the motor-car industry, brought about a decisive change. For it was soon found that rubber would thrive even on the infertile lateritic soils in the Malay peninsula. Between 1906 and 1910 the value of rubber produced annually in the F.M.S. increased from £399,000 to £5,923,000.[35] A few years later it had wrested first place from tin among the country's exports and this lead has been consistently maintained to the present day.

This great expansion of rubber planting was accompanied by an equally rapid influx of alien labour, for the indigenous Malays showed no more interest in abandoning their traditional subsistence economy in order to work for wages on European estates than they had previously evinced in tin mining. But although large numbers of Chinese workers were at first employed on tapping, the planting community as a whole found that Tamils from southern India were more amenable to the regimentation of estate life, and in the decade 1901–11 the number of Indians in the F.M.S. rose from 58,211 to 172,465.

Apart from the problem of finding a suitable labour force, the high cost of

[33] Such movements to and fro within the Malaysian world had been going on since time immemorial, but after the introduction of British protection the number of Sumatran immigrants into Malaya greatly increased. See below, pp. 634–5.

[34] The F.M.S. derived its revenue primarily from the export duty on tin and (later) rubber.

[35] Wright and Reid, p. 292.

jungle clearing has in many parts of the tropics proved to be the most critical factor limiting the spread of plantations. But in western Malaya, which was already provided with a good network of roads and railways, and where a great deal of ready money was available for investment, the difficulties in this respect were not serious. Within a few years the more favourable sites along the existing roads and railways through the foothill zone[36] of the western F.M.S. were ear-marked for rubber, and the demand for still more land went hand in hand with the extension of the trunk railway and tributary roads through Johore to Singapore, and northwards from Perak and Province Wellesley into southern Kedah. Nor apparently was activity to be limited to the west, which had hitherto been the only part of Malaya to attract outside attention. Even in Kelantan in the remote north-east the Duff Development Company began planting as early as 1901, and in 1907 work began on the new eastern railway between Gemas and Kota Bharu.

It was in these conditions of ever-widening horizons that the British authorities decided to extend still farther the area under their jurisdiction in the peninsula, a step which was in part precipitated by the discovery that the Siamese were permitting German engineers to survey a railway route from Bangkok through the Kra isthmus to the Siamese Malay states lying immediately to the north of the F.M.S. By the Bangkok Treaty of 1909 the Siamese, in exchange for certain financial benefits and a modification of British extra-territorial rights in their country, transferred to the British their rights of suzerainty over Kedah, Perlis, Kelantan and Trengganu, and undertook to forbid any foreign power to build a canal across the Kra isthmus.

Thus an area containing over 600,000 Malays[37] was added to the British sphere, though the former Malay state of Patani nearby, which at an earlier stage had been deprived of its sultan and incorporated into the Siamese provincial system, remained under the rule of Bangkok. Five years later, in 1914, the rapidly growing importance of Johore as the geographical link between Singapore and the F.M.S. was recognized by a new agreement bringing it under closer British supervision on virtually identical terms with the four new unfederated states in the north.

IV. MALAYA BETWEEN THE WARS

At the time when these agreements were concluded there seemed every reason to believe that the five unfederated states would be incorporated in the F.M.S. within a few years. But in fact the high hopes of continued economic expansion were only partially realized. Following the distractions of the First World War came the threat of overproduction in Malaya's two main commodities, rubber and tin, resulting mainly from increased competition in neighbouring parts of South-east Asia, such as French Indochina, Siam, Burma and the outer territories of the Netherlands Indies. With the introduction of international

[36] Where drainage is better than in the coastal margins.

[37] Besides nearly 50,000 Chinese and nearly 7,000 Indians, mostly in Kedah.

restriction schemes in both rubber and tin during the 1920s and 30s to tackle this problem, the pace of Malaya's advance inevitably slackened and, from a geographical point of view, this meant that the expected extension of the economic frontier into the eastern part of the country did not in fact take place.

Furthermore, in addition to some long-overdue diversification of the country's economy by developments in palm-oil and pineapple cultivation, substantial changes occurred meanwhile in the organization of production in both rubber and tin. Ever since the rubber boom of 1910–12 more and more Malay peasants had been attracted by the idea of growing a few rubber trees to provide a cash income to supplement their traditional subsistence farming,[38] and in many ways these small-holdings proved better able than the heavily capitalized European and Chinese estates to withstand the severe drop in prices during the crisis years. Thus, by 1937 188,836 tons out of a total Malayan rubber production of 503,494 tons came from small-holdings, a majority of which were owned by Malays.[39]

On the other hand the proportion of Asian ownership in the tin-mining industry declined for, as the areas capable of being exploited by primitive Chinese methods gradually became exhausted, various more efficient mechanical means, which required a heavy capital outlay, were introduced mainly by Europeans. Accordingly between 1920 and 1936 the Chinese share in tin mining dropped from 64 per cent to 36 per cent while that of the Europeans rose correspondingly.[40]

The period in which these important economic changes occurred was also marked by a major alteration in British colonial policy with respect to Malaya.[41] After the First World War the doctrine of indirect rule acquired an enhanced prestige and a sense almost of guilt developed in British administrative circles over the way in which the unsophisticated and easy-going Malays had been outnumbered and outclassed by the more thrusting Chinese and Indians in the S.S. and the western F.M.S. Admittedly the establishment of Malay Reservations in 1913, which eventually came to include most of the relatively limited area in the Malay states suitable for paddy growing, did much to preserve the Malay way of life even in this part of the peninsula, for all permanent alienation of land to non-Malays was prohibited within the Reservations. But in spite of this enactment such states as Perak, Selangor and even Negri Sembilan in the western tin and rubber belt gave the impression of belonging primarily to their much more numerous Chinese and Indian inhabitants, a fate from which the British administration during the inter-war period resolved, if possible, to spare the unfederated states.

So far as Johore was concerned its Sultan, who adopted a policy of encouraging

[38] Also many Sumatran Malays and Javanese (from the Cultuurgebied) were attracted to Malaya by the prospects of small-holder cultivation of rubber.

[39] See Mills, pp. 212–13.

[40] Non-Chinese investments in tin in 1936 amounted to *c.* £14 million, and in rubber to £55 million. About three-quarters of these totals were British. See Callis, p. 49.

[41] On the whole subject of British colonial policy see Emerson (A) and Mills.

the immigration of Indonesians in preference to other alien labourers, succeeded in fostering economic development without entirely losing the Malaysian character of his state. But among the British officials it was such almost exclusively Malay states as Kelantan and Trengganu which came to be regarded somewhat nostalgically as the 'real Malaya', whose character must at all costs be preserved.

The effect of this policy was inevitably to perpetuate the political fragmentation of the peninsula, for although in 1931 the Governor/High Commissioner, Sir Cecil Clementi, put forward tentative plans for a Pan Malayan Union to embrace the whole country, his Malayophile policy merely succeeded in ranging the powerful economic interests – European, Chinese and Indian – in both the F.M.S. and the S.S. implacably against any such unification.

In fact, however, the problem was further complicated by the intense rivalry which still persisted between the S.S and the F.M.S. themselves, and the widespread belief in both areas that their respective economic interests were mutually exclusive. In retrospect these arguments seem to have been largely beside the point. Apart from the fact that Penang since the Second World War has been able to continue as a free port within the Federation of Malaya, it is evident that ever since the beginning of the present century the interests of the F.M.S. and the S.S. were tending to draw closer together. For while with the development of better port facilities, and the formulation of more nationalistic economic policies in the neighbouring lands of South-east Asia,[42] the hinterlands served by both Singapore and Penang gradually decreased in area,[43] the corresponding loss in trade from these sources was more than made good by the growing volume of trade with the Malay peninsula. Furthermore, through the activities of the big managing agencies[44] and other commercial houses, with their headquarters in Singapore, even closer ties developed between the commercial interests of the S.S. and the planting and mining interests of the F.M.S., a process which was accelerated by the economic changes of the inter-war years.

Such tendencies towards economic integration indeed have been present in some degree from the very beginning of British interest in Malaya. It was out of the proceeds acquired by trading and other activities in the S.S. that the early tin miners were able to establish themselves in the Malay states, and practically the whole of the tin mined in the country was smelted in Singapore and Penang. Moreover, in their turn the profits derived from tin both paid for the first roads

[42] The reference here is to the more nationalistic economic policies extended by the metropolitan powers to their South-east Asian dependencies.

[43] Singapore's first great loss was the China trade taken over by Hong Kong after 1842; later much of its Indochina trade was lost when the French opened direct shipping services between France and Saigon/Haiphong; and similarly the improvements to Makasar and Belawan harbours in the Indies entailed further losses. By the 1930s Singapore was the main entrepôt only for Malaya, western Borneo and south-eastern Sumatra. Mills, pp. 112–13.

[44] There have been about a dozen of these major agencies, which also built up very extensive commercial interests in other parts of South-east Asia. See Allen and Donnithorne, p. 52.

and railways, and found an outlet in developing the rubber industry and in establishing Singapore as the greatest rubber market in the world. Only this remarkably fortunate sequence of events, associated as it was with the favoured geographical position of Singapore and the easy accessibility of the western tin belt from the great oceanic highway through the Straits, can explain why such an intrinsically infertile country as Malaya has been able to become by far the richest territory in the whole of South-east Asia.

In a very real sense, therefore, pre-war Malaya, in spite of its seven separate governments, was already one country and the major regional differences which existed there lay not between the S.S., the F.M.S. and the five unfederated states, but rather between the western tin and rubber belt, stretching from Singapore to southern Kedah, with its highly developed economy, elaborate communication network and numerous towns inhabited mainly by alien immigrants, and the largely undeveloped eastern two-thirds of the peninsula, including Pahang and eastern Johore as well as Kelantan and Trengganu, where the traditional subsistence economy and rural stetlement pattern of the Malays remained for the most part unaffected by foreign intrusions.

This contrast between east and west was undoubtedly the outstanding feature in the geographical pattern of pre-war Malaya, though the political map gave little indication of the fact. At least in the western third of the country the low watershed divides between the several riverine states had lost all material significance with the clearing of the jungle, the construction of roads and railways and the exploitation of resources whose distribution knew no political boundaries. Yet to all outward appearances the states remained the basis of the administrative system, and in this way the convenient fiction that Malaya was still essentially the Malays' own country was preserved.

The facts of demography, however, told a different story. As early as 1921 the combined number of Chinese and Indians in the peninsula had already overtaken that of the 'Malays', even though this last category was stretched to include all Malaysian immigrants as well as the locally born Malays. Moreover, expecially during the 1930s a growing proportion of Chinese was beginning to settle permanently in Malaya. Thus in this respect, as in many others, the country was already losing some of the more striking characteristics of the pioneer fringe and showing signs of settling down to a more stable pattern of existence. In retrospect, therefore, it seems doubly unfortunate that the opportunity of promoting some sense of common Malayan nationhood was not seized at this juncture while communal tensions were still at a minimum.

A policy of this kind, moreover, would have been a logical complement to some form of administrative unification, and certainly such a process of rationalization was long overdue. For, apart from the wastage involved in maintaining seven separate administrations[45] in a country the size of England, with a popu-

[45] Or ten if the four components of the F.M.S. were regarded as separate states.

lation smaller than that of London, these arrangements entailed serious strategic disadvantages. Thus both the creation of the Singapore naval base and the immense capacity of Malaya's rubber and tin for earning foreign exchange made the peninsula a major objective in Japan's impending drive to the south. To guard against this threat the greatest possible co-ordination of peninsular defence was essential,[46] and it is significant that the first use in an official title of the all-embracing name 'Malaya', over-riding the sectional differences of S.S., F.M.S. and unfederated states, came with the establishment of Malaya Command in 1922.[47] Unfortunately, however, it needed much more than this to withstand the Japanese advance of 1941, and the prior commitments of the Allies in other theatres left Malaya quite inadequately prepared for the decisive strategic rôle which it was thereupon called to play.

SELECT BIBLIOGRAPHY

Allen and Donnithorne
Crawfurd
Daly
Dale (A) (B)
Dobby (A) (B) (C) (D) (H)
Emerson (A)
Fisher (E)
Hodder (C) (D)
Kunst
Mills
Newbold
Ooi (A) (B)
Parkinson (A) (B)
Pelzer (A)
Purcell (C) (D)
Richardson
Robequain (D)
Roberts, G. (A) (B)
Scrivenor (A) (B)
Skeat and Blagden
Steel and Fisher
Swettenham
Vlieland (A) (B)
Wales (B)
Wheatley (A) (B) (C) (D) (E) (F) (G) (H)
Wheeler
Winstedt (A) (B) (C) (D) (E)
Wright and Reid

Handbook of the Federated Malay States

On the geology and geomorphology of Malaya, Scrivener (A) (B) and Richardson are pioneer works, as are the papers by Dale on climate, while more wide-ranging physical studies are found in Dobby (D) (H), in Ooi (B) and the introductory section of Vlieland (A).

On historical geography the several papers by Wheatley are indispensable, as are the historical studies by Winstedt. Also important are the contributions of Wright and Reid, Purcell, and Parkinson, while Swettenham, Mills and Emerson (A) are major studies on British colonial practice. I have also drawn extensively on my own earlier work in Steel and Fisher.

See also the Select Bibliographies in Chapters 18 and 19.

[46] Note that Malaya's land frontier with Siam, and also the direct peninsular approach to Singapore both lay under the jurisdiction of unfederated states, where British control was relatively tenuous.

[47] See Emerson (A), p. 371.

CHAPTER 18

Malaya: Economic Geography

Between 1945 and 1948 Malaya made a remarkable economic recovery from the crippling effects of the Japanese occupation during the Second World War and, notwithstanding the Communist-led terrorist activities which began in 1948 and were not finally suppressed until 1960, this recovery has been further consolidated and maintained in the years which have followed. During the same period major changes have occurred in the political geography of the country. The former divisions into S.S., F.M.S. and unfederated states disappeared, and in their place were established first the Malayan Union (1946) and later the Federation of Malaya (1948), to include the whole of Malaya apart from Singapore, which in the meantime was constituted a separate Crown Colony. But although this political separation was decided upon because Singapore 'is a centre of entrepôt trade and has economic and social interests distinct from those of the mainlands',[1] the economies of the two units remained very closely inter-linked even after the Federation achieved its independence in 1957 and internal self-government was granted to the State of Singapore in 1959. For this reason the two territories have been treated as a single country in this and the following chapter. This practice seemed to be justified by the inclusion of both within the wider Federation of Malaysia in 1963, but it has since been called in question by the separation of Singapore from the latter in 1965.

Meanwhile, with its Malay population primarily engaged in subsistence production, the Chinese and Indians of the tin and rubber belt concentrated on production for export, and the inhabitants of Singapore and Penang maintaining a far-ranging entrepôt trade, Malaya's economy is hardly less plural than its society, and it will be convenient to consider each of these main components separately.

I. SUBSISTENCE ECONOMY AND FOOD PRODUCTION

As in all the other more advanced regions of South-east Asia, rice forms the staple article of diet in Malaya, not only for the Malays themselves, but equally for the immigrant Chinese and Indians. But partly because of the British policy of seeking to preserve the Malay way of life by including most of the land best suited for paddy within the bounds of the Malay Reservations, and partly because both plantation agriculture and market gardening have hitherto yielded

[1] *Malayan Union and Singapore: statement of policy on future constitution*, Cmd. 6724, p. 3, para. 5. The social and political aspects of this problem are dealt with in Chapter 19.

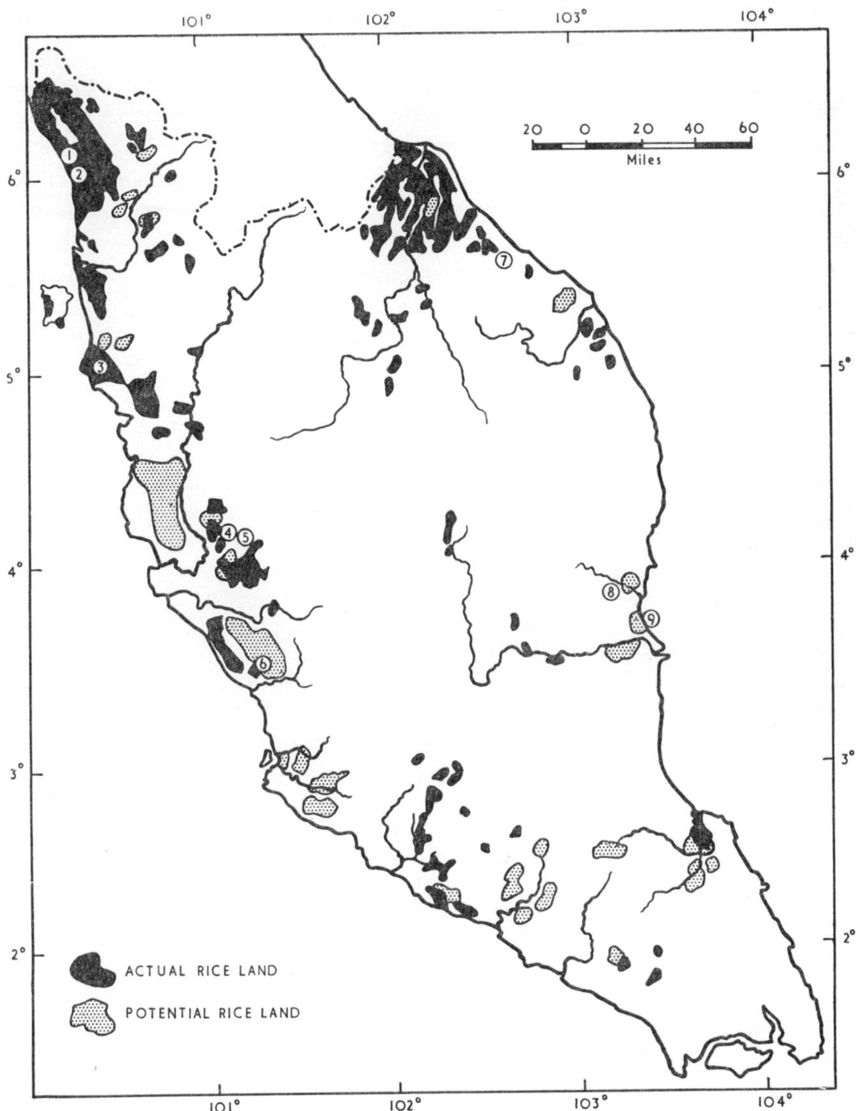

FIG. 85—Malaya: rice-land, actual and potential

Numbers refer to settlement schemes, as follows:—1. South Perlis. 2. Kubang Pasu, Kedah. 3. Krian, Perak. 4. Sungei Manik, Perak. 5. Changkat Jong, Perak. 6. Tanjong Karang, Selangor. 7. Besut, Trengganu. 8. Paya Besar, Pahang. 9. Pahang Tua, Pahang.

far higher cash returns than paddy growing, the latter has remained almost entirely in the hands of the Malays and immigrant Malaysians. Moreover, with only minor exceptions until very recently, this cultivation has been carried out on a subsistence basis, with the result that, while the rural Malays provide for their own needs of the staple foodstuff, a large part of the Chinese and Indian consumption has had to be met by imports. Thus before the war Malaya grew only about one-third of the rice consumed within the country and although belated attempts were made after 1939 to remedy this potentially dangerous state of affairs,[2] Malaya suffered from an acute rice shortage during and after the Japanese occupation.[3] Since then continued attempts to stimulate production have met with notable success and today the country grows some two-thirds of the rice consumed by a population which has meanwhile increased considerably in number.

TABLE 77

MALAYA: LAND USE

All figures in thousand acres for the years stated

Cultivation	*Federation of Malaya*		*Singapore*	
Rubber	(1953)	3,728	(1955)	16
Rice	(1957–8)	902	(1957–8)	7
Coconuts	(1955)	500		n.a.
Oil palm	(1954)	110		
Bananas	(1955)	57		
Sweet potatoes and yams	(1948–52 av.)	47	(1948–52 av.)	2
Cassava	(1957)	37		
Pineapples	(1955)	35		
Tea	(1957)	10		
Maize	(1957)	7		
Tobacco	(1957)	5		
Ground nuts	(1957)	2		
Sugar cane	(1957)	2		
Total cultivated (including others, 1957)		5,269		35

Source: Based mainly on *Production Yearbook*, Vol. 12, 1958, F.A.O., Rome, Sections I, IV and V.

According to the Census of 1957, paddy growing accounted for 398,295 out of a total gainfully employed population in the Federation of 2,126,112 thus coming second after rubber cultivation which had a labour force returned as 614,387.[4] More recent figures, for 1959, show paddy to have covered an area of 934,000 acres (approximately 17 per cent of the total cultivated acreage

[2] Although this policy was well-intentioned, its effects have sometimes been criticized. Thus the Malays' rice economy has been described as one 'of poverty and chronic debt . . . not much above the appalling poverty of most of Asia' (Silcock, (B) p. 1) and 'Government attempts to make Malaya more self-supporting in rice were largely attempts to resist a current flowing towards higher standards . . .' (*Ibid.*, p. 3).

[3] This helped to exacerbate communal tensions since the Malays generally had their own sources of rice, while the Chinese and Indians did not.

[4] In 1947 470,592 were engaged in paddy cultivation and 505,108 in rubber cultivation.

in the country), and to have yielded an output of 700,000 tons. On the basis of the official conversion figure of 63 per cent paddy to rice, this gave a total of 443,000 tons of rice, against an import in the same year of 438,600 tons coming mostly from Thailand and Burma.[5]

Of the locally grown paddy all but a small amount from an area of 61,000 acres, was wet paddy. Moreover, although it might be expected that former cultural contacts with such peoples as the Menangkabau Malays and the Javanese would have familiarized the peninsular Malays with at least the rudiments of terraced cultivation, this practice is conspicuous by its absence, and virtually all the rice grown is limited to the lowest-lying parts of the peninsula near to the coast and/or the river flood-plains. As Fig. 85 suggests, much the largest totals came from the alluvial lowlands of Kedah, Province Wellesley and Krian (Perak) in the north-west, and Kelantan in the north-east, the remainder being grown in widely scattered but generally much smaller tracts in the more southerly parts of the peninsula.

The average yield of paddy, which stood at 37 bushels per acre in 1954–5, has on balance continued to rise, and is well above the average for South-east Asia, a remarkable achievement, as Dobby points out,[6] when one considers that the climate of Malaya is distinctly less suitable for rice than is that of the tropical monsoon lands farther north. But in contrast to these areas, Malaya's rice growing is generally more intensive; plots are comparatively small and often severely fragmented, the industry is organized on a subsistence rather than a commercialized basis and there are few giant mills of the type which characterize the great rice bowls of Burma, Thailand and Southern Vietnam.

In spite of the recent increase in output, however, the government is determined that Malaya shall produce a still higher proportion of the rice which it consumes, both by extending the area under paddy and by improving the efficiency of cultivation in existing areas. So far as the former is concerned it has already been seen that physical geography imposes serious limits and the total potential area not yet under cultivation was estimated in 1950 at 763,000 acres, or rather less than the area already under wet paddy.[7] Furthermore, much of this potential rice land is of very uncertain value, mainly because of the problem posed by acid peat in most of the remaining lowland areas. And in any event, however, the costs of clearing the jungle and, where necessary, of providing drainage or irrigation facilities, as well as communications and amenities, are everywhere heavy, and in the absence of any serious consciousness of land

[5] A little also came from Indochina. The total rice output of 495,500 tons, from an acreage of 909,000, in 1958 was a record, but the amount of rice imported in that year was approximately the same as in 1954–5. In 1959 output declined, but in 1960 it rose still further to 560,200 tons. Note that these figures refer to Malaya as a whole. The Federation of Malaya now produces about 69 per cent of the rice it consumes, but Singapore relies prepoderantly on imported rice. Of the imports in 1959, 359,600 tons went to the Federation and 79,000 tons to Singapore.

[6] On rice cultivation in Malaya, see Dobby (H), pp. 106–11, and also Dobby (L) and (M), for two detailed regional accounts.

[7] See Federation of Malaya *Draft Development Plan* (1950), p. 39, para. 142.

hunger among the Malays there remains the further difficulty of finding colonists to occupy the new lands once they are ready for cultivation.

Nevertheless, the irrigation of some 50,000 acres of paddy land at Tanjong Karang in Selangor was completed and the land settled by 1953, and work is now proceeding on the much larger Trans-Perak River Irrigation Scheme, west of Kampar, where it is planned to transform some 180,000 acres of jungle into a new rice bowl for Malaya. To judge from experience in both these areas and elsewhere,[8] it seems probable that mechanization, which has already revolutionized the technique of jungle clearing, may also provide at least part of the answer to the problem posed by the shortage of labour willing to undertake paddy cultivation. However, while satisfactory methods of mechanized ploughing and harrowing have been devised, the more complicated tasks of planting and harvesting continue to present difficulties in this respect.

As regards the areas already devoted to paddy, the nature of peasant cultivation and land tenure is such that mechanization can do comparatively little to raise the output per acre, and the emphasis is rather on improving existing drainage and irrigation, increasing the use of fertilizers and introducing such better strains of paddy as scientific research makes available. As a result of continued efforts along these lines the yield per acre is undoubtedly rising, and further improvements are expected from the proposed extension of double cropping.

Besides the production of paddy, the subsistence economy of the Malays also includes the cultivation of fruit trees, especially of coconut palms which are valued for shade and thatching materials as well as for cooking and illuminant oil. More important, and equally intimately associated with the traditional coastal and riverine pattern of Malay settlement, is the emphasis on both sea and freshwater fishing which provides the second main staple in the diet. While, as Firth has shown,[9] some Malay villages, especially along the north-east coast, are pre-eminently concerned with fishing, it is more typical for the latter to be practised as a supplementary activity of agriculture. Although the total catch almost certainly exceeds the reported figures, these have shown a notable increase in recent years. In 1959 the total weight of sea-fish landings was recorded as 118,600 tons in the Federation and 10,663 tons in Singapore, and in addition some 20,000 tons of freshwater fish were caught.[10] The practice of fish culture in artificial ponds and flooded rice fields is also spreading, and owes much to the Tropical Fish Culture Research Institute in Malacca.

To complete this account of the traditional Malay, economy mention should also be made of the great variety of cottage and handicraft industries which

[8] For an interesting account of another scheme at Padang Terap in Kedah (20,000 acres) see Courtenay (A), pp. 46–7. As in the other well-established paddy areas the cultivators here are Malays, but at Changkat Jong (Perak) and Tanjong Karang (Selangor) some Chinese are now growing rice.

[9] Firth (A), p. 197.

[10] These figures include the work of 19,408 Chinese as well as 41,411 Malays who in 1957 were returned as fishermen within the Federation. There were also approximately 950 fishermen in Singapore.

include mat and cloth weaving, boat building, timber sawing, flour milling and the manufacture of thatch, pottery and utensils. As in other parts of South-east Asia such activities form an essential part of the rural economic pattern and though, since they scarcely figure in official statistics at all, they are apt to be overlooked by the casual observer, their potential importance as a possible foundation for more elaborate rural industrialization should not be forgotten.

Until recently subsistence production in Malaya was almost solely the concern of the Malays. The Chinese and Indians came to the country in order to make money, which they did mainly as labourers, clerks and traders.[11] But from the time of the depression of the early 1930s the practice began among unemployed Chinese tin or rubber workers of squatting illegally in outlying areas away from police surveillance, and seeking to make a living from the cultivation of vegetables, rice and fruit and the rearing of a few pigs and poultry. During the economic dislocation and accompanying food shortage of the Japanese occupation the numbers of such squatters greatly increased, and when the war ended the total was in the vicinity of half a million.

When the wave of Communist terrorism broke out in 1948 the squatter problem achieved a new prominence for, owing to their location on the fringe of the jungle and their consciousness of possessing no legal title to their land, these people were easily coerced into providing food for the terrorists. In order therefore to put a stop to this practice, the British decided to resettle the squatters – in all representing nearly 10 per cent of the Federation's population – in a series of 'New Villages', situated for the most part along the main roads where they would be separated from the terrorists and under effective police supervision.[12]

While the occupants of some of the New Villages have been employed as mining or plantation labour, the main basis of their economy in most cases is subsistence farming and market gardening. The provision of suitable sites for villages of this kind and the granting of proper titles to the surrounding agricultural land has involved considerable encroachment within the Malay Reservations, and this in its turn provoked some resentment among the Malays who were also inclined to be disgruntled by the fact that the Chinese inhabitants of the New Villages had obtained better housing and amenities at the expense of the country as a whole.[13]

The long-term economic consequences of this resettlement policy may prove to be of great importance. Although there was a temporary decrease in the output of market-garden produce while the transfer of population was going on, production has since risen and a significant increase in subsistence farming – including rice cultivation – on the part of non-Malays seems to be a permanent legacy

[11] The Chinese were also active in various forms of commercial agriculture; see below, p. 611. The wages of estate and mining coolies were usually at least four to five times as great as those for labourers in Madras or southern China. Zinkin (A), p. 156.

[12] See Dobby (N), for a detailed account of the problem.

[13] Conversely some of the Chinese involved resent what they appear to regard as almost a form of internment. On the New Villages, see Dobby (N) and Sendut.

of this episode. Hitherto the Chinese in Malaya have been far too ready to discard their traditions as 'farmers of forty centuries' and, in keeping with the spirit of the pioneer fringe, to skim quick profits from the soil by raising such exhaustive cash crops as tapioca and by over-tapping their rubber, in a way which has all too often resulted in the lasting impoverishment of trees or land. But in large measure this attitude has been the outcome of the impermanence of their tenure, and the present revolutionary changes in this respect may lead to an equally pronounced change in farming methods which would make the Chinese even more serious competitors of the Malays than they have been hitherto. For indeed it has long been evident in the small but concentrated areas of market gardening in the vicinity of the main towns that the Malayan Chinese can be a very skilful cultivator, working wonders from the most unpromising patch of tin tailings as long as his tenure seems reasonably secure. Thus the growing participation of the Chinese in food production, which is but one symptom of the increased permanence of Chinese settlement in the country, may make for new difficulties in the future. In these circumstances such local irritants as the Muslim Malay's disapproval of the Chinese addiction to pig-rearing are apt to be exaggerated into major causes of friction and care will be needed if relations are to remain harmonious.

II. PRODUCTION FOR EXPORT: PLANTATIONS AND MINES

Rubber cultivation is by far the most important industry in Malaya, accounting for some two-thirds of the country's total net exports and a similar proportion of the cultivated area, and supporting directly or indirectly between one-third and one-half of its population. Indeed Malayan rubber has been referred to as the most valuable single industry in the whole Commonwealth, the industry which saved the United Kingdom from bankruptcy after the war by earning more dollars in the critical five years of 1947–51 than all the industries and trades of the metropolitan country put together.[14]

Moreover, although in several recent years Indonesia was the world's largest producer, Malaya also has greatly increased its output since the war, and has once again moved into first place. In 1960 it accounted for 708,377 tons out of a world total of approximately 2 million tons.

As can be seen from Fig. 86 rubber cultivation is still overwhelmingly concentrated in a relatively narrow belt of country within 40 miles of the west coast, stretching from central Kedah southwards without serious interruption to Singapore. Within that area European estates are located wherever possible on the better-drained foothills, but much of the Asian small-holder cultivation occurs in the low-lying coastal margins. In the eastern states of Pahang, Kelantan and

[14] Robinson (A), pp. 133–4.

[15] Malayan rubber production in 1928 was 258,906 tons; 1930 420,985 tons; 1932 385,961 tons; 1934 465,765 tons.

TABLE 78

FEDERATION OF MALAYA: RUBBER PRODUCTION

Type of holding	*Area* (000 *acres*)		*Production* (000 *long tons*)		
	1940	1959	1940	1953	1960
Estates	2,082	1,942	332	341	414
Small-holdings (less than 100 acres)	1,330	1,500 (est.)	213	232	294
Total . .	3,412	3,442 (est.)	545	573	708

Note: In 1955 Singapore had 15,820 acres under rubber with a total output of 1,670 tons.

Source: *Federation of Malaya Reports, Official Year Book* 1961, and *Rubber Statistical Bulletin.*

Trengganu, on the other hand, rubber occupies only approximately 2 per cent of the total area, mostly along the railway and near the mouth of the Pahang river, thus again emphasizing that transport facilities rather than natural conditions are the over-riding factor in determining its location.

The distinction between estate and small-holder production is all-important, though the official practice of grouping together all units of less than 100 acres as small-holdings tends to obscure the true position. In the early stages of the industry it was generally assumed that only heavily capitalized European estates could afford the high expenditure entailed by jungle clearing, the installation of coagulating plant, and the long delay of six or seven years before the trees came into production. Normally such estates occupied between 1,000 and 2,000 acres, and much the greater part of these are still European owned, the rest being mainly in Chinese hands.[16] More typically, however, the Chinese have concentrated on small holdings, and small estates of from 50 to 500 acres,[17] while at the same time the Malays have greatly increased the acreage of rubber cultivated in small lots of a few acres as an adjunct to subsistence farming.

On the basis of the accepted distinction between estates and small-holdings

[16] In order to reduce expenses there has been a tendency since the Second World War to concentrate in larger units of about 5,000 acres under a single European manager, with perhaps one or two assistants. Meanwhile, Asians are being trained for management. Allen and Donnithorne, p. 129.

[17] The Chinese share in estate ownership is now tending to increase, partly at European expense. *Ibid.*, pp. 130–31.

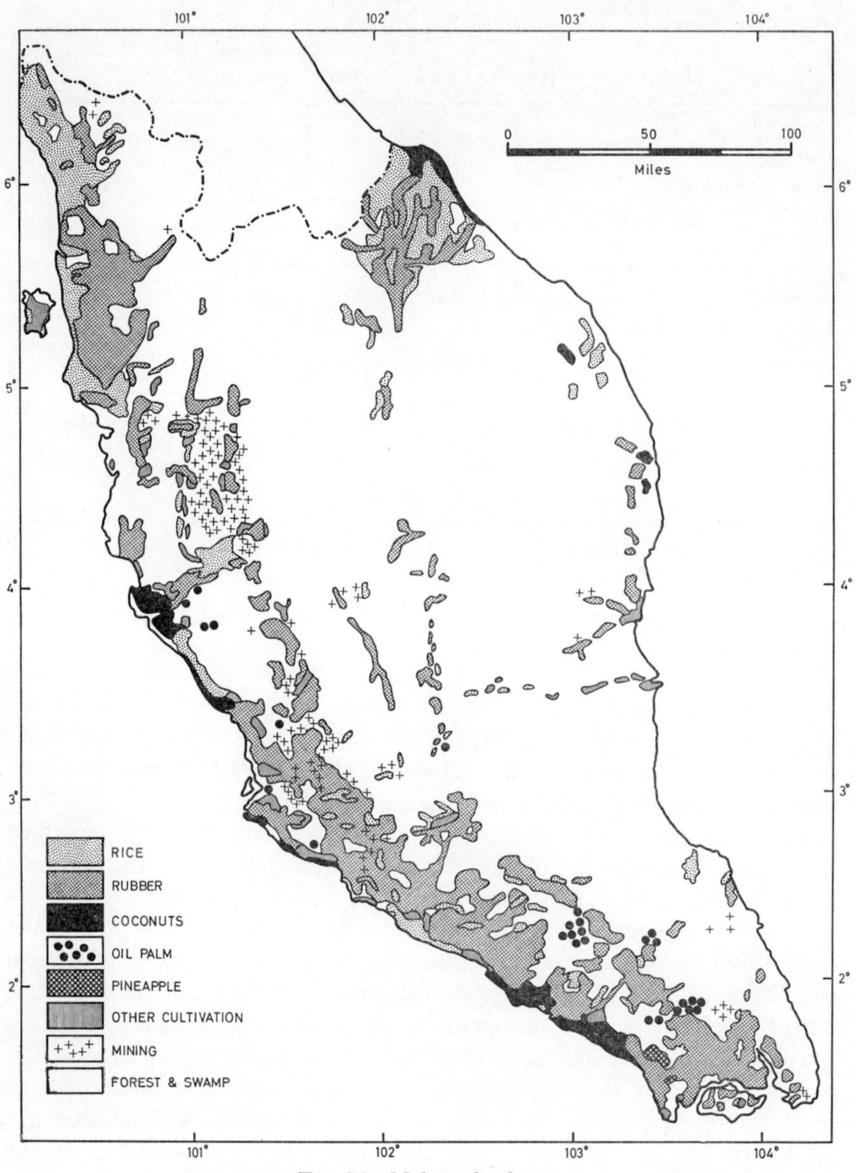

FIG. 86—Malaya: land use

the latter, a considerable proportion of which are Malay owned, gradually increased their share from about 35 per cent of the total in the mid 1930s to over 47 per cent in 1950, but more recent years have seen some falling off. In 1955 the total labour force on rubber estates in the Federation amounted to 278,200 of whom rather more than 50 per cent were Indians (representing about 60 per cent of the gainfully employed Indian population of the country), about 30 per cent Chinese, 12 per cent Malay, and the rest mainly other Malaysians. The numbers engaged in small-holding cultivation in the same year were approximately half a million, though a high proportion of these included part-time Malay cultivators who were also engaged in paddy farming and fishing. Among these Malay small-holders the practice of co-operative tapping and selling of latex to nearby estates for processing is gaining ground.

It can be seen, therefore, that non-European small-holdings have developed as it were in the lee of the large estates, for without the communications, processing and marketing facilities and research which the latter provided for their own requirements the small-scale producers would never have been able to establish themselves in so highly competitive an industry.

So far as the relative positions of estates and small-holders in the future is concerned, it is difficult to make any very confident predictions. In the early post-war years many of the estates, with their great capital reserves, were able to strengthen their competitive position by very extensive replanting with high-yielding material, which most of the small-holders, 60 per cent of whose trees were over 30 years old, could not afford to do. However, in 1952 a new small-holders' replanting organization was set up with government assistance, and since independence further schemes have continued to help the small-holders.

In the long run, if the pressure for higher wages continues,[18] the estates may lose some of their at present considerable competitive advantage. Moreover socio-political considerations similar to those in other parts of South-east Asia may ultimately favour the predominance of the small-holder in rubber production. Whether natural rubber will continue in the meantime to maintain its position against the competition of the synthetic product is even more problematical. The 1955 Report of the World Bank Mission to Malaya stated:

> 'Cost-data from a representative cross-section of rubber estates indicate that the production of high-yielding rubber on well-managed estates could continue to compete profitably with synthetic rubber even if prices of the latter were to fall well below present levels.'[19]

The Report went on to recommend that the highest possible priority be given to the replanting of estates and small-holdings with new high-yielding stock, and this advice has since been generally accepted by the government. The best clonal seedlings hitherto developed have yielded 1,500 lbs. per acre but from material now being tested it is hoped to get as much as 2,500 lbs. Yet if the recent history of synthetics provides any guide for the future, it would seem that

[18] Rubber makes a considerable demand on labour. Tapping must be by hand, and takes place all the year round. On an average one tapper is needed for every six acres. Dobby (H), p. 113.

[19] International Bank for Reconstruction and Development: *The economic development of Malaya*, p. 34.

Malaya's policy of continued over-concentration on rubber entails exceedingly grave risks. For even if the future for rubber were not overhung with such uncertainty, the extent to which Malaya has become dependent on this one major cash crop would give cause for concern, and in recent years the need further to diversify the economy has become more than ever apparent. The difficulty is that there appears to be no other crop remotely comparable in value to rubber which can be so extensively and efficiently grown on the prevailing lateritic soils which have proved satisfactory for rubber. Thus the oil palm, for whose produce the market appears good, is generally restricted in Malaya to coastal and riverine alluvials which are characteristically scarce, and in any case in demand for rice, and though the acreage under oil palms has increased from 78,000 in 1947 to 127,000 in 1959, the value of oil exported in 1959 was only $M60 million compared with the Federation's net export of $M1829 million's worth of rubber and latex.

Hitherto cultivation of the oil palm in the Federation has been limited solely to large estates, but attempts are now being made to encourage small-holders also to grow it. Meanwhile the government has been investigating the possibilities of developing cocoa as a new small-holders' crop, but although its prospects seemed good on the better soils it was not until 1953 that the first commercial planting of Amelonada cocoa began in Trengganu (441 acres planted by late 1955)[20] and more research will be needed before the Malay peasantry can be recommended to take it up on a large scale.[21]

For the time being, therefore, greater importance resides in two older-established commodities, namely coconuts and pineapples. Of these, the former occupy about 518,000 acres, some 80 per cent of which is in small and scattered Malay holdings, producing an estimated total of 172,800 tons of copra in 1960. But there are in addition many large estates, most of them in tracts of coastal alluvium in Perak and elsewhere, which yielded 40,000 tons of copra in the same year. In 1960 the value of copra and coconut-oil exports from the Federation amounted to just over $M24 million. Pineapples, likewise important before the Second World War, are significant as the only known commercial crop which can be satisfactorily grown on the peaty soils typical of much of lowland Malaya. The industry, which was developed by Chinese packers catering for the British metropolitan market, suffered a severe setback during the occupation but cultivation has since been extended from its original locale in Johore into both Selangor and Perak. Out of a total acreage of 34,850 in 1955 approximately half was in small-holdings; exports (canned) were valued at $M26 million in 1960.

By comparison with rubber, the remaining agricultural exports are thus all-

[20] If cocoa is taken up on a large scale the main areas may well be in eastern Malaya, where experimental planting is already taking place. See *Report on the potentialities for the cultivation of cocoa in Malaya*, H.M.S.O., London, Col. No. 230, 1948.

[21] Owing to the absence of a dry season, Malayan cocoa is subject to blight. Other possible export crops include tea and derris (an insecticide), but the output of these is at present very small.

told of very minor significance, and in fact Malaya's only other important export product is tin, of which the country is still the leading source, producing, in 1960, 51,979 out of a world total[22] of 135,500 long tons. This Malayan production, valued at approximately $M507 million, is, however, not yet up to the pre-war level (69,366 tons in 1927, 77,224 in 1937 and 80,651 in 1940) owing primarily to the serious damage sustained by the elaborate and expensive capital equipment used in the larger European-owned mines. For the same reason, the Chinese share in production, 40·5 per cent in 1955, was somewhat higher than pre-war, since the simpler type of gravel-pump equipment which could be more quickly restored after 1945 is almost exclusively restricted to Chinese concerns.

With the exception of some 3·7 per cent of production which comes from lode mines, mainly at Sungei Lembing near Kuantan on the east coast, all the present output is derived from alluvial sources. All-told about 50 per cent is obtained by dredging, which is for the most part confined to European-owned mines, compared with 40 per cent by gravel pumping which is practised by both European and Chinese mines. Other methods include 'hydraullicking', and even some occasional small-scale hand-panning by the Chinese.[23] In the industry as a whole the latter provide over 70 per cent of the labout force which in the 1957 census was recorded as 50,737. The broad geographical distribution of production has not greatly changed since the close of the 19th century. Thus over 70 per cent of the output still comes from the areas centring in Taiping and Ipoh in Perak and Kuala Lumpur in Selangor, and most of the remainder from nearby localities in the western foothill zone. However, there are signs of exhaustion in some of the old-established centres, and so long as prices remain low no serious prospecting is likely to be undertaken elsewhere.

Official estimates nowadays put the average life of existing mining centres at not more than another twenty years, given present levels of production, though it should be noted that former prophecies of exhaustion have been repeatedly belied both by the discovery of fresh deposits and by improvements in extraction, notably the introduction of dredging.

Ease of access, and later the availability of coal and electric power, have

[22] These figures are for tin in concentrates. World totals do not include the Communist bloc. Malayan figures refer to the Federation.

[23] The gravel-pump method, which represents a modernization of the early Chinese open-cast methods, involves digging an open pit, from whose sides the tin-bearing gravels are removed by hand. The gravels are then mixed with water within the pit, and this mixture is pumped to the top of a long sloping sluice which stands on scaffolding high above the ground. As the mixture flows down the incline, the tin is separated out from the gravel. Dredging requires much more costly equipment and did not become widespread until the 1920s. The tin dredges themselves have been likened to 'Noah's Arks of corrugated iron', Purcell (B), p. 88. To use them a large pit has to be excavated in the tin-bearing gravels, and then filled with water to make an artificial lake. In this the dredge floats, its continuous chain of buckets scooping up the gravels, from which the tin is separated on board. Both gravel pumps and dredges use either steam or electric power. Hydraulicking is a modified and intensified form of gravel pumping. The spreads of discarded gravels (from any type of working) are known as tin tailings; these are normally considered to be of very little value for cultivation.

combined to make the western side of the country much the most economical area in which to operate. Whether the development of the Malayan national electricity grid[24] will ultimately pave the way for a greater extension of mining east of the Main Range will depend partly on the outcome of new prospecting, and partly on the state of the market. Hitherto the great asset of Malaya (as of Indonesia) as a tin producer has been its low mining costs, and when the geographical circumstances of Malaya are compared with those of its main rival, Bolivia, this is not surprising. But from the point of view of the United States, which is by far the largest consumer, Bolivia may well appear to be a more convenient source of supply and, in view of the recent international restriction of output, the Malayan tin industry seems unlikely to do much more than maintain its present level of production in the foreseeable future.[25]

As in respect of commercial agriculture so also in mining, one commodity completely dominates the scene, and by comparison with the value of the tin output the production of other minerals is small. Of these iron, whose export value has risen from $M9 million in 1950 to $M140 million in 1960, ranks first. The ore, which is good-quality haematite, has until recently been coming largely from the Bukit Besi mine in Trengganu (2 million out of a total of 3¾ million tons in 1959), but before the war there were also important mines in Johore (Batu Pahat and Endau), and total production then was around 2 million tons. The industry was developed entirely by Japanese capital at that time, and much the greater part of the output is still exported to Japan. Moreover, recent prospecting has led to new discoveries in Perak, and in 1960 this state was the largest source of the Federation's total output of 6 million tons.

Malaya's only worked coalfield, covering an area of about five square miles at Batu Arang, some 28 miles from Kuala Lumpur, is of very minor significance.[26] The coal, which has a calorific value of 9,000 B.T.U., is unsuitable for coking, and the 1959 output of 75,000 tons, valued at just under $M2½ million, represents a distinct decline from the 415,777 tons of 1950 and the peak figure of 780,000 tons in 1940. Originally the coalfield was developed for the use of the railway, but the main consumer now is the cement industry.

Other mineral production includes some 27,000 oz. of (raw) gold, mostly from Raub in Pahang, a little tungsten (both wolfram and scheelite) from Kedah and Trengganu and, rather more promising, some 365,000 tons of bauxite, valued at some $M6½ million, which comes from Telok Ramunia in Johore and is exported to Japan and also to Australia. Magnetic recovery of both ilmenite and monazite from tin-mining dumps is also becoming more important and the output of ilmenite has risen from 19,000 tons in 1949 to 73,000 tons, valued at nearly $M2 million in 1959.

[24] At present this serves the western states only; any extension into the east will depend on developing new hydro-electric power stations, e.g. that at Cameron Highlands, see below, p. 623.

[25] For data on smelting, see below, pp. 620–1.

[26] The Enggor coalfield in Perak was worked only from 1925 to 1928.

This account of the extractive industries of Malaya may be completed by a brief reference to forestry. Although natural forests of one kind or another cover much of the greater part of the country's surface, only 15·9 per cent of the area is officially classified as productive forest and at present large quantities of timber and firewood have to be imported from Sumatra and Thailand. Nevertheless it is now planned to achieve self-sufficiency in timber and already there is a small but significant export of certain Malayan hardwoods, the total sawn timber export of 142,259 tons in 1955 being worth $M26,700,000.[27] The most important local consumer is the Malayan Railways, which use large quantities of termite-resisting keruing and kampas for sleepers.

III. TRANSPORT, MANUFACTURING AND TRADE

From the preceding pages it will be clear that the commercialized sector of the Malayan economy is overwhelmingly concentrated within the western third of the country, and the regional variations in the density of the motor road network shown in Fig. 88 correspond fairly closely to the differences in degree of economic development between one part of the peninsula and another.[28]

More detailed analysis shows that the basic pattern of circulation has been determined by the prior development of the two main ports of the former S.S., namely Singapore and Penang. During the second half of the 19th century export produce, consisting mostly of tin, moved from the foothills by river, and later by the first Malayan railways to such west-coast ports as Telok Anson, Port Weld, Port Swettenham and Port Dickson.[29] From these in turn it was carried by small coastal craft to one or other of the two major S.S. ports where, after preliminary processing, it was reloaded on to ocean-going vessels for export overseas. At the same time mining equipment, together with rice and essential consumer goods for the miners, moved in the opposite direction from Singapore and Penang to the western Malay states.

Both of these great ports, more especially Singapore, served a much wider area than the Malay peninsula, for both were at the same time nodal points for local South-east Asian shipping – much of it Chinese owned – and regular ports of call for ocean-going passenger and cargo vessels sailing between Europe and India on the one hand and the Far East and Australia on the other.

To a recognizable extent this pattern has survived to the present day, though, so far as the peninsular hinterland is concerned, the spectacular development of road transport during the present century has led to a relative decline in the importance of coastal shipping as the link between the tin-and-rubber-belt and the major ports.[30] Moreover, beginning in the early years of the century, the

[27] For data on sawmilling, see below, pp. 621–3. In 1960 the Federation's exports of sawn timber were worth $M55 million.

[28] The particularly elaborate road network in Malacca (Settlement) results from the earlier European development of that area.

[29] Later lines were also built to other small ports, Kuala Selangor, Malacca, Prai (opposite Penang) and to Singapore itself. See Dobby (D).

[30] However, coastal shipping is still of considerable importance.

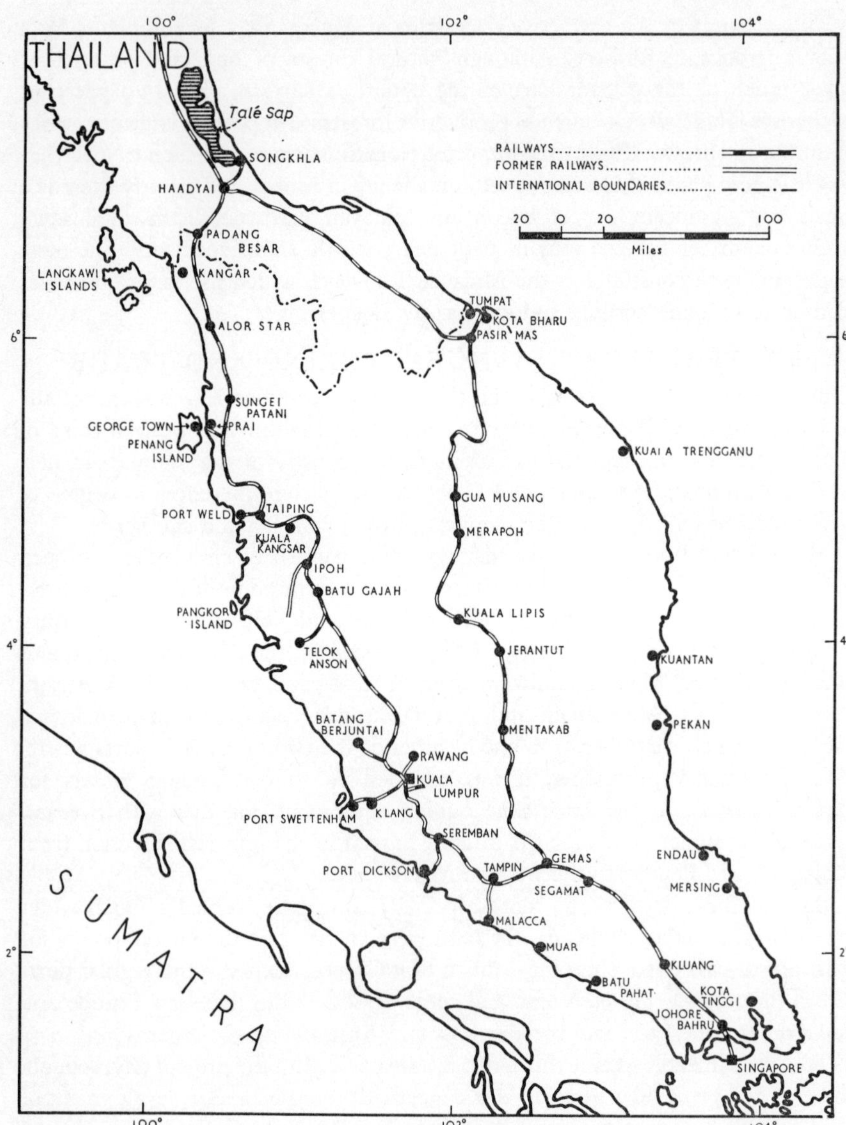

FIG. 87—Malaya: railways

F.M.S. in a somewhat prophetic outburst of local patriotism, embarked on a policy of developing Port Swettenham as 'the Federation's own port', and especially since 1945 this port has far outstripped all the lesser centres of the west coast and is now on the way to catching up with Singapore and Penang.

While there was much to be said for providing good harbour facilities near to

Kuala Lumpur, the site of Port Swettenham in a mangrove swamp only a few feet above sea-level has proved far from ideal. However, the policy of seeking to develop Port Swettenham as a 'national port' for the old F.M.S. has since been continued by the new Federation of Malaya and, whatever the local disadvantages of site, the overall situation of Port Swettenham, virtually mid-way between Singapore and Penang, has obvious attractions. Thus today Port Swettenham is being developed as the Federation's front door on to the Straits highway.[31]

The relative importance of the various ports serving Malaya in 1953 is shown in Table 81, from which it can be seen that, while Penang and Port Swettenham respectively handled 33·3 and 18·0 per cent of the Federation's exports (by value) and 30·6 and 25·9 of its imports, Singapore still led with 42·4 per cent of the exports and 38·3 per cent of the imports. So far as the traffic *via* Singapore is concerned, nearly 45 per cent of the goods moving from the Federation went by coastal shipping, but in the reverse direction 76 per cent were transported overland by road or rail.

Ever since the 1920s road transport has been gaining in importance at the expense of the railways, and especially during the 1930s competition between the two became a serious problem. The excellence of the Malayan highway system, the relatively short hauls involved, and the initiative of Chinese contractors in building up fleets of lorries and small 'mosquito' buses have all continued to favour the former, and the balance was further tipped in that direction both by the Japanese removal of track from several of the railway routes during 1942–5 and by the subsequent concentration of terrorist attacks on trains. Although the eastern railway line was reopened throughout in 1953, the Malacca and Tronoh branches have not been restored, and the effect of the emergency in curtailing train speeds constituted another setback for the railway, though this is now a thing of the past.[32]

Meanwhile several extensions have been made to the road network, notably the new east-west link between Temerloh and Maran, and still others have followed under the 1956–60 Development Plan.[33] In addition to competition from road transport the railways now have to face the new rivalry of the aeroplane, which *inter alia* reduces the travelling time between the two capitals to a mere two hours. Furthermore, if the experience gained in the campaign against the terrorists is turned to good account, there will probably be further advances, perhaps including the use of helicopters in the less developed parts of the country.

As in the case of shipping so also with air transport, Singapore is by far the

[31] As provided for in the 1956–60 Development Plan 'an adequate port for Kuala Lumpur' is being built at North Klang, *i.e.* near the existing Port Swettenham but in a much better site. For this purpose the U.S.A. in 1958 granted a loan of $M30 million.

[32] More recently rail services have been further improved by the introduction of diesels.

[33] In 1958 the U.S.A. also granted the Federation a loan of $M30 million towards the cost of highways and bridges proposed under this Plan. In 1960 the Federation had 128,200 motor vehicles and Singapore 81,700. These totals do not include motor cycles etc. Taken together, these give Malaya much the highest total of any South-east Asian country, although its population is much smaller than that of most of its neighbours.

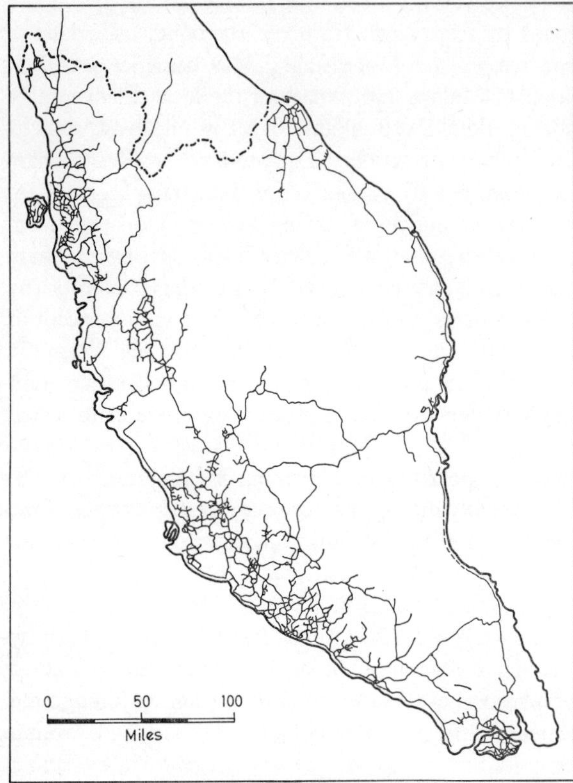

FIG. 88—Malaya: roads

main centre in all Malaya, and the principal point of contact between local and international services.

Thus in 1960 2,174 internal and 4,054 external aircraft landings were recorded at Paya Lebar, the new international airport seven and a half miles from the city centre, which was opened in 1955. Nevertheless, as noted in Chapter 6, Singapore's importance as a focus of air routes in South-east Asia is challenged by Bangkok, though its unrivalled dock facilities as well as its geographical position continue to ensure its pre-eminent status among the seaports of the region.

Some of the most paradoxical features of the Malayan economy are to be found in respect of its industrial sector. For although, as the World Bank Report points out, the 9 per cent of the Malayan working population recorded in the 1947 Census as engaged in secondary industries is a high figure for Asia,[34] the fact remains that until very recently these industries were limited mainly to simple processing (mainly of rubber and tin), the servicing of mining and transport equipment, and such public utilities as power stations, railways and harbours. Moreover, even today factory industry is still not so highly developed as it is, for example, in Hong Kong, and while by South-east Asian standards Malaya is well above average in this respect, it is at first sight surprising that greater progress has not been made, at least in Singapore, with its prosperous and enterprising Chinese community and its remarkable facilities for marketing and distribution.

[34] Exceeded only by Japan, India and Hong Kong. International Bank of Reconstruction and Development: *The economic development of Malaya*, p. 301. The total has risen since, as noted below.

However, there are other factors, both economic and political, to be taken into account. For the most part the raw materials produced in Malaya do not provide the basis for any major industrialization, and the shortage of coal has also been a drawback. Again, Malaya's has hitherto been a colonial economy in the literal sense of that term, and so long as the country, in the absence of any serious population problem, proved able to provide full employment for its people, by labour-intensive production of rubber and tin and the multifarious activities of its ports, there was no inducement for the colonial authorities to follow a policy of deliberately fostering local factory industry, as happened in both Hong Kong[35] and Java. While it is true that some such industry might perhaps have been expected to develop even without any form of official encouragement or protection,[36] the smallness of the Malayan market has been a limiting factor and, in the increasingly nationalistic climate of South-east Asia, Malayan manufactures will have to face the competition of state-aided industries catering for larger markets in neighbouring lands.

Until very recently, therefore, industry has been largely restricted to a few familiar lines. Among the industries processing local raw materials first place goes to tin smelting and until 1955, when a new works was opened at Butterworth (Province Wellesley), virtually all the tin produced in the country was smelted at either Singapore or Penang.[37] Nevertheless, in numbers of people involved, saw-milling is much more important and in the Federation alone 4,941 people were employed (1955) in 373 sawmills, most of them Chinese owned. Besides further sawmills, there were 10 rubber mills employing some 2,360 workers in Singapore,[38] and other processing includes pineapple canning (using locally manufactured tins), the extraction of coconut oil, and the refining of imported mineral oil.

Secondly, under servicing and maintenance industries may be included various foundries and engineering works, notably those of United Engineers in Singapore, motor and vehicle repair shops, and above all the naval and civilian shipyards of Singapore and the central workshops of Malayan Railways at Sentul near Kuala Lumpur. Both the latter also undertake assembly and construction work, and the assembly of cars and lorries began in Singapore with the establishment of the Ford plant just before the depression of the 1930s.

[35] In June 1959 Hong Kong had 192,843 factory workers and a further 100,000 workers in cottage industries. These figures are larger than those for Malaya (see Table 79) though Hong Kong's total population is only 2,900,000.

[36] The obvious places for such industry, namely Singapore and Penang, were both committed to free trade under the pre-war Straits Settlements administration. The same policy was continued in Singapore until 1959, though it is planned to change it under the new regime there.

[37] Penang and Singapore have done much less smelting of non-Malayan tin since 1945 than they did before 1941, when approximately one-third of the total they treated came from overseas. Since the renewal of tin restriction in 1957 the main smelter in Singapore has been closed down. See Courtenay (B), p. 230.

[38] The Indonesian policy of promoting rubber milling in its own territories has caused some setbacks to the Singapore industry since 1955.

For the rest, the pre-war industrial development was limited to food processing (notably flour milling, brewing and the manufacture of soft drinks and biscuits) and the production of such simple consumer goods as soap, cigarettes, matches and cheap footwear, the last from the two Bata factories, respectively at Klang and Singapore, and two Chinese factories also at Klang.

Since the war, however, the need for further industrialization has received much more attention and an expansion, particularly of consumer-goods industries, has begun. Thus in 1953 the first yarn-spinning mill was opened in Singapore to provide cotton yarn, staple fibre yarn and acetate viscose spun yarn. Among its employees the factory introduced a number of skilled operatives from Hong Kong who were admitted in order to train locally recruited labour. Other new industries in Singapore, most of them comparatively small, are engaged in the manufacture of batteries, rubber goods, boot polish, fruit juice, soya-bean milk, glass-ware, metal-ware, rope, plywood, paint, paper, hats, shoes and pencils, as well as printing and the processing of aluminium.

While most of the larger Malayan towns contain at least some small processing and maintenance establishments of one kind or another, the only two areas that can be regarded in any real sense as industrial centres are Singapore and the Kuala Lumpur district,[39] though it seems probable that similar developments will follow fairly quickly in Ipoh and elsewhere.[40]

While the most rapid expansion is taking place in the consumer-goods industries of Singapore, some of whose most imposing new factories have been set up on the Colonial Development Corporation's industrial estate at Bukit Timah, by far the largest single establishment on the island is H.M. Naval Dockyard, which employs some 8,500 workers. At Kuala Lumpur the railway workshops have a labour force of approximately 2,000 and a similar but growing number of other industrial workers are employed mainly in food-processing and consumer-goods factories, repair shops and small foundries. Much the largest of these establishments is the Lever Brothers soap, detergent and edible oil factory opened in 1952[41], while at Rawang a few miles north of Kuala Lumpur, a new cement factory has an output of 106,000 tons a year.

Both Singapore and the Kuala Lumpur/Klang area are well supplied with power. Thus Singapore, which until recently was dependent on the St. James' thermal-electric power station, with a capacity of 37,000 kW, now has a new station at Pasir Panjang, whose installed capacity of 100,000 kW in 1955 has since been increased to 150,000 kW. For many years Kuala Lumpur relied on the local Batu Arang coalfield for much of its fuel, and on the Connaught Bridge thermal-electric power station near Klang. Since the war the capacity of the

[39] The main new industrial centre in the Kuala Lumpur area is at Petaling Jaya. However, similar industrial estates are being planned in other large towns, and in 1958 the first big textile mill in the Federation was opened at Tampo in Johore.

[40] In both the Federation and Singapore the industrial labour force is predominantly Chinese and Indian. On new developments in Singapore, see below, p. 628, note 51.

[41] This consumes 6,000 tons of locally produced palm oil annually.

latter has been raised to 80,000 kW, as part of an all-round increase in power production and the establishment of a Malayan National Grid in 1953. The other major power stations at present in operation include Bungsar (26,500 kW), Malim Nawar (30,000 kW) and Batu Gajah (24,450 kW), all of them thermal, and the two hydro-electric units at Chenderoh (27,000 kW) and Ulu Langat (2,288 kW). It is planned to supplement these by the two new thermal stations,

TABLE 79

MALAYA: EMPLOYMENT

Category	*Federation of Malaya (Based on 1957 Census)*	*Singapore (March 1961) (Workers only)*
Agriculture, forestry, hunting and fishing	572,800	1,888
Agriculture products requiring substantial processing	672,000	—
Mining and quarrying	58,500	512
Manufacturing	135,400	44,295
Building/Construction	68,100	10,372
Commerce	195,200	8,570
Transport, storage and communications	74,800	21,308
Services	319,700	13,407
Total (including others)	2,126,100	105,990 (to which should be added 54,816 industrial clerks, shop assistants and clerks)

Sources: *Federation of Malaya Official Year Book*, 1961, p. 166. Singapore: *Monthly Digest of Statistics*, Vol. 1, No. 2, February 1962, pp. 15–30.

TABLE 80

MALAYA: EMPLOYMENT IN MANUFACTURING AND PROCESSING INDUSTRIES

Federation of Malaya			*Singapore*	
	1955	1957		1955
Textiles, rope, clothing and footwear	n.a.	25,567	Shipbuilding, repairing and marine engineering	10,813
Sawmilling	4,941	10,086	Engineering works and manufacture of non-electrical machinery	4,767
Food manufacturing	4,737	17,596	Motor-vehicle repairs	4,540
Engineering works and foundries	3,440	13,002	Printing and publishing	2,291
Motor-vehicle repairs	3,090	10,575	Rubber milling	2,281
Printing and publishing	2,936	4,319		
Tin smelting	664	n.a.		

Sources: *Federation of Malaya Annual Report*, 1955. *Population Census, Federation of Malaya* 1957 (Fell). *Colony of Singapore Annual Report*, 1955.

at Malacca and Penang (40,000 and 20,000 kW respectively), and work is in progress on a large new hydro-electric station at Cameron Highlands which will ultimately have a capacity of 200,000 kW.

So far as overseas trade is concerned Tables 82 and 83 speak for themselves, though a few points may call for special emphasis. Perhaps the most striking feature is the excessive dependence of the Federation on rubber and tin (respectively accounting for 67 and 18 per cent of its exports), which still constitutes the greatest single economic weakness of the country. Secondly, the importance of the U.S.A. as a market for these two commodities may be inferred from the high place of that country on the 'destinations' list of both the Federation and Singapore, while the relatively small amount of imports from the U.S.A. has resulted from import and exchange control, designed to preserve Malaya as the Sterling Area's leading earner of U.S. dollars.[42] In 1961 the U.S.S.R. replaced the U.S.A. as the second importer of Malayan rubber.

The vast scale of the entrepôt trade of Singapore and the importance of this city as the rubber market of South-east Asia is likewise apparent. But the tables also show that imports of tin for smelting (except from the Federation) have fallen off and it is noteworthy that while both Singapore, and to a lesser extent Penang, continue to handle a high proportion of the export trade of both Indonesia and Thailand, their share in the import trade of these two countries is tending to decline.

Traditionally there have been two kinds of entrepôt trade in Singapore and Penang. In the simpler form goods imported in bulk are merely handled in transit and receive no treatment. But much the greater part of the trade is complex and involves the sorting, grading, handling and often processing of tropical produce and the breaking down of bulk imports of Western manufacture into assorted parcels suited to the needs of small Asian traders. This second more profitable type nowadays seems to be increasingly threatened by the current tide of economic and political nationalism in South-east Asia, though losses in this respect may be partly offset by an increase in the trans-shipment trade. Thus in 1955, despite a drop in its entrepôt trade, the total net tonnage of shipping entered and cleared at Singapore amounted to the record figure of 53,160,000 tons.[43]

[42] Since independence, the Federation of Malaya has remained within the Sterling Area and the same arrangement is to be followed in respect of Singapore. Meanwhile Malaya has received substantial economic aid from the United Kingdom during the post-war years. Such aid for development includes approximately £50 million allocated to the Federation and Singapore by the Colonial Development Corporation (locally operating under the name of Malayan Developments Ltd.) between 1948 and 1956, and various smaller sums provided by other donor nations under the Colombo Plan. However, the United Kingdom has made much larger contributions towards the cost of the emergency in the Federation, and in this connexion the latter has also received loans from both Singapore ($M30 million) and Brunei ($M40 million). Since obtaining its independence the Federation has received development loans totalling $M60 million from the U.S.A. (see above, notes 31 and 33) and a further loan of $M100 million from Brunei.

[43] *Colony of Singapore, Annual Report*, 1955, p. 151. However, this records entrance and clearance as separate transactions. In 1961 33,998 tons entered and 31,818 tons cleared.

IV. RECENT TRENDS IN THE ECONOMIC GEOGRAPHY OF MALAYA

In the preceding sections of this chapter the several component strands of the Malayan economy have each been examined in turn and it now remains to consider the relationships which exist between them. Until well into the present century, as was shown in Chapter 17, the subsistence farming of the Malays, the primary production of the Chinese and Indians in the tin and rubber belt, and the entrepôt trade of the cosmopolitan ports of the old S.S. existed to a considerable extent independently of one another in different parts of the country. Moreover, so far as mining, planting and trading were concerned, each had been developed by non-natives whose activities had prospered in the prevailing atmosphere of economic liberalism in which the country had been opened up during the 19th century.

In characteristically British fashion economic activity had been carried on with a careful eye to comparative costs, but with an apparent disregard of the dangers of lopsided development which this entailed. The most striking example of this is, without doubt, the neglect of local food production,[44] though the equally pronounced dependence of a heavily forested country like Malaya on imported timber is hardly less anomalous.

Nevertheless, as in the case of the metropolitan country itself, this type of development yielded remarkable economic returns. On the eve of the Second World War British Malaya, which led the world in the production of both rubber and tin, and in addition contained the greatest entrepôt port in the whole of South-east Asia, had a volume of overseas trade almost equal to that of the Netherlands Indies. And when it is recalled that Malaya's total population was only a tenth of that of the Indies, it is hardly surprising that its income per head was three times that of Java and roughly equal to that of Japan, economically by far the most advanced country in Asia. Notwithstanding the large sums remitted to India and China each year, on an average about £500,000 and £2,000,000 respectively, and the immeasurable benefits derived directly and indirectly by Great Britain, Malaya was much the wealthiest area in South-east Asia and this differential has increased rather than diminished since the war.

Since 1945 many changes which were already afoot before the war have proceeded at an accelerated rate. The twin needs of rehabilitation and adjustment to the new economic and political conditions of the post-war world led to a measure of planning hitherto without precedent in Malaya, and both the Federation and Singapore have produced development plans within the wider framework of the Colombo Plan.

[44] Notwithstanding Professor Silcock's strictures quoted in note 2, above, the lack of food production in Malaya hitherto has been a serious weakness in the country's economy, and when it is seen against the background of uncertainty regarding the future of natural rubber, this weakness becomes even more disturbing. See below, p. 626.

Most of the projects which these involved have already been mentioned in passing. Thus the first Singapore Plan provided for the building of the new power station and airport, as well as improvements in the docks, an extended programme of social services and industrialization. In the Federation the original emphasis of the 1950–1955 Plan was placed mainly on replanting rubber, extending the paddy acreage, increasing the supply of electricity and restoring the railway system, but the Plan was later extended to include the resettlement of squatters and the establishment of the Rural and Industrial Development Authority. The latter, usually known as R.I.D.A., was set up mainly, in the words of the Colombo Plan Report of 1954, 'to generate a spirit of self-help among smallholders, small business-men and fishermen to enable them to improve their standards of living. Its activities cover the provision of training facilities in such matters as domestic science, mechanized farming, industrial crafts, and commerce and accounting. Loans are also given to help farmers, business-men and fishermen to improve their trades and crafts, and to small communities to carry out schemes for improved local amenities, such as roads and water supplies.'[45]

In the meantime considerable progress has taken place under the Federation's 1955–60 Development Plan. This envisaged an allocation of roughly 60 per cent (of a total capital expenditure amounting to *c.* \$M1,000 million) on the economic sectors, in which the most noteworthy items were \$M254 million for transport and communications, \$M160 million replanting grants for rubber, over \$M80 million for further development of electric power and \$M40 million on drainage and irrigation projects for rice cultivation; various forms of assistance were also given to the mining industry.[46]

Thus, while the Federation, as a fully independent state has been no less anxious than its neighbours to hasten the transition from a 'colonial' to a more advanced type of economy, its leaders have been well aware of the need for careful planning at this stage and intend to do all in their power to help the major export industries, on whose earnings the long-term success or failure of the whole economy depends. Accordingly the recommendations of the World Bank Commission notably in respect of rubber replanting, have been accepted, and at the same time renewed efforts are being made to diversify cash-crop production and to reduce dependence on imported food.

Sound as this attitude may be, however,[47] many grave problems remain. Thus, notwithstanding the high average per capita income of the population as a whole, the difference in wealth between the indigenous and the non-indigenous population remains wide, and the rural Malay, though better off than most other

[45] *The Colombo Plan, Third Annual Report*, H.M.S.O., London, Cmd. 9336, p. 64, para. 25. See also 'Helping the Malayans to help themselves', T.B.C.R., Summer 1954, p. 19.

[46] See Spencer, O. A., pp. 43–4. 1961 saw the launching of both the Federation's Second Five Year Plan (1961–65) and the Singapore Development Plan (1961–64).

[47] Though the writer confesses to a lingering doubt as to whether it is wise for Malaya to remain so heavily dependent on rubber. See above, p. 625.

Asian peasants, lives at a standard well below that of the bulk of the Chinese and Indians, whether traders, clerks, industrial workers or even estate and mining labourers.[48]

This situation in turn is closely bound up with the problem of reducing Malaya's dependence on imported food. If the latter could be solved by a large-scale opening-up of new rice areas, under a system of mechanized cultivation with a high output per man to provide both a substantial surplus for sale and a good livelihood to the cultivators, it would not matter much whether the cultivators in question were Malays, Chinese or Indians. But, in view of the shortage of suitable land, such an approach is possible on only a limited scale, and much of the hoped-for increase in rice production will probably have to come from a further intensification of cultivation on the part of the Malay peasantry. And there is scant prospect that this will lead to any revolutionary improvement in their living standards in view of the smallness of the traditional peasant holdings.

Admittedly, much can be done to encourage further small-holder cultivation of cash crops as an adjunct to subsistence farming, to develop rural handicraft industries and other means of mopping up seasonal unemployment in the countryside, and to promote peasant co-operatives of various kinds. This, indeed, is very largely what R.I.D.A. is attempting to do, and although its activities are not specifically limited to the Malays, the latter, by virtue of their predominantly rural distribution, are the greatest beneficiaries.

But while R.I.D.A. is soundly conceived as a means of raising the living standards of the rural Malays, and would be an almost ideal solution to the problem, if the urban, mining and estate workers were also of the same community and culture, it remains to be seen whether it will bridge the economic gap between town and countryside in the context of the Malayan plural society. For the products of the Malays' handicraft industries will not commend themselves to the more sophisticated Chinese and Indian purchasers, who will prefer factory-made goods,[49] and unless very great increases take place in the Malays' output of cash crops their economy will still remain in large measure separate from and at a lower level than that of the non-Malays.

The economic relationship between Malays and non-Malays within the Federation is in some respects similar to that between the Federation as a whole and Singapore. Notwithstanding the policy of boosting the Federation's ports at the expense of Singapore, the latter is increasingly aware that its economic future is ineluctably bound up with that of the peninsula, as the world at large departs more and more from the principles of 19th-century liberalism, which provided its very *raison d'être* as the entrepôt of South-east Asia. With a population now growing at the fantastic rate of nearly 40 per 1,000 per annum,

[48] The Malays are better off than most other Asian peasants, because the productive activities of their non-Malay fellow-countrymen are taxed to provide services for all.

[49] *Cf.* the difficulties which Java faces in selling similar handicraft manufactures to the outer territories. See Chapter 10.

Singapore, in somewhat belated imitation of Hong Kong,[50] has turned towards industrialization as the most obvious answer to its problems, and in this connexion it regards the Federation as a principal market for its goods.

This is a situation which should call for the closest possible collaboration between the two governments. For while the Federation itself, in common with all other countries in South-east Asia, wishes to increase its manufacturing activities, it is clear that in many respects Singapore is geographically and economically among the most favoured locations for industry in the whole of Malaya. Furthermore, Singapore's only alternative to such an industrial expansion would seem to be to dispose of a growing proportion of its predominantly Chinese population to nearby areas to find whatever employment they could, and an influx of this kind would scarcely be welcome to the Malays of the Federation.[51]

For quite apart from the communal complications, the Federation is also faced with the problem of rising numbers, and its own rate of increase, 35/1,000 per annum, is not far below that of Singapore. True, there is as yet no absolute shortage of land for settlement in the Federation, and, indeed, provided that the market for Malayan export produce remained unsated, vast areas in the eastern two-thirds of the country could be planted with rubber, and many others might well be found to contain mineral deposits no less intrinsically valuable than those of the west. But the proviso is a big one, and even were it to be fulfilled, development would be a costly matter, involving heavy outlays on jungle clearance and the provision of communications and utilities of all kinds.

Nevertheless, since the setting up of the Federal Land Authority in 1956, and more particularly since the formation, after independence, of Rural Development Committees at the District level, much has already been done to bring hitherto uncultivated jungle tracts into productive agricultural use.[52]

While much of the land in question is within the western states, a large and growing proportion is east of the Main Range, notably in Pahang, and the typical peasant holding in such development areas is a ten-acre plot which can provide both subsistence crops for the family and a substantial cash crop as well. Among the latter rubber remains by far the most popular, and much is now being done to assist the peasant to improve the quality of his product.

Thanks partly to the work of the former British pioneers, partly to the peaceful nature of the transfer of political control, and certainly not least to the statesmanlike policies of Tunku Abdul Rahman's administration, the Federation of Malaya at the time of its merger with Singapore, Sarawak and Sabah in 1963 was a

[50] Hong Kong began its industrialization much earlier, and was greatly assisted by its proximity to the China market and by Western control of the Chinese customs. With the post-1949 decline of both its entrepôt trade and the China market for its manufactures, Hong Kong is extending its manufacturing activities and seeking new outlets for them; Malaya is itself regarded as one of the most promising of these.

[51] The Singapore government has since announced proposals for creating a new industrial town at Jurong, and it hopes to increase the rate of gross investment from *c.* 11 per cent to *c.* 20 per cent of the national income. *The Times*, July 4 and 21, 1960.

[52] See Tinker (D), pp. 318–322, and *Lembaga Kemajuan Tanah Persekutuan.*

thriving and prosperous land. Whether the standards which it has achieved can be further advanced and simultaneously extended over the new Federation of Malaysia as a whole will be intimately bound up both with the latter's success in developing a sense of national cohesion in the face of internal differences and external distractions, and with the developing state of the world's demand for its export products.

TABLE 81

FEDERATION OF MALAYA: CHANNELS OF TRADE, 1953

All values in $M million

Imports

464·1	via Penang, of which	21·6	from Singapore
377·7	„ Port Swettenham	5·6	„ „
33·9	„ Malacca	11·9	„ „
128·8	„ Other ports	94·2	„ „
441·2	„ Road, rail, air	423·3	„ „
1,445·7	Total		

Exports

617·0	via Penang, of which	37·6	to Singapore
349·0	„ Port Swettenham	62·6	„ „
53·3	„ Malacca	51·9	„ „
184·5	„ Other ports	152·4	„ „
394·4	„ Road, rail, air	373·1	„ „
1,598·2	Total		

Sources: *Federation of Malaya, Annual Report*, 1953; *Colony of Singapore, Annual Report*, 1953.

TABLE 82

FEDERATION OF MALAYA: TRADE

All values in $M million

Imports

Commodities	1955	1959
Rice	125·6	132·18
Other foodstuffs	352·1	378·0
Beverages and tobacco	79·7	80·37
Tin concentrates	64·0	58·96
Rubber (including latex)	59·4	97·23
Copra	11·4	10·92
Mineral fuels	125·8	128·90
Chemicals	88·0	119·55
Textile yarn, fabrics and finished goods	105·1	99·39
Clothing and footwear	29·0	26·82
Base metals	52·7	46·17
Electrical machinery	40·5	61·54
Other machinery	58·6	78·47
Transport equipment	74·3	100·84
Total (including others)	1,543·0	1,739·31

Sources	1955	1960
United Kingdom	295·3	462·4
Indonesia	133·3	324·6
Thailand	160·2	249·5
Singapore*	586·9	192·2
Japan	n.a.	172·3
Australia	52·1	99·9
U.S.A.	17·9	89·1
China (mainland)	24·7	83·5
Hong Kong	n.a.	81·6
Germany (Fedl. Repub.)	n.a.	76·9
Netherlands	n.a.	48·2
India	28·3	45·2
Burma	41·0	30·0
Total (incl. others)	1,543·0	2,150·6

Exports

Commodities	1955	1959
Food, beverages and tobacco	93·9	89·41
Copra and coconut oil	52·3	43·13
Palm oil and kernels	40·8	60·84
Rubber (all types)	1,584·3	1,691·61
Wood, lumber, etc.	28·6	20·49
Tin concentrates	191·4	294·65† (tin concentrates and tin blocks, ingots, etc. combined)
Tin blocks, ingots, etc.	231·4	
Iron ore	32·6	99·83
Total (including others)	2,360·0	2,473·13

Destinations	1955	1960
Singapore*	985·4	633·9
United Kingdom	323·4	382·4
Japan	89·7	370·0
U.S.A.	326·7	303·1
Germany (Fedl. Repub.)	125·3	226·1
France	101·6	113·4
U.S.S.R.	n.a.	110·9
Italy	79·3	107·5
India	45·1	82·4
Australia	n.a.	58·0
Poland	n.a.	54·5
Belgium/Luxembourg	n.a.	46·2
Canada	33·7	39·2
Netherlands	31·5	39·0
Spain	n.a.	36·4
Czechoslovakia	n.a.	36·3
Argentina	n.a.	32·3
Total (incl. others)	2,360·0	2,927·4

* includes value of commodities imported or exported via Singapore for which the country of source or destination is not known.

† tin and tin alloys, unwrought.

Sources: *Federation of Malaya, Annual Report*, 1955, *Yearbook of international trade statistics, U.N.*, 1960.

TABLE 83

SINGAPORE: TRADE

All values in $M million

Imports

Commodities

	1955	1959
Rubber	608·6	1,379·93
Motor spirit	165·6	200·67
Liquid fuel	150·4	365·59
Rice	92·3	87·34
Cotton fabrics	91·1	82·29
Other fabrics	76·8	92·94
Spices	67·7	90·68
Machinery (non-electrical)	64·4	87·66
Iron and steel manufactures	53·7	58·28
Total (including others	2,865·4	3,908·31

Sources

	1955	1960
Indonesia	1,018·9	999·3
Fedn. of Malaya	985·4	852·9
United Kingdom	395·3	363 1
Japan	194·2	298·1
Sarawak	n.a.	198·5
U.S.A.	130·9	156·1
Thailand	112·6	145·8
China (mainland)	91·2	139·8
Australia	91·5	106·0
Hong Kong	92·0	89·6
Germany (Fedl. Repub.)	n.a.	74·1
Iran	n.a.	59·1
Netherlands	n.a.	58·8
Total (incl. others)	3,850·8	4,077·7

Exports

Commodities

	1955	1959
Rubber	1,384·1	1,537·04
Tin	202·2	38·87
Motor Spirit	130·0	184·79
Spices	63·3	92·46
Liquid fuel	58·0	176·77
Cotton fabrics	35·3	59·61
Other fabrics	28·8	46·72
Rice	20·4	52·09
Machinery (non-electrical)	17·4	67·00
Iron and steel manufactures	7·7	31·41
Total (including others)	2,781·8	3,440·26

Destinations

	1955	1960
Fedn. of Malaya	586·9	843·0
United Kingdom	437·6	286·8
U.S.A.	396·7	242·2
Japan	198·6	156·7
Australia	158·3	135·4
Indonesia	188·4	121·1
Thailand	59·8	107·3
France	n.a.	91·4
China (mainland)	10·8	86·9
Sarawak	n.a.	85·6
Italy	n.a.	82·4
North Borneo	n.a.	78·9
Germany (Fedl. Repub.)	n.a.	78·7
India	n.a.	69·5
U.S.S.R.	n.a.	61·9
Hong Kong	52·5	60·0
Netherlands		57·8
Total (incl. others)	3,368·7	3,477·1

Source: *Colony of Singapore, Annual Report,* 1955, and *Yearbook of international trade statistics, U.N.,* 1960.

SELECT BIBLIOGRAPHY

Allen, D. F.
Allen and Donnithorne
Anderson
Bauer (A) (B)
Blaut
Burkill
Courtenay (A) (B)
Dobby (B) (D) (G) (H) (L) (M) (N)
Dobby *et al.*
Dykes
Firth (A) (B)
Fisher (E)
Fryer (G)
Ginsburg and Roberts
Grist (A)
King, A. W.
Kirby
Mackenzie, K. E.
Mills
Mills *et al.*
Ooi Jin-Bee (A) (B)
Purcell (B)
Robinson (A)
Robequain (D)
Rowe
Silcock (B)
Spencer, O. A.
Steel and Fisher
Tinker (D)
Vandenbosch and Butwell
Zinkin (A)

Federation of Malaya, Draft Development Plan
'Helping the Malayans to help themselves', *T.B.C.R.*, Summer, 1954
International Bank for Reconstruction and Development, *The economic development of Malaya*
The Far Eastern Territories, Vol. V of An economic survey of the colonial territories
Federation of Malaya, Annual Reports
Colony of Singapore, Annual Reports
Colombo Plan Reports
Economic Surveys of Asia and the Far East
Straits Times
Monthly Digest of Statistics (Singapore)
Federation of Malaya Official Year Book, 1961
Lembaga Kemajuan Tanah Persekutuan

On economic geography in general and especially on agricultural geography many of the works by Dobby, notably (D) (G) (H) (L) (M) (P), and Dobby *et al.* are pioneer studies. These may be supplemented by the works of Blaut, Fryer (G), Ooi (A) (B), Ginsburg and Roberts, and both the papers and the thesis by Courtenay.

No less valuable to the economic geographer are the several studies by economists, notably Allen and Donnithorne, Bauer (A) (B), Rowe, and Silcock. (B), and the works by the agricultural specialists Anderson, Burkill, and Grist (A).

A noteworthy overall survey of the economic problems facing Malaya is contained in the I.B.R.D. report, while the various governmental publications listed provide a wealth of detailed source material.

See also the Select Bibliography in Chapter 19.

Addendum: See also Ooi Jin-bee: *Land, people and economy in Malaya*, London, 1963.

CHAPTER 19

Malaya: Social and Political Geography

As a result of the geographical and historical forces which have been considered in the two preceding chapters, the population of Malaya today exhibits in an intensified form the ethnographic complexity which is a major characteristic of South-east Asia as a whole. In addition to numerous lesser groups, three main ethnic components, derived respectively from eastern, south-eastern and southern Asia have met in this focal peninsula at the maritime cross-roads of Monsoon Asia. But the meeting has not been followed by any general intermingling, and an account of the present-day population must therefore begin by considering each of the ethnic groups in turn.

I. MAIN ETHNIC GROUPS

First in logical order but in most other respects the least important of all are the aboriginal peoples,[1] whose number was recorded by the 1947 Census as 34,737. Of these, 29,648 were classed as nomads, living mainly by hunting and food gathering in the interior jungles, notably of the northern half of the country, while the remainder followed the more settled life of the primitive cultivator.[2] Members of the latter group may in the course of time be accepted into the Malay society by the simple process of adopting the Muslim religion and there is little doubt that such a practice has become increasingly common in recent times. Although, until the Communist terrorists began to exploit their remarkable skill in jungle craft by employing them as guides, the aborigines took no part in the economic and political development of the country, many are now being given agricultural land, and the community has a representative in the Federation Parliament.

Nevertheless, while it has for many years been customary to regard the far more numerous 'Malays' (2,543,569 in 1947) as the true 'natives of the country'

[1] The aborigines include several different ethnic groups. The most primitive are the Negrito Semang, and the most advanced are the Jakun who have been variously assessed as Proto- or Deutero-Malay in origin. Intermediate in level of advancement but less clear in ethnic type are the Senoi-Temiar, who speak a language of the Mon-Khmer family. The Senoi-Temiar are often known as Sakai, but this term, which is a Malay word meaning subject, is applied indiscriminately by the Malays to all aboriginal peoples. See Del Tufo, pp. 119–21. See also below, p. 636, note 7.

[2] Traditionally shifting cultivation, and although this is now illegal it is still practised in outlying areas. It is thought that the 1947 Census underestimated the number of nomads.

TABLE 84

MALAYA: MAJOR ETHNIC GROUPS, 1947 AND 1957

Area	*Malaysians*		*Chinese*		*Indians and Pakistanis*		*Total (including others)*	
	1947	1957	1947	1957	1947	1957	1947	1957
Johore	323,680	444,618	354,770	392,568	55,044	71,758	738,251	926,850
Kedah	377,075	475,563	115,928	144,057	51,347	68,037	554,441	701,964
Kelantan	412,918	463,118	22,938	28,861	4,940	5,963	448,572	505,522
Malacca	120,327	143,128	96,144	120,759	19,717	23,623	239,356	291,211
Negri Sembilan	110,560	151,408	114,406	150,055	38,082	55,052	267,668	364,524
Pahang	135,772	179,088	97,329	108,226	14,744	22,082	250,178	313,058
Penang	136,163	165,092	247,366	327,240	57,157	69,778	446,321	572,100
Perak	360,631	484,530	444,509	539,334	140,176	182,225	953,838	1,221,446
Perlis	55,185	71,272	11,788	15,771	1,684	1,598	70,490	90,885
Selangor	187,324	291,411	362,710	488,657	145,184	204,005	710,788	1,012,929
Trengganu	207,874	256,246	15,865	18,228	1,761	2,987	225,996	278,269
Total Federation of Malaya	2,427,834	3,125,474	1,884,534	2,333,756	530,638	707,108	4,908,086	6,278,758
Singapore	115,735	197,066	730,133	1,090,585	68,978	124,084	940,824	1,445,929
Total Malaya	2,543,569	3,322,540	2,614,667	3,424,343	599,616	831,192	5,848,910	7,724,687

Sources: Based on 1947 Census (Del Tufo), and 1957 Census (Fell).

the former Census Superintendent, C. A. Vlieland, attempted to modify this view. Before the founding of the Straits Settlements the peninsular Malays certainly formed the overwhelming majority of the population, but the country was very sparsely inhabited, and according to Newbold's calculations of 1835–9 the total Malay population of the peninsula (excluding Patani) could not have exceeded 300,000. This, admittedly, was only a rough estimate, and we are on much surer ground with the official figures for 1891, which gave a total of 232,000 Malays in the four states later joined together as the F.M.S. On this basis Vlieland argued that natural increase alone could not have raised this figure to more than 350,000 by 1931, when in fact the Malay population of the F.M.S. was returned as 594,000. Hence the balance of 224,000 (and probably a larger proportion than this) must have been made up by immigration during the intervening period. However, more recent work by Tunku Shamsul Bahrin suggests that Vlieland's assumed natural growth rates were too low, and for this and other reasons he concludes that Indonesian immigration during the period concerned was much lower than Vlieland implied.[3]

Migration to and fro across the Malacca Straits had nevertheless been going on for centuries before that time, and there is abundant evidence to suggest that the introduction of law and order under British protection was quickly followed by an increase in the flow of migrants into the west-coast states of the peninsula.

[3] See Vlieland (B), p. 64 and the thesis by Tunku Shamsul Bahrin, Chapter 5.

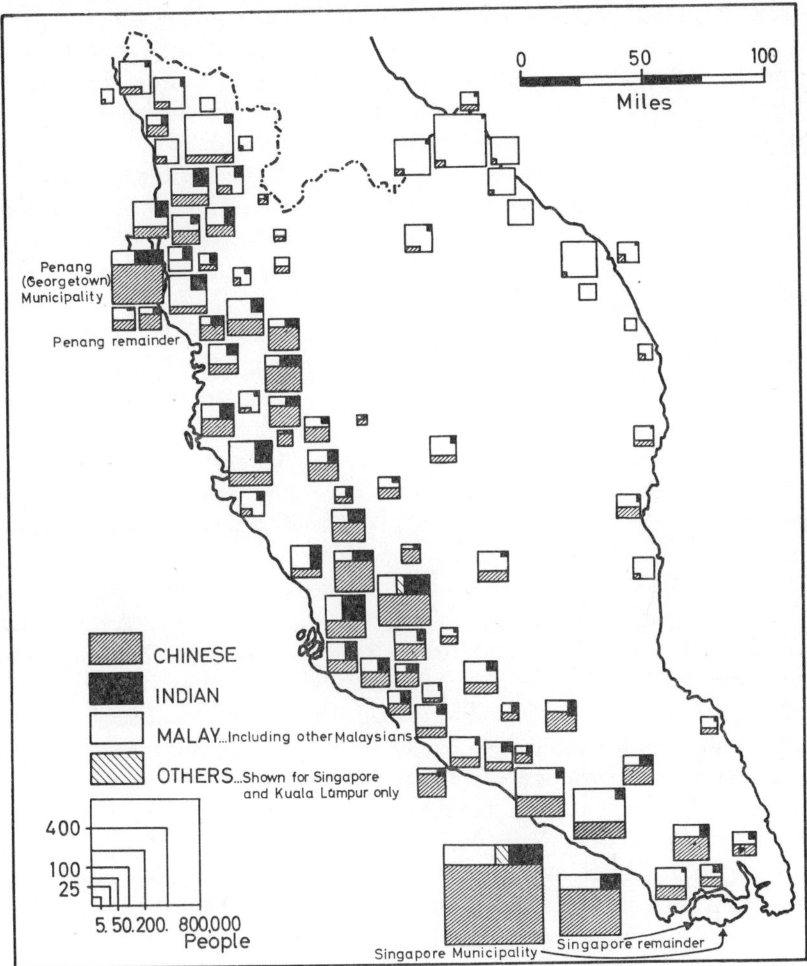

FIG. 89—Malaya: communal distribution, 1947

Note: In this map each square is proportionate in area to the total population in each Census District. Each square is divided internally to show the proportions of Malays (including other Malaysians), Chinese, and Indians (including Pakistanis) within the Census District concerned, the Chinese component being shown in the lower left, the Indian in the upper right and the Malay in the middle of the square.

This map may be compared with Fig. 98, p. 688, which shows the corresponding data, on a state basis, from the 1957 Census.

Moreover, until the Second World War several factors combined to sustain this flow except in times of acute economic crisis. Thus the 'Malays', while receiving 'a preferential treatment which enabled [them] to maintain [their] chosen life of ease unaffected by the stress and strain of life that are the lot of the immigrant'[4] Chinese and Indians, nevertheless benefited indirectly from the productive efforts of these aliens which supported a far higher per capita expenditure on public services than was the case in the Netherlands Indies. And since the British were increasingly anxious to strengthen the Malays *vis-à-vis* the Chinese and Indians, no obstacles were raised against either the immigration or the assimilation of Indonesians.

To say this, however, is not to accept Vlieland's conclusion (1934) that 'only a negligible fraction of the Malay population [of the peninsula] consists of descendants of pre-nineteenth century immigrants and . . . more than half of it has less than 50 years' prescriptive rights to the title 'owners of the soil'. The Malays are, in fact, merely immigrants of generally longer standing than the other immigrant races represented in the peninsula and are in no sense an autochthonous population.'[5] Were this conclusion proved to be valid it would assuredly weaken the arguments in favour of Malay paramountcy which was the cornerstone of modern British policy in Malaya after 1927. However, as Tunku Shamsul Bahrin has shown[6] the situation varies greatly in different parts of the country. Vlieland's remarks apply primarily to the States of the tin and rubber belt which carried only a very small Malay population in the early 19th century. In the northern and north-eastern States, including Patani, the Malay population seems to have grown essentially by its own natural increase throughout the period under consideration, and these are still the areas showing the thickest clustering of Malays today, despite the fact that they must have provided many of the 'immigrants' into the Western States during the past century.

In the 1947 Census the 'Malays' of popular parlance, who should strictly be called Malaysians, are divided into the two categories of Malays and Other Malaysians,[7] the distinction being purely that of birthplace in or outside Malaya.[8] On this basis the figures show that immigrants form 43·2 per cent of the total Malaysian population of Selangor, 31·4 per cent in Johore, 16·2 per cent in Perak and 36·7 per cent in Singapore. In no other state or settlement does the proportion exceed 10 per cent, and in Trengganu and Kelantan the figures drop to 0·21 and 0·11 per cent respectively. Everywhere the percentages of other Malaysians show a decline in comparison with the previous Census (1931) and in the meantime there has been both a falling-off of immigration and a further assimilation of those who had already arrived.

In the case of immigrants from Sumatra assimilation is almost automatic for,

[4] Vlieland (B), p. 64. [5] *Ibid.*, pp. 64–5. [6] *Loc. cit.*

[7] In the 1957 Census (Federation only) the 3,125,000 Malaysians included 2,802,900 Malays, 281,200 Indonesians and 41,400 aborigines.

[8] In the great majority of cases, therefore, 'Other Malaysians' are immigrants from Indonesia.

since many of the peninsular Malays themselves are descended from immigrants from the Menangkabau, Djambi, Riauw, Siak and Kampar districts of Sumatra, there are scarcely any discernible differences between the inhabitants of the lands on opposite sides of the Straits. In both areas, in short, the people, besides being virtually identical in physical type, speak the same Malay language and are firm, if rarely extreme, adherents of the Muslim religion.

The Javanese, as also the Bandjarese from southern Borneo, present rather more of a problem,[9] but even in their case the bond of Islam is enough to overcome other differences and they find no difficulty in adopting Bazaar Malay as a *lingua franca*. Thus, notwithstanding the apparent diversity of the Malaysian population as shown in Table 85, the distinctions in question count for far less than those present among both the Chinese and the Indian populations of Malaya, and for this reason the common practice of including all together, regardless of birthplace, as Malaysians can be justified.

This total for Malaya as a whole had risen by 1957 to 3,322,530 and, if Newbold's estimates can be relied upon, this implies a ten-fold growth, by immigration and natural increase, in little over a century, a rate almost comparable with that of Java, though the numbers involved are altogether smaller. Geographically, as may be inferred from Fig. 89, this growth has resulted in a marked filling out of the earlier distribution pattern, but not in any major change in its lineaments.

Thus the Malays are still concentrated mainly along the coasts and the lower

TABLE 85

MALAYA: MALAYSIAN POPULATION, 1947

Malays	(born in Malaya)	2,199,598
Javanese	,, ,, Java	187,755
Sundanese	,, ,, Java	751
Boyanese	,, ,, Sumatra	20,429
Achinese	,, ,, Sumatra	1,143
Menangkabau	,, ,, Sumatra	10,866
Korinchi	,, ,, Sumatra	2,412
Palembangan	,, ,, Sumatra	1,116
Djambi	,, ,, Sumatra	980
Other Sumatran peoples	,, ,, Sumatra	9,806
Bandjarese	,, ,, Borneo	62,356
Bugis	,, ,, Celebes	6,962
Total other Malaysians, including lesser groups not separately enumerated		343,971
Total Malaysians		2,543,569

Source: Based on 1947 Census.

[9] Many of the Javanese immigrants have come to Malaya after spending some time as labourers, etc., in Sumatra, particularly in the *Cultuurgebied*. See above, p. 266, note 62.

courses of the rivers, with a clear preponderance in the better rice lands of the north and north-east, and now also in the rice and rubber small-holding districts of western Johore. The pattern is essentially rural, with the village (*kampong*) not the town[10] as the major unit of settlement. Indeed, in the strict sense of the term there are no indigenous Malay towns, and even the traditional state capitals are little more than overgrown villages, to which a larger mosque, a Sultan's palace (*istana*) and, more recently, a handful of administrative buildings and a sprinkling of Chinese shops have been added.[11]

Whether the relationship is one of cause or effect, there can be no doubt that this rural way of life has been accompanied by a somewhat parochial outlook on the part of the great many of the peninsular Malays. In the traditional scheme of things Malaya never constituted a political unit, and until recently the Malay's primary loyalty has been to the sultan of the particular state in which he himself was born or now resides.[12] Under British protection the administrative structure of the states was completely transformed and their importance, at least superficially, enhanced. The old nobility, the semi-independent territorial chiefs of former days, were largely absorbed into the Civil Service while the sultans were transmogrified into minor constitutional monarchs.[13] Yet ever since the roads and railways superseded the coast and the rivers as the principal means of communication, the divisions between the states have tended to lose their geographical significance.[14]

Through all these changes, however, the rural Malays were, until recently, carefully shielded from the realities of the 20th-century world. Protected by British paternalism, they were encouraged to carry on winning their livelihood as nearly as possible in their traditional unhurried manner, while the more hard-headed immigrants transformed at least the western third of Malaya from a tangle of jungle into one of the most intensively exploited regions in the whole of South-east Asia.

In this process it is unquestionably the Chinese who have played the decisive rôle. Although a trickle of Chinese immigration and related settlement antedates the arrival of the British in the S.S. the flood tide of this migration into Malaya occurred in the second half of the 19th and the early decades of the 20th centuries. As in other parts of South-east Asia so also in Malaya, the Chinese immigrants came almost exclusively from the southern provinces of Kwangtung, Fukien and Kwangsi and their motives in so doing were entirely economic.

Thus, in spite of real differences in the status accorded them in the S.S. and the protected states respectively, the Chinese always regarded Malaya as a

[10] Only 14·1 per cent of the Malay population was classed as urban in 1947.

[11] Kuala Trengganu, Kota Bharu, Alor Star and Kangar are still more or less traditional-style capitals, though in the states of the former F.M.S. the old centres had ceased to be capitals by the end of the 19th century. But see below, p. 651.

[12] In 1947 only 5·9 per cent of Malays were enumerated outside their state or settlement of birth. Del Tufo, p. 87.

[13] Freedman, p. 24.

[14] Both the coast and the rivers are still much used by Malay country boats.

single country – as for the purpose of immigration regulations it always was under British rule – and though the great majority landed in Singapore, many subsequently followed wherever opportunity seemed to beckon, notably in the western states where the scope in tin mining and in petty trading of all kinds appeared to be unlimited.[15] Beginning with relatively few exceptions at the bottom, a surprisingly high proportion later climbed the occupational ladder to establish themselves in due course as skilled craftsmen, market gardeners, clerks and shopkeepers, while others have entered the professions or achieved both importance and affluence as business-men of high standing. All told the Chinese stake in the country's wealth is enormous, and their capital holdings – almost exclusively entrepreneur investments – were second only to those of the British before the war when they were estimated by Callis to be of the order of $ (U.S.) 200 million.[16]

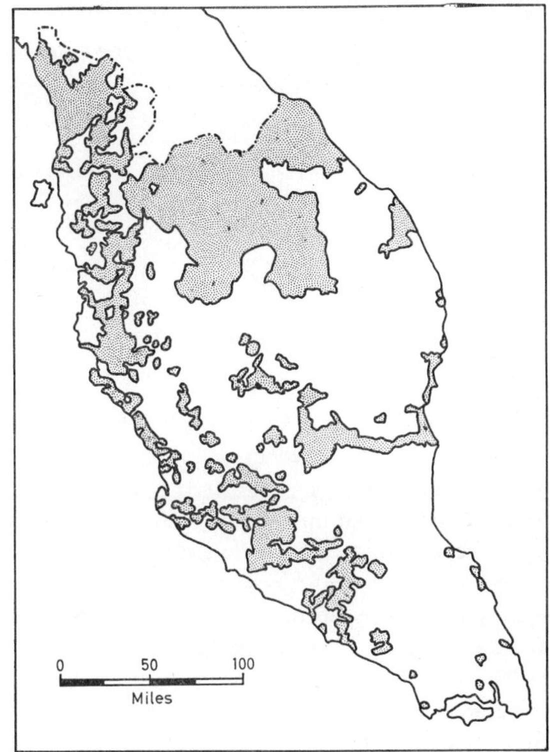

FIG. 90—Malaya: Malay reservations

In short the Malayan Chinese, ranging from labourers and small cultivators to dollar millionaires and the leading members of the Chinese Chamber of Commerce, form a complete capitalist society in themselves and, apart from their former exclusion from the administrative civil service,[17] are found in abundance in every major occupation necessary for the effective running of the country. In contrast to the rural Malays, some 53·7 per cent of the Chinese were

[15] Once tin mining was firmly established the Chinese organized their own recruitment of further labour from China.

[16] Callis, *op. cit.* See also Thompson and Adloff, p. 40, note 75.

[17] A proportion of Chinese and Indians have at last been admitted into the Malayan Civil Service since the Second World War, but prior to that the Service was exclusively British and Malay.

TABLE 86

MALAYA: CHINESE POPULATION, 1947

	Penang	*Malacca*	*Perak*	*Selangor*	*Negri Sembilan*	*Pahang*	*Johore*	*Kedah*	*Singa-pore*	*Total**
Hokkien .	107,052	36,588	80,536	108,473	21,527	15,478	117,304	31,432	289,167	827,411
Cantonese .	55,251	13,239	166,531	99,925	37,052	29,496	49,060	24,640	157,980	641,945
Hakka . .	21,867	23,277	97,869	96,908	35,282	21,304	77,109	16,400	40,036	437,407
Tiechiu .	48,901	7,202	33,091	21,198	2,518	2,770	54,530	33,319	157,188	364,232
Hainanese .	8,912	11,758	12,285	18,153	7,234	7,421	28,237	3,325	52,192	157,649
Kwongsai .	339	588	23,033	6,214	6,020	18,266	14,197	1,440	742	71,850
Hokchiu .	3,092	602	19,013	4,690	2,434	717	5,483	2,190	9,477	48,094

* Including Perlis, Kelantan and Trengganu also.

Source: Based on 1947 Census.

classed as urban,[18] and a majority of the remainder are engaged in the production of either tin, rubber or pineapples, or in market gardening to supply food for the towns. As can be seen from Fig. 89 the community is widely distributed throughout the country though, as would be expected, it shows a marked concentration in the tin and rubber belt and in the two great port cities.

Yet although to the Chinese Malaya forms a single geographical unit, the community itself is by no means homogeneous. In the first place there are major divisions of 'tribe',[19] primarily though not entirely a matter of spoken language, for the mountainous provinces of southern China from which the immigrants come are an area of great complexity in this respect. Altogether nine 'tribes' were separately enumerated in the 1947 Census, and data concerning the seven largest of these are included in Table 86 which shows how widely these divisions extend.

While almost any generalization is difficult on this subject, a few observations may usefully be made concerning both their geographical and occupational distribution. The Hokkien, who form the largest component in the former S.S. and also in Johore and Selangor, were the first 'tribe' to come in large numbers to Malaya, and remain predominantly urban and commercial in outlook. In most parts of the Malay States the largest group is the Cantonese, who are generally more versatile and important as tin miners, shopkeepers and agriculturists. The Hakka, also known as Kheh, run a close second in most of the States where, again, they are active in both mining and agriculture, while the Hainanese (Hailam) are particularly prominent in domestic service, and the Tiechiu, though less numerous, may be compared with the Cantonese in the range of their activities.

[18] *I.e.* in 1947, when the figure for the Federation alone was 43·1 per cent.

[19] 'Tribe' in this connexion is a concept which seems to have originated with the Malayan Census authorities. The distinctions are 'admittedly based on an inconsistent blend of political, geographic and linguistic, rather than ethnographic criteria'. Vlieland, quoted in Del Tufo, p. 74. The general pattern as shown in Table 86 had not greatly changed in the Federation in 1957.

In many areas, both rural and urban, these 'tribal' groups of Chinese are clearly segregated and, as Dobby observes, they must in early days have been as foreign to one another in speech and customs as they were to the Malays themselves.[20] For although nearly all the Chinese are normally regarded as subscribing to what the Census calls the 'national religion of China', the several spoken languages of the main 'tribes' are mutually unintelligible and there are deep-seated traditional differences in other respects as well.

Nor is this the only kind of social cleavage which exists within the Chinese community. Like other immigrant groups, the Malayan Chinese exhibit a stratification based in part on the length of domicile in the adopted country. In this respect the Baba Chinese of Malacca, some of whom can trace their ancestry in Malaya back several centuries, form a distinctive community and speak a language which is more Malay than Chinese. Ethnically the Baba community is a mixture of Chinese and Malay, for before the 19th century virtually no Chinese females emigrated to Malaya, and the small Chinese merchant community in Malacca thus inter-married with the local Malay population.[21]

During the 19th century this community spread into both Penang and Singapore, and thereafter it increased appreciably in number, partly as a result of fresh immigration. Many of its members acquired a knowledge of English, some became Christians, and almost all of those born in the S.S. were extremely proud of their British citizenship. In the present century descendants of this Straits Chinese community, as it came to be called, have formed a distinct and in some respects a select group, which has tended to stand aloof from the great mass of more recent immigrants and their immediate descendants.[22]

During the main period of immigration, between 1850 and 1930, Chinese society in Malaya remained extremely unstable. For the most part the immigrants were young men who came with the intention of staying for only a limited period of perhaps ten or fifteen years until they had acquired enough money to return home as comparatively wealthy individuals. In fact, however, a substantial proportion normally decided to remain permanently, but even so between 1921 and 1931, for every 100 who arrived, 80 returned to China. In these circumstances the epithet 'birds of passage' was not inappropriate, and among Europeans the belief was widely held that the Chinese immigrants as a whole would never of their own volition develop any lasting attachment to Malaya. From this premise it was easy to argue that the government had no responsibility for educating the Chinese as prospective Malayan citizens, and further to justify all measures aimed at preserving the traditional Malay way of life, so that this at least might survive even if the tin and rubber economy should ultimately pass away.

[20] Dobby (H), p. 130.

[21] In spite of the Islamic opposition to intermarriage, which has been the most powerful single factor preventing more extensive fusion.

[22] But see below for changes since the Second World War.

With the great exodus of unemployed Chinese who returned to the mother country during the crisis years of the early 1930s this belief seemed at first to be confirmed. But before long the tide began to flow back once again, and, notwithstanding the immigration quota system introduced in 1933, the Chinese population of Malaya increased by 244,708 on balance of migration between 1931 and 1941. Moreover, while economic conditions in Malaya were improving, the political and military situation in China itself deteriorated, and accordingly the inducement to return home was declining even before the Second World War put a virtual stop to sea-borne traffic between the two countries.

Thus between 1931 and 1947 the percentage of locally born among the Malayan Chinese rose from 31·2 to 62·5, and the ratio of females per 1,000 males from 513 to 833.[23] Today it is beyond dispute that the vast majority of Chinese in Malaya are there to stay and, on the basis of length of domicile, their claims to a permanent stake in the country are thus as great as were those of many of the Malays at the beginning of the present century. On the grounds of numerical strength their claim is even stronger for, with a total of 2,614,667 in 1947, and 3,424,333 in 1957, they have in recent years moved into first place, ahead of the Malays, in Malaya as a whole.

Of the three main Asian communities in Malaya the Indian has remained by far the smallest. Owing to the appalling casualties among Indian labourers employed by the Japanese during the occupation, the total of 599,616 Indians recorded in the 1947 Census shows a substantial decline from the 1931 figure of 621,847, but this has since been made good by immigration and natural increase and in 1957 the total (including Pakistanis) was estimated at 831,193.

Like the Chinese, the Indians in Malaya exhibit a somewhat bewildering series of stratifications, based in part on length of stay, in part on occupation, and in part on their place of origin. The last of these has been still further complicated since 1947 by the partition of the Indian subcontinent between India and Pakistan, though the name 'Indian' may conveniently be used to cover the nationals and descendants of both now living in Malaya.[23]

A major distinction can, however, be fairly easily made between the large group of immigrants from southern India, most of whom (or whose parents) emigrated to Malaya in the present century as rubber tappers,[24] and a much smaller but very diverse collection of peoples from northern India (and Pakistan), the original nucleus of which came over in the early days of the S.S. as labourers, clerks, traders and middlemen of various kinds. This northern 'Indian' group, which grew rather slowly throughout the 19th century by further small-scale immigration, is in some respects comparable to the Straits Chinese. Thus, besides the high proportion of its members who are engaged in small trading activities, it has its wealthy merchants who run the Indian Chamber of Commerce and a

[23] In 1957 the corresponding figure for the Federation alone was 926.

[24] However Tamil migration on a small scale can be traced back to the early 19th century, when labour was imported for the sugar and coffee plantations of the S.S.

considerable proportion of men who are prominent in most walks of professional life. Also included in the northern 'Indian' category are the Punjabi and Sikh policemen and watchmen who have long been a distinctive feature of the Malayan urban scene.

Today, however, well over 90 per cent of the total 'Indian' population of Malaya belongs to the southern Indian group, the main influx of which coincided with the rubber boom in the early years of the present century. The coolies, largely Tamils[25] from the old Madras Presidency, were originally indentured for a three-year period at the expense of individual planters. In 1910 the Kangany system was introduced, under which selected people, usually foremen, were licensed to recruit labour in their native villages, and between the two World Wars this was supplemented by the Indian Immigration Fund, maintained by contributions from all Malayan employers of southern Indian labour, which provided free passages for intending workers. However, in 1938 the Indian government put a stop to the assisted emigration of Indian labourers to Malaya, though it still remained possible for Indians already domiciled there to bring their wives to the country.[26]

Owing to its nearness to their homeland, Penang was the main port of entry for the southern Indian immigrants. Nearly half the total 'Indian' population in Malaya is found in Selangor and Perak, and most of the remainder live in the other west-coast states and settlements or in Singapore; 39 per cent of the total in Malaya as a whole were returned as urban in 1947.

Compared with the Chinese, the 'Indian' labourers were an even more transitory group and before the Second World War the average duration of their stay in Malaya was under three years. Since then, however, there have been signs of greater permanence, and the 1947 Census showed that 49·8 per cent of the Indian community had been born in Malaya, as against 21·1 per cent in 1931, and that the sex ratio had meanwhile improved from 482 to 637 females per 1,000 males. Moreover, so far as the Federation alone was concerned, this ratio rose still further to 743 in 1957, though it should be noted that such a figure remains significantly below its Chinese counterpart.

Again, relatively few of the southern Indian labourers have ever risen to any position of eminence in Malaya, and in this respect the difference between them and the Chinese is particularly significant. For the latter, who came to Malaya entirely on their own initiative, unassisted and unprotected by their own authorities, nevertheless built up the early tin industry and also branched out into almost every other kind of economic activity imaginable. This remarkable self-reliance of the Chinese was in fact one reason why they were less popular than the more docile Indians as labour on European-run estates, and also why, in spite of the bitter animosity shown to them as a group by the Japanese, they weathered the occupation with far smaller losses.

[25] Also Telugus and Malayalis. See Table 87.

[26] See Kondapi, pp. 43–4, and Thompson and Adloff, pp. 74–5

The southern Indians, on the other hand, with the exception of a small proportion who work as clerks or storekeepers, and the members of the Chettyar[27] caste who have earned an unenviable reputation as money-lenders, have remained in the purely labouring jobs. Thus some 60 per cent of the gainfully employed 'Indians' in Malaya still work on the rubber estates, and large numbers are also employed as workers on road and railway construction and maintenance.

Both the southern and the northern group of 'Indians' may be sub-divided on linguistic grounds as Table 87 shows, and there is also the Hindu/Muslim division which roughly but by no means exactly corresponds with the new national difference between Indians and Pakistanis.[28]

TABLE 87

MALAYA: INDIANS AND PAKISTANIS, 1947

Main Linguistic Groups

Tamil	460,985	Sikh	10,132
Telugu	24,093	Punjabi	20,460
Malayali	44,339	Pathan	3,166
Other 'southern Indian'	15,968	Bengali	3,834
		Other 'northern Indian'	16,639
Total 'southern Indian'	545,385	Total 'northern Indian'	54,231
	Total Indians	559,616	

Source: Based on 1947 Census.

Nevertheless neither these differences nor those of caste are as pronounced as those which exist between the several Chinese 'tribes'. To the rest of the population of Malaya the only difference which seems to matter is that between 'Bengalis' and 'Klings', by which cryptic and nowadays somewhat resented terms Bazaar Malay seeks to distinguish between northerners and southerners.

Other Ethnic Groups

The rest of Malaya's polyglot population recorded in the 1947 Census calls only for brief treatment. The 22,762 Ceylonese, 16,783 of whom were Tamils, may logically be included with the Indian population and the 20,203 Siamese were mostly domiciled in the immediate vicinity of the international boundary between the two countries. Among the Asian peoples there remained the small but much respected Arab community of 5,718, 80 per cent of whom lived in Singapore and Johore, but the once influential Japanese population (6,431 in 1931) had dropped to a mere 254.[29]

[27] For details of the post-war economic position of the Chettyars see Thompson and Adloff, p. 108.

[28] The general pattern shown in Table 87 had not greatly changed in the Federation in 1957.

[29] However, there has been some increase on this figure since 1947.

Eurasians and Europeans respectively totalled 19,171 and 18,958[30] in 1947. Most of the Eurasian families, as their surnames show, date back to the Portuguese and Dutch periods though they have spread from Malacca into Singapore, Penang and most of the main towns of the peninsula, and nowadays habitually speak English.[31] Although the community is too small to play anything like so important a rôle as that of its counterpart in the old Netherlands Indies, several of its members occupy influential positions, while the majority are employed in office work of various kinds. Most of the Europeans are Britons engaged in government service, planting, mining and the various ramifications of business and commerce. That their numbers are so large in comparison with those in most other tropical ex-dependencies is a measure of both the wealth and importance of Malaya. And in 1947 the proportion of Europeans proper (0·32 per cent) and of Europeans plus Eurasians (0·65 per cent) were both appreciably higher than the corresponding figures (respectively 0·07 per cent and 0·40 per cent in 1930) in the former Netherlands Indies. More recent data are given in Table 88.

II. THE MALAYAN PLURAL SOCIETY

In the course of the last few decades the relationships between these several component elements in the Malayan plural society have undergone a profound change. With the trend towards greater stability, marked by the rise in the percentage of locally born, in all three major ethnic groups, the communities concerned have developed a much greater degree of internal cohesion. In the pioneer environment of Malaya many of the traditional divisions brought with them by the immigrants have tended to lose their significance. Thus Indonesians from all parts of the archipelago have become simply 'Malays', while both 'Indians' and Chinese have acquired a new measure of solidarity with the growth of national consciousness in their respective homelands. And though this has been complicated by the India/Pakistan issue on the one hand and the Communist/Kuo Min Tang struggle on the other, there is no doubting the permanent effect of either the decline in the importance of caste among the Indians overseas or the increase in the teaching of Kuo Yü (the Chinese national language) in the Chinese schools.

Thus, whereas in the past each community was so divided within itself that '*divide et impera*' was a superfluous injunction, today almost every issue in Malaya, however apparently innocuous, is apt to give rise to unexpected communal overtones. In view of the changing structure of the population and the rising tide of nationalism throughout Asia such a development was probably inevitable, but it was the deliberate playing off of one community against another by the

[30] 41,886 and 22,694 respectively in 1957.

[31] In 1854 A. R. Wallace noted that the Eurasians of Malacca still spoke Portuguese. Robequain (D), p. 135.

TABLE 88

MALAYA: CHANGING ETHNIC COMPOSITION OF POPULATION, 1931–57

All figures are percentages

Community	*Federation of Malaya*			*Singapore*			*All Malaya*		
	1931	1947	1957	1931	1947	1957	1931	1947	1957
Aborigines . .	0·8	0·70	0·7	0·0	0·00	0·0	0·7	0·60	0·0
Malays . .	42·4	43·35	44·6	6·8	7·67	n.a.	37·8	37·60	n.a.
Other Malaysians .	6·0	5·41	4·5	5·0	4·63	n.a.	5·9	5·29	n.a.
All Malaysians .	49·2	49·46	49·8	11·8	12·30	13·6	44·4	43·49	43·0
Chinese . .	33·9	38·40	37·2	74·9	77·61	75·5	39·2	44·70	44·3
Indians and Pakistanis . .	15·1	10·81	11·3	9·1	7·33	8·6	14·3	10·25	10·6
Europeans . .	0·3	0·20	0·7	1·5	0·99	0·7	0·4	0·32	0·5
Eurasians . .	0·2	0·20	0·7	1·2	0·97	0·7	0·4	0·33	0·3
Total (incl. others)	100·0	100·0	100·0	100·0	100·0	100·0	100·0	100·0	100·0

Sources: Based on 1947 Census (Del Tufo), and 1957 Census (Fell).

Note: Aborigines are included in All Malaysians throughout.

Japanese, followed immediately by the post-war declaration of Britain's intention to promote democratic self-government, which together brought things to a head. The irony is that this should have come about precisely at the time when the Chinese had at last overtaken the Malays to become the largest single community in the country (Table 88).

In these circumstances, further complicated as they soon were by economic difficulties and the outbreak of Communist terrorism, which was in some respects an extension of the Chinese civil war onto Malayan soil, it is understandable that the British authorities felt it expedient to restrict immigration into the country after 1946. More recently the Immigration Ordnances introduced in both Singapore and the Federation of Malaya in August 1953 virtually stopped the inflow of Chinese and Indians, apart from wives and children of persons already resident in Malaya.

Thus the vital question now turns upon the relative rates of natural increase of the major communities in Malaya and in this respect the evidence available is not entirely conclusive. Tables 89 and 90 show the crude birth- and death-rates and the resultant rate of natural increase in Singapore and the Federation since the War. By comparison with pre-war figures the most striking feature is that throughout Malaya the death-rate has been almost halved within a mere two decades, and in Singapore today it is only slightly above that in most parts of Western Europe. But birth-rates remain extremely high among all the communities, and there is as yet little sign of any pronounced drop as a result

TABLE 89

FEDERATION OF MALAYA:

VITAL STATISTICS, 1947, 1953 AND 1955

Crude birth- and death-rates, natural increase rates, per 1,000 in all cases

	Birth-rate			*Death-rate*			*Natural increase*		
	1947	1953	1955	1947	1953	1955	1947	1953	1955
Malaysians . .	41·4	45·1	45·1	24·3	14·5	14·0	17·1	30·6	31·1
Chinese . . .	44·0	42·1	40·6	14·3	10·2	9·0	29·7	31·9	31·6
Indians and Pakistanis	49·1	44·2	43·9	15·8	10·9	9·5	33·3	33·3	34·4
Total (including others) .	43·0	43·7	43·0	19·4	12·4	11·5	23·6	31·3	31·5

Sources: 1947 Census, and *Federation of Malaya Annual Reports.*

TABLE 90

SINGAPORE: VITAL STATISTICS, 1947, 1953 AND 1955

	Birth-rate			*Death-rate*			*Natural increase*		
	1947	1953	1955	1947	1953	1955	1947	1953	1955
Malaysians . .	48·09	53·15	56·29	17·83	14·49	13·15	30·26	38·66	43·14
Chinese . . .	46·10	48·48	46·49	12·84	9·87	8·26	33·26	38·61	38·23
Indians and Pakistanis	44·76	45·36	46·99	12·73	9·33	7·55	32·03	36·03	39·44
Total (including others) .	45·88	48·68	47·76	13·34	10·31	8·73	32·54	38·37	39·03

Sources: 1947 Census, and *Colony of Singapore Annual Reports.*

of urbanization though most urban birth-rates are a little lower than those in rural areas.[32] Until recently, therefore, the view has been widely held that since urban death-rates were distinctly lower than rural death-rates, natural increase would favour the Chinese as the most urbanized of the main communities. However, the figures shown in Tables 89 and 90 do not entirely bear this out, and the situation contains too many variables such as, for example, the rate of improvement in rural hygiene, for any confident predictions to be made.[33] The statistics of total populations by community in 1957 imply that the Chinese and Malays are increasing at virtually identical rates, and there is as yet no reason to assume that this neck-and-neck race will not continue indefinitely. The 'Indians' now appear to have made up most of the ground lost during the War, but it is highly unlikely that they will ever challenge the lead of either of the other two main groups.

In the meantime, the total rate of natural increase of the population as a whole (*c.* 39 per 1,000 in Singapore and *c.* 32 per 1,000 in the Federation) can only be described as formidable, and in view of the relatively low average age of both populations no sudden decrease is to be expected.[34] All-told it would appear that the population of Malaya has increased some twenty-fold during the past 150 years, and the average density per square mile (158 in 1958) of this formerly almost uninhabited peninsula is now well above the average for South-east Asia.

In a geographical sense this growth has continued to be very unevenly distributed, and the resultant pattern is extremely complex. Dobby has spoken of Malaya's 'cellular' rather than 'plural' society, with different cultural, linguistic, ethnic and economic communities living in their separate ways in different parts of the peninsula.[35] In the past this was undoubtedly true and it is still fair to say that the north and the north-east including Patani are thickly populated and overwhelmingly Malay, the rest of the east also predominantly Malay though much more sparsely inhabited, and only the tin and rubber belt completely mixed. But it also remains to be noted that the tin and rubber belt is the economic and political centre of gravity of the country, with the highest density of population and by far the greatest concentration of wealth. And within this region not only are all the ethnic groups living together in the closest geographical proximity, but both Chinese and Malays are also to some extent spreading the range of their economic activities into fields which were formerly regarded as the special preserves of the other.

Nevertheless, it is still true that while the Chinese and 'Indians' are both urban and rural in their distribution, the Malays belong overwhelmingly to the latter category. This situation is illustrated in Table 91, based on the 1947 and

[32] As Tables 89 and 90 show, Singapore's crude birth-rate is higher than that of the Federation, though this difference is related to the abnormally high proportion of young and early middle-aged persons now living in Singapore.

[33] For a more detailed analysis see Smith, T. E., Chapter 6.

[34] A Family Planning Association has been formed in Singapore with government assistance; it advises those who seek its help.

[35] Dobby (H), p. 136.

TABLE 91

MALAYA: TOWN AND COMMUNITY, 1947 AND 1957

Percentage of community classed as urban	1947	1957	*Percentage of urban population belonging to each community*	1947	1957
Malaysians	14·1	22	Malaysians	17·4	23
Chinese	53·7	73	Chinese	68·3	64
Indians and Pakistanis	39·0	42	Indians	11·4	11

Source: Based on 1947 Census (Del Tufo) and 1957 Census (Fell).
Note that 1957 figures are Federation only.

1957 Censuses which classified agglomerations of over 1,000 inhabitants as towns. On this basis the Chinese percentage has since risen considerably as a result of the resettlement programme, for most of the New Villages come within the urban category.[36] But although the percentage of Malaysians in towns is still the lowest, its rate of increase is now the most rapid of the three communities, and this trend is clearly indicative of the great changes which the Malaysians have been experiencing in recent years.

On the basis of the Census criterion the urban percentage of the total population rose from 29·5 in 1931 to 35·1 in 1947, and in the Federation alone to 42·5 in 1957. However, if a figure of 10,000 be taken as the urban criterion, the percentage in the Federation alone was only 26·2 in 1957, though in Malaya as a whole it was approximately 34. In either case, therefore, it is evident that Malaya has a much higher urban percentage than any other country in Asia except Japan. Yet, as has already been seen, this is not accompanied by a correspondingly high degree of industrialization for in Vlieland's words, 'the urban population exists to serve the needs of a large rural producing component' – a state of affairs radically different from, if not the converse of, those existing in Europe and North America.[37] In fact the high degree of urbanization in Malaya has arisen through the centralization of the administrative, supply, marketing and transport services required by a rural population engaged largely in production for export, and manufacturing industry is still only at a relatively early stage.

Nearly all the main towns (Table 92 and Figs. 89 and 91) and certainly the four largest were originally the creation of non-Malays during the past two hundred years, and even Malacca and Johore Bahru are preponderantly non-Malaysian in their population today. Moreover, all but one shown in the table are situated in the tin and rubber belt and all but three of them originated as either ports or mining towns. The latter, which have sprung up in the past hundred years, are all, with the exception of Kuala Lumpur, remarkably alike in their rectangular street plans and the monotony of all but their most recent architecture, though some of the newer buildings are distinctly enterprising.

[36] See above, p. 609.
[37] Vlieland (B), p. 74.

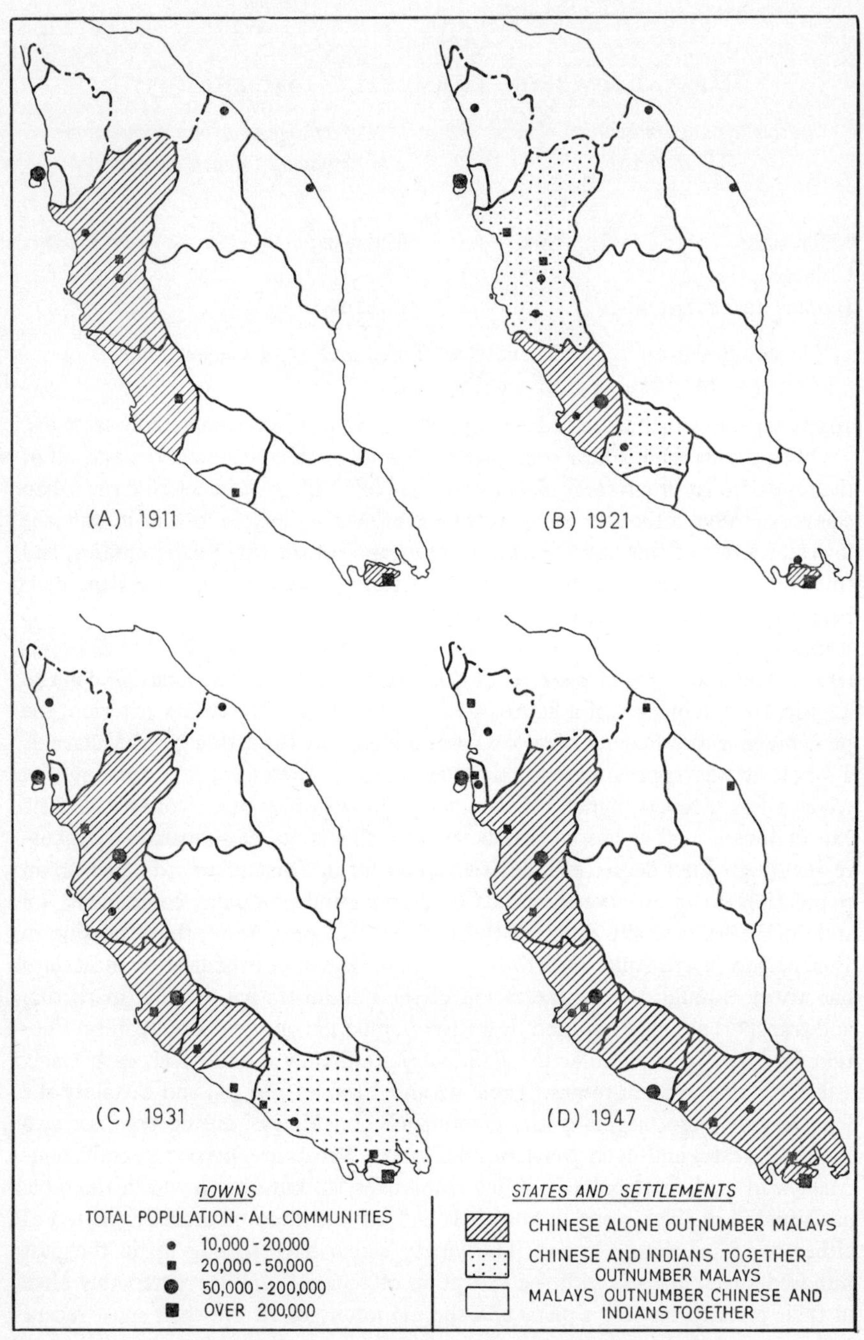

FIG. 91—Malaya: urbanization and community, 1911–1947

TABLE 92

MALAYA: POPULATION OF PRINCIPAL TOWNS

Town	1947	1957	*Town*	1947	1957
Singapore . .	679,659	912,343	Johore Bahru .	38,826	74,909
Kuala Lumpur .	175,961	316,230	Malacca . .	54,507	69,848
Penang (Georgetown)	189,068	234,903	Alor Star . .	32,404	52,915
Ipoh . . .	80,894	125,770	Seremban . .	35,274	52,091
Klang* . . .	33,506	75,649	Taiping . .	41,361	48,206

Sources: Based on 1947 Census (Del Tufo), and 1957 Census (Fell).
* Note: In 1957 Klang included Port Swettenham.

Since the closing years of the 19th century several of these towns, namely Taiping and later Ipoh in Perak, Kuala Lumpur in Selangor, Seremban in Negri Sembilan and Johore Bahru have served as capitals of the Malay states in question,[38] though in some cases the Sultans' residences still remain at the older river-mouth *kampongs* as they do in Kelantan and Trengganu where there has been no change in the position of the capitals. In this situation is epitomized the crucial problem of the relationship between the Malays and the other communities inhabiting the country today. For so long as the Malay culture remains primarily rural, no town or city properly so called can be a wholly representative focus for the Malay way of life.[39] Meanwhile, since independence the capital of Pahang has again been moved, from Kuala Lipis to Kuantan, and that of Selangor is also to be moved, from Kuala Lumpur to Klang.

III. KUALA LUMPUR AND SINGAPORE

Kuala Lumpur, the capital of the Federation, provides the test case. Already since the 1880s the capital of Selangor, the town which had been no more than a handful of squalid miners' huts in the seventies was made the F.M.S. capital in 1896, mainly because of its central position within the tin belt as it then was. As the years went by, the rapidly extending road network was made to focus on the town, which was meanwhile laid out in a spacious manner with impressive government buildings in pseudo-Muslim style. From a mere 25,000 in 1900, its population grew in step with the economic development of the F.M.S. at large, and today it is in the vicinity of 325,000. But notwithstanding the domes of the old Secretariat and the minarets of the railway station, 62 per cent of the population is Chinese, another 17 per cent Indian, and both Malays and Other Malaysians combined account for only 15 per cent of the total.

In fact the Malay percentage of Kuala Lumpur's population is not strikingly

[38] Kuala Lipis in Pahang is similar in character to these, though it lies outside the tin and rubber belt proper. See above, note 11. Prior to Kuala Lipis, Pekan was the capital of Pahang.

[39] *Cf.* the situation in Wales, where again the indigenous culture is rural, and the only real cities, *i.e.* those of the South Wales coalfield, contain a high proportion of migrants from other parts of the British Isles.

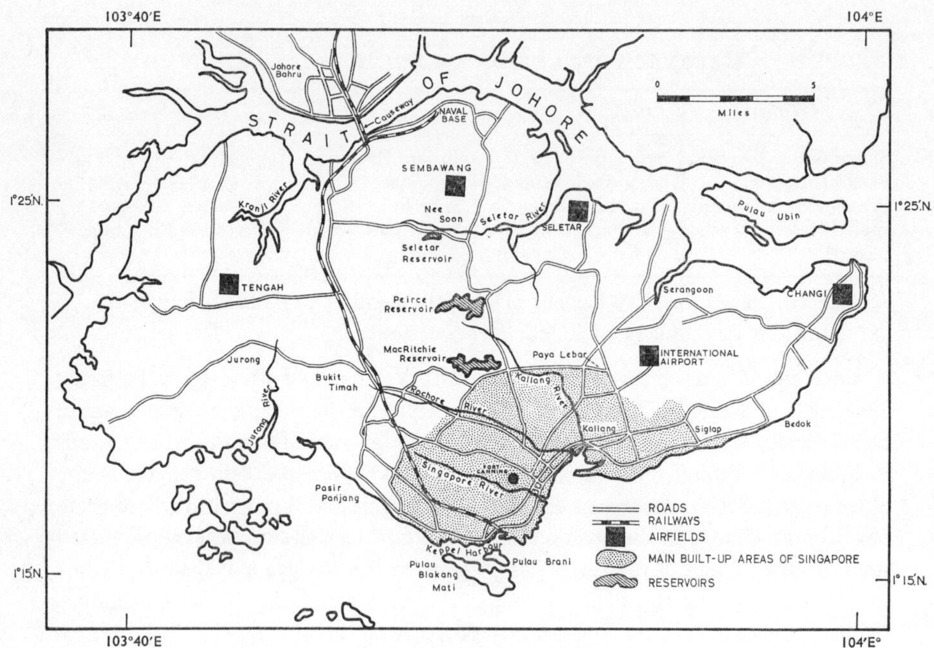

FIG. 92—Singapore island

higher than that of Singapore municipality (11 per cent), and the main difference in the ethnic ratios of the two cities lies in Singapore's lower proportion of Indians (8 per cent) and still greater preponderance of Chinese (78 per cent).[40] But there are other and no less important differences between the two cities, and in particular the much larger size of Singapore, and the general character of its architecture are more characteristic of the great ports of the China coast, like Shanghai and Hong Kong, than of the Malay peninsula nearby.

Singapore has been excellently planned and in this respect, as in so many others, its primary debt is to Raffles who laid it out with painstaking care, and allocated separate residential zones to each of the main communities which he hoped to see established there. Thus the original European nucleus was on a spacious and well-drained site near government headquarters at Fort Canning, though in modern times European houses have become much more widely dispersed in the hillier areas farther north. By contrast, the main Malay area lies to the east of the city centre in a typical *kuala* locality, between the Rochore river and the coast. Within this neighbourhood both Kampong Java and Kampong Boyan grew up in the 19th century besides the earlier Malay, Buginese and Arab settlements. The Chinese, on the other hand, were allotted a central area adjacent to the early mercantile core, and the Indians also at first established

[40] Note that these Singapore percentages refer to 1947.

themselves alongside this, before spreading out in more recent times in company with the Chinese, into the area adjoining the docks and the railway terminus.

Such a summary description however does less than justice to the extraordinary variety of the Singapore scene. As befits its nodality both in relation to South-east Asia and also to world-wide shipping routes, Singapore is in every sense a cosmopolitan city, and beside the more numerous Chinese, Indians and Malaysians, its resident and floating population probably includes citizens of every important country in the world. In this respect, notwithstanding its 19th-century origin and predominantly East Asian colouring, it is perhaps best compared with Constantinople (Istanbul), whose geographical situation also is in many respects strikingly similar. Certainly the contrast between Singapore and the much quieter, almost garden-city capital of the Federation is still apparent, notwithstanding the rapidity with which the latter is growing.

In addition to the port and city proper, moreover, the naval base on the northern coast of the island serves still further to emphasize the extra-Malayan interests of Singapore. Although from the outset Raffles intended Singapore to be a great naval station, it was not until after the First World War that this plan was put into effect. Two factors combined to bring about the change. In the first place the increase in size of capital ships had resulted in the strategically dangerous situation that no British naval dock- or repair-yards capable of handling the Royal Navy's larger vessels existed at any point between Malta and Sydney. And secondly, the termination of the Anglo-Japanese Alliance meant that neither India nor Australasia could be regarded as entirely secure against naval attack in the future.

Under the terms of the Washington agreements of 1921 it was laid down that the British Empire (along with the United States and Japan) should maintain the *status quo* with regard to fortifications and naval bases within the Pacific realm. But by definition the latter was bounded on the west by the 110th meridian (E), and Singapore therefore lay outside its terms of reference. Following the Imperial Conference in 1923, the decision was taken to establish a new base at Singapore, capable of handling the largest capital ships afloat. Work on this task began two years later, with New Zealand, Hong Kong and the Malay States as well as the United Kingdom contributing to the cost, and Australia undertaking to develop Darwin as a link between Singapore and Sydney. The base was built on the Johore Straits, immediately to the east of the new causeway, three-quarters of a mile long, which carries the road, railway and water pipe-line between Johore Bahru and Singapore Island. A few miles to the east the R.A.F. established the Seletar air base.

Rarely if ever have the strategic functions of any base been so completely misunderstood by the general public as were those of Singapore. Yet, writing in 1938, Brigadier (then Major) D. H. Cole gave a sober appraisal of its significance when he stated:

> 'It is nothing more than a means by which, in the last resort, Britain could utilize part of her naval strength to protect the British and Dominion interests in the south-west quadrant of the Pacific.'[41]

That the Japanese would be able to acquire an air base at Saigon within bombing range of Singapore, and that practically the whole of Britain's striking power would be pinned down thousands of miles away before the first shot was fired in the Pacific War, were circumstances which could scarcely have been foreseen, but in the event they reduced the utility of the Singapore base to vanishing point in the campaigns of 1941–2.

Despite the profound changes in military techniques and the post-war advance of Communist power half-way down the Indochinese peninsula in a manner which to many recalled Japan's line of progress in 1941, there has been no official inclination to play down the strategic importance of Singapore in recent years. Indeed, following the decision to withdraw the headquarters of the British Far Eastern Fleet from Hong Kong, and the ending of British control over the naval and air bases of Ceylon in 1957, Singapore, with its naval base and four military airfields, remains the only major focus of British armed strength east of Cyprus.[42]

In view of these manifold external interests,[43] it is hardly surprising that the supporters of a policy of Malay paramountcy should always have opposed any suggestion that Singapore should become the capital of a united Malaya, and since the war these views have been even more strongly held by both British officials and Malay nationalist leaders. Yet Singapore's ties with the rest of Malaya are deep and abiding. Ever since the 1820s it has been Malaya's principal city, and although its banks, warehouses and docks grew up to serve South-east Asia as a whole, they perform more duties today for the Malay peninsula than for any other single country. Moreover, while Kuala Lumpur is the focus of the Malayan road network and in some sense also of the railway system, Singapore is the major centre of coastal shipping routes, which continue to play a vital part in the pattern of circulation, and it still remains the leading port handling the Federation's overseas trade.

Finally, Singapore is Malaya's only great metropolis, with a population approximately treble that of Kuala Lumpur. As a major point of call for international air and shipping lines, Singapore forms an excellent 'head-link'[44] with the outside world, and notwithstanding the setting up of a new division of the

[41] Cole, D. H., *Imperial Military Geography*, 9th edition, 1938, pp. 168–9.

[42] The graving dock at the naval base can take ships up to 1,000 ft. length and 125 ft. depth, which covers all existing British warships. There are four floating docks, with nominal lifting powers ranging from 800 to 15,500 tons, and facilities for refitting warships up to and including cruisers. The two main air stations are Changi, the H.Q. of the Far East Air Force, and Seletar, an R.A.F. maintenance base. *The Times*, April 16, 1956.

[43] The office of the (British) Special Commissioner for South-east Asia was also set up in Singapore after the Second World War. The main task of this commission was to co-ordinate policy in Malaya and the British Borneo territories. See below, p. 683.

[44] See Spate (B), pp. 622–31.

University of Malaya in Kuala Lumpur,[45] an important part of that institution remained in Singapore, which is also the locus of the new Nanyang Chinese University.

Yet mention of the University of Malaya recalls the crucial problem which remains unsolved. For, out of a total student population in September 1958 of 1,615, drawn from the whole of the country, 1,021 were Chinese, 221 Indians, 140 Ceylonese and only 181 Malaysians.[46]

IV. THE POLITICAL PATTERN

When the Second World War came to an end, the British, whose decision to grant Dominion status to the Indian Empire had implicitly sealed the fate of colonialism throughout South-east Asia as well, were faced with a peculiarly awkward problem in Malaya. For, as a result partly of its political fragmentation into S.S., F.M.S. and unfederated States, and more fundamentally of its ethnic heterogeneity, this vital peninsula at the heart of South-east Asia appeared, in contrast to the surrounding countries, to lack any really cohesive national movement.

In view of the manner in which the British recognized the nationalist aspirations of both Ceylon and Burma, as well as of the altogether more powerful Indian empire, there was no reason to dispute the sincerity of their repeated professions of willingness to grant independence to Malaya also, as soon as the latter should prove capable of exercising it effectively. And indeed it was evident that in such a course of action lay the metropolitan power's only real chance of maintaining any lasting economic and strategic interests in this critical region. The difficulty, however, was to find a means of putting this policy into operation.

In theory the most desirable course would have been to abolish the old political sub-divisions which had contributed so much to the country's wartime collapse and, within the framework of a newly unified state, to seek to build up a sense of Malayan nationality and loyalty among all the permanent population, regardless of ethnic origin. But the obstacles to the realization of such a policy were formidable. Although the relative importance of the 'Indian' population, never in any case very great, seemed to be declining with the fall in numbers,[47] the intensified rivalry between Malays and Chinese, which had developed under the stress of the occupation and of the more rapid increase of the Chinese, made it extremely difficult to achieve inter-communal harmony. Moreover, it was widely believed that if truly representative government were to be introduced under these conditions, the Chinese by virtue of their numerical ascendancy would dominate the country's politics as they already dominated its economic

[45] The Kuala Lumpur division of the University of Malaya was opened in September 1957.

[46] In 1961 the University split into two separate institutions, namely the University of Malaya (Kuala Lumpur) and the University of Singapore.

[47] The number of 'Indians' has since risen again, but not perhaps to a sufficient extent to invalidate this argument.

life. And in such circumstances the outlook for the Malays would be bleak indeed.

The simplest way of allaying the Malays' fear of being outpaced in their own country by the Chinese was to avoid the complete unification of Malaya, and instead to divide the country in such a manner as to leave the Malays in the lead in one part of it. Thus, as outlined on page 604, the whole of the former Federated and unfederated Malay States, together with Malacca, Penang and Province Wellesley were formed into the Malayan Union of April 1946, while Singapore, with its 'economic and social interests distinct from those of the mainland', was kept apart as a separate Crown Colony 'at least for the time being'.[48]

Clearly the most critical of these distinctive interests of Singapore was the preponderantly Chinese character of its population, though, as has already been seen, the Malay percentage in the city was little lower than that in Kuala Lumpur or indeed in most of the main peninsular towns (Fig. 89). Altogether, however, Singapore in 1947 contained some 730,000 Chinese, representing 27·9 per cent of the total Chinese population in Malaya, and by excluding these from the Malayan Union it became possible to leave the Malays as appreciably the largest single community within the latter. Nevertheless, as Table 88 shows, they did not even then form an absolute majority, and this meant that, while Singapore island was left with its mainly Chinese population, the Malayan Union retained all the problems of a plural society, and it still remained to be seen whether or not the latter could be welded into a coherent Malayan nation.

That it was the original intention of the British to promote 'Malayan' – and not exclusively Malay[49] – nationhood in the Union was evident from the whole character of the institutions proposed. Under the Union constitution the Malay rulers were relegated to a subordinate position, and it was made clear that the British Crown was to provide the focus of loyalty for all the inhabitants of this newly united – if simultaneously decapitated – country. A common Malayan Union citizenship was proposed, which would be open to all persons born in Malaya, irrespective of race or creed, and to all foreign-born persons who had resided there for ten out of the fifteen years preceding 1942.[50]

However, these proposals, which would have admitted almost the whole Chinese and 'Indian' population, as well as all the Malays, to political rights, were opposed by the Malays who also strongly resented the lowering of the status of their rulers. Accordingly, after intense and prolonged controversy,

[48] *Malayan Union and Singapore: statement of policy on future constitution*, Cmd. 6724, p. 3, para. 5. With Singapore were included Christmas Island (pop. 1,306 in 1940) and the Cocos (Keeling) Islands (pop. 1,142). The Cocos (Keeling) Islands, which are important for their airfield and cable station *en route* to Australia, were ceded to Australia in 1955, and similar arrangements were made in 1958 for Christmas Island, which contains some minor phosphate deposits. Labuan became part of North Borneo when the latter became a Crown Colony in July 1946.

[49] In local parlance a 'Malayan' is anyone who makes Malaya his home.

[50] Carnell (A), p. 507.

the Malayan Union was replaced in February 1948 by a new Federation of Malaya. Under the new constitution the jurisdiction of the rulers was restored, and a new federal citizenship introduced on terms which excluded a majority of the non-Malaysian population.

This change, while meeting most of the Malay objections to the Union, understandably failed to satisfy many Chinese, and though there is no evidence to suggest that it was responsible for the terrorist movement which broke out a few months later, the feeling of again being treated as second-class citizens in a country which had been largely built up by their efforts explains why the Chinese community as a whole were unwilling to offer the wholehearted co-operation which the government needed if the campaign against the terrorists were to be quickly suppressed.

For this reason, therefore, the British authorities soon found themselves compelled once again to reconsider their course of action, and to seek more effective ways of promoting a sturdy sense of Malayan nationhood, without which progress of any kind seemed impossible. The new policy which took shape after 1949 started from the premise that, so long as political power remained primarily the preserve of the Malays and economic strength no less the monopoly of the Chinese, the deadlock would be complete. Accordingly, besides setting up a new system of inter-racial primary schools, in which all communities were to be 'Malayanized' by education in English and Malay, the government concentrated its attention on building up the economic strength of the Malays, notably by means of R.I.D.A.,[51] while at the same time trying to persuade them to accept a wider basis of citizenship which would admit a much higher proportion of non-Malays to political rights.

All things considered, this policy has met with encouraging success. With a view to contesting the first federal elections in 1955, the three leading communal organizations, the United Malays National Organization, the Malayan Chinese Association and the Malayan Indian Congress, formed an Alliance which won a sweeping victory, gaining 51 out of the 52 elected seats on the Legislative Council. On the strength of this, the new government pressed for a speedy transfer of sovereignty, and on August 31, 1957, when the end of the 'Emergency' was in sight, the Federation of Malaya achieved its independence. Besides remaining a member of the Commonwealth and of the Sterling Area, though not of S.E.A.T.O., independent Malaya signed a defence treaty with Britain whereby the latter is permitted to lease a number of military bases, and to station British and other Commonwealth troops on Malayan soil for purposes of local and regional defence.[52]

Notwithstanding the current stability of the popularly elected government,

[51] See above, pp. 626–7. Meanwhile the Communist 'Emergency' was tackled by the methods described on pp. 575 and 609.

[52] *I.e.* the defence of Hong Kong, the Federation of Malaya, Singapore and the British Borneo territories, but *not* the other S.E.A.T.O. territories.

however, many serious problems remain unsolved, and in particular it seems that the Malayan Chinese Association, however representative it may be of the older Chinese, has less appeal to a majority of the younger generation.[53] Whether the loyalties of this increasingly important section of the population can be won by the new regime remains to be seen. Under the new constitution all persons, regardless of race, who are born in the Federation after independence become citizens by law, and it is still possible for others to obtain citizenship if they have resided there for at least eight out of the preceding twelve years. But at the same time there is no mistaking the fact that the Malays are treated in some ways as preferred citizens. Thus the constitution guarantees them the main share in the public service, and their privileged rights in respect of land tenure have been made permanent. Moreover, Malay is the state language, and neither Chinese nor Indian languages may be used in Parliament; and although it is stated that Malaya is a secular state it is nevertheless specified in the constitution that Islam is the state religion. What these arrangements will mean in practice time alone will show, but they are not wholly consistent with the aim suggested by one Indian member of parliament of making the Federation into an 'Asian Switzerland'.

Admittedly the provisions of the new constitution are not the only obstacles which stand in the way of such a consummation. For while there is a superficial similarity in the character of Malaya and Switzerland as multi-lingual states, each of whose major component groups has close affinities with still larger groups outside, the parallel cannot be taken much further. For Switzerland's is not a plural society, and many of the recent immigrants to Malaya have not yet had the time in which to develop loyalties to their land of domicile strong enough to counteract the ties of blood and culture which bind many of them to their original homelands.

In this context it remains to add that, while Mr. Nehru explicitly told the Indians in Malaya that they must choose between the two nationalities open to them, the willingness of the Peking regime as expressed in 1955, to adopt a similar policy towards the Chinese in Indonesia has not as yet been extended to Malaya.[54] And, in view of the much greater influence which the Chinese wield in the latter country, it is by no means certain that Peking has any intention of applying this policy there.

In these circumstances the reluctance of the Malays in the Federation to grant full political parity to the already economically stronger Chinese is at least understandable, as likewise has been their past reluctance to enter into closer political relationships with Singapore such as the latter has repeatedly suggested.

Here, admittedly, more was involved than the unwillingness of the Federation Malays to add another million or so Chinese to their population and thus lose even the measure of Malay preponderance which they still possessed. In

[53] See also Carnell (E), pp. 315–30.

[54] See above, p. 386.

particular the British government remained no less unwilling to contemplate losing control over the Singapore base, having already lost those in Ceylon. In these circumstances, the most it was prepared to offer prior to 1963 was that Singapore should become internally self-governing while Britain retained control over its external relations and defence, and internal security was safeguarded by a joint British-Singapore council on which a representative of the Federation had the casting vote.[55]

This new status came into effect in June 1959, following a general election in which the left-wing People's Action Party won 43 out of the 51 seats in the new Legislative Council. The P.A.P., which claimed to oppose both Communism and imperialism, was in favour of a merger with the Federation, which it tried to woo, *inter alia* by making Malay and not Chinese the national language of Singapore. But its original policies in respect of socialization and its aims of developing Singapore as the main industrial centre within a united Malaya were not popular in government circles in Kuala Lumpur, while its related plan to press for the withdrawal of British bases after the merger had been effected ran counter to expressed British policy and raised the further question of how to provide alternative sources of income for the 10 to 25 per cent of its population who depend directly or indirectly on the employment afforded by the British armed services.

Until 1962, therefore, the Federation and Singapore continued to go their separate ways. The Federation government strove at home to close the socio-economic gap dividing the rural Malays from the largely urban Chinese and Indians, and abroad to foster greater cohesion within South-east Asia as a whole. Significantly its first overtures in the latter connexion were made to the ethnically similar[56] states of Indonesia and the Philippines, but in view of Indonesian reactions the original plan to establish a treaty relationship was dropped in favour of a looser Association of South-east Asian States, (A.S.A.) consisting initially of the Federation of Malaya, Thailand and the Philippines, which was set up on 31 July 1961.

While economic as well as political motives were involved it seemed that anxiety regarding the growing might of China was one of the driving forces behind this movement towards regional co-operation. At the same time, however, a related though not an identical fear tended to prevent the Federation from agreeing to Singapore's suggestion that the two Malayan states should merge. In this respect the Federation faced a dilemma. From a purely local point of view there was no doubt that the Federation would have found it much easier to pursue its chosen and eminently reasonable policies within the confines of

[55] Under the 1959 constitution Singapore was styled a State, not a Crown Colony, and had a Malayan-born Head of State, with the title of Yang di-pertuan Negara. The senior British representative was styled the United Kingdom Commissioner for Singapore and Commissioner-General for South-east Asia. This office replaced that of Special Commissioner for South-east Asia. See p. 654, note 43.

[56] *I.e.* similar to (though not identical with) the Malays.

the territory which it already possessed than to run the risk of jeopardizing their success by agreeing to a merger with Singapore. Meanwhile, however, the Singapore administration actively encouraged the population of that island, overwhelmingly Chinese in ethnic composition though it is, to develop a Malayan consciousness and culture, representing in effect a fusion of all the major elements found within Malaya as a whole. For it is only within some such wider context that the population of this dynamic city state can find a satisfying outlet for their energies and thus be prevented from looking elsewhere for a focus for their loyalties, as in fact a significant proportion have already begun to do.

Indeed the lack of any comprehensible *raison d'être* for Singapore as an isolated city state was the basic cause of the serious political instability there after the mid-1950s, and this in turn was reflected in chronic labour disputes which threatened to undermine the very basis of its economy. Certainly, as the history of both Danzig and Trieste shows, the city state has become an anachronism in the modern world, and the more recent experience of Britain in Cyprus is no more encouraging as regards the strategic value of bases inpolitically disturbed territories.

It was against this background that in July 1962 the Prime Minister of the Federation of Malaya, Tunku Abdul Rahman, after discussions with the Prime Minister of Singapore, Mr. Lee Kuan Yew, put forward statesmanlike proposals for a new Federation of Malaysia to include both of these states, together with the British colonial and protected territories in northern Borneo. But although all except Brunei agreed to join the new Federation, which was accordingly established in September 1963, the crucial problem of the relationship between Kuala Lumpur and Singapore was not solved thereby, and in August 1965, Singapore accepted the federal government's demand that it should secede.

While it is too early to assess the full significance of this separation, it provides an ironic comment with which to end this account of Malaya. For it is surely the greatest of all that country's many paradoxes that the supreme memorial to Sir Stamford Raffles, the first and most illustrious of Britain's numerous Malayophile proconsuls, should be this predominantly Chinese metropolis which the rest of Malaya has now so emphatically rejected.[57]

SELECT BIBLIOGRAPHY

Butwell
Callis
Carnell (A) (B) (C) (D) (E)
Cole, D. H.
Cornish
Del Tufo
Dobby (B) (D) (H) (N) (O)
Freedman
Fryer (A)
Ginsburg and Roberts
Hodder (C) (D) (E)
Kondapi
Olver
Parkinson (B)
Pelzer (A)
Purcell (B) (C) (D) (F)
Roberts, G. (A) (B) (D)
Robequain
Silcock (A)
Skeat and Blagden
Smith

[57] For further discussion of the formation and prospects of the Federation of Malaysia see below, 681–7.

Steel and Fisher
Thompson and Adloff
Vandenbosch and Butwell
Vlieland (A) (B) (C)
Wint (C)

British Dependencies in the Far East, 1945–1949
Federation of Malaya, Annual Reports
Singapore, Annual Reports
Malayan Union and Singapore, Statement of policy on future constitution, Cmd. 6724, 1946
Singapore Constitutional Conference, Cmd. 9777, 1956
Straits Times
Federation of Malaya Official Year Book, 1961

The social geography section of this chapter was written before the Report on the 1957 Census (Fell) became available, and although some modifications have since been made in the light of the latter, the basic material remains that provided by the 1947 Census Report (Del Tufo), supplemented particularly by the works of two other demographers, namely Vlieland (the Superintendent of the 1931 Census) and Smith.

On the aboriginal population Skeat and Blagden is a major source, as are Purcell (C) (D) on the Chinese and Kondapi on the Indians, while Dobby (A) (B) (C) (D) (H) (N) (O), Fryer (A), Hodder (C) (D) (E) and Ooi (B) all make important contributions to the social geography of Malaya, as does Freedman to its sociology.

On pre-war political geography the thesis by Dobby was a pioneer study, while on the post-war political situation the papers by Carnell (A) (B) (C) (D) (E) are indispensable, as is Purcell's book (F), and again I have made considerable use of my own material in Steel and Fisher.

It will be apparent from the above list and the corresponding ones in Chapters 17 and 18 that the specifically geographical literature on Malaya is particularly rich. For this the credit must go largely to the work of the Departments of Geography in the Universities of Malaya and of Singapore, whose joint publication *The Journal of Tropical Geography* is particularly important in this connexion.

Addenda.

Note the following new works on Malaya: physical geography: Carter, Nossin, and Ho, Robert; historical geography: Wheatley (K); history: Cowan (B); economic development: *Federation of Malaya Second Five Year Plan*, *Singapore Development Plan;* social and political geography: Sandhu (A) (B), Sendut, McGee and the thesis by Tunku Shamsul Bahrin; general geography: Fryer (H).

CHAPTER 20

Northern Borneo

I. THE PHYSICAL AND HISTORICAL SETTING

Besides the Federation of Malaya and Singapore, the historic British sphere in Malaysia also included the larger area of some 80,000 square miles comprising Sarawak, North Borneo and Brunei.[1] However, while Malaya and Singapore had both by 1959 obtained complete or qualified independence, the Borneo territories remained at a less advanced stage of political evolution, and this in turn was a reflection of the way in which they had been largely by-passed by the economic and social forces which were transforming the Malayan scene.

Geographical facts alone cannot wholly explain this retardation of Northern Borneo *vis-à-vis* the Malay peninsula. Thus, while the latter obviously owes a great deal to its focal position within South-east Asia, the northern fringe of Borneo, flanking both the South China Sea and the main route south from China and Japan, via the Sulu Sea, to eastern Indonesia and Australia, can hardly be described as remote.

Moreover, while Northern Borneo contains only a low percentage of good agricultural land, much of the territory is no less suitable intrinsically for rubber cultivation than is the Malay peninsula, and it has in addition an abundance of forest products and a variety of mineral deposits. On the other hand the region certainly suffers from the almost complete absence of good harbours along the north-west coast, except for the offshore island of Labuan, and although the situation in this respect is very much better along the more remote north-east coast, both shores, like that of eastern Malaya, suffer from exposure to the NE monsoon which presents great hazards to navigation during the 'winter' months.[2]

Despite its apparent arbitrariness, the 19th-century division of Borneo into a British and a Dutch sphere was geographically sound. For as we have already seen, South-east Asia is a region in which the land divides but the sea unites,

[1] With the inclusion of Sarawak and North Borneo (renamed Sabah) in the Federation of Malaysia in 1963, as noted above, p. 660, it is no longer appropriate to refer to them as parts of British Borneo. The term Northern Borneo is therefore used in this chapter to include these two territories, together with Brunei.

[2] The north-west coast also experiences rough seas from the SW monsoon, and most stations there get their maximum rainfall between May and September. Total amounts are mostly from 100 to 180 in. per annum. For further consideration of the climate of Northern Borneo, which may be characterized throughout as equatorial monsoon, see above, Chapter 7.

and the boundary between the two political spheres follows the main NW/SE water-parting or related uplands for most of its length.

Thus delimited, Northern Borneo lies wholly to the north of the structural core of the island, and the main pattern of its relief is determined by the axes of Tertiary folding, running in a series of parallel curves from E/W in western Sarawak, through NE/SW in eastern Sarawak and Brunei, to NNE/SSW in the old North Borneo, beyond which the line is continued via the Sulu arcs into the western Philippines. While the surface rocks within this belt contain some older material, Mesozoic and more especially Tertiary formations predominate, with sandstones and limestones as perhaps the most characteristic of all. Associated with this structure is the occurrence of petroleum in the gentler folds on the northern flanks of the main ranges, and also of coal in a series of small basins in Sarawak, Labuan and North Borneo. In addition to these two, some half a dozen different metallic minerals, including gold, have also been located, though hitherto few of these have been mined commercially and even those only on an extremely limited scale. Apart from a small area along the north-east coast of North Borneo, however, there are no indications of recent volcanic activity and, except for riverine and coastal alluvium elsewhere, most of the soils are maturely laterized.

Throughout much the greater part of its length the relief of Northern Borneo exhibits a fairly regular three-fold pattern. Thus behind the generally low-lying and mangrove-fringed shore is a coastal plain, typically about 20 to 40 miles wide and generally very flat, and composed largely of imperfectly consolidated material deposited by the major rivers. At least one-third of this coastal plain is regularly subjected to either tidal or riverine flooding, though even so the extent of the swamp belt here is on a much smaller scale than in the west and south of the island which lie in Indonesian territory.

Behind the coastal plain is an intermediate zone, sometimes referred to as 'the hill country' or even 'the downs', though both names are rather misleading. However, apart from a few small areas immediately adjacent to some of the rivers, this belt is generally free of swamp; and although its average altitude is mostly well below 1,000 ft. it is fairly frequently capped by isolated hills reaching several times that height, which mark subsidiary lines of folding parallel to that of the main range, or in some cases form a series of spurs branching off from the latter towards the coast.

The interior highlands in turn form the third physiographic region, and here summit levels range mostly between 4,500 ft. and 7,500 ft. This mountainous divide between Northern Borneo and Kalimantan does not represent a continuous range throughout its whole length, and in particular many gaps occur in the west, notably between the Bukit Kelingkang and the Upper Kapuas mountains. The latter, however, continue without a break into the Iran range on the southern borders of central Sarawak, and this line is prolonged northwards into North Borneo where, as the Crocker range, it runs parallel with and much nearer to the coast, and culminates in the spectacular granitic peak of Kinabalu (13,455 ft.).

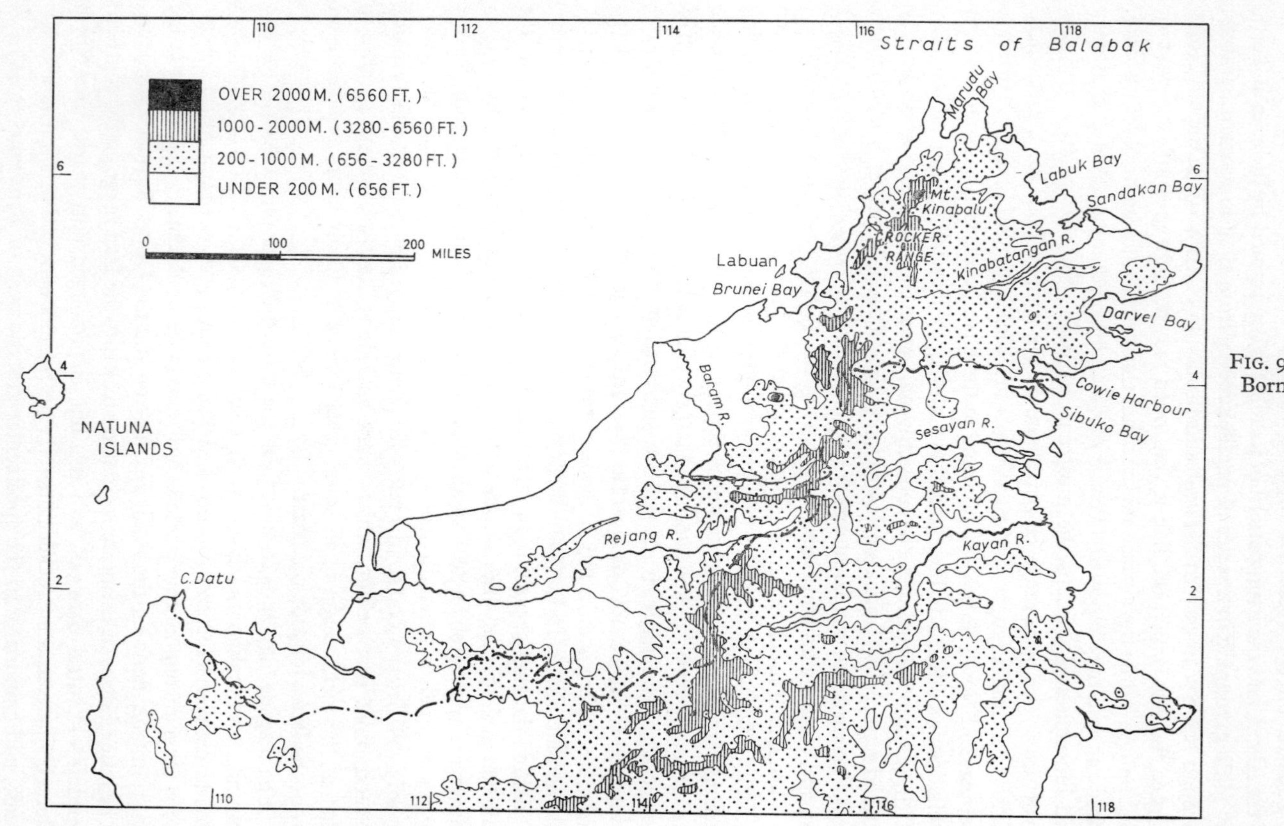
OVER 2000 M. (6560 FT.)
1000-2000 M. (3280-6560 FT.)
200-1000 M. (656-3280 FT.)
UNDER 200 M. (656 FT.)
0
100
200
MILES
Straits of Balabak
Marudu Bay
Labuk Bay
Sandakan Bay
Mt. Kinabalu
ROCKER RANGE
Kinabatangan R.
Labuan
Brunei Bay
Darvel Bay
Baram R.
Cowie Harbour
Sibuko Bay
Sesayan R.
NATUNA ISLANDS
Rejang R.
Kayan R.
C. Datu
110
112
114
116
118
6
4
2

FIG. 93—Northern Borneo: relief

In other respects, also, North Borneo shows important differences in relief from that of Brunei and Sarawak. On the one hand north of Brunei bay the north-west coast takes on a bolder character, and the high relief on land is matched by the greater depth of the adjacent sea, which marks the outer edge of the Sunda Shelf. Thus the coastal lowlands are rarely more than 10–20 miles wide, though many of the small alluvial plains behind the seaward strip of mangroves provide good agricultural land. Moreover, inland from the Crocker range is a series of lower but roughly parallel ridges, separated one from another by wide valleys, the lower portions of which have been drowned to form the magnificent rias of the north-east coast. In particular, Sandakan bay provides an excellent natural harbour, giving easy access to the fertile Kinabatangan valley, which extends over some 4,000 square miles. These various alluvial lowlands, together with the volcanic terrains of the Simporna peninsula, explain why North Borneo appears to have much the best agricultural potential of the three territories in question.

Apart from Kinabalu, no other summit in Northern Borneo reaches 8,000 ft., and although the main mountain backbone contains much undeniably rugged country, it is above all its character as a water-parting which makes it so effective a divide between the opposite sides of the island. For in view of the almost continuous cover of dense equatorial rain forest, rivers provide the only effective inland routes, and although jungle paths interconnect the head-waters of many of the rivers in the hill country, there are very few such links across the major divides of the remote interior. But while exceedingly useful for native craft, the Borneo rivers are of much more limited use for larger shipping since, besides the prevalence of falls and rapids at the point where they leave the hill zone, nearly all of them are impeded by both shifting sandbanks and dangerous bars near their mouths. The two largest rivers, the Rejang in Sarawak and the Kinabatangan in North Borneo, are both strike streams, and each is approximately 350 miles long; the former is navigable by small ocean-going vessels as far as Sibu, 60 miles upstream, and by shallow-draught river craft for a further 100 miles, while the latter is used by launches for a distance of 120 miles from the coast.

These physical conditions are closely mirrored in the indigenous settlement pattern of Northern Borneo. Although there is evidence of a succession of migrations, both from the Indo-Pacific peninsula and from other parts of Malaysia, the average density of population today (16 per square mile) is very low, and at the time when British administration began a century ago the areas in question were even more sparsely inhabited than they are today. Various groups of predominantly Nesiot Dyaks, notably the Sea Dyaks (Ibans), Land Dyaks, Dusuns, Kayans, Kenyahs, Kajangs and Muruts, form the indigenous population, and are thinly scattered to some extent over the coastal lowlands and also over the lower hill country inland, where they normally practise shifting cultivation and live in long-house villages on or near the banks of the rivers. In the coastal zone however the Dyak population is both interspersed and intermingled with the so-called Malays, derived principally in the past from Sumatra.[3] But although the typical darker colouring and more Mongoloid physiognomy of the latter is much in evidence here, the operative distinction between Malay and Dyak is primarily a matter of adherence or non-adherence to Islam.

Among many of the coastal Malays, moreover, there is a good deal of Chinese blood,[4] and it is now clear that very extensive trading contacts existed between Northern Borneo and China at least from the 10th to the 13th century, and that this commerce was accompanied by inter-monsoonal if not indeed permanent Chinese residence in certain areas.[5] Thereafter it seems likely that extensive parts of northern Borneo came under the influence first of Sri Vijaya and later of Madjapahit, before transferring their allegiance to Malacca early in the 15th century. Between 1405 and 1425 Brunei is recorded as sending tribute to China, but later in that century it fell increasingly under the domination of Malacca, and its ruler was converted to Islam.

After the Portuguese conquest of Malacca many Muslim traders, wishing to avoid contact with the Europeans, transferred their activities to Brunei[6] which, for the greater part of the 16th century experienced something of a golden age. With its capital occupying a well-defended site on a creek leading into the largest embayment on the whole north-western coast of Borneo, Brunei was well placed to extend its influence over much of the adjacent coastline. In fact, however, its Sultan did far more, and succeeded in bringing such distant territories as Sambas and Pontianak, and the islands of Balabak and Palawan also, under his rule. According to Pigafetta, the historian who accompanied Magellan, Brunei town contained some 25,000 families in 1521, and whether this be true or not there is some archæological evidence to suggest that the town was considerably larger at that time than it is today.[7]

Nevertheless, the hey-day of Brunei was short lived. Although for a time it enjoyed friendly relations with the Portuguese, it was twice sacked by the Spaniards from the Philippines, and after the end of the 16th century it proved unable to maintain control over its outlying dependencies. The Dutch, with their greater command of the sea, established at least nominal authority over the south-west, south-east and east coasts of the island while the north-east came under the control of the increasingly powerful Filipino Sultanate of Sulu. Thus by the end of the 18th century Brunei's territories had been reduced to the lands

[3] Some of these peoples in the north-east are descendants of relatively recent immigrants – including former pirates – from the Philippines.

[4] This should not be confused with the presence of recent Chinese immigrants. See below, pp. 672, 676 and 681.

[5] *Sarawak Annual Report*, 1956, pp. 145–6.

[6] Originally Brunei was only one of several principalities dotted along the coasts of Borneo. But by the time when the first Europeans visited the island it had become the largest, and most of the others recognized its overlordship. The name Borneo, which is a European corruption of Brunei, applies to the whole island; the Indonesian name Kalimantan is usually applied only to the part which lies within the Republic of Indonesia.

[7] See below, p. 681.

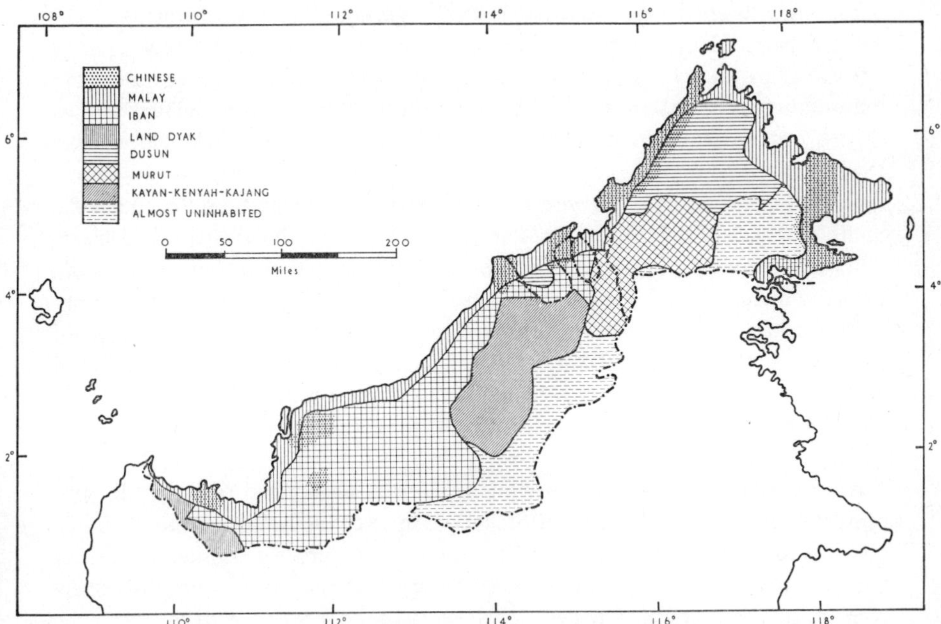

FIG. 94—Northern Borneo: ethnic groups

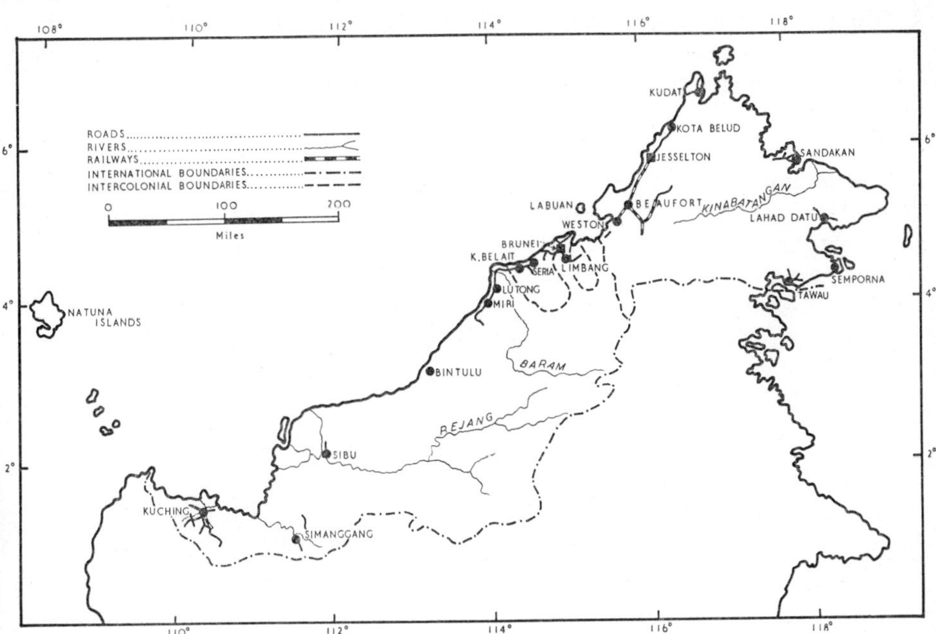

FIG. 95—Northern Borneo: roads and railways

bordering the north-west coast, that is the present Sarawak, Brunei and the western part of North Borneo. Moreover, internal corruption was acute, piracy was rife along the coast and the Sultan's authority counted for little or nothing in the outlying parts of the state. It was against this background that the first serious British intervention in the affairs of Northern Borneo took place after 1839.

In fact, however, British interest in the key area where the Sulu Sea meets the South China Sea had been aroused as early as 1762, when the Spanish declaration of war against England had led to the despatch of a naval expedition from Bengal which captured Manila in October of that year. Although by the Treaty of Paris in 1763, Manila was restored to Spain, the East India Company retained control over the island of Balambangan, which it had acquired from the Sultan of Sulu as a by-product of this expedition, and for a time the Company maintained a post on the island[8] which it hoped to develop as a base for trade with China.

After various setbacks this attempt was finally abandoned early in the 19th century, and with the founding of Singapore in 1819 the latter became the headquarters for the British trade with China. However, piracy continued to present a major threat to commerce in the South China Sea, and this was not fully overcome until steam-powered patrol vessels were brought into use. It was with the two-fold purpose of stamping out piracy and finding suitable coaling stations for naval and commercial vessels between Singapore and the China coast that the British again turned their attention to the northern coast of Borneo, which by the Anglo-Dutch treaty of 1824 lay within their sphere.

In this activity the pioneer rôle was played by the adventurer James Brooke who, after visiting Sarawak[9] in a private capacity in 1839, assisted the local viceroy to quell an uprising at Kuching and was rewarded with a feudal title to that territory, over which he was officially installed as Rajah (under the Sultan of Brunei) in 1841. In accepting this unusual status Brooke was genuinely concerned to put a stop both to coastal piracy and to the chaos and oppression within the territory in question. In the long run he succeeded in both of these aims, though the former was achieved only with the help of the Royal Navy and the British annexation of Labuan in 1846, while the latter involved Brooke and his successor[10] in a policy of territorial expansion at the expense of their own overlords, which progressively extended the original diminutive holding around Kuching to the shores of Brunei Bay. The three main stages in this advance, which took

[8] The East India Company's trading station at Balambangan was founded in 1773 and abandoned in 1775. Thereafter the Company tried to set up a station at Labuan (1775) but this also was short lived, and the attempt to re-establish the Balambangan station in 1803 was soon abandoned. See Hall (B), pp. 425–8 and Harrison, pp. 143–4.

[9] At that time still part of the Sultanate of Brunei.

[10] Sir Charles Brooke, who reigned for nearly 50 years. The third Rajah, Sir Charles Vyner Brooke, succeeded his father in 1917 and remained in office until July 1, 1946, when Sarawak became a British Crown Colony. See below, p. 672.

place in 1861, 1882 and 1883–1904, can be traced in the administrative map of the country today, since they correspond almost exactly to the Second and Third, the Fourth, and the Fifth Divisions respectively, while the First Division, a mere 7,000 square miles, represents the original territory acquired in 1842.

In this process the once extensive territories of Brunei were at first steadily whittled away, and after 1890 split into two by the inclusion of the Limbang valley in Sarawak. Moreover, Brunei was meanwhile subjected to encroachment from the opposite side as a result of the activities of the British North Borneo Company.

The origin of the latter mav be traced to American initiative, for it was the U.S. Consul at Brunei, C. Lee Moses, who first, in 1865, obtained for himself from the Sultan cessions of most of the territory which today comprises (British) North Borneo. His claim to this territory, originally valued mainly for its timber, minerals and potential plantation land, was eventually made over by Moses to the American Trading Company, under the chairmanship of J. W. Torrey of Hong Kong. However, the situation was complicated by the rival claim of Sulu to the north-eastern coastal regions of Borneo, and in 1872 the Sultan of Sulu granted to W. C. Cowie, a British citizen, a site in Sandakan Bay from which to carry on trade with the Sulu islands. About this time the American Trading Company's rights were acquired by Baron Overbeck, the Austrian Consul-General in Hong Kong but, having failed to interest either his government or the Vienna capitalists in North Borneo, Overbeck later joined forces with the Englishman Alfred Dent, of Dent Brothers, Hong Kong, to whom he eventually sold his interests in the venture.

Meanwhile on realizing that the title, derived from Brunei, was contested by Sulu, Dent, with the co-operation of Cowie, obtained from the Sultan of Sulu another title to the whole territory between Pandassan and Sibuko Bay. Although this claim was disputed by the Dutch, Spanish and German governments, the British government agreed in 1881 to the incorporation by Royal Charter of the British North Borneo Company, with an authorized capital of £2 million.

By the terms of the Charter it was stipulated that the foreign relations of the area under the Company's administration should be conducted through the British government, and that no territory should be disposed of without the latter's consent. In the event the territory was subsequently extended by several minor acquisitions on its western border, where after 1904 it adjoined that of Sarawak from the coast to the international boundary in the interior.

In 1888, at a time when the colonial scramble in South-east Asia was nearing its climax, the British government established a protectorate over the territories under the jurisdiction of the British North Borneo Company, and in the same year British protectorates were also declared over both Sarawak and Brunei. The latter which, weakened by continuing internal mismanagement, had been reduced almost to vanishing point, undertook in 1906 to accept a British Resident acting under the direction of the High Commissioner for the Malay States, and thereafter its affairs were more closely aligned with those of peninsular Malaya.

Similarly Labuan, after being transferred from 1889 to 1905 to the administration of the British North Borneo Company, was incorporated within the Straits Settlements in the latter year, though this arrangement was again changed in 1912 when the island was constituted a separate Settlement within the S.S. but under its own Resident.

These administrative changes were symptomatic of a growing uncertainty regarding the long-term prospects of the island. Originally Labuan had been acquired to serve both as a naval station for use in the anti-piracy campaign and as an intermediate bunkering port for steamships on the run from Singapore to Hong Kong. Moreover, it had also been expected that Labuan, with its fine natural harbour along an otherwise ill-provided coast, and its status as a free port comparable with Singapore and Hong Kong, would become the entrepôt for the whole fringe of Northern Borneo and perhaps also for other areas farther east.

In the event, however, although it fulfilled its rôle against piracy so well that the garrison was withdrawn in 1867,[11] Labuan achieved little success in other respects. Owing to the steady increase in the size and efficiency of the steamship, the need for a coaling port here soon ceased to exist, and meanwhile the slowness with which the hinterland was opened up meant that there was insufficient traffic to justify the detour from the direct sailing route between Singapore and Hong Kong.

While the sparseness of the indigenous population goes some way to explain the lack of economic progress within Borneo itself, the absence of any important known mineral,[12] once coal had ceased to be required in major quantities locally, was a more serious handicap. Thus compared with Malaya, where the profits obtained from tin mining had sparked off the great economic revolution which transformed the western third of the peninsula after the second half of the 19th century, Northern Borneo appeared to be totally lacking in anything which could provide such a stimulus. And when in the early years of the 20th century rubber seemed to offer new and encouraging prospects, the fact that western Malaya was already well provided with roads, railways and ports meant that most British growers concentrated their attention there, rather than in the Borneo territories which were sadly deficient in all these respects.

In short, in this respect as in several others, Northern Borneo may be regarded as suffering from much the same liabilities as eastern Malaya, and in fact both areas seem to have been regarded as reserve territories which might be brought into production at some future date if ever the demand for estate land in western Malaya should outrun the supply.[13]

[11] Ginsburg, Kaplan and Roberts, p. 25.

[12] Oil was not discovered until shortly before the First World War.

[13] A similar situation existed in the Netherlands Indies, where first Java and then the Sumatran Cultuurgebied and the oilfields were intensively exploited, while the greater part of the remaining territories were left almost completely undeveloped by Western enterprise. See above, pp. 290–1.

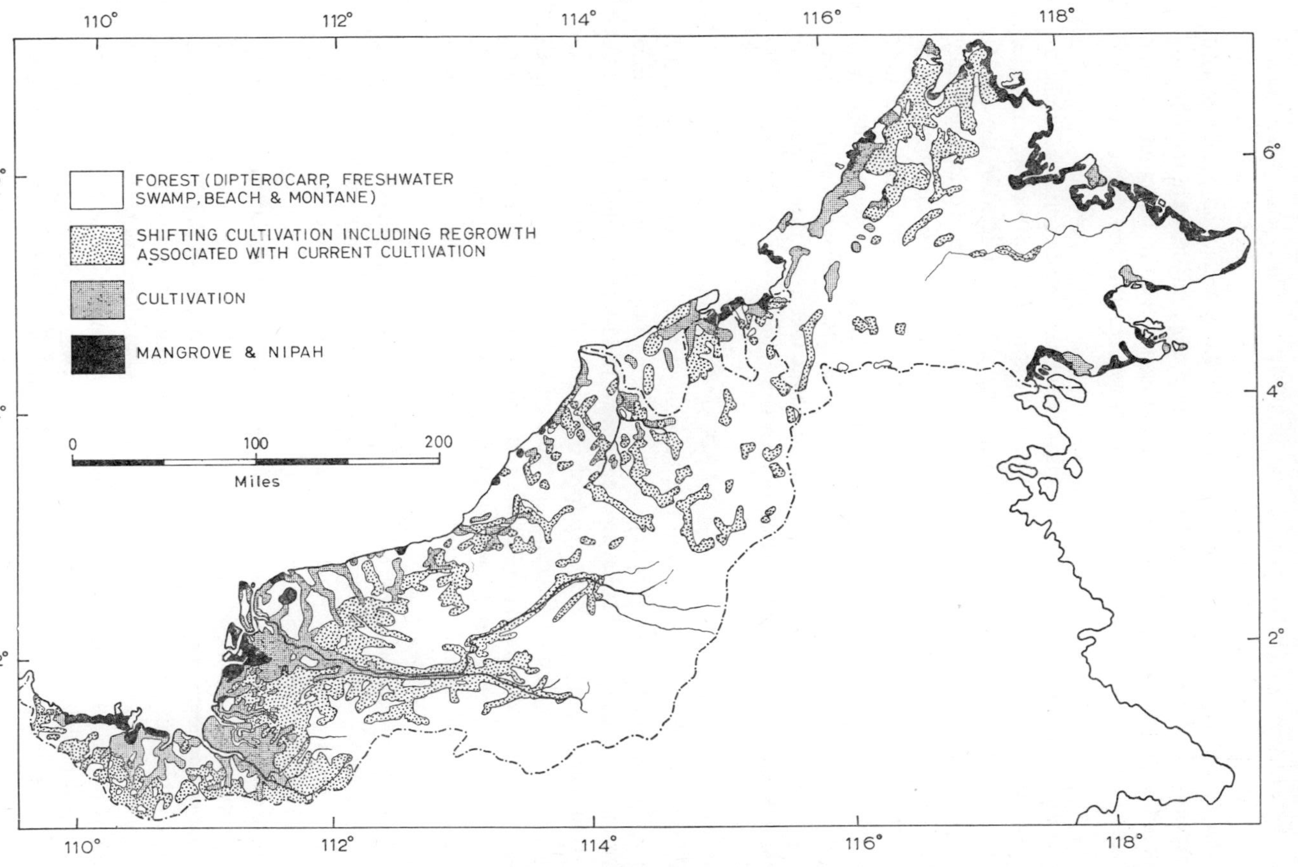

FIG. 96—Northern Borneo: land use

Nevertheless in more recent times the discovery of oil in Northern Borneo has introduced a new element into the situation. Admittedly, the amounts produced prior to the Second World War were not enough to initiate any more general economic expansion, but the big increase since 1945 might, were it to be sustained – though the reverse now seems more likely – lead to something like the kind of development that occurred in Malaya as a result of the 19th-century 'tin rush'.

Initially, however, the main preoccupation of the three British administrations since the Second World War was to restore their respective territories to working order after the material and spiritual damage inflicted by the war. It was in these circumstances that the decisions were taken to replace the family rule of the Brookes in Sarawak and the Chartered Company administration in North Borneo by the more usual Crown Colony system, and at the same time Labuan was constituted a part of the new North Borneo Colony. But despite this long overdue move towards greater standardization, the effect of past differences is still apparent in the social and economic life of the three territories, as the following consideration of each in turn will show.

II. SARAWAK

Throughout the 105 years of the Brooke family's rule, the improvement of the peoples' welfare was the primary concern of the administration. In accordance with the original aims of James Brooke, piracy, head-hunting and oppression by the former ruling class were stamped out, and under his two successors the country continued to be run rather in the manner of a vast family estate. Large-scale agricultural exploitation on Western capitalist lines was not encouraged, the 'White Rajahs' preferring instead to preserve the indigenous pattern of peasant cultivation and, so far as possible, to shield the country from over-rapid economic development.

Nevertheless this was not a policy of stagnation. From the very beginning James Brooke realized that the extreme sparseness and backwardness of the population were the two greatest obstacles to progress, and he accordingly looked with favour on the immigration of Chinese settlers in the belief that they would provide a new and much-needed dynamic element in Sarawak society.

Despite a serious Chinese rebellion in 1867, which followed the first important influx of Chinese from the nearby Sambas district of Dutch Borneo, the official attitude towards the Chinese underwent no fundamental change, though it took many decades before the numbers of immigrants increased very substantially.[14] But in 1899 a settlement of Foochow Chinese was established at Sibu, thanks to the persistence of Charles Brooke, whose aim was to encourage the Chinese colonists to teach better farming practices to the local population. In spite of some initial difficulties the settlement eventually prospered and another followed later at Baram.

[14] As late as 1871 there were only some 5,000 Chinese there. See Purcell (D), pp. 421–39

During the present century the numbers of Chinese grew steadily and today they account for 30·8 per cent of the total population, a figure which is well above the average for Northern Borneo as a whole. Although a considerable proportion are engaged in small-holder cultivation, both of rice and more especially of the two main cash crops, rubber and pepper, many have taken to clerical, handicraft and above all commercial activities, while still others find employment both as skilled and unskilled labour in the oil industry.

The latter, centring at Miri close to the Brunei frontier, forms the only important outpost of Western capitalist enterprise in Sarawak. The petroleum deposits here were first worked on a serious scale in 1913[15] and by 1926 production had reached a figure of 633,000 metric tons a year. To handle this oil a refinery was built at Lutong six miles to the north-east, by Sarawak Oilfields Ltd., a subsidiary of Royal Dutch/Shell. By the 1930s the output of the Miri fields was already beginning to decline, but meanwhile a new field had been discovered across the Brunei border at Seria, some 35 miles away, and its product has ever since been pumped to Lutong for refining and export. Moreover, as Lutong harbour cannot accommodate large vessels, the oil is transferred to the tankers by means of a submarine pipe to a point some three miles offshore.[16]

Since the Second World War the output of the Miri oilfields has declined to a mere trickle, valued at $M3,758,000 out of the total of $M357,101,464 exported from Lutong in 1956.[17] Despite considerable expenditure on further prospecting, mainly beneath the shallow seas adjacent to the Miri field,[18] no fresh discoveries have been made, so that today, apart from the minor profits made from refining and shipping the much larger product of its neighbour, the Sarawak petroleum industry appears to be virtually a thing of the past.

Except for the immediate vicinity of Miri and Lutong, population in the eastern half of Sarawak, even within the coastal zone, is very sparse. In general, as Fig. 96 implies, the density is greatest in the south-west, where considerable areas near the coast have over 25 persons to the square mile and this is clearly related to the earlier establishment of Western rule in this corner of the country. It is here also that the two largest towns are situated, namely the capital, Kuching (population 56,000) and the second largest port[19] of Sibu (20,000), on the lower Rejang. Both of these are within 600 miles of Singapore, through which the greater part of the country's overseas trade is routed, the only major exception to this being the 30 per cent or so of the oil shipped from Lutong direct to Indonesia for refining.[20]

[15] Though small-scale operations began in 1911.

[16] See Ginsburg, Kaplan and Roberts, p. 57.

[17] In 1956 the output from the Miri field was 70,616 long tons. Sarawak and Brunei oil exported via Lutong in the same year totalled 5,578,761 tons, most of it being crude oil. The Lutong refinery output (long tons) was: gasoline 476,284, kerosene 79,000, gas oil 5,282, diesel fuel 1,211,202, naphtha 102,754, isobutane concentrate 11,158, Lutong residue 635,356.

[18] In 1954 Sarawak extended its boundaries over the adjacent continental shelf.

[19] Sibu and Kuching are general merchandise ports; Lutong is concerned solely with oil.

[20] Another 26 per cent goes to Singapore.

Apart from petroleum no other mineral has ever played an important rôle in the Sarawak economy. Thus despite the fact that it was gold (in the Bau district of the south-west) which attracted the first Chinese settlers from over the border, no large finds were ever made, and the total export of gold in 1956 was valued at only $M60,000. More recently bauxite has been worked for export, also in the south-west, and in 1962 a Japanese concern obtained a concession to mine coal in the Silantek area.

For the rest, the country's economy is almost entirely agricultural, with cash-crop production confined mostly to a relatively small part of the coastal zone, side by side with subsistence wet-rice and sago cultivation, and more primitive shifting tillage extending deeper into the interior.

By cropped area rice leads with some 268,000 acres under cultivation, though only about 83,000 acres of this is wet rice, and even that is mostly grown by very primitive methods. Thus the total output is only about 50–60 per cent of the country's requirements and 45,710 tons of rice were imported, mainly from Thailand, in 1960.

In view of the much lower rice yield from the *ladang* method of cultivation, which is generally practised by the Sea Dyak population, many people have argued that the latter should be encouraged to change over to wet cultivation as quickly as possible. But as Hodder points out[21] much of the land occupied by these peoples is quite unsuited to such methods, and the need there is rather to improve the traditional practices of dry cultivation. Certainly there is scope for much to be done in this respect, for in many areas growing population and steady deterioration of the soil is leading to a progressive shortening of the fallow period, in some cases from twelve to as little as two years, which in turn serves both to aggravate the impoverishment of the soil and to ruin potentially valuable reserves of timber.

Second in acreage (*c.* 300,000) and much the most important of the cash crops is rubber, the total export of which, namely 49,961 tons in 1960, was worth $M122·4 million. While Sarawak's rubber output, 95 per cent of which comes from small-holdings of less than five acres each, is the largest of the three Northern Borneo territories, the total amount is less than one-tenth of that of Malaya, and furthermore practically all the trees are low yielding and over age. In recent years a new replanting scheme has been put into operation, under which it is planned to grant government subsidies to replant at least 10,000 acres within the next five years.

While rubber production has done little more than regain its pre-war level, the annual output of pepper increased six-fold between the late 1930s and 1956, largely because of the unexpectedly high prices for this commodity resulting from the great decline in Indonesian and Indochinese production. Thus by 1956 Sarawak, with a total export of 19,800 tons valued at $M24·6 million, had become the world's leading exporter, but by 1960 exports had fallen to some

[21] Hodder (B), p. 78.

4,100 tons, worth $M17·2 million, while Indonesia's had risen to 34,400 tons.

Compared with these two, the remaining agricultural exports are of minor importance, though both sago (sago flour exports $M2·8 million in 1960) and coconuts are significant in the subsistence economy, and respectively occupy some 150,000 and 25–50,000 acres.

Finally it remains to mention timber, which ranked third in value ($M43·6 million) among the exports (*i.e.* after oil and rubber) in 1960, and the associated but much smaller item of forest products, chiefly jelutong ($M0·8 million), rattan and damar, which are collected from a wide area of the interior. At least 15,000 square miles of commercially significant timber exist within Sarawak, though an even larger area of formerly dense forest has undergone serious degeneration as a result of shifting cultivation.

Notwithstanding the post-war development of air communications focusing on Kuching, and to a lesser extent on Sibu and the Miri oilfields, the outstanding material needs of Sarawak today are better overland transport and improved port facilities. In the former connexion, serious thought is now being given to the planning of a 'national' road system, the first part of which to be built has been the new 82-mile link between Kuching and Simanggang,[22] the headquarters of the Second Division. But the cost of road making through the Sarawak jungle is very heavy, and in view of the sparseness of the population to the north and east of the Second Division it will probably be many years before any important developments take place in those areas.

So far as shipping facilities are concerned, the main proposal at present under consideration is the building of a new deep-sea port at Kuching, which would almost certainly lead to a substantial increase in the volume of overseas trade, at least partially at the expense of the present traffic via Singapore.

For the rest the main tasks calling for attention in the economic field are the greater diversification of agriculture, the production of more food, particularly rice, and the replanting of both small-holding and estate rubber with high-yielding material. While all of these, together with ambitious anti-malarial measures, figured in the recent Development Plan for 1955–60, available funds, from local sources and from Colonial Development and Welfare funds, were together sufficient only for relatively modest progress.[23] So long as Sarawak remained on its own and had nothing more to offer the world than its hitherto not very impressive list of exports, no major economic development could be expected there. For this reason its inclusion within the Federation of Malaysia has understandably raised hopes of a more promising future, but quite apart from the present distraction of Indonesian 'confrontation' it would be unwise to expect

[22] This was completed in 1962. *Inter alia* it provides access to the Silantek coalfield.

[23] Out of an originally planned spending of $M99·4 million during 1955–60, $M54·2 million was earmarked for communications, $M14·8 million for medical and health measures and $M10·7 million for agriculture. From 1951 to 1960 grants received from Colonial Development and Welfare funds amounted to $M27·7 million. In 1960 a loan of $M20·57 million was subscribed by the Brunei government.

any spectacularly rapid transformation of what is intrinsically a relatively poor country.

III. NORTH BORNEO (SABAH)*

The administration of the British North Borneo Company which survived until 1946 was no less anachronistic than that of the paternalistic régime of the Brookes in Sarawak, though it differed sharply from the latter in its aims. Thus the purpose of the Chartered Company was to exploit North Borneo as a profitable commercial venture and, although it never exercised its rights to trade or to undertake productive enterprise on its own account, it had sought to establish the necessary conditions, in the form of harbours, transport, labour supplies and general administration, to attract others to develop the country's resources which were taxed in various ways to provide profits for the shareholders.[24]

Yet in spite of this avowedly commercial aim, North Borneo was not noticeably more successful as a producer of export commodities than was Sarawak. Compared with the latter its area and population are roughly two-thirds as great, but its exports in 1960 stood at only $M222·6 million, against Sarawak's $M488·3 million. Moreover, even if the whole of the Brunei-produced oil is deducted from the Sarawak total, the latter is only a little lower ($M203·0 million) than that of North Borneo, though on a *per capita* basis North Borneo is ahead with $M490 as against Sarawak's $M272.

Besides the difference in the form of its administration, North Borneo has hitherto been somewhat less closely linked with Singapore than has Sarawak. While this applies to some extent even to the west-coast region, the tendency was much more pronounced along the north-east coast, whose contacts with Hong Kong, southern China and the Philippines were closer, and this divergence of outlook between the two coastal zones has been apparent throughout the country's history.

Of the original stations established by the early 1880s, namely Sandakan, Penungah, Silam, Kudat, Semporna, Kotah Belud, Gaya and Papar, all except the last three were in the north-east part of the country and from 1884 onwards[25] the largest of these, namely Sandakan, served as the seat of the administration.

In view of the extreme sparseness of population throughout the company's territories one of the administration's first acts was to appoint an immigration commissioner to encourage prospective labourers and agricultural settlers to come direct to North Borneo from southern China. Thanks to the financial and other inducements offered, this policy proved unexpectedly successful, and indeed the labour market quickly became saturated with Chinese immigrants.[26] In the meantime another current of Chinese migration had begun from Singapore, and since these Straits Chinese were familiar with Bazaar Malay they were

[24] See Kahin (A), especially pp. 51–5.

[25] Until 1946. See below, p. 678. Before 1884 Kudat was the capital.

[26] Purcell (D), p. 434.

* See p.662.

better able than the China-born to establish themselves as local traders. Thus in the mid 1880s a considerable return flow to China took place, but this setback proved only a temporary phenomenon, and since that time there has been substantial further migration of Chinese from both sources.

After some initial experiments with a wide range of commercial crops, including sugar, coffee, cocoa, coconuts, ramie and rubber, the first major success, which in fact put the territory on its feet, was achieved with the cultivation of cigar-wrapper tobacco in emulation of the Deli planters of Sumatra. By 1889 78 companies had taken up land, nearly all for this purpose, and the value of the crop rose from £400 in 1887 to over £100,000 in 1891. But the boom proved short lived, and by 1894 the resultant financial difficulties gave rise to a proposal that British North Borneo should be federated with Sarawak.

Although this plan, which was probably suggested by the contemporary movement towards federation in the Malay States,[27] came to nothing, Malayan experience in respect of the economic progress which followed railway construction was adduced in support of similar developments in North Borneo. Accordingly, between 1896 and 1900 a metre-gauge line was built from Weston, on the shores of Brunei Bay facing Labuan, to Beaufort, and this was later extended (1900–1905) both to Jesselton, farther north on the west coast, and to Melalap in the interior. However, in the absence of any mineral wealth remotely comparable in value to Malayan tin, no very spectacular developments followed, and the proposed extension of the railway through the interior to Cowie Harbour never materialized.

Nevertheless, the existing railway proved very useful during the rubber boom of the early 20th century, when the Chartered Company offered land on extremely favourable terms alike to estates and small-holders, and since that time the greater part of the country's rubber has been cultivated in the western coastal and foothill zone through which the railway runs. Despite the severe setback after 1931, rubber has continued until very recently to be the most important of North Borneo's exports though it is now outstripped by timber.

The history of mining on the other hand has been one of repeated disappointments. Thus although coal was worked for a time in several localities, namely at Weston, behind Cowie Harbour, on Sebatik Island, and also on Labuan, none of these ever attained major importance and all have ceased production since the early 1930s. Gold mining, likewise, came to nothing, and although there has been extensive prospecting for oil, no workable deposits have ever been discovered.

At the time when the Second World War broke out, therefore, North Borneo still remained very much a backwater, important only for a relatively small production of rubber and timber. Meanwhile the Settlement of Labuan, of which so much had originally been expected, had actually declined in population, from 8,411 in 1901 to 7,497 in 1934, and served merely as a minor collecting centre for the produce of the neighbouring coast.

[27] See above, p. 597.

This comparative isolation was rudely shattered by the war, for owing to its important strategic position the Japanese were determined to establish a firm hold over North Borneo and in due course the Allied counter-offensive resulted in widespread devastation. Following the restoration of British authority and the reconstitution of the territory as a British Crown Colony in 1946, Jesselton on the west coast replaced Sandakan as capital, a change which was symptomatic of the trend towards a closer co-ordination of British policy in South-east Asia through the office of the Special Commissioner for South-east Asia in Singapore, for Jesselton has always been in closer touch with the latter than has Sandakan. By 1960, however, Sandakan had been largely rebuilt, and with a population of 28,805 was appreciably larger than Jesselton which numbered only 21,704.

While Jesselton at the northern terminus of the railway line is the main outlet for rubber, most of which is shipped to Singapore, Sandakan remains the principal centre of the timber export trade, which is directed mainly towards Japan, Hong Kong and Australia. Apart from these two, no other town exceeds 10,000 in population, though Tawau, Kudat and Beaufort are of local significance. Labuan continues to serve as a trans-shipment port for the Brunei Bay area, and in 1956 was once again constituted a free port.

As in Sarawak economic development is virtually limited to a narrow and far from continuous zone within about 20 miles of the coast. Population density is highest in the strip served by the railway, where a figure of 25–50 to the square mile obtains, and a second smaller patch of similar density exists in the vicinity of Sandakan. But elsewhere the average falls to around or below 10, and indeed extensive areas, particularly in the north-eastern interior, are virtually unoccupied.

Compared with Sarawak, North Borneo has a somewhat higher, though none the less quite inadequate road mileage, and it also contains most of the fifty or so estates in all British Borneo. As in neighbouring areas the Chinese, numbering 104,542 or 23·0 per cent in 1960, completely dominate the commercial life of the country, and in spite of having suffered exceptionally severely during the Japanese occupation are now increasing at a proportionately faster rate than the indigenous inhabitants.

As a group the most important economic activities are agricultural, though the total area under rice, *c.* 75,000 acres, is little more than half that devoted to rubber. Nevertheless some two-thirds of this rice acreage is under wet cultivation, notably in the alluvial zone immediately behind the west coast. Mainly because of the harmful effects of *ladang* cultivation on the country's timber reserves, the government has tried hard to stop this type of farming, though it still continues to be practised over a substantial area. With a total output of 50,000 tons of wet paddy (from 46,000 acres) and a further 14,900 tons of dry paddy in 1960 North Borneo supplied only about two-thirds of its requirements of rice. But the country contains considerable areas well suited for wet cultivation which are at present largely or wholly unused, and new drainage and irrigation schemes are afoot in the Papar and Tuaram valleys and the Klias peninsula. Besides rice, sago, cassava, maize, sugar and coconuts are cultivated for local consumption, though there is little or no production of these for cash.

The acreage planted with rubber is approximately 172,000, which in 1960 yielded some 22,034 tons, valued at $M49·5 million, or nearly a quarter of the colony's total exports. Although approximately half of this is grown on estates and the rest largely on Chinese small-holdings, not more than 40 per cent is from high-yielding stock and many of the trees are over 20 years old. However, great strides have been made in replanting in recent years, thanks to the activities of the Rubber Fund Board and meanwhile exports have risen from 19,900 tons in 1956 to 22,000 tons in 1960.

In addition to rubber, copra is now an important export, but although over 45,000 acres are planted with coconuts, three-quartets of the 1960 export figure of $M40·2 million was accounted for by the reshipment of copra from nearby parts of Indonesia which were seeking to by-pass the official copra marketing arrangements in that country.[28] Of the once numerous tobacco estates only the solitary Darvel Tobacco Plantation in the volcanically enriched Lahad Datu area still remains in production and was responsible for the export of 460,695 lb. of high-grade cigar wrapper worth $M5·3 million in 1956; some 800,000 lb. of inferior tobacco are also grown by small-holders for local consumption.

The abacá industry, represented by six estates totalling 4,500 acres, all on rich basaltic soils in the Semporna peninsula, was originally built up before the war by the Japanese as an extension of their activities in the Philippines. Besides the setback occasioned by the war, however, abacá has recently suffered further reverses from virus disease, but it is nevertheless still believed that there is considerable scope for expanding production. The same view is also held regarding cocoa though at present cultivation of this crop is confined to a total area of 2,800 acres at Tawau.

Second only to agricultural products is the export of timber, which in 1960 was valued at $M90·7 million. Before the Second World War North Borneo ranked third in the Commonwealth (after Canada and Burma) as a timber exporter, and though output declined catastrophically as a result of the war, it has trebled since 1956. All-told North Borneo contains over 2 million acres of commercial forest within 20 miles of the coast, and besides the timber handled by its 61 sawmills, there is a useful export of rattans, gutta percha, damar, tannin bark, firewood and birds' nests.

Despite the smallness of the number of estates and other productive enterprises in North Borneo, the problem of maintaining an adequate labour pool calls for constant attention. For this reason the government, besides permitting the temporary entry of skilled and semi-skilled Chinese workers from Hong Kong and Singapore, concluded an agreement with the Philippines in 1955 to promote the recruitment of workers from that country also. As yet the results of

[28] See above, p.321, note 23.

this latter step have proved disappointing, but there has recently been a considerable influx of labour from various parts of eastern Indonesia, notably Celebes and Timor.

Apart from the need to make good the devastation caused by the war, development plans for North Borneo since 1946 have concentrated, like those in Sarawak, on diversifying agriculture, increasing the output of rice and improving the existing transport system. In particular, new wharves have been built at Sandakan, Jesselton and Labuan,[29] the railway between the latter and Beaufort has been improved, a programme of earth-road construction, to open up new areas for development, was begun in 1954 and overall progress is impressive.

Besides coastal shipping and longer-distance services linking the main ports with Singapore, Hong Kong and also, in the case of Sandakan, with Australia, Manila and Japan, most of the main centres are nowadays interconnected by fairly frequent air services, and there are daily flights from Jesselton to Brunei, Sarawak and Singapore. Although as in Sarawak Indonesian 'confrontation' is tending here also to divert attention from the tasks of economic development, Sabah appears to offer appreciably better prospects in this respect than does Sarawak.

IV. BRUNEI

Having been reduced by the simultaneous expansion of Sarawak and British North Borneo to two minute fragments, together comprising a mere 2,226 square miles, Brunei appeared in the opening years of the present century to be an area of very little importance, economic or otherwise, and in these circumstances the British decision to administer it, with the aid of a few Malayan government servants[30] as a minor appendage of the Malay peninsula was understandable.

Yet by a curious turn of fortune, this surviving rump of the once extensive Sultanate has since been found to contain practically the whole of the considerable petroleum deposits known to lie within Northern Borneo, and this fact has given a new significance to its position as a protected state *vis-à-vis* the two former Crown Colonies which flank it on either side.

Although, as we have seen, petroleum was first worked at Miri in Sarawak in 1911/12, it was not until 1929 that the much richer field was discovered at Seria in Brunei. Even with the comparatively small pre-war production of oil (707,219 tons in 1938) Brunei was quickly able to pay off its 'national debt' (a loan from the Straits Settlements government) and for the rest to use the proceeds of its

[29] Aid for the construction of these wharves has come from U.S. counterpart funds. Other aid to North Borneo is from Colonial Development and Welfare funds and further sums for development have been obtained from the sale of former Japanese assets in the country. The combined totals from all three sources were $M16·5 million for the three years 1953–6 inclusive. Development proposals for the period 1959–64 are estimated at $M71 million.

[30] Selected members of the Malayan Civil Service and the various Malayan technical departments were periodically seconded to Brunei.

new-found wealth in agricultural improvements of various kinds. Since 1945, however, the British interest in obtaining Sterling Area supplies of oil has led to a spectacular increase in production, which for a short time exceeded 5 million tons a year, or roughly a quarter that of all Indonesia's oilfields put together. With the income derived from such great natural wealth in a country of only 60,000 people, Brunei is now in an extremely strong financial position[31] but, since the known oil reserves are enough for only another 15 years or so, it is wisely refraining from a policy of mere spending for spending's sake. Since 1956 oil production has begun to fall and in 1963 amounted to only 3½ million tons.

Inevitably the oil industry dominates the whole Brunei scene. Thus 24,000 people, or nearly one third of the total population, are found in the two oilfield towns of Seria and Kuala Belait, both of which are extremely cosmopolitan and contain numerous Chinese, Europeans and Indians, as well as Malays and Dyaks. To preserve the oilfield from marine erosion a 6½-mile dike has been built along this exposed coastline, but in fact several of the existing wells operate undersea at distances of a mile or so from the land.

Apart from oil, practically the only commercial production comes from four estates and a few small-holdings, with a total of 30,575 acres of rubber. Rice occupies a much smaller acreage (6,789), but two-thirds of this is wet, and it is also supplemented by considerable cultivation of sago. In any case, however, the total rural population is only about 40,000, the remaining 17,000 living in the largest urban concentration, namely Brunei town.

Besides a cosmopolitan trading quarter, which also houses a cutch factory, Brunei town contains the picturesque 'Kampong Ayer' (*c.* 9,000 people), the direct survival of the old Malay capital described by Pigafetta. Brunei town is the principal centre of Islamic/Malay political consciousness in the whole of Northern Borneo, and a desire to exploit this fact to create an exclusively North Bornean federation goes far to explain the lack of popular support here for the Federation of Malaysia.

While Kuala Belait is now connected by a direct weekly shipping service to Singapore, Brunei town has its own airport providing daily links with all parts of Malaysia. But, as noted above, the petroleum, which forms over 99 per cent of the country's exports, is shipped exclusively via Sarawak.

V. THE MOVE TOWARDS FEDERATION[32]

Although the British government had long exercised a measure of control over the external relations of Sarawak and North Borneo, it was only with the change in the status of these two territories in 1946 that they came under the direct control of the Colonial Office. To some observers, and particularly to the Dutch

[31] In 1956 Brunei's crude-oil exports of 5,526,504 long tons were worth $M309,308,891. In such circumstances the country is fully able to pay for all its own development projects without recourse to Colonial Development and Welfare funds.

[32] See Fisher (Q), pp. 667–72, and Carnell (B), pp. 12–14.

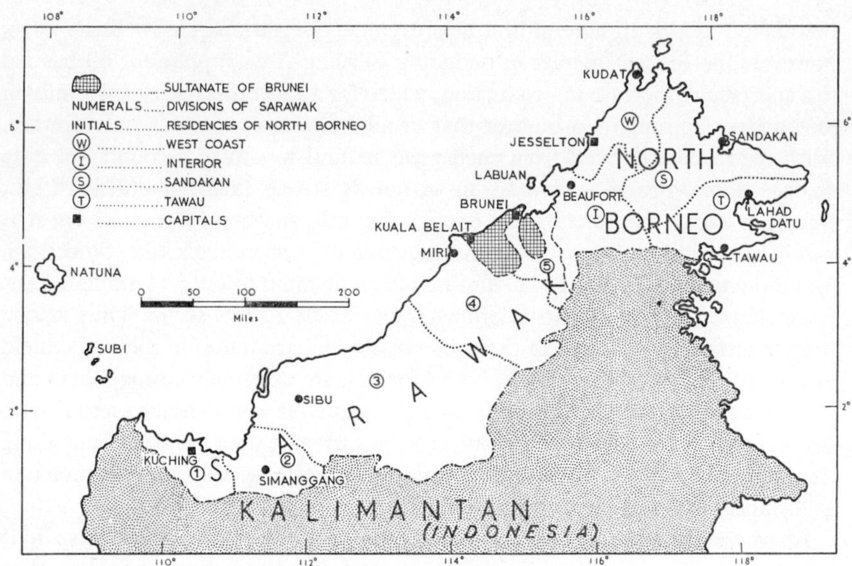

FIG. 97—Northern Borneo: political divisions

who had been frustrated in their post-war attempts to recoup their losses in western Indonesia by strengthening their hold over the less advanced areas farther east, this transformation of two protected states into British Crown Colonies seemed both retrograde and hypocritical.

Yet in fact the British intention was not to tighten the imperial shackles, but rather to foster economic and social progress and to prepare the way for self-government. For, notwithstanding the constitutional changes introduced in Sarawak in 1941,[33] neither it nor North Borneo seemed likely to achieve these goals so quickly under the old regimes, and in particular neither could command the financial resources needed to repair the damage caused by the war and to initiate new schemes of welfare and economic development.

At the same time, moreover, the scale of rehabilitation and reconstruction which the situation demanded was so extensive that it provided an opportunity for carrying out at least a measure of administrative rationalization throughout the whole of British Borneo. Thus before the war each of the territories had its own currency as well as its own postage stamps, and each recruited its civil servants wholly independently of the others, though the combined population of the whole area was less than a million. Since 1946 much of the wastage involved in such practices has been eliminated; all three territories now use the Malayan dollar, and have entered into a customs agreement, a common Supreme Court has been set up and various forms of technical co-operation have been introduced.

[33] In 1941 to celebrate the centenary of Brooke rule the Rajah abrogated his absolute powers and enacted a new constitution with a non-elected Supreme Council.

In these circumstances and in view of the move towards unification in peninsular Malaya in 1946, the question of closer political association between the three Borneo territories has inevitably arisen.[34] Indeed the creation of the Special Commission in South-east Asia,[35] with the prime task of co-ordinating British policy in the Malayan Union, Singapore, Brunei, Sarawak and North Borneo, led many people to believe that even more far-reaching changes were contemplated, and this view was underlined when the Special Commissioner[36] was specifically instructed to advise the Secretary of State for the Colonies 'from time to time' on the question of 'closer political co-operation' between these lands as a whole.

In fact some form of regional federation appears to have been seriously considered as a preliminary to the creation of a new Dominion of British South-east Asia.[37] Although various other proposals have since been suggested, the one apparently favoured in the immediate post-war period was the most far-reaching, aiming as it did at the merger of all the British Malaysian territories together with Hong Kong.

On historical, economic and strategic grounds such a grouping had much to commend it. The various British possessions in the region had all been acquired originally as part of a policy which in the 19th century had made the South China Sea into a British lake, and all were closely interlinked by British and local shipping, and by a host of commercial ties focusing in the two great port cities of Singapore and Hong Kong. Unfortunately, however, that very fact, quite apart from the precarious balance of numbers (Table 93), implied that a grouping which included Hong Kong would be dominated by the Chinese element.

However, a federation of all the remaining territories, namely the Malayan Union/Federation, Singapore, Brunei, Sarawak and North Borneo, would have contained a clear majority of Malaysians, a fact which to many observers appeared to be strongly in its favour. For while it had so far proved difficult to unite a predominantly Chinese Singapore with the rest of the Malay peninsula, the inclusion of the further 875,533 Malaysians and only 355,494 Chinese of the three Borneo territories might help to assuage the fears of the peninsular Malays and so make possible a solution along these lines. In this way an answer might be found to the problem of Singapore's future rôle, for only as part of a substantially larger territory than at present could that great port city today find its *raison d'être*. And at the same time the inclusion of the Borneo lands, with their useful petroleum reserves, would contribute a much-needed element of diversity to the over-specialized economy of Malaya.

Against this, however, several arguments could be raised. Thus it has been argued that the potential voting strength of the Borneo population was not nearly

[34] See above, pp. 604 and 660. [35] See above, p. 654, note 43.

[36] This title was subsequently changed to Commissioner-General in South-East Asia.

[37] *Cf.* the proposals for the British West Indian federation which have taken shape since the Second World War. See Carnell (B). However, these have since been abandoned.

so favourable to the Malays as the above figures suggest, for of the Malaysians total only a minority were 'Malays' even in the liberal interpretation of that term, and furthermore the Chinese population was known to be increasing at a proportionately faster rate than that of the Malays and other indigenes in all the Borneo territories.

Secondly the growth of Communist terrorism in the Malay peninsula after 1948 inclined some British observers to argue that it might be wisest to isolate the more backward – but potentially valuable[38] – territories of Borneo from possible infection of this kind. Notwithstanding various disturbances in Sarawak shortly afterwards,[39] this view has been widely held ever since and is further reinforced by the desire of many of the politically conscious Malays in Brunei and other parts of Northern Borneo to prevent any fresh influx of Chinese, whether Communist or otherwise, from Singapore and the Malay peninsula. Equally important, and notwithstanding the basic Malaysian cultural affinities which both Borneo and Malaya share, many of the non-Muslim peoples, who form the majority of the indigenous inhabitants of North Borneo and Sarawak, have entertained doubts about the desirability of these territories joining forces with the predominantly Muslim Federation of Malaya.

Nevertheless in Northern Borneo, as well as in Singapore and the Federation of Malaya, opinion moved quickly after 1960, and there was growing belief that the advantages of federation would far outweigh its possible disadvantages, most

TABLE 93

FEDERATION OF MALAYSIA; SINGAPORE; AND BRUNEI: POPULATION

Political Unit	*Sources* (1960)	*Malaysians*	*Chinese*	*Total (including others)*
Federation of Malaya	estimated	3,460,956	2,552,276	6,909,009
Singapore . .	estimated	227,300	1,230,000	1,634,100
Brunei . .	census	59,203	21,798	83,877
Sarawak . .	census	509,852	229,154	744,529
North Borneo .	census	306,498	104,542	454,421
Malaysia . .	estimated	4,563,809	4,037,767	9,825,936

[38] At least in respect of oil and possibly also in providing strategic *points d'appui*, *e.g.* Labuan as a future alternative to Singapore.

[39] The most serious was the murder of the new Governor of Sarawak on December 3, 1949 by two Malays who opposed the ending of the Brooke family's rule. However this anti-cessionist movement seems to have subsided since that time.

of which, in any case, could be avoided or overcome with reasonable care and tolerance. It was presumably in the light of such considerations that in 1962 the British government gave its approval to the proposals of Tunku Abdul Rahman[40] for the setting up of the new Federation of Malaysia in 1963. And, in spite of the criticisms, not only from the Communist bloc, that these proposals represented a form of British-sponsored neo-colonialism, and the almost contrary fears on the part of others who believed that the interests of the Borneo indigenes were being sacrified to the ambitions of their more advanced neighbours on the opposite shore of the South China Sea, the Federation of Malaysia provided the most constructive way of ending the political retardation of Sarawak and North Borneo[41] and of enabling them to achieve meaningful independence as integral parts of a unit of sufficient size and economic diversity to be truly viable.

TABLE 94

NORTHERN BORNEO: SELECTED DATA

	Sarawak	*North Borneo*	*Brunei*
Area, square miles	47,498	29,387	2,226
Population	744,529	454,421	83,877
Density per square mile	16	16	38
Chinese as percentage of total	30·8	23·0	25·9
Capital	Kuching	Jesselton	Brunei
Wet paddy, acres	83,000	46,000	3,643
Dry paddy, acres	185,000	n.a.	2,766
Rice output, tons	n.a.	42,000	4,830
Rice import, tons	45,710	21,000	6,730
Rubber export/production, tons	49,961	22,034	1,023
Rubber export, $M million	122·4	49·5	1·7
Rubber planted, acres	*c.* 300,000	172,000	34,634
Timber export, $M million	43·6	90·7	n.a.
Oil export, $M million	28·7	—	300·4
Total exports, $M million	488·3	222·6	326·9
Total imports, $M million	44·9	195·0	78·5

Data for Sarawak and North Borneo are for 1960 throughout. Data for Brunei are for 1958, except population data which are for 1960.

Sources: *Sarawak Annual Report, 1960, North Borneo Annual Report, 1960, State of Brunei Annual Report, 1958, and Brunei Census of Population, 1960, Preliminary Release.*

[40] See above, p. 660.

[41] Note: North Borneo has since changed its name to Sabah.

TABLE 95

NORTHERN BORNEO: TRADE

(All figures in $M million)

A. SARAWAK

Imports	1956	1960	*Exports*	1956	1960
Mineral oils	321·5	251·0	Mineral oil products	356·7	287·0
Food	52·3	59·4	Rubber	68·6	122·4
Manufactures	35·1	30·1	Pepper	24·6	17·2
Machinery and vehicles	19·9	26·1	Timber	19·1	43·6
Beverages and tobacco	10·9	6·9	Sago flour	2·4	2·8
Chemicals	9·5	15·2	Jelutong	1·6	0·8
Raw materials	5·0	11·0	Bauxite	n.a.	5·0
Total (including others)	464·4	444·9	Total (including others)	487·0	488·3
Total (excluding oil)	142·5	205·0	Total exluding petroleum re-exports)	130·3	203·0

B. NORTH BORNEO

Imports	1956	1960	*Exports*	1956	1960
Provisions	19·3	22·3	Rubber	40·3	49·5
Machinery and transport equipment	16·1	30·0	Timber	26·2	90·7
Metal manufactures	5·0	12·1	Copra (including re-exports)	23·3	40·2
Textiles and clothing	8·3	9·2	Tobacco	3·4	5·3
Rice	8·3	8·4	Cutch	2·1	1·6
Oils	5·9	15·8	Abacá	2·1	5·2
Tobacco manufactures	4·3	12·8	Dried and salt fish	0·9	0·7
Motor vehicles	3·3	7·4	Firewood	0·3	0·6
Building materials	2·8	2·8			
Sugar	2·6	3·5			
Total (including others)	117·4	195·9	Total (including others)	119·4	222·6

C. BRUNEI

Imports	1956	1960	*Exports*	1956	1958
Food	16·2	13·2	Crude oil	309·3	300·4
Mineral fuels, etc.	2·5	3·0	Plantation rubber	3·9	1·7
Chemicals	5·0	4·9	Natural gas	0·7	0·6
Manufactured goods	29·4	14·3	Jelutong	0·3	0·5
Total (including others)	105·2	78·5	Total (including others)	314·3	326·9

DIRECTION OF TRADE

SARAWAK, 1959

Imports from: Brunei 295·1, U.K. 37·8, Singapore 22·3, Thailand 17·5, China 13·0, Hong Kong 10·2, Japan 10·0 (North Borneo 0·4)

Exports to: Singapore 209·5, Australia 80·1, Japan 74·4, U.K. 56·5, Netherlands 33·2, U.S.A. 26·7, Indonesia 17·9 (North Borneo 0·6), (Brunei 5·0).

NORTH BORNEO, 1959

Imports from: U.K. 31·8, Indonesia 20·1, Philippines 17·7, U.S.A. 14·7, Hong Kong 12·1, Thailand 8·9, Singapore 8·8.

Exports to: Japan 70·5, U.K. 20·0, Singapore 19·4, Hong Kong 11·8, Australia 9·4, U.S.A. 7.·8

Sources: Based mainly on *Yearbook of international trade statistics, U.N.*

Such at least were the high hopes of 1963, but the subsequent hostility of Indonesia's anti-Malaysian 'confrontation'[42] had already borne harshly upon northern Borneo even before the withdrawal of Singapore from the new Federation[43] cast further doubts upon the latter's capacity to survive. To those, like the writer, who believed that, by providing in this critical focal area at the heart of South-east Asia a stable framework within which further economic and political advance could be made, the Federation of Malaysia represented an inspiring consummation of 150 years of British rule, the events of 1965 appear as a tragic setback. One can only hope that the peoples concerned will be able to devise some new and more workable formula for maintaining and strengthening the closer association which the 1963 Federation was designed to provide.

SELECT BIBLIOGRAPHY

Baring-Gould and Bampfylde
Broek (K)
Carnell (B)
Fisher (Q)
Ginsburg, Kaplan and Roberts
Helbig (B)
Hodder (B)
Kahin (A)
Olver
Posewitz
Purcell (D)
Robequain (D)
Rutter
Tregonning (A) (B)

The Far Eastern Territories, Vol. V of An economic survey of the colonial territories
British Dependencies in the Far East, 1945- 1949
Brunei Annual Reports
North Borneo Annual Reports
Sarawak Annual Reports
Handbook of Sarawak
Colombo Plan Reports
Economic Surveys of Asia and the Far East
Americana Encyclopædia
Netherlands East Indies (N.I.D.), Vols. I and II.

Addenda: Note the new histories by Runciman (B) and Tregonning (C). See also the author's two articles on Malaysia *viz.* 'The geographical setting of the proposed Malaysian Federation,' *J.T.G.*, 17, 1963, 99–115 and 'The Malaysian Federation, Indonesia and the Philippines: a study in political geography, *G.J.*, 129, 1963, 311–328.

[42] See above, p. 390.
[43] See above, p. 660.

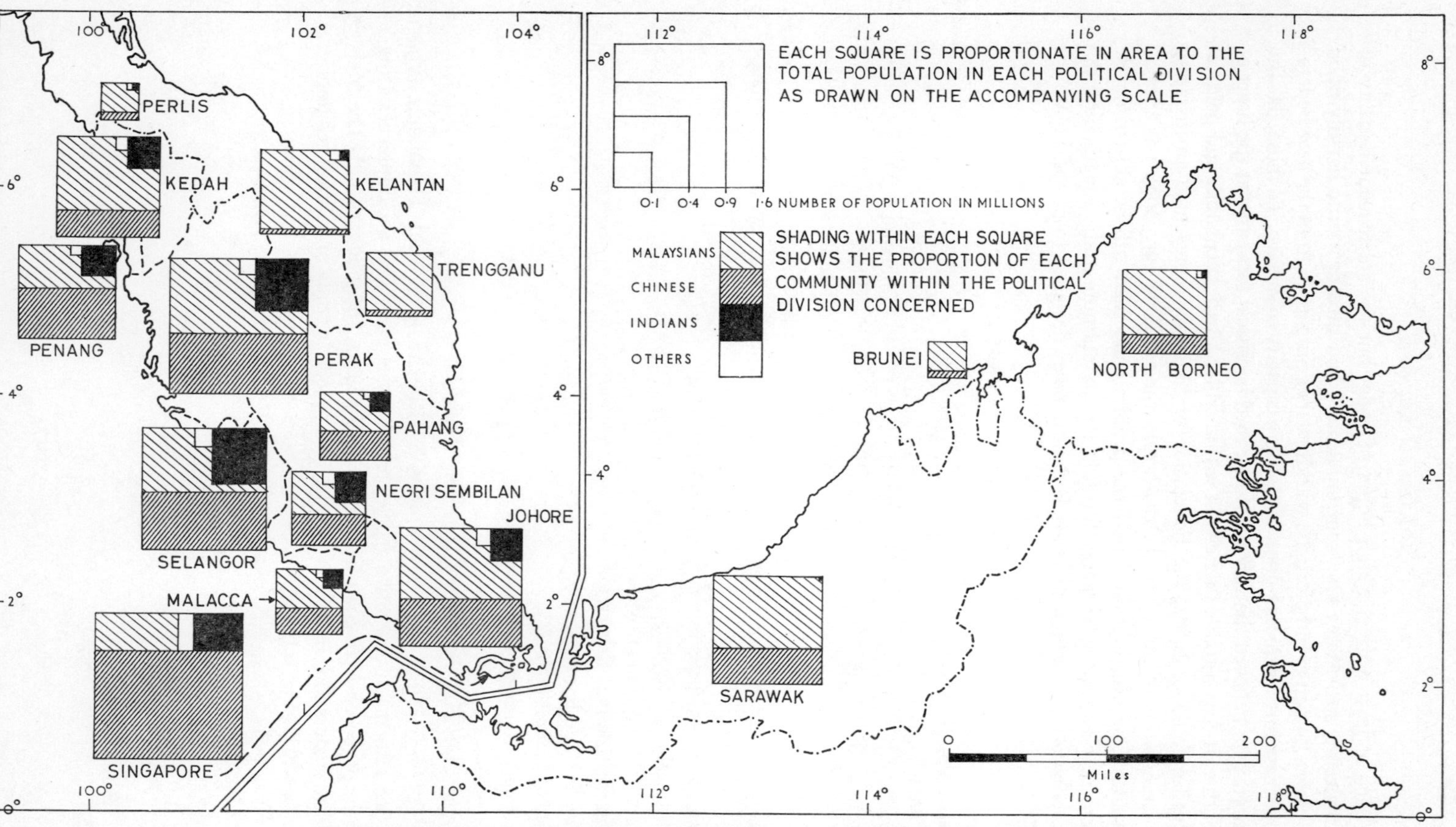

FIG. 98—Federation of Malaysia; Singapore; and Brunei: population by community

PART V

The Tropical Archipelago: The Philippines

CHAPTER 21

The Republic of the Philippines

I. INTRODUCTION

In relation to the rest of South-east Asia the Philippines occupies a marginal position. Indeed its structural links with the offshore island chains to the north are so strong and its historic ties across the Pacific so firmly established that some scholars prefer to exclude the archipelago from the South-east Asian realm altogether.

On the other hand, its separation from the rest of Malaysia and the mainland is, geologically speaking, a very recent phenomenon and its vegetation and fauna as well as its ethnic composition show very strong affinities with these neighbouring lands. Thus, while its position on the borders of the south-west Pacific has given rise to many distinctive traits which distinguish the Philippines from the other South-east Asian lands, these are for the most part only variations on themes which are common to that region as a whole, and in respect of physique, climate, population density, colonial antecedents and the legacy which these last have left in present-day economic and social patterns, the Philippines surely belongs within the South-east Asian realm.

Yet the fact remains that it has no indigenous civilization really comparable with those of the historic mainland kingdoms or the western islands of Indonesia, and largely as a result of this absence the period of colonial rule under Spain and more especially under the United States has wrought a much greater transformation in its way of life than that which has occurred in any of the neighbouring lands, with the possible exception of Malaya. For the time being, therefore, some element of doubt remains; the Philippines is indubitably in South-east Asia, but whether it is also in the fullest sense of South-east Asia only time will show.

II. PHYSICAL GEOGRAPHY

With a total area of 115,708 square miles the Philippines is slightly smaller than the British Isles, but thanks to its elaborate geographical sub-division it has a coastline very nearly as long as that of the United States. All-told 880 of the islands are inhabited and 462 have an area of not less than one square mile.[1] Nevertheless, the two largest, Luzon (40,422 square miles, or about four-fifths

[1] Official handbooks claim that there are 7,100 islands, though most of these are merely isolated pieces of rock or coral.

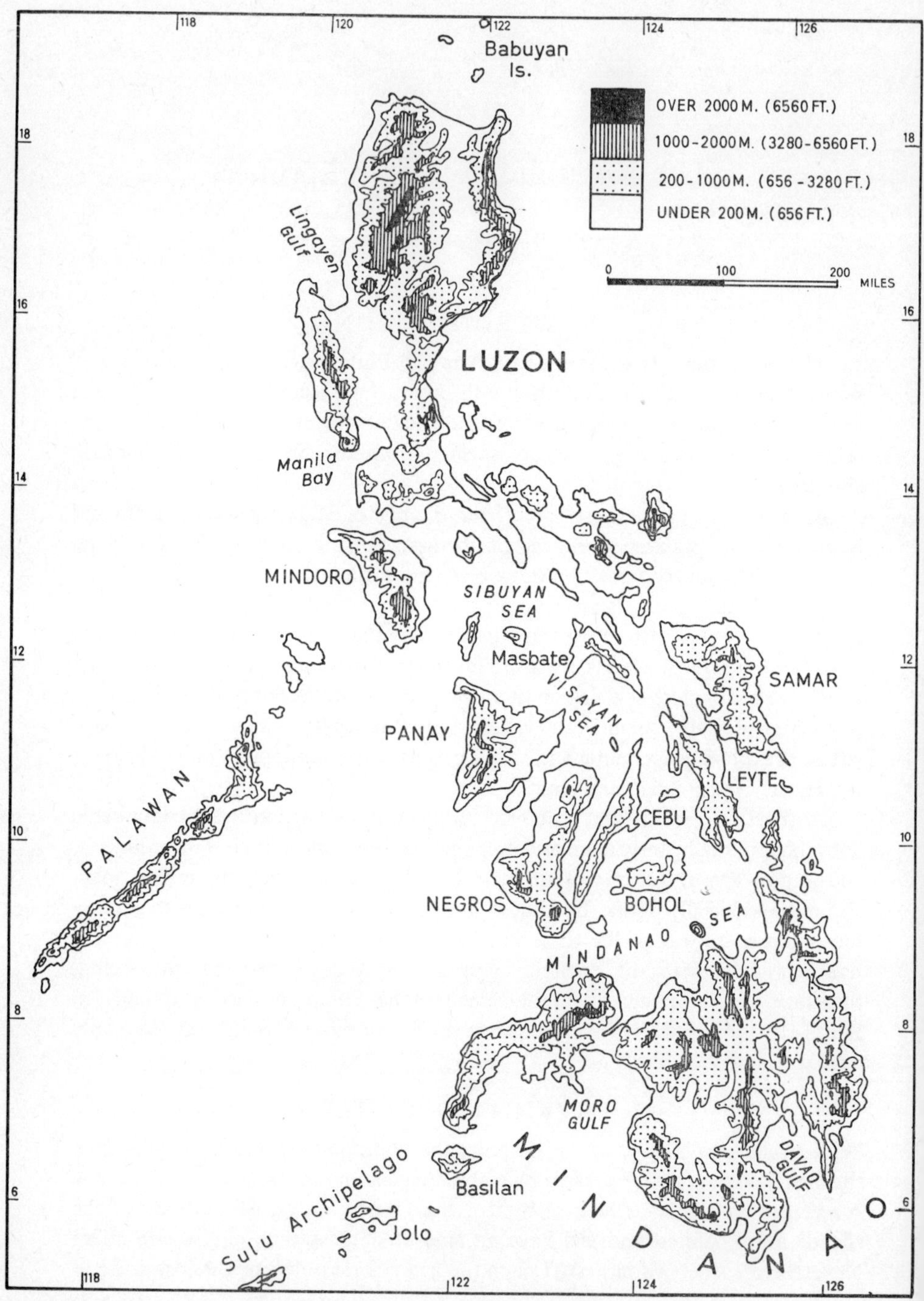

FIG. 99—The Philippines: relief

the size of Java) and Mindanao (36,538 square miles) together comprise 67 per cent of the total area, and a further nine, ranging from Samar (5,050 square miles) to Masbate (1,255 square miles) and including also Negros, Palawan Panay, Mindoro, Leyte, Cebu and Bohol, cover another 27 per cent.

Of the larger islands, Luzon and Mindanao are respectively the most northerly and the most southerly, the remainder either belonging to the Visayan group surrounding the 'mediterranean' sea of the same name in between or, in the case of Mindoro and Palawan, extending in a NE/SW direction from opposite central Luzon to the Balabak Straits off the north-eastern tip of Northern Borneo.

This general complexity of outline results in the main from the focal position occupied by the archipelago in respect of the Tertiary mountain building movements in the borderland between South-east Asia and the Western Pacific. Thus, the two parallel N/S lines of folding in north-central Luzon appear to represent a resurgence of the offshore arcs running through Formosa and the Ryu-kyus to Japan, while the more westerly of the two similar sets of N/S folds in interior Mindanao is clearly an extension of those in the Minahasa peninsula of Celebes. In between these two areas of longitudinal folding, however, the dominant trends in southern Luzon and the eastern Visayas swing approximately NW/SE, which is roughly at right angles to the equally pronounced NE/SW line through Palawan and the western Visayas and the parallel series through the western tip of Mindanao and the Sulu islands, both of which are linked with the folds of Northern Borneo.

With these as their principal axes, the islands resemble the upper portions of submarine mountain ranges. Nearly all have rugged interior uplands, rising usually to between 4,000 and 8,000 ft. (though Mt. Apo in Mindanao reaches 9,690 ft. and Mt. Pulog in Luzon 9,600 ft.), and even in the largest islands the coastal plains are rarely as much as ten miles wide. Apart from a few exposures of the ancient basement complex, mostly in Luzon, Mindoro and Panay, Tertiary sedimentaries and Tertiary-Quaternary eruptives are everywhere the dominant rocks. Besides a much larger number now extinct, over a dozen volcanoes are still regarded as active, the best known being the extremely violent Hibok-Hibok on Camiguin island to the north of Mindanao, but only a relatively small proportion of the volcanic ejecta in the country are basic in composition.

Like Japan, which it closely resembles in both structure and scale, the Philippines is seriously deficient in extensive areas of lowland. Of those which do exist the most important is the central plain of Luzon, whose rôle is analogous to that of the Tokyo plain in Japan. In addition, Luzon also contains the Cagayan valley in the north-east and the Bicol plain in the south-east, while elsewhere western Negros, south-eastern Panay and the Agusan and Cotobato lowlands of Mindanao also provide good agricultural land.

Two facts go far to determine the climatic pattern of the Philippines, namely the overall position of the islands both in latitude and in relation to the SW

TABLE 96

THE PHILIPPINES, SELECTED TEMPERATURE AND RAINFALL FIGURES

Station	*Jan.*	*Feb.*	*Mar.*	*Apr.*	*May*	*Jun.*	*Jul.*	*Aug.*	*Sep.*	*Oct.*	*Nov.*	*Dec.*	*Average*	*Total*
Manila 15° N, 120° E	78	79	81	83	84	83	82	82	81	80	79	77	81	
47	0·9	0·6	0·9	1·2	5·1	9·9	16·9	16·3	14·0	7·7	5·8	2·3		81·6
Baguio 16° N, 121° E	64	66	68	69	69	68	67	67	67	67	66	64	67	
c. 5000	1·2	1·0	2·5	5·2	14·0	14·2	50·2	47·1	39·7	14·3	2·9	2·7		195·1
Surigao 10° N, 126° E	78	79	80	81	81	82	82	82	81	80	79	78	80	
16	22·0	14·3	13·3	9·9	6·1	5·0	6·7	4·8	6·3	10·3	16·8	24·5		140·1
Basco Batanes 20° N, 122°E	72	73	75	79	81	83	83	82	81	80	77	73	78	
near S.L.	9·6	4·6	4·8	4·4	9·3	6·3	11·4	14·8	13·7	14·0	14·0	14·9		121·8
Zamboanga City 7° N, 122° E	80	80	81	81	81	81	80	81	81	81	81	81	81	
23	2·1	2·2	1·5	2·0	3·5	4·2	4·9	4·0	4·7	5·6	4·2	3·4		42·3
Dadiangas, Cotabato 6° N, 125° E														
near S.L.	2·0	2·5	3·2	2·2	4·3	4·7	3·6	4·5	3·4	3·8	3·2	2·7		39·9

monsoon and the NE trade winds, and the almost complete continuity of the mountain systems from north to south.

While in the southern extremity of the archipelago temperatures show an approximation to the equatorial régime, the whole country may fairly be classed as tropical. As in Indonesia, however, maritime influences make for greater evenness throughout the year than is normal for the latitude, so that mean monthly temperatures at Basco in the Batanes (20° 30′ N) vary only from 72° in January to 83° in June, at Manila (14° 40′) from 77° in December to 84° in May, and at Zamboanga City (6° 55′) from 79° in February to 80° in May.[2]

Rainfall, on the other hand, shows considerable diversity both in total amounts and in the pattern of seasonal incidence. In a few inland rain-shadow areas, such as the Cagayan valley of Luzon and parts of Mindanao, the annual total is less than 60 in., the lowest reading of all being 39·9 in. at Dadiangas in the southern interior of Mindanao. But elsewhere much heavier rain is normal, with totals mostly over 80 in., and in many areas at least double that figure.

Nevertheless, at nearly all stations there is a wide variation between the wettest and the driest month, the details in this respect depending on the general aspect and the local relief of the place in question. As a rule the western fringes of the archipelago receive much the greater part of their rainfall from the SW monsoon, between late June and the end of September, and while the amount of this

[2] *Cf.* the temperature ranges of such mainland stations as Akyab 14°, Rangoon 10°, Mandalay 20°, Saigon 6° and Hanoi 21°. See above, Table 48, p. 422.

varies widely according to the degree of exposure, virtually all such areas are very dry during the winter months, when they are effectively sheltered from the prevailing NE winds. Thus, for example, Manila gets only 5·9 in. for the five months December–April, out of an annual total of 81·6 in., with July and August (respectively 16·9 and 16·3 in.) as its two wettest months.

On the eastern side of the archipelago the wettest period of the year is usually from November to March, when the prevailing winds are from the NE. But while the winds over the South China Sea at this time of the year may not unreasonably be referred to as monsoonal,[3] those over the eastern Philippines represent the normal trade-wind circulation in such latitudes. Admittedly, even as far east as this, that circulation is much modified during the summer months when the SW monsoon is at its height over the South China Sea and not infrequently extends right across to the eastern side of the Philippines, thus replacing the onshore winds which in any case are usually weak and erratic at this season. Nevertheless, the climate along the eastern side of the Philippines does resemble the normal trade-wind type, and in contrast to the west these areas have no true dry season.[4] A subsidiary source of rainfall in the eastern Philippines north of Mindanao is provided by typhoons which occur most frequently in late summer and autumn, and whose effects are most strongly felt in the exposed coastal regions of eastern Luzon and Samar, but only very exceptionally to the south of this.

Between the outward facing zones of east and west, the rainfall in the interiors of Luzon and Mindanao and the inner portions of the Visayas is transitional in pattern and generally smaller in total volume. While in the northern two-thirds of this intermediate zone a short dry season occurs in the early part of the year, the southernmost areas, namely Bohol, eastern Leyte and central Mindanao, have a somewhat more even distribution with no real dry season, but the total amount of rain is nevertheless much smaller than that along the east coast.[5] Despite much local variation in this respect it is true to say that the transitional zone contains the only parts of the country where total rainfall in either half of the year is liable to be inadequate for rice cultivation without irrigation.

For the rest, the only important variations in climatic type are in the higher mountains. In general, as is shown by the accompanying figures for Baguio (*c.* 120 miles to the north of Manila) these upland climates have similar rhythms to the adjacent lowlands, though with heavier rainfall, and with temperatures roughly 3° lower for every 1,000 ft. above sea-level.

To the casual observer the Philippines may appear singularly favourable as a

[3] See above, p. 29.

[4] See the figures for Surigao, Table 96. While it may be argued that the Philippines should be excluded from the tropical monsoon category altogether, the archipelago is probably best regarded as marginally monsoonal.

[5] This division follows Kolb (p. 40). Note that the concave stretch of the east coast of Luzon has a significantly lower rainfall than the rest of the eastern Philippines, and for this reason is included in Kolb's second transitional type.

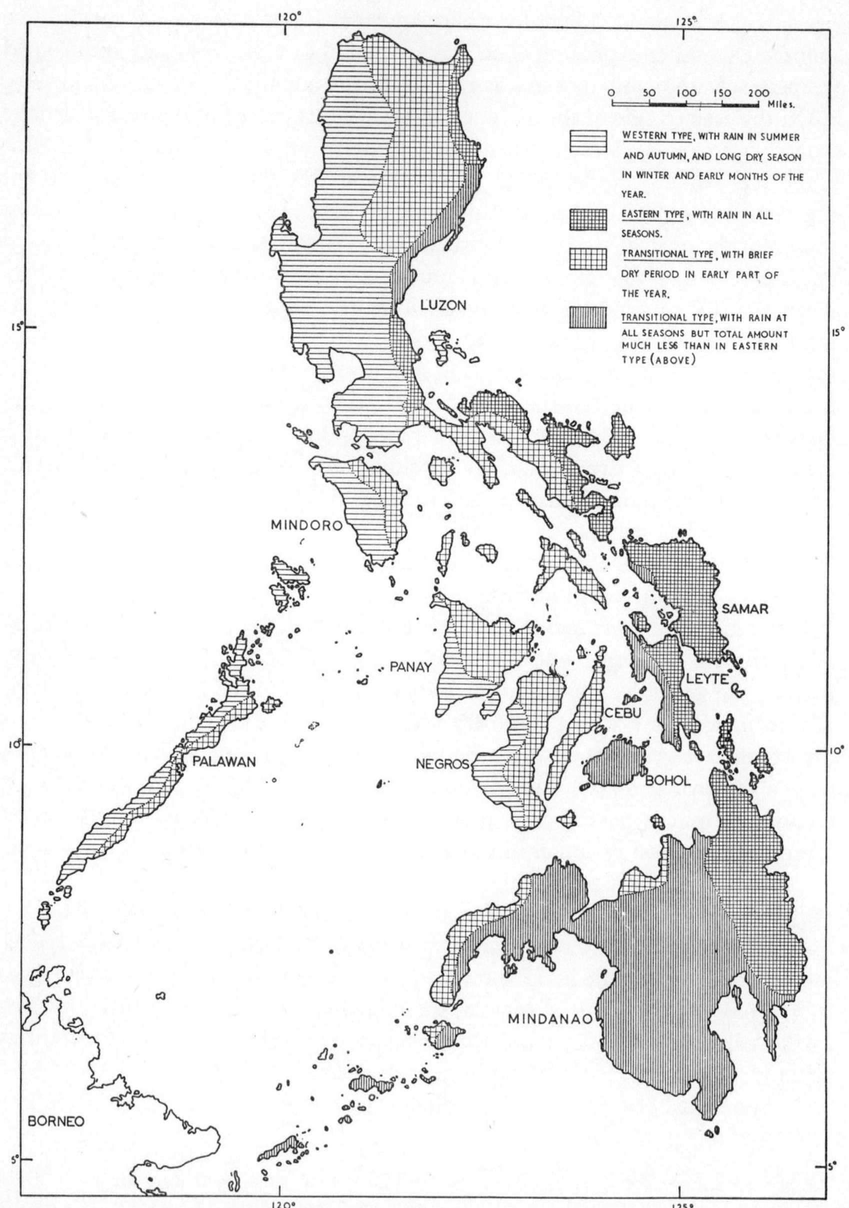

120°
125°
0 50 100 150 200 Miles.
WESTERN TYPE, WITH RAIN IN SUMMER AND AUTUMN, AND LONG DRY SEASON IN WINTER AND EARLY MONTHS OF THE YEAR.
EASTERN TYPE, WITH RAIN IN ALL SEASONS.
TRANSITIONAL TYPE, WITH BRIEF DRY PERIOD IN EARLY PART OF THE YEAR.
TRANSITIONAL TYPE, WITH RAIN AT ALL SEASONS BUT TOTAL AMOUNT MUCH LESS THAN IN EASTERN TYPE (ABOVE)
LUZON
15°
MINDORO
SAMAR
PANAY
LEYTE
CEBU
10°
PALAWAN
NEGROS
BOHOL
MINDANAO
BORNEO
5°

FIG. 100—The Philippines: climatic types

home for man. From almost every angle of approach the first appearance of the natural landscape is one of palm-fringed shores rarely obstructed by any significant mangrove swamps, and backed inland by a luxuriant growth of forest. Further inland on the slopes of the mountain ranges which are never far removed from the shore, the vegetation changes gradually from true rain forest to a mixed tropical evergreen type, but it is only on the upper slopes of the often extremely beautiful volcanic cones that the crenellated outline of the forest trees is replaced by a smooth skyline.

Faced with such a prospect it is not difficult to understand the enthusiasm which inspired Justice George A. Malcolm to describe the Philippines as 'the most favoured group of tropical islands in the world. On the fertile land of these islands, nature has bestowed her bounties in harmonious combination. . . . The natural resources of the Philippines are so varied and represent so much wealth as hardly to be within the comprehension of mere man.'[6]

Yet these appearances are in large measure deceptive. In the first place most of the very limited patches of lowland lie within the zone of least plentiful and least reliable rainfall. Over these areas, especially where the dry season is very prolonged, tall but almost useless tropical grass (*Imperata cylindrica*, locally known as *cogon*) and intermittent patches of bamboo form the dominant vegetation, and such *cogonales* have also spread over other marginal areas as a result of shifting cultivation.

Moreover, the soils are by no means exceptionally fertile, apart from the small proportion derived from basic volcanic ejecta and those along the coasts of Cebu and a few other parts of the Visayas which have been formed from recently uplifted coral reefs. Outside Luzon and Mindanao the rivers are too small to provide any extensive tracts where fertility is renewed by seasonal flooding, and most of the sedentary soils show clear evidence of laterization. Thus, while it is often stated that at least 40 million acres, or 54 per cent of the country is cultivable,[7] compared with the 27·3 per cent at present cultivated, and that the islands could with ease support 70–80 million people, the fact remains that, outside Mindanao, most of the best lands are already in use, and any substantial increase in upland cultivation would run a grave risk of promoting soil erosion, both there and in the plains below.

However, while the physique thus imposes real limits on the agricultural potential of the islands, the long coastline has been of great value in facilitating movement and, as in the Indonesian archipelago, navigation within the inner seas presents few hazards except for the occasional typhoon. But in the Philippines, whose layout recalls that of Japan rather than that of Indonesia, no great expanses of sea separate the islands one from another; even in Luzon and

[6] Former Justice of the Supreme Court of the Philippine Commonwealth. Quoted in *Facts about the Philippines*, p. 6.

[7] This much higher proportion than Japan's 16 per cent is related to the tropical temperatures which permit of cultivation at higher altitudes.

Mindanao no point is as much as 75 miles from the coast, while elsewhere the maximum distance is less than 30 miles. Thus both the individual islands and the archipelago as a whole are much more easily manageable units than their Indonesian counterparts and the task of administrative unification has accordingly presented far less difficulty.[8]

III. THE HUMAN GEOGRAPHY OF PRE-COLONIAL AND COLONIAL TIMES

The peopling of the Philippines has occurred as the result of a series of migrations from the continental mainland and the Indonesian archipelago, the earliest movements taking place before the post-glacial rise in sea-level destroyed the continuity of the land bridges, and the more recent ones following by sea along the lines of islands which survived this change. As elsewhere in South-east Asia, successive invasions led to some displacement of population from the coastlands to the interior, though much intermingling also occurred between the newcomers and the pre-existing peoples in the former regions.

Although the sequence of migrations is not wholly clear, it may be assumed that the present-day Negrito Aëtas represent the descendants of the earliest human occupants of the islands. These extremely primitive peoples, probably numbering less than 50,000, nowadays survive only in minute groups in the Zambales mountains and Sierra Madre of Luzon, and a few interior districts in Mindanao and the Visayas, and like their counterparts in Malaya and Indonesia practise a hunting and gathering economy.

Probably many thousands of years after the arrival of the Negritos came the first of many waves of Nesiot peoples, some of them presumably via Borneo and others, including the confusingly named Indonesian A and B invaders, directly across the sea from the Chinese or Tonkinese mainland. The introduction of *caiñgin* or shifting cultivation is generally attributed to the Nesiot peoples and this practice,[9] nowadays with a greater emphasis on maize than on dry rice, is still in use among some 500,000 tribespeople, of predominantly Nesiot origin, in the interiors of Mindanao, Palawan, some of the larger Visayas and parts of Luzon.

However, the best-known Nesiot peoples of the northern interior of Luzon, namely the Bontocs and Ifugaos[10] are sedentary cultivators of wet rice, who at the cost of a prodigious expenditure of human energy have built magnificent terraced fields extending in places several thousand feet up the mountain sides. These practices, which are capable of supporting very high densities of population

[8] An interesting consequence of this geographical pattern is that the inner seas of the Philippines have always been regarded as the latter's territorial waters and not as the high seas. This situation finds a parallel in Japan's Inland Sea, but is in marked contrast to that in Indonesia prior to the latter's claim of December 13, 1957 (see above, p. 379), which has not been conceded by most other maritime powers.

[9] Though now illegal, shifting cultivation is still practised.

[10] Often referred to collectively as Igorots, a general – and in origin deprecatory – term meaning mountain people.

locally in mountainous countryside, must originally have been learned from the mainland Chinese, and it is significant that they are found exclusively within the northern half of Luzon. Yet the people who follow them are in other respects backward and, though in recent years they have abandoned head-hunting, the great majority, like the other Nesiot inlanders farther south, are still animists.

The last major migrations to the Philippines were of Pareœan peoples who first began to penetrate from western Indonesia via Borneo, Palawan and the Sulu archipelago to the coast lands of the Visayas, southern Luzon and Mindanao in the last few centuries B.C. These movements probably continued throughout the greater part of the pre-European period, and represented in effect the outer ripples of the great Pareœan wave spreading slowly eastwards throughout the whole Malaysian island realm.

So far as the Philippines was concerned, the shores of the Visayan Sea served as the centre from which further diffusion took place by sea, the invaders arriving in small bands under their own chieftains and establishing themselves usually in favourable river-mouth localities around the coasts. Today the Pareœan element comprises the largest single component in the population nearly everywhere[11] except in the remoter interiors of the two largest islands though, owing to the relative recency of the migrations, the proportion which it forms in the total ethnic make-up of the modern Filipino population is probably less than among the Javanese or the coast peoples of Sumatra.

While the later Pareœan groups were the bearers of an Indianized culture, evidence of which survives in the prevalent methods of lowland rice cultivation, in art and architectural styles and in the vocabulary of the numerous regional languages,[12] it seems improbable that any direct Indian settlement occurred in the islands or that the latter ever formed part of Sri Vijaya or Madjapahit in any meaningful manner, as has traditionally been claimed.[13]

However, with the arrival of Islam, likewise via northern Borneo, in the late 15th century, the islands became rather less of a cultural backwater than they had been hitherto. During the course of the next hundred years the faith obtained a firm hold in Sulu, Palawan and Mindanao, and even as far north as Luzon Muslim warrior chieftains began to set themselves up as territorial rulers (datos and rajahs) in the fashion which had already become familiar in other parts of Malaysia. Nevertheless, when in 1565, some 44 years after Magellan had claimed the archipelago for Spain,[14] Legaspi established the first permanent settlement there, the Philippines was still a relatively empty region, with a population of

[11] This applies to the Muslim Moros (see below, p. 725) no less than to the Christian Filipinos.

[12] Some of which were formerly written in Indian-style scripts. All the languages in the archipelago, except those of the Negritos, belong to the Malayo-Polynesian group.

[13] As described above, pp. 116–7, recent historical research is casting increasing doubts on the latter connexion. But some trading links doubtless existed between the Philippines and Indonesia in pre-Islamic times.

[14] Several unsuccessful attempts at establishing settlements had been made during these 44 years.

only half a million, virtually no political organization except at the local level, and only a thin and far from ubiquitous veneer of Islam superimposed on a wholly pagan base.

It was largely because the Philippines presented such a *tabula rasa* that the Spaniards were able so effectively to stamp their own culture on the islands, and indeed had they not established their rule there in the 16th century other peoples might well have done so instead. Thus the Chinese had long shown interest in the islands, and in 1405 the Ming Emperor had even sent an officer to govern Luzon.[15] Though nothing appears to have come of this venture politically, individual Chinese traders were well established in the islands before the Spaniards took over, and thereafter two Chinese pirate leaders, namely Limahong (1574) and Koxinga (1662), attempted unsuccessfully to capture Manila. The Japanese also were active as traders and buccaneers in Philippine waters from the 15th century until 1637, and in 1592 the Spanish Governor felt it prudent to pay the tribute demanded by Hideyoshi.[16] But within less than half a century the growing influence of Spain in the surrounding seas played a major part in causing the Japanese to adopt the introvert policies which thereafter eliminated them from the scene until the closing decades of the 19th century.

In seeking a base for Spanish power in the Philippines, Legaspi turned in the first instance to Cebu, the long narrow island which had earlier attracted Magellan's attention both because it lay in the latitude of the main west-bound sailing route across the Pacific (between 10° and 12° N), and also because of its key position in relation to the focal Visayan Sea. But though Legaspi did establish a settlement at Cebu City, the activities of the Portuguese based on the Moluccas led him to shift his attention, first to Panay (1569) and then to Luzon, where in 1570 he captured the small Muslim stronghold of Manila.

Despite its eccentric position relative to the archipelago as a whole, Manila had a magnificent natural harbour, well sheltered from typhoons and not far removed from the northern entrance to the Visayan Sea. Since, moreover, it stood at the gateway to the largest and most productive lowland in the region, Legaspi's decision to build a new Spanish city there to serve as the seat of administration for the whole archipelago (1572) proved well founded. Within a few years Manila had eclipsed Cebu, and before the end of the century had become the greatest port in eastern Asia, frequented by the ships of China, Japan, India, the Middle East and the rest of the Malaysian lands.

Meanwhile Legaspi had extended Spanish control outwards from Manila over most of the coastal regions in the northern two-thirds of the archipelago.[17] And while he organized both the military conquest and the civil administration which followed, the Augustinian friars led by his cousin Urdaneta,[18] were no less

[15] Purcell (D), p. 582. [16] At that time the *de facto* ruler of Japan.

[17] The unification of the Spanish and Portuguese thrones 1580–1640 put a stop to the Portuguese threat to the Visayas.

[18] It was Urdaneta who discovered the eastward sailing route using the Westerlies. See above, pp. 131–2.

ardent in spreading the Catholic faith. Thanks to the superficiality of the Islamic hold in the north and centre, the missionaries met with little resistance there, but in Palawan, Sulu and most of Mindanao the Muslim faith was too firmly established for the Spaniards ever to dislodge it or even indeed to bring the population under their own effective administration.[19]

Thus, although they made a settlement near Zamboanga in western Mindanao in 1596, they were driven out of it in 1599 by the local Muslim population, whom they referred to as Moros (*i.e.* Moors). Thereafter, despite many further attempts to subdue the far south, the Spaniards did not fully succeed in breaking the power of the Moros and preventing the raids of Muslim pirates even as far north as Manila, until the middle of the 19th century when the coming of the steamship eventually decided the issue.

Administratively the Philippines formed a single Governorship within the Vice-Royalty of New Spain, which centred in Mexico and included also the adjacent parts of Central America and the Caribbean, and this position as an outpost of a dependency, two whole oceans removed from the mother country, goes far to explain the comparative neglect from which the islands suffered.

In the absence of any spectacular wealth in precious metals[20] or spices, so remote a region offered little scope for economic development even if the Spaniards had not been wedded to restrictive mercantilist dogmas. In these circumstances, therefore, the missionary activity of the friars, who by the 17th century included Franciscans, Jesuits and Dominicans as well as the original Augustinians, tended to dominate the scene, and the Philippines, under Spanish rule has aptly been called 'the empire of the friars'. For the most part the economy was one of great landed estates such as the Spaniards had already set up in the Americas, and huge areas were made over in this way to religious organizations and individual conquistadores. However, the number of the latter who settled in this remote archipelago remained very small, and hardly any of them brought European wives. Thus the greater part of the landowning class consisted of *caciques*, the descendants of the traditional territorial chieftains whom the Spaniards effectively confirmed in power and with whose families they intermarried freely.

While, as noted in Chapter 5, the Spaniards introduced many new crops, particularly from the Americas, they did almost nothing to stimulate economic progress in any other way. Overseas trade, which slowly dwindled after the early 17th century,[21] remained a governmental monopoly until into the 19th century and in any case most of the galleon traffic, via Mexico to Spain, consisted of Chinese produce for which Manila served merely as the trans-shipment port. Moreover, while the Church provided a fairly extensive system of rudimentary schooling and also some higher education extending even to the university

[19] See Spencer, J. E. (A), Fig. 92, p. 286.

[20] There was a little gold but it did not become commercially important until the 1930s.

[21] Manila lost its pre-eminence to Batavia in the 17th century.

level,[22] practically the only opportunities for qualified Filipinos lay in the lower ranks of the administration, in teaching and in the service of the Church.

In its almost complete lack of an indigenous commercial middle class the Philippines differed little from the other Spanish colonial territories or even from the mother country itself. But the Philippines was nevertheless part of South-east Asia, and despite all the restrictions of Spanish policy the commercial enterprise of the Chinese found some opportunities in these islands with which they had been familiar for so long. Indeed it was primarily Chinese initiative which lay behind the original development of Manila as an entrepôt, and in the early days of Spanish rule the numbers of Chinese in the country grew rapidly, notwithstanding the massacres of 1603 and 1639. Subsequently, however, the greater commercial opportunities afforded in the more progressive Dutch colonies tended to reduce the flow to the Philippines,[23] but the Chinese community still continued to increase slowly. By 1850 it included some 30,000 in Manila and another 20,000 in the rest of the archipelago, together with a much larger number of mestizos, and all-told its share in the internal commerce of the islands was very great.

After the revolt of the Spanish American colonies, beginning in 1808, the Philippines became even more isolated than it had been before. The last Manila galleon sailed to Mexico in 1811 and thereafter the commercial as well as the administrative links with Spain were re-routed via the Cape of Good Hope. About the same time a gradual relaxation began of the rigid restrictions on foreign trade, but otherwise the Spaniards failed to appreciate the measure of the changes required if the Philippines was to be prevented from following the lead of the American colonies.

With the opening of the Suez canal foreign commercial interests increased, and more and more Filipino students began to attend Spanish and other European universities. It was this group which provided the nucleus of the first nationalist organization, the Liga Filipina, founded in 1891 by the Chinese mestizo José Rizal y Mercado. But while Rizal and his associates sought to work through constitutional reform, mounting popular resentment against the wealth and privilege enjoyed by the friars, the Church and the *caciques* eventually precipitated the insurrection of 1896. Although this was temporarily suppressed, the nationalists again took up arms against the Spaniards when the latter became involved in the war of 1898, which resulted a year later in the transfer of the islands to American rule.

Despite the obvious defects which had served to hasten its end, the Spanish occupation of the Philippines had nevertheless left much of permanent value. In the course of three centuries the congeries of little coastal settlements had

[22] The College of Santo Tomas, Manila, was founded in 1619 and became a university in 1645. Others followed during the period of Spanish rule, long before anything of a comparable nature was established in any other part of South-east Asia.

[23] Purcell (D), p. 602.

been organized into a single political entity whose people, once the most isolated and retarded, had become the most Westernized in all South-east Asia. Moreover, thanks in the main to the introduction of law and order by the Spaniards, the population had grown from an estimated 500,000 in the late 16th century to 1,500,000 in 1800 and to nearly 7,000,000 by 1899.

When, therefore, the Americans took over from Spain, they found firm foundations on which to build. But although considerations of wartime strategy had prompted Dewey's seizure of the islands, it was by no means clear that the United States would wish to retain control over them. Apart from a vague and ill-founded belief that Manila might be revived as a great Far Eastern entrepôt,[24] economics scarcely entered into the discussion, and the eventual decision to annex was made mainly on strategic grounds. As such it represented a triumph for Theodore Roosevelt and the other adherents of Mahan who had consistently worked for the establishment of a series of forward naval bases in the western Pacific. Yet while there was every reason to believe that if the United States had not annexed the islands, the Germans or the Japanese would have done so instead, the sorely troubled anti-colonial conscience of the Americans was only salved by a solemn declaration that the aim of their government was not selfish interest but rather the promotion of the 'happiness, peace and prosperity of the people of the Philippine Islands'.

Under the Republican party, then and for many years afterwards in power in the United States, the policy adopted towards the Philippines was paternal but benevolent, and the emphasis it placed upon the expansion of health and educational services and the promotion of economic progress continued throughout the whole period of American rule.

Outstanding success was achieved in the first two of these aims, the death-rate falling from 28 per 1,000 in 1905 to under 19 in 1939 and the literacy rate meanwhile rising from 18 to 48 per cent. In the economic field however, the achievements were less satisfactory. Admittedly, the growth in population from 7,635,000 in 1903 to 16,000,303 in 1939 was matched by an increase in the area under cultivation from 6,988,200 to 16,533,900 acres over the same period, and the value of foreign trade expanded even more dramatically from $34 million in 1899 to $297 million in 1941.[25] But against this the Americans, believing that development would best be promoted by providing a framework of transport and other basic utilities and for the rest relying on the free play of economic forces, made no serious attempt to alter the established pattern of land-holding, and the *caciques* thus maintained their traditional pre-eminence in the economic and political life of the country.

In order to prevent non-Filipinos from setting up a plantation economy, which was at variance with American anti-colonial ideals, the administration

[24] Hong Kong was by this time too well established in this rôle for Manila, with fewer geographical advantages, to offer serious competition.

[25] Zinkin (A), p. 162.

limited to 2,532 acres the amount of public land which could be held by corporations. For this reason American rubber capital avoided the islands, finding its outlets instead chiefly in Malaya and Sumatra,[26] and most of the production of the other commercial staples which developed after the inclusion of the Philippines within the United States tariff area in 1909 remained largely in Filipino hands.[27]

Nevertheless, this so-called free-trade policy was not an unmixed blessing. For while it led to a great increase in the output of sugar, abacá, coconut oil and copra, which together formed three-quarters of the total exports, much of this production was very inefficient, and survived only by virtue of its privileged market position compared with that of most of its competitors.

Moreover, the expansion of cash-crop cultivation took place at least partially at the expense of food production, so that the Philippines became increasingly dependent on imports from overseas.[28] Further, the free-trade policy gave little scope for the development of manufacturing industry, and indeed with 80 per cent of the exports destined for the United States and a similar proportion of imports coming from that country, the Philippines showed a higher degree of economic dependence on the metropolitan power than any other colonial territory in all South-east Asia.

Finally, although the average *per capita* income was greatly increased under American rule, this fact was of little account to a large section of the rural population. For a wholly disproportionate share of the wealth was in the hands of a small upper stratum, consisting mainly of the *cacique* families, together with many Chinese and a few Spaniards and Americans. Nearly 70 per cent of the retail trade was controlled by the Chinese and Japanese,[29] over 70 per cent of the rice mills were owned by Chinese, and at least 80 per cent of the overseas trade was conducted by non-Filipino concerns.

Admittedly, these defects had arisen in spite of, rather than because of, American intentions, and in any case they did not invalidate the latter's notable achievements in other respects. But when in 1907 the first elective legislative assembly was set up, it was clear that American benevolence could not assuage the nationalist sentiments which had been aroused under the Spanish regime. From the outset, Manuel L. Quezon's Nacionalista party, which demanded immediate independence, dominated the scene and continued so to do throughout the rest of the period of American rule.

On this issue the two political parties in the United States differed significantly, and it was under the Democrats that both the Jones Act of 1916 and the Tydings-McDuffie Act of 1934 were passed. The latter provided for a ten-year transitional period of Commonwealth government, under which the United States would

[26] Pelzer (C), p. 105.

[27] Apart from their large share of small-holder cultivation, Filipinos today own over 50 per cent of the invested capital in their own country, a situation which is without parallel in the other former colonial lands of South-east Asia. See Higgins (B).

[28] This dates from Spanish colonial times.

[29] See below, pp. 726–7.

retain control over foreign policy and defence, but in other respects the Philippines, with its own elected President, would enjoy almost unfettered home rule. The Commonwealth was inaugurated in November 1935 with Quezon as President and with every prospect of outright independence in 1946.

Despite the preparation for self-government which the Filipinos had received at United States' hands, the Commonwealth speedily showed that a Latin-American style economy breeds Latin-American style democracy. The power of the landlords and a few related business interests was immense and corruption a byword, and there was growing concern as to whether the Philippine export trade could survive once the country lost its privileged access to the huge American market.

Nevertheless, nationalist demands were more nearly satisfied in the Philippines than in any other Asian dependency, and when the Japanese attacked on December 8, 1941, Filipino as well as the American troops fought a magnificent defensive action for five months against far superior forces. Moreover, even after the Japanese victory, it was still clear that the Filipinos thought of themselves as a free people, and for this reason the Japanese in October 1943 set up a supposedly independent republic under the Presidency of José P. Laurel, the lawful President (Quezon) and Vice-President (Osmeña) having been evacuated by the Americans shortly before the surrender in order to head the government-in-exile in Washington.

After the Americans had recaptured the Philippines in the closing phases of the war, the Commonwealth government returned to Manila under President Osmeña, and notwithstanding the appalling chaos and devastation in the islands the United States kept its pledge to grant full independence. Elections were quickly held, and on July 4, 1946 the Republic of the Philippines was inaugurated, with Manuel A. Roxas as its first President.[30]

IV. THE REPUBLIC OF THE PHILIPPINES: ECONOMIC GEOGRAPHY AND ECONOMIC PROBLEMS

From its very inception the new Republic of the Philippines has had to grapple with a host of difficult problems. In so far as United States' action could help, notably in the more urgent tasks of rehabilitation and in softening the blow to the export trade caused by withdrawal from the American tariff area, such assistance was immediately forthcoming. All-told the Philippines received some $2,500 million from the United States during 1945–55,[31] and the Philippines Trade Act of 1946 (the Bell Act) provided for the continuation of reciprocal free

[30] Roxas died in April 1948, and was succeeded by Vice-President Elpidio Quirino; the latter was re-elected President in 1949. President Quezon died in 1944.

[31] This figure (from Vandenbosch and Butwell, p. 105) includes such items as back pay for the Philippines armed forces, redemption of guerrilla currency, war-damage compensation, etc. Specifically economic aid for the period 1946–57 has been estimated by the *New York Times* at $848 million. The amount in 1957 alone was $33·9 million.

trade until July 1954, after which date tariffs on both sides would rise annually by 5 per cent of the normal rate, the latter eventually coming into effect in 1974.[32] Later, in 1954 the Bell Act was revised in the Philippines' favour by the Laurel-Langley agreement, whereby duties on Philippines produce entering the United States were to be raised more slowly, while those on American goods entering the Philippines were to go up more quickly.

Thanks to this help the Philippines, which from 1942 to 1945 had suffered the worst devastation in all South-east Asia, had by 1957 made a more impressive economic recovery than most of its neighbours. But it is arguable that a more drastic reorientation of the export trade, though painful to certain economic interests in the country, would in the long run have been more beneficial, and in addition to this there are other deep-seated problems, both economic and social, which still remain to be solved.

At the root of nearly all the country's difficulties lie the twin problems of population pressure and land tenure. Between 1939 and 1960[33] the total population rose from 16,000,303 to 27,455,799, and the difference between a birth-rate of 26·94 and a death-rate of 9·31 per 1,000 (1958) implies an annual natural increase of 15·63 per 1,000. While this will necessitate the creation of some 300,000 new jobs a year, the current population density of 240 per square mile does not of itself suggest overcrowding, though it is admittedly above the South-east Asian average. However, this figure covers a very wide range of densities, from a mere 36 in Palawan, 83 in Mindoro and 147 in Mindanao to around 800 in Cebu and the central plains of Luzon, exclusive of Manila and its suburbs.[34]

This very great unevenness is only partially a reflection of differences in innate agricultural potentiality, for while prolonged and substantial growth of population has occurred in the focal areas of Spanish colonization, the increase has been much less striking in the Muslim and pagan areas which remained outside the range of effective administration until recent times.[35] By the end of the Spanish period congestion was already becoming apparent in central Luzon and Cebu, and today Bohol and the Ilocos provinces of north-west Luzon must also be regarded as areas in which virtually all the available land is under cultivation. Nevertheless, large tracts of potentially good land elsewhere remain undeveloped, notably in Mindanao, which occupies 32 per cent of the total area, but contains only 19·5 per cent of the country's population.

However, while such unevenness in population density is found in other parts of South-east Asia, the acute tenancy problem which aggravates it here results directly from the Spanish colonial system and has no parallel anywhere else in the region. In general terms about one-third of the farms are occupied by tenants, one-sixth are part owned and part rented, and only half are in the hands

[32] Special arrangements were also made for goods under quotas.

[33] Both these were census years. In between them the 1948 Census showed a total of 19,234,000.

[34] The average for Luzon is 260. All these figures are estimates.

[35] Mindanao was under U.S. military government until 1913.

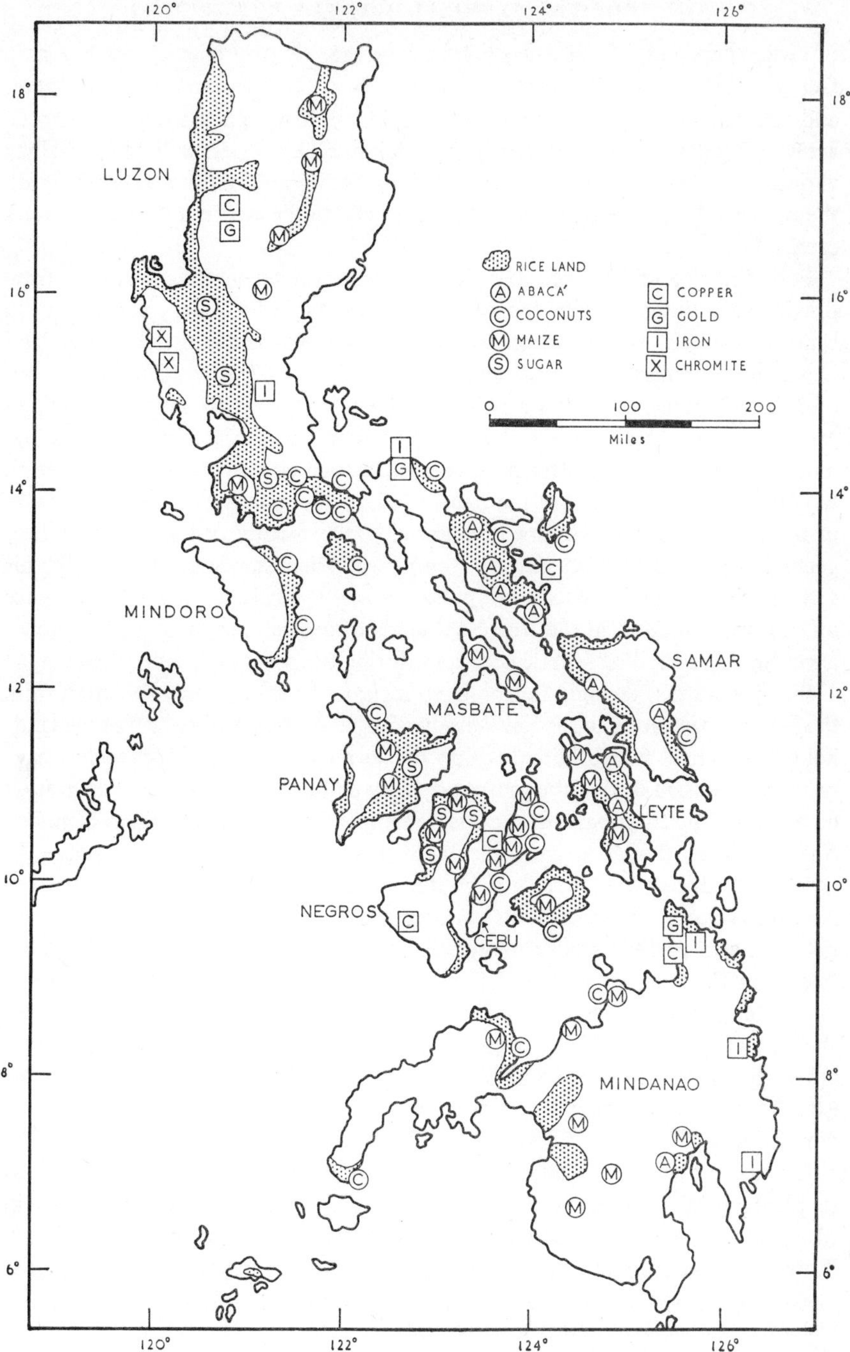

FIG. 101—The Philippines: economic development

of owner-occupiers. In size the holdings average slightly over 10 acres, but in fact over half are smaller than 5 acres, another third between 5 and 12 acres and the remainder, just over one-eighth in number, range from 12 to 5,000 acres and together cover over half the total area. These larger holdings belong variously to business corporations, religious bodies and, most numerous of all, the *caciques*,[36] but the great majority are let out to tenants in lots of a few acres each.

Both the size of holdings and the percentage of tenancy vary greatly from province to province, with the smallest farms, typically 4 or 5 acres only, in central Luzon, in four provinces of which over 60 per cent of the cultivated land is worked by tenants. By tradition 50 per cent of the crop is paid in rent, but often much more disappears owing to the need to repay advances made at exorbitant rates by the landlords, and the tenant farmer is fortunate if he has more than 30 per cent left for his own use. In such circumstances it becomes all too easy to get into a state of permanent indebtedness to the *cacique*, and this in turn rules out any possibility of improving the quality of farming, which in general is extremely low, even by South-east Asian standards. Caught in this vicious circle, the impoverished peasantry may conclude that only violence offers a way out, and in the congested lands of central Luzon agrarian disturbances have occurred on several occasions during the past two hundred years.

Possible ways of tackling this problem include the transfer of population from the overcrowded areas to the less densely peopled islands, and reform of the landholding practices which obtain within the former. Both these approaches have received attention during the present century and indeed spontaneous migration on a small scale from parts of the Visayas to northern Mindanao dates from late Spanish times, though it was much accelerated by American road-building in that island during the period of military administration. But migration from Luzon has posed a more difficult problem, partly because of the greater expense involved and partly because many tenants have found it impossible to break free from the *caciques* to whom they were indebted. Other obstacles to more extensive migration have been the language barriers,[37] the frequent hostility shown by the Moros and the pagan peoples of central Mindanao to settlers from other regions,[38] the heavy incidence of malaria in the interior uplands of all the islands, and the traditional preference for village life as opposed to individual pioneering.

It was in order to overcome these difficulties that the government first turned to planned colonization, and seven agricultural colonies were established in Mindanao, with others in Bohol and the Cagayan valley, between 1913 and 1917. Between 1918 and 1934 30,000 settlers received free transport, mostly to Minda-

[36] *Cacique* holdings are mostly less than 250 acres. For an excellent account of this problem as a whole see Pelzer (C), Chapter 4.

[37] See below, pp. 727–31.

[38] It must be admitted that this is largely the result of past excesses, particularly in land-grabbing, committed by the Christian Filipinos.

nao, and substantially larger numbers migrated without any such help. Thereafter growing fear of Japanese influence in Davao[39] provided a further stimulus to the settlement of Mindanao, and under the Commonwealth government the National Land Settlement Administration was set up, which made a promising start by establishing some 11,000 people in the Koronadal valley in 1939–41.

However, the scale of such operations was minute compared with the size of the problem to be tackled, and greater interest attached to the possibilities of improving tenancy conditions elsewhere. Yet apart from the purchase by the United States of some 425,000 acres of friar lands early in the century very little was done until 1933, when the Rice Share Tenancy Act was passed to protect share tenants against the worst excesses of exploitation. And even though the act still permitted rents up to 50 per cent of the total crop, and interest rates of 10 per cent per annum, the *caciques* who dominated the government succeeded in rendering it largely ineffective in many parts of the country. Later, the Commonwealth government also purchased a few large estates in Luzon for resale to the tenant occupiers, but the total area involved was small and, like the resettlement schemes of the same era, this activity was brought to an abrupt end by the Japanese invasion.

In these circumstances, therefore, it is not surprising that many of the inhabitants of central Luzon saw in the war an opportunity for overturning the established order. Thus was born the Hukbalahap[40] (Huk) guerrilla movement which, besides its activities against the Japanese, also claimed to have exterminated some 20,000 Filipinos, mostly landlords and their supporters, during the occupation period. And after the war ended, the Huks with an estimated membership of approximately 100,000 centred in the four 'Huklandia' provinces of Pampanga, Nueva Ecija, Tarlac and Bulacan close to Manila, continued the struggle against the Philippine government on such a scale as to threaten the very survival of the new Republic by 1950.

While the leadership of the movement was undoubtedly Communist, the mass of its support came from the impoverished countryfolk who were attracted by its promise of free land for the landless. This was recognized by Ramon Magsaysay, the Secretary of Defence who was charged with the task of crushing the rebellion, and his success in doing so after 1951[41] led to his election as President in 1953.

Magsaysay's immediate policy was for the government itself to grant what the Huks had promised, and to this end he set up the Economic Development Corps (E.D.C.O.R.) which sponsored four Huk resettlement schemes, three of them in Mindanao and the other in the Cagayan valley. But after becoming President he

[39] See below, p. 727.

[40] Abbreviation of *Hukong Bayan Laban Sa Hapon*, *i.e.* People's Anti-Japanese Army.

[41] In 1950–51 the rebellion spread beyond central Luzon to Leyte, Negros, Panay, Mindoro and Mindanao. But it was largely broken by the end of 1951 though its leader, Luis Taruc, did not surrender until 1954. For a full account of the Huk problem see Scaff, *op. cit.*

introduced a wider ranging series of measures for rural improvement and development. Between 1954 and 1956 7,000 (non-Huk) families from Luzon were resettled, each on 25-acre plots, in Mindanao and Palawan, and at the same time rural banks and other agricultural credit facilities were rapidly multiplied, and new Farmers Co-operative Marketing Associations (F.A.C.O.M.A.) set up throughout the country. Hand in hand with these activities Magsaysay also developed the agricultural extension services and under the new Five Year Plan of 1954 schemes were drawn up for extending the area under controlled irrigation from 1·3 to 1·76 million acres, primary attention being given to the needs of central Luzon.

The most important but also the most controversial of Magsaysay's measures, however, was the Land Reform Act of 1955, designed to establish a 'democratic agricultural economy' by limiting the size of the large estates and arranging for government purchase of excess land and its resale to tenants. But once again *cacique* interests succeeded in reducing the scope of the changes originally proposed, and even before Magsaysay's death in March 1957 it was apparent that the reform was failing to achieve the results intended. With the death of Magsaysay, the prospect of effecting fundamental reforms in the pattern of land tenure receded and, despite the great improvements in rural conditions since 1953, it is by no means certain that the corner has been turned in the struggle for better living standards for the millions of landless Filipinos.[42]

The Five Year Plan of 1954 also sought to remove other weaknesses in the Philippines economy, notably its excessive dependence on a limited range of exports, all of them primary produce, and its generally retarded industrial development. Of a total projected public investment of 1,552 million Pesos, 257 million were allocated to agricultural improvement (including irrigation), 383 million to industrial projects and 772 million to public utilities, and it was expected that private investment in all fields would raise the total figure to 4,700 million Pesos for the five-year period.

Like the rest of South-east Asia, the Philippines is primarily agricultural, with some 70 per cent of its gainfully employed population engaged in farming, which in turn accounts for 42 per cent of the national income. Details of the country's agriculture are summarized in Table 97.

Between 1940 and 1960 the total area under crops rose from 12,690,000 to 18,767,000 acres, the latter figure representing some 25 per cent of the surface area of the country. When due allowance is made for the double cropping of some of the better agricultural lands, it appears that about two-thirds of the area listed as cultivated is actually under crops in any given year.

Notwithstanding an increase of approximately 33 per cent in the islands' paddy production between 1937 and 1956, the yield per acre went up only from 23·0

[42] Magsaysay did no more than make a start; and as yet probably less than 10 per cent of the farm population is affected by F.A.C.O.M.A. and the agricultural credit facilities.

to 23·5 bushels, and the current figure is still the lowest national average in the whole of South-east Asia.

In part, this results from the fairly considerable share (15 per cent or more) provided by dry upland cultivation, whose yields are extremely poor. Elsewhere, apart from the 70,000 acres or so of irrigated terrace cultivation in the northern

TABLE 97

THE PHILIPPINES: AGRICULTURAL PRODUCTION

Commodity	*Output* (000 *tons*)			*Area* (000 *acres*)		
	1937	1946	1960	1940	1946	1960
Rough rice . . .	2,421	1,623	3,740	5,140	4,078	8,170
Maize (shelled) . .	438	331	1,165	2,256	1,401	4,560
Root crops* . . .	334	434	1,412	446	366	714
Vegetables . . .	n.a.	n.a.	2,275	121	74	393
Fruit and nuts† . .	n.a.	n.a.	719	580	479	846
Meat and poultry products‡ . . .	237	77	n.a.			
Total food crops (including others) . . .			n.a.	8,622	6,479	14,846
Sugar§	1,076	63	1,809	568	72	598
Coconuts . . .				2,597	2,372	2,618
Copra . . .	522	204	1,075			
Coconut oil . .	213	40	42			
Abacá	201	30	94	722	674	413
Tobacco (leaf) . .	36	14	64	143	67	237
Total export crops (including others) . . .				4,068	3,214	3,924
Total all crops . .				12,690	9,693	18,769

* Root crops include mainly sweet potatoes and manioc.

† Fruit and nuts include bananas, pineapples, citrus fruits, peanuts etc.

‡ Livestock (1960) include: buffaloes 3,696,400; cattle 1,110,500; pigs 6,572,000; goats 617,100; sheep 14,900; horses 217,400; domestic fowl 52,335,100; ducks 2,230,700.

§ Sugar total includes centrifugal and muscovado sugar.

Source: *Facts about the Philippines*, and *Philippine agricultural situation*, 3, 2, June 1961.

interior of Luzon, rice is exclusively a lowland crop, and the normal method of cultivation, involving the use of the buffalo-drawn plough and transplanting by hand, and relying mainly on impounded rain water, are not much different from those in most other parts of the Malaysian lands. Only a small area, about 30 per cent of the total under rice, has controlled irrigation, introduced either in Spanish or more recent times, and it is here that the highest yields are obtained.

TABLE 98

THE PHILIPPINES: LAND USE

	Per cent
Commercial forest	38·3
Non-commercial forest	14·9
Marsh and swamp	2·0
Open grassland	17·5
Cultivated	27·3

This includes a substantial part of the plains of central Luzon which is the main rice-surplus region, supplying much of the needs of Manila, parts of the Visayas and Davao, as well as its own local demand, and it was intended that recent plans for extending the irrigated area here and elsewhere would make the country completely self-sufficient in rice by 1959.[43] Other important rice-growing areas are south-eastern Luzon, Panay, Leyte, Samar and Lanao and Cotabato in south-western Mindanao.

However, while rice is the leading grain in the Philippines as a whole, it covers only 43·5 per cent of the total cropped area, which represents a lower proportion than that in any other South-east Asian state. Fundamentally this is because, thanks to the Spanish-American connexion and the relatively limited development of wet-rice cultivation there in pre-colonial times, the Filipinos have been more willing than their neighbours to adopt maize as the staple foodstuff wherever natural conditions were not really favourable for rice. This applies particularly to the areas of porous soils on the coral limestones of some of the Visayan islands, where, moreover, rainfall is generally only moderate in total amount. These include parts of Leyte and Negros, and more especially Cebu, which alone accounts for a quarter of the total maize output but now requires an additional import of 150,000 tons a year, mostly from Mindanao. All these traditional maize-staple areas are now relatively overcrowded, and those of their peoples who have migrated in recent times to northern Mindanao and elsewhere have continued to rely on maize as the principal food grain in their new homes. Moreover, as in many neighbouring lands, maize has been widely adopted

[43] Manila also imports about 60,000 tons of rice from other islands, notably Palawan and Mindanao. Imports of foreign rice, chiefly from Thailand, continued in 1959.

by the shifting cultivators and is also very popular as a dry hillside crop among the Bontocs and Ifugaos. Since 1937 the expansion in maize production has been even more spectacular than that of rice, and today it provides the chief item in the diet of over 25 per cent of the total population. Nevertheless, these are among the most impoverished members of the community, and their situation is likely to deteriorate in those areas where continuous cropping with maize is already leading to serious soil erosion.

Among the other food crops shown in Table 97, the roots include mainly sweet potatoes (approximately 500,000 acres) which are rather more common in the northern half of the archipelago, and manioc (nearly 200,000 acres), which conversely is more popular in the southern half, and forms the staple food in the Sulu islands. Of the 846,000 acres under fruit and nuts, more than half grows bananas, with mangoes, pineapples, citrus fruits and peanuts covering most of the remainder. There is also a wide range of vegetables grown for subsistence on nearly every farm, but commercial production of these is very small, being mainly confined to a few Chinese market gardens in the vicinity of the larger towns.

Besides the above crops,[44] other sources of food are provided by livestock and fish. Meat and poultry products figure rather more prominently in the Filipino diet than is customary elsewhere in South-east Asia, but even so they are less important than fish, of which the average annual *per capita* consumption is about 50 lb. Except in the remote interiors almost all Filipinos engage in some coastal or river fishing, and in recent years there has been a notable increase in the raising of fish in rice fields and fish ponds, the latter of which now occupy well over 250,000 acres and yield an annual catch exceeding 50,000 tons. Commercial sea fishing, on the other hand, has yet to regain the pre-war volume of production. Formerly almost exclusively in Japanese hands, it has since 1945 become mainly a Filipino preserve,[45] though some Japanese have recently been permitted to resume operations.

Despite the large increase in overall food production since the war the Philippines has become more dependent than ever on imports of dairy produce and cereals, which together in 1959 comprised some 8·4 per cent of total imports as against 4·5 per cent for all food imports in 1939. Admittedly this is still less than half the value of the islands' own exports of sugar and desiccated coconut, so that on balance the Philippines is a net exporter of foodstuffs. But the government is determined to reduce dependence on foreign sources of food, even though this may involve a further reduction in the acreage available for export crops.[46]

[44] Some of the 'export' crops noted below are also produced partly for home consumption; this applies particularly to 'muscovado' sugar and coconut oil.

[45] Very little of the Japanese equipment survived however, and shortage of equipment is the main reason for the drop in output.

[46] At the same time the Rice Enrichment Program has been initiated to combat malnutrition leading to beri-beri. *Cf.* the action of the Burmese government noted above, pp. 456–7.

Between 1940 and 1960, while the food-crop acreage rose by 72 per cent, the area under export crops fell by 3 per cent, and the ratio of export to food crops declined from 32/68 to 21/79. But this decrease resulted mainly from difficulties in the marketing of abacá, and so long as the Philippines continues to depend primarily on agricultural products as earners of foreign exchange, it cannot afford to reduce the total acreage under such crops much further, even though it may well seek both to diversify the range of crops and to increase the yield per acre.

In fact, the area under sugar has increased slightly and the same is also true of that under coconuts, though greater efficiency in production has increased the output of both, particularly coconuts, which in 1959 accounted for some 29·4 per cent of the total exports, against sugar's 21·3 per cent. This represents an almost exact reversal of the immediate pre-war situation (sugar 40·9 per cent, coconut products 24·0 per cent in 1939) and it is certainly desirable to avoid heavy dependence on sugar. For this was the crop which in the past benefited most from duty-free entry into the United States, and as this advantage disappears the Philippines, which is only a relatively minor producer, will become particularly vulnerable to competition from other sources. In respect of coconut products, as well as abacá, on the other hand, the Philippines is the world's largest producer, but here also the long-term outlook is uncertain, owing to the competition of detergents and synthetic cordage fibres respectively.

The geographical distribution of these three main export crops calls for little explanation. The chief sugar-growing regions are in western and north-eastern Negros, which alone produces over 60 per cent of the total, and the central plain of Luzon, where much of the sugar land is under controlled irrigation. It is in these two areas, both of which have numerous estates of 200 acres or more, and to a lesser extent in northern Cebu and eastern Panay, that most of the 'centrals' refining white (or 'centrifugal') sugar are situated. However, there is a much more widespread production of brown (or 'muscovado') sugar, mainly for local consumption, and all-told small-holders have a large share in the cultivation of the export as well as the subsistence product. Coconuts are even more widely distributed throughout the coastal districts especially south of latitude 15° where the typhoon danger is less than in northern and central Luzon. The largest single producer is southern Luzon, where extensive estates, as well as the otherwise more typical small-holder cultivation, are found. But the total output of the Visayas is greater, and Cebu has replaced Manila as the chief centre for the collection and processing of copra.

Abacá (*Musa textilis*) on the other hand, which besides being similarly vulnerable to typhoons cannot tolerate either prolonged drought or excessive soil water, is much more concentrated in its distribution, with south-eastern Luzon, south-eastern Mindanao and the eastern Visayas as the principal centres. Prior to the Second World War, production in Mindanao was dominated by the large block of Japanese-owned estates around Davao, but these have since been replaced mainly by Filipino small-holdings.

Other commercial production includes cigar tobacco, the one crop in which Spanish interests continue to predominate. But while the output, which comes primarily from the Cagayan valley of northern Luzon, has been maintained in recent years, foreign sales have dwindled with changing smoking habits, and there has been a considerable import of Virginia tobacco from the U.S.A.[47] Pineapple production seems to have some prospect of further expansion, and an attempt is now being made to grow cotton for the local textile industry.

From a long-term point of view the agricultural prospects of the Philippines are not discouraging, provided that the land tenure problem can be solved. Over the country as a whole there is no shortage of cultivable land and, freed from the burden of debt, the Filipino farmer could substantially raise the yield per acre of all crops, as indeed the estates are doing already. So far as export crops are concerned, however, external factors are at least as important as those which lie within the republic's power to control, and for this reason the diversification of exports resulting from recent developments in lumbering and mining is a step in the right direction.

With nearly two-fifths of its area classed as commercial forests, the Philippines has an abundance of standing timber, the greatest reserves being in the interiors of Mindanao, Negros, Samar, Palawan and Mindoro, with exploitation at present centred mainly in Mindanao, Negros and Mindoro. Most of the commercially useful trees are dipterocarps, the best known being the lauan or 'Philippine mahogany'. The lumber industry now employs some 80,000 workers and over 350 sawmills are in operation; meanwhile Filipino capital in the industry has overtaken that of the Chinese, though American concerns are still in the lead. In 1956 the total cut amounted to 1,824 million board feet, of which 714 million were exported. By 1960 exports of 76 million board feet of lumber and 1,488 million board feet of logs together accounted for 18 per cent of total exports, compared with only 2·6 per cent in 1939.

The post-war expansion in mineral production has been no less rapid, and from a long-term point of view is at least equally significant. Although some small-scale panning of gold was practised by the Filipinos and Chinese before the arrival of the Spaniards, minerals were of almost negligible importance in the Philippine economy prior to the so-called gold rush of 1933–6. Thereafter, gold remained the principal mineral for some years, with production reaching a peak of nearly 900,000 oz. in 1937, but after that a decline set in and the industry suffered severe damage during the war. Despite some recovery since that time, output is still less than half that of 1937, and meanwhile copper has surpassed it in total value.

The main surviving gold workings are around Baguio (central Luzon), where

[47] This has since been largely replaced by local production of Virginia tobacco, particularly in La Union, Ilocos Sur and Ilocos Norte. See Cutshall (C).

several mines use modern equipment either for dredging or lode-working, but reserves are widespread elsewhere, notably in Camarines Norte (south-eastern Luzon), Masbate and Surigao (north-eastern Mindanao). Copper likewise is mined in south-eastern Luzon, but the most important single working is at Toledo in Cebu, followed by the Sipalay mine in Negros Occidental.

The other two minerals already of economic importance are chromite, of which the Masinloc district in the Zambales mountains contains the largest refractory-grade deposits in the world, and iron which occurs both in the form of high-grade hæmatite in Balucan (central Luzon) and Camarines Norte, and in lower-grade lateritic deposits in Surigao. The Philippines now produces 23 per cent of the world's chromium ore while, as regards iron, the hæmatite workings at present account for most of the 1½ million tons of ore mined annually, but the vast lateritic deposits, containing 48 per cent iron, are potentially of much greater significance. Unfortunately these ores are difficult to refine, but they have nevertheless excited considerable interest recently, particularly in Japan.[48]

TABLE 99

THE PHILIPPINES: MINERAL RESERVES, AND PRODUCTION 1960

Mineral	*Reserves of ore, million metric tons*	*Production, metric tons unless otherwise stated*	*Value, million Pesos*
Copper (metal)	22	44,010	59·067
Gold	15	410,618 oz.	28·743
Silver		1,133,843 oz.	2·043
Chromite, refractory	10	606,013	27·288
„ metallurgical		128,426	6·649
Iron (ore)	1,200	1,138,770	20·706
Mercury (metal)	n.d.	3,041 flasks*	1·300
Lead (metal)	n.d.	122	0·066
Zinc (metal)	n.d.	4,978	2·847
Manganese (ore)	0·2	17,381	1·148
Coal	40	147,857	3·438
Total (including others)			244·242

* 1 flask = 76 lb.

Source: Bureau of Mines, cited in *Facts about the Philippines* and *Journal of Philippine Statistics*, 14, 1, January-March, 1961.

[48] Japan is anxious to obtain new sources of iron ore to replace its former supplies from Manchuria, Korea, etc.

So far as local industrialization is concerned, however, the almost complete absence of coal, apart from a little lignite which is worked in Cebu, represents a serious liability, as does the equally pronounced dearth of local oil. Nevertheless, although most of the electric power at present generated is thermal, the physical character of the islands offers all the advantages possessed by Japan for the generation of hydro-electricity, without the drawback of the winter freeze. Thus, in planning for further industrialization, the Philippines is turning to hydro-electric power as the chief prime mover, and it is estimated that the potential in this respect is at least 3½ million kW, compared with an installed capacity (both thermal and hydro) of 292,000 kW in 1955.[49]

Already four major hydro-electric stations have been set up, namely Ambuklao in Mountain Province, northern Luzon (75,000 kW), Caliraya-Lumot, Laguna, central Luzon (36,000 kW) and Maria Cristina I and II, both in Lanao, Mindanao (25,000 kW each). Five other large projects are under construction, the largest being at Binga, Mountain Province (100,000 kW), and at present Manila and its suburbs, which constitute the chief industrial focus, has 92,000 kW of hydro-electric as well as 146,000 kW of thermal-electric power at its disposal.

Until the Commonwealth period manufacturing industry in the Philippines comprised only domestic handicrafts and the processing of certain primary products. While the former probably employs at least half a million people full-time, as well as many more intermittently, its only important contribution to the export trade, namely embroideries, has declined in recent years, though there may still be a market in neighbouring lands, as well as at home, for such articles as hats and rattan furniture.[50]

In 1935 the total employed in 'modern factories' which consisted mainly of rice mills, sawmills, and sugar, abacá, coconut-oil, and desiccated-coconut plants, was estimated at 120,000, but under the Commonwealth régime a series of consumer-goods and other plants was set up by government initiative, and despite serious war-time damage, the number and range of these have been extended since independence.

Such establishments now in operation, mostly in or around Manila, include factories manufacturing cotton and other textiles, shoes, cigarettes and plywood, as well as distilleries and canneries, while other large-scale concerns are the fertilizer plant set up in association with the Maria Cristina power station, the Iligan steel mills and cement plants, the largest of which is in Cebu, where both coal and limestone are locally available. In addition to these, many private and generally smaller-scale factories, again mainly in Manila, now manufacture or

[49] This represents a big advance over the 72,500 kW of 1941. Total electricity generated in 1949 was 229·9 m. kWh, as against 1,078·6 m. kWh in 1955.

[50] Cottage industries in general experienced a decline during the inter-war years but have seen something of a revival since 1946. Though less advanced than in some other parts of South-east Asia, they could be extended to make a useful contribution by mopping up seasonal unemployment in the countryside. See Hart, Donn V., p. 364, and Spencer, J. E. (B), p 14.

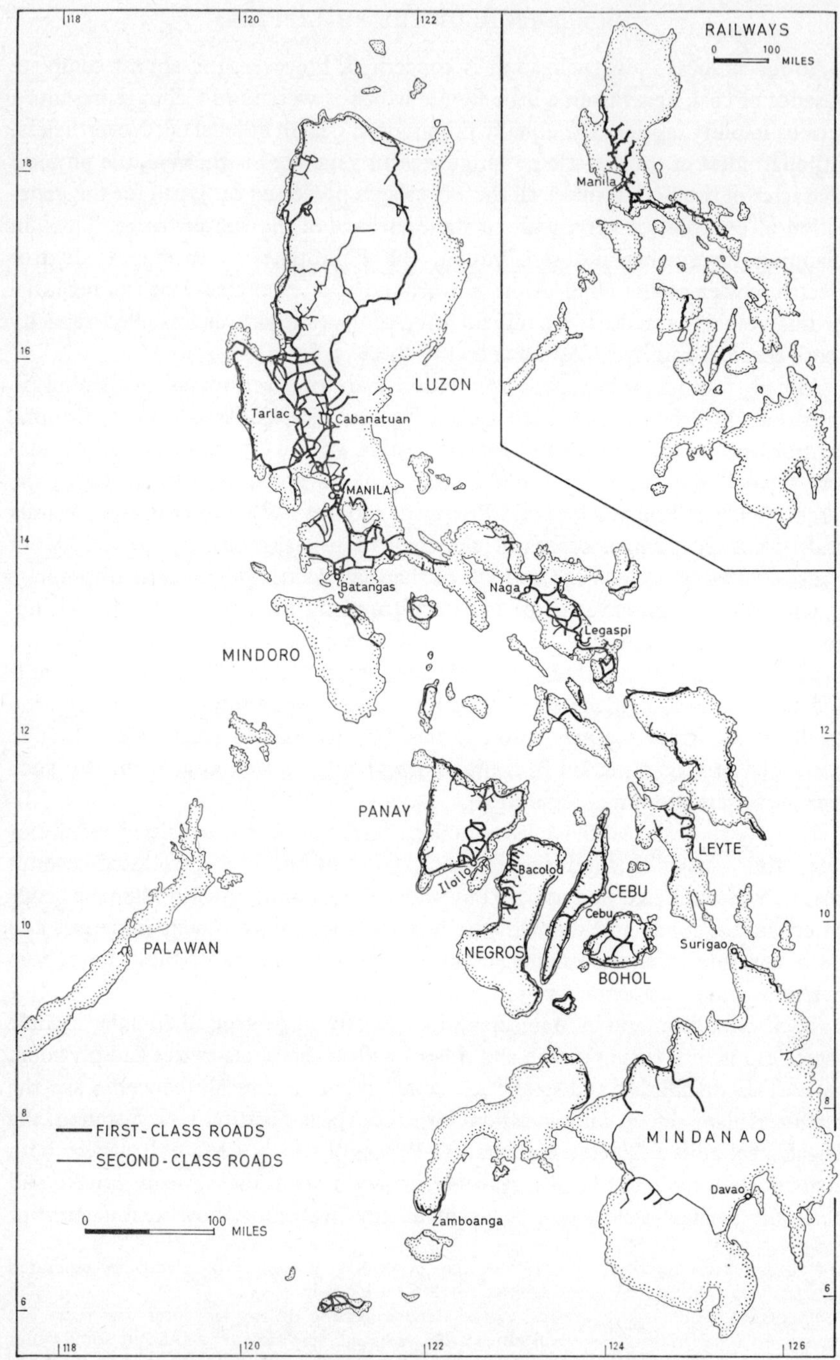

FIG. 102—The Philippines: roads and railways
Note: The railway in Cebu is no longer in operation

assemble a variety of consumer goods and food preparations,[51] and all-told it is claimed that over 800 new 'industries' have been set up in the Philippines since 1945. But many of these, depending on both imported equipment and imported raw materials, have not proved a paying proposition, and early in 1958 the government announced its intention of stopping the establishment of further packaging and processing plants, while still continuing to encourage such manufactures as could make use of locally produced raw materials.

Because of its character as an archipelago, the Philippines, like Indonesia, has always depended primarily on sea transport and, notwithstanding the building of railways and modern highways and the more recent introduction of air services, the volume of inter-island shipping continues to grow.

However, the transport system as a whole was badly disorganized by the war, and even today the effects of this are plainly evident. Thus, for example, the railway mileage has been reduced from 840 to about 700, the pre-war line in Cebu has been completely abandoned and the volume of both passenger and freight traffic remains below that of 1941. Apart from the solitary line from Iloilo to Capiz in Panay, the railway system is now confined exclusively to central and southern Luzon, that is from San Fernando to Legaspi, though extensions to the Cagayan valley in the north-east and to Matnog in the far south of the island are under consideration.

As Fig. 100 shows, all the main islands have at least the rudiments of a highway system, and with some 10,238 miles of surfaced roads outside the towns, and 123,698 registered motor vehicles in 1956, the Philippines compare favourably with most other parts of South-east Asia in respect of road transport. Nevertheless, only central Luzon is really well provided for, and over the country at large there is an urgent need for many more minor roads to link outlying villages with local market towns.

On the other hand, the great expansion of air services since 1945 has done much to break down regional isolation within the archipelago, and in 1956 Philippine Air Lines maintained 80 internal flights daily, and carried a total of 370,000 passengers and 6,816 short tons of freight.[52] P.A.L. also has regular flights to Hong Kong, and the situation of the Philippines at the junction of long-distance air routes from southern Asia, the United States, Australia and the western Pacific has helped to make Manila airport one of the three most important in South-east Asia.

Despite the wartime loss of some 80 per cent of the inter-island fleet, including all the larger vessels, however, maritime transport still remains of paramount importance. Thanks to American action in making available war-surplus ships, an 'inter-island core fleet' of 125 vessels, aggregating 88,000 tons has been recon-

[51] In December 1954 Caltex opened an important new oil refinery at Batangas on Manila Bay.

[52] By 1960 the number of passengers carried on domestic flights had risen to 763,000, and freight to 11,500 tons.

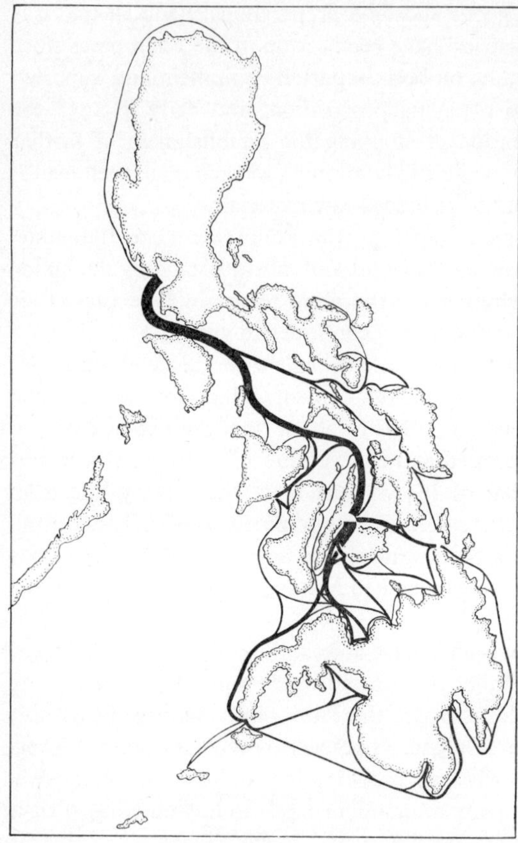

FIG. 103—The Philippines: shipping routes

stituted, and though this is smaller than its pre-war counterpart it provides regular services between all the main parts of the archipelago.[53]

So far as inter-insular shipping alone is concerned, Cebu forms the greatest single focus, but Manila which ranks second in this respect is much the most important international port, and serves as the main entrepôt for the archipelago. This situation represents a carry over from the pre-1834 period when Manila was the sole port of entry, and today over 7 million net registered tons of shipping annually enter its great international harbour which has been built along the shores of Manila Bay north of the Pasig river, while most of the inter-insular traffic is handled by a separate harbour lying to the south of the river.

Between 85 and 90 per cent of all the Philippines' imports enter via Manila, but though it also handles the greater part of the abacá, tobacco and iron ore exports, as well as much of the coconut oil, copra and sugar, particularly from Luzon itself, its share of the total exports is only about 30 per cent. For since most of these are very bulky, they tend increasingly to find their outlet via the large regional ports, such as Cebu, which ships over half the copra, Iloilo, the main centre for sugar from nearby Negros, and, on a smaller scale, Davao and Zamboanga, the two leading ports of Mindanao.

As Fig. 103 shows, the central artery of the inter-island shipping system is

[53] This is not a single concern like the old K.P.M. of Indonesia (see above, pp. 298–301). It is owned by twelve separate companies, and the size and efficiency of the ships are not comparable with those of the K.P.M. In addition there are large numbers of country craft not included in these figures. For further details on shipping, see Wernstedt.

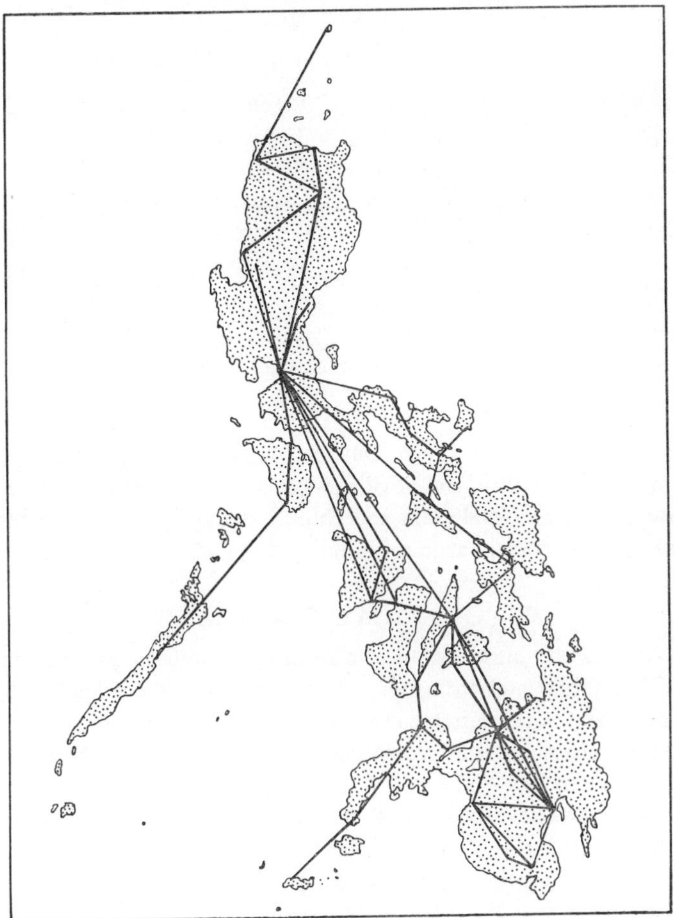

FIG. 104—The Philippines: air routes

formed by the route connecting Manila and Cebu, which besides being the two chief ports are also the two largest cities, and the respective regional foci of Luzon and the Visayas. But ever since the Spaniards made Manila the capital, its importance has far outstripped that of Cebu, and Luzon has acquired a growing preponderance in the life of the country. This dominance of the largest island, which may be compared with that of Honshu in Japan, is evident from both the road and railway map (Fig. 102) and the accompanying table of urban population. And indeed the analogy with Japan may be extended further to embrace the close parallel which exists between Mindanao and Hokkaido, the large peripheral islands, traditionally occupied by peoples different from the main mass of the population and still only in the frontier stage of development. However, in its retarded urbanization the Philippines resembles the rest of

TABLE 100

THE PHILIPPINES: PRINCIPAL TOWNS, 1960

Town	Population	Town	Population
Manila (Luzon)	1,145,723	Bacolod City (Negros)	119,768
Quezon City* (Luzon)	397,374	Tarlac (Luzon)	98,131
Cebu City (Cebu)	259,194	Batangas „	82,819
Davao City (Mindanao)	231,833	Cabanatuan City (Luzon) „	70,898
Iloilo City (Panay)	150,976	Legaspi „	60,768
Pasay City* (Luzon)	132,178		
Zamboanga City (Mindanao)	131,411		

* Note: Both Quezon City (the new capital) and Pasay City form parts of Greater Manila.

South-east Asia rather than Japan. Outside Manila and a few leading provincial towns it is pre-eminently a land of villages or *barrios*, the larger of which characteristically possess a central plaza and church, dating from Spanish times, and often also a more recently acquired public school, cinema and Chinese-owned rice mill.

V. POLITICAL GEOGRAPHY

Notwithstanding the introduction of a form of republican government with a bicameral legislature and strong presidential powers closely modelled on that of the United States, the extreme centralization characteristic of the old Spanish régime still survives, and the 54 provinces remain completely subordinate to the central government in Manila.

In official parlance Quezon City is now the capital, but this is as yet merely one of the newer suburbs, some ten miles from the centre of Manila, whose total population is of the order of two million. With its many striking contrasts, between the surviving Malaysian-style dwellings of the fishing population of Navotas, the old walled city of Intramuros, where unfortunately few of the historic Spanish colonial buildings escaped the devastation of 1945, the traditional Chinese quarter in Tondo, and the modern business, administrative and residential districts, with their medley of reinforced concrete, heavy 'American-civic' and varied domestic styles, the architecture of Manila aptly epitomizes the cultural history of the Philippine islands. But the equally sharp contrast between the lines of glistening automobiles and ultra-expensive hotels, apartments and restaurants of the modern centre, and the poverty and squalor of the appallingly congested slums hard by is no less a part of the Manila scene, and it also symbolizes a reality of nation-wide significance.

Nevertheless, while the dominance of a single great Western metropolis is a feature which the Philippines shares with most other South-east Asian states, the character of Philippine nationhood differs in important respects from that of all its neighbours.

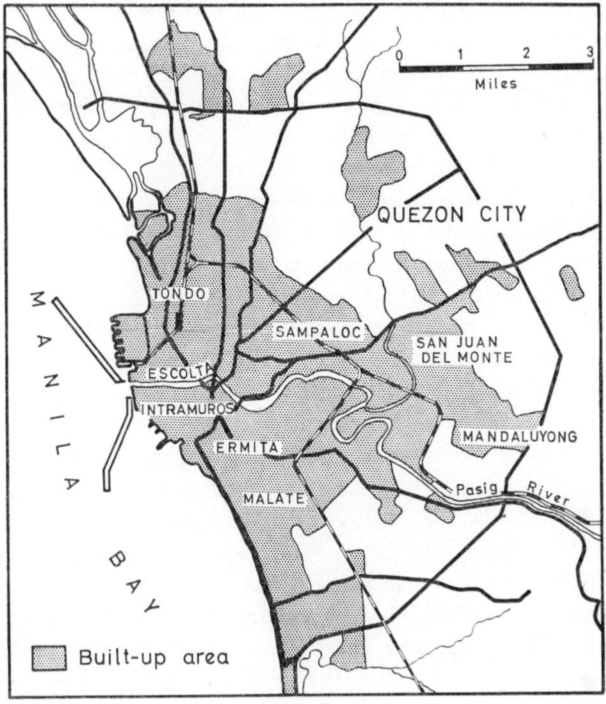

FIG. 105—Manila

By far the strongest force making for national unity is the common Roman Catholic culture, derived from Spain, and shared by all the lowland peoples except the Moros. As Table 101 shows, nearly 80 per cent of the total population are Roman Catholics, about 2 per cent are converts of American Protestant missions, and another 8 per cent belong to the Aglipayan or Filipino Independent Church, which is doctrinally modernistic but retains much of the organization and ritual of the Roman Catholic Church from which it broke away in 1902.

TABLE 101

THE PHILIPPINES: RELIGIONS, 1948

Roman Catholic	15,941,000
Aglipayan	1,456,000
Muslim	792,000
Protestant	444,000
Pagan/animist	354,000
Iglesia ni Cristo	88,000
Buddhist	43,000
Total (including others)	19,234,000

Although even among the established Roman Catholic population many of the old pre-Christian beliefs still survive in modified form, loyalty to the Church is real and abiding, and today most of the priests are themselves Filipinos. Nevertheless, Filipino national consciousness emerged only as a result of opposition to Spanish rule, and, in particular, to the privileged position of the Church as the most powerful of all the great landowners. Significantly, however, this opposition which did not differ fundamentally in spirit from the widespread resentment of clerical privilege in metropolitan Spain, was led mainly by individuals who were themselves partially Spanish in origin.

In contrast to their position in most other South-east Asian lands, the mestizos of the Philippines have never been ranked as a distinct community,[54] and for this reason their number has never been recorded, though it is clear that a substantial proportion of the population has some admixture of Spanish and/or Chinese blood. In general, this mixed element has corresponded fairly closely to the wealthier[55] and hence the better educated strata in Philippine society. But unlike the Eurasians of Indonesia, the mestizos of the Philippines have not been separated from the mass of the population by any religious barrier, and indeed after the predominantly Protestant United States replaced Spain as the ruling power, the Roman Catholic religion tended to become an even stronger bond of unity between all members of the Filipino population, whatever their ethnic origin. Thus, the earlier mestizo leaders, Rizal and Aguinaldo, were succeeded by others of mixed blood, including many of the leading politicians during the first half of this century, and even Magsaysay who claimed to be 'a son of the people' and used Tagalog instead of English (or Spanish) in his public speeches, was partly Chinese and Spanish as well as Filipino in ancestry.

This dependence upon a mestizo élite, which is without parallel except in certain parts of Latin America, constitutes one of the most important factors distinguishing the Philippines from the rest of South-east Asia. Almost equally distinctive, however, has been the manner in which independence was achieved. For while as elsewhere in the region the common sufferings of the Second World War served greatly to strengthen national consciousness, the fact that the United States had previously set a date for independence, which it subsequently honoured, meant that the final separation occurred without the bitterness which marked such changes in many other parts of South-east Asia.[56]

For this reason the Philippines was willing to consider on its merits and ultimately to accept the case for retaining some defensive link with the former

[54] In this respect their position has been similar to that of the Eurasians in Indonesia under Dutch rule, though this parallel breaks down in other respects, as noted below.

[55] Whether their better position was due to superior vigour in any way associated with the European and/or Chinese admixture must remain an open question. See above, pp. 58–61.

[56] Notwithstanding a certain controversy over the question of wartime collaboration, which, however, was probably no more serious than in most of the occupied countries of Europe.

metropolitan power. Thus, in 1947 twelve American-built army, naval and air bases were leased for 99 years to the United States, which also undertook to continue training the Philippine armed forces.[57] Later, the Philippines made its acceptance of the San Francisco Peace Treaty with Japan conditional upon the conclusion of the Philippines-United States Mutual Defence Treaty in 1951, and after the Geneva Agreement of 1954,[58] when Communist China appeared to present a danger no less grave than that of a resurgent Japan, the Philippines played an active part in the setting up of S.E.A.T.O., which was in fact negotiated at Manila in September of that year. Thus, of all the South-east Asian states the Philippines is among the most explicitly aligned with the West, and notwithstanding occasional friction with its erstwhile mentor, the United States, there appears to be little likelihood of any major change in this respect.

Yet while the behaviour of the Philippines *vis-à-vis* the outside world is indicative of considerable political maturity, it would be a mistake to deduce from this that the internal problem of national unification has already been solved, and indeed there are several factors which at present operate in the opposite direction.

In the first place, the Philippines has in its 800,000 Moros of Sulu and Mindanao and 500,000 pagans[59] (including Negritos) substantial indigenous communities, most of whose members are conscious of no loyalties except to their own local or tribal leaders. Moreover, both these groups still harbour suspicions and resentment against the Christian Filipinos as a result of the treatment they have received in the past, and there is some evidence that the tendency to over-rapid Filipinization, which first became apparent under the Commonwealth regime, has intensified such feelings. Thus, while few people today would attempt to justify the Bacon Bill of 1926, which aimed at separating Mindanao and Sulu from the rest of the archipelago and retaining them permanently under United States' rule,[60] the central government will need to exercise great care in its handling of the indigenous minorities, particularly in those areas where resettlement schemes and other forms of economic development by Christian Filipinos are undertaken.[61]

However, notwithstanding the close maritime communications which link Mindanao and Sulu with the fellow-Muslim areas of Indonesian Borneo (Kalimantan), there is little indication that the Moros desire political ties with these neighbouring lands,[62] and there is no fundamental reason why the small

57 There have been some disputes, which are still unresolved, about sovereignty rights over these bases, but the principle of allowing the U.S.A. to use them is not in dispute. They involve an annual U.S. expenditure of some $60 million in the country.

58 See above, p. 556.

59 Some who are classed as pagans have in fact been converted to Christianity by either Protestant or Roman Catholic missions.

60 Hayden, p. 13.

61 Although the 200,000 Moros in Sulu still account for 90 per cent of the population of those islands, the 500,000 or so in Mindanao are now outnumbered by Christian Filipinos. In both areas a small but growing minority of educated Moros now regards itself as an integral part of the Philippine nation. See Hunt, pp. 332–3.

62 However, in 1962 a claim to North Borneo by the heirs to the former Sultan of Sulu was taken up by the Philippines government under President Macapagal. As noted in Chapter 20, the population of North Borneo is predominantly non-Muslim, and the

beginnings which have already been made at assimilating Moros and pagans with the rest of the Filipino nation should not be successful, providing that reasonable tact and understanding are shown towards them.

The same, however, seems less likely to happen in respect of the only important alien minority, namely the Chinese, even though the numbers of these, officially given as 132,650 in 1955[63] are lower than in any other major state in South-east Asia.

The relatively small number of Chinese in the Philippines results from the limited opportunities available to them under the Spanish regime, and the subsequent decision of the United States to extend to the islands its own immigration laws, despite the expressed desire of many American business concerns in the islands for the admission of Chinese labour.[64] In fact, however, many Chinese entered illegally both before and after the introduction in 1940 of an annual immigrant quota of 500,[65] and even though the total numbers remained small, the Chinese controlled over 70 per cent of the country's retail trade (and a still higher proportion in Manila where nearly half of them lived) and owned 75 per cent of the country's 2,500 rice mills, while their investments totalling $100 million were second only to those of United States citizens, immediately prior to the outbreak of the Pacific War.[66]

Under both colonial regimes the Chinese had been regarded as aliens, and after 1946 the new republic made no attempt to assimilate them. On the contrary, widespread jealousy and fear, occasioned by the activities of the Chinese as money-lenders, their skill as traders and the apparent support extended by some of them to the Huk movement, led the government to adopt various measures to curb their power in the country. In effect both the reduction in the annual immigration quota of any alien group from 500 to 50, and the constitutional provision that 60 per cent of the permanent employees in any business concern must be Philippines citizens, though general in their application, operated mainly against the Chinese. Moreover, the authorities have exerted much closer supervision over Chinese schools and in 1954 a law was passed with the ultimate purpose of excluding the Chinese completely from the retail trade.

Indeed, but for the desire to avoid difficulties with the United States, whose policy towards Formosa the Philippines on strategic grounds firmly supports, it would appear that even more drastic action might have been taken against the Chinese minority. But already the latter has suffered a severe setback, and the decision to nationalize the rice and maize industry by 1963 will hit them still

Philippines claim is based on its interpretation of the agreement made in 1878 between the Sultan of Sulu and the British syndicate headed by Dent and Overbeck. In the Philippines view the Sultan merely leased his territories in North Borneo, but in the British view he ceded them in perpetuity.

[63] Excluding mestizos. *Cf. The Times* estimate of 200,000 for 1956, above, Table 9, p. 181.

[64] See Purcell (D), p. 622.

[65] This number was the maximum permitted to any nationality.

[66] U.S. investments were estimated at $200 million–$280 million, largely in processing industries, public utilities and mines. See Callis, *op. cit.*

harder.[67] Presumably Filipino confidence in their ability to manage without Chinese middlemen rests upon the fact that the Philippines has a much larger 'indigenous' white-collar class than any of its South-east Asian neighbours. But it should not be forgotten that within this group there is a high proportion of Chinese admixture, and indeed the total number of Filipinos who show recognizable evidence of such miscegenation is probably not far short of a million.[68]

By comparison with the number of Chinese, the 1938 total of 25,837 Japanese residents in the Philippines (of whom two-thirds were in Davao alone) appeared very small. Yet this was the largest Japanese colony in all South-east Asia, and its economic interests – in abacá, fishing, lumbering, retail shopkeeping, and factory industry – were much more extensive than these figures might suggest. Moreover, the Japanese were planning to extend their activities still further once the Philippines obtained their independence, but the outcome of the war and the subsequent repatriation of all Japanese residents put an end to such hopes.

During the first post-war decade hostility towards Japan remained intense.[69] After prolonged haggling a reparations agreement was eventually ratified in July 1956, whereby Japan undertook to pay the Philippines $500 million in capital goods, plus $50 million in cash and services, and to grant long-term development loans of $250 million. But although this settlement was followed by the Philippines' ratification of the Peace Treaty, anxiety remained lest it should once again open the door to Japanese economic imperialism, and meanwhile there is scant possibility of any resumption of Japanese migration to the islands. For the rest, the most numerous aliens in the country are the 5,195 Americans and 1,512 Spaniards whose presence is an obvious legacy of recent history.

Apart from the problems occasioned by the minority communities, both indigenous and alien, it remains to consider the linguistic and socio-economic cleavages which still impair the unity of the Filipino population itself. With some 87 recognized languages and dialects, the Philippines presents an even greater degree of linguistic complexity, area for area, than does Indonesia. Moreover, under Spanish rule both primary education and missionary activity were normally conducted in the vernacular tongues, and today less than 2 per cent of the population, belonging almost exclusively to the upper social stratum, habitually speak Spanish.

The Americans, on the other hand, sought to make English a real *lingua franca*, and with such success that the Philippines has been called the third-

[67] As in Indonesia and Thailand, recent anti-Chinese policies in the Philippines have caused the Chinese community to invest its money in Hong Kong and Singapore instead of locally.

[68] However, as already noted above, p. 724, such mestizos are among the most ardently Filipino in sentiment.

[69] The Philippines is almost unique in South-east Asia in not feeling that it owes its independence at least partly to the Japanese. Since 1958–9 relations between the Philippines and Japan have begun to improve, and progress in this respect continues.

FIG. 106—The Philippines: languages

See opposite.

largest English-speaking nation in the world.[70] But while some 37·2 per cent of the population were listed as English speakers in 1948, and English is normally used in Government, education, commerce, and by most of the press and radio, few Filipinos regularly speak it in the home.

It was for this reason the President Quezon, who had originally favoured the use of English, subsequently decided in favour of adopting one of the indigenous languages as the national speech.[71] For although such a step would necessarily provoke much short-term controversy between different parts of the country, the continued survival of a series of regional languages, with their associated loyalties, clearly constituted a far greater obstacle to national unity. By virtue of the numbers of people already speaking them, the choice lay between the Ilocano language of north-western Luzon, a standardized Visayan language, and Tagalog, which besides being indigenous to the country round Manila had also become somewhat more widely known owing to its use by traders operating well outside that region. In the event, a modified form of Tagalog was adopted as the national language in 1937, since when it has ranked with English and Spanish as one of the three official languages, and is nowadays taught in all schools. As a result its use has spread rapidly (Table 102), though as yet it remains less widely spoken than the Visayan group as a whole.

Meanwhile a small but powerful 'Hispanista' element among the upper class has campaigned since 1945 for the revival of Spanish, partly as a means of emphasizing Filipino separateness from the United States, and partly in order to strengthen political ties with the Latin-American bloc, and in 1957 the teaching of Spanish was made obligatory in all secondary schools. Though there appears to be no possibility that Spanish will ever become the first language of more than a small minority of the population, it remains uncertain whether the official promotion of Spanish as well as of Tagalog will ultimately lead to any decline in the use of English, and it is to be hoped that the rivalries of linguistic politics will neither obstruct the cause of national unity nor undermine the great asset

[70] This is nevertheless misleading. The Philippines is the third-largest country in which English is the most widely spoken language. But there are more English speakers in Canada and Australia than in the Philippines.

[71] See Bernstein, p. 19.

Fig. 106—Key to linguistic map of the Philippines

1. ISINAI. 2. GADDANG. 3. IGOROT. 4. IFUGAO. 5. ILONGOT. 6. IBANAG. 7. TINGGIAN. 8. BONTOK. 9. KALINGA. 10. APAYAO. 11. ILOCANO. 12. IVATAN. 13. SAMBALI. 14. PANGASINAN. 15. PAMPANGO. 16. TAGALOG. 17. BIKOL. 18. DUMAGAT. 19. MANGYAN. 20. KALAMIANO. 21. KUYUNON. 22. AGUTAINA. 23. PANAYANO. 24. AKLAN. 25. HARAY-A. 26. CEBUANO. 27. SAMARENO. 28. SUBANON. 29. MARANAO. 30. BUKIDNON. 31. MANOBO. 32. MAGINDANAO. 33. ATA. 34. MANGGUANGAN. 35. BAGOBO. 36. TIRURAY. 37. BILA-AN. 38. TAGAKA-OLO. 39. KULAMAN. 40. MANDAYA. 41. TAGBANUA. 42. YAKAN. 43. JOLOANO AND SAMAL. ? LANGUAGE UNKNOWN.

which the country possesses in its command of the leading international language of today.

In the last analysis, however, it is the class division,[72] between a small upper stratum consisting of *caciques*, officials and business and professional men, and the great mass of the peasantry who exist at an altogether lower standard of

TABLE 102

THE PHILIPPINES: PRINCIPAL LANGUAGES, 1937 AND 1948

1937		1948	
(a) Christian Filipinos		English	7,156,420
Tagalog (C Luzon)	2,250,000	Spanish	345,111
Ilocano (N Luzon)	1,300,000	Tagalog	7,126,913
Pampanga (N Luzon)	390,000	Visayan group	8,506,946
Pangasinan (N Luzon)	350,000	(of which):	
Ibanog (N Luzon)	120,000	Hiligaynon	2,435,577
Bicol (S Luzon)	830,000	Cebuano	4,856,017
Visayan group	5,330,000	Samareno	1,215,352
(b) Moro groups	490,500	Ilocano	2,642,095
(of which):		Pampanga	707,290
Maguindanao	160,000	Pangasinan	664,336
Samal	88,000	Others	2,440,722
Sulu	125,000		
(c) Pagan groups (including Negritos)	584,500		
(of which):			
Ifugao (Luzon)	100,000		
Bontoc "	40,000		
Ibaloi "	30,000		
Kalinga "	30,000		
Lepanto "	30,000		
Bukidnon	35,000		
Bukidonon (Mindanao)	35,000		
Manobo (Mindanao)	30,000		
Subanun (Mindanao)	27,000		
Tagbanua (Palawan)	20,000		

Sources: Keesing (A), Chapter 9, and *Facts about the Philippines*.

[72] The socio-economic aspects of this are considered above, pp. 708–10.

living which constitutes the greatest threat to the internal stability of the Philippine Republic. At most, the former element comprises no more than a million people, and even if the hitherto small but now growing middle class of small tradesmen, skilled workers, lower-grade civil servants and school-teachers be counted in, the broad outlines of the picture are not significantly changed.

In contrast to the other newly independent states of South-east Asia, all of which have adopted universal suffrage, despite a generally low level of literacy, the franchise in the Philippines is restricted to the literate 60–70 per cent of the adult population,[73] which means, in effect, that the most impoverished members of the community, namely the landless peasants, are virtually unrepresented in Congress. It was the supreme significance of Magsaysay that he represented a break with the established Philippine tradition of government by the wealthy minority, and on the way in which this precedent is regarded by the ruling élite during the next few years the whole future of the Republic is likely to depend.

VI. CONCLUSION

Alone among the former colonial lands of South-east Asia the Philippines has been linked in recent centuries with the Americas rather than with Europe. In the moulding of its culture and society, Spanish influence, via the intermediary of the New World colonies, has been all-important, and in both these respects the country today shows much closer affinities with Mexico and the Andean republics than with any of its South-east Asian neighbours. Moreover, while the United States subsequently made an invaluable contribution through the dissemination of English-language education and the introduction of a democratic form of government, its relative neglect of economic development and its extreme reluctance to tamper with the existing but archaic social order have meant that its impress on the life of the country has not gone as deep as is often supposed. Thus, outside Manila and a few other towns, the Philippines is still only superficially Anglo-Americanized, and in the long run its Hispano-American heritage may prove to be the more significant determinant of its character.

Be that as it may, the Filipinos with their cosmopolitan traditions and the highest standard of literacy[74] in all South-east Asia are often disposed to regard themselves as forming a natural bridge between East and West and, more specifically, as constituting the natural leaders of the region in which they live. Thus, shortly after independence their permanent representative at the United Nations, General Romulo, proposed the formation of a Pan-Malayan Union, to include the Philippines, Indonesia and Malaya, and in 1950 President Quirino sought to establish a regional organization embracing the whole vast realm stretching from Pakistan to Australia.

These endeavours met with no success. For, apart from the obvious difficulties

[73] *I.e.* both sexes, over 21.

[74] In living standards the Philippines ranks second highest (*i.e.* after Malaya) in South-east Asia. See above, Table 10.

TABLE 103

THE PHILIPPINES: OVERSEAS TRADE BY COUNTRIES

(All figures f.o.b., in 000 Pesos)

A. Exports

Country of destination	*Value* 1956	1959
United States	482,395	585,160
Japan	160,849	233,280
Netherlands	78,610	82,500
Germany	27,606	29,200
Colombia	21,865	4,610
Belgium and Luxemburg	16,147	11,830
Sweden	15,718	4,480
United Kingdom	13,785	17,340
Denmark	12,399	9,400
Hong Kong	11,271	3,250
Norway	8,243	4,560
Venezuela	7,049	12,860
Korea	5,448	14,350
Spain	4,838	6,840
Italy	3,612	7,790
Total (including others)	902,200	1,058,990

B. Imports

Country or origin	*Value* 1956	1959
United States	600,905	463,530
Japan	102,391	179,940
Indonesia	44,757	87,400
Germany	34,485	47,390
Canada	32,109	28,030
United Kingdom	30,579	42,990
Malaya and Singapore	29,251	11,590
Netherlands	20,461	26,800
Belgium and Luxemburg	18,247	12,530
Hong Kong	14,723	15,750
Saudi Arabia	14,509	11,030
Australia	9,999	20,620
France	7,313	8,880
Argentina	5,731	3,960
India	5,413	4,120
Total (including others)	1,012,900	1,018,280

Source: Central Bank of the Philippines, cited in *Facts about the Philippines* and *Yearbook of International Trade Statistics*, U.N.

involved in organizing any such regional arrangements, none of the neighbouring peoples regard the Filipinos as truly representative of South-east Asia. On the contrary, their mestizo élite, their Western traditions and their supposed rejection of Asian values are all suspect, and it is widely believed that their surviving military and commercial ties with the United States[75] and their failure to trans-

TABLE 104

THE PHILIPPINES: OVERSEAS TRADE BY COMMODITIES

(*All figures f.o.b., in 000 Pesos*)

A. Exports

	1956	1959
Copra	268,601	276,146
Sugar (centrifugal)	201,219	225,273
Logs and lumber	97,656	160,888
Abacá (unmanufactured)	69,940	77,726
Coconut oil (inedible)	47,952	44,968
Chromite ore	27,632	33,509
Desiccated coconut	25,716	36,332
Iron ore	22,907	18,123
Copper concentrate	21,269	32,150
Pineapple (canned)	10,973	16,045
Total (including others)	902,200	1,056,458

B. Imports

	1956	1959
Machinery (non-electrical)	154,362	156,653
Textile yarns, fabrics and made-up articles	119,215	77,281
Mineral fuels, lubricants, etc.	104,780	118,780
Base metals	88,786	100,987
Dairy products, eggs and honey	59,184	37,817
Transport equipment	58,047	54,609
Cereals and cereal preparations	52,322	46,241
Electrical machinery, apparatus and appliances	39,150	58,664
Paper, paperboard and manufactures	36,404	39,332
Metal manufactures	29,531	30,434
Total (including others)	1,012,900	1,018,278

Source: Bureau of Commerce, cited in *Facts about the Philippines* and *Yearbook of International Trade Statistics, U.N.*

[75] Under the Bell Act U.S. citizens have equal rights with Philippines citizens to exploit natural resources and to operate utilities in the Philippines.

TABLE 105

THE PHILIPPINES: MANUFACTURING INDUSTRY, 1953–8

	Number of establishments reporting		*Value of production (million Pesos)*	
	1953	1958	1953	1958
Foods, manufactures	386	547	381·6	276·5
Beverages	106	68	133·9	157·5
Tobacco products	87	68	148·7	215·8
Textiles	43	68	56·3	178·3
Wearing apparel and other made-up goods and footwear	315	400	96·5	69·6
Wood and cork products, except furniture	338	341	106·3	110·0
Furniture and fixtures	99	211	3·7	9·5
Paper and paper products	32	161	17·9	92·5
Leather products, except footwear and other apparel	28	20	2·7	2·0
Rubber products	13	18	11·2	73·9
Chemicals and chemical products	224	400	78·3	315·1
Animal and vegetable oils and fats	19	13	79·8	58·3
Non-metallic mineral products	68	113	49·0	84·0
Metal products	153	301	26·8	115·0
Electrical machinery, appliances, apparatus and supplies	22	59	6·0	18·1
Transportation equipment and assembly plants	9	38	15·2	54·0
Miscellaneous manufactures	293	159	26·1	29·3
Electricity, gas and heat	347	135	60·3	115·6
Total	2,582	3,119	1,300·3	1,975·0

Source: based on *Handbook Philippine Statistics, 1903–1959*, pp. 51–5.

form the structure of society, a step which is elsewhere considered to be an integral part of the national revolution, are indicative of continued subservience to Western capitalism.

While such an attitude may sometimes recall the parable of the mote and the beam, it has been a formidable obstacle to the closer collaboration which successive Philippine governments have desired to achieve with neighbouring states. Yet in the long run such ties will assuredly develop.[76] As the old trading links with the United States gradually weaken and as the Filipinos begin to work out solutions to their own problems, which at bottom have so much in common with those of their neighbours, the accidents of history will take second place to the facts or geography, and the Philippines will find its destiny ever more closely bound to that of the rest of South-east Asia.

SELECT BIBLIOGRAPHY

Araneta
Ball
Bernstein
Berreman
Bowman
Buss (B)
Cressey
Cuaderno
Cutshall (A) (C)
Fernando and Africa
Forbes
Ginsburg (B)
Golay (A) (B)
Hart, D. V.
Hayden
Higgins (B)
Hunt
Jenkins
Jones and Mehnert
Keesing (A) (B)
Kolb
Krieger
Mendinueto
Pelzer (C) (E)
Purcell (D)
Robequain (D)
Ronall
Roosevelt
Scaff
Spencer, J. E. (A) (B) (C)
Stephens
Vandenbosch and Butwell
Wernstedt (A) (B)
Wurfel (A) (C)
Zinkin (A)

Bataan Monthly
Facts about the Philippines
Far Eastern quarterly: Special number on the Philippines, 4, 1945
The Philippines, 1953
The Philippines, Review of commercial conditions
Colombo Plan Reports
Economic Surveys of Asia and the Far East
Americana Encyclopædia
Encyclopædia Britannica
Handbook Philippine Statistics, 1903–1959
Philippine agricultural situation
Journal of Philippine statistics
Population of the Philippines by provinces and municipality
Population growth and manpower in the Philippines

The standard work on the geography of the Philippines is Kolb's excellent study in German. On land use and population problems the major works by Pelzer (C) and by Spencer (B) are fundamental, and may be supplemented by the other writings of these two authors listed above, while various other aspects

[76] As noted on page 659, Malaya, Thailand and the Philippines in July 1961 jointly established A.S.A. However, the Philippines' claim to North Borneo (see above, p. 725, note 62) led to a cooling of relations with Malaysia and hence to a decline of interest in A.S.A.

of economic geography are well handled by Cutshall (A) (C) and Wernstedt (A) (B).

On administration and governmental policy, largely or wholly during the period of United States control, Forbes, Hayden and Roosevelt are all of great value, while in the general field of social studies the works by Bernstein, Keesing (A) (B), Krieger, and Hunt should also be consulted. Among the wealth of published material on post-war economic matters should be noted the works by Araneta, Golay (A) (B), Hart, D. V., Higgins (B), Jenkins, and Wurfel; and on more specifically political problems the studies by Scaff, Buss (B), and Fernando and Africa are all useful.

Addenda: Note the important new study by Golay (C). Note also Cutshall, Alden, *The Philippines: nation of islands*, New York, 1964, and the many useful articles that have appeared in the *Philippine Geographical Journal* (Manila).

PART VI

Epilogue

CHAPTER 22

South-east Asia and the World

I. THE AFTERMATH OF WAR

Few parts of the world have experienced such profound political and social changes during the past quarter of a century as has South-east Asia. Within the space of a few months following the first Japanese attacks in December 1941, the Western imperial powers, which since the middle of the 19th century had drastically refashioned the map of virtually the entire region, were ignominiously expelled, and although three years later the tables were turned again and the Japanese compelled to relinquish all their gains, the Western powers returned only for a brief interlude to wind up their affairs before withdrawing for ever. At the time of writing, this process is almost complete and, with the setting up of the Federation of Malaysia in September 1963, the sole surviving traces of Western rule in South-east Asia are the diminutive half-island of Portugese Timor and the even smaller British-protected Sultanate of Brunei.

Moreover, partly because of their wartime experiences, which were unparalleled in other colonial lands, many of the South-east Asian peoples have been particularly thorough-going in their rejection of Western affiliations. Thus, while the South Asian successor states – India, Pakistan and Ceylon – remained in the Commonwealth, Burma opted out in 1948, the new national states of Indochina – Cambodia, Laos and Vietnam – found little satisfaction in the offer of associated statehood within the French Union, of which their membership was tacitly allowed to lapse after the Geneva Agreement of 1954, and in 1956 the Indonesian government unilaterally withdrew from the Netherlands-Indonesian Union of 1949. Of the newly independent states, only Malaysia, as a member of the Commonwealth, and the Philippines, by virtue of its economic and defence agreements with the United States, now maintain any really significant links with their erstwhile metropolitan powers.

Accordingly, where formerly there existed a series of colonial dependencies, each tied politically and in varying degree also economically to a particular Western power, and relying – though in the crucial test unavailingly – on that same Western power for the preservation of its security, the South-east Asia of recent years has comprised a growing number of independent, but at the same time weak and inexperienced states, each with its painter cut, standing self-consciously alone as it prepares to chart its individual course on turbulent and unfamiliar seas.

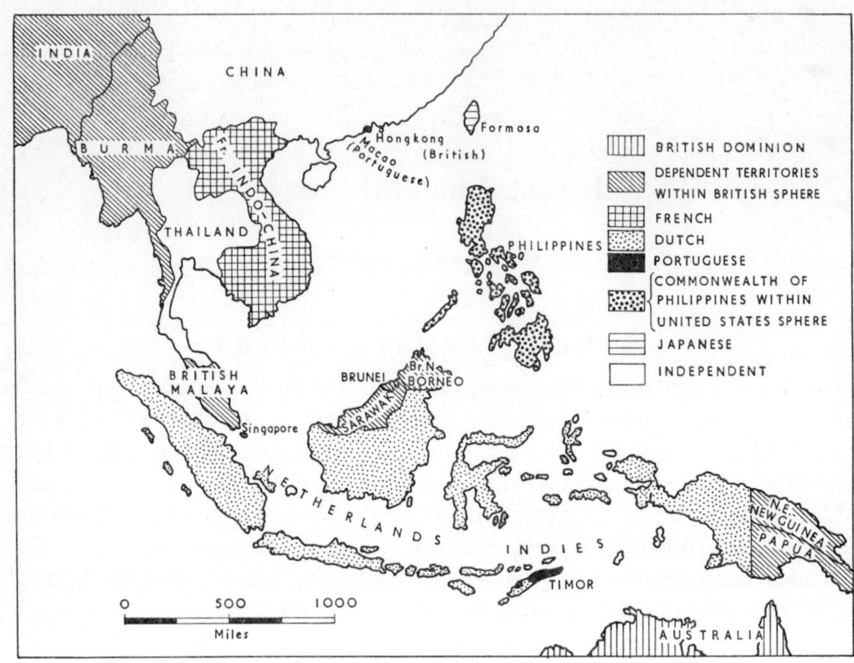

FIG. 107—South-east Asia: imperial alignments, 1939

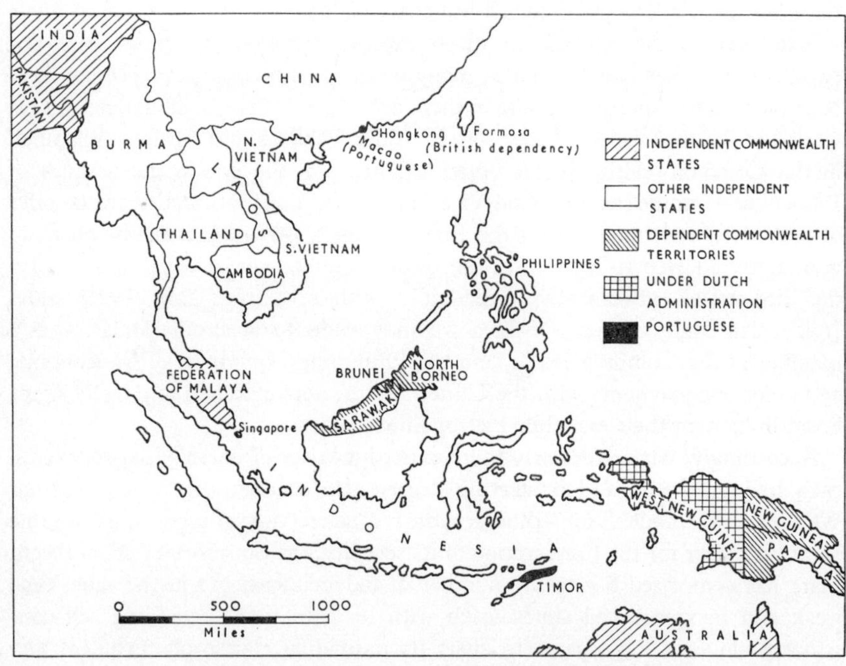

FIG. 108—South-east Asia: political alignments, 1961

The attempts of the several South-east Asian states to tackle the problems which confront them in this post-war era have provided the central theme of the greater part of this book. As has been implied in Chapter 6, the basic economic problem of restoring and if possible improving upon pre-war living standards, while at the same time promoting new industrial and other activities in order to reduce excessive dependence on primary production, and the no less urgent political problem of building up a cohesive sense of national unity among populations which are both multi-lingual and multi-racial, are common to every one of the newly independent states, and indeed also in large measure to Thailand, Singapore and the British Borneo territories as well.

Yet despite this academic similarity in the problems to be solved, the approach to them has differed significantly from country to country. For although the communal difficulties, for example of Indonesia and Burma, may be similar in kind, they differ sharply in detail, and it no more follows that a solution appropriate to the one will work in the other than it can be assumed that what is good for Malayan rubber is equally applicable to Siamese rice. Indeed it is only to the detached observer outside that the overall economic and political similarities seem to outweigh local differences of emphasis and setting, to say nothing of the traditional rivalries which still tend to divide the several states one from another. And from the point of view of the individual governments the magnitude of the tasks calling for immediate attention within their own borders has been so great as to leave little time to spare for consideration of how neighbouring governments were dealing with the situation in their particular territories.

Thus during the first fifteen years which followed the Second World War very little was done towards promoting any form of South-east Asian regional organization, though such a possibility had been fairly widely discussed, particularly in the United States, during the closing stages of the war. Admittedly, on July 27, 1947, a 'Manifesto of representatives of the countries of Southeast Asia' was issued at Bangkok on behalf of spokesmen from Indonesia, Malaya, Vietnam, Cambodia, Laos and Thailand, but it amounted to little more than a vague declaration of mutual support against Western colonialism which, understandably at that time, was still regarded as the principal obstacle to the realization of nationalist aims in most parts of the region. But the manifesto was never translated into any permanent political form, nor did anything ever come of either General Romulo's proposed Pan Malayan Union to embrace the Philippines, Indonesia and Malaya,[1] or of the even more nebulous attempts in the early post-war years to bring together Burma. Thailand, Laos and Cambodia in a so-called Buddhist bloc,[2] though it is perhaps significant that even at this stage the cultural-geographical cleavage between the Malay archipelago and the

[1] See above, p. 731. Though there were signs of a revival of such ideas in 1962–3.

[2] The possibility that this should also include Ceylon was suggested, but Vietnam remained outside its scope, for Buddhism in this connexion referred only to Theravada Buddhism.

Buddhist countries of the mainland was already revealed as a possible obstacle to the realization of any wider regional unity. However, with the progressive withdrawal of Western political control after 1947, the main preoccupation shifted from the maintenance of solidarity against the 'colonialists' to the more urgent matter of taking over from them,[3] and in these changing circumstances local interest in regional association tended to decline during the 1950s.

In the event, the measure of success or failure which the respective South-east Asian governments achieved during that decade in their attempts simultaneously to preserve the new states as going concerns while gradually remodelling both their economies and their socio-political structures has differed in several respects from what was expected by many – perhaps indeed most – observers in the years immediately following the war.

Taken as a whole, the position today, if distinctly less bleak than it appeared after the widespread Communist-inspired revolts of 1948, still falls short in the two vital respects of living standards and political stability of what might not unreasonably have been hoped for after ten to fifteen years of independence.[4] In particular, the continuing instability of both Indonesia and Vietnam has come as a surprise to those who assumed that the comparatively long and involved history of nationalism in these two countries implied a higher level of political sophistication among their peoples than was to be expected in most of the neighbouring states. On balance, both Indonesia and Vietnam have lost ground economically since the war, as also, and perhaps even more unexpectedly, has Burma,[5] whose export trade, from being the third largest in the region in 1937, had fallen to fifth place in 1960. (Table 13.) On the other hand Thailand, the Philippines and the Federation of Malaya have all registered positive advances in economic prosperity since 1937, and unquestionably these three countries, together perhaps with Cambodia, are also in the lead in respect of political stability and the preservation of internal law and order.

No doubt the experience of Thailand and the Philippines in running their own affairs since before the Second World War[6] goes far to explain their comparatively quick return to stability after the Japanese occupation. But if few would deny that the setbacks in Indonesia and likewise in Laos and Vietnam can be traced back to their protracted struggles for independence after 1945, resulting from the reluctance of the Dutch and the French respectively to bow to the winds of

[3] Though the Indonesian President appeared until 1962 to be more concerned with getting rid of the remaining vestige of Dutch rule in West New Guinea than with the tasks awaiting attention in the vastly more important territories over which Indonesia had been granted full sovereignty in 1949. See above, Chapter 11, especially pp. 389–390.

[4] Not all the states have had so long. Complete independence came to the Indochinese states only in 1953–4, and to the Federation of Malaya in 1957. As noted above, it has not yet come to Singapore, the British Borneo territories or Portuguese Timor.

[5] *Cf.* Spate (C), p. 34.

[6] Under the Commonwealth status of 1935 the Philippines was largely self-governing. (See above, p. 705.) Thailand has never been a colony, though it was not until 1932 that constitutional government replaced the old absolutist system. (See above, p. 503.)

change, it is also possible to argue that the contrast within the erstwhile British sphere, between the continuing confusion in Burma and the remarkable success story of the Federation of Malaya, derives basically from the fact that, whereas independence was conceded to the former before the ravages of war had been repaired, the exceptionally complex communal situation in Malaya delayed any comparable move there for another ten years, during which time both security and prosperity were effectively restored.

While, however, it is easy to make such observations after the event, it does not follow that the critical decisions taken by the various governments were necessarily ill-conceived at the time when they had to be made. For although it is abundantly clear that the extent of the damage, both material and spiritual, occasioned by the war and the associated Japanese occupation was such as to make extremely difficult the task of any post-war government, it was not unreasonable to believe that greater success was likely to be achieved by harnessing the new-found sense of national unity, wherever this existed, to the task of reconstruction, than by attempting meanwhile to postpone independence and, in so doing, running the risk of a complete breakdown of nationalist confidence in Western intentions.[7] And all things considered, it was not unreasonable to believe that the national élites which had emerged into the political limelight by the end of the war were capable of tackling their countries' problems in the years that lay ahead, had they been left in peace to do so.

But whether, in view of the focal and exposed geographical position which South-east Asia occupies in the world at large, it was reasonable in 1945 to expect that these countries would be left in peace is more arguable, and had there in fact been a more widespread appreciation in the West of the implications of the Balkan analogy, to which reference was made in Chapter 1, it is possible that different decisions might have been taken on more than one occasion, though not necessarily with any more satisfactory results. Be that as it may, however, the one event which more than any other has darkened the whole South-east Asian scene since the capitulation of Japan in 1945 was something which no Western statesmen could reasonably be expected to have foreseen in the immediate post-war years, and indeed not even the Soviet leaders themselves appear at that time to have believed that a Communist regime might assume control over China before the decade had run its course.

It was in fact in October 1949 that the new Chinese People's Republic was formally established, by which time the Philippines and Burma had achieved their independence, Malaya had been launched on its new course towards that goal with the constitutional change from Union to Federation in 1948, and the Round Table Conference to arrange the transfer of sovereignty from the Netherlands to Indonesia was already in session at the Hague. While it is pointless to speculate on what might have happened in these various cases had the

[7] The dangers inherent in the latter course were clearly illustrated in Burma during 1945–7.

Communists taken over in China three years earlier, there is no denying that the establishment of the new regime in Peking profoundly affected the course of events thereafter in all parts of French Indochina, and most especially so in the Vietnamese lands. For by a strange irony it happened that this one major European dependency in South-east Asia in which no solution to the nationalist question was yet in sight embraced in Vietnam the only part of that region which enjoyed close cultural affinities with China itself, and in which nationalism had important links with Communism.[8] Thus from 1949 onwards the nationalist struggles in Indochina were increasingly confused by the two inter-related but by no means identical factors of Communist penetration and the mounting rivalry between the two power blocs respectively led by the United States and the Soviet Union.

In these circumstances the French tried to enlist the moral support of other Western Powers in their opposition to the Vietminh, by stressing the Communist rather than the nationalist character of the latter, though in fact the two were inextricably intertwined. And since by this time the United States had already been alarmed by the series of Communist terrorist outbreaks which began in many widely separated parts of South-east Asia in 1948,[9] it was disposed to listen sympathetically to the French appeals. However, when it became obvious that, notwithstanding the prodigious financial assistance they had received over several years from the United States, the French had no prospect of defeating the Vietminh, the Geneva settlement was hurriedly patched up in July 1954, and thereafter the United States, which had taken no part in the Geneva talks, made its own arrangements for filling the power vacuum which was expected to develop south of the 17th parallel.[10] With the formulation of Mr. John Foster Dulles's plans to meet this situation, the emphasis in United States policy *vis-à-vis* South-east Asia appeared, at least in part, to have swung away from traditionalist American support of colonial nationalism towards a new but no less distinctively American version of geopolitics directed above all to the containment of Communism on a global scale.[11]

Yet, however regrettable this tempering of idealism by power politics may appear in retrospect to have been, it was probably inevitable that, no matter what form of government had existed in China, geopolitical considerations could

[8] The embryonic nationalist movements in Cambodia and Laos, like those in the rest of South-east Asia, looked to India rather than China for inspiration, and were in no sense allied to Communism. See below, pp. 747–8.

[9] *I.e.* before China became a Communist state. It is said that these outbreaks were planned at a Communist conference at Calcutta in April 1948. They were aimed at undermining 'bourgeois nationalism' by interrupting economic recovery and progress.

[10] See above, p. 556.

[11] The doctrine of containment originated several years before Mr. Dulles began to apply it in South-east Asia. The seminal idea was first propounded in an article by X (George F. Kennan) entitled 'The Sources of Soviet Conduct' in *Foreign Affairs*, 25, 4, 1947, pp. 566–82. The N.A.T.O. alliance, the new U.S. policy towards Japan after 1948, and the economic support of the French war effort in Indochina were all aspects of the containment policy. See also below, p. 749.

not for long have been excluded from the South-east Asian scene. To expect a series of new, weak and inexperienced states to be left undisturbed in an area such as this, which throughout its history has been a meeting place of external rivalries of one kind or another, was fundamentally unrealistic. For politics no less than nature abhors a vacuum, and the successive expulsion of the Western armies, the defeat of Japan and the final withdrawal of Western power all within little more than a decade not merely created such a vacuum but doubly underlined its existence.

II. WESTERN DIFFERENCES, THE NEW RÔLE OF INDIA, THE FORMULATION OF THE COLOMBO PLAN AND THE CREATION OF S.E.A.T.O.

Before going on to examine in more detail the nature of the new American moves, it is profitable to pause for a moment to consider the widening rift which had begun to appear several years earlier between the respective South-east Asian policies of the British Commonwealth and the United States. And in order to appreciate the true significance of this rift it is necessary to go back still farther to consider certain geopolitical concepts which emerged during and immediately after the Second World War, but whose origins lie in the basic geographical difference between the traditional Commonwealth habit of viewing South-east Asia in terms of its Indian Ocean affinities and the no less firmly rooted American practice of regarding the region as forming part of the Asian rim of the Pacific Ocean. Or to put the issue in the slightly different terms used at the beginning of this book, it is necessary to consider the external as well as the internal implications of the two alternative Western names for South-east Asia, to wit Further India and the Far Eastern tropics.[12]

So far as the Commonwealth is concerned, the initiative in policy making *vis-à-vis* South-east Asia had already ceased to lie solely in metropolitan British hands before the end of the Second World War, as soon, in fact, as it became clear that India, the centre-piece of the British empire in Asia, would be granted its independence after the war. However, there was no lack of constructive thinking along these lines both in India and elsewhere within the Commonwealth, and indeed the need for forward planning to fill the places which would be left by the impending departure of both the Japanese and the Western colonial powers was accurately foreseen as early as 1943 by the Indian scholar, K. M. Panikkar, whose book on this theme, *The Future of South-East Asia*, was incidentally the first to popularize the use of that term as a regional name. Understandably Panikkar viewed South-east Asia as 'Further India', and the central argument of his book, which did not anticipate a Communist take-over in China or even any rapid growth in the industrial strength[13] of that country,

[12] See above, p. 3.

[13] Though he did take into account the wartime growth of Chinese military power, its interests in mainland South-east Asia and the possible consequences of the population pressure within its borders. See Panikkar (A), pp. 30–1 and 103–5.

was that the defence of India depended primarily upon sea power and that, in the era of national independence which he rightly expected to follow the war, it would be essential to preserve the continuity of the Indian Ocean defence system built up by the British during the preceding century and a half. Only on the basis of a regional organization for the whole Indian Ocean theatre, of which an independent India must be the foundation, could safety be assured, and in the absence of a stable and responsible government in India 'Further India will remain the cockpit of colonial ambitions, incapable of defending itself, and a prey to the predatory urge of any power which is strong enough to attack it'.[14]

However, Panikkar did not limit his horizon to purely strategic considerations, and besides making use of historic arguments, he also stressed the importance of the economic links which would be likely to develop between a rapidly industrializing India and a South-east Asia which would inevitably for a long time remain largely an exporter of many of the primary products that India itself required. And while he emphasized that the continuing industrialization of India would provide scope for the co-operation of Indian and British financial interests, as well as giving rise to growing competition between the manufactures of the two countries in the markets of other Indian Ocean lands, it is clear that he was also concerned with the prospect of India's largely replacing Japan, particularly in the markets of South-east Asia. Thus, if 'a truly satisfactory economy is to develop in this area after the war, it can only be if India and South-East Asia work out a "Co-prosperity sphere" based on their interdependence'.[15]

Although the course of events in South-east Asia since the war has included much that could not have been foreseen by Panikkar, no-one reading his 1943 book today can fail to be impressed by his extraordinary prescience. Thanks to the great wartime expansion of Indian industry, that country has changed from being pre-eminently an exporter of primary produce to a very important exporter of manufactured goods. Indeed as early as 1950 it was the world's first exporter of cotton piece goods (by yardage), and although this was an exceptional year India has consistently ranked more recently as one of the three or four largest suppliers of cotton textiles, the most obvious markets for which are in the lands bordering the Indian Ocean, where Indian traders have long been firmly established.

Moreover, while at first sight it might seem that Panikkar's strategic views were completely at variance with Mr. Nehru's post-independence policy of non-alignment, there is in fact a considerable element of continuity here also, for it is precisely Panikkar's same Indian Ocean region which Nehru has been most concerned, for the sake of India's own security, to keep outside the orbit of either of the great power blocs. And indeed, as long ago as 1944, Nehru himself, commenting on the possibility of a post-war 'regional grouping of the countries

[14] *Ibid*, pp. 11–12.
[15] Panikkar (A), p. 16. See also *ibid.*, pp. 33 and 55.

bordering on the Indian Ocean on either side of India', stated that 'India will develop as the centre of economic and political activity in the Indian Ocean area, in southeast Asia and right up to the Middle East. Her position gives an economic and strategic importance in a part of the world which is going to develop rapidly in the future'.[16]

Nevertheless it would be wholly wrong to assume that either Nehru or Panikkar, or indeed any other Indian statesman, conceived of his country's links with these lands only in terms of economics and strategy. For in fact innumerable Indians from Tagore onwards have derived inspiration from the memory of India's civilizing mission in Further India during the first millennium of our era, and furthermore all the main pre-war nationalist parties in South-east Asia outside Vietnam had tended to model themselves on the Indian *swaraj* movement.[17] Thus, after Japan's wartime failure to maintain its reputation as the champion of 'Asia for the Asiatics', India has attempted with considerable success to assume the rôle of spokesman for the former colonial lands of South-east Asia.

In the meantime another state within the old British Indian Ocean region, namely Australia, has also tried in curiously parallel ways to help fill the gap created by the Japanese capitulation in 1945. Like India, if on a more limited scale, Australia also experienced rapid industrial expansion during the Second World War, and has since shown a similar interest in the potential market which South-east Asia affords for its manufactured goods. And like India again, though in a way which has surprised many Europeans, particularly the Dutch, Australia has actively sympathized with post-war nationalist aspirations in the area which it now calls not the Far East but the Near North, for Australians now appreciate that the corollary of White Australia can only be Asia for the Asians. But, more important than all this, Australia, to an even greater extent than India, has been concerned to see that a potential aggressor, whether it be a resurgent Japan or a newly expansionist China, should be halted as far as possible from its own shores.

To these two similar, though not identical, strands of opinion *vis-à-vis* South-east Asia in the early post-war period may be added those of many other Commonwealth countries as well, and certainly not least that of Britain itself, whose own forward-looking attitude towards Burmese and Malayan nationalism stood out in sharp contrast to the much more cautious policies of the other European powers with colonial interests in this region. Thus it was not surprising that this substantial measure of Commonwealth agreement found expression in the launching of the Colombo Plan in January 1950, that is almost immediately after

[16] Nehru, p. 550 (fourth edition).

[17] This Indian-style nationalism was essentially democratic and non-Communist as were its various South-east Asian counterparts, though Vietnamese nationalism, which took its cue from China, came increasingly under Communist influence. See above, pp. 533–538 and 744.

the Communist victory in China but at a time when the memory of the recent Japanese invasion still remained sharp.

The origin of this plan has been variously attributed to Mr. D. S. Senanayake of Ceylon and to Sir (then Mr.) Percy Spender of Australia, but besides these it seems that it owes something not only to Panikkar's ideas as expressed in 1943, but also to a further memorandum which he prepared and passed to the British and Australian Ambassadors to China while he himself was serving as Indian Ambassador to that country, during the final collapse before the Communist take-over in 1949.[18]

Although membership of the Colombo Plan, which represents in effect a kind of mutual aid association for economic development, significantly in South *and* South-east Asia, was never restricted to Commonwealth countries, the Indian sub-continent was clearly its main focus, and the geographical pattern was essentially that of the old Indian Ocean region, with its traditional links with Britain, Australia and other parts of the Commonwealth. Indeed the original plan may be fairly described in effect, if not entirely in intention, as an economic counterpart to Panikkar's strategic blueprint of 1943, at a time when emphasis on economic development had become more acceptable within the region than talk of military preparedness.

The United States, however, had meanwhile approached the post-war problems of South-east Asia from a different angle. To the Americans China rather than India had always been the key country in Asia, and immediately following the war it had been the American intention to build up China as a friendly power and potential counterweight to the U.S.S.R., while holding Japan severely in check and relegating it to at best a subsidiary rôle in the new East Asia. But the failure of China to play its assigned part, combined with the inability of Japan, with its greatly reduced industrial capacity, to support the post-war increase in its population, forced the United States to make the first of a series of 'agonizing reappraisals' of its foreign policy. Thus in 1948 the decision was taken to replace China by Japan as the major focus of American influence in Asia and, partly in order to relieve the burden on the United States tax-payer of indefinitely supporting 80 million ex-enemies, and partly in order to prevent these same 80 million from following the 550 million Chinese[19] on the road to Communism, Japan was to be rebuilt, in the words of General Draper, as 'the workshop of the Far East'.

Inevitably such a policy implied the rapid re-emergence of Japan as a major competitor in overseas markets for manufactured goods, to an extent that ran counter to the economic assumptions on which the early post-war policies of the Commonwealth countries towards South-east Asia had been based. For whatever gains Japan might hope to make in more distant markets, it was felt that its most obvious opportunities lay nearer at hand in the territories of the former

[18] See Wint (B), p. 13. and Panikkar (D), pp. 55–6.

[19] By 1960 the population of Japan was estimated at 93·2 million and that of mainland China at 645·5 million.

Co-prosperity sphere. And this situation assumed an even more controversial aspect after China joined the Communist bloc, for since the United States thereafter expected the Japanese to renounce any attempts to trade with the northern half of the old Co-prosperity sphere, their attention was bound to focus more than ever on the possibilities that might remain within the southern half, that is in South-east Asia.[20]

Coming as they did so quickly after the events of 1942–5, such developments aroused considerable misgiving both in South-east Asia and in the British Pacific Dominions, and this was further intensified as the United States proceeded with its plans to conclude a peace treaty with Japan which, along with 47 other states[21] it did in 1951, and then two years later to call upon the Japanese to reverse their American-inspired decision of 1945 to renounce armaments of all kinds, and in effect to play a more active part in the new American containment policy, designed to close the ring around the entire Soviet bloc, and in so doing to prevent the further territorial expansion of Communism.

It is against this background that the more specifically South-east Asian plans announced by Secretary Dulles after the Geneva Settlement should be seen. As has already been noted in Chapters 15 and 16, these included the replacement of French military power in Southern Vietnam by the building up of powerful American-trained indigenous forces there, together with the attempted bolstering up of the economies both of Southern Vietnam and also of the supposed buffer states of Laos and Cambodia next door, by means of prodigious outpourings of American aid funds. Meanwhile the co-operation was sought of all countries with South-east Asian interests which were willing to participate in extending the containment strategy into this part of the world.

Thus it was that in September 1954 S.E.A.T.O. came into being, with the Philippines, Thailand and Pakistan providing links, though markedly discontinuous ones, between the Pacific island chain extending through Japan and Formosa in the north-east and the N.A.T.O.[22] powers in Europe. And in the hope of plugging some of the more obvious gaps within South-east Asia itself, the S.E.A.T.O. powers initially 'designated' Cambodia, Laos and Southern Vietnam as areas against which they would regard an attack as 'endangering their own peace and security'.[23]

Besides the United States and the three Asian powers already mentioned, the S.E.A.T.O. group also included France and the three Commonwealth powers, Australia, New Zealand and the United Kingdom. For, while the collapse of the

[20] See above, pp. 194–8.

[21] Among these were Australia, New Zealand and the Philippines, all of which however had refused to sign the treaty until they had been given specific guarantees of United States help in the event of any future Japanese attack. See Fisher (P), p. 544.

[22] Since that time the C.E.N.T.O. group has been organized in the Middle East as the successor to the Baghdad Pact group.

[23] As noted on p. 572, the position of Laos and Cambodia in relation to S.E.A.T.O. was modified in 1962.

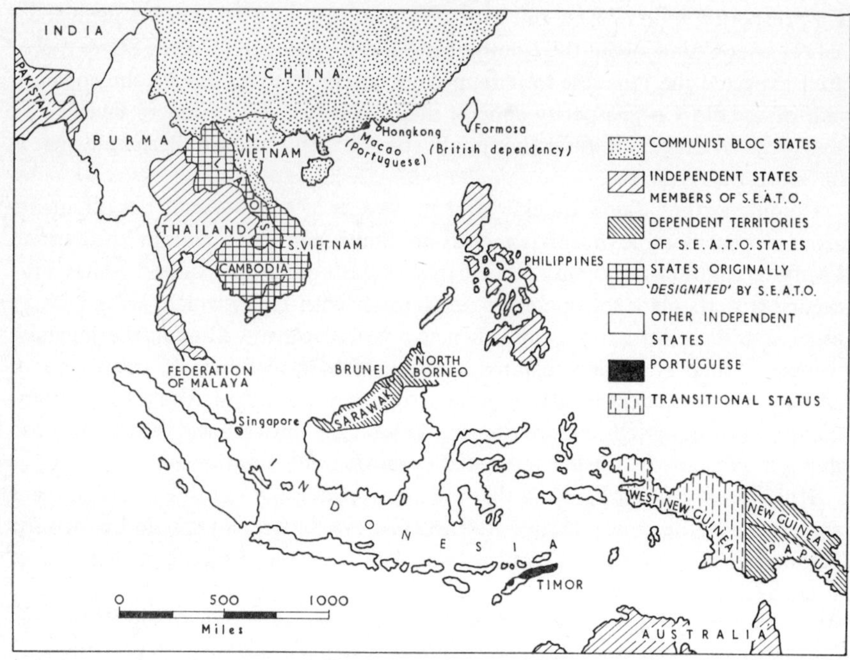

FIG. 109—South-east Asia: strategic alignments, 1954–62

French position in Indochina can scarcely be said to have reduced the differences between the Commonwealth and the United States attitudes towards South-east Asia, it did at least underline the need for acting more closely together within the limits which such continuing differences permitted.

Moreover, at the same time as the S.E.A.T.O. alignment was taking shape, its two South-east Asian members, Thailand and the Philippines, together with Japan, were admitted as members of the Colombo Plan, which by this time included Cambodia, Laos, Vietnam, Burma, Nepal, Indonesia, Singapore and the United States in addition to the original founder members.[24] But if the Colombo Plan group now included virtually the whole of South and South-east Asia, the strong opposition in particular of India to the concepts which S.E.A.T.O. represented implied a serious breach in Commonwealth unity so far as strategic planning was concerned. And in its turn this helped to maintain some degree of divergence between the Commonwealth members of S.E.A.T.O. on the one hand and the U.S.A. on the other. For, in seeking at least to take into account the attitudes of India and of the considerable body of similarly non-aligned opinion both in other parts of the Commonwealth and outside, the United

[24] The United States, Cambodia, Laos and Vietnam joined in 1951, Burma and Nepal in 1952, Indonesia in 1953 and the remainder in 1954. The Federation of Malaya became a full member in 1957 and Singapore in 1959.

Kingdom and its other Commonwealth partners have frequently taken up positions somewhat different from that of the United States which, particularly during the Dulles era, has sometimes seemed too ready to view South-east Asian problems solely in terms of the global Communist/Free World antithesis.

III. THE NEW RÔLE OF JAPAN AND THE PATTERN OF OUTSIDE AID TO SOUTH-EAST ASIA

Nevertheless in other respects important progress has been made in narrowing the differences between the United States and the Commonwealth, and in particular the latter is now much less critical of the American view that Japan should participate more extensively in South-east Asian trade. Once again it is interesting to quote a wartime comment of Panikkar, to the effect that 'the exclusion of Japan from the economy of South-east Asia is neither possible nor desirable'.[25]

No doubt this change derives partly from the growing belief that Communist China presents a far greater potential threat than post-war Japan to the security of South-east Asia and hence of Australia, New Zealand and the whole Indian Ocean region. But much more is involved here than merely strategic considerations, and as the passage of time has both dulled the fears and bitterness of 1942–5 and revealed the magnitude of the changes that have since been taking place in Japan, the arguments in favour of closer economic links between that country and South-east Asia have come to be considered on their merits, which in fact are very great.

Thus, apart from the significant degree of complementariness in the produce of temperate industrialized Japan and the tropical primary-producing lands of South-east Asia – the Far Eastern tropics – there should also be a tremendous opportunity for Japanese skills and services in these neighbouring lands to the south. For since in the cultivation of their basic foodstuff, namely rice, Japan has developed the most advanced techniques in the world, and has infinitely more experience than any Western nation, it is the obvious country to supply the kind of agricultural expertise which is most needed there. And in industry likewise, Japan, as an Asian country which has itself 'been through the mill', and in so doing adapted Western methods to Oriental conditions, now possesses precisely the sort of knowledge which South-east Asia requires at this stage in its evolution.[26]

It was this basic complementariness of the Japanese and the South-east Asian economies which in pre-war days had provided much of the rationale of the old Greater East Asia Co-prosperity Sphere, but the post-war changes in

[25] Panikkar (A), p. 110.

[26] A minor but significant reason why many South-east Asians have often preferred Japanese to European machinery has been that much of it was designed for people of comparably short stature to themselves.

both the economic and the political position of Japan have combined to make mutual trade between that country and South-east Asia a much more attractive proposition for the latter today than it was in the 1930s. For while Japan now constitutes no military threat to its neighbours,[27] which therefore have no cause to fear that closer commercial links might again prepare the way for political penetration and ultimate conquest, the country's great expansion in engineering and other advanced types of industrial production also means that it is primarily interested in finding markets for capital goods and better quality consumer goods, which will not compete with South-east Asia's own developing industries, since these are mostly of a less advanced type.

Admittedly the significance of these changes took time to make itself felt in South-east Asia, and it was not until some years after the conclusion of the Japanese Peace Treaty in 1951 that significant progress began to be made, though the treaty in fact marked a turning point. For although its terms included no formal stipulation about reparations, Japan did recognize its obligation to contribute substantial reparations to those Asian countries which it had invaded and, as its own reconstruction got under way, it began to honour these undertakings in a series of bilateral agreements, beginning with that between itself and Burma in 1955.[28]

While the pattern of these reparation settlements has varied somewhat from country to country, it has been common for a major part of the payment to take the form of an allocation for goods and technical services, and to be spread over a decade or more. Initially such arrangements aroused some suspicion, both locally and elsewhere, that Japan might try to use the payment of reparations as a means of re-establishing something like the old 'co-prosperous' relationship with the South-east Asian countries, to the detriment of their own plans for industrialization. But in fact there seems to be little cause for anxiety on this score, and Japan's ability to supply much-needed capital equipment, for example for the key hydro-electric installations at Lawpita in Burma and Danhim in Southern Vietnam, clearly represents a major contribution to the industrial programmes in both these countries.

Besides the important rôle played by reparations in restarting Japanese trade with the South-east Asian countries since the early 1950s, the readiness of the United States to allow aid funds which it granted to the latter to be spent on Japanese goods has also been a significant factor, though the further expansion of such trade must nowadays be effected by more normal commercial means. Be that as it may, the scale of Japanese economic enterprise in South-east Asia has already more than regained its pre-war level, as may be inferred from a comparison of Tables 106 and 107. Between 1952 and 1960 the value of Japan's

[27] Note also that since 1948 Japan has made a strikingly successful attempt to reduce its formerly high birth-rate.

[28] See above, pp. 481–2. Details of other reparations agreements, respectively with Indonesia, Southern Vietnam and the Philippines, are given on pp. 317, 566, note 75, and 727. See also Table 108, Part II.

TABLE 106

PRE-WAR TRADE OF SOUTH-EAST ASIAN COUNTRIES WITH CERTAIN OTHER COUNTRIES

South-east Asian country and year to which data refer		*United Kingdom*		**Other European metro-politan power*		*U.S.A.*		*Japan*		*India*		*China*		*British Malaya*	
		c	*d*	*c*	*d*	*c*	*d*	*c*	*d*	*c*	*d*	*c*	*d*	*c*	*d*
Burma	*a*	17%	2	—	—	6%	4	8%	3	56%	1	†	†	3%	5
1939–40	*b*	13%	2	—	—	1%	6	4%	5	59%	1	†	†	6%	4
Thailand	*a*	11%	3	—	—	5%	7	15%	2	6%	6	4%	9	26%	1
1938–9	*b*	1%	5	—	—	11%	2	1%	6	1%	7	†	†	57%	1
French Indochina	*a*	3%	6	56%	1	5%	4	3%	8	†	†	7%	3	3%	7
1938	*b*	2%	8	53%	1	9%	4	3%	5	3%	6	3%	7	10%	2
British Malaya	*a*	15%	3	—	—	3%	5	2%	10	3%	6	6%	4	—	—
1939	*b*	11%	2	—	—	43%	1	9%	3	4%	5	†	†	—	—
Netherlands Indies	*a*	8%	5	19%	2	10%	3	25%	1	3%	7	2%	9	8%	6
1937	*b*	5%	4	20%	1	19%	3	4%	5	1%	9	1%	8	19%	2
Philippines	*a*	2%	4	—	—	68%	1	6%	2	†	†	2%	6	2%	7
1939	*b*	3%	3	—	—	76%	1	6%	2	†	†	1%	5	1%	6

This table shows the proportion and ranking of the trade (import and export) of each South-east Asian country named (*extreme left*) with certain other countries named (*top line*).

(*a*) refers to imports (*b*) to exports
(*c*) to percentages (*d*) to order of ranking

Thus, for example, in 1939–40 17 per cent of Burma's imports came from the U.K., which represented the leading source of Burma's imports, while 1 per cent of Burma's exports went to the U.S.A., which ranked sixth among the countries to which Burmese exports were consigned.

*Note that 'Other European metropolitan power' refers to Holland in the case of the Netherlands Indies and to France and other French dependencies in the case of French Indochina.

†Indicates amounts or rankings of negligible importance.

imports from this region as a whole rose from $229·7 million to $602·8 million, representing over 13 per cent of all Japanese imports in the latter year, while the value of its exports to South-east Asia increased even more spectacularly, from $151·6 million to $629·6 million or nearly 15 per cent of the corresponding total.

Today, wherever one looks in South-east Asia, Japanese manufactures and evidence of Japanese economic and commercial enterprise can be seen on all hands, from the three-wheel taxis of Bangkok and the Kubota suction pumps and power tillers in the Burmese rice lands to the Maruzen-Toyo oil refinery at Singapore and the developing Japanese interest in the expanding iron ore production of the Federation of Malaya and the recently explored Silantek coalfield in Sarawak. But while Japanese trade with the region has grown in this way, and indeed is nowadays limited only by the relatively restricted purchasing power of the South-east Asian countries themselves, the hoped-for expansion of Indian trade with South-east Asia has not come about. Indeed between 1952 and 1960 the value of Indian imports from South-east Asia fell

TABLE 107

POST-WAR TRADE OF SOUTH-EAST ASIAN COUNTRIES WITH CERTAIN OTHER COUNTRIES

All data relate to 1959

South-east Asian country		*United Kingdom*		**Other European ex-metro-politan power*		*U.S.A.*		*Japan*		*India‡*		*China§*		*Singa-pore*		*Federa-tion of Malaya*	
		c	*d*	*c*	*d*	*c*	*d*	*c*	*d*	*c*	*d*	*c*	*d*	*c*	*d*	*c*	*d*
Burma	*a*	19%	2	——	—	5%	5	21%	1	11%	3	8%	4	——	—	3%	10‖
	b	9%	6	——	—	1%	14	4%	7	17%	2	†	†	——	—	11%	4‖
Thailand	*a*	10%	3	——	—	17%	2	25%	1	1%	n.a.	†	†	8%	4	3%	9
	b	3%	6	——	—	25%	1	12%	4	†	†	†	†	14%	3	14%	2
Cambodia	*a*	1%	11	29%	1	8%	5	13%	3	†	†	6%	6	——	—	12%	4‖
	b	1%	9	31%	1	25%	2	4%	5	†	†	2%	6	——	—	10%	4‖
Southern Vietnam	*a*	3%	8	18%	3	26%	1	21%	2	2%	9	†	†	†	†	†	†
	b	3%	7	32%	1	9%	4	3%	8	†	†	†	†	6%	6	†	†
Federation of Malaya	*a*	22%	1	——	—	3%	10	7%	5	3%	10	4%	7	10%	4	——	—
	b	13%	2	——	—	12%	4	13%	3	2%	9	1%	15	22%	1	——	—
Singapore	*a*	8%	3	——	—	3%	7	6%	4	2%	11	3%	6	——	—	20%	2
	b	8%	3	——	—	9%	2	6%	4	2%	17	3%	8	——	—	21%	1
Sarawak	*a*	9%	2	——	—	1%	10	2%	7	†	†	3%	5	5%	3	†	†
	b	11%	4	——	—	5%	6	14%	3	†	†	†	†	39%	1	†	†
North Borneo	*a*	20%	1	——	—	9%	4	6%	6	1%	14	3%	9	5%	8	1%	15
	b	11%	2	——	—	4%	6	40%	1	†	†	1%	12	11%	3	†	†
Indonesia	*a*	7%	5	4%	8	16%	1	15%	2	2%	11	13%	3	2%	11	†	†
	b	22%	2	1%	14	15%	3	4%	6	†	†	6%	4	23%	1	4%	7
Philippines	*a*	4%	5	——	—	46%	1	18%	2	†	†	†	†	†	†	†	†
	b	2%	5	——	—	55%	1	22%	2	†	†	†	†	†	†	†	†

This table is set out to correspond as closely as possible with Table 106.
(*a*) refers to imports (*b*) to exports
(*c*) to percentages (*d*) to order of ranking
*'Other European ex-metropolitan power' refers to Holland in the case of Indonesia and to metropolitan France in the cases of Cambodia and Southern Vietnam.
†Indicates amounts of rankings of negligible importance.
‡India in this table does not include Pakistan (as it does in Table 106).
§China refers to Chinese People's Republic.
‖Singapore and Federation of Malay combined.
Source: Based on data in *Yearbook of International Trade Statistics*, U.N., 1959.

from \$105·8 million to \$85·9 million, and that of exports to the region from \$110·0 million to \$53·8 million, so that in 1960 the total value of Indian trade with South-east Asia was little more than one-ninth that of the corresponding Japanese trade.[29]

This trend suggests that the close trading links between South-east Asia and Japan, such as the United States has tended to favour, have proved a good deal more effective than the corresponding commercial ties between South-east Asia

[29] These figures for Indian and Japanese trade may not be absolutely complete. They are based on the data given on pp. 282 and 329 in the 1960 *Yearbook of International Trade Statistics* (U.N.) and include all the South-east Asian countries there listed as trading partners of either India or Japan respectively.

and India implicit in the original concept of the Colombo Plan. Notwithstanding the very great British contribution to the economic development of India in the early years after the Second World War,[30] and the further massive assistance it has received, particularly from the United States in more recent times, the immense task of raising the extremely low living standards of this vast country of over 400 million people has been all engrossing, and it is scarcely surprising that India has not been able to match the economic and commercial dynamism of the new Japan, largely rebuilt and re-equipped as the latter has been, thanks above all to American influence.

Without wishing in any way to underrate the Colombo Plan, therefore, one must concede that, as originally conceived by its Commonwealth founders, its contribution in terms of capital aid to the South-east Asian countries as such could only have been a relatively modest one. For while its field of activity specifically included both South and South-east Asia, the immense needs of the former inevitably tended to absorb much the greater part of the available funds. Moreover, when it is realized that the population of India alone represents very nearly one-third of the total under-developed world (excluding China) and five times that of all the developed Commonwealth countries (including the United Kingdom) put together, it was clear that the aims of the Colombo Plan could not possibly have been accomplished purely in Commonwealth terms alone, but would need to be strongly supported by outside powers. Thus, while Commonwealth countries, including the Asian members themselves, have made invaluable contributions in technical assistance, the fact remains that of the total sums invested in the development plans of the Colombo Plan region since 1951, over £11,500 million came from internal sources, and of the £3,500 million capital aid from Colombo Plan donors, the amounts contributed by the United States have far exceeded the combined totals of all the Commonwealth donors.

So far as aid to South-east Asia is concerned, Table 108 gives some idea of the relative importance of the sums involved, though the absence of strictly comparable data from all the various donor countries makes it almost impossible to produce a reliable statement of the overall position, and the information on bilateral aid provided in the table is confined to that from Western (and Indian) sources during only part of the post-war period.[31] Nevertheless this information

[30] Mainly in the form of release of India's accumulated sterling balances. One official estimate puts the British contribution during the first five years after the war at £750 million (see Wint (B), p. 12) and this was not the end of the story. From 1951 to 1960 further capital assistance to India included £A 11 million from Australia, $C 147 million from Canada, £2 million from New Zealand, £66 million from the United Kingdom, and $2,557 million from the United States.

[31] Only economic aid by governments and the United Nations agencies is included in this table, though in addition the United States has provided substantial military aid to certain countries in the region, and there have also been extensive investments of private capital. For fuller details of aid, including – where applicable – that from the Communist bloc, which in total is smaller than that from the West, see the appropriate regional chapters above.

TABLE 108. INTERNATIONAL

PART I:

Contributing country or agency	Recipient: British Borneo territories		Burma		Cambodia		Federation of Malaya		Indonesia	
(1) Bilateral aid	A	B	A	B	A	B	A	B	A	B
Australia	0·2	—	1·4	—	0·5	—	1·0	—	4·9	—
Canada	0·1	—	0·8	—	0·5	—	0·7	—	0·6	−6·3
India	—	—	9·2	21·0	—	—	—	—	0·1	—
Netherlands	—	—	—	—	—	—	—	—	—	−22·1
New Zealand	0·2	—	0·4	—	—	—	0·2	—	1·5	—
United Kingdom	6·5	1·8	0·4	—	—	—	28·4	3·1	0·1	—
U.S.A.	0·6	—	4·9	0·1	121·6	—	1·0	—	39·8	33·8
Total bilateral aid received from all countries named	7·6	1·8	17·1	21·1	122·3	—	31·2	3·1	47·0	5·4
(2) Multilateral aid										
U.N.I.C.E.F.	0·3	—	3·0	—	0·1	—	0·1	—	4·0	—
I.B.R.D.	—	—	—	6·2	—	—	—	—	—	—
Other U.N.T.A.	1·0	—	4·2	—	1·6	—	1·0	—	5·1	—
Total multilateral aid received	1·2	—	7·1	6·2	1·8	—	1·1	—	9·0	—
Grand total of aid received	8·8	1·8	24·2	27·3	124·1	—	32·3	3·1	56·0	5·4
Total population (millions)	1·1		20·1		4·6		7·7		85·1	
Total aid received per head (U.S. dollars) (gifts only)	8·0		1·2		27·0*		4·2		0·7	

All aid figures are in million U.S. dollars, except amounts per head of population which are in U.S. dollars.

A	Gifts.
B	Loans.
E.D.F.	Development Fund of the European Economic Community.
I.B.R.D.	International Bank for Reconstruction and Development.
U.N.I.C.E.F.	United Nations Children's Fund.
U.N.E.P.T.A.	United Nations Expanded Programme of Technical Assistance. See below, Part II, p. 758.
Other U.N.T.A.	Regular Programmes of Technical Assistance of the United Nations and its Specialized Agencies.

AID TO SOUTH-EAST ASIA

1954–8

Countries

Laos		*West New Guinea*		*Philippines*		*Thailand*		*Southern Vietnam*		*Total aid contributed to South-east Asia*	
A	B	A	B	A	B	A	B	A	B	A	B
0·6	—	—	—	0·2	—	0·3	—	1·0	—	10·1	—
0·1	—	—	—	—	—	—	—	0·2	—	2·7	−6·3
—	—	—	—	—	—	—	—	—	—	9·3	21·0
—	—	86·8	−7·1	—	—	—	—	—	—	86·8	−29·2
—	—	—	—	—	—	—	—	—	—	2·3	—
—	—	—	—	0·2	—	0·1	—	—	—	35·7	4·9
152·7	—	—	—	109·4	−0·8	94·3	11·8	794·2	35·2	1318·5	80·1
153·4	—	86·8	− 7·1	109·8	− 0·8	94·7	11·8	795·4	35·2	1465·5	70·5
—	—	—	—	1·8	—	1·2	—	0·2	—	10·7	—
—	—	—	—	—	2·4	—	17·3	—	—	—	25·9
0·8	—	0·1	—	2·6	—	3·3	—	0·9	—	20·6	—
0·8	—	0·1	—	4·4	2·4	4·6	17·3	1·1	—	31·3	25·9
154·2	—	86·9	−7·1	114·2	1·6	99·3	29·1	796·5	35·2	1496·8	96·4
1·7		0·7		22·7		21·3		12·3		177·3	
90·7*		124·1		5·0		4·2		64·8*		8·4	

* To these totals should also be added significant contributions from France. (In 1954–8 France contributed approximately $100 million in grants and loans to Laos, Cambodia and Southern Vietnam together, and in 1960 it supplied $12 million in grants and $4 million in loans in the same three states.)

† Multilateral contributions of less than $50,000.

‡ Totals may be slightly higher than the figures shown. Note: Some inconsistencies exist in other totals, owing to rounding.

Sources: Based (except for certain totals) on *Statistical Yearbook, U.N.*, 1959, Table 159, and *Statistical Yearbook, U.N.*, 1961, Table 156.

TABLE 108. INTERNATIONAL

PART II:

Contributing country or agency	British Borneo territories		Burma		Cambodia		Federation of Malaya		Indonesia	
	Recipient									
(1) Bilateral aid	A	B	A	B	A	B	A	B	A	B
Australia	0·3	—	0·7	—	1·0	—	1·1	—	1·4	—
Canada	0·1	—	0·3	—	0·1	—	0·2	—	1·1	—
Netherlands	—	—	—	—	—	—	—	—	—	—
New Zealand	0·2	—	0·1	—	—	—	0·1	—	0·2	—
United Kingdom	3·6	−0·1	—	—	—	—	9·5	−1·4	—	—
U.S.A.	—	—	1·6	1·4	24·6	—	0·2	0·8	10·6	2·3
Total bilateral aid received from all countries named above	4·2	−0·1	2·7	1·4	25·7	—	11·1	−0·6	13·3	2·3
(2) Multilateral aid										
E.D.F.	—	—	—	—	—	—	—	—	—	—
I.B.R.D.	—	—	—	2·4	—	—	—	2·7	—	—
U.N.I.C.E.F.	†	—	0·9	—	†	—	†	—	0·5	—
U.N.E.P.T.A.	0·1	—	0·8	—	0·3	—	0·3	—	1·0	—
Other U.N.T.A.	†	—	0·2	—	0·2	—	0·1	—	0·4	—
Total multilateral aid received	0·1‡	—	1·9	2·4	0·5	—	0·4	2·7	1·9	—
Grand total of aid received	4·3‡	−0·1	4·6	3·8	26·2*	n.a.	11·5	2·1	15·2	2·3
Total population (millions)	1·3		20·7		5·0		6·9		92·6	
Total aid received per head (U.S. dollars) (gifts only)	3·3‡		0·2		5·2*		1·7		0·2	

For explanation of signs and abbreviations see Part I, pp. 756–7.

ADDENDUM

The following data, based upon *Fact Sheets on the Colombo Plan*, Nos. 4 and 7, Central Office of Information, London, 1961, are included for comparison. All aid figures are in million U.S. dollars, except amounts per head of population which are in dollars.

Total U.S. aid of all kinds to South-east Asia, 1951–mid-1960 . . . . 3,258·9
(This includes Burma 95·8, Cambodia 195·8, Indonesia 417·2, Laos 233·1, Federation of Malaya 21·5, Singapore, North Borneo and Sarawak 0·9, Philippines 633·0, Thailand 260·0, Vietnam 1,401·6.)

Total U.S. aid to whole Colombo Plan area (i.e. South and South-east Asia) . . . . . 7,378·1

AID TO SOUTH-EAST ASIA

1960

Countries

Laos		*West New Guinea*		*Philippines*		*Singapore*		*Thailand*		*Southern Vietnam*		*Total aid contributed to S.E. Asia*	
A	B	A	B	A	B	A	B	A	B	A	B	A	B
—	—	—	—	0·2	—	0·2	—	0·8	—	0·5	—	6·2	—
—	—	—	—	0·1	—	—	—	0·1	—	0·5	—	2·5	—
—	—	21·9	—	—	—	—	—	—	—	—	—	21·9	—
—	—	—	—	—	—	—	—	—	—	—	—	0·6	—
—	—	—	—	—	—	0·3	−0·5	—	—	—	—	13·4	−2·0
33·0	—	—	—	18·8	8·0	0·2	—	26·5	16·5	185·7	—	301·2	29·0
33·0	—	21·9	—	19·1	8·0	0·7	−0·5	27·4	16·5	186·7	—	345·7	27·0
—	—	0·1	—	—	—	—	—	—	—	—	—	0·1	—
—	—	—	—	—	1·5	—	—	—	8·7	—	—	—	15·3
—	—	†	—	0·5	—	†	—	0·2	—	†	—	2·1‡	—
0·3	—	†	—	0·5	—	0·1	—	0·7	—	0·2	—	4·3	—
0·1	—	†	—	0·5	—	†	—	0·3	—	0·2	—	2·0‡	—
0·4	—	0·1‡	—	1·5	1·5	0·1	—	1·2	8·7	0·4	—	8·5‡	15·3
33·4	n.a.	22·0‡	—	20·6	9·5	0·8	−0·5	28·6	25·2	18·7*	n.a.	354·2‡	42·3
1·8		0·7		27·5		1·6		25·5		14·1		197·7	
16·3*		31·4‡		0·7		0·5		1·1		13·3*		1·8	

Total capital aid commitments of United Kingdom to South-east Asia, 1951–mid-1960 . . . 219·5
(This includes Federation of Malaya and Singapore 168·0, North Borneo 35·3 and Sarawak 16·2.)

Total U.K. aid commitments to whole Colombo Plan area . . . . 458·9

Total Japanese capital aid to whole Colombo Plan area, 1954–60 . . . . 21·1

Total Japanese reparations payments to South-east Asia up till mid-1960 . . . . . . *c.* 227
(These include Burma 99·7, Indonesia 31·7, Philippines 95·6 and Vietnam 0·08.)

is sufficient to show that the varying amounts of economic aid granted by the West to the several parts of South-east Asia since 1954 are in no sense proportionate to the respective economic needs of the lands in question at this time. Thus, for example, while Burma and Indonesia have remained among the most seriously depressed parts of the region, the amounts of aid per head ot population which they have been receiving are far lower than those granted to any other country shown in the table, and meanwhile by far the largest *per capita* contributions (apart from the very exceptional case of West New Guinea) have gone to the two countries, Laos and Southern Vietnam, which have a common frontier with the only Communist state in South-east Asia, namely Northern Vietnam.

However, this is by no means the whole of the story. During the critical years preceding 1954 the pattern of Western aid to South-east Asia had shown a very different emphasis,[32] and besides the immediate post-war contributions of the United States and the United Kingdom towards the rehabilitation of their respective South-east Asian dependencies, both Burma and Indonesia as well as other South-east Asian states received considerable help from various sources, notably again from the United States and, on a rather smaller scale, from the various Commonwealth donors under the Colombo Plan prior to 1954.

Moreover, there is every reason to believe that the Americans would have continued to help in this way, had these countries been willing to continue accepting their aid. But, as the division between the Western powers and the Communist bloc seemed to be assuming a more portentous character in South-east Asia after 1953–4, attitudes towards aid tended to change, and while some states, such as Cambodia, sought to emphasize their non-alignment by accepting help from both East and West, others, like Burma and also for a time Indonesia, were unwilling to risk compromising their neutrality by accepting specifically Western aid.[33] Although this latter posture commonly permitted the acceptance of some aid via the Colombo Plan, the receipt of direct aid from the United States was more often considered to be incompatible with it, and as may be inferred from Table 108, this meant that Burma and Indonesia cut themselves off from by far the most important available source.

When the volume of United States aid to South-east Asia is compared with that of the United Kingdom, it is easy to appreciate the resentment which Americans have sometimes felt at the readiness of many Britons to criticize their policies in this part of the world. And while the divergence between British and American viewpoints would seem to be greater at the popular than at the official level, the matter is nevertheless important enough to call for more detailed consideration at this stage.

[32] A partial indication of this may be gained from the addendum to the table, but even this does not include the critical five years immediately following the Second World War.

[33] More recently Indonesia has changed its attitude in this respect to one resembling that of Cambodia. See above, p. 316.

As we have already seen[34] this divergence goes back at least to the early post-war period, when the South-east Asian policies of both were overshadowed by the respective aims of the United States in China and of the United Kingdom in India. Thus, while the United States certainly did not neglect its South-east Asian responsibilities, which at this time were still limited to the Philippines, its primary concern in Asia was to see that China should at long last have a real chance to develop as an independent modern state. With this end in view, therefore, the United States contributed vast sums towards stabilizing the situation in China, by helping it to break out of the appalling poverty which had been its condition long before the Japanese invasion and all that had followed since 1937 had added still further to its people's distress. Likewise the British government, while undertaking immediate relief and rehabilitation work in Malaya, British Borneo and for a time also in Burma, was more preoccupied with the situation in India, even though the latter had gained rather than lost economically as a result of the war. And here the sense of embarrassment felt by the British Labour government, that a territory which had been under British rule for so long as India had been should nevertheless be so abysmally poor, added to their determination to do what they could to provide it with the economic means to make a success of political independence.

In the event, China after 1945 proved to have been too deeply undermined for the American solution to work, and the shock of the consequent Communist take-over in 1949 has coloured American thinking towards Asia ever since. Thus its policy makers have tended to be obsessed by the need to develop counter-measures against Communist infiltration in neighbouring lands, and to complete the containment strategy by bringing as many as possible of the uncommitted countries peripheral to the Sino-Soviet bloc into the series of defensive organizations to which we have referred on p. 749.

In contrast to this, many Britons, faced with no such collapse of their plans in India, but only with a growing realization of the magnitude of the economic assistance which would be needed if that country was ever to break permanently out of its crippling poverty, have tended to regard the American preoccupation with the 'Communist menace' as a distraction from the all-important task of economic reconstruction, even though in fact the Americans have for many years been supplying much the greater part of the Western aid devoted to this latter purpose. In this respect moreover many Britons, perhaps unduly sensitive about their own national decline in power, have been sympathetic to the official and very characteristically Indian view that to divert any significant part of the country's limited resources into military preparations was both economically unsound and, thanks to the supposedly impregnable Himalayan defences, strategically unnecessary. However, while events have shown that the British were right in thinking that anti-Communism would not be a popular rallying cry in most parts of Asia, and least of all in India, it is by no means so clear that

[34] See above, pp. 745–751.

it has also been right implicitly to play down the political and strategic dangers with which these countries have been faced.

IV. THE REASONS WHY AID IS NEEDED

Whatever may prove to be the relative merits of British and American viewpoints in this respect, however, both have been equally at fault so far as South-east Asia is concerned. For in tending to view the latter as a mere extension either of the temperate Far East or of India, they have failed properly to appreciate the fact that South-east Asia's problems differ fundamentally from those of both of these neighbouring regions.

Here, even at the risk of being misunderstood, one must begin by pointing out that in normal times poverty has had nothing like the same significance in South-east Asia as it has had for centuries both in India and in China. That is not to pretend that the prevailing standards of nutrition, housing or medical services in most parts of the region are anything but low, but it is to draw a real and valid distinction between the carefree bearing typical of most South-east Asian peoples and the much more austere outlook of their counterparts in the acutely congested lands of India and China. Thus, while in contrast to the characteristic Indian reaction to centuries of poverty, which has taken the form of an almost overpowering sense of apathy and resignation,[35] and the corresponding response of the Chinese – in an altogether less exhausting climate – which manifests itself as an apparently instinctive compulsion to work oneself to the bone in order at all costs to survive, the more typical attitude of the South-east Asian peasant, at least until recently, has been no less obviously related to his experience that, in the words of the Siamese proverb, 'there is fish in the river and rice in the field' and that, this being so, it is generally wisest to take things easily in this humid tropical climate, where to obtain a reasonable modicum of comfort does not call for any great abundance of material possessions.

Significantly this attitude of mind, which finds satisfaction in simple things and, so far from being a manifestation of either asceticism or innate idleness, is in fact accompanied by a real appreciation of the dignity of human life and the harmony of nature, is equally prevalent among the Hindu Balinese, the Buddhist Siamese and the Muslim Malays. But while all these may fairly be described as Indianized peoples, and while moreover this same attitude to life is not shared by the much more hard-headed Vietnamese, whose culture is basically Sinitic, it would seem that cultural history alone does not explain the difference which exists today. For the typical South-east Asian attitude is completely unlike the Indian, and would appear to owe at least as much to the geographical circumstances of lack of population pressure, combined with an enervating but not

[35] The task of overcoming this apparently ingrained attitude represents probably the greatest difficulty with which India has been faced since independence, and although there are some indications of a change it would be foolish to assume that this problem can easily be solved.

normally unpleasant climate. And by a parallel argument the toughness of the Vietnamese, particularly the northerners, may be explained in terms not only of Sinicization but also of long-standing pressure of people on the land comparable to that of China proper, and perhaps also in part of a climatic regime which is unique in South-east Asia in possessing a recognizable cool season.[36]

In addition to the special case of Vietnam, it is also necessary to recall that a few other instances of high population density already existed in South-east Asia before the Second World War, notably in Java and parts of Luzon, and although the congestion there originated much more recently than that in northern Vietnam, it also had come to be accompanied by a real sense of poverty. Nevertheless, in contrast to the situation in China and India, such congestion and such an awareness of poverty were the exception rather than the rule in the South-east Asian countryside, and furthermore, as both the Netherlands Indies and the Philippines transmigration schemes were demonstrating, sufficient land existed elsewhere within both countries to absorb the excess population from the congested areas.

Likewise it is also true that severe poverty and degradation existed in the slums of the larger South-east Asian towns, but here again it was rarely comparable in degree, and certainly not in extent, to that in the corresponding cities of China or India. However, it was in the towns that the damage, disruption and general demoralization produced by the Second World War were felt in their most intense form, though few rural areas dependent on export production or on imported food escaped serious dislocation, and in the guerrilla fighting of one kind or another which has taken place in many states after 1945 the rural areas often suffered worst.

Without attempting to assess the geographical variations in the extent of the material and psychological damage caused by the war and its aftermath, one can state unequivocally that repair of the physical devastation, above all of harbours, transport systems, productive plant and basic social services, was the most urgent task requiring to be undertaken in all parts of the region after August 1945, and indeed without this there could be little possibility of political stability whatever form of government was subsequently adopted. But while the continuance of fighting – in new forms – in Indonesia, Indochina and Burma greatly delayed such rehabilitation there, events have shown that in the other countries where no such obstacles at first blocked the way,[37] it was perfectly possible to restore the pre-war level of prosperity within a few years, and wherever this has been done there is now no likelihood that any sense of economic hardship will drive the people towards Communism.[38]

[36] Such a climate is found in Northern but not in Southern Vietnam. See above, pp. 533–4.

[37] Though the widespread outbreaks of Communist-inspired terrorism in many parts of South-east Asia, beginning in 1948, seriously delayed this process, as indeed it was their purpose to do.

[38] For, as we have seen, the nationalist movements in all parts of South-east Asia except Vietnam were as non-Communist in origin as that in India itself.

In these more fortunate countries, with which Cambodia and the British Borneo territories may also be included, the possibility that a sense of economic hardship might impel the local population willingly to adopt a Communist form of government seems remote, and in so far as such a political revolution represents a serious possibility in other South-east Asian countries, the basic causes, except perhaps in Indonesia, lies not in any intrinsic lack of economic opportunity.

To be more specific, the disappointing economic position of Burma, Laos and Southern Vietnam today, as compared with the progress made by some of their neighbours since the war, is primarily the result and not the cause of their long-continued political instability, though even so the likelihood of an internal Communist revolution in the first two of these is probably small. In Singapore, meanwhile, although no comparable economic setback has occurred, political frustration, together with some associated apprehension about long-term economic prospects, has produced a state of chronic instability among the predominantly Chinese population, and here a Communist coup has of late seemed a distinct possibility.[39] In Indonesia, however, where the problem of overpopulation in Java is in every sense crucial, it is much less easy to say whether political instability is more a cause or a symptom of economic difficulty. In this connexion, moreover, it is significant that in Java, though not in the outer islands where there is no such overcrowding, the Communist party already has massive popular support in the countryside, a situation which is without parallel elsewhere in South-east Asia, except in the similarly congested lands of Northern Vietnam, where such support has already proved decisive.

Nevertheless, if it must be concluded that, except possibly in Indonesia, the granting of further economic aid can of itself do little to arrest whatever danger may exist of internal Communist revolution within the South-east Asian countries, it by no means follows that the latter have no problems caling for continued economic assistance from outside, or that there is no other tlhreat to their future security and well-being. It will be best to examine each of these questions in turn.

Inevitably it was only to be expected that the achievement of political independence would be accompanied by significant changes in the economic patterns of the new states, for however much the forms of economic activity introduced by the Europeans may have indirectly benefited the local peoples, they were in the main designed to serve European rather than indigenous interests. Unfortunately, however, nationalist sentiment sometimes leads to no less serious distortions of the facts than those of which the West is frequently accused. In particular, the myth of the immense natural wealth of South-east Asia is extremely slow to die, and when this supposed abundance is contrasted with the relatively low living standards of the local peoples it is easy to present the colonial record as one of rapacious exploitation.

[39] Although the establishment of the Federation of Malaysia in 1963 appeared to reduce this danger, the exclusion of Singapore from it in 1965 may produce new complications.

Yet in fact it cannot be too strongly stressed that South-east Asia is rich only in comparison with the other humid tropical regions, and that the initial task of developing its economic potentialities involved a heavy outlay of capital, which only the Western powers have hitherto been able to provide, but from which their successors should now derive considerable benefit. Moreover, in so far as Westerners may nevertheless be fairly accused of having driven many a hard bargain with South-east Asians in the past, the remedy now lies largely in the latters' own hands. Thus even where Western capital remains in control of South-east Asian enterprises, reasonable legislation can ensure that the local employees get a fair share of the rewards, without going to such extremes as to drive the foreigner out altogether and so kill the goose that lays the golden eggs. Here, as in many other respects, the contrast between current policies in Malaya and in Indonesia represents an instructive example of the difference between a positive and a negative approach.

Whatever the extent of past economic exploitation, however, a much more lasting consequence of Western colonial rule has been the unbalanced nature of the economic development which it initiated, both in the economic sense of over-specialization on a handful of export commodities, which the West happened to want at the time, and in the geographical sense of concentrating such economic activities in a few scattered areas while leaving the rest virtually undeveloped. So far as the former of these two aspects is concerned the resultant problems of excessive dependence on a very limited range of exports are well known, and especially when the market price for these fluctuates as widely as that for most kinds of South-east Asian produce has tended to do both before and after the Second World War, it is clearly in these countries' interests to diversify their economies wherever this can effectively be done. Unfortunately for them, however, this is not as simple as it sounds. The accumulated experience, particularly of the peasant cultivator, in producing one crop is not readily transferable to another requiring quite different and unfamiliar methods of cultivation, nor is it usually easy to compete on the world market for such a crop against an already well established producer.

When to these difficulties are added the recurrent rumours that new advances in Western synthetic production may be about to undermine the position of this or that South-east Asian product, it is not surprising that many of the local peoples feel that their economies are still precariously based, and perhaps indeed that their whole future today, no less than in colonial times, depends on the machinations of outside forces and interests over which they have no control. In this connexion the West could certainly do more to help, and indeed it is arguable that a really effective international system of commodity price stabilization would in the long run be of greater benefit to South-east Asia as a whole than the continuance of economic aid in its present form.[40]

[40] This, however, would be of least help to those countries whose needs are greatest, and in fact the need for selective aid would certainly remain.

The effects of the geographical unevenness of colonial economic development, though less widely discussed, present no less serious problems. In fact the most extreme case, namely that resulting from the prolonged over-concentration of the Dutch upon Java, lies at the root of what is by far the greatest socio-economic problem in the whole of South-east Asia today,[41] and one which if it is to be solved at all will call for an infinitely greater effort than Indonesia has yet attempted, as well as for correspondingly generous assistance from outside. But although the problem of uneven development in Indonesia is unique in scale, it can be paralleled in kind in virtually every country in South-east Asia, and the basic reason why the grossly disparate development, for example, of the western third and the eastern two-thirds of Malaya does not present a comparably acute problem to that in Indonesia is merely that it has not gone on for so long and hence that population density has not yet built up to danger point even in the more intensively developed western zone.

In Malaya, therefore, as also in most neighbouring states, there is still time to avert the unfortunate experience of Java by spreading the pattern of economic development more evenly over the whole country, and in fact not only in Malaya but also in the Philippines, Thailand and elsewhere serious efforts are being made to promote new land settlement schemes in this connexion.[42] However, the opening up of new areas in the humid tropics requires a considerable expenditure of capital, on which no spectacular returns are likely to be forthcoming for a long time, and thus it is very tempting to pander to uninformed public opinion by concentrating instead on the building of imposing new factories, which may nevertheless be little more than nationalist status symbols, within the already developed zones, while neglecting the more fundamental tasks of pioneering elsewhere.

Here again the West is not without its share of the blame, for its glib equating of machinery and gadgets with efficiency and progress has had a profound effect on popular attitudes in the under-developed lands. This, of course, is not to say that the South-east Asian states should not strive to develop industrial production of any kind. On the contrary, a substantial expansion of appropriate kinds of industry represents one of the most constructive ways of diversifying their economies and deserves all possible support from outside. But such activity should be based on sober assessment of needs and opportunities rather than on mere patriotic sentiment and a desire to show that South-east Asians are the equal of Westerners because they also can produce steel and manufacture motor cars. For however much one may sympathize with this desire for proper recognition, the way to impress the hard-headed men of the West is surely by the pursuance of realistic policies rather than by flamboyant window dressing.

In this connexion, therefore, it is of primary importance to take due account of local circumstances, which in all cases are very different from those of the West and even from those of neighbouring Asian lands, though of all the coun-

[41] See above, p. 338. [42] See Tinker (D), and above, pp. 525 and 628.

tries which have successfully industrialized it is probably Japan whose experience is most relevant to South-east Asia's problem today.[43] Notwithstanding the much more extensive sources of indigenous capital which could be drawn upon to finance its large-scale factory industries, Japan also relied very heavily on expanding and gradually modernizing the small-scale domestic industries of its rural areas. This latter unspectacular but inexpensive line of advance is particularly appropriate to the needs of South-east Asia today, not least because, as in Japan, it can go hand in hand with the further development of agriculture by making use of the large fund of rural labour which is under-employed for most of the year, but cannot yet be spared from the land during the peak farming periods.

In addition to this it is certainly desirable to establish new factories, notably to process locally produced raw materials and to manufacture the simpler kinds of consumer goods for which the local demand is highest, and here, in the absence of such capital reserves as Japan could draw upon in the 19th century, the South-east Asian countries will need to rely largely on outside help. Precisely which forms of industry each country should develop must obviously depend on local conditions, and if in fact these should make it economically worth while to set up steel mills or car plants,[44] this may reasonably be done. But for the time being such ventures will remain the exception rather than the rule, if for no other reason than that neighbouring Asian countries, like India, China and, above all, Japan, with their much larger home markets as well as much greater industrial experience, will usually be able to supply these kinds of product much more cheaply and efficiently than the mostly small and generally less experienced South-east Asian countries can hope to do themselves.

When one considers all the many tasks still remaining to be accomplished, it is clear first that Western aid of one kind or another will continue to be needed in most parts of South-east Asia for many years to come, and secondly that to give the impression, however indirectly, that such aid is somehow designed to prevent the advance of Communism will strike most South-east Asians at best as an irrelevance and at worst as a cloak for some other undisclosed but presumably sinister motive. With only few exceptions the ordinary man in the street, and still more so his counterpart in the rice field, has had little opportunity as yet of assessing for himself the benefits of democratic self-government. Long years of paternalist colonial rule have been followed in breathless succession by war and the Japanese occupation, then in many areas by a further struggle against a last-ditch colonial stand, and finally by indigenous rule which has necessarily been feeling its way and in some cases has not yet risen above the level of inefficiency and corruption. In these circumstances, therefore, the ordinary citizen will be inclined to judge his government less on the basis of any constitutional

[43] See above, p. 751.

[44] *E.g.* if suitable local supplies of coal or iron give a particular area a real competitive advantage in the former, or if the local market is large enough to justify the latter.

niceties than on the opportunities which it affords him of living his life in peace, while enjoying perhaps a few more material comforts than he was accustomed to in the past, together with such unfamiliar benefits as improved medical services and better education for his children.

Yet it would be wrong to think that interest in the basic policies which the new national governments should adopt is wholly lacking even in the remote countryside, and particularly among the townsfolk it is in fact developing rapidly. Characteristically some form of Socialism,[45] usually in close association with the co-operative principle, is most commonly preferred, partly because, according to the teachings of so many Indian political and social reformers, this is believed to harmonize with indigenous traditions, and partly also because capitalism is almost instinctively bracketed with colonialism as another aspect of alien exploitation which must at all costs be resisted.

In so far as some Westerners have tended by contrast to regard Socialism as a mere half-way house to Communism, the effect in South-east Asia has been less to discredit either of these doctrines than to cast doubts on Western intentions, and although in recent years fewer Westerners have continued to make this mistake, such suspicions once aroused are not so quickly dispelled. Indeed, in those countries where old-style landlordism continues to be a serious social evil, suspicion may well be reinforced by other factors, for if it can be made to appear that Western aid is finding its way into the hands of an oppressive and reactionary landlord class, it is easy to argue that, so far from contributing to a solution of the country's problems, it is serving instead to perpetuate them. And while the United States, which has been the main target for such criticism, has in fact done its best to try to persuade recipient countries to carry out necessary land reforms, no one has yet explained how to practise the virtues of non-interference by attaching no strings to the aid which is given, while simultaneously telling the recipients how they should spend it, and making sure that they do as they are told.

V. THE ENIGMA OF CHINA

All such lesser criticisms aside, however, the most remarkable thing about the whole question of Western attitudes towards South-east Asia and indigenous reactions to them has centred in the confusion which has existed over the significance of the Chinese Communist revolution of 1949. For while to the West in general and to the United States in particular this has seemed to represent primarily a massive strengthening of the forces of world Communism, to the politically conscious population of South-east Asia its principal significance is felt to lie rather in the possibility that the newly reconstructed China, with its ruthless organization, expanding industries and rapidly growing population may some day seek in one way or another to resume its traditional rôle as the dominant power in the whole Oriental world.

[45] The terms Socialism and Communism are used in the English and not in the Marxist sense.

Admittedly, to pretend that the issue can be expressed in terms of such an alternative as this is to be guilty oneself of serious over-simplification, which must serve still further to confuse rather than to clarify the problem. For, as the U.S.S.R. has already shown, Communist states are apt to include in thier national objectives much that derives from earlier times, and to make use of whatever means are to hand – whether specifically Communist or not – in order to achieve them. And while the fact that China has already begun to follow the U.S.S.R.'s example in this respect has precipitated the Sino-Soviet split, which may significantly reduce the effectiveness of Communism as a world force, it also opens up a whole range of potentially explosive possibilities in respect of the former tributary states of South-east Asia.

Be that as it may, the information contained in many of the foregoing chapters of this book suggests that the South-east Asian peoples may have good reason to be apprehensive about what the emergence of the new China may portend for them. For close upon 4,000 years the Chinese peoples have been expanding territorially, and predominantly towards the south, from the site of the first specifically Chinese kingdom in the Wei-ho and middle Hwang-ho valleys. During the first 3,000 years or so of this expansion, its main effect upon South-east Asia was to set in motion other migrations of related and mostly southern Mongoloid peoples, successive waves of whom followed the predominantly longitudinal grain of the country into mainland South-east Asia, and ultimately settled in various parts either of that peninsula or of the island world beyond.[46] And although it was only in the more accessible north-east, that is in the original Annamite kingdom of Nan Yüeh, that the Chinese ever attempted to impose direct political control over any of these peoples, they began, once they had effectively absorbed the southern coastal provinces of Kwangtung and Fukien, gradually to turn their attention towards the South-east Asian kingdoms bordering upon the South China Sea.[47]

As we have already seen in Chapter 3, one consequence of this new interest overseas was the establishment of Chinese suzerainty – in the form of a distinctive tributary relationship – over many of the South-east Asian kingdoms, at various dates prior to the arrival of the Europeans in the 16th century, and moreover, after the Annamite lands had broken away from direct Chinese control in 939, they also came under this less direct form of Chinese overlordship. In addition to this, however, the expansion of the Chinese to the southern and south-eastern coasts was subsequently followed by a more direct form of contact between China and the Nan Yang, in the form of southern Chinese emigration to various parts of that region. Precisely when permanent migration, as opposed to the temporary sojourn of Chinese traders, began it is not easy to say, but it was certainly under way before Ming times, and despite the attempts of later rulers

[46] See Chapter 3 and also see Fisher (U).

[47] The effective absorption of Fukien did not take place until some centuries after the conquest of Nan Yüeh. See Chapter 3.

to check it, the drift continued throughout the period of the Manchu dynasty,[48] notwithstanding the fact that the growing maritime influence of the Europeans in the Nan Yang was little by little cutting away the tributary links which nominally bound much of the region to China. Finally, as we saw in Chapter 5, the establishment of the British link between Singapore and Hong Kong in the 19th century, together with the widening economic opportunities under European colonial rule in more and more parts of South-east Asia, brought about a vast increase in the volume of Chinese emigration to that region, while finally removing the last formal vestiges of Chinese suzerainty over any part of it.

Although to the Europeans this last development was accounted of relatively little importance at the time, its psychological effect on China went very deep, and it is abundantly clear from the writings of both Sun Yat-sen[49] and Chiang Kai-shek[50] that they had not forgotten China's former claims to suzerainty in this part of Asia, even if at the time there was nothing they could do about them. But since the Communist take-over in 1949, all China has come under much more effectively centralized control than it has been at any time since its internal weakness was revealed by the Opium War of 1839–42, and with its industrial and military strength vastly greater than they have ever been in the past,[51] many people both inside and outside South-east Asia are wondering whether the withdrawal of Western power from that region is about to be followed by a Chinese attempt to re-establish some form of political ascendency over it.

Anxiety on this score is deepened, moreover, when it is borne in mind that China's position *vis-à-vis* South-east Asia has been transformed since the early 19th century in another way, namely by the presence in that region today of some 12 million ethnic Chinese, who remain as the end product of the migrations referred to above, and furthermore occupy many of the most important posts in the countries concerned, where they are concentrated above all in and around the key economic and strategic centres. For although one might assume that the leading commercial and professional members of these overseas Chinese communities would be utterly antipathetic to the Communist regime in China, blood is apt to prove thicker than ideology, and while a great many overseas Chinese undoubtedly do remain loyal to their country of domicile, there are also others who, having suffered long years of petty humiliation as a result of the past inability of their mother country to back them up, now feel themselves strangely drawn towards a regime which has at least made China a force to be reckoned with in the outside world.

It is above all this uncertainty concerning the loyalties, national at least as much as doctrinal, which in recent years has caused growing apprehension on the part of South-east Asian governments about the long-term aims of China itself.

[48] See above, p. 95.
[49] Sun Yat-sen, *op. cit.*, pp. 34 *et seq.*
[50] Chiang Kai-shek, *op. cit.*, pp. 32–9.
[51] See Fisher, (O), pp. 584–587, (U), p. 657, and (V) pp. 12–16.

For while most of them have little fear that their own nationalist faith will be undermined by Communist subversion, which is wholly alien to its Indian-inspired ethos, and, except perhaps in the few acutely depressed areas noted above,[52] are conscious of nothing which might lead their own people to abandon the prevailingly Socialist and at least partly democratic path in favour of a doctrinaire Communist approach modelled on the Chinese, they feel no such confidence about their Chinese minorities, who, even in pre-Communist days, they tended to dislike and to distrust, basically because of their greater capacity for making money.

Moreover, whereas very soon after India became independent, Mr. Nehru specifically advised the members of the much smaller Indian communities in South-east Asia to choose between remaining citizens of India or throwing in their lot with the countries in which they lived, Communist China has continued to follow the *jus sanguinis* and not the *jus soli*, and in the new Chinese Constitution drawn up in 1953, provision was made for the overseas Chinese communities to be represented by thirty deputies in the National People's Congress.

In these circumstances it is entirely understandable that, while most of the South-east Asian countries continued to follow the Indian lead in foreign policy and accordingly rejected the S.E.A.T.O. alliance in 1954, nearly all of them, with their historic memories of former tributary status and with their Chinese minorities capable of being manipulated as potential fifth columns, have been much more suspicious of China's intentions than India has been, at least prior to the latter's own recent experience of Chinese invasion.

The extent of these suspicions was clearly revealed for the first time at the Afro-Asian conference at Bandung in 1955, apparently much to the surprise of the Chinese representative, Mr. Chou En-lai. As noted on p. 386, Chou attempted to allay these suspicions by suggesting a Nehru-type solution, whereby the overseas Chinese might be allowed to choose between retaining Chinese nationality or applying for that of the country in which they lived, and indeed a treaty with Indonesia to this effect was signed shortly afterwards.

While this went some way towards removing Indonesian suspicions, and soon afterwards China began to develop much closer trading links with Indonesia than with any other part of South-east Asia except Northern Vietnam,[53] no comparable treaty has since been signed with any other neighbouring state, and indeed several of these, together with Indonesia itself, have since introduced various measures to curb the economic power of the Chinese within their midst.[54] Moreover, although the eventual conclusion of what seemed to be a reasonable settlement of the border dispute between China and Burma in 1960

[52] See above, p. 763. Note also, however, the special urban case of Singapore which is considered below, p. 752.

[53] See Table 107 and above, pp. 559–562.

[54] See above, pp. 387–8, 525–6, 564 and 726.

helped to quieten apprehensions both there and in neighbouring countries, the Chinese incursions into Indian territory, beginning in 1959 and culminating in the large-scale invasion of October–November 1962, have meanwhile been working more powerfully in the opposite direction.

VI. A.S.A., MALAYSIA AND THE FUTURE

It is against this background that in the early 1960s the first significant moves for over a decade began to be made towards closer regional co-operation between certain of the South-east Asian states, at the initiative of the Prime Minister of the Federation of Malaya, as has already been briefly noted on pp. 659–60. For while the Federation had every reason to congratulate itself on the success with which it had won the loyalties of a large proportion of its own Chinese population, it had been increasingly perturbed by the mounting signs of political instability among the predominantly Chinese population of Singapore next door, who had been left with no comparable opportunity to maintain or develop any satisfying sense of identity with the part of South-east Asia in which they live. And whether or not it was excusable in the international circumstances of 1946–8 to allow this great metropolitan focus at the vital cross-roads of South-east Asia to be placed in a state of political suspense through excluding it 'for the time being' from the new Malaya, the risks in so doing were magnified out of all recognition by the Communist victory in China in 1949.[55] Thus since that time a growing number of Singapore Chinese have begun to look for political inspiration towards their ancestral but newly revitalized motherland and, unless this trend is quickly reversed, the stability of all South-east Asia may before long be fatally undermined as a result.

Although it was not designed exclusively for this purpose, and indeed had many other points in its favour,[56] the new Federation of Malaysia appeared to provide the most effective framework within which the Singapore problem might still at this late stage be solved. But besides seeking through this federation to weld all the erstwhile British Malaysian territories into a politically united and economically prosperous unit at the geographical centre of South-east Asia, the Tunku simultaneously attempted to extend the area of co-operation still further, by means of the new Association of South-east Asian States (A.S.A.) in which the Federation of Malaysia was to be partnered by both Thailand and the Philippines.

[55] It is however possible, perhaps even probable, that, if Singapore had not been excluded at that time, the Federation of Malaya would have been so over-loaded with Chinese that it would never have been able to establish the harmonious relations which now obtain between its three main communal groups. See above, p. 659. But it is certainly true that many of Singapore's people, Chinese, Indian and Malay, have felt themselves to belong to Malaya—in the wider sense—in precisely the same way as their counterparts who were within the Federation of Malaya.

[56] See above, pp. 684–5.

While local speculation to the effect that A.S.A. might become the nucleus of a 'South-east Asian Common Market' was certainly premature, the main emphasis in this loose association of neighbouring states was avowedly economic and cultural, and to this extent it might fairly be regarded as a South-east Asian response to the current trends towards such closer regional co-operation in many parts of the world. But it was also significant that the three countries concerned were the only independent states within South-east Asia which retained any formal defensive agreements with the West[57] and, as can be seen from Fig. 110, the combined Malaysian and A.S.A. territories formed a kind of inner arc within South-east Asia, embracing the southern, western and eastern margins of the South China Sea.

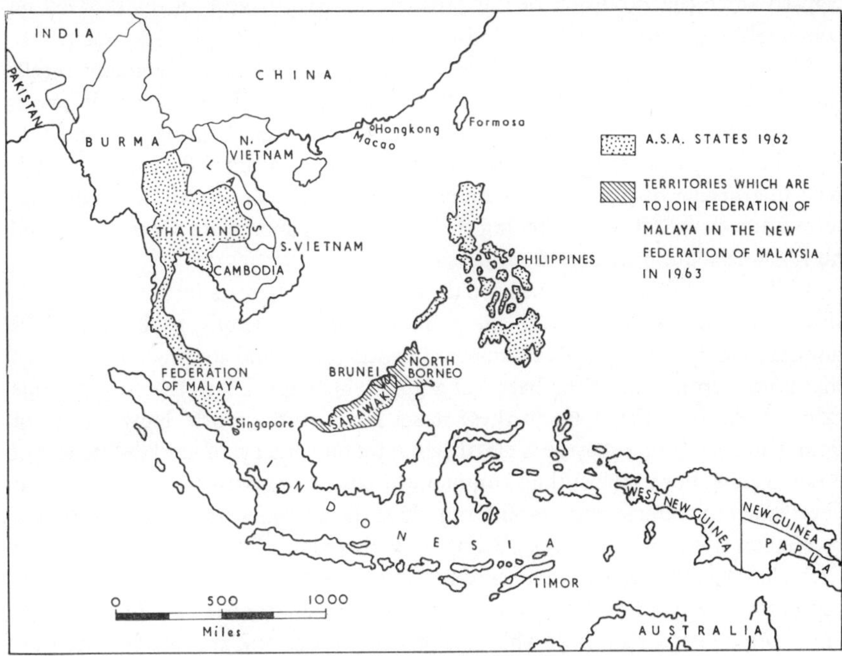

FIG. 110—South-east Asia: A.S.A. and the Federation of Malaysia as originally proposed in 1962

Moreover, contrary to most of the early post-war essays in regional association within South-east Asia, the A.S.A. alignment cut completely across the old ethnic and religious divides, in that its members belonged respectively to the three main religious groups – Buddhist, Muslim and Christian – present in the non-Sinicized parts of South east Asia.[58]

[57] Thus Thailand and the Philippines are both members of S.E.A.T.O., and the Federation of Malaya has its own defence treaty with the United Kingdom. See above, p. 657.

[58] These three are the predominant religions respectively of Thailand, the Federation of Malaya and the Philippines.

However the promise of greater regional stability suggested by these developments in 1961–2 has since been belied, first by the Philippines' espousal of Sulu's claims to North Borneo, which led to a deterioration of relations with Malaysia in 1963, and more recently by the tremendous setback which the latter has suffered through the secession of Singapore in 1965. And when to these are added the further threat to Malaysia from Indonesia's 'confrontation' policy, and the even greater threat to the stability of mainland South-east Asia arising out of the unresolved conflict in Vietnam, it is clear that the twenty years which have elapsed since the expulsion of the Japanese in 1945 have been marked by no comparable resolution of internal differences within South-east Asia itself.

The continuance of such rivalries within South-east Asia inevitably recalls the Balkan analogy with which this book began, and almost irresistibly one is reminded of how, after Turkish rule had at long last been brought virtually to an end in South-eastern Europe in 1912, the Balkans again fell victims to their own internecine disputes, in a manner which proved disastrous to their long-term interests by fatally weakening their capacity in later years to resist new and no less menacing pressures from outside.

While both India and Japan have developed new interests in South-east Asia since the Second World War these have remained wholly pacific and it is unquestionably China, with its massive armed forces and its proclaimed belief that power grows out of the barrel of a gun, which appears as the only possible external threat to the peace in these lesser lands to the south. How serious or imminent this danger may be is clearly a matter on which profound differences of opinion exist, but in the author's opinion the course of events in recent years has done much to confirm and nothing to reduce the anxieties he has repeatedly expressed on this score since 1955.[59] For while there is every reason to believe that China is steadily increasing its industrial strength, and hence, *inter alia*, its capacity to wage war, its achievements in agriculture since the middle 1950s have manifestly fallen far short of what was officially predicted, and much more than bad weather lies behind this miscalculation.

Yet in striking contrast to both India and Japan, China, while growing more rapidly in numbers than both of these put together, has been extremely slow to admit the existence of any population problem,[60] and although the birth control campaign of 1962–3 suggests that the Peking government may at long last have modified its orthodox Marxist views on this subject, such a change, even if it has taken place and is effectively translated into action, can do little to relieve the acute pressure on resources from which China will be bound to suffer during the next two decades. Viewed against the background of its age-old demographic

[59] See Fisher (U), (M), (O) and (V).

[60] *E.g.* see the comment: 'Under the socialist system the problem of "over-population" simply does not exist', in an article entitled 'More on Nehru's philosophy in the light of the Sino-Indian boundary question', in *Peking Review*, 44, November 2, 1962, p. 14. (Translation of an article in *Renmin Ribao*, October 27, 1962.)

push to the south, this situation gives every reason for alarm, for if China is able greatly to increase its industrial strength, while failing to solve its food problem, the temptation to use its new-found power in order to acquire more *lebensraum* in the leading food-surplus region in Asia may prove irresistible. And while it is arguable that China might be able to obtain all the food and raw materials it desires from South-east Asia by peaceful trading, its inability as yet to match Japan in capturing South-east Asian markets may tempt its leaders to seek some form of political control over the region in order to control its trade in much the same way as Japan planned to do under the Greater East Asia Co-prosperity Sphere.

In this context, moreover, it is perhaps doubly ironic that, while the ending of the era of Western dominance in this region may thus be about to open the way for a resumption in 20th-century terms of China's ancient aspirations to suzerainty over South-east Asia, these last two decades have meanwhile witnessed the refashioning and subsequent weakening of India's similarly ancient but much more tenuous cultural links with South-east Asia, this time in the form of moral leadership associated with political non-alignment, which derives largely from the Gandhian doctrine of non-violence.

To the Western observer contemplating the Asian scene after the Chinese invasion of 1962 had compelled Mr. Nehru to admit that India itself had been 'out of touch with reality', this situation is profoundly disturbing. Indeed, to judge from Chinese propaganda, it would seem that jealousy of India's moral leadership in South-east Asia, and a related desire to demonstrate that it is China which is now the strongest power in this part of the world, were leading motives behind this invasion. Consider, for example, the following distortion:

> 'First, the goal pursued by this ambitious Nehru is the establishment of a great empire unprecedented in India's history. The sphere of influence of this great empire would include a series of countries from the Middle East to Southeast Asia and far surpass that of the colonial system set up in Asia by the British empire. . . . The Indian ruling circles have used every means to interfere in the internal and external affairs of countries around India, to control their economy and trade and demand their absolute obedience.'[61]

Although the Chinese made no attempt to press home their advantage beyond the Himalayan frontier zone, their revelation of India's weakness served to intensify already evident South-east Asian doubts about the wisdom of following that country's lead, and the continuing decline in Indian prestige within this region has become one of the most significant trends during the early 1960s. However, except in those states which had already accepted formal defensive agreements with the West, the prevailing South-east Asian reaction has been to accept the inevitability of some form of future Chinese predominance within the

[61] *Renmin Ribao*, quoted in *Peking Review*, 44, November 2, 1962, p. 11. This passage is preceded by a reference to Nehru's comments on post-war regional association of Indian Ocean states, as quoted above, p. 747.

region, and to seek, in the different ways dictated by the different geographical circumstances notably of Burma, Cambodia and Indonesia,[62] to mitigate or to exploit the consequences of this in their own respective national interests.

Nevertheless, while S.E.A.T.O. has thus failed to function as a rallying point for a concerted effort by the South-east Asian states to preserve their newly-won freedom, this does not mean, as so many Westerners appear to assume, that the South-east Asian peoples view the prospect of greater Chinese influence with equanimity, or that the assertion of the S.E.A.T.O. powers' interest in preserving the territorial integrity of the region has been of no avail. What, however, it does suggest is that the time is already overdue for a complete rethinking of Western policy towards this entire region, involving both a refocusing of attention on the latent threat of Chinese power rather than on the ideological issue of the 'Communist menace', and a new attempt to harness the positive forces of indigenous nationalism in the support of the real long-term interests of the people themselves.

As we saw in the opening chapter of this book, South-east Asia is more than a mere zone of transition between India and China, and while its civilization has drawn extensively from both of these greater neighbours, and from other more distant ones as well, the South-east Asian peoples have not been borrowers only, but have also contributed their own individual seasoning to the mixture. And if the characteristic South-east Asian syncretism and insouciance may appear to some to be essentially negative traits, they nevertheless underlie the positive and supremely important virtues of tolerance of one's fellow men and appreciation of the everyday joys of living.

To anyone who has witnessed the surprising unimportance of racial prejudice in the day-to-day behaviour of the multi-coloured population of an ordinary Malayan town, or who has learned to appreciate both the natural dignity and the infectious gaiety of the village folk in all parts of South-east Asia, such an assertion will represent neither an expression of expatriate sentimentality nor an obscurantist plea for preserving old-fashioned modes of life as sociological museum pieces after they have outlived their usefulness. On the contrary, it is an affirmation that, if South-east Asia has already learned much from the West and is eager to learn more, it also has much to teach in return.

Within a remarkably short time since Western education has been available to more than a privileged but minute élite, the South-east Asian peoples have abundantly demonstrated their capacity to absorb, and more important to discriminate in what they absorb, and in addition to the growing number of really able indigenous statesmen who hold or have held office in various parts of the region today, it is not nowadays a cause for surprised comment that a South-east Asian official should since 1962 have served the world at large as Secretary-General of the United Nations.

What South-east Asia needs above all else today is a reasonable space of time

[62] And also, *mutatis mutandis*, of Northern Vietnam.

in which to work out its own answers to the many and pressing internal problems with which it is faced, without having to divert either its energies or its far from unlimited resources to the demands of defence and security. Notwithstanding the familiar difficulties involved in reconciling outside assistance with the sometimes over-sensitive pride of newly independent states, it should surely not be beyond the wit of the world's statesmen to provide these predominantly pacific lands with the protection which they need, but which for obvious geographical and demographic reasons they can never wholly provide for themselves. For, aside from all considerations of Western self-interest – whether economic or strategic – the world would be tragically the poorer if these gracious lands beside the South China Sea should ever be submerged beneath a new imperial tide from the north.

SELECT BIBLIOGRAPHY

Benham
Butwell (B)
Chiang Kai-shek
Du Bois
Fifield
Fisher (M) (Q) (T)
Harris (A)
Ho Ping-ti
Ishii
King, John Kerry
Lattimore
McGee
Norodom Sihanouk, Prince
Panikkar (A) (D) (E)
Pauker (A)
Roucek
Roxby
Sjahrir
Sovani
Sun Yat-sen
Tinker (D)
Van Mook
Wiens
Wint (A) (B) (C) (D)
Zelinsky

Yearbook of International Trade Statistics, U.N., 1959 1960.
Statistical Yearbook, U.N., 1959, 1961.
Peking Review

In addition to the works listed above, this chapter draws indirectly on a wide range of the materials included in preceding select bibliographies. I should also mention that I have again made extensive use of my own earlier work, particularly Fisher (M) and (U).

Addenda: Harris (B), Purcell (H) and Sarkisyanz. *The Colombo Plan Basic Information*, Colombo Plan Bureau, 1962. See also Freeberne, Michael, 'Birth Control in China,' *P.S.* 18, 1964, 5–16, Fisher, Charles A.; 'The Chinese threat to South-east Asia: fact or fiction?', *Royal Central Asian Journal*, 51, 1964, 251–267, and Paauw, Douglas S., 'Economic progress in Southeast Asia', *J.A.S.*, 23, 1963, 69–92. See also Buchan, Alastair (ed.), *China and the peace of Asia*, London, 1965.

Bibliography

I. ARTICLES, BOOKS AND PAMPHLETS

(arranged alphabetically by Authors)

ABDULGANI, ROESLAN, *In search of an Indonesian identity*, Djakarta, n.d.

ABRAHAMSEN, HELEN M., *The Philippine Islands – a guide*, Palo Alto, 1954.

Academica Sinica, Staff members, Institute of Geophysics and Meteorology, (A) 'On the general circulation over eastern Asia', Part I, I, **9**, 1957, 432–446. (B) *idem*, Part II, I, **10**, 1958, 58–75.

AFRICA, JOSÉ L., see Fernando, Enrique.

ALERS, H. J. H., *Dilemma in Zuid-Oost-Azie*, Leiden, 1955.

ALISJAHBANA, TAKDIR, 'The Indonesian language – by-product of nationalism', *P.A.*, **22**, 1949, 388–391.

ALLEN, D. F., *Report on the major ports of Malaya*, Kuala Lumpur, 1951.

ALLEN, G. C., AND DONNITHORNE, AUDREY G., *Western enterprise in Indonesia and Malaya*, London, 1957.

ALLEN, ROBERT LORING, 'Burma's clearing account agreements', *P.A.*, **31**, 1958, 147–163.

Americana Encyclopædia.

ANDERSON, GORDON, 'Rubber and the future of Malaya', *E.W.*, **48, 1**, 23.

ANDREWS, J. M., *Siam: second rural economic survey*, 1934–35, Bangkok, 1935.

ANDRUS, J. R., *Burmese economic life*, Stanford, 1947.

APPLETON, G., *Buddhism in Burma* (Longman's Burma Pamphlets No. 3), 1943.

ARANETA, SALVADOR, 'Basic problems in Philippine economic development', *P.A.*, **21**, 1948, 280–284.

ARDIZZONE, MICHAEL, *A nation is born*, London, 1956.

Asian Affairs, Special number on problems of economic development in South-east Asia, **1**, March 1956.

Asian Annual, London.

Asia's battle against floods, U.N.O., 1950.

Atlantic Monthly, with special section on Burma, **201**, February 1958.

AYAL, ELIEZER B., 'Some crucial issues in Thailand's economic development', *P.A.*, **34**, 1961, 157–164.

AZIZ, M. A., *Japan's colonialism and Indonesia*, The Hague, 1955.

BAKER, J. N. L., *A history of geographical discovery and exploration*, London, 1931.

BALL, W. MACMAHON, *Nationalism and communism in East Asia*, Melbourne, 1952.

Bank Indonesia Annual Report, Djakarta.

BARING-GOULD, S., AND BAMPFYLDE, C. A., *A history of Sarawak under its two white rajahs*, London, 1909.

BARNOUW, ADRIAAN J., 'Cross currents of culture in Indonesia', *F.E.Q.*, **5**, 1946, 143–151.

See also VAN NAERSSON, F. H.

BAUD, JONKHEER A. T., 'Nationalism – Indonesia compared with Indochina', *W.R.*, January 1947, 29–33.

BAUER, P. T., (A) *Report on a visit to the rubber growing smallholders of Malaya, July–September* 1946, Colonial Research Publications, No. 1, London, H.M.S.O., 1948.

(B) 'The prospects of rubber', *P.A.*, **20**, 1947, 381–390.

BEKKER, CONRAD, 'Historical patterns of culture contact in Southern Asia', *F.E.Q.*, **11**, 1951, 3–16.

BELL, SIR HESKETH, *Foreign colonial administration in the Far East*, London, 1928.

BENHAM, FREDERIC, *The Colombo Plan, and other essays*, London, 1956.

BERNSTEIN, DAVID, *The Philippine story*, New York, 1947.

BERREMAN, GERALD D., *The Philippines: a survey of current social, economic and political conditions*, Cornell Southeast Asia Program, Data Paper No. 19, Ithaca, 1956.

BERTLING, C. TJ., 'Les populations d'Indonésie', *R.Ps.P.*, **9**, 1954, 28–51.

BIRDWOOD, LORD, 'The defence of South East Asia', *I.A.*, **31**, 1955, 17–25.

BLAUT, J. M., 'The economic geography of a one-acre farm on Singapore island', *M.J.T.G.*, **1**, 1953, 37–48.

BOEKE, J. H., (A) *The structure of Netherlands Indian economy*, New York, 1942.

(B) 'Economic conditions for Indonesian independence', *P.A.*, **19**, 1946, 394–401.

BORTON, HUGH, see Jones, F. C.

BOULGER, D. C., *The life of Sir Stamford Raffles*, London, 1897.

BOUSQUET, G. H., *A French view of the Netherlands Indies*, (trs. Lilienthal, Philip E.), Oxford, 1940.

BOWEN, I., *Population*, London and Cambridge, 1954.

BOWMAN, ISAIAH, *The New World*, 3rd. edition, New York, 1928.

BRAAK, C., (A) 'The climate of the Netherlands East Indies', in Rutten (A), 50–64, reprinted in Honig and Verdoorn, 15–22.

(B) 'Earthquakes', in Rutten (A), 75–79.

(C) *Klimakunde von Hinterindien und Insulinde* (Band IV, Teil R, of Köppen, W., and Geiger, R., eds., *Handbuch der Klimatologie*, Berlin, 1931).

BRADDELL, DATO, SIR ROLAND, 'Malayadvipa: a study in early Indianization', *M.J.T.G.*, **9**, 1956, 1–20.

BRAIBANTI, RALPH, 'The Southeast Asia Collective Defense Treaty', *P.A.*, **30**, 1957, 321–341.

BRIGGS, LAWRENCE PALMER, (A) 'A sketch of Cambodian history', *F.E.Q.*, **6**, 1947, 345–365.

(B) 'The Hinduized states of Southeast Asia: a review', *F.E.Q.*, **7**, 1948, 376–393.

(C) 'Siamese attacks on Angkor before 1430', *F.E.Q.*, **8**, 1948, 3–33.

(D) 'The Khmer empire and the Malay peninsula', *F.E.Q.*, **9**, 1950, 256–305.

(E) *The ancient Khmer empire*, Philadelphia, 1951.

British dependencies in the Far East, 1945–1949, London, H.M.S.O., Cmd. 7709, 1949.

BRO, MARGUERITTE HARMON, *Indonesia – land of challenge*, London, 1955.

BRODRICK, ALAN HOUGHTON, (A) *Little China*, London, 1942.

(B) *Beyond the Burma Road*, London, 1945.

(C) *Little Vehicle*, London, 1949.

BROEK, JAN O. M., (A) 'The economic development of the outer provinces of the Netherlands Indies', *G.R.*, **30**, 1940, 187–200.

(B) *The economic development of the Netherlands Indies*, New York, 1942.

(C) 'Indonesia and the Netherlands', *P.A.*, **16**, 1943, 329–338.

(D) 'Diversity and unity in Southeast Asia', *G.R.*, **34**, 1944, 175–195.

(E) 'Man and resources in the Netherlands Indies', *F.E.Q.*, **5**, 1946, 121–131.

(F) 'Regionalism in the postwar world', *P.G.*, **4**, 1946, 1–9.

(G) 'East Indonesia: problems and prospects', *F.E.S.*, **20**, 1951, 65–7.

(H) 'Resources of the tropics III: Southeast Asia', *Focus*, **4**, February 1954.

(K) *The ports of Borneo*, Technical Report No. 1, May 1957, Department of Geography University of Minnesota, Minneapolis, (mimeo.).

See also LOEB, EDWIN M.

BROUWER, H. A., (A) '*Geology of the Netherlands Indies*, New York, 1925.

(B) 'Geology of the Netherlands Indies', in Rutten (A), 101–125.

Brunei Annual Report, London, H.M.S.O.

Brunei Census of Population, 1960, Preliminary Release.

BUNCHANA ATTHAKER, 'A decade of economic progress', *Thai News*, August 1961.

BURGER, D. H., *Structural changes in Javanese society: the supra-village sphere*, (trs. Palmier, Leslie H.), Cornell Modern Indonesia Project, Ithaca, 1956, (mimeo.).

BURKILL, I. H., *Dictionary of economic products of the Malay peninsula*, 2 vols., London, 1935.

Burma facts and figures (Longman's Burma Pamphlets No. 9), 1946.

Burma petroleum industry, The (Longman's Burma Pamphlets No. 10), 1946.

Burma rice (Longman's Burma Pamphlets No. 4), 1944.

Burma, Review of commercial conditions, London, H.M.S.O., 1953.

'Burma, the sixth anniversary', Special number of the *Burma Quarterly*, **4**, January 1954.

'*Burma's fight for freedom, Independence commemoration*', Department of Information and Broadcasting, Rangoon, n.d.

BUSS, CLAUDE A., (A) *The Far East*, New York, 1955.

(B) 'The Philippines', in Mills, Lennox A., *et. al.*, 18–78.

(C) 'International relations in Southeast Asia', *ibid.*, 371–433.

BUTWELL, RICHARD A., (A) 'A Chinese university for Malaya', *P.A.*, **26**, 1953, 344–348.

(B) *Southeast Asia Today – and tomorrow*, London and Dunmow, 1962.

BUTWELL, RICHARD, and VON DER MEHDEN, FRED, 'The 1960 election in Burma', *P.A.*, **33**, 1960, 144–157.

See also VANDENBOSCH, AMRY.

BUU LOC, 'Aspects of the Vietnamese problem, *P.A.*, **25**, 1952, 235–247.

BUXTON, L. H. DUDLEY, *The peoples of Asia*, London, 1925.

CABATON, A., *Java and the Dutch East Indies*, London, 1911.

CADY, JOHN F., 'Burma', in Mills, Lennox A., *et al.*, 126–173.

Cai-san, une expérience de réforme agraire et de réimplantation dans le "grenier à riz" de la republique du Viet-Nam, Saigon, n.d.

CALDER, RITCHIE, *Men against the jungle*, London, 1954.

CALLIS, HELMUT G., *Foreign capital in Southeast Asia*, New York, 1942 (mimeo.).

CAMPBELL, DOUGLAS HOUGHTON, *An outline of plant geography*, London, 1926.

CARNELL, FRANCIS G., (A) 'Malayan citizenship legislation', *I.C.L.Q.*, October 1952, 504–518.

(B) 'Closer association in British South-east Asia', *E.W.*, 1953, 12–14.

(C) 'Communalism and communism in Malaya', *P.A.*, **26**, 1953, 99–117.

(D) 'Constitutional reform and elections in Malaya', *P.A.*, **27**, 1954, 216–235.

(E) 'The Malayan elections', *P.A.*, **28**, 1955, 315–330.

(F) 'Southeast Asia in the modern world', *I.Q.*, **13**, 1957, 101–120.

CARR-SAUNDERS, A. M., *World Population*, Oxford, 1936.

CARTER, J., 'Mangrove succession and coastal change in south-west Malaya', *I.B.G.*, **26**, 1959, 79–88.

CATOR, W. J., *The economic position of the Chinese in the Netherlands Indies*, Oxford, 1936.

CHALONER, W. H., 'The history of the rubber industry', *Manchester Guardian*, January 15, 1957, 8.

Chambers's Encyclopædia.

CHAPMAN, F. SPENCER, *The jungle is neutral*, London, 1949.

Chatham House study group report: *Collective defence in South East Asia*, London, 1956.

CHESNEAUX, JEAN, *Contribution à l'histoire de la nation Vietnamienne*, Paris, 1955.

CHHIBBER, H. L., *The physiography of Burma*, Calcutta and London, 1933.

CHIANG KAI-SHEK, *China's destiny* (with notes and comments by Jaffe, Philip), New York, 1947.

China, Geographical Handbook Series, B.R. 530, 530A and 530B, Naval Intelligence Division, 3 vols., 1944–5.

China Quarterly, No. 9, January – March 1962, Special Survey of North Vietnam.

CHRISTIAN, JOHN LE ROY, (A) 'Anglo-French Rivalry in Southeast Asia', *G.R.*, **31**, 1941, 272–282.

(B) *Modern Burma*, Berkeley, 1942.

CLARK, COLIN, *The conditions of economic progress*, 3rd edition, London, 1957.

CLARK, W. D., 'The Asian revolution', *I.A.*, **34**, 1958, 273–279.

CLEMENTIN, J. R., 'The nationalist dilemma in Vietnam', *P.A.*, **23**, 1950, 294–310.

CLEMENTS, F. W., 'The World Health Organization in Southern Asia and the Western Pacific', *P.A.*, **25**, 1952, 334–348.

CLIFFORD, SIR HUGH, *Further India*, London, 1904.

Coal and iron resources of Asia and the Far East, United Nations, E.C.A.F.E., Bangkok, 1953.

COAST, JOHN, 'The clash of cultures in Bali', *P.A.*, **24**, 1941, 398–405.

CŒDÈS, G., *Les états Hindouisés d'Indochine et d'Indonésie*, Paris, 1948.

COLE, D. H., *Imperial military geography*, London, 9th edition 1938, 12th edition 1956.

COLE, FAY-COOPER, *The peoples of Malaysia*, New York, 1945.

COLLETT, O. J. A., *Terres et peoples de Sumatra*, Amsterdam, 1925.

Collier's Encyclopædia.

COLLIS, MAURICE, *Siamese White*, London, 1936.

Colombo Plan Annual Report, London, H.M.S.O.

Colony of Singapore Annual Report, Singapore.

CONDOMINAS, GEORGES, 'Aspects of a minority problem in Indochina', *P.A.*, **24**, 1951, 77–82.

COOKE, B. C. A., *Burma, Overseas Economic Surveys*, London, H.M.S.O., 1957.

COOLHAAS, W. PH., *Insulinde, mensch en maatschappij*, Deventer, n.d.

COON, CARLETON S., *The history of man*, London, 1955.

CORNISH, VAUGHAN, *A geography of imperial defence*, London, 1922.

COUGHLIN, RICHARD J., 'The status of the Chinese minority in Thailand', *P.A.*, **25**, 1952, 378–388.

COUPLAND, SIR REGINALD, *Raffles of Singapore*, London, 1946.

COURTENAY, P. P., (A) 'Water control and irrigation in North Malaya', *G.*, **44**, 1959, 46–47.

(B) 'International tin restriction and its effects on the Malayan tin mining industry', *G.*, **46**, 1961.

COWAN, C. D., (A) 'Indonesia and the Commonwealth in South-East Asia', *I.A.*, **34**, 1958, 454–468.

(B) *Nineteenth century Malaya*, London, 1961.

CRAW, SIR HENRY, 'The Burma Road', *G.J.*, **99**, 1942, 238–246.

CRAWFURD, JOHN, (A) *History of the Indian archipelago*, London, 1820.

(B) *Journal of an embassy to the Courts of Siam and Cochin-China*, London, 1828.

(C) *Descriptive dictionary of the Indian Islands*, London, 1856.

CREDNER, WILHELM, *Siam, das Land der Thai*, Stuttgart, 1935.

CRESSEY, G. B., *Asia's lands and peoples*, New York, 1945.

CROSBY, SIR JOSIAH, (A) *Siam: the crossroads*, London, 1945.

(B) *Siam*, Oxford Pamphlets on Indian Affairs No. 26, 1945.

CROWE, P. R., (A) 'The trade wind circulation of the world', *I.B.G.*, **15**, 1949, 37–56.

(B) 'The seasonal variation in the strength of the trades', *I.B.G.*, **16**, 1950, 23–47.

CROZIER, BRIAN, 'The international situation in Indochina,' *P.A.*, **29**, 1956, 309–323.

CUADERNO, M., 'The Bell Trade Act and the Philippine economy', *P.A.*, **25**, 1952, 323–333.

CUTSHALL, ALDEN, (A) 'The Philippine Islands', in Pearcey, G. Etzel, *op. cit.*, 1st edition, 430–442, 2nd edition, 628–642.

(B) 'Indonesia and Malaya', *ibid*, 2nd edition, 579–596.

(C) 'Tobacco production in the Philippines', *Transactions of the Illinois State Academy of Science*, **52**, 1 and 2, 1959.

DALE, W. L., (A) 'Wind and drift currents in the South China Sea', *M.J.T.G.*, **8**, 1956, 1–31.

(B), 'The rainfall of Malaya', Part I, *J.T.G.*, **13**, 1959, 23–37, Part II, *J.T.G.*, **14**, 1960, 11-28.

DALY, D. D., 'Surveys and explorations in the native states of the Malay peninsular, 1875–1882', *Proceedings of the Royal Geographical Society*, July 1882, 396.

DANG CHAN LIEU, 'Annamese nationalism', *P.A.*, **20**, 1947, 61–65.

DARBY, H. C., 'The medieval sea-state', *S.G.M.*, **48**, 1932, 136–149.

DATTA, S. K., *Asiatic Asia*, London, 1932.

DAVIS, KINGSLEY, *The population of India and Pakistan*, Princeton, 1951.

DE JOSSELIN DE JONG, P. E., 'Malayan and Sumatran place-names in classical Malay literature', *M.J.T.G.*, **9**, 1956, 61–70.

DE MEEL, H., (A) 'Impediments to economic progress in Indonesia', *P.A.*, **24**, 1951, 39–51.

(B) 'Demographic dilemma in Indonesia', *P.A.*, **24**, 1951, 266–283.

DE NEUMAN, A. M., *Industrial development in Indonesia*, 1955.

DE TERRA, HELLMUT, 'Component geographic factors of the natural regions of Burma', *A.A.A.G.*, **34**, 1944, 67–96.

DEVILLERS, PHILIPPE, 'The struggle for the unification of Vietnam', *C.Q.*, No. 9, 1962, 2–23.

DE VRIES, E., 'Problems of agriculture in Indonesia', *P.A.*, **22**, 1949, 130–143.

DE WAAL, A. M., 'Industrialisatie van Indonesië,' *G. Tijd.*, 217–227.

DE YOUNG, JOHN E., *Village life in modern Thailand*, Berkeley and Los Angeles, 1955.

DEASEY, GEORGE F., 'Localization of Sumatra's oil palm industry', *E.G.*, **18**, 1942, 153–158.

DEL TUFO, M. V., *Malaya. A report on the* 1947 *Census of Population*, London, 1949.

Digest of colonial statistics, London, H.M.S.O.

DOBBY, E. H. G., (A) 'Settlement and land utilization, Malacca', *G.J.*, **94**, 1939, 466–478.

(B) 'Singapore – town and country', *G.R.*, **30**, 1940, 84–109.

(C) 'Settlement patterns in Malaya', *G.R.*, **32**, 1942, 211–232.

(D) 'Some aspects of the human ecology of South-east Asia,' *G.J.*, **108**, 1946, 40–54.

(E) 'Winds and fronts over Southeast Asia', *G.R.*, **35**, 1945, 204–218.

(F) 'Our immediate problem of rice cultivation regarded in Southeast Asia', *Proceedings of I.G.U. Regional Conference, Japan*, 1957, Tokyo, 1959, 593–595.

(G) *Agricultural questions in Malaya*, Cambridge, 1949.

(H) *Southeast Asia*, London, 1st edition 1950, 5th edition 1956.

(K) 'Malayan prospect', *P.A.*, **23**, 1950, 392–401.

(L) 'The Kelantan delta', *G.R.*, **41**, 1951, 226–255.

(M) 'The north Kedah plain', *E.G.*, **27**, 1951, 287–315.

(N) 'Resettlement transforms Malaya', *E.D.C.C.*, **3**, 1952, 163–189.

(O) 'Recent settlement changes in South Malaya', *M.J.T.G.*, **1**, 1953, 1–8.

(P) 'Malaya's rice problem', *P.A.*, **27**, 1954, 58–60.

DOBBY, E. H. G., AND OTHERS, 'Padi landscapes of Malaya', *M.J.T.G.*, **10**, 1957, 3–143.

DODD, E. E., *The new Malaya*, London, 1946.

DONNISON, F. S. V., *Public administration in Burma*, London, 1953.

DONNITHORNE, AUDREY G., 'Western business in Indonesia today', *P.A.*, **27**, 1954, 27–40.

See also ALLEN, G. C.

DOOTJES, F. J. J., 'Deli – the land of agricultural enterprises', *B.C.I.A.*, **2**, 1938, 45–55.

DOUWES DEKKER, N. A., *Tanah air kita*, The Hague and Bandung, n.d.

DU BOIS, CORA, *Social forces in Southeast Asia*, Minneapolis, 1949.

DUMONT, RENÉ, *Types of rural economy*, London, 1957.

DUYVENDAK, J. J. L., *China's discovery of Africa*, London, 1949.

See also VAN HELSDINGEN, W. H.

DYKES, F. J. B., *Mining in Malaya*, London, 2nd edition 1919.

EAST, W. G., AND MOODIE, A. E. (eds.), *The changing world*, London, 1956.

EAST, W. G., AND SPATE, O. H. K. (eds.), *The changing map of Asia*, London, 1st edition 1950, 4th edition 1961.

Eastern and western world, Selected readings, with a foreword by Hofstra, S., The Hague, 1953.

Economic Bulletin for Asia and the Far East, United Nations, Department of Economic Affairs, Bangkok, quarterly.

Economic survey of Asia and the Far East, United Nations, Department of Economic Affairs, Bangkok, annual.

Economic survey of Burma, Rangoon, annual.

Economisch weekblad voor Nederlandsch-Indië, Bijzonder nummer: Industrie in Nederlandsch-Indië, Batavia, May 1941.

ELDRIDGE, F. B., *The background of eastern sea power*, London, 1948.

ELIAS, W. H. J., *Indië onder Japanschen hiel*, The Hague, 1946.

ELSBREE, WILLARD H., *Japan's role in Southeast Asian nationalist movements, 1940–1945*, Harvard, 1953.

EMERSON, RUPERT, (A) *Malaysia: a study in direct and indirect rule*, New York, 1937.

(B) 'Problems of representative government in Southeast Asia', *P.A.*, **26,** 1953, 291–302.

EMERSON, RUPERT; MILLS, LENNOX A.; AND THOMPSON, VIRGINIA, *Government and nationalism in Southeast Asia*, New York, 1942.

Encyclopædia Britannica.

Facts about the Philippines, Manila, 1957.

FAIRBAIRN, GEOFFREY, (A) 'Aspects of the Burmese political scene', *P.A.*, **29,** 1956, 211–222.

(B) 'Some minority problems in Burma', *P.A.*, **30,** 1957, 299–311.

FALL, BERNARD B., (A) 'Local administration under the Viet-Minh', *P.A.*, **27,** 1954, 50–57.

(B) 'Indochina since Geneva', *P.A.*, **28,** 1955, 3–25.

(C) 'The political-religious sects of Viet-Nam', *P.A.*, **28,** 1955, 235–253.

(D) *The Viet-Minh régime*, New York, revised edition 1956 (mimeo.).

(E) 'The international relations of Laos', *P.A.*, **30,** 1957, 22–34.

(F) 'Viet-nam's Chinese problem', *F.E.S.*, **27,** 1958, 65–72.

(G) 'South Viet-Nam's internal problems', *P.A.*, **31,** 1958, 241–260.

(H) 'Power and pressure groups in North Vietnam', *C.Q.*, No. 9, 1962, 37–46.

Far Eastern Quarterly, Special numbers:

(A) Southeast Asia, **2,** November 1942.

(B) The Philippines, **4,** February 1945.

(C) The Netherlands Indies, **5,** February 1946.

(D) French Indochina, **6,** August 1957.

Far Eastern Territories, The (Vol. V of *An economic survey of the colonial territories*), London, H.M.S.O., Colonial No. 281-5, 1954.

FARMER, B. H., *Pioneer peasant colonization in Ceylon*, Oxford, 1957.

FAUCONNIER, HENRY, *The Soul of Malaya*, London, 1931. (Penguin books, 1948.)

Federation of Malaya (formerly Malayan Union) Annual Report, London, H.M.S.O., and Kuala Lumpur.

Federation of Malaya, *Annual Report of the Drainage and Irrigation Department*, Kuala Lumpur.

Federation of Malaya, *Draft Development Plan*, Kuala Lumpur, 1950.

Federation of Malaya: Summary of revised constitutional proposals, London, H.M.S.O., Cmd. 7171, 1947.

Federation of Malaya Official Year Book 1961, Kuala Lumpur, 1961.

Federation of Malaya, Second Five-Year Plan 1961–65, Kuala Lumpur, 1961.

FEITH, HERBERT, (A) 'Towards elections in Indonesia', *P.A.*, **27**, 1954, 236–254.

(B) *The Indonesian elections of* 1955, Cornell Modern Indonesia Project, Ithaca, 1957 (mimeo.).

FELL, H., *1957 Population Census of the Federation of Malaya*, 14 vols., Kuala Lumpur, n.d.

FERNANDO, ENRIQUE, AND AFRICA, JOSÉ L., *Chances for survival of democracy in the Philippines*, Philippine council of the I.P.R., Manila, 1950.

FIELD, FREDERICK V., *Economic handbook of the Pacific area*, New York, 1934.

See also GREENE, KATRINE C.

FIFIELD, RUSSELL H., *The diplomacy of Southeast Asia: 1945–1958*, New York, 1958.

See also PEARCEY, G. ETZEL.

FINKELSTEIN, LAWRENCE S., 'The Indonesian federal problem', *P.A.*, **24**, 1951, 284–295.

FIRTH, RAYMOND, (A) 'The coastal people of Kelantan and Trengganu, Malaya', *G.J.*, **101**, 1943, 193–205.

(B) *Malay fishermen: their peasant economy*, London, 1946.

FISCHER, LOUIS, *The story of Indonesia*, London, 1959.

FISHER, CHARLES A., (A) 'The Thailand–Burma railway', *E.G.*, **23**, 1947, 85–97.

(B) 'Crisis in Indonesia', *P.Q.*, **18**, 1947, 295–312.

(C) 'The Eurasian question in Indonesia', *I.A.*, **23**, 1947, 522–530.

(D) 'The concept of Asian unity – a geographer's view', *A.H.*, **1**, 1948, 3–12.

(E) 'The railway geography of British Malaya', *S.G.M.*, **64**, 1948, 123–136.

(F) 'Continental and maritime components in Japanese expansion', *G.J.*, **115**, 1950, 1–19.

(G) 'The Greater East Asia Co-prosperity Sphere', *G.J.*, **115**, 1950, 179–193.

(H) 'Eurasian resettlement in Indonesia', *E.W.*, **5**, 1951, 9–11.

(K) 'West New Guinea in its regional setting', *The Year Book of World Affairs*, **6**, London, 1952, 189–210.

(L) 'Les Hollandais et l'Indonésie', *P.E.*, **19**, 1954, 45–58.

(M) 'Crisis in South-east Asia', *Q.Q.*, **63**, 1956, 104–118.
(N) 'South-east Asia', in East, W. G., and Spate, O. H. K., *op. cit.*, 312–343.
(O) 'Communist China', in East, W. G., and Moodie, A. E., *op. cit.*, 568–598.
(P) 'The prospect for Japan', *ibid.*, 535–565.
(Q) 'The Malaysian realm', *ibid.*, 652–680.
(R) 'Mainland South-east Asia', *ibid.*, 624–651.
(S) 'Burma, Thailand and Indochina', in Pearcey, G. Etzel, *op. cit.* (2nd edition), 562–572.
(T) 'Southeast Asia: the Balkans of the Orient?', *G.*, **47**, 1962, 347–367.
(U) 'The choice before South-east Asia', *Listener*, 14 April, 1955, 645–6 and 657.
(V) *The compleat geographer*, (Inaugural lecture) Sheffield, 1959.

See also STEEL, R. W.

FITZGERALD, C. P., *Revolution in China*, London, 1952.

FORBES, W. CAMERON, *The Philippine Islands*, Harvard, 2nd edition, 1945.

FORDE, C. DARYLL, *Habitat, economy and society*, London, 1934.

France-Asie, Numéro spécial: Présence du Cambodge, Saigon, November–December 1955.

France-Asie, Numéro spécial: Présence du Royaume Lao, Saigon, March–April 1956.

FREEDMAN, MAURICE, (A) 'The plural society of Malaya', *T.B.C.R.*, Summer 1955, 24–25.
(B) 'The growth of a plural society in Malaya', *P.A.*, **33**, 1960, 158–167.

FREEMAN, OTIS W., (ed.), *Geography of the Pacific*, New York, 1951.

FREYRE, GILBERTO, 'Human factors behind Brazilian development', *Progress*, **42**, 1951–2, 3–12.

FRUIN, TH. A., *Het economische aspect van het Indonesische vraagstuk*, Amsterdam, 1947.

FRYER, D. W., (A) 'The "Million City" in Southeast Asia', *G.R.*, **43**, 1953, 474–494.
(B) 'Indonesia's economic prospects', *F.E.S.*, **23**, 1954, 177–182.
(C) 'Recovery of the sugar industry in Indonesia', *E.G.*, **33**, 1957, 171–187.
(D) 'Economic aspects of Indonesian disunity', *P.A.*, **30**, 1957, 195–208.
(E) *Indonesia*, Longman's Australian Geographies No. 5, Melbourne, 1957.
(F) 'Jogjakarta – economic development in an Indonesian city state', *E.D.C.C.*, **7**, 1959, 452–464.
(G) 'Food production in Malaya', *A.G.*, **6**, 1954, 35–38.
(H) *Malaya*, Longman's Australian Geographies, No. 14, Melbourne, 1962.

FURNIVALL, J. S., (A) *Netherlands India*, Cambridge, 2nd edition 1944.
(B) *The tropical Far East*, Oxford pamphlets on world affairs No. 71, 1945.
(C) 'Capitalism in Indonesia', *P.A.*, **20**, 1947, 66–69.

(D) *Colonial policy and practice, a comparative study of Burma and Netherlands India*, Cambridge, 1948.

(E) 'Twilight in Burma: reconquest and after', *P.A.*, **22**, 1949, 3–20.

(F) 'Twilight in Burma: independence and after', *P.A.*, **22**, 1949, 155–172.

GADGIL, D. R., 'Some requirements for technical progress in Asia', *P.A.*, **24**, 1951, 178–184.

GARBELL, M. A., *Tropical and equatorial meteorology*, London, 1947.

Garuda Indonesian Airways Plan, 1951–1955, n.d.

GEIGER, R., See Braak, C. (C).

GERBRANDY, P. S., *Indonesia*, London, 1950.

GINSBURG, NORTON S., (A) 'The great city in Southeast Asia', *A.J.S.*, **40**, 1955, 455–462.

(B) (ed.) *The pattern of Asia*, Englewood Cliffs, 1958.

GINSBURG, NORTON S., AND ROBERTS, CHESTER F., *Malaya*, Seattle, 1958.

GINSBURG, NORTON S. (general ed.), KAPLAN, IRVING, AND ROBERTS, CHESTER F. (eds.), *Area handbook on British Borneo*, Human Relations Area Files, Chicago, Preliminary edition, 1955.

GISCARD D'ESTAING, EDMOND, 'L'industrialisation de l'Indochine', *C.I.G.*, Amsterdam, 1938, 2 Section III C, 535–539.

GOLAY, FRANK H., (A) 'Economic consequences of the Philippine Trade Act', *P.A.*, **28**, 1955, 53–70.

(B) 'The Philippine monetary policy debate', *P.A.*, **29**, 1956, 253–264.

(C) *The Philippines, public policy and national economic development*, Ithaca, 1961.

GOUROU, PIERRE, (A) *Les paysans du delta tonkinois*, Paris, 1936.

(B) 'L'industrie villageoise dans le delta du Tonkin', *C.I.G.*, Amsterdam, 1938, 2 Section III A, 249–251.

(C) 'Densité de la population et utilisation du sol en Indochine française', *C.I.G.*, Amsterdam, 1938, 2 Section III C, 417–420.

(D) *L'utilisation du sol en Indochine française*, Paris, 1940.

(E) 'For a French Indo-Chinese federation', *P.A.*, **20**, 1947, 18–29.

(F) *L'avenir de l'Indochine*, Paris, 1947.

(G) 'Notes on China's unused uplands', *P.A.*, **21**, 1948, 18–29.

(H) *The tropical world* (trs. Laborde, E. D.), London, 1953.

(K) *L'Asie*, Paris, 1953.

GRAHAM, W. A., *Siam*, 2 Vols., London, 1924.

GREENE, KATRINE C., AND PHILLIPS, JOSEPH D., *Transportation and foreign trade* (Part II of *An economic survey of the Pacific area*, General ed., Field, F. V.), New York, 1942.

GREGORY, J. W. (ed.), *The structure of Asia*, London, 1929.

GREGORY, J. W. and C. J., 'The Alps of Chinese Tibet', *G.J.*, 61, 1923, 153–178.

GRIST, D. H., (A) *Agriculture in Malaya*, London, 1936.

(B) 'The rice problem', *M.J.T.G.*, **5**, 1955, 20–25.
(C) *Rice*, London, 1953.
GROSLIER, BERNARD P., *Angkor et le Cambodge au XVI*^{e} *siècle*, Paris, 1958.
GROSLIER, BERNARD, and ARTHAUD, JACQUES, *Angkor art and civilization*, London and New York, 1957.
GULL, E. M., *British economic interests in the Far East*, Oxford, 1943.
HADDON, A. C., *The wanderings of peoples*, Cambridge, 1927.
HAGEN, EVERETT E., *The economic development of Burma*, Washington, 1956.
HALL, D. G. E., (A) *Burma*, London, 1950.
(B) *A history of South-East Asia*, London, 1955.
HALLETT, HOLT S., 'Exploration survey for a railway connection between India, Siam and China', *S.G.M.*, **2**, 1886, 78–92.
HAMILTON, WALTER, *The East Indian gazetteer*, London, 1815.
HAMMER, ELLEN J., (A) 'Blueprinting a new Indochina', *P.A.*, **21**, 1948, 252–263.
(B) 'The Bao Dai experiment', *P.A.*, **23**, 1950, 46–58.
(C) *The struggle for Indochina*, Stanford, 1954.
(D) *The struggle for Indochina continues*, Stanford, 1955.
(E) 'Progress report on South Viet Nam', *P.A.*, **30**, 1957, 221–235.
Handbook of the Netherlands Indies, Buitenzorg, 1930.
Handbook on Netherlands New Guinea, Rotterdam, 1958.
Handbook Philippine Statistics, 1903–1959, Manila, 1960.
Handbook of Sarawak, Singapore, 1949.
HARE, F. KENNETH, *The restless atmosphere*, London, 1953.
HARRIS, H. G., AND WILLBOURN, E. S., *Mining in Malaya*, London, 1936.
HARRIS, RICHARD, (A) 'The unrecognized frontier', *Listener*, 6 September, 1962, 339–342.
(B) *Independence and after*, Oxford, 1962.
HARRISON, BRIAN, *South-east Asia – a short history*, London, 1954.
HART, DONN V., 'Projects and progress in the Philippines', *P.A.*, **27**, 1954, 353–366.
HART, G. H. C., (A) 'Recent developments in the Netherlands Indies', *G.J.*, **99**, 1942, 81–102.
(B) *Towards economic democracy in the Netherlands Indies*, New York, 1942.
HARTSHORNE, RICHARD, 'The functional approach in political geography', *A.A.A.G.*, **40**, 1950, 95–130.
HARVEY, G. E., (A) *History of Burma from the earliest times to the beginning of the English conquest*, London, 1925.
(B) *British rule in Burma*, London, 1946.
(C) 'The Wa people of the Burma-Chinese border', *St. Antony's Papers*, No. 2, Oxford, 1957, 126–135.
HATTA, MOHAMMAD, (A) 'Indonesia's foreign policy', *F.A.*, **31**, 1953, 441–452.
(B) 'Indonesia between the power blocs', *F.A.*, **36**, 1958, 481–490.

(C) *The co-operative movement in Indonesia*, with an introduction by Roesli Rahmin, ed. George McT. Kahin, Ithaca, 1957.

HAYDEN, JOSEPH RALSTON, *The Philippines – a study in national development*, New York, 1950.

HEINE-GELDERN, ROBERT, (A) 'Conceptions of state and kingship in Southeast Asia', *F.E.Q.*, **2**, 1942, 15–30.

(B) 'Prehistoric research in the Netherlands Indies', in Honig, P., and Verdoorn, F., *op. cit.*, 129–167.

See also LOEB, E. M.

HEINISCH, HEINZ H., *Südostasien*, Berlin, 1954.

HELBIG, KARL M., (A) *Am Rande des Pazifik*, Stuttgart, 1949.

(B) *Die Insel Borneo in Forschung und Schrifttum*, Hamburg, 1955.

'Helping the Malayans to help themselves', *T.B.C.R.*, Summer 1954, 19.

HENDRY, JAMES B., 'American aid in Vietnam', *P.A.*, **33**, 1960, 387–391.

HIGGINS, BENJAMIN, (A) 'Indonesia's development plans and problems', *P.A.*, **29**, 1956, 107–125.

(B) 'Development problems in the Philippines: a comparison with Indonesia', *F.E.S.*, **26**, 1957, 161–169.

(C) *Indonesia's economic stabilization and development*, New York, 1957.

HIGGINS, BENJAMIN AND JEAN, 'Indonesia: now or never', *F.A.*, **37**, 1948, 156–165.

HO PING-TI, *Studies in the population of China, 1368–1953*, Harvard, 1959.

HO, ROBERT, *Environment, man and development in Malaya* (Inaugural Lecture), Kuala Lumpur, 1962.

HOANG VAN CHI, 'Collectivisation and rice production', *C.Q.*, No. 9, 1962, 94–104.

HODDER, B. W., (A) 'Population and economic development in Southeast Asia', *G.*, **41**, 1956, 131–132.

(B) 'The economic development of Sarawak', *G.S.*, **3**, 1956, 71–84.

(C) 'Biogeographical aspects of settlement in Malaya', *M.J.T.G.*, **5**, 1955, 12–19.

(D) *Man in Malaya*, London, 1959.

(E) 'Racial groupings in Singapore', *M.J.T.G.*, **1**, 1953, 25–36.

Holland: East Indies Colonial Possessions, Admiralty Naval Intelligence Department, London, 1887.

HOLLAND, WILLIAM L., 'Japan and the new balance of power in the Far East', *I.A.*, **28**, 1952, 292–297.

HONEY, P. J., (A) 'The historic unity of Viet Nam', *E.W.*, **10, 11**, 1956, 11–12 and 49.

(B) 'The position of the D.R.V. leadership and the succession to Ho Chi Minh, *C.Q.*, No. 9, 1962, 24–36.

HONIG, P., AND VERDOORN, F. (eds.), *Science and scientists in the Netherlands Indies*, New York, 1945.

HUDSON, G. F., *The Far East in world politics*, Oxford, 1937.

HUNT, CHESTER L., 'Moslem and Christian in the Philippines', *P.A.*, **28**, 1955, 331–349.

HYMA, ALBERT, *The Dutch in the Far East,* Ann Arbor, 1942.

Indisch Verslag, annual (pre-war).

Indo-China, Geographical Handbook Series, Naval Intelligence Division, B.R. 510, 1943.

Indo-China – a French point of view, Paris, 1950.

Indo-China – a geographical appreciation, Foreign Geography Information Series, No. 6, Department of Mines and Technical Surveys, Geographical Branch, Ottawa, 1953.

'Indochinas Christen', *Z.G.*, **26**, 1955, 242–248.

'Indo-China: the unfinished struggle', *W.T.*, **12**, 1956, 17–26.

'Indonesia after the elections', *W.T.*, **12**, 1956, 330–339.

Indonesia, Review of commercial conditions, London, H.M.S.O., 1951.

'Industrialization of Indonesia, The', *I.R.*, **1**, 1951, 185–189.

INGRAM, JAMES C., *Economic change in Thailand since* 1850, Stanford, 1955.

International Bank for Reconstruction and Development, *The economic development of Malaya*, Singapore, 1955.

International Bank for Reconstruction and Development, *A public development program for Thailand*, Baltimore, 1959.

IRELAND, ALLEYNE, *The Far Eastern tropics*, London, 1905.

ISHII, RYOICHI, *Population pressure and economic life in Japan*, London, 1937.

JACOBY, ERICH H., *Agrarian unrest in Southeast Asia*, New York, 1949.

JAFFE, PHILIP, see Chiang Kai-shek.

JARRETT, H. R., 'The oil palm industry and its changing place in the economy of Sierra Leone', *G.*, **42**, 1957, 50–59.

JENKINS, SHIRLEY, 'Financial and economic planning in the Philippines' *P.A.*, **21**, 1948, 33–45.

JONES, F. C., BORTON, HUGH, AND PEARN, B. R., *The Far East*, 1942–1946 (*Survey of International Affairs*), Oxford, 1955.

JONES, L. W., Sarawak – *Report on the Census of Population taken on 15th June 1960*, Kuching, 1962.

JONES, STEPHEN B., AND MEHNERT, KLAUS, 'Hawaii and the Pacific – a survey of political geography', *G.R.*, **30**, 1940, 358–375.

JONES, W. H. S., *Malaria: a neglected factor in the history of Greece and Rome*, London, 1907.

JONKERS, A., 'Het bevolkingsvraagstuk van Java en de landbouwkolonisatie', *Indonesië*, **1**, 1947, 28–42.

JOSEY, ALEX, 'Indonesia faces the future', *E.W.*, **10**, 1956, 23–24.

JUMPER, ROY, 'Mandarin bureaucracy and politics in South Viet Nam', *P.A.*, **21**, 1948, 33–45.

KAHIN, GEORGE MCT., (A) 'The state of North Borneo, 1881–1946', *F.E.Q.*, **7**, 1947, 43–65.

(B) 'Indirect rule in Eastern Indonesia', *P.A.*, **22**, 1949, 227–238.

(C) *Nationalism and revolution in Indonesia*, Ithaca, 1952.

See also HATTA, MOHAMMED (C).

KATTENBURG, PAUL M., *A central Javanese village in* 1950, Cornell Southeast Asia Program Data Paper No. 2, Ithaca, 1951 (mimeo.).

KAYE, WILLIAM, 'A bowl of rice divided: the economy of North Vietnam', *C.Q.*, No. 9, 1962, 82–93.

KEESING, FELIX M., (A) *The Philippines: a nation in the making*, Shanghai, 1937.

(B) 'Cultural trends in the Philippines', *F.E.Q.*, **4**, 1945, 102–108.

KENDREW, W. G., *The climates of the continents*, Oxford, 1937.

KENNEDY, RAYMOND, (A) *The ageless Indies*, New York, 1942.

(B) 'Contours of culture in Indonesia', *F.E.Q.*, **2**, 1942, 5–14.

(C) *Islands and peoples of the Indies*, Washington, 1943.

KEYFITZ, N., (A) 'The population of Indonesia', *E.K.I.*, October 1953.

(B) *Population: the dynamic factor in Indonesian development*, National Planning Bureau, Djakarta, 1953.

KHAN, M. HALIM, 'The rise and decline of cash crops in Java', *I.G.J.*, **1**, 1961, 47–55.

KING, A. W., 'Plantations and agriculture in Malaya, with notes on the trade of Singapore', *G.J.*, **93**, 1939, 137–148.

KING, F. H., *Farmers of forty centuries*, New York, 1926.

KING, JOHN KERRY, *Southeast Asia in perspective*, New York, 1956.

KIRBY, S. W., 'Johore in 1926', *G.J.*, **71**, 1928, 240–260.

KIRK, WILLIAM, (A) 'Some factors in the historical geography of Burma', *J.M.G.S.*, **54**, 1947–1949, 16–26.

(B) 'Indian Ocean community', *S.G.M.*, **67**, 1951, 161–177.

KLEIN, W. C. (ed.), *Nieuw Guinea*, The Hague, 1954.

KLEIWEG DE ZWAAN, J. P., *De rassen van den Indischen archipel*, Amsterdam, 1925.

KOLB, ALBERT, *Die Philippinen*, Leipzig, 1942.

KONDAPI, C., *Indians overseas*, 1838–1949, New Delhi, 1951.

KÖPPEN, W., See Braak, C. (C).

KOTESWARAM, P., 'The easterly jet stream in the tropics', *T*, **10**, 1958, 43–57.

KOTESWARAM, P., RAMAN, C. V., AND PARTHASARTHY, S., 'The mean jet stream over India and Burma in winter', *I.J.M.G.*, **4**, 1953, 111–122.

KREBS, NORBERT, *Vergleichende Länderkunde*, Stuttgart, 1952.

KRIEGER, HERBERT W., 'Races and peoples in the Philippines', *F.E.Q.*, **4**, 1945, 95–101.

KROM, N. J., *Hindoe-Javaansche geschiedenis*, The Hague, 1926.

KUNO, YOSHIO S., *Japanese expansion on the Asiatic continent*, 3 Vols., Berkeley, 1937.

KUNST, J., *The peoples of the Indian archipelago*, Leiden, 1946.

LABORDE, E. D., See Gourou, Pierre, (H), and Robequain, Charles, (D).

LANCASTER, DONALD, *The emancipation of French Indo-China*, Oxford (London), 1961.

LANDON, K. P., (A) *Siam in transition*, Oxford, 1939.

(B) 'Siam', in Mills, Lennox A., *et al.*, 246–272.

LANSANG, JOSÉ A., 'The Philippine-American experiment: a Filipino view', *P.A.*, **25**, 1952, 226–234.

LASKER, BRUNO, (A) *Peoples of Southeast Asia*, New York, 1944.

(B) 'Southeast Asia enters the modern world', *Forum*, **106**, November 5, 1946.

LATTIMORE, OWEN and ELEANOR, *The making of modern China*, London, 1945.

LEACH, E. R., *Social science research in Sarawak*, Colonial Research Studies, No. 1, London, H.M.S.O., 1950.

LÊ THÁNH KHÔI, *Le Viêt-Nam*, Paris, 1955.

LE BAR, FRANK, and SUDDARD, ADRIENNE eds., *Laos* (Human Relations Area Files), New Haven, 1960.

LE MAY, REGINALD, *The culture of South-East Asia*, London, 1954.

LEE, DOUGLAS H. K., *Climate and economic development in the tropics*, New York, 1957.

LEE, Y. L., (A) 'Some aspects of shifting cultivation in British Borneo', *Malayan Forester*, **24**, 1961, 102–109.

(B) 'Some factors in the development and planning of land use in British Borneo', *J.T.G.*, **15**, 1961, 66–81.

(C) 'Land settlement for agriculture in North Borneo', *T.E.S.G.*, **52**, 1961, 184–191.

(D) 'Historical aspects of settlement in British Borneo', *P.V.*, **2**, 1961, 187–212.

(E) 'The long house and Dayak settlements in British Borneo', *O.G.*, **6**, 1962, 39–60.

(F) 'The port towns of British Borneo', *A.G.*, **8**, 1962, 161–172.

(G) 'The population of British Borneo', *P.S.*, **15**, 1962, 226–243.

LEGGE, JOHN D., *Problems of regional autonomy in contemporary Indonesia*, Cornell Modern Indonesia Project, Interim Report Series, Ithaca, 1957 (mimeo.).

LEHMANN, HERBERT, 'Das Antlitz der Stadt in Niederländisch Indien', in *Länderkundliche Forschung, Festschrift Norbert Krebs*, Stuttgart, 1936.

LEIFER, MICHAEL, 'Cambodia and her neighbours', *P.A.*, **34**, 1961–2, 361–374.

Lembaga Kemajuan Tanah Persekutuan (*Federal Land Development Authority*) *Report*, Kuala Lumpur, 1961.

LÉVY, ROGER, (A) *Extrême-Orient et Pacifique*, Paris, 1948.

(B) *Regards sur l'Asie*, Paris, 1952.

(C) 'Indochina: a keystone in Asia – A French view', *I.Q.*, **8**, 1952, 31–38.

LEWIS, NORMAN, *A dragon apparent*, London, 1951. (Pan books, 1957.)

LIMBOURG, MICHAEL, *L'économie actuelle du Viet-nam démocratique*, Hanoi, 1956.

LINTON, RALPH (ed.), *Most of the world*, New York, 1949.

LOBECK, A. K., *Physiographic diagram of Asia*, New York, 1945.

LOEB, EDWIN M., AND BROEK, JAN O. M., 'Social organization and the long house in South-east Asia', *Am. An.*, **49**, 1947, 414–425.

LOEB, EDWIN M., AND HEINE-GELDERN, ROBERT, *Sumatra, its history and people*, Vienna, 1935.

LOFTUS, A. J., *Notes of a journey across the isthmus of Kra, January–April*, 1883, Singapore, 1883.

LOGEMANN, J. H. A., 'The Indonesian problem, *P.A.*, **20**, 1947, 30–41.

LUCE, G. H., 'Economic life of the early Burman', *J.B.R.S.*, **30**, 1940, 283–335.

LYDE, L. W., *The continent of Asia*, London, 1933.

MACDONALD, MALCOLM, *The Asian revolution*, Singapore, 1953.

MACGILLIVRAY, SIR DONALD, 'Malaya – the new nation', *I.A.*, **34**, 1958, 157–163.

MACKENZIE, COMPTON, *Realms of silver*, London, 1954.

MACKENZIE, K. E., *Malaya, Overseas Economic Survey*, London, H.M.S.O., 1951.

MACKIE, J. A. C., 'Indonesia's government estates and their masters', *P.A.*, **34**, 1961–2, 337–360.

MACKINDER, SIR HALFORD J., *Democratic ideals and reality*, London (Pelican edition), 1943.

MADGE, C., 'Country life in Siam', *The Times*, January 7, 1955, 9.

MAJUMDAR, R. C., (A) *Suvarna-dvipa*, Dacca, 1936.
(B) *Hindu colonies in the Far East*, Calcutta, 1944.

Malaya: the making of a nation, Central Office of Information Reference Pamphlets No. 27, London, 1957.

Malayan Union and Singapore: Statement of policy on future constitution, London, H.M.S.O., Cmd. 6724, 1946.

Malaysian Heritage, Ministry of Culture, Singapore, 1962.

MARSHALL, HARRY I., *The Karens of Burma* (Longman's Burma Pamphlets No. 8), 1945.

MAUNG MAUNG, (A) 'Burma looks ahead', *P.A.*, **25**, 1952, 40–48.
(B) *Burma in the family of nations*, Amsterdam, 1956.

MAYR, ERNST, 'Wallace's line in the light of recent zoogeographic studies', in Honig and Verdoorn (eds.), 241–250.

MCCARTHY, JAMES, *Surveying and exploring in Siam*, London, 1902.

MCCUNE, SHANNON, (A) 'The diversity of Indochina's physical geography', *F.E.Q.*, **6**, 1947, 335–344.
(B) 'Korea, Indochina and Siam: historic Asiatic buffers', in Pearcey, G. Etzel, *op. cit.* (1st edition), 358–372.

MCGEE, T. G., 'Aspects of the political geography of Southeast Asia', *P.V.*, **1**, 1960, 39–58.

MEHNERT, KLAUS, See Jones, Stephen B.

MEIJER RANNEEFT, J. W., *De weg voor Indië*, Amsterdam, 1946.

MENDE, TIBOR, *South-East Asia between two worlds*, London, 1955.

MENDINUETO, S. R., 'Industrial Philippines, *C.I.G.*, Amsterdam, 1938, 2 Section III C, 564–566.

MERRILL, E. D., 'The vegetation of Malaysia', *F.E.Q.*, **2**, 1942, 66–76.

METCALF, JOHN E., *The Agricultural economy of Indonesia*, U.S. Department of Agriculture, Washington, 1952.

METZGEMAEKERS, L., 'The Western New Guinea problem', *P.A.*, **24**, 1951, 131–142.

MICAUD, CHARLES A., 'French Indochina', in Mills, Lennox A., *et al.*, 216–245.

MILLER, A. AUSTIN, *Climatology*, London, 1937.

MILLER, E. WILLARD, 'Industrial resources of Indochina', *F.E.Q.*, **6**, 1947, 396–408.

MILLS, LENNOX A., *British rule in Eastern Asia*, Oxford, 1942.

MILLS, LENNOX A., and associates, *The new world of Southeast Asia*, Minneapolis, 1949.

See also EMERSON, RUPERT.

MINTZ, JEANNE, *Indonesia – a profile*, Princeton, 1961.

Modern Thailand, Royal Thai Embassy, Washington, n.d. (mimeo.).

MOERDOWO, R., 'Indonesia's language question', *E.W.*, **10**, 1956, 22 and 35.

MOHR, E. J. C., (A) 'Climate and soil in the Netherlands Indies', in Honig, P., and Verdoorn, F., *op. cit.*, 250–254.

(B) 'The relation between soil and population density in the Netherlands Indies', *Ibid.*, 254–262.

(C) *The soils of equatorial regions, with special reference to the Netherlands Indies* (trs. Pendleton, R. L.), New York, 1944.

MOLENGRAAF, G. A. F., 'Modern deep-sea research in the East Indian archipelago', *G.J.*, **57**, 1921, 95–121.

MOREHEAD, F. T., *The forests of Burma* (Longman's Burma Pamphlets No. 5), 1944.

MORGAN, ROBERT, *World sea fisheries*, London, 1956.

MORRISON, IAN, 'Aspects of the racial problem in Malaya', *P.A.*, **22**, 1949, 239–253.

MOUNTJOY, ALAN B., 'Vegetable oils and oilseeds', *G.*, **42**, 1957, 37–49.

MURPHEY, RHOADS, (A) 'The ruin of ancient Ceylon', *J.A.S.*, **16**, 1957, 181–200.

(B) 'New capitals of Asia', *E.D.C.C.*, **5**, 1957, 216–243.

(C) 'Economic conflicts in South Asia', *Conflict Resolution*, **4**, 1960, 83–95.

MURRAY, HUGH, *An encyclopædia of geography*, London, 1834.

MUS, PAUL, (A) 'The role of the village in Vietnamese politics', *P.A.*, **22**, 1949, 265–271.

(B) *Viêt-Nam, sociologie d'une guerre*, Paris, 1952.

MYSBERGH, J. H., 'The Indonesian élite', *F.E.S.*, **26**, 1957, 38–42.

National Income of Burma, The, Ministry of National Planning, Rangoon, 1951.

NAUNTON, W. J. S., 'The development of synthetic rubber and its future', *N.S.*, March 21, 1957, 12–14.

'Nederlands Nieuw Guinea en de wereld', *Internationale Spectator*, October 18, 1950, 7–11.

NEHRU, JAWAHARLAL, *The discovery of India*, London, 1946, 4th edition, 1956.

Netherlands East Indies, Geographical Handbook Series, B.R. 518 and 518A, Naval Intelligence Division, 2 vols., 1944.

NEWBOLD, T. J., *Political and statistical account of the British Settlements in the Straits of Malacca*, 2 Vols., London, 1839.

NGUYEN NGOC BICH, 'Vietnam – an independent viewpoint', *C.Q.*, No. 9, 1962, 105–111.

NOOTEBOOM, C., 'Indonesie als gebied van scheepvaart', Koninklijke Vereeniging Indisch Instituut, 28*ste Indische Vacantiecursus voor Geografen*, Amsterdam, 1949, 5–9.

NORODOM SIHANOUK, PRINCE, 'Cambodia neutral: the dictate of necessity', *F.A.*, **36**, 1958, 582–586.

North Borneo Annual Report, London, H.M.S.O.

NOSSIN, J. J., 'Relief and coastal development in north-eastern Johore (Malaya)', *J.T.G.*, **15**, 1961, 27–38.

OLIVER, J., 'Bamboo as an economic resource in southern Asia', *G.*, **41**, 1956, 49–56.

OLVER, A. S. B., 'The Special Commission in South-East Asia', *P.A.*, **21**, 1948, 285–290.

OOI JIN-BEE, (A) 'Mining landscapes of Kinta', *M.J.T.G.*, **4**, 1954.

(B) *Rural development in tropical areas, with special reference to Malaya*, *J.T.G.*, **12**, 1959.

(C) 'The rubber industry of the Federation of Malaya', *J.T.G.*, **15**, 1961, 46–65.

ORMELING, F. J., *The Timor problem*, Groningen, 1957.

PALMER, C. E., (A) 'Tropical meteorology', in *Compendium of Meteorology*, American Meteorological Society, Boston, 1951, 859–880.

(B) 'Tropical meteorology', *Q.J.R.M.S.*, **78**, 1952, 126–169.

PALMIER, LESLIE H., (A) 'Modern Islam in Indonesia: the Muhammadiyah after independence', *P.A.*, **27**, 1954, 255–262.

(B) 'Indonesia and the West', *I.A.*, **31**, 1955, 182–191.

(C) 'Aspects of Indonesia's social structure', *P.A.*, **28**, 1955, 117–131.

(D) 'Sukarno, the nationalist', *P.A.*, **30**, 1957, 101–119.

(E) *Indonesia and the Dutch*, Oxford (London), 1962.

See also BURGER, D. H.

PANIKKAR, K. M., (A) *The future of Southeast Asia*, New York, 1943.

(B) *India and the Indian Ocean*, London, 1945.

(C) *Asia and Western dominance*, London, 1953.

(D) *In two Chinas*, London, 1955.

(E) *The Afro-Asian states and their problems*, London, 1959.

PANNEKOEK, A. J., 'Eenige hoofdlinien van het relief van Java', Koninklijke Vereeniging Indisch Instituut, 27*ste Vacantiecursus voor Geografen*, Amsterdam, 1948, 11–18.

PARKINSON, C. NORTHCOTE, (A) *A short history of Malaya*, Background to Malaya Series, No. 1, Singapore, 1954.

(B) *Britain in the Far East – the Singapore naval base*, Background to Malaya Series, No. 7, Singapore, 1955.

PARMER, J. NORMAN, *Colonial labor policy and administration. A history of labor in the rubber plantation industry in Malaya 1910–1941*, New York, 1960.

PARRY, J. H., *Europe and a wider world*, 1415–1715, London, 1949.

PAUKER, GUY J., (A) 'Southeast Asia as a problem area in the next decade', *W.P.*, **11**, 1959, 325–345.

(B) 'Indonesia's eight year development plan', *P.A.*, **34**, 1961, 115–130.

PEARCEY, G. ETZEL, FIFIELD, RUSSELL H., and associates: *World political geography*, New York, 1948. (2nd edition: Pearcey, G. Etzel, and associates, New York, 1957.)

PEARN, B. R., *Burma background* (Longman's Burma Pamphlets No. 1), 1943. See also JONES, F. C.

PEEKEMA, WIBO G., 'Colonization of Javanese in the outer provinces of the Netherlands East Indies', *G.J.*, **101**, 1943, 145–153.

PEET, G. L., *Political questions in Malaya*, Cambridge, 1949.

PELZER, KARL J., (A) *Die Arbeiterwanderungen in Südostasien*, Hamburg, 1935.

(B) *Population and land utilization* (Part 1 of *An economic survey of the Pacific area*, General ed., Field, F. V.), New York, 1941.

(C) *Pioneer settlement in the Asiatic tropics*, New York, 1945.

(D) 'Tanah sabrang and Java's population problem', *F.E.Q.*, **5**, 1946, 133–142.

(E) 'Rural problems and plans for rural development in the Republic of the Philippines', Working paper for the 28th study sessions of the *International Institute of Differeing Civilization*, The Hague, September 7–10, 1953.

(F) 'The agrarian conflict in East Sumatra', *P.A.*, **30**, 1957, 151–159.

(G) 'The impact of science on Southeast Asia', Background paper for the sixth national conference of the *U.S. National Committee for UNESCO*, San Francisco, November 6–9, 1957 (mimeo.).

(H) 'Agriculture in the humid tropics', *Ninth Pacific Science Congress*, Bangkok, November 18–30, 1957 (mimeo.).

(K) 'Geography and the tropics', in Taylor, Griffith, *op. cit.*, 311–344.

PENDLETON, R. L., (A) 'Laterite and its structural uses in Thailand and Cambodia', *G.R.*, **31**, 1941, 177–202.

(B) 'Land use in northeastern Thailand', *G.R.*, **33**, 1943, 15–41.

PENDLETON, R. L., with the assistance of Kingsbury, Robert C., and others, *Thailand, aspects of landscape and life*, New York, 1962.

See also PRESCOTT, J. A. and PENDLETON, R. L.

See also MOHR, E. J. C.

PETERSON, A. D. C., (A) 'Britain and Siam: the latest phase', *P.A.*, **19**, 1946, 364–372.

(B) 'The birth of the Malayan nation', *I.A.*, **31**, 1955, 311–316.

(C) *The Far East, a social geography*, London, 3rd. edition, 1957.

'Philippine islands: economic problems of independence', *W.T.*, **4**, 1948, 488–496.

Philippines (The), Review of commercial conditions, London, H.M.S.O., 1950.

Philippines (The), 1953, Department of Commerce and Industry, Manila, 1953.

PIRES, TOMÉ, *The Suma Orientalis* (trs. Cortesao, A), 2 Vols., Hakluyt Society, London, 1944.

Population growth and manpower in the Philippines, U.N. Population Studies, No. 32, New York, 1960.

Population of the Philippines by provinces and municipality, Special Bulletin, No. 1, Manila, 1960.

Population of Indonesia, The, Djakarta, 1956.

POSEWITZ, THEODOR, *Borneo: its geology and mineral resources*, London, 1892.

PRESCOTT, J. A., and PENDLETON, R. L., *Laterite and lateritic soils*, Commonwealth Agricultural Bureaux, Farnham Royal, 1952.

'Presidential policy in the Philippines', *W.T.*, **12**, 1956, 512–523.

Proceedings of the Fourth Pacific Science Congress, Java, 1929, Vol. IV, Batavia, 1930.

PURCELL, VICTOR, (A) 'A Malayan Union', *P.A.*, **19**, 1946, 20–40.

(B) *Malaya – outline of a colony*, London, 1946.

(C) *The Chinese in Malaya*, Oxford, 1948.

(D) *The Chinese in Southeast Asia*, Oxford, 1951.

(E) *The colonial period in Southeast Asia*, New York, 1953 (mimeo.).

(F) *Malaya – communist or free ?*, London, 1954.

(G) 'Indo-China and the prospect in South-East Asia', *Year Book of World Affairs*, **9**, 1955, London, 126–148.

(H) *The revolution in Southeast Asia*, London, 1962.

Pyidawtha – the new Burma, Economic and Social Board, Government of the Union of Burma, Rangoon, 1954.

RAFFLES, SIR THOMAS STAMFORD, *A history of Java*, London, 1817.

RAHMIN, ROESLI, See Hatta, Mohammed (C).

RAJCHMAN, MARTHE, See Hudson, G. F.

RAMAGE, C. S., 'Relationship of general circulation to normal weather over southern Asia and the western Pacific', *J.M.*, **12**, 1955, 252–262.

RAWLINGS, G. S., *Malaya*, Oxford Pamphlets on Indian Affairs, No. 29, 1945.

RAWSON, R. REES, 'Two new railways in South-east Asia', *G.J.*, **108**, 1946, 85–88.

RECLUS, ÉLISÉE, edited Keane, A. H., *India and Indo-China* (*The universal geography*, Vol. 8), London, 1875–1894.

REEVE, W. D., *Public administration in Siam*, Oxford, 1951.

RENOUVIN, PIERRE, *La question d'Extrême-Orient*, 1840–1894, Paris, 1946.

Report of the Commission of Enquiry, North Borneo and Sarawak, London, H.M.S.O., Cmnd. 1794, 1962.

Report of the Committee New Guinea (Irian) 1950, 4 parts, Secretariat of the Netherlands-Indonesian Union, 1950.

Report on Netherlands New Guinea for the Year 1953, presented by the Netherlands Government to the Secretary-General of the United Nations, pursuant to Article 73(e) of the Charter, The Hague, Foto Btz., 99725a.

RICHARDS, C. J., *The Burman – an appreciation* (Longman's Burma Pamphlets No. 7), 1945.

RICHARDS, P. W., *The tropical rain forest*, Cambridge, 1957.

RICHARDSON, J. A., 'Outline of the geomorphological evolution of British Malaya', *G.M.*, **84**, 1947, 129–144.

RIEHL, H., *Tropical meteorology*, New York, 1954.

RIEHL, H., ALAKA, M. A., JORDAN, C. L., and RENARD, R. J., *The jet stream* (Meteorological monographs, American Meteorological Society, **7**, **2**), Boston, 1954.

ROBEQUAIN, CHARLES, (A) *L'Indochine française*, Paris, 1935.

(B) 'Le développement industriel de l'Indochine française', *C.I.G.*, Amsterdam, 1938, 2 Section III C, 590–593.

(C) *The Economic development of French Indo-China* (trs. Ward, Isabel A.), London, 1944.

(D) *Malaya, Indonesia, Borneo, and the Philippines* (trs. Laborde, E. D.), London, 1954.

ROBERTS, GUY, (A) 'East to the Indies', *Geographical Magazine*, **8**, 1946, 347–358.

(B) 'South to the Indies', *Geographical Magazine*, **8**, 1946, 403–412.

(C) 'From Europe to the Spice Islands', *Geographical Magazine*, **8**, 1946, 473–482.

(D) 'Making Malaya a nation', *Geographical Magazine*, **8**, 1946.

ROBERTS, S. H., *History of French colonial policy*, 1870–1925, 2 Vols., London, 1929.

ROBINSON, J. B. PERRY, (A) 'Progress and prosperity in Malaya', *The Listener*, **54**, July 28, 1955, 133–134.

(B) *Transformation in Malaya*, London, 1956.

RONALL, JOACHIM O., 'Spanish revival in the Philippines', *E.W.*, **11**, 1957, 20–21.

ROOSEVELT, THEODORE, *Colonial policies of the United States*, New York, 1937.

ROUCEK, JOSEPH S., 'The development of political geography and geopolitics in the United States', *Australian Journal of Politics and History*, **3**, 1959, 204–217.

Round Table Conference at the Hague, Facts and Documents, The Hague, 1949.

ROWE, J. W. F., *Markets and men*, Cambridge, 1936.

ROXBY, PERCY M., 'The expansion of China', *S.G.M.*, **46**, 1930, 65–80.

'Rubber Industry, The', *Manchester Guardian*, January 15, 1957, 7–17.

RUNCIMAN, STEVEN, (A) 'Siam searching for security', *The Times*, February 11, 1955, 9.

(B), *The White Rajahs*, Cambridge, 1960.

RUTTEN, L. M. R., (A) (ed.) *Science in the Netherlands East Indies*, Amsterdam, 1929.

(B) *De geologie van Nederlandsch Indië*, The Hague, 1932.

RUTTER, O., *British North Borneo*, London, 1922.

SANDHU, KERNIAL SINGH, (A) 'Chinese colonization of Malacca', *J.T.G.*, **15**, 1961, 1–26.

(B) 'The population of Malaya', *J.T.G.*, **15**, 1961, 82–96.

Sarawak Annual Report, London, H.M.S.O.

SARKISYANZ, EMANUEL, *Südostasien seit 1945*, Munich, 1961.

SASORITH, KATAY D., *Le Laos*, Paris, 1953.

SAUER, C. O., *Agricultural origins and dispersals*, New York, 1952.

SCAFF, ALVIN H., *The Philippine answer to communism*, Stanford, 1955.

SCHAKEL, PIETER (van Balluseck, D. J.), *Wij, deelgenoten*, Amsterdam, 1945.

SCHILLER, A. ARTHUR, *The formation of federal Indonesia*, 1945–1949, The Hague, 1955.

SCHMIDT, W., *Die Mon-Khmer Völker*, Vienna, 1906.

SCHRIEKE, B., *Indonesian sociological studies*, 2 parts, The Hague, 1955 and 1957.

SCRIVENOR, J. B., (A) 'The physical geography of the southern part of the Malay peninsula', *G.R.*, **11**, 1921, 351-371.

(B) *The geology of Malaya*, London, 1931.

SENDUT, HAMZAH, 'The resettlement villages in Malaya', *G.*, **47**, 1962, 41–46.

SHABAD, THEODORE, 'Economic developments in North Vietnam', *P.A.*, **31**, 1958, 36–53.

SHAH, IKBAL ALI, *Viet Nam*, London, 1960.

Siam – General and medical features, Far Eastern Association of Tropical Medicine, Bangkok, 1930.

Siam – Nature and industry, Ministry of Commerce and Communications, Bangkok, 1930.

SIEGFRIED, ANDRÉ, *Suez and Panama*, London, 1940.

SILCOCK, T. H., (A) 'Policy for Malaya, 1952', *I.A.*, **28**, 1952, 445–451.

(B) *The economy of Malaya*, Background to Malaya Series, No. 2, Singapore, 1954.

SIMMONS, J. S., and others, *Global epidemiology: a geography of disease,* Vol. I, Part I, *India and the Far East.*

Singapore Annual Report, London, H.M.S.O.

Singapore Constitutional Conference, London, H.M.S.O., Cmd. 9777, 1956.

SION, JULES, *Asie des moussons* (*Géographie universelle,* Vol. 9, Parts I and 2), Paris, 1928 and 1929.

SITSEN, PETER H. W., *Industrial developments of the Netherlands Indies,* New York, n.d.

SJAHRIR, SOETAN, *Onze strijd,* Amsterdam, 1946.

SKEAT, W. W., AND BLAGDEN, C. O., *Pagan races of the Malay peninsula,* 2 Vols., London, 1906.

SKINNER, G. WILLIAM, 'Chinese assimilation and Thai politics', *J.A.S.,* **16,** 1957, 237–270.

SLEUMER, W., *Het rijk der Nederlanden,* Amsterdam, 1946.

SMITH, T. E., *Population growth in Malaya,* Oxford, 1952.

SMOLSKI, T., 'Les statistiques de la population indochinoise', *Congrés international de la population,* Paris, 1937, Vol. IV.

Social welfare in Indonesia, Djakarta, 1956.

SOKOL, A. E., (A) 'Communications and production in Indonesian history', *F.E.Q.,* 7, 1948, 339–353.

(B) 'Indonesia', in Freeman, Otis W., *op. cit.,* 460–494.

SOVANI, N. V., *Economic relations of India with South-east Asia and the Far East,* Poona, 1949.

SOWASH, WILLIAM BURTON, 'Colonial rivalries in Timor', *F.E.Q.,* 7, 1948, 227–235.

SPATE, O. H. K., (A) 'Beginnings of industrialization in Burma', *E.G.,* **17,** 1941, 75–92.

(B) 'Factors in the development of capital cities', *G.R.,* **32,** 1942, 622–631.

(C) *Burma setting* (Longman's Burma Pamphlets No. 2), 1943.

(D) 'The Burmese village', *G.R.,* **35,** 1945, 523–543.

(E) *India and Pakistan,* London, 1954.

(F) 'Changing native agriculture in New Guinea', *G.R.,* **43,** 1953, 151–172.

(G) 'Problems of development in New Guinea', *G.J.,* **122,** 1956, 430–440.

SPATE, O. H. K., AND TRUEBLOOD, L. W., 'Rangoon: a study in urban geography', *G.R.,* **32,** 1942, 56–73.

See also EAST, W. G.

SPENCER, JOSEPH E., (A) *Asia East by South,* New York, 1954.

(B) *Land and people in the Philippines,* Berkeley, 1954.

(C) 'The Philippine Islands', in Freeman, Otis W., *op. cit.*

SPENCER, J. E., AND THOMAS, W. L., 'The hill stations and summer resorts of the Orient', *G.R.,* **38,** 1948, 635–651.

SPENCER, THE HON'BLE OSCAR A., 'Malaya's Development Plan, 1956–60'' *E.W.,* **9,** August 1957, 43–44.

STAMP, L. DUDLEY, (A) *Asia – a regional and economic geography*, 9th edition, London, 1957.
(B) 'Burma: an undeveloped monsoon country', *G.R.*, **20**, 1930, 86–109.
(C) 'The Irrawaddy river', *G.J.*, **95**, 1940, 329–359.
(D) 'Siam before the War', *G.J.*, **99**, 1942, 209–224.

State of Brunei Annual Report, London, H.M.S.O.

State of Singapore Development Plan 1961–1964, Singapore, 1961.

Statistical pocket book of Indonesia, Batavia, 1941.

Statistical Pocketbook of Indonesia, Djakarta, 1960.

Statistical Year Book of Thailand, new series, Bangkok, 1952.

Statistical Yearbook of Viet-nam, Saigon.

STAUFFER, H., 'The geology of the Netherlands Indies', in Honig, P., and Verdoorn, F., *op. cit.*, 320–335.

STEEL, R. W., AND FISHER, C. A. (eds.), *Geographical essays on British tropical lands*, London, 1956.

STEINBERG, DAVID J., and others, *Cambodia*, Human Relations Area Files, New Haven, 1957.

STEPHENS, ROBERT P., 'The prospect for social progress in the Philippines', *P.A.*, **23**, 1950, 139–152.

STEVENSON, H. N. C., *The hill peoples of Burma* (Longman's Burma Pamphlets No. 6), 1944.

STODDARD, LOTHROP, *The rising tide of color*, New York, 1922.

Straits Times Annual, Singapore.

SUDDARD, ADRIENNE, See LE BAR.

SUESS, E., *The face of the earth*, 4 Vols. (trs. Sollas, H. B. C., and Sollas, W. J.), Oxford, 1904–1909.

SUKARNO, 'Pantja-Sila – the basic philosophy of the Indonesian state', *I.R.*, **1**, 1951, 11–17.

SUPOMO, R., 'Indonesia's ten years of independence and struggle', *E.W.*, **9**, 1955, 26–27.

SWETTENHAM, SIR FRANK, *British Malaya*, London, 1929.

TADAW (SAW HANSON) 'The Karens of Burma', *J.B.R.S.*, **42**, 1959, 31–40.

TAYLOR, GRIFFITH (ed.), *Geography in the twentieth century*, London, 1953.

Ten years of Japanese burrowing in the Netherlands East Indies, Netherlands Information Bureau, New York, 1944.

TER BRAAKE, ALEX L., *Mining in the Netherlands East Indies*, New York, 1944.

TER HAAR, B., *Adat law in Indonesia*, New York, 1948.

Thailand, Review of commercial conditions, London, H.M.S.O., 1949.

THOMAS, WILLIAM L., JR., *Land, man and culture in mainland Southeast Asia*, published privately, Glen Rock, 1957.

THOMPSON, B. W., 'An essay on the general circulation of the atmosphere over South-east Asia and the western Pacific', *Q.J.R.M.S.*, **77**, 1951, 569–597.

THOMPSON, VIRGINIA, (A) *French Indo-China*, London, 1937.

(B) 'The relationship between the density of population and the method of land utilization in colonial regions, French Indo-China', *C.I.G.*, Amsterdam, 1938, 2 Section III C, 507–517.

(C) *Thailand, the ne w Siam*, New York, 1941.

(D) *Labor problems in Southeast Asia*, New Haven, 1947.

(E) 'Regional unity in Southeast Asia', *P.A.*, **21**, 1948, 170–175.

(F) 'The Vietnamese community in France', *P.A.*, **25**, 1952, 49–58.

THOMPSON, VIRGINIA, AND ADLOFF, RICHARD, *Minority problems in Southeast Asia*, Stanford, 1955.

See also EMERSON, RUPERT.

THOMPSON, WARREN S., (A) *Population problems*, New York, 1953.

(B) *Population and progress in the Far East*, Chicago, 1959.

THORENAAR, A., *Overvloed in Insulinde*, Amsterdam, 1946.

THORNTHWAITE, C. W., 'The climates of the earth', *G.R.*, **23**, 1933, 433–440.

TIBBETTS, G. R., 'The Malay peninsula as known to the Arab geographers', *M.J.T.G.*, **9**, 1956, 21–60.

TIMMERMANS, P. G. M., 'Industrialisatie van Java', *T.E.G.*, **28**, 1937, 126.

TINKER, HUGH, (A) 'Burma's northeast borderland problems', *P.A.*, **29**, 1956, 324–346.

(B) 'Nu, the serene statesman', *P.A.*, **30**, 1957, 120–137.

(C) *The Union of Burma*, London, 1957.

(D) 'Community development: a new philosopher's stone?', *I.A.*, **37**, 1961, 309–322.

TOHIR, KASLUN, *Sekitar Masalah Rakjat*, Djakarta, 1953.

TOYNBEE, A., *Civilization on trial*, Oxford, 1948.

TREGONNING, KENNEDY G., (A) 'North Borneo, 1957', *P.A.*, **31**, 1958, 65–73.

(B) 'The partition of Brunei', *J.T.G.*, **11**, 1959, 84–89.

(C) *North Borneo*, London, H.M.S.O., 1960.

TREWARTHA, G., 'Climate as related to the jet stream in the Orient', *E*, **12**, 1958, 205–214.

TRUEBLOOD, LESTER W., 'The complexity of India and Burma', in Pearcey, G. Etzel, *op cit.* (1st edition), 325–340.

See also SPATE, O. H. K.

TRUED, M. N., 'South Viet-nam's industrial development center', *P.A.*, **33**, 1960, 250–267.

TUCKER, G. B. 'Evidence of a mean meridional circulation in the atmosphere from surface wind observations', *Q.J.R.M.S.*, **83**, 1957, 290–302.

UMBGROVE, J. H. F., (A) *The pulse of the earth*, The Hague, 1942.

(B) *Structural history of the East Indies*, Cambridge, 1949.

UNESCO: *Proceedings of the UNESCO Symposium on typhoons, Tokyo, 1954*, Tokyo, 1955.

UNGER, L., 'The Chinese in Southeast Asia', *G.R.*, **34**, 1944, 196–217.

UNGPHAKORN, PUEY, (A) 'The prospects of tin', *P.A.*, **21**, 1948, 150–161.
(B) 'Thai prudence cushions the recession', *The Times Review of Industry*, June 1958, 82.

United Nations: Demographic Yearbook.

United Nations: Future population estimates by sex and age, Report III The population of Southeast Asia (including Ceylon and China: Taiwan) 1950–1980, New York, 1958.

United Nations: Statistical Yearbook.

United Nations: Yearbook of International Trade Statistics.

Vademecum voor Nederlands-Nieuw-Guinea, Rotterdam, 1956.

VAGELER, P., *An introduction to tropical soils*, 1933.

VAILE, ROLAND S., 'Southeast Asia in world economics', in Mills, Lennox A., *et al.*, 343–370.

VAN ASBECK, F. M. BARON, 'Indonesië in Azië', *Indonesië*, **1**, 1947, 2–27.

VAN BEMMELEN, R. W., *The geology of Indonesia*, 2 Vols., The Hague, 1949.

VANDENBOSCH, AMRY, (A) *The Dutch East Indies, its government, problems and politics*, Berkeley, 1942.
(B) 'Indonesia', in Mills, Lennox A., *et al.*, 79–125.

VANDENBOSCH, AMRY, AND BUTWELL, RICHARD A., *Southeast Asia among the world powers*, Lexington, 1957.

VAN DER KROEF, JUSTUS M., (A) 'Indonesia and the origins of Dutch colonial sovereignty', *F.E.Q.*, **10**, 1951, 151–169.
(B) 'The Hinduization of Indonesia reconsidered', *F.E.Q.*, **11**, 1951, 17–30.
(C) *Indonesia in the modern world*, 2 Parts, Bandung, 1954 and 1956.
(D) 'Indonesia's "New Life" movement', *E.W.*, **11**, 1957, 316–317.
(E) 'Indonesia's economic future', *P.A.*, **32**, 1959, 46–72.

VAN DER MOLEN, G. H. J., 'Indonesia and the Republic of the South Moluccas', *International Relations*, **1**, 1958, 393–400.

VAN DER VEUR, PAUL W., 'The Eurasians of Indonesia: castaways of colonialism', *P.A.*, **27**, 1954, 124–137.

VAN GOUDOEVER, W. A., (A) *Malino maakt historie*, Batavia, 1946.
(B) *Denpasar bouwt een huis*, Batavia, 1947.

VAN HALL, C. J. J., *Insulinde: de inheemsche landbouw*, Deventer, n.d.

VAN HELSDINGEN, W. H., AND HOOGENBERK, H. (trs. and abridged by Duyvendak, J. J. L.), *Mission interrupted*, Amsterdam, 1945.

VAN LEUR, J. C., *Indonesian trade and society*, The Hague, 1955.

VAN MOOK, H. J., (A) *The Netherlands Indies and Japan*, London, 1944.
(B) *The stakes of democracy in Southeast Asia*, New York, 1950.

VAN NAERSSON, F. H. (trs. Barnouw, A. J.), *Culture contacts and social conflicts in Indonesia*, Southeast Asia Institute, Occasional Papers, No. 1, New York, 1947.

VAN NIEUWENHUIZE, C. A. O., (A) 'The Dar ul-Islam movement in western Java', *P.A.*, **23**, 1950, 169–183.
(B) 'Taking stock in Indonesia', *P.A.*, **25**, 1952, 76–79.

VAN RIPER, JOSEPH E., 'The Malay Archipelago and Oceania', in Pearcey, G. Etzel, *op cit.* (1st edition), 416–429.

VAN STEENIS, C. G. G. J., 'Maleische vegetatieschetsen', *T.K.N.A.G.*, Reeks 2, deel 52, 1935.

VAN VALKENBURG, S., 'Java: the economic geography of a tropical island', *G.R.*, **15**, 1925, 563–583.

VAN VUUREN, L., (A) *De beteekenis van Straat Malakka*, Utrecht, 1925.

(B) *Die Niederlande und ihr Kolonialreich*, Utrecht, 1932.

(C) 'Geographical aspect of the Netherlands East Indies', in Rutten (A), 1–37.

VAN WIJNEN, D. J. (ed.), *Pangkalpinang – werkelijkheidszin der minderheden*, Batavia, 1946.

VERDOORN, J. A., 'Indonesia at the crossroads', *P.A.*, **19**, 1946, 339–350.

'Viet-Nam', *Focus*, **1**, February 15, 1951.

VISMAN, FRANS H., *The situation in Java*, Netherlands Information Bureau, New York, 1945.

VLEKKE, B. H. M., (A) *Nusantara: a history of the East Indian Archipelago*, Harvard, 1943.

(B) 'Indonesia in retrospect', *P.A.*, **22**, 1949, 290–294.

(C) *Indonesia in* 1956, *political and economic aspects*, The Hague, 1957.

VLIELAND, C. A., (A) *British Malaya: A report on the* 1931 *Census and on certain problems of vital statistics*, London, 1932.

(B) 'The population of the Malay peninsula', *G.R.*, **24**, 1934, 61–78.

(C) 'The 1947 Census of Malaya', *P.A.*, **23**, 1950, 169–183.

Volkstelling 1930 (*Census of* 1930 *in Netherlands India*), 7 Vols., Batavia, 1933.

VON DER MEHDEN, FRED, see BUTWELL, RICHARD.

WALES, H. G. QUARITCH, (A) *Towards Angkor*, London, 1937.

(B) 'Archaeological research on ancient Indian colonization in Malaya', *J.R.A.S.M.B.*, **18**, 1940, 1–85.

(C) *The making of Greater India*, London, 1951.

WALLACE, A. R., *The Malay archipelago*, 3rd edition, London, 1872.

'Waning power of France in Vietnam, The', *W.T.*, **12**, 1956, 50–58.

WATSON, SIR MALCOLM, 'The geographical aspects of malaria', *G.J.*, **99**, 1942, 161–172.

WATTS, I. E. M., (A) *Equatorial weather*, London, 1955.

(B) 'The rainfall of Singapore island', *M.J.T.G.*, **7**, 1955.

Weather in the China Seas and in the western part of the North Pacific Ocean, 2 vols., Air Ministry Meteorological Office, London, H.M.S.O., 1937.

Weekly Overseas Mail, Special supplement on Thailand, September 15, 1951.

WEHL, DAVID, *The birth of Indonesia*, London, 1948.

WEIDENREICH, FRANZ, 'Early man in Indonesia,' *F.E.Q.*, **2**, 1942, 58–65.

WERNSTEDT, FREDERICK L., (A) *The role and importance of Philippine inter-island shipping and trade*, Cornell Southeast Asia Program, Data Paper, No. 26, Ithaca, 1957 (mimeo.).

(B) 'Cebu: focus of Philippine interisland trade', *E.G.*, **32**, 1957, 336–346.

WERTHEIM, W. F., (A) 'The Indo-European problem in Indonesia', *P.A.*, **20**, 1947, 290–298.

(B) 'Changes in Indonesia's social stratification', *P.A.*, **28**, 1955, 41–52.

(C) *Indonesian society in transition*, The Hague, 1956.

WEYER, G. A. P., *Holland and the Netherlands Indies, some economic aspects*, Netherlands Information Bureau, New York, 1945.

WHEATLEY, PAUL, (A) 'Langkasuka', *T'oung Pao* (Leiden), **44** (Livr. 4–5), 387–412.

(B) 'A curious feature on early maps of Malaya', *Imago Mundi* (Stockholm), **11**, 1954, 67–72.

(C) 'The Malay peninsula as known to the Chinese of the third century A.D.', *J.R.A.S.M.B.*, **28**, 1955, 1–23.

(D) 'Belated comments on Sir Roland Braddell's *Studies of ancient times in the Malay peninsula*', *J.R.A.S.M.B.*, **28**, 1955, 78–96.

(E) 'The Golden Chersonese', *I.B.G.*, No. 21, 1955, 61–78.

(F) 'Tun-sun', *J.R.A.S.M.B.*, **29**, 1956, 17–30.

(G) 'The Malay peninsula as known to the West before A.D. 1000', *M.H.J.*, **3**, 1956, 2–16.

(H) 'Chinese sources for the historical geography of Malaya before A.D. 1500', *M.J.T.G.*, **9**, 1956, 71–78.

(K) *The golden Khersonese*, Kuala Lumpur, 1961.

WHEELER, L. RICHMOND, *The modern Malay*, London, 1928.

WHITTAM, DAPHNE E., 'The Sino-Burmese boundary treaty', *P.A.*, **34**, 1961, 174–183.

WHITTINGHAM-JONES, B., 'Patani appeals to U.N.O.', *E.W.*, April, 1948.

WICKIZER, V. D., AND BENNETT, M. K., *The rice economy of Monsoon Asia*, Stanford, 1941.

WIDJOAMIDJOJO, RADEN ABULKADIR, 'Islam in the Netherlands East Indies', *F.E.Q.*, **2**, 1942, 48–57.

WIENS, HEROLD J., *China's march towards the tropics*, Hamden, 1954.

WIKKRAMATILEKE, R., (A) 'Mukim Pulau Rusa: land use in a Malayan riverine settlement', *J.T.G.*, **11**, 1958, 1–31.

(B) 'Trends in settlement and economic development in eastern Malaya', *P.V.*, **3**, 1962, 27–50.

WILLBOURN, E. S., See Harris, H. G.

WILLIAMSON, J. A., *Europe overseas*, London, 1925.

WILLMOTT, DONALD E., *The national status of the Chinese in Indonesia*, Cornell Modern Indonesia Project, Ithaca, 1956 (mimeo.).

WINSEMIUS, J., 'Een algemeen planologisch schema voor Nieuw Guinea's ontwikkeling op lange termijn', *T.K.N.A.G.*, **72**, 1955, 118–129.

WINSTEDT, SIR RICHARD O., (A) 'A history of Johore', *J.R.A.S.M.B.*, **10**, 1932.

(B) 'A history of Malaya', *J.R.A.S.M.B.*, **13**, 1935.
(C) *Britain and Malaya*, 1786–1941, London, 1944.
(D) *The Malays: a cultural history*, Singapore, 1947.
(E) *Malaya and its history*, London, 1949.
WINT, GUY, (A) *South-east Asia and its future*, (Background Books), London, 1951.
(B) *What is the Colombo Plan?* (Background Books), London, 1952.
(C) *The British in Asia*, 2nd edition, London, 1954.
(D) *Spotlight on Asia*, London, 1955.
WITTFOGEL, KARL A., *Oriental despotism*, New Haven, 1957.
WOLF, CHARLES, JR., 'Problems of Indonesian constitutionalism', *P.A.*, **23**, 1950, 314–318.
WOOD, W. A. R., *History of Siam*, London, 1926.
WOODMAN, DOROTHY, *The Republic of Indonesia*, London, 1955.
World Health Organization, *Malaria eradication*, Geneva, 1958.
WORMSER, C. W. (ed.), *Wat Indië ontving en schonk*, Amsterdam, 1946.
WRIGHT, ARNOLD, AND REID, THOMAS H., *The Malay peninsula*, London, 1912.
WURFEL, DAVID, (A) 'The Philippine Rice Share Tenancy Act', *P.A.*, **27**, 1954, 41–49.
(B) 'Agrarian reform in the Republic of Vietnam', *F.E.S.*, **26**, 1957, 81–92.
(C) 'Philippine agrarian reform under Magsaysay', *F.E.S.*, **27**, 1958, 7–15.
WURZBURG, C. E. *Raffles of the eastern isles*, London, 1954.
WYATT, WOODROW, *Southwards from China*, London, 1952.
ZELINSKY, WILBUR, 'The Indochinese peninsula: a demographic anomaly', *F.E.Q.*, **9**, 1950, 115–145.
ZIMMERMAN, C. C., (A) *Siam: rural economic survey*, 1930–31, Bangkok, 1931.
(B) 'Some phases of land utilization in Siam', *G.R.*, **27**, 1937, 378–393.
ZINKIN, MAURICE, (A) *Asia and the West*, London, 1951.
(B) *Development for free Asia*, London, 1956.

List of abbreviations used

A.A.	*Asian Affairs*
A.A.A.G.	*Annals of the Association of American Geographers*
A.G.	*Australian Geographer*
A.H.	*Asian Horizon*
A.J.S.	*American Journal of Sociology*
A.M.	*Atlantic Monthly*
Am. An.	*American Anthropologist*
B.C.I.A.	*Bulletin of the Colonial Institute of Amsterdam*
B.Q.	*Burma Quarterly*

C.I.G.	*Congrès International de Géographie*
C.Q.	*China Quarterly*
E.	*Erdkunde*
E.D.C.C.	*Economic Development and Cultural Change*
E.G.	*Economic Geography*
E.K.I.	*Ekonomi dan Keuangan Indonesia*
E.W.	*Eastern World*
F.A.	*Foreign Affairs*
F.E.Q.	*Far Eastern Quarterly* (now *Journal of Asian Studies, q.v.*)
F.E.S.	*Far Eastern Survey*
G.	*Geography*
G.J.	*Geographical Journal*
G.M.	*Geological Magazine*
G.R.	*Geographical Review*
G.S.	*Geographical Studies*
G.Tijd	*Geographische Tijdschrift*
I.A.	*International Affairs*
I.B.G.	*Institute of British Geographers, Transactions and Papers*
I.C.L.Q.	*International and Comparative Law Quarterly*
I.G.J.	*Indonesian Geographical Journal*
I.J.M.G.	*Indian Journal of Meteorology and Geophysics*
I.Q.	*India Quarterly*
I.R.	*Indonesian Review*
J.A.S.	*Journal of Asian Studies*
J.B.R.S.	*Journal of the Burma Research Society*
J.M.	*Journal of Meteorology*
J.M.G.S.	*Journal of the Manchester Geographical Society*
J.R.A.S.M.B.	*Journal of the Royal Asiatic Society, Malayan Branch*
J.T.G.	*Journal of Tropical Geography* (formerly *Malayan Journal of Tropical Geography*)
M.H.J.	*Malayan Historical Journal*
M.J.T.G.	*Malayan Journal of Tropical Geography* (now *Journal of Tropical Geography*)
N.S.	*New Scientist*
O.G.	*Oriental Geographer*

P.A.	*Pacific Affairs*
P.E.	*Politique Étrangère*
P.G.	*Professional Geographer*
P.Q.	*Political Quarterly*
P.S.	*Population Studies*
P.V.	*Pacific Viewpoint*
Q.Q.	*Queen's Quarterly*
Q.J.R.M.S.	*Quarterly Journal of the Royal Meteorological Society*
R.Ps.P.	*Revue de Psychologie des Peuples*
S.G.M.	*Scottish Geographical Magazine*
S.T.	*Straits Times*
T.	*Tellus*
T.B.C.R.	*The Times, British Colonies Review*
T.E.G.	*Tijdschrift voor Economische Geographie*
T.E.S.G.	*Tijdschrift voor Economische en Sociale Geografie*
T.K.N.A.G.	*Tijdschrift van het Koninklijk Nederlandsch Aardrijkskundig Genootschap*
W.P.	*World Politics*
W.R.	*World Review*
W.T.	*World Today*
Z.G.	*Zeitschrift für Geopolitik*

II. NEWSPAPERS, NEWS MAGAZINES, NEWS REPORTS AND STATISTICAL BULLETINS

Economist
Guardian (formerly *The Manchester Guardian*)
New York Times
Times
Times of Viet-Nam
Bulletin Statistique du Laos
Cambodge d'aujourd'hui
International Tin Council Statistical Bulletin
Indonesian Information
Journal of Philippine Statistics

Listener
Mededelingen Nieuw Guinea Instituut, Rotterdam
Monthly Digest of Statistics (Singapore)
Neving-Nieuws
News from Viet-Nam (Saigon)
Peking Review
Philippine Agricultural Situation
Progress
Report on Indonesia
Republic of Viet-Nam Information Bulletin
Rubber Statistical Bulletin
Straits Times
Thai News
Thong-ke Nguyet-san (Monthly Bulletin of Statistics, Republic of Vietnam, Saigon)
Union of Burma Central Statistical and Economic Department, *Bulletin of Export Trade* and *Bulletin of Import Trade*
Vietnam (Hanoi)
Vietnam Advances (Hanoi)

III. CARTOGRAPHIC

It is impossible to list all the topographical and other maps consulted but the following atlases are of particular interest:

Atlas de l'Indochine, Hanoi, 1928
Atlas Semesta Dunia, The Hague, 1952
Atlas van Tropisch Nederland, Batavia, 1938
Historical and Commercial Atlas of China (Hermann, A.), Harvard, 1935
Oxford Economic Atlas of the World, 1954
Philip's Historical Atlas, Medieval and Modern (Muir, R., Philip, G., and McElroy, R.), London, 1927
The Advanced Atlas of Modern Geography (Bartholomew, J.), London, 1950
Atlas des Colonies Françaises, Paris
An Explanatory Atlas of the Far East (Hudson, G. F., and Rajchman, Marthe), London, 1942
An Historical Atlas of the Indian Peninsula (Davies, C. Collin), Oxford, 1949.
An Outline Atlas of Eastern History (Sellman, R. R.), London, 1954.
Westermanns Atlas zur Weltgeschichte, Brunswick, 1956.
Chinese People's Republic Atlas of the Provinces, Peking, 1952.
Geschiedkundige Atlas van Nederland – De Kolonieën, The Hague, 1924
Stanford's London Atlas of Universal Geography, Folio edition, London, 3rd edition, 1904

IV. THESES

(unpublished)

COURTENAY, P. P., *Penang – the economic geography of a free port*, Ph.D. thesis, University of London.

DOBBY, E. H. G., *The political geography of Malaya*, Ph.D. thesis, University of London.

FRYER, D. W., *Indonesia, the economic geography of an underdeveloped country*, Ph.D. thesis, University of London.

LIM, J. J., *The geography of padi growing in parts of South-east Asia*, B.Litt. thesis, University of Oxford.

BAHRIN, TUNKU SHAMSUL, *The Indonesians in Malaya*, M.A. thesis, University of Sheffield.

Sources of maps included in the text

Nearly all of the maps used in this book have been drawn specially for its under the author's general direction, by either Mr. J. E. Hall or Mr. Neil Hislop, to whom sincere thanks are offered both for their patience and for their skill. Many of these maps are entirely original works, others represent compilations of material drawn from various sources, while a third category includes those based partly or exclusively on single maps prepared by other authorities.

Of the maps in the first category a few have appeared in other published works by the author, and these are listed at the end of the table below. The various works upon which composite maps have been based are included in the book lists at the end of the chapters concerned. The sources of maps in the third category are given in detail in the table which follows.

Maps based partly or wholly on existing maps by other authorities:

Fig. 2. After Philip's *Comparative Wall Atlas of Asia*, ed. Unstead, J. F., and Taylor, E. G. R. Figs. 5, 26, 27, 28, 30, 31, 38, 39, 42. After *Atlas von Tropisch Nederland.* Fig. 6. Mainly after Braak (C). Fig. 8. After Mayr. Fig. 9. Mainly after Broek (D). Fig. 16. After Jones and Mehnert. Fig. 21. After Unger. Fig. 32. After Pannekoek. Figs. 29, 33, 46–51. Based partly on *Atlas Semesta Dunia.* Figs. 35 and 52. After *Report on Indonesia.* Fig. 37. After Vlekke. Fig. 40. After Van Valkenburg. Fig. 45. Transport based on *Atlas Semesta Dunia*, production after Halim Khan. Fig. 53. After Kahin (C). Fig. 57. After *Mededelingen Nieuw-Guinea Instituut.* Fig. 58. After Winsemius. Fig. 62. After Gregory, J. W., and C. J. Fig. 64. After Stamp (B) (modified). Fig. 65. After Spate and Trueblood. Fig. 71. Based on *Thailand*, 1:2,500,000, Hydrographic Service Department, Thonburi, 1955. Fig. 73. Mainly after Fryer (A). Fig. 77. Mainly after *Carte economique de l'Indochine*, 1:2,000,000, Service géographique de l'Indochine,

1937. Fig. 78. Based partly on *Cambodge-Laos-Vietnam, Croquis physique et routier*, Dalat, 1954. Fig. 79. After *Zeitschrift für Geopolitik*. Fig. 80. After *Atlas de l'Indochine*. Fig. 82. Based on *Geological map of Malaya*, Survey Department, Federation of Malaya, No. 38, 1948. Fig. 85. Based on Ooi (B). Fig. 86. After *Land Utilization Map*, Survey Department, Federation of Malaya, No. 29, 1953. Fig. 88. Based on *Malaya*, 1:760,230, 1948, new edition 1960, Survey Department, Federation of Malaya, No. 172. Fig. 90. After I.B.R.D. *The economic development of Malaya*. Fig. 94. Mainly after Ginsburg, Kaplan and Roberts. Fig. 96. Based on Lee, Y. L. (B). Figs. 100 and 102. After Kolb. Fig. 103. After Wernstedt (A). Fig. 105. After Fryer (A). Fig. 106. After Hayden.

The following maps originally prepared by the author for publication elsewhere are reproduced by kind permission of the publishers concerned:

Figs. 17, 18. *The changing map of Asia*, ed. East, W. G., and Spate, O. H. K., (Methuen & Co., Ltd.). Fig. 24. *Geographical Journal*, 115, 1950 (Royal Geographical Society.). Fig. 35 (redrawn). *The changing world*, ed. East, W. G., and Moodie, A. E. (George G. Harrap & Co., Ltd.). Figs. 84, 89, 91. *Geographical essays on British Tropical Lands*, ed. Steel, R. W., and Fisher, C. A. (George Philip & Son, Ltd.).

Index

abacá (Musa textilis), North Borneo, 679; Philippines, 714–715
acacia leucophloea, see pilang
Acapulco, 131
Aëta peoples, 66, 698
Afro-Asian Conference, Bandung, 1955, 380, 386, 771
Aglipayan church, 98, 723
agriculture, see each country
Agusan lowlands, 693
aid, economic, 311, 316, 480, 505, 516–517, 561, 565–566, 569, 570, 619, 624, 675, 680, 705, 752–768
air masses, see climate
Air Musi (river), 220, 305
air transport, Burma 466; Indonesia, 354–355; Malaya, 620; New Guinea, 400; Philippines, 719; Thailand, 493, 517
Akyab, 22, 29, 34, 36, 465, 473; population, 466; temperature and rainfall, 422
Albizzia, 46
Alfurs, 66, 242–243
Alor, 14, 210
Amarapura, 434
Ambon (Amboyna), 24–25, 33, 37, 128, 130, 135, 229, 286, 306, 364; Ambonese, 395; Dutch settlement, 255; Massacre, 95n., 136; temperature and rainfall, 214
Ambuklao hydro-electric station, 717
A.B.C.D. powers (Americans, British, Chinese, Dutch), 195
Amherst, 422
Anamba, 147
Angkor (Siemreap), 46, 82, 86, 89n, 93, 110–112, 114–115, 155, 419n, 489, 491, 537
Anglo-Siamese Treaty of Commerce and Navigation (1925), 502
Anjer, 300
ankylostomiasis, 56
Annam, 82, 84, 91, 122, 123, 140, 154, 407, 552–553, see also Indochina, States of; Annamites, 68, 81, 88–89, 112–113, 122–123, 140, 152, 532–533, 539, 552, 557; Annamite chain, 55, 96, 113, 122, 409, 412, 417, 425, 429, 534; Annamite empire, 531–533; French rule, 153, 533
anopheles, see mosquitoes
anthracite, 20, 420, 560
Anti-Fascist Peoples Freedom League (A.F.P.F.L.), Burma, 198, 447–448, 469
antimony, 420, 459, 544
apatite deposits, 560
Apo, Mt (9,690 ft), 693
Arabs, Indonesia, 384–385; Malaya, 644
Arakan, 149, 433, 435, 463; Arakanese, 432, 472–473; Arakan ranges, 11, 16, 36, 426, 429; Arakan Yoma, 412, 424, 430, 465
Aranya Prades, 491
areca, 46
aroids, 79
Arracan Flotilla Company (A.F.C.), 442–443, 465
arrowroot, 72
Aru, 17, 210
Asahan (river), 220, 260; project, 330, 343, 347
Assam, 63, 83, 412
Association of South-east Asian States (A.S.A.), 525–526, 659, 734, 772–774
Ataran (river), 413, 471
Atjeh, 96, 100, 118, 135, 145, 147, 157, 217, 251, 254, 353, 591; Atjehnese, 7n, 68, 157, 240–241, 254, 268, 370; Dutch rule, 261, 284, 288, 298, 300; ranges, 217
Aung San, 447
Australia, 12, 46, 66, 747, 751, 755–759; Australoids, 65–66, 69, 79
Ava, 92, 113, 120, 149, 154, 415, 433
Ayuthia, 92, 114, 121, 136, 140, 488, 490, 495, 518, 537, 592; population, 519

Baclieu-Camau, development project, 564
Bacolod City, population, 722
Bacson-Hoabinhian culture, 79
Badui, 66, 239–241
Bagan Siapiapi, 335
Baguio, 25, 715, 716; temperature and rainfall, 694
Bahasa Indonesia, 368–369
Baie d'Along, 420
Balabak, 666; Straits, 693
Balambangan, 668
Bali, 17, 53, 74, 96, 209, 229–230, 239, 255, 336, 370; Balinese, 7n, 68, 239, 242–243, 264; Dutch rule, 261, 283, 286; popula-

Bali (*cont.*)
tion, 206, 289–290; roads, 352; towns, 352
Balikpapan, 304, 306, 328n
Balkans, 9, 10, 774
Balucan, 716
Balu Chaung, 463, 464
bamboo, 45, 46
bananas, 72, 79, 713; Malaya, 601
Banda, 135, 136, 210, 229, 255, 286; Bandanese, 264; population, 290; Sea, 11, 14, 17
Bandjarese, 242–243, 251, 265, 370
Bandjarmasin, 96, 221n, 283, 286, 306, 339, 342
Bandung, 211, 223, 296, 305, 337; industries, 297, 344; temperature and rainfall, 214, 228, see also Afro-Asian Conference
Bangka, 12, 20, 210, 220, 222, 256, 265; tin, 260, 329
Bangkok, 121, 185–187, 415, 445, 489, 490, 492, 495, 499, 523, 526; Bight of, 417, 495; Chinese quarter (Sampong), 519; communications, 517; growth and morphology, 518–520; industries, 504, 512–514; Klong Ong Ang (canal), 519; population 519; temperature and rainfall, 422, 486
Bangrak quarter (Bangkok), 519
Bang-yi-khan, 514
Bank Industri Negara (Indonesia), 324
Banméthuot, 564, 565
Banpong, 464, 517, 523
Bantam, 130, 134, 135, 256, 263, 280, 300
Bao Dai (Emperor of Annam), 554, 555, 557
Baram, 672
Barito (river), 221, 339
barley, 80
Basco Batanes, temperature and rainfall, 694
Bassac (river), 539–541
Bassein, 438, 443, 465, 469; population, 466
Bataafsche Petroleum Maatschappij (B.P.M.), 328
Bataks, 67, 240–241, 244–245, 249, 264; plateau, 217
Batangas, 328n, population, 722
Batang Hari (river), 220
Batavia, see Djakarta
Batjan, 209
Battambang, 155, 489; French annexation, 491
Batu Arang, 616, 622
Batu Gajah, 623
Batu Pahat, 616
bauxite, 51; Indonesia, 330, 343; Malaya, 616; Riau archipelago, 285, 330; Sarawak, 674; Sumatra, 220, 285
Bawdwin, 442, 459
Bawlake State, 471
Beaufort, 677, 678
Belawan (Belawan Deli), 305n
Belitung, 12, 20, 146, 210, 220, 222, 256, 265; tin deposits, 260, 329
belukar, 47
Bengal, Bay of, 33, 83, 126, 139, 151, 412
Benkulen, 136, 146; mountains, 217
Ben Thuy, 545
Berau peninsula, 33
beri-beri, 56
Besisi peoples, 99
Besitang, 300
Bhamo, 31, 36, 415, 433, 443, 463n, 477
Biak, 396n, 399
Bicol Plain, 693
Binga, 717
Bintan, 220, 330
birds of paradise, 49
Bogor (Buitenzorg), 228, 343n, 344
Bohol, 693, 695, 706, 708
Bojolali, 337
Bolovens, 409
Bombarai peninsula, 234
Bontoc peoples, 67, 698, 714
Borguin car assembly plant, 347
Borneo (Kalimantan), 7n, 12, 14, 15, 17, 19, 21, 31, 37, 51, 67, 69, 72, 106, 116, 137, 147, 165, 209, 234, 255, 331, 380–381, see also Indonesia, and for remainder of island see Northern Borneo, Brunei, North Borneo and Sarawak area, 208, 662; climate, 223; communications, 349; Dutch rule, 285–286; Land reclamation projects, 339–340, 347; population, 290; rivers, 221; structure and relief, 220–223; towns, 349; vulcanism, 223
Borobudur, 108
Boun Oum, Prince 572
Boven Digoel, 393
Brahmans, 84
Brahmaputra (river), 412
Brantas (river), 228, 247
British Burma Petroleum Company (B.B.P.C.), 441
British North Borneo Company, 669
Bronze Age, 80–81
Brooke family in Sarawak, 672; Charles, 672; James, 668, 672
Brunei, 3n, 157, 662n, 665–666, 680–681, 686
Buddhism, 84–87, 91–92, 98, 474, 762; Theravada Buddhism, 91–92, 96, 115, 535, 537
Buddhist bloc, 523, 741
Budi Utomi movement, 296

buffalo, 75, 496, 500
Buginese, 68, 242–243, 255, 264
Bukit Asem, 220, 330
Bukit Barisan, 217
Bukit Besi, 616
Bukit Kelingkang, 663
Bukit Rantemario, 230
Bukit Timah, 622
Bukit Tinggi (Fort de Kock), 214–215
Bulacan, 709
Bung Borophet Lake, 512
Bungsar, 623
Burma, 3, 8, 11, 12, 14, 15, 16, 20, 26, 31, 35, 38, 46, 51, 55, 63, 68, 83, 89, 91, 95, 113, 120, 128, 135, 139, 149, 154, 160, 169, 187, 195, 412, 490, 739, 740, 741, 743, 750, 753, 754, 756, 758, 760, 763, 764, 772, see also Mainland States; administrative problems, 467–477; agriculture, 433–438, 450–457; boundary disputes, 477–478; British annexation and rule, 149, 154, 430–448; Delta region, 435–439; Dry zone, 433–435, 440–441; economic development and problems (Pyidawtha), 448–467; Indian immigrants, 438–439, 445–446, 474–477; Independence (1947), 160, 198, 447–448; indigenous peoples, 432–433, 438, 467–473; industrial development, 461–464; irrigation, 434, 452–454; languages, 470, 474; mining, 442, 459–461; natural regions, 431; overseas trade and export production, 459, 479–481; population, 82–83, 172–174, 430, 466; relief and structure, 430–432; towns and cities, 439–441, 443, 444–445, 446; transport and communications, 16, 155, 464–466, (pre-war) 442–445
Burma Road, 464
Burmah Oil Company, 441
Burmans, 7, 81, 89, 90, 100, 106, 113, 141, 432–433, 468–469, 471
Buru, 14, 210, 229, 255, 264
Butterworth, 621

Cabanatuan City, population, 722
caciques, 701–704, 708–710, 730
Cagayan plain, 693; valley, 708, 715, 719
Caisan, development project (South Vietnam), 564–565
Calcutta, 445, 465
Caliraya-Lumot hydro-electric station, 717
Caltex Oil Company, formerly Nederlandsche Pacific Petroleum Mij, 238
Carmarines Norte, 716
Camau, 419
Cambodia, 3, 12, 20, 35, 91, 94, 99, 112, 114, 121, 123, 128, 155, 418, 537–549, 567–577, 739, 741, 743n, 749, 750, 754, 756, 758, 760, 764, see also Indochina, States of; agriculture, 537, 567; Cambodians, 7, 100, 537; Chinese minority, 570; foreign aid and development plans, 569–570; French protectorate, 152; land use, 575; neutrality, 572; overseas trade, 575–576; population, 567–568; relations with Thailand, 523, 569; roads, 550; selected production data, 574
Cameron Highlands, 25, 623; temperature and rainfall, 587
Camiguin island, 693
camphor, 45, 84
Canada, 679, 755–759
Cantonese, 640
Cao Dai sect (founded 1925), 553
Cap St. Jacques, temperature and rainfall, 422
Cape Varella, 532
Capiz, 719
Cardamom mts., 425, 487, 534
Carstenz-top (16,400 ft.), 232
cassava, 72; Indonesia, 332, 334; Java, 281; Malya, 606
Casuarina, 48, 211
Cebu, 131, 189, 693, 700, 712, 720; city, 721–722; population, 706
Celebes (Sulawesi), 14, 33, 43, 49, 53, 67, 69, 72, 84, 116, 162, 209, 229, 234, 239, 370, 380–381; agriculture, 231; development under Dutch rule, 286; minerals, 232; population density, 206, 232, 290; rainfall, 231; relief, 230–232; size and area, 203–208; volcanic activity, 211, 230–231
cellulose, 331
Central Treaty Organization (C.E.N.T.O.), 749
Ceylon, 3n, 91, 130, 136, 137, 165, 739; British occupation, 144; independence, 198
Chainad, 487, 496, 508
Chakkri, P'ya, 121
Champa, kingdom of, 103, 112–113, 120, 122–123, 554
Chams, 68, 112, 113, 122–123, 532
Chao Phraya (river), see Menam
charcoal, 330
Chau Doc, 419
Chauk, 460, 465
Cheli, 522
Chenderoh, 623
Cheng Ho, 95, 119
Chenla, kingdom of, 103, 109
Chettyar moneylenders, 183, 438, 451n, 474; in Indochina, 541, 549

Chiang Kai-shek, 8, 770
Chiengmai, 434, 486, 488, 491, 517, 518; population of, 519; temperature and rainfall, 422
Chin hills, 407, 412, 430
China, 3, 5, 9, 12, 15, 16, 29, 63, 67, 81, 100, 102, 114, 123, 144, 154, 179, 189, 194, 199, 357, 386, 451, 476–478, 482, 522–526, 559–561, 569, 573–574, 628n, 743–745, 761, 764, 768–772, 774–775; cultural influence, 83–95, 769–770
Chindwin (river), 16n, 408, 415, 430, 460–461; navigation, 443
Chinese peoples, 180–185, 193, 199, 267–269; Burma, 439, 468, 474–477; Cambodia, 570; Indochina, 138, 267–268, 531, 541; Indonesia, 386, 387; Malaya, 604, 609–610, 636, 639–642, 656–657; Philippines, 726–727; Thailand, 497, 501–503, 521, 526; Vietnam, 564
Chins, 68, 432, 438, 468, 470–472; Chin Special Division, 472
Chittagong, 34
Cho Bo, 419
Chola, 84n, 115–116
Cholburi, population, 519
cholera, 54, 56, 57
Cholon, 541, 549; industries, 542
Chou En-lai, 658
Christianity, 98, 130–131, 133, 264, 267, 375, 385, 394, 432, 469, 472; Protestants, 264–266, 375, 469; Roman Catholics, 130, 140, 265–266, 375, 562, 553, 558, 701–702, 722–724
chromite, Philippines, 716
Chulalongkorn (Rama V), King of Siam (1868–1910), 490, 519
Chumphon, 517
Chungking, 464
cinchona, 258, 331; Java, 281
Clementi, Sir Cecil, 601
climate, 21–42, see also under separate countries, air masses, 26–42; climatic types, 40–42; human reactions, 26, 54–55; monsoons, 28–42; rainfall, 26–41; relative humidity, 26; sunshine, 26; temperature, 22–27; typhoons, 38–39; winds, 28–42
coal, Borneo, 223, 260, 330; British Borneo, 663, 670, 677; Burma, 460, 461; Indochina, 544; Indonesia, 330; Malaya, 616; New Guinea, 234; Philippines, 716; Sumatra, 220, 260, 330; Thailand, 516; Vietnam (South), 566
Cochinchina, 122, 123, 537–549, 557; ceded to France, 152; rice cultivation, 539–541
cockatoos, 49
cocoa, Indonesia, 322–323; Malaya, 614; New Guinea, 398; North Borneo, 677, 679
coconut and coconut palm, 46, 48, 70, 72, 162, 169; North Borneo, 677, 679; Java, 281; Indonesia, 320–322; Malaya, 606, 608, 614; Outer Territories, 284; Philippines, 704, 714; Sarawak, 675; Thailand, 500, 508
coffee, 138, 143, 261, 286; Arabian, 162; Indochina, 542; Indonesia, 322–323, 332; Java, 281; *liberica* variety, 162; North Borneo, 677; South Vietnam, 565
Colombo Plan, 316, 342, 480, 625, 748, 755, 760
Commissioner-General for South-east Asia (Special Commissioner for South-east Asia), 654n, 659n, 683
Commonwealth (British), 447, 610, 657; Post-war policy towards South-east Asia, 739, 745–748, 755–756, 760
Communism, Communists, 373n, 376, 377, 378n, 379n, 387, 447n, 525, 555–562, 565, 571–572, 574, 604, 609, 646, 659, 684, 709, 710
Confucianism, 87
continental shelf, 19
co-operatives, 313–314, 330, 710, 768
copal, 330
copper, 137; Philippines, 715–716
copra, 169, 171, 285–286, 679
coral, 17–19; atolls, 17; reefs, 17
Cotobato, 693
cotton, 324; Burma, 434, 441, 455; Indochina, 545; Siam, 493; Thailand, 496, 500, 503–504, 508
Cowie Harbour, 677
Cowie, W. C., 669
Cretaceous system, 11, 12, 14
Crocker Range, 663
Cultuurgebied (Sumatra), 228, 290, 310, 376, see also Indonesia and Sumatra; crop distribution, 285; Dutch economic development, 260–261, 284–285, 288; population, 266–267
Cuong De, Prince, 553

Dadiangas Cotabato, temperature and rainfall, 694
Daga (river), 465
Dai-co-viet, kingdom of, 112
Dajak Ketjil (river), 221n
Dalat, 550, 566
Dalla, 443
Daman, 137
damar, 330, 675
Damar, 210, 679

Dangrek (range), 520, 534
Danhim (river), 566, 752
Dap Cau, industries, 545
Darlac, 409
Darul Islam, 373, 384
Darvel Tobacco Plantation, 679
Davao, 709, 720
Dawng Phya Fai, 418
D.D.T. (insecticide), 56
deciduous monsoon forest, 46
Deli plantations, 265, 285
Demak, 247n
Denpasar, 301
Dent, Alfred, 669
Deutero-Malays, see Parœeans
Dhanyaburi, 496
diamonds, Borneo, 222
Dieng plateau, 228, 330
Digul (river), 232
Dili, 404
Dindings, 116, 157, 593
dipterocarpaceae, 45, 46, 715
disease and health, 54–58
Diu, 137
Djakarta (Batavia), 136, 139, 147, 186, 211, 228, 298, 337, 342, 355, 373, 395; Djakartans (Batavians), 240–241; Dutch rule, 302–304; morphology, 302–304; rainfall, 228; temperature, 22, 214
Djambi (Melayu), 220, 248n, 306, 342, 637
Djapara, 247n
Djateng, 324
Djatiluhur, drainage project, 338
Djatim, 324
Djokjakarta, 148, 187, 256, 294, 300, 305, 362; temperature and rainfall, 214
Djuwiring, 342
Dom Muang airport (Bangkok), 517
Dong Trieu, 544
Doumer, Governor-General of Indochina, 550
Douwes Dekker, E. F. E., 205, 385
Dordrecht Oil Company, 261
Drake, Sir Francis, 134
Dran, 565
Duff Development Company, 599
Dulles, John Foster, 9, 744, 751
Dumai, 328n
Dusuns, 665
Dvaravati, kingdom of, 105, 488
Dyaks, 67, 72, 242–244, 264, 534, 665
dysentery, 56

East India Company (E.I.C.), 134, 139–141, 144, 668; foundation, 134; influence of Raffles, 144–147; relations with Dutch, 134–136
Ecija, 709
Economic Commission for Asia and the Far East (E.C.A.F.E.), 505, 508
Economic Development Corps (E.D.C.O.R.), Philippines, 709
Eiland (river), 232
Elephant mts., 425, 534
Emmahaven, 305n
Endau, 616
Enggano, 210, 240–241
Ethical Policy, 256, 271–273, 275
eucalypts, 46
Eurasians, 130, 138, 183–184, 199, 269–270; Burma, 468; Indonesia, 385–386; Malaya, 645
European influence in South-east Asia, 126–200; British, 134, 139–155, 156–157; Dutch, 133, 134–139, 148–149, 157–158, 252–273; French, 139–141, 152–156; Portuguese, 126, 127–133, 137; Spanish, 126, 127–133
Europeans, 183–184
evergreen rain forest, 44–45, 211

Faifo, 541n
Fakfak, 396n
Farmers Co-operative Marketing Associations (F.A.C.O.M.A.), Philippines, 710
fauna, 48–50
Federated Malay States (F.M.S.), 597–603
Federation of Malaya, see Malaya
Filipinos, 7, 133, 699, 702
fish and fishing industry, Burma, 457, fishing, 49–50, 78; Indonesia, 334–336; Malaya, 608; Philippines, 713; species, 49; Thailand, 496, 511–512
Fleuve Antérieur, 419
Fleuve Postérieur (Bassac), 419
Flores, 210, 266, 370; population density, 290
Food and Agricultural Organization of the United Nations (F.A.O.), 171, 339, 511n
Foreign Operations Administration (U.S.A.), 342
Formosa, 3n, 43
Fort Canning, 652
framboesia, see yaws
Funan, kingdom of, 103–105, 107, 110, 115, 533, 554

Gajo, 67, 240–241, 244
garuda bird, 97, 368
Garuda Indonesian Airways, 355, 378
Garut, 297
Gawlun, 477n
Gaya, 676
Gedongtataän, 293–294

Geelvink Bay, 399
Gemas, 599
Geneva Agreements, 1954, 556, 739, 744, 749; 1962, 575
gentians, 48
Giesting, 287n
Goa, 137, 402
gold, 20, 157; Borneo, 222; Burma, 442; Celebes, 232; Indochina, 544; Malaya, 616; New Guinea, 398; Philippines, 715–716; Sarawak, 674; Sumatra, 220
'*gotong rojong*', 77, 296, 313, 381, 448n
graphite, Indochina, 544
Greater East Asia Co-prosperity Sphere, 194, 198, 748–749, 751, see also Japan
Gresik, 116, 247n, 342
ground nuts, Burma, 455; Cambodia, 574–575; Indonesia, 332–334; Java, 281; Laos, 574–575; South Vietnam, 574–575; Thailand, 497, 508
Gunong Dempo, 217
Gunong Karang, 228
Gunong Kerbau, 583
Gunong Kerintji, 217, 223
Gunong Leuser, 217
Gunong Lompobatang (Piek van Bonthain), 230
Gunong Merapi, 226
Gunong Mohomeru, 223
Gunong Ophir, 217
Gunong Raja, 221
Gunong Saputan, 230
Gunong Slamet, 228
Gunong Tahan, 583
Gunong Tjarene, 228
Gweinoi (river), 413, 486
Gweiyai (river), 486

Haadyai, 514
Hainan, 502; Hainanese, 640
Haiphong, 155, 187, 415, 544–545, 549–550, 554
Hakka Chinese, 640
Halmahera, 14, 229, 245, 264, 392
Ham Rong, 545
Hangfang, 477n
Hanoi, 420, 422, 544, 549–550
Ha Tien, 547
Hatta, Mohammed, 313, 314, 379
health, see disease and health
Henzada, 466
Hibok-Hibok, 14n, 693
Hideyoshi, 700
Hiep Hoa, 566
High Plateaux development project (South Vietnam), 564–565
Himalayas, 11, 15
Hinduism, 84–87, 96, 98, 762
Hlaing (river), 416, 439, 443
Hmawza (Prome), 106
Hoa Hao sect (founded 1939), 553
Ho Chih Minh, 553, 554–555, 557; Creation of Vietminh, 554
Hokkien Chinese, 640
Ho Ling kingdom, 247
Hollandia, 396–399
Homo Soloensis, 64
Hon Gay, 544
Hong Kong, 146, 594–595, 621, 669, 670, 678, 770
Honshu, 15n
Hpimaw, 477n
Hué, 123, 153, 550; temperature and rainfall, 422
Hukawng valley, 55, 407, 412
Hukbalahap (Huk) guerilla movement, 709–710
humid tropics, 5
Hung Hoa, 420
hydraulic civilization, 93, 107n, 194, 531
hydro-electricity, Burma, 464; Indonesia, 338, 350; Malaya, 622–623; South Vietnam, 566; Thailand, 516

Iberian conquests, 117, 127–133, 134
Idenburg-top, 232
Idenburg (river), see Taritatu
Ifugao, 67; Ifugaos, 698, 714
Iligan, 717
ilmenite, Malaya, 616
Ilocano, 68; language, 729–730
Ilocos, 706
Iloilo, 719, 720, 722
indaeng, see monsoon forest
Indagiri (river), 220n
India, 3, 5, 9, 15, 29, 64, 81, 83, 136, 141, 176, 189, 194, 199, 739, 745–747, 755, 761, 772–777; cultural influence, 83–95
Indians in South-east Asia, 180–185, 199; Burma, 438–439, 445–446, 474–477; Malaya, 609, 636, 642–644
Indian subcontinent, 5, 65
indigenous peoples, 8, 63–100, 182, 189, 193; Burma, 432–433, 438, 467–473; Indochina, 534–537; Indonesia, 238–252; languages, 98–100; Malaya, 633–645; political history, 102–125; religions, 85–92, 96–97, 264–266; Thailand, 488–489, 520–522
Indo Burma Petroleum Company (I.B.P.C.), 441
Indochina, the states of, 20, 51, 68, 154, 169, 187, 192, 195, 529–578, see also individual states; agriculture, 531, 539–

542; alien peoples, 531, 549; Annamite Empire, 530–533; economic development, 539–545; French rule, 537–556; indigenous peoples, 534–537; Indo-Chinese Union, 538; industry, 542–545; irrigation, 537, 546; Japanese occupation, 553–554; languages, 563; minerals, 542–545; natural regions, 530; overseas trade and export production, 547–548; plural society, 548–549; population, 531–533, 534, 537, 558; post-war administration, 554–556; rice cultivation, 539–541, 546; Roman Catholicism, 538, 553, 557–558; Songkoi delta, 531–532, 545–546; towns, 541, 549; transport and communications, 536, 550–552

Indonesia, 3, 11–14, 22, 25–26, 37, 46, 53, 56, 65–66, 97, 126, 137, 162, 169, 183, 192, 195, 205, 659, 739, 742, 743, 750, 754, 756, 758, 760, 763, 764, 766, 774n, see also separate islands, and for conditions under Dutch rule see Netherlands Indies; agriculture, 276–287, 317–326, 332–337; alien peoples, 267–270, 344, 384–387; climate, 211, 214–217; co-operatives, 313–314; economic development and problems, 310–317, 337–350; Eurasians, 385–386; forestry, 330–331; hydro electricity, 338, 350; independence (1949), 160, 310; indigenous peoples, 238–267; industrial development, 341–350; land reclamation, 339–340; languages, 246, 252, 368–369; minerals, 326–330; outer territories, 172, 283–286, 377–381, 390; overseas trade and export production, 316–332, 356–358; Pareœans, 239–245; period of Dutch rule, 252–309; political parties, 373–377; population, 173, 175, 287–298, 337–338, 340–341, 384, 388; relief, 209–237; religions, 249–251, 266, 369–372; R.U.S.I., 362–364; Sumitro Plan, 341–344; towns and cities, 301–307; transport and communications, 298–301, 350–355; unitary state, 364–390; vegetation, 211–213

Indo-Europeesch Verbond, 385, 393, 398

Indo-Pacific peninsula, 15, 16, 43, 90, 102, 117, 127, 151, 155, 195, 420, 426, 665; Anglo-French rivalry, 149–156; history, 109–115, 120–124

Indosinia, 12, 409

Indragiri, 591

in-kanyin, 457

Insein, 461n

International Bank for Reconstruction and Development (I.B.R.D.), 465, 505n, 514n, 613, 620n

Intramuros (Manila), 722

Ipoh, 597, 649; tin production, 615

Iran Range, 663

iron, 20, 420; Borneo, 222, 330; Celebes, 232, 330; Indochina, 544; Malaya, 616; Moluccas, 330; Philippines, 716; Thailand, 514

Irrawaddy (river), 16, 151, 409–416, 430; British navigation rights, 153, 442–443; delta, 121, 156, 177, 179, 192, 435, 436–439; valley, 113, 472

Irrawaddy Flotilla Company (I.F.C.), 442–443, 465

Irrigation, 74, 82, 89n, 93, 189; Bali, 283; Indochina, 546; Java, 279; Malaya, 608; North Borneo, 678; Philippines, 710, 712; Thailand, 495–497, 508–509

Islam, 92, 96, 98, 119, 127, 131, 133, 249–252, 762; Indonesia, 369–370, 384; Malaya, 592n, 658; Philippines, 699

ivory, 84

jackfruit, 72

Jajasan Kelapa Minahasa, 321

Jajasan Kopra, 320–321

Jakun peoples, 67, 99, 590

Janggala-Kadiri, 247

Japan, 3n, 5n, 137, 144, 176, 179, 194, 199, 353; armies, 3; Greater East Asia Co-prosperity Sphere, 194, 198, 748–749, 751; industry, 464, 481–482, 767; occupation of South-east Asia, 194–198, 310, 330, 344, 505, 521, 739, 741, 746–749, 761; pre-war trade with South-east Asia, 196–197, 503; post-war trade with South-east Asia, 751–755, 774–775; reparations, 317, 481–482, 566n, 727, 752

Japanese, 95, 183n, 184, 194–198, 324, 447, 464, 569

Java, 5, 11–19, 32–33, 43, 46, 53, 55, 67, 74, 76, 91, 94, 96, 106–107, 116, 126, 144–148, 162, 189–192, 205, 209, 258, see also Indonesia; agriculture, 229, 276–282; climate, 228–229; Dutch exploitation, 258–261; early man, 64; entrepôt centre, 138; indigenous peoples, 264n, 279; land classification, 325; minerals, 229; plantation agriculture, 259–260; population, 172, 206, 258, 289–298; relations with outer territories, 380–381; structure and relief, 223–228; towns, 301–305; transport and communications, 300, 345

Javanese, 7n, 68, 239–241, 370

Jayavarman VII (1181–1219), 112

Jelebu, 587

jelutong, 675

Jesselton, 677, 678, 680
Johore, 585, 591, 597; ethnic groups, 634, 640; iron mines, 616; pineapple cultivation, 614; soils, 587; under British rule, 157
Johore Nahru, 649, 651
Jones Act (1916), 704
Jurassic system, 12
jute, Burma, 455

Kachins, 68, 409, 432, 468, 471–472, 477; Kachin State, 467, 472
Kahanjan (river), 339
Kai, 210, 370
Kaimana, 396n
Kajangs, 665
Kaladan (river), 463
Kalewa, 460, 463
Kalimantan, see Borneo
Kampar, 591, 608, 637
Kampar (river), 220n
kampas, 617
Kampong Ayer, 681
Kampong Boyan, 652
Kampong Java, 652
Kanbalu, 461n
Kanburi, 504
Kandan Village Irrigation Project, 454
Kantarawaddy, 471
kapok, Java, 281; Indonesia, 324
Kapuas mountains, 663; river, 221, 339
Karens, 68, 432, 434, 438, 447, 468–471; Karen State, formerly Kawthulay Special Region, 426, 467, 471
Kaskong, 35
Kawthulay Special Region, see Karen State
Kayah State, 454, 464, 467, 471
Kayans, 665
Kedah, 108, 487, 522, 590, 592, 596, 616; British protection, 491; ethnic groups, 634; soils, 587
Kediri, 226, 227, 247
Kedu, 227
Kelantan, 487, 522, 590n, 592, 597, 601, 616, 636, 651; British protection, 491; ethnic groups, 634; soils, 587
Kelantan (river), 585
Kendeng Highlands, 228
Kengtung, State of, 468, 521
Kennan, George F., 744n
Kenyahs, 665
keruing, 617
Keyfitz, Dr. Nathan, 341
Kh. Khiow, 418
Kha peoples (Mois in Annam; Penongs in Cambodia), 67, 534
Khao Huagang, 517
Khemarat, 418, 573
Khmers, 68, 83, 90, 113, 114, 117, 123, 432, 537; collapse of empire, 114–115, 120, 121, 537; historic boundaries, 110
Khone falls, 418, 535, 537, 573
Kinabalu, Mt., 223, 663, 665
Kinabatangan valley, 665
Klamono, 393, 398
Klang, 622
Klias peninsula, 678
Klong Ong Ang (canal), 518
Knappen, Tibbetts, Abbett Engineering Company, 461
Koh Hongs, 501n
Koh Sichang island, 518
Kompong Som, 569
Kompong Thom, 420, 544
Koninkijke Nederlandsche-Indische Luchtvaart Maatschappij (K.N.I.L.M.), 301, 355
Koninklijke Paketvaart Maatschappij (K.P.M.), 262, 298–301, 353–354
Kontum, 409, 564
Korat, 493, 499, 500, 503; plateau, 417, 418, 486, 488–489, 535, 573
Korea, 3n
Koronadal valley, 709
Kota Baru, 335, 599
Kotah Belud, 676
Koxinga, 700
Kra, 15, 413, 487, 491, 501, 517, 599; canal project, 153, 156, 525
Krakatau, 14n
Kratié, 418, 550
kretek cigarettes, see under tobacco
Kuala Belait, 681
Kuala Lipis, 651n
Kuala Lumpur, 597, 616, 618, 649, 651–652, 655, 659; industry, 622; population, 651; temperature and rainfall, 587
Kuala Selangor, 617n
Kuala Trengannu, 587
Kuantan, 598, 615
Kubus, 69, 240–241
Kuching, 668, 673, 675
Kudat, 676, 678
Kumon mts., 408
Kunming, 550
Kuo Min Tang, 502, 553
Kuo Yü, 183n
Kupang, 22, 26, 214
Kutaradja, 214, 300
Kutei, 260
Kyaukse, 434
Kyebogy, 471

Labuan, 37, 157, 663, 668, 670, 680; ceded to British, 147; population, 677
Lae, Captain Kong, 573
Laguna hydro-electric station, 717
La Han, General, 554
lalang, 47, 50
Lampang, 504, 516
Lampongers, 240–241
Lampung, 293, 294, 298
Lampun (Haribunchai), 105, 488
Lanao, 712, 717
Lan Chang, kingdom of, 113, 120, 122, 488, 525
Langkasuka, kingdom of, 103, 590
Lang-son valley, 414
Lanywa, 460
Lao Issarak movement, 523, 571
Laokay, 554
Laos, 3, 12, 16, 29, 35, 46, 68, 113, 121, 154, 155, 409, 412, 567–577, 739, 741, 742, 743n, 749, 757, 759, 760, 764, see also Indochina, States of; foreign aid, 570–571; hill peoples, 571, 488; land use, 575; Lao peoples, 521, 571; Mekong development projects, 573; political situation, 571–573; population, 570; relations with Thailand, 523–525; selected production data, 574
Larut hills, 583; tin field, 596
Lashio, 36, 444, 464; temperature and rainfall, 422
Laurel, José P., 705
Lawpita, 464, 752
leaching, 50–52
lead, 20, 420; Burma, 442, 459; Indochina, 544; Philippines, 716
Lebensraum, 10, 478, 775
Ledo Road, 464
Lee Kuan Yew, 660
Legaspi, 699–700, 719, 722
Lengkong, 324
Lepanto copper mine, 716
leprosy, 57
Leyte, 693, 695, 712
Lhasa, 36
lianes, 45, 47
Liga Filipina, 702
lignite, see coal
Limahong, 700
Limbang valley, 669
Lingga archipelago, 210
Loc Ninh, 550
Loikan Area Irrigation Project, 454
Lolo peoples, 68, 468, 535
Lombok, 43, 53, 67, 210, 229–230, 244, 251, 255; under Dutch rule, 286; population, 290
long house, 72
Lopburi, 420, 491, 518, 525
Lovek, 114
Luang Prabang, 29, 113, 122, 418, 535, 539, 554, 571; temperature and rainfall, 422
Lubus, 240–241
Lutong, 673
Luzon, 15n, 19, 43, 74, 82, 131, 189, 695, 697, 700, 709, 719, 721; area, 691; farm size, 708; population density, 706; temperature, 22
Lyautey, Marshal, 576

McMahon line, 478
Macao, 137, 404
Macapagal, Diosdado, 725n, 774
Madiun, 226
Madjapahit, 93, 115–119, 123, 127, 145, 147, 206, 248, 368, 393, 529, 666, 699
Madurese, 7n, 68, 239–241, 264n
Madura, 76, 223, 228, 240, 280, 336, see also Java and Indonesia
Mae-hongson, 488
Mae Moh, 516
Magelang, 342
Magellan, voyages of, 131, 134, 666
Magsaysay, Ramon, 709–710, 724
Mahakam (river), 221
Mahakam valley coal mines, 330
Mahan, A.T., 703
mainland states, see also individual countries; climate, 420–426; drainage, 409–412, 414–420; minerals, 420; structure and relief, 407–420; vegetation, 426–429
maize, 70, 133; Cambodia, 574–575; Indochina, 535, 541; Indonesia, 332–334; Java, 281; Laos, 574–575; Malaya, 606, North Borneo, 679; Outer Territories, 283; Philippines, 712–713; Thailand, 500, 508; Vietnam (North), 574; (South), 574–575
Makasar, 17, 136, 146, 211, 230, 255, 298, 301, 306, 342; Makasarese, 7n, 68, 242–243, 264; temperature and rainfall, 214
Makian, 209
Malacca, 649, 656; Baba Chinese, 641; British occupation, 144, 146, 593; Dutch seizure (1641), 254; ethnic groups, 634, 645; kingdom of, 118–119, 128, 130, 133, 135–137, 156, 162, 249–252, 263; population, 651; Portuguese seizure (1511), 591–592, 666; Straits of, 9n, 12, 63, 103, 106, 130, 141, 228, 592
Malang, 226, 337

malaria, 55–56, 192
Malaya (*i.e.* former Federation of Malaya and State of Singapore), 3, 12, 16, 17, 20, 39, 43, 51, 55, 59, 69, 83, 100, 117, 149, 161, 164, 183, 187, 192, 205, 739, 741–743, 750n, 753–754, 756, 758, 761; agriculture and land use, 604–617; British administration, 592–603, 655–659; Chinese settlers, 609–610, 639–642; climate, 586–587; economic development, 597–599, 604–631; 'Emergency', 604, 609, 657; Federated Malay States (F.M.S.), 597–603; Federation of Malaya, formation in 1948, 604; independence in 1957, 160, 523, 604, 626, 657–660; fishing, 608; independence (1957), 160, 523, 626, 657–660; Indians, 642–644; indigenous peoples, 633–645; industry, 620–623; irrigation, 608; Malayan Union, 604, 655–656; minerals and mining, 589, 615–617; New Villages, 609, 649; overseas trade, 624, 629–630; plural societies, 645–651; population, 175, 596, 602, 634–637, 646–649; ports, 617–619; relations with Indonesia, 381; rice, 605, 606–608; rubber, 598–600, 610–614; soils, 117, 588; Straits Settlements, 593–595, 600–601; structure and relief, 583–585; towns, 593–596, 617–619, 649–655; transport and communications, 617–620; Union of Malaya, 1946, 604; vegetation, 587–588, see also Singapore
Malays, 7, 68, 264, 633, 634–639, 666; population figures, 634, 637; way of life, 638–639
Malaysia, Federation of, 659–660, 684–686, 764n, 772–774
Malcolm, Justice George A., 697
Mali Kha (river), 415
Malim Nawar, 623
Malupi, 465
Manchu dynasty, 95
Mandalay, 22, 32, 36, 154, 187, 415, 434, 435, 444–445, 463; population, 466; temperature and rainfall, 422
Mandarin road, 550
manganese, Burma, 459; Indonesia, 330; Philippines, 716
Mangkunegara, 256n
mangroves, 46, 47, 103, 228
Manila, 131, 133, 186, 556, 668, 694, 701–702, 717, 720–723
manioc, 713
Manokwari, 214, 396n, 398
Man peoples (Yaos), 68, 535
Mao Tse-tung, 557
Maran, 619
Maria Christina I and II hydro-electric stations, 717
Martaban, Gulf of, 415
Martaban Fishing Company, Burma, 457
Martapura, 260
Marxism, Marxist, 448, 482
Masbate, 693, 716
Masinloc, 716
Masjumi, 373–377, 381
Masulipatam, 136
Matana, Lake, 230
Mataram, 227, 247, 254–256, 263
Matnog, 719
Mawchi, 442, 459
Max Havelaar, 258
Medan, 187, 285, 301, 305, 342
Meervlakte trough, 233
Meester Cornelis (Djatinegara), see Djakarta
Meklong (river), 486; delta, 417
Mekong (river), 16, 68, 103, 105, 110, 151, 154, 192, 409, 417–419, 517, 529, 537; delta, 122, 123, 152, 156, 177, 179, 413, 529–533, 539–541, 546, 552, 565; development projects, 573; navigation, 492, 552–553; population, 532, 533, 535; valley, 113, 152, 412, 535, 571
Melalap, 677
Melanesia, 38; Melanesoids, 66, 79
Menado, 214, 255, 306
Menadonese (Minahasans), 7n, 68, 242–243, 265
Menam (Chao Phraya) (river), 16, 68, 110, 121, 192, 411, 417, 486, 489, 517; basin, 114; delta, 156, 177, 487, 495–496, 518; development project, 508–509; navigation, 492
Menangkabau, 7n, 248–249, 637; Highlands, 217; peoples, 240–241, 251, 265, 268, 370
Mentawei, 210, 240–241
Meo peoples, 296n, 535
Me Ping (river), 412, 417; Yan Hee project, 514, 516
Merak, 353
Merauke, 232, 263, 396, 399
Merbok estuary, 591
merdeka, 360
Mergui, 34, 465
Mesolithic peoples, 79
Miao peoples, 68
millet, 70, 80
Minahasa, 211, 230, 266, 286, 693
Minas oilfields, 328
Minbu, 434
Mindanao, 15n, 17, 133, 145, 693, 695, 697,

701, 710, 712, 725; area, 691; population density, 706
Mindat, 465
Mindoro, 693, 715; population density, 706
minerals, 20–21, see also separate entries and under each country
Ming dynasty, 94
Mingaladon, 466
Miri, 673, 675, 680
Mogaung, 464
Mogok, 442
Moi peoples, 67, 99, 564
Moluccas (Maluku), 14, 66, 68, 99, 116, 127, 130, 134, 209, 269, 370, 393, 395; British occupation, 144; population, 290
Mongkol Borey, 550
Mongkut (Rama IV), King of Siam (1851–1868), 489–490
Möng Pan, 521
Mons (Peguans or Talaings), 68, 90, 105, 110, 113, 114, 121, 432, 435, 468, 472
monsoon, see climate
monsoon forest, 46, 47, 211
Moros, peoples, 68, 701, 708, 725–726
Moses, C. Lee, 669
mosquitoes, 54–56, 533
Motir, 209
Moulmein, 34, 114, 153, 441, 464, 469, 490; population, 466
Mu valley, 434; Irrigation Project, 452
Muda (river), 585
Multatuli (E. Douwes Dekker), 205, 258
Muong peoples, 535
Muruts, 665
Muslims, see Islam
Myanaung, 415
Myingyan, 461n, 463
Myitnge, 461n
Myittha (river), 461
Myitkyina, 415, 444, 477

Nagas, 68, 432, 468, 471–472, 476; Naga hills, 407, 412, 430
Nahdatul Ulama (N.U.), 374–377
Nakhorn Ratsima, 422, 519
Nakhornsrithamrat, 504, 519
Nakorn Pathom, 518
Nam Dinh, 544, 545
Nam Hou valley, 571n
Nam Mun (river), 418, 425, 487, 499
Nam Patene, 544, 570
Nam Si (river), 418, 425, 487, 499
Namti, 463n
Namtu, 442
Namwan Assigned Tract, 477
Nan (river), 486
Nan Chao, 89, 113, 488
Nan Yang, Nan Yo, 7, 90–95, 180–185, 770
Nan Yüeh, 7, 88, 414, 769
Naradhivas province, 522
Nassau Range, 232
Natuna, 147
Nederlandsche Handels Maatschappij (N.H.M.), 148
Nederlandsche Nieuw Guinea Petroleum Mij, 393
N.A.T.O., see North Atlantic Treaty Organization
Negri Sembilan, 583, 592, 597, 600, 634
Negrito peoples, 7, 66, 79
Negros, 693, 715, 720
Nehru, Jawaharlal, 658, 746–747, 771, 775
Neolithic cultures, 80–81
Nesiots, 66–67, 103, 698–699
Netherlands, 755–759, see also Europeans
Netherlands Indies, see also Indonesia, individual islands and Cultuurgebied; administrative divisions, 299; agriculture, 276–287; export production, 278; fishing, 280–281; irrigation, 278–279; Java population transmigration, 292–298; manufacturing industries, 297–298; outer territories, 283–286; plantation estates, 281, 284–285; population, 288–290; rice cultivation, 277–279, 283; towns, 301–307; transport and communications, 298–301
Netherlands-Indonesian Union, 310–311, 739
New Guinea, West (Irian Barat), 3n, 11n, 12, 16–19, 21, 26, 38, 43, 49, 66, 69, 99, 145, 206, 208–210, 234–235, 379, 757, 760; air routes, 399–400; British, Dutch and German annexations, 158; Dutch claims and rule, 261, 287, 392–395; economic development, 396–402; language, 401; overseas trade, 402; population, 206, 396; transfer to Indonesian sovereignty, 403; relief, 232–234; roads, 300, 396, 397; vegetation, 233–234
Ne Win, General, 448, 482
New Zealand, 751, 755–759
Ngandong, 64
Ngo Dinh Diem, 558, 562–563, 567
Nguyen family, 122–123
Nhatrang, 422
Nias, 210, 240–241, 264
nickel, Celebes, 232, 330
Nienhuys, Jacobus, 261

Ninhoa, 565
Nmai Kha (river), 415
Nongkhai, 493, 517, 571
Nongson, 566
North Atlantic Treaty Organization (N.A.T.O.), 744, 749
North Borneo, 3n, 662n, 665, 676–680, 686, 754, see also Northern Borneo
Northern Borneo, 221, 662–687, 740, 742n, 756, 758, 761, 774, see also Brunei, North Borneo, and Sarawak; British policy, 668–670; Chinese, 672–673; climate, 662n; economic development, 670–672; indigenous peoples, 665–667; natural resources, 662; population, 665, 684; prospects for federation, 681–686; roads and railways, 671; structure and relief, 663–665; trade, 686
Northern Vietnam, see Vietnam, Northern
N.U., see Nahdatul Ulama
Nueva, 709

oil (mineral), see petroleum
oil palm (*Elæis guineensis*), 168, 171, 284, 322; Malaya, 606, 614
Oosthaven, 300, 305
opium, 141; poppy, 535
Opium War (1839–1842), 151, 152, 770
Orang Akit, 66, 240–241, 244
Orang Laut, 240–241
Orang Mamak, 240–241
Outer territories, see under Indonesia
Overbeck, Baron, 669
Owen Stanley Range, 232

Padang, 214, 249, 305, 342n, 379
Padang Besar, 491
Padauk, 457
paddy, see rice
Padung, 297
Pagan, 103, 113, 434
Pahang, 149, 589, 592, 616; British protection, 597; ethnic groups, 634
Pahang (river), 585, 610
Pakanbaru, 328n
Pak Chang, 504
Pakistan, 3, 5, 739
Pak Lay, 426
Paknampo, 417, 492n, 512
Pakokku, 415
Paku Alam, 256
Palaung peoples, 67, 99, 432, 468
Palawan, 133, 666, 693, 698, 706, 710
Palembang, 294, 301, 304, 305, 328n, 342, 376; kingdom of, 107, 108–109, 115, 118, 220, 247, 249
palmyra, 46
Palu, Gulf of, 230
Pa Mong, 573
Pampanga, 709
Panarukan, 300
Panay, 693, 700, 712, 719
Pandassan, 669
pandeng, see monsoon forest
Pandjang, 353
Pangkalansusu, 300
Panikkar, K. M., 8, 745–748
Pan-Malayan Union, 741
Pan-Möng, 468
Pantja Sila, 375
Papar, 676, 678
papaya, 72
Papuans, 66
parakeets, 49
Parian, 722
Parkindo, 375
Pareœans, 66–68, 88, 98, 103, 105; Burma, 432; Indonesia, 239–245; Malaya, 590; Philippines, 699
Partai Katolik Indonesia, 375
Partai Komunis Indonesia (P.K.I.), 376, 377, 378n, 379n
Partai Nationalis Indonesia (P.N.I.), 373–377, 381
Partai Socialis Indonesia, 373, 375n
Pasei, 249
Pasig (river), 720
Pasir Ikan, 344
Pasir Panjang, 622
Pasundan, 96
Pasuran, 32, 214, 300, 304
Patani (Pattani), 103, 112, 116, 136, 520 521, 590–592, 599
Pathet Lao, 556, 571–572
Patkai hills, 407, 412
Pau, 555
Paya Lebar airport, 620
peanuts, 133
Pechaburi, 487, 491
Pegu, 466; kingdom of, 120; province of, 433, 435, 444; river, 416, 439, 443, 464
Peguans, see Mons
Pegu Yoma, 408, 426, 430, 435, 439, 441, 469
Pelni, 353
Pemali (river), 264n
Penang, 37, 146, 149, 156, 595, 601, 617, 619, 656; British acquisition (1786), 592; entrepôt trade, 624, 629; population, 595; temperature and rainfall, 587

Penungah, 676
People's Action Party (P.A.P.), Malaya, 659
People's Volunteer Organization (P.V.O.), Burma, 447
Perak, 149, 584, 592, 597, 600, 616; British protection, 597; coconut production, 614; ethnic groups, 634, 643; pineapple cultivation, 614
Perak (river), 585
Perlak, 92
Perlis, 522, 597; British protection, 491; ethnic groups, 634
Petaling Jaya, 622n
petroleum and oilfields, 8, 20, 21, 171, 237; Borneo, 328; British Borneo, 663, 673; Brunei, 680–681; Burma, 420, 441, 459–460; Indonesia, 326–329, 347; Java, 229, 261; New Guinea, 234, 398; North Borneo, 672; Sarawak, 673; Seram, 287; Sumatra, 261, 328–329
Philippines, 3, 11, 14, 16, 19, 25, 26, 29, 33, 37, 46, 48, 53, 55, 67, 96, 98, 100, 126, 131, 133, 161, 169, 179, 182, 187, 194, 205, 659, 742, 743, 753, 754, 757, 759, 766, 774; agriculture and land use, 710–715; American annexation and rule, 703; area, 691; climate, 693–696; hydro-electric power, 717; Independence (1946), 60, 198, 705; industry, 717; land tenure, 706–710; languages, 727–730; minerals, 715–716; overseas trade, 732–733; population, 172, 175, 703, 706–708; post war economic development, 709–722; problem of minority communities, 725–727; relations with West, 724–725; relief, 692; religions, 723–724; Spanish occupation and rule, 699–703; soils, 697; towns, 722–723; transport and communications, 718–721
Philippines Air Lines, 719
Philippines Trade Act (Bell Act), 1946, 705–706
Phnom Dang Rek, 418
Phnom-Penh, 114, 187, 419, 542, 549, 550, 569–570
Phong Saly, 556, 571, 572
phosphate, 229, 544
Phuket, 34, 117, 422, 501
Phulan, 26
Phu Phong, 542
Phy Tho, 561
Pia Ouac, 544
Pibul Songgram, 484, 503, 505, 522–523, 525
Pigafetta, 666
pilang, 46
pineapples, Malaya, 606, 614; Philippines, 713, 715
Ping (river), 486
Pintu Barat (Westervaarwater), 228
Pithecanthropus erectus, 64
Pitsanulok, 417, 518
P.K.I., see Partai Komunis Indonesia
Pladju, 328
Plaine des Joncs (Mekong delta), development project, 564
Plared, 342
Paknam, 490
Plato, 7
Pleiku, 564, 565
Pliocene, 14
plural society, 9, 184–185
P.N.I., see Partai Nationalis Indonesia
pomelo, 72
Ponnagyun, 463
Pontianak, 26, 268, 286, 306, 342, 666; temperature and rainfall, 214–215
Popa, Mt., 408, 415
population, 59, see also individual countries; Chinese immigrants, 180–185; death rate, 57, 173; density, 61, 71, 76, 176, 177, 192; distribution, 6, 178; figures, 172, 174–175, 177; growth, 71, 172–179; immigration, 179–185; Indian immigrants, 180–185; migration, 63, 65; pressure, 61, 763, 766; social organization, 69–79
Port Dickson, 617
Port Swettenham, 598, 618–619
Port Weld, 617
Porte d'Annam, 420, 531
Portuguese, 404, see also European influence
Poso (lake), 230
Prai, 617n
Prapança, 116
Préah Vihéar, 523
Pre-Cambrian, 12
Priangan, 226, 251, 256, 280; Highlands, 236, 305
Pridi Banomyong, 503, 505
Probolinggo, 304
Progo (river), 247
Prome, 106, 434, 444, 465
Proto-Australoids, 65
proto-Malays, see Nesiots
Province Wellesley, 149, 162, 593, 596, 634, 656
Pulau Laut, 335
Pulog, Mt., 693
Pyidaungsu (Union) Party, Burma, 448
Pyidawtha, 448–467
pyinkado, 457

Pyinmana, 463
Pyus, 68n, 90

Quang Nam, 103, 532
Quang Ngai, 532
Quangtri, 552
Quang Yen basin, 544
Quaternary era, 12, 19
Quezon, Manuel L., 704–705
Quezon City, 722
Qui Nhom, 422, 565
quinine, 163

Rach Gia, 547
Raffles, Sir Thomas Stamford, 144–147, 148, 172, 593, 595, 653, 660
Rahman, Tunku Abdul, 660, 684, 772
Raheng, 490, 499
railways, 151, 155; Burma, 443–444, 464–465; Indochina, 536, 550–552; Indonesia, 300, 353; Malaya, 618–619; Thailand, 490–491, 517
Ram K'amheng, 114
ramie, 324
Rangoon, 31, 186, 415, 438, 439–441, 443–445; industry, 462–463; population, 466; port, 465; river, 440–441; temperature and rainfall, 422
rattan, 45, 330, 675, 679
Raub, 616
Rawang, 622
Rawar peoples, 240–241
Redjong-Lebonger peoples, 240–241
Rejang (river), 221, 665, 673
religion, see separate entries
Rembang plateau, 211; highlands, 228
Republic of the United States of Indonesia (R.U.S.I.), 362
resin, 45
rhododendrons, 48
Riau archipelago, 210, 220, 235, 285, 343
rice, 70–76, 80, 137, 162; British Borneo, 673; Burma, 435–437, 456–457; Cambodia, 567, 574–575; cultivation, 53, 74–76, 82, 89, 169; improvement of strains, 171; Indochina, 531, 535, 539–541; Indonesia, 332–334, 338; Java, 277–279, 293; Laos, 574–575; Malaya, 604–608; North Borneo, 678; paddy, 72, 76; Philippines, 711–712; Sarawak, 674; Siam, 493; Thailand, 493–500, 507–512, 513; varieties, 73–74; Vietnam (North), 574, (South), 566, 574–576; world production, 171
rivers, see separate entries
Rizal y Mercado, José, 702
roads, Burma, 444–445; Indochina, 550–552; Indonesia, 345, 348–349, 351–352; Malaya, 619–620; New Guinea, 396–397; Thailand, 492–493, 516–517; Vietnam (South), 565
Rochore (river), 652
Roi-et, 493
Rokan, 591
Romulo, General, 741
Roosevelt, Theodore, 703
Rouffaer (river), see Tarika
Roxas, Manuel A., 705
rubber, 156, 157, 163–168, 171, 237; Borneo, 286; British Borneo, 673; Burma, 441; Cambodia, 567, 574–575; Cultuurgebied, 261, 284; Indochina, 542; Indonesia, 272, 317–320, 347; Java, 281; Malaya, 598–599, 600, 602, 606, 610–614; North Borneo, 677, 679; Sarawak, 674; Thailand, 497, 500–501, 506–508; Vietnam (South), 565, 574–576
Rural and Industrial Development Authority (R.I.D.A.) (Malaya), 626–627, 657
rust fungus, 162

Sabang, 263
Sagaing, 444
sago palm, 46, 70, 675, 679
Sahul-land, Sahul Shelf, 12, 209, 210
Saigon, 22, 26, 123, 152, 187, 415, 549, 569, 654; French settlement, 541; industries, 542, 566; Japanese Headquarters, 554; population, 567; rivalry with Hanoi, 549, 555; temperature and rainfall, 422
Sailendra dynasty, 108–109
Saingdin falls, 463, 464
Sakai peoples, 72, 240–241, 244
Salween (river), 16, 151, 154, 409–417, 443, 464, 468
Samar, 693, 695
Sambas, 666, 672
Sambor, 573
Sam, 556, 571, 572
Sampit, 342
Sampuranhariman falls, 343
Sampuransegara falls, 343
Samsen-Dusit, 519
Samutsakhorn, 519
Sandakan, 214, 396n, 665, 669, 678, 680
San Fernando, 719
Sangihe, 266
Saparua, 255
Saraburi, 514

Saramanti, 412
Sarawak, 3n, 83, 157, 662n, 665, 672–675, 686, see also British Borneo
Sarit, Marshal, 525
Sarmi, 396n
Sasaks, 67, 242–243, 245
Savannakhet, 418, 552
sawah, Borneo, 339; Java and Madura, 279, 325
Sawankalok, 110, 114, 488, 491, 499
Schophuys, H. J., 339–340, 347
Schwaner Gebergte, 221
S.E.A.T.O., see South-east Asia Treaty Organization
Sebatik Island, 677
Second World War, 3, 56, 182, 195, 208, 491; Burma, 446–448, 478; Indochina, 553–554; Japanese occupation, 158, 165, 194–198; Malaya, 604; Thailand, 505; aftermath in South-east Asia, 739–745, 763
sedentary cultivation, 72–73, 75–76, 78
Seikkyi, 441
Selangor, 585, 592, 597, 600, 608, 614, 634, 636, 640, 643
Semangs, 66, 69, 99, 590
Semarang, 258, 297, 300, 303, 342
Semeru mountains, 223
Semporna, 676
Senanayake, D. S., 747
Senoi-Temiar, 69, 99, 590, 633n
Sentul, 621
Sept Pagodes, 544
Seputih (river), 220
Seram, 14, 21, 210, 229, 255, 286–287
Seremban, 649
Seria, 673, 680–681
Seriam, 675n
Seroei, 396n
sesamum, Burma, 455; Thailand, 508
Shajeungdhrao, 491
Shan plateau, 12, 20, 25, 36, 409, 442, 488, 523
Shans, 89, 100, 113, 120, 432, 434, 438, 467–469, 477
Shan States, 154, 439, 459, 467, 469, 488
Shan-Tenasserim highlands, 12
shifting cultivation, 7, 46–47, 70–72, 76, 78, 82, 281, 499–500
shipping, Burma, 465n; Indonesia, 353–354; Malaya, 619; New Guinea, 396
Shwedaung, 459
Shwegun, 443
Siak, 260, 591, 637; valley, 328
Siam (see Thailand, post-1939), 120–122, 128, 135, 139, 149, 155, 161
Sibolga, 342
Sibu, 665, 673, 675
Sibuku Bay, 669
Siemreap, see Angkor
Sierre Madre, 698
Sihanoukville, 569
Si-Kiang (river), 411–412, 414
Silam, 676
silk and sericulture, 133; Thailand, 503–504
silver, 20, 420; Burma, 442, 459; Celebes, 232; Indochina, 544
Simanggang, 675
Simeulue, 240–241
Singapore, 3n, 15, 117, 145, 149, 151, 156, 185, 187, 195, 262, 379, 445, 465, 525, 593, 601, 617, 652–655, 742n, 750, 754, 759, 770, 772, see also Malaya, Federation of; airport, 620; city, 652–653; development and settlement by British, 146–147, 593–594, 602; entrepôt trade, 624; ethnic groups, 634; industry, 622–623; naval base, 161, 653; population, 595, 646–648; port, 617–619; relations with Federation of Malaya, 627–628, 656–659; temperature and rainfall, 587; trade, 355, 631
Singgora (Songkhla), 108, 487
Singhasari, 109, 116, 227, 247
Singkawang, 268
Singkep, 20, 210, 220, 329
Sittang (river), 113, 408, 415–416, 430; navigation, 443; valley, 120, 433; Yamethin District Irrigation Project, 452
Siva-Buddha, 87, 98, 116n
Sjahrir, Sutan, 375n
Socialism, 373, 375n, 448, 482, 570n, 768, 771
soils, 50–53, 71, see also individual countries
Solo River, 228, 247, 300
Song-bo (river), 419
Song-chu (river), 420
Song-ka (river), 420
Songhkla, 501n, 517, 519
Song-koi (river), 16, 152, 410, 419, 420, 529; agriculture, 531–532; delta, 112, 531–532, 552; history of navigation, 153; irrigation works, 547; population density, 531–532, 545–546
Song-ma (river), 420
Sorong, 393, 396–398
South China Sea, 7, 12, 17n, 126, 137, 141, 221
South-east Asia, 3, 5, see also individual countries and aspects area and extent, 11; early relations with India and China, 83–94; economic change and economic

South-east Asia (*cont.*)
development, 161–171, 762–768; geographical unity, 3–10; human geography, 5, 58–61; living standards, 762; Japanese rule, 194–198; orogenesis, 11; overseas trade, 200; political geography (pre-European period), 102–124; population growth, 172–184; prehistory, 79–83; relief, 15–20; regional association, 741, 772; structure, 11–14; towns and cities, 86, 185–188; Western influence, 7, 126–200
South-East Asia Command (S.E.A.C.), 3
South-East Asia Treaty Organization (S.E.A.T.O.), 523, 525, 556, 572–573, 725, 749, 750, 771, 773, 774, 776
Southern Vietnam, see Vietnam, Southern
South-West Pacific Commission, 394
soya beans, 332–334
Spaniards in South-east Asia, see European influence, and individual countries
Special Commissioner for South-east Asia, see Commissioner-General for South-east Asia
Spender, Sir Percy, 748
spices, 79, 84, 128, 130–131, 137, 162, 247, cinnamon, 137; cloves, 128, 134, 136, 137; European demand, 127–128, 142; ginger, 128; nutmeg, 128n, 134, 136–137; pepper, 137, 332, 500, 674
Spinifex squarrosus, 48
Srakeo delta, 417
Sri Vijaya, kingdom of, 108–109, 112, 115–117, 137, 147, 206, 247–248, 393, 591, 666, 699; downfall, 248, 249n
Stanvac oil company, 328n
Steenkool, 396n
Straits Settlements (S.S.), 156, 593–595, 600–601, see also under separate entries
subsistence cultivation, 162, 182, 189, 192
Suez canal, 156, 260, 435, 595
sugar, 70, 138, 143, 162; Indochina, 535; Indonesia, 324; Java, 281; North Borneo, 677, 679; Philippines, 704, 714; plantations, 138; Siam, 493; Thailand, 508; Vietnam (South), 575
Sukarno, 310, 367, 369–370, 375–376, 378–379
Sukothai, 110, 114, 488, 518
Sukur, 322, 343
Sulawesi, see Celebes
sulphur, 229, 330
Sultan Agung (1613–1645), 254
Sulu, 133, 666, 669, 699, 725
Sumatra (Sumatera), 7n, 12, 14, 16, 17, 19, 31, 34, 37, 53, 55, 66, 69, 91, 94, 106, 118, 128, 136, 145, 162, 165, 192, 205, 234, 331; see also Indonesia and Netherlands Indies; agriculture, 220; Asahan project, 343, 347; communications, 298–301, 348; Cultuurgebeid, 219–220, 284–285; geology, 218; history, 248–249; minerals, 220, 285; population, 206, 290; rubber, 164, 284–285; soils, 218–219; structure and relief, 217–220; vulcanism, 217–219
Sumba, 210, 290
Sumbawa, 210, 290; Sumbawans, 264
Sumitro plan, 341–344
Sundas, 11, 14, 16, 19, 66, 116, 209, 229, 395, see also individual islands; roads, 353; towns, 353
Sunda-land, Sunda shelf, 12, 14, 17, 19, 20, 48, 51, 53, 210, 220, 221, 583
Sunda Straits, 118, 135, 217, 263, 300
Sundanese, 68, 239, 240–241, 251, 264n, 370
Sungei Golok, 491
Sungei Lembing, 615
Sungei Ujong, 597
Sun Yat-sen, 8, 557, 770
Supanburi, 518
Surabaja, 116, 187, 247n, 258, 298, 300, 303, 342; industries, 297; morphology, 305; temperature and rainfall, 214
Surakarta, 148, 226, 256, 294, 300, 305, 324, 343
Surat, 136, 140
Surigao, 694, 716
Surin province, 507
swamp, 19, 47, 48, 106
sweet potatoes, 72, 133; Indonesia, 332 334; Malaya 606; Philippines, 713
Syriam, 140, 441, 460, 465

Tachin (river), 417
Tagalog, 68, 729–730
Tagore, Rabindranath, 747
Taikkyi Hydro-Electric Power Project, 464
Taiping, 587, 596, 615, 649
Taklee, 514
Taksin, P'ya, 121
Talaings, see Mons
Talaud, 266
Talé Sap, 407
Tali, 89
tamarind, 72
Tambelan, 147
Tan Ap, 550

Tandjung Periuk, 262, 304
Tanimbar (Timor Laut), 210
Tanjong Karang, 608
tannin, 47
Taoism, 87
Tapanuli, 284
Tapiro, 66
Tarakan, 301
Tarikaikea (Mamberano) (river), 233
Tariku (Rouffaer) (river), 233
Taritatu (Idenburg) (river), 233
Tarlac, 709, 722
taro, 70, 72
Taunggyi, 459
Taungup, 465
Tavoy, 34, 114, 121, 466
Tawau, 678, 679
Tay-Dinh, 553
tea, 163; Indochina, 542; Indonesia, 322–323; Java, 281; Malaya, 606; Vietnam (South), 565
teak, 46, 141, 156, 211, 426; Burma, 435, 441, 457; Java, 281, 330n; Thailand, 497, 499
Technical Assistance Organization (U.N.O.), 342
Tegal, 297, 304, 338
tegalan, 76, 279
Telok Anson, 617
Telok Ramunia, 616
Temerloh, 619
Tempe (lake), 336
temperate zone, 5
temperature, see climate
Tenggenese peoples, 67, 239–241
Tenasserim, 20, 34, 55, 105, 114, 121, 149, 409, 412, 426, 430, 441, 465; minerals, 442, 459
Tenasserim (river), 413
Ternate, 128, 131, 133, 134, 135, 209, 229, 255, 290
terracing, 74–75; Bali, 281
Tertiary, 12, 14, 15, 20, 210
Thabeikkyin, 415
Thai Airways Company, 517
Thailand (see Siam, pre-1939), 3, 12, 15, 20, 26, 29, 35, 46, 51, 55, 68, 94, 114, 120–122, 128, 135, 149, 155, 169, 187, 412, 446, 740–742, 740, 753–754, 757, 759, 766; agricultural regions and land use, 495-501, 507–511; alien minorities, 501–502, 521, 526; climate, 486–487; fishing industry, 511–512; hydro-electric power, 516; indigenous peoples, 488–489, 520–522; industrial development, 503–504, 512–516; inland waterways, 492; Inter-War years, 501–505; irrigation, 495–497, 508–509; natural regions, 485–486; overseas trade and export production, 493, 506–507, 510–511, 513; political geography, 489–493, 518–526; population, 174, 487, 493, 495, 505–506; post-War foreign policy, 522–526; relief, 486–488; rice production, 493–500, 507–512, 513; towns, 518–520; transport and communications, 490–493, 494, 516–518
Thailand–Burma railway, 413n, 464, 517, 523
Thai-Lao-Shan peoples, 68, 90, 105, 113
Thai-Meo Autonomous Zone, 561, 571
Thai peoples, 7, 81, 88, 89, 100, 105, 112, 114, 117, 121, 488, 497, 505; Indochina, 535; Thailand, 520–522
Thakhek, 550
Thamaing, 462
Thanbyuzayat, 464, 523
Thanh-Hoa, 561
Than Thien, 532
Thaton, 105, 113
Thayetmyo, 424, 461n, 463
Theing Wang Razi, 407
Theravada Buddhism, see Buddhism
Thilawa, 441
Thonburi, 121, 518n
Three Pagodas Pass, 464, 517
Tibet, 16, 37, 67; Tibetan plateau, 5, 36
Tidore, 128, 135, 209, 229, 255, 290
Tiechiu, 640
timber, 171; Burma, 457–459; Indonesia, 330–331; Malaya, 617; North Borneo, 679; Philippines, 715; Thailand, 499
Timor, 3n, 11n, 49, 68, 130, 137, 205, 209, 210, 248, 266, 290, 355, 370
Timor (Portuguese), 404
tin, 8, 20, 157, 171, 256, 420; Bangka, 260, 285; Belitung, 260, 285; Burma, 442, 459; Indochina, 544; Indonesia, 272, 329; Malaya, 285, 596–597, 600–601, 615–616, 621; Singkep, 285; Sumatra, 220, 285; Thailand, 497, 501
Tinh Tuc, 544
Tjabatjan, 338
Tjilatjap, 305, 343
Tji Liwung (river), 302, 304
Tjirebon, 228, 256, 300, 301, 338
Tjisaät, 342
Toala, 69
Toba, Lake, 218
Toba highlands, 249
tobacco, 133; Cambodia, 574–575; Cultuurgebied, 261; Indonesia, 322–323; Java, 281; kretek cigarettes, 324; North

tobacco (*cont.*)
Borneo, 677; Philippines, 715; Thailand, 497, 499, 500, 504, 508; Vietnam, 574–575
toddy, 46
Tongkah, 501
Tokugawa seclusion, 95, 194
Tondo, 722
Tonkin, 20, 29, 68, 79, 122, 123, 140, 152, 179, 413, 539, 545, 547, 554, 576; Gulf of, 410, 535; delta, 426, 534; Mineral wealth, 542–544; rainfall, 421
Tonlé Sap, 419, 529, 537, 550; development scheme, 573; lowlands, 419, 537
topography, see South-East Asia, relief
Toradja peoples, 67, 72, 242–244
Tordesillas, Treaty of, 127
Torrey, J. W., 669
Tosari, 214
Toungoo, 453; kingdom of, 120
Tourane, 552n, 571
Towuti (lake), 230, 350
trade, see individual countries, overseas trade
Transindochinois, 550
Trans-Perak River Irrigation Scheme, 608
Trengganu, 491, 522, 584, 590, 592, 597, 601, 614, 616, 634, 651
Tronoh, 619
tropical red earth, 52
tropical ulcers, 57
Tsan-po (river), 411–412
Tuaram valley, 678
Tuban, 116, 247n
tuberculosis, 57
tubers, 70
Tumasik, 249, 591
tungsten, 420; Burma, 442, 459; Malaya, 616
Tuy Hoa, 566
Twante Canal, 437, 443
Tydings-McDuffie Act (1934), 704
typhoons, see climate
typhus, 56

Ubol, 491, 493
Ubon, 525
Ubonrat-thani, 519
Udatin Coy, 346
Udon, 491, 493, 517
Ulu Langat, 623
Umbilin, 220, 260, 330
Union of Burma airways, 466
Union of Socialist Soviet Republics (U.S.S.R.), 316n, 480, 561
United East India Company (Dutch), see Vereeingde Oostindische Compagnie
United Kingdom (U.K.), Post-war policy towards South-East Asia, 745–751, 755–760; on British policy pre-war and post-war, see also under Burma, Malaya and British Borneo
United Nations Organization, 316, 339n, 342, 402, 476n, 755–756
United States of America (U.S.A.), 158; post-war policy towards South-east Asia, 556, 558, 562–566, 569, 570, 619n, 624, 745–751, 755–761; on United States policy pre-war and post-war, see also under Philippines
U Nu, 447–448, 456
Urdaneta, 131, 700
Utan peoples, 240–241
Uttaradit, 491, 499

Vaico (river), 419
Vajiravuhd (Rama VI) King of Siam, 519
Van der Heide, J. H., 495–496
Van Kol, 295
vegetation, 42–48
Vereenigde Oostindische Compagnie (V.O.C.), 135–139, 142, 143, 270; dissolution of company, 142; foundation, 135; history, 254–257; use of Chinese labour, 138–139
Victoria Point, 34, 422
Vien Chang, see Vientiane
Vientiane (Vien Chang), 122, 417, 422, 489, 517, 535, 552, 571, 572
Viet Bac Autonomous Zone, 562
Vietcong, 574
Vietminh (Democratic Republic of Vietnam), 554, 556, 571; creation by Ho Chih Minh, 554; land reform programme, 559–560
Vietnam, 3n, 37, 38, 55, 68, 98, 100, 120, 123, 739, 741–743, 750, see also Vietnam, Northern and Vietnam, Southern and Indochina, States of; creation of state by Japanese, 554; war with Vietminh, 555–556
Vietnam, Northern, 22, 26, 29, 35, 179, 189, 559–562, 760, 764, 771, see also Vietnam, and Indochina, States of; Chinese influence, 559–562; economic development, 559–562; ethnic groups, 559; formation of state, 556; industry, 560–561; land redistribution, 559–560; overseas trade, 577; population, 558; problems of partition, 557–558; selected production data, 574; Thai-Meo Auto-

Vietnam, Northern (*cont.*)
nomous Zone, 561, 571; Viet Bac Autonomous Zone, 562
Vietnam, Southern, 3, 12, 35, 562–567, 749, 754, 757, 759, 760, 764, see also Vietnam, and Indochina, States of; agriculture, 564–566; Chinese minority, 564; development projects, 564–567; formation of state, 556; land use, 575; overseas trade, 576–577; population, 558; problems of partition, 557–558; refugee problems, 562; selected production data, 574
Vietnamese Revolutionary Association, 553
Viettri, 545
Vinh, 545
Vinh Long, 419
Visayas, 695, 698, 708, 712; peoples, 68
V.O.C., see Vereenigde Oostindische Compagnie
Vogelkop, 21, 232, 234, 396
volcanoes, 14; soils derived from, 53
Volksraad, 269n, 273, 296
Vorstenlanden, 289, 301
Vyadhapura, 105

Wa peoples, 67, 99, 432, 477
Wadjak skulls, 64, 65
waduks, 279
Wallace's line, 43, 44, 48, 49, 209, 210, 235, 392
Wang (river), 486
Ward, Sir Thomas, 496
Warindra, 491
Waru, 343
Weber's line, 49, 210, 235, 392
Weltevreden, see Djakarta
West New Guinea, see New Guinea, west
Weston, 677
Wetar, 14, 210
wheat, 80
Wittfogel, Karl, 93, 94, 107n, 531
World Health Organization (W.H.O.), 56, 512
winds, see climate
wolfram, 544
Wonokromo, 328n
World Bank, see International Bank for Reconstruction and Development

Xom Cuc, 550

Yamethin District Irrigation Project, 452
yams, 70, 72, 79
Yang-tze Kiang (river), 411–412
Yan Hee project, 514, 516
yaws, 56
Ye, 444, 464
Yen Bay, 419
Yenangyat, 460n
Yenangyaung, 460
Yom (river), 486
Yunnan, 12, 20, 151, 409, 488, 497, 521, 522, 538, 550; plateau, 413, 529

Zambales mountains, 698, 716
Zamboanga City, 694, 701, 720, 722
Zeyawaddy, 461n
zinc, 420; Indochina, 544; Burma, 442, 459; Philippines, 716

90°
100°
110°
CHINA
20°
BURMA
Hanoi
LAOS
NORTHERN VIETNAM
Hong
Macao (Port.)
Vientiane
Rangoon
HAINAN
THAILAND
SOUTH CHINA SEA
Bangkok
SOUTHERN VIETNAM
CAMBODIA
10°
Phnom penh
Saigon
PENANG Is.
Jesselton
FEDERATION OF MALAYSIA
BRUNEI
N.
STRAITS OF MALACCA
SUMATRA
Kuala Lumpur
NATUNA Is.
Kuching
SARAWAK
0°
SINGAPORE
BORNEO (KALIMANTAN)
Djakarta
JAVA SEA
JAVA
10°
LOMBOK
100°
110°